International Directory of
COMPANY
HISTORIES

International Directory of

COMPANY

HISTORIES

VOLUME 113

Editor

Tina Grant

ST. JAMES PRESS
A part of Gale, Cengage Learning

Detroit • New York • San Francisco • New Haven, Conn • Waterville, Maine • London

International Directory of Company Histories, Volume 113

Tina Grant, Editor

Project Editor: Miranda H. Ferrara

Editorial: Virgil Burton, Donna Craft, Louise Gagné, Peggy Geeseman, Julie Gough, Sonya Hill, Keith Jones, Matthew Miskelly, Lynn Pearce, Laura Peterson, Holly Selden, Justine Ventimiglia

Production Technology Specialist: Mike Weaver

Imaging and Multimedia: John Watkins

Composition and Electronic Prepress: Gary Leach, Evi Seoud

Manufacturing: Rhonda Dover

Product Manager: Jenai Drouillard

Cover Photograph: Bahrain Financial Harbour, ©Rizami Annuar, Dreamstime.com

For product information and technology assistance, contact us at **Gale Customer Support, 1-800-877-4253.**
For permission to use material from this text or product, submit all requests online at **www.cengage.com/permissions.**
Further permissions questions can be emailed to **permissionrequest@cengage.com**

Gale
27500 Drake Rd.
Farmington Hills, MI, 48331-3535

LIBRARY OF CONGRESS CATALOG NUMBER 89-190943
ISBN-13: 978-1-4144-4109-2
ISBN-10: 1-4144-4109-6

This title is also available as an e-book
ISBN-13: 978-1-55862-776-5   ISBN-10: 1-55862-776-6
Contact your Gale, a part of Cengage Learning sales representative for ordering information.

BRITISH LIBRARY CATALOGUING IN PUBLICATION DATA
International directory of company histories, Vol. 113
Tina Grant
33.87409

Printed in the United States of America
1 2 3 4 5 6 7 14 13 12 11 10

Contents

List of Abbreviations

€ European euro
¥ Japanese yen
£ United Kingdom pound
$ United States dollar

A

AB Aktiebolag (Finland, Sweden)
AB Oy Aktiebolag Osakeyhtiot (Finland)
A.E. Anonimos Eteria (Greece)
AED Emirati dirham
AG Aktiengesellschaft (Austria, Germany, Switzerland, Liechtenstein)
aG auf Gegenseitigkeit (Austria, Germany)
A.m.b.a. Andelsselskab med begraenset ansvar (Denmark)
A.O. Anonim Ortaklari/Ortakligi (Turkey)
ApS Amparteselskab (Denmark)
ARS Argentine peso
A.S. Anonim Sirketi (Turkey)
A/S Aksjeselskap (Norway)
A/S Aktieselskab (Denmark, Sweden)
Ay Avoinyhtio (Finland)
ATS Austrian shilling
AUD Australian dollar
Ay Avoinyhtio (Finland)

B

B.A. Buttengewone Aansprakeiijkheid (Netherlands)
BEF Belgian franc

BHD Bahraini dinar
Bhd. Berhad (Malaysia, Brunei)
BND Brunei dollar
BRL Brazilian real
B.V. Besloten Vennootschap (Belgium, Netherlands)

C

C. de R.L. Compania de Responsabilidad Limitada (Spain)
C. por A. Compania por Acciones (Dominican Republic)
C.A. Compania Anonima (Ecuador, Venezuela)
C.V. Commanditaire Vennootschap (Netherlands, Belgium)
CAD Canadian dollar
CEO Chief Executive Officer
CFO Chief Financial Officer
CHF Swiss franc
Cia. Compagnia (Italy)
Cia. Companhia (Brazil, Portugal)
Cia. Compania (Latin America [except Brazil], Spain)
Cie. Compagnie (Belgium, France, Luxembourg, Netherlands)
CIO Chief Information Officer
CLP Chilean peso
CNY Chinese yuan
Co. Company
COO Chief Operating Officer
Coop. Cooperative
COP Colombian peso

Corp. Corporation
CPT Cuideachta Phoibi Theoranta (Republic of Ireland)
CRL Companhia a Responsabilidao Limitida (Portugal, Spain)
CZK Czech koruna

D

D&B Dunn & Bradstreet
DEM German deutsche mark (W. Germany to 1990; unified Germany to 2002)
Div. Division (United States)
DKK Danish krone
DZD Algerian dinar

E

E.P.E. Etema Pemorismenis Evthynis (Greece)
EC Exempt Company (Arab countries)
Edms. Bpk. Eiendoms Beperk (South Africa)
EEK Estonian Kroon
eG eingetragene Genossenschaft (Germany)
EGMBH Eingetragene Genossenschaft mit beschraenkter Haftung (Austria, Germany)
EGP Egyptian pound
Ek For Ekonomisk Forening (Sweden)
EP Empresa Portuguesa (Portugal)

ESOP Employee Stock Options and Ownership
ESP Spanish peseta
Et(s). Etablissement(s) (Belgium, France, Luxembourg)
eV eingetragener Verein (Germany)
EUR European euro

F

FIM Finnish markka
FRF French franc

G

G.I.E. Groupement d'Interet Economique (France)
gGmbH gemeinnutzige Gesellschaft mit beschraenkter Haftung (Austria, Germany, Switzerland)
GmbH Gesellschaft mit beschraenkter Haftung (Austria, Germany, Switzerland)
GRD Greek drachma
GWA Gewerbte Amt (Austria, Germany)

H

HB Handelsbolag (Sweden)
HF Hlutafelag (Iceland)
HKD Hong Kong dollar
HUF Hungarian forint

I

IDR Indonesian rupiah
IEP Irish pound
ILS Israeli shekel (new)
Inc. Incorporated (United States, Canada)
INR Indian rupee
IPO Initial Public Offering
I/S Interesentselskap (Norway)
I/S Interessentselskab (Denmark)
ISK Icelandic krona
ITL Italian lira

J

JMD Jamaican dollar
JOD Jordanian dinar

K

KB Kommanditbolag (Sweden)
KES Kenyan schilling
Kft Korlatolt Felelossegu Tarsasag (Hungary)
KG Kommanditgesellschaft (Austria, Germany, Switzerland)
KGaA Kommanditgesellschaft auf Aktien (Austria, Germany, Switzerland)
KK Kabushiki Kaisha (Japan)
KPW North Korean won
KRW South Korean won
K/S Kommanditselskab (Denmark)
K/S Kommandittselskap (Norway)
KWD Kuwaiti dinar
Ky Kommandiitiyhtio (Finland)

L

L.L.C. Limited Liability Company (Arab countries, Egypt, Greece, United States)
L.L.P. Limited Liability Partnership (United States)
L.P. Limited Partnership (Canada, South Africa, United Kingdom, United States)
LBO Leveraged Buyout
Lda. Limitada (Spain)
Ltd. Limited
Ltda. Limitada (Brazil, Portugal)
Ltee. Limitee (Canada, France)
LUF Luxembourg franc

M

mbH mit beschraenkter Haftung (Austria, Germany)
Mij. Maatschappij (Netherlands)
MUR Mauritian rupee
MXN Mexican peso
MYR Malaysian ringgit

N

N.A. National Association (United States)
N.V. Naamloze Vennootschap (Belgium, Netherlands)
NGN Nigerian naira
NLG Netherlands guilder
NOK Norwegian krone
NZD New Zealand dollar

O

OAO Otkrytoe Aktsionernoe Obshchestve (Russia)
OHG Offene Handelsgesellschaft (Austria, Germany, Switzerland)
OMR Omani rial
OOO Obschestvo s Ogranichennoi Otvetstvennostiu (Russia)

OOUR Osnova Organizacija Udruzenog Rada (Yugoslavia)
Oy Osakeyhtiö (Finland)

P

P.C. Private Corp. (United States)
P.L.L.C. Professional Limited Liability Corporation (United States)
P.T. Perusahaan/Perseroan Terbatas (Indonesia)
PEN Peruvian Nuevo Sol
PHP Philippine peso
PKR Pakistani rupee
P/L Part Lag (Norway)
PLC Public Limited Co. (United Kingdom, Ireland)
PLN Polish zloty
PTE Portuguese escudo
Pte. Private (Singapore)
Pty. Proprietary (Australia, South Africa, United Kingdom)
Pvt. Private (India, Zimbabwe)
PVBA Personen Vennootschap met Beperkte Aansprakelijkheid (Belgium)
PYG Paraguay guarani

Q

QAR Qatar riyal

R

REIT Real Estate Investment Trust
RMB Chinese renminbi
Rt Reszvenytarsasag (Hungary)
RUB Russian ruble

S

S.A. Sociedad Anónima (Latin America [except Brazil], Spain, Mexico)
S.A. Sociedades Anônimas (Brazil, Portugal)
S.A. Société Anonyme (Arab countries, Belgium, France, Jordan, Luxembourg, Switzerland)
S.A. de C.V. Sociedad Anonima de Capital Variable (Mexico)
S.A.B. de C.V. Sociedad Anónima Bursátil de Capital Variable (Mexico)
S.A.C. Sociedad Anonima Comercial (Latin America [except Brazil])
S.A.C.I. Sociedad Anonima Comercial e Industrial (Latin America [except Brazil])

S.A.C.I.y.F. Sociedad Anonima Comercial e Industrial y Financiera (Latin America [except Brazil])

S.A.R.L. Sociedade Anonima de Responsabilidade Limitada (Brazil, Portugal)

S.A.R.L. Société à Responsabilité Limitée (France, Belgium, Luxembourg)

S.A.S. Societe Anonyme Syrienne (Arab countries)

S.A.S. Societá in Accomandita Semplice (Italy)

S.C. Societe en Commandite (Belgium, France, Luxembourg)

S.C.A. Societe Cooperativa Agricole (France, Italy, Luxembourg)

S.C.I. Sociedad Cooperativa Ilimitada (Spain)

S.C.L. Sociedad Cooperativa Limitada (Spain)

S.C.R.L. Societe Cooperative a Responsabilite Limitee (Belgium)

S.E. Societas Europaea (European Union Member states

S.L. Sociedad Limitada (Latin America [except Brazil], Portugal, Spain)

S.N.C. Société en Nom Collectif (France)

S.p.A. Società per Azioni (Italy)

S.R.L. Sociedad de Responsabilidad Limitada (Spain, Mexico, Latin America [except Brazil])

S.R.L. Società a Responsabilità Limitata (Italy)

S.R.O. Spolecnost s Rucenim Omezenym (Czechoslovakia

S.S.K. Sherkate Sahami Khass (Iran)

S.V. Samemwerkende Vennootschap (Belgium)

S.Z.R.L. Societe Zairoise a Responsabilite Limitee (Zaire)

SAA Societe Anonyme Arabienne (Arab countries)

SAK Societe Anonyme Kuweitienne (Arab countries)

SAL Societe Anonyme Libanaise (Arab countries)

SAO Societe Anonyme Omanienne (Arab countries)

SAQ Societe Anonyme Qatarienne (Arab countries)

SAR Saudi riyal

Sdn. Bhd. Sendirian Berhad (Malaysia)

SEK Swedish krona

SGD Singapore dollar

S/L Salgslag (Norway)

Soc. Sociedad (Latin America [except Brazil], Spain)

Soc. Sociedade (Brazil, Portugal)

Soc. Societa (Italy)

Sp. z.o.o. Spólka z ograniczona odpowiedzialnoscia (Poland)

Ste. Societe (France, Belgium, Luxembourg, Switzerland)

Ste. Cve. Societe Cooperative (Belgium)

T
THB Thai baht
TND Tunisian dinar

TRL Turkish lira
TTD Trinidad and Tobago dollar
TWD Taiwan dollar (new)

U
U.A. Uitgesloten Aansporakeiijkheid (Netherlands)

u.p.a. utan personligt ansvar (Sweden)

V
V.O.f. Vennootschap onder firma (Netherlands)

VAG Verein der Arbeitgeber (Austria, Germany)

VEB Venezuelan bolivar

VERTR Vertriebs (Austria, Germany)

VND Vietnamese dong

VVAG Versicherungsverein auf Gegenseitigkeit (Austria, Germany)

W–Z
WA Wettelika Aansprakalikhaed (Netherlands)

WLL With Limited Liability (Bahrain, Kuwait, Qatar, Saudi Arabia)

YK Yugen Kaisha (Japan)

ZAO Zakrytoe Aktsionernoe Obshchestve (Russia)

ZAR South African rand

ZMK Zambian kwacha

ZWD Zimbabwean dollar

A.N. Deringer, Inc.

64 North Main Street
Saint Albans, Vermont 05478
U.S.A.
Telephone: (802) 524-8110
Toll Free: (800) 523-4357
Fax: (802) 524-5970
Web site: http://www.anderinger.com

Private Company
Incorporated: 1919
Employees: 500
NAICS: 488510 Freight Transportation Arrangement

■ ■ ■

A.N. Deringer, Inc., is a private company based in Saint Albans, Vermont, that provides international logistics. While its core competency is U.S. Customs brokerage, Deringer offers a variety of supply chain services, including duty drawback (refunds from U.S. Customs), U.S. Department of Agriculture (USDA) meat inspection, warehousing and distribution, freight forwarding, cargo insurance, and customs and logistics consulting.

The company serves such markets as consumer goods, electronics, food and beverage, furniture and home furnishings, paper and forestry products, textiles and apparel, transportation and industrial machinery, and rubber and plastic. Deringer operates about 35 offices in the United States, with branches at the major U.S.-Canada border crossings in Vermont, Maine, New York, Michigan, North Dakota, and Washington, and a few other states with important coastal and inland ports

of entry. In addition, Deringer works with a network of agents to provide global service to its customers, primarily in the Western Hemisphere, Europe, and the Pacific Rim.

ORIGINS

The man behind the A.N. Deringer name was Alfred Neel Deringer, born in Lima, Ohio, in 1889. As a young man, he became involved in the customs business through his employment with Toledo, Ohio-based Raymond P. Lipe Company, a hay and grain wholesaler. In 1912, two years before the start of World War I, Deringer was dispatched to Canada to establish and run a buying office. In 1915 Deringer came to Saint Albans to manage a new warehouse that made use of the community's rail infrastructure to accept Canadian hay and send it to ports to be shipped to France to feed the mules and horses of the Allied armies.

Nearly a year after the conclusion of the war, and shortly before his 30th birthday, Deringer struck out on his own in August 1919 to put to good use the knowledge he had accumulated in exporting goods. Forming a partnership with a Raymond P. Lipe colleague, Herb Schultz, and Saint Albans resident Jack Hurley, Deringer opened his own hay and grain grading and dealership, taking over the Raymond P. Lipe Company's operation, under the A.N. Deringer name at the Saint Albans rail yard.

Deringer did not limit himself to the hay and grain dealership. Because he was well versed in the steps required to transport goods over borders, he also offered his services as a customs broker. In 1928 the company

COMPANY PERSPECTIVES

Developing solutions for our customers is the reason Deringer is in business. We seek to serve customers who want a mutually rewarding, profitable partnership. Our principal focus is our customer markets.

was granted power of attorney as a customhouse brokerage, and two years later became one of the first customs brokers to be licensed by the U.S. Treasury Department, granted corporate license number 22. In that same year, 1930, Deringer expanded into the insurance business, opening an insurance agency, focusing on selling U.S. Customs Bonds to its importing clients and then expanding to commercial and personal lines, to achieve some level of diversity.

VENTURING BEYOND VERMONT: 1941

Deringer focused on its region, as did other customs brokers, mostly concerning itself with rail shipments initially, and then truck shipments as the interstate system was developed, between the United States and Canada. The company warehoused the goods during customs inspection, completed the necessary import and export documents, addressed any legal or trade issues, and shepherded the goods over the border. In 1941 the company expanded outside of Vermont, acquiring Lovell's Customhouse Brokerage in Rouses Point, New York, albeit the new facility was located just 20 miles from Saint Albans.

Deringer remained a regional customs service provider and local insurance broker during the post-World War II years. In 1951 the company acquired property in Highgate Springs, Vermont, and added offices in Calais and Vanceboro, Maine, in 1952. During the following decade, offices opened in Champlain, New York, in 1967, and Alexandria Bay, New York, two years later. Deringer's nephew, Ken Holzscheiter, who had joined the company along with his older brother, Albert J. Holzscheiter, opened the Alexandria Bay office. By this time, Alfred Deringer had retired, and in September 1969 his wife, Helen, took over as company president. A few months later, in January 1970, Albert Holzscheiter was named general manager and essentially ran the company. Alfred Deringer died later that year.

The Holzscheiter brothers, whose mother was Alfred Deringer's sister, had grown up in Toledo, Ohio,

their father a restaurateur. From an early age they knew there was a career opportunity waiting with their uncle, and almost an expectation that they would join A.N. Deringer. Albert Holzscheiter joined the company first, while brother Ken completed a degree in economics and a major in international business from the Wharton School of Business at the University of Pennsylvania. Ken Holzscheiter went to work at A.N. Deringer in 1963, but just six months later, in March 1964, he was drafted, and spent two years in the military before resuming his career at his uncle's company.

ACCIDENT CLAIMS BROTHER: 1971

Under the direction of Albert Holzscheiter, Deringer expanded further. Offices were opened in Fort Covington, New York, in 1971, land was purchased in Houlton, Maine, and plans were made to build facilities at Champlain and Highgate Springs, New York, and Calais, Maine. Ken Holzscheiter was still branch manager at Alexandria Bay in July 1973 when his brother was tragically killed on a flight between Burlington, Vermont, and Boston's Logan Airport, which was enveloped that morning by low clouds and fog. The aircraft's landing gear clipped a seawall, causing a crash that took the lives of all 83 passengers and six crew members. Ken Holzscheiter was then asked by his aunt to take over as Deringer's general manager.

Despite the difficult circumstances under which he assumed control, Ken Holzscheiter was well prepared to further the growth of Deringer. The company moved into its permanent headquarters in Saint Albans in 1975. New offices opened in Boston in 1974; Bangor, Maine, in 1977; Ogdenburg, New York, in 1979; and Burlington, Vermont, in 1980. In addition, Jackman, Maine-based Pacific Customs Brokers was purchased in 1974. The insurance business was bolstered by a pair of acquisitions: Enosburg Falls, Vermont-based Asselstine Insurance Agency in 1976, followed two years later by S.S. Watson Insurance Agency with offices in Saint Albans and Milton, Vermont.

For decades, customs brokers like A.N. Deringer focused on their portion of the Canadian border, but in the 1980s the company began looking to enter new markets. In 1983 W.R. Filbin & Co. was acquired, adding offices in Detroit, Port Huron, Grand Rapids, and Sault Ste. Marie, Michigan; and Buffalo, New York. In 1985 three acquisitions were completed: Hartford, Connecticut, customs broker Brian R. Glynn CHB Inc.; ITC Compucustoms Corp. of New York City; and Boston's Air-Sea Brokers. Deringer closed the decade with the purchase of the William A. Marshall customs brokerage located in Bridgeport, Connecticut.

KEY DATES

1919: Alfred Neel Deringer and partners open a customs insurance agency under the A.N. Deringer name.
1930: Company is licensed as customs broker.
1969: Alfred Deringer retires.
1983: W.R. Filbin & Co. is acquired.
2001: Terrorist attacks against the United States change customs procedures.

WESTERN EXPANSION: 1994

Further external growth continued in the 1990s. The Chicago and Cincinnati offices of Milne & Craighead Custom Ltd. were acquired in 1991, and Boston's H.P. Lambert & Co. Inc. a year later. Deringer looked to the central and western portions of the Canadian border in 1994, purchasing three more Milne & Craighead offices, located in Portal, North Dakota; Sweetgrass, Montana; and Blaine, Washington. The New York and Miami offices of Maron Shipping Agencies, Inc., were purchased in 1997, and Duluth, Minnesota-based Buchanan Customs Brokers was added in 1998. During this period Deringer also opened branch offices in Pembina, North Dakota, in 1995, and Eastport, Idaho, in 1996.

To expand its business to support the Asia Pacific trade route and larger international markets, Deringer opened offices in Los Angeles in 1999, Atlanta in 2001, and Houston in 2001. Deringer also sought to serve the global needs of its growing customer base. The company had always been oriented toward trucking. Deringer began to add expertise in air, rail, and water transportation in order to become a one-stop shop for its customers, who at this time wanted more than just someone to help them cross a border. Deringer thus commenced to transform itself into a logistics company rather than just a customs broker.

The end of the 1990s also brought a new chief executive, with longtime employee Wayne Burl succeeding Ken Holzscheiter. Burl held the post until 2006, when he went into partial retirement but continued to contribute as a vice president. His replacement was Ken Holzscheiter's son, Jacob, who became only the fifth president in Deringer's history. He was well prepared for the job, a licensed customs broker with nearly two decades of experience at the company, during which time he had been involved in nearly all aspects of the business.

INCREASED SECURITY MEASURES: 2001

The new century also brought fresh concerns about secure borders that required Deringer to embrace new technologies in order to do its job. The watershed event was the terrorist attacks against the United States of September 11, 2001. The old ways of doing business were no longer tolerated. For decades, Deringer had provided the paperwork for a truck crossing the Canadian border, and when the truck arrived, the customs station merely reviewed the paperwork, looked briefly at the cargo, and waved it through.

After September 11, however, trucks were not even allowed to approach the border without prior approval. A wealth of information about the shipment had to be delivered electronically ahead of time, including the name of the driver, the recipient of the cargo, and an itemized breakdown of the shipment that would allow Customs and Border Protection personnel to look for variances and better spot potential alteration or tampering of the cargo. In 2003 Deringer was certified as a full participant in the Customs-Trade Partnership Against Terrorism (C-TPAT) program administered by U.S. Customs and Border Protection, the agency charged with securing the borders for the Department of Homeland Security.

New rules to protect the border required a more sophisticated supply chain, opening up an opportunity for the company to focus more on becoming a logistics service provider. In 2009 Deringer introduced a new supply chain and online purchase order management program, eShipPartner Supply Chain Manager, to streamline the shipment process and provide customers with the ability to track an item from purchase order through delivery.

Deringer also expanded its market reach by opening an office in Seattle, Washington, in 2005, and adding network partners around the globe to better serve customers. In addition, it played an important role in shaping trade policy by participating in Customs and Border Protection pilot programs. In 2009 it became one of four brokers selected to participate in a self-assessment pilot. Border security was certain to remain a major priority for all governments, and Deringer was poised to continue to serve as an important player in the development of new policies that would affect the business for years to come.

Ed Dinger

PRINCIPAL DIVISIONS

Electronics and Electrical Equipment; Fabricated Metal Parts; Food and Beverage; Furniture and Home Furnishings; Paper and Forestry Products; Textiles, Apparel, and Accessories; Transportation Equipment and Industrial Machinery; Rubber and Plastics.

PRINCIPAL COMPETITORS

FedEx Corporation; Livingston International Inc.; Norman G. Jensen, Inc.

FURTHER READING

Barna, Ed, "The Business of the Border," *Vermont Business Magazine,* July 2, 2008.

Burl, Wayne, "A.N. Deringer," *Journal of Commerce,* January 12, 2004, p. S117.

"Deringer Announces New Supply Chain Management Tool," *St. Albans Messenger,* February 23, 2009, p. 2A.

Kelley, Kevin, "The Shipping News Is Pretty Good," *Vermont Business Magazine,* November 1, 2004.

Robinson, Sue, "Deringer Takes Care of Shipping," *Burlington Free Press,* September 24, 2001, p. 1D.

Simmon, Virginia Lindauer, "Borderline Business," *Business Digest of Greater Burlington,* November 1998.

Albert Trostel and Sons Company

———— ■ ————

330 East Kilbourn Avenue, Suite 750
Milwaukee, Wisconsin 53202
U.S.A.
Telephone: (414) 223-1560
Fax: (414) 225-0025
Web site: http://www.trostel.com

Wholly Owned Subsidiary of Everett Smith Group Ltd.
Incorporated: 1909
Employees: 5,200
Sales: $627 million (2008 est.)
NAICS: 316110 Leather and Hide Tanning and Finishing; 325211 Plastics Material and Resin Manufacturing; 339991 Gasket, Packing, and Seals Manufacturing

■ ■ ■

Albert Trostel and Sons Company is a holding company for Trostel, Ltd., Trostel Specialty Elastomers Group, Inc., and Eagle Ottawa, LLC. The company, founded as a leather tannery, manufactures leather components for the automotive industry, cast urethane and thermoplastic products, and seals and molded rubber products. Its customers include the major global automobile manufacturers, as well as companies in the tool industry, forklift manufacturers, and other makers of industrial parts, components, engines, and equipment. Its Trostel, Ltd., subsidiary is headquartered in Lake Geneva, Wisconsin. It makes precision molded seals, rubber products, and other components for a variety of industries. Trostel, Ltd., also has facilities in Whitewater, Wisconsin, and in Reynosa, Mexico.

Trostel Specialty Elastomers Group (SEG) also runs facilities in Lake Geneva. It makes a variety of cast and molded plastics. Eagle Ottawa, headquartered in Auburn Hills, Michigan, is a major global supplier of leather components for the automotive industry. It has plants in Mexico, South Africa, China, England, and Hungary, as well as in the United States. Albert Trostel was for many years one of the world's largest leather tanners, supplying leather for most of the boots worn by U.S. troops during World War II. It diversified significantly in the 1970s. The company is privately held by the Everett Smith Group, which also owns a cluster of other industrial component companies.

ROOTS IN LEATHER TANNING

Albert Gottlieb Trostel founded the company that bears his name in Milwaukee in 1858. Trostel was born in Germany in 1834 and came to the United States when he was 18 years old. By that time, Trostel had apprenticed at a leather tannery for several years, so he came to his new country with solid skills. He went to work for a tanner in Milwaukee, and by 1858 he had formed his own tannery business, in partnership with another German immigrant, August Gallun.

Milwaukee was at the time a thriving industrial city, rivaling Chicago for growth and promise. It had a large German immigrant community, and was also home to people from all over Europe. The city had access to water and to cattle hides. It was also close to forests of oak and hemlock, from which chemical tanning agents

COMPANY PERSPECTIVES

Trostel designs and manufactures custom seals and precision molded rubber products through product innovation and material expertise. These skills, along with our technical capabilities, give you confidence that your products will deliver superior performance and value. We welcome you to partner with us for all your custom applications. Let us show you what we can do.

were derived. Milwaukee was becoming the center of the tanning industry in the United States as Trostel and his partner were building their company.

The early company prospered despite two disastrous fires. The Civil War provoked a huge demand for leather for soldiers' boots, and for harnesses and straps for carriages and wagons. Trostel and Gallun had no difficulty selling their leather, which they sold under the brand name Blue Star. Business was so good that they moved into larger quarters in 1861. They called the new facility Star Tannery. Star Tannery caught fire in 1865. The building and much of its brand new machinery had to be replaced.

Trostel and Gallun bought a new property in 1876, which they called Empire Tannery. Empire also was destroyed by fire. It burned down in 1881, and was rebuilt the next year. Trostel and Gallun at the same time bought another neighboring tannery. This one also had at one time been burnt and rebuilt, so they called their new facility Phoenix Tannery.

The two partners ran three different tanneries in the city. Meanwhile, Albert Trostel married Gallun's older sister Charlotte. Although the two men got along, the marriage led to friction between the women in the family, and for this reason, the partnership split in 1885. Gallun took the Empire Tannery and the company offices, while Trostel took the two other tanneries. Trostel's tanneries specialized in leather for harnesses, boots, and upholstery.

The company continued to expand. By the early 1890s, it had sales of some $500,000. Trostel bought a canal from a much larger competitor in 1895, and then built a large new plant. By the late 1890s, Trostel's tanneries employed approximately 600 people. When Albert Trostel died in 1907, the business went to his sons, Gustav and Albert. The company incorporated in 1909 as Albert Trostel and Sons.

WORLD WAR I AND THE GREAT DEPRESSION

Gustav Trostel, Albert's oldest son, had been educated at a German-English school in Milwaukee, and in his teens went back to his father's homeland to apprentice in a German tannery. He was well prepared to take over the family business when his father died. He and his wife lived in an elaborate mansion of German design that remained a Milwaukee landmark into the 21st century. Gustav's younger brother Albert O. Trostel was also known for his imposing home. He had married an heiress to the Schlitz brewery, Clara Uihlein. Her grandfather was said to be the city's wealthiest man, and later her fortune would have much impact on the Trostel tannery.

The business was flourishing at the time it incorporated, with capital stock valued at $2.7 million. A few years later, the start of hostilities in Europe posed difficulties for German Americans like the Trostels. The Trostel wives were prominent among German Americans who raised money for German war casualties in 1916. However, public sentiment turned against Germany in Milwaukee, and the public support of the Trostels for their ancestral land became uncomfortable.

Nevertheless, the war provided good business for tanneries. Trostel and Sons expanded its plants in 1919. They also began making a special leather called purple Trostan calf. This came to be used for army officers' dress boots, as well as civilian shoes. By the midst of the war years, Trostel had become one of the largest tanneries in the world.

The demand for leather fell precipitately after World War I ended. Inflation caused great difficulties as well. By 1923 the economy seemed to have stabilized, and leather production increased. The end of the 1920s saw steadily rising markets and increasing prosperity all around. However, the stock market crash of 1929 and the ensuing Great Depression hit the Milwaukee area particularly hard. Trostel and Sons ran into financial difficulties that exposed the interwoven accounts of the various Trostel families and the company itself.

TANGLED FAMILY AND BUSINESS FINANCES

Gustav Trostel, his brother Albert O., and Adolph Finkler, husband of their sister Ida Trostel, were all directors of Trostel and Sons. By 1932, with the nation's economy staggering, the company urgently needed to borrow money. However, it could not do so without untangling the personal finances of the Trostels. Some had lent the company money, and some had borrowed from it. Finkler had borrowed $700,000 from the

KEY DATES

1858: German immigrants Trostel and Gallun found their first tannery in Milwaukee.
1885: Partners Trostel and Gallun split.
1909: Company incorporates as Albert Trostel and Sons.
1933: Founder's son Albert O. Trostel resigns; his son Albert O., Jr., becomes president.
1938: Everett G. Smith hired as financial analyst.
1946: Leather Packings Division founded.
1952: Leather Packings Division becomes Trostel Packings, Ltd., and moves to Lake Geneva, Wisconsin.
1961: Trostel and Sons acquires Michigan tannery Eagle Ottawa.
1997: Trostel Packings changes name to Trostel, Ltd.
2003: Eagle Ottawa expands into China.

company, while his brother-in-law Albert O. Trostel had taken out loans from the company equaling almost $2 million. At the same time, Gustav and Ida had lent the company $70,000 and $35,000 respectively. Clara Uihlein Trostel, Albert's wife, had lent the company $2.5 million. A meeting of attorneys for all the interested parties straightened out the debt situation, with the largest creditors, Clara and Gustav, forgiving the company its debt to them.

Soon after this meeting, brother Albert O. withdrew from the family business. He formally resigned in 1933, asking that his son Albert O. Trostel, Jr., take his place. Albert, Jr., became vice president of Trostel and Sons when he was only 25 years old. His mother Clara became a director of the company. Part of the arrangement made in 1932 settling the debts of the various family members to the company stipulated that Clara could not lend any more money to Trostel and Sons. However, the company's situation was so bad that it could not pay for hides, and therefore could not produce tanned leather.

Since Clara could not directly lend the company money, she instead bought calf hides in Chicago and gave them to the company in return for a share in their finished price. Clara began to take even more direct action to keep the company afloat. She pushed the company to sell some of its property. This move was not popular with her brothers-in-law. However, Clara had enough proxy votes, and a position on the board, so that she and her son could make the sale happen. The

company then raised enough money to pay delinquent taxes by selling a warehouse.

The company was still not solvent, however, and had to borrow money from Gustav Trostel's life insurance several times. In 1936 Gustav Trostel and brother-in-law Adolph Finkler both died in the month of May. Less than six months later, Albert O. Trostel also died. Albert and Clara's mansion, once Milwaukee's most expensive piece of real estate, had suffered a terrible fire a year earlier, and the family had abandoned it. The burned wreck was sold to a demolitionist for only $500. The fortune the first Albert Trostel had built was gone, and the whole second generation of Trostels was out of the family business.

MOVING INTO NEW PRODUCTS

After the death of her husband, Clara Trostel resigned her directorship, but she remained concerned about the company her son was then leading. In 1938 she recommended that Trostel and Sons hire a financial analyst. The company hired her choice, a Dartmouth classmate of her husband Albert O., named Everett G. Smith. Smith became treasurer of the company in 1940, and eventually moved to an ownership position.

Albert O. Trostel, Jr., began working as general manager for the family company when he was just out of college. He was president of the firm when he was not yet 30. Although young, he knew the leather business thoroughly, and had the education and insight to move the company in promising new directions. He realized that some of Trostel's techniques were out of date, and he traveled to Europe and employed European consultants in order to bring in more modern processes.

Trostel's travels in Europe also acquainted him with global politics. He foresaw the coming of World War II, and made sure his company was prepared. Trostel and Sons had made a variety of leathers, including fine calf-skin used for women's shoes and purses. In 1939 Albert Trostel decided to move the company into side leather, which was sturdy enough for soldiers' boots. Just as in World War I, when the company had been a major supplier of officers' boots, Trostel was again the leading supplier of leather for American combat boots. Trostel supplied the Russian army as well.

The company also began making leather for industrial applications. Trostel and Sons borrowed money and sold land in order to invest $2 million in equipment that would help it gear up for war production. It was able to make leather seals and gaskets, which were used for military vehicles. Trostel also formed a joint venture with a company in Colombia in 1944. Leather supplies worldwide had been stricken by the war, and Trostel needed a South American supplier. By the end of the war, Trostel had recovered from the disasters of the Great Depression. It was a profitable company with a new line of products it had developed for the war, and an overseas partner.

EMPHASIS ON MECHANICAL LEATHER

Albert Trostel, Jr., was keen to make sure the company took advantage of its comfortable postwar position to plan for the future. The so-called "mechanical leather" components the company had manufactured for the war effort became the focus of a new company division in 1946. This was called the Leather Packings Division. Within a few years, the company was also making similar machine parts out of synthetic rubber. In 1952 the Leather Packings Division incorporated as Trostel Packings Ltd., and moved into larger quarters in the town of Lake Geneva, Wisconsin.

The Lake Geneva plant made a variety of polyurethane products, including shoe insoles and carpet padding. Eventually it moved into cast and molded plastics. Trostel Packings became one of the largest suppliers of carburetor cups, a component of automobile manufacturing. The plastic casting business grew so much that it branched off as its own Polymer Compounding Division in 1959. Meanwhile, the tanning business was still growing. Trostel and Sons was one of the world's largest producers of side leather in the 1950s. Its plants employed the most up-to-date equipment, and the company was an innovator in the industry.

However, the U.S. tanning industry came under increasing pressure from overseas manufacturers in the 1960s. Trostel and Sons made several moves to keep its tannery competitive. It opened a plant in Milan, Kentucky, in 1961, in order to take advantage of lower labor costs in the mostly non-unionized South. Albert Trostel, Jr., died in 1962, and Everett Smith became president. Shortly before Trostel's death, the company was approached by executives of a foundering Michigan tannery called Eagle Ottawa. Although the Michigan company was not doing well at the time, Smith believed it had promise, with product lines in furniture-grade leather and in automotive upholstery.

Trostel and Sons acquired Eagle Ottawa in 1961. The two companies remained somewhat separate until 1966, when Eagle Ottawa's offices moved to Milwaukee. By that time, the company was doing well, and was a major supplier of boot leather for U.S. soldiers in the Vietnam War. By the end of the decade, the Trostel plants in Milwaukee and Tennessee were losing money.

The company's equipment was too outdated for it to move into the specialty leather lines that might have sold well. The tannery, once the largest in Wisconsin and one of the largest in the United States, closed for good in 1969.

FURTHER DIVERSIFICATION

The company moved in significant new directions in the 1970s. Everett Smith acquired partial ownership in Trostel and Sons in 1971, as did the head of its Eagle Ottawa subsidiary, Anders Segerdahl. At that point, a holding company, Everett Smith Investments was established to hold Trostel and Sons, Trostel Packings, Eagle Ottawa, and eventually a handful of other companies.

Eagle Ottawa pursued the automotive market in the 1970s, although in many ways this was a trying decade for that industry. The big U.S. automakers were suffering from the encroachment of foreign competitors, and the industry was shifting dramatically to making smaller, more fuel-efficient cars. Eagle Ottawa secured business with the Ford Motor Company, making car upholstery. By the end of the 1970s, Eagle Ottawa was one of Ford's largest leather suppliers. Soon the company had contracts with the other U.S. automakers as well.

Trostel Packings, on the other hand, was losing money at the beginning of the decade, and could not afford to invest in updated equipment. The company refined its focus by the end of the decade, and began producing precision molded parts. These had applications in the auto industry and other machinery industries. During the 1980s, the company began making an array of advanced plastic and rubber components. This business was good, and Trostel Packings opened a new plant in nearby Whitewater, Wisconsin. Meanwhile, its sister company Eagle Ottawa had made such inroads into automotive leather that it opened a new tannery in Iowa in 1984. A few years later, Eagle Ottawa opened another facility, in Juarez, Mexico. This put it closer to the Mexican plants of U.S. auto companies.

INTERNATIONAL MOVES

By the early 1990s, Albert Trostel and Sons was still in the leather tanning business, but entirely through its Eagle Ottawa subsidiary. Eagle Ottawa grew more enmeshed with the global automotive market, and expanded overseas. After opening its plant in Mexico, Eagle Ottawa entered the European market with acquisitions in England. The first was a tannery located in Warrington, called Pierpoint and Bryant. Eagle Ottawa acquired it in 1992 and renamed it Eagle Ottawa, Ltd.

Preface

The St. James Press series *The International Directory of Company Histories* (*IDCH*) is intended for reference use by students, business people, librarians, historians, economists, investors, job candidates, and others who seek to learn more about the historical development of the world's most important companies. To date, *IDCH* has profiled more than 10,860 companies in 113 volumes.

INCLUSION CRITERIA

Most companies chosen for inclusion in *IDCH* have achieved a minimum of US$25 million in annual sales and are leading influences in their industries or geographical locations. Companies may be publicly held, private, or nonprofit. State-owned companies that are important in their industries and that may operate much like public or private companies also are included. Wholly owned subsidiaries and divisions are profiled if they meet the requirements for inclusion. Entries on companies that have had major changes since they were last profiled may be selected for updating.

The *IDCH* series highlights 25% private and nonprofit companies, and features updated entries on approximately 35 companies per volume.

ENTRY FORMAT

Each entry begins with the company's legal name; the address of its headquarters; its telephone, toll-free, and fax numbers; and its web site. A statement of public, private, state, or parent ownership follows. A company with a legal name in both English and the language of its headquarters country is listed by the English name, with the native-language name in parentheses.

The company's founding or earliest incorporation date, the number of employees, and the most recent available sales figures follow. Sales figures are given in local currencies with equivalents in U.S. dollars. For some private companies, sales figures are estimates and indicated by the abbreviation *est.* The entry lists the exchanges on which the company's stock is traded and its ticker symbol, as well as the company's NAICS codes.

Entries generally contain a *Company Perspectives* box which provides a short summary of the company's mission, goals, and ideals; a *Key Dates* box highlighting milestones in the company's history; lists of *Principal Subsidiaries*, *Principal Divisions*, *Principal Operating Units*, *Principal Competitors*; and articles for *Further Reading*.

American spelling is used throughout *IDCH*, and the word "billion" is used in its U.S. sense of one thousand million.

SOURCES

Entries have been compiled from publicly accessible sources both in print and on the Internet such as general and academic periodicals, books, and annual reports, as well as material supplied by the companies themselves.

CUMULATIVE INDEXES

IDCH contains three indexes: the **Cumulative Index to Companies**, which provides an alphabetical index to companies profiled in the *IDCH* series, the **Index to Industries**, which allows researchers to locate companies by their principal industry, and the **Geographic Index**, which lists companies alphabetically by the country of their headquarters. The indexes are cumulative and specific instructions for using them are found immediately preceding each index.

SPECIAL TO THIS VOLUME

This volume of *IDCH* contains entries on Dr. Seuss Enterprises L.P., which manages the estate of popular children's book author Theodore Seuss Geisel, and alternative rock music record producer Matador Records Inc.

SUGGESTIONS WELCOME

Comments and suggestions from users of *IDCH* on any aspect of the product as well as suggestions for companies to be included or updated are cordially invited. Please write:

The Editor
International Directory of Company Histories
St. James Press
Gale, Cengage Learning
27500 Drake Rd.
Farmington Hills, Michigan 48331-3535

St. James Press does not endorse any of the companies or products mentioned in this series. Companies appearing in the *International Directory of Company Histories* were selected without reference to their wishes and have in no way endorsed their entries.

Notes on Contributors

Gerald E. Brennan
Writer and musician based in Germany.

M. L. Cohen
Novelist, business writer, and researcher living in Paris.

Ed Dinger
Writer and editor based in Bronx, New York.

Paul R. Greenland
Illinois-based writer and researcher; author of three books and former senior editor of a national business magazine; contributor to *The Encyclopedia of Chicago History*, *The Encyclopedia of Religion*, and the *Encyclopedia of American Industries*.

Robert Halasz
Former editor in chief of *World Progress* and *Funk & Wagnalls New Encyclopedia Yearbook*; author, *The U.S. Marines* (Millbrook Press, 1993).

Evelyn Hauser
Researcher, writer and marketing specialist based in Germany.

Frederick C. Ingram
Writer based in South Carolina.

Carrie Rothburd
Writer and editor specializing in corporate profiles, academic texts, and academic journal articles.

Christina M. Stansell
Writer and editor based in Louisville, Kentucky.

Frank Uhle
Ann Arbor-based writer, movie projectionist, disc jockey, and staff member of *Psychotronic Video* magazine.

Ellen D. Wernick
Florida-based writer and editor.

A. Woodward
Wisconsin-based writer.

been stricken by the war, and Trostel needed a South American supplier. By the end of the war, Trostel had recovered from the disasters of the Great Depression. It was a profitable company with a new line of products it had developed for the war, and an overseas partner.

EMPHASIS ON MECHANICAL LEATHER

Albert Trostel, Jr., was keen to make sure the company took advantage of its comfortable postwar position to plan for the future. The so-called "mechanical leather" components the company had manufactured for the war effort became the focus of a new company division in 1946. This was called the Leather Packings Division. Within a few years, the company was also making similar machine parts out of synthetic rubber. In 1952 the Leather Packings Division incorporated as Trostel Packings Ltd., and moved into larger quarters in the town of Lake Geneva, Wisconsin.

The Lake Geneva plant made a variety of polyurethane products, including shoe insoles and carpet padding. Eventually it moved into cast and molded plastics. Trostel Packings became one of the largest suppliers of carburetor cups, a component of automobile manufacturing. The plastic casting business grew so much that it branched off as its own Polymer Compounding Division in 1959. Meanwhile, the tanning business was still growing. Trostel and Sons was one of the world's largest producers of side leather in the 1950s. Its plants employed the most up-to-date equipment, and the company was an innovator in the industry.

However, the U.S. tanning industry came under increasing pressure from overseas manufacturers in the 1960s. Trostel and Sons made several moves to keep its tannery competitive. It opened a plant in Milan, Kentucky, in 1961, in order to take advantage of lower labor costs in the mostly non-unionized South. Albert Trostel, Jr., died in 1962, and Everett Smith became president. Shortly before Trostel's death, the company was approached by executives of a foundering Michigan tannery called Eagle Ottawa. Although the Michigan company was not doing well at the time, Smith believed it had promise, with product lines in furniture-grade leather and in automotive upholstery.

Trostel and Sons acquired Eagle Ottawa in 1961. The two companies remained somewhat separate until 1966, when Eagle Ottawa's offices moved to Milwaukee. By that time, the company was doing well, and was a major supplier of boot leather for U.S. soldiers in the Vietnam War. By the end of the decade, the Trostel plants in Milwaukee and Tennessee were losing money.

The company's equipment was too outdated for it to move into the specialty leather lines that might have sold well. The tannery, once the largest in Wisconsin and one of the largest in the United States, closed for good in 1969.

FURTHER DIVERSIFICATION

The company moved in significant new directions in the 1970s. Everett Smith acquired partial ownership in Trostel and Sons in 1971, as did the head of its Eagle Ottawa subsidiary, Anders Segerdahl. At that point, a holding company, Everett Smith Investments was established to hold Trostel and Sons, Trostel Packings, Eagle Ottawa, and eventually a handful of other companies.

Eagle Ottawa pursued the automotive market in the 1970s, although in many ways this was a trying decade for that industry. The big U.S. automakers were suffering from the encroachment of foreign competitors, and the industry was shifting dramatically to making smaller, more fuel-efficient cars. Eagle Ottawa secured business with the Ford Motor Company, making car upholstery. By the end of the 1970s, Eagle Ottawa was one of Ford's largest leather suppliers. Soon the company had contracts with the other U.S. automakers as well.

Trostel Packings, on the other hand, was losing money at the beginning of the decade, and could not afford to invest in updated equipment. The company refined its focus by the end of the decade, and began producing precision molded parts. These had applications in the auto industry and other machinery industries. During the 1980s, the company began making an array of advanced plastic and rubber components. This business was good, and Trostel Packings opened a new plant in nearby Whitewater, Wisconsin. Meanwhile, its sister company Eagle Ottawa had made such inroads into automotive leather that it opened a new tannery in Iowa in 1984. A few years later, Eagle Ottawa opened another facility, in Juarez, Mexico. This put it closer to the Mexican plants of U.S. auto companies.

INTERNATIONAL MOVES

By the early 1990s, Albert Trostel and Sons was still in the leather tanning business, but entirely through its Eagle Ottawa subsidiary. Eagle Ottawa grew more enmeshed with the global automotive market, and expanded overseas. After opening its plant in Mexico, Eagle Ottawa entered the European market with acquisitions in England. The first was a tannery located in Warrington, called Pierpoint and Bryant. Eagle Ottawa acquired it in 1992 and renamed it Eagle Ottawa, Ltd.

KEY DATES

1858: German immigrants Trostel and Gallun found their first tannery in Milwaukee.
1885: Partners Trostel and Gallun split.
1909: Company incorporates as Albert Trostel and Sons.
1933: Founder's son Albert O. Trostel resigns; his son Albert O., Jr., becomes president.
1938: Everett G. Smith hired as financial analyst.
1946: Leather Packings Division founded.
1952: Leather Packings Division becomes Trostel Packings, Ltd., and moves to Lake Geneva, Wisconsin.
1961: Trostel and Sons acquires Michigan tannery Eagle Ottawa.
1997: Trostel Packings changes name to Trostel, Ltd.
2003: Eagle Ottawa expands into China.

company then raised enough money to pay delinquent taxes by selling a warehouse.

The company was still not solvent, however, and had to borrow money from Gustav Trostel's life insurance several times. In 1936 Gustav Trostel and brother-in-law Adolph Finkler both died in the month of May. Less than six months later, Albert O. Trostel also died. Albert and Clara's mansion, once Milwaukee's most expensive piece of real estate, had suffered a terrible fire a year earlier, and the family had abandoned it. The burned wreck was sold to a demolitionist for only $500. The fortune the first Albert Trostel had built was gone, and the whole second generation of Trostels was out of the family business.

MOVING INTO NEW PRODUCTS

After the death of her husband, Clara Trostel resigned her directorship, but she remained concerned about the company her son was then leading. In 1938 she recommended that Trostel and Sons hire a financial analyst. The company hired her choice, a Dartmouth classmate of her husband Albert O., named Everett G. Smith. Smith became treasurer of the company in 1940, and eventually moved to an ownership position.

Albert O. Trostel, Jr., began working as general manager for the family company when he was just out of college. He was president of the firm when he was not yet 30. Although young, he knew the leather business thoroughly, and had the education and insight to move the company in promising new directions. He realized that some of Trostel's techniques were out of date, and he traveled to Europe and employed European consultants in order to bring in more modern processes.

Trostel's travels in Europe also acquainted him with global politics. He foresaw the coming of World War II, and made sure his company was prepared. Trostel and Sons had made a variety of leathers, including fine calf-skin used for women's shoes and purses. In 1939 Albert Trostel decided to move the company into side leather, which was sturdy enough for soldiers' boots. Just as in World War I, when the company had been a major supplier of officers' boots, Trostel was again the leading supplier of leather for American combat boots. Trostel supplied the Russian army as well.

The company also began making leather for industrial applications. Trostel and Sons borrowed money and sold land in order to invest $2 million in equipment that would help it gear up for war production. It was able to make leather seals and gaskets, which were used for military vehicles. Trostel also formed a joint venture with a company in Colombia in 1944. Leather supplies worldwide had

company, while his brother-in-law Albert O. Trostel had taken out loans from the company equaling almost $2 million. At the same time, Gustav and Ida had lent the company $70,000 and $35,000 respectively. Clara Uihlein Trostel, Albert's wife, had lent the company $2.5 million. A meeting of attorneys for all the interested parties straightened out the debt situation, with the largest creditors, Clara and Gustav, forgiving the company its debt to them.

Soon after this meeting, brother Albert O. withdrew from the family business. He formally resigned in 1933, asking that his son Albert O. Trostel, Jr., take his place. Albert, Jr., became vice president of Trostel and Sons when he was only 25 years old. His mother Clara became a director of the company. Part of the arrangement made in 1932 settling the debts of the various family members to the company stipulated that Clara could not lend any more money to Trostel and Sons. However, the company's situation was so bad that it could not pay for hides, and therefore could not produce tanned leather.

Since Clara could not directly lend the company money, she instead bought calf hides in Chicago and gave them to the company in return for a share in their finished price. Clara began to take even more direct action to keep the company afloat. She pushed the company to sell some of its property. This move was not popular with her brothers-in-law. However, Clara had enough proxy votes, and a position on the board, so that she and her son could make the sale happen. The

Next came an automotive leather sewing firm, Callow and Maddox, based in Coventry. Like Eagle Ottawa itself when Trostel acquired it, Callow and Maddox was struggling financially at the time of the sale. However, it was strategically placed to work with leather from the Warrington tannery, and gave Eagle Ottawa a strong base for sales to the European automotive market. Shortly after securing its European base, Eagle Ottawa opened a subsidiary in South Africa.

While Eagle Ottawa focused on automotive leather, Trostel Packings had become a multifaceted plastics company, its heritage in leather tanning no longer evident. In 1997 Trostel Packings changed its name to Trostel, Ltd. In fact it no longer made packings of any kind. Most of its business was in seals for the appliance and auto industries. At the same time as the name change, the company spun off its casting business into a separate company called Trostel Specialty Elastomers Group, or Trostel SEG. This company made cast and molded plastic devices that were used in the automotive, hand tool, appliance, and material handling industries.

GLOBAL GROWTH IN THE 21ST CENTURY

Everett Smith, who had been with the company since 1938, died in 1997. Anders Segerdahl, who had been head of Eagle Ottawa and was also a part owner of Albert Trostel and Sons, took over the chief executive position. The company carried on in the next decade much as it had in the 1990s, with global growth. Expanding its European presence, Eagle Ottawa opened a subsidiary in Hungary in 2001. In 2003 it began a joint venture with a Chinese partner.

At that time, Eagle Ottawa had grown to revenues of around $550 million. By the end of the decade, Albert Trostel and Sons overall had estimated sales of approximately $627 million. Trostel, Ltd., and Trostel SEG had state-of-the-art research and manufacturing facilities in Lake Geneva and Whitewater, Wisconsin, and Trostel Mexico in Reynosa, Mexico. Eagle Ottawa was a truly global company, one of the world's leading automotive leather suppliers.

Trostel's holding company, Everett Smith Group, by that time also held Maysteel, OEM Worldwide, Inc., and Dickten Masch Plastics. The collection of Milwaukee tanneries founded by industrious German immigrants had evolved in multiple ways, some leading away from leather. Nevertheless, the Albert Trostel and Sons companies were still essential players in the supply chain of industries spanning the globe.

A. Woodward

PRINCIPAL SUBSIDIARIES

Eagle Ottawa, Inc.; Trostel Ltd.; Trostel SEG.

PRINCIPAL COMPETITORS

Seidel Tanning Corporation; Thiele Tanning Co.

FURTHER READING

"Albert Trostel, Jr., 53," *New York Times*, February 3, 1962, p. 16.

Dawson, Brad, "Trostel Units Reach Five-Year Deals with Union Staff," *Rubber and Plastics News*, August 25, 2003, p. 3.

Knoche, Eldon, "Everett G. Smith Ran Leather, Steel Firms," *Milwaukee Journal Sentinel*, October 14, 1997, p. 6.

Meyer, Bruce, "Trostel Is Expanding Unit," *Urethanes Technology*, April/May 2001, p. 16.

Rodengen, Jeffrey L., and Richard F. Hubbard, *The Legend of Albert Trostel and Sons*, Fort Lauderdale, FL: Write Stuff Enterprises, 2004.

Amazon.com, Inc.

—■—

1200 12th Avenue South, Suite 1200
Seattle, Washington 98144
U.S.A.
Telephone: (206) 266-1000
Web site: http://www.amazon.com

Public Company
Incorporated: 1994
Employees: 24,300
Sales: $24.51 billion (2009)
Stock Exchanges: NASDAQ
Ticker Symbol: AMZN
NAICS: 454113 Mail-Order Houses

■ ■ ■

Based in Seattle, Washington, Amazon.com, Inc., is an Internet retailing powerhouse, evolving from online bookstore to the purveyor of a wide variety of goods by itself and through third parties. Amazon.com offers programs to help these sellers increase sales through their Web sites and provide fulfillment of their orders. Developers are also served through Amazon Web Services, which offers technology infrastructure services. Additionally, Amazon.com is the manufacturer of the popular Kindle e-reader and generates income through self-publishing, co-branded credit cards, online advertising, and other marketing and promotional services. Almost half of the company's sales (48 percent) originate outside of North America, and about 40 percent take place in the final quarter of the calendar year, spurred by holiday sales. Amazon.com maintains

25 fulfillment centers strategically located in nine states, the United Kingdom, Germany, France, China, and Japan.

COMPANY ORIGINS: 1994

Throughout the 1990s, the popularity of the Internet and the World Wide Web swept across the world, and personal computers in most businesses and households got hooked up in some form or another to Internet providers and Web browser software. As use of the Internet became more prevalent in society, companies began looking to the Web as a new avenue for commerce. Selling products over the Internet offered a variety of choices and opportunities.

One of the pioneers of e-commerce was Jeff Bezos, founder of Amazon.com. In 1994, Bezos left his job as vice president of the Wall Street firm D. E. Shaw, moved to Seattle and began to work out a business plan for what would become Amazon.com. After reading a report that projected annual Web growth at 2,300 percent, Bezos drew up a list of 20 products that could be sold on the Internet. He narrowed the list to what he felt were the five most promising: compact discs, computer hardware, computer software, videos, and books. Bezos eventually decided that his venture would sell books over the Web, because of the large worldwide market for literature, the low price that could be offered for books, and the tremendous selection of titles that were available in print.

Bezos chose Seattle as the company headquarters due to its large high-tech workforce and its proximity to a large book distribution center in Oregon. Bezos then

COMPANY PERSPECTIVES

Amazon, a Fortune 500 company based in Seattle, Washington, is the global leader in e-commerce. Since Jeff Bezos started Amazon in 1995, we have significantly expanded our product offerings, international sites, and worldwide network of fulfillment and customer service centers. Today, Amazon offers everything from books and electronics to tennis rackets and diamond jewelry.

worked to raise funds for the company while also working with software developers to build the company's Web site. The Web site debuted in July 1995 and quickly became the number one book-related site on the Web.

In just four months of operation, Amazon.com became a very popular site on the Web, making high marks on several Internet rankings. It generated recognition as the sixth-best site on Point Communications' "top ten" list and was almost immediately placed on Yahoo!'s "what's cool list" as well as Netscape's "what's new list." The site opened with a searchable database of over one million titles. Customers could enter search information, prompting the system to sift through the company database and find the desired titles. The program then displayed information about the selection on a customer's computer screen and gave the customer the option to order the books with a credit card and have the books shipped in a just a few days.

Unlike its large competitors, such as Barnes & Noble and Borders, Amazon.com carried only about 2,000 titles in stock in its Seattle warehouse. Most orders through Amazon.com were placed directly through wholesalers and publishers, so no warehouse was needed. Amazon.com would simply receive the books from the other sources and then ship them to the customer. At first, the company operated out of Bezos's garage, until it was clear that it was going to be a success, necessitating a move to a Seattle office, which served as the customer support, shipping, and receiving area. Because of the Internet, a small venture could realize a broad scope quickly; within a month of launching the Web site, Bezos and Amazon.com had filled orders from all 50 states and 45 other countries.

As a pioneer in the world of Internet commerce, Amazon.com strived to set the standard for Web businesses. With that goal in mind, Bezos went to work on making the Web site as customer friendly as possible

and relating the site to all types of customers. For those people who knew what book they were looking for and just wanted quick performance and low cost, Amazon. com offered powerful search capabilities of its expanded 1.5 million-title database.

The company also began offering 10 to 30 percent discounts on most titles, making the prices extremely attractive. For other customers who were just looking for something to read in a general area of interest, Amazon.com offered topic areas to browse, as well as lists of best sellers, award winners, and titles that had been recently featured in the media. Finally, for people who could not decide, Amazon.com offered a recommendation center. There customers could find books based on their mood, reading habits, or preferences. The recommendation center also offered titles based on records of books customers had purchased in the past, if they were return customers to the site.

Other hits with customers were the little touches, such as optional gift wrapping of packages and the "eye" notification service, which sent customers e-mails alerting them when a new book in their favorite subject or by their favorite author came into stock. The site also offered customers the ability to contribute their reviews to a customer comment section and peruse the reviews of others.

GOING PUBLIC: 1997

After less than two years of operation, Amazon.com became a public company in May 1997 with an initial public offering (IPO) of three million shares of common stock. With the proceeds from the IPO, Bezos went to work on improving the already productive Web site and on bettering the company's distribution capabilities.

To help broaden the company's distribution capabilities and to ease the strain on the existing distribution center that came from such a high volume of orders, Bezos announced in September 1997 that Amazon.com would be opening an East Coast distribution center in New Castle, Delaware. There was also a 70 percent expansion of the company's Seattle center. The improvements increased the company's stocking and shipping capabilities and reduced the time it took to fill customers' orders. The Delaware site not only brought Amazon.com closer to its East Coast customers, but also brought it closer to East Coast publishers, which decreased the company's receiving time. With the new centers in place, Bezos set a goal for the company of 95 percent same-day shipping of in-stock orders, getting orders to the customers much faster than before.

Another growth area for Amazon.com was the success of its Associate program. Established in July 1996,

```
┌─────────────────────────────────────────────┐
│                                               │
│              KEY DATES                        │
│                   ▪                           │
│  ─────────────────────────────────────────   │
│  1995:  Amazon.com debuts on the Web.         │
│  1997:  The company goes public; Amazon.com   │
│         becomes the first Internet retailer   │
│         to secure one million customers.      │
│  1998:  Amazon.com enters the online music    │
│         and video business; companies are     │
│         acquired in the United Kingdom and    │
│         Germany.                              │
│  1999:  The firm expands into selling toys,   │
│         electronics, tools, and hardware;     │
│         Jeff Bezos is named *Time* magazine's │
│         "Person of the Year."                 │
│  2003:  First annual profit is posted.        │
│  2007:  Kindle e-book reader is introduced.   │
│                                               │
└─────────────────────────────────────────────┘
```

the program allowed individuals with their own Web sites to link to Amazon.com, placing ads for relevant books on their own sites that allowed visitors to click and purchase from Amazon.com. Associates were sent reports on their sales and made a 3 to 8 percent commission from books sold on their sites. The Associates program really began to take off in mid-1997, when Amazon.com formed partnerships with Yahoo! Inc., and America Online, Inc. Both companies agreed to give Amazon.com broad promotional capabilities on their sites, two of the most visited sites on the Web. As the success continued, Amazon also struck deals with many other popular sites, including Netscape, GeoCities, Excite, and AltaVista.

As the company continued to grow in 1997, Bezos announced in October that Amazon.com would be the first Internet retailer to reach the milestone of one million customers. With customers in all 50 states and now 160 countries worldwide, what had started in a Seattle garage was now a company with $147.8 million in yearly sales.

FURTHER EXPANSION: 1998

The company continued to grow. By February 1998, the Associate program had reached 30,000 members, who now earned up to 15 percent for recommending and selling books from their Web sites. Four months later, the number of associates had doubled to 60,000.

The company's customer database continued to grow as well, with cumulative customer accounts reaching 2.26 million in March, an increase of 50 percent in just three months and of 564 percent over the previous year. In other words, it took Amazon.com 27 months to serve its first million customers and only six months to serve the second million. This feat made Amazon.com the third-largest bookseller in the United States. Financed by a $75 million credit facility secured in late 1997, Amazon.com continued to reshape its services in 1998. To its catalog of over 2.5 million titles, the company added Amazon.com Advantage, to help the sales of independent authors and publishers, and Amazon.com Kids, a service providing over 100,000 titles for younger children and teenagers.

Amazon.com also expanded its business through a trio of acquisitions in early 1998. Two of the companies were acquired to further expand Amazon.com's business in Europe. Bookpages, one of the largest online booksellers in the United Kingdom, gave Amazon.com access to the U.K. market. Telebook, the largest online bookseller in Germany, added its German titles to the mix. Both companies not only gave Amazon.com access to new customers in Europe but also gave existing Amazon.com customers access to more books from around the world. The Internet Movie Database (IMDB), the third acquisition, was used to support plans for its move into online video sales. The tremendous resources and information of IMDB served as a valuable asset in the construction of a customer-friendly and informative Web site for video sales.

Another big change in 1998 was the announcement of the company's decision to enter into the online music business. With over 125,000 music titles available, the new site debuted in June 1998 and offered many of the same helpful services available at the company's book site. The database was searchable by artist, song title, or label, and customers were able to listen to more than 225,000 sound clips before making their selection.

GROWTH CONTINUES: 1999

In 1999 the company launched an online auction service titled Amazon Auctions. It also began offering toys and electronics and then divided its product offerings into individual stores on its site to make it easier for customers to shop for certain items. By the holiday season of that year, sales had climbed to $1.6 billion proving that the founder's efforts to create an online powerhouse had indeed paid off. In 1999 Bezos reached the upper echelon of the corporate world when *Time* magazine honored him with its prestigious "Person of the Year" award.

While Amazon.com's growth story was remarkable, Bezos's focus on market share over profits had made Wall Street uneasy and left analysts speculating whether the company would ever be able to turn a profit. Sales continued to grow as the company added new products to its site, including lawn and patio furniture and kitchen wares. The company, however, continued to post net losses. Moreover, the "dot-com boom" of the late 1990s came to a crashing halt in the early years of the new millennium as many start-ups declared bankruptcy amid intense competition and weakening economies.

Bezos remained optimistic, even as Amazon.com's share price faltered. During 2001 the company focused on cutting costs, laying off 1,300 employees and closing a distribution facility. The company also added price reduction to its business strategy, which had traditionally been centered on vast selection and convenience. Amazon.com inked lucrative third-party deals with such well-known retailers as Target Corporation and America Online. By now, products from Toysrus.com Inc., Circuit City Stores Inc., the Borders Group, and a host of other retailers were available on the Amazon.com site.

Amazon.com's strategy worked. In 2001 sales grew to $3.12 billion, an increase of 13 percent over the previous year. During the fourth quarter, Amazon.com reached a milestone that many had regarded as unlikely: It secured a net profit of $5 million. In 2002 the company launched its apparel store, which included clothing from retailers The Gap and Lands' End. Overall, the company reported a net loss of $149 million for the year, an improvement from the $567 million loss reported in 2001. In the fourth quarter of 2002, however, the firm secured a quarterly net profit of $3 million, the second net profit in its history.

TURNING A PROFIT

While securing quarterly net profits was a major turning point for the young company, a July 2002 *Business Week* article observed, "after seven years and more than $1 billion in losses, Amazon is still a work in process." Indeed, the company's foray into providing the "Earth's Biggest Selection" had yet to prove it could provide profits on a long-term basis.

Amazon.com was beginning to win the confidence of investors, who began to bid up the price of Amazon stock, which had fallen as low as $6 in 2001 but rebounded to $58 a share by the end of 2003. Revenues increased 34 percent to $5.3 billion in 2003, and the company posted its first annual profit ($35.3 million). The following year sales approached $7 billion, and the company netted $588.5 million.

To continue its strong growth, Amazon remained innovative. In 2005 it introduced Amazon Prime, a two-day delivery service for all in-stock products at an annual flat fee of $79. The Amazon Pages program allowed customers to purchase online access to specific sections of a book, and the Amazon upgrade program provided optional online access with the purchase of traditional printed books. Not every investment in technology had a direct payoff. For example, a search engine called A9, begun in 2004 to challenge Google, failed to take root, but the effort helped to bolster Amazon's infrastructure.

With revenues of $8.49 billion and earnings of $432 million in 2005, Amazon supplanted AT&T on the prestigious Standard & Poor's S&P 500-stock index. Some investors were not pleased, however, with Amazon's heavy investment in technology, the cost of which cut the company's operating margins to 4.1 percent, compared to more traditional retailers such as Wal-Mart (5.9 percent) and Barnes & Noble Inc. (5.4 percent). Undaunted, Bezos initiated a stock repurchase plan in 2006 and continued to spend on new technology.

THE KINDLE DEBUTS

One of Amazon's major investments was the development of its first consumer electronics product, the Kindle e-book reader, developed by subsidiary Lab126 and released in the United States in November 2007. Amazon was hardly the first company to offer such a device, but its launch was greeted with enthusiasm by consumers. Despite the initial retail price of $399, the Kindle sold out within six hours of its release. A key to the device's success was it ease of use and ability to operate independent of a computer. Building on the success of the device, Amazon introduced a more robust yet thinner version, Kindle 2, in February 2009, and later in the year an international version followed. The more devices Amazon sold, of course, the greater the demand for the e-books it also offered.

In addition to the Kindle, Amazon opened up other new revenue streams by taking advantage of its investment in technology. In 2006 Amazon unveiled Ec2 (Elastic Compute Cloud), a service that made the computing power of its servers available to Web developers. Amazon also helped third-party merchants to increase their business through an initiative launched in 2006 called Fulfillment by Amazon. In essence, merchants shipped their products to an Amazon warehouse and stepped aside while Amazon processed the online orders, shipped goods to customers, processed returns, and even handled customer service. As a result of making online purchasing more consistent and reliable across the board, Amazon benefited from the general improvement in the online customer experience.

Sales continued to grew at a strong clip, reaching $10.7 billion in 2006, $14.83 billion in 2007, and

$19.2 billion in 2008, when net income reached $645 million. Even a recession in 2009 could not derail Amazon as it did other retailers. Sales improved to $24.5 billion and net income to $902 million in 2009, as Amazon was able to take advantage of its broad selection and low prices, coupled with strong service.

Book publishers, on the other hand, were not especially pleased with Amazon. On Christmas Day 2009, Amazon for the first time in its history sold more digital books than printed ones. Fearful that Amazon would gain even more influence in the pricing of digital books than it already had, publishers began cutting deals with other device makers and retail partners to undercut Amazon's leverage. Amazon was hardly successful in every category it pursued, luxury items being a notable disappointment, but there was no doubt that the company would remain a potent force in book selling and niche retailing for years to come.

Robert Alan Passage
Updated, Christina M. Stansell; Ed Dinger

PRINCIPAL SUBSIDIARIES

Lab126; Zappos.com, Inc.; Brilliance Audio, Inc.; Imdb Inc.

PRINCIPAL COMPETITORS

Barnes & Noble, Inc.; eBay Inc.; Wal-Mart.com USA LLC.

FURTHER READING

Ante, Spencer E., "At Amazon, Marketing Is for Dummies," *Business Week,* September 28, 2009, p. 53.

———, "Trying to Avert a Digital Horror Story," *Business Week,* January 11, 2010, p. 50.

"Chewing the Sashimi with Jeff Bezos," *Business Week,* July 15, 2002.

Hazleton, Lesley, "Jeff Bezos: How He Built a Billion Dollar Net Worth before His Company Even Turned a Profit," *Success,* July 1998, pp. 58–60.

Hof, Robert D., "Jeff Bezos' Risky Bet," *Business Week,* November 13, 2006, p. 52.

"How Amazon Cleared the Profitability Hurdle," *Business Week,* February 4, 2002.

Martin, Michael, "The Next Big Thing: A Bookstore," *Fortune,* December 9, 1996, pp. 168–70.

O'Brien, Jeffrey M., "Amazon's Next Revolution," *Fortune,* June 8, 2009, p. 68.

Quitter, Josh, "How Jeff Bezos Rules the Retail Space," *Fortune,* May 5, 2008, p. 126.

Vogelstein, Fred, "Mighty Amazon," *Fortune,* May 26, 2003, p. 60.

Zito, Kelly, "Amazon CEO Tells of Life at the Top," *San Francisco Chronicle,* December 23, 1999, p. B1.

Aon Corporation

—■—

200 East Randolph Street
Chicago, Illinois 60601
U.S.A.
Telephone: (312) 381-1000
Fax: (312) 381-6032
Web site: http://www.aon.com

Public Company
Incorporated: 1980 as Combined International Corporation
Employees: 36,200
Sales: $7.59 billion (2009)
Stock Exchanges: New York
Ticker Symbol: AON
NAICS: 524210 Insurance Agencies and Brokerages

■ ■ ■

Chicago, Illinois-based Aon Corporation is one of the world's largest insurance brokerages, maintaining more than 500 offices in over 120 countries. Clients include corporations, professional organizations, governments, insurance companies, and independent agents and brokers. Individuals are also served through personal lines, specialty units, and affinity groups. Aon divides its business between two segments: Risk and Insurance Brokerage Services and Consulting. The former generates about 83 percent of Aon's total revenues and includes the retail brokerage of insurance products as well as reinsurance brokerage, while the latter provides health and benefits, retirement, compensation advice,

and outsourcing services to clients in the United States and Canada.

COMPANY ORIGINS IN THE EARLY 20TH CENTURY

The corporate structure of Aon originated in 1980, when the Combined International Corporation was set up as a holding company for the acquisition-hungry Combined Insurance Company of America. The latter company had been formed in 1947 through the merger of the Combined Mutual Casualty Company of Chicago and Combined Insurance Company of America of Pennsylvania. Both companies belonged to self-made millionaire and self-help proponent W. Clement Stone. Stone controlled a number of insurance companies operating in various states at the time. He had begun his insurance career at the age of 16. Stone was born on Chicago's south side in 1902. His father died when he was two years old, and by age six, Stone was earning money as a paperboy to help his dressmaker mother. At age 13 the entrepreneurial Stone had his own newsstand. At 16 he embarked on an insurance career, selling policies for an agency his mother had started in Detroit, Michigan.

In 1922, at the age of 20, Stone set up a Chicago-based insurance agency with a $100 investment. During the 1920s the Combined Registry Company, which acted as agent for about six insurers, grew rapidly, employing 1,000 agents nationwide by 1930. The Great Depression hit the company hard, however, and Stone was forced to reduce the number of agents to 135. In 1939 Stone acquired his first insurance company, the

American Casualty Company of Dallas, later known as the Combined American Insurance Company of Dallas. That same year he organized the Combined Mutual Casualty Company of Chicago, followed by the Combined Casualty Company of Philadelphia, renaming it the Combined Insurance Company of America, and paving the way for the 1947 merger.

When the Combined Insurance Company of America got its start just after World War II, the company wrote accident and health insurance, hospitalization, and noncancelable accident and health insurance. An army of door-to-door salesmen carried Combined's policies directly to homes and businesses. At the end of 1947 Combined had assets of $2.2 million.

MID-CENTURY EXPANSION

In December 1949 the company acquired the Boston Casualty Company, an accident and health insurer, and renamed it Hearthstone Insurance Company of Massachusetts. In 1954 Combined acquired the First National Casualty Company of Fond du Lac, Wisconsin. During the 1950s, Combined and its subsidiaries grew substantially. Between 1949 and 1959, premiums increased an average of 17 percent annually while assets jumped from $2.9 million to $20.3 million. The company relied on direct sales of low-cost accident and health policies, which were a good risk for Combined.

Stone's personal philosophy—the "positive mental attitude," or PMA—was the cornerstone of the company's day-to-day operations. Stone, wearing a flamboyant bow tie, was known to enter the boardroom shouting, "Is everybody happy?" Salespersons lived by such slogans as "What the mind can conceive and believe, the mind can achieve" and "When you have nothing to lose and everything to gain by trying, by all means try." Employees were encouraged to greet each day with the upbeat maxim "I feel healthy. I feel happy. I feel terrific."

Sales pitches were memorized and repeated by the company's door-to-door representatives. Stone remarked years later: "It's impossible to fail when you follow this step-by-step set-up." Indeed, Combined Insurance Company's sales continued to expand throughout the 1960s. By 1969 Combined's written premiums totaled $187 million, up from $27 million a decade earlier; assets were $225 million, up from $20.3 million.

In 1965 Combined began selling low-cost, low-benefit life insurance, which gradually became a significant segment of the company's business. In 1968 the company acquired the Commerce and Industry Insurance Company of New York, a fire and property insurer that sold to preferred commercial, institutional, and industrial clients. The Commerce and Industry shares were exchanged for 50,000 shares of the American Home Assurance Company of New York six months later.

WEATHERING LEADERSHIP CHANGES AND RECESSION

In January 1970 Matthew T. Walsh, former executive vice president and international sales manager, became president of Combined Insurance when the 67-year-old W. Clement Stone assumed the new offices of chairman and CEO. Walsh had been with the company since 1946. At the same time, Clement Stone, the 41-year-old son of the founder, became president of Combined's European operations. Although W. Clement Stone stepped down from the day-to-day running of the company, his influence directed the company. Throughout the next decade, Combined pushed overseas.

Having penetrated English-speaking markets including Canada, Great Britain, Australia, and New Zealand in the 1960s, Combined entered West Germany in 1977, France in 1979, and Japan in 1980. Combined tailored its policies to fit conditions in these countries. In New Zealand, for example, where socialized medical programs cover virtually the entire cost of hospitalization and doctors' bills, Combined sold supplemental policies that protected against loss of income in case of illness or accident. By 1980, 17 percent of the company's revenues came from outside the United States.

In December 1971, just two years after assuming the presidency of Combined Insurance, Matthew T. Walsh resigned. Walsh said he was leaving because his years at Combined had given him the financial means to do the things he enjoyed most. W. Clement Stone resumed the president's chair until a replacement could be found. Clement Stone took the reins as president and

KEY DATES

1922: W. Clement Stone establishes the Combined Registry Co. to act as an agent for six insurance companies.

1939: Stone makes his first acquisition.

1980: Combined International Corporation is established as a public holding company.

1987: Company changes its name to Aon Corporation.

1997: Aon becomes the world's largest insurance broker by acquiring Alexander and Alexander Services Inc. for $1.23 billion.

2001: Aon loses 176 employees in New York City terrorist attack.

2004: Restructuring effort is launched.

chief operating officer in 1972 and became CEO in 1973.

The recession of 1973 sent stock prices plummeting. Between 1970 and 1977 Combined's price dropped about 66 percent. Nevertheless, growth continued at an impressive rate during the decade. Because Combined focused on the low end of the insurance market, the company did not suffer from problems that faced other insurers during the late 1970s. While those companies struggled with skyrocketing health costs and accident settlements, Combined prospered. Between 1969 and 1979 assets grew to $1.57 billion, or about 16 percent annually.

NEW HOLDING COMPANY: 1980

By the end of the 1970s, Combined Insurance Company was looking for acquisitions. In 1980 the company formed the publicly owned Combined International Corporation to act as a holding company, in order to avoid state-by-state regulation. The holding company was monitored by the Securities and Exchange Commission and was not subject to scrutiny by each state's insurance commission. In 1981 the new Combined International Corporation made its first acquisition when it bought the Union Fidelity Corporation along with its Nashaming Valley Information Processing unit, for $105.5 million.

Union Fidelity was an accident and health insurer that excelled at direct-response marketing and sold 75 percent of its policies through direct-mail and newspaper campaigns. The unit was expected to give

Combined's door-to-door marketers a needed boost. Combined suffered from the rising costs of recruiting and maintaining a large battalion of field representatives, and the company's domestic sales had been flat for the two years prior to the acquisition.

In March 1982 Clement Stone abruptly resigned as president and CEO of Combined, citing personal reasons. His father once again resumed control of the company. After his resignation, Clement Stone received a $3.4 million consulting contract. At age 79, W. Clement Stone was once again caretaker of the company he had founded. At the same time, the company was troubled by stagnation in domestic premiums. Although the slump in growth was offset in the short term by excellent investment results, a plan to deal with rapidly changing markets was needed.

Combined solved its leadership problems with the acquisition of the Ryan Insurance Company in August 1982. Combined spent $133 million for the 18-year-old specialty insurer and brokerage, which had been a pioneer in credit life insurance for auto dealerships and extended mechanical warranty insurance agreements. Founder Patrick G. Ryan then became president and CEO of Combined. Stone remained chairman. Although W. Clement Stone had called an unexpected adjournment that lasted for five hours at the special shareholders meeting that had been called for the purpose of approving the acquisition, Stone finally approved the deal, and Combined at last had a new leader.

Pat Ryan's management style differed considerably from W. Clement Stone's. Ryan, while himself a good motivator, was generally described as less flamboyant and more diplomatic. The new CEO of Combined demonstrated his approach by announcing a major acquisition just two months after taking charge of the company's operations. Combined purchased the Chicago-based insurance brokerage Rollins Burdick Hunter Company for $109 million. Rollins Burdick, which was well known for its large corporate clients, absorbed Combined's other brokerage operations, making it the eighth largest insurance broker in the United States. The acquisition provided Combined with a source of fee income that was not readily susceptible to decline because of the less competitive nature of corporate insurance.

In 1982, although revenue rose 27 percent, net earnings dropped 19 percent. Ryan began to cut costs and integrate Combined's greatly diversified operations. In 1983 revenues grew 18 percent and operating earnings jumped 47 percent. The Ryan Insurance subsidiary stretched its extended warranty insurance to appliances, and Union Fidelity took advantage of the growing need for supplemental health insurance.

In April 1986 Combined bought the Life Insurance Company of Virginia for $557 million. The acquisition further widened Combined's product line, notably adding an array of interest-sensitive universal life products for upscale markets. In January 1987 the Rollins Burdick Hunter unit bought five regional operations: Allen, Hart, Franz and Zehnder of Los Angeles; Schroeter, White and Johnson of Oakland, California; Pilot Insurance Agency of Winston-Salem, North Carolina; Todorovich Agency of St. Louis, Missouri; and the agency operations of Springhouse Financial Corporation of Philadelphia, Pennsylvania.

AON NAME ADOPTED: 1987

In March 1987 Combined International Corporation's shareholders voted to change the name of the company to Aon Corporation, *aon* being a Gaelic word connoting oneness or bringing together. Patrick Ryan said the name change was necessary to eliminate confusion between the holding company and its subsidiary, Combined Insurance Company of America. Continuing its diversification, Aon bought the employee benefits consulting firm Miller, Mason and Dickenson for $12 million in the summer of 1988 and in September bought the nation's ninth-largest reinsurance agent, Reinsurance Agency.

In January 1989 Aon restructured its subsidiary Rollins Burdick Hunter Company, setting up a holding company to oversee four units: Rollins Burdick Hunter Company, the brokerage; Rollins Specialty Group, a newly created unit concentrating on brokerage services for financial institutions, associations, and affinity groups; Miller, Mason and Dickenson, the newly acquired employee benefits consultant; and Aon Risk Services, a reinsurance brokerage operating through Aon Reinsurance Agency, formerly Reinsurance Agency.

In 1990 Stone left the board of directors and the company he had founded. Ryan continued his growth-through-acquisitions strategy through the early 1990s, maintaining the company's focus on life and health insurance, life underwriting and specialty insurance, and insurance brokerage. In 1991 Aon acquired Hudig-Langeveldt and the following year, Frank B. Hall.

By 1994 Aon had reached sales of more than $4 billion, almost twice the annual sales of the late 1980s. Net income also had doubled, to $360 million. Ryan, however, felt the company needed to shift its focus, eliminating its slow-growing life insurance and annuities business and beefing up its brokerage and specialty insurance businesses. Within a year, Aon had sold off all of its direct life insurance companies. It also added hostile takeover insurance for small and medium-sized businesses to its specialty insurance offerings.

WORLD'S LARGEST INSURANCE BROKERAGE: 1996

Aon became the largest insurance brokerage in the world in 1996, primarily through its purchase of Alexander & Alexander Services Inc. Aon acquired the New York-based brokerage for $1.23 billion. Aon's 1997 purchase of The Minet Group also helped pull the company into the lead. Its number one position was short-lived, however, as the rival brokerage Marsh & McLennan Cos. knocked them out with the purchase of Johnson & Higgins in 1997. Aon's size remained impressive with revenues of $5.8 billion in 1997 and 400 offices in 80 countries.

The company extended its global reach in 1998, with numerous overseas purchases. The most prominent acquisitions included Spain's Gil y Carvajal, France's Groupe Leblace de Nicolay, and Bain Hogg of Britain. Seven other purchases were made, primarily in Europe and Latin America. In addition to its purchases, Aon opened new offices and subsidiaries throughout the world, such as Aon Korea. The following year, Aon continued its international acquisitions, buying the Italian insurance firm Nikols Sedgwick Group, among others.

Expenses related to its acquisitions caught up with Aon in 1999. Although sales had exceeded $7 billion, net income fell to $352 million in 1999, down from $541 million in 1998. Integrating the new businesses and updating their technology were among the largest costs, although a restructuring of Aon's brokerage and consulting businesses added $120 million in costs. The collapse of the workers' compensation pool set up by the insurance firm Unicover Managers Inc. also led to $72 million in expenses for Aon, as the company settled litigation related to its underwriting of those pools.

All told, Aon spent $2.4 billion on acquisitions in the final three years of the 1990s. In 2000 the company suspended its acquisitions program and focused attention on improving profitability and its stock price. In an effort to gain efficiencies and cut costs, Aon laid off 3,000 workers in 2000. A year later it announced that it planned to divest its underwriting unit by spinning it off to shareholders. Because of Wall Street's tepid interest in insurance stocks, the plan never came to fruition, however, and Aon continued to struggle with the effects of an unwieldy collection of uncoordinated assets.

TERRORIST ATTACKS KILL 176 EMPLOYEES: 2001

Aon Corporation also had to contend with tragedy in 2001. The company's office in New York City was located in the upper floors of the World Trade Center's

Twin Towers. On September 11, 2001, terrorists crashed jetliners into the structures, which subsequently collapsed, resulting in the deaths of 176 Aon employees. Rather than abandon lower Manhattan, the company moved into temporary quarters and then reopened in new offices several blocks away in the summer of 2003.

Following the September 11, 2001, attacks most insurance companies prospered through large rate increases, but Aon continued to struggle. More restructuring to reduce overhead was implemented in 2004. The organization was now structured according to geography rather than major lines of business. Aon also made another attempt to cut loose its insurance underwriting business, either through spin-off or sale. More significantly, in October 2004 Ryan announced his retirement as chief executive.

While a search for a new CEO was conducted, Aon had to contend with charges of fraud and anticompetitive practices from regulators in New York, Connecticut, and Illinois. Aon had accepted what were called contingent commissions from insurers, a common practice that was now cast as accepting secret payments from insurers for steering business to them. Aon settled the matter in March 2005 by agreeing to pay $190 million in restitution to policyholders. As a result of the controversy, Aon's stock lost one-third of its value, and the company looked for a new CEO outside of the organization to reassure investors. The man selected was a surprise, 42-year-old Gregory C. Case, a McKinsey & Co. consultant. Prior to McKinsey, the Harvard Business School graduate had also spent time at the Federal Reserve and as an investment banker.

Although Ryan remained as executive chairman, Case was given free rein and quickly moved to clean house, replacing Ryan's executive teams with new faces. Putting his consulting experience to good use, he also proved adept at recognizing redundancies in the organization and brought greater efficiencies to bear to significantly reduce overhead. Moreover, he played the regulatory problems to Aon's benefit. Forced to be more transparent with clients about what they were actually paying for, Aon marketers gained a competitive edge. The company was able to capture a good deal of business from its chief rival, Marsh & McLennan, and eventually succeeded Marsh as the industry leader. Case also succeeded in divesting Aon's underwriting operations, selling Combined Insurance Companies of America to the ACE Group of Companies for $2.56 billion, and Sterling Life Insurance Companies to Munich Re for $352 million. Both deals closed in April 2008.

RYAN RETIRES: 2008

With the money it received from the sale of Combined and Sterling, Aon was able to buy back stock to bolster the share price and build up its Risk and Brokerage Services business with the November 2008 acquisition of Benfield Group Ltd., a major independent reinsurance intermediary. While the details of this transaction were being worked out, Ryan announced his retirement from Aon. He was not, however, retiring from the insurance industry. Following a stint as the head of Chicago's unsuccessful effort to host the 2016 Summer Olympic Games, he formed Ryan Specialty Group in 2010 to become involved in the wholesale insurance marketplace.

After enjoying steady growth from 2005 to 2008, Aon had to contend with a global recession in 2009. While revenues improved slightly to $7.6 billion, net income dropped from $1.46 billion in 2008 to $747 million in 2009. As market conditions improved, however, the company appeared well positioned to regain lost momentum.

Thomas M. Tucker
Updated, Susan Windisch Brown; Ed Dinger

PRINCIPAL SUBSIDIARIES

Allied Group Holdings LLC; Aon Advisors, Inc.; Aon Advisory Services Inc.; Aon Benfield Global, Inc.; Aon Group, Inc.; Aon Finance US LP.

PRINCIPAL COMPETITORS

Arthur J. Gallagher & Co.; Marsh & McLennan Companies, Inc.; Willis Group Holdings Ltd.

FURTHER READING

"Aon's Game Plan for Future," *Business Insurance*, December 18, 2000, p. 2.

"Aon to Spin Off Underwriting Biz," *Crain's Chicago Business*, April 23, 2001, p. 38.

Arndorfer, James B., "Post-Acquisition Expenses Put Brakes on Aon," *Crain's Chicago Business*, April 24, 2000, p. 9.

Daniels, Steve, "Aon Fasts as Rivals Feast," *Crain's Chicago Business,* May 6, 2002, p. 1.

———, "Aon Spinoff Sputters as Market Sags," *Crain's Chicago Business,* July 22, 2002, p. 3.

———, "Odd Man In: Does Aon CEO Have the Chops?" *Crain's Chicago Business,* April 11, 2005, p. 1.

Fritz, Michael, "The Man Who Made Aon a Global Power," *Crain's Chicago Business,* June 2, 1997, p. 1.

Garino, David, "Clem Stone Discovers That Positive Thinking Sells Insurance Policies," *Wall Street Journal,* February 27, 1969.

"Healthy Policy: Combined Insurance Thrives at Low End of Market," *Barron's,* February 4, 1980.

Johnsson, Julie, "Acquisitions Bolstering Insurer Aon's Bottom Line," *Crain's Chicago Business,* April 26, 1999, p. 28.

Machan, Dyan, "Devouring Risk," *Forbes,* August 23, 1999, p. 106.

Martin, Sara, and Joanne Wojcik, "Aon Settles Fraud Suits," *Business Insurance,* March 7, 2005, p. 1.

Roberts, Sally, "Aon Founder Seeks to Build New Insurance Venture," *Business Insurance,* February 15, 2010, p 1.

Strahler, Steven R., and Steve Daniels, "Pat Ryan Express Jumps the Tracks," *Crain's Chicago Business,* November 18, 2001, p. 1.

Weber, Joseph, "A Scandal Turns into a Blessing," *Business Week Online,* January 23, 2008.

Arcapita Bank B.S.C.

Batelco Commercial Center
Building 14, Block 304
Al Khalifa Avenue
Manama,
Bahrain
Telephone: (+973) 1721-8333
Fax: (+973) 1721-7555
Web site: http://www.arcapita.com

Private Company
Incorporated: 1997 as First Islamic Investment Bank
    B.S.C.
Employees: 305
Sales: $648.5 million (2008)
NAICS: 523110 Investment Banking and Securities
    Dealing

■ ■ ■

Arcapita Bank B.S.C. is a Bahrain-based international investment bank operating out of offices in Bahrain, Atlanta, London, and Singapore. Arcapita focuses on corporate investment, real estate investment, asset-based investment, and venture capital. Target sectors in the corporate investment realm include consumer, health care, energy, technology, and manufacturing. Real estate sectors include health care, senior living, residential, warehousing, retail, resort, and residential. The bank's asset-based investment team focuses on the oil and gas, utility, and transport infrastructure industries. On the venture capital side, Arcapita focuses on U.S. health care, information technology, and industrial technology.

What differentiates Arcapita from the vast majority of the world's investment banks is its adherence to Islamic law. Arcapita abides by the Shari'ah principles of Islamic law that provide guidance in all aspects of a Muslim's life. Aside from avoiding investments in companies related in any way to alcohol, tobacco, gambling, adult entertainment, or pork products, Arcapita has to contend with a ban on earning interest on borrowed money, which is considered usury.

To stay within the confines of Shari'ah, Arcapita typically acquires specific assets of a company, which it then leases back to the borrower at a profit. At the conclusion of the lease, the borrower is able to pay a fee to acquire title to the assets. To ensure that its investments meet religious criteria, Arcapita submits each deal for approval from a four-person Shari'ah advisory panel that at one time consisted of a retired judge from Saudi Arabia's Supreme Court as well as religious scholars from Bahrain and Pakistan. Since its inception, Arcapita has been led by its chief executive officer, Atif A. Abdulmalik.

ARCAPITA FOUNDED: 1997

Traditional Islamic banking focused on Murabaha accounts in which a bank avoided forbidden interest charges by purchasing assets from a borrower, who then bought it back in installments that included a profit margin for the bank. Atif A. Abdulmalik and the cofounders of First Islamic Investment Bank sought to modernize the concept, recognizing that there were numerous medium-risk investment opportunities, especially in the United States, that could comply with Shari'ah principles.

Abdulmalik was educated in the United States, graduating with a degree in accounting, finance, and management from Saint Edward's University in Texas. He then became a certified public accountant in Maryland and an executive with Investcorp Bank E.C., a New York-based investment firm backed by Middle Eastern investors. Abdulmalik and his cofounders then approached a wealthy Saudi Arabian family, who agreed to fund the new enterprise, and in April 1997 First Islamic Investment Bank was licensed in Bahrain.

First Islamic established a branch in London, England, called Crescent Capital Investments (Europe) Limited, as well as in Atlanta under the name Crescent Capital Investments Inc. The Atlanta subsidiary was also established by former Investcorp executives, who opted for Atlanta rather than New York in order to be "a big fish in a smaller pond," in the words of its president, David Crosland. Two of Crescent's first six acquisitions were Atlanta companies. The firm's intent was to be "actively passive" investors, to help existing management teams formulate a strategy and provide the necessary funds for growth, but beyond that to take a hands-off approach. Crescent also looked to hold a company from three to five years.

First Islamic's initial U.S. investment through Crescent was the $215 million acquisition in 1998 of a pair of leading kayak and canoe manufacturers, Perception Group, Inc., and Dagger Canoe Company. They were then merged to form WaterMark Paddlesports Inc. As a result of this U.S. investment, First Islamic reported net income of $12 million in 1998.

HIGH-TECH ACQUISITIONS: 1999

Crescent also looked to the high-technology field, another area that presented no conflicts with Shari'ah tenets. In May 1999 Crescent invested $178 million in Computer Generation Incorporated, an Atlanta company that tracked telephone or Internet usage for billing purposes. Later in 1999 Crescent paid $63.9 million for a majority stake in DVT Corporation, an optical sensors firm. Crescent was able to build value in both companies and sell them at a profit before the collapse of the technology sector.

A major acquisition completed in 2000 by Crescent was Minneapolis-based Caribou Coffee Co. at $80 million. The small coffee store chain was looking for an infusion of cash to continue in its effort to compete against Starbucks. A year later, following the terrorist attacks against the United States of September 11, 2001, Caribou found itself the subject of an Internet-fueled boycott because of its Muslim ownership, despite the clear difference between the conservative and devout nature of Islamic investing and the radical, political Islam espoused by the extremists behind the attacks on New York's World Trade Center and the Pentagon in Washington, D.C.

First Islamic also had to contend with some of its Middle Eastern investors who withdrew their money, fearful that assets would be seized in the name of antiterrorism. First Islamic persisted, however, and continued to invest in the United States, which continued to offer a multitude of investment opportunities. The Middle East, on the other hand, had a limited number of investment opportunities that were being chased by too many parties to provide sufficient returns.

21ST-CENTURY ACQUISITIONS

One of the opportunities in the United States that presented no religious conflicts was the senior living sector. In March 2002 First Islamic formed a joint venture with Virginia-based Sunrise Assisted Living, Inc., to acquire stakes in 12 assisted living properties in such markets as New York, Los Angeles, Chicago, Detroit, Philadelphia, and Virginia. First Islamic and its investors owned an 80 percent interest in the venture.

Other significant U.S. investments in the early years of the 21st century included Cirrus Industries, a Minnesota single-engine aircraft manufacturer, and Destination Outdoors Inc., a kayak and marine products manufacturer, in 2001; Smart Document Solutions, a health document processor, in 2002; and American Pad & Paper, a Texas-based provider of paper-based office products in 2003. The firm in 2004 added TLC Health Care Services and paid $190 million for the Loehmann's off-price retail chain. The Church's Chicken restaurant chain was acquired as well. First Islamic had rejected other restaurant investments because of the presence of pork. A chicken eatery was a natural fit, albeit one Church's recipe had to be altered, with turkey replacing pork as an ingredient.

While the majority of its investments were made in the United States through Crescent in Atlanta, First Islamic did not neglect Europe or the Middle East. In 2004, for example, the firm created a $300 million joint

KEY DATES

1997: First Islamic Investment Bank B.S.C. is formed.
1998: First investments are made in United States.
2005: First Islamic is renamed Arcapita Bank.
2007: Singapore office opens.
2010: ARC Real Estate Income Fund is formed.

venture to develop a themed residential community around Bahrain's Riffa Golf Course, and a $500 million joint venture to develop a golf-themed resort in Dubai.

First Islamic also became more active in Europe during this time. It acquired interests in wind farms developed in the United Kingdom by a branch of Germany's RWE, as well as a U.K. water supply company, South Staffordshire Plc. Also in 2004 First Islamic completed its first European corporate acquisition, buying a significant stake in a French kitchen and bathroom retailer, VGC SA.

ARCAPITA NAME ADOPTED: 2005

First Islamic was also making plans to rename its operation. Not only were there other banks that made use of the phrase "First Islamic Investment," the crescent moon was a common symbol of Islam and as a result "Crescent" could be found in the names of many financial institutions as well as other companies. Hence in March 2005, First Islamic was renamed Arcapita Bank B.S.C., and Crescent Capital in Atlanta became Arcapita Inc., while the London branch took the name Arcapita Limited.

Following the name changes in 2005, Arcapita divested some of its holdings, including DVT Corporation and a pair of U.S. real estate portfolios acquired in 2000. Also in 2005 Arcapita initiated plans on three new major residential developments in the Middle East that would include a new corporate headquarters for the firm. It also teamed up with Elysian Development Group in the United States to develop a 60-story high-rise tower in Chicago.

Later in 2005 Arcapita acquired majority control of Falcon Gas Storage Company Inc., a major U.S. owner of natural gas storage capacity. Moreover, Arcapita Inc. in Atlanta launched a venture capital fund under the Arcapita Ventures banner to invest in later stage health care and information technology companies, primarily located in the southeastern United States. In 2005 Ar-

capita Bank reported net income of $104.3 million, a 48 percent increase over the prior year's $70.5 million.

Arcapita completed a major deal in Europe in early 2006, paying about $200 million for Roxar AS, a provider of technology services and equipment to the oil and gas industry. Arcapita divested its Sunrise assisted living assets in 2006 and then in the summer replenished its coffers further, raising about $400 million to double its capital, a move that also allowed the firm to borrow as much as $1.5 billion. This was more than enough to fund opportunities the firm hoped to pursue in China and India.

In the meantime, Arcapita acquired a Finnish building materials manufacturing company, Paroc Holding Sverige, A.B., for EUR 650 million. As 2006 came to a close it completed the $4.2 billion acquisition of Viridian Group plc, a Northern Ireland-based electricity utility.

SINGAPORE OFFICE OPENED: 2007

To support its Asian aspirations, Arcapita opened a branch in Singapore in 2007. Not only did Arcapita seek area investments, it hoped to take some of its U.S. and European portfolio companies into Asia. Arcapita established an investment trust that it planned to take public on the Singapore Exchange, but market uncertainty ultimately led Arcapita to make a private placement instead.

Arcapita meanwhile continued to pursue opportunities in the United States. In early 2007 Arcapita Inc. acquired Tennessee-based Sanus Holdings, LLC, a major dental practice management company with 50 dental clinics focusing on providing care to underprivileged children that did business as FORBA. Late in the year Arcapita added Varel International, Inc., a fast-growing Texas manufacturer of drill bits for the oil and gas industry doing business in 22 countries. Also of note in 2007 was Arcapita's profitable divestiture of Roxar.

A new area of emphasis was infrastructure investments, including warehousing as well as utilities and sewage treatment. In 2008 Arcapita acquired Pinnacle, a leading Eastern European warehousing company. The firm also formed a joint venture with ProLogis to develop a $1 billion network of warehouses in Saudi Arabia and the Persian Gulf. Arcapita then added to this sector by acquiring French logistics provider Compagnie Europeenne de Prestations Logistiques, which operated 23 sites in France and Germany.

In 2010 Arcapita formed the $500 million ARC Real Estate Income Fund to invest in warehouses as well as health care and education-related assets in the Middle East. Arcapita also remained interested in residential projects, in late 2008 launching development of a residential golf project in Qatar.

A significant development for Arcapita in 2009 was the sale of Church's Chicken, providing a return that was two-and-a-half times its investment. Church's also greatly benefited from Arcapita's ownership, moving into new markets in the United States and expanding into Latin America, the Arabian Gulf, the United Kingdom, Russia, and India. Global system sales increased to more than $1.2 billion and earnings increased 60 percent. It was this kind of mutually beneficial deal that Arcapita was likely to strike in the future as it continued to pursue investment opportunities guided by adherence to the Shari'ah principles of Islamic law.

Ed Dinger

PRINCIPAL SUBSIDIARIES

Arcapita Inc.; Arcapita Limited; Arcapita Pte. Limited.

PRINCIPAL COMPETITORS

Oak Hill Capital Partners; PAI Partners; Summit Partners.

FURTHER READING

Dunkley, Clare, "Coming Home to Roost," *Middle East Economic Digest,* December 10, 2004, p. 38.

———, "Developing the Backyard," *Middle East Economic Digest,* December 23, 2005, p. 53.

Kerr, Simeon, "Arcapita Seeks to Get Its Hands Dirty," *Financial Times,* May 13, 2008, p. 13.

Monroe, Matt, "Crescent Rising in Atlanta," *Atlanta Business Chronicle,* March 5, 2001.

Paul, Péralte C., and Shelia M. Poole, "Branching Out, with Limits," *Atlanta Journal-Constitution,* July 30, 2006, p. E1.

Siddiqi, Moin, "Gulf Super Rich Seek Secure Home for Trillion-Dollar Assets," *Middle East,* April 2009, p. 32.

Tripathi, Salil, "Islamic Banks Adopt Global Portfolio," *Asian Business,* December 1997, p. 58.

Useem, Jerry, "Banking on Allah," *Fortune,* June 10, 2002, p. 154.

B. Braun Medical Inc.

■

824 12th Avenue
Bethlehem, Pennsylvania 18018
U.S.A.
Telephone: (610) 691-5400
Fax: (610) 691-6249
Web site: http://www.bbraunusa.com

Wholly Owned Subsidiary of B. Braun Melsungen
Incorporated: 1956 as Burron Medical Products
Employees: 4,099
NAICS: 423440 Other Commercial Equipment Merchant Wholesalers

■ ■ ■

Based in Bethlehem, Pennsylvania, B. Braun Medical Inc. is the U.S. subsidiary of B. Braun Melsungen, a German medical supply company. Braun produces health care products for drug delivery, intravenous therapy, pain control, clinical nutrition, dialysis, and vascular intervention. Products include syringes and caps, needle-free systems, vascular access products, vascular interventional products, containers, filtering devices, dialysis products, irrigation/urology sets, duplex and premixed drugs, infusion pump systems, pain control products, and nutrition products such as concentrated dextrose, fat emulsion, and amino acid combinations.

COMPANY FOUNDED: 1956

Although a subsidiary of a German company, B. Braun Medical was established in Bethlehem, Pennsylvania, as

Burron Medical Products, the name an amalgamation of the last names of the cofounders, George K. Burke Sr. and his father-in-law, Anthony J. Ronca. Burke was the driving force of the company. Born in Philadelphia, Pennsylvania, in 1927, he was orphaned at a young age and raised by relatives. After a stint in the Navy, he earned a degree in biochemistry from Pennsylvania State University in 1950. He then worked for Johnson & Johnson and Bethlehem-based R.K. Laros Company. In 1956 he struck out on his own, forming Burron Medical Products with financial backing from Ronca, a Bethlehem building contractor.

Burron was a one-product company, focusing on the development and manufacturing of the revolutionary mostly plastic disposable syringe, a version of which Burke invented. He filed papers with the patent office in October 1958 and received his patent in February 1961. The syringe held numerous advantages, including the time saved from repeated sterilization of hypodermic needles and syringes, and the elimination of cross contamination. It found a ready market and established Burron Medical in the health care industry. Burke also developed locking mechanisms used to connect intravenous pumps and other devices.

Burron suffered a devastating fire in 1974 that burned for three days. Insurance did not fully cover the loss, but Burke decided to rebuild in Bethlehem to make sure his 200 workers were employed. They reciprocated by helping to rebuild the plant and going without pay for nine months. The industry was changing, however, and Burron faced stiff competition from high-volume producers of syringes, making it imperative for the company to diversify. Burke decided to sell the business to a company with deeper pockets, National Patent Development Corporation of New York City, which bought Burron in 1976. Burke stayed on to run the business until he retired in 1977 at the age of 50.

BURRON SOLD TO BRAUN: 1979

National Patent held onto Burron until 1979, when it was sold to the West German company B. Braun Melsungen. Like Burron, Braun was a family concern, but much older. It was founded in Melsungen, Germany, in 1839 by Julius William Braun. What started out as a pharmacy grew into a medical products company. In 1909 B. Braun introduced the first sterile resorbable suture, followed by the first commercially prepared intravenous (IV) solution in 1929.

At the same time Burke was developing his disposable syringe, B. Braun began selling the first disposable plastic syringe. Despite its innovativeness, however, the company was generating just $24 million a year, none of which came from the U.S. market. A new chief executive took over in 1979, Ludwig Georg Braun, who was in his early 30s at the time. One of his priorities was to break into the hospital supplies market in the United States.

Diether Otto, a B. Braun executive, was dispatched to the United States to find an acquisition to lay a foundation for a U.S. business. Otto considered six U.S. companies, but settled on Burron, in large part because of its location in Pennsylvania's Lehigh Valley, which possessed German cultural roots and a work ethic that meshed well with the German company. In November 1979 B. Braun bought Burron for $6.25 million.

Although Otto became chairman of Burron, he retained the company's management and was the only German at the company. Serving as chief executive was Frank W. Petrie, who had joined Burron in 1973 and succeeded Burke. Nevertheless, B. Braun shifted Burron's emphasis away from syringes, which was then little more than a commodities business, and toward higher margin specialty hospital products. The new strategy proved effective. In a matter of five years Burron

increased annual revenues from $6 million to about $30 million, and the workforce grew from 230 employees to 700. After losing money, Burron also began turning a profit.

NEW WAREHOUSE OPENS: 1985

Burron quickly outgrew its 126,000-square-foot plant. Although the company could have relocated to an area where labor was less costly, it opted to remain in Bethlehem. In the early 1980s Burron launched a multiphase $35 million, 500,000-square-foot expansion program on a 30-acre site in Lehigh Valley Industrial Park. The first phase was a $3 million, 60,000-square-foot packaging and final production warehouse that opened in 1985. Further parts of the expansion program were completed in 1989 and 1992.

One of Burron's most successful new products, introduced in the late 1980s, was a passive needle-free intravenous delivery system, Safsite, the first product of its kind. Several years later the company brought out Ultrasite, a capless, positive pressure valve that prevented the drawback of fluid, thus greatly reducing catheter blockages. Another organic driver of growth was the 1991 creation of subsidiary Central Admixture Pharmacy Services, Inc., which created a nationwide network of pharmacies to provide safe pharmacy admixtures. This allowed hospital pharmacies and outpatient surgery center pharmacies to improve patient care and expand services without having to take on the expense of additional staff.

NAME CHANGED: 1992

Burron also grew through acquisitions. In the summer of 1992 it acquired the Medical Products division of Minneapolis-based Angeion Corporation, which primarily made accessory devices used in cardiovascular procedures. Also in 1992 Burron changed its name to B. Braun Medical Inc. A year later Petrie retired, leaving behind a company that had increased annual sales to the $100 million mark. Replacing him as chief executive was 47-year-old Richard B. Trchak, executive vice president, who had come over from National Patent when Burke sold the business, stayed after the sale to B. Braun, and since 1986 had served as chief financial officer.

In 1996 Caroll H. Neubauer took over as chairman and CEO. Although born in New Jersey, he was a dual citizen of Germany and the United States. His father was a German veterinarian who worked in the United States. Neubauer was educated in both countries, attending boarding school in Germany and earning law degrees from Albert-Ludwigs University in Germany

```
┌─────────────────────────────────────────┐
│                                           │
│              KEY DATES                    │
│                   ■                       │
│  ─────────────────────────────────────   │
│  1956: Burron Medical Products is founded.│
│  1976: Company is acquired by National    │
│        Patent Development Corporation.    │
│  1979: B. Braun Melsungen acquires Burron.│
│  1992: Named is changed to B. Braun       │
│        Medical Inc.                       │
│  2006: Plant expansion program is         │
│        launched.                          │
│                                           │
└─────────────────────────────────────────┘
```

and Georgetown University in Washington, D.C. He became general counsel at B. Braun and director of human resources before taking charge of the U.S. operation in October 1996. He retained his seat on the parent company's board of directors, thus influencing decisions that impacted the U.S. company.

In 1997 Neubauer was able to advocate for an important Braun acquisition, the $320 million purchase of Irvine, California-based McGaw Inc. from IVAX Corp. McGaw was a pioneer in the intravenous solution field. Not only did the deal add $340 million in revenues, but it also transformed Braun into a full-line supplier of intravenous therapy in the United States. Because of the size of McGaw, there was some consideration of moving Braun's headquarters to California, but again Neubauer used his influence, insisting that the company remain in the Lehigh Valley, with jobs that would have gone to California coming instead to Pennsylvania.

POSITIVE DEVELOPMENTS IN THE 21ST CENTURY

Unlike other industries Braun did not turn to outsourcing as the new century dawned. In fact, the sterilization of finished products, something that had been previously outsourced, was brought back to the Lehigh Valley. At the home facility, with improved equipment and better training, the company was able to significantly lower the error rate, which proved to be a major competitive advantage in the hospital marketplace.

Braun was able to expand its business with Premier, a nationwide alliance of 1,500 hospitals and health systems. In 2001 Braun signed a contract to sell more of its safety products to Premier. Two years later Braun signed a five-year contract with Premier worth about $4 billion to supply a full line of infusion products. Another factor favoring Braun's prospects in the new century was the November 2000 passage of the Needlestick Safety and Prevention Act that required health care facilities to minimize accidental needlesticks by adopting

safer medical devices, such as Braun's needle-free delivery products.

Braun enjoyed other positive developments in the early years of the 21st century. The company reached an agreement in 2003 with New Jersey-based Vyteris Inc. to market and distribute a transdermal lidocaine system on a worldwide basis for dermal anesthesia used in the preparation for a number of invasive procedures, including venipunctures, blood draws, and immunizations. A year later Braun was granted a patent on its wireless communications pump technology for the administration of intravenous solutions. Not only did the technology reduce medication errors, it was more efficient and streamlined reporting for hospitals and other health care providers.

In 2005 Braun introduced ultraviolet (UV) resistant tubing, eliminating the degradation of drugs caused by sunlight, as well as CefTRIaxONE, a new intravenous antibiotic preparation. A new suite of infusion therapy products were added in 2007, as well as a new anesthesia product, the Stimuplex Pen, a noninvasive percutaneous nerve mapping device.

Braun also increased revenues through agreements with Novation, the supplier of VHA Inc. and the University HealthSystem Consortium. In 2007 Braun added an outpatient market sales and marketing organization to drive the sale of its surgical sutures in the non-acute marketplace, in particular the surgery center and oncology markets.

NEIGHBORING PLANT ACQUIRED: 2006

To keep pace with an expanding array of products and increasing demand, Braun made plans to expand its Lehigh Valley operation. Helped by $6.7 million in state aid, the $100 million, two-phase plan was expected to add at least 300 jobs and as many as 500. In 2006 Braun paid $9.4 million for a 26-acre former Sure Fit slipcover plant, which had closed two years earlier. Although the plant was not suitable for the kind of manufacturing performed by Braun, it was perfectly located next to Braun's Hanover Township facility.

The expansion plan called for the Sure Fit facility to be torn down to make way for a smaller plant. More space would also be added to the main Braun plant. Another smaller plant was also planned to produce intravenous solution bags. Such a facility was a longer-term effort, due in large measure to the approval process required by the U.S. Food and Drug Administration that could take as long as five years.

Moreover, Braun had to deal with zoning issues. To produce the solution bags, a tower as tall as 110 feet was required, but Hanover Township had a 50-foot height limit on all structures, essentially to control the size of office towers. Because the plant could provide 250 jobs and was not able to produce solutions without the tower, a zoning variance was granted. With the new facilities Braun was well positioned to enjoy further growth and deepen its roots in Pennsylvania's Lehigh Valley.

Ed Dinger

PRINCIPAL SUBSIDIARIES

B. Braun OEM; Central Admixture Pharmacy Services, Inc.

PRINCIPAL COMPETITORS

Antares Pharma Inc.; Baxter International Inc.; Phar-MEDium Healthcare Corporation.

FURTHER READING

Blumenau, Kurt, "B. Braun Adds at Least 300 Jobs," *Morning Call,* November 10, 2006, p. A1.

Deogun, Nikhil, "Ivax to Sell Its McGaw Intravenous Unit to German Company in Strategy Shift," *Wall Street Journal,* June 2, 1997, p. B6.

Kunsman, Ken, "Burron Is Changing Name to B. Braun Medical," *Morning Call,* March 18, 1993, p. B11.

Kupper, Thomas, "Braun Medical Grows with Industrial Parks," *Morning Call,* June 19, 1996, p. B10.

Salamone, Anthony, "A Medical Marvel—B. Braun Keeps on Succeeding Despite Shaky Economy," *Express-Times,* September 28, 2003, p. D1.

Shope, Dan, "Braun Chief Finds Roots in the Valley," *Morning Call,* February 8, 1998, p. D1.

Wirth, Paul, "Germans' Gamble in Burron Pays Handsomely," *Morning Call,* July 8, 1984, p. D1.

Banco Azteca, S.A., Institución de Banca Múltiple

———— ■ ————

Insurgentes Sur 3579, Torre 2
Mexico City, D.F. 14000
Mexico
Telephone: (52 55) 8582-7000
Fax: (52 55) 8582-7656
Web site: http://www.bancoazteca.com.mx

■ ■ ■

Wholly Owned Subsidiary of Grupo Elektra, S.A. de C.V.
Incorporated: 2002
Employees: 18,207
Sales: MXN 17.77 billion ($1.34 billion) (2009 est.)
Stock Exchanges: Mexico City
NAICS: 522110 Commercial Banking; 522210 Credit
Card Issuing; 522220 Sales Financing; 522291
Consumer Lending; 522310 Mortgage and Other
Loan Brokers

Banco Azteca, S.A., Institución de Banca Múltiple, is
the financing arm and a wholly owned subsidiary of
Grupo Elektra, S.A. de C.V., a holding company
controlled by Ricardo Salinas Pliego, a billionaire who is
one of Mexico's richest men. Organized to finance
purchases made on credit at Elektra's chain of furniture,
home appliance, and consumer electronics outlets,
Banco Azteca has grown to become one of the nation's
largest Mexican-owned banks. It has expanded to other
Latin American countries in the same way as it has done
in Mexico: by extending credit to low-income customers
all but ignored by established banks. Banco Azteca is
listed on Mexico City's stock exchange, but its stock is
not quoted.

BANCO AZTECA FOUNDED: 2002

Banco Azteca was founded in 2002 by Salinas and given
a name reflecting his TV Azteca S.A. company, owner of
the second-largest television network in Mexico. It was
the first Mexican-owned bank to be chartered since the
nation's 1994 financial crisis that resulted in the
nationalization of the entire banking sector. The new
institution began by offering three types of services:
consumer credit, savings accounts, and forwarding the
remittances of Mexicans working in the United States to
their family members in Mexico.

Banco Azteca built its business on the 1.6 million
Elektra customers who over the years had borrowed a
total of close to $500 million to finance their purchases.
Grupo Elektra had been Latin America's largest
consumer finance company as well as its largest specialty
retailer. Elektra had also been managing an annual
volume of between $800 million and $1 billion sent
home from the United States in the form of remittances
by Mexican workers. For savings accounts the bank
formed an alliance with Banca Serfin, a bank that had a
product called Mi Guardadito, meaning roughly, "My
Stash." Banca Serfin had been managing nearly a million
of these small savings accounts, almost half of which
held less than MXN 50 (about $6).

Banco Azteca began operating with nearly 900
branches throughout Mexico. Approximately 600 of
these were in Elektra stores. There were 90 more in Salinas y Rocha outlets and 61 in Bodega De Remates

KEY DATES

2002: Ricardo Salinas Pliego founds Banco Azteca.
2004: The bank begins issuing debit cards and mortgage and auto loans.
2005: Banco Azteca issues credit cards and opens branches in Panama.
2008: The bank makes its first South American appearance, opening branches in Peru and Brazil.
2009: Banco Azteca ranks second among Mexican banks in number of savings accounts.

units, two other retail chains owned by Grupo Elektra. Another 136 were in the stores of THE ONE, a clothing chain also owned by Grupo Elektra. Before the first year was over the new bank was offering the same installment plans as Grupo Elektra's chains, which were in the process of phasing out their own consumer financing departments. Banco Azteca had also received authorization to extend loans that did not depend on store purchases and had begun to offer one-year personal loans of up to $350.

MAKING CREDIT AVAILABLE TO MILLIONS

Although Banco Azteca was taking on customers who had very little earning power and, in many or most cases, no banking history, it used Elektra's experience to weed out poor risks. The giant retailer monitored credit applicants by sending out thousands of motorcycle-riding agents to visit their homes and examine their pay receipts and utility bills. These same agents were responsible for collecting payments if clients were unable to make payments at Banco Azteca branches. In the case of nonpayment and unwillingness to restructure personal loans, a separate team collected collateral such as television sets and refrigerators. The merchandise would then be resold by a group of Elektra-owned used-goods stores.

Elektra's database held the payment histories of four million existing and former customers. The retail chain claimed a default rate of only 3 percent on installment loans made to families with as little income as $250 a month, despite annual interest rates of at least 40 percent and often much more. As a bank, Azteca was eligible to borrow money at an interest rate of about 8 percent a year, while Elektra had been paying 13 percent for access to funds.

At that rate, microlenders like Banco Azteca found it easy to pay back their own loans. They sometimes found that they could finance their activities from their own cash flow without borrowing money. Their customers were unsophisticated consumers who had little or no experience dealing with banks and focused on the weekly payment instead of interest rates. The need to make weekly payments kept them coming back to the bank branch and, Grupo Elektra executives hoped, to an adjacent group-owned store.

In its first month of operation Banco Azteca claimed to have opened approximately 160,000 new accounts. This number represented less than 1 percent of the almost 17 million households in what was called the popular sector: the 80 percent of Mexican households with monthly incomes of less than MXN 12,000 (about $1,400). Traditional banks considered the profit margin to be earned by serving such customers too low to justify reaching out to them.

EXPANDING OPERATIONS

A year after opening its doors, Banco Azteca reported that it had two million accounts totaling about $400 million in deposits. It also reported a similar amount in personal loans. The bank's chief executive said that Azteca had about 1.5 million loans outstanding, at an average of $250 to $260 per account. The bank was also granting in-store credit to customers of several smaller, non-Elektra retailers.

In 2003 Banco Azteca received permission to open a pension fund, which took the name Afore Azteca and became a separate subsidiary of Grupo Elektra. At the beginning of the following year it began to issue debit cards, extend mortgage and auto loans, and buy and sell dollars for pesos. Mortgage loans were offered for the purchase of houses subsidized by a federal government agency. Management sought to persuade companies to pay their employees directly through the bank's branches, thereby allowing these workers to use cards at automated teller machines (ATMs). By late 2005 it had such agreements with 25 companies.

Banco Azteca introduced its own credit card, which required weekly payments, in 2005. Also that year, Seguros Azteca, a separate insurance subsidiary of Grupo Elektra, was founded. The bank began to operate outside Mexico for the first time, opening branches in Panama. By early 2007 Banco Azteca had seven million customers, four-fifths of whom had never had opened a bank account before, and more than $3 billion in assets.

INTERNATIONAL GROWTH

By mid-2008 Banco Azteca was present in Guatemala and Honduras as well as Panama. During the year the bank made its first appearance in South America, with branch openings in Peru and Brazil. In 2009 Banco Azteca entered El Salvador as well. The Elektra chain was also growing abroad. Salinas forecast that in 2015 some 40 percent of the revenues of Grupo Elektra would be coming from outside Mexico.

Grupo Elektra's entry into Brazil, a country of almost 200 million people comparable in area to the contiguous 48 states of the United States, was noteworthy because both the retail and banking sectors there were characterized by already developed markets and well-heeled local competitors. The group made its first move cautiously, opening 19 combined store-bank branches in the northeastern state of Pernambuco, which was located in one of Brazil's poorest regions.

Salinas predicted that the group could have 2,000 outlets in Brazil in the next five years. Economic analysts were skeptical. Brazil already had centralized systems of credit information as extensive as Grupo Elektra's own, available to all banks and retailers, and at lower cost. According to the nation's central bank, Banco Azteca's rate of interest for personal loans in early 2009 was the third highest among 96 financial institutions in Brazil. Among 49 institutions offering credit for consumer purchases, Banco Azteca was also third highest.

Salinas was looking north as well as south of Mexico, casting an eye on acquiring Circuit City Stores, Inc., the struggling second-largest electronic goods retail chain in the United States and Canada. He was seemingly handicapped by an earlier agreement with the Securities and Exchange Commission in which he settled allegations of fraud by paying a fine and agreeing not to direct any firm quoted on a U.S. stock exchange until 2011. Salinas planned to get around the restriction by taking Circuit City private. However, in 2009 Circuit City's senior creditors opted for liquidation, causing Salinas to lose $39 million already invested in the chain.

DOMESTIC STANDING

Among banks in Mexico, Banco Azteca passed BBVA Bancomer in 2006 in terms of the number of demand deposits. These deposits constituted 97 percent of Azteca's capital in 2009 and were highly profitable, since the bank was paying only 4.5 percent annual interest to the depositors, which was not much higher than the inflation rate.

By mid-2009 Banco Azteca had 7.4 million savings accounts, second only to BBVA Bancomer in number and representing more than one-third of such accounts in Mexico. Guardadito was the bank's main savings ac-

count product. Such an account could be opened with only MXN 50 (about $4) and might, unlike those of other banks, come with a debit card, but it paid only .25 percent in annual interest.

In terms of number of branches, Banco Azteca ranked third in Mexico, all open every day of the year for 12 hours a day. It authorized 13,000 credit approvals a day and performed 7.3 million operations a week. However, as the world financial crisis caused the Mexican economy to fall into recession, the bank did not rate well by some other measures.

With its emphasis on microlending, Banco Azteca ranked only 10th among Mexican banks in size, as measured by total assets. At the end of 2009, the portion of its credit portfolio in arrears was 8.4 percent. This figure was considerably higher than for the banking system as a whole, although it compared favorably to that recorded by such microlending peers as Banco Ahorro Famsa and BanCoppel.

ADDITIONAL PRODUCTS AND SERVICES OFFERED

Banco Azteca had 1,580 point of sale locations in Mexico at the end of 2008. Of these, 827 were located in Elektra stores and 55 in Salinas y Rocha stores. The other 698 were in independent stores. The bank had eight million active accounts at the end of 2007.

In addition to Guardadito, Banco Azteca was offering Guardadito en Dólares, a savings account in dollars for customers living near the U.S. border and in the states of Baja California and Baja California Sur. Guardakids was a savings account for children that could be opened with only MXN 10 (less than $1). Ganaré Más ("I'll Earn More") was a fixed-term product that offered better returns but required a minimum balance of MXN 1,000 (about $80).

Guardadito accounted for 23 percent of Banco Azteca's deposits of MXN 42.41 billion ($3.14 billion) at the end of 2008. The chief source of deposits, accounting for 68 percent, was Inversión Azteca. This demand deposit product offered a variety of interest rates, depending on the length of the deposit. The minimum deposit was MXN 1,000.

Installment loans to buy merchandise sold by Elektra and Salinas y Rocha accounted for 72 percent of Banco Azteca's credit portfolio at the end of 2008. They were available for periods ranging from 13 weeks to two years. The average loan period was 58 weeks. Personal loans were available to a limit of MXN 30,000 ($2,255). The average life of these loans was 62 weeks.

Another 22 percent of Banco Azteca's credit portfolio consisted of commercial and services loans. Some of these were to corporate clients for short-to-medium periods. Another product was designed for small-scale manufacturers, merchants, and service providers. Still another consisted of microcredit for sole proprietors at the bottom of the economic base.

Mortgage loans were available for terms of five to 20 years, with a 10 percent down payment required. Auto loans were made for a period of up to five years for new cars and four years for used ones. They required a down payment of 20 percent.

Banco Azteca's revenues reached MXN 17.8 billion ($1.32 billion) in 2008, slightly more than the previous year when taking the inflation rate into account. However, the growing financial crisis took a heavy toll on its net profit, which fell from MXN 664 million ($60.92 million) in 2007 to MXN 36 million ($2.67 million). Revenue totals in 2009 were largely unchanged at MXN 17.77 billion ($1.34 billion), but net profit climbed to MXN 477 million ($35.86 million).

Robert Halasz

PRINCIPAL SUBSIDIARIES

Banco Azteca del Perú S.A.; Banco Azteca do Brasil S.A. (Brazil); Banco Azteca (Panama) S.A.; Servicios Ejecutivos y Laborales, S.A. de C.V.

PRINCIPAL COMPETITORS

Banco Ahorro Famsa, S.A., I.B.M.; Banco Comparamos S.A., I.B.M.; BanCoppel, S.A.; Financiera Independencia, S.A.B. de C.V.; Grupo Financiero BBVA Bancomer, S.A. de C.V.; Grupo Financiero Banamex, S.A. de C.V.

FURTHER READING

"Azteca Exports Winning Formula," *Banker,* July 2008, p. 100.

Conger, Lucy, "A Bank for Mexico's Working Families," *New York Times,* December 31, 2002, pp. W1, W7.

Epstein, Keith, and Geri Smith, "The Ugly Side of Micro-Lending," *Business Week,* December 24, 2007, pp. 39–46.

Perdomo-Riveros, Cristóbal, and Rafael Borbón, "La Banca popular en México," *Reforma,* March 10, 2003, p. 8.

Smith, Geri, "Buy a Toaster, Open a Bank Account," *Business Week,* January 13, 2003, p. 54.

Tegel, Simeon, "The Company Store," *Latin Trade,* September 2002, p. 38.

"Underwear and Overdrafts; Mexican Banking," *Economist,* November 25, 2006, p. 76.

Banco do Brasil S.A.

SBS Edificio Sede III
24th Floor
Brasília, DF 70073-901
Brazil
Telephone: (+55-61) 3310-5920
Fax: (+55-61) 3310-3735
Web site: http://www.bb.com.br

Public Company
Incorporated: 1808
Employees: 89,369
Total Assets: BRL 488.18 billion ($207.2 billion) (2008)
Stock Exchanges: São Paulo
Ticker Symbol: BBAS3
NAICS: 522110 Commercial Banking

■ ■ ■

With a history dating back over 200 years, Banco do Brasil S.A. is Brazil's largest financial group. The company has approximately 16,000 locations in Brazil, over 24 million clients, and operations in over 20 countries. Along with traditional retail banking, the company is involved in insurance, bonds, asset trading, portfolio management, financial securities advising, and market analysis and research. During 2010, Brazil's government owned just over 65 percent of the company.

EARLY HISTORY

The history of Banco do Brasil intertwines with that of Brazil itself. A Portuguese colony since 1500, Brazil was for centuries held under tight commercial restraint,

forbidden any industry except for shipbuilding and sugar manufacturing. Even salt, in this coastal country, was imported from Portugal.

Restrictions were relaxed in the early part of the 19th century as Portugal faced war after ignoring Napoleon's demand that all European ports be closed to the British. With no prospect of fighting off Napoleon, Portugal's prince regent, Dom Joáo, his family, and 15,000 subjects fled across the Atlantic Ocean to Brazil. Joáo established a monarchy in Rio de Janeiro and improved trade relations between Brazil and Europe. He created the Banco do Brasil on October 12, 1808, before Portugal had its own bank, as the bank for the Portuguese Court. It was Portugal's principal depository for years.

The bank built schools and hospitals, investing heavily in the country well into the late 1800s. Banco do Brasil also equipped Brazil's navy in its battles for independence from Portugal in the 1820s. When Brazil became a republic in 1889, the bank was a major player in restoring stability to the country's economy. Brazil had been left in a shambles after the Portuguese conflict, which caused the fall of the monarchy. During the period of rebuilding, Banco do Brasil became the country's main bank, the government's financial agent, and both a commercial and development bank focusing on rural areas, exports, and domestic business.

STIMULATING AGRICULTURAL DEVELOPMENT

In the last decades of the 19th century, there was another switch in the country's structure, when Brazil's

COMPANY PERSPECTIVES

Mission: To be the solution in services and financial intermediation, to meet the expectations of customers and shareholders, to strengthen the commitment between employees and the Bank, and to contribute towards the development of the Country.

slaves became wage earners. In 1888 Banco do Brasil signed an agreement with the government to ensure the availability of credit for agriculture. The new financing encouraged immigrant settlement in rural areas and was the beginning of an organized push to develop agriculture. The bank opened a branch in 1908 in Manaus, the heart of the Amazon region, to stimulate rubber production. Financial incentives brought people from all over the world, but especially from Italy, to Brazil's rich and plentiful coffee plantations. The flood of immigrants continued at the dawn of the 20th century.

Internally, Banco do Brasil was cleaning its house. The bank began giving public exams to new employees. So rigid were the tests that in 1909, 10 out of the 35 candidates could not even complete the exam. Of the remainder, only nine passed.

In 1937 the bank created its Agricultural and Industrial Credit Division (CREAI). The division provided the country with a credit program to encourage and support agricultural and industrial development. With the assistance of CREAI, Companhia Siderúrgica Nacional, Brazil's first steel mill, was built in the 1940s.

CREAI was involved in almost every aspect of Brazilian agriculture, from rice, cashew nuts, and fruit, to sugarcane and coffee. CREAI's agricultural activities eventually turned Banco do Brasil into one of the world's largest agricultural banks. In 1941 Banco do Brasil laid the foundation for foreign trade support, opening a branch office in Asunción, Paraguay, and then later that same year opening its export and import division.

During World War II, Banco do Brasil provided the troops' payroll as well as war reparations and money transfers to the Brazilian Expeditionary Force. To help operations, three offices were opened in Italy and mobile units were sent to the front lines. The bank also set up a special system through which soldiers could withdraw or deposit cash using passbook entries.

Banco do Brasil's foreign activities continued long after the war, and in 1953 it established a foreign trade division. However, it was in 1969, with the opening of its branch in New York, that the bank really became international.

A DECADE OF CHALLENGES: 1960–69

The 1960s were a time of upheaval for all Brazilian banks. In 1964 the government, with increasing inflation on its hands, faced the deficiencies of the country's financial institutions. At the time, short-term lending was the business of commercial banks, which gave them dominance over other financial institutions. Long-term financing was carried out by state institutions, but with growing inflation, these loans were no better than "donations," according to Oswaldo R. Colin, chairman of the board for Banco do Brasil.

The 1964 Banking Reform Law totally restructured the banking system. New types of securities became available, special credit services were offered, and medium- and long-term investments were favored. Banks began to compete by offering increased services such as guaranteed overdraft checking rights and credit cards, and competition, especially among commercial banks, heated up.

The Banking Reform Law and resolutions that followed initiated a move away from small, specialized banks toward larger institutions offering a variety of services. In 1950, for example, Brazil had 404 banks, but by 1972, there were only 128. In the late 1960s and 1970s the number of branches grew from about 4,000 to 11,000.

MOVING INTO NEW MARKETS: 1970–89

In 1975 Banco do Brasil created a fund for scientific research, backing many health and agricultural projects such as the manufacture of artificial arteries, vaccines against measles, hydroelectric turbines suited for rural areas, and better methods for extracting sugar from cane.

Supporting Brazil's business community, especially small businesses, had become a major concern for the bank by the end of the 1970s, and in 1979 the bank created a program that provided financial assistance and technical guidance to small businesses. In 1982 the bank offered a fund to increase agricultural activity, diversify crops, and foster cottage industries. Other projects included building dams, schools, health centers, and small hospitals.

Banco do Brasil entered the credit card business in 1987, signing with Visa International and announcing

KEY DATES

1808: Dom João establishes Banco do Brasil.
1964: The Banking Reform Law restructures Brazil's banking system.
1969: Company opens a branch in New York.
1987: Banco do Brasil enters the credit card business.
1994: Brazil's currency changes to the real.
1996: Company posts losses; the government gives Banco do Brasil a BRL 8 billion capital infusion.
2000: Internet banking is launched.
2006: Banco do Brasil lists on the New Market section of the Bovespa stock exchange.
2008: Company acquires Banco do Estado Piaui, as well as a majority stake in Banco Nossa Caixa.
2009: A majority stake in Banco Votorantim is purchased.

plans to issue one million cards that first year. Prior to Visa, the bank offered no credit card and up until the mid-1980s handled most of its business through deposits. Being the largest country in Latin America, with 140 million people, Brazil represented an attractive new market for Visa.

In 1988 a new finance minister, Mailson Ferreira da Nobrega, came into power and Banco do Brasil's president, Camilo Calazans, was replaced by the finance ministry's general secretary, Mario Berard. The move came on the heels of the forced resignation of Brazil's central bank president. Brazil had a direct election of a president in 1989, which was the first such election since 1960. Fernando Collor de Mello was elected that year but resigned in 1992 amid a corruption scandal that led to impeachment proceedings.

A NEW CURRENCY: 1994

During the early 1990s, Banco do Brasil faced challenges related to Brazil's changing political environment. The company's profits had long benefited from extraordinarily high inflation rates but that began to change during this time period. Fernando Henrique Cardoso became the country's minister of finance in 1993 and introduced the Plano Real, or Real Plan, that was designed to reduce inflation by launching a new currency called the real. Cardoso was elected president of Brazil in 1994 and remained at the helm until 2003.

Under Cardoso's regime, Banco do Brasil was given the task of changing all currency in Brazil to the new Brazilian real in 1994. The company claimed it was the largest physical currency exchange to ever take place in the world. By July 1, 1994, the company had distributed BRL $3.8 billion to 31,000 bank branches across Brazil.

At the same time, Cardoso initiated a major restructuring effort at Banco do Brasil in an attempt to reduce overstaffing and eliminate bad debt. During 1995 the company launched a voluntary dismissal program that resulted in the reduction of over 13,000 jobs. It also began to shutter unprofitable branches. During the first half of 1995 the company posted losses of $2.61 billion. Losses continued in 1996 as the company worked to overhaul its financial structure. It received a BRL $8 billion capital infusion from the government that year after writing off a significant amount of bad loans.

Banco do Brasil returned to profitability in 1997, having cut costs and offering new credit options to clients in capital markets as well as in the retail and insurance sectors. It also focused on developing its new Technological Center and received an ISO 9002 certification in credit analysis. Banco do Brasil launched Internet banking in 2000.

LOOKING TOWARD THE FUTURE

Banco do Brasil spent the early years of the new millennium changing its organizational and share ownership structure. On a corporate level, the company adopted an executive board structure with a board of officers and committee levels. It also structured its business operations into three segments: wholesale, retail, and government.

At the same time, the company transferred its preferred shares into common shares, which would allow Banco do Brasil to be listed on the New Market section of the Bovespa stock exchange. The New Market traded common shares of companies considered to have high corporate governance levels. As a result of listing on this section, Banco do Brasil was required to provide minority shareholders with a host of new rights, including annual meetings with market analysts, financial statements provided in English, and financial information made available on the Internet. The company was listed on the New Market in 2006, offering its shares to the public in 2006 and again in 2007.

As one of the largest financial institutions in Latin America, Banco do Brasil began to purchase state-owned regional banks to bolster its holdings. During 2007 it acquired Banco do Estado de Santa Catarina (BESC). It purchased Banco do Estado Piaui in a $37.2 billion deal in 2008. In addition, it added the São Paulo state-owned Banco Nossa Caixa to its arsenal. In early 2009 the company announced plans to buy nearly 50 percent of Banco Votorantim for $2.35 billion. The deal strengthened Banco do Brasil's motor vehicle financing arm.

Brazilian President Luiz Inácio Lula da Silva called for the resignation of Banco do Brasil's CEO in April 2009, claiming the interest rates the bank was charging its credit clients were too high. CEO Antônio Francisco Lima Neto stepped down and was replaced by Aldemir Benedine.

While the financial crisis in the United States spread across the globe, Brazil and its large banks remained profitable. During 2008 Banco do Brasil posted a record BRL 9.7 billion in net profit. Newly elected CEO Benedine outlined a plan of expansion for the future that included making inroads into the United States, Japan, Paraguay, and Portugal. While the economic health of the United States and other important markets remained in question, Banco do Brasil believed it was well positioned for growth in the years to come.

Updated, Christina M. Stansell

PRINCIPAL SUBSIDIARIES

BB Gestão de Recursos–Distribuidora de Títulos e Valores Mobiliários S.A.; BB Banco de Investimento S.A.; BB Banco Popular do Brasil S.A.; BB Leasing S.A.; BESC Distribuidora de Títulos e Valores Mobiliários S.A. (99.62%); BESC Financeira S.A. (99.58%); BESC Leasing S.A. (99%); Banco do Brasil AG; BB Leasing Company Ltd.; BB Securities LLC; BB Securities Ltd.; Brasilian American Merchant Bank; Cia. de Seguros Aliança do Brasil; Brasilveículos Companhia de Seguros (70%); Brasilcap Capitalizações S.A. (49.99%); Brasilprev Seguros e Previdência S.A. (49.99%); Brasilsaúde Companhia de Seguros (49.92%); Seguradora Brasileira de Crédito à Exportação (12.09%).

PRINCIPAL COMPETITORS

Banco Bradesco S.A.; Caixa Econômica Federal; Itaú Unibanco Multiplo S.A.

FURTHER READING

"Banco do Brasil Approves Absorption of State-Owned Bank," *Global Insight Daily Analysis*, November 12, 2008.

"Banco do Brasil Completes Acquisition of Votorantim Stake," *Global Banking News*, October 1, 2009.

"Banco do Brasil Share Sale Approaches," *Gazeta Mercantil*, June 10, 2002.

"Banco do Brasil Takes Skeleton out of the Closet," *Financial Times*, August 3, 1995.

"Brazil: Banks Expand Their Horizons," *Economist Intelligence Unit-Business Latin America*, January 25, 2010.

Jelmayer, Rogerio, "Brazil Fires Bank's CEO, Citing Rates," *Wall Street Journal*, April 9, 2009, p. A6.

Jelmayer, Rogerio, and Tom Murphy, "Banco do Brasil Plans Acquisition," *Wall Street Journal*, January 10, 2009, p. B8.

Katz, Ian, "Brazil's Banks Discover a Profit Machine," *Business Week*, October 23, 1995.

Moffett, Matt, "Bearding the Beast: Brazil's New President Has Monster to Tame," *Wall Street Journal*, October 5, 1994, p. A1.

"The Pain after the Profits," *Financial Times*, April 19, 1996, p. 17.

Beall's, Inc.

1806 38th Avenue East
Bradenton, Florida 34208
U.S.A.
Telephone: (941) 747-2355
Fax: (941) 746-1171
Web site: http://www.beallsinc.com

Private Company
Founded: 1915
Employees: 11,000
Sales: $1.23 billion (2008 est.)
NAICS: 452111 Department Stores (Except Discount Department Stores); 453112 Discount Department Stores

■ ■ ■

Based in Bradenton, Florida, Beall's, Inc., is a privately owned holding company for Beall's Department Stores, Inc.; Beall's Outlet Stores, Inc.; and Burke's Outlet Stores, Inc. Beall's Department Stores are located throughout Florida, offering a wide variety of apparel for women, men, children, and juniors, as well as home décor, housewares, and bed and bath merchandise. The Beall's Outlet stores, offering off-price merchandise, are found in about 150 locations in Florida, 30 in Georgia, and 20 in Arizona.

The outlet concept is also operated under the Burke's name in other Sunbelt states, including Alabama, Arkansas, California, Louisiana, Mississippi, North Carolina, New Mexico, Nevada, South Carolina, Tennessee, and Texas. While the three operating companies make their own buying, merchandising, and advertising decisions, they share back office functions, including finance, human resources, distribution, and information systems. Although the Beall family controls the company, employees own a portion of it through a 401(k) plan.

FIRST BRADENTON STORE OPENS: 1915

Beall's was founded by Robert M. Beall when he was 22 years old. Originally from Georgia, he moved to Florida in the wake of a boll weevil plague that devastated Georgia's cotton crop. After briefly running a store in Ocala, Florida, Beall bought the Globe general merchandising store in Palmetto in 1914. A year later he moved the business across the Manatee River to the ground floor of the St. James Hotel in Bradenton. There it became a "dollar limit" clothing store, aptly named The Dollar Limit, with nothing priced over a dollar. With only $2,500 at his disposal, Beall used all of his money on inventory, opting to use the packing cases for his stock as makeshift tables. The dollar format proved popular but inflation caused by World War I made it unprofitable. In 1918 Beall raised the maximum price to $5 and the store was renamed the V (Five) Dollar Limit.

In 1925 Beall acquired some nearby property and opened a larger V (Five) Dollar Limit Store. A few years later, however, the stock market crashed, plunging the country into the Great Depression. Business suffered and during the 1930s Beall's bank seized control of the store. Beall continued to run it, saved his money, and in 1940 bought back the business. In that same year, his son, Egbert Ruffin "E. R." Beall, joined him. The younger Beall was a 1939 University of Florida graduate. A year after he went to work for his father, the United States became involved in World War II and he joined the Army Air Corps. He was not discharged until 1946, the same year the family store was renamed Beall's Department Store.

SECOND STORE OPENS: 1956

Following a brief recession, the U.S. economy boomed during the postwar years, Florida's population began to swell, and Beall's Department Store prospered. E. R. Beall, who had attended the Wharton School of Finance, was eager to expand the business, and in 1956 he opened a second Beall's Department Store in West Bradenton at the Westgate Shopping Center. His father, in the meantime, continued to manage the original store until shortly before his death in 1979. Despite his advancing years he clung to his daily routine of walking the day's deposit to the bank, never aware that, by this time, the police were accompanying him in the background. The downtown store was finally closed in 1986.

E. R. Beall took advantage of the growth of the Publix supermarket chain in the 1950s and 1960s to add more department stores. As a Publix supermarket opened in a shopping center, a Beall's "junior" department store (so called because of the smaller format) often followed. A third department store opened in Venice, Florida, in 1961, followed by stores in several other small Florida towns served by Publix. By the end of the decade Beall's was operating six stores. The third generation of the Beall family became involved in the business in 1970, when E. R. Beall's son, Robert M. Beall II, joined the company.

ROBERT BEALL II NAMED CEO: 1980

A 1965 graduate of the University of Florida who had served in the Reserve Officers Training Corps, Robert

Beall became a second lieutenant in the U.S. Army, completing his military service in Washington, D.C. He then earned a master of business administration degree from New York University and became a trainee and assistant buyer at Bloomingdale's. He would also work at another major New York department store, B. Altman & Co.

It was in 1970 that his father telephoned and asked if he would return home to Florida to open a seventh Beall's department store in Dunedin, Florida. Robert Beall agreed and began his tenure with the business established by his grandfather and namesake. He rose through the ranks of the organization to become chief executive officer in 1980, providing the energy and expertise needed to take the company to new heights.

Robert Beall II took over a chain of 20 department stores with combined annual revenues of $38 million. In order to continue growing the business, however, it was clear that Beall's had to upgrade its distribution operation, which shared space with the Bradenton headquarters store and did not possess even a conveyor belt. A new 18,000-square-foot distribution center was then opened. While it offered more space, it remained a rudimentary operation that still relied on workers processing merchandise by hand. In August 1983 a 17,000-square-foot addition was completed, bringing with it a conveyor system, electronic scanning, and computerized ticketing capabilities.

Improved distribution allowed Beall's to accelerate the pace of its growth. By the end of 1984 the chain totaled 34 department stores and annual revenues were in the $70 million range. Also contributing to the balance sheet were a pair of specialty ventures, a two-store off-price division called Just Labels and a three-unit junior apparel division doing business as Junior Images. Neither proved to have staying power and eventually closed. This was not to be the case, however, for the Beall's Outlet concept introduced in 1987.

EMPLOYEES GAIN OWNERSHIP STAKE: 1986

The outlet stores were developed to take advantage of the emergence of outlet malls in Florida. The outlet stores also allowed Beall's to move into urban markets, including Jacksonville, Orlando, and Tampa. By the end of the 1980s, annual revenues for Beall's approached $200 million. Another important factor in the company's growth surge was its employees, who became even more motivated in their work in 1986 when Beall's implemented a 401(k) plan that incorporated a stock purchase option in which the company matched employee contributions up to $300 per pay period to

KEY DATES

1915: Robert M. Beall opens Dollar Limit Store in Bradenton, Florida.
1946: Business renamed Beall's Department Store.
1956: Second department store opens.
1987: Beall's Outlet chain launched.
2006: First non-family member named chief executive officer.

LARGER STORES IN THE 21ST CENTURY

Long known for their small footprints, about 35,000 square feet, Beall's stores began moving into much larger locations in the new century. The new locations were about double the size, with expanded shoe, housewares, and gift departments in order to better compete against the likes of Wal-Mart and Target. Beall's also took advantage of a retailer that proved less nimble than other discount merchandisers, Kmart, acquiring several former Kmart stores in Florida and converting them to the Beall's Department Store format. Another factor in Beall's success was its Florida focus, which gave it a better idea of what customers wanted than its national competitors. In keeping with this advantage, Beall's added a Florida Marketplace section that offered select gifts, housewares, and food items.

The department stores were expanding into Central Florida and the Panhandle area and also increasing sales by enlarging their footprints, all despite a downturn in the economy. The outlet stores under the Beall's and Burke's names were also adding locations throughout the southern edge of the United States. In the first three years of the 21st century, 200 new stores were added, bringing the total to more than 400 stores in 13 states.

Outlet sales increased to $300 million in 2002 and $400 million in 2003. Smaller outlet stores began to expand to offer a greater range of clothing as well as books, CDs, DVDs, and toys. The company was also testing a Beall's Home Outlet concept along with Coastal Home by Bealls, offering home fashions with a tropical feel associated with Florida's coastal and resort communities. Another test format was Bealls Kids, a clothing store serving the children's market.

Revenues topped $900 million in 2004. A fourth generation of the Beall family was working for the company, Matt Beall, the son of Robert M. Beall II. A graduate of the MBA program at Stetson University, the younger Beall had worked as a buyer at Ross stores before starting a three-year orientation program at Beall's. His father, well into his 60s, was ready to cut back on his responsibilities, but with Matt Beall not yet seasoned enough to take charge, the first non-family member was named chief executive officer in 2006. The choice came down to longtime executives Steve Knopik, president of Beall's Inc., and Conrad Szymanski, president of Beall's Outlet, Inc. Knopik was chosen for the post, and a year later Szymanski left the company.

Also in 2007 Beall's moved into a new corporate headquarters. Annual sales topped the $1.2 billion mark in 2008. There was every reason to believe that the company would continue to grow in the years to come. Moreover, with a fourth generation of the Beall family

buy shares of Beall's stock. Beyond that, the company paid 25 cents on the dollar. In all, it was an attractive benefit, and a large percentage of Beall's employees took the opportunity to become shareholders. As a result, they developed a keen interest in the company's performance.

The major driver in the growth of Beall's was the outlet stores. As the company saturated the Florida market, it began to look for out-of-state opportunities. In 1992 it opened its first outlet store in Arizona, a state similar to Florida in that both had a large retiree population. Other Sunbelt states were to follow, with the outlet stores operating under both the Beall's and Burke's Outlet banners. Annual sales from the outlet stores reached $100 million in 1995 and $200 million just four years later.

Despite the success of its department stores and outlet stores, Beall's remained willing to test new concepts, a practice that had served it well since the beginning. More involved in urban markets, Beall's found that it had to change its approach to the young men's and juniors markets. Unlike the rural communities where Beall's appealed to grandmothers, who bought clothing to send out of state, Beall's faced young adult customers who shopped for themselves. In addition to updating styles and adding shelf space to carry more apparel, Beall's in the early 1990s tested a concept called Outlets, a moderately priced juniors and young men's apparel specialty store concept. Although Outlets failed to take roots, it demonstrated Beall's refusal to grow complacent.

A more successful sideline established in the 1990s was My Gift Cottage, a gifts and collectibles retailer that by the start of the new century generated $13 million in annual sales from 29 stores located in Florida and Georgia as well as an Internet site. Beall's increased total sales to $456.3 million in 2000. The year 2000 was also noteworthy because it brought the death of 85-year-old E. R. Beall.

learning the business, the company was likely to remain an independent chain.

Ed Dinger

PRINCIPAL SUBSIDIARIES

Beall's Department Stores, Inc.; Beall's Outlet Stores, Inc.; Burke's Outlet Stores, Inc.

PRINCIPAL COMPETITORS

Kohl's Corporation; Target Corporation; Wal-Mart Stores, Inc.

FURTHER READING

Albright, Mark, "Beall's Reaches Outside Family for New CEO," *St. Petersburg Times,* August 8, 2006.

"Beall, Son of Store Founder, Dies at 82," *Tampa Tribune,* March 24, 2000, p. 4.

"Bradenton, Fla.-Based Retail Chain Looks toward Expansion," *Bradenton Herald,* July 25, 2002.

Coletti, Richard J., "Baby Beall's?" *Florida Trend,* October 1992, p. 73.

"For Beall's, Bigger Is Always Better," *Bradenton Herald,* February 14, 2005.

Jones, Rochelle, "Division of Bradenton, Fla.-Based Retail Chain See Sales Top $400 Million," *Bradenton Herald,* July 25, 2003.

"Moving Forward at Bealls," *Bradenton Herald,* October 15, 2006.

Sanchez, Dana, "Beall's Push to Expand Existing Florida Stores Reaps Dividends on Grand Scale," *Bradenton Herald,* January 20, 2005.

Belships ASA

Lilleakerveien 4
P.O. Box 23 Lilleaker
Oslo, 0216
Norway
Telephone: (+47) 22 52 76 00
Fax: (+47) 23 50 08 82
Web site: http://www.belships.com

Public Company
Incorporated: 1935 as Belships Company Limited Skibs-A/S
Employees: 42
Sales: $585.57 million (2009)
Stock Exchanges: Oslo
Ticker Symbol: BEL
NAICS: 483111 Deep Sea Freight Transportation; 541614 Process, Physical Distribution, and Logistics Consulting Services; 488510 Freight Transportation Arrangement; 488320 Marine Cargo Handling

■ ■ ■

Belships ASA is an international shipping company based in Oslo, Norway. The firm is active in three general areas of international shipping: dry cargo, product tankers, and ship management. Belships's dry cargo shipping division operates primarily through the company's subsidiary, Elkem Chartering. Elkem operates a fleet of some 25 dry bulk vessels with capacities of between 10,000 and 60,000 dry weight tons (dwt). Belships also uses vessels that it contracts, or charters, from other ship owners for specific periods. Belships dry cargo division transports primarily semifinished goods for industry and raw materials, such as ore, coal, and grain. Dry cargo accounted for 89 percent of Belships's 2008 revenues.

Belships's product tanker division transports petroleum and vegetable oils on a chartered 48,000 dwt tanker. The tanker division accounted for 6 percent of 2008 revenues. Belships's ship management division provides technical and maritime management services for vessels owned by other shippers. It operates primarily through the Oslo-based Belships Management AS and Belships Management (Singapore) Pte Ltd. The Shanghai subsidiary also specializes in providing international vessels with Chinese crews. Ship management accounted for about 4 percent of the company's revenues in 2008.

ORIGINS

The story of Belships ASA began in 1918 when Christen Smith, a retired officer of the Norwegian navy, launched his own shipping company in Oslo. World War I concluded and normal shipping between Europe and the rest of the world resuming finally, the time looked promising. Belships's first action was to place orders for two new ships. Work on the first, the M/V *Belgot*, was completed in 1920. Smith had already found a charterer (a partner who had contracted to take lease on the vessel and use it for a specified period) when the *Belgot* was delivered that same year.

However, by the time the charter had expired one year later in 1921, the world shipping industry was in

KEY DATES

1918: Christen Smith establishes Belships A/S.
1922: Belships specializes in locomotive and railcar transport.
1937: Belships is reorganized, and the Lorentzen Brothers take over its management.
1972: Belships sells its last heavy lift ship and exits that market sector.
2002: Company acquires controlling interest in Elkem Chartering A/S.

the grip of a serious downturn. Nearly half of the entire Norwegian merchant fleet was sitting in harbor with nothing to ship. Competition for the little remaining cargo was so fierce that shipping rates fell dramatically until they were approximately 25 percent of their average just one year earlier. With no one interested in chartering the vessel and no cargo available to ship, Smith had little choice but to lay the *Belgot* up in dock until market conditions improved. When the *Belgot*'s sister ship, the M/V *Belfri*, was delivered in 1921, there was no one interested in chartering it and it too went straight to the docks to wait for better days.

TRANSPORTING LOCOMOTIVES

Smith was an experienced and extremely competent seaman, but more importantly he proved a natural entrepreneur attuned to shipping opportunities that were not obvious to others. By the 1920s the use of railroads for commercial and passenger needs had burst the bounds of Europe and was spreading quickly across the globe. While railroads were being laid on every continent, the locomotives and coaches themselves were manufactured almost exclusively in England and the United States. They were being shipped worldwide, but they were shipped in pieces that had to be assembled upon arrival at their final destinations, a situation that could frequently be problematic for the purchasers. Smith found an effective means of loading fully assembled locomotives and other railroad cars onto ships and transporting them to India, Argentina, Australia, and Egypt. Among the main problems that the company had to overcome was lifting the large, extremely heavy cars onto ships, securing them so that the ships would remain seaworthy, and unlading the unusual cargo once it arrived in its foreign port.

Once the appropriate crane technology had been worked out, the company started outfitting existing

ships and new vessels with it. By the end of its first decade Belships was operating six vessels that were capable of transporting heavy railroad vehicles. The ships were not limited to such cargoes. They could also take on different kinds of dry cargo, and because they were equipped their own advanced cranes, they were able to load and unload quickly, even in relatively primitively equipped ports.

As the 1930s began, it was clear that Smith had blazed a trail into a completely new area of shipping. By then the company had become the world leader in the transport of heavy materials. It had also begun taking on the large oil refinery elements for petroleum plants that were just then being built in the Far East and Latin America. Undeterred by the challenges brought by the Great Depression, Smith pursued a bold strategy of growth. He acquired a series of loans, and in 1935, while the Depression was still in a critical phase, reorganized the company as Belships Company Limited Skibs-A/S. In 1937 the firm was listed on the Oslo stock exchange.

WARTIME PRODUCTION

At the outbreak of hostilities in 1939, Norway, like Sweden, declared its neutrality. Its commanding presence on the North Sea and the North Atlantic, however, made it a coveted target of the German navy, and in April 1940 the Nazis invaded the country. The Norwegian royal family escaped to Britain at the last moment, where they established an anti-Nazi government-in-exile. Commercial vessels that were in Norwegian harbors were captured by the Germans, but those that were on the open sea at the time did not return to home port, making instead for England.

Such Belships vessels played a particularly critical role in the British war effort, suitable as they were for shipping heavy war materiel such as tanks, aircraft, and artillery pieces. So important were they that the name *Belships* entered merchant marine speech as the name for a heavy lift ship. The term became so entrenched that only after a protracted legal battle, the conclusion of which was that such vessels were officially designated as "heavy lift ships," was the company able to secure trademark protection for its name in England.

Christen Smith, who died in the summer of 1940, was not able to see his company through the war or to witness the start of its new age of prosperity in the following years. After the war ended in 1945, the Allied command returned control of the Belships fleet to its former Norwegian shareholders, primarily the three Lorentzen brothers, Jørgen Johannes, Axel, and Frithjof, who had entered the firm at the time of its prewar reorganization. The Lorentzens were a family long active in Norwegian shipping, but their area of expertise had been ship-broking (bringing together ship owners and customers with cargo) rather than the technical side of the industry (operating and maintaining vessels). When the Lorentzen brothers took over Belships' management, they infused the firm with a solid profit orientation. The postwar market offered abundant opportunities to do business. Western Europe was in the middle of rebuilding its ravaged cities and economies. Heavy lift ships were in high demand, and hence Belships was increasing the size of its fleet. The outbreak of the Korean War in 1950 created even greater demand for ships. The strong climate for shipping continued through the decade.

NEW MARKETS, NEW CRISES

By the 1960s, however, the rebuilding of Europe was largely accomplished, and the need for the Belships heavy lift ships declined dramatically. As a result, the company decided to abandon this segment of the shipping market, the segment that had made its fortunes for some 35 years, entirely. By the early 1970s it had sold off its last heavy lift ship fleet. In the meantime, Belships had been building a presence in most of the other important segments of the shipping industry, including dry cargo, refrigerated ships, tankers, and automobile transport. The company had just placed orders for several new vessels in the latter half of the 1970s when skyrocketing grain prices and the first oil crisis combined to pitch the world into the worst recession since the 1930s.

The oil crisis, in particular, had a serious impact on Belships. Rejecting aid for shippers being offered by a special project sponsored by the Norwegian government, the firm decided instead to attempt to get through the crisis on its own. It sold off its large tanker fleet, taking large losses in the process abandoning the large tanker market completely in the process. At the end of the 1970s, shipping companies thought they could see the light at the end of the tunnel. Little did most shippers realize that far from recovering, the crises of the 1970s had ushered in a long period of instability that would dominate their industry for the next three decades.

CONSOLIDATION AND ENTRY INTO NEW SECTORS

During the brief period of raised hopes toward the end of the 1970s, Belships seized the opportunity to consolidate, concentrating its operations on handysize bulk vessels, a class of ships generally between 15,000 and 35,000 dwt used primarily to ship dry bulk cargo, such as grain, coal, or ore. As a result of the decline dur-

ing the preceding years, prices for idle ships were cheap, and Belships was quickly able to acquire a handysize fleet. Unfortunately, freight rates were also correspondingly low at first. Within several years, however, the market recovered somewhat and the fleet became a profitable venture. Another problem for the company was fluctuating foreign currency exchange rates, brought about by shifting values of the currencies used by Belships' clients and its base currency, the Norwegian krone. For a time in the early 1980s, this foreign currency exposure made Belships' share price unstable and some of its major stockholders attempted to buy out other investors as part of an effort to stabilize the shares. Few stockholders, however, were willing to sell.

The dry bulk segment remained strong through the 1980s and into the 1990s, reaching an all-time peak around 1995. By then the company had begun to expand its focus somewhat, hedging its exposure in the shipping market by adding product tankers once again and larger bulk vessels called panamax vessels to its fleet. However, another of the recurring declines in the market struck again as the millennium was drawing to a close. Belships might not have been hit as hard by the recession, if one of their main strategic objectives of the 1990s had not been foiled.

FAILED TAKEOVER ATTEMPT

In the 1990s, Belships was involved in trying to assume control of Western Bulk Carriers, a company with a large and profitable fleet of handysize bulk vessels. Belships locked up a 43 percent share of Western Bulk Carriers in 1991, in erstwhile partnership with a Norwegian engineering company, Kvaerner ASA, which held approximately 30 percent. The following year, Belships and Kvaerner performed a complicated reorganization, in which Western Bulk Carriers became simply Western Bulk and was listed on the Oslo stock exchange. Its business prospered, and by 1996 Western Bulk was one of the most profitable operators in the handysize sector. Belships then made plans to acquire a controlling share, and in July 1997 made an offer to purchase shares held by other stockholders. Belships's offer, which was some 50 cents below the current market value of Western Bulk's stock, was rejected by nearly all its shareholders. Just one month later, another shareholder, Oslo-based Sjoinvest Holding A.S., took over Western Bulk on its own. Sjoinvest, which had quietly acquired its own 26 percent of the company, had also won the confidence of other shareholders, most notably Kvaerner. Unwilling to play the role of a silent partner, Belships sold its Western Bulk holdings in September 1998.

Without Western Bulk's secure, regular income, Belships entered a decade of increased financial uncertainty. It reported losses in both 1997 and 1998, the result of weakened shipping markets, the crisis in Asia, and low interest worldwide in acquiring its secondhand vessels. The negative pattern continued in 1999 in all sectors in which Belships was active, product carriers, gas carriers, and dry bulk. It anticipated an upturn as the 2000s began, an outlook that was based on a negotiations it had begun with Shell Coal International in 1999. Closing that agreement would bring Belships a lucrative 17-year charter to shuttle coal from Australia to a power plant in Madras, India. Unfortunately, the finalization of the contract was dragged out until the latter half of 2000, probably the result of Shell's divestiture of Anglo Coal Australia, for whom Belships began finally shipping in late 2002.

After a slight market recovery, during which Belships acquired a controlling interest in another dry bulk shipper, Elkem Chartering A/S, in early 2002, world shipping slumped once again, the result of the U.S. preparations for the start of its war in Iraq. As a consequence, the firm reported losses in both 2002 and 2003. At the end of 2004, when the market stabilized and shipping rates rocketed, Belships reported $14 million in profits. It stayed in the black over the next two years, albeit without such strong showings; profits were slashed in half. One reason for the drop was the flooding of the market with new vessels, heralding a buyers' market and a decrease in the fees shippers could charge. In the same period, Belships abandoned the gas carrier sector completely to focus on dry bulk shipping, a sector where it predicted steady growth. The company was confident enough in the strengthening market to order five new handymax vessels from a Chinese shipyard in June 2007.

The U.S. housing crisis and the subsequent crisis in the world financial sector in 2008 wreaked havoc on shipping companies. Belships did not take a loss, but its profits dropped by some 88 percent from the previous year. The company by then was focusing more and more of its operations in the Far East. It had established a subsidiary in Shanghai that provided Chinese crews for international shippers. China had become more than a source of labor, it was also an important client nation, as well as a source of technical and maritime management expertise. So positive were its experiences in Asia that Belships established a technical management subsidiary in the Chinese city of Tianjin and planned expansion into other Asian nations, in particular Vietnam.

Gerald E. Brennan

PRINCIPAL SUBSIDIARIES

Belships Management AS (Oslo); Belships Management (Singapore) Pte Ltd.; Elkem Chartering (50%); SNC Management Co. Ltd (Shanghai; 50%).

PRINCIPAL DIVISIONS

Dry Cargo; Product Tankers; Shipping Management.

PRINCIPAL COMPETITORS

Aker ASA; Dongnama Shipping Co., Ltd.; Essberger Group of Companies; Hanjin Shipping Co., Ltd; John T. Mitsui O.S.K. Lines; Wilh. Wilhelmsen ASA.

FURTHER READING

"Belships Eyes China 'With Awe,'" Chinadaily.com.cn, April 14, 2008.

Frank, Jerry, "Belships Gets Back into Black," *Lloyd's List*, August 23, 2004, p. 2.

———, "Dry Bulk Revival Benefits Belships," *Lloyd's List*, November 15, 2004, p. 2.

———, "Dry Cargo Rates Boom Puts Belships Back into the Black," *Lloyd's List*, February 24, 2004, p. 2.

Hughes, David, "Dry Bulk Market Proves Resilient, Says Galbraith," *Business Times Singapore*, September 1, 2006.

"Market Conditions Hamper Belships' Run of Success," *Lloyd's List*, November 9, 2005, p. 12.

Berentzen-Gruppe AG

Ritterstrasse 7
Haselünne, 49740
Germany
Telephone: (+49 5961) 502-0
Fax: (+49 5961) 502-268
Web site: http://www.berentzen-gruppe.de

Public Company
Founded: 1758
Incorporated: 1865 as I. B. Berentzen
Employees: 629
Sales: EUR 199.1 million ($292.7 million) (2008)
Stock Exchanges: Frankfurt am Main Bremen-Berlin Hamburg Munich Dusseldorf Stuttgart Xetra
Ticker Symbol: BEZ3
NAICS: 312140 Distilleries; 312111 Soft Drink Manufacturing; 424820 Wine and Distilled Alcoholic Beverage Merchant Wholesalers

■ ■ ■

Berentzen-Gruppe AG is a leading German manufacturer of spirits. In addition to its flagship brands, Berentzen and Puschkin Vodka which are sold in many countries around the world, the distillery also produces brandy, whiskey, and other spirits under regional brands names and for private labels, and distributes an additional range of brand name spirits and wine in Germany. The company's nonalcoholic beverage subsidiary Vivaris Getränke produces mineral spring water and soft drinks, and is one of the largest distributors of Pepsi-Cola in Germany. Based in Ha-

selünne in northern Germany, Berentzen has subsidiaries in the Czech Republic, Slovakia, Poland, Norway, and Great Britain. German Investment firm Aurelius AG owns 75 percent of Berentzen-Gruppe AG.

FAMILY DISTILLERY GROWS IN 18TH AND 19TH CENTURIES

In 1758 there were 26 distilleries in the small northwestern German city of Haselünne. One of them was run by Johann Bernhard Berentzen, a blacksmith and councilman who distilled the increasingly popular grain schnapps on the side. His son, Johann Bernhard II, a miller, continued to run the distillery as a side business until his death in 1815. His oldest son Johann Bernhard III, also a miller, took over the distillery and ran it together with his mother. In 1838 he acquired a property in Haselünne's city center that included a house as well as a distillery.

A hardworking and deeply religious man, Johann Bernhard III enlarged the premises as bordering parcels of land were put up for sale, and his property increased to a considerable size. In 1847 his 18-year-old son Bernhard Heinrich joined the family business. Together with his mother, who took care of purchasing the grain, and his brother Josef, who oversaw the technical side of the business, Heinrich Berentzen took on a leading role within a few years.

Berentzen's clear Kornschnaps, which was also available in anise-flavored and bitter varieties, became very popular in the whole region and was shipped by horse-drawn carriage in wooden barrels to a growing number of customers. In addition to spirits, the Berentzens also produced vinegar. In 1857 Heinrich Berentzen married the daughter of a brewer and distiller who also produced compressed yeast from grain. In the following year the Berentzens set up a compressed yeast production that was mainly overseen by Heinrich Berentzen's wife Helene.

INDUSTRIAL PRODUCTION AFTER 1865

In 1865 the company I. B. Berentzen was officially registered as a general partnership, and three years later Heinrich and Josef Berentzen took over the business as partners. With industrialization underway in the late 19th century, the Berentzens transformed their distillery into a mechanized, steam-engine-driven factory which was continuously expanded and equipped with the most modern machinery available. Berentzen's spirits were shipped to most of northwestern Germany, including Bremen and Hamburg, and to Westphalia.

After her husband's death in 1886, Helene Berentzen carried on the business. When she died in 1890, her only son Johannes Bernhard was only 17 years old. After finishing his education, Johannes took over the family business in 1893 and transformed it into the limited liability company I. B. Berentzen G.m.b.H. Three years later the distillery was connected to the railroad. The company's grain schnapps, Berentzen Vom Alten Fass, became a best seller in the 1890s and was officially registered as a brand name by the German Patent Office in 1899.

RAPID GROWTH IN EARLY 20TH CENTURY

Under Johannes Berentzen, who proved to be a clever and provident businessman, the family enterprise enjoyed a period of rapid growth. In 1901 a second distillery was set up at the Sautmannshausen family farm in the Haselünne heathland. By 1907 the two distilleries were putting out over 100 million liters of spirits per year. An advertising poster for the branded grain schnapps claimed that Berentzen Vom Alten Fass made a perfect replacement for Cognac and should be enjoyed by every German. The company also distilled Hünensteiner, a branded Jenever, and started manufacturing fine liquors.

Dry yeast production became an important second pillar of the Berentzen family enterprise in the early years of the 20th century. Berentzen invested heavily in new yeast production technologies, set up a malt production facility, and added cellar and storage space. When an increasingly fierce competition broke out in the market for dry yeast that threatened profitability, Johannes Berentzen was a driving force in forming a syndicate of yeast manufacturers. In 1907 the company produced over one million pounds of wheat-based dry yeast.

The third pillar of the Berentzen family business, vinegar production, also reached new heights. In 1904 a brand-new vinegar factory was built in Haselünne. The family also ran a thriving wine wholesale business. However, the outbreak of World War I brought the company's growth to a sudden halt when many of Berentzen's workers were drafted into the military.

LEADERSHIP CHANGES BETWEEN WORLD WARS

While the production of spirits was prohibited after World War I ended in 1918, Berentzen manufactured nonalcoholic beverages until the company received permission to resume distillery operations. In the 1920s Johannes Berentzen's oldest sons joined the family business. Heinrich Berentzen became general manager in 1920, followed by his brother Anton who took over responsibility for the family farm in 1921. In 1925 Dr. Johannes B. Berentzen, who had studied chemistry after serving in the military during World War I, became the new technical director of the family enterprise.

It was due to Johannes B. Berentzen that the company's yeast production survived the ruinous price wars of the 1920s. Following the chemist's initiative, Berentzen's yeast factory replaced malt with molasses as raw material for a higher-quality dry yeast. To use the full capacity of its malt production facilities the

KEY DATES

1758: Johann Bernhardt Berentzen's distillery is officially registered in Haselünne.

1899: The distillery's grain schnapps Berentzen Vom Alten Fass is registered as a brand name.

1958: Subsidiary Emsland-Getränke, a nonalcoholic beverage maker, is founded.

1960: Emsland-Getränke acquires a production and distribution license for Pepsi-Cola.

1976: The wheat-schnapps-and-apple-juice mix Berentzen Apfelkorn is launched.

1988: I. B. Berentzen merges with distillery Pabst & Richarz to form Berentzen-Group.

1994: The company's stock is listed at the Frankfurt and Bremen stock exchanges.

1998: Berentzen takes over German distiller Dethleffsen.

2008: German investment firm Aurelius AG acquires a majority in Berentzen-Gruppe AG.

company started selling malt to other distilleries. Johannes B. Berentzen also initiated the setting up of a small malt extract factory. In addition to dry yeast, the company's baking aid, Dr. Berentzen's Bäckomalt, became a best-selling malt product for bakeries.

The formation of a joint organization of German yeast manufacturers after the Nazis came to power in the early 1930s put an end to the fierce price competition. On the other hand, the company was confronted with an increasingly aggressive competition in the spirits market. In 1937 the company was transformed into a general partnership owned by Johannes Berentzen and his children. The onset of World War II was a major shock for the senior Berentzen, however, and he died in 1942. Heinrich Berentzen died only a few weeks later.

POSTWAR RECONSTRUCTION AFTER WORLD WAR II

Johannes B. Berentzen was drafted into the military at the beginning of World War II in 1939, but he returned from the battlefield after being seriously injured and steered the company through the difficult war years. After the war had ended, the company produced yeast and malt products, vinegar, alcohol for medical and industrial use, and nonalcoholic beverages on a small scale. In February 1948 Anton Berentzen took over the Sautmannshausen farm, which was legally separated from the rest of the business.

Johannes B. Berentzen became the sole owner of I. B. Berentzen. After currency reform in 1948 Berentzen rebuilt the heavily damaged production facilities in Haselünne. The company continued to purchase spirits from the Sautmannshausen farm for a time. In the early 1950s, however, Berentzen leased a distillery in Gladbeck, Westphalia, which produced the necessary spirits for the company's growing range of schnapps and liquors. Thanks to their high quality, Berentzen's products were listed by retailers and the hospitality trade in spite of massive competition. Johannes B. Berentzen died in 1954 at age 54.

NEW LEADERSHIP AND NEW SPIRITS AFTER 1954

After Johannes B. Berentzen's death, his sons, Dr. Johannes B. Berentzen and Friedrich Berentzen, took over the company, which by the mid-1950s was grossing DEM 4 million in annual sales. In 1955 the company built a new distillery in Haselünne that provided the basic spirits which were then processed to schnapps and liquor. To increase the amount of alcohol the new distillery was allowed to produce, which was strictly regulated by the German government, Berentzen founded Brennerei Hillringhaus und Berentzen, a joint venture with the Wuppertal-based distillery Dr. Fritz Hillringhaus, which transferred its allowed output volume to the new company.

In the 1950s Berentzen began to expand its range of spirits, adding Senator brand wheat schnapps, Berentzen Exquisit brandy, the herb liquor Dr. Kern's Klosterkräuter, and other novelties. In the 1960s the company strengthened its sales force and invested more in advertising campaigns. As a result, Berentzen was able to increase its market share considerably.

FOCUS ON SOFT DRINKS AFTER 1958

In the late 1950s Berentzen made the strategic decision to enter the promising growth market for nonalcoholic beverages. A legally independent subsidiary for soft-drink manufacturing, Emsland-Getränke, was founded in 1958. To free additional funds for the new venture, Berentzen gave up its baker's yeast and vinegar factories; eventually production of its malt-based baking aid was shuttered as well. In a major coup for Berentzen's new subsidiary, Emsland-Getränke acquired a concession for bottling and distributing Pepsi-Cola in West Germany in 1960.

Starting out by supplying specialized beverage retailers and restaurants in the northern German Emsland

and Ostfriesland regions and the city of Oldenburg, the company successfully established itself in spite of the strong competition. Berentzen's total sales skyrocketed during the 1960s, quadrupling from DEM 6.5 million in 1961 to DEM 26.7 million at the end of the decade. When soft-drink production reached the limits of the former yeast factory, the company built a brand-new factory at the outskirts of Haselünne in 1970.

In the 1970s and 1980s Emsland-Getränke acquired several regional beverage wholesalers and another soft-drink manufacturer in Burgsteinfurt, expanding its market to the North Sea and Westphalia. The company also added a number of soft drinks to its product range that were marketed under the Emsland brand. After the company discovered a suitable spring on its premises in the early 1980s, Emsland-Getränke also produced mineral water. The company's output more than doubled from about 140,000 hectoliters (3.6 million gallons) in 1975 to roughly 328,000 hectoliters (8.6 million gallons) in 1982.

APPLE SCHNAPPS BECOMES BEST SELLER IN 1976

Up until the mid-1970s Berentzen was mainly known for its grain schnapps. Three-fourths of the distillery's spirits sales were generated by its flagship product Echter Berentzen, which was distributed from northern Germany to the Ruhr. However, the launch of the new apple-flavored grain schnapps Berentzen Apfelkorn in 1976 ushered in a new era for the company. Due to its fruity but not overly sweet taste and its relatively low alcohol content, the novelty, soon nicknamed Appelkorn by consumers, became the most successful new product launch in the West German spirits market. With the number of Berentzen Apfelkorn bottles sold moving up swiftly from 2.6 million in 1976 to 25.2 million three years later, the company joined the national league of German distillers.

When sales began to drop in the contracting German spirits market of the late 1970s and early 1980s, Berentzen set its sights on the markets abroad. In 1978 the company started exporting its Appelkorn to Western Europe, mainly to the Netherlands and Denmark but also to Switzerland and Austria, Spain, Italy, and Great Britain. In 1981 the first Berentzen Apfelkorn was shipped to the United States, and by the middle of the decade it was being exported to over 50 countries.

FORMATION OF BEVERAGE GROUP BEGINS IN 1988

The year 1988 marked another milestone in the company's history when I. B. Berentzen merged with the German distillery and brandy manufacturer Pabst & Richarz, which was founded in 1861 and specialized in the private-label production of spirits and liquors, to form Berentzen-Group. The merger created Germany's second-largest distillery and was the first of a number of acquisitions in the 1990s and early 2000s.

In 1992 Berentzen took over Doornkaat AG, the manufacturer of one of Germany's most well-known grain schnapps brands. With the acquisition of Strothmann Brennereien, another major grain schnapps manufacturer, in 1995 Berentzen became the German market leader in that segment. Finally, in 1998 Berentzen made it to the top of the spirits market by taking over Dethleffsen, one of the company's main competitors and a major German manufacturer of rum, herb schnapps, and other spirits and liquors.

An important step in expanding Berentzen's portfolio of brand-name spirits was the acquisition of the well-known brand Puschkin Vodka in 1990. The mid-1990s also saw the company expand its nonalcoholic beverage distribution by acquiring two German mineral water manufacturers. The nonalcoholic beverage subsidiary was later reorganized under the new holding Vivaris Getränke GmbH.

PUBLIC OFFERING IN 1994

To raise the necessary capital for the company's ambitious expansion plans, Berentzen went public in 1994. While the Hans and Friedrich Berentzen and the Pabst, Richarz, and Wolf families retained voting rights, 50 percent of the publicly traded preferred shares with no voting rights were floated at the Frankfurt and Bremen stock exchanges. Following its international expansion strategy to set off declining spirits sales in Germany, the company took over the leading Czech spirits distributor Eurobrands in 1997. Four years later the company acquired a 30 percent stake in the state-owned Norwegian spirits producer Arcus.

To revive domestic sales, Berentzen launched new products, including a range of fruit-flavored and cream liquors, and a line of mixed alcoholic beverages called Alcopops. While the former were quickly copied by the competition, however, the latter flopped in the market, despite the company's high marketing investments. To make things worse, rising taxes on alcoholic beverages with a lower alcohol content further diminished sales and profits. As a result Berentzen started producing losses in the late 1990s.

In response, the company launched a major restructuring program to cut costs, acquired the distribution rights for additional well-known spirits brands such as the Spanish Licor 43 and the Norwegian

Aquavit, and added Australian wine to its line of wholesale items. To better penetrate the hospitality market, Berentzen acquired the beverage marketing firm Columbus Vertriebs GmbH in 2004, which also distributed Budweiser beer in Germany. However, with price wars raging in all market segments, and with the number of competing products on the rise, Berentzen continued to produce losses. The sale of Berentzen's stake in the Norwegian Arcus group in 2005 temporarily pushed the company back into profits.

FAMILY MANAGEMENT ENDS 2006

After the acquisition of the spirits division of major competitor Eckes fell through in 2003 while the downward trend in sales persisted, Hans Berentzen's son Jan B. Berentzen stepped down as head of the company's executive board after 11 years in 2006 and was succeeded by Axel Dahm, putting a nonfamily member at the helm for the first time in the company's history. Dahm's strategy to revive the Berentzen brand with massive investment in television advertising, however, did not yield the desired results.

In 2008 Berentzen's shareholders sold a 75.1 percent stake in Berentzen-Gruppe AG to Munich-based investment firm Aurelius AG. To get Berentzen out of the red quickly, the new management closed down two bottling lines in Haselünne, cut the company's workforce by one-fifth, spun off the company's sales division, and gave up roughly one-third of its low-margin private-label spirits production. After years of losses, the company reported an operating profit in mid-2009. Aiming at leading the German spirits market, Berentzen-Gruppe launched a marketing campaign to reposition the Berentzen brand in 2010 and focused international activities on the Czech Republic, the Netherlands, Russia, and the United States.

Evelyn Hauser

PRINCIPAL SUBSIDIARIES

Kornbrennerei Berentzen GmbH; Berentzen Distillers International GmbH; Dethleffsen Spirituosen GmbH; Puschkin International GmbH; Vivaris Getränke GmbH & Co. KG; Strothmann Spirituosen Verwaltung GmbH & Co. KG; Jürgen Weber GmbH; Landwirth's GmbH; Winterapfel Getränke GmbH; Zinnaer Klosterspirituosen GmbH; Doornkaat AG; Noris Weinbrennereien GmbH; Berentzen Distillers CR s.r.o. (Czech Republic); Berentzen Distillers Slovakia s.r.o.; Sechsämtertropfen G. Vetter Spolka z o.o. (Poland); Pabst & Richarz Vertriebs GmbH (27%); Sucra AS (Norway); Double Q Whiskey Company Ltd. (Great Britain); Pierre Louge & Cie. GmbH; Der Berentzen Hof GmbH; Mampe-Markenvertrieb GmbH.

PRINCIPAL COMPETITORS

Bacardi Ltd.; Diageo plc; Henkell & Soehnlein Sektkellereien KG; Krombacher Brauerei Bernhard Schadeberg GmbH & Co. KG; Pernod Ricard; Rotkäppchen-Mumm Sektkellereien GmbH; The Coca-Cola Company.

FURTHER READING

"Axel Dahm to Take Over at Berentzen (Personalien: Berentzen)," *Europe Intelligence Wire*, October 2, 2006.

"Berentzen Alters Strategy," *Europe Intelligence Wire*, March 30, 2007.

"Berentzen Family to Withdraw from Company Management," *Europe Intelligence Wire*, June 8, 2005.

"Berentzen schafft unerwartet deutliche Ergebniswende," *Börsen-Zeitung*, February 6, 2010, p. 12.

"Berentzen to Be Sold to Aurelius," *Europe Intelligence Wire*, July 23, 2008.

"Drinks Group Berentzen Aims for Return to Profit in 2006," *Europe Intelligence Wire*, August 11, 2005.

"Eckes Fails to Sell Alcoholic Drinks Division," *Europe Intelligence Wire*, May 13, 2003.

"Germany: Berentzen Back in the Black," *Frankfurter Allgemeine Zeitung*, January 28, 1999, p. 26.

"Germany: Vivaris, Pepsi Continue Cooperation," *Lebensmittel Zeitung*, December 1, 2000, p. 17.

I. B. Berentzen Chronik eines Hauses, Haselünne, Germany: I. B. Berentzen, 1983.

"Neue Berentzen-Tochter," *Lebensmittel Zeitung*, December 12, 1997, p. 14.

"Norway: Arcus in Private Hands," *Frankfurter Allgemeine Zeitung*, June 23, 2001, p. 22.

Schloz, Harald, *So schmeckt Lebensfreude, Seit 250 Jahren*, Haselünne, Germany: Berentzen-Gruppe AG, 2008.

"Subsidiary of Holsten Taken Over by Berentzen," *Europe Intelligence Wire*, February 3, 2004.

"Tempo statt Tradition," *manager magazine online*, August 1, 2004.

Bharat Electronics
Limited

—■—

Nagavara, Outer Ring Road
Bangalore, 560 045
India
Telephone: (+91 080) 2503 9300
Fax: (+91 080) 2503 9305

Public Company
Incorporated: 1992
Employees: 12,372
Sales: $1.01 billion (2009)
Stock Exchanges: Bangalore Mumbai National
Ticker Symbols: BEL; 500049
NAICS: 334511 Search, Detection, Navigation, Guid-
    ance, Aeronautical, and Nautical System and Instru-
    ment Manufacturing; 334419 Other Electronic
    Component Manufacturing

■ ■ ■

Bharat Electronics Limited (BEL) is India's leading
developer and producer of electronics-based components
and systems for the military and defense sectors. BEL is
classified as a Public Sector Unit (PSU) and in this
capacity holds near-monopoly status in the supply of
electronics, including sonar, radar, communication
systems, missile guidance and gunfire control systems,
naval systems, tank electronics, and electro-optics to
India's military. BEL's Defense Products division accounts for roughly 83 percent of its total revenues of
$1.01 billion in 2009. BEL itself accounts for nearly 9
percent of the Indian government's defense budget.

In addition to its defense operations, BEL has
diversified into the civilian sector, producing a range of
products including microwave and transmitting tubes,
electronic voting machines, set-top boxes and broadcasting equipment for the telecommunications and television industries, solar-powered traffic lights, and security
systems. The company has also expanded beyond India,
developing exports to countries around the world.

BEL's headquarters and primary manufacturing
facility are in Bangalore. The company also operates
through a network of six strategic business units, with
factories in Panchkula, Kotdwara, Taloja, Pune, Machilipatnam, and Chennai (Madras). In support of its
defense technology, BEL began setting up a new central
research laboratory in 2010, focused on electronic
warfare systems. BEL also operates through subsidiary
BEL Optronics Devices, specialized in high-voltage
power supply equipment and imaging products, and a
26 percent stake in X-ray tube joint venture GE BE (P)
Ltd.

BEL is a public company, listed on the Mumbai
and New York stock exchanges. The Indian government,
which holds approximately 40 percent of the company,
gave BEL Navratna status in 2007. Navratna companies
enjoy a greater degree of autonomy in their operations
than other government-controlled companies. V.V.R.
Sastry is BEL's chairman and managing director.

ORIGINS

After gaining independence from Great Britain in 1947,
the Indian government placed a priority on building its
military and defense capacity. This effort became

COMPANY PERSPECTIVES

Vision. To be a world-class enterprise in professional electronics. Mission. To be a customer focused, globally competitive company in defence electronics and in other chosen areas of professional electronics, through quality, technology and innovation.

particularly important in light of the country's long-running conflict with Pakistan and the efforts of both countries to develop nuclear weapons capability. In 1954 the Indian government founded a new company focused on producing electronic components and systems for its defense sector. The company, called Bharat Electronics Limited (BEL), began construction of a factory in Bangalore in 1954. Bharat is the Hindi name for the Republic of India.

By 1956 BEL had launched production of its first products, which included radio and microwave transmitters, receivers, relays, and related components. BEL's operations expanded to include the production of vacuum tubes in 1961, and germanium-based semiconductors in 1962. The company continued to invest in building its range of technologies, which enabled it to enter the production of radar components and equipment by 1966. Other products added during the 1960s included transmitting tubes in 1967, and high-frequency broadcasting systems in 1968. The company also built a dedicated printed circuit board factory that year, and launched production of silicon-based semiconductors and integrated circuits.

The 1970s represented a major period of expansion for BEL's product lines. The company leveraged its radar operations into new areas, such as the production of X-ray tubes in 1970, and then black-and-white picture tubes in 1972. BEL had begun supplying radar systems to the Indian Navy by 1973. The company went on to become one of the few defense specialists in India to supply all three branches of India's military, as well as its police, coast guard, and other security operations.

DECENTRALIZATION AND EXPANSION

BEL took advantage of the Indian government's decentralization policies in the 1970s to expand its manufacturing network. This expansion gave the company both additional and more specialized produc-

tion capacity, as well as a strategic presence near India's Air Force and other military branches. The first of the new factories opened in Ghaziabad in 1974, and specialized in producing radar systems and communications equipment for the Air Force. The company opened a third facility in Pune in 1979, dedicated to producing imaging systems. In 1982 the Pune facility began producing magnesium manganese dioxide batteries in support of BEL's Space Electronics division. By then, BEL had achieved sales of more than INR 1 billion.

The company added operations in Machilipatnam in 1983, when it took over ASCO (Andhra Scientific Co.), which had fallen into financial difficulties. Other business units followed through the decade, including Madras and Panchkula in 1985, and Kotdwara, Taloja, and Hyderabad in 1986. The addition of these facilities allowed the company to expand its operations into a variety of areas, including traveling wave tubes, digital communication equipment, broadcast and television equipment, space electronics, tank electronics, and low-power television transmitters.

BEL's efforts increasingly turned toward boosting its technology capability during the 1980s. The company created a dedicated Naval Equipment Division, which then focused its product development on this core market. This was followed by the opening of the company's first Central Research Laboratory, in Bangalore in 1988. The company's research and development investments soon paid off, as the company added a range of television, microwave, and FM transmitters.

In 1990 the company launched its own satellite communications and simulation systems operations, as well as automatic testing equipment for the army, and ship handling simulators for the navy. Following this successful expansion, the company added a second Central Research Laboratory, in Ghaziabad in 1992.

PUBLIC OFFERING IN 1992

The year 1992 marked the beginning of BEL's transition from state-owned company to public company. In 1992 BEL listed its shares on the Bangalore, Bombay, and National stock exchanges. The company's initial public offering reduced the government's ownership of the company to 80 percent. In 1994 the government completed a secondary offering, this time selling another 41.4 percent of BEL. The Indian government nonetheless retained a controlling stake in the company.

BEL struggled through a period of reduced government defense spending during the first half of the 1990s. In order to reduce its reliance on that sector, the company launched a new diversification strategy. This included the setting up of two joint ventures in 1994. The first of these was an X-ray tube joint venture with

KEY DATES

1954: Bharat Electronics Limited (BEL) is founded in Bangalore to develop electronics components for the Indian military and defense sectors.

1974: BEL opens its second production unit in Ghaziabad.

1988: The company's first Central Research Laboratory opens, in Bangalore.

1992: BEL goes public on the Bangalore, Bombay, and National stock exchanges.

2003: The company is recognized as the Bangalore stock exchange's Best Company.

2007: The Indian government awards BEL status as a Navratna company.

the U.S.-based General Electric Company, in which BEL became a minority partner. The second was an image intensifier joint venture, BE Delft, with Netherlands-based M/S Delft. BEL later acquired full control of BE Delft, which changed its name to BEL Optronics in 2003.

BEL added a third joint venture with U.K.-based Multitone, creating BEL Multitone in 1996. This company then launched production of pagers for the Indian and other markets. In the meantime, BEL continued to face losses in parts of its defense operations, including at the Machilipatnam and Kotdwara plants. This encouraged the company to step up its diversification efforts. BEL expanded its production in the second half of the decade to include a variety of civilian applications, including solar cells and systems, railway communication systems, and fish finders.

BEL also stepped up its investments in developing its production capacity for the electronics sector. This led to the construction of a new silicon wafer facility in Bangalore in 1997. BEL's diversification drive enabled it to build its total sales to more than INR 12 billion by the middle of the decade. In the second half of the decade, as India became caught up in the economic crisis that swept through much of the Asian region, the company suffered a series of setbacks in its sales. The company had once again begun to grow by 2000, building its sales past INR 17 billion for the year.

BEST COMPANY IN 2003

BEL stepped up its diversification in the new century. The company gained a major new contract from the lo-

cal government of Andhra Pradesh to build a statewide broadcast and communications network in 2001. The success of this venture helped BEL secure an even larger contract, for the construction of the national POLNET network to coordinate communications and data exchange among the country's police departments.

The success of these ventures helped the company raise its total revenues past INR 25 billion in 2003, and to nearly INR 28 billion the following year. The company's profits rose strongly as well, topping INR 1.26 billion, and then INR 1.5 billion. This performance earned the company recognition in 2003 as the Bangalore stock exchange's Best Company, the first time a government-controlled PSU had won that honor.

BEL continued developing new civilian operations, often extending the expertise generated by its defense work. This led the company to launch the production of set-top boxes for the television and telecommunications markets in 2006. BEL had also begun producing solar-powered, LED-based traffic lights by then, winning major orders from New Delhi, Hyderabad, Bangalore, and elsewhere.

The pursuit of diversification included an effort to develop the company's export operations. BEL had established its first international links in the 1980s, setting up a purchasing office in New York in 1980 in order to secure its components supply. The company added a second purchasing office in Singapore in 1998. BEL began developing its international sales network at the same time. This effort hit a setback in the late 1990s, however, when the U.S. and European governments put a block on the company's goods.

NAVRATNA COMPANY IN 2007

However, BEL's exports made increasing gains as its list of markets grew in the 21st century. By the end of the first decade, the company's defense wing had developed communications equipment supply contracts in such markets as Suriname, Indonesia, Botswana, and Malaysia. Indonesia, Switzerland, and Egypt became customers for BEL's radar systems, while Russia and Brazil acquired the company's electronic warfare systems.

BEL's civilian wing expanded even more strongly on the international market. By the end of the decade, BEL's markets included South Africa, Singapore, Turkey, Israel, the United Kingdom, the United States, France, Germany, Zimbabwe, Uganda, Sri Lanka, and Kenya. BEL also developed a contract manufacturing business for the export market, securing contracts with GE Medical Systems and Eton Corporation in the United States, for example, in 2005.

By the end of the decade, BEL's civilian products and exports combined to represent some 17 percent of the group's total revenues, which had in the meantime risen past INR 41 billion in 2007 to near INR 46 billion in 2009. This achievement brought the company a new award in 2007, the highly coveted status as one of India's Navratna companies. The select list of Navratna companies, of which there were fewer than 20 in 2010, were granted special autonomy in their investment, export, and expansion decisions by the Indian government.

BEL celebrated its new status with a pledge to boost its share of civilian operations. In 2009 the company announced plans to enter a variety of new areas, including railways, airports, ports, and homeland security operations. The company also intended to develop expertise in instrumentation for the nuclear power and other industries, while also investing in renewable energy initiatives. This effort was expected to raise the share of its civilian operations to as much as 30 percent of its total revenues by 2013.

BEL backed up this effort with plans to expand its research and development operations. At the beginning of 2010, the company announced an increase in its research spending to as high as INR 700 million per year. The new strategy in the meantime had begun to provide success, as the group won a contract to provide a coastal surveillance system for the Indian Coast Guard. BEL began pilot testing the new system in March 2010.

Despite the success of the company's growing civilian operations, its defense division remained its core business. The company gained a number of major defense contracts at the end of the decade, including the contract to develop a state-of-the-art gunfire control system for the Indian Navy, starting in January 2010. BEL also made moves to expand its electronic warfare operations, setting up a dedicated central research laboratory for this area in February of that year. BEL expected its revenues to rise past INR 50 billion by the end of the year, and to reach as high as INR 100 billion by 2013.

M. L. Cohen

PRINCIPAL SUBSIDIARIES

BEL Optronics Devices Ltd. (92.79%); GE BE (P) Ltd. (26%).

PRINCIPAL DIVISIONS

Defense Products; Civilian Products.

PRINCIPAL OPERATING UNITS

Panchkula; Kotdwara; Taloja; Pune; Machilipatnam; Chennai.

PRINCIPAL COMPETITORS

Abengoa S.A.; BAE Systems PLC; China Aerospace Science and Technology Group Corp.; European Aeronautic Defence and Space Company EADS N.V.; General Dynamics Corp.; Honeywell International Inc.; Lockheed Martin Corp.; Northrop Grumman Corp.; Siemens AG.

FURTHER READING

Agarwal, Ahish, "BEL Good for Investors with a Time Frame of 2–3 Years," *Economic Times*, December 14, 2009.
"BEL Develops Advanced Gunfire Control System for Indian Navy," *Information Company*, January 29, 2010.
"BEL Implements Major Shift in R&D Policy," *Financial Express*, January 18, 2010.
"BEL to Diversify Product Portfolio," *Financial Express*, April 29, 2009.
"BEL to Set Up Lab on Futuristic Tech in Electronic Warfare," *India Business Insight*, February 11, 2010.
"Bharat Electronics," *Communications Today*, March 10, 2009.
Kerur, Bhargavi, "BEL's Surveillance System to Secure Costs," *DNA*, February 2, 2010.

Bio·IT World

Bio-IT World Inc.

———————— ▪ ————————

250 First Avenue, Suite 300
Needham, Massachusetts 02494-2887
U.S.A.
Telephone: (508) 628-4700
Fax: (508) 628-4766
Web site: http://www.bio-itworld.com

*Wholly Owned Subsidiary of Cambridge Healthtech
    Institute, Inc.*
Incorporated: 2001
Employees: 35
NAICS: 511120 Periodical Publishers

■ ■ ■

A subsidiary of Cambridge Healthtech Institute based in
Needham, Massachusetts, Bio-IT World Inc. is a
publisher and conference producer that focuses on the
convergence of the life sciences and information
technology (IT) that allows for the accelerated development of new drugs and treatments. Special emphasis is
placed on predictive biology, drug discovery, informatics,
personalized medicine, and clinical trials. Areas of
emphasis include cheminformatics, clinical research,
computational modeling, correlation of biological data,
discovery informatics, genomic analysis, IT infrastructure, predictiveness, pharmacogenomics, semantic
web (data sharing and social networking), systems biology, target data, and text mining of published literature
and internal documents.

The company publishes *Bio-IT World* magazine six
times a year, available in print and a less-expensive
digital edition, and newsletters. Additionally, it produces
podcasts and Webcasts, offers white papers and special
reports, and covers breaking news on its Web site.
Bio-IT World also sponsors an annual conference and
exposition in Boston, Massachusetts, bringing together
biotech and pharmaceutical firms, the academic research
community, and IT firms with possible solutions as well
as venture capital firms looking for investment
opportunities. Bio-IT World has also organized conferences and expositions in San Diego, Hong Kong, and
Europe.

ORIGINS

Bio-IT World was formed as a business unit in
September 2001 by International Data Group, Inc.
(IDG), a Boston-based media, research, and exposition
company, best known as the publisher of *Computerworld*. IDG's roots date back to the 1950s as the
computer industry was just beginning to take root. The
company's founder, Patrick J. McGovern, was a teenager
fascinated by computers in 1953 when he used $20
saved from his paper route to build a crude computer
out of bell wire and flashlight bulbs. His computer was
unbeatable in tic-tac-toe and earned him a scholarship
to the Massachusetts Institute of Technology.

After graduation McGovern became associate
publisher for the first national computer magazine,
Computers and Automation. In 1964 he formed Information Data Corporation to conduct market research for
IBM's computer rivals, the goal being to study how
computers were being used and where the industry was

likely headed. He took advantage of his own research, which indicated that computer systems managers were not able to keep up with the latest developments in computers, nor keep tabs on others were doing with computers. As a result, McGovern put his publishing experience to use by launching *Computerworld* in 1967, as well as forming IDG to serve as a holding company for his research and publishing businesses.

McGovern began producing conferences and expositions in the late 1970s in response to the increasing importance of telecommunications technology, resulting in the ComNet (Communications Networks) trade show and the IDG World Expo Corporation. Additional magazines were added in the 1980s, including *Macworld Magazine* to cover news related to Apple's new Macintosh computer. Facing increasing competition at home, IDG expanded internationally, launching computer magazines in Europe, the Soviet Union, and China. With the demise of Communism, IDG added publishing operations in former Soviet Bloc nations in the 1990s. It also looked to Africa, publishing *PC World Africa*, as well as launching *PC World* editions in several countries. A variety of publishing assets were added in the 1990s.

IDG LOOKS FOR NEW NICHES

In 1997 IDG looked for new opportunities by exploiting the growth of the digital industry, focusing on the intersection of technology, the Internet, entertainment, and media. The company took a similar approach four years later when its research revealed that the biosciences and bioinformatics markets would be major drivers of revenue growth in the technology industry over the next 10 years. Moreover, IDG believed that the life sciences market would make increasing use of IT, creating a "Bio-IT" nexus.

Thus, IDG formed Bio-IT World Inc. in 2001 becoming the first technology publisher to serve the participants in this emerging market. This was not an especially easy task given that life science and IT professionals relied on different terminology and concepts, in effect speaking different languages.

Named to serve as chief executive of the company was Dr. Morris R. Levitt, a veteran of publishing and conferences in the life sciences. He founded *Medical Laser Industry Report* and the annual medical laser market conferences. He also served as an executive vice president at Advanstar Healthcare, where he oversaw *Pharmaceutical Technology, Pharmaceutical Executive,* and other medical titles.

Even before Bio-IT World launched *Bio-IT World* magazine in 2002, it held its first trade show in January of that year in Hong Kong under the unhyphenated "BioIT World" banner. By starting in Asia, the new company hoped to establish that its commitment extended beyond the United States or a limited region. The first issue of the magazine was published in March 2002 in conjunction with the related World Expo Bio-IT World Conference & Expo held at Boston's World Trade Center.

The monthly started with a controlled circulation of 25,000 life science professionals involved in such areas as drug discovery and development, bioinformatics, genomics, and proteomics. Serving as editor in chief was Kevin Davies, former science editor and program administrator at the Howard Hughes Medical Institute. He was also the author of books on gene research, the founding editor of *Nature Genetics,* and the editor in chief of Cell Press.

MAGAZINE ENJOYS SUCCESSFUL DEBUT

Bio-IT World enjoyed a successful debut, despite conditions in which most tech publications were experiencing poor ad sales. Of the 96 pages in the first issue, nearly a third were ad pages, and sales continued to climb in the April and May issues. Among the advertisers were major companies that normally shied away from publications, including Apple, IBM, and Hewlett-Packard. Moreover, the publication was able to attract as advertisers others interested in making themselves known to this cross-section of life science and IT researchers and executives, such as venture capital firms, law firms, and state economic development agencies. Due in some measure to the magazine's early success, a number of rival publications emerged to pursue the same market.

In addition to the successful launch of the magazine, the Bio-IT World trade show also did well,

KEY DATES

2001: Bio-IT World Inc. is formed as a business unit by International Data Group, Inc.
2002: First trade show is held; *Bio-IT World* magazine is launched.
2005: *Pharmaceutical Discovery* magazine is acquired.
2006: Cambridge Healthtech Institute, Inc., acquires Bio-IT World Inc.
2009: First trade show is held in Europe.

attracting more than 100 exhibitors and about 3,500 people to the two-day event. Because it was bringing together divergent groups, the trade show emphasized seminars and other educational events as a way to demonstrate how IT could help life science firms in their development efforts. Boston was a good location not only because of its proximity to IDG's headquarters, but also because the Boston and Cambridge area was home to a host of technology and biotechnology companies as well as major research universities.

Because of the success of the Boston show, Bio-IT World decided to host another expo in San Diego in November 2002 at the San Diego Convention Center. By holding the event on the West Coast, the company hoped to attract attendees who missed the Boston show, in particular the national research labs that were largely located in the western part of the country. Like Boston, San Diego was an ideal location because Southern California was home to a large number of biotech firms.

COMBINING LIFE SCIENCE AND TECHNOLOGY

While the marriage of IT and biotech and pharmaceutical companies appeared to be a good one from the point of view of magazine publishers and trade show operators, it was not embraced by all of the key players. Technology entrepreneurs and investors, on one hand, were clearly interested, especially after the dot-com bubble burst. Scott Kirsner in the October 28, 2002, issue of the *Boston Globe* explained the reasoning: "Pharma and biotech companies are among the least sophisticated users of technology. The cost of creating new drugs keeps going up. Our band of brilliant technologists can help." The companies themselves, however, were not convinced that the technologists knew enough about the life sciences to offer much help, and elected instead to continue writing their own software to serve their own specific needs.

The technology advertisers in *Bio-IT World*, as well as the editorial pages of the magazines, pleaded the case for bringing the two together, making use of the tactic that proved so successful in the late 1990s when corporations, terrified of falling behind the competition, spent heavily on technology. One column in *Bio-IT World* warned life sciences companies to "beware the fate of the horse and buggy."

ADDITIONAL PUBLICATIONS LAUNCHED

Bio-IT World did not enjoy explosive growth, but the results still exceeded its conservative projections. One year after its launch, the magazine published its largest issue to date, 124 pages, half of which were advertising. By then the magazine had a better understanding of its target audience and its mailing list was refined. In fact, it became one of the most popular of IDG's rental lists. It was also clear that despite the reluctance of life science companies to join forces with technology companies, the convergence of life science and technology was undeniable and favored the long-term prospects of Bio-IT World Inc. and its operations.

The company added to its business in 2003 with the launch of *Health-IT World News*, a twice-weekly electronic publication targeting technology professionals and health care, pharmaceutical, regulatory, and supplier executives. It covered product development, clinical trials, treatments, and related technology. In the spring of 2004 a monthly digital, *Health-IT World*, was added as well. Both were distributed free to qualified professionals. Bio-It World also launched an electronic weekly called *PharmaWeek* to track pharmaceutical industry news and trends. In 2005 Bio-It World acquired *Pharmaceutical Discovery* magazine from Advanstar Communications and made plans to relaunch it in the spring of 2006.

CHANGE IN OWNERSHIP

Bio-It World changed ownership in February 2006, when majority control of the media and events company was sold to Newton, Massachusetts-based Cambridge Healthtech Institute. IDG retained a minority stake in the business. Cambridge Healthtech was primarily a conference producer for the life sciences industry, making Bio-IT's trade show an obvious fit, but the addition of the company's media properties, *Bio-IT World*, *Pharmaceutical Discovery*, and *PharmaWeek*, was welcomed as well.

Cambridge Healthtech was a relatively young company, established in 1992 with just eight employees.

A year later it produced a dozen conferences, a number that grew to 40 in 1994. Over the years, the company hosted events in Europe and Asia and conducted meetings related to many areas of biotechnology that were also within the purview of Bio-IT World. With the addition of the Bio-IT World Expo, Cambridge Healthtech was producing more than 90 conferences a year. The company also moved its headquarters from Newton to Bio-IT World's home in Needham, Massachusetts.

Bio-IT World did well under new ownership. The flagship magazine continued to be published, albeit reduced to six times a year. The expo was taken to Europe in 2009 for the first time when Bio-IT World Europe was held. The parent company also continued to grow, and with the further integration of IT and the life sciences, there was every reason to expect that greater opportunities awaited Bio-IT World in the years to come.

Ed Dinger

PRINCIPAL COMPETITORS

Advantage Business Media; Jameson Publishing; Penn-Well Corporation.

FURTHER READING

"BIOTECHNICA 2009 Expands Its Coverage," *Blood Weekly,* July 9, 2009, p. 527.

Cohen, David S., "Bio-IT World San Diego: New Show to Focus on Bioinformatics Market," *Tradeshow Week,* October 28, 2002, p. 4.

"IDG Sells Bio-IT World Inc. to Cambridge Healthtech Institute," *Business Publisher,* March 16, 2006, p. 1.

"International Data Group Forms New Business Unit," *Business Publisher,* November 30, 2001, p. 1.

Kirsner, Scott, "Bio-IT Firms Get Nowhere—In a Rush," *Boston Globe,* October 28, 2002, p. C1.

"New IDG Unit to Launch 'Bio-IT World' in March," *Business Publisher,* January 16, 2002, p. 1.

Van Camp, Scott, "IDG, Others Target Trendy Sector," *Adweek Magazine's Technology Marketing,* May 2002, p. 6.

BorsodChem Zrt.

Pf. 208, Bolyai Ter. 1
Kazincbarcika, H-3702
Hungary
Telephone: (+36 06) 48 511 211
Fax: (+36 06) 48 511 511
Web site: http://www.borsodchem.hu

Private Company
Incorporated: 1949 as Borsodi Vegyi Kombinát
Employees: 3,958
Sales: EUR 918 million ($1.39 billion) (2006)
NAICS: 325188 All Other Inorganic Chemical
    Manufacturing; 325211 Plastics Material and Resin
    Manufacturing

■ ■ ■

BorsodChem Zrt. is one of Eastern Europe's leading producers of raw materials for the plastics industry. The Kazincbarcika, Hungary-based company focuses on two primary categories. The first is Isocyanates, including TDI (toluene di-isocyanate) and MDI (methylene di-para-phenylene isocyanate), both essential components of polyurethane. MDI-based polyurethanes are used for such applications as adhesives, sealants and coatings, and in the production of footwear, as well as for thermoplastic polyurethanes used in appliances, automobiles, and the construction industry. TDI-based polyurethanes are used especially for the production of flexible foams, used in furniture, car seats, and similar products.

BorsodChem's second main business unit is Vinyls, which produces polyvinyl chloride (PVC) resins and compounds, as well as chlorinated polyethylene, and hydrochloric acid and caustic soda, among others. BorsodChem announced plans to sell off its PVC operations in 2009, however. The company also produces a small amount of semifinished and finished plastic products.

BorsodChem operates in the Czech Republic through subsidiary BC-MCHZ, which produces aniline and nitric acid, among other products, for BorsodChem's isocyanates production. The company's BC Polska unit, formerly Petrochemia-Blachownia, produces benzene and toluene and other aromatic hydrocarbons. BorsodChem is owned by First Chemical Holding Vagyonkezelo Kft, an investment vehicle controlled by Permira and Vienna Capital Partners. The company expects to add China's Yantai Wanhua Polyurethanes, part of Wanhua Industrial, as a minority shareholder following a debt restructuring in 2010. Kay Gugler is BorsodChem's CEO and chairman.

COMMUNIST ORIGINS IN 1949

The site of the future BorsodChem already served as a chemical manufacturing plant in the years before Communist control of Hungary. An earlier business, called the Imperial Chemical Factory, had been established in 1928, under the auspices of famed Hungarian inventor Kálmán Kandó. The factory was located in Berente, a small village in the county of Borsod-Abaúj-Zemplén, in northern Hungary near the Slovakian border.

KEY DATES

1928: Imperial Chemical Factory is founded in Berente, in the county of Borsod-Abaúj-Zemplén, Hungary.

1949: Borsodi Vegyi Kombinát (BVK) is founded.

1960: The Berente factory becomes part of BVK and is retooled for polyvinyl chloride (PVC) production.

1984: BVK launches a phosphene gas plant as a first step toward isocyanate (MDI and TDI) production.

1991: BVK is restructured as a state-owned joint-stock company, BorsodChem, and launches production of MDI.

1996: BorsodChem is listed on the Budapest and London stock exchanges.

2001: BorsodChem launches production of TDI.

2006: Permira and Vienna Capital Partners (VCP) acquire 100 percent of BorsodChem.

2009: BorsodChem announces plans to sell off its PVC business.

2010: Permira and VCP reach an agreement to add Yantai Wanhua as a minority shareholder in BorsodChem.

Following World War II, the Hungarian government created a new industrial town, Kazincbarcika, by combining a number of the area's villages, including Berente. The government created a new holding company in 1949 to take over parts of the country's chemical industry. This company then took over several local industrial operations, including Borsod Industrial Trust, Borsod Coke Works, and Sajomentí Chemical works in 1952. These were merged to form the Borsodi Vegyi Kominát, or Borsod Chemical Complex (BVK), in 1954.

One of BVK's earliest operations was the production of fertilizers, which began in 1955. From the outset, the company's factory produced 132,000 metric tons of calcium nitrate per year. The factory also initially produced 110 metric tons of ammonia each day. A refitting of the factory the following year, however, eliminated the ammonia unit. Instead, the company focused on its calcium nitrate operations, which it began marketing under the Agronit brand name.

BVK broadened its product base again in 1960, when it took over the operations of the former Imperial Chemical Factory in Berente. The site was then retooled

to launch production of olefin, a new type of plastic fiber that had been developed in the late 1950s. Olefin, a major breakthrough in plastics technology, became more commonly known as polypropylene and polyethylene. In 1963 BVK formed a new company, Chemical Works of Berente, and launched construction of its Olefin I factory, incorporating technology from Shin-Etsu Chemical Company of Japan. The Berente factory, using technology from Uhde Hoescht, became the first in Hungary to produce PVC resin, with an initial capacity of 6,000 metric tons per year.

HUNGARY'S PLASTICS LEADER IN THE SEVENTIES

BVK continued to expand its chemicals operations. The group added mercury-pool cathode capacity, used for the production of chlorine and chlorine-based compounds, which were important components of the PVC production process. This permitted the group to add a hydrochloric acid production unit in 1963. The company also later added caustic soda production as well. Two years later, the company added production of caporlactam, a primary material in the production of polyamide fibers such as nylon. BVK then added its own polyamide production, launching its Bonamid brand in 1968.

BVK added a PVC-processing facility in 1970, launching the production of PVC-based shutters. In 1971 the company expanded its PVC production unit to 30,000 metric tons per year. This expansion came in support of the group's entry into the PVC profiles market, with the addition of a factory in Szekszárd, in southern Hungary. The new plant produced doors and wall elements. Closer to home, BVK added a plastic-processing facility in Miskolc, the capital city of Borsod-Abaúj-Zemplén County.

BVK continued its expansion through the 1970s. In 1975 the company added a new factory for the production of drainpipes, rigid films, and PVC profiles. By then, BVK had become Hungary's largest plastics producer, responsible for half of the country's total production.

The rising demand for plastics led to further investments by BVK. These included a 160,000 metric-ton-per-year vinyl-chloride factory, and a third PVC plant, as part of the group's Olefin II project, boosting its PVC resin capacity to 150,000 metric tons per year, in 1978. In that year, the company also launched production at a new 110,000 metric ton (per year) chloralkali electrolysis facility, based on technology imported from Italy.

PRIVATIZED IN 1991

BVK added several new operations through the 1980s. In 1982 BVK began producing PVC dry blend, a mix of PVC resin and plasticizer used for the production of softer plastics. The following year, BVK launched the production of PVC window. BVK entered the pharmaceutical market as well, setting up a tryptamine factory in 1984. BVK also continued to produce fertilizer, introducing new granulated fertilizers launched in 1988.

By then, however, BVK had taken the first step toward its future focus on isocyanates. This came with the opening of a phosgene plant in 1984. Phosgene, a highly poisonous gas most notoriously known for its use during World War I, was an important component in the production of isocyanates, including toluene diisocyanate (TDI) and methylene di-para-phenylene isocyanate (MDI). Both TDI and MDI in turn were the primary raw materials for the production of polyurethane plastics. Polyurethane had a broad range of uses, including foams used for furniture, automobile seats, and insulation, as well as for footwear, gel pads, and many other products.

BVK next began building its own isocyanate factory, incorporating technology from Japan's Mitsui Toatsu Chemicals Company. This facility launched production in 1991, starting with a capacity of 25,000 metric tons per year. BVK initially focused on the production of MDI, used in the production of flexible polyurethanes for such purposes as adhesives, sealants, and coatings, but also for footwear.

In the meantime, the collapse of the Soviet Union and the installation of a new democratic government also led to a breakup of the country's state-owned industrial holdings. The election of a center-right government in 1990 set to the stage for the country's privatization effort. As Hungary's largest chemical concern, BVK became a major part of the privatization process.

As a first step, the government converted the company into a joint-stock company, called Borsod-Chem Rt., in 1991. The government maintained ownership of the company during the difficult years of the transition to a market-based economy. In the middle of the 1990s, however, Hungary's economy had begun to grow again. This enabled the government to complete BorsodChem's privatization, with a public offering on the Budapest and London stock exchanges in 1996.

ADDING ISOCYANATE CAPACITY IN 2001

By then, BorsodChem had completed a number of plant upgrades. These included the implementation of a new environmental protection policy, along with the addition of a wastewater treatment plant, in 1992. In this way the company began to counteract the decades of notoriously lax environmental controls of the Communist era. BorsodChem also invested in upgrading its production lines, including launching an ISO 9002 Quality Assurance program in 1994.

In 1995 BorsodChem also launched an expansion of its polyurethanes business, raising output at its MDI plant to 60,000 metric tons per year. The new facility also incorporated advanced environmental techniques, which enabled it to reuse waste by-products to produce other products, including chlorine and caustic soda. The company also completed an expansion of its vinyl-chloride factory in 1999, the upgrade enabling the company to raise its production levels to 220,000 metric tons per year.

BorsodChem's public offering fueled the group's expansion into the other major isocyanates category, with the construction of a TDI factory it began in 1998. This facility, built in Kazincbarcika and completed in 2001, added another 60,000 metric tons per year to BorsodChem's isocyanate capacity.

BorsodChem had also made its first moves beyond Hungary during this time. The company added a Polish sales subsidiary in 1997, then later acquired Petrochemia-Blachownia, a producer of benzene and toluene and other aromatic hydrocarbons. In 2000 the company acquired a stake in MCHZ, based in the Czech Republic, a producer of aniline and nitric acid used in the production of isocyanates. BorsodChem continued to build its shareholding in MCHZ, acquiring 100 percent control in 2008.

NEW OWNERS IN 2010

BorsodChem itself had gained new shareholders in the new century. In 2000 a company registered in Ireland and called Milford Holdings began buying up Borsdo-Chem's shares, gaining nearly 25 percent of the company by September of that year. Soon after, however, it became clear that Milford Holdings had been set up as a front for Russia's Gazprom, which sought to gain control of BorsodChem's own 25 percent share of the TVK chemicals pipeline.

In response, BorsodChem sold its TVK to Hungarian energy giant MOL, in order to keep the pipeline out of Russian hands. This led Milford to sell its share of the company in 2003 to VCP Industrie Beteiligungen, also known as Vienna Capital Partners (VCP). VCP, which had already acquired a separate stake in Borsod-Chem, and which itself had been suspected of acting on behalf of Gazprom, thereby raised its control of Borsod-

Chem to more than 88 percent. In 2004, however, VCP decided to sell off 63 percent of BorsodChem, this time through a listing on the Warsaw Stock Exchange, maintaining a minority stake in the company.

In the meantime, BorsodChem continued to expand strongly in the first half of the decade, building its revenues from EUR 453 million in 2001 to nearly EUR 700 million by 2006. This growth caught the eye of another investment group, Permira, which, through its Luxembourg-based fund Kikkolux SARL, gained options to acquire 53 percent of the company in 2005. By 2006 Permira and VCP had bought out the company's minority shareholders and removed its stock exchange listings.

BorsodChem then launched a new and ambitious expansion program, spending more than EUR 500 million through the end of the decade. This enabled the company to add a new 120,000 metric ton-per-year membrane-cell chlorine plant in 2006. The company also added a second TDI production unit, with a capacity of 160,000 metric tons per year, and launched construction of a 200,000 metric ton-per-year nitric acid facility in 2007.

BorsodChem's ambitious expansion came as part of an effort to raise the group's isocyanate production capacity in order to enable the company to compete on a European level, beyond its core Central and Eastern European markets. The investment drive came at a cost, however, as the company suffered the effects of the economic downturn while also struggling under an increasingly heavy debt load. By 2009 the company's debt had topped EUR 1.1 billion, more than its last reported revenues of EUR 918 million ($1.3 billion) in 2006. This led the company to announce in April 2009 that it planned to sell off its PVC business.

The company also went in search of a new strategic investor in order to bolster its flagging financial situation with a new capital injection. Help came in the form of Yantai Wanhua Polyurethanes, part of China's Wanhua Industrial, which sought to gain an entry into the European plastics market. The deal soon appeared to stall, after Wanhua insisted on taking majority control of BorsodChem by squeezing out Permira. By October 2009, Wanhua had dropped this effort, contenting itself with a minority share.

Talks continued into 2010, as BorsodChem negotiated with the Hungarian government to restructure its debt. In February 2010, the companies announced that they had reached an agreement, whereby Permira, VCP, and Wanhua agreed to underwrite EUR 140 million in new funding, bringing in Wanhua as a minority shareholder. BorsodChem hoped to resolve the issue of its shareholding structure, and its debt load, in order to refocus its efforts on building its position as one of Eastern Europe's leading chemical companies.

M. L. Cohen

PRINCIPAL SUBSIDIARIES

BC Polska Sp. z o.o.; BC-Ablakprofilgyártó és Forgalmazó Kft.; BC-Energiakereskedo Kft. (BC-Energy Trade Ltd.); BC-KC Formalin Kft.; BC-Ongropack Kft.; BorsodChem Italia s.r.l.; BorsodChem-MCHZ s.r.o. (Czech Republic); Petrochemia-Blachownia; Polimer Szolgáltató Kft.

PRINCIPAL DIVISIONS

Isocyanates; Vinyls.

PRINCIPAL COMPETITORS

Solvay S.A.; BASF; Arkema Inc.; PPG Industries Inc.; LG Chem Ltd.; Tangshan Sanyou Group Company Ltd.; Ineos Norge A.S; Tosoh Corp.; Hengyang Xinhua Chemical Metallurgy Company Ltd.

FURTHER READING

"BorsodChem Owners to Raise Capital Jointly with Wanhua," *Budapest Business Journal*, February 1, 2010.

"BorsodChem to Require Less Money to Complete Necessary Developments," *Budapest Business Journal*, February 12, 2010.

"Can Hungary's BorsodChem Still Be Saved?" *Portfolio.hu*, January 22, 2010.

"China's Wanhua Retreats, Surrenders Goal to Have Permira Exit from Hungary's BorsodChem," *Budapest Business Journal*, October 15, 2009.

"Dynea and BorsodChem Expand Capacity in Kazinbarcika," *Chemie.de*, February 7, 2005.

"Permire Agrees on Debt Restructure for BorsodChem," *AltAssets*, February 8, 2010.

Sakoui, Anousha, and Martin Arnold, "Permira Agrees Deal on BorsodChem's Debt," *Budapest Business Journal*, February 5, 2010.

Bruker Corporation

40 Manning Road
Billerica, Massachusetts 01821-3915
U.S.A.
Telephone: (978) 663-3660
Fax: (978) 667-5993
Web site: http://www.bruker.com

Public Company
Incorporated: 1991 as Bruker Federal Systems, Inc.
Employees: 4,400
Sales: $1.107 billion (2008)
Stock Exchanges: NASDAQ
Ticker Symbol: BRKR
NAICS: 334516 Analytical Laboratory Instrument
   Manufacturing

■ ■ ■

Billerica, Massachusetts-based Bruker Corporation is the parent for a group of companies divided between Bruker Scientific Instruments Division and Bruker Energy & Supercon Technologies (BEST) Division. The Bruker Scientific Instruments Division includes Bruker AXS, which produces analytical X-ray systems, optical emission spectrometers, and combustion analyzers for a wide range of research and industrial customers, including life sciences, nanotechnology, forensics, pharmacy, and petrochemistry. Another of the units, Bruker BioSpin, offers analytical magnetic resonance instruments and the superconducting high and ultrahigh field magnets used in magnetic resonance imaging (MRI) machines and nuclear magnetic resonance (NMR) machines.

Bruker Daltonics manufactures mass spectrometry (MS) instruments used by life science, pharmaceutical, biochemical, and chemical researchers to analyze the chemical structure of a compound. The company also produces chemical, biological, radiological, and nuclear (CBRN) detection devices for homeland security. Bruker Optics employs infrared and Raman molecular spectroscopy technology to provide academic and industrial researchers with analytical and process analysis instruments.

The BEST Division manufactures high-performance superconductor wire products and devices for physics and energy research, and includes operations in Germany and the United Kingdom in addition to the United States. Bruker is a public company listed on the NASDAQ. All told, it employs more than 4,000 people working out of 90 locations across the globe.

WEST GERMAN ORIGINS

Despite the Bruker name, the man behind the founding of Bruker Corporation was Gunther Laukien, a German-born scientist who earned an undergraduate degree in physics from the University of Tubingen in 1951. He then performed studies in NVIR spectroscopy, receiving his PhD from the same school in 1955. As early as 1951 Laukien learned about the spin echo phenomenon that was at the root of magnetic resonance technology. In 1958 he published a seminal paper on high-frequency NMR.

Despite the demands of an academic career as both professor and head of the Institute of Physics at Karlsruhe's Technical University, Laukien decided in 1960 to build high-resolution devices using magnetic resonance for analytical chemistry purposes. Unlike in the United States, West German universities did not allow active professors to commercialize their research. Hence, the company he launched in September 1960 took the name of a partner, Dr. Emil Bruker, and became known as Bruker Physik AG.

Bruker was little more than a garage start-up, producing laboratory magnets and power supplies. However, within three years the company boasted a staff of 30, producing NMR and electron paramagnetic resonance (EPR) instruments, and the company purchased land to build a larger facility. Laukien formed another company in the mid-1960s called Spectrospin AG to absorb the NMR spectrometer department of a financially troubled company, Trub Tauber, which was doing pioneering work in the field. The two companies worked cooperatively.

Bruker Physik then focused all of its attention on magnets and power supplies that were used by Spectrospin to develop cutting-edge high-resolution instruments. Their collaboration resulted in the HFX 90, the first fully transistorized, commercially available NMR instrument, unveiled in 1967. A year later Yale University acquired the first HFX 90 in the United States, leading to the opening of a sales office in Elmsford, New York.

Bruker made advances in other areas as well. Work in pulse NMR technology led to the development of the first high-power radio-frequency amplifier that could both pulse and decouple, resulting in a form of broadband decoupling that led to the 1969 introduction of the first FT-NMR spectrometer system with broadband proton decoupling capabilities. Bruker also pursued pulse spectrometry, developing the minispec 20 NMR spectrometer, the first such instrument suitable for industrial applications.

LAUKIEN ABANDONS ACADEMIA: 1971

Well respected in the NMR field, Bruker began to grow into a global concern. Unable to adequately perform his dual roles as professor and president of Bruker, Laukien decided in 1971 to focus all of his attention on running the company. Bruker had already taken steps in 1969 to expand into the Soviet Union. Next, an office opened in Israel, followed in the 1970s by sales offices in Australia, Japan, South Korea, and Taiwan. Bruker also made inroads in the People's Republic of China. Participating in the Swiss Industrial Exhibition in Beijing in 1975, Bruker sold a pair of WH 90 spectrometer systems to the Chinese.

Bruker's research and development efforts in the 1970s continued to lead to innovative products. Taking advantage of technologies it developed for NMR spectrometers, Bruker worked with Professor Ludwig Genzel, a pioneer in Fourier transform (FT) infrared spectrometry (IR), to develop the company's first FT-IR spectrometer, the IFS 100, the design of which separated the electronics from the optics bench. Launched in 1974, it was a highly successful product line for Bruker, leading to the 1981 introduction of a benchtop version for industrial use, a development that opened up new applications for the technology and generated further instrument sales. In 1998 this business would be spun off as Bruker Optics.

INTERNAL AND EXTERNAL EXPANSION

Also in the 1970s, Bruker applied its NMR work to the MRI field, forming a medical division in 1976 called Bruker Medizintechnik. At first the subsidiary only produced mobile defibrillators, but by the end of the 1970s it was offering NMR-based tomography systems for clinical and preclinical use. This work led to the 1983 introduction of one of the first whole body MRI tomographs. Eventually Bruker elected to focus on preclinical systems, resulting in the creation of the Bruker BioSpin MRI unit.

In addition to internal developments, Bruker expanded through external means. In 1978 the IBM Instruments division of IBM Inc. invested in Bruker and the two companies began working together to optimize IR, NMR, and TD-NMR instruments for specific applications, as well as to develop instruments for gas and liquid chromatography and polar graphs. After a decade of fruitful endeavors, Bruker bought out IBM's interests and folded the systems into its regular operations.

Another acquisition, involving a company named Dr. Franzen Analysentechnik, was completed in 1980 and allowed Bruker to become involved in mass spectrometry. The young spin-off company run by Dr. Jochen Franzen had developed the first tabletop mass

KEY DATES

1960: Gunther Laukien founds Bruker Physik AG in West Germany.
1971: Laukien quits academic career to run company.
1980: Dr. Franzen Analysentechnik company acquired, allowing Bruker to become involved in mass spectrometry.
1991: Laukien's son Frank, forms Bruker Federal Systems, Inc., in the United States.
1997: Gunther Laukien dies, leaving his heirs a group of loosely connected companies.
1999: Laukien businesses are reorganized into four companies.
2003: Bruker Daltonics and Bruker AXS are merged to form Bruker BioSciences Corporation.
2008: Bruker BioSciences merges with last of family companies; changes name to Bruker Corporation.

spectrometer. Renamed Bruker-Franzen Analytik GmbH, the unit would develop the first mobile detection system, which found a ready military and civilian market. Further research led to mass spectrometry, which found applications in molecular biology and medicine, and later in pharmaceutical, life sciences, clinical, and other research.

A subsidiary, Bruker Saxonia, was formed in Leipzig, Germany, in 1990 with scientists from the former Academy of Science. Bruker-Franzen made a major contribution to the field in 1994 when it introduced the first charge-coupled device (CCD) detector for X-ray diffraction, which greatly increased the quality of the data obtained while significantly reducing sample analysis time. In 1997 Bruker-Franzen Analytik GmbH was renamed Bruker Daltonik GmbH to honor the pioneering work of John Dalton on the atomic structure of matter.

GROWTH IN THE UNITED STATES

While Bruker was expanding in manifold directions, one of Laukien's sons, Frank H. Laukien, received an education in the United States. He earned a bachelor of science degree in physics from the Massachusetts Institute of Technology and a PhD in chemical physics from Harvard University. He remained in the Boston area and in February 1991 formed a company called Bruker

Federal Systems, Inc., which worked on the development of a chemical and biological warfare agent detector.

Bruker Federal Systems, Inc., later took over the Bruker Daltonik GmbH operations and changed its name to Bruker Daltonics. In 1997, the Laukien family acquired the analytical X-ray division of Siemens AG, which operated manufacturing plants in Karlsruhe, Germany, and Madison, Wisconsin, in the United States. The U.S. assets were packaged into a new subsidiary, Bruker AXS, which was headed by Frank Laukien, while a family company in Germany operated the Karlsruhe plant.

Gunther Laukien died in 1997, leaving his widow and four sons the owners of a group of loosely connected companies. The family engineered a series of transactions to consolidate the businesses while providing liquidity for themselves. In 1999 the businesses were consolidated into four independent operating companies: Bruker AXS (which in that same year combined the U.S. and German assets into a U.S.-based company), Bruker Daltonics, Bruker BioSpin, and Bruker Optics. The next step was to take Bruker Daltonics public in the United States. Papers were filed in April 2000, and in August of that year 15 percent of the company was sold in an initial public offering of stock that raised $104 million.

BRUKER AXS TAKEN PUBLIC: 2001

Madison, Wisconsin-based Bruker AXS acquired Nonius Group, a maker of specialized analytical X-ray systems, from a Dutch company, Delft Instruments, and in December 2001 made a public offering as well, receiving a price of $6.50 per share, resulting in net proceeds of nearly $53 million. Aside from allowing family members to cash in some of their holdings, the reorganization combined systems and created synergies between the Bruker companies, resulting in improved product development. They also sold to the same customers, so that sales increased, as did profitability.

The Bruker family pursued consolidation further in July 2003 when Bruker Daltonics and Bruker AXS were merged into a single company through a $103.6 million stock and cash transaction, resulting in Bruker Bio-Sciences Corporation. Not only did the combined operation achieve even greater efficiencies, the larger company, which posted $260 million in revenues for the year, attracted more attention from investors. The Laukien family continued to hold a controlling 58 percent stake in the company. In conjunction with the merger, two operating subsidiaries were formed under the Bruker Daltonics and Bruker AXS names.

Revenues approached $300 million for Bruker Bio-Sciences in 2005. A third family-owned company was brought into the fold in April 2006 when Bruker Optics was acquired for $135 million, 59 percent of which was in cash and the balance in stock. In effect, the transaction allowed Laukien family members to convert some of their Bruker Optics stock into cash, while the rest of their shares were exchanged for stock in Bruker BioSciences. Bruker Optics brought about $80 million to the balance sheet of Bruker BioSciences.

BRUKER CORPORATION NAME ADOPTED: 2008

The last of the Bruker entities, the Bruker BioSpin group of U.S. and German companies, joined Bruker BioSciences in February 2008 in a $914 million transaction that included $388 million in cash and $526 million in stock. Upon completion of the deal, Bruker Bio-Sciences changed its name to Bruker Corporation. Frank Laukien served as president, CEO, and chairman for a company that on a consolidated basis generated more than $1 billion in sales and net earnings of $98.9 million in 2007.

Bruker was a major player in its field, and in 2008 continued to introduce innovative new products and solutions. While revenues topped $1.1 billion for the year, difficult economic conditions that adversely impacted sales from industrial customers prevented the company from meeting its goals, as net income fell to $64.5 million. As a result, the company implemented cost-cutting measures in the second half of the year, including salary and hiring freezes. Nevertheless, Bruker continued to invest in product development to pursue more profitable areas as well as new growth markets, such as Latin America, India, and China.

The company also grew through acquisitions. In 2008 Bruker bought JUWE Laborgeraete GmbH, a German manufacturer of advanced combustion analysis systems, and S.I.S. Surface Imaging Systems GmbH, a German company involved in advanced atomic force/scanning probe microscopy. In the spring of 2009

Bruker acquired the research instruments business of Varian Medical Systems, Inc.

Business continued to lag in the first half of 2009, but picked up in the third quarter as academic and government customers, the beneficiaries of economic stimulus funds, began to invest in new equipment, a trend that was sustained into 2010.

In the meantime, the Laukien family members continued to cash in some of their interests. In September 2009 two family members sold $128 million in a public stock offering. There was every reason to believe, however, that the Laukien family would continue to maintain majority control and run the company for the foreseeable future.

Ed Dinger

PRINCIPAL DIVISIONS

Bruker Scientific Instruments Division; Bruker Energy & Supercon Technologies.

PRINCIPAL COMPETITORS

Oxford Instruments plc; Shimadzu Corporation; Thermo Fisher Scientific Inc.

FURTHER READING

Aoki, Naomi, "Bruker Daltonics in $103.6M Deal Merging with Bruker AX to Create New Parent," *Boston Globe,* April 8, 2003, p. C1.

Bushnell, Davis, "Bruker Daltonics Files for IPO," *Boston Globe,* April 30, 2000, p. 5.

Douglas, Craig M., "Bruker Cashes Out Laukiens," *Boston Business Journal,* June 5, 2009.

Gallagher, Kathleen, "Madison Tech Firm Going Public," *Milwaukee Journal Sentinel,* July 28, 2001, p. 1.

Richgels, Jeff, "History of Bruker AXS Inc.," *Madison (Wis.) Capital Times,* August 29, 2002, p. 5E.

Spoth, Tom, "Bruker Group Combines Two Units in $135M Deal," *Lowell (Mass.) Sun,* April 19, 2006.

Calpine Corporation

717 Texas Avenue, Suite 1000
Houston, Texas 77002
U.S.A.
Telephone: (713) 830-2000
Fax: (713) 830-2001
Web site: http://www.calpine.com

Public Company
Incorporated: 1984
Employees: 2,049
Sales: $6.5 billion (2009)
Stock Exchanges: New York
Ticker Symbol: CPN
NAICS: 221112 Fossil Fuel Electric Power Generation;
221119 Other Electric Power Generation

■ ■ ■

Calpine Corporation is a leading independent power company that owns and operates natural gas-fired and geothermal power plants in North America. Through its network of 77 operating power plants, the company's generation capacity was 24,802 megawatts during 2009. Calpine sells wholesale power, steam, capacity, and renewable energy credits to utilities, independent electric system operators, industrial and agricultural companies, retail power providers, municipalities, and power marketers.

Through its Geysers assets, located in northern California, the company has the largest geothermal power portfolio in the United States. Calpine produced 21 percent of all renewable energy produced in California during 2008. The company, which emerged from Chapter 11 bankruptcy protection in 2008, claims to have the lowest carbon footprint of any U.S. independent power producer in the industry.

ORIGINS

Calpine was founded by three executives from the San Jose, California, office of New York-based Gibbs & Hill, Inc., an environmental engineering firm specializing in power engineering projects. Peter Cartwright, the senior member of the small group, had spent five years at Gibbs & Hill, serving as the vice president and general manager of the company's western regional office. Prior to that, Cartwright earned his bachelor of science degree in geological engineering from Princeton University in 1952 and his master of science degree in civil engineering from Columbia University in 1953. His academic training eventually provided entry into General Electric Co.'s nuclear energy division, where he spent 19 years working on plant construction, project management, and new business development.

When Cartwright left Gibbs & Hill in 1984 to start Calpine, he was joined by Ann Curtis and John Rocchio, two Gibbs & Hill executives who became vice presidents of the newly formed Calpine. The company received financial backing from Guy F. Atkinson Co., which later sold its 50 percent stake in the firm, and from Electrowatt Ltd., a Switzerland-based utility, industrial products, and engineering services company. An oversized Swiss cowbell on display at corporate headquarters in San Jose, as well as the "alpine" in the company's name, were testaments to Calpine's Swiss lineage.

COMPANY PERSPECTIVES

COMPANY PERSPECTIVES

Using advanced technologies, Calpine generates electricity in a reliable and environmentally responsible manner for the customers and communities it serves.

Initially, Calpine provided engineering, management, finance, and maintenance services to the then emerging independent power production industry, which was entering a new era of competition as regulatory constraints loosened. Calpine built turnkey power plants, which were facilities ready for immediate use, for its clients, registering its first annual profit two years after its founding.

SHIFT IN FOCUS

Calpine went on to record a string of profitable years, but much of the company's consistent success was achieved while pursuing a substantially different corporate objective than it had proclaimed at its outset. Cartwright was inspired by the impressive gains of his clients, the operators of Calpine's turnkey power plants, who were registering tantalizing financial growth. He became convinced that the greatest prospects for financial growth were to be found as a power plant operator, rather than serving the operators. Accordingly, in 1989 Cartwright altered Calpine's business focus by concentrating the company's energies on the acquisition, development, ownership, operation, and maintenance of gas-fired and geothermal power generation facilities.

As Calpine set out to fulfill its new role as a power plant developer and operator, the company's growth was measured not only by its financial totals, but also by the number of plants it owned and by the amount of electricity it produced, expressed by the megawatt (one megawatt is sufficient to light 1,000 households). Based on these criteria, Calpine achieved only moderate progress during its first years as a power plant developer and operator. By 1992, the company produced approximately 297 megawatts of electricity at four plants, enabling it to collect nearly $40 million in revenue for the year.

Calpine's production capacity represented sufficient electricity to power more than a quarter million homes. However, relative to its stature at the end of the decade and relative to the more than $200-billion-a-year power generation industry, the company was a diminutive national force during the early 1990s, its anonymity not helped by its standing as a privately held, wholly owned subsidiary of a foreign parent company.

DEREGULATION LEADS TO EXPANSION: 1990–95

Calpine was nevertheless beginning to distinguish itself during the early 1990s. The company was most widely recognized for its geothermal plants, ranking "as one of the top four or five in the business," according to Tsvi Meidav, president of a geothermal engineering company, quoted in the July 20, 1992, issue of *Business Journal–San Jose*. "They [Calpine] are most outstanding in the area of engineering and very strong in operations maintenance," Meidav added. Calpine was determined to pursue expansion more aggressively. Toward that end, the company announced plans in 1992 to complete an initial public offering of stock in three to five years and to triple its capacity by 1994.

Calpine's commitment to aggressive expansion occurred at an opportune time. As the company grew, more than tripling its annual revenue volume by collecting $132 million in 1995, the dynamics of the U.S. electric industry were about to be dramatically changed. In what would spark a national movement, the California legislature announced in 1996 that it would deregulate the state's electric industry and allow customers to choose their electricity supplier. The state legislation touched off a wave of similar resolutions across the country as deregulation spread state by state.

Within a year of California's announcement, nearly a dozen states had announced that they would deregulate their electric industries as well, with 24 other states taking the action under consideration. As the movement toward deregulation intensified, members of the U.S. Congress tried to accelerate the national trend by introducing a bill that would bypass state legislatures and promulgate nationwide electric deregulation.

As an independent power company, Calpine stood to benefit enormously from the fervor for deregulation that swept across the country during the late 1990s. The company's foundation as a service provider to power plant operators and its subsequent development into a power plant operator itself engendered a vertically integrated enterprise primed for the new competitive era. Calpine presided over every stage of a plant's development, handling each phase from conceptual design, financing, and construction, to operation, fuel management, and power marketing.

With this synergistic approach to the business of producing electricity, the company was capable of offering highly competitive rates that did not sacrifice profitability. Accordingly, Cartwright and his senior

KEY DATES

1984: Calpine is organized with the financial help of Switzerland-based Electrowatt, Ltd.

1989: Calpine broadens its business focus to include plant operation and ownership.

1996: Calpine gains independence and completes initial public offering of stock.

1999: Company announces plan to increase capacity to 25,000 megawatts by 2004.

2001: Profits increase by 82 percent; power production nearly doubles.

2002: Energy market conditions deteriorate; Calpine puts expansion plans on hold.

2005: Company files Chapter 11 bankruptcy.

2008: Calpine emerges from bankruptcy.

2009: The Otay Mesa 600megawatt gas-fired generation plant goes online.

2010: Calpine receives permit to build the nation's first power plant with a federal limit on greenhouse gas emissions.

executives welcomed the changes that were transforming their industry, particularly because they had anticipated these changes and, unlike many of their competitors, had moved aggressively to take advantage of the changes. The effect of their anticipatory actions was most evident in one pivotal transaction completed in 1996.

ACCELERATING GROWTH: 1996–99

Although Cartwright and his team completed scores of deals during the 1990s, outstanding among these was a purchase from Siemens Westinghouse Power Corp. In 1996 Calpine placed an order with Siemens Westinghouse for 46 gas-fired turbines. The acquisition represented a gamble considering that many of the turbines involved in the deal were purchased before the company had commitments to build new power plants, but Cartwright pressed ahead despite the risk. He had launched an ambitious plan at the beginning of 1996 to develop 6,300 megawatts of new capacity before the end of the decade, expansion that required new equipment to actualize.

Although the purchase of 46 turbines shocked outside observers, the timing of the deal later justified Cartwright's gamble. The purchase was made before the tidal wave of support for deregulation reached its acme

and before the majority of utilities realized more industry capacity was needed. Consequently, at the time of the Calpine-Siemens Westinghouse deal, power generation equipment was less expensive and easier to obtain than it would be once the movement toward deregulation took hold.

The combination of Calpine management's foresight in anticipating a growing demand for capacity and its willingness to gamble heavily paid handsome dividends. Commitments for new power plants arrived, thereby necessitating the acquisition of the turbines and prompting industry pundits to hail the turbine purchase as the primary cause for Calpine's glowing success at the dawn of the new century. Less than three years after the deal, companies were clamoring for turbines, with demand exceeding supply to the point that some companies were selling their turbine delivery slots, essentially exchanging their place in line for cash.

RAPID EXPANSION

The decisive Siemens Westinghouse purchase coincided with another important corporate event in 1996, one that saw the Swiss cowbell at company headquarters lose its relevance. Electrowatt Ltd. informed Cartwright that it was narrowing its strategic focus on its industrial business, a decision that paved the way for Calpine's independence. In response to the news from Switzerland, Cartwright prepared Calpine for its debut as a publicly traded company, completing an initial public offering of stock in September 1996. The stock sale netted the company $82 million and gave management an 11 percent ownership stake in Calpine.

Calpine evolved from a relative unknown in the power industry to a recognizable, burgeoning national force during the mid-1990s. Between the end of 1992 and the end of 1997, the company completed transactions involving 13 gas-fired cogeneration facilities and two steam fields, more than quadrupling its total power generating capacity and substantially diversifying its fuel mix. Calpine achieved its growth by taking on the posture of an aggressive acquirer, resulting in $855 million of total indebtedness by the end of 1997.

For Cartwright, the debt taken on was the price to pay for rapidly expanding in the promising business climate of the late 1990s, a sacrifice that greatly elevated his company's stature. Between 1992 and 1997, Calpine's net interest in power generation facilities increased from 297 megawatts to 1,981 megawatts, fueling a 48 percent compound annual growth rate in revenue that enabled the company to announce $276.3 million in revenue in 1997. Equally impressive, the value of Calpine's assets increased from $55 million in

1992 to $1.4 billion in 1997. The company's greatest surge in growth, however, was yet to come.

AMBITIOUS PLANS FOR THE 21ST CENTURY

Calpine entered the 1990s endeavoring to slip past $40 million in sales. The company ended the decade approaching the $1-billion-in-sales mark. Much of this growth was achieved between 1997 and 1999, when the company's revenue volume swelled from $276 million to $847 million as the number of plants in which it held interests increased from 23 to 44. Deregulation was in full swing during the last years of the 1990s, prompting Cartwright to develop expansion plans that promised to exponentially increase the size of his company within the coming five years.

With a flurry of acquisitions and development projects that nearly doubled the size of the company's power plant portfolio, Cartwright fleshed out Calpine's presence in California, New England, New York, and Texas. By the end of the decade, he had targeted the Southeast, and Florida in particular, as the company's next major growth area for gas-fired generation.

Cartwright's short-term plans for the first years of the 21st century were of staggering proportions. Building on a total capacity of 4,273 megawatts in 1999, Cartwright hoped to increase the company's capacity to 25,000 megawatts by 2004. To help finance such expansion, the company secured a $1 billion revolving loan backed by a syndication of more than 20 banks in late 1999. The line of credit provided the means for the construction of approximately six plants, but Cartwright's plans called for far more than six additional plants.

As the company entered the 21st century, 10 new power plants were under construction, representing nearly 6,000 megawatts of additional capacity. In addition, the company announced plans for developing 12 more plants in the near future, which represented another 7,990 megawatts of capacity. During 2001, profits increased by 82 percent over the previous year, power production nearly doubled, and the company was able to raise over $10 billion to fuel an expansion.

OVERCOMING CHALLENGES: 2002–07

During 2002 the company's aggressive expansion plans were interrupted by problems in the energy industry due in part to the collapse of Enron Corp., an energy wholesaler that was forced to declare bankruptcy amid scandal and federal charges against many of its executives. Electricity deregulation was in question at this time and California was dealing with supply and demand issues and rising energy prices. Enron had tried to hide huge losses that stemmed from price fluctuations in the wholesale energy trading market, and the downfall of the company and its executives became one of the most infamous business collapses in U.S. history.

With market conditions in the energy industry deteriorating, Calpine was forced to retool its strategy. Its debt load had grown substantially, to $12.7 billion in 2001. The company put the brakes on many of its projects in an attempt to lessen its debt. It continued to build those plants that were already in the midst of construction, however, and debt grew to $17.2 billion by 2005.

The increasing debt levels proved too much for Calpine and in December 2005 the company filed for Chapter 11 bankruptcy protection. CEO Cartwright, who was named Business Leader of the Year by *Scientific American* magazine that year for his focus on promoting low carbon energy, was forced to resign from the company shortly before the filing. Robert P. May was named his replacement and oversaw the company's reorganization process.

By May 2007, the company had sold eight power plants, initiated a cost cutting program that included cutting one-third of its employees, restructured seven of its wholesale power sales contracts, and cut debt by $1.2 billion. By the end of 2007, the company's reorganization plan was approved and Calpine emerged from bankruptcy in early 2008 with $8 billion in debt, 77 plants, and approximately 24,000 megawatts of generating capacity.

LOOKING TOWARD THE FUTURE

Jack Fusco was named Calpine's CEO in August 2008. During this time the company focused on expanding its business in its core markets while expanding its foothold in Canada through the opening of its Greenfield Energy Centre in Ontario. During 2009 the company's Otay Mesa 600-megawatt gas-fired generation plant went online and was under contract to supply San Diego Gas and Electric Co.

The company posted positive financial results during fiscal 2009 with net income increasing to $149 million from $10 million recorded in 2008. The company's projects for 2010 included upgrading its turbines and expansion at The Geysers (a geothermal plant 100 miles north of San Francisco) as well as at its Los Esteros Critical Energy Facility. In February 2010, the company received approval to construct the first power plant in the United States with a federal limit on greenhouse gas emissions. Construction on the 600-megawatt Russell City Energy Center located in Haywood, California, was slated to begin later in the year.

Calpine, which claimed to be the largest independent power producer in the nation with the lowest carbon footprint, appeared to have overcome its financial challenges. While the recession in the U.S. economy and fluctuating U.S. power demand threatened to undermine the company's expansion efforts, Calpine was confident that it was on track for future success in the U.S. energy industry.

Jeffrey L. Covell
Updated, Christina M. Stansell

PRINCIPAL SUBSIDIARIES

Calpine Foundation; Calpine Freestone, LLC; Calpine Fuels Corporation; Calpine Generating Company, LLC; Calpine Geysers Company, L.P.; Calpine Gilroy 1, Inc.; Calpine Gilroy 2, Inc.; Calpine Gilroy Cogen, L.P.; Calpine Global Investments, S.L. (Spain); Calpine Global Services Company, Inc.; Calpine Greenfield (Holdings) Corporation; Calpine Greenfield Commercial Trust (Canada); Calpine Greenfield LP Holdings, Inc.; Calpine Greenfield ULC (Canada); Calpine Greenleaf Holdings, Inc.; Calpine Greenleaf, Inc.; Calpine Hidalgo Energy Center, L.P.; Calpine Hidalgo Holdings, Inc.; Calpine Hidalgo, Inc.; Calpine International Holdings, LLC; Calpine Investment Holdings, LLC; Calpine Jupiter, LLC; Calpine Kennedy Airport, Inc.; Calpine Kennedy Operators Inc.; Calpine KIA, Inc.; Calpine King City 1, LLC; Calpine King City 2, LLC; Calpine King City Cogen, LLC; Calpine King City, Inc.; Calpine King City, LLC; Calpine Leasing Inc.; Calpine Long Island, Inc.; Calpine Magic Valley Pipeline, Inc.; Calpine Monterey Cogeneration, Inc.; Calpine MVP, Inc.; Calpine Newark, LLC; Calpine Northbrook Corporation of Maine, Inc.; Calpine Northbrook Holdings Corporation; Calpine Northbrook Investors, LLC; Calpine Northbrook Project Holdings, LLC; Calpine Northbrook Southcoast Investors, LLC; Calpine Oneta Power I, LLC; Calpine Oneta Power II, LLC; Calpine Oneta Power, L.P.; Calpine Operating Services Company, Inc.; Calpine Operations Management Company, Inc.; Calpine Pasadena Cogeneration, Inc.; Calpine Peaker Holdings, LLC; Calpine Philadelphia, Inc.; Calpine Pittsburg, LLC; Calpine Power Company; Calpine Power Management, Inc.; Calpine Power Management, LP.

PRINCIPAL OPERATING UNITS

Calpine Merchant Services; Power Operations; Marketing and Sales.

PRINCIPAL COMPETITORS

The AES Corporation; Mirant Corp.; RRI Energy Inc.

FURTHER READING

Anderson, Mark, "Cogen Plant's Under Way," *Sacramento Business Journal*, December 10, 1999, p. 11.

Baker, David R., "Calpine Betting State Needs Juice," *San Francisco Chronicle*, September 5, 2004.

"Calpine Dedicates Otay Mesa Plant," *Power Market Today*, December 14, 2009.

"Calpine Obtains Permit to Build Nation's First Power Plant with Federal Limit on Greenhouse Gas Emissions," *Global Warming Focus*, February 15, 2010.

"Calpine's New CEO Says Price Levels of Gas, Wind Are Not a Worry," *Global Power Report*, September 11, 2008.

Fricker, Mary, "Energy Giant Retrenches," *Santa Rosa (CA) Press Democrat*, March 31, 2002, p. E1.

Gosmano, Jeff, "Calpine's Eye-Popping Streak Set Off by Canny Turbine Buys," *Natural Gas Week*, August 30, 1999, p. 1.

Keegan, Jeffrey, "Building Calpine's Financing Future," *Investment Dealers' Digest*, December 13, 1999.

McLane, Tegan M., "Calpine Execs Steamed Up to Power Up," *Business Journal–San Jose*, July 20, 1992, p. 1.

Smith, Rebecca, "Calpine Announces Chapter 11 Filing," *Wall Street Journal*, December 21, 2005.

———, "Calpine Bankruptcy Plan Is Cleared," *Wall Street Journal*, December 20, 2007.

———, "Plugging into Calpine," *Wall Street Journal*, May 16, 2007.

Speaker, Scott C., "Calpine Eyes the Sunshine State," *Natural Gas Week*, September 13, 1999, p. 10.

Spring, Nancy, "Calpine's New CEO: Jack Fusco; Ready for the Future," *Electric Light & Power*, September 1, 2008.

Celio France S.A.S.

21 rue Blanqui
Saint Ouen, F-93406 Cedex
France
Telephone: (+33 01) 40 12 98 94
Fax: (+33 01) 48 74 59 54
Web site: http://www.celio.com

Private Company
Founded: 1978 as Cléo 3000
Employees: 2,500
Sales: EUR 485 million ($712.90 million) (2009)
NAICS: 448110 Men's Clothing Stores

■ ■ ■

Specializing in the men's ready-to-wear retail sector, Celio France S.A.S. is one of France's top menswear retailers. The group's more than 700 stores feature four collections each year developed by the company's own design staff. France is Celio's largest market, with nearly 250 stores. The company operates internationally as well, however, through its Belgium-based subsidiary Celio International, with stores in Belgium, Spain, and Italy.

The company has developed a strong franchise business, with stores in more than 40 countries, representing 10 percent of its total network. The company is also a partner in the Celio Future Fashion Ltd. joint venture in India, which operates 43 shop-in-shop boutiques and expects to open as many as 50 self-standing Celio stores by the end of 2010. Celio remains controlled by founders Marc and Laurent Grosman,

who also own the Jennyfer chain of young women's clothing stores. Celio's sales reached approximately EUR 485 million ($713 million) in 2009.

FOUNDING A MENSWEAR CHAIN IN 1978

Celio has its roots in a small ready-to-wear business founded by Maurice Grosman in Paris in the years following World War II. Grosman had been orphaned during the war after his entire family was deported and murdered at Auschwitz. Grosman himself survived only because, on the day of the deportation, an attack by a schoolmate landed him in the hospital. After the war, Grosman, then 15 years old, was reunited with an aunt. He had hoped to pursue his studies but instead had to go to work in order to support himself.

Grosman's working career later led him into the retail sector, where he opened a small women's clothing shop in Paris called Cléo 3000. In 1978 he was joined by his sons Laurent and Marc, who decided to extend the family's business into the men's clothing area.

Initially, the Grosmans focused on sales of branded clothing. As Laurent Grosman explained to *Le Figaro*: "In fact, we sold what we ourselves were wearing, or what we wanted to wear." This led the brothers to develop a collection markedly different from the relatively conservative retail menswear sector at the time, which focused largely on men's suits. The Grosmans instead introduced a range of colorful prints and casual clothing, quickly catching the eye of Parisian shoppers. Before long, the brothers had opened a second boutique

COMPANY PERSPECTIVES

■

Masculinity, seduction, openness, generosity and service: these are the five pillars that guide Celio in its customer relations. Since its inception, the brand has created a style that is both casual and trendy, which speaks to men. Good intuition that has borne fruit, as half of all French men now own Celio clothes! With four collections per year, designed by our team of stylists, our clothes are more than ever the stars of the brand. These are the ingredients which have made and continue to make Celio a worldwide success story.

and by the middle of the decade were operating several stores in Paris.

At first, these operations all bore different store names. In 1985, however, the brothers decided to adopt a single brand name, Celio, formed by rearranging the letters of their father's original store. The decision to develop the Celio brand was accompanied by the Grosman brothers' new strategy: that of developing their own clothing collection for their stores, a rarity in the French retail sector at that time. The Celio style, which emphasized cotton polo shirts and bright colors, proved an immediate success.

FOREIGN EXPANSION IN 1992

Celio expanded rapidly through the second half of the 1980s. By 1987, the company had opened its first store outside of Paris, in Mérignac, next to Bordeaux, expanding the chain to 13 stores. Just two years later, the company already boasted 34 stores in its chain. In 1990, Celio launched the first of several highly successful advertising campaigns. Based on the tagline "la mode je m'en fous!" ("fashion, who cares!"), the campaign backed the company's ambitious expansion effort. By 1992 the company boasted 100 stores in France.

That year also marked Celio's first steps into the international markets, with the opening of stores in Belgium and Spain. While Celio's operations in these markets came through the opening of company-owned stores, the company also put into place a franchise model for its wider international growth. The first of the franchised stores opened in 1993, in Beirut, Lebanon. The company reached a new franchise agreement in 1996, this time introducing the Celio brand to the French West Indies.

By then, its French operations had already topped 150 stores. These included a new larger store format rolled out in 1996 in a prime location across from Paris's Palais Garnier. The new store featured more than 1,000 square meters of floor space.

The Grosmans had also begun developing broader retail interests during this time. In 1997, the company launched a more upscale complement to its Celio brand, called Dooble. That chain, however, failed to replicate the Celio brand's success, building to just four stores by 2000. The company's international expansion suffered a setback as well. In 1996 the company entered the Swiss market, opening a shop in Geneva. That experiment ended just two years later, however, and the company pulled out of Switzerland.

ACQUISITIONS IN 2000

The Celio store concept remained strong, however, as the company expanded into Portugal in 1998 and then Italy in 1999. In that year, the company signed a new franchise agreement introducing the brand into Poland. By 2000 the company's franchise operations had reached Israel, Saudi Arabia, Greece, Japan, and China, among other markets.

In France, Celio made an attempt to capture a share of the fast-growing sporting wear market, launching its own retail format for that sector, Celio Sport, in 1998. The new brand grew strongly, at first, growing to 23 store by 2000. At the same time, the company sought to gain an entry into the family clothing sector, joining with Etam, a leading women's ready-to-wear retailer, to establish the WMK (Women, Men and Kids) chain in 1998.

By 2000 WMK had opened 12 stores, focusing initially on locations in out-of-town shopping zones. In that year, however, WMK shifted to a center of town strategy, which proved far more costly to implement. By 2002 the partners agreed to break up the chain, with Celio buying out the city center locations.

In the meantime, Celio had refocused its effort to enter the upscale sales bracket. The company decided to abandon the Dooble chain in 2000. In its place, Celio acquired the 65-store Laurent Cerrer men's clothing chain that year. By the end of 2000, Celio had completed a second acquisition, that of the 35-store Appel's chain in Belgium. These stores, previously women's ready-to-wear shops, were then converted to Celio, Celio Sport, and Laurent Cerrer stores. The following year, the Grosman brothers turned over the company's day-to-day leadership to Christian Pimont, former CEO of Monoprix.

Pimont's arrival signaled a new expansion of the Celio chain, which reached 170 stores by 2003. The

KEY DATES

1978: Marc and Laurent Grosman add a menswear collection to their father's women's clothing store in Paris.
1985: The Grosmans rebrand their men's clothing stores as Celio.
1992: Celio opens its first international stores in Belgium and Spain.
2000: Celio acquires clothing chains Laurent Cerrer in France and Appel's in Belgium.
2007: Celio launches a new upscale store, Celio Club.
2009: Celio's e-commerce-enabled Web site goes live.

company's international operations also grew strongly, in part through the development of a new in-store boutique format, placing the Celio brand in more than 60 multibrand clothing stores. Celio had also opened a large-scale flagship store, on Paris' prestigious Champs Elysées, in 2002.

CELIO CLUB IN 2008

Celio's franchise network grew strongly during the decade, with new markets that included Malta in 2001, the Philippines in 2002, and Algeria in 2005. By then, Celio had established a presence in 20 countries. The company's total retail operations had grown to 375 stores, generating sales of more than EUR 400 million per year. By then, too, the Grosmans had entered the women's clothing sector, when they bought up the struggling French young women's retailer Jennyfer in 2005. That company and its 350 stores, however, retained their autonomy under Celio's parentage.

In 2006 Celio carried out a relaunch of its brand, developing a new visual style and store format, as well as redeveloping its clothing collection to capture current trends. The company also expanded its number of collections from its previous winter/summer schedule to four new collections, plus a special holiday collection, per year.

In 2007 Celio decided to discontinue the Laurent Cerrer brand. The 70 Laurent Cerrer stores were re-branded, with approximately half placed under the Celio name. At the same time, the company developed a new upscale brand concept, Celio Club. The new brand presented an urban business concept, targeting the active

25 to 35 year old segment. By the end of 2007, Celio had already opened 35 Celio Club stores. Encouraged by the success of the new brand, Celio extended it to Belgium in 2008, opening five Celio Club stores there. In that year, the company moved the headquarters of Celio International, which guided the group's international operations, to Brussels.

INDIA EXPANSION IN 2010

Celio's foreign operations gained new momentum in 2008, after the company formed a joint venture with India retailer Pantaloon Retail to form Celio Future Fashion Inc. in 2008. In addition to placing Celio in-store boutiques in Pantaloon and other retail stores, the new company began rolling out a number of self-standing Celio stores. By the end of 2009, the company had already opened 11 stores and 43 in-store boutiques. In February 2010, the company announced plans to add another 15 self-standing stores in Mumbai (Bombay), Delhi, Chennai (Madras), Hyderabad, Bangalore, and Chandigarh by the end of the year.

Celio had also begun adopting new technologies in the second half of the decade. The company launched a redesigned Web site, featuring its own blog, and developed an SMS-based arm to explore ways to market Celio via mobile phone technology. Celio revamped its Web site, launching an e-commerce-enabled site in November 2009. By then, the company had instituted an in-store "flashcode" service. This marketing device allowed customers to receive 10 percent discounts by using their mobile phones to take photographs of specialized electronic billboard displays. Celio's celebrated the 25th anniversary of its brand as one of the world's top men's fashions specialists.

M. L. Cohen

PRINCIPAL SUBSIDIARIES

Celio International S.A. (Belgium); Celio Future Fashion Ltd. (India; 50%).

PRINCIPAL DIVISIONS

Menswear; Sportswear.

PRINCIPAL OPERATING UNITS

Celio; Celio Club.

PRINCIPAL COMPETITORS

Old Navy Inc.; NEXT PLC; Tommy Hilfiger Corp.; Arcadia Group Ltd.; H and M Hennes and Mauritz

B.V. and Company KG; Edgars Stores Ltd.; Valentino Fashion Group S.p.A.; Esprit Holdings Ltd.; Vivarte S.A.S.; Primark Holdings Ltd.; Burberry Group PLC.

FURTHER READING

"Celio Chamboule Sa Direction," *Fmag*, February 5, 2010.

"Celio on an Expansion Spree," *Fibre2Fashion.com*, March 3, 2010.

"Celio Streamlines Collection Design with Infor.," *just-style.com*, July 11, 2008.

"Celio to Expand in India," *Fashion United*, February 12, 2010.

"Celio Uses Flashcodes for Extra Discounts in Winter Sales," *Telecompaper Europe*, January 16, 2009.

"Comment le Reseau Celio Distribue le Fond de Hotte du Père Noël," *Les Echos*, January 9, 2008.

"The French Franchise Celio in Full International Expansion," *Franchise News*, November 14, 2008.

Jourgeaud, Bénédicte, "Celio: au Bonheur des Hommes," *Le Figaro*, January 19, 2009.

"Le Groupe Celio Se Fait Plus 'Ville,'" *La Libre*, September 24, 2008.

Maliszewski, Catherine, "Celio Lifte Son Style," *Le Figaro*, October 15, 2007.

Roquecave, Jean, "Celio Augmente Ses Capacités de Production de 30%," *Les Echos*, February 27, 2002, p. 24.

Chemring Group plc

———————————————— ■ ————————————————

1550 Parkway, Whiteley
Fareham, PO15 7AH
United Kingdom
Telephone: (+44 01489) 881880
Fax: (+44 01489) 881123
Web site: http://www.chemring.co.uk

Public Company
Incorporated: 1905 as British Foreign & Colonial
    Automatic Light Controlling Company Limited
Employees: 3,070
Sales: £505 million ($800 million) (2009)
Stock Exchanges: London
Ticker Symbol: CHG
NAICS: 332995 Other Ordnance and Accessories
    Manufacturing

■ ■ ■

Chemring Group plc is a leading producer of military
decoys and countermeasures for the U.S. and European
defense markets, as well as a fast-growing producer of
pyrotechnics and energetics—that is, specialized fuels for
the aerospace, defense, and other industries. Chemring
operates through four primary divisions: Countermeasures; Pyrotechnics; Munitions and Missiles; and
Explosive Ordnance Disposal. The Counter-measures
division produces flares, naval decoys, and other anti-
missile countermeasures, used for such purposes as
confusing heat-seeking missiles. The company's
Pyrotechnics division develops flares, distraction and

screening grenades, battlefield simulation products,
rockets, line throwers, and ejection seating systems.

The Munitions and Missiles division develops and
manufactures medium- and large-caliber ammunition,
energetics materials including propellant rocket motors,
warheads, fuses, aerial delivery and recovery systems,
and mines. The company's Explosive Ordnance Disposal
division provides anti-mine countermeasures, such as
Portable Explosive Mine Breaching Systems, as well as
detonators and related products. Chemring is listed on
the London Stock Exchange and generated revenues of
£505 million ($800 million) in 2009. David Price is the
company's chief executive officer.

ORIGINS: 1905

Chemring plc traces its origins to the beginning of the
20th century and the founding of a company called
British Foreign & Colonial Automatic Light Controlling
Company Limited, based in Bournemouth, England. As
its name implied, Automatic Light Controlling initially
specialized in developing electrical controls for the
automatic switching of gas-based street lighting systems.
By 1908, the company had developed its own street
lighting system featuring timer-based lighting and
extinguishing controls.

By the 1930s, the company's flagship line had
become its Gunfire brand of automatic light controllers.
In the 1950s the company expanded its product range
to include gas controllers, also marketed under the
Gunfire brand. The company also began developing its
own lighting devices, leading to the addition of an
operation producing silver-coated filaments.

Automatic Light Controlling nevertheless remained a modestly sized company. The company had begun to struggle by the end of the 1960s, particularly in its mechanical engineering operations. That division slipped into losses, prompting the company to shut it down in 1970. Automatic Light Controlling turned its attention instead to expansion into other areas.

One of these was a small operation developing countermeasures for the British military. Countermeasures included decoys and other devices designed to divert or distract enemy detection efforts. This activity began with World War II, when the company supplied anti-radar devices comprising aluminum foil bundles that could be launched from British aircraft in order to fool German radar stations along the British Channel. The company's investments in silver-coated filaments during the 1950s provided a new boost for its growing countermeasures activity as the company redeveloped that technology into the production of chaff, used as anti-radar decoys.

BECOMING CHEMRING: 1974

By 1973 Automatic Light Controlling had announced its intention to pursue acquisitions in order to expand its product range, continuing the shift away from its former specialty. This led to the acquisition of rival radar reflector producer Vacuum Reflex, based in Surrey. Vacuum Reflex also brought the company a range of specialized protective clothing, including life jackets, for both military and civilian use. Following that purchase, Automatic Light Controlling went public in 1974, listing its shares on the London Stock Exchange and changing its name to Chemring Ltd.

The shift in focus enabled Chemring to report new growth into the end of the 1970s. The company's revenues topped £1.5 million in 1976. The following year, the company passed the £2 million mark. By 1980, Chemring's sales had reached £3.3 million.

War over the Falklands Islands brought a new boost for Chemring as the company ramped up production of aluminum and glass chaff, used as a countermeasure against the surface-skimming missiles used to attack British naval vessels. In order to meet the British navy's needs, the company set up a new purpose-built factory.

ACQUIRING PAINS WESSEX: 1986

Toward this end, the company completed a major acquisition in 1986, of pyrotechnics group Pains Wessex. Pains Wessex had been founded by James Pain in 1850, although the Pain family traced its involvement in the manufacture of gunpowder and pyrotechnics to as early as the late 16th century. Through the first half of the 20th century, James Pain & Sons grew into one of the United Kingdom's leading manufacturers of fireworks and other pyrotechnics products, such as naval smoke signals and military flares.

British Match, through its subsidiary Bryant & May, acquired James Pain as part of a diversification drive in 1960. Two years later, Bryant & May acquired a second pyrotechnics company, Wessex Aircraft Engineering Company, also known as WAECO, which specialized in producing smoke generators for determining wind direction. In 1964, the two companies were merged together to form Pains Wessex Ltd.

Pains Wessex expanded through the 1970s, in part through the acquisition of Schermuly, based in Dorking, in 1973. This acquisition brought Pains Wessex new expertise in the marine pyrotechnics field, including the development and production of line throwing rockets. In the meantime, Pains Wessex found itself part of a far larger international group following the merger between consumer products giant Wilkinson Sword and British Match in 1973.

KEY DATES

1905: British Foreign & Colonial Automatic Light Controlling Company Limited is founded in Bournemouth, England.
1974: Automatic Light Controlling goes public and changes name to Chemring Ltd.
1986: Chemring acquires Pains Wessex, a major U.K. pyrotechnics specialist.
1992: Chemring acquires Haley & Weller and becomes the leading U.K. pyrotechnics producer.
1993: Chemring enters the United States with the acquisition of Alloy Surfaces Company.
2001: Chemring becomes the U.S. leader in defense decoys with the purchase of Kilgore Flares.
2005: Chemring creates new energetics division; acquires Comet in Germany, Troon Investments and Leafield in the United Kingdom, and Technical Ordnance in the United States.
2009: Chemring acquires Hi-Shear Technology Corporation in the United States.
2010: Chemring acquires Allied Defense Group in the United States.

Wilkinson Match, as the company became known, struggled through the 1970s, in part because of its failed effort to repeat its European success in the United States. In 1978, Wilkinson Match was acquired by Allegheny International, based in Pittsburgh, Pennsylvania. Allegheny then proceeded to break up Wilkinson Match into its various business units. As part of Allegheny, Pains Wessex also restructured to focus purely on its higher-value defense and marine pyrotechnics operations. As a result, the company's fireworks production division was sold off as a separate company, Pains Wessex Fireworks, in 1981. The sale of Pains Wessex to Chemring came amid the sale of what remained of the former Wilkinson Match to Swedish Match that same year.

FOCUS ON DEFENSE

Chemring paid £14 million ($25 million) to acquire Pains Wessex, a move that allowed the company to expand into the production of infrared decoys, as well as giving it control of the Schermuly flares brand name. Chemring and Pains Wessex also had a long history of cooperation, often collaborating on projects such as the Sea Gnat, a decoy system deployed by much of the NATO naval force. Chemring supplied the chaff for this project, while Pains Wessex produced the projectiles and their explosive propellants.

The addition of Pains Wessex also positioned Chemring to become a major supplier during the Persian Gulf War in 1991. As it had during the Falklands conflict, Chemring expanded its production, supplying infrared decoys, flares, and other countermeasures products. The company also debuted its portable anti-mine system, called the Rapid Anti-Personnel Minefield Breaching System.

Chemring's successful contribution to the war effort came despite its relatively small size. By the early 1990s the company's total revenues barely topped £30 million. The company then positioned itself to begin a long stream of acquisitions that helped transform it into a major countermeasures and pyrotechnics group. This effort started off with the purchase in 1991 of Octavious Hunt, a leading producer of smoke pesticides, for £1.5 million. Chemring also acquired Horace Sleep that year, which then became part of the company's Vacuum Reflex protective clothing unit.

These purchases came as part of Chemring's effort to reduce its dependence on the defense sector, which had begun to shrink following the collapse of the Soviet Union. Nevertheless, the company continued to invest in building its defense operations. In 1991 the company bought up the marine pyrotechnics division of Kilgore Corp., part of Allegheny International. In 1992 the company took over its major British rival, Haley & Weller. That company, founded in 1949 as a fireworks producer, had later focused on pyrotechnics. Its merger into Chemring allowed the company to become the primary supplier of pyrotechnics to England's Ministry of Defence.

ENTERING THE UNITED STATES: 1993

Chemring's success during the Persian Gulf War had also raised its profile in the United States. In 1993 the company moved to capitalize on its growing popularity there with the acquisition of its first U.S.-based operation, Alloy Surfaces Company Inc., based in Chester Township, Pennsylvania. The addition of Alloy positioned Chemring as a major supplier of infrared decoy flares to the U.S. military.

Through much of the 1990s Chemring's acquisition strategy nevertheless focused largely on consolidating its leadership position in the United Kingdom, as well as developing a presence in the Australia and New Zealand markets. The company acquired a long string of companies during the decade, including U.K. companies

Graseby plc and Kembrey plc in 1994, and Lewin & Warner Ltd. in 1995. The company's entry into Australia came with the purchase of Ronstan Trading Trust in 1995, which followed on the purchase of New Zealand-based Hutchwilco in 1994. By the middle of the decade, the company's revenues had risen past £70 million.

Chemring launched a restructuring in the late 1990s in order to refocus around a smaller range of operations. The company's defense business focused on countermeasures and military pyrotechnics and explosives, while its non-defense based operations narrowed to focus on marine safety, the Kembrey wiring harnesses business, and a small chemical coatings operation. After disposing of its non-core businesses, the company's revenues fell back to £65 million.

Chemring's restructuring paved the way for the company's major expansion at the dawn of the 21st century. Among the company's most significant acquisitions during this period was that of Kilgore Flares Company, based in Tennessee and part of Alliant Techsystems. Chemring paid $23 million for Kilgore, which produced magnesium/Teflon-based flares. The addition of Kilgore Flares with its Alloy Surfaces business made Chemring the single largest supplier of decoy flares to the U.S. military.

ADDING ENERGETICS IN THE 21ST CENTURY

Chemring faced a number of setbacks at the beginning of the decade. The company suffered a major explosion at its new Kilgore facility, followed by the refusal of its insurance company to settle its claim to the full amount. Another blow to the company came in 2002 when the BBC aired a broadcast alleging that the company's defense division, then called PW Defence, had illegally manufactured anti-personnel landmines, which had been banned since 1997. The accusations caused a significant drop in Chemring's share price. Chemring denied the allegations.

The beginning of the century nevertheless represented a period of significant growth for the company. This was in part as a result of the increased military activity by both the United States and the United Kingdom, including the invasions of Afghanistan and Iraq. By 2003, Chemring's revenues had climbed to £120 million ($200 million). This growth came despite a new company streamlining which resulted in the sale of its Kemberly wiring harnesses and its Alloy chemical coatings businesses. By this time, the United Kingdom represented just 24 percent of the company's total sales.

This streamlining paved the way for Chemring's extension into a new business area, that of energetics, that is, the propellant and explosive systems used to fuel rockets, missiles, and related devices. The move into energetics came following the arrival of David Price as the company's new chief executive. The company then completed its first acquisition in this area, in 2005, of Troon Investments Ltd., for £22 million. That operation included a production facility on the Ardeer Peninsula in North Ayrshire that had formerly been part of British chemicals giant ICI. Chemring changed the name of its new subsidiary to Nobel Energetics Ltd., adopting the name of the inventor of dynamite.

Soon after, Chemring completed several more acquisitions, including Germany's Comet GmbH; U.K.-based Leafield Engineering and Leafield Marine; and Technical Ordnance, based in the United States. Together, these acquisitions helped raise the total revenues of the company's new energetics division to more than £75 million ($110 million) before the end of its first year in operation, boosting total group revenues to more than £187 million ($290 million) by 2006.

DUAL FOCUS

The success of the energetics division encouraged the company to jettison its marine division starting in 2006. The company then launched a new string of acquisitions. These included Simmel Difesa SpA, based in Italy, which supplied fuses, safety and arming systems, warheads, and other energetics subsystems, in March 2007. In November of that year, the company added Richmond Electronics and Engineering Ltd., based in Norfolk, England, a company producing disrupters and other explosives neutralization equipment. The Richmond acquisition came as part of the company decision to establish operations in the Explosive Ordnance Disposal (EOD) sector.

Chemring's attention turned again to the United States in 2008, as it completed a new series of acquisitions there. These included Martin Electronics, based in Florida, a producer of fuses, medium- and large-scale ammunition, training grenades, and other products. The company also acquired Titan Dynamics Systems, Inc., a Texas-based producer of battlefield effect simulators; Scot Inc., based in Illinois, a producer of propellants for ejector seat systems; and Niitek, based in Virginia, which developed mine detection systems. These purchases helped raise the company's total revenues above £350 million ($560 million). By then, energetics had become the group's largest division.

Despite the decline in the global economy, the company's acquisitions continued through 2009 and into 2010. In November 2009, for example, the company acquired Hi-Shear Technology Corporation, based in Los Angeles. This acquisition, at a cost of $132 million, also enabled the company to expand its energetics division into new high technology, high-margin sectors, such as antiballistic missile systems and space and satellite separation technologies.

At the beginning of 2010, Chemring had found its next acquisition target, announcing its $59 million purchase of Allied Defense Group in January of that year. This purchase provided Chemring with a major boost to its production of ammunition. From its origins as a manufacturer of street lighting timers, Chemring had grown into the world's leading producers of countermeasures, and one of the fastest-growing players in the energetics sector.

M. L. Cohen

PRINCIPAL SUBSIDIARIES

Alloy Surfaces Company, Inc. (USA); BDL Systems Limited; Chemring Australia Pty Ltd.; Chemring Countermeasures Limited; Chemring Defence Germany GmbH; Chemring Defence UK Limited; Chemring Energetics UK; Chemring Marine Limited; Chemring Nobel AS (Norway); CIRRA S.A. (France); Kilgore Flares Company LLC (USA); Pirotecnia Oroquieta S.L. (Spain); Simmel Difesa S.p.A. (Italy); Technical Ordnance, Inc. (USA).

PRINCIPAL DIVISIONS

Countermeasures; Pyrotechnics; Munitions and Missiles; Explosive Ordnance Disposal.

PRINCIPAL COMPETITORS

Alliant Ammunition and Powder Company L.L.C.; Alliant Defense L.L.C.; ATK Space Systems; BAE Systems plc; NAVANTIA S.A.; Northrop Grumman Corp.; Rheinmetall AG; RUAG Holding; Thales Group.

FURTHER READING

"Chemring Blasts into Space," *Investors Chronicle*, September 24, 2009.

"Chemring Can See beyond Iraq," *Investors Chronicle*, June 26, 2007.

"Chemring Expands into Space," *Acquisitions Monthly*, October 2009, p. 43.

"Chemring Pounces on Ejector Seat Maker," *Acquisitions Monthly*, June 2008, p. 40.

Hofmann, Julian, "Chemring Continues to Fizzle," *Investors Chronicle*, January 20, 2009.

———, "Chemring Shrugs Off Budget Fears," *Investors Chronicle*, June 23, 2009.

———, "Chemring's Stellar Year," *Investors Chronicle*, January 19, 2010.

Kavanagh, Michael, "Chemring in Swoop on MEI," *Financial Times*, June 25, 2008, p. 24.

Lemer, Jeremy, "Acquisitions Help Chemring to Record Revenues," *Financial Times*, June 24, 2009, p. 22.

Odell, Mark, "Chemring Goes in Search of Acquisitions," *Financial Times*, February 4, 2004, p. 24.

The Chubb Corporation

15 Mountain View Road
Warren, New Jersey 07059-6711
U.S.A.
Telephone: (908) 903-2000
Fax: (908) 903-2027
Web site: http://www.chubb.com

Public Company
Incorporated: 1882 as Chubb & Son
Employees: 10,600
Sales: $11.08 billion (2009)
Stock Exchanges: New York
Ticker Symbol: CB
NAICS: 523210 Security and Commodity Exchanges; 524113 Direct Life Insurance Carriers; 524130 Reinsurance Carriers; 524114 Direct Health and Medical Insurance Carriers; 233110 Land Subdivision and Land Development; 551112 Offices of Other Holding Companies; 524126 Direct Property and Casualty Insurance Carriers; 524128 Other Direct Insurance (Except Life); 525190 Other Insurance Funds

■ ■ ■

The Chubb Corporation is best known as a provider of specialty insurance policies for upscale clients, both individuals and organizations. The company formerly did business in health and life insurance, real estate development, consulting, and financial subsidiaries, but exited these areas in the early 1990s. What distinguishes Chubb from its competitors is its focus on niche products, such as policies covering liability for corporate officers and directors or insuring stage or theater productions. Strongest in the United States, Chubb has 120 offices in 28 countries and its policies are offered by 8,500 independent agents and brokers.

STEADY GROWTH DURING THE FIRST 75 YEARS

Chubb was formed over a century ago with the partnership of Thomas Chubb, a New York underwriter of cargo and ship insurance, and his son Percy Chubb. The two formed Chubb & Son in 1882. Their venture was initially funded with $100,000 collected in $1,000 portions from each of 100 prominent merchants. Soon after its formation, Chubb & Son was one of the 100 founders of the New York Marine Underwriters (NYMU). Chubb first operated as a representative of NYMU and Sea Insurance Company Limited of England. Chubb's principal property and casualty affiliate, NYMU, was reorganized in 1901 as Federal Insurance Company.

During its first 40 years of business, Chubb & Son grew quickly, acting as an agent for several insurers. The company established itself as a respected underwriter of insurance for ships and cargo. During the 1920s, the company explored new areas. In 1921 Chubb & Son began to represent U.S. Guarantee Company. Through that company, Chubb began to underwrite fidelity, surety, and casualty insurance. In 1923 Chubb opened its first branch in Chicago. In March 1929 Chubb and another transportation insurance agent, the Marine Office of America, organized the Associated Aviation

Underwriters, the largest aviation insurance-underwriting group in the United States. Seven companies represented by Chubb and eight insurers represented by the Marine Office joined to form the association.

During the Depression, Chubb's growth slowed as the insurance industry suffered. Nevertheless, in April 1930 Chubb & Son bought a 9,000-square-foot plot in Manhattan to house its companies and allow room for expansion. In 1939 Chubb founded Vigilant Insurance Company, a wholly owned fire and marine subsidiary. The economy recovered during World War II, and Chubb & Son's business began to grow more quickly.

In December 1941 Chubb gave employees with more than six months of service their first Christmas bonuses. The workers each received half of their bonus in cash, and half in the form of war bonds. Also in December 1941, Chairman Charles A. Seibert, a 55-year veteran of the company, announced his retirement. The company acquired The Colonial Life Insurance Company of America in 1957, and in 1959 Chubb & Son reincorporated under the laws of New York.

REORGANIZATION AND ACQUISITIONS

The Chubb Corporation saw many changes in the late 1960s. In 1967 the company's management formed The Chubb Corporation to act as a holding company. Chubb & Son became a wholly owned subsidiary of The Chubb Corporation, as did Chubb & Son's subsidiaries. The property and casualty companies within the Chubb group of insurance companies fell under the management of Chubb & Son, the branch responsible for the company's domestic property and casualty insurance companies and U.S. branches of foreign insurers. The primary property and casualty insurance company managed by Chubb & Son remained Federal Insurance Company.

In July 1967 Chubb acquired Pacific Indemnity Corporation of Los Angeles. In November 1967 Carl Fisher, president and chief executive officer of Pacific Indemnity, was elected senior vice president and director of Chubb. In January 1969 First National City Corporation (later Citicorp) agreed to acquire The Chubb Corporation. In April 1969, however, the two corporations confirmed that the U.S. Department of Justice was examining the antitrust implications of the merger. Later that month, the two companies agreed to postpone the merger until the summer of 1969 in order to allow the Department of Justice to complete its study of the transaction. On June 13, 1969, the Department of Justice announced its intention to bring suit to bar the acquisition. Three hours later, First National City Corporation canceled the planned merger.

In September 1969 William M. Rees, then president of The Chubb Corporation, was elected chief executive officer and became responsible for all operations excluding investment. Investment responsibilities and general corporate policy and development remained with Chairman Percy Chubb II.

In 1970 Chubb acquired Bellemead Development Corporation, a Delaware real estate company with land holdings primarily in New Jersey and Florida. This acquisition was Chubb's first major move into the real estate field. Chubb confirmed that its real estate consultants placed a value of more than $25 million on Bellemead's properties if sold individually on the open market.

In 1971 Chubb acquired United Life & Accident Insurance Company and founded Chubb Custom Market. Chubb Custom Market became involved heavily in the entertainment industry. The subsidiary specialized in insurance for the film industry, and insured such movies as *E.T.: The Extra-Terrestrial, Tootsie, The Verdict,* and *Missing.* When Dustin Hoffman developed laryngitis and was unable to perform for three days during the filming of *Tootsie,* Chubb covered the additional expense. In addition to insuring films, Chubb Custom Market provided entertainment coverage for television productions, special entertainment events, and Broadway shows. In 1983 Chubb insured 75 percent of the productions on Broadway. Chubb's coverage was popular because of its comprehensive nature, which included theft, injuries, and equipment failure.

HEAD OFFICE RELOCATED TO NEW JERSEY

On June 9, 1971, American Financial Corporation, a Cincinnati, Ohio-based financial holding company, sold 875,000 shares of Chubb stock to Salomon Brothers in

KEY DATES

1882: Thomas and Percy Chubb form Chubb & Son.
1901: Chubb's principal property and casualty affiliate reorganizes as Federal Insurance Company.
1939: Chubb founds Vigilant Insurance Company.
1957: The company acquires The Colonial Life Insurance Company of America.
1967: The company's management forms The Chubb Corporation to act as a holding company for Chubb & Son and its subsidiaries.
1970: Chubb acquires Bellemead Development Corporation.
1984: Chubb acquires Volunteer State Life Insurance Company.
1998: Chubb sells a substantial portion of its Bellemead Development portfolio and forms Chubb Re.
2002: The terrorist attacks of September 11, 2001, asbestos claims, and Enron collapse result in huge payouts.
2005: Hurricanes Katrina and Rita cost Chubb $536 million.

a transaction valued at more than $54 million. American Financial had begun to acquire the stock in 1969 and had planned to attempt a buyout of Chubb. Salomon Brothers resold the shares, which represented a 14 percent stake in Chubb, to the public later in the day.

In 1973, Chubb, through the international division of Chubb & Son, joined First National City Corporation's subsidiary, FNC Comercio, in buying a majority interest in Companhia de Seguros Argos Fluminense, a Brazilian multiple-line insurance company.

The Chubb Corporation formed Chubb Life Insurance Company of America in 1978 to serve as an intermediate holding company for life insurance subsidiaries. In 1981 the company began to consolidate the activities of The Colonial Life Insurance Company of America and United Life & Accident Insurance Company at Chubb Life's headquarters in Concord, New Hampshire. This consolidation was completed in 1984.

In 1983 The Chubb Corporation completed and relocated to a new head office on 185 acres in Warren,

New Jersey. The following year, Chubb focused its efforts on growth in its international division. The company sought to increase its international property and casualty insurance business and to expand its worldwide coverage for U.S. multinationals.

The company's strategy for distinguishing itself was not to offer universal contracts or preformulated programs, but instead to create policies tailored to meet the needs of its clients. Chubb set a goal of maintaining 20 percent annual growth of its international business. In 1984 Chubb acquired Volunteer State Life Insurance Company of Chattanooga, Tennessee, and discontinued its money-losing medical malpractice insurance policies.

During the summer of 1987, a nine-person delegation from the People's Republic of China spent two days at the company's Warren, New Jersey, headquarters. The company's relations with China dated to before World War II, when Chubb owned and operated the Cathay Insurance Company. The delegation, consisting of government officials and representatives from the People's Insurance Company of China, studied Chubb's safety and loss control problems.

Also in 1987, Chubb acquired Sovereign Corporation, a life insurance holding company. Profits were significantly lower that year due to higher catastrophe losses from the Chicago rainstorms, Edmonton tornadoes, and a hurricane in Bermuda.

CORPORATE IMAGE SUFFERS AND IS REBUILT

Through a New York firm called Good Weather International Incorporated, Chubb began advertising rain insurance in 10 states in May 1988. Drought insurance was also offered to midwestern farmers by the Chubb subsidiary, Federal Insurance Company. Chubb usually reserved the authority to approve each policy that its independent agents sold, but in this case Good Weather was given the authority to approve Chubb policies. Because rain insurance was a small part of Chubb's business, with Chubb issuing $5 million of coverage to approximately 200 farmers in 1987, the company set a total limit of $30 million of coverage.

Response was moderate until early June, when lack of rain threatened farmers with the most serious drought in over 50 years. On June 14 and June 15, 1988, Good Weather received over 6,600 applications seeking $275 million worth of coverage, and applications kept coming after the deadline. While farmers worried about the drought, Good Weather and Chubb worried about the flood of applications. The figures were not totaled until the end of June.

In the confusion, agents had signed up at least

$350 million of coverage for nearly 9,000 farmers. The drought continued, and on July 15 of that year Chubb notified 7,616 farmers that they had been denied coverage. In a goodwill effort, Chubb offered to return double the original premiums to farmers who had applied on June 14 or 15. The effort was unsuccessful. After this experience, Chubb decided to discontinue drought insurance.

In July 1988 Dean R. O'Hare, chairman and chief executive officer of The Chubb Corporation and Federal Insurance Company since May, was elected chairman and chief executive officer of Chubb & Son. In August 1988 Chubb agreed to let American National General Agencies Incorporated (ANGA) take over its entertainment insurance underwriting responsibilities on the East Coast. Headquartered in Los Angeles as a wholesale entertainment insurance broker, ANGA branched into New York to assume the underwriting function for production risks through Chubb Custom Market.

In 1989 Chubb took great measures to reestablish a positive corporate image. Its efforts were successful, and 1989 was a good year for the company overall. In April 1989 Chubb Life Insurance of America joined the Geese Theatre Company, a nonprofit touring theater group working exclusively in prisons, in establishing a theater residency program in Concord, New Hampshire. Chubb generated more good press later that year when it won the Insurance Marketing Communications Association Special Award from members. The competition was mounted to recognize and award superior marketing communications work in the property and casualty industry.

OUTPERFORMING THE INDUSTRY

Hurricane Hugo and the California earthquake had a significant impact on Chubb's 1989 domestic earnings, however. Although earnings still increased, the catastrophes took a substantial bite out of profits. International operations continued to contribute greatly to the company's financial success, and revenues from international operations that year approached $500 million, about 12.5 percent of the year's $4 billion total. Chubb worked to increase its international activities and set a goal of generating 25 percent of total revenue from international operations by 2000.

The softening of the property and casualty insurance market in the early 1990s affected Chubb less than some of its competitors. The company's focus on specialty products helped Chubb outperform the industry through those years. Chubb had showed great improvement in life and health insurance during 1989,

and anticipated that earnings would continue to increase as group health operating conditions improved. At $4.2 billion, earnings for 1990 reached a new high, setting the company's fifth consecutive year of record earnings.

The success was attributed to conservative underwriting, a large network of branch offices (71 with plans to open four more), and a solid balance sheet. With the failure of many large financial institutions shaking public confidence in the late 1980s, a clear ability to cover liabilities with liquid assets became essential to maintaining a reliable reputation. Chubb fulfilled this requirement well.

At the same time, a downturn in the economy and unfavorable regulatory conditions began to reveal potential vulnerabilities in Chubb's real estate and commercial insurance businesses. Commercial overbuilding in the 1980s glutted the market, and regulatory scrutiny following the savings and loan failures led banks to curtail real estate lending. Unable to counteract these changes, Chubb's real estate holdings and development ventures began to lose money.

Chubb said in its 1990 annual report that it saw these market conditions as more than a cyclical downturn, and that it would begin to view real estate holdings as long-term investments. The company predicted that conditions in the real estate market would even worsen as companies economized on space as a result of consolidating and downsizing their operations. In fact, Chubb reported a steady decline in net income from real estate after 1989, and a loss of about $2 million a year in 1993 and 1994.

GROWTH IN INTERNATIONAL BUSINESS

Simultaneously, potential changes in environmental and health care regulations initiated by the Clinton administration and state legislatures presented challenges for Chubb and the insurance industry in general. On the environmental side, uncertainties relating to toxic waste and asbestos claims made on policies written decades earlier posed an increasingly large threat to profitability.

Chubb began to lobby actively for regulatory reform, hoping to narrow the widening judicial interpretations of such regulations as Superfund toxic waste cleanup rules. In 1994 Chubb settled its most costly asbestos exposure claim to date from an insurance policy issued in 1956 to Fibreboard Corporation by Pacific Indemnity Corporation, a Chubb subsidiary.

New legislation in New York and New Jersey significantly changed the way the company would handle health insurance in that region. The legislation created community-based rating and limited restrictions on preexisting conditions. Whereas other insurers left that market, Chubb restructured its offerings, encouraging clients to move to managed care policies, and remained effective in the region, which accounted for 80 percent of Chubb's group health business.

In the mid-1990s Chubb increased its international expansion and accelerated the growth of its domestic network. The company's London branch, at the center of the world insurance market, had doubled in size since its formation in the early 1980s. In 1993 Chubb added offices in Birmingham, Reading, and Manchester, England, to take advantage of profitable opportunities in more local business. When the company determined that London lacked the service-oriented insurance products required for that city's growing affluent population, it focused upon personal insurance, which represented 23 percent of Chubb's total business.

In Germany, the new opportunities created by the formation of the European Community and the deregulation of the European insurance industry led Chubb to promote its commercial lines. As a commercial powerhouse, Germany provided an attractive new market for foreign insurers.

In 1994 premiums from international business passed 20 percent of the total, approaching the company's goal of 25 percent for the year 2000. Chubb opened offices in Beijing, Hamburg, Munich, London, and Glasgow. In the United States, Chubb opened a new office in Fresno, California. By 1995, the company, which had 20 domestic branches in 1965, had grown to 89 branches worldwide. The company projected hiring 1,300 new underwriters a year for the next five years. Some analysts questioned if quality operations could be maintained at such a high growth rate in a soft market, but by 1999, the number of offices worldwide was 132.

A NARROWER FOCUS

Chubb's gains were impressive, particularly in light of the fact that the early to mid-1990s were hard years for property and casualty insurers. With too many companies chasing too little business, and premiums that had stagnated at 1987 levels, the industry was rocked in 1994 by a series of underwriting losses: the California earthquake, snowstorms in the Northeast, flooding in the southern and western United States, and a series of environmental cleanup claims. Insurers paid out $15 billion in disasters in 1994 alone, leading the industry as a whole to institute a 4.9 percent premium hike in 1994 and a 6.6 percent hike in 1995.

Over the next several years, Chubb began to shed some of its businesses, following a trend in the insurance industry to concentrate on a single segment. Chubb chose to focus on its property and casualty lines. In 1996 it severed its 114-year relationship with Sun Alliance, the United Kingdom's largest insurer, as part of this refocusing. In 1998 it sold a substantial portion of its Bellemead Development portfolio to PW/MS Acquisition for $737 million, and its life insurance business to the Jefferson-Pilot Corporation for $875 million. It used proceeds from the sales to buy back about 30 percent of the company's outstanding shares during 1997 through 1999.

Chubb made news repeatedly in 1997 for having issued President Clinton a personal liability umbrella policy in the early 1990s and for later assuming half of the legal costs of his defense in the suit brought against him by Paula Jones. Some argued that the president appeared to be receiving preferential treatment from Chubb and State Farm, who paid the other half of his legal costs, but both companies insisted that they were paying his defense costs as a matter of policy.

Chubb also was noted for its leadership in tackling issues unique to the nascent online publishing industry. Beginning in 1997, it began to offer multimedia coverage, or liability insurance for the multimedia business. Such coverage, as defined by Chubb, included the unauthorized use of ideas, an area not touched upon by normal liability insurance. An example would be the stealing of someone's video-game scenario.

NEW VENTURES AND ACQUISITIONS

The company continued to grow through new ventures and acquisition throughout the late 1990s. In 1998, in a move to enter the global reinsurance market, it formed Chubb Re, Inc., and became a low-cost reinsurance provider. In December it purchased a 28 percent stake in Hiscox, the integrated Lloyd's of London insurer. Chubb also expanded its umbrella liability policy, offering liability insurance for food processors, suppliers, and franchisers. In 1999 it purchased Executive Risk Inc., the third-largest insurer of executives and directors, in a $750 million stock deal.

The commercial and property insurance markets continued to struggle through hard times. The industry's overcapacity created a bad pricing environment for insurers and slowed revenue growth, and the strength of the company's personal and specialty lines was not sufficient to counterbalance its losses in standard commercial insurance in 1998 and 1999. Announced earnings for 1998 were short of expectations, despite rate increases in commercial premiums, and stock prices tumbled. To make matters worse, catastrophic losses were heavy in both 1998 and 1999 as a result of Hurricane Floyd, which caused the largest number of claims from a single event in the company's history to date.

Chubb set itself the task of turning its standard commercial lines around in the year 2000, by continuing its "pricing and pruning" strategy of premium increases, while continuing to grow in its personal and specialty businesses. Analysts as a group were positive that the company, with its solid history and experience, would pull through its hard times. In January 2000, *Fortune* magazine named the company to its list of "The 100 Best Companies to Work for in America." In August 2000 Chubb received an operating license to open a branch in Shanghai, which the company estimated would bring in about $200 million in business each year. Despite midyear rumors that the company was ripe for a takeover, the company insisted it was not for sale.

The tech boom of the late 1990s produced a number of new millionaires, and potential clients. It made Chubb's niche of insuring the personal possessions of the wealthy all the more attractive to competitors. Insurance giant American International Group, Inc. (AIG), entered the business in 2000, offering much higher coverage and writing riskier types of policies, while reportedly poaching talent from Chubb. Part of AIG's aim was to draw very affluent families to its other products. However, it had a reputation as being much more penurious than Chubb when it came to paying out claims, leading some to doubt its prospects.

21ST-CENTURY CHALLENGES

A number of major crises were brewing. After the September 11, 2001, terrorist attacks on the United States, Chubb paid out more than $500 million in claims, even though President George W. Bush characterized them as acts of war. In 2002 there were also sizable claims related to asbestos. Chubb had to pay surety claims following the collapse of Enron Corp., which inspired a wave of shareholder lawsuits at other companies. This resulted in more payouts, but also more demand for liability coverage for corporate executives and directors

In the fall of 2002 Chubb's chief financial officer, Weston Hicks, left unexpectedly after a year and a half on the job. He joined rival Alleghany after he learned that he was passed over to succeed Dean R. O'Hare, who departed Chubb in November 2002 after 40 years with the company and 14 years as CEO. O'Hare was instead succeeded by John Finnegan, former chairman and president of General Motors Acceptance Corp. Ac-

cording to *Best's Review*, O'Hare was credited with increasing the share of international business from less than 3 percent of total revenues when he became CEO in 1988 to more than 20 percent by the time he left.

The company had recently launched a joint venture in India with a local financial services firm, Housing Development Finance Corporation (HDFC). However, Chubb's conservative nature did not suit its local partner's appetite for riskier lines in the booming market and the company sold back its 26 percent interest after five years in 2007.

In 2005 Hurricanes Katrina and Rita cost Chubb $536 million. The company was preparing to shift its reinsurance business to a new Bermuda-based joint venture called Harbor Point. Its partner was Stone Point Capital, a private-equity firm.

The company opposed the participation of rival property and casualty insurance companies (most conspicuously AIG) in the federal recovery program that followed the credit collapse of 2008, saying it considered such bailouts to be anticompetitive. Chubb's conservative approach helped it weather the difficult conditions. Flush with more than $500 billion in capital reserves at the end of 2009, the company faced falling premiums in its commercial lines, noted *Barron's*.

Revenues slipped 6 percent to $11.1 billion in 2009. However, the company was able to report near-record per-share earnings, as all three of its business units (Chubb Personal Insurance, Chubb Commercial Insurance, and Chubb Specialty Insurance) were doing relatively well in a still recovering economy.

Leslie C. Halpern
Updated, Katherine Smethurst;
Carrie Rothburd; Frederick C. Ingram

PRINCIPAL SUBSIDIARIES

Federal Insurance Company; Chubb Atlantic Indemnity Ltd. (Bermuda); Bellemead Development Corporation; Chubb Financial Solutions, Inc.; Chubb Financial Solutions LLC; Chubb do Brasil Companhia de Seguros (Brazil; 99%).

PRINCIPAL OPERATING UNITS

Chubb Personal Insurance; Chubb Commercial Insurance; Chubb Specialty Insurance.

PRINCIPAL COMPETITORS

ACE Ltd.; Aetna Life and Casualty Co.; Lloyd's; State Farm Insurance Companies; The St. Paul Companies; Zurich American Insurance Co. Inc.

FURTHER READING

Bary, Andrew, "Pulling Away from the Pack," *Barron's*, January 18, 2010, p. B19.

"Chubb Vanguard Swoops in Ahead of WTO Accession," *South China Morning Post*, October 2, 2000, p. 3.

Gallagher, Kathleen, "Industry Problems Make Insurer's Stock Under-valued," *Milwaukee Journal Sentinel*, February 14, 1999, Business p. 4.

Green, Meg, "The Specialists; The Chubb Corp. Credits Its Success to Excelling in the Niche Markets It Knows Well, Rather than Growing by Writing Mediocre Business Outside Its Specialties," *Best's Review*, January 2004, pp. 26–27.

Greenwald, Judy, "Chubb Selects Outsider as Chief," *Business Insurance*, November 11, 2002, p. 1.

"HDFC, Chubb Decide to Part Ways," *Times of India*, May 16, 2007.

"Is the President Getting Special Insurance Treatment for the Paula Jones Lawsuit?" *Insight on the News*, July 21, 1997, p. 24.

Kalawsky, Keith, "Is Chubb Exiting Lawsuit Hell? Profit Jumps 20%," *National Post's Financial Post & FP Investing*, August 1, 2003, p. IN3.

Moreau, Dan, "Chubb Thinks Small, but All Its Little Pieces Add Up," *Kiplinger's*, May 1995, pp. 38–40.

Ostermiller, Marilyn, "Exit Lines; Dean R. O'Hare Recently Stepped Down as Chubb's Chairman, Leaving behind a Legacy of Global Expansion and Underwriting Profits," *Best's Review*, January 2003, pp. 46–47.

Pilla, David, "Chubb's O'Hare: Despite Disasters, Future Looks Good," *A.M. Best Newswire*, December 13, 2001.

Rodengen, Jeffrey L., Elizabeth Fernandez, and Elijah Meyer, *Chubb: Celebrating 125 Years*, Fort Lauderdale, FL: Write Stuff Enterprises Inc., 2008.

Treaster, Joseph B., "A New Fight for a Rich Slice of the Insurance Pie," *New York Times*, Bus. Sec., October 15, 2000, p. 14.

Coalition America Inc.

———————————■———————————

2 Concourse Parkway, Suite 300
Atlanta, Georgia 30328-5581
U.S.A.
Telephone: (404) 459-7201
Web site: http://www.coalitionamerica.com

Private Company
Incorporated: 1995
Employees: 125
Sales: $107 million (2006 est.)
NAICS: 621999 All Other Miscellaneous Ambulatory
    Health Care

■ ■ ■

A private company based in Atlanta, Georgia, Coalition America, Inc. (CAI), bills itself as a "healthcare savings company." It uses proprietary technology to lower medical and dental costs for clients representing more than 12,000 health plans, including medical and dental insurance carriers, health maintenance organizations, self-insured employers, Taft Hartley plans for private-sector unionized employees, and third-party administrators. It also lowers costs for physicians, labs, pharmacies, and other care providers.

Cost-containment services include discounts arranged through about 300,000 proprietary contracts, provider negotiation to increase savings for clients by taking advantage of their combined size, reimbursement scheduling to determine fair hospital and fair physician reimbursement, and consumer negotiation to discount consumer out-of-pocket medical expenses. CAI also of-

fers enhanced claim editing services to help clients to review both in-network and out-of-network claims and avoid miscoding and overpayment; real-time fraud detection services; and fraud, waste, and abuse screening and special investigation services.

In addition, CAI owns National Preferred Provider Network (NPPN), a major preferred provider organization (PPO) that includes more than 550,000 physicians, about 4,000 acute facilities, and nearly 100,000 ancillary care provider locations. The network is made available to insurance carriers, Taft-Hartley plans, self-administered employers, third-party administrators, and other managed care organization. CAI was founded and is led by brothers Sean and Scott Smith, chairman and chief executive officer, respectively.

COMPANY FOUNDED: 1995

Identical twins born 15 minutes apart, Sean and Scott Smith both graduated with honors from the University of Kentucky, where they received degrees in finance in 1991. After college they both found employment as sales representatives at Medical Review Systems (MRS), a medical bill review company where both distinguished themselves. Recognized as a top producer in 1993, Sean Smith became vice president of an MRS division, Validated Network, Inc. His brother played a key role in the conversion of MRS data files from a commercial software system to a proprietary in-house platform, a project completed in 1995, the same year that the Smith twins, still in their mid-20s, elected to strike out on their own.

In March 1995 Sean and Scott Smith founded CAI in Atlanta as an S corporation. They had long harbored a dream to start a business, the object of which was unknown until their experience at MRS. The goal for CAI was to bring technology to bear to improve efficiency in the health care industry and provide a variety of cost-containment solutions. "This is a very dynamic industry, but a very low-tech industry," Sean Smith explained to the *Atlanta Journal-Constitution*, adding, "There's a lot of paper that gets pushed from one side of the desk to the other."

While Sean Smith provided the vision for the company, Scott Smith supplied his knowledge of computer systems to make the concept a reality. They set up shop in their three-bedroom apartment and worked the first eight months without pay. CAI then enjoyed steady growth so that three years later the company employed 50 people and posted revenues of $7.6 million. The success of the Smith brothers won them regional honors in the 1998 Ernst & Young Entrepreneur of the Year contest.

MCONLONG FORMED: 1999

CAI expanded its capabilities and furthered its goal of creating a paperless transaction environment by forming a partnership with Scott Arlotta. He was a former chief information officer at a major PPO, Plan Vista Solutions, and also had experience at a Blue Cross Blue Shield of New Jersey workers compensation subsidiary. In April 1999 Arlotta and CAI established MCOnlong, LLC, an automated electronic claims processor serving PPOs and health care purchasers based in Harriman, New York. The company developed a proprietary Internet claims repricing and discounting system.

From its inception through 1999 CAI grew at a 2,106 percent clip. It was a performance that earned the company a spot on *Inc.* magazine's list of America's 500 fastest-growing companies, cracking the top 100 at No. 96. When the Smith brothers spoke with the *Atlanta*

Journal Constitution in 1998, they indicated a desire to take CAI public by 2000 or perhaps be acquired by a larger high-technology company. Despite the company's strong performance, neither option came to pass, as the high-tech sector led by Internet ventures collapsed. Involved in the recession-proof health care field and providing cost-cutting services that became only more desirable during tough times, CAI skirted the shakeout but continued to plot its own course.

In 2001 CAI introduced the ProviderNow services. It was an Internet-based health care provider information application that could be searched from a variety of fields, including name, ZIP code, area of specialty, or hospital. Later that year, CAI added the Solutions Plus! and Savings Plus! services. While both reduced administrative tasks and cut costs through Internet claim repricing, Solutions Plus! focused on PPO's primary network claims while Savings Plus! focused on out-of-network claims and supplemental PPO access. CAI also forged a strategic alliance with Prim Capital Corporation during this time to provide these services to Prim's customers and affiliates. Offering financial planning, investment and risk management solutions to many of the United States' largest employer groups and *Fortune* 1000 companies, Prim was well positioned to drive growth for CAI.

LODESTONE SOLUTIONS ESTABLISHED: 2001

On another front in 2001, CAI formed Lodestone Solutions LLC with health care veteran Francisco Cline to provide data management services and database products tailored for health care companies. Holding a degree in molecular biology from Bucknell University as well as a master's in finance and health services management from Duke University, Cline had previous experience at a biotechnology hedge fund and launched the first product of medical device start-up BioMed. Drawing on a variety of sources, Lodestone gathered detailed data on physicians, group practices, hospitals and others. The information was then cross-checked to eliminate errors and speed up claims processing. The physician directories could also be used for patient referrals and as a marketing tool to reach target groups. Lodestone clients soon included the likes of Abbott Laboratories, Baxter Healthcare, ChoicePoint, GE Medical, and GlaxoSmithKline.

Early in the new century CAI restructured its operations in an effort to ensure the company remained a leader in medical claim savings. By this point MCOnline had emerged as a top PPO network management and integration service provider. CAI decided in 2003 that it would be better served if MCOnline and its technology were taken in-house and integrated into CAI.

As a result, CAI was able to improve accuracy of the data used to provide repricing and other services. A year later, in April 2004, a similar step was taken when CAI acquired Lodestone and brought in-house its data management, data hygiene, and data enhancement capabilities. CAI payor clients enjoyed immediate benefits. Lodestone's technology helped them to increase auto-adjudication rates (eliminating the involvement and expense of a claims examiner) and lower the number of manual edits involved in the adjudication process. Later, CAI's PPO clients enjoyed the benefits of Lodestone's capabilities as well.

Because of its range of services, CAI was able to attract a number of major clients. For example, Humana Inc., one of the United States' largest publicly traded health benefits companies, expanded its relationship with CAI in 2004, using CAI to receive repricing information on out-of-network medical claims. CAI also continued to increase what it could offer clients through strategic alliances. In 2005 CAI helped clients to save on radiology and diagnostic services by contracting with MedLink Healthcare Networks, Inc., a managed service organization that made available to payors a low-cost yet high-quality network of radiologists. Also in 2005 CAI teamed up with The TriZetto Group, Inc., to use the latter's repricing and adjudication service, both in-network and out-of-network, for health plans and benefit administrators.

ECHO HEALTH ESTABLISHED: 2005

Another strategic partnership established in 2005 was with ECHO Health, Inc., a medical payment consolidator that generated significant cost savings by generating payments electronically and reducing the explanation of benefits to a single report. In this way, postage and printing was reduced, as was paperwork and banking

fees. To help clients electronically transmit and reprice medical bills, in-network or out-of-network, CAI partnered with Advanced Medical Pricing Solutions and Eldorado Computing, Inc.

CAI's strong performance in the early 2000s caught the attention of the major accounting firm Deloitte & Touche, LLP. CAI was named to the firm's prestigious Technology Fast 50 list for Georgia companies, based on the percentage of revenue growth from 2001–05. With a 55 percent increase during the period, CAI received a No. 36 listing in 2006. A year later the company again made the Fast 50, this time posted at No. 40.

In November 2007 CAI reached a deal to acquire National Preferred Provider Network (NPPN) from MedAvant Healthcare Solutions for $23.5 million in cash. The transaction, which closed in February 2008, included several subsidiaries that comprised NPPN: PlanVista Solutions Corporation; Medical Resource, LLC; National Network Services, LLC; and National Provider Network, Inc. The deal allowed MedAvant to pay down debt and focus on its core information technology used to process transactions in the health care industry. For CAI, on the other hand, the acquisition of NPPN added 300,000 direct providers contracts. The combined heft of CAI-NPPN created greater medical cost savings for its clients, who now had significantly improved bargaining power.

NPPN ACQUISITION

NPPN was slightly older than CAI, founded in Middletown, New York, in 1993 by Ronald J. Davi, a former health care executive with such major insurers as AIG, Metropolitan Life, and Travelers Insurance Company. With Davi serving as chief executive, just three years later the company was providing health care services to more than 4.5 million people located in all 50 states from a network of 280,000 physicians, over 3,300 hospitals, and 18,000 ancillary facilities. Boasting one of the country's most extensive PPO networks, NPPN was acquired for $25 million in cash in 1998 by HealthPlan Services Corporation, a Florida-based company that administered health and other benefit plans on an outsourced basis. Davi left NPPN a short time later.

NPPN was the country's largest independent PPO at the start of the new century. The company expanded its offering in 2000 when it introduced an Internet-based claims repricing system that allowed a payer to reprice claims online and receive claims that were auto-adjudicated. NPPN also added network and data management and e-commerce services. Because of its expanding scope, NPPN adopted a new name in 2000, becoming Plan Vista Solutions, Inc. In 2002 the company added bill negotiation services as well. Health-Plan Services, in the meantime, struggled and sold off all of its units with the exception of Plan Vista and in 2001 changed its name to PlanVista Corporation, a reflection of the company's sole focus. The PlanVista PPO was then sold to MedAvent in 2004 and resumed using the NPPN name. It was expand through acquisitions before being acquired by CAI.

The addition of NPPN had a immediate impact on CAI, which reported improved medical costs savings for its clients in 2008. The company appeared to be well positioned for the future, which was anything but certain in the health care field. A new administration in Washington promised health care reform, an effort that consumed most of 2009 and carried on into 2010. What changes would be made and how they would impact CAI were yet to be seen, but it was likely that cost-containment services would remain an important component of the health care field no matter what the result.

Ed Dinger

PRINCIPAL SUBSIDIARIES

Lodestone Solutions, LLC; NPPN.

PRINCIPAL COMPETITORS

Health Decisions Inc.; Prime Health Services LLC; Rising Medical Solutions, Inc.

FURTHER READING

"CAI Buys Lodestone Solutions," *Atlanta Business Chronicle,* April 1, 2004.

"Coalition America Taps Two Services," *Employee Benefit News,* September 1, 2001.

"Entrepreneurs of the Year," *Atlanta Journal-Constitution,* June 17, 1998, p. D20.

Forgrieve, Janet, "Tampa, Fla.-Based Employee Administration Firm Sells Units, Cuts Debt," *Tampa Tribune,* October 25, 2000.

"MedAvant Announces Agreement to Sell National Preferred Provider Network (NPPN) to Coalition America," *Prim-eZone Media Network,* November 8, 2007.

"Snapshots," *Inc.,* October 17, 2000, p. 121.

"This Generation Is All Business," *Business Week,* March 1, 1999.

Danfoss A/S

Nordborgvej 81
Nordborg, DK-6430
Denmark
Telephone: (+45) 74 88 22 22
Fax: (+45) 74 49 09 49
Web site: http://www.danfoss.com

Private Company
Founded: 1933 as Dansk Køleautomatik- og Apparat-Fabrik
Incorporated: 1961
Employees: 31,717
Sales: DKK 10.78 billion ($2.06 billion) (2008)
NAICS: 332911 Industrial Valve Manufacturing; 332919 Other Metal Valve and Pipe Fitting Manufacturing; 333410 Ventilation, Heating, Air-Conditioning, and Commercial Refrigeration Equipment Manufacturing; 333415 Air-Conditioning and Warm Air Heating Equipment and Commercial and Industrial Refrigeration Equipment Manufacturing; 423690 Other Electronic Parts and Equipment Merchant Wholesalers

■ ■ ■

Danfoss A/S is Denmark's largest company and one of the world's leaders in the development and production of electronic and mechanical components for a broad array of industrial and consumer applications. The company is organized into three divisions. The Refrigeration & Air Conditioning Division develops and manufactures automatic controls, consumer and commercial compressors, electronic controls and sensors, and heat exchangers for household refrigerators and freezers as well as for commercial refrigeration units, such as grocery stores coolers and air conditioning systems. The division has factories in 17 countries in Europe, North America, and Asia.

The Heating Division develops and produces components, such as valves, thermostats, controls, and burner parts for individual heating systems in residential and commercial buildings; components for district heating plants; and heat pumps, as well as a line of water control equipment components. The division manufactures its products in 15 countries.

The Danfoss Motion Controls Division manufactures gear motors, frequency converters for speed control in motors, and wide variety of electronic power modules in factories in Europe, Asia, and the United States. Danfoss is a global company with nearly 200 full or partial subsidiaries involved in both production and distribution in Europe, Asia, and North and South America. It has 17 subsidiaries in the United States alone, most notably Sauer-Danfoss Inc. in Illinois. Danfoss A/S is owned by the family of founder Mads Clausen. The majority of the company shares are administered by the Bitten and Mads Clausen Foundation, a nonprofit organization.

FOUNDING AN INDUSTRIAL COMPANY IN RURAL DENMARK

Danfoss played a critical role in the industrialization of Denmark. Its history has its roots in Denmark's agricultural past. The founder of the company that became Danfoss A/S, Mads Clausen, was born in 1905 near the Danish town of Elsmark, not far from the city of Nordborg, where the company would eventually have its headquarters. Although he grew up on a farm, he was more interested in machines than agriculture. While still in high school, he began inventing various devices, including a regulator, which he tried unsuccessfully to patent. In 1928, however, he received his first patent for an automobile jack of his own design. It was a dubious honor in rural Denmark of the 1930s, one that earned him the scorn of the local farmers who took to calling him Mads Patent.

Clausen left high school without graduating to do an apprenticeship in an engineering works. He subsequently attended the technical college in Odense, Denmark, graduating with a degree in mechanical engineering in 1927. One of his jobs afterward was at a company where he became acquainted with refrigeration technology. While there, an idea for a company took seed. The valves used in refrigeration facilities at the time were manufactured primarily in the United States. However, strict Danish import regulations made them expensive and difficult to obtain precisely at a time when Europe was reeling under the impact of the Great Depression. Clausen's plan was to design, manufacture, and market his own refrigeration valves in Denmark. He returned home in 1933 and set up a company in his parents' attic in Elsmark. That location would later house the Danfoss company museum.

PRODUCING REFRIGERATION VALVES FOR DENMARK

Clausen's first products were two refrigeration valves he designed. The name he invented for them was Danfoss: "Dan" from *Danmark,* the Danish word for "Denmark" and "foss" from *fosse,* the Danish word for "flow." With product to sell, Clausen established his company, Dansk Køleautomatik- og Apparat-Fabrik (Danish Refrigeration and Apparatus Manufacturer) in 1933. The young company, with Clausen as its sole employee, was soon

manufacturing a line of air release valves and thermostatic radiator valves. Sales were good the very first year. Clausen sold 466 valves, bringing DKK 12,682 in revenues.

In 1934 Clausen added automatic AV and AVS valves to his product line and his sales increased fourfold from the previous year. The following year, the firm hired its first four employees and obtained its first piece of heavy production equipment, a lathe. By 1938 the company was making broad variety of valves, including automatic spring valves, ball float valves, thermostats, pressure-controlled valves, diaphragm valves, suction valves, room thermostats, constant-pressure valves, and drying filters. Its rapid success necessitated the construction in 1936 of a separate production facility where its seven employees (including Clausen's own father) could manufacture the expanding product line. By 1939, barely three years later, the workforce had tripled, reaching 26 employees. On the eve of World War II, Clausen expanded his business beyond the borders of Denmark for the first time when he signed his first foreign deal, which authorized the Itho Company to act as his agent in the Netherlands. Clausen realized early on the importance of establishing markets abroad.

Although Denmark declared its neutrality at the start of World War II, this did not prevent the country's invasion by Germany in April 1940. Nonetheless, Denmark enjoyed a limited degree of sovereignty not known in other nations under the Nazi yoke. Furthermore, because the country made only token resistance when the Germans came, it was spared the devastating destruction of buildings and crucial infrastructure that other countries suffered. Production at Clausen's company continued more or less as normal at first, mainly by means of production licensed to companies in Sweden, which had managed to maintain its neutrality.

In 1940 Clausen hired his first design engineer to oversee research and development (R&D). R&D, however, experienced some setbacks during the war. Some new projects, the invention of a thermostatic radiator valve in 1943, were carried out successfully. Others had to wait. Shortly after the invasion, for example, a project to produce a special thermostat that was able to maintain the temperature of a room at 18 degrees Celsius had to be canceled temporarily. A number of other inventions begun during the war could not go into production until after the cessation of hostilities. Operations continued steadily up to 1945, however. In 1943, the year of the firm's 10th anniversary, 179 employees were producing 37 different products, and the factory had grown to a total 1,400 square meters. Clausen's valve sales were brisk during

KEY DATES

1933: Dansk Køleautomatik- og Apparat-Fabrik is founded.
1950: Danfoss Convention is held in Nordborg, Denmark.
1961: Reorganized into a share company.
1966: Founder Mads Clausen dies.
1975: The Bitten and Mads Clausen Foundation is founded.
2008: Company acquires majority share of Sauer-Danfoss Inc. in United States.

the war years, although client nations were limited to Germany, its occupied countries, Fascist Spain, and neutral Sweden.

RAPID GROWTH IN THE POSTWAR YEARS

In 1946, a year after the defeat of the Axis powers, Mads Clausen changed the name of his company to Danfoss, the brand name his products had borne since 1933, and set out on a process of expansion. His first move was to open an office in the Danish capital of Copenhagen. Sales were strong from the start. As a result of the bitterly cold winter in 1946–47, there was constant interest in a control system for oil burners that Danfoss had developed. Other significant new products followed, some of which had been waiting in the wings since the war period, including a new line of thermostatic radiator valves. To handle the high demand, Danfoss built a series of temporary wooden structures and doubled the size of its production facilities in 1947.

The company made a dramatic leap to the Western Hemisphere when it established its first fully owned foreign subsidiary in Buenos Aires, Argentina, in 1949. The following year the firm organized the Danfoss Convention in Nordborg, where the company and its network of agents and distributors representing some 21 countries developed marketing strategies for the coming years. Mads Clausen and his wife continued their planning in 1950, when they made a study tour of North America, collecting ideas from their U.S. and Canadian counterparts.

The 1950s launched a period of frenetic growth at Danfoss that would last some two decades. By 1950 the company was employing 500 workers, many of them women, in part because demand for workers far outstripped the available labor pool after the war, but also because Mads Clausen believed that women performed the fine assembly work he needed better than men could. One year later, in 1951, the Danfoss workforce had doubled, and only a year later it had doubled again, reaching 2,000. In 1952 the firm added a brand new factory with 12,000 square meters in floor space. Among the product innovations of the period was a newly designed thermostatic radiator valve and a line of compressors, a sector Danfoss entered for the first time.

GOING GLOBAL AND THE FOUNDER'S DEATH

Until the mid-1950s Danfoss had done all if its manufacturing in Denmark, and most of that on the island of Als, where the company had its headquarters. In 1956 it opened a subsidiary just across the German border in the city of Flensburg, Danfoss Automatic Schalter und Regelapparate GmbH, which produced hermetic compressors. It quickly established subsidiaries in other countries as well. Danfoss Proprietary Ltd. Australia was founded in 1958, Danfoss Inc. in New York in 1959, Danfoss Manufacturing Company Ltd. in Japan in 1961, and Danfoss Industrial Espanola S.A. in Spain in 1965. Danfoss also made its first foreign acquisition in 1960 when it purchased Stamp-Hermetik GmbH of Offenbach, Germany. By that time the firm's Danish works, primarily in and around Nordborg, were employing more than 5,000 workers, making Danfoss Denmark's largest company.

When Mads Clausen died in August 1966, the leadership of the company passed to his wife Bitten, then 54 years old. During their marriage, Bitten had been her husband's closest confidante, offering her opinion on many important Danfoss decisions. Thus when she took over as the chairman of the board, although it was a period of continuing expansion, Danfoss was in good hands. In 1971, when Mrs. Clausen stepped down from the chairmanship, the company underwent a significant reorganization. Danfoss was divided into five separate groups: Group Management, Compressors, Automatic Controls, Hydraulics & Burners, and International Sales. At the same time Bitten Clausen founded the Bitten and Mads Clausen Foundation, group entrusted with a majority of the firm's Class A shares.

NEW PRODUCTS AND A MOVE EAST

In 1972 Danfoss sales topped the DKK 1 billion mark for the first time in its history, while its workforce numbered more than 11,000. One year later, when the company celebrated its 40th anniversary, the 50 millionth compressor left the assembly line. The 1970s saw Danfoss expand its product lines. Flowmeters went into production for the first time in 1975, automatic control systems for natural gas in 1976, oil preheaters together with a new line of radiator thermostats in 1978, and TWIN compressors for heat pumps in 1980.

The 1980s witnessed continued growth at Danfoss. It sales topped DKK 5 billion in 1985, and the firm had a total of 13,285 workers, 9,275 employed in Denmark. There was a good deal of activity in the upper echelons of Danfoss during the decade as well, with three changes in CEO, and two in chairman of the board. In 1989 Bitten Clausen gave up her membership on the board.

With the fall of Communism in 1989, Danfoss, like so many other companies in Western Europe, set their sights on the lands that lay behind the former Iron Curtain. In 1992–93 alone, the firm established production and sales subsidiaries in Russia, Poland, and Slovenia. More significantly, in 1997, Danfoss built its first factory in the People's Republic of China, a country it would term in 2004 its "second home market." Danfoss also established new operations in France, Germany, Norway, France, and South Africa in the 1990s. By 1997 it owned so many foreign companies that the employee balance tipped once and for all: more than half of Danfoss's employees, or 18,257, worked outside Denmark.

EXPLOSIVE GROWTH IN 2000

In 1999 Danfoss announced that it was negotiating the merger of Danfoss Fluid Power A/S and Sauer-Sundstrand Corp., an Illinois-based manufacturer of hydraulic components for mobile equipment. The merger was completed in early 2000. At the same time related operational areas of the Danfoss Group were spun off and merged into the new company Sauer-Danfoss Inc. Subsequently Sauer-Danfoss was listed on the New York and Frankfurt stock exchanges, with Danfoss holding a 38.5 percent share. That same year, Danfoss took important steps into the retail cooling and air conditioning systems sector with the acquisition of another U.S.-based company, Energy Controls International of Baltimore, Maryland, as well as Woodley Electronics Group Ltd. in the United Kingdom.

In 2001, in the wake of this expansion, the Danfoss Group underwent a major reorganization into three basic operational segments: Refrigeration & Air Conditioning, Heating & Water, and Motion Controls. The reorganization streamlined the group, bringing together business areas that were far-flung but under unified management. Another important move was a major change to the company charter, which up to then had provided for majority ownership of the company by the Bitten and Mads Clausen Foundation. In August 2001, however, Danish authorities gave their approval to its amendment which would remove the restriction that the foundation remain the majority holder of Danfoss stock and hence made it possible for the company to go public at some time in the future if it so chose.

Danfoss's remarkable growth continued after the reorganization, with 37 companies in Denmark and elsewhere in the world joining the group between 2001 and 2008. It consolidated its holdings in China, which it saw as its primary foreign market, and built a new factory there in 2004. In 2006 the firm made the largest acquisition in its history when it bought Scroll Technologies, an American producer of commercial scroll compressors for DKK 1.15 billion, or about $188.32 million. Despite the large outlay, 2006 also concluded with the best operating result in the Group's history with sales increasing by 18 percent to DKK 19.4 billion, about $3.46 billion, and pretax profits jumping by 39 percent.

During this time, not only had Danfoss established a solid foothold in the United States via its group of subsidiaries, the United States had also become the firm's second-largest market. In 2008 Sauer-Danfoss Inc. was reporting sales of more than DKK 10 billion ($1.7 billion) annually and about 9,800 of Danfoss's 31,717 employees. In July of that year Danfoss acquired a further 17.5% of the shares in Sauer-Danfoss, giving it 55% and majority control of the firm. In 2009 it upped its holdings to 76 percent.

As the end of the decade approached, the trend eastward continued. In May 2009 Danfoss announced the closure of its Flensburg, Germany, compressor factory and moved production to China and Slovakia, where wages were significantly lower. A month later it put a new factory and sales office in Bucharest, Romania, into operation. One of the newest Danfoss subsidiaries was founded in spring 2009, when the Danfoss Ventures and Bitten and Mads Clausen Foundation funded the launch of IXA Danfoss A/S to develop and market equipment to measure gases, such as carbon dioxide and nitrogen dioxide, which damaged the environment.

Gerald E. Brennan

PRINCIPAL SUBSIDIARIES

Danfoss GmbH (Germany); Danfoss Redan A/S; Danfoss Saginomiya (Japan; 50%); Danfoss Semco A/S Fire Protection (50%); Danfoss Turbocor Compressors Inc.

(USA; 50%); Devi A/S; Sauer-Danfoss Inc. (USA).

PRINCIPAL DIVISIONS

Refrigeration & Air-Conditioning; Heating; Motion Control.

PRINCIPAL COMPETITORS

Bristol Compressors International, Inc.; Carrier Corporation; Emerson Electric Co.; Goodman Global, Inc.; Honeywell International Inc.; Lennox International Inc.; Nordyne Inc.; Tecumseh Products Company; Trane Inc.; VDL Groep; Yazaki Corporation.

FURTHER READING

Boje, Per Johansen, and Hans Christian, *An Entrepreneur: The Story of Mads Clausen and Danfoss,* Odense University Press, 1995.

Hansen, Hanne Steen, "Danfoss - Arven fra Mads," *J. H. Schultz Information A/S*, 1994.

Darden Restaurants, Inc.

———————■———————

1000 Darden Center Drive
Orlando, Florida 32837
U.S.A.
Telephone: (407) 245-4000
Fax: (407) 245-5389
Web site: http://www.darden.com

Public Company
Incorporated: 1995
Employees: 179,000
Sales: $7.22 billion (2009)
Stock Exchanges: New York
Ticker Symbol: DRI
NAICS: 722110 Full-Service Restaurants

■ ■ ■

Operating 1,800 units throughout the United States and Canada, Darden Restaurants, Inc., is the largest full-service restaurant operating company in the world. The company serves more than 400 million meals per year through its restaurant outlets, which include Red Lobster, Olive Garden, LongHorn Steakhouse, The Capital Grille, Bahama Breeze, and Seasons 52.

Founded in 1968, Red Lobster is one of the nation's largest seafood and casual dining restaurant chains. Launched in 1982, Olive Garden quickly became one of the largest chains of casual but full-service Italian restaurants. Opened in 1981, LongHorn Steakhouse is a moderately priced western-style steak house with more than 300 locations across the eastern half of the United States. The Capital Grille is an upscale steak house founded in 1990, with 40 units located primarily in major urban areas across the country. Bahama Breeze was introduced in 1996 and had 24 restaurants in operation during 2009. Seasons 52, a fresh grill and wine bar that debuted in 2003, had eight locations in 2009.

THE FIRST RED LOBSTER RESTAURANTS: 1968–70

William B. Darden, who was reared in Waycross, Georgia, opened at the age of 19 a Depression-era Waycross lunch counter that he called "The Green Frog," promising "Service with a Hop." He went on to own some local motel and hotel properties and all or part of about 20 Howard Johnson restaurants. Inspired by the great popularity of seafood in two of his eight restaurants, including one in Orlando and the other in Jacksonville, Darden opened his first Red Lobster restaurant in Lakeland, Florida, in 1968. Its manager was Joe R. Lee, a native Georgian who later became chief executive officer of Darden Restaurants.

Darden wanted to market a chain of moderately priced, family style, full-service seafood restaurants. He chose to open in Lakeland because it was as far from the ocean as possible in Florida, and he wanted to test his concept outside of coastal areas. The first Red Lobster was a booming success, so much so that Darden and his partners had to work full shifts to meet the objective of getting food to the table within 10 minutes of the order.

There were three Red Lobster restaurants in operation by 1970, all in Central Florida, and two more under construction. The three units, which despite their

COMPANY PERSPECTIVES

Our core purpose is to nourish and delight everyone we serve.

name specialized in the fried fish and hush puppies favored by southerners, averaged $800,000 each in annual sales. Earnings were solid, but the company lacked the cash to grow. For General Mills, a diversified food products giant, acquiring Red Lobster Inns of America in 1970 made sense because fish sales for General Mills accounted for about $80 million in revenue, or one-ninth of its total sales. Darden was hired to oversee the chain and open a restaurant headquarters in Orlando. He later became a General Mills vice president and senior consultant, retired in 1984, and died in 1994.

General Mills upgraded Red Lobster into a mid-priced seafood dinner house that was a model of corporate efficiency. Lee, who rose to become president of Red Lobster in 1975, carried a slide rule with him everywhere in the early 1970s to calculate prices and portion weights, and to quantify whatever else could be quantified. He also carried a thermometer in order to assure that entrees had been cooked to the proper temperature before being served. In 1971 Red Lobster established an in-house department for purchasing seafood on a worldwide scale. The company also established, long before the rest of the industry, a computerized point-of-purchase system to track how much of any given item was selling where.

RAPID GROWTH: 1970–82

Red Lobster grew rapidly in each year of operation. By the end of fiscal 1971 there were 24 restaurants with total sales of $9.1 million, and by the end of fiscal 1972 there were 47 restaurants with sales of $27.1 million. When Lee was named president of Red Lobster in 1975, there were 97 restaurants with 9,500 employees. In 1976 the General Mills subsidiary opened a microbiology laboratory in Orlando to ensure the quality of its products. Red Lobster ended that fiscal year with 174 units in 26 states and total sales of $174.1 million.

Because of higher costs, attributed in large part to increased fuel bills for truck transportation and fishing boats caused by the Arab oil embargo of 1973–74, Red Lobster again felt the need to upgrade in the mid-1970s. It carpeted the floors, redecorated the interiors, and added a few fresh dishes to its predominantly frozen menu, and it sharply increased prices to pay for the

improvements. The strategy worked. By the end of 1980, Red Lobster, with 260 units and almost $400 million in annual sales, had reached ninth place among fast-food companies and accounted for more than half of total sales by seafood fast-food companies. Although a sit-down chain, frequently with lounges, Red Lobster was considered "fast food" by some analysts because most entree items were frozen.

By 1982, however, Red Lobster was rated as the nation's largest "dinner house" restaurant chain (a restaurant offering table service and a full lunch and dinner menu). With an average annual return on invested assets of 22.3 percent before taxes, it was one of the most profitable chains in its field, and its growth had come entirely without franchising.

WIDER CHOICES: 1982–89

Red Lobster provided General Mills with $75 million in operating earnings during fiscal 1982. By early 1983 there were 350 establishments in 36 states. The first of dozens of franchised Red Lobsters in Japan opened in Tokyo in 1982, and the first Canadian unit opened in 1983. Securities analysts attributed the chain's success in large part to Red Lobster's position as the only nationwide seafood dinner chain and its extraordinary quality control measures. According to a Red Lobster executive, while seafood could be 16 days old and still legally be sold as fresh, Red Lobster's seafood, although frozen, was "fresh frozen" at five regional warehouses, each with a quality control laboratory.

Red Lobster decided to pursue a new direction in 1982. The chain's research, according to Lee, indicated that its customers resented waiting in line yet did not like being hustled out. They wanted a more casual dining experience, with an atmosphere conducive to drinks, appetizers, and finger food to share instead of massive entrees. Accordingly, a prototype unit opened in Kissimmee, Florida, in 1984, with a seafood bar serving up oysters, shrimp, clams, calamari, and other appetizers with drinks, and a glass-enclosed grill where fresh seafood was broiled over mesquite-wood flames. Red Lobster restaurants had deliberately been built without windows so that diners would not spend time looking out while seated, but the new unit had picturesque views. Servers were instructed to relax instead of speeding diners through the dinner cycle.

In 1984 General Mills authorized a $104 million remodeling program for Red Lobster, the largest capital spending item in the parent company's history to date. All 370 units were to be overhauled. The menu was to be 40 percent longer to include such items as seafood salads and pastas, and six to eight fresh fish entrees,

KEY DATES

1968: William B. Darden opens his first Red Lobster restaurant in Lakeland, Florida.
1970: General Mills, Inc., acquires the Red Lobster chain.
1975: Joe R. Lee is named president of Red Lobster; 97 restaurants are in operation.
1981: LongHorn Steakhouse opens its first restaurant in Atlanta.
1982: General Mills opens its first Olive Garden restaurant in Orlando.
1990: The Capital Grille opens its first restaurant in Providence, Rhode Island.
1995: General Mills spins off its restaurant operations as Darden Restaurants, Inc.
1996: Darden opens its first Bahama Breeze restaurant in Orlando.
2003: Darden opens its first Seasons 52 restaurant in Orlando.
2007: RARE Hospitality International Inc., owner of LongHorn Steakhouse and The Capital Grille, is acquired.

North American standbys such as Florida stone crab, Maine flounder, and Alaska salmon. By 1995 Red Lobster was purchasing seafood from 44 countries.

The array of options allowed the chain to draw in new customers by featuring bargain specials. Close contact between the chain's buyers and thousands of entrepreneurial fishing operations, and delivery by overnight air express services, enabled much of the catch to reach units daily while still fresh. The price of Red Lobster dinner entrees ranged from about $7 to $19 in 1995. Lunch entrees ranged from about $4.30 to $7. Red Lobster also offered a lower-priced children's menu.

Questionnaires and focus groups also convinced Red Lobster of the importance of good service to securing follow-up trade. It held a four-day training course for servers before each restaurant opened and then required the staff to attend follow-up monthly classes. After 1986 servers were encouraged to display individuality in serving customers rather than relying on mechanical recitations of what the restaurant had to offer. A maroon apron under which servers wore clothing of their own choice replaced the uniform of shirts and slacks. Servers were also motivated by Red Lobster's reputation for good benefits, flexible hours, chances for advancement, and the hope of earning more than $100 in tips on good nights.

twice as many as in the past. Dinner prices were lowered to draw more customers, with the expectation that patrons would make up for the difference by increased spending on appetizers and alcoholic beverages.

Red Lobster continued to reinvent itself and reward its parent company in subsequent years, passing $1 billion in North American sales during 1988. By then it was the second-largest revenue producer for General Mills, trailing only the cereals division and accounting for about one-fifth of the parent company's business. A food industry analyst told the *New York Times*, "They have a concept that works extremely well, but they also constantly refresh their franchise. … If Cajun food is hot, they'll put five Cajun entrees on the menu. Whatever's hot, they'll do it."

A GROWING MENU: 1990–95

By this time Red Lobster was offering more than 100 seafood items every day. To supply its units it was buying about 58 million pounds of seafood every year, searching the world's oceans for the latest novelty. These included popcorn shrimp, caught off the shores of Brazil, slipper lobster from Thailand, and Pacific orange roughy, a whitefish from New Zealand to supplement

THE OLIVE GARDEN AND CHINA COAST: 1982–95

Fearing saturation in the seafood market, however, General Mills had decided years earlier to expand its restaurant group, which included York Steak House as well as Red Lobster. In 1982, following five years of painstaking research and about $28 million for development funds, the company opened the first Olive Garden restaurant in Orlando. By the end of 1985 there were eight such units, and by mid-1989 there were 145, making it the fastest-growing business for General Mills and probably the fastest-growing major chain in the United States.

A 1991 *Forbes* article found the dinner portions, averaging only $10, enormous, but called the salad soggy with dressing and the chicken bland, and likened the fettuccine alfredo to something out of a TV dinner. The public, however, flocked to these outlets. Average sales per Olive Garden were $2.8 million that year, compared with $3 million for Red Lobster, and both were high for the industry. Olive Garden ended fiscal 1992 with $808 million in sales and 341 outlets. It reached the $1-billion-a-year sales mark in 1993.

In 1995 the menu included not only Italian specialties such as veal piccata, baked lasagna, and chicken marsala, but also a variety of veal, beef, and seafood dishes. Dinner entree prices ranged from about $7 to $14.25, and lunch entree prices ranged from about $4.25 to $8.75. A limited-menu Olive Garden Café concept in food court settings at regional shopping malls was being tested. There were seven such units in late 1995.

The success of Olive Garden encouraged General Mills to expand its ethnic food format. After three years of development and test marketing, the restaurant group launched China Coast in 1990 as the first national Chinese food chain. This eatery opened with an eight-page menu, described in *Newsweek* as "about as long as the list of emperors in the Ming Dynasty."

The interiors were festooned with bamboo, paper lanterns, and Chinese-character wall scrolls, and the servers wore Chinese-style jackets. Eventually the China Coast chain grew to 51, but it failed to thrive and was ordered closed in 1995. During fiscal 1995 China Coast's sales came to only $71 million, and Wall Street analysts estimated that it lost $20 million that year. Thirty China Coast restaurants were converted into Red Lobster or Olive Garden units.

DARDEN RESTAURANTS FORMED: 1995

General Mills decided in 1995 to spin off its restaurant operations into a new company so that it could concentrate more on its consumer food products. Lee, the chairman and chief executive officer, named the new company Darden Restaurants in honor of his mentor and Red Lobster's founder. Stockholders received one share of Darden Restaurants common stock for each share of General Mills common stock they held. In their last fiscal year under the auspices of General Mills, the constituent units of Darden Restaurants had combined net income of $108.3 million.

Investors failed to rally around Darden Restaurants, whose stock ended its first day of trading on the New York Stock Exchange below the $12 to $13 a share expected by analysts. One securities analyst said that the restaurants had been accounting for only one-quarter of the operating profits of General Mills while absorbing half of the company's capital spending for expansion and renovation. Nevertheless, its market capitalization of $1.8 billion made it second in size only to McDonald's among the nation's publicly traded restaurant companies.

Darden Restaurants indicated in early 1996 that the China Coast experience would not keep it from trying other ethnic formats. In March of that year it began test marketing Bahama Breeze Caribbean Grille, in Orlando,

with a menu drawn from Spanish, French, African, Dutch, Indian, and American influences. Entrees, priced between $5 and $15, were to include Bahamian conch chowder, slow-roasted ribs, Caribbean paella, jerk chicken, and rum-glazed yellowtail dolphin, offered with Caribbean-island beer and other drinks. Lee predicted that, whether Bahama Breeze went into operation or not, Darden Restaurants would add at least two chains to its repertoire by 1998.

Executives of Darden Restaurants expressed confidence that they were on the right track toward long-term robust growth. Casual dining, according to the company, was the fastest-growing segment of the full-service restaurant market, with sales increasing at more than twice the overall market's rate since 1988 and representing, in 1995, 32 percent of full-service restaurant sales, or $29 billion. The trend toward casual dining, the company argued, was reflected in the less formal dress code in the workplace and would continue in years to come. Moreover, the company noted that 40- to 60-year-olds were the most frequent visitors to casual dining restaurants, and that the population aged 45 and older was expected to grow by 40 million through 2010.

At the end of fiscal 1995, Darden Restaurants was operating 1,250 restaurants, with locations in every state except Alaska. A total of 73 were in Canada. Red Lobster restaurants were being remodeled, with weathered wood accented by nautical artifacts for a wharf-side effect, to be completed by the end of fiscal 1997.

OVERCOMING MARKET SATURATION: 1997–2000

Despite the company's positive outlook for the future, Darden Restaurants began to experience financial setbacks in 1997 due to market saturation. The company was forced to shut down some of its poorly performing restaurants. Lee commented on the restructuring in a 1997 *Nation's Restaurant News* article, claiming, "There are some situations where we oversaturated and there were some areas where the market changed." The article also stated, "Lee described the closings and write-offs as a strategic move to increase positive cash flow." By the end of the fiscal 1997, 48 restaurants were closed, which included 26 outlets in Canada, and the company posted a $91 million loss as a result of the restructuring charges.

Determined to get Darden Restaurants back on track, management focused on reviving the Red Lobster and Olive Garden chains and also looked to its Bahama Breeze concept to bolster sales. After its lackluster performance in 1997, the company rebounded and secured profits of $102 million in 1998. The following year, the company established the Culinary Institute of Tuscany in Italy. The facility was created to train Olive Garden chefs in an authentic Italian environment.

New Red Lobster restaurants were opened with open floor plans and larger bar areas. Olive Garden restaurants also received a new look and were designed to resemble a Tuscan farmhouse. Darden Restaurants also began testing a new restaurant concept titled Smokey Bones BBQ Sports Bar and opened its first unit in Orlando in late 1999. The restaurant could seat 300 and had a U-shaped bar in the center. Decorated to resemble a mountain lodge, the outlet catered to sports fans, with 40 televisions throughout the restaurant and monitors at each table.

Having successfully overcome the sluggish sales of 1996 and 1997, Darden began to actively pursue new store openings. By the end of 1999, there were 669 Red Lobster restaurants, 464 Olive Garden outlets, 6 Bahama Breeze units, and 1 Smokey Bones BBQ Sports Bar. Additional store openings were slated for the upcoming year. Profits for 1999 reached $140.5 million on revenues of $3.46 billion.

Darden Restaurants entered the new millennium on solid financial ground. Sales increased 7 percent over the previous year while earnings climbed to $173.1 million. During the year, Red Lobster and Olive Garden achieved their 10th and 23rd consecutive quarter of sales increases, respectively. The company as a whole recorded its 14th consecutive quarter of earnings increases. The company posted its best financial year to date in fiscal 2001.

During the year, sales reached $4 billion, while earnings increased to $197 million. The number of Bahama Breeze restaurants rose to 21, while nine Smokey Bones outlets were in operation. Expansion for the sports concept was swift. By 2003, the concept had doubled in size for the third consecutive year. In addition to its financial gains, the company was named by *Fortune* magazine as one of the top 50 companies for minorities for the third year in a row.

SUCCESS DURING TOUGH ECONOMIC TIMES

During 2003, both Red Lobster and Olive Garden achieved record results. That year the company began to test a new concept. Called Seasons 52, the Orlando-based concept featured fresh and healthful menu items and had an extensive wine list. Growth for this concept was slow, however. By 2009 there were just nine outlets, located in Florida, New Jersey, and Atlanta, Georgia.

Despite a slowdown in the casual dining market, Darden Restaurants continued to secure positive results.

In 2004 the company posted revenues of $5 billion. While sales at Red Lobster and Olive Garden remained strong, the company opted to shutter six unprofitable Bahama Breeze locations that year.

Clarence Otis Jr. was named CEO in 2004 and chairman in 2005. The company's financial success continued but its Smokey Bones chain, which had grown rapidly over the past several years, started to show signs of weakness and its same-store sales began to decline in 2006. During 2007, the company continued to shutter unprofitable Bahama Breeze locations as well as 54 Smokey Bones restaurants.

With Red Lobster and Olive Garden posting strong results in the competitive seafood and Italian markets, Otis began looking for ways to bolster the company's holdings. Bahama Breeze continued to restructure in an attempt to secure same-store sales growth, and Smokey Bones had proved unprofitable. The chain, once thought to be the company's growth engine, was sold in 2008.

Otis then set his sights on the steak-house market. The CEO orchestrated a $1.4 billion deal in late 2007 to purchase RARE Hospitality International Inc., operator of 287 LongHorn Steakhouses and 28 upscale Capital Grille restaurants. LongHorn Steakhouse opened its first restaurant in Atlanta in 1981 while Capital Grille was launched in Providence, Rhode Island, in 1990.

LOOKING TO THE FUTURE

The RARE purchase, while giving the company a new area for growth, came at a time when the casual dining industry was struggling. The U.S. economy was in a downward spiral and consumer spending was falling, leaving many casual dining operators scrambling to get customers through their doors. Many offered significant discounts but Darden Restaurants opted to avoid that strategy. As Otis told MSNBC.com in early 2010, "We're a very strong brand, and we wanted to make sure that, even as we respond tactically, we didn't reduce those brands to the point where price was the primary attribute that we reinforced in people's minds."

The strategy of Darden Restaurants appeared to pay off. Combined same store sales for Olive Garden, Red Lobster, and LongHorn declined by 1.4 percent during 2009, but that was well below the 5.6 percent average decline seen at other casual restaurants. Even so, the company faced challenges in the future, including market saturation of the causal dining sector. With growth of industry sales expected to slow in the coming years, Darden Restaurants would need to maintain the health of its restaurants while looking for new growth opportunities.

Nevertheless, the company was optimistic about its future and believed it was on track for success in the years to come. It opened a new state-of-the-art Restaurant Support Center (RSC) in 2009 complete with a fitness and wellness center and facilities that brought the support staff for each of its brands under one roof. CEO Otis spoke at the opening ceremony, telling employees, "Today marks a new era in Darden's history. Our new home is the embodiment of our goal to create a great company—a winning company financially and a special place to be; a place where our employees can pursue their personal and professional dreams."

Robert Halasz
Updated, Christina M. Stansell

PRINCIPAL SUBSIDIARIES

GMRI, Inc.; RARE Hospitality International, Inc.; N and D Restaurants, Inc.; Darden SW LLC; Florida SE, Inc.

PRINCIPAL COMPETITORS

Brinker International, Inc.; DineEquity, Inc.; OSI Restaurant Partners, LLC.

FURTHER READING

Cobb, Catherine R., "Darden Stakes Claim in New Category with Rare Purchase," *Nation's Restaurant News*, August 27, 2007.

"Darden Expanding Four Chains," *Food Institute Report*, June 25, 2001, p. 2.

"Darden Posts FY '97 Loss of $91 Million after Restructuring," *Nation's Restaurant News*, June 30, 1997, p. 12.

"Darden Restaurants Opens New, State-of-the-Art Corporate Headquarters," *PR Newswire*, September 30, 2009.

"Darden Turns Olive Garden and Red Lobster Around," *Food Institute Report*, November 8, 1999.

"Darden Ups 2nd-Q Earnings as It Digs Out of Early Slump," *Nation's Restaurant News*, January 15, 1996, p. 12.

Gindin, Rona, and Richard L. Papiernik, "Darden Tests More BBQ Units; Analysts Eye Strategic Growth," *Nation's Restaurant News*, March 20, 2000, p. 1.

Harris, John, "Dinnerhouse Technology," *Forbes,* July 8, 1991, pp. 98–99.

Holmes, Tamara E., "Clarence Otis Named CEO of Darden Restaurants," *Black Enterprise*, November 1, 2004.

Horovitz, Bruce, "Casual Dining Chains Hunger for Change," *USA Today*, October 14, 2008.

Krummert, Bob, "A Bell-Ringer for Darden," *Restaurant Hospitality*, September 1, 2007.

Lavecchia, Gina, "Bahama Mama," *Restaurant Hospitality*, November 1998, p. 64.

Linn, Allison, "Restaurant Chain Sees Recession Bets Pay Off," MSNBC.com, February 25, 2010.

McGill, Douglas, "Why They Smile at Red Lobster," *New York Times,* April 23, 1989.

Miller, Annette, and Karen Springen, "Egg Rolls for Peoria," *Newsweek,* October 12, 1992, pp. 59–60.

Papiernik, Richard, "Darden Faces Up to Its Problems, Finds Its Own Solutions," *Nation's Restaurant News*, March 31, 1997, p. 11.

Deere & Company

1 John Deere Place
Moline, Illinois 61265
U.S.A.
Telephone: (309) 765-8000
Fax: (309) 765-5671
Web site: http://www.deere.com

Public Company
Incorporated: 1868
Employees: 51,300
Sales: $23.11 billion (2009)
Stock Exchanges: New York
Ticker Symbol: DE
NAICS: 333111 Farm Machinery and Equipment Manufacturing; 333112 Lawn and Garden Tractor and Home Lawn and Garden Equipment

■ ■ ■

Deere & Company, a leading manufacturer of agricultural machinery under the brand name John Deere, is based in Moline, Illinois, and is listed on the New York Stock Exchange. The company divides it business among three segments: Agriculture and Turf, Construction and Forestry, and Credit. Deere is a world leader in the manufacture of farm equipment, including a full range of tractors, loaders, combines, harvesters, seeding and application equipment, balers and mowers, and irrigation equipment. Additionally, it offers golf course equipment, residential and commercial walk-behind and riding mowers, garden tractors, outdoor power equipment, and landscape and nursery products.

Deere is also the world's largest manufacturer of timber harvesting equipment and attachments, and a major North American manufacturer of earthmoving, material handling, and other construction equipment. Finally, Deere's credit segment finances the purchase or lease of its new and used equipment and manages a portfolio of about $23 billion. Deere owns and operates 18 factories in the United States and Canada, and leases and operates another five locations. The company also operates plants around the world, including Brazil, China, France, Germany, India, Israel, New Zealand, Russia, and Spain.

EARLY HISTORY

Born in 1804 in Vermont, John Deere was a blacksmith renowned for his craftsmanship and inventiveness. After a business depression in the 1830s, Deere, like many young Easterners, migrated west. He settled in Grand Detour, Illinois, where his blacksmith business thrived. He soon saw that the cast-iron hand plow that pioneers had brought from the East did not work well in midwestern soil, which clung to the plow's bottom and made it necessary for the farmer to scrape off the soil every few feet. Deere developed a plow with a polished and specially shaped moldboard and share, which scoured itself after lifting the soil.

This first plow was made from a broken saw blade, but the tool quickly became so popular with Deere's customers that he began to make plows before he got orders for them, a revolutionary practice in those days. In 1848 Deere ordered a shipment of rolled steel from England. This move enabled him to expand his business, and three years later, he was able to get steel made to his specifications from Pittsburgh, Pennsylvania, mills. In 1848 Deere moved his business to Moline, Illinois, near the Mississippi River, which provided water power and convenient transportation. By 1850 he was producing 2,300 plows a year.

Known to say, "I will never put my name on a plow that does not have in it the best that is in me," Deere continued to improve his plows and to tailor them for different soil conditions. In 1868 the business was incorporated as Deere & Company. In 1869 Deere named his son, Charles Deere, vice president and treasurer of the company. When John Deere died in 1886, Charles succeeded him as president.

Charles Deere focused on the company's distribution system, establishing wholesale branches to market and distribute Deere equipment to the independent dealers who sold it. The product line was also expanded. The Gilpin Sulky Plow, launched in 1874, had the capacity to plow three acres in 12 hours, and in 1898 the new Deere Gang Plow, which used four horses instead of three and could plow six acres in 12 hours, was introduced. In the early 1900s, Deere plows were powered by steam engines. By the time Charles Deere died in 1907, the company was manufacturing a range of cultivators, steel plows, corn and cotton planters, and other tools.

GROWING THROUGH ACQUISITIONS

William Butterworth, a son-in-law of Charles Deere who was responsible for bringing together under the John Deere name other farm equipment companies with whom Deere had done business, became the next president, in 1907. As president, Butterworth engineered the 1911 acquisition of the Van Brunt Manufacturing Company of Horicon, Wisconsin, which

produced the first working broadcast seeder and grain drill. Also in 1911, Deere & Mansur Works, which had been established in 1877 by the company to make corn planters, was merged with Deere, as was Joseph Dain's hay-making tool company. In 1918 Deere bought Waterloo Gasoline Engine Company in Waterloo, Iowa, one of the first makers of tractors. During World War I, the demand for food motivated many more farmers to begin to use tractors, and agriculture gradually lost its dependence on animal power. Deere sold 8,000 Waterloo Boy tractors in 1918. In 1923 Deere introduced its own tractor, called the Model D, the first tractor to bear the John Deere brand name.

In 1928 Charles Deere Wiman, John Deere's great-grandson, became president of the company. Wiman concentrated on engineering and product development, and the company grew rapidly. In the 1930s, when the John Deere Combination Unit was introduced, the farmer could bed, plant, and fertilize cotton 10 times faster than four men with four mules. The four-row tractor corn planter allowed one man to plant and fertilize between 40 and 50 acres a day. In 1937, despite the Great Depression, Deere reached $100 million in gross sales.

During World War II Burton F. Peek was president. Peek served during the two years that Wiman held the post of colonel of ordnance, in Washington, D.C. Peek and Wiman, when the latter returned to Deere, focused on innovation in product design, and by the end of the war Deere was a leader. In 1952 Deere was the first farm equipment manufacturer to modify the self-propelled combine for picking and shelling corn. Three years later, Deere was one of the 100 largest manu- facturing companies in the United States.

MAJOR PERIOD OF POSTWAR GROWTH

After Wiman died in 1955, his son-in-law, William A. Hewitt, became president and CEO. He led the company into a major growth period. Seeing that Deere's decentralized operations needed to be coordinated, Hewitt accomplished this by increasing communication between different branches of the company. During the mid-1950s, while Deere's competitors were expanding abroad, Hewitt seized the opportunity to manufacture overseas. In 1956 he sent one of Deere's factory leaders, Harry Pence, to look for possible acquisitions overseas. The first was a small German tractor company called Heinrich Lanz, which was in financial trouble and could be bought cheaply. Other acquisitions or plant constructions followed in France,

KEY DATES

1837: Blacksmith John Deere invents polished-steel plow.
1868: Deere & Co. is officially incorporated.
1918: Company makes its first tractor.
1931: Deere opens its first foreign plant in Canada.
1956: A period of international expansion begins.
1978: Sales reach $4 billion.
1983: Deere begins to import Hitachi construction equipment.
2001: Research center opens in India.
2003: Home Depot begins carrying John Deere riding mower.

Spain, Argentina, Mexico, and South Africa. Deere also continued to expand in Canada, Western Europe, and Latin America.

In the late 1950s, Vice President Elwood Curtis persuaded Hewitt to diversify into finance. In 1958 Deere donated its capital stock in Moline National Bank to the John Deere Foundation, and, freed of antitrust constraints, the John Deere Credit Company was established to help finance farm equipment dealerships. Ten years later, Deere acquired Fulton Insurance Company in New York. Insurance and finance were to become important Deere operations when equipment sales slumped.

Hewitt diversified and expanded Deere to help balance the company's farm equipment operations. Since tractor sales were dependent on the income of farmers, sales fluctuated according to weather, agricultural prices, and government policy. Although agricultural machinery still accounted for most of Deere's sales, in the late 1950s, Deere began to make machinery for construction, along with equipment for street and road maintenance and logging. In 1963 the company began to manufacture and market lawn care and garden equipment. This branch of the company grew rapidly. By 1969 there were 3,700 independent John Deere dealers in the United States and Canada.

LABOR PROBLEMS HURT COMPANY

Although the 1960s were a decade of growth and diversification for Deere, it was also a turbulent time. Earnings decreased markedly in 1966 and 1967, mainly because of overseas operations. In 1968, the company suffered losses due to unfavorable weather, low crop prices, and a six-week strike. The United Auto Workers (UAW) demanded a contract from Deere similar to that won from Caterpillar Tractor Company, one of Deere's competitors. Deere refused, and the strike finally ended when the UAW proposed an inverse seniority plan, which gave senior workers up to 95 percent of their pay if they volunteered to be laid off for one year. This allowed older workers, who were closer to retirement, to take time off while collecting UAW supplemental unemployment benefits. The plan went into effect in late 1967, and in three years Deere laid off 1,698 people, about 70 percent of them with high seniority.

Throughout the 1960s, Deere expanded its lawn and garden product line to include snowmobiles, hand tools, portable heaters, lanterns, chain saws, and other products. In 1972 Deere introduced the John Deere bicycle in an effort to take advantage of a rapidly expanding market. This was also the first year Deere made a profit overseas, as the demand for farm machinery increased both within the United States and abroad. In 1975, overseas plants accounted for $681 million in sales and the company expected to grow more in foreign operations than domestically. That year, Deere also began a seven-year, $1.8 billion capital program to increase the capacity of its factories and plants by 30 percent.

During the 1970s, Deere repeatedly had conflicts with the UAW, as the firm began to mechanize further its manufacturing operations, cut back costs, and lay off workers. In 1976 a six-week strike reduced inventory at a time when the demand for equipment remained strong, and Deere lost a significant amount. In October 1979 UAW members went on strike again, demanding more paid time off and cost-of-living wage increases. Deere argued that its workers already had more paid time off than employees at similar companies and changes would be too costly. Consequently, Deere factories were shut down for three weeks, until a new contract was agreed upon.

In 1978 Hewitt committed $350 million to overseas expansion. Nonetheless, that year overseas operations took serious losses due to foreign-exchange fluctuation and high start-up costs for its new line of German tractors. In the late 1970s Deere added 20 products to its construction equipment sector and doubled the size of its Davenport, Iowa, plant, with the expectation that the construction industry would grow twice as fast as the farm equipment industry. By 1982, however, because of high interest rates, the construction equipment business was in a slump.

IMPACT OF FARM RECESSION
BEGINS: 1982

In 1982 Deere also experienced the first effects of the farm recession. Hewitt retired as head of the company and later became the U.S. ambassador to Jamaica. Robert Hanson, a longtime Deere employee, became president and CEO; he was the first chief executive to be unrelated to the Deere family, and he took up the post at a challenging time. The country was in the midst of a recession and farm equipment sales were low. The company's dealers were overstocked and its plants were running at about 50 percent capacity. To help its dealers survive, Deere incurred a large amount of short-term debt. Hanson cut capital spending by 30 percent, much of it in labor costs, and Deere began its dramatic reduction of salaried employees. Between 1980 and 1983, the company laid off about 40 percent of its employees.

In 1982 the newly robotized Waterloo tractor plant lost money, only a year after it began production. Although the plant required fewer workers, the demand for tractors was so low that the plant had to run at a fraction of its capacity and overhead was high. In fact, manufacturing operations lost money continually until 1986. To recoup some of the losses, Deere continued to develop its financial sector.

The company acquired Central National Life Insurance Company during this time, and expanded its John Deere Credit Company to include leasing operations. Deere was active in helping farmers to finance tractor purchases, offering credit incentives. Deere won the loyalty of many farmers this way. This helped sales at a time when many farmers were tightening their budgets. Farmers' net incomes had decreased about 75 percent in the past decade, basically because of overproduction, which, in turn, cost the government a great deal in surplus storage. In 1983 President Ronald Reagan introduced a payment-in-kind program, which paid farmers not to plant a certain number of acres, to alleviate the overproduction problem.

Deere's investment in overseas expansion had not paid off, and in 1983 the company still held a small share of the European market. In an effort to strengthen its links with Japan, Deere began to import Hitachi construction equipment.

Despite Deere's financial troubles, the recession hit Deere much less severely than it did its competitors, and Hanson found ways for the company to make money in sectors other than farm implements. In 1984 Deere acquired a rotating-combustion-engine business from the Curtiss-Wright Corporation, and Deere also bought all rights to Farm Plan, an agricultural financing service.

Sales in farm equipment continued to decrease markedly. The company survived mainly from its sale of lawn tractors, European sales, and its financial operations. In 1985 Deere continued to cut back on labor costs when it simplified the design of its basic engine and reorganized its factory system, laying off 480 workers.

In 1985 a $100,000 John Deere tractor sold for about $70,000. About 20 percent of the dealers in the Midwest closed. This attrition helped the stronger dealers to survive. With sales at $4 billion, Deere lost money before taxes.

In 1986 Deere won an $11 million military contract to develop an implement for repairing bomb-damaged runways. Also that year, 12,000 UAW members struck four key plants, seeking a new contract that would protect employees against cutbacks and maintain a cost-of-living adjustment. Deere shut down its remaining UAW plants, and the UAW accused the company of a lockout. Deere's dealers had enough inventory to last several months at the rate they were selling them, and the strike allowed Deere to reduce inventory and overhead. Deere said it could not afford the proposed labor contract, and the strike lasted five-and-a-half months before Deere and the UAW could come to an agreement.

Deere lost $99 million in 1987, mainly due to depressed sales and the effect of the strike. Hanson continued to push Deere into manufacturing parts such as hydraulic cylinders for other companies, and he also expanded credit operations. Although the lawn care business continued to do well, the company still depended on the farm implements sector for 60 percent of its sales.

In 1987 Hans W. Becherer was named president of Deere and Hanson remained CEO. In 1988 the farm economy began to recover from its slump because of the lower dollar and the improvement of the North American agricultural economy. As the main survivor in the industry, Deere had increased its market share during the recession from 45 to 55 percent. In 1988 sales increased 30 percent to $5.4 billion and net income reached a record $315 million, a one-year turnaround of $414 million. Sales of tractors rose 90 percent and sales of harvesting machinery tripled. As the recession lifted, many farmers were ready to buy new equipment.

Deere offered its largest selection of new agricultural products ever in 1988 and 1989, spending about $16 million to display its 44 new combines, tractors, and balers in Denver, Colorado, and Palm Springs, California. In 1988 Deere formed a joint venture with Hitachi called Deere-Hitachi Construction Machinery, which would produce and market earth excavators.

IMPROVING CONDITIONS

In August 1989 Becherer was named CEO of Deere, becoming chairman as well in June 1990 when Hanson retired. Although Deere enjoyed profits of $411.1 million in 1990, it then lost $20.2 million in 1991 and made only $37.4 million in 1992. Sales fell in both 1991 and 1992. The difficulties stemmed in part from the early 1990s recession, which hit Deere's $1 billion construction equipment business particularly hard, and in part from farmers' reluctance to buy new equipment despite an improved farm sector economy.

In response, Deere poured money into a $120 million 1991 restructuring program and into research and development; $280 million in 1992 alone. The result was the company's 1992 introduction of the 6000/7000 series of tractors, touted as Deere's most significant new products since 1960. The line consisted of six new tractors with horsepower ranging from 66 to 145 and featuring the largest cabs in the industry, cabs that included comfortable seats, stereo cassettes, air conditioning, and better visibility thanks to 29 percent more glass. Deere's revitalized new product development efforts did not let up, however. Just two years later, the company introduced the 8000 series tractors, including the 8400 model, which was the world's first 225-horsepower row-crop tractor.

Meanwhile, Deere continued to seek ways to bolster its nonfarming sectors. It acquired several other manufacturers of power mower and mower products for the consumer and commercial markets, including the Homelite division of Textron, Inc. With this acquisition, Deere's lawn and ground care equipment business, which became known as the Worldwide Commercial & Consumer Equipment Division, generated almost as much revenue as the Industrial Equipment Division.

Although Deere had long been active manufacturing its farm product overseas, the company had not been as aggressive as its competitors in selling tractors and other farm equipment outside the United States and Canada. The mid-1990s saw Deere become much more active in this area.

Starting in 1994 Deere enjoyed three consecutive years of record sales and profits. Farmers, whose coffers were overflowing as a result of high commodity prices, were finally replacing their old equipment with the innovative new models Deere introduced earlier in the decade. Sales outside the United States and Canada were becoming increasingly important to the company's success, increasing more than 75 percent from 1993 to 1996, going from $1.55 billion to $2.75 billion.

Deere remained vulnerable to the inevitable economic downturn but was now somewhat more diversified than the Deere of the late 1980s in both product line and geographically. In April 1996, Ukraine bought 1,049 of Deere's combines at a price of $187 million, the company's largest single agricultural equipment sale to date. Sales were also booming in Argentina and Australia. China, which harvested seven-eighths of its acreage by hand, seemed to provide the greatest room for growth.

At home, Deere had to contend with new competition from Peoria-based Caterpillar Inc., which had launched its own line of agricultural equipment in the late 1980s. Nonetheless, Deere's revenues grew by $1 billion a year between 1993 and 1997, with profits growing by $100 million annually. *Crain's Chicago Business* credited a six-year labor agreement signed with the UAW in 1997 that lowered starting pay. A growing economy, new product lines, and new joint ventures in China, Brazil, and India also contributed to the company's improved outlook.

By the fall of 1998, some of the lowest grain prices in 20 years ended the company's recovery, and unsold machinery began to pile up on dealers' lots. Deere responded with temporary layoffs and placed its hopes on its new lawn care business, although agricultural equipment remained at the core of the business. Diversification was also an important survival strategy for rivals Case Corp. and Caterpillar Inc., which extended their financing and distribution capabilities, respectively, into other fields.

NEW CHALLENGES IN THE NEW MILLENNIUM

Robert Lane, a longtime employee, was named president and chief operating officer in January 2000, succeeded Becherer as Deere CEO in June. In June of that year, the company's new $30 million, highly automated plant near Williamsburg, Virginia, began turning out lightweight, versatile Gator utility vehicles, which were also produced in Ontario. There were 10 variants, including a military version designed to be dropped by parachute, priced between $6,000 and $12,500. In July, Deere's finance arm received approval to charter its own federal savings bank, which would take over the existing credit card program.

In spite of weaknesses in certain markets, Deere posted worldwide net income of $485.5 million for the 2000 fiscal year on sales of $13.1 billion. *Fortune* magazine picked Deere as the United States' most admired company in the industrial and farm equipment category. Although it continued to pick up market share in farm equipment, by March 2001 falling grain prices and slowness in Deere's lawn care and construction businesses made its immediate outlook uncertain. The company soon announced new production cutbacks, as well as an early retirement program for 2,500 office workers.

JOHN DEERE LANDSCAPES
FORMED: 2001

Seeking to expand into related businesses, Deere acquired irrigation products manufacturer Richton International Corporation for $170 million in 2001. Richton's supply distribution business was combined with another new purchase, McGinnis Farms, Inc., to create a landscaping and irrigation supply division called John Deere Landscapes. Difficult economic conditions also led to consolidation. In the summer of 2002 Deere closed plants in Williamsburg, Virginia, and Jeffersonville, Indiana, in a cost-cutting move.

An unexpected new market opened up for Deere in the early 2000s in a roundabout manner. In 2001 the company opened a research center in India to develop a tractor that could break into the Indian market where some 300 million farmers were still mostly relying on oxen to pull plows. A stripped-down inexpensive tractor, reliable but void of comforts, was developed. In the meantime, an Indian tractor maker, Mahindra & Mahindra, began selling its bare-bolts tractors in the United States, targeting the growing ranks of farming hobbyists, who like Indian farmers valued price and functionality over frills. Thus, in 2002 Deere began selling a modified version of its Indian tractor to the American hobbyist market.

Deere reached out to the mass market channel as well. In 2003 Deere for the first time began selling its riding mowers in the mass market through an agreement with big-box retailer The Home Depot, in the process gaining access to 100,000 new customers that had been long neglected by Deere's dealer network. In the past Deere had shied away from this market, essentially ceding it to Sears, in order to maintain dealer relationships. In order to placate dealers, Deere made the new line available to them at the same price offered to Home Depot. Moreover, the dealers became the service center for repairs, thus providing dealers with sales opportunities from a new group of customers. Lowe's, another mass market home center chain, also began carrying the new Deere line in 2004.

In the early 2000s, Deere pursued still more new opportunities. It invested about $40 million in wind energy turbines in the midwestern United States in 2005 and a year later increased that amount to about $300 million. Wind energy offered promise on several fronts. Not only did it provide diversity and act as a hedge against the cyclical nature of demand for farm and construction equipment, it helped to support the finances of farmers, who could in turn purchase more Deere equipment. Farmers were able to lease land and air rights for $5,000 to $7,000 a year per turbine, each of which could generate as much as 1.65 megawatts of electricity and gross nearly $240,000 in electricity sales.

LANE STEPS DOWNS: 2009

A surge in global demand for Deere products resulted in record earnings of $1.69 billion in 2006 and led to the company chairman and chief executive, Robert W. Lane, being named CEO of the Year by *Industry Week* magazine. There was a changing of the guard as well as a reorganization of the business in 2009. The Agricultural Equipment Division and Commercial & Consumer Equipment Divisions were merged to create the Worldwide Agriculture and Turf Division, and the six U.S. sales branch offices were consolidated into two centers. Later in 2009 Samuel R. Allen was named Deere's ninth CEO. Allen had first joined the company as an engineer in 1975 and worked his way up through the managerial ranks. Although Lane remained chairman, a succession plan called for Allen to assume that post as well. He took the reins of a history-rich company that still retained a good deal of hope for the future.

René Steinke
Updated, David E. Salamie;
Frederick C. Ingram; Ed Dinger

PRINCIPAL DIVISIONS

Agriculture and Turf; Construction and Forestry; Credit.

PRINCIPAL COMPETITORS

Caterpillar Inc.; CNH Global N.V.; Kubota Corporation.

FURTHER READING

Arndorfer, James B., "Deere Hunts Construction Equipment Dealerships, but Buyout Push Sparks Legal Shootout," *Crain's Chicago Business,* November 20, 2000, p. 1.

Bankston, John, "John Deere Announces Plans to Scale Back Production," *Augusta Chronicle,* March 22, 2001.

Barboza, David, "Aiming for Greener Pastures; Farm-Equipment Makers Step Up Efforts to Diversify," *New York Times,* April 14, 1999, p. C1.

Broehl, Wayne G., Jr., *John Deere's Company: A History of Deere & Company and Its Times,* New York: Doubleday, 1984.

Christie, Jim, "Inventor John Deere—Relied on Skill, Determination to Provide the World with Farming Solutions," *Investor's Business Daily,* December 3, 1999, p. A4.

Crown, Judith, "Cat Stalking Deere in New Market: Bobcat Territory," *Crain's Chicago Business,* October 20, 1997, p. 3.

"Deere Names Samuel Allen New CEO," *Rental Equipment Register,* June 1, 2009.

Deveny, Kathleen, "As John Deere Sowed, So Shall It Reap," *Business Week,* June 6, 1988, p. 84.

Eaton, Leslie, "William Hewitt, 83, Responsible for Overseas Expansion of Deere," *New York Times,* May 22, 1998, p. A23.

Flint, Jerry, "Root, Hog! Or Die," *Forbes,* November 4, 1985, p. 170.

Frazier, Mya, "John Deere Cultivates Its Image," *Advertising Age,* July 25, 2005, p. 6.

Gross, Lisa, and Jill Bettner, "Planting Deep and Wide at John Deere," *Forbes,* March 14, 1983, p. 119.

Historical Highlights: 150 Years of John Deere Contributions to Agriculture, Moline, Ill.: Deere & Company, 1990.

Mero, Jenny, "John Deere's Farm Team," *Fortune,* April 14, 2008, p. 119.

Murphy, H. Lee, "Farm Crisis Ruins Deere's Sales Harvest: Heavy Equipment Revenues Tumble as Cat Sharpens Claws," *Crain's Chicago Business,* March 8, 1999, p. 4.

———, "New Markets Help Boost Deere Harvest: Company Taps into Emerging Areas," *Crain's Chicago Business,* March 23, 1998, p. 26.

The Story of John Deere, Moline, IL: Deere & Company, 1989.

Tita, Bob, "Deere Investing in Wind Power," *Crain's Chicago Business,* April 17, 2006, p. 20.

Weiner, Steve, "Staying on Top in a Tough Business in a Tough Year," *Forbes,* May 27, 1991, pp. 46, 48.

Délifrance S.A.

99 rue Mirabeau
Ivry sur Seine, F-94200
France
Telephone: (+33 01) 49 59 75 00
Fax: (+33 01) 49 59 75 47
Web site: http://www.Délifrance.com

Wholly Owned Subsidiary of Grand Moulins de Paris S.A.
Incorporated: 2003
Employees: 2,200
Sales: EUR 240 million ($276 million) (2006)
NAICS: 311812 Commercial Bakeries

■ ■ ■

Délifrance S.A. is one of the world's leading manufacturers of French-style frozen bread, pastry, patisserie, and other bakery goods for the wholesale market. Based in Ivry-sur-Seine, near Paris, Délifrance produces nearly 1,000 different breads, pastries, cakes, and snacks for the professional, restaurant/catering, and consumer markets. Délifrance, which pioneered the frozen bread dough market, markets its products across several technologies: Ready to Prove (RTP), Ready to Bake (RTB), Thaw and Serve (T&S), Oven Prove, Part-baked, Fully-baked.

The company also produces a line of consumer-oriented part-baked bread products using Modified Atmosphere Packaging, which provides for long shelf-life. Délifrance operates subsidiaries in 16 countries, in France, Belgium, the Netherlands, the United Kingdom, Switzerland, Spain, Portugal, Russia, Germany, Austria, Greece, Italy, Singapore, and Lebanon. The company also operates factories in France, as well as in the Netherlands, the United Kingdom, and Belgium.

On the international market, Delifrance is well-known for its Délifrance-branded bakery kiosks and fast-food café-style restaurants. The company directly oversees franchised operations in Switzerland, the United Kingdom, the Netherlands, and Belgium. The company also supplies the extensive network of Délifrance restaurants operated by Singapore-based Délifrance Asia Pte, an independently owned company. Délifrance Asia operates more than 230 restaurants and bakeries in Brunei, China, Hong Kong, Indonesia, Malaysia, the Philippines, Sri Lanka, and Thailand.

Délifrance is owned by Grands Moulins de Paris S.A. (GMP), France's leading flour-milling group, and generated annual revenues of approximately EUR 240 million ($276 million) in 2006. GMP is itself controlled by Nutrixo Groupe, part of the industrial arm of French cooperative group Champagne Céréales SA. Hubert François is president of Délifrance as well as of GMP.

NANCY MILLER IN THE 19TH CENTURY

The Délifrance brand was introduced in 1982. The company's origins, however, may be traced back to the 19th century. France's flour production remained the province of small-scale, largely artisan millers into the early decades of that century. Starting from the 1830s, however, a number of entrepreneurs began introducing more modern milling methods, imported from the United States and elsewhere. Among them was Émile Bouchotte, who opened a mill in Metz in 1837.

COMPANY PERSPECTIVES

Délifrance has built its success on 3 values at the very heart of the company: PASSION. Men and women driven by a passion for the product and innovation. CUSTOMER. We put the customer at the centre of our thinking. To satisfy multiple distribution channels—retail, food service, craft bakery, wholesalers and industrials—Délifrance develops technologies and packaging that meet their specific needs. Délifrance products are convenient and easy to prepare for any type of customer. CRAFT. We use our know-how to bring the best of these qualities to our customers.

Following the German annexation of that city, Bouchotte moved to Nancy, where he acquired the lease of an existing mill, Grands Moulins de Nancy, which had been set up under a partnership between Louis-Antoine Vilgrain and Léon Simon. Vilgrain and Simon operated several other flour mills in the Lorraine region at that time. Bouchotte died in 1885, whereupon Vilgrain and Simon took over the Nancy mill. They then merged all of their operations together into a single joint-stock company called Grands Moulins de Nancy.

Vilgrain traveled to Budapest in 1893, where he discovered a new milling technology recently developed in what was then considered the center of the European milling industry. The Hungarian system replaced the traditional grindstone with a cylinder-based system. The new technology not only provided a major boost in productivity but also in quality, producing a finer and purer flour. As a result, Grands Moulins de Nancy soon gained recognition in France for the quality of its flours.

BUILDING GRANDS MOULINS DE PARIS IN THE TWENTIES

Ernest Vilgrain, born in 1880, took over the direction of the company from his father at the turn of the century. The younger Vilgrain led the company on an acquisition drive, buying up mills in France's eastern region. By the beginning of World War I, Grands Moulins de Nancy had already become one of the largest flour millers in France. As such, the company played a crucial role in supporting France's military effort during the conflict. Ernest Vilgrain himself served as the undersecretary of provisions during the war.

In this role, Vilgrain became a somewhat controversial figure and was later accused of using his position

in order to gain a monopoly over the supplier of grain to the French government. Vilgrain also profited from dissension within the somewhat closed world of France's wheat industry by secretly acquiring La Société des Grands Moulins Réunins, a grouping of nine flour companies and a total of 13 flour mills, founded by Lucien Baumann, a member of one of the country's most prominent wheat families. Vilgrain renamed the company as La Société d'Entreprise Meunière.

In 1919 Ernest Vilgrain led the creation of a new company, merging Grands Moulins de Nancy and La Société d'Entreprise Meunière with the operations of two other miller families, Boussac and Herteux. Vilgrain called the new company Grand Moulins de Paris (GMP) and then launched construction of a new mill along the Seine river in Paris's XIII arrondissement. That mill, completed in 1921, became the first in France to feature fully automated production, boosting both production and the purity of its flour. By 1924 the company had added a second modern mill, in Bordeaux. In this way, GMP emerged as France's leading flour miller.

BREAD PRODUCTS IN THE SIXTIES

GMP played a major role as a supplier to the French military, and to the population as a whole, through the years of World War II. The postwar period was also marked by the introduction of new intensive agricultural techniques. Stimulated by the French government, France's agricultural sector became one of the world's most heavily industrialized. As a result, the country posted dramatic increases in wheat yields. The growth in supply provided GMP with the raw materials for its own expansion. In 1955 the company began its first flour exports, to other European markets as well as to developing markets.

At the same time, GMP had begun to take a closer interest in the ultimate destination for much of its production: bread. Already in 1929 the company had backed the establishment of l'École de Boulangerie de France (Bakery School of France), the first of its kind in the country.

Into the 1960s, GMP also began developing a wider range of products for the bakery sector. This led to the launch of the company's first premixed bread flours in 1968, which represented something of a revolution for the French baking industry. By then, the company had come under the complete control of the Vilgrain family, now under the direction of Jean-Louis Vilgrain. By then, the company had joined forces with several other flour producers, including Champagne

KEY DATES

1919: Founding of the Grand Moulins de Paris (GMP).
1982: GMP launches frozen bread products brand and franchise format Délifrance.
2001: GMP and Délifrance become part of Nutrixo.
2003: Délifrance incorporates as Délifrance S.A.
2009: Nutrixo acquires Sofrapain and Le Pain Croustillant, which become part of Délifrance.

Céréales, to form France Farine in 1965. That company then launched Francine, France's first national flour brand.

GMP continued to play the role of innovator to the French bread sector, introducing its first frozen bread dough in 1978. This new product line responded to a major trend in France's bread market: the emergence of the large-scale supermarket chains. GMP's frozen bread products permitted these companies to avoid the installation of complete bakeries at their stores.

LAUNCHING THE DÉLIFRANCE BRAND IN 1982

The move into premixed and frozen dough products provided the foundation for GMP's next foray. During the 1970s, the company began developing its own bakery and café concepts, in order to introduce French-style baked goods to the international markets. Among the company's initial targets was the United States, where it launched subsidiary Vie de France. By 1976, the company had added subsidiary operations in the Netherlands, followed by an entry into Belgium in 1978.

The growth of these operations encouraged the company to develop a wider range of bread products, and in 1982 GMP launched a new brand for the range, called Délifrance. Soon after, the company decided to extend the Délifrance brand as a franchised bakery and restaurant concept. Taking the lead in this operation was Alexandre Vilgrain, who had joined the family business in 1979 and had been responsible for developing its interests in Africa and Asia.

This international experience encouraged Alexandre Vilgrain to launch the Délifrance concept beyond Europe. The Asian markets appeared especially promising during this time. Bread had not formed part of the

traditional diet in most Asian countries. Into the 1980s, however, adoption of Western customs and habits led to increasing demand for Western-style breads. Recognizing this trend, Alexandre Vilgrain established Délifrance Asia in Singapore in 1983.

Initially, that company focused on the wholesale market, supplying Délifrance products to hotels, supermarkets, airlines, and other outlets. Then, in 1985, the company opened its first Délifrance Café, located at Singapore's Clifford Centre. By 1987 Délifrance Asia had opened its first cafés in Hong Kong and China, focusing on the Shanghai market for the latter. GMP extended its own range of Délifrance operations during the decade as well. The company entered the United Kingdom in 1988, setting up a sales subsidiary, as well as extending the Délifrance café franchise.

MANAGEMENT BUYOUT IN 1998

By the end of the 1980s, GMP's main Parisian site had become a highly coveted piece of property as the 13th arrondissement underwent a construction boom that included a number of important landmarks, including the site of the new French national library. In 1989 the Vilgrain family, which held GMP through their holding company Jean-Louis Vilgrain, agreed to sell GMP to fast-rising French conglomerate Bouygues for FRF 2 billion (approximately $300 million). The Vilgrains maintained control of parts of their empire, including their international trade operations, Vie de France in the United States, and the fast-growing Délifrance Asia network.

Bouygues's purchase of GMP appeared to have been made to gain control of GMP's Parisian property. Nonetheless, GMP itself grew strongly under Bouygues. Starting in 1990, the company launched a major modernization of its operations. This included the construction of a new state-of-the-art facility in Gennevilliers, northwest of Paris, which was completed in 1997. By then, Bouygues had completed the sale of the former GMP mill to the city of Paris, which built a new extension of its university on the site.

Following that sale, Bouygues, then in the process of an extension into the mobile telecommunications market, reached an agreement to sell MDP to a management buyout led by Hubert François and backed by Axa Private Equity Fund and Charterhouse, among others. That deal was completed in 1998.

INTERNATIONAL GROWTH INTO 2000

By then, Délifrance's operations had been extended to 11 factories producing breads, pastries, and desserts, both for the group's growing franchise business abroad as well as for the restaurant, bakery, and supermarket sectors in France. By then, Délifrance had also extended its range of operations to include Spain and Portugal, starting in 1992. By the end of the decade, Délifrance already represented 30 percent of GMP's total revenues of FRF 2.4 billion (approximately $400 million).

Following the buyout, Délifrance launched a new expansion effort. The company introduced a new line of ready-to-eat foods for the consumer market, called PEP's, in 1999. That year also marked the group's entry into Switzerland. At the same time, Délifrance launched franchise operations in the Scandinavian markets, establishing a subsidiary in Sweden. Partnerships provided the company with an entry into other markets, including Greece in 1999 and Lebanon in 2000.

During this time, Délifrance Asia had also grown into a major revenue source for the group. That company had established operations in Australia and Malaysia at the beginning of the 1990s and then entered the Philippines in 1995. Throughout this time Délifrance Asia had remained controlled by the Vilgrain family until 1996, when it went public on the Singapore Stock Exchange. The offering helped fuel the group's further expansion, including an entry into a Thailand in 1996 and the launch of its own franchise business, starting with Sri Lanka in 1999. In that year, Délifrance Asia was taken private again, after PAMA Group acquired control of the company. Délifrance changed hands again, in 2007, when it was acquired by Auric Pacific Group Ltd.

JOINING NUTRIXO IN 2001

In the meantime, GMP had lost its leadership of the French flour milling market, falling to the number two position at the beginning of the 21st century. The company, however, worked to correct this situation. In 2001 GMP and its venture-capital backers agreed to a merger with the number four player, Euromill, a subsidiary of Champagne Céréales, and Inter-Meunerie, part of the Nouricia cooperative. The new company became a subsidiary of Champagne Céréales under the name of Nutrixo. GMP remained a separate subsidiary, with 50 percent of its shares controlled by its management and employees.

Délifrance formally incorporated as Délifrance S.A. in 2003 while remaining a subsidiary of GMP. The company benefited in a number of ways by being part of Nutrixo and the larger Champagne Céréales. For one, Délifrance enjoyed access to its parent companies' grain and flour supplies, ensuring both its own raw materials supply and its quality. At the same time, Nutrixo's

acquisition drive strengthened Délifrance's own operations.

These acquisitions included Appétit de France, which operated three factories producing frozen bread specialties, acquired in 2004. In 2006 Nutrixo acquired one of Délifrance's major rivals in France's Nord region, Krabansky, adding two more factories to the group's larger industrial network, as well as expanding the company's range of frozen bread products.

Similarly, in 2007 the acquisition of Toufflet Gourmet expanded the group's frozen patisserie range. This was followed by the takeover of two companies held by the United Kingdom's Premier Foods, Sofrapain, based in France, and Le Pain Croustillant, based in the United Kingdom. These acquisitions were completed in 2009 and then placed under Délifrance's operations.

Délifrance complemented the expansion of its industrial backbone with an extension of its international sales and franchising operations. In particular, the company began exploring the Eastern European markets at the end of the decade, creating a subsidiary in Poland in 2006. In 2007 the company added two new markets: Hungary and Russia. The company's Asian franchise operations, controlled by Délifrance Asia, continued strong growth by adding operations in Brunei in 2008. This boosted that company's total operations to more than 230 locations by the end of the decade. Délifrance had become an ambassador for French bread around the world.

M. L. Cohen

PRINCIPAL SUBSIDIARIES

Appétit de France; Délifrance Asia Wholesale (Singapore); Délifrance Belgium; Délifrance Deutschland GmbH (Germany); Délifrance Hellas (Greece); Délifrance Hungaria (Hungary); Délifrance Iberica S.A. (Spain); Délifrance Italia s.r.l. (Italy); Délifrance Middle East (Lebanon); Délifrance Netherlands; Délifrance Norden AB; Délifrance Osterreich GmbH (Austria); Délifrance Portugal; Délifrance Roccia LLC (Russia); Délifrance Suisse (Switzerland); Délifrance UK Ltd.; Krabansky S.A.

PRINCIPAL DIVISIONS

Savory Products; Viennoiserie; Bread; Brioche; Pastry.

PRINCIPAL OPERATING UNITS

Appétit de France; Krabansky.

PRINCIPAL COMPETITORS

Unilever N.V.; Dr. August Oetker KG; Orkla ASA; Aryzta AG; Danisco A/S; Vandemoortele S.A./NV; Sara Lee UK Holdings Ltd.; Bimbo S.A.; Europastry S.A.

FURTHER READING

Dedieu, Franck, "Les Grands Moulins de Paris," *L'Expansion*, March 1, 2006.

"Délifrance Back in Brunei," *Borneo Bulletin*, August 27, 2008.

Ducuing, Olivier, "Nutrixo S'Offre le Boulanger Industriel Nordiste Krabansky," *Les Echos*, March 30, 2006, p. 18.

Jitpleecheep, Sukanya, "Délifrance Seeks to Double Outlet Total," *Bangkok Post*, November 12, 2002.

"Rapprochement Trois dans la Meunerie Française," *Les Echos*, April 6, 2001, p. 16.

Delta Apparel, Inc.

322 South Main Street
Greenville, South Carolina 29601
U.S.A.
Telephone: (864) 232-5200
Web site: http://www.deltaapparelinc.com

Public Company
Incorporated: 1999 as Delta Apparel, Inc.
Employees: 6,500
Sales: $355.2 million (2009)
Stock Exchanges: New York
Ticker Symbol: DLA
NAICS: 315211 Men's and Boys' Cut and Sew Apparel Contractors; 315221 Men's and Boys' Cut and Sew Underwear and Nightwear Manufacturing; 315223 Men's and Boys' Cut and Sew Shirt (Except Work Shirt) Manufacturing; Men's and Boys' Cut and Sew Apparel Contractors; 315228 Men's and Boys' Cut and Sew Other Outerwear Manufacturing; 315231 Women's and Girls' Cut and Sew Lingerie, Loungewear, and Nightwear; 315991 Hat, Cap, and Millinery Manufacturing

∎ ∎ ∎

Delta Apparel, Inc., is a manufacturer of casual and athletic clothing and headwear. When spun off from Delta Woodside in 2000, the Greenville, South Carolina-based company primarily made T-shirts for the screen-printing industry and others. In 2003 it acquired Georgia's M. J. Soffe Co., which added a popular line of cheerleader shorts and other branded casual apparel

items. Additional brands were added in subsequent years, as the company built up low-cost manufacturing capacity in Honduras, Mexico, and Costa Rica.

The two main segments of Delta Apparel's business, activewear and retail ready, operate according to different schedules. Activewear, which includes sportswear such as sweats and, primarily, unadorned T-shirts, is manufactured in bulk runs according to the company's own specifications and forecasts, and warehoused for eventual sale. Such brands include the basic Delta Pro Weight, the heavier Delta Magnum Weight, and more fitted Quail Hollow labels.

Delta Apparel has been increasingly involved in the higher margin retail ready side of the business, which is more fashion-oriented and is produced to customer specifications for delivery within several weeks. The company owns such brands as Soffe, Intensity Athletics (a supplier of uniforms for sports teams), Junk Food, To The Game, and Kudzu. It also supplies products under contract for leading international brands such as Nike and adidas.

Delta Apparel is vertically integrated, maintaining low-cost textile and cut-and-sew operations abroad as well as facilities in the United States for faster turnarounds and for politically sensitive customers such as the military. It also subcontracts some work to suppliers in India and China. The company has five U.S. distribution centers. In contrast to many of its industry rivals, Delta Apparel prefers to deal directly with a large number of customers (12,000 of them in 2009). This insures it against dependence on any one customer and reduces its exposure to large credit lines.

ORIGINS

Delta Apparel, Inc., was formed in a 2000 spin-off of the T-shirt business of Delta Woodside Industries, Inc., of Greenville, South Carolina. Delta Woodside had been formed in 1983 by Bettis Rainsford and Erwin Maddrey II. In the next decade and a half Delta Woodside bought numerous textile plants and apparel companies located chiefly in South Carolina and Georgia, including parts of J. P. Stevens & Co., and employed 6,000 people at its peak. In a rare diversification move, Delta Woodside acquired Virginia's Nautilus International, Inc., in 1993.

Delta Woodside built up significant apparel operations through the acquisitions of Woodside Mills, Inc. (1984), Maiden Knitting Mills (1985), and Royal Manufacturing (1985). A 1986 purchase from J. P. Stevens & Co. added apparel producer StevecoKnit and Delta Fabrics, the latter a prominent fabric producer dating back to 1903. In the late 1990s, Delta Woodside was refocusing to increase its appeal to investors. It began by selling its StevecoKnit Fabrics Division in 1998 and the next year divested the Nautilus exercise machine business.

Experiencing better results from Delta Mills Marketing Co., its core cotton-fabrics operation, than from its two clothing lines, Delta Woodside also looked for buyers for Duck Head Apparel Co., a maker of casual clothing, and Delta Apparel Co., which primarily produced T-shirts. When this proved unsuccessful, in 1999 Delta Woodside resolved to spin them off. Weakness in the bond market (coinciding with a steep drop

in promotional business related to the dot-com bust) delayed the offerings a few months but in June 2000 both Delta Apparel and Duck Head Apparel became independent companies traded on the American Stock Exchange (the parent company remained on the New York Stock Exchange).

The companies involved were posting improving results. In the full year ended July 2000, Delta Woodside posted a $17 million profit after losing $38 million the year before. Duck Head reduced its annual loss from $47.7 million to $7.4 million as sales slipped 25 percent to $53.3 million. Delta Apparel made $4.7 million after losing $19.2 million the previous year, as sales rose 7.2 percent to $114.5 million in fiscal 2000.

Before the year was up, the management of both newly independent companies faced a proxy battle led by dissident shareholder Bettis Rainsford, who had previously been Delta Woodside's treasurer and chief financial officer. However, Delta Apparel Chairman E. Erwin Maddrey II and President and Chief Executive Officer Robert W. Humphreys remained in place. Humphreys, who had taken over Delta Apparel in April 1999 when it was still a division of Delta Woodside, succeeded Maddrey as chairman in June 2009.

In 2002 the *Atlanta Journal-Constitution* noted the extent of Delta Apparel's operations. It was producing 84 million T-shirts a year. It had 2,900 employees, only 700 of them at its U.S. factories; the rest were in Mexico and Honduras. It counted 1,200 customers, virtually all of them in the United States.

ENTERING BRANDED APPAREL: 2003

Until 2003, Delta Apparel primarily supplied screen printers and embroiderers. In a deal that closed in October 2003, Delta Apparel acquired M. J. Soffe Co., a maker of branded athletic and casual clothing, which brought it into the retail marketplace. Soffe's colorful cheerleader shorts were popular among college students. Sporting goods stores accounted for about half of Soffe's sales. Its products were also sold in department stores such as Belk, Kohl's, and J.C. Penney, and at college bookstores.

Milton J. Soffe had launched the company in Haymount, Georgia, in 1946 to sell hard goods to local military exchanges. It eventually began making laundry bags and in 1971 began screen-printing T-shirts for the Air Force. The popularity of jogging in the 1970s helped Soffe sustain its own line of athletic clothes and revenues were up to $15 million by the end of the decade. Company President Jim Soffe told the *Fayetteville Observer* he sold the business to facilitate his

```
┌─────────────────────────────────────────────┐
│                                               │
│              KEY DATES                         │
│                   ◆                            │
│                                               │
│   1946:  M. J. Soffe Co. founded in Haymount, │
│          Georgia.                             │
│   1983:  Delta Woodside Industries, Inc.,     │
│          formed.                              │
│   2000:  Delta Apparel, Inc., spun off from   │
│          Delta Woodside Industries, Inc.      │
│   2003:  Delta buys M. J. Soffe Co., maker of │
│          branded athletic and casual clothing.│
│   2005:  Delta Apparel's yarn manufacturing   │
│          facility in Edgefield, South         │
│          Carolina, sold to Parkdale           │
│          America, LLC, for $10 million.       │
│   2007:  Delta opens Ceiba Textiles plant in  │
│          Honduras.                            │
│                                               │
└─────────────────────────────────────────────┘
```

retirement planning, although he planned to stay with it for another few years.

At the time it was acquired by Delta Apparel, Soffe had grown to annual revenues of about $100 million and employed 1,400 people at three North Carolina plants. The sewing plant in Maxton was closed soon after the acquisition, but the company maintained the two remaining plants, in Bladenboro and Rowland, in order to meet demand for "Made in U.S.A." products from military and labor union customers.

The deal was ultimately worth $58 million, including performance incentives paid later. Delta Apparel soon integrated Soffe with its facilities in Maiden, North Carolina, and Honduras. In addition to nearly doubling its fiscal 2003 revenues of $129.5 million, the purchase brought higher-margin, more fashion-oriented lines into Delta Apparel's business mix.

Delta Apparel took over the supply of cotton T-shirts for Soffe, which in turn began making polyester-cotton fleece products for the company's other brands. This helped offset the seasonality of the cotton T-shirt business, which was becoming more competitive as a pair of major distributors merged.

The vertically integrated company found that some functions were best left to others. With the price of cotton rising, Delta Apparel sold its yarn manufacturing facility in Edgefield, South Carolina, to Parkdale America, LLC, in January 2005 for $10 million. Proceeds were earmarked to reduce debt. The company agreed to buy yarn from Parkdale for five years.

In August 2005 Delta Apparel acquired Liquid Blaino Designs, Inc., which traded as Junkfood Clothing. Founded in Los Angeles in 1998, Junkfood

had successfully harnessed an enduring wave of nostalgia by licensing trademarks such as Twister and My Little Pony for its line of hip, retro T-shirts that sold for $22 to $48 each in high-end department stores. Its revenues were $27 million a year. The deal was ultimately worth a total of $27 million.

The year after the Junkfood acquisition, the *Atlanta Journal-Constitution* commented on the company's progress thus far. While it had a relatively low profile, being followed by only one analyst, its shares were worth seven times their value at the time of the spin-off. It differed from its peers in preferring to deal with many smaller customers (12,000 of them at the time), to avoid the risk of extending large credit lines or becoming too dependent on any particular one. It was also unique in maintaining its own manufacturing capacity when outsourcing was the industry norm. Delta Apparel did buy some products from contractors in Pakistan and China.

OFFSHORE TEXTILE MANUFACTURING INITIATIVE: 2006

When the company did farm out work, it stuck to the Caribbean Basin, which had textile-trade agreements with the United States and could offer quicker times to market than Asia. In 2006 the company formulated its Offshore Textile Manufacturing Initiative. While it maintained finishing and distribution facilities in the United States, the company resolved to produce more of its fabrics abroad.

In October 2006 Delta Apparel bought FunTees, Inc., which made custom knit T-shirts for branded sportswear companies, paying $20 million. The acquisition brought with it cut-and-sew operations in El Salvador and Mexico, along with a sales and marketing office in Concord, North Carolina.

In September 2007 the company closed a Fayette, Alabama, textile manufacturing facility it had acquired five years earlier for $2 million. At the same time the company was preparing its new Ceiba Textiles plant near San Pedro Sula, Honduras. The 300,000-square-foot facility began operations in November 2007. It was expected to save Delta Apparel at least $1 million per year in fabric costs.

The company shuttered its Fayetteville, North Carolina, textile manufacturing plant in May 2009, shifting its work to Ceiba Textiles in Honduras and its sole remaining U.S. textile production plant in Maiden, North Carolina. M. J. Soffe's fabric production was moved to Maiden, North Carolina, and Honduras after January 2009, with the loss of 100 jobs. About 550 workers remained at Soffe's Fayetteville plant, however.

Delta Apparel was not immune to the global economic downturn of 2008 and lost $508,000 during the year. The fast-growing Junk Food business was affected by the move of its production into the Maiden, North Carolina, facility. In the fiscal year ended June 27, 2009, Delta Apparel posted net income of $6.5 million as revenues rose 10 percent to $355.2 million.

The company continued to build its retail-ready segment by adding growing brands. It bought Gekko Brands for $5.7 million in March 2009. Based in Phenix City, Alabama, Gekko had been formed in 1986 by Neil Stillwell as a maker of collegiate headwear.

In September 2009 Delta Apparel announced it had become the licensed producer of the Realtree Girl and Realtree Outfitters brands. Realtree, owned by Jordan Outdoor Enterprises, Ltd., and known for its camouflage patterns, had worked with Delta Apparel's recently acquired To The Game business since the mid-1990s. In December 2009 Delta Apparel bought Art Gun Technologies, LLC. Art Gun, launched just nine months earlier, provided software for companies to offer customized apparel online.

Delta Apparel began its 2010 fiscal year with strong results, driven by both organic growth and the addition of its headwear lines. The Soffe business had recently placed its products in Disney stores and theme parks and added a license for PGA products. Humphreys predicted Delta Apparel would reach sales of $500 million by 2013.

Frederick C. Ingram

PRINCIPAL SUBSIDIARIES

M. J. Soffe, LLC; Junkfood Clothing Company; To The Game, LLC; Delta Apparel Honduras, S.A.; Delta Campeche, S.A. de C.V. (Mexico); Delta Cortes, S.A. (Honduras); Campeche Sportswear, S de RL de CV (Mexico); Textiles La Paz, LLC; Ceiba Textiles, S de RL (Honduras); Atled Holding Company Honduras, S de RL (Honduras); LaPaz Honduras, S de RL.

PRINCIPAL DIVISIONS

Delta Apparel; M.J. Soffe; Junkfood Clothing; FunTees; To The Game.

PRINCIPAL OPERATING UNITS

Activewear; Retail Ready.

PRINCIPAL COMPETITORS

Fruit of the Loom, Inc.; Gildan Activewear, Inc., Russell Brands, LLC.

FURTHER READING

Barksdale, Andrew, "107 Jobs at M. J. Soffe to Be Eliminated," *Fayetteville (N.C.) Observer,* January 29, 2009.

Bell, Adam, "Concord T-Shirt Maker Bought: About 90 Jobs Staying in Cabarrus County after Sale to Ga. Company," *Charlotte Observer,* September 7, 2006.

Clinebell, Michael, "Delta, M.J. Soffe Apparel Companies Knit Assets Together," *Fayetteville (N.C.) Observer,* February 21, 2004.

———, "Fayetteville, N.C.-Based Subsidiary Boosts Georgia T-Shirt Maker's Bottom Line," *Fayetteville (N.C.) Observer,* November 2, 2004.

Greenwood, Al, "Delta Apparel in Georgia Has New Leadership," *Fayetteville (N.C.) Observer,* August 18, 2004.

Hirschman, Dave, "The Georgia 100: No. 10: Delta Apparel; Low-Cost Structure Fits T-Shirt Maker Well; Duluth Firm Uses Factories Outside U.S.," *Atlanta Journal-Constitution,* May 19, 2002, p. 11.

Luke, Robert, "Hot Brands Drive Explosive Growth," *Atlanta Journal-Constitution,* May 21, 2006, p. F8.

Malone, Scott, "Delta Woodside Plans to Spin Off Apparel Units," *WWD,* October 6, 1999, p. 27.

Doprastav A.S.

Drienova 27
Bratislava, 826 56
Slovakia
Telephone: (+421 02) 4827 1500
Fax: (+421 02) 4827 1568
Web site: http://www.doprastav.sk

Wholly Owned Subsidiary of DDM Group
Founded: 1953
Employees: 3,095
Sales: SKK 11.83 billion ($506 million) (2008 est.)
NAICS: 237310 Highway, Street, and Bridge Construction; 237110 Water and Sewer Line and Related Structures Construction; 237990 Other Heavy and Civil Engineering Construction

■ ■ ■

Doprastav A.S. is the largest construction and engineering company in Slovakia, and through the DDM Group one of the leaders in the Czech-Slovak region. Doprastav focuses primarily on large-scale construction and civil engineering projects, including roads and motorways, railways, bridges, water treatment and environmental installations, infrastructure and other public works projects, as well as commercial, industrial, and related construction projects. Roadway and street construction, including a leading role in the construction of Slovakia's freeway network, is the group's largest activity, accounting for nearly 50 percent of its total revenues of SKK 11.8 billion ($506 million).

Doprastav is organized into several regional divisions, including the Zilina and Zvolen divisions, the Prague Branch, the Bratislava-Mlynske nivy division, and the Bratislava-Petrzalka division. Other divisions include Mechanization and Transport; the Technical and Testing Service; and Prestressing Technologies. The company's Prefa division produces concrete, as well as reinforced and prestressed concrete elements; precast bridge girders and related components; supporting frameworks; and road panels, noise barriers, and safety barriers. In addition, the Steel Structures division manufactures and installs steel structures, bridge bearing and movement joints, as well as machine components, along with providing corrosion protection services and systems.

Since 2000, Doprastav has also controlled Metrostav, based in the Czech Republic, which together with Slovakia-based DOAS SA, form the DDM Group, a privately held confederation of companies. While primarily active in Slovakia and the Czech Republic, Doprastav competes on an international level, with projects in markets including Hungary, Poland, and Azerbaijan. Dušan Mráz and Ivan Sestak lead Doprastav.

BUILDING SLOVAKIA'S
ROADWAYS SINCE 1953

Doprastav originated as part of the efforts of the Communist Czechoslovak government to rebuild and expand the country's infrastructure following World War II. During this period, the government created a number of state-run construction and engineering firms that operated largely on a local or regional basis. In 1953,

COMPANY PERSPECTIVES

Doprastav is a modern construction company having over half a century of history, which is able to offer a complex execution of all kinds of construction works. During its professional growth it gained a special expertise to become the largest, the strongest and the most stabile construction company in Slovakia, the results of which are visible everywhere in the Slovak Republic. The advantages of Doprastav include the experience, the expertise and the professional potential of its staff, the capacity of its machinery, the quality of its construction methods (know-how) and perfect understanding of the demands of construction market, the demands, which it can satisfy, and it is able to meet the individual needs and requirements of each customer. The trademark Doprastav represents a guarantee for each investor that its project will be completed on time and in the quality, which is comparable with the world standard.

however, the government founded a new state-run business focused on developing the country's roadway network on a national level. Doprastav established its headquarters in Bratislava, the historic capital of Slovakia. The name "Dopra," which translates as "Trans" in English, clearly established the company's focus.

Roadway construction in Slovakia had historically taken a back seat to the development of the highway and roadway network in the richer Czech region of what was then Czechoslovakia. Under Communist rule, efforts were made to address the imbalance in the economies and infrastructures of the two states. The government began drawing up ambitious plans to develop a network of highways, including corresponding bridges and tunnels, that would provide north-south and east-west travel across all of Slovakia, as well as provide links to the Czech region and to Czechoslovakia's neighbors.

The D1 Motorway represented the most ambitious of the government's highway projects. That project had originated in the 1930s as part of a plan to build a highway linking Prague to Bratislava and then to the country's border near the future Ukraine. In the event, construction took place only on the Czech side. World War II halted construction on the D1. Work on the Czech side started up again in the mid-1960s, while

EXPANDING OPERATIONS AND MATERIALS

In the meantime, Doprastav had been developing its expertise both in roadway construction and in the construction of bridges, tunnels, and related transportation infrastructure. The company expanded its operation by opening a second office in Zvolen, in central Slovakia, in 1961. The company also branched out beyond road building in the late 1950s. In 1958, for example, the company added the construction of water treatment facilities, acquiring another state-owned firm, Vodstav (*vod* being the Slovak for "water"). Despite the large-scale construction of housing projects during this period, Doprastav remained concentrated on building Czechoslovakia's infrastructure.

In the 1960s Doprastav began adding to its range of expertise by incorporating new building material technologies. This led the company to become the first in the Slovak region to begin producing prefabricated and prestressed concrete bridge elements in 1962. Doprastav created a dedicated bridge construction division in 1967. By then, the company had also launched the production of bitumen, a major component of asphalt road construction, establishing a subsidiary in Bratislava in 1965.

By the end of the 1960s Doprastav had positioned itself to play a major role in the construction of Slovakia's motorway network, which got started in 1969. By 1972 the first leg of the D1 had opened, a 153-kilometer stretch connecting Bratislava to Sverepec. This was followed in 1973 by the opening of the 60-kilometer link between Vazec and Ivachnova.

BEYOND SLOVAKIA IN 1974

During this period Doprastav participated in the construction of another important highway, the D2 Motorway connecting Bratislava north to Brno and south to the Hungarian border. The first leg of this road was completed in 1973, providing a 29.3-kilometer link between Malacky and Bratislava. This was followed later in the decade with the completion of the 27.2-kilometer Malacky-Kuty extension.

Throughout its early years, Doprastav's operations had focused on the Slovak region. Starting in 1974, however, the company began participating in Czech road-building and infrastructure projects as well. Over the next two decades, the company expanded its international operations further, contributing to projects

KEY DATES

1953: Doprastav is founded in Bratislava to build roads in the Slovak region of Czechoslovakia.

1962: Doprastav launches the production of prefabricated and prestressed concrete bridge sections.

1969: Doprastav begins construction of the Slovak motorway network.

1988: Doprastav is reorganized as a state-owned enterprise.

1994: Doprastav converts to a joint stock company and begins its privatization process.

2001: Doprastav wins the bid to acquire Metrostav from the Czech government and forms the DDM Group as a holding company.

2008: Doprastav establishes a branch office in Poland and begins construction of the Laliki Tunnel project.

2010: Doprastav wins a railway contract in Budapest, Hungary.

in such markets as Egypt, South Yemen, East Germany, and Iraq. As pointed out by Doprastav's chairman, Ivan Sestak, in an interview featured in *Forbes Global*, these projects "were more or less politically motivated."

By then, Doprastav had begun to prepare for the post-Communist era. A first step toward its future privatization came in 1988, when the company status changed to that of a state-owned enterprise. The collapse of the Soviet Union and the Eastern Bloc soon after, and the subsequent breakup of Czechoslovakia, introduced a new phase in Doprastav's history.

In the early 1990s, the government of newly independent Slovakia launched the privatization of parts of the formerly state-controlled industrial holdings. Doprastav became one of the early beneficiaries of the privatization effort. At the beginning of 1994 Doprastav's employees, led by Sestak, formed a new joint stock company called DOAS A.S., which acquired 11.4 percent of Doprastav. The privatization process continued through the year, and in 1995 the Slovakian government agreed to sell a 51 percent stake in Doprastav to DOAS. Sestak, who had joined Doprastav in 1967, became the company's director general.

RESTRUCTURING

Although one of the leading construction companies in Slovakia, Doprastav remained quite small by European

standards at the time of its privatization. This was in part because of a freeze placed on most new highway and infrastructure spending by the Slovakian government since the breakup of Czechoslovakia. As a result, Doprastav's sales at the time of its privatization stood at just SKK 800 million (approximately $22 million), only slightly more than the company's total debt of SKK 700 million.

Doprastav also inherited the notoriously inefficient organizational structure that characterized many enterprises of the former Communist Bloc. The company's administration, for example, consisted of more than 400 employees. At the same time, the company's operations were hampered by outdated and poor quality construction equipment and machinery, another legacy of the Communist era.

Sestak set out to modernize the company, shedding more than 75 percent of its administrative personnel. At the same time, the company carried out wage increases in order to stimulate the productivity of its existing workforce while attracting new employees amid a shortage of qualified labor in the post-Communist era. This allowed the company to hire more than 500 employees in 1996 alone. Doprastav also launched a major investment into new construction equipment and machinery.

This effort was aided by the launch of a new wave of investment by the Slovak government into the country's infrastructure during the second half of the 1990s. Doprastav became a major beneficiary of the Slovak government's new spending program, winning the contracts for a number of high-profile road projects, including a 45-kilometer stretch of the western Slovakian motorway. As a result, Doprastav's sales increased dramatically, topping SKK 8.17 billion ($233 million) by 1998.

FORMING DDM GROUP: 2001

Doprastav ranked as the third-largest Slovakian construction firm in the late 1990s. The company's strong growth, along with the bankruptcy of one of its largest competitors, enabled the company to claim domestic leadership in the next decade. A major part of this growth came through the company's successful bid to acquire Metrostav from the Czech government in 2001.

Metrostav had been founded in 1971 in order to build the Prague subway network, which also enabled it to gain expertise in tunnel construction. In the 1980s the company expanded into other infrastructure areas, including highway and railroad construction. Doprastav and Metrostav first began working together in 1996, when the companies formed a highway and tunnel construction joint venture active in both Slovakia and the Czech Republic.

This gave Doprastav the lead in the bidding for Metrostav's privatization. The company initially acquired a 62.5 percent stake in Metrostav, paying CEK 950 million ($49 million). Soon after the Metrostav acquisition, Doprastav restructured its organization. As part of this restructuring, the company merged with DOAS and Metrostav under a new holding company, called DDM Group.

The addition of Metrostav not only allowed Doprastav to claim the lead in Slovakia, but also raised its profile to the rank of second-largest construction company in the Czech-Slovak region. This new clout also enabled Doprastav to expand its range of operations during the early years of the new century. The company entered the railroad construction sector, as well as the construction of retail buildings. The company's major projects in this latter category included stores for Tesco as that U.K.-based chain expanded into the region, as well as the furniture group Ikea.

SLOVAK CONSTRUCTION LEADER IN THE 21ST CENTURY

Doprastav's new scale enabled it to compete for a growing range of high-profile projects as well. For example, in 2003 the company was part of a consortium, including Hochtief VSB and ZS Brno, which won the bid to build a new terminal for Prague's Ryzyne Airport. The company also began exploring other international opportunities, joining the bidding for projects in Hungary, Serbia, and Romania, among other markets.

At the same time, the company remained a major presence in the Slovakia infrastructure market. The company completed a number of large-scale projects in the middle of the decade. In 2004 the company completed work on another roadway, the Budča-Kováčová section of the R1 Expressway. By the end of that year, the company had also completed a new wastewater treatment facility in Trenain.

In 2005 the company's projects included the Apollo Bridge spanning the Danube River in Bratislava, as well as two sections of the D1 Motorway, linking Ladce and Sverepec, and Bratislava to Viedenska Cesta-Pristavny. The company also successfully bid for the contract to build the Hricovské Podhradie–Kysucké Nové Mesto section of the D3 Motorway. By the end of 2006, Doprastav's revenues neared SKK 12.8 billion ($583 million), raising the total revenues of the DDM Group past EUR 1.5 billion ($1.8 billion).

Doprastav continued throughout 2007 to build on its efforts both to diversify its operations and to expand internationally. The company's industrial construction operations secured contracts to build factories for Samsung and Hansol in Voderady. At the same time, the group won its bid to construct a nearly seven-kilometer highway linking the Azerbaijan capital city of Baku to the country's Heydar Aliyev International Airport. That road opened in 2008. By then, Doprastav had extended its operations into Poland, where it opened a branch office in 2008, and launched construction of the Laliki Tunnel project. The company also formed a partnership with Poland's Polimex-Mostostal to bid on other construction projects in that country.

By the end of the decade, Doprastav had become a major contender in the Central European construction market. This was underscored in 2010 with its successful bid, in a consortium with Subterra of the Czech Republic, for a major railway project in Budapest, Hungary. This project including the rebuilding of a 20-kilometer railway between Budapest and Tarnok, as well as the construction of a railway station at Budapest Kelenfold, and a link between that station and the city's new Metro subway line. Doprastav had survived the shakeup of the former Soviet Bloc to become Slovakia's construction leader in the 21st century.

M. L. Cohen

PRINCIPAL SUBSIDIARIES

DOPRA–VIA, a.s. (40%); Doprastav Alfa, s.r.o.; Doprastav Development, a.s.; Doprastav DI, a.s.; Doprastav RO S.R.L. (Romania); Doprastav Services, s.r.o.; Euro City Park, a.s. (80%); GEOstatik, a.s. (70%); PK Doprastav, a.s.; PRO TP 01 a.s.; TBG Doprastav, a.s. (40%); Železničné stavebníctvo Bratislava, a.s. (22.34%).

PRINCIPAL DIVISIONS

Zilina; Zvolen; Prague; Bratislava-Mlynske nivy; Bratislava-Petrzalka; Mechanization and Transport; Prefa; Steel Structures.

PRINCIPAL OPERATING UNITS

Technical and Testing Service; Prestressing Technologies.

PRINCIPAL COMPETITORS

Bilfinger Berger AG; Eurovia SA; Hochtief AG; Holcim; Hornex; JFE Holdings Inc.; NCC AB; Skanska AB; Skanska CZ; Royal BAM Group N.V.; RWE AG.

FURTHER READING

Danko, Slavomir, "Doprastav Rides Government's Highway Plan to Profits," *Slovak Spectator*, May 7, 1998.

"Doprastav Acquires a Majority Stake in Metrostav for CEK 950 Mil," *Ekonomicke Zpravodajstvi*, August 31, 2000, p. 6.

"Doprastav Does Not Plan Further Penetration to the Czech Republic," *Hospodarske Noviny*, September 15, 2000.

"Doprastav Expanding and Extending," *Slovak Spectator*, March 18, 2002.

"Doprastav Projects SK392 Million Profit," *Slovak Spectator*, September 20, 2004.

"Doprastav to Pay about CEK 950 Mil for the Acquisition of Metrostav," *Hospodarske Noviny*, August 29, 2000.

"Interview with Ing. Ivan Sestak, Chairman of DDS Group," *Forbes Global*, May 27, 2002.

"Metrostav Is Profitable under Doprastav Too," *Access Czech Republic Business Bulletin*, June 19, 2006.

"Slovak Firms Succeed in Tender for Construction of D1 Section," *Czech News Agency*, February 18, 2009.

Dr. Seuss Enterprises L.P.

———————■———————

1200 Prospect Street, Suite 751
La Jolla, California 92037
U.S.A.
Telephone: (858) 459-9744
Web site: http://www.seussville.com

Private Company
Incorporated: 1993
Employees: 10
Sales: $15 million (2009 est.)
NAICS: 533110 Lessors of Nonfinancial Intangible Assets (Except Copyrighted Works)

■ ■ ■

Dr. Seuss Enterprises L.P. represents the estate of Theodor Seuss Geisel, the beloved children's author and illustrator. The firm's income includes royalties from the many books Geisel published, as well as licensing fees from films, television programs, stage shows, apparel, toys, games, and other products derived from his creations. It is owned and headed by Audrey Geisel, the author's widow, who donates a sizable portion of income to charity.

ROOTS

Theodor Seuss Geisel was born on March 2, 1904, in Springfield, Massachusetts, where his German immigrant father ran a brewery and later oversaw a park and zoo. After completing high school he enrolled at Dartmouth, serving as editor of the comedy magazine *Jack-O-Lantern*, and then entered Oxford University with the intention of becoming an English professor. He soon grew bored with his studies, however, and decided to leave school.

As a child Geisel had shown a talent for cartooning, and had particularly enjoyed the rhyming bedtime stories of his mother, Henrietta Seuss Geisel. With the encouragement of fellow Oxford student Helen Marion Palmer, who had seen him drawing in the margins of his notebooks, he decided to seek a career writing and cartooning.

Geisel and Palmer married in 1927 and moved to New York, where he began publishing cartoons and essays for such magazines as *Judge* and the *Saturday Evening Post*. Having sometimes used his middle name as a pseudonym in college, he wrote a satirical piece in *Judge* as Dr. Theophrastus Seuss, then shortened it to Dr. Seuss for other work that included illustrating two volumes of jokes in 1931.

FIRST CHILDREN'S BOOK PUBLISHED: 1937

Geisel also won a job drawing ads for the Standard Oil Company's well-known Flit insect spray around this time, which paid well and made his idiosyncratic style familiar to millions of Americans. The money allowed the Geisels to travel, and on one ocean passage, annoyed by the constant throbbing of the ship's engines, he was inspired to write a children's book whose words had its rhythmic pulse, as well as place names and imagery from his childhood home of Springfield. Despite Geisel's established reputation as an illustrator, 27 publishers turned the book down, and the frustrated author was thinking of burning the manuscript when he chanced to meet an old Dartmouth chum on the street in New York who had just been hired as a juvenile editor. Within an hour, Geisel had signed a contract with Vanguard Press.

Published in 1937, *And to Think That I Saw It on Mulberry Street* was followed a year later by *The 500 Hats of Bartholomew Cubbins*, after which Geisel moved to Bennett Cerf's newly formed publishing firm, Random House. He branched out with an adult cartoon book in 1939, *The Seven Lady Godivas*, but its relative failure ensured that he would henceforth primarily work as a children's author.

During World War II Geisel joined Frank Capra's Signal Corps film unit to work on projects for propaganda and recruitment purposes, and also created political cartoons for the newspaper *PM*. His screenplays for two shorts, *Hitler Lives?* (1946) and *Design for Death* (1947) won Academy Awards, and he later also wrote scripts for the Oscar-winning cartoon short *Gerald McBoing-Boing* (1951) and feature-length *The 5,000 Fingers of Dr. T* (1953), which attempted to transfer the Seussian visual style to a live-action format. Although it became something of a cult favorite, *Dr. T* was a major disappointment for the author and led him to decline future offers from Hollywood.

Now based in California, where in 1948 Geisel and his wife had purchased a former observation tower overlooking the ocean just north of San Diego in La Jolla, he resumed turning out such children's classics as *Thidwick the Big-Hearted Moose* (1948) and *Horton Hears a Who!* (1954).

THE CAT IN THE HAT DEBUTS IN 1957

Challenged by a mid-1950s *Life* magazine article decrying the dull "Dick and Jane" primers used to educate

young readers, Geisel decided to create one himself. The result was a book with a vocabulary of just 236 words, *The Cat in the Hat* (1957), which was initially published in hardcover by Houghton Mifflin and then in a trade edition by new Random House imprint Beginner Books. Over time Geisel would contribute a number of titles to the latter, including some written under the pen name Theo LeSieg and illustrated by others. He would also serve as the publishing unit's president.

More Seuss classics soon followed, including *How the Grinch Stole Christmas* (also 1957), and *One Fish Two Fish Red Fish Blue Fish* and *Green Eggs and Ham* (both 1960). The latter, which would go on to be Geisel's best-selling title ever, was the result of a bet with Bennett Cerf that the author could not write a book with a vocabulary of just 50 words.

Although he had given up on films after the disappointing *5,000 Fingers of Dr. T*, Geisel was lured to the small screen by some of his former Signal Corps associates including animation legend Chuck Jones. A string of eight animated programs including *How the Grinch Stole Christmas*, *Horton Hears a Who*, and *The Cat in the Hat* ran on CBS and later ABC between 1966 and 1982, with several winning Emmy Awards and *Grinch* becoming especially popular through annual rebroadcasts.

GEISEL MARRIES DIMOND IN 1968

In October 1967 Geisel's wife Helen, who had been battling cancer, committed suicide. Audrey Dimond, who had served as Geisel's editor and collaborator and herself had published several children's books, became romantically involved with Geisel. The following year he married Dimond, who was 18 years his junior. Although his life's work was dedicated to children, Theodor and Helen Geisel had never had a child, and because the author was generally uncomfortable around youngsters Dimond sent her own 9- and 14-year-old daughters to a boarding school.

A number of Seuss books had contained fairly overt social messages, like the anti-prejudice *The Sneetches and Other Stories* of 1961, and Geisel's second wife encouraged him in this area, which resulted in such titles as the pro-conservation *The Lorax* (1971) and antiwar *The Butter Battle Book* (1984). The author continued working into his mid-80s, with his acclaimed last book, *Oh, the Places You'll Go!*, published the year before his death on September 24, 1991.

In his lifetime Geisel had written and illustrated 44 children's books and written 14 others, which had been translated into more than a dozen languages and report-

1904: Theodor Seuss Geisel is born in Springfield, Massachusetts.
1937: As "Dr. Seuss," Geisel publishes his first children's book.
1957: Geisel publishes classic *The Cat in the Hat* to help children learn to read.
1968: Geisel marries Audrey Dimond.
1991: Theodor Geisel dies at 87, leaving his wife in charge of the Seuss legacy.
1993: Audrey Geisel founds Dr. Seuss Enterprises L.P. to license properties.

edly sold a total of more than 200 million copies. He had earned an estimated $500 million during his lifetime, with four of his books on *Publishers Weekly*'s list of the top-10 best-selling children's books of all time. In addition to his Academy Awards, Emmys, and a number of other honors, Geisel had received an honorary Pulitzer Prize in 1984, although he had never won the coveted Caldecott or Newbery awards for children's literature.

DR. SEUSS ENTERPRISES IS FOUNDED IN 1993

Theodor Geisel had long been represented by entertainment powerhouse International Creative Management (ICM), which would continue to represent his estate, and two years after his death Audrey Geisel founded Dr. Seuss Enterprises L.P. (DSE) to oversee his ongoing business interests, which included sizable royalty payments from his perennially popular books. She would be its CEO, with the author's longtime agent Herbert Cheyette serving as vice president. A sizable portion of the firm's profits would be funneled to charity through Audrey Geisel's Dr. Seuss Foundation, which supported literacy causes and annually donated many thousands of Seuss books to public schools.

Over the years Theodor Geisel had fielded many requests to license his characters for commercial products, but rejected most and even canceled others, including a 1987 Cat in the Hat toy he did not like the prototype for. Soon after his death unauthorized toys and clothing featuring Seuss imagery began to appear, however, and in June 1993 DSE won the first in a series of judgments against their manufacturers. Convinced by attorneys and representatives of ICM that the Seuss trademarks could fall into the public domain if no

authorized items were produced, Audrey Geisel decided to seek licensees.

Character clothing from the likes of Warner Brothers and Disney had recently become hugely popular, and in 1994 the firm licensed San Francisco-based Esprit de Corp. to create a line of Seuss-inspired apparel, footwear, and accessories, which would initially focus on children's items before expanding to include an adult line. Approximately $10 million (wholesale) worth of the clothes were shipped to Esprit and Penney's stores in the first year.

In 1994 DSE also licensed the worldwide multimedia rights to Seuss's works to Living Books, a Random House/Broderbund company. One CD-ROM version of a Seuss book would be released each year, featuring an interactive version of the original story with added voices and other effects.

DAISY-HEAD MAYZIE FIRST "NEW" SEUSS BOOK IN 1995

In 1994 TNT cable began airing many of the classic Seuss TV programs along with a new documentary on the author. Production also began on a new cartoon based on a recently unearthed 1960s script called "Daisy-Head Mayzie." Geisel's rough sketches were used to create a half-hour television version, as well as a book that was issued in January 1995, credited to Dr. Seuss. The critics were not kind to either, with the general consensus being that both fell short of the author's high standards.

In the fall of 1995 Audrey Geisel gave the University of California at San Diego a reported $20 million to endow its library, which would be renamed the Geisel Library. The papers of the late author would be housed there, some of which were relocated from sister institution the University of California at Los Angeles. It was the largest gift to the school to that date. In his lifetime Theodor Geisel had also supported his alma mater Dartmouth, reportedly being that institution's most generous donor.

During 1995 DSE launched a Web site in conjunction with Random House, Seussville.com, and in the fall *The Secret Art of Dr. Seuss* was published, which featured previously unseen paintings and sculptures. Another new title, *My Many Colored Days*, was published in 1996 by Alfred A. Knopf. Geisel had written the story in 1973 sans illustrations, which were created by artists Steve Johnson and Lou Fancher. In 1996 DSE also successfully filed suit against the author and publishers of a book called *Cat NOT in the Hat*, halting publication of a book that used Seussian rhymes to satirize the O. J. Simpson murder trial.

In just three years DSE's annual revenue had grown to an estimated $7 million to $10 million. Seuss products were hugely popular, with a special promotional Cat in the Hat toy offered by Macy's selling 200,000 copies in three weeks, the fastest for a product of its type in that firm's history.

SEUSS-INSPIRED NICKELODEON TV SHOW DEBUTS IN 1996

Other deals of 1996 had included a board game, abridged versions of four Seuss books for preschoolers, and *The Wubbulous World of Dr. Seuss*, a Cat in the Hat-hosted Nickelodeon puppet series created by Jim Henson Productions, which began airing in October. Plans were now also afoot for Hallmark greeting cards, a movie, a theme park, and two Broadway shows. Some observers noted that the flood of Seuss product was verging on overexposing the brand, but the firm countered that it turned down many more offers for licenses than it granted and had refused to authorize lucrative items like lunch boxes, glasses, clocks, and children's cereal.

In 1997 Audrey Geisel partnered with the U.S. Department of Health and Human Services to launch a childhood immunization campaign, in which six posters with Seuss characters were distributed to places such as schools and medical centers. DSE also joined with the National Education Association and other partners to sponsor Read across America Day, which would feature annual readings at libraries, schools, and bookstores around the United States on or near Ted Geisel's birthday of March 2.

Efforts of 1998 included a series of limited-edition prints of Seuss images and the translation of *The Sneetches* into Serbo-Croatian so that 500,000 copies could be distributed in ethnically divided Bosnia and Herzegovina. The Grinch character, which had not been heavily licensed, was suddenly everywhere for the Christmas shopping season in Dayton Hudson and Hallmark stores.

In 1999 a small theme park called Seuss Landing opened in Orlando, Florida, within Universal Islands of Adventure. Other offerings of the year included a book of Geisel's political cartoons from World War II.

GRINCH MOVIE A HIT IN 2000

On Thanksgiving Day in 2000 *Dr. Seuss' How the Grinch Stole Christmas,* opened in theaters. Although reviews of the live-action, Jim Carrey-starring film were mixed, it took in $260 million at the domestic box office and later proved popular on home video. DSE was

reportedly paid $5 million up-front and 4 percent of the gross receipts, with Audrey Geisel given script approval. Numerous movie-related books and toys were produced, as well.

November 2000 also saw *Seussical the Musical* open on Broadway. The child-friendly stage show merged elements from some 20 Seuss stories, but was poorly reviewed and closed in six months. A touring production later found an audience around the country, however, and an abridged version became popular with school and community theater groups.

In 2001 DSE licensed Manhattan Toys to make hand puppets and plush toys based on Seuss characters, and in 2002 the firm reached an agreement with NewKidCo International to create Seuss-based video games; licensed Racing Champions the right to make Seuss-inspired toy vehicles; and signed Vandor to make children's furniture.

In the summer of 2002 the new $6.2 million Dr. Seuss National Memorial Park opened in the author's hometown of Springfield, Massachusetts. It featured bronze figures from the stories and a statue of Geisel made by one of Audrey Geisel's daughters. Funding came in part from her mother and Random House.

CAT IN THE HAT FILM RELEASED IN 2003

In November 2003 a new $109 million feature film based on *The Cat in the Hat* was released. The Universal/Dreamworks/Imagine Entertainment, Mike Meyers-starring film got poor reviews, however (including from Audrey Geisel), and took in only $100 million at the U.S. box office. For 2003, *Fortune* magazine estimated DSE's earnings at $16 million.

In 2004 the 100th anniversary of Theodor Geisel's birth was celebrated with a traveling show that played 40 cities around the United States, two new biographical books, a star on the Hollywood Walk of Fame, a U.S. postage stamp, several museum shows, and more. Various new licensed products appeared including scarves, puppets, clothing, a calendar, and a board game.

In 2005 plans for a computer-animated film version of *Horton Hears a Who* were announced by 20th Century Fox Animation and Blue Sky Studios. Fox had won a bidding war with other studios in part by agreeing to give Audrey Geisel executive producer credit and creative approval. During the year DSE also signed Pepper's Ghost to handle Seuss licensing in the United Kingdom and Europe.

In 2006 a new Seuss-branded Aquafresh toothpaste and toothbrush line debuted, and the firm signed Nick

Graham's 100 Minute Co. to market the 50th anniversary of *The Cat in the Hat* and *How the Grinch Stole Christmas*, which fell in 2007. The firm also cut a licensing deal for preschool developmental toys with Small World Toys.

GRINCH MUSICAL A BROADWAY HIT IN 2006

A revival of 1998's smaller-scale *Dr. Seuss' How the Grinch Stole Christmas! The Musical* opened on Broadway in the fall of 2006 to strong ticket sales, becoming the number one show in December and recouping its investment with ticket sales of $15 million in 11 weeks. The special holiday show would be revived in future years.

In 2007 DSE partnered with Random House and the nonprofit First Book to create Project 236 (named after the number of vocabulary words in *The Cat in the Hat*) to raise awareness about reading and distribute children's books to low-income families. A book would be donated to charity for reach mailed or e-mailed birthday greeting sent to Dr. Seuss, with upward of one million expected.

The firm also successfully forced ABC Studios to change the name of a comedy about an amnesiac from "Sam I Am" (the name of a character in *Green Eggs and Ham*) to *Samantha Who?*, out of concerns that it would confuse viewers. In the fall, a license with I Can Do That! Games yielded three Seuss-derived games.

HORTON HEARS A WHO FILM RELEASED IN 2008

In March 2008 the digitally animated *Horton Hears a Who* was released. With vocal talent including Jim Carrey, Steve Carell, and Carol Burnett, the $85 million film did $154 million in business in U.S. theaters, and received the best reviews for a Seuss feature adaptation to date.

During the year DSE also partnered with Conservation International and Random House to reissue *The Lorax* with an added message about environmental protection and a pledge to donate more than 10 percent of the profits to The Lorax Project, which supported ending deforestation in Madagascar, Brazil, and China. Other DSE deals of this period included a license issued to kidthing to distribute digital versions of Seuss classics online with added interactive content; another with Trend Lab to produce children's furnishings and bed-

ding; and one with Hosung NY Inc., for eco-friendly plush toys and infant accessories.

In 2010 production began on a new animated TV series, *The Cat in the Hat Knows a Lot about That!*, which was slated to debut in the fall on PBS and the Canadian Treehouse network. The $15 million-budgeted program would take the book's characters through a series of new adventures, with the voice of the Cat provided by Canadian comic actor Martin Short. A complementary book series was planned by Random House, which would be overseen by Geisel's longtime editor Kate Klimo.

Nearly two decades after Theodor Seuss Geisel's death, Dr. Seuss Enterprises L.P. was busy with a slate of licensing deals that ranged from films, television programs, and theatrical shows to clothing, toys, games, and other products. As caretakers of the legacy of America's best-selling children's author, the firm appeared set for many years of profitable activity.

Frank Uhle

PRINCIPAL COMPETITORS

Charles M. Schulz Creative Associates; The Jim Henson Company; MTV Networks; Turner Broadcasting System; The Walt Disney Company; Warner Brothers Entertainment, Inc.

FURTHER READING

France, Mike, "A Cat-in-the-Hat Attack," *Business Week*, October 21, 1996, p. 85.

Green, Frank, "Famed Feline to Be Cat on the Shirt," *San Diego Union-Tribune*, March 3, 1994, p. C1.

Hellman, Mary, "Dr. Seuss Book Due for Release This Week," *San Diego Union-Tribune*, January 5, 1995, p. B1.

Lewis, Connie, "Mrs. Geisel Can You Tell, How Dr. Seuss Is Alive and Well," *San Diego Business Journal*, November 24, 2003, p. 1.

Morgan, Judith, and Neil Morgan, *Dr. Seuss & Mr. Geisel: A Biography*. New York: Random House, 1995.

Morgante, Michelle, "'Dr. Seuss' Has 100th Birthday," *Associated Press Newswires*, February 25, 2004.

Smith, Dinitia, "The Creatures of a Purist Go Commercial," *New York Times*, February 13, 1997, p. 19C.

Story, Paula, "Infamous Holiday Spoilsport Now Has Line of Christmas Goodies," *Associated Press Newswires*, December 21, 1998.

Walder, Joyce, "Mrs. Seuss Hears a Who, and Tells about It," *New York Times*, November 29, 2000, p. 2B.

Elcoteq SE

19 Rue Eugene Ruppert
Luxembourg, L-2453
Luxembourg
Telephone: (+352) 2483 3210
Fax: (+352) 2483 3290
Web site: http://www.elcoteq.com

Public Company
Incorporated: 1984 as Lohja Microelectronics
Employees: 18,830
Sales: EUR 3.44 billion ($4.93 billion) (2008)
Stock Exchanges: Helsinki
Ticker Symbol: ELQAV
NAICS: 334412 Printed Circuit Board Manufacturing

∎ ∎ ∎

Elcoteq SE is one of the world's top 10 electronics manufacturing services (EMS) providers. Registered in Luxembourg but originally a Finnish company, Elcoteq specializes in providing contract manufacturing and contract design services for the telecommunications and communications markets. The company has long been a leading supplier of mobile telephone handsets and components for Nokia and Ericsson, among others. Elcoteq also produces flat-panel televisions and set-top boxes, among other consumer products, as well as base stations, microwave broadcasting systems, and related infrastructure and communications network equipment.

Handsets and other personal communications products components remains the group's largest product category, accounting for 65 percent of its EUR 3.44 billion ($4.9 billion) revenues in 2008. Home communications added 15 percent and communications networks 20 percent that year. Europe, where the company is the EMS leader, remains the group's core market, at 48 percent of revenues. The Americas and Asia-Pacific regions account for 30 percent and 22 percent, respectively. Elcoteq is listed on the Helsinki Stock Exchange. Jouni Hartikainen is the group's CEO and president, while cofounder and largest shareholder Antti Piippo is chairman.

ORIGINS IN 1984

Elcoteq originated as a division of Lohja Corporation, one of Finland's largest companies, as it attempted to develop televisions based on flat-panel display technologies at the beginning of the 1980s. Lohja Microelectronics, as the new division was called, was created in 1984 in order to produce the control electronics for the displays. Antti Piippo, who had gained experience working with the electronics division of another major Finnish company, Aspo, was placed in charge of the new division.

Lohja struggled to produce a commercially viable flat-panel display. With few orders coming from its parent company, the Lohja Microelectronics division was forced to seek out additional customers in other markets. This search brought Lohja into contact with two fast-rising players in the nascent mobile telecommunications market, Nokia and Ericsson. Both companies had been developing handsets incorporating the Nordic Mobile Telephone standard, but lacked the manufacturing capacity to produce their handsets on a large scale.

COMPANY PERSPECTIVES

Vision and Strategy. Elcoteq's vision is to be the world's leading provider of integrated electronics manufacturing services to communications technology companies. The cornerstones for the implementation of the strategy are a service offering that meets the needs of the global customer base, profitable growth in selected market areas and continuous improvement of operational efficiency.

Strategy. Elcoteq has three core strategic themes: expanding the service offering, focused growth and operational excellence. Expanding the service offering plays a key role in the IEMS strategy. Customers expect their partners to take on a larger role in the management of complex product structures throughout the entire supply chain. As competition tightens and product lifecycles shorten, especially in the Personal Communications Business Area, Elcoteq targets to offer its customers a broader service offering globally.

Lohja Microelectronics spotted the potential for entering the electronics manufacturing services (EMS) sector, providing the production expertise and capacity to carry out the manufacturing of Nokia's and Ericsson's handset designs. As a result, Nokia and Ericsson became the primary customers for Lohja Microelectronics. Lohja Microelectronics in turn provided the foundation for the development of the two companies into two of the world's top mobile telecommunications brands. Through the 1980s, however, Lohja Microelectronics remained only a small part of Lohja Corporation, generating revenues of less than $15 million.

MERGER CREATES ELCOTEQ IN 1990

The division's fortunes were to change dramatically in the next decade. In 1990 Lohja Corporation and another leading Finnish company, Wartsila, agreed to merge in order to thwart a takeover of the latter company by a Swedish investor group. The merged company took on the name of Metra. As part of the lead-up to the merger, Lohja restructured parts of its businesses, including reincorporating its microelectronics division into a separate company called Elcoteq.

With the merger completed, Metra launched a new restructuring, disposing of a number of non-core opera-

tions, including its television and electronics units. Piippo, who remained as head of Elcoteq, recognized the opportunity to build a new company dedicated to the EMS market just as that market entered a boom in the 1990s. In 1991 Piippo, joined by coworkers Henry Sjöman and Jorma Vanhanen, launched a buyout of Elcoteq.

The parallel growth of both the EMS sector and the mobile telecommunications industry during the early 1990s provided the foundation for Elcoteq's own growth. By 1992 the company had grown to nearly 200 employees at its Lohja, Finland, location. Rising orders from its two main customers led Elcoteq to expand its own production capacity.

Toward this end, Elcoteq decided to add its first overseas factory. Rather than turn to the lower-wage markets in the Far East, Elcoteq looked closer to home. In 1992 the company opened a factory in nearby Tallinn, Estonia, then just emerging from decades of Soviet rule. Estonia offered a stable political market as well as wages that averaged some five time lower than those in Finland. The company continued to ramp up production levels at the Tallinn site, which became the company's main European production facility. In 1996 the company also added a repair center at the Tallinn facility.

GAINING SCALE AND GOING PUBLIC

Elcoteq made a series of expansion moves in the 1990s. The company added a new printed circuit board subsidiary, Printeq-Piirilevyt Oy, in Finland in 1993. The company acquired two rival Finnish operations in 1994, Jorvas Partners and the Helsinki-based electronics assembly unit from ABB Industry. The following year, the company added two new factories in Finland, at Salo and in Lohja.

By 1997 Elcoteq had added a subsidiary in Germany, and had also launched a new production unit in St. Petersburg, Russia. The expansion of the Tallinn factory also continued, raising its total area to 17,000 square meters, with a total workforce of more than 1,300. This expansion positioned Elcoteq for the next major step in the international mobile telecommunications sector, the introduction of the GSM (Global System for Mobile Communications) digital mobile telephone standard.

GSM became the standard adopted across Europe and throughout much of the world, leading to the first true surge in demand for mobile telephones. Elcoteq became one of the earliest EMS players to enter this market, launching production of its first GSM-based

KEY DATES

1984: Lohja Corporation of Finland launches a microelectronics division in support of its flat-panel television production.

1990: Lohja Microelectronics changes its name to Elcoteq as Lohja and Wartsila merge to form Metra.

1991: Elcoteq is spun off from Metra in a management buyout.

1997: Elcoteq goes public on the Helsinki Stock Exchange.

2001: Elcoteq loses a $4 billion contract to produce handsets for Ericsson.

2005: Elcoteq is one of the first companies in Europe to become a Societas Europaea (SE).

2009: Amid falling revenues and profits, Elcoteq adopts a new divisional structure based on three core business areas.

handset for Ericsson in 1997. Elcoteq went public that year, listing on the Helsinki Stock Exchange. Piippo, who remained the group's largest shareholder, had guided the company's growth from revenues of just FIM 76 million at the beginning of the decade to more than FIM 1.7 billion.

STUMBLING IN 2001

Riding high on the boom in the mobile handset market, Elcoteq launched a new expansion drive. The company added new production facilities in Pecs, Hungary, and in Monterrey, Mexico, in 1998. The group also acquired the elevator electronics business of Kone Corporation, as well as the printed circuit board (PCB) business of ABB Transmit, both in Finland, that year. Elcoteq moved into China in 1999, acquiring a factory in Dongguan. The following year, the company added a Beijing subsidiary as well. By then, Elcoteq had set up a subsidiary in Denmark. Stephan Elektronik, based in Uberlingen, Germany, was acquired in 2000. This purchase also added operations in Switzerland. By the end of the year, Elcoteq had also launched production at a new factory in Wroclaw, Poland.

Elcoteq had also been taking steps to diversify its EMS offerings away from its reliance on mobile handsets. By the end of 2000, the company had established business units overseeing the manufacture of network equipment and industrial electronics, in addition to its handsets business. Handsets remained by far

the group's largest area of operation, however, and Nokia and Ericsson combined to represent 86 percent of the group's total revenues.

This reliance on just two major companies left Elcoteq vulnerable at the beginning of the new century. In 2001 the company was caught by surprise after Ericsson decided to dispose of its own manufacturing operations. When Singapore-based Flextronics International then acquired Ericsson's factories, it also acquired the rights to manufacture all of Ericsson's handsets. As a result, Elcoteq suffered the loss of a nearly $4 billion handset contract. Elcoteq's share price dropped overnight from $41.37 to $11.82. By September, as the telecommunications industry, along with the world economy, slipped into a recession, Elcoteq's share price had dropped to just $3.25.

BROADENING FOCUS

Elcoteq set out to restore its growth. Rather than diversify away from its core communications expertise, the company decided instead to broaden its range of services to the sector. As a result, the company began investing in building up operations targeting after-sales services on the one hand, and on providing research, design, and engineering services on the other.

Toward this end, the company made a new acquisition in 2001, buying up the mechanical engineering operations of Adtranz Schweiz. In 2002 the company formed a research and development joint venture, Imbera Electronics, with Aspocomp. The company also paid $10.8 million to acquire 75 percent of Benefon Research and Development Center, which was merged into its own subsidiary, Elcoteq Design Center Oy. Elcoteq also invested in the new product introduction sector, acquiring U.S.-based NPRC Inc. in 2003, as well as 70 percent of GKI, based in China and previously held by IBM. The acquisition of GKI, with operations in Shenzhen and Beijing, helped give Elcoteq a major presence in what was shortly to become the world's fastest-growing telecommunications market.

Elcoteq also set out to broaden its customer base beyond its historical reliance on Nokia and Ericsson. The company successfully developed relationships with a number of new partners, including Siemens, Lancom, Strix, and Marconi. In the case of Marconi, the company also agreed to take over its production facility in Offenburg, Germany. Similarly, a contract with Tellabs led to the takeover of that company's factory in Espoo, Finland. Other new customers added in the middle of the decade included Research in Motion, developers of the popular Blackberry handset, and Vitelcom Mobile Technology.

JOINING SOCIETAS EUROPAEA IN 2005

The renewed growth of the global telecommunications, communications, and electronics industries in the middle of the decade led Elcoteq to launch another expansion phase. In 2004 the company expanded its operations in Russia with the construction of a new factory in St. Petersburg. The company then entered India and Brazil, adding new production facilities in those countries, in Bangalore and Manaus, respectively.

As part of a new service contract to manufacture television set-top boxes for Thomson in 2004, the company acquired that company's production unit in Juarez, Mexico. By then, the company had decided to refocus its business around the telecommunications and communications sectors, selling off its industrial electronics business unit to Enics AG in Switzerland in 2004.

In the meantime, the explosive growth of the mobile telephone sector in Central and Eastern Europe, where fixed-line penetration remained low compared to Western Europe, encouraged Elcoteq to expand its presence there. Toward this end, the company established a new regional headquarters in Budapest, Hungary, in 2005. The company also launched production at its new St. Petersburg plant that year.

Also in 2005, Elcoteq became one of the first companies in Europe to convert its corporate status to that of a Societas Europaea, or SE. In order to reinforce its transition from a Finnish company to a European corporation, Elcoteq moved its headquarters to Luxembourg the following year.

STRUGGLING IN THE RECESSION OF 2008

Elcoteq's revenues rose to a peak of nearly EUR 4.3 billion for its 2006 fiscal year. However, in the second half of the decade the company confronted new pressures on its growth. Penetration rates for mobile telephone use neared saturation in most of the company's core markets, leading to large fluctuations in Elcoteq's manufacturing volumes. By the end of the decade, the launch of new high-speed mobile networks created new demand for multimedia-enhanced and Internet-capable handsets. This development also stimulated a new market based on shorter product life cycles, and increasingly lower prices, further cutting into the company's revenue growth.

Elcoteq was also affected by a trend toward vertical integration among many of its EMS competitors. This led these companies to begin manufacturing many of the components they had previously purchased from Elcoteq, further depressing the company's sales volumes. As a result, Elcoteq's revenues began to slip, dropping back to EUR 4 billion in 2007. Worse for the company was the collapse of its profits. At the end of 2007, the company posted a net loss of more than EUR 108 million. The following year, which saw the spread of severe global economic distress, offered little relief for the company as its sales slumped to EUR 3.4 billion, for a net loss of nearly EUR 66 million.

In response, Elcoteq streamlined much of its manufacturing network, shifting a greater bulk of its production to low-wage facilities in China and India. The company also shut down its factories in Lohja, Finland; Juarez, Mexico; Richardson, Texas; and a facility in Arad, Romania, acquired in 2006. In 2009 the company announced a plan to shed more than 5,000 jobs globally.

NEW SERVICES FOR 2010

Elcoteq's difficulties continued through that year. By August 2009, the company was forced to sell its Tallinn, Estonia, factory to Ericsson, which paid EUR 30 million ($34 million) for the facility. In September the company turned to a new investor, Kaifa, a unit of China Electronic Corp., which injected $71 million into the company in exchange for a 30 percent stake in the company.

With its revenues forecast to drop below EUR 2.6 billion for the year, Elcoteq put into place a new divisional structure. The company planned to build its future growth around three core business areas: personal communications, including mobile handsets; home communications, including set-top boxes and flat-panel televisions; and communications networks.

Elcoteq also moved to expand its range of services beyond manufacturing. For example, in 2008 the company acquired a contract to provide final assembly services for flat-panel televisions for Philips. This contract included the takeover of a Philips factory in Juarez, Mexico. In 2010 the company also signed an agreement with Nokia to provide aftermarket sales services to Nokia's customers. Elcoteq hoped its new service-focused strategy would enable it to retain its position among the world's leading EMS companies in the years to come.

M. L. Cohen

PRINCIPAL SUBSIDIARIES

A.S. Elcoteq Tallinn (Estonia); Elcoteq Inc. (USA); Elcoteq Magyarorszag Kft. (Hungary); Elcoteq S.A. de C.V. (Mexico).

PRINCIPAL COMPETITORS

Alcatel-Lucent Deutschland AG; Flextronics International Ltd.; Hitachi Ltd.; Jabil Circuit Inc.; Johnson Matthey PLC; Siemens AG; Panasonic Electric Works Company Ltd.; Simclar International Ltd.; Sumitomo Electric Industries Ltd.; STMicroelectronics S.A.; Toyota Industries Corp.

FURTHER READING

Buetow, Mike, "Elcoteq Slashes 5,000 Jobs, Closing Plants," *Circuits Assembly*, February 2009, p. 8.

———, "Weak Pecs: Elcoteq to Cut Staff, Seeks Cash," *Circuits Assembly*, September 2009, p. 12.

Buetow, Mike, and Chesley Drysdale, "More Cuts Ahead of Elcoteq," *Circuits Assembly*, February 2008, p. 10.

Drysdale, Chesley, "Elcoteq Halts Sale of Russian Unit to Flextronics," *Circuits Assembly*, August 2008, p. 12.

"Elcoteq Buys Thomson's Mexican Fab Operations," *CircuiTree*, February 2005, p. 83.

"Elcoteq Warnings Cast Pall over Nokia," *RCR Wireless News*, September 18, 2006, p. 29.

"Ericsson Closes Buy of Elcoteq Business in Tallinn," *Corporate IT Update*, August 3, 2009.

"Finland's Elcoteq to Provide After Market Support for Nokia," *Worldwide Computer Products News*, January 27, 2010.

Serant, Claire, "Elcoteq Decides to Alter Product Mix," *EBN*, April 2, 2001, p. 88.

Wilson, Drew, "Estonia's Economy Offsets Labor Shortage," *Electronic Engineering Times*, March 10, 2008, p. 25.

EmblemHealth Inc.

---

55 Water Street
New York, New York 10041-8190
U.S.A.
Telephone: (646) 447-5000
Toll Free: (877) 444-6506
Fax: (646) 447-3011
Web site: http://www.emblemhealth.com

Private Company
Incorporated: 2006
Employees: 5,400
Sales: $8.61 billion (2008)
NAICS: 524114 Direct Health and Medical Insurance
Carriers; 621491 HMO Medical Centers

■ ■ ■

EmblemHealth Inc., through subsidiaries Group Health Inc. (GHI) and Health Insurance Plan of New York (HIP), is the largest health insurer based in New York, serving more than 3.4 million members. There are more than 106,000 participating providers in 150,000 locations throughout New York, New Jersey, and Connecticut. Formed as a holding company for GHI and HIP, both not-for-profit organizations, Emblem-Health offers a full range of medical, hospital, dental, mental health, vision, and prescription drug plans. GHI has the most members areawide of the two; HIP has the most in New York City. Plans to merge GHI and HIP into one for-profit company were announced in 2007 but remained unrealized as of early 2010.

HISTORIES OF GHI AND HIP: 1937–47

GHI dates from 1937, when it was organized as Group Health Association of New York, a nonprofit association. In 1940 it offered its first prepaid plan, which included surgical and obstetrical coverage. Two years later it became the first medical insurance carrier to offer paid-in-full benefits and discounted rates with participating providers. GHI was also responsible for a number of firsts in the state of New York, including being the first to cover in-hospital medical care; the first to cover preventive-medicine measures such as yearly physical examinations; and the first to cover outpatient psychiatric care. In 1951 GHI introduced one of the first comprehensive dental coverage plans in the United States.

HIP, incorporated in 1947 as a nonprofit body, began with considerably more fanfare. New York City had, in 1946, signed an agreement by which the city would contribute half the cost of enrollment in HIP for all its employees earning no more than $5,000 a year, with the rest to be deducted from the employee's paycheck. The cost for the city and employee in 1948 came to 2 percent of annual pay each.

The HIP plan, which also covered the employee's spouse and unmarried children, allowed each insured person to choose from medical groups that had contracts with HIP, and within the chosen group to select a personal physician. However, at least 75 percent of the employees in a department agency or unit would have to sign to establish the necessary employee group membership. The cost of hospitalization was covered by

COMPANY PERSPECTIVES

EmblemHealth is committed to providing affordable, quality health coverage in ways that respect and respond to people's fundamental needs. We pursue our mission by providing a choice of products and network so members have access to the medical care they need at prices they can afford. We do this by improving the health of members through wellness programs that foster prevention and healthier living and by using technology to ease access to information and services.

a separate Blue Cross or similar contract, which was required of all HIP members.

HIP was also seeking agreements with private employers. All persons employed in the city and earning no more than $5,000 a year were eligible, but 75 percent of eligible employees in a business concern would have to join in order to create a membership group. Because of the need for sizable groups, employees of small firms and the self-employed were effectively outside coverage.

THREE DECADES OF GROWTH AND CHALLENGES: 1950–80

HIP began life in 1947 with an initial group of 2,100 members. By the summer of 1948 its enrollment had reached 58,700, of which almost three-quarters were city employees. Counting dependents, the number of persons covered reached 122,000. There were 659 participating physicians in 25 medical groups. Each group, in addition to its general practitioners, contained at least one specialist in each of 12 medical specialties.

Municipal employees still composed 60 percent of HIP's membership in early 1956, when the number of members was 485,000 in New York City and adjacent Nassau County, Long Island. They were served by 950 physicians in 31 groups, most of which now owned their own centers. HIP membership reached the half-million mark later in the year.

There was an increasing demand for alternative health insurance plans to be offered to New York City employees and, as a result, in 1965 these employees received the option of GHI or Blue Shield coverage. Moreover, the city government assumed the entire cost of basic insurance coverage in 1967. When the city decided in 1971 to drop Blue Shield, it was covering

112,000 city employees and retirees and their families. GHI was covering 110,000, and HIP covered 144,000.

With 740,000 members in 1972, HIP was the second-largest prepaid group health-insurance organization in the United States. Nevertheless, it had lost more than 30,000 subscribers in four years and was described as financially troubled in a *New York Times* news story. Its situation did not improve later in the decade, for a 1980 New York State Insurance Department report stated that "HIP has recently gone to the brink of disaster," due to what the document described as its ambitious expansion program.

The same report declared that GHI, whose membership had fallen to fewer than 2.2 million subscribers from nearly 2.9 million in 1975, was also financially troubled. One problem was that, like HIP, GHI had perhaps expanded unwisely. In 1970 the insurer had amended its charter to become a service company as well as an insurer. This was followed by a failed venture to provide hospitalization insurance in competition with Blue Cross.

Another mistake proved to be the acquisition of an already troubled hospital in Flushing, Queens. Moreover, an acquired retail optical chain quickly fell into the red. In the *New York Times* article that alluded to HIP's own problems, a former GHI vice president told reporter David Bird that the GHI expansion program was "an asinine rape of the company. They used subscriber money to buy services that lost money."

WORSENING FINANCES: 1980–2005

New York City, in addition to providing basic health insurance coverage to municipal workers, was also offering more options in the 1980s than were available in the past, although at additional cost through payroll deductions. GHI was covering 64 percent of the 435,000 municipal employees, and HIP 35 percent, in 1986. That year for-profit health maintenance organizations (HMOs) were allowed to compete with GHI and HIP for members. In 1987 GHI once again introduced hospital insurance programs, which it said would coordinate inpatient care with its outpatient medical-surgical services.

If GHI had its problems, HIP faced a blizzard of complaints in the following decade, including poor record keeping, lack of continuity of care for patients referred to outside specialists or hospitals, and delays in paying the bills of these patients. Moreover, the insurer was losing money, partly because expansion into New Jersey and southern Florida during the 1980s proved disastrous. It sold its 18 centers in New Jersey in 1997

KEY DATES

1937: Founding of Group Health Association of New York, later GHI.

1947: Founding of Health Insurance Plan of Greater New York (HIP).

1986: For-profit HMOs begin competing with HIP and GHI to cover city workers.

2006: HIP and GHI join forces under a new health insurance company, EmblemHealth.

to a for-profit company that was short of capital, and as a result this network was closed by state regulators. The ill-advised venture cost HIP $40 million, and in 2000 New Jersey was seeking $83 million for unpaid medical bills. HIP Health Plan of Florida, which served members who had retired there, was sold so cheaply in 2000 that business analysts estimated the parent company would recover only a fraction of the $80 million it had invested.

In addition, HIP was losing members in New York. Although the lowest-cost HMO in the metropolitan area, it had a reputation for assembly-line care. To dispel this image, in 1996 it gave its members a choice of access to 14,000 out-of-network doctors, but this decision threatened hardship for its 46 health centers in New York City, Long Island, and Westchester County, and the 1,400 physicians who worked there. These groups were still serving about 90 percent of HIP's members in 1999.

Of dubious benefit to the insurer were the 140,000 Medicaid enrollees who, in 2003, made HIP the largest private insurer of such recipients in the state of New York. HIP, and also GHI and other nonprofits, were by nature committed to this government-sponsored program. By contrast, the largest for-profit insurers in the region, such as Oxford Health Plans and Aetna U.S. Healthcare, were not covering Medicaid recipients on the ground that they were unprofitable.

GHI was considered to be doing much better than HIP. In a 2005 *Crain's New York Business* article, Gale Scott credited the company with keeping "its premiums affordable and payments to health care providers competitive." GHI had even, at the bidding of state functionaries, taken over a smaller, deficit-ridden HMO and turned it around financially. It had 2.6 million members in the tri-state area and a broader network than HIP, with 130,000 locations and ties to almost every hospital in New York City.

FORMATION OF EMBLEMHEALTH IN 2006

Amid much consolidation by for-profit competitors in the industry, HIP and GHI came together in 2006 under the parentage of newly created EmblemHealth Inc. With four million customers and some $7 billion in annual revenue, EmblemHealth became the largest such company in the region. EmblemHealth was seeking to become a commercial company that could raise large amounts of cash by selling stock for the first time. HIP and GHI said that they would retain separate identities and operations under a single governing foundation.

Such a union was attractive to New York state officials and many legislators because billions of dollars from an initial public offering of stock would go to the state, as in the case of a recent conversion to for-profit status by Empire Blue Cross and Blue Shield. It was expected that more than 20 percent of EmblemHealth's stock would be sold. The proceeds from this offering, as well as any remaining stock, would be transferred to two bodies that had been created by the state of New York in connection with the 2002 conversion of Empire to for-profit status.

New York City municipal officials, conversely, were very much opposed to the merger, claiming that rates hikes were inevitable and the combined forces violated antitrust legislation. A federal judge rejected an attempt by lawyers for the city to block the creation of EmblemHealth. Enabling state legislation was passed in 2007, but the city continued to contest the merger in court.

EmblemHealth's attempt to take the new company public still required approval by the insurance department of the state of New York. At a 2008 hearing, opponents maintained that allowing the company for-profit status would cause premiums to rise sharply. EmblemHealth officials argued that only such a change in the company's status would allow it to compete with large corporations. They pledged not to discontinue any health benefit program or coverage category and to continue to cover members enrolled in all government-sponsored and/or government-financed programs. No action was taken in 2008 or 2009, a year in which the prospect of a stock offering was unattractive because the national economy was in recession.

EMBLEMHEALTH IN 2008

EmblemHealth lost $117.02 million in 2008 after two profitable years. It entered the year with two flagship plans. PPO, the highest level of coverage, offered members the choice of seeing physicians in or out of network. EPO was a network-only plan. Both were available for groups of two or more eligible employees in businesses that had headquarters anywhere in the state of New York.

During the year EmblemHealth introduced a number of other plans. InBalance PPO and EPO included deductibles and co-insurance for out-of-network services and certain in-network services in order to reduce plan costs. ConsumerDirect PPO and EPO imposed higher than usual deductibles, offset by health savings-account tax advantages. CompreHealth and CompreHealth EPO were the most affordable plans, offering a coordinated-care network of physicians and physician group practices.

HIP's subsidiaries included Connecticut of New York, Inc., an insurer with 240,000 members in Connecticut and western Massachusetts that was purchased by HIP in 2004. HIP had 43,000 contracted doctors and other providers in over 72,000 locations in New York, Connecticut, and Massachusetts. Both HIP and GHI had prescription, drug, dental, and vision plans as well as medical ones. The future of their nonprofit status remained uncertain in 2010.

Robert Halasz

PRINCIPAL SUBSIDIARIES

EmblemHealth Services Company LLC; Group Health Incorporated; Health Insurance Plan of New York.

PRINCIPAL COMPETITORS

Aetna, Inc.; WellPoint Inc.

FURTHER READING

Benson, Barbara, "HIP Stanches Bloodletting," *Crain's New York Business,* September 1, 1997, pp. 1, 30.

———, "GHI and HIP Make Their Move," *Crain's New York Business,* October 3, 2005, p. 34.

Best, Jessica, and Betty Flood, "Debate Rages over Proposed HIP-GHI Conversion," *Insurance Advocate,* February 11, 2008, pp. 6–7.

Bird, David, "Health Insurer in Danger as Its Growth Plans Fail," *New York Times,* January 26, 1980, pp. 23, 26.

"City Workers Get Health Insurance," *New York Times,* October 25, 1946, p. 25.

Drew, Christopher, and Melody Petersen, "Expansive Ambitions Dig Deep Hole for Health Plan," *New York Times,* July 14, 2000, pp. A1, B6.

Engel, Leonard, "Dollars and Doctors," *Nation,* October 14, 1950, pp. 336–38.

Pérez-Peña, Richard, "Many Sides Await Deal on Insurer," *New York Times,* December 22, 2003, pp. A1, B4.

Robaton, Anna, "HIP Centers Suffer as Insurer Sets Up Physician Network," *Crain's New York Business,* December 20, 1999, pp. 4, 43.

Schmitt, Eric, "Few City Workers Chose to Switch Health Plans," *New York Times,* November 23, 1986, p. D2.

Scott, Gale, "For GHI, Growth Is Coming in Small Pieces," *Crain's New York Business,* August 22, 2005, pp. 15–16.

YOUR FRIEND ON THE ROAD

F.L. Roberts & Company, Inc.

---■---

93 West Broad Street
Springfield, Massachusetts 01105-2525
U.S.A.
Telephone: (413) 781-7444
Fax: (413) 781-4328
Web site: http://www.flroberts.com

Private Company
Incorporated: 1920
Employees: 550
Sales: $200 million (2009 est.)
NAICS: 447110 Gasoline Stations with Convenience
        Stores

■ ■ ■

F.L. Roberts & Company, Inc., is a family owned and operated group of companies based in Springfield, Massachusetts. Under a variety of names, the company operates 23 gas station-convenience stores in Massachusetts, another six units in Connecticut, and three truck refueling facilities in Massachusetts. Roberts also operates 21 car washes in Massachusetts and Connecticut under the Golden Nozzle Car Wash banner, and eight Jiffy Lube oil change franchised operations in Massachusetts.

In addition, Roberts operates a wholesale fuel delivery business, serving retail gas stations, farms, constructions sites, golf courses, hospitals, schools, and municipalities. The company's fleet program allows drivers to use credit cards locally at company convenience store locations, many of which offer diesel fuel, as well

as thousands of service locations across the United States. Roberts provides fleet customers with detailed reporting each month, including month-to-date and year-to-date accounting.

Finally, Roberts owns and operates the Whately Diner Fillin' Station, considered one of the top diners in the country. Located in Whately, Massachusetts, it is close to an Interstate 91 exit, making it a popular stop for truckers as well as local residents. F.L. Roberts is run by the third generation of the Roberts family, with the fourth generation assuming positions of responsibility and poised to carry on the family tradition.

COMPANY FOUNDED: 1920

The person behind the F.L. Roberts name was Frank Lawrence Roberts, who started the company in 1920. He had been an employee of the Fisk Tire and Rubber Company, but after being passed over for promotion he became angry enough to quit and start his own business. Roberts opened an automotive and tire store at the corner of Main and Adams streets in Springfield. He was in business for several years when the Texaco Oil Company approached him about carrying motor oil. Roberts agreed, but lacking inside shelf space, he resorted to stacking the product outside the store, where it quickly found a ready supply of customers. Next, he added gasoline pumps outside the store and began selling Texaco fuel.

While Frank Roberts may have gone into business in a pique of anger, he proved to be a natural entrepreneur. He opened more gas stations in the area, and by the mid-1930s he ran a chain of 15 gas stations.

Additionally, he began carrying fuel oil for home heating. In the 1940s, Frank's son, Abbott S. Roberts, joined the company after completing his military service during World War II. The younger Roberts brought more sophistication to the family business as a graduate of the University of Pennsylvania. He helped to expand the fuel and motor oil business during the postwar era and eventually replaced his father as the head of F.L. Roberts.

THIRD GENERATION JOINS COMPANY

In the 1970s the third generation of the family joined the business when Abbott's son, Steve, went to work for the company. Later in the decade Steve's brother Seth followed suit. The newcomers quickly made their mark on the company. Steve Abbott grew frustrated with the fuel oil business in the early 1970s and persuaded his father to sell the business and use the proceeds to open more gas stations. After Seth joined the company, the brothers opened more gas stations and also added other complementary ventures. The repair garages closed, and the gas stations evolved into convenience stores offering self-service gasoline. In one case, the company had to go to court to convert some of its stations to a self-service format, because West Springfield had an ordinance limiting the number of self-service gas stations within its limits.

The Roberts family, in keeping with the entrepreneurial spirit of the company's founder, was not averse to pursuing other business opportunities as well. At one point the company ran a small hotel, a discount tobacco store, and two diners. The Whately Diner proved to have staying power. The structure was built in 1960 by the famous New Jersey diner manufacturer, the Kullman Company, which was responsible for the design and construction of some of the country's most beautiful diners. The Whately Diner, an example of Kullman's Princess model, was originally located in Chi-

copee, Massachusetts, and known as the Princess Diner. The Roberts family bought it in the early 1970s and relocated it to Whately, where it became known as one of the top diners in the United States and attracted a host of celebrity customers. It would also be used for a scene in the film *In Dreams*.

Roberts expanded in a variety of directions in the 1980s. The company won a contract in 1982 to operate all 10 gas stations along the Massachusetts Turnpike, beating out the likes of Mobil Oil Co. and Standard Oil Co. of Ohio. Prior to that time, each station was run by a different operator. Five years later the turnpike authority renewed the contract. The stations were especially lucrative, and by 1990 contributed $22 million to the company's balance sheet, or 16 percent of $137.5 million in total revenues. Mobil made a concerted effort to win the contract and succeeded in 1990, bringing an end to the turnpike business for Roberts.

QUICK LUBE DIVISION ADDED: 1989

The car washes Roberts opened under the Golden Nozzle Car Wash brand proved to be a more lasting venture. Many of them were combined with the company's gas stations and convenience stores, or located nearby. In 1989 Roberts became involved in the quick lube business, which the company believed was on the verge of rapid growth. Forming a subsidiary called Minit-Lube of New England Inc., Roberts became a franchisee of the Salt Lake City, Utah-based Quaker State Minit-Lube chain and began opening Minit-Lube outlets in Springfield and other communities in Western Massachusetts. Again, Roberts preferred to cluster its operations, enabling the company to cross market the gas stations, car washes, and quick lube shops, and create such tie-ins as discount coupons to one service for using another.

Roberts was also very active in real estate development in Western Massachusetts in the 1980s. It codeveloped the $20 million Riverdale Plaza in West Springfield in the mid-1980s. In 1986 Roberts moved its headquarters to Springfield's North End, revitalizing an area that had once been a focus for manufacturing, employing as many as 20,000 people at its peak in the 1940s. By this time, however, manufacturing jobs had migrated elsewhere, leaving behind shuttered buildings. Roberts took over the former Moore Drop Forge building, renovated it, and then began looking to attract other businesses to the neighborhood, which continued to hold potential because of its easy access to Interstate 91.

It was the highway, constructed in the early 1960s, that brought an end to the working class, residential community that had taken root in the North End. The Springfield Redevelopment Authority bought many of these homes and demolished them for industrial development. Roberts bought land and buildings from the Authority, as well as from private owners, to develop an office park, targeting office and light manufacturing tenants, especially those who might be interested in establishing regional headquarters in Western Massachusetts. The plan was to build three midsize office towers, but the real estate market slumped in the late 1980s, and Roberts decided to focus on businesses with which it was more familiar. In April 1989 it sold Riverdale Plaza to Prudential Realty for $28 million.

GAS STATIONS SOLD: 1993

In the early 1990s Roberts reorganized its gas station-convenience store operations, which totaled 50 units. The stores had been operated under the names of oil company suppliers BP, Mobil, and Texaco, as well as the Golden Nozzle name. In the summer of 1990, Roberts signed a distribution contract with BP America Inc. and most of the stores were switched over to the BP banner. With the slumping economy crimping its finances, Roberts then decided to cut its holdings. In 1993 it sold 23 of its gasoline retail locations to Philadelphia, Pennsylvania-based Sun Company, which operated gas stations under the Sunoco name. Twenty of the units were in the Springfield area and three in Connecticut. For Sun, the deal allowed it to further a strategy of growing its gasoline retail marketing in the Northeast, while Roberts received the necessary funds to return its business to fiscal health.

Roberts focused on its core operations during the remainder of the 1990s. Several more gas station-convenience stores were added, and in 1999 the company converted its four Q-Lube (formerly Minit-Lube) franchises to Jiffy Lube, the result of a merger

between Quaker State and Pennzoil Co., which controlled the 1,500-unit Jiffy Lube chain. As part of the deal that created PennzEnergy Co., more than 500 Q-Lube stores across the country adopted the Jiffy Lube name. In some cases, Jiffy Lube and Q-Lube stores were nearby competitors. Such was the case for Roberts in three Western Massachusetts locations where PennzEnergy owned and operated Jiffy Lube stores within three miles of a Roberts-owned Q-Lube. To rectify the conflict, PennzEnergy sold these and five other Jiffy Lube stores to Roberts in November 1999.

The new century brought challenges, opportunities, and honors to the Roberts family. A war in Iraq led to uncertainty over oil supplies, resulting in record-high gasoline prices. For small operators like Roberts, already narrow margins were sliced thinner. The company was fortunate that the Roberts name was well known and respected in Western Massachusetts, allowing it to convert some of its gas station-convenience stores to the Roberts name rather than a major fuel supplier.

In July 2008 the company dropped the Exxon name on a convenience store in Springfield, adopted the Roberts banner, and began selling less-expensive unbranded gasoline. Other units would follow suit, but Roberts realized that in some markets, such as Boston, the Roberts brand did not translate as well and the company was better off using the Exxon, Sunoco, or Mobil name. Moreover, stores located near highway exits could attract more business with a brand name and were not converted.

TRUCK STOP PERMIT OBTAINED: 2007

A poor economy hurt other company ventures. Family restaurants of all types experienced a severe decrease in business, coupled with rising costs, and the Whately Diner, despite its popularity, was no exception. In 2007 the eatery implemented cost-cutting measures. Rather than lay off employees, however, it reduced employee hours. A major truck stop development plan was also adversely impacted. In December 2007 Roberts received the necessary permits to convert a former Lee, Massachusetts, Diesel Dan's truck stop, an eight-acre property located off Exit 2 of the Massachusetts Turnpike, into a $21.5 million travel plaza that would include a 93-room hotel and 210-seat family restaurant, as well as a gas station, convenience store, and car wash. The poor economy prevented Roberts from breaking ground on the projects before the permits expired. A credit crunch then made it nearly impossible to obtain financing on the project. The town remained supportive, and Roberts hoped to finally break ground in 2010.

The Roberts family and its 90 years of effort were also recognized in the new century. The Western Massachusetts Entrepreneur Hall of Fame inducted the family in 2007. While few family-owned businesses were able to survive into the third generation, the Roberts had a fourth generation preparing to carry on the tradition: Jana Roberts and a new Frank L. Roberts.

Ed Dinger

PRINCIPAL OPERATING UNITS

Gas Stations and Convenience Stores; Golden Nozzle Car Wash; Whately Diner.

PRINCIPAL COMPETITORS

Cumberland Farms, Inc.; 7-Eleven, Inc.; Sunoco, Inc.

FURTHER READING

"Abbott S. Roberts; Headed Oil Company," *Springfield (Mass.) Union-News,* March 31, 1995, p. 18.

Blomberg, Marcia, "6 Entrepreneurs Picked for Hall," *Springfield (Mass.) Republican,* May 24, 2007, p. C9.

———, "Roberts Loses Turnpike Contract," *Springfield (Mass.) Union-News,* May 2, 1990, p. 1.

Goldberg, Marla A., "F.L. Roberts Buys 8 Jiffy Lube Franchises," *Springfield (Mass.) Union-News,* November 4, 1999, p. B8.

Kinney, Jim, "Price Fuels Switch to Generic Gasoline," *Springfield (Mass.) Sunday Republican,* September 21, 2008, p. D4.

Lindsay, Dick, "Planners Examine Truck Stop Project," *Berkshire Eagle,* February 24, 2009, p. B1.

Robbins, Carolyn, "F.L. Roberts Renews Luster of Old Sites," *Springfield (Mass.) Sunday Republican,* September 4, 1988, p. G1.

———, "F.L. Roberts Will See 23 Gas Stations," *Springfield (Mass.) Union-News,* February 26, 1993, p. 21.

Falke Group

——————■——————

Oststrasse 5
Schmallenberg, D-57392
Germany
Telephone: (+49 2972) 799 1
Fax: (+49 2972) 799 319
Web site: http://www.falke.com

Private Company
Founded: 1895 as Franz Falke-Rohen
Employees: 2,717
Sales: EUR 201 million ($295 million) (2008 est.)
NAICS: 315111 Sheer Hosiery Mills; 315119 Other
  Hosiery and Sock Mills; 315191 Outerwear Knit-
  ting Mills; 315299 All Other Cut and Sew Apparel
  Manufacturing

■ ■ ■

Falke Group is one of Europe's largest knitted hosiery manufacturers and the German market leader in men's socks. In addition to socks for men, women, and children, Falke produces a broad range of branded women's hosiery as well as bodies and shirts. The company also makes a line of functional sportswear for men and women, including trousers, athletic shirts, blazers, sweaters, and socks, with a special focus on running, Yoga, and fitness sports. Falke's fashion subsidiary manufactures men's sweaters and knit apparel that are marketed under the Falke and Burlington labels. In addition to its own brand-name products, the company produces socks under license for the Esprit label and under private label for retailers and other manufacturers.

Falke's products are sold in major department and specialty stores in Europe and in the United States. The company also runs a flagship store in Berlin and Falke Sports Shops in Berlin and Frankfurt am Main. Falke's German subsidiary LTW Leinefelder Textilwerke manufactures high-quality specialty yarns. Based in Schmallenberg near Cologne, the company has production subsidiaries in Germany, Portugal, Hungary, and South Africa. Falke Group is privately owned by Otto and Paul Falke Jr., the fourth generation of Falke family managers.

SOCKS MANUFACTURING STARTS IN 1895

Before Franz Falke-Rohen established his own enterprise in Schmallenberg in Germany's midwestern Sauerland region, the roofer learned about knitting as a seasonal worker at Strickerei Stern, a local knitting company. Working at the knitting factory during the winter season when it was too cold to do roofing work, he quit roofing to work full time at Strickerei Stern. Thanks to his suggestions on how to improve the production technologies, Falke-Rohen was soon promoted. In 1895, however, he decided to leave Stern and to found his own enterprise.

Starting out with eight workers, Falke-Rohen began producing wool socks for men and children at his knitting mill. In its first years the mill manufactured about two dozen socks per day. To purchase the yarn needed, the company founder traveled to the market in Essen, a city in the Ruhr, once every few days. Since there was no train station in Schmallenberg, Falke-Rohen carried

COMPANY PERSPECTIVES

We believe in our daydreams. Firmly believing in our visions of modern living and aesthetics, we prefer to make them a public statement instead of hiding behind impersonal anonymity. The perfect design, of course, has many faces but only one—depending on personal tastes and tendencies—catches our special liking.

yarn in his backpack while walking back 18 kilometers from the nearest train station.

When the demand for Falke-Rohen's socks began to stagnate in 1900, his oldest son, Franz Falke Jr., made up for the lost family income by becoming an umbrella maker and by selling his own product door-to-door. In 1902, however, he followed in his father's footsteps and took over the knitting mill, with all of his seven siblings working in the family business. Beginning in 1906 Falke Jr., purchased the yarn directly from manufacturers and won additional customers. Around the same time the knitting mill began to sell part of its output under the Falke name.

FASTER GROWTH AFTER WORLD WAR I

After World War I, the Falkes acquired J. Meisenberg, a local manufacturer of wool yarn and hair yarn made from animal hair with a staff of 30 in 1918. With wool not available as a raw material after the war, the company used gorse fibers and rags instead. Although the company recovered only slowly after the war, Falke Jr., with no experience or knowledge in yarn making, managed to modernize and grow the yarn business considerably within a few years. By 1924 the Meisenberg factory's workforce had grown to 230.

In 1920 the Falkes built a brand-new sock factory in Schmallenberg which was equipped with state-of-the-art machinery. In addition to socks the company started manufacturing knee-highs that, beginning in 1927, were produced by automated circular knitting machines. By the time the company founder died in 1928, about 800 people worked at the factory.

KNIT APPAREL MANUFACTURING BEGINS IN 1939

Franz Falke Jr., who became the majority shareholder after his father's death, opened a new chapter in the company's history in 1939 when he ventured into knitwear. When his schoolmate, Arthur Stern, a Jew, fled Nazi Germany, Stern sold the knitwear factory in Schmallenberg to Falke Jr., the very factory where his father had learned the knitting craft. Founded in 1810, Salomon Stern Knitwear Company, which employed some 100 workers in the late 1930s, was renamed Franz A. Falke GmbH and soon expanded its market beyond the Sauerland region.

During World War II Falke manufactured socks and knit sweaters for the military and for the German population. After openly criticizing the Nazis, Falke Jr. was arrested shortly before the end of the war but managed to escape, according to the company's chronicle *Die Falke Gruppe*. The two factories in Schmallenberg suffered only minor damage during the war. After the end of World War II, in the second half of the 1940s, the company logo was created. While the colors changed from gray, blue, and red in 1950 to pastel pink in 1956 to red in 1963, the basic design, the silhouette of a hawk sitting on the letters "falke" in a square, remained the same for 30 years.

GENERATION CHANGE AND NEW START IN 1951

Franz Falke Jr. died in 1951. His sons, Paul and Franz-Otto Falke, both in their early 30s, who had been prepared for running the family business after they returned from the war, took over the company. Paul Falke focused mainly on the yarn business while the younger Franz-Otto oversaw the socks and knitwear manufacturing. Both agreed on two major strategic goals: creating a strong brand through investment in marketing and growing the business by venturing into new geographic markets.

Falke's knitwear business received a major boost when the company was awarded an order for 150,000 sweaters by the British Allied Forces in 1951. The large contract not only kept the company busy for the next two years. The incoming cash provided Falke with the necessary funds to invest in modern machinery. In 1954 the company purchased a hosiery knitting machine that knit the parts of a garment in the exact shape of the pattern. As knitwear made its entry into fashion, the demand for Falke's high-quality sweaters for men and women rose.

Due to improved manufacturing technologies and the introduction of synthetic fibers, yarn quality was greatly improved in the 1950s. Falke's wool yarns became softer and tearproof, while the use of synthetic yarns in socks extended their durability. By 1954 Falke had become one of Europe's largest hair yarn

KEY DATES

1895: Franz Falke-Rohen establishes a knitting mill in Schmallenberg.

1939: The company takes over Salomon Stern Knitwear Company.

1974: A production subsidiary is set up in South Africa.

1987: The first line of Falke men's sportswear is launched in the United States.

2008: The company acquires the men's apparel brand Burlington.

manufacturers. One of the company's innovative products was a multicolored yarn that combined threads of different colors.

HOSIERY AND COMBINABLE KNITWEAR

A major step in Falke's history was the acquisition of Uhli-Feinstrumpfwerke, a manufacturer of fashion stockings based in Lippstadt, in 1958. After the financially struggling company's product line had been changed to mostly seamless fashion stockings and panty hose in the early 1960s, Uhli started generating profits again. In 1965, at the height of the miniskirt fashion wave, the company launched Uhli-Fling, the first fashion stockings line containing the stretchable synthetic fiber Lycra.

Concentrating on a high-priced upscale product range, Falke stayed away from the ruinous price wars in the low-priced market segment. While a pair of basic nylons was available for DEM 1.45, a pair of Uhli Flings, available in a broad range of colors, cost DEM 18.90. In addition to nylons and pantyhoses, Falke developed the Uhli-Dress-Program, a line of sporty but elegant and brightly colored women's wear made from Helanca, a textured polyamide fiber, in the 1960s.

In the mid-1960s Falke's knitwear division in Schmallenberg introduced a new design concept. Most all of their garments were to be combinable with each other in material and color. To communicate this concept to its customers and to promote sales, the company introduced shop-in-shop shelf systems for retails stores where the whole Falke apparel line was presented. The new concept made the Falke brand more visible for consumers and helped increase sales.

IMPROVED YARNS AND HOME TEXTILES AFTER 1960

As the use of textile floor coverings came into fashion in the mid-1960s, Falke's yarn division started manufacturing needle felt in hard and soft qualities. Soaked in resin and dried at a high temperature, the multilayered felt was extremely durable. The product line would remain one of Falke's staples into the 21st century. As synthetic fiber products such as nylon and Perlon took the textile industry by storm in the late 1960s, they became a serious competition for Falke's yarns. The company decided to focus on improving the quality of its yarns and invested in yarn finishing technology. In addition, Falke adopted space-dyeing, a technology first developed in the United States, to dye nylon yarns.

As the company constantly expanded production capacity and added new sales units, Falke's revenues climbed steeply during the economic boom of the 1950s and 1960s. By 1969 Falke had become Europe's fifth-largest manufacturer of space-dyed nylon yarns and reported DEM 200 million in total sales. Also that year the company was renamed Falke Feinstrumpfwerke.

SPECIALIZATION, INTERNATIONALIZATION, AND LICENSE PRODUCTION AFTER 1970

In the 1970s market conditions became more difficult for the German textile industry. While German textile workers demanded higher wages, lower-cost imports began to erode price levels. Again, Falke decided to continue its high-price strategy and to defend its market position. The company focused on selected market niches, launched innovative new products, expanded its market presence through brand-name license production, and expanded beyond Germany.

In 1974 Falke began to set up production subsidiaries abroad. The company established Franz Falke Textiles (FFT) in Belleville at the outskirts of Kapstadt, South Africa, in that year, and built a factory for finishing and dyeing synthetic yarns for the country's carpet manufacturing industry. A second production facility in South Africa was set up in Rosslyn near Pretoria in the early 1980s where Falke produced nylons and pantyhose. In 1981 the company opened a finishing factory for socks and hosiery in Tovar, Portugal. Additional production facilities were later set up in Hungary.

A major step in expanding Falke's presence on the shelves of upscale department stores was the cooperation with world-renowned designers on the basis of exclusive licensing agreements. The first license agreement had been sealed as early as in 1954 when Falke began manufacturing nylons under the Christian Dior label. However, it was in the mid-1970s that the company followed this strategy more intensely. Beginning in 1976 Falke produced men's knitwear carrying the Giorgio Armani label. In the 1980s the company signed additional license agreements with Moschino, Jeff Sayre, Yves Saint Laurent, Kenzo, and Christian Dior for a variety of products.

Computer-aided design and electronically controlled manufacturing greatly expanded creative capabilities in Falke's socks production in the 1980s, making almost any pattern or variation possible. The company introduced the woolen sock line Bristol and the Walkie hiking socks as well as new lines of tennis socks and knee-highs for joggers. Falke decided to give up its women's knitwear range in 1985 and to concentrate solely on menswear.

BRAND BUILDING AND SPORTS TEXTILES

Intensifying its marketing efforts helped Falke strengthen its market position and increase brand awareness and sales. Beginning in 1989 the company launched a series of international image campaigns, associating vision, imagination, creativity, and high performance with the Falke brand. Falke also continued to follow its licensing strategy in the 1990s. While several licenses of the 1980s expired, new partners were found in the designer labels Boss, Joop!, and Esprit. In 1992 the first Falke flagship store featuring Falke outerwear opened in Cologne, followed by additional stores in Berlin and Vienna in the late 1990s when the number of the Falke's shop-in-shops had grown to 80.

After Falke had already begun to focus on the niche market for sports socks in the 1970s and 1980s, the company took another major step when it began to cooperate with experts and coaches from Cologne's College of Sports in developing customized socks and knee-highs for different types of sports. The result was the Ergonomic Sport System line with ergonomically designed socks and knee-highs shaped differently for the left and right foot for hikers, skiers, horseback riders, sailors, athletes, and soccer players. Beginning in 1993 Falke got involved in sports sponsoring, mainly boxing and Formula One racing.

RESTRUCTURING AND INTERNATIONALIZATION AFTER 1990

When Paul Falke died shortly after his 70th birthday in 1990, his son, Paul Falke Jr., together with Franz-Otto

Falke's son Franz-Peter Falke, took over company management. Franz-Otto Falke retired from active involvement in the family business in 1995. In that year the company reorganized its export business under the umbrella of the newly established Falke International GmbH. Falke International together with the company's hosiery and socks production companies, Falke Feinstrumpfwerke and Franz Falke-Rohen Strumpfwarenfabriken, were united under the new Falke KG. In 1991 Falke set up a hosiery production plant in Dorfchemnitz in Saxony, Eastern Germany. Six years later the company acquired Leinefelde Textile Works GmbH, a manufacturer of high-quality specialty yarns in the Eastern German state of Thuringia.

As the fall of the Berlin Wall in 1989 and the following liberalization of global trade opened up new markets, Falke intensified its internationalization efforts. New sales subsidiaries were set up in Austria, Switzerland, the Netherlands, and the United Kingdom. In addition to Western Europe, Falke exported its products to Eastern European countries such as Poland, Bulgaria, Croatia, and Russia.

Beginning in the late 1980s Falke also expanded massively in the United States. The company's U.S.-sales office Falke Fashion, Inc., launched its first line of men's sportswear under the Falke brand in fall 1987. In the following year another U.S. subsidiary for private-label sportswear manufacturing, named Falke Private Brands, was founded. In 1992 Falke launched its first women's hosiery collection in the United States.

At the turn of the 21st century Falke focused on its role as a leading international sportswear manufacturer. In 2005 the company successfully launched a line of cutting-edge functional sportswear for which Falke received several design awards. In 2008 the company acquired the Burlington brand, a competitor in the upscale segment of the men's socks market from U.S.-based International Textile Group. By 2008 the share of Falke's foreign sales had reached 42 percent, compared with 29 percent in 2001. To focus even more on its apparel business in the future, the company sold its two yarn factories in 2003 and 2009. In 2010 Falke launched another novelty, a maritime fashion collection for infants.

Evelyn Hauser

PRINCIPAL SUBSIDIARIES

Falke KGaA; Falke Fashion.

PRINCIPAL COMPETITORS

Fogal AG; Kayser-Roth Corporation; Kunert AG; Soxland International, Inc.; Wolford AG; Odlo Sports Group AG.

FURTHER READING

Die Falke Gruppe: Die Geschichte. Die Marke. Die Arbeit, Schmallenberg, Germany: Falke Gruppe, 2001.

"Esprit International Signs Hosiery Licensee in Europe," *WWD,* August 17, 1989, p. 3.

"Falke Betting on Sports Underwear," *Süddeutsche Zeitung,* May 8, 2002, p. 33.

"Falke Forms Private Label Division in U.S.," *Daily News Record,* July 6, 1988, p. 2.

"Falke Group Launches Line of Sportswear," *Daily News Record,* February 19, 1987, p. 20.

Foster, Carol, "Falke Offering Collection of Women's Hose in U.S.," *Footwear News,* November 30, 1992, p. 23.

Probe, Anja, and Elke Dieterich, "Made in Schmallenberg," *TextilWirtschaft,* October 18, 2007, p. 32.

"Underwear Brand Falke to Launch into Sportswear," *Marketing Week,* June 30, 2005, p. 8.

Walsh, Peter, "Falke Private Label to Be Sold in Europe," *Daily News Record,* November 13, 1990, p. 9.

Wollenschläger, Ulrike, "Wirth kauft die Falke-Garnsparte," *TextilWirtschaft,* December 18, 2003, p. 10.

#1 SHOE AND GLOVE IN GOLF

Foot-Joy Inc.

—■—

333 Bridge Street
Fairhaven, Massachusetts 02719
U.S.A.
Toll Free: (800) 225-8500
Fax: (800) 867-0004
Web site: http://www.footjoy.com

Wholly Owned Subsidiary of Acushnet Company
Incorporated: 1857 as Burt and Packard Shoe Company
Employees: 5,000
Sales: $2.4 billion (2008 est.)
NAICS: 339920 Sporting and Athletic Good Manufacturing

■ ■ ■

Foot-Joy Inc. (informally known as FootJoy) is a Fairhaven, Massachusetts-based subsidiary of Acushnet Company, a major golf equipment company which in turn is part of Fortune Brands, Inc. Serving the market for men, women, and juniors, FootJoy produces the leading brand of golf shoes worn by professional as well as recreational golfers. In addition, FootJoy offers casual and athletic shoes, as well as high-tech socks designed to provide impact cushioning and moisture control. Foot-Joy is also a market leader in golf gloves, made from leather as well as synthetic materials and designed for different weather conditions. FootJoy jackets and vests are designed to withstand wet, windy, cool, and warm conditions. Miscellaneous items include fleece hats and ear bands, bucket hats, baseball hats, umbrellas, shoe care products, shoe trees, shoe bags, and duffels. FootJoy

also offers repair services for its Classic line of leather golf shoes, the company's longtime flagship product that was discontinued in 2009 when the company's Brockton, Massachusetts, plant was closed, leaving all production to a plant located in China.

19TH-CENTURY ROOTS

FootJoy's lineage dates to the mid-19th century when Brockton, Massachusetts, was a major center for shoe-making in the United States. The Burt and Packard Shoe Company was established there in 1857 and soon changed its name to Field and Flint Company, which billed itself as "Boot Makers to Gentlemen." In 1910 the company branched out to begin producing golf shoes, a relatively new footwear category. For years golfers had relied on makeshift shoes to provide sure footing when hitting shots, primarily made by adding metal hobnails to regular heavy boots. It was not until the 1890s that specialized golf shoes began to appear in the United Kingdom, either in the form of shoes with rubber knobs or overshoes fitted with spikes that could be slipped over regular shoes. Spiked wing tip oxford shoes were then introduced.

In the 1920s Field and Flint made its mark on the golf shoe category with the introduction of the Classic line sold under the FootJoy name. The Classic was a welted shoe that employed an arching leather strip to join the upper with the bottom, similar to saddle shoes that employed a saddle-shaped piece of leather on the upper to help retain shape during activity. It also improved comfort by including a cork-filled cavity in the bottom to mold the shoe to the foot. It was a meticulously made shoe, requiring 164 steps to produce. In 1927 the FootJoy Classic became the official golf shoe for the Americans in the Ryder Cup, a biennial tournament for teams from the United States and Europe.

By 1945 most of the golfers on the U.S. PGA Tour wore FootJoys, a distinction that the company would retain. It was also during the 1940s that FootJoy made significant inroads with recreational golfers. Although well-dressed golfers had been wearing golf shoes for years, many players continued to rely on rubber-soled sneakers or even street shoes. Many continued to buy regular retail shoes and insert their own spikes. Field and Flint salesman Ernie Sabayrac opened up the market for FootJoys in the 1940s by persuading golf course pro shops, which had limited themselves to the sale of clubs and balls, to begin carrying golf shoes.

Sabayrac was also responsible for the addition of apparel to pro shops. He began displaying wares out of the trunk of his car at golf tournaments, thus planting the seeds for what would become the highly successful PGA Merchandise Show. The PGA would name an award in his honor for lifetime contributions to the golf industry. In short order most golfers turned to specialized spiked golf shoes. It was also in the 1940s that the first golf shoes for women were introduced, although they were little more than smaller sizes of the shoes designed for men.

CHANGE IN OWNERSHIP: 1957

Ownership of Field and Flint changed hands in 1957 when the Stone and Tarlow families bought the company. They had deep ties to the Brockton shoe industry, having formed Stone and Tarlow Co. in 1917. Under the leadership of Richard and William Tarlow, FootJoy production was moved to the Stone and Tarlow plant in Brockton. More importantly, they elected to limit sales to pro shops, creating an air of exclusivity that proved beneficial to sales and produced higher

margins, as FootJoy became an internationally recognized brand. To better align the company with the brand, Field and Flint was renamed Foot-Joy Inc. in 1970.

The Stone and Tarlow families sold a controlling interest in FootJoy to General Mills, Inc., in 1975 for about $6 million. Two years later General Mills acquired a 100 percent interest, and folded the business into the General Mills Fashion Group, although the Tarlow brothers continued to run the company. Under General Mills, FootJoy began moving most of its production overseas. The Brockton plant, however, remained viable because of the workmanship required to hand craft the Classic line of golf shoes. Over the plant entrance a sign read, "Through these halls pass the greatest shoemakers in the world."

With the backing of General Mills, FootJoy expanded beyond golf shoes. In 1979 the company began producing golf gloves, a product that had taken longer to catch on with golfers. According to FootJoy research, development of gloves for golfing purposes did not begin until the late 1890s. Instead, golfers had relied on calluses to prevent blistering due to repeated swings, and club handles to provide the necessary tackiness for a steady swing. It was not until the 1930s that professionals began to don gloves at tournaments, but many major players of the day never wore gloves.

By the 1960s, however, the gloveless player had become the rare exception, as golf gloves evolved from fingerless or backless versions to modern models based on research and development. FootJoy worked with Pittards plc, a United Kingdom leather dresser, to develop the Sta-Sof line of golf gloves made from cabretta leather and using the Pittards technology to provide water and stain resistance, breathability, and durability, as well as a soft feel. By 1981 Sta-Sof became the world's best-selling golf glove. FootJoy also added a line of socks in 1981, which subsequently became the top-selling brand in its category, establishing a third major product line for FootJoy.

ACUSHNET ACQUIRES COMPANY: 1985

In January 1985 General Mills announced it was focusing on its core business and selling its fashion lines, including FootJoy. Fearful that new owners might relocate or close the plant, FootJoy employees urged the Tarlow brothers to buy back the company. The Tarlows led a management team that made a bid for a leveraged acquisition but in the end could not match the $53 million in cash offered by New Bedford, Massachusetts-based Acushnet Inc. in the spring of 1985. Other suitors

KEY DATES

1857: Burt and Packard Shoe Company is founded in Brockton, Massachusetts, then renamed Field and Flint Company.
1910: Company begins making golf shoes.
1957: Stone and Tarlow families acquire the company.
1970: Field and Flint is renamed Foot-Joy Inc.
1975: General Mills, Inc., acquires FootJoy.
1979: FootJoy gloves are introduced.
1985: FootJoy is sold to Acushnet.
1997: Outerwear product line is added.
2009: Brockton plant closes.

included Spalding and Converse Inc.

A subsidiary of Fortune Brands, Acushnet was founded in Acushnet, Massachusetts, in 1910 by Phillip W. "Skipper" Young, a graduate of the Massachusetts Institute of Technology, and a pair of college friends. Originally a partnership called Peabody, Young & Weeks, it adopted the Acushnet Processing Company name, which it retained even after moving to New Bedford. The company produced reclaimed uncured rubber using a recovery process developed by Young. After the bottom fell out of the rubber market in the 1920s, Acushnet began producing a variety of molded rubber products, such as hot water bottles and bathing caps. It also turned its attention to golf balls, due primarily to Young's passion for the game and his growing irritation over wayward shots. Young X-rayed the balls to see if the cores were properly centered, and discovering that they were not, he began to develop a revolutionary new "dead center" golf ball marketed under the Titleist name.

Like FootJoy, the sale of Titleist balls was limited to pro shops to increase margins. Acushnet maintained its place as a leader in golf ball technology after World War II and branched into other areas of the game as well. In 1968 the company name was changed from Acushnet Processing to Acushnet Company, Inc. The Bulls Eye putter was acquired in the 1960s, followed by other clubs and golf bags. Golf carts were added to the mix in 1975. A year later, Acushnet was acquired by American Brands, a consumer products conglomerate that grew out of the American Tobacco Company and in 1997 changed its name to Fortune Brands, Inc. Acushnet continued to produce rubber products along with its golf division until 1994, when the rubber division was spun off as a separate company.

While Acushnet did not close the Brockton plant, it did bring in a new general manager, Robert B. Forbush, and the Tarlow brothers were reduced to consultants who soon left the company. Forbush was a Brockton native, who after graduating from Harvard and Columbia worked in marketing at Hershey Foods Corp. before joining Acushnet in 1977. There he worked his way up through the ranks to become Titleist vice president for worldwide marketing. His tenure at the helm of FootJoy lasted almost five years, during which time the company introduced the popular Dry-Joy line of waterproof golf shoes, helping revenues to increase 50 percent to $100 million. In late 1989 Forbush resigned, citing philosophical differences with Acushnet's management, who decided to consolidate some of FootJoy's operations with Titleist.

RUMORS OF PLANT CLOSING: 1995

The reorganization was completed in 1990, resulting in a single operating unit called Titleist-Foot-Joy Worldwide. FootJoy kept up with changes in the marketplace in the 1990s. Because metal spikes caused damage to the grounds, many golf courses in the United States began to ban their use, prompting the development of spikeless shoes that relied on rubber knobs. FootJoy also had to contend with changing economics. In 1995 Titleist/FootJoy (Thailand) Ltd. was established to manufacture golf gloves.

In that same year, rumors circulated that the Brockton plant might be closed. Brockton mayor Jack Yunits quickly contacted FootJoy to assemble a package of incentives, including tax breaks and land grants, to help the company open a modern new plant in the community that with increased productivity could remain competitive. The enduring popularity of the expensive Classic line was also a key element in FootJoy's ability to survive in Brockton, where scores of shoe companies had once flourished but by this time had gone out of business.

In the mid-1990s FootJoy controlled nearly half of the consumer market for golf shoes. Its closest rival, Etonic, owned just an 11 percent share, but sales of Classics were overshadowed by the younger Soft-Joy line. To maintain its place, FootJoy stayed on the cutting edge in a number of areas. In 1996 it introduced a new laser fitting system as well as a new non-membrane waterproof technology, DryJoys Leather System. The DryJoys line added the IntelliGel Fit-Bed system to provide temperature responsive arch support. Later in the decade FootJoy introduced its Dry ICE (interactive cooling environment) technology and interchangeable traction rings that could be fitted over spikes to providing differing degrees of gripping power depending on course conditions.

FootJoy also added specialty gloves, Winter-Sof and Rain Grip, in 1996, and a year later expanded into new product categories. DryJoys Performance Outerwear was introduced, as was a women's fashion category called The FootJoy Europa Collection. In 1998 a complete line of FootJoy products was added, including gloves, socks, outerwear, and accessories. Moreover, FootJoy sought to modernize its image, in 1998 updating its logo and graphics. The company also unveiled a new humorous television advertising campaign featuring "SignBoy," a fictional character who carried leaderboard signs at PGA events and regaled famous golfers with the virtues of FootJoy products. Actor Matt Grieser developed something of a cult following among the golfing set and made regular appearances at charity golf events.

BROCKTON PLANT CLOSES: 2009

Further product development greeted the new century. FootJoy introduced golf sandals, in this case playing catch-up with start-up company Bite Footwear. Advances were also made in regular golf shoes, including improvements to waterproofing and laser fitting technology, the introduction of the Reelfit dial-up lacing system for a custom fit, fresh styling for women, and a shoe line geared to the junior market. FootJoy also marketed padded practice gloves, but interest soon declined and the product was pulled.

The company enjoyed better success with the ultrathin Sta-Soft Premiere golf glove it added in 2000. A year later the Women's Sta-Cooler golf and sport glove lines were introduced. In 2004 FootJoy unveiled new waterproofing technology for its outerwear products, and the following year entered the performance knits category by adding the FootJoy Golf Mock. TechSof performance socks became available in 2008, featuring left and right shaped socks to provide greater comfort and performance.

Although FootJoy's flagship golf shoe remained the gold standard in the category, the Classic's $300 price tag led to diminishing sales. As the economy tumbled into recession in 2008, resulting in a corresponding dip in corporate spending on golf, FootJoy announced in December of that year that the workforce at the Brockton plant had to be reduced. The plan was to institute a hiring freeze to allow empty positions to go unfilled, followed by buyouts and then layoffs.

A few weeks later, however, as February 2009 came to a close, FootJoy decided that demand for Classics was no longer high enough to justify the Brockton operation and the decision was made to close the plant and cease production of the Classic line. Manufacturing was then limited to the company's plant in China, marking the end of an era for FootJoy, which would continue to provide repair services for Classics, so well made that they enjoyed long lives and were beloved by their owners. What would remain for years to come would be the FootJoy name, and the golf-related products it continued to adorn.

Ed Dinger

PRINCIPAL COMPETITORS

Callaway Golf Company; Etonic Worldwide LLC; Nike, Inc.

FURTHER READING

Abelson, Jenn, "FootJoy to Shutter Last Shoe Factory in Brockton," *Boston Globe*, February 28, 2009, p. B5.

Allegrini, Elaine, "Once Known as 'Shoe City,' Brockton Loses Its Last Factory," *Brockton (Mass.) Enterprise*, March 1, 2009.

Allis, Sam, "Requiem for a Heavyweight," *Boston Globe*, April 26, 2009, p. B2.

Boyle, Maureen, "FootJoy Plant that Makes Golf Shoes in Brockton Is Closing," *Enterprise*, February 27, 2009.

Carton, Barbara, "Foot-Joy Chief Ties Departure to Reduced Role," *Boston Globe*, December 4, 1989, p. 57.

DeMello, Margo, *Feet and Footwear: A Cultural Encyclopedia*, Santa Barbara, CA: ABC-CLIO, LLC, 2009.

French, Desiree, "Acushnet Will Buy Foot-Joy for $53M," *Boston Globe*, April 26, 1985, p. 83.

Radsken, Jill, "Pride 'n Joy," *Boston Herald*, June 11, 1997, p. 47.

"Richard N. Tarlow, 72, Former Head of Foot-Joy Inc.," *Boston Globe*, October 22, 1995, p. 43.

Genuine Parts Co.

2999 Circle 75 Parkway
Atlanta, Georgia 30339
U.S.A.
Telephone: (770) 953-1700
Fax: (770) 956-2211
Web site: http://www.genpt.com

Public Company
Incorporated: 1928
Employees: 29,000
Sales: $10.1 billion (2009)
Stock Exchanges: New York
Ticker Symbol: GPC
NAICS: 421120 Motor Vehicle Supplies and New Part Wholesalers; 441310 Automotive Parts and Accessories Stores; 421830 Industrial Machinery and Equipment Wholesalers; 422120 Stationery and Office Supplies Wholesalers; 421210 Furniture Wholesalers; 421610 Electrical Apparatus and Equipment, Wiring Supplies, and Construction Materials Wholesalers

■ ■ ■

Genuine Parts Co. is the largest member and majority owner of the National Auto Parts Association (NAPA). The company operates as one of the largest automobile parts suppliers in the United States, overseeing 58 NAPA Auto Parts distribution centers across North America that offer over 380,000 products. Just over half of the company's revenues are generated by its Automotive Parts Group division, with about 29 percent coming from its Industrial Parts Group, which operates under the Motion Industries name. This division serves over 120,000 customers throughout North America and offers over four million industrial replacement parts including bearings, hydraulic and pneumatic components, and mechanical power transmission items. The company's Office Products Group sells general office supplies, business machines, and office furniture while the Electrical/Electronic Materials Group provides a variety of products ranging from adhesives and static control products to magnet wire and varnish and resins.

FROM ONE STORE TO NATIONWIDE DISTRIBUTOR: 1928–69

Genuine Parts Company was founded by Carlyle Fraser in 1928 when Fraser bought a small auto parts store in Atlanta. The store had six employees and capital of $40,000 when he acquired it. Sales reached $75,000 the first year, although the store lost about $2,500. Independent garages for car repair were spreading with incredible rapidity, providing Genuine with a swiftly growing market for its parts. Genuine bought auto parts from manufacturers such as Tenneco and sold them to parts stores, called jobbing houses, which sold them to the independent garages. From the beginning, Genuine pushed swift, reliable service as a way to outflank the competition. The firm also used its relationship with NAPA, the trade association cofounded by Fraser in 1925. NAPA set standards and sold parts to jobbers.

Genuine's business was in some respects helped by the Great Depression. Many people could not afford to buy new cars, so they held onto aging automobiles and bought the replacement parts needed to repair them when they broke down. In 1936 about $2 was spent on parts for the average one-year-old car, whereas a three-year-old car required $10 in parts. During the 1930s, company sales went from $339,000 to $3.18 million.

Genuine continued to grow during World War II. Consumers again held onto their older cars, sometimes having little choice because automakers were devoting much of their capacity to the war effort. By the same token, the War Production Board allocated resources to parts manufacturers only to build "functional" parts for cars. This restriction meant, for instance, no fenders or door hardware were available to sell to those needing them. With auto sales slacking, the average vehicle was 7.28 years old in 1946, compared with 4.77 years old in 1941 before the United States entered the war. As a result, $19 in parts were bought for the average car in 1945. In the year of its 20th anniversary in 1948, the company had $20 million in sales. That same year the company went public, selling 150,000 shares of common stock at $11 per share (thanks to a series of stock splits, an investor who had bought one share in 1948 would have had 205.04 shares by April 1997).

With the prosperity of the 1950s and the increasing number of families with two cars, Genuine expanded at a tremendous pace. It opened NAPA operations in Boston in 1950, Omaha in 1955, Jacksonville and Miami in 1956, Denver in 1957, and Minneapolis in 1959. By 1962 the firm owned 97 retail stores and 12 warehouses along the East Coast and in the South and had annual sales of about $80 million. Rebuilt parts accounted for 15 percent of sales. Although it still bought parts from manufacturers, Genuine did some parts rebuilding itself, including clutches, brake shoes, and pumps. To increase its slice of that business, in 1968 the firm acquired Atlanta-based John Rogers Co., a rebuilder of auto engines. In 1969 Genuine diversified out of the auto business for the first time, buying Beck &

Gregg Hardware Co., a 103-year-old distributor of home appliances, building goods, and sports products (this business was sold in 1985).

By the late 1960s, Genuine was a nationwide distributor, supplying 2,500 independent jobbers and owning 33 of the 55 NAPA distribution centers, which then served 4,000 jobbers throughout the United States. The first NAPA brand parts were introduced in 1966. Genuine also supplied parts for trucks, tractors, power boats, and power tools.

DIVERSIFICATION AND EXPANSION: 1970–79

Expansion outside the United States began in 1972, when Genuine acquired auto parts distributor Corbetts, Ltd., which was based in Calgary, Alberta. Corbetts served more than 100 jobbing stores. Genuine also began an expansion into Europe in 1973, but this proved to be a short-lived endeavor as the European operations were sold off in 1978.

The OPEC oil embargo in 1973 played havoc with the auto parts market. With the rise in gasoline prices, consumers drove less and needed fewer auto parts in the short term. The oil shortage, however, also led to recession in 1973 and 1974. Car owners held onto their older cars, driving up sales and prices of auto parts in the longer term. Nearly 90 million cars were being driven in the United States, and approximately 60 percent of them were over three years old, making them likely candidates for car parts. An increasing number of these vehicles were small cars, whose parts tended to wear out faster than those of larger cars. Although cars were being driven for fewer total miles than ever before, more of those miles were in urban areas, resulting in greater wear on the parts. Do-it-yourself sales soared, and mass marketers such as Sears Roebuck and J.C. Penney began increasing parts orders from distributors. Genuine's sales reached $500 million in 1973, twice as much as its nearest competitor, APS. That figure, however, represented just 2 percent of the fragmented auto parts market.

Auto parts were becoming more elaborate and expensive as a result of technology advances and stricter pollution standards. In 1975, attempting to diversify, Genuine picked up a wholesale office supplies firm, S.P. Richards Co. In 1976, under the leadership of CEO Wilton Looney, Genuine also expanded into the industrial parts business with the acquisition of Motion Industries, Inc. Looney believed that industrial parts would be recession-proof in the same way that auto parts were: during recessions industrial firms would buy

KEY DATES

1925: Carlyle Fraser is one of the cofounders of the National Auto Parts Association (NAPA).
1928: Fraser founds Genuine Parts Company after buying a small auto parts store in Atlanta.
1948: Company goes public.
1966: The first NAPA brand parts are introduced.
1972: Company expands into Canada with the purchase of auto parts distributor Corbetts, Ltd.
1976: Expansion into industrial parts ensues with the acquisition of Motion Industries.
1982: The firm acquires Dallas-based General Automotive Parts Corp.
2006: Sales surpass $10 billion for the first time in company history.

replacement parts for existing machinery rather than purchasing new equipment. In 1979 the firm bought a Michigan-based industrial parts distributor, Michigan Bearing Company, to expand that segment of its business.

In 1978 Genuine installed a computerized point-of-sale system for billing customers, tracking inventories, and automatically ordering replacements for parts that were sold. The system, developed with Data General Corp., cost $24,000 to $30,000 per complete system, and grew to include 900 jobbers by 1982. This system gave Genuine an important advantage over competitors, because no other independent distributor could match the services Genuine could offer.

STAYING AHEAD THROUGH ACQUISITIONS AND RETOOLING: 1980–85

Genuine's sales reached $1.6 billion in 1981, of which 63 percent came from the distribution of parts, 22 percent came from industrial replacement parts, and 8 percent from office-supply products. The firm had 55 U.S. distribution centers for auto parts and four in western Canada, selling to about 5,200 jobbers, of which it owned about 350. Genuine ran six distribution centers and 160 branches for industrial parts, selling to 50,000 customers. Office supplies were being sold to more than 5,000 retailers in 15 states. Genuine's leading item overall was spray paint used for touch-ups, which accounted for 8 percent of sales. Exhaust products,

filters, hoses and belts, and batteries accounted for between 3 and 6 percent of sales each.

The number of vehicles in the United States continued to rise, reaching 160 million by the end of 1981, with an average age of 6.5 years. Parts for imported cars accounted for only about 10 percent of inventory, despite rapidly growing import sales in the United States. Since the imported parts broadened inventory, the trend to buy imports was seen as increasing Genuine's advantage against smaller, less well-financed competitors.

In 1982 Genuine bought General Automotive Parts Corp. of Dallas in a stock swap valued at about $250 million. General Auto had stores in 12 states in the southwest, north, and central regions of the United States. Genuine also was opening about five outlets a year, most in major cities. To better supply them, it opened NAPA distribution centers in Dallas, Houston, and San Antonio in 1983, and Portland, Maine, in 1984.

A recession hit the United States in 1982 and hurt Genuine's supposedly recession-proof industrial parts business. The recession was severe enough to temporarily shut down some factories, and closed factories do not buy parts. As a result of its diversification, about 35 percent of Genuine's sales came from operations other than auto parts, up from 10 percent 10 years earlier.

NAPA was an increasingly important part of Genuine's business. NAPA's 72 distribution centers sold parts to 5,200 NAPA jobbers, who sold parts to local mechanics. Genuine owned 55 of the distribution centers, and 350 of the 5,200 jobbing sites. Genuine thus had 85 percent of NAPA's sales, although that accounted for only 5 percent of the nationwide market for replacement parts. About 85 percent of Genuine's 100,000 auto and truck parts bore the NAPA brand name. Genuine used its NAPA connection to give it leverage over the 5,200 NAPA jobbers. If a jobber began buying less than 85 percent or so of its parts from Genuine, the firm might open another NAPA shop in the same area. If jobbers kept Genuine happy, they would find little direct competition and excellent service. Genuine delivered parts overnight to most of its customers, enabling them to keep their inventories, and thus costs, low. Genuine began refurbishing its image in the mid-1980s, raising awareness of the NAPA brand name and redesigning its stores. Most of the firm's nearly 500 stores installed brighter lighting, updated the layout of sales floors, and added a blue-and-yellow color scheme that drew attention to the NAPA logo.

OVERCOMING CHALLENGES: 1985–89

Replacement part sales sagged in the mid-1980s, barely keeping pace with inflation. Car and truck sales had slumped in 1982 and 1983, meaning fewer cars needed parts several years later. Cars were being built better and generally started to need replacement parts after four years rather than three. Customers increasingly brought their cars back to their dealers for repairs, and the dealers got parts directly from the manufacturers. As Japanese cars steadily acquired U.S. market share, parts suppliers were slow to begin carrying them in sufficient numbers. Warm winters in 1988 and 1989 were partly to blame for the drop in sales as well because alternators, batteries, and other parts tended to fail during very cold weather. At the same time, Genuine's competition was heating up. Specialty shops such as Midas and Jiffy Lube were expanding rapidly, and retail chains were increasing their automotive operations.

To help compensate, Genuine tried to increase its efficiency and started a new marketing campaign. Genuine signed agreements with Midas, Montgomery Ward, and others to supply some of their auto parts. To make jobbers aware that it carried foreign parts, Genuine put out a catalog focusing on imported car parts. By 1990 most of the 6,000 retailers who bought parts from Genuine were connected by computer to one of the firm's 64 NAPA distribution warehouses. In addition to getting parts to jobbers quickly, Genuine used the computer system to keep track of who was selling how many parts and why.

Changes in the auto industry did have some benefits: If cars needed parts less often, the parts continued to increase in cost, with some costing twice what they had 20 years earlier. At the same time, Genuine's other businesses continued to grow at higher rates. Sales for the industrial group were $547 million in 1988, with profits of $35.7 million. Office product sales came to $450 million, with profits of $36.7 million.

CONTINUED GROWTH, MAJOR ACQUISITIONS: 1990–99

In late 1993 Genuine strengthened its industrial parts business by acquiring Berry Bearing Company for about $300 million worth of stock. Bearings were seen as a stable seller in a recessionary economy as firms delayed purchases of new equipment. Expansion into Mexico began in 1994 when Genuine formed a joint venture with Auto Todo, based in Puebla, Mexico, to distribute automotive replacement parts in that country. In 1995 NAPA entered into an agreement with Penske Corporation to become the exclusive parts supplier for more

than 850 Penske Auto Centers. That same year, S.P. Richards bolstered its operations through the acquisition of Horizon USA Data Supplies, Inc., a Reno, Nevada-based wholesaler of computer supplies.

Another development in the mid-1990s was the revamping of hundreds of NAPA stores, including the creation of superstores with about 8,000 square feet of space, in an effort to attract more do-it-yourselfers. Coinciding with this remodeling program, which continued into the late 1990s, was an advertising campaign emphasizing the same theme, that NAPA stores served more than just auto repair shops. By year-end 1996, there were 5,700 NAPA stores, 750 of which were owned by Genuine Parts. Revenues surpassed the $6 billion mark for the first time in 1997, the company's 70th year in operation.

The late 1990s featured a series of acquisitions as Genuine sought to increase its pace of growth and return to the double-digit annual increases in sales and earnings the company had enjoyed in earlier years. Perhaps most significantly, Genuine entered a new, and potentially higher growth, line of business through the July 1998 acquisition of EIS, Inc., a distributor of electrical and electronic materials, in a deal valued at about $180 million. Also based in Atlanta, EIS achieved $522.4 million in sales in 1999, its first full year as a subsidiary of Genuine.

In December 1998 Genuine spent about $231 million to buy the 80 percent of Montreal-based UAP Inc. that it did not already own. Since 1989 Genuine had held a minority stake in UAP, a distributor of auto and industrial parts with annual sales of $555 million. In January 1999 Genuine further expanded its auto parts group by acquiring another Atlanta-based firm, Johnson Industries, Inc. With annual revenues of $120 million, Johnson served new-car dealers and owners of large vehicle fleets, such as Federal Express.

Also in 1999, Genuine acquired Brittain Brothers, Inc., a NAPA distributor based in Oklahoma City that served more than 190 stores in Oklahoma, Missouri, Arkansas, and Texas. Meanwhile, S.P. Richards gained its first presence in Canada through the 1998 purchase of Norwestra Sales, Inc., which was based in Vancouver, British Columbia, and was expected to serve as a base for a Canada-wide operation. This spate of major deals enabled Genuine to post a 21 percent increase in net sales for 1999, to $7.98 billion. The late 1990s also saw Genuine Parts develop e-commerce capabilities in each of its four product groups.

Despite continued softness in the automotive aftermarket, Genuine managed to post net sales of $8.37 billion for 2000, marking 51 straight years of sales gains. Profits edged up as well, hitting $385.3 million, giving the company 40 consecutive years of profit improvement. Dividends also rose that year, the 45th consecutive year of dividend increases. With one of the best track records in American business, an increasingly diversified range of operations, and a more aggressive approach to growth, Genuine Parts entered the new millennium on solid ground.

SUCCESS IN THE NEW MILLENNIUM

While sales in 2001 slowed temporarily, Genuine enjoyed success during the early years of the 21st century. The company's Industrial Parts group, operating as Motion Industries, opened 27 new branches in 2001. That same year Coach and Motor Company of Detroit was acquired, and the company's S.P. Richards Company subsidiary expanded its foothold in Canada by opening a branch in Toronto. Sales and profits rebounded in 2002 and Genuine paid dividend increases for the 46th consecutive year.

During 2003, the company added NAPA Hawaii to its fold, which served 36 NAPA Auto Parts stores across the Hawaiian islands and Samoa. Thomas Gallagher was named CEO in 2004 and added chairman to his title the following year. Under new leadership, Genuine continued to prosper. The company reported record levels of sales and profits during the year. Genuine's Motion Industries and EIS units experienced significant growth that year, due in part to strong demand in the U.S. manufacturing sector. Sales increased by 11 percent and 13 percent, respectively.

In 2006 sales surpassed $10 billion for the first time in company history. The company's Industrial Parts and Electrical/Electronic Materials group continued to experience solid growth while the Automotive Parts Group experienced a downturn in sales due to rising gas prices and a slowdown in consumer spending. The company decided to sell off its Johnson Industries subsidiary at this time and completed the transaction in 2008.

The company continued its steady expansion during this time period by making strategic acquisitions. During 2005 Genuine purchased a 25 percent stake in Altrom Canada Corp. In 2008, Motion Industries bought Drago Supply Company, which sold safety, construction, welding, janitorial, and industrial supply products through eight locations in Texas, Arkansas, and Louisiana. It also acquired Mill Supply Corp. and Monroe Rubber and Plastic Supply. These three acquisitions added nearly $100 million to the company's annual revenues. Motion Industries continued its expansion in late 2009 with the purchase of BC Bearing

Group's North American assets, which included 53 branches in Western Canada.

Genuine began to feel the effects of the economic downturn in the United States during 2008; company sales fell by 9 percent in 2009 while net income fell by 16 percent over the previous year. As demand for industrial parts fell, Genuine's Motion Industries business was hit hard. Sales in that segment dropped by 18 percent. The Electrical/Electronic Materials segment's sales also fell dramatically, dropping by 26 percent over the previous year.

Despite the challenging economic times, Genuine remained financially strong with low debt levels. During 2009, the company made a total of six acquisitions that bolstered its Automotive and Industrial parts business. While a turnaround in its key markets was expected to be slow, CEO Gallagher was optimistic about the company's future. With its long-standing history of success and a solid strategy in place, Genuine appeared to be well positioned to face this economic downturn head on.

Scott M. Lewis
Updated, David E. Salamie; Christina M. Stansell

PRINCIPAL SUBSIDIARIES

Balkamp; Eis, Inc.; Eis Dominican Republic, LLC; Genuine Parts Finance Company; GPC Procurement Company; National Automotive Parts Association; Motion Industries, Inc.; Hub Tool & Supply, Inc.; S.P. Richards Company; S.P.R. Procurement Company; Shuster Corporation; Drago Supply Company; 1st Choice Auto Parts, Inc.; The Flowers Company; General Tool & Supply; Genuine Parts Holdings, Ulc (Canada); Genuine Parts Investment Company; Gpc Mexico, S.A. De C.V.; Eis De Mexico; Eis Holdings (Canada), Inc.; Motion Industries (Canada), Inc.; Motion–Mexico S. De Rl De CV; S. P. Richards Co. Canada, Inc.; Uap Inc. (Canada); Garanat Inc. (Canada); Uapro Inc. (Canada); United Auto Parts (Eastern) Ltd. (Canada); Services Financiers Uap Inc. (Canada); Gpc Global Sourcing Ltd. (China); Genuine Parts Sourcing (Shenzhen) Company Ltd. (China); Altrom Canada Corp.

PRINCIPAL OPERATING UNITS

Automotive Parts Group; Industrial Parts Group; Office Products Group; Electrical/Electronic Materials Group.

PRINCIPAL COMPETITORS

Advance Auto Parts Inc.; AutoZone Inc.; General Parts Inc.

FURTHER READING

Bond, Patti, "Genuine Parts to Diversify by Acquiring EIS in a $200 Million Deal," *Atlanta Journal*, May 22, 1998, p. F1.

———, "More Than Autos," *Barron's*, December 18, 2000, p. 34.

Cronkleton, Robert A., "New Concept Unveiled in NAPA Store," *Kansas City Star*, February 8, 1995, p. B3.

"Genuine Parts Company Announces Proposed Acquisition of NAPA Distributor," *Reuters Significant Developments*, September 3, 2003.

"Genuine Parts Company Reports Record Results for 2004," *Business Wire*, February 22, 2005.

Jelter, Jim, "Genuine Parts Profit Up 8%, Making Up for Slack in Autos," *Dow Jones Chinese Financial Wire*, July 19, 2007.

Kanell, Michael E., "Parts Firm Names CEO," *Atlanta Journal-Constitution*, August 17, 2004.

Lee-Young, Joanne, "Family-Run BC Bearing Sells North American Assets to Atlanta-Based Auto Parts Company," *Vancouver Sun*, December 22, 2009.

Luke, Robert, "Genuine Parts Growth Lag an Incentive for Changes," *Atlanta Constitution*, January 19, 1999, p. E1.

———, "Genuine Parts Makes Still Another Acquisition," *Atlanta Journal/Constitution*, October 31, 1998, p. H1.

———, "Genuine Parts Shops for Growth, Acquisition," *Atlanta Constitution*, October 30, 1998, p. E2.

"Motion Industries Acquires Port Arthur, Texas-Based Drago Supply," *Industrial Distribution*, October 1, 2008.

Gourmet Services, Inc.

Gourmet Services, Inc.

82 Piedmont Avenue N.E.
Atlanta, Georgia 30303-2518
U.S.A.
Telephone: (404) 876-5700
Web site: http://gourmetservicesinc.com

Private Company
Incorporated: 1975
Employees: 2,500
Sales: $182.5 million (2008 est.)
NAICS: 722310 Food Service Contractors

■ ■ ■

Privately held, Atlanta, Georgia-based Gourmet Services, Inc. (GSI), is the largest African American owned and operated foodservice management company in the United States. GSI offers dining programs to colleges and universities, the company's original focus, including such branded concepts as Carvel, Chick-fil-A, Domino's, McDonald's, Moe's, and Planet Smoothie. With an emphasis on historically black colleges and universities, GSI serves such institutions as Alabama State University, Bethune-Cookman University, Hampton University, and Winston-Salem State University. (Additionally at Hampton University, GSI operates a side venture, the Campus Couture boutique, which sells apparel and accessories.)

GSI's business and industry clients include CNN, New York Life, Time Warner/Turner, UPS, and Wachovia Bank. Other sectors served include government, correctional facilities, and public school systems. Over the

years GSI has provided catering services to the president of the United States and other prominent officeholders, as well as *Fortune* 500 companies, the Super Bowl, and the Olympic Games held in Atlanta in 1996. GSI also offers hotel management and vending services, including the Shop 24 Convenience Store concept that in addition to food items offers miscellaneous merchandise.

FOUNDER BORN: 1938

Gourmet Services was founded by its longtime chief executive officer and chairman, Nathaniel R. Goldston III. An African American, Goldston was born in 1938 in Omaha, Nebraska, where both of his parents were employed in the foodservice industry, his mother in the public school system and his father as the catering and banquet manager at local hotels and restaurants, including Omaha's luxurious Blackstone Hotel. During high school, Goldston went to work for his father as a busboy at the Blackstone, eventually becoming dining room captain. He also caddied at an area golf course where he once carried the clubs for famed financier Warren Buffett.

In the late 1950s Goldston enrolled at the University of Denver to study food management. Prior to his junior year, Goldston was informed that an anonymous donor had paid his tuition. Although he never confirmed the identity of his benefactor, he suspected that it was the Swanson family, who made their fortune in frozen foods and had befriended his father at the Blackstone. The gift made a significant impression on Goldston, and later he would give generously, personally and through foundations, to provide scholarships for deserving college students.

COMPANY PERSPECTIVES

We are a foodservice industry leader, serving a diverse clientele including school districts, colleges and universities, and corporations. We're proud to say that we've been in business for more than 30 years. Our longevity is due to our ability to build lasting relationships based on a simple formula of delivering high-quality products and superior service that add definitive value to, and exceed the expectations of, the clients we are fortunate enough to serve.

After graduating from college in 1962, Goldston was hired by Missouri-based Catering Management Inc. Over the next dozen years he worked his way up through the ranks to become a district manager, regional vice president, and senior vice president before he reached what he perceived as a race-related ceiling in his career. Convinced that he could never become company president, he decided in late 1974 to strike out on his own and start a foodservice business. It was hardly an ideal time to take such a gamble, given that it was the holiday season and his wife was pregnant.

Nevertheless, Goldston and two others, including Catering Management colleague Brenda Branch, formed GSI in 1975, setting up offices in Charlotte, North Carolina, to focus on fulfilling the foodservice needs of black colleges, a sector that was neglected by the industry. Goldston invested all of his life savings to start the company and was able to receive an advance on the first month's fees from the company's initial clients. By the end of 1975, GSI held contracts with six black colleges, resulting in $2.3 million in revenues for the year.

MOVE TO ATLANTA: 1976

On a business trip in 1976 Goldston was seated next to Atlanta Mayor Maynard Jackson on his flight. The mayor extolled the virtues of Atlanta and urged Goldston to relocate GSI to his city. Not only had Atlanta become a good place for African American businessmen, it was home to several major black colleges, and was well positioned as a transportation hub. The argument was compelling and later in the year Goldston moved GSI to Atlanta.

The move to Atlanta proved to be a wise long-term decision, but in the early 1980s growth stalled and GSI struggled through a three-year period, described by Goldston as the "indigestion years." Although earnings

dwindled and GSI was unable to obtain local funding, the company managed to stay in business. By mid-decade GSI had shored up its finances. In 1985 it employed 1,000 people and was generating about $15 million in annual revenues, drawn from 19 accounts that included colleges as well as corporate clients such as Northwestern Bell Telephone Company and Atlanta-based Coca-Cola Bottling Company. All told, GSI was doing business in 17 states and the Virgin Islands.

GSI was also involved in very profitable joint ventures with white-run companies, including a partnership to serve the New Orleans airport and another to serve Atlanta's city-run golf courses. Through another partnership GSI became involved in the correctional facilities sector, winning contracts with the Fulton and DeKalb County jail systems in Georgia. GSI's partners provided the capital and track record to land the contracts. "No way would we have done it by ourselves," Goldston told the *Wall Street Journal*. In June 1988 *Black Enterprise* reported GSI's gross sales at $21.3 million, earning the company the No. 33 ranking of the top 100 African American owned businesses, one of only six in Georgia to hold that distinction.

IRS AUDITS COMPANY

Although joint venture partners played an important role in GSI's success, one of them sullied the company's reputation by association in the second half of the 1980s and threatened the financial stability GSI had worked so hard to achieve. The partner was LeCroy Cafeterias, which created L&G Catering Services Inc. with GSI to serve correctional facilities. In 1985 L&G won a foodservice contract with the DeKalb County jail system, this despite being the fifth-highest of the six bidders. The contract was then renewed without bid through the end of 1988, arousing suspicion and eventually leading to a federal extortion indictment for Jack T. LeCroy, owner of LeCroy Cafeterias, who was charged with making payoffs to the Fulton County sheriff and a loan to the DeKalb County sheriff.

GSI also came under suspicion as a result, and had to contend with an Internal Revenue Service audit. GSI's clients, in particular the historically black colleges and universities, remained loyal. "They believed in us and didn't turn their backs on us when it would have been easy for them to do so," Goldston recalled in an interview with the *Atlanta Journal-Constitution*. "I'm indebted to HBCUs for that."

In the 1990s Goldston was joined by his son, Nathaniel R. Goldston, who went by his middle name, Russell. He had worked for his father since the age of 12, minus any salary, washing dishes and emptying trash

```
┌─────────────────────────────────────────┐
│                                         │
│            KEY DATES                     │
│              ───■───                     │
│  ┌───────────────────────────────────┐  │
│  1975:  Company is founded in Charlotte, North │
│         Carolina.                        │
│  1976:  Headquarters are moved to Atlanta, Georgia. │
│  1985:  Company wins correctional facility contract │
│         through a joint venture partnership. │
│  1999:  Joint venture wins Atlanta Public Schools │
│         contract.                        │
│  2007:  Vending services added.          │
│                                         │
└─────────────────────────────────────────┘
```

cans during the summer. He studied at the hotel management school at Cornell University, graduating in 1989. He then went to work for GSI, learning the operation from a number of perspectives. In 1992, *Black Enterprise* reported that he was then working as the foodservice director at Morehouse College to learn the operations aspect of the company.

Russell Goldston's wife, Leslie, a well-trained chef, was also employed by GSI, serving as director of catering in the Atlanta region. Nathaniel Goldston, 53 at the time of the *Black Enterprise* report, indicated a desire to retire in about five years. That step was not taken, however, as his son eventually left the company and Nathaniel Goldston remained CEO through the rest of the 1990s and the first decade of the new century. Another of his children, daughter Kim Goldston-Martin, would also go to work for GSI in the marketing department in 1996 and later became senior vice president of corporate development.

ATLANTA SCHOOL CONTRACT
WON: 1999

By the end of the 1990s GSI was generating more than $40 million a year in revenues, much of which was provided by 17 historically black colleges and universities. A key partner in the company's success was Aramark Corporation, a giant foodservice company based in Philadelphia, Pennsylvania. Together the two companies won foodservice contracts at Atlanta-area college, health care, and correctional facilities. They also became involved in the public school sector in the late 1990s, forming a joint venture called Aramark-Gourmet Service Inc. In 1999 this unit made the winning bid to manage Atlanta's $23 million food service program, covering 57,000 students in 150 schools and a pair of high school day care centers. In the fall of 2001, Aramark-Gourmet won a contract to serve the Detroit public school system and its 163,000 students in 268 schools.

The Atlanta school contract proved nettlesome, however. Rather than fully privatize the school food program, the city merely outsourced the program's management. As a result, the cafeteria workers remained employees of Atlanta Public Schools and Aramark-Gourmet had to contend with managing a troubled program without the ability to hire or fire. Moreover, individual cafeterias retained the right to create their own menus and order their own food, hardly a cost-effective way to run the program. In 2002, an audit concluded that Aramark-Gourmet lost $1.27 for every meal served. The company was also criticized for the quality of the meals and the poor management of government surplus foods, a large amount of which had to be discarded. The company won several annual extensions on the contract and believed it was on the verge of turning around the program when it was outbid for the contract for the 2004 school year.

According to trade publication *Food Management*, GSI generated an estimated $146 million in revenues in 2002, earning the company the No. 12 ranking in the magazine's Top 50 foodservice contractors. (Aramark, in contrast, held the top spot with $5.7 billion in sales volume.) GSI brought in a new president in 2003 to take charge of the day-to-day running of the business, although Goldston remained CEO and chairman. William Simms, an executive with an insurance and market planning background, was hired. According to *Food Management*, he introduced some new menu concepts, including Planet Smoothie, Dietz & Watson Sandwich Factory, and Zero Subs, which helped to drive revenues to $169 million in 2003, allowing the company to reach No. 10 on the *Black Enterprise* Top 50.

FIRST HOTEL MANAGEMENT
CONTRACT: 2007

As the decade unfolded, GSI continued to pursue new opportunities. In 2005 it worked with Morehouse School of Medicine to introduce new healthful and organic-based menus, and also teamed up with Preferred Meal Systems of Illinois to create a line of pre-plated meals for elementary school students. In 2007 a new president was installed, Raymond J. McClendon, who possessed more than 30 years of consulting experience in a variety of industries. In that same year, GSI signed a five-year lease to manage its first hotel operation, the St. James Hotel in Selma, Alabama. Also in 2007 GSI forged a relationship with Universal Vending Services to incorporate vending services into its managed units. The company also made inroads with corporate accounts during this period, adding such new clients as CNN, UPS, and Wachovia.

Revenues totaled $171 million in 2007, and increased to $182.5 million in 2008. Due to a struggling economy, many people were eschewing four-year colleges and universities for community colleges. GSI followed the market, strengthening its community college business. Because much of the student population was older, the company offered pre-plated entrees and a greater variety of fare to cater to their tastes. GSI also sought diversification, and in the fall of 2008 introduced the Campus Couture at Hampton University, offering men and women's clothing, jewelry, handbags, belts, and other accessories. It was that willingness and ability to adapt to changing conditions that promised to keep GSI prosperous in the years to come.

Ed Dinger

PRINCIPAL OPERATING UNITS

Colleges and Universities; Business and Industry; K-12 School Support; Correctional Facilities.

PRINCIPAL COMPETITORS

AVI Food Systems, Inc.; Centerplate; Sodexo, Inc.

FURTHER READING

Carter, Rochelle, "School Watch: Food Company Still Not Fulfilling Cafeteria Contract," *Atlanta Journal-Constitution,* November 23, 2000, p. JD4.

Coleman, Seth, "Food Service Entrepreneur Savors His Success," *Atlanta Journal-Constitution,* July 9, 1999, p. JJ3.

Corvette, David, and Gail Epstein, "Feds Reportedly Investigating Fulton Sheriff," *Atlanta Journal-Constitution,* September 10, 1988, p. A1.

"Dynasties. (Black Executives)," *Black Enterprise,* June 1992.

Epstein, Gail, "Food Vendor Lent Money to DeKalb Sheriff," *Atlanta Journal-Constitution,* March 1, 1990, p. A1.

"Food Management's Top 50 Management Companies," *Food Management,* September 2007.

Grossman, Laurie M., "Black Entrepreneurship (A Special Report)," *Wall Street Journal,* April 3, 1992.

Kimbrough, Ann Wead, "10 Red-Hot Years Have Failed to Sate the Gourmet Appetite for Success," *Atlanta Journal-Constitution,* February 18, 1985, p. E17.

"Partners in Growth," *Fortune,* April 30, 2007.

Reid, S. A., "A Fortune, Inspiration to Share," *Atlanta Journal-Constitution,* December 17, 2006, p. D1.

Harrah's Entertainment, Inc.

One Caesars Palace Drive
Las Vegas, Nevada 89109
U.S.A.
Telephone: (702) 407-6000
Fax: (702) 407-6037
Web site: http://www.harrahs.com

Private Company
Incorporated: 1971 as Harrah's
Employees: 80,000
Sales: $8.907 billion (2009 est.)
NAICS: 713210 Casinos; 721120 Casino Hotels

■ ■ ■

Tracing its roots to a small Reno, Nevada, bingo parlor, Harrah's Entertainment, Inc., is one of the largest providers of casino entertainment in the world. Operating primarily under the Harrah's, Caesars, and Horseshoe brands in the United States, Harrah's also manages casinos on Indian reservations and owns the London Clubs International collection of casinos and the World Series of Poker. Its properties include land-based casinos, riverboat and dockside casinos, casino clubs, and racetracks.

Harrah's facilities consist of three million square feet of gaming space, some 39,000 hotel rooms, as well as convention, restaurant, and non-gaming entertainment venues. At the end of 2008, Harrah's owned or managed 53 casinos in six countries: the United States, Canada, the United Kingdom, South Africa, Egypt, and Uruguay. Most of its business is conducted through its wholly owned subsidiary, Harrah's Operating Company, Inc.

CALIFORNIA ORIGINS

William Fisk Harrah was the son of a Venice, California, lawyer and real estate operator who also had served as mayor of that seaside community. The senior Harrah went bankrupt during the Great Depression and was left with only one asset: a leased building on the Venice pier jutting into the Pacific Ocean. There he operated a nickel-and-dime game of dubious legality, loosely based on bingo, in which players sat in a circle and rolled marbles toward a number. After Bill Harrah was caught cheating on a college chemistry exam in 1930, he went to work running the game and soon concluded he could do better than his father, who sold it to him for $500. He got rid of the shills his father had hired, refurbished the premises, and grossed as much as $50,000 a year.

In the wake of a state crackdown on gambling, Harrah moved in 1937 to Reno, Nevada, where gambling had been legalized six years earlier. There he bought a bingo parlor that was poorly located and failed in three months. In 1939 he reopened in the two-block gambling heart of Reno. Three years later he opened a casino, equipping it with a blackjack table, a craps table, and 20 slot machines.

The enterprise flourished during the free-spending World War II years, and in 1946 Harrah's Club opened in quarters that had been expanded by the purchase of neighboring properties. Harrah added roulette to the card and dice tables and served liquor to the players. His spotlessly clean, glass-fronted, plush-carpeted casino was a contrast to the rough frontier-type betting parlors of the time and was the first to be lined with one-way mirrors to oversee the dealers and cashiers handling the chips and cash. By 1948 the gross annual revenue of Harrah's Club was more than $1.5 million and its net profit, after taxes, was about $100,000.

RENO AND LAKE TAHOE CASINO-HOTELS: 1955–70

In 1955 Harrah bought a dingy casino housed in a Quonset hut on the southern shore of Lake Tahoe, just east of the California state line, for $500,000. He built a false front around it and reopened it as Harrah's Tahoe. Four years later he relocated the casino across the highway, in the world's largest single structure devoted to gambling at that time. The new casino was a highly integrated operation that included a 10-acre parking lot and an 850-seat theater-restaurant featuring star entertainers.

Blizzards habitually buried the area each winter, but Harrah assembled a fleet of snowplows to clear the mountain roads, which were doubled in width at his own expense. Not averse to the low-budget trade, he established a vast bus network to bring in customers from 31 California cities and opened a child-care center for gambling parents to leave their offspring. The Lake Tahoe casino was said to have turned a profit of more than $1 million in its first year.

The annual gross from Harrah's two casinos was estimated at $40 million in 1961, and four years later William Harrah was described as the world's largest gambling operator. With 2,500 employees, he was the largest employer in Nevada except for the Atomic Energy Commission. A lover of fast cars, he established Rolls Royce, Ferrari, and Jeep dealerships, and assembled the world's largest automobile collection, which the

Internal Revenue Service allowed him to write off as a business expense.

With both his casinos booming, Harrah next turned to the hotel business. He constructed the highest building in Reno, a 24-story hotel across the street from his casino. Completed in 1968, it cost about $7 million. Next he erected a luxurious 18-story hotel that opened in 1973 on his Lake Tahoe property. Every room included a view of the lake and two marble-finished bathrooms.

PUBLIC COMPANY: 1971–79

In part to finance these ventures and to support his lifestyle (he was married six times), Harrah took his company public in 1971, raising $4 million after taxes and expenses by offering 13 percent of the stock at $16 per share. No Wall Street firm would handle the offering, but it was oversubscribed, and within a year the stock had soared to $71 per share. Overcoming the financial sector's misgivings about the gambling industry, Harrah's in 1973 became the first casino company to be listed on the New York Stock Exchange.

Harrah's net sales increased from $77.9 million in 1970 to $195.6 million in 1979, and net income grew from a low of $4.3 million in 1971 to a record $16.9 million in 1978. One securities analyst called Harrah's the most tightly controlled and best-managed casino company in the world. Its two casinos, operating around-the-clock every day of the year, accounted for about 10 percent of Nevada's gambling volume. Games of chance included baccarat, poker, and keno, as well as the roulette, blackjack, craps, and bingo tables, and 3,733 slot machines. The 1,600 seats at the theater-restaurants in Reno and Lake Tahoe were filled nearly every night. The two hotels enjoyed a 92 percent occupancy rate. Nearly 250,000 customers came every year by bus.

By the late 1970s, however, Harrah's was beginning to encounter difficulties from the opening of competing hotel-casinos in Reno and environmental constraints on further development in the Lake Tahoe area. The company scrapped plans to open a new Reno hotel-casino just across the street from the existing one and a combination hotel-casino and theme park just outside the city. When Harrah died in 1978, he left his heirs almost six million shares of stock in his company, but no cash to pay estate taxes of $35 million or a $13 million debt to a Reno bank.

At this point a buyer for Harrah's emerged in the form of family-oriented Holiday Inns, Inc., a Memphis-based company previously run by pious Baptists opposed to gambling. Even before Harrah's death,

KEY DATES

1937: William Harrah moves his casino operations from California to Reno, Nevada.

1946: Harrah's Club opens, the first casino in the country to use one-way mirrors to oversee dealers.

1971: Harrah's goes public, offering 13 percent of the stock at $16 per share.

1973: Harrah's becomes first casino company to be listed on the New York Stock Exchange.

1980: Holiday Inns, Inc., acquires Harrah's for $310 million; Harrah's Marina Hotel Casino opens in Atlantic City.

1989: The holding company Promus is created, which becomes the parent firm of Harrah's.

1993: Harrah's establishes riverboat casinos division to take advantage of new forms of legalized gambling.

1995: Promus is divided into two separate public corporations; the casino division becomes Harrah's Entertainment, Inc.

2005: Harrah's buys Caesars Entertainment.

2008: Harrah's is acquired by joint venture of Apollo Management and TPG Capital and taken private.

however, Holiday Inns executive Michael Rose was seeking his participation in a joint venture in Atlantic City, New Jersey, where gambling had been legalized in 1977. In 1979 the company bought a stake in a casino adjacent to the Holiday Inn on the Las Vegas Strip. It was renamed Holiday Casino. Holiday Inns also announced plans to build two casino-hotels in Atlantic City.

HOLIDAY INNS SUBSIDIARY: 1980–90

In February 1980 Holiday Inns acquired Harrah's, which was still about 70 percent owned by William Harrah's estate, for $310 million in cash and notes. Rose, who became chief executive officer of Holiday Inns the next year, sold most of Harrah's 1,400 automobiles for $100 million and gave the rest to a Reno museum.

Then a wholly owned subsidiary of Holiday Inns, Harrah's became the operator of a casino opened in 1980 on marshland a mile and a half north of Atlantic

City's boardwalk and named Harrah's Marina Hotel Casino. It had 506 guest rooms, a casino with capacity for 6,300 patrons, and an array of other spaces, including restaurants and bars, a Broadway-sized theater, conference and meeting rooms, a high-rise garage for 2,100 cars, and an entertainment center for children and teenagers. A 264-suite tower was added later. Harrah's Marina (later renamed Harrah's Atlantic City) proved to be consistently profitable. In 1985, for example, the facility earned $48.8 million before taxes, by far the best performance of any of the 11 Atlantic City casinos at that time.

In 1984 Harrah's, in partnership with real estate developer Donald J. Trump, opened the tallest building on the Atlantic City boardwalk to date, the 39-story Harrah's Trump Plaza hotel and casino. The joint venture, built by the Trump organization on Trump land but with Harrah's money, collapsed in acrimony when the competing Trump's Castle made its debut the following year directly across the street from Harrah's Marina. In 1986 Trump bought Harrah's half-share in Trump Plaza (Harrah's name had been removed) for $59.1 million.

Meanwhile, Harrah's continued to pursue developments in the west. Harrah's opened Bill's Lake Tahoe Casino in 1987 on a 2.1-acre site adjacent to Harrah's Lake Tahoe. The following year Harrah's Laughlin was opened in Laughlin, Nevada, on a natural cove on the Colorado River, with 464 hotel rooms and 26,500 square feet of casino space. Late in 1988 a second Laughlin hotel tower was completed.

In 1989 Holiday Corp., formerly Holiday Inns, became the Promus Cos., Inc. The following year Rose sold the Holiday Inns hotel chain to Bass PLC of Great Britain for $2.23 billion. Holiday shares were then converted, on a one-for-one basis, to Promus shares, with Holiday's Embassy Suites, Hampton Inn, and Homewood Suites hotel divisions remaining as Promus units. Harrah's continued to thrive as the company's casino-entertainment division.

GEOGRAPHIC DIVERSIFICATION: 1991–99

In 1991 Philip Satre was named president and COO for Promus. Satre came to work for Bill Harrah as an attorney in 1980, handling his corporate account. Satre's vision for the growth of Harrah's was based on expanding the presence of gaming beyond Nevada and Atlantic City. Casino gambling had been legal only in Nevada and New Jersey until 1989, but between 1989 and 1996 it was legalized in some form in 21 additional states.

In 1993 Harrah's established a new division for riverboat casinos and opened the first of these facilities along the Illinois River in Joliet, Illinois. A second Joliet floating casino opened the following year. During this period Harrah's also established riverboat casinos along the Mississippi River in Vicksburg and Tunica, Mississippi; the Red River at Shreveport, Louisiana; and the Missouri River in North Kansas City, Missouri. A second Tunica riverboat opened in 1996.

In 1992 Harrah's announced the creation of a new division for operating casinos on Indian lands. In 1988 Congress had passed a law legalizing games of chance on Indian reservations in any state where such games were allowed for churches, temples, and veterans and other groups. By August 1993 no fewer than 73 tribes in 19 states were offering or would soon be offering full-scale casino gambling. Harrah's Ak-Chin, near Phoenix, opened in December 1994. A year later the Upper Skagit Indians and Harrah's opened a casino entertainment complex about 70 miles north of Seattle.

In 1995 the Promus Cos. divided into two separate corporations, with the casino division becoming Harrah's Entertainment, Inc., and the hotel division Promus Hotels Corp. Rose remained chairman of both companies and Satre continued as president and CEO of Harrah's. By the end of February 1996, Harrah's Entertainment offered 16 casinos with 592,500 square feet of space, 16,377 slot machines, 898 table games, 63 restaurants, and 21,905 parking spaces. There were 5,736 hotel rooms at the end of 1995. Gaming volume came to $20.6 billion that year, compared with $8.5 billion in 1991.

The riverboat division was Harrah's most lucrative in 1995, accounting for 43 percent of its $354 million operating profit, followed by Atlantic City (22 percent), Southern Nevada (18 percent), and Northern Nevada (16 percent). Of Harrah's $1.55 billion in revenues that year, the riverboat operations accounted for 38 percent, followed by Atlantic City (22 percent), Northern Nevada (20 percent), and Southern Nevada (19 percent). Net income was $78.8 million.

Over the next few years, Las Vegas saw an unprecedented growth in billion-dollar destination properties. Gaming companies built opulent, themed mega-casinos such as the Venetian, Mandalay Bay, Monte Carlo, and Bellagio, which opened to rave reviews. Instead of expending billions to build something new, Harrah's continued to concentrate on a buyout formula. In 1998 Harrah's bought Showboat, Inc., for $1.2 billion in stock and debt. It also acquired Sam's Town, a struggling casino in Missouri. Then in 1999 Harrah's and the Rio Hotel and Casino merged, allowing Harrah's to align itself with one of the first large destination properties in Las Vegas.

BRAND RECOGNITION AND DATA-DRIVEN MARKETING

With the acquisition of these properties and the continued profitable partnerships with Indian gaming casinos scattered across the country, Harrah's became the first nationwide casino business. It also developed what no other gaming company had before: brand recognition. A key marketing tool was the Harrah's Gold Card.

Cards were given to the millions of people who played at one of the casinos or had stayed at a Harrah's property. In addition to enabling the company to follow trends in play and the popularity of certain games, the Gold Card was used to gather information on guests for marketing purposes and to reward them based on volume of play.

Building on the success of its Gold Card program, in 1997 Harrah's launched Total Gold, good at any Harrah's property. This nationwide brand loyalty program allowed gamblers to earn points for playing the slots at smaller facilities, such as its riverboat casinos. Members could then redeem these points for cash or discounts on food and lodging at Harrah's more well-known, larger properties, such as those in Las Vegas and Atlantic City. The system also offered a huge amount of data about Harrah's customers to anyone who would analyze it

The man who would take advantage of that data was Gary Loveman. A professor at Harvard Business School, Loveman first worked for Harrah's in 1997 as a consultant. He joined the company in 1998 as chief operating officer, taking a sabbatical from Harvard. His charge, as he explained in a 2003 *Harvard Business Journal* article, was "to change Harrah's from an operations-driven company that viewed each casino as a stand-alone business into a marketing-driven company that built loyalty to all Harrah's properties."

Loveman began analyzing the information in the program's database and conducted surveys and focus groups. He quickly discovered that cardholders were spending only 36 percent of their gambling budget at Harrah's. The data also showed that just over a quarter of the gamblers visiting Harrah's accounted for 82 percent of revenues. These moneymakers, it turned out, were not the high rollers targeted by Harrah's and its competitors. Rather, they were middle-aged and older adults who enjoyed playing the slots and had the time and money to do so.

Based on these data, Loveman set out to design a marketing program that would attract those former teachers, machinists, and doctors, and keep them playing at Harrah's. Also aiding Harrah's brand recognition campaign was the 1999 decision by the U.S. Supreme Court to lift a ban on gambling advertising that featured people inside casinos. After the ruling, Harrah's aired two ads in nine cities showing the joys of playing slot machines. The spots ended with the tagline, "You know you gotta get to Harrah's, oh yeah."

CONTINUED GROWTH AND GREATER PROFITABILITY: 2000–04

By 2000 Harrah's was operating 21 casinos in 17 U.S. markets. Moreover, half of the U.S. population lived within a three-hour drive of a Harrah's owned or managed property. In an industry that many characterized as mature, Harrah's continued to see increases in revenues. Company-wide revenues grew 15 percent in 2000, to $3.5 billion.

That same year, Harrah's introduced Total Rewards, its new loyalty program. This expanded program offered three levels of rewards, based on how much a member played. Each level was awarded certain benefits, but those for the higher Platinum and Diamond tiers were progressively greater. The new system solved the three problems the data had identified: The program was different from those offered by other casinos, rewards were consistent across the different Harrah's properties, and there were incentives for cardholders to do all their gambling at Harrah's.

In 2002 Loveman was named president. When Phil Satre announced his retirement the following year, Loveman was appointed CEO. That year, the company brought in about 90 percent of its $4.3 billion in revenue through its 41,000 slot machines and 1,100 table games. This was a much higher percentage than its competitors, who depended more on hotel rooms, show tickets, and restaurants for their sales. According to a *Fortune* article in March 2004, Harrah's was second to Caesars in sales, but generated about six times Caesars' $46 million in profit.

The company continued to expand during the first half of the decade, primarily through acquisitions. In 2000 it purchased Players International, followed in 2001 by the purchase of Harveys Casino Resorts. Its Joliet, Illinois, riverboat was replaced with a huge barge containing a more Las Vegas-like casino. In 2002 Harrah's became the full owner of Harrah's New Orleans Casino and added the $100 million Rincon Casino near San Diego to its collection of properties operated for Indian tribes. In 2004 the company acquired Horseshoe Gaming Holding Co. Although it sold the Horseshoe Casino in 2005, it retained the Horseshoe brand and the World Series of Poker.

During this same period, private-equity firms became more active as players in various casino deals. Colony Capital, for example, bought four of the properties spun off from Harrah's merger with Caesars. One reason for the interest was the rich flow of cash from the casinos. More critical was the growing understanding that a firm's many limited partners did not need to be vetted and licensed by the various states in order for the firm to run gaming operations.

MAJOR CHANGES

In 2005 Harrah's acquired Caesars Entertainment for $9.3 billion in cash and stock in the largest merger in the history of the industry to date. Caesars was the 1998 spin-off of Hilton Hotel's casino arm. At the time of the purchase, Caesars had annual revenues of $4.5 billion compared to Harrah's $4.4 billion.

The acquisition gave Harrah's a greater presence in Las Vegas with a total of seven properties on the Strip. These included Caesars Palace, as well as Bally's, the Flamingo, and Paris Las Vegas. The deal also expanded Harrah's customer database from 25 million to 40 million. That number then included the high rollers from Caesars, a customer demographic not associated with Harrah's. The big benefit for Harrah's was the potential to improve the financial performance of Caesars by integrating the Total Rewards program and other information technology systems throughout the facilities.

Harrah's also expanded along the Mississippi River. Following the destruction of casinos by Hurricane Katrina in 2005, states passed laws allowing casino owners to build more and larger facilities. Harrah's also increased its presence in the international arena. The company announced plans for projects in the Bahamas, Spain, and Slovenia, although for various reasons none was completed. In 2006 it purchased London Clubs International plc. A year later it bought Macau Orient Golf.

In October 2006 Harrah's received and accepted a private buyout offer from Hamlet Holdings, a joint venture of private-equity firms Apollo Management and TPG Capital. The purchase was completed in January 28, 2008, at a price of $30.7 billion. The new owner then took Harrah's Entertainment, Inc., private. Three months later, Harrah's announced it would change the company name to Caesars Entertainment Corp. Later in 2008 Harrah's announced it was delaying the name change because of the slowing economy.

Harrah's was operating under a huge debt, taken on by the owners to finance the buyout. According to a May 4, 2009, *BusinessWeek* article, the company's annual interest payment was $2.1 billion. During 2008, Apollo and TPG wrote down their holdings by over 25 percent. The company also initiated cost cuts that ranged from cutting managers' pay, to changing snacks in the VIP lounges in the casinos, and stopping construction projects. During 2009, bondholders agreed three times to forgive some debt, exchanging billions of dollars in debt for lesser amounts in new, longer-term notes.

The recession was felt immediately in the gaming industry. In Las Vegas, convention business dropped more than 25 percent during 2009 and gambling revenue in Atlantic City fell move than 10 percent. For the year, the company's revenues declined 12 percent. Harrah's pulled back on various expansion plans as revenues from its casinos and hotels dropped and it worked to reduce its debt load. Those plans, including the name change, appeared to be only on hold. Late in 2009, Harrah's announced the appointment of a new president of strategy and development. Early in 2010 Harrah's bought the mortgage of the Planet Hollywood Resort and Casino on the Las Vegas Strip. The huge casino company indicated it would look to overseas markets for growth. It remained to be seen if this bet would pay off in the years to come.

Robert Halasz
Updated, Suzanne L. Rowe; Ellen D. Wernick

PRINCIPAL SUBSIDIARIES

Harrah's Operating Co., Inc.

PRINCIPAL COMPETITORS

Boyd Gaming Corporation; Las Vegas Sands Inc.; MGM Mirage; Wynn Resorts Ltd.

FURTHER READING

Audi, Tamara, Peter Lattman, and Jeff McCracken, "Harrah's Changes Its Game," *Wall Street Journal*, October 27, 2008, pp. C1, C5.

Bush, Michael, "Why Harrah's Loyalty Effort Is Industry's Gold Standard," *Advertising Age*, October 5, 2009, p. 8.

"Diamonds in the Data Mine," *Harvard Business Review*, May 2003, p. 109.

Fitch, Stephane, "Stacking the Deck," *Forbes*, July 5, 2004, pp. 132–34.

Getmanikow, George, "Holiday Inns Discards Family Image for Stake in Gambling Industry," *Wall Street Journal*, January 11, 1980, pp. 1, 31.

Illia, Tony, "Personalities Motivate Harrah's Chief," *Las Vegas Business Press*, September 2, 2002, p. 12.

Johnston, David, *Temples of Chance*, New York: Doubleday, 1992.

Knightly, Arnold M., "State of Harrah's," *Las Vegas Business Press*, June 15, 2009, pp. P6–P8.

Land, Barbara, and Myrick Land, *A Short History of Reno*, Reno and Las Vegas: University of Nevada Press, 1995.

"The Legacy of William Harrah," *Harrah's People*, Spring 1995, pp. 4–11.

Loveman, Gary, "Diamonds in the Data Mine," *Harvard Business Review*, May 2003, pp. 109–13.

Mandel, Leon, and William Fisk, *Harrah*, New York: Doubleday, 1982.

McDowell, Edwin, "Promus Proposes to Divide Its Units into Two Companies," *New York Times*, January 31, 1995, pp. D1, D7.

Palmeri, Christopher, "Take a Haircut Now, Avoid Bankruptcy?" *BusinessWeek*, May 4, 2009, p. 27.

Pogash, Carol, "From Harvard Yard to Vegas Strip," *Forbes*, October 7, 2002, pp. 48–52.

Schlosser, Julie, "Teacher's Bet," *Fortune*, March 8, 2004, pp. 158–64.

Indian Oil Corporation Ltd.

———————————•———————————

3079/3, J B Tito Marg
Sadiq Nagar
New Delhi, 11004-9
India
Telephone: (91 11) 2626-0000
Web site: http://www.iocl.com

Public Company
Incorporated: 1964
Employees: 33,000
Sales: INR 2.4 trillion ($46 billion) (2009)
Stock Exchanges: Bombay
Ticker Symbol: 530965
NAICS: 324110 Petroleum Refineries; 324191 Petroleum Lubricating Oil and Grease Manu-facturing

■ ■ ■

The Indian Oil Corporation Ltd. is the largest company in India in terms of sales and is the nation's leading company in the *Fortune* Global 500 listing. During the early 2010s the company accounted for approximately 50 percent of petroleum consumption in India, where it distributed products via approximately 35,000 different locations. Indian Oil's operations include 89 Indane liquified petroleum gas (LPG) bottling plants, 101 aviation fuel stations, and 167 bulk storage terminals and depots.

ORIGINS

Indian Oil owes its origins to the Indian government's conflicts with foreign-owned oil companies in the period immediately following India's independence in 1947. The leaders of the newly independent state found that much of the country's oil industry was effectively in the hands of a private monopoly led by a combination of British-owned oil companies Burmah and Shell and U.S. companies Standard-Vacuum and Caltex.

An indigenous Indian industry barely existed. During the 1930s a small number of Indian oil traders had managed to trade outside the international cartel. They imported motor spirit, diesel, and kerosene, mainly from the Soviet Union, at less than world market prices. Supplies were irregular, and they lacked marketing networks that could effectively compete with the multinationals.

Burmah-Shell entered into price wars against these independents, causing protests in the national press, which demanded government-set minimum and maximum prices for kerosene (a basic cooking and lighting requirement for India's people) and motor spirit. No action was taken, but some of the independents managed to survive until World War II, when they were taken over by the colonial government for wartime purposes.

During the war, the supply of petroleum products in India was regulated by a committee in London. Within India, a committee under the chairmanship of the general manager of Burmah-Shell and composed of oil company representatives pooled the supply and worked out a set price. Prices were regulated by the government, and the government coordinated the supply of oil in accordance with defense policy.

THE INDIAN OIL INDUSTRY EVOLVES

Wartime rationing lasted until 1950, and a shortage of oil products continued until well after independence. The government's 1948 Industrial Policy Resolution declared the oil industry to be an area of the economy that should be reserved for state ownership and control, stipulating that all new units should be government-owned unless specifically authorized. India, however, remained effectively tied to a colonial supply system. Oil could be afforded only if imported from a country in the sterling area rather than from countries where it had to be paid for in dollars. In 1949 India asked the oil companies of Britain and the United States to offer advice on a refinery project to make the country more self-sufficient in oil. The joint technical committee advised against the project and said it could be run only at a considerable loss.

The oil companies were prepared to consider building two refineries, but only if these refineries were allowed to sell products at a price 10 percent above world parity price. The government refused, but within two years an event in the Persian Gulf caused the companies to change their minds and build the refineries. The companies had lost their huge refinery at Abadan in Iran to Prime Minister Mussadegh's nationalization decree and were unable to supply India's petroleum needs from a sterling-area country. With the severe foreign exchange problems created, the foreign companies feared new Iranian competition within India. Even more important, the government began to discuss setting up a refinery by itself.

Between 1954 and 1957 two refineries were built by Burmah-Shell and Standard-Vacuum at Bombay, and another was built at Vizagapatnam by Caltex. During the same period the companies found themselves in increasing conflict with the government, which came into disagreement with Burmah Oil over the Nahor-

katiya oil field shortly after its discovery in 1953. It refused Burmah the right to refine or market this oil and insisted on joint ownership in crude production. Burmah then temporarily suspended all exploration activities in India.

Shortly afterward, the government accused the companies of charging excessive prices for importing oil. The companies also refused to refine Soviet oil that the government had secured on very favorable terms. The government was impatient with the companies' reluctance to expand refining capacity or train sufficient Indian personnel. In 1958 the government formed its own refinery company, Indian Refineries Ltd. With Soviet and Romanian assistance, the company was able to build its own refineries at Noonmati, Barauni, and Koyali. Foreign companies were told that they would not be allowed to build any new refineries unless they agreed to a majority shareholding by the Indian government.

In 1959 the Indian Oil Company was founded as a statutory body. At first, its objective was to supply oil products to Indian state enterprise. Then it was made responsible for the sale of the products of state refineries. After a 1961 price war with the foreign companies, it emerged as the nation's major marketing body for the export and import of oil and gas.

Growing Soviet imports led the foreign companies to respond with a price war in August 1961. At this time, Indian Oil had no retail outlets and could sell only to bulk consumers. The oil companies undercut Indian Oil's prices and left it with storage problems. Indian Oil then offered even lower prices. The foreign companies were the ultimate losers because the government was persuaded that a policy of allowing Indian Oil dominance in the market was correct. This policy allowed Indian Oil the market share of the output of all refineries that were partly or wholly owned by the government. Foreign oil companies would only be allowed such market share as equaled their share of refinery capacity.

INDIAN OIL CORPORATION IS FORMED

In September 1964 Indian Refineries Ltd. and the Indian Oil Company were merged to form the Indian Oil Corporation. The government announced that all future refinery partnerships would be required to sell their products through Indian Oil. It was widely expected that Indian Oil and India's Oil and Natural Gas Commission (ONGC) would eventually be merged into a single state monopoly company. Both companies grew vastly in size and sales volume but, despite close

```
┌─────────────────────────────────────────────┐
│                                               │
│              KEY DATES                        │
│                   ■                           │
│  ┌─────────────────────────────────────────┐ │
│  │                                           │ │
│  │ 1959:  Indian Oil Company is founded as  │ │
│  │        a statutory body to supply oil    │ │
│  │        products to Indian state          │ │
│  │        enterprise.                        │ │
│  │ 1964:  Indian Refineries and Indian Oil  │ │
│  │        Company merge to form the Indian  │ │
│  │        Oil Corporation.                   │ │
│  │ 1976:  The Burmah-Shell and the Caltex   │ │
│  │        refineries are nationalized.       │ │
│  │ 2002:  The Indian petroleum industry is  │ │
│  │        deregulated.                       │ │
│  │ 2007:  The company merges with its       │ │
│  │        marketing subsidiary, IBP Co.     │ │
│  │        Ltd.                               │ │
│  │ 2009:  Indian Oil merges with Bongaigaon │ │
│  │        Refinery & Petrochemicals Ltd.;   │ │
│  │        Indian Oil celebrates its 50th    │ │
│  │        anniversary.                       │ │
│  │                                           │ │
│  └─────────────────────────────────────────┘ │
└─────────────────────────────────────────────┘
```

KEY DATES

1959: Indian Oil Company is founded as a statutory body to supply oil products to Indian state enterprise.

1964: Indian Refineries and Indian Oil Company merge to form the Indian Oil Corporation.

1976: The Burmah-Shell and the Caltex refineries are nationalized.

2002: The Indian petroleum industry is deregulated.

2007: The company merges with its marketing subsidiary, IBP Co. Ltd.

2009: Indian Oil merges with Bongaigaon Refinery & Petrochemicals Ltd.; Indian Oil celebrates its 50th anniversary.

links, they remained separate. ONGC retained control of most of the country's exploration and production capacity. Indian Oil remained responsible for refining and marketing.

During this same decade, India found that rapid industrialization meant a large fuel bill, which was a steady drain on foreign exchange. To meet the crisis, the government prohibited imported petroleum and petroleum product imports by private companies. In effect, Indian Oil was given a monopoly on oil imports. A policy of state control was reinforced by India's closer economic and political links with the Soviet Union and its isolation from the mainstream of western multinational capitalism. Although India identified its international political stance as nonaligned, the government became increasingly friendly with the Soviet Bloc, because the United States and China were seen as too closely linked to India's major rival, Pakistan. India and the USSR entered into a number of trade deals. One of the most important of these trade pacts allowed Indian Oil to import oil from the USSR and Romania at prices lower than those prevailing in world markets and to pay in local currency, rather than dollars or other convertible currencies.

For a time, no more foreign refineries were allowed. By the mid-1960s government policy was modified to allow expansions of foreign-owned refinery capacity. The Indian Oil Corporation worked out barter agreements with major oil companies in order to facilitate distribution of refinery products.

In the 1970s the ONGC of India, with the help of Soviet and other foreign companies, made several important new finds off the west coast of India, but this increased domestic supply was unable to keep up with demand. When international prices rose steeply after the 1973 Arab oil boycott, India's foreign exchange problems mounted. Indian Oil's role as the country's monopoly buyer gave the company an increasingly important role in the economy. While the Soviet Union continued to be an important supplier, Indian Oil also bought Saudi, Iraqi, Kuwaiti, and United Arab Emirate oil. India became the largest single purchaser of crude on the Dubai spot market.

NATIONALIZATION CONTINUES

The government decided to nationalize the country's remaining refineries. The Burmah-Shell refinery at Bombay and the Caltex refinery at Vizagapatnam were taken over in 1976. The Burmah-Shell refinery became the main asset of a new state company, Bharat Petroleum Ltd. Caltex Oil Refining (India) Ltd. was amalgamated with another state company, Hindustan Petroleum Corporation Ltd., in March 1978. Hindustan had become fully Indian-owned on October 1, 1976, when Esso's 26 percent share was bought out. On October 14, 1981, Burmah Oil's remaining interests in the Assam Oil Company were nationalized, and Indian Oil took over its refining and marketing activities. Half of India's 12 refineries belonged to Indian Oil. The other half belonged to other state-owned companies.

By the end of the 1980s India's oil consumption continued to grow at 8 percent per year, and Indian Oil expanded its capacity to about 150 million barrels of crude per annum. In 1989 Indian Oil announced plans to build a new refinery at Pradip and modernize the Digboi refinery, India's oldest. However, the government's Public Investment Board refused to approve a 120,000 barrels-per-day refinery at Daitari in Orissa because it feared future overcapacity.

By the early 1990s Indian Oil refined, produced, and transported petroleum products throughout India. Indian Oil produced crude oil, base oil, formula products, lubricants, greases, and other petroleum products. It was organized into three divisions. The refineries and pipelines division had six refineries, located at Gwahati, Barauni, Gujarat, Haldia, Mathura, and Digboi. Together, the six represented 45 percent of the country's refining capacity. The division also laid and managed oil pipelines. The marketing division was responsible for storage and distribution and controlled about 60 percent of the total oil industry sales. The Assam Oil division controlled the marketing and distribution activities of the formerly British-owned company.

Indian Oil also established its own research center. Located at Faridabad, near New Delhi, the facility focused on testing lubricants and other petroleum products. It developed lubricants under the brand names Servo and Servoprime. The center also designed fuel-efficient equipment.

CHANGES IN THE OIL INDUSTRY

The oil industry in India changed dramatically throughout the 1990s and into the new millennium. Reform in the downstream hydrocarbon sector (the sector in which Indian Oil was the market leader) began early in 1991 and continued throughout the decade. In 1997 the government announced that the Administered Pricing Mechanism (APM) would be dismantled by 2002.

To prepare for the increased competition that deregulation would bring, Indian Oil added a seventh refinery to its holdings in 1998 when the Panipat facility was commissioned. The company also looked to strengthen its industry position by forming joint ventures. In 1993 the firm teamed up with Balmer Lawrie & Co. and NYCO SA of France to create Avi-Oil India Ltd., a manufacturer of oil products used by defense and civil aviation firms. One year later, Indo Mobil Ltd. was formed in a 50-50 joint venture with Exxon Mobil. The new company imported and blended Mobil brand lubricants for marketing in India, Nepal, and Bhutan. In addition, Indian Oil was involved in the formation of 10 major ventures from 1996 through 2000.

Indian Oil also entered the public arena as the government divested nearly 10 percent of the company. In 2000 Indian Oil and ONGC traded a 10 percent equity stake in each other in a strategic alliance that would better position the two after the APM dismantling, which was scheduled for 2002. According to a 1999 *Hindu* article, Indian Oil Corporation's strategy at this time was "to become a diversified, integrated global energy corporation." The article went on to claim that "while maintaining its leadership in oil refining, marketing and pipeline transportation, it aims for higher growth through integration and diversification. For this, it is harnessing new business opportunities in petrochemicals, power, lube marketing, exploration and production … and fuel management in this country and abroad."

In early 2002 Indian Oil acquired IBP, a state-owned petroleum marketing company. The firm also purchased a 26 percent stake in financially troubled Haldia Petrochemicals Ltd. In April of that year, Indian Oil's monopoly over crude imports ended as deregulation of the petroleum industry went into effect. As a result, the company faced increased competition from large international firms as well as new domestic entrants to the market. During the first 45 days of deregulation, Indian Oil lost INR 7.25 billion, a signal that the India's largest oil refiner would indeed face challenges as a result of the changes.

RAPID EXPANSION BEGINS

In early 2003 Indian Oil entered the retail fuel market in Sri Lanka, moving forward with plans to acquire more than 100 filling stations from the state-owned Ceylon Petroleum Corporation. The company earmarked $100 million for its subsidiary, Lanka IOC, to revamp the filling stations and acquire an ownership interest in a joint storage venture. In December the Indian government revealed plans to sell a portion of its shares in both ONGC and Indian Oil to domestic investors, as part of a plan to generate $2.9 billion in state assets.

Indian Oil expanded within the petrochemicals sector in 2004. In August of that year the company revealed plans to commission a $276 million linear alkyl benzene plant at its Baroda, India-based refinery. In addition, the company signed a memorandum of understanding with National Petrochemical Company to build the world's largest cracker operation in Assaluyeh, Iran. "Cracking" is the process used to obtain ethylene from natural or coal gas. It also was in 2004 that an oil storage terminal was commissioned for the company's IOML business at Mer Rouge port in Mauritius. Late in the year Indian Oil announced it would invest $33.5 million investment in Haldia Petrochemicals Ltd.

During the early 2000s Indian Oil began pursuing new business opportunities as part of a plan to increase its sales to $60 billion by 2011. One example was an exploration and production sharing agreement the company made with the National Oil Corporation of Libya. Plans also were made to double Indian Oil's investment in Mauritius, where $35 million was earmarked to establish a new laboratory and improve storage facilities. In Haryana, India, expansion within the refining sector prompted a capacity doubling at Indian Oil's Panipat plant. In October 2005 the Union Cabinet approved a proposal calling for the merger of Indian Oil with its IBP Co. Ltd. subsidiary. Finally, the company ended the year by announcing it would invest $495 million to construct a refinery and petrochemical facility in Shanghai, China, in partnership with Sinopec.

EXPANSION ACCELERATES

Developments at Indian Oil unfolded at a rapid pace in 2006. That year the company merged with its IndianOil

Blending Ltd. operation. In October the company announced plans to nearly double its crude oil refining capacity by 2011–12. That same month, a $1.1 billion expansion of Indian Oil's Panipat refinery was announced.

In addition to a $3.1 billion refinery and petrochemical plant in West Bengal, plans were in the works to construct a refinery in Paradip, Orissa, India, a $4.9 billion refinery in Turkey, and a $3.5 billion refinery in Nigeria. Finally, in late November 2006 a proposal to merge with Bongaigaon Refinery & Petrochemicals Ltd. was approved by the boards of both companies. Indian Oil's merger with its marketing subsidiary, IBP Co. Ltd., was completed in 2007. That year the company offered to acquire Petkim Petrokimya Holdings AS, Turkey's state-operated chemicals company. In addition, an auto care services business concept called SERVOXpress Centres was introduced. The company ended the year by revealing plans for a refining and petrochemicals joint venture with Egyptian General Petroleum Corp., which called for the construction of a $9 billion integrated refining and petrochemical plant.

In 2008 Indian Oil commissioned its first LPG pipeline from Panipat to Jalandhar, India, and rolled out its SERVO lubricants brand in the Arabian country of Oman. Indian Oil's merger with Bongaigaon Refinery & Petrochemicals Ltd. came one step closer to fruition when the latter company's shareholders approved the deal in early 2008. Also that year, a joint effort with Hindustan Petroleum Corp. and Bharat Petroleum Corp. was announced, calling for the investment of $600 million to establish ethanol plants in Brazil.

GOLDEN JUBILEE

Indian Oil began 2009 by announcing plans to establish the country's second hydrogen fuel-dispensing station by 2010, in timing with the Commonwealth Games in Delhi. With a goal of showcasing the country's concern for environmental affairs, the station would be used by approximately 100 government vehicles. Following receipt of government approval, the amalgamation of Indian Oil and Bongaigaon Refinery & Petrochemicals Ltd. finally occurred on March 25, 2009. A major milestone was reached when Indian Oil celebrated its 50th anniversary. The occasion was recognized by a Golden Jubilee celebration lasting from June 30 to September 1, 2009.

A major leadership change occurred in early 2010 when Brij Mohan Bansal was named chairman of Indian Oil, succeeding Sarthak Behuria. A company board member since 2005, Bansal had assisted the company in the areas of planning and business development. Under his leadership the company moved forward with plans to expand and diversify its operations, including initiatives related to biofuels and renewable/nuclear energy. Following 50 years of operations, Indian Oil appeared to have excellent prospects for continued success during the 21st century's second decade.

Clark Siewert
Updated, Christina M. Stansell; Paul R. Greenland

PRINCIPAL SUBSIDIARIES

Chennai Petroleum Corporation Ltd.; IndianOil Technologies Ltd.; IndianOil (Mauritius) Ltd.; IOC Middle East FZE; Lanka IOC plc.

PRINCIPAL DIVISIONS

Refineries; Marketing; R&D Centre; Pipelines; Assam Oil; IBP.

PRINCIPAL COMPETITORS

Bharat Petroleum Corporation Ltd.; Hindustan Petroleum Corporation Ltd.; Royal Dutch Shell plc.

FURTHER READING

"Business Line: Deregulation of Oil Sector: Is Government Prepared?" *Chemical Business Newsbase*, March 17, 2002.

"Business Line: IOC Monopoly over Import Ends," *Chemical Business Newsbase*, March 11, 2002.

"Indian Oil Corp. Harnessing New Business Opportunities," *Hindu*, April 2, 1999.

"India's IOC Seeks to Be among World's Top 100 Companies," *AsiaPulse News*, March 27, 2002.

"IOC Acquisition of Haldia Petro: Biting Off More Than It Can Chew?" *Business Line*, March 31, 2002.

"IOC Gets Government Nod for Merging BRPL with Itself," *PTI—The Press Trust of India Ltd.*, March 25, 2009.

"IOC Plans Hydrogen Station near Games Village in Delhi," *AsiaPulse News*, January 5, 2009.

"IOC's $60 Billion Global Dream," *Asia Africa Intelligence Wire*, April 25, 2005.

International Electric Supply Corp.

6606 LBJ Freeway, Suite 184
Dallas, Texas 75240
U.S.A.
Telephone: (972) 387-3600
Fax: (469) 374-0353
Web site: http://www.rexelusa.com

Wholly Owned Subsidiary of Rexel, S.A.
Incorporated: 1866 as Willcox & Gibbs Sewing Machine
   Co.
Employees: 4,700
Sales: EUR 2.44 billion ($3.5 billion) (2009 est.)
NAICS: 423690 Other Electronic Parts and Equipment
   Merchant Wholesalers

∎ ∎ ∎

International Electric Supply Corp., formerly known as Rexel Inc., is the holding company for the U.S. operations of Rexel, S.A., the world's largest electrical parts supplier. In the 1990s Rexel accumulated a controlling interest in Willcox & Gibbs, which had for more than a century supplied sewing machine parts before diversifying into electrical supply in the late 1950s. The company, renamed Rexel, Inc., became the basis for the U.S. operations. Since then, it has been built up through acquisitions of smaller players in the highly fragmented industry.

Rexel became the largest player in the country in 2006 through the purchase of GE Supply (later known as GexPro), which it maintained as a sister company to Rexel, Inc., under newly formed U.S. holding company

International Electric Supply Corp. In 2009 the United States accounted for sales of EUR 2.44 billion, about a quarter of Rexel's global revenues.

A CENTURY IN THE SEWING MACHINE TRADE

Established in 1859, Willcox & Gibbs Sewing Machine Co. was incorporated in New York seven years later. It was engaged in the sale of sewing machines and accessories for industrial applications, manufactured by others under contract. The company had assets of $2.6 million in 1923, of which $1.4 million consisted of inventories. There were 128 employees in 1930 and 218 stockholders in 1931. Dividends were paid consistently for many years, dating back to at least 1927. During the Great Depression, however, inventories were reduced and no dividends were paid during much of that time.

Willcox & Gibbs purchased Metropolitan Sewing Machine Corp. in 1935 and opened an English subsidiary in 1937. The company did not disclose annual income until 1939, when it reported net income of $28,960, followed by $12,466 in 1940. In 1941 Willcox & Gibbs opened its first manufacturing plant, in Nyack, New York. Its net income varied during the decade from $74,125 in 1945 to $286,867 in 1948. In 1950 the company had 545 employees, 299 holders of its common stock, and net income of $259,748.

Willcox & Gibbs first reported its sales total in 1952, when it earned $149,709 on net sales of $4,861,135, a figure not surpassed until 1957. It ran a deficit in 1953 and ceased, except during 1956–57, to pay dividends on common stock until 1985. Seeking to

KEY DATES

1859: Sewing machine manufacturer Willcox & Gibbs is established.

1958: Willcox & Gibbs begins to diversify with acquisition of Thermatron Co., maker of heat-sealing equipment.

1976: Willcox & Gibbs files for Chapter 11 bankruptcy reorganization.

1983: Covered elastic yarn manufacturer Regal Manufacturing Company is acquired.

1986: Canada's Rubyco, Inc., is acquired, making Willcox & Gibbs the world's largest supplier of covered yarn.

1992: Covered yarn subsidiary Worldtex Inc. is spun off; Rexel, S.A., acquires initial stake in Willcox & Gibbs via sale of Southern Electric Supply Co.

1995: Rexel, S.A., raises stake in Willcox & Gibbs to 47 percent; Willcox & Gibbs is renamed Rexel, Inc.

2006: Rexel, S.A., acquires GexPro (then GE Supply) from General Electric Co., becoming the largest electrical supply distributor in the United States.

end its dependence on the low-profit sewing machine business, in 1958 it acquired Thermatron Co., which produced and sold electronic equipment for heat-sealing and welding of soft plastic products. In 1960 Willcox & Gibbs opened a plant in Orangeburg, New York, and also added a Swiss subsidiary. That year it earned $161,036 on sales of more than $8.4 million and had 548 employees and 526 stockholders.

DIVERSIFIED AFTER 1958

Willcox & Gibbs grew by acquisition and diversification during the 1960s. In 1960 it acquired the European and U.S. rights to the automatic doffing machine, developed to supplant the manual operation of removing full bobbins of yarn and replacing them with empty plastic or paper tubes on the spindles of the spinning frame. It sold the North American rights to this machine to the Draper Corp. in 1961 for a share of the receipts from its sale or lease.

The company acquired Raybond Electronics, a manufacturer and distributor of high frequency wood gluing and laminating equipment, in 1966. During the

same year it acquired Faratron, a manufacturer of high frequency sealing and curing equipment; the manufacturing and distributing rights to a sealing machine used to package such items as phonograph records, toys, and candy; and the U.S. manufacturing and distributing rights to a British technique electronically joining the uppers of shoes.

Willcox & Gibbs dropped "Sewing Machine" from its name in 1967, the year its net sales reached $17 million and its net income $675,000. Also in 1967, the company acquired Stanelco Industrial Services, manufacturer and distributor of high frequency plastic welding and induction heating equipment, and Tele-Sonic, designer and manufacturer of bag opening and filling machinery, bag sealers, and overwrap machinery. In January 1968 the company acquired the rights to a new moldless process of fusing polystyrene beads directly inside a shipping container.

PUBLIC IN 1969

In 1968 sewing machines for industrial use accounted for about half of company income. This included not only the machines manufactured by Willcox & Gibbs and its U.K. subsidiary, but also distribution of the machines manufactured by G.M. Pfaff A.G. of West Germany. The Thermatron division was manufacturing equipment joining soft plastic products and other materials through the dielectric heating process. Stanelco-Thermatron Ltd., a U.K. subsidiary, was producing induction-heating equipment for metals and plastic welding equipment.

Raybond, also a subsidiary, was making equipment for the bonding of wood, such as furniture or flooring. Tele-Sonic and other divisions were engaged in making packaging equipment. Four divisions were involved in the manufacture of high-frequency heat sealing, curing, and drying machinery, making the company the nation's foremost producer in this field.

In 1969, the first year its stock was listed on the American Stock Exchange, Willcox & Gibbs acquired two companies making swatch cards and sample books for the wall covering, textile, garment, carpeting, upholstery, and drapery industries, making this division the largest operation of its kind in the United States. A third acquired company manufactured and imported trimmings and decorative buttons.

The following year Willcox & Gibbs acquired Sunbrand Corp., which became a subsidiary selling some 50,000 items for the apparel industry. After losing $1.7 million in 1969, Willcox & Gibbs recovered the following year, earning $338,912 on net sales of $26.7 million. The company had four plants in New York, two in California, one in Atlanta, and two in England.

REORGANIZED IN 1976

Willcox & Gibbs continued to acquire small companies in related businesses through the early 1970s. In 1972 Willcox & Gibbs sold its Dielectric Division, which included Stanelco-Thermatron, for cash, notes, and stock. Sales rose each year, but in 1974 the company lost $1.5 million on net income of $40.5 million. The following January, John K. Ziegler, the company's vice-president for finance, moved up to president and chief executive officer. That year Willcox & Gibbs lost $11.4 million on net income of $48.8 million. This outcome was attributed mainly to abnormally low profit margins on sales of industrial sewing equipment.

In June 1976, soon after the American Stock Exchange suspended trading in its shares, Willcox & Gibbs borrowed $28.2 million to consolidate its debts. When the company's creditors refused to accept a delay in payments, however, it filed for reorganization in November 1976 under Chapter 11 of the federal bankruptcy act. A new $10 million loan allowed the company to continue business without interruption, but it owed $38 million and had negative net worth of $27 million.

During the following years Willcox & Gibbs persuaded its creditors to settle for what turned out to be only 20 cents on the dollar, paid in cash, preferred stock, and warrants. Trading of the company's stock on the American Stock Exchange resumed in June 1979. For 1978 Willcox & Gibbs reported net income (after an extraordinary credit) of $1.3 million on net sales of $63.8 million, followed in 1979 by net income of $2.1 million on net sales of $69.7 million. In 1980 its properties included plants in Atlanta, Brooklyn, Dallas, El Paso, Los Angeles, Miami, and Pittsburgh, as well as in Fall River, Massachusetts, and Inwood, New York. Overseas, the company had properties in Paris, London, and High Wycombe, England.

COVERED YARN IN 1983

In 1982 Willcox & Gibbs sold its domestic sewing machine operations to a new Japanese-owned company, Pfaff-Pegasus of U.S.A. Inc., for about $2.5 million and a 29 percent interest. In the same year it also sold almost all of its operations in England and France to G.M. Pfaff of West Germany for $2.1 million in cash and notes. These divestitures reduced its debt by $8.3 million. However, in 1983 the firm purchased Regal Manufacturing Co., the leading producer of covered elastic yarn, chiefly for pantyhose, for $3.2 million in cash and a promise of added payments over seven years.

Later that year it paid $20 million in cash and notes, plus payments contingent on profits, for

Consolidated Electric Supply Inc. and its affiliates, a major wholesale distributor of electrical components and supplies to building contractors in Southern California and southern Florida. The addition of Regal, and especially Consolidated, which had annual sales larger than the prior Willcox & Gibbs, hiked the revenues of the amalgamated company from $74.9 million in 1983 to $207.8 million in 1984 at a total cost of only $29 million. Net income, excluding extraordinary credits, rose from $1.3 million to $5.1 million.

In addition to its acquisitions and its manufacture of cards and books for the textile, apparel, and wall covering industries by the Reliance Sample Card division, the company then consisted of its Sunbrand division, which continued to distribute sewing machines and parts, serving as exclusive U.S. distributor for Pfaff and Pfaff-Pegasus and also marketing a wide range of other products to the apparel and related industries, including pressing and cutting equipment; the Unity Sewing Supply division, a wholesale distributor of sewing equipment replacement parts; and the Montrose Supply & Equipment division, distributing parts and equipment to the textile and apparel industries, mainly to companies engaged in knitting operations.

CONTINUED EXPANSION

Willcox & Gibbs continued to expand in 1984 by acquiring Inter-City Wholesale Electric Inc., another distributor in the thriving housing market of Southern California, and Eildon Electronics Ltd., a Scottish company producing hardware and software for automated apparel manufacturing. In 1985 it acquired Leadtec Systems, Inc., another supplier of computer-based automation equipment for the apparel industry, and its stock moved up to the New York Stock Exchange. For the year net income, excluding an extraordinary credit, came to $6 million on net sales of $224.7 million. Of this total, distributing electrical products accounted for about 60 percent, distributing apparel equipment for about 20 percent, and manufacturing for about 20 percent.

In 1986 Willcox & Gibbs acquired Rubyco, Inc., the largest Canadian manufacturer of covered yarn, for about $6.4 million and thus became the world's largest manufacturer of this product. The following year it purchased three electrical supply companies in the South. Clark Consolidated Industries, Inc., a big Ohio electrical parts distributor, was bought in January 1989 for about $17.3 million. In 1989 sales rose for the seventh straight year, to a record level of $547.7 million. Net income came to a record $17.9 million.

COVERED YARN SPUN OFF IN 1992

In the company's most expensive acquisition to date, Willcox & Gibbs purchased Filiz Lastex, S.A., of Troyes, France, a producer of covered yarn, in 1990 for $44.9 million. However, in 1992 the company spun off its covered yarn subsidiary, Worldtex Inc., into a separate company. Willcox & Gibbs shareholders received one share of Worldtex for each share of the parent company's stock in a tax-free transaction. That year, following a meager 1991 in which the company earned only $248,000, Willcox & Gibbs lost $4.9 million on net sales of $359 million.

Willcox & Gibbs returned to the black in 1993, reporting net income of $9.1 million on net sales of $521.5 million. In April 1993 it paid $13.6 million for Sacks Electrical Supply Co., and in December acquired another distributor of electrical parts and supplies, Summers Group Inc., for $91 million in cash and notes. To finance the purchase, Willcox & Gibbs sold 3.5 million shares of newly issued common stock to a French firm, Rexel, S.A., for $31.4 million in cash and agreed to allow Rexel to appoint five of the company's nine directors. In March 1994 Ziegler resigned as chairman, president, and chief executive officer, turning over the presidency to Alain Viry, a former Rexel executive.

By taking a controlling interest in Willcox & Gibbs, Rexel, the world's largest distributor of electrical parts, was taking direct aim at the $40 billion U.S. market. Through subsidiary Compagnie de Distribution de Material Electrique B.V., it had first acquired 27 percent of Willcox & Gibbs in 1992, in exchange for $9.9 million in cash and all its stock in Southern Electric Supply Co.

Viry told *International Business* in 1994 that his goal was to free Willcox & Gibbs's assets by reducing the receivables cycle to a maximum of 45 days and decreasing inventory. He also said he planned to improve the purchasing system and to find better ways to invest the additional cash he expected to generate. Since Rexel was not interested in serving the apparel industry, it sold this segment of Willcox & Gibbs's business to WG, Inc., for about $44 million in cash, stock, and warrants, and moved the company's headquarters from Manhattan's garment district to Coral Gables, Florida.

FOCUS ON ELECTRICAL PARTS AND SUPPLIES IN 1994

By the end of 1994 Willcox & Gibbs was engaged only in the wholesale distribution of electrical parts and supplies, operating 171 electrical distribution locations in 19 states and the Bahamas. During that year substantially all of the company's operating subsidiaries were merged into Southern Electric Supply Co., a unit in the eastern region, and Summers Group Inc., a unit in the western region.

Each of the company's locations served an average of 400 customers in an area of approximately 50 miles in radius and carried about 15,000 items. Its clientele consisted of electrical contractors engaged in construction work and industrial customers who needed materials for the manufacture of equipment and for maintenance and repairs. The product line included electrical fixtures, cable, cords, boxes, covers, wiring devices, conduit, raceway duct, safety switches, motor controls, breakers, panels, lamps, fuses, and related supplies and accessories. It also included materials and special cables for computers and advanced communications systems.

In addition, the company had two divisions focused on specialty markets. The DataCom division distributed products used to interconnect voice, data, and video systems. The Cummins division distributed supplies to the utility industry. These two divisions were responsible for about 8 percent of the company's sales in 1994.

In 1995 Rexel, S.A., raised its stake in Willcox & Gibbs to 44 percent and changed the name of the company to Rexel, Inc. Net sales rose to $1.07 billion and $1.12 billion in 1994 and 1995, respectively. Net income jumped from $8.9 million in 1994 to a record $19.8 million in 1995. The company's long-term debt was reduced from $112 million to $50 million during the year. By October 1995 Rexel, S.A., had raised its stake in Rexel, Inc., to about 47 percent. Rexel, S.A., was then a subsidiary of France's Pinault-Printemps-Redoute group.

CHANGES IN 1997

In April 1997 Rexel, Inc., CEO Alain Viry left to head Compagnie Française de l'Afrique Occidentale, the international trading unit of Pinault-Printemps-Redoute S.A. of which Rexel, Inc., was an indirect subsidiary. Viry was succeeded by Gilles Guinchard, who had previously led another Rexel, S.A., division. Through its subsidiary International Technical Distributors Inc., in 1997 Rexel, S.A., raised its holding in Rexel, Inc., from 50.6 percent to 93 percent.

Rexel, Inc., continued to make opportunistic acquisitions. It added Arkansas's Davies Electric Supply Co. in 1995. In January 1997 it closed the acquisition of Southland Electrical Supply of Lexington, Kentucky, which had annual sales of $62 million. It then made two West Coast acquisitions, Pacific Electrical of San

Leandro, California, and Taylor Electric of Portland, Oregon. The pair added annual revenues of about $140 million.

In the same year Rexel sold its utility products unit, Cummins Utility Supply, to a management-led group for $30 million. Cummins had revenues of $107 million in 1996, about 10 percent of Rexel, Inc.'s, total. Rexel also added Tampa, Florida's Chemco Electric Supply Inc., which had annual sales of about $23 million. Norcal Electric Supply Inc. and Valley Electric Co. were acquired two years later.

In 2000 Rexel, S.A., had revenues of about $7 billion, 70 percent of which came from outside France. The United States, where Rexel had 5,000 employees, accounted for about $2 billion of the total. During the year Maryland's Branch Group was acquired. This was followed two years later by the purchase of All-Phase Electric Supply Co. of Dayton, Ohio. In July 2001 Rexel, S.A., bought Westburne Inc., a leading distributor in Canada with extensive operations in the United States.

CHANGE IN OWNERSHIP IN 2005

Meanwhile, there was a change in ownership at the ultimate parent company of Rexel, Inc. In 2005 Pinault-Printemps-Redoute S.A. sold its 73.5 percent stake in Rexel, S.A., as it prepared to take over the Gucci Group. The EUR 1.9 billion transaction valued the entire company at EUR 3.7 billion ($4.9 billion). The new owners were Clayton, Dubilier & Rice; Merrill Lynch Global Private Equity; and Eurazeo.

Rexel, Inc.'s, 2006 acquisitions included that of Capitol Light and Supply (CLS) of Hartford, Connecticut. CLS had revenues of $235 million and 520 employees in 22 locations from its electrical distribution side. Also included was a retail lighting business with locations in three-dozen states. Rexel also bought DH Supply Co., which had six locations around Atlanta, Georgia.

Also in 2006, Rexel, S.A., acquired GE Supply from General Electric Co. for $725 million, becoming the largest electrical supply distributor in the United States. It operated the new acquisition, renamed General Supply & Services, Inc., or GexPro, under newly created Dallas-based holding company International Electric Supply Corp., which would oversee Gexpro and Rexel Inc. as divisions. Shelton, Connecticut-based GexPro had annual revenues of $2.4 billion and 2,500 employees when acquired. Rexel Inc. had total pro forma U.S. revenues of $5.3 billion for 2006. It had more than 7,200 employees in more than 45 states. It

continued to make small acquisitions such as that of Casa Grande, Arizona's Tri-Valley Electric Supply Inc., acquired in 2007.

As Rexel's U.S. business arm, International Electric Supply Corp focused on the industrial and commercial sides of the market, although residential sales made up one-quarter of its business. The U.S. revenues of Rexel, S.A., including contributions from Rexel, Inc., and Gex-Pro, fell 30 percent in the midst of the global financial crisis, to EUR 2.44 billion ($3.5 billion) in 2009. The company looked to improve profitability by, in the words of Rexel Inc. CEO Jean-Charles Pauze in a press release, "capturing new market opportunities, upgrading its business model, continuing to enforce cost discipline and generating solid free cash flow." As part of Rexel S.A., the largest electrical distributor in the United States and in the world, International Electric Supply held certain advantages over its competitors in weathering the economic downturn of the early 2000s.

Robert Halasz
Updated, Frederick C. Ingram

PRINCIPAL DIVISIONS

General Supply & Services, Inc.; Rexel, Inc.

PRINCIPAL COMPETITORS

Graybar Electric Co.; Consolidated Electrical Distributors, Inc.; W.W. Grainger, Inc.; WESCO Distribution, Inc.; Sonepar USA.

FURTHER READING

Allen, Margaret, "'Business-Friendly' Terrell Nabs Rexel Warehouse," *Dallas Business Journal,* June 15, 2001, p. 1.

Funk, Dale, "Rexel Buys Tri-Valley Electric," *Electrical Wholesaling,* July 2007.

———, "Waterman on the New Rexel," *Electrical Wholesaling,* January 2008, pp. 40–41.

Marcial, Gene G., "Sparks Fly at Rexel," *Business Week,* November 3, 1995, p. 128.

Oestricher, Dwight, "Willcox & Gibbs Name Change Signals Stronger, Focused Co.," *Dow Jones News Service,* May 31, 1995.

Salimando, Joe, "'Change' Is Byword for New EVP/COO," *Power Outlet,* Vol. 1, No. 1 (2001), pp. 32–34.

Silverman, Suzann D., "The Waiting Game," *International Business,* June 1994, pp. 102, 104.

Stephens, Caleb, "Room for Growth; Rexel to Use Former Roberds Warehouse as Regional Hub," *Dayton Business Journal,* February 18, 2005.

Inventec Corp.

———— ■ ————

Inventec Building
66 Hou-Kang Street
Shin-Lin District
Taipei, 111
Taiwan
Telephone: (+886 2) 2881 0721
Fax: (+886 2) 2882 3605
Web site: http://www.inventec.com.tw/english

Public Company
Incorporated: 1975
Employees: 4,053
Sales: TWD 350.62 billion ($10.68 billion) (2008)
Stock Exchanges: Taiwan
Ticker Symbol: 2356
NAICS: 334111 Electronic Computer Manufacturing;
    334210 Telephone Apparatus Manufacturing;
    333313 Office Machinery Manufacturing

■ ■ ■

Taiwan-based Inventec Corp. is a leading designer and manufacturer of technology products, which it produces on behalf of other companies. In addition to making the iPod for Apple Computer, the company also produces notebook computers, mobile devices, network applications, enterprise servers, and storage products. During the early 2010s roughly 40 percent of Inventec's sales were attributed to Hewlett-Packard, with Toshiba accounting for another 30 percent.

FORMATION AND EARLY YEARS

Inventec traces its establishment back to July 1, 1975, when the company was formed with $1 million in capital. Several important milestones were reached during the 1980s. Among these was the establishment of Inventec's Tokyo branch office in 1982.

By 1984 Inventec had become the largest manufacturer of calculators in Taiwan. Early recognition came when Sears, which at the time was the largest department store in the world, honored Inventec with its Partners in Progress Award in both 1987 and 1988. In addition, Philips presented the company with its Best Supplier Award in 1988. The following year Inventec began manufacturing word processors and Chinese-English electronic dictionaries. In addition, its Malaysia and Inventec Besta subsidiaries were formed.

During the first half of the 1990s, Inventec expanded its production capabilities to include a variety of new devices. In addition, the company's corporate footprint grew via the formation of new subsidiaries. Telephone and fax machine production commenced in 1990, and the company established a new subsidiary in Shanghai the following year. Recognition continued as Inventec was honored with a supplier award from Zenith, as well as the Supplier Excellence Award from Texas Instruments.

Inventec received ISO-9001 Quality Certification in 1992. The following year, the company began manufacturing personal digital assistants (PDAs) and formed new subsidiaries in Beijing, Nanjing, and Tianjin. Growth continued in 1994, when another subsidiary was formed in Xian.

<table><tr><th></th></tr></table>

COMPANY PERSPECTIVES

Inventec is a cutting edge technology company which designs, develops and manufactures the best e-products for commercial, individual and home customers.

NOTEBOOK PRODUCTION BEGINS

The production of Pentium series multimedia notebook computers began in 1995. That year the company ramped up its capacity by opening new factories. Inventec's Lin Kou Factory was established to produce and assemble computer peripherals, while its Hou Gang Factory was developed for the production of electronic dictionaries. Finally, in 1996 a second factory opened its doors in Taipei for the purpose of manufacturing graphic calculators and PDAs.

Inventec went public in 1996. The following year, the company established new subsidiaries in Scotland and the United States. Production levels of personal notebook computers were healthy enough to prompt the construction of a third factory in Taipei that year.

In late 1998 Compaq Computer Corp. authorized Inventec to develop new technology for the company's workstations, servers, and enterprise personal computers. That year Inventec's notebook computer production totaled about 750,000 units, and was projected to reach 1 million units in 1999. In an effort to further the company's ability to produce high-end servers and desktop computers and bolster its research and development capabilities, Digital Taiwan was acquired.

In January 1999 Inventec's monthly sales totaled $145 million, eclipsing those of competitor Quanta Computer Inc. for the very first time. In March the company partnered with British Telecommunications PLC to launch the Easicom 1000, a telephone with a pull-out keyboard and LCD display that had both e-commerce and e-mail functionality. The device enabled those without traditional Internet service to send and receive e-mails and make purchases from select retailers.

It also was in 1999 that the company formed several new businesses. Inventec Multimedia & Telecom Corp. was formed for the purpose of producing multimedia and communications products. In addition, the development of Inventec Micro-Electronics Corp. furthered the evolution of the company's calculator

business. The company ended the 1990s by receiving ISO-14001 Certification.

A NEW MILLENNIUM

By the new millennium, Inventec had become one Asia's leading consumer electronics manufacturers. In 2000 the company made its first wireless Internet access device, which incorporated technology from the French company Wavecom S.A. New product introductions that year included graphic calculators, as well as wireless Internet-enabled cellular phones with advanced messaging capabilities.

In 2000 the company formed Inventec Appliances Corp. for the production of information appliances. Notebook computer sales to Compaq totaled $2.68 billion that year. Inventec's Shanghai Hongqiao Factory opened its doors in 2001. In addition, the company entered the book publishing and distribution business via the formation of Inventec Tomorrow Studio Corp.

Although Inventec had received numerous supplier-related honors by this time, several noteworthy recognitions were received in 2001. That year the Chinese Association for Industrial Technology Advancement presented the company with an Excellence in Innovation Award. In addition, Taiwan's Ministry of Economic Affairs honored Inventec with a Gold Medal National Invention Award.

GROWING CUSTOMER BASE

After making notebook computers exclusively for Compaq, Inventec began producing the devices for Toshiba in early 2002. This followed a significant decline in notebook computer shipments to Compaq in 2001, when sales totaled $1.8 billion. Specifically, Toshiba chose Inventec to produce its high-end Tecra business notebook computer. In addition to notebooks, Inventec had become the exclusive supplier of servers to Compaq by 2002.

By this time Inventec's operation in Beijing had become the largest foreign-owned software enterprise in mainland China, with revenues of approximately $1.6 million and a workforce of 2,000 people. Progress continued at Inventec during the second half of 2002, when the company became Hewlett-Packard's largest original equipment manufacturing partner. Inventec received an order to produce approximately 2 million DeskNote thin client notebook computers for Hewlett-Packard in 2003.

In October 2002 Inventec revealed plans to invest $40 million in E28 Co., a provider of telecommunications software and hardware in mainland China. The

```
┌─────────────────────────────────────────────┐
│                                               │
│              KEY DATES                        │
│              ───────◆───────                  │
│  ┌─────────────────────────────────────────┐ │
│  │ 1975: Inventec is formed with $1 million  │ │
│  │       in capital.                         │ │
│  │ 1984: The company ranks as the largest    │ │
│  │       manufacturer of calculators in      │ │
│  │       Taiwan.                             │ │
│  │ 1995: Production of Pentium series        │ │
│  │       multimedia notebook computers       │ │
│  │       begins.                             │ │
│  │ 1996: Inventec goes public.               │ │
│  │ 2010: The company is among the world's    │ │
│  │       largest notebook computer           │ │
│  │       manufacturers, producing more       │ │
│  │       than 30 million units annually.     │ │
│  └─────────────────────────────────────────┘ │
└─────────────────────────────────────────────┘
```

deal allowed the company to make greater inroads into the burgeoning Chinese marketplace. In addition, Inventec also announced that it would increase its investment in mainland China by $18 million, via the establishment of a new manufacturing facility in Pudong, Shanghai.

During this period, Inventec shuttered its LinKou plant in northern Taiwan. In addition, the company began making plans to establish a new factory in Mexico while reducing production at its plants in Scotland and Houston, Texas. Inventec's new Shanghai Pudong Campus came online in 2003. One final development that year was the formation of a $12 million personal computer assembly plant in Pujiang, China, as well as a research and development unit focused on personal computers for corporate users.

RECORD FINANCIAL PERFORMANCE

Progress continued at a strong pace in 2004, when Inventec's revenues reached a record $4 billion. That year, a new business operation named Inventec Enterprise System Corp. was formed. In addition, a new factory was established in the Czech Republic, enabling the company to better serve the European market.

Worldwide, Inventec's workforce numbered about 4,000 people by mid-2004. In addition to its facilities in Taiwan, the company's global footprint extended to China, Europe, and the United States. By late 2004 Inventec had relocated the majority of its notebook personal computer production to mainland China.

It was around this time that construction was completed on a plant in Pudong, Shanghai, China, where a new Shanghai-area headquarters also was established. The company's main office in Taipei began concentrating more on research and development-related

projects. Following increased demand for personal digital video and audio products, subsidiary Inventec Appliances Corp. also began scaling up operations at its plants in Nanjing in Pudong, China. The company ended the year with healthy sales, thanks in part to the popularity of the iPod and iPod mini music players, which the company had begun producing on behalf of Apple Computer.

CONTINUED GROWTH

In 2005 Inventec celebrated its 30th anniversary. That year Acer Inc. chose the company as one of its notebook computer manufacturing partners. With the addition of Inventec, Acer indicated it would have the ability to ship approximately 10 million notebook computers in 2006.

Another important milestone took place in 2005 when Inventec Appliances Corp. went public. The company ended the year by announcing plans to invest approximately $3 million in a U.S. joint venture with an Indian firm. Via this tie-up, Inventec sought to test the market for server-related software and products in India.

Inventec continued to make strong progress in 2006. That year Hewlett-Packard, which had surpassed Dell as the leading personal computer maker worldwide, chose the company to produce a combination notebook computer/game console in 2007. In addition, a strategic investment was made in the technology firm NetXen Inc. Recognition continued as Inventec placed 17th in *Business Week*'s Information Technology 100 ranking. The company ended 2006 on a high note, generating record revenues of more than $6 billion.

Beyond its focus on computer manufacturing, by the middle of the decade, Inventec also was marketing Dr.eye, one of the most popular translation software applications in China. The company offered three different versions of the application (student, business, and professional), with which it competed against offerings from the several other companies, including IBM, for a share of the $30 billion global translation software market. One specific tactic used by Inventec was a free trial campaign, which the company rolled out at colleges and universities on the Chinese mainland.

CHALLENGES

In early 2007 Inventec established a consumer electronics products joint venture with Singapore-based Huan Hsin Holdings Ltd. Around the same time, the company's board approved a plan to purchase a facility in Taipei that would serve as a research and development complex, and its Pudong Notebook R&D Center commenced operations.

Inventec was faced with a setback in April 2007 when prosecutors raided the offices of subsidiary Inventec Appliances. Seventeen company managers and their relatives were arrested on allegations of insider trading. Officials charged that company executives sold approximately 8 million shares of stock in January and February 2006, profiting from the sale immediately before decreased revenues were revealed.

Several key developments took place in 2008. That year, Inventec established a distribution agreement with Brightpoint Inc. The deal called for Brightpoint to distribute Inventec's Velocity Mobile phones and accessories throughout Europe and other parts of the world. On a related note, Inventec also brought its Taipei Mobile Computing Center online in 2008.

It also was in 2008 that Inventec was selected by the Chinese personal computer manufacturer Lenovo Group as one of its laptop manufacturers. That year, Inventec shipped more than 16 million notebook computers. The company ended the year with record revenues of more than $10 billion.

INDUSTRY LEADER

Progress continued in 2009, when Inventec partnered with the location-based information and services technology provider Pharos Science & Applications Inc. Specifically, the tie-up called for Inventec to produce a new line of smart phones with advanced navigation features. The Pharos Traveler 117, Traveler 127, Traveler 137, and Traveler 619 handsets included the Windows Mobile operating system, with Global Positioning System capabilities.

Another development in 2009 occurred in March, when word surfaced that Inventec was discussing the establishment of a new laptop factory in West China with Hewlett-Packard. The new plant was expected to have the capacity to produce more than 4 million laptops annually. It also was in 2009 that Inventec increased its ownership interest in Japan-based KOHJINSHA Co. Ltd to 61.69 percent.

By early 2010 Inventec was positioned to benefit from the burgeoning e-book market. In Taiwan the production value of such devices was expected to increase from $30 billion to $42 billion by 2012. The company already had contributed to research and development initiatives related to e-book readers.

Over more than three decades, Inventec had established itself as a leading technology manufacturer. By 2010 the company was producing more than 30 million notebook computers annually, as well as more than 3 million servers and 5 million smart phones. Inventec ranked as one of the world's largest notebook computer manufacturers and appeared to be positioned for continued success during the second decade of the 21st century.

Paul R. Greenland

PRINCIPAL SUBSIDIARIES

Inventec Appliances (44.15%); Inventec BESTA (32.7%); Inventec Multimedia & Telecom (48.67%); Inventec Enterprise Systems Corp.; E28 Limited (42%); Kohjinsha Co. Ltd. (61.69%); Inventec Huan Hsin Technology Co. Ltd. (49%).

PRINCIPAL COMPETITORS

Hon Hai Precision Industry Co. Ltd.; Quantum Computer Inc.; Wistron Corporation.

FURTHER READING

"Acer Adds Inventec as Fourth Contract Partner in NBs," *Asia Africa Intelligence Wire,* October 31, 2005.

"Inventec to Increase Its Mainland Investment," *Asia Africa Intelligence Wire,* December 31, 2002.

"Prosecutors Raid Inventec Appliances for Insider Trading," *Taiwan Economic News,* April 13, 2007.

"Taiwan E-Book Output Value to Hit TWD42bn in 2 Yrs," *SinoCast Daily Business Beat,* February 8, 2010.

"Taiwan's Notebook PC Makers Expanding Operations in China," *Asia Africa Intelligence Wire,* November 8, 2004.

Ivan Allen Workspace L.L.C.

1000 Marietta Street Northwest, Suite 224
Atlanta, Georgia 30318
U.S.A.
Telephone: (404) 760-8700
Fax: (404) 760-8673
Web site: http://www.ivanallen.com

Private Company
Incorporated: 1900 as Fielder & Allen Co.
Employees: 800
Sales: $40 million (2005 est.)
NAICS: 453210 Office Supplies and Stationery Stores

∎ ∎ ∎

Ivan Allen Workspace L.L.C. is a privately held, Atlanta, Georgia-based full-service office furniture dealer, representing a wide range of manufacturers but primarily Allsteel Inc. As the leading "comprehensive interior solution provider" in the southeastern United States, the company offers seating, tables, storage, and office systems products, as well as lighting, organization products, and ergonomic accessories. Services include floor plan and workstation design, installation and project management, maintenance, and asset storage management. Ivan Allen is run by the fourth generation of the Allen family.

BUSINESS ESTABLISHED: 1900

The man who gave Ivan Allen Workspace its name was born Isaac Anderson Allen in Dalton, Georgia, in 1876

(some sources say 1877). When he was three his mother renamed him Ivan Earnest in honor of his father, Earnest Allen, who had died. As a young man, Allen began to study law but was soon waylaid by an Atlanta man, James Fielder, who gave him an opportunity to sell typewriters, a relatively new invention. Allen managed to sell a dozen machines in Dalton, prompting him in 1895 to move to the larger market of Atlanta, where he became a typewriter salesman earning $40 a month. In 1900 he teamed up with Fielder and secured financial backing from his mother to start an office equipment store under the name of Fielder & Allen Co., which a century later would evolve into Ivan Allen Workspace.

In addition to typewriters, Fielder & Allen carried furniture, fixtures, drafting instruments, and office supplies. Not only did the business flourish in Atlanta and within a dozen years claim to be the South's largest office supply house, but Allen flourished there too, becoming a very active and esteemed resident. He became president of the Atlanta Convention Bureau and the Atlanta Chamber of Commerce, and helped to found the Atlanta Rotary Club and an art museum. He was also a member of the Elks, Masons, and Shriners. During World War I he was active in promoting bond drives and after the war won election to the Georgia Senate. Later he headed a commission that led to a reorganization of the state's government.

Allen and one of his trusted employees, Charles Marshall, bought out Fielder in 1919, and the business was renamed Ivan Allen-Marshall Company. In 1933 Allen brought his son, Ivan Allen Jr., into the business after he graduated from the Georgia Institute of Technology. Like his father, Allen Jr. made a commitment to community service and politics. In the 1930s he became an aide to Georgia's governor. During World War II the younger Allen served as a quartermaster in Atlanta, while the senior Allen served the Roosevelt administration as a sugar-rationing administrator.

COMPANY CHANGES NAME: 1953

Allen Jr. rejoined the governor's office in 1945, but when Marshall fell ill and was forced into retirement, his father, now 70 years of age, asked him to take charge of the office supply business. In 1946 Allen Jr. was named president of the firm and two years later Marshall died and willed his half of the business to Allen Jr. The company continued to operate under the Ivan Allen-Marshall name until 1953, when Marshall was dropped and the company became known as Ivan Allen Company. Allen Sr., in the meantime, retired from the business and continued to serve the community until his death in 1968.

Allen Sr. had placed the office supplies business in good hands. In just five years after his taking the reins in 1946, sales grew fivefold. He also anticipated the need for a one-stop shopping concept and brought together office supplies, furniture, and space design services under one roof. Not only was it an idea that helped make Ivan Allen Co. the leading office supply company in the Southeast, it anticipated the office supply superstores that would emerge years later, such as Staples and Office Depot. Allen also proved progressive in employment, hiring African Americans and women to managerial positions at a time when such decisions were rare and often times controversial. At one point Allen considered selling the company, unsure that the next generation would be able to run it, but he ultimately determined to keep it in the family.

Allen's interest in politics may have also led to his thoughts of selling the business. After flirting with a run at the governorship in 1958, he became president of Atlanta's Chamber of Commerce in 1960, establishing a platform to run for mayor the following year. Having positioned himself as a segregationist in his gubernatorial campaign, Allen had had a change of heart and advocated school integration. As the president of the Chamber of Commerce he had brokered an agreement to desegregate Atlanta's lunch counters. As a result, Allen was able to secure almost all of the city's black vote, representing about 40 percent of the electorate, and was able to defeat his segregationist opponent, Lester Maddox, who later became Georgia's governor.

COMPANY SPREADS THROUGHOUT SOUTH

To take charge of Ivan Allen Company, Allen turned to a man named Billy Glenn, who had joined the company in 1952. Glenn became president, a position he held until the early 1970s. Under his leadership the Ivan Allen Co. was expanded to second-tier cities throughout the South. Allen, in the meantime, spent two eventful terms as Atlanta's mayor, forging a reputation as perhaps the most influential leader in the history of the city.

Allen left office in 1970 and returned to the office supply business, assuming the chairmanship while his son, Ivan Allen III, replaced Glenn as president and chief executive officer. Like his father and grandfather before him, Allen III became a prominent civic leader, active in a number of causes and playing an important role in Atlanta's successful bid for the 1996 Olympics.

The company enjoyed steady growth over the next two decades, topping $40 million in annual revenues in 1980 and reaching a peak of $116 million in 1988 from some two dozen outlets in Georgia (six in the Atlanta market), Alabama, Tennessee, and the Carolinas. Changes were in the air, however. Since the mid-1980s the idea of creating an office supply retail discount chain began to take shape, and in 1986 three companies sharing a similar concept made their start in three different parts of the United States: Office Depot in Florida, Office Club in California, and Staples in Brighton, Massachusetts. The office supplies field began to quickly consolidate, leading to stiffer competition. Ivan Allen's business began to suffer, with sales dipping to $94.2 million in 1990.

IVAN ALLEN III DIES: 1992

Ivan Allen Co. and all of Atlanta were shocked in May 1992 when 53-year-old Allen III died of a self-inflicted gunshot wound while on a weekend visit to a family farmhouse. Allen Jr., now in his 80s, decided the time had come to sell the family business. A deal was reached to split the company and sell the contract office furniture division to Steelcase Inc. and the manufacturing division to a Dutch company, Koninklijke KNP BT, Europe's second-largest paper producer with close to $7 billion in annual revenues.

KEY DATES

1900: Ivan Allen and James Fielder found Fielder & Allen Co.
1919: Business is renamed Ivan Allen-Marshall Company.
1953: Company renamed Ivan Allen Company.
1998: Staples acquires Ivan Allen's office supply business.
2002: Company renamed Ivan Allen Workspace.

At the eleventh hour, in September 1994, following 15 months of negotiations, Allen Jr. scuttled the sale of the company. He said that a day after the deal had been announced a painting depicting the three Ivan Allens fell from its frame and trapped him in his office chair, reminding him of what his father had said the other time he had considered selling the company. Perhaps of more importance was his fear that the sale might lead to layoffs of loyal longtime employees under new ownership. Whatever the reasons, Allen elected to keep the business in the family.

Another son of Allen Jr., H. Inman Allen, was persuaded to leave his real estate companies in the hands of others and take over as chairman and CEO of Ivan Allen Co. He then added the presidency as well in a 1996 corporate reorganization, eager to take a more direct role in the running of the company. The restructuring could not, however, change business conditions. As the office supplies industry consolidated further, leaving three major chains (Staples, Office Depot, and OfficeMax) and regional survivor W. B. Mason Company in the Northeast, Ivan Allen was no longer able to compete effectively.

After already failing in one attempt, Staples reached an agreement in October 1998 to acquire Ivan Allen's $60 million-a-year supply business including manufactured products and 15 divisional sales offices in Georgia, Alabama, Tennessee, and the Carolinas. Staples also acquired the use of the Ivan Allen name for the next two years, the offices operating as Staples/Ivan Allen until a transition was complete to the Staples name.

Ivan Allen retained its office furniture division, which also generated about $60 million in annual sales. Composed of 13 Steelcase dealerships spread across the Southeast, the business was rechristened Ivan Allen Furniture. Ownership was vested to the three daughters of Inman Allen. A much smaller concern, it moved out of its home since the 1960s, establishing a new downtown headquarters in 2000.

The new century brought a number of significant changes to Ivan Allen. The company began repositioning itself as a comprehensive interior solution provider. Early in 2002 it helped to redesign the interior of an Atlanta business training facility, D.W. Brooks Conference Center, and began bidding for other projects. Late in the year Ivan Allen Furniture Co. decided to rebrand itself as Ivan Allen Workspace. A year later, in July 2003, Ivan Allen Jr. died at the age of 92. Well into his 80s he had made the daily drive to the company's downtown headquarters before advancing Parkinson's disease forced him to stay home.

LOUISE ALLEN NAMED CEO: 2005

More changes followed for Ivan Allen Workspace. In 2005 the fourth generation of the Allen family took charge when Inman Allen's daughter, 31-year-old Louise Allen, was named chief executive. She had worked with Goldman Sachs in San Francisco and Thomson Financial before deciding to return home in 2004. She began learning more about the family business and developed a strategy for growing the business that she presented to her father, who was enthusiastic about the plan and which led to the company's board voting to make her the new CEO. Her father stayed on as chairman. Two years later another significant change took place when Ivan Allen ended a 60-year partnership with Steelcase and forged a new alliance with Allsteel, Inc., a move that was made because Louise Allen believed Allsteel was a better fit for her vision for the company. In addition, Allsteel agreed to make an investment in Ivan Allen Workspace and help establish showrooms in the Southeast, moves that helped assure the company's success for years to come.

Ed Dinger

PRINCIPAL COMPETITORS

Facility Group, Inc.; Interior Architects, Inc.; SBLM Architects, P.C.

FURTHER READING

Barry, Tom, "Ivan Allen Jr. Helped Build, and Heal, Atlanta," *Atlanta Business Chronicle,* November 11, 2002.

Emerson, Bo, and Martha Woodham, "An Atlanta Family Dynasty," *Atlanta Journal,* Mary 19, 1992, p. D6.

Ezell, Hank, "Ivan Allen Ends Talk to Sell Company," *Atlanta Journal-Constitution,* September 15, 1994, p. 1.

Kempner, Maria, and Matt Saporta, "Staples to Acquire Part of Ivan Allen," *Atlanta Journal-Constitution,* October 14, 1998, p. D3.

Salter, Charles, and Susan Laccetti, "Ivan Allen III, Son of Former Atlanta Mayor, Is Dead at 53," *Atlanta Journal,* May 18, 1992, p. A1.

Saporta, Maria, "Another Allen to Operate Business," *Atlanta Journal-Constitution,* May 14, 2005, p. F1.

———, "Ivan Allen Jr. 1911–2003," *Atlanta Journal-Constitution,* July 8, 2003, p. A12.

Suggs, Ernie, and Tom Bennett, "Shaper of Modern Atlanta: Ivan Allen Jr.: 1911–2003," *Atlanta Journal-Constitution,* July 3, 2003, p. A1.

Japan Tobacco Inc.

—————— ■ ——————

2-1, Toranomon 2-chome
Minato-ku
Tokyo, 105-8422
Japan
Telephone: (81 3) 3582-3111
Fax: (81 3) 5572-1441
Web site: http://www.jti.co.jp

Public Company
Incorporated: 1949 as Japan Tobacco and Salt Public
  Corporation
Employees: 15,590
Sales: ¥6.83 trillion ($69.55 billion) (2009)
Stock Exchanges: Tokyo Osaka Nagoya Kukuoka Sapporo
Ticker Symbol: 29140
NAICS: 312221 Cigarette Manufacturing; 312111 Soft
  Drink Manufacturing; 311412 Frozen Specialty
  Food Manufacturing; 325412 Pharmaceutical
  Preparation Manufacturing

■ ■ ■

Japan Tobacco Inc., known as JT, is the world's third-
largest tobacco company. JT controls about 65 percent
of the Japanese cigarette market. Its leading brands are
Mild Seven, which is Japan's number-one seller, as well
as Seven Stars, Caster, Cabin, Peace, Pianissimo, Hope,
and Frontier. The company also owns international
rights to the key brands Winston, Salem, and Camel,
which it acquired from R.J. Reynolds in 1999. The
company gained the Benson & Hedges and Silk Cut
brands through its $15 billion purchase of Gallaher

Group plc in 2007. The company's Global Flagship
Brands include Winston, Camel, Mild Seven, Benson &
Hedges, Silk Cut, LD, Sobranie, and Glamour. These
eight brands are marketed through the company's JT
International subsidiary, headquartered in Geneva,
Switzerland.

In addition to its tobacco holdings, JT is a diversified company with substantial interests in pharmaceutical development and sales, and in the sale and distribution of processed foods, beverages, and seasonings. The
company markets drugs that fight cancer and HIV, and
operates joint ventures with pharmaceutical companies
in Japan, the United States, and Europe. Its food division acquired Katokichi Co. Ltd., known as TableMark
Co. Ltd., and Fuji Foods Corp. in 2008. JT was a state-
owned monopoly until 1985. The Japanese government
still owns nearly half of the company, with the rest
publicly traded on the Tokyo Stock Exchange.

ROOTS IN THE 19TH CENTURY

The tobacco industry in Japan can be traced back to
1869, when Yasugoro Tsuchida, a Tokyo merchant,
began the production of rolled cigarettes on a small
scale. This represented the introduction of locally
produced cigarettes and came less than 20 years after the
first introduction of cigarettes to Japan as imports from
Britain and the United States. In 1883 Iwatani Co. Ltd.,
a trading company, began the production and sale of
Japan's first popular cigarette brand, Tengu.

In 1888 the government responded to the increase
in tobacco smoking by placing a special tax on the
products, with varying rates for rolled tobacco and

cigarettes. Around this time the Murai Brothers Company began producing and selling Sunrise cigarettes and importing Hero cigarettes from the United States. In 1896 the company expanded into the Tokyo market, thus prompting a price war with Iwatani Co. Ltd.

Japan at the time was undergoing an accelerated period of industrialization. The Tokyo Stock Exchange opened in 1878, the Bank of Japan began operations in 1882, and the state-owned Yamato Iron and Steel Works began operation in 1901. In 1895 Japan established itself as a military power with the defeat of China in the Sino-Japanese War. Operations such as these needed funding, and the government realized that a tobacco monopoly such as existed in several European countries could be a lucrative source of revenue. In 1898 a tobacco bureau was established within the ministry of finance to operate this monopoly.

In 1905 a salt monopoly was added to the bureau's responsibilities. The bureau began marketing Cherry cigarettes in 1904, a brand still sold in Japan in the 21st century. In 1906 it began producing and selling its most popular brand at the time, Golden Bat. In 1900 Japan became one of the first countries in the world to pass a law forbidding the use of cigarettes by minors, those under the age of 18.

For the next 30 years tobacco and salt production in Japan continued to be administered by this bureau within the ministry of finance. Profits went directly into state coffers and were regarded as a kind of tax by the authorities. The prices charged by the government on tobacco were relatively low while those on salt were minimal, and the monopoly was in some ways used as a means of controlling the nation's economy, providing a regular source of income for the government.

POSTWAR PRODUCTION

By 1940 Japan was heading toward war with the Allied powers. The supplies of raw tobacco leaves from the West, notably from North and South America, were becoming less and less reliable. The government was forced to implement rationing of cigarettes in 1943.

Following Japan's defeat and subsequent occupation, the Allied powers restructured the country's economy. They kept the monopoly in place as a source of income for the cash-starved Japanese government.

In 1949 the government bureau traditionally responsible for tobacco production became a public company, known as the Japan Tobacco and Salt Public Corporation. Although still a wholly government-owned concern, tobacco production and sales in Japan were then to be operated on a commercial basis and as a self-accountable business concern. The company began afresh, and in 1949 commenced the retailing of two brands, Peace and Corona.

In 1950 rationing of tobacco products was halted, and in 1952 finished tobacco products were exported from Japan for the first time, mostly to Southeast Asia nations. In 1954 a new consumption tax was established on sales of cigarettes with the proceeds going directly to the government rather than the Japan Tobacco Corporation.

In 1957 the company introduced the Hope brand and also set up a research center to study the effects of cigarette smoking on health. This came at a time when scientists in the United States were beginning to publicize the link between smoking and lung cancer. Japan, with its lower incidence of cancer, was more concerned with its very high rate of stroke and stress-related deaths, and the research center studied the causes of these illnesses.

The Japanese population continued to take up smoking at a prodigious rate, and by 1967 Japan Tobacco's best-selling cigarette brand, Hope, was also the world's best-selling brand. In the following year the company established a factory for producing cigarette papers and filters to cater to increased demand for them in Japan. Following reports of the health risks of smoking both from the West and to a lesser extent within Japan, Japan Tobacco began to issue health warnings on its cigarette boxes. The warnings were fairly low-key, however, and only advised the smoker not to overindulge in the habit.

Since establishing the salt monopoly in 1905, the Japanese government had entrusted Japan Tobacco in its various forms with full responsibility for the country's salt supply. The salt business had traditionally been conducted with the aim of maintaining stable salt supplies and prices. With no salt mines in Japan, Japan Tobacco had to import most of its salt, mainly from China and Korea. In 1972 Japan Tobacco introduced a new method of producing salt in which seawater was separated from fresh water by membranes, with the salt allowed to permeate across the membrane. This method

KEY DATES

1898: The Japanese government establishes a tobacco bureau.

1949: The company is incorporated as Japan Tobacco and Salt Public Corporation.

1967: Japan Tobacco's best-selling cigarette brand, Hope, is also the world's best-selling brand.

1985: The company begins exporting cigarettes.

1987: Import tariffs are eased, opening the Japanese market to foreign tobacco companies.

1994: The Japanese government sells one-third of Japan Tobacco to the public.

1999: Japan Tobacco buys non-U.S. operations of R.J. Reynolds.

2002: The company purchases retail bakery store chain Saint-Germain Co. Ltd.

2007: Gallaher Group plc is acquired.

2008: Majority stakes in Katokichi Co. Ltd. and Fuji Foods Corp. are purchased.

was introduced into all Japan Tobacco salt-making facilities.

CONTINUED GROWTH

In 1973 Japan Tobacco began the sale of Marlboro cigarettes under license from Philip Morris Co. Ltd. of the United States. As the largest tobacco company in the world, Philip Morris was determined to make inroads into the lucrative Japanese market but was bewildered by Japan's complex distribution system. Most of Japan Tobacco's products were sold in small kiosks and vending machines, presenting an importer of cigarettes with a difficult and arduous task in breaking into the market. A competitor would require a huge capital investment to set up such a network, and supply staff and maintenance staff would be required. Japan Tobacco at the time controlled almost 100 percent of Japan's cigarette market.

In the 1980s Japan Tobacco faced increasing pressure from foreign cigarette manufacturers to allow them to sell their products more freely on the Japanese market. The Japanese government was under pressure to cut its huge trade surplus with the United States and therefore exerted pressure on Japan Tobacco to cooperate with foreign importers and allow them the use of distribution channels, notably Japan Tobacco's large network of automatic vending machines. Philip Morris and R.J. Reynolds were the first to make inroads, with

Lark, a Philip Morris brand especially designed for the Japanese market, becoming a best seller.

RESTRUCTURING BEGINS IN 1985

In 1985 Japan Tobacco underwent a fundamental restructuring. The government reorganized the company by privatizing it and reestablishing it as Japan Tobacco Inc. (JT), a joint stock company with its shares fully owned by the Japanese government. In the face of increasing competition from foreign imports, the move was intended to make the company more competitive, while still giving the government a monopoly on cigarette manufacturing in Japan. In 1987 import tariffs on cigarettes were lifted, making it possible for importers to sell cigarettes at approximately the same price as Japan Tobacco.

At that time, as a consequence, both Japan Tobacco's total sales and its share of the Japanese market started to decline. The company's management realized that the new Japan Tobacco would have to diversify in order to sustain growth. Japan Tobacco International Corporation (JATICO) was established in 1985 to export cigarettes. First year sales were 7.5 billion cigarettes, as compared with the 270 billion sold domestically. The United States and Southeast Asia were the chief targets of JATICO's products.

JT entered the pharmaceutical business in 1986, with the formation of JT Pharmaceutical Co. Ltd. This subsidiary took advantage of the parent company's extensive research and development facilities. The main areas of the pharmaceuticals business on which the company first focused were over-the-counter (OTC) cough remedies and nutritional supplement drinks. One of the company's successes was Kakimaro, marketed as a hangover remedy. Through international strategic alliances, JT Pharmaceutical also entered the field of OTC drugs.

Through other subsidiaries formed between 1985 and 1990, JT entered the food, fertilizer and agribusiness, and real estate businesses. The latter made use of JT's real estate holdings which, like many Japanese companies in the real estate boom years of the late 1980s, it used to its full financial advantage through office letting, land sales, and renting.

FENDING OFF COMPETITION THROUGH EXPANSION

By the mid-1990s, JT was the fourth-largest cigarette maker in the world. It faced increasing competition at home from European and U.S. imports and at the same time eyed the opening of the potentially huge market in

China. The company's pharmaceuticals division grew rapidly, and JT invested some hundreds of billions of yen in diversified interests such as the beverage business, real estate, and health clubs. Tobacco remained the pillar of the company, however, accounting for almost 90 percent of the firm's revenue.

A significant proportion of Japan's population continued to smoke, and the kind of class-action lawsuit that dogged U.S. tobacco companies was unheard of in Japan. Although growth in domestic cigarette sales was small, company managers maintained an optimistic outlook. Consequently, the Japanese government arranged to sell one-third of the company to the public in 1994 to raise money.

The government had previously privatized portions of other state-owned companies, including the telecommunications company Nippon Telegraph & Telephone and its East Japan Railways. The shares were first offered to large investors and then made available through a lottery system to individual investors. In the midst of a falling stock market, however, response to the public offering was dull.

JT went ahead with various diversification projects in the mid-1990s. In 1996 the company entered a joint venture with the British company Grand Metropolitan plc, owner of Burger King, to expand the Burger King franchise in Japan. Burger King was a distant third in the Japanese burger market, but both firms saw plenty of room for expansion. In 1997 JT acquired the food operations of the Asahi Chemical Industry Co., Ltd. This gave JT access to a wider market for its food business. Previously, the firm had reached primarily commercial customers with its frozen foods, but the Asahi purchase gave the company some well-known consumer brands.

The company also sold beverages through a network of vending machines. JT reorganized its vending machine operating companies in order to widen its beverage market. In 2000 it launched the popular canned coffee brand Roots. In pharmaceuticals, the company also pursued joint ventures and made acquisitions. One significant acquisition was that of the Torii Pharmaceutical Co. Ltd. in 1998. JT bought up 53 percent of the company and then beefed up the company's marketing.

R.J. REYNOLDS ACQUISITION: 1999

The largest coup for JT was its acquisition in 1999 of the non-U.S. operations of R.J. Reynolds. The company paid out $7.8 billion for the international operations of Reynolds. The deal established JT as the world's third-largest tobacco company (behind Philip Morris and British American Tobacco), and made Japanese history by being the largest foreign acquisition by a Japanese company at that time. JT gained the three leading brands of Reynolds, Camel, Winston, and Salem. These brands were big sellers in places where JT had made few inroads, including Eastern Europe and the former Soviet Union. Sales of brands with a global presence were growing at an estimated 5 percent annually, while overall cigarette sales growth was just 1 percent.

The acquisition was expensive and cut heavily into JT's earnings, but the company saw its future in global expansion. Although JT had not been sued over health issues, an awareness of the health risks of smoking was beginning to penetrate Japan. The company looked to the opening of China's market to cigarettes as a source of revenue and hoped to concentrate other foreign sales in Pacific Rim countries that still had growing markets for tobacco.

By 2000 the company was marketing its leading Mild Seven brand in Malaysia, Thailand, and Singapore. The company gained a new president in late 2000, Katsuhiko Honda. Honda had negotiated the acquisition of the R.J. Reynolds brands. International sales made up close to 40 percent of the company's business by this time. The company also worked closely with its two global rivals, Philip Morris and British American Tobacco.

Documents leaked by *Advertising Age* in 2001 showed that the three top companies had agreed to work together to limit their marketing around the world. Japan Tobacco and the others proposed to voluntarily limit advertising in publications with a substantial readership under age 18, to keep tobacco ads 100 meters away from schools, and to restrict their advertising in other ways.

LOOKING TOWARD THE FUTURE

Japan Tobacco continued to look for ways to bolster its business during the early years of the new millennium. The company's food division experienced growth thanks in part to several acquisitions. The first came in 2002 when the company bought the retail bakery store chain Saint-Germain Co. As the domestic food market was expected to shrink eventually, the company planned for international expansion and increased its size through two acquisitions in 2008, Katokichi Co. Ltd. and Fuji Foods Corp.

These acquisitions came at a time when JT had been hit hard by a scandal after some of its frozen dumplings sold on store shelves in China were found to have been laced with pesticides. The company worked quickly to revamp its image but the JT name was tarnished. The company therefore transferred all of its processed food, frozen food, and seasoning operations to the Katokichi name. Katokichi changed its name to TableMark Co. Ltd. in 2010.

Meanwhile, JT worked to grow its share of the Japanese cigarette market. It faced many challenges including the risk of tax increases on cigarettes in Japan, stricter smoking regulations, and rising costs of tobacco, transportation, and packaging materials. The company ended its licensing contract to manufacture and market the Marlboro brand in 2005.

JT's boldest move of this time period was the $15 billion acquisition in 2007 of Britain's Gallaher Group plc. The deal, which was touted as the largest foreign acquisition in Japan's history to date, gave JT a foothold in the Western European cigarette market and the rights to the Silk Cut and Benson & Hedges brands. The purchase strengthened the company's International division, which announced the formation of a new Global Flagship Brands portfolio shortly after Gallaher was integrated. The portfolio included Winston, Camel, Mild Seven, Benson & Hedges, Silk Cut, LD, Sobranie, and Glamour.

In March 2008 JT secured the first increase in domestic market share since its privatization in 1985. Its market share increased again in 2009, a sure sign the company's strategy was paying off. The company continued to eye international expansion as crucial to its future growth and understood that gaining a foothold in emerging markets including Russia would be necessary in order to successfully compete in the industry. JT also looked to secure quality tobacco leaves and acquired Tribac Leaf Ltd., a U.K.-based processor of tobacco leaves, in 2009. It also partnered with two U.S. leaf suppliers to form JTI Leaf Services LLC, a joint venture based in Virginia.

During 2009 the company's pharmaceutical operations were strong after the company secured a licensing deal with Merck & Co. Inc. for its osteoporosis drug. It also had several drugs that were licensed out to Switzerland's Roche and U.S.-based Gilead Sciences in Phase III clinical trials. These included an antidyslipidemic compound, which was used to raise good cholesterol levels, and an anti-HIV compound.

While JT would no doubt face future challenges, the company believed it had a well-rounded portfolio of tobacco, food, and pharmaceutical holdings and that its position as the world's third-largest tobacco company was secure. By focusing on expanding its global footprint and strengthening its domestic operations, JT appeared to be well positioned to compete in the years to come.

Dylan Tanner
Updated, A. Woodward; Christina M. Stansell

PRINCIPAL DIVISIONS

Domestic Tobacco; International Tobacco; Pharmaceutical; Foods.

PRINCIPAL COMPETITORS

British American Tobacco plc; Imperial Tobacco Group plc; Philip Morris International Inc.

FURTHER READING

Bentley, Stephanie, "Euro Launch for Japanese Cigarettes," *Marketing Week*, August 16, 1996, p. 7.

Coleman, Joseph, "Big Tobacco Still Calls the Shots in Japan," *Marketing News*, August 4, 1997, p. 12.

Dawson, Chester, "Smoke Alarm," *Far Eastern Economic Review*, June 22, 2000, pp. 50–52.

"The Importance of Acting with Noblesse Oblige," *Wall Street Journal Asia*, July 20, 2009.

"Japan Tobacco Aims to Lead Food Sector Realignment," *Nikkei Report*, December 25, 2007.

"Japan Tobacco Expanding Overseas as Domestic Sales Stall," *Nikkei Report*, June 16, 2009.

Kageyama, Yuri, "Japan Tobacco Acquires Britain's Gallaher Group for $15 Billion," *Associated Press Newswires*, April 18, 2007.

McKegney, Margaret, and Normandy Madden, "Tobacco Report Reveals Global Retreat," *Advertising Age*, August 13, 2001, pp. 1, 27.

"Smoke Gets in the Eyes as Marlboro Man Tries to Crack China Market," *South China Morning Post*, December 29, 2005.

"Tobacco Giant to Buy Fuji Foods," *Just-Food*, January 18, 2008.

Updike, Edith Hill, "Burger King Wants to Build a Kingdom in Asia," *Business Week*, November 25, 1996, p. 52.

Komatsu Ltd.

———————■———————

2-3-6, Akasaka
Minato-ku
Tokyo, 107-8414
Japan
Telephone: (81 03) 5561-2616
Fax: (81 03) 3505-9662
Web site: http://www.komatsu.com

Public Company
Incorporated: 1921
Employees: 39,855
Sales: ¥2.02 trillion ($20.42 billion) (2009)
Stock Exchanges: Tokyo
Ticker Symbol: 6301
NAICS: 333120 Construction Machinery Manufacturing; 333131 Mining Machinery and Equipment Manufacturing; 334413 Semiconductor and Related Device Manufacturing

■ ■ ■

Komatsu Ltd. is the world's second-largest manufacturer of construction and mining equipment, after Caterpillar Inc. More than 86 percent of the company's revenues are generated from the sale of construction, mining, and utility equipment, including bulldozers, dump trucks, forklift trucks, hydraulic excavators, mobile debris crushers, motor graders, tunnel-boring machines, and wheel loaders. Through a large network of subsidiaries, Komatsu also produces a variety of other products, including metal forging and stamping presses, sheet metal machinery, machine tools, thermoelectric semiconductor devices, and prefabricated commercial-use structures. The company has manufacturing facilities across the globe. Its U.S. facilities are in Illinois, Indiana, South Carolina, Tennessee, and Texas.

19TH-CENTURY ORIGINS

Komatsu had its origins in 1894 when the Takeuchi Mining Company was founded. A major expansion occurred in 1917, during World War I, when the Komatsu ironworks was established to manufacture mining equipment and machine tools to expand the mining operations. The name Komatsu came into existence in 1921 when the ironworks separated from the mining company to become Komatsu Ltd. Tashiro Shiraishi, an engineer, was the founder and first president, serving until 1925. In the 1920s and 1930s the firm grew as a major manufacturer of machine tools and pumps, including development of a metal press in 1924 and the firm's first farm tractor in 1931. Production of steel materials began in 1935.

By 1929 the number of employees had risen to 742, from its original 1921 workforce of 121 employees, but during the depth of the Great Depression in 1933 it dropped to 505 workers. The firm soon increased production and by 1936 increased its staff to 601. Mitsugi Nakamura served as president during the Depression and war years, from 1934 to 1946.

During World War II the firm expanded by supplying the navy with antiaircraft artillery shells and bulldozers. Komatsu's first major product after the war was a redesigned bulldozer, which came off the assembly line in 1947. One year later diesel engines were

COMPANY PERSPECTIVES

We at Komatsu believe our corporate value is the total sum of trust given to us by society and all stakeholders. In order to increase corporate value in a lasting way, we work to enhance all aspects of Quality and Reliability with regard to not only our business activities but also our efforts for the environment and cooperation with society.

produced. From 1947 to 1964 President Yoshinari Kawai provided key leadership in rebuilding the company and making it a global multinational corporation.

The Korean War gave the Japanese economy a boost with orders from the United States to supply its troops in Korea. At that time the firm had plants in Awazu, Osaka, Kawasaki, Himi, and Komatsu, Japan. Forklift trucks, dump trucks, and armored cars were added to the line in 1953, with shell mold castings introduced the following year. By 1959 defense production included armored personnel carriers and self-propelled cannons.

International activities increased in 1955 when both construction equipment and presses were shipped outside the country. In 1958 operations began in India with an agreement between the firm and the Indian government to manufacture tractors. Three years later, another license agreement was signed with a U.S. manufacturer, Cummins Engine Company, to make and sell diesel engines.

SIGHTS ON CATERPILLAR: 1960–69

By the early 1960s the firm had grown such that a new headquarters was required, and the Komatsu Building was constructed in Tokyo. Ryoichi Kawai became president in 1964, the same year the firm received the Deming Prize for quality, named after William Edwards Deming, the American quality guru whose writings on quality control between 1950 and 1952 became the bible of Japanese manufacturing.

The 1960s saw an economic buildup for Japan as a result of the Vietnam War, and Komatsu's expansion continued at a rapid pace. In the latter part of the decade a new engine plant began production in Japan, a radio-controlled bulldozer was introduced, and a technical research center was established. In 1967 the

company established its first overseas subsidiary, N.V. Komatsu Europe S.A., which was based in Belgium.

President Kawai made it clear that the company's goal was to surpass Caterpillar. Each year, Kawai presented his managers with a clear set of priorities modeled after Caterpillar's performance. The yearly priorities were then worked into detailed plans of action, known as Plan, Do, Check, Act (PDCA). Kawai's growth strategy was clearly successful. Over the next 20 years, Komatsu grew from a local manufacturer to a serious competitor in the global construction market. As a result, Komatsu's management style became widely studied and emulated.

GLOBAL EXPANSION: 1970–89

In 1970 the firm began its first direct investment in the United States, with the establishment of Komatsu America Corporation. Other foreign operations soon followed, in Singapore, Australia, Mexico, Brazil, and China. Komatsu began producing bulldozers in Brazil in 1975, marking the company's first production of construction equipment outside of Japan.

In 1981 Komatsu was awarded the Japan Quality Control Prize, to honor the company's outstanding production quality. The following year Shoji Nogawa became president. The 1980s brought expansion of global operations. In 1985, after a number of incentives from the state of Tennessee, Komatsu purchased a 55-acre empty plant in Chattanooga, a purchase that reflected a decision by the firm to challenge its principal rival, Caterpillar, in its home market. This move gained Komatsu its first U.S. manufacturing facility. Canadian operations expanded as well, as two plants were built, in Quebec and in Ontario. European operations included an interest in the West German construction firm of Hamomag AG, a licensing agreement with FAI S.p.A. of Italy, and a plant in the United Kingdom.

The year 1987 marked expansion in other areas, such as the establishment of two financial subsidiaries in Europe, the marketing of plastics injection molding machinery, and the development of a telephone with a data terminal. At the same time, the construction market was changing, and Komatsu's sales began to slump. From 1985 to 1987, construction equipment sales dropped each year. As a result, the company president, Shoji Nogawa, was dismissed by Chairman Ryoichi Kawai, and changes were instituted. In 1988 an international business division was set up in the Tokyo headquarters. The division had three regional groups that would be the main focus of the firm's international business operations: the Americas, Europe, and Japan. The goals of the division included development of joint

KEY DATES

1894: The Takeuchi Mining Company is founded.

1917: Takeuchi Mining establishes Komatsu Iron Works to manufacture machine tools and mining equipment for in-house use.

1921: The ironworks are separated from the mining company to form Komatsu Ltd.

1947: Komatsu begins manufacturing a redesigned bulldozer, marking the expansion into construction equipment.

1953: Production of forklift trucks and dump trucks begins.

1967: The first overseas subsidiary, Komatsu Europe, is established in Belgium.

1970: The first U.S. subsidiary, Komatsu America Corporation, is created.

1975: The first production of construction equipment outside of Japan begins, at a plant in Brazil.

1985: U.S. manufacturing activities begin with the purchase of a plant in Tennessee.

1995: Production of construction equipment begins at plants in China.

2008: Company launches the world's first hybrid hydraulic excavator.

ventures around the world and overseas purchase of parts.

In 1988 the company established a new subsidiary, Komatsu Trading International, to increase imports to Japan, in response to the Japanese government's commitment to reduce its trade surplus by importing more foreign products. As a result, logging machinery from Canada, backhoe loaders from Italy, and high-powered motor boats from Norway were brought into Japan for sale in the domestic market under importer agreements between Komatsu and companies in the respective countries.

Also in 1988, Komatsu sharpened its competitive edge in the U.S. market by forming a joint venture with Dresser Industries, Inc., called Komatsu Dresser Company. Included within the venture were Komatsu's two U.S. subsidiaries and Dresser's construction machinery division, thereby forming the second largest maker of construction machinery in the United States. The combination enabled Komatsu to move assembly of its construction equipment to the United States, using Dresser plants that were running at 50 percent capacity while Komatsu was unable to fill all of its orders.

NEW TARGETS: 1990–95

A new president, Tetsuya Katada, took over in 1989. Katada decided that Komatsu's management had been hampered to some extent by the company's goal of catching Caterpillar. Whereas this strategy had worked remarkably well in expanding the company while the global market was growing, now that worldwide demand for construction equipment was down, Komatsu did not have the flexibility to adapt. Katada believed that the creativity of Komatsu's middle managers had been sacrificed while everyone was concentrating on Caterpillar, and that managers had grown afraid to question the direction of the company. Katada's solution was to stop comparing Komatsu to Caterpillar. He encouraged managers to think of Komatsu as a "total technology enterprise" and to find new products and markets that fit the wider definition of the company. Komatsu's new goal became the somewhat broader "Growth, Global, Groupwide," with a more concrete aim to double sales by the mid-1990s.

Katada's success became clear quickly. Sales had been declining since 1982, but after Katada initiated the new business strategy, sales began to climb again. Komatsu's non-construction business grew by 40 percent between 1989 and 1992. Nevertheless, the Komatsu Dresser Company lost money, because of deteriorating markets for heavy equipment and problems with the merger. The Dresser and Komatsu product lines were to remain distinct under the merged company, but this resulted in dealers within the company directly competing with each other. Dresser managers also reported problems communicating with their Komatsu counterparts. This was to some extent remedied when Komatsu began bringing its American employees to Japan to learn more about Japanese culture and work. Steep appreciation of the Japanese yen also ate into Komatsu's profits. In 1993 Komatsu introduced cost-cutting measures, including some cuts in its workforce and streamlining of its manufacturing facilities in Japan.

The firm had shown a quick response to the 1992 integration of Europe by the European Common Market. British operations included purchase agreements with the British firm of Perkins Engines Ltd. for diesel engines to power Komatsu excavators. The U.K. plant in Birtley was the main production facility for European construction equipment. Other parts came from Spain, France, Belgium, and Germany. An additional agreement with the Italian firm of FAI to manufacture under license mini-hydraulic excavators added to a strong

European presence. Komatsu also began expanding its production of large trucks in the United States and Brazil in 1993, and increased its imports of parts from Brazil, South Korea, Indonesia, and China.

Komatsu also continued its longstanding relationship with Cummins Engine Company. In 1993 the companies formed two joint ventures to manufacture and sell diesel engines. A Japan-based unit was created to make Cummins' small engines, and a unit based in the United States was formed to produce Komatsu's large engines.

There were a number of ownership changes that affected the Komatsu Dresser venture in the early to mid-1990s. In August 1992 Dresser Industries spun off its industrial businesses, including its 50 percent stake in Komatsu Dresser, to its shareholders, forming Indresco, Inc. Then in September 1993 Komatsu increased its stake in the venture to 81 percent by buying out part of Indresco's interest. Finally, in 1994 Komatsu purchased Indresco's remaining stake, taking full control of Komatsu Dresser. In January 1996 the U.S. subsidiary was renamed Komatsu America International Company.

MOVING INTO NEW MARKETS: 1993–98

A key to Komatsu's continued growth was its diversification into new markets, including nonconstruction businesses. Electronics became Komatsu's second most important business area. To increase its presence in this area, Komatsu made a strategic alliance with Applied Materials, Inc., a U.S. manufacturer of computer display panels, in 1993. Komatsu invested tens of millions of dollars in a 50 percent share of a new joint venture with the U.S. company. By 1995 the venture, called Applied Komatsu Technology Inc., had become a competitive force in the Japanese market for computer liquid crystal displays. Meanwhile, in 1994 Komatsu expanded into the local area network (LAN) equipment market by beginning production of two types of hubs and a print server.

Komatsu also began to focus more on business ventures related to recycling. In 1994 the company began a joint venture with Japan Samtech Co. Ltd., a leading Japanese maker of incinerators. In 1995 Komatsu entered an agreement with a leading plastics recycler in the United States, Pure Tech International, to begin building and marketing recycling plants in Japan. Komatsu also continued to press for an expansion of its core construction business worldwide in the mid-1990s. Construction in Komatsu's domestic market boomed in 1995 and 1996, sadly because of the massive Kobe earthquake in January 1995. Around the world, Komatsu had 15 plants in 10 countries outside Japan as of 1995, and the company entered new joint ventures in Thailand, Vietnam, and China in that year. In June 1995 Satoru Anzaki became the new president of Komatsu, and former president Kataka became chairman.

From fiscal 1995 to fiscal 1998 Komatsu enjoyed four consecutive years of increasing net profit and sales. The company was aided by the booming U.S. economy and a surge in spending on infrastructure projects in the burgeoning market of east Asia. This period was highlighted by a continued drive into new markets and the formation of several more joint ventures.

In January 1996 Komatsu joined with Mannesmann Demag AG to form the German venture Demag Komatsu GmbH, which was charged with developing and producing super-large hydraulic excavators for the global mining industry. Komatsu had already entered the mining market through its former joint venture with Dresser, which brought to the company the Haulpak line of mining trucks. Further involvement in this sector came through the March 1996 acquisition of controlling interest in Modular Mining Systems, Inc., maker of electronic mine management systems.

Then in April 1997 Komatsu created Vernon Hills, Illinois-based Komatsu Mining Systems, Inc., as the international headquarters for its rapidly growing mining equipment business. Also created in 1997 and also based in Vernon Hills was Komatsu Utility Corporation, which took over the manufacturing of backhoe loaders, compact excavators, compact wheel loaders, and compact bulldozers and the marketing of these products to the utility, construction, and rental markets.

The desire to capture a greater share of the increasing market for construction machinery in Southeast Asia led Komatsu in mid-1996 to create Komatsu Asia & Pacific Pte. Ltd. in Singapore to coordinate and expand its operations in the region. That year the company also began manufacturing construction equipment in Thailand, giving it two production bases in Asia, the other being in Indonesia. In early 1998 Komatsu joined with Larsen & Toubro Ltd. of India to form Bangalore-based L&T-Komatsu Ltd., which would make Komatsu hydraulic excavators and sell them in India and bordering countries. Around this same time, Cummins Engine and Komatsu formed a third joint venture, a Japan-based firm called Industrial Power Alliance, Ltd. This venture was an extension of the previous ones and was formed to research and develop next-generation industrial diesel engines. Cummins Engine shortened its name to Cummins Inc. in 2001.

DECLINING FORTUNES AND RESTRUCTURING EFFORTS: 1997–2000

The late 1990s and early 2000s brought a sharp decline in Komatsu's fortunes. One factor was fallout from the Asian economic crisis that erupted in mid-1997 and that brought a halt to the rapid growth in Southeast Asia. At the same time, the already struggling Japanese economy went into its steepest postwar recession, prompting Komatsu customers to slash their orders for construction equipment. In addition, Komatsu's electronics business was hit hard by the deterioration in the price of and the demand for silicon wafers. Record results from the still buoyant U.S. and European economies were not enough to keep Komatsu from falling into the red for the fiscal year ending in March 1999, the first full-year loss in the company's history. Net sales declined that year by 3.8 percent.

Komatsu responded by launching a restructuring of its domestic construction equipment manufacturing operations in November 1998. Three factories were closed over the course of the next two years, resulting in a 20 percent reduction in production floor space. Komatsu also halted production at its semiconductor plant in Hillsboro, Oregon, announcing that it would concentrate its production in Japan and Taiwan. In a further pullback in its electronics business, Komatsu in November 1999 sold its stake in Applied Komatsu Technology, the flat panel display joint venture, to its partner, Applied Materials. Komatsu also reorganized its management structure during 1999 by slashing the number of board members from 26 to 8 and appointing a person from outside the company to the board. These moves were designed to speed up the decision-making process and enhance the objectivity and transparency of management. Katada and Anzaki remained chairman and president, respectively.

Although Komatsu returned to profitability in fiscal 2000 and 2001, the recovery would prove short-lived. During these two years, the company established additional joint ventures. In February 2000 an agreement was reached with Linde AG of Germany on global collaboration in the production and marketing of forklift truck and related products. Komatsu joined with Ushio Inc. of Japan in August 2000 to form a joint venture called Gigaphoton Inc. to develop, manufacture, and sell excimer lasers used as lithography tools in the production of semiconductors. In December 2000 Komatsu acquired Hensley Industries, Inc., a U.S. maker of construction and mining equipment components.

Also in 2000, Anzaki hired Keith Sheldon, a retired General Motors Corporation manager, for the new position of global financial officer. Sheldon's task was to overhaul Komatsu's system of financial management and lay the foundation for revamping the company through takeovers and spin-offs of noncore operations. For a Japanese company to hire a foreigner for such a high-level position was quite bold, and it was indicative of Anzaki's desire to transform Komatsu into a more American- or European-style company. In a similar vein, Anzaki a few years earlier had begun trying to boost the company's return on equity in clear imitation of U.S. and European multinationals. Finally, during fiscal 2001 Komatsu announced that it planned to introduce a stock option scheme for 47 top employees. In June 2001 Masahiro Sakane, an executive vice president, was appointed president, succeeding Anzaki, who became chairman.

RESTRUCTURING CONTINUES: 2001–03

Construction machinery orders in Japan declined precipitously in fiscal 2002 as the government greatly reduced its spending on public works projects. Demand also was falling in the now struggling U.S. and European economies. The main bright spot was China, which continued to grow. Komatsu was hit further by a drastic decline in the semiconductor market. Revenues for the year declined 5.5 percent, and the company fell back into the red, posting a net loss of ¥80.6 billion, or $606 million.

Responding to this dismal performance, Komatsu announced a major restructuring in October 2001. Aiming to reduce annual fixed costs by ¥30 billion ($250 million) by 2004, the company said it would reduce its workforce by 2,200 workers, or about 10 percent. Komatsu also took a ¥26 billion write-off to shut down its Oregon semiconductor plant. In an attempt to reignite sales growth in its core construction machinery operations, the company said it would attempt to capture a larger share of the rental equipment, used equipment, and machinery repair markets.

Further restructuring efforts came in 2002. The firm's U.S. construction, mining, and utility operations were merged within the Komatsu America Corp. subsidiary; included were Komatsu America International, Komatsu Mining Systems, and Komatsu Utility. The move was intended to cut costs and improve efficiency.

By 2003 it was clear that Komatsu was taking aggressive action in an attempt to spark a turnaround. Indeed, by the end of that year profits appeared to be rebounding. The company established Komatsu Forklift Co., Ltd., in China that year to bolster sales of forklift trucks.

GLOBAL FOCUS LEADS TO SUCCESS: 2004–07

Komatsu found success in 2004 and 2005 due to its focus on international ventures. Global demand for construction and mining machinery had surged and the company was prepared to take advantage. Infrastructure projects in developing markets known as the BRICs, which included Brazil, Russia, India, and China, was also fueling demand.

During 2004 the company established Komatsu Forest AB by acquiring Partek Forest AB, a manufacturer and distributor of forestry equipment in Sweden. It also created Komatsu Industries Ltd. in China to serve as a sales company for industrial machinery. Komatsu Power Generation Systems Ltd. was also launched in China to manufacture power generators. The company also established a forklift manufacturing subsidiary in China that year.

By fiscal 2004 and 2005, Komatsu was securing record operating profits. The company focused on bolstering its industrial machinery holdings but opted to sell off some of its noncore businesses. As such, it jettisoned its polysilicon business in 2005. Komatsu Electronic Metal, its silicon wafer business, was sold to Sumco Corp. in 2006.

During 2007 the company opened two new plants in Japan and one in India. The following year it established a subsidiary in Russia to oversee the construction of its first plant in the region. The facility was slated to begin production in June 2010. Komatsu also focused on emerging technologies and launched the world's first hybrid hydraulic excavator in 2008. In addition it equipped its construction machinery with monitoring devices that used Global Positioning System communications to track in real time how much the machine was used and its fuel consumption. This feature allowed Komatsu to forecast future demand for its machines.

A CHANGING MARKETPLACE: 2008 AND BEYOND

By 2008 a financial crisis in the United States led to a global economic downturn that began to weaken demand for construction and industrial equipment. Overall, the company saw its sales fall dramatically in the United States, Japan, and in Europe. Demand in emerging markets including China, India, and Brazil also fell temporarily. During fiscal 2009, Komatsu saw its revenues decline by nearly 10 percent and its net income plummet by 62.3 percent over the previous year. It was forced to shutter six of its manufacturing facilities and implement a strict cost-cutting program.

While a recovery in the United States, Japan, and Europe was expected to be slow, Komatsu began to show signs in early 2010 that it had overcome the challenges and was well positioned to capitalize on improvement in the BRIC construction industries. When asked in October 2009 how the global market had changed over the past two years, Komatsu President and CEO Kunio Noji told the *Nikkei Report*, "The construction machinery industry has entered an era in which the market is led by emerging countries." Indeed, by gaining a solid foothold in countries including China and India, Komatsu was optimistic it was on track for success in the years to come.

Joseph A. LeMay
Updated, Angela Woodward;
David E. Salamie; Christina M. Stansell

PRINCIPAL SUBSIDIARIES

Komatsu Construction Equipment Sales and Service Japan Ltd.; Komatsu Rental Japan Ltd.; Komatsu Used Equipment Corp.; Komatsu Cummins Engine Co., Ltd.; Industrial Power Alliance, Ltd.; Komatsu Diesel Co., Ltd.; Komatsu Castex Ltd.; Komatsu Cabtec Co., Ltd.; Komatsu Safety Training Center Ltd.; Komatsu Logistics Corp.; Komatsu Utility Co., Ltd.; Komatsu Forklift Japan Ltd.; Komatsu Industries Corporation; Komatsu Machinery Corporation; KOMATSU NTC LTD.; Komatsu Engineering Corp.; KELK Ltd.; Komatsu Business Support Ltd.; Komatsu Tokki Corporation; Komatsu House Ltd.; Komatsu General Services Ltd. GIGAPHOTON INC.; Komatsu America Corp.

PRINCIPAL COMPETITORS

Caterpillar Inc.; CNH Global N.V.; Deere & Company.

FURTHER READING

Darnbrough, Jessica, "World's First Hybrid Excavator Debuts," *Australian Mining*, September 1, 2008.

Kelly, Tim, "Squash the Caterpillar; Komatsu Is a Smaller Rival to Caterpillar in a Global Battle, but It's Making Its Mark in China," *Forbes Asia*, April 21, 2008.

"Komatsu CEO: Japan Still Firm's Tech Innovation Center," *Nikkei Report*, October 27, 2009.

"Komatsu Recovery Hinges on Emerging Countries," *Nikkei Report*, June 18, 2009.

"Komatsu Sees Brisk China Construction Gear Sales," *Reuters News*, June 26, 2009.

Konishi, Yusuke, "Komatsu Roars Back as Global Firm," *Nikkei Weekly*, October 31, 2005.

Kruger, David, and Ichiko Fuyuno, "Komatsu Heads for the Trenches," *Far Eastern Economic Review*, November 22, 2001, pp. 58–61.

Marsh, Peter, "Digging for Ideas in the West," *Financial Times*, May 2, 2000, p. 14.

Rahman, Bayan, "Komatsu Weighs Up the Situation," *Financial Times*, December 6, 2001, p. 3.

Uesaka, Yoshifumi, "Komatsu Moves Ahead of Peers," *Nikkei Weekly*, March 1, 2010.

Williams, Michael, and Douglas Appell, "Komatsu Hopes Overhaul Can Lift It Out of Slump," *Asian Wall Street Journal*, September 18, 2000, p. 13.

Kwik Trip Inc.

———————■———————

1626 Oak Street
La Crosse, Wisconsin 54603
U.S.A.
Telephone: (608) 781-8988
Fax: (608) 781-8950
Web site: http://www.kwiktrip.com

Private Company
Incorporated: 1965
Employees: 8,070
Sales: $3 billion (2008 est.)
NAICS: 445120 Convenience Stores; 447110 Gasoline
    Stations with Convenience Stores

■ ■ ■

Kwik Trip Inc. is a midwestern chain of approximately 400 Kwik Trip or Kwik Star conveniences stores, doing business in Wisconsin, Minnesota, and Iowa. Based in La Crosse, Wisconsin, Kwik Trip stands out among other convenience store chains in the degree to which it is vertically integrated. Kwik Trip runs its own baking plant, which provides baked goods for all its stores. Its commissary provides the stores with fresh sandwiches, Kwik Trip's own brand of frozen pizza, and other prepared foods. The company also runs a dairy plant, producing its own milk and coffee creamer, an ice cream plant, an ice and water plant, and its own warehousing, trucking, and vehicle maintenance divisions. Kwik Trip processes its own credit card, allowing it to save on fees it would otherwise pay to card issuers such as Visa and MasterCard.

Kwik Trip's convenience stores are generally about 5,000 square feet. They carry an array of grocery and snack items, and sell gas and tobacco, filling a niche left open by large-format grocery chains and general merchandisers such as Wal-Mart. Kwik Trip Inc. also operates some 40 Tobacco Outlet Plus stores. The company's combined stores serve approximately four million customers every week. The chain is privately held by members of the Zietlow family. Kwik Trip also shares a substantial amount of profits with its employees. Founded in 1965, the chain was still expanding in the 2010s.

A NEW NOTION FOR THE NORTH

Kwik Trip was founded in 1965 by John Hansen. Hansen grew up in Bangor, Wisconsin, and graduated with a degree in agricultural science from the University of Wisconsin in 1960. Early in his career, he worked for the National Livestock and Meat Board in Chicago. Later he worked for a company called John Morrell and Co. His job required frequent travel, and he spent some time in the South. Hansen took note of the convenience stores that were popular in the southern states.

These small groceries offered customers an easy way to pick up just a few food items, beer, or cigarettes, so that a shopping trip was not an extended affair. At the time these stores were mostly a southern fixture, and had not yet spread to the Midwest. Hansen, by this time married and with young children, and was becoming less willing to spend time away from his family. He began to speculate about opening a southern-style convenience store in Wisconsin. He thought the time was right, and that having his own store would allow him to stay at home with his wife and children rather than spend time on the road.

Hansen went into partnership with Gateway Foods, a local grocery wholesaler. The company's first store was a former IGA grocery store in Eau Claire, Wisconsin. Hansen and his wife decided to call the store Kwik Trip. They made Kwik Trip's first sign themselves out of plywood and red paint. They set to work to make the new store flourish. Hansen worked from 7:00 a.m. until 11:00 p.m., including weekends and holidays. For the first year, the store did not turn a profit.

The building also required numerous renovations to distinguish it from an ordinary grocery. The Eau Claire building was a long rectangle, with a door in front and parking along the side. Hansen installed windows and rearranged the entrance so that customers could walk in directly from the parking lot. For the Eau Claire store, he used sliding doors, although this turned out to be a poor choice for frigid Wisconsin.

Numerous changes to the interior made Kwik Trip easy for shoppers to navigate, and set it apart from larger stores. Hansen renovated and remodeled so that the new store had a central checkout stand instead of individual checkout lanes. He made the shelving lower, changed the lighting, and turned what had been the old IGA's meat department into walk-in beer coolers. Hansen endeavored to make the store noticeably different. At the same time, he was careful to keep prices similar to pricing at regular groceries. Kwik Trip's aim was to provide a quicker, easier shopping experience that did not leave the customer feeling gouged by higher prices.

EARLY EXPANSION

With its first year behind it, Kwik Trip began to be financially viable. Within a few years, the company began to expand. Kwik Trip started selling gasoline as well as groceries. By 1971, there were five Kwik Trip

stores. Gateway's interest in Kwik Trip ended in 1972, when two of its executives became partners with Hansen and bought out the grocery chain. One partner, Don Zietlow, eventually became president of Gateway, and later, sole owner of Kwik Trip. The other partner was D. B. Reinhart. By 1974, Kwik Trip ran nine stores. Hansen continued to put in long hours running the company, and to relax he farmed. Although his company was young and growing and required a full-time commitment, Hansen found time to work a farm with some 200 head of animals.

Kwik Trip grew from nine stores in 1974 to 50 stores less than a decade later. At the same time that stores were being added, the company also added production facilities, allowing Kwik Trip to manufacture and distribute many of its own products. It began by opening a commissary in 1975. This allowed the company to prepare foods such as sandwiches for sale in its stores. Eventually the commissary, located in La Crosse, also made hot foods as well.

Kwik Trip opened a corporate support center in La Crosse in 1980. This served a variety of functions. It was a centralized distribution center, which made deliveries of prepared food and other products to Kwik Trip stores six days a week. The support center also took on some other duties that other convenience store chains might have outsourced. Kwik Trip cleaned its own rugs for all its stores at its central support center. It also installed a facility to ripen its own bananas, so fruit could be sent to its stores at the peak of freshness. The support center made ice, and also took care of all kinds of equipment repair. All these factors let the convenience store chain control its costs to a high degree.

ADDING A DAIRY

Next Kwik Trip began operating its own dairy. The company's first dairy, opened in 1981, was located in New Caledonia, Minnesota. The dairy bought raw milk from Wisconsin and Minnesota farmers, and pasteurized, processed, and bottled it for distribution to Kwik Trip stores. In 1984 the dairy moved to La Crosse. Milk was one of Kwik Trip's biggest sellers, so it made sense for the company to run its own milk production plant and keep control of its costs as much as possible. For a while, the company bought its coffee creamer from an outside vendor in individual serving portions. Eventually Kwik Trip started making its own creamer, which it made up in half-gallon containers that sat in countertop units at the stores' coffee bars. The company estimated that using its own creamer saved Kwik Trip approximately $500,000 a year.

Next came a Kwik Trip central bakery. This opened in 1985, and made pastries, bread, buns, donuts, cook-

KEY DATES

1965: John Hansen opens first store in Eau Claire, Wisconsin.
1972: Founder Hansen takes two new partners.
1981: Company opens own dairy.
1985: Kwik Trip opens its own centralized bakery.
1986: Chain grows to 100 stores.
1989: Hansen and Don Zietlow become sole owners of company.
2000: Zietlow buys out Hansen's share.
2010: Chain grows to 400 stores.

ies, and other desserts. Baked goods comprised about 5 percent of sales, and the company reaped savings by making and distributing its own. Its dairy delivered milk to the bakery, and Kwik Trip's own fleet of trucks shipped out finished goods. This tight operation helped Kwik Trip to keep its costs low. By the early years of the 21st century, the company was manufacturing and distributing nearly 80 percent of the products it sold. There were some products, such as soda, that the company tried to make in house, only to find that consumers preferred national brands.

The company tested new products carefully, using focus groups and surveys. With some products, such as pizza, the company could make and sell its own brand without stocking competitors' labels. In the case of snack foods such as potato chips, the stores offered national brands such as Frito-Lay, but also sold the Kwik Trip brand at a much lower price. With an eye on cost and customer preference, the company moved carefully into more and more cities and towns. From 50 stores in 1983, the chain grew to 100 units by 1986.

NEW OWNERSHIP IN 1989

John Hansen had pioneered the company in 1965, with the backing of Gateway Foods. Don Zietlow bought into the business in 1972, along with another partner. Zietlow grew up on a farm near La Crosse, and then worked as a truck driver. He began working at Gateway in 1963. He worked as a frozen foods buyer, and then was promoted to manager of meat merchandising. By 1989, Zietlow had become president of Gateway. That year, another grocery wholesaler, Scrivner Inc., acquired Gateway. At that point, Zietlow bought out the third partner's interest in Kwik Trip. He then sold half of his new share to Hansen. At that point, their two families

became sole owners of Kwik Trip Inc. Zietlow left his job at Gateway and became more involved in the operation of Kwik Trip.

The task ahead of Hansen and Zietlow in the 1990s was to manage the company's growth. Kwik Trip had added stores at an increasingly rapid pace. It had also brought along an array of support services and production facilities. With almost 200 stores in 1989, the company had to make sure it could survive as a bigger, more complex chain. The company hoped to add some 20 stores a year in the early 1990s. It explored new markets as it added new services and revamped store design.

RESTRUCTURING MANAGEMENT

Some changes were made to the company's management structure in the 1990s. Executive departments of marketing, human resources, buying, training, and credit were established. That way, the more than 3,000 employees had the kind of support and information they needed to do their jobs well. Furthermore, the company could hire people with specialized skills to devote to systems such as computer and information technology.

The company explored promising markets, and began moving into metropolitan St. Paul, Minnesota. A major investment was made in a new warehouse facility. The company broke ground on a new warehouse and distribution center in 1995. The new facility was almost double the size of the old facility. The chain had about 250 stores at the time, and it built the distribution center so that it could handle 500 stores. This gave Kwik Trip comfortable room to grow.

The company also expanded its office headquarters as it added employees, divisions, and stores. It invested $2 million in 1997 in a new office building, the fourth headquarters in its history. The next year, Kwik Trip rolled out a new store floor plan. The new design gave maximum impact to the most profitable items. It included a hot beverage counter, with more room for coffeemakers and cappuccino machines. Existing stores also got upgrades.

The company reconfigured its gas pumps in 1998, allowing its machines to handle "pay at pump" credit and debit cards. Since the company had its own Kwik Card credit card, software used at other gas stations had to be customized for Kwik Trip. These multiple renovations and improvements were expensive. The company aimed to fund its growth through its own profit, which was targeted at $32 million for 1998.

ANOTHER OWNERSHIP CHANGE
IN 2000

John Hansen, the company's founder, had co-owned Kwik Trip since 1989 with Don Zietlow. They worked together throughout the 1990s to continue the chain's growth. By the end of the decade, the chain had grown to about 300 Kwik Trip or Kwik Star stores (its Iowa stores were renamed Kwik Star in 1995) plus a chain of about 50 tobacco outlets, several Hearty Platter restaurants, and all the associated infrastructure such as the dairy, bakery, commissary, and computer support center. Hansen retired from Kwik Trip in 2000. He sold his interest in the company to Zietlow for $120 million. Hansen went on to found another business, while Zietlow was alone at the helm of Kwik Trip.

With his purchase of Hansen's share of the company, Zietlow also assumed $160 million in company debt. He then borrowed $300 million as he set about assessing where the company needed to grow or cut back in ensuing years. The company came up with a long-term strategic marketing plan to allow it to grow in its most profitable areas. Kwik Trip determined that sales of gas and cigarettes would tend toward less profit as time went on.

More effort was therefore devoted toward the company's foodservice business. It developed new products and also focused its marketing more on food. Customer focus groups identified products that should sell well. Kwik Trip added more hot and cold prepared foods to its lineup. As always, vertical integration was key to the company's strategy. It continued to develop its own proprietary food products, such as its Urge brand frozen pizza, so that its best sellers were also its highest profit items. By around 2005, with over 300 stores, Kwik Trip manufactured approximately 80 percent of the products it sold.

RESEARCH AND INNOVATION

The company kept abreast of competitors by doing lots of research. Its technology was always up to date, and its executives traveled to investigate what other chains and other markets were like. This included a study trip to London in 2007. European stores, in many ways ahead of American convenience stores, offered good pointers for innovations. Furthermore, European grocery chains such as Tesco were actively investigating moving into U.S. markets. Kwik Trip made sure it understood how European convenience chains operated.

The company also opened a new food research facility. It spent $14 million on a new food commissary in 2007 in order to handle increasing demand for its sandwiches, salads, pizza, and other prepared foods. The commissary included a test kitchen, stocked with equip-

ment similar to that actually installed in Kwik Trip stores. The company standardized its procedure for testing new products, to make sure quality was consistent and to allow staff from different areas to provide input. Employees at every level were asked to give suggestions. When the test kitchen opened, its new director already had a 28-page list of ideas.

Zietlow was 73 in 2008. He considered retiring, while the Kwik Trip chain continued to plot future growth. The company had close to 400 stores in 2008, with expectations to keep building as many as 20 stores a year. It also planned to expand its bakery and build a new ice cream and yogurt plant. Although the U.S. economy hit hard times toward the end of the first decade of the new century, the recession did not seem to affect Kwik Trip's plans. The company went ahead with a $23 million project that doubled the size of the bakery and tripled its production capability.

By 2009 Kwik Trip employed some 1,600 people in its headquarters and various facilities in La Crosse. The company added jobs even as many midwestern employers downsized and laid off workers. Late in 2009 the company unveiled a new store design. Zietlow told *Convenience Store News* (August 10, 2009) that the chain's sales had "grown quite well, despite the recession." Therefore, the company would invest some $30 million in refits of its existing stores while it rolled out new ones. The company claimed 400 stores and $3 billion in annual sales in 2010, and seemed well positioned for continued growth.

A. Woodward

PRINCIPAL COMPETITORS

7-Eleven, Inc.; Hy-Vee, Inc.; Speedway SuperAmerica LLC.

FURTHER READING

Calahan, Steve, "CEO: Kwik Trip Poised for Growth," *La Crosse (Wis.) Tribune*, November 3, 2006.

———, "Kwik Trip Bakery Expansion Helps Position Company for the Future," *La Crosse (Wis.) Tribune*, June 7, 2009.

———, "Kwik Trip Is Still Family-Owned and Still Growing," *La Crosse (Wis.) Tribune*, May 4, 2008.

———, "Kwik Trip Plans to Continue Expanding Its Support Center Facilities," *La Crosse (Wis.) Tribune*, May 8, 2008.

Donohue, Bill, "The Central Nervous System of Kwik Trip," *Convenience Store Decisions*, November 2004, p. 64.

Hebets, Shahla, "On the Road with Kwik Trip," *Convenience Store Decisions*, December 2006, p. 8.

"Kwik Trip Makes Splash in Twin Cities," *Kwik Connection*, June 1995, pp. 1, 7.

Longo, Don, "Kwik Trip Bows New Look," *Convenience Store News*, August 10, 2009, p. 14.

Laïta S.A.S.

Zone Industrielle Kergaradec
60 Avenue du Baron Lacrosse
Brest, F-29806 Cedex 9
France
Telephone: (+33 02) 98 42 54 25
Fax: (+33 02) 98 42 46 10
Web site: http://www.laita.fr

Private Company
Incorporated: 2009
Employees: 1,850
Sales: EUR 1.1 billion ($1.5 billion) (2009 est.)
NAICS: 424430 Dairy Products (Except Dried or Canned) Merchant Wholesalers; 424490 Other Grocery and Related Product Merchant Wholesalers

■ ■ ■

Laïta S.A.S. is France's third-largest producer and distributor of dairy products, behind Lactalis and Sodiaal. Laïta represents the merger of the industrial dairy production facilities of three of the largest dairy cooperatives in France's northwest region, Coopagri Bretagne, Terrena, and Even, in 2009. However, Laïta has existed since 1990 as the commercial arm for the dairy products of the three cooperatives. As such, Laïta has developed a number of strong brands, including Paysan Breton, the leading French butter brand, which has since diversified into a wide range of prepared foods and ready-to-eat meals; Mamie Nova, covering a line of yogurts and sour cream products; Regilait, France's leading powdered milk brand, which also produces concentrated milk products; and Madame Loïk, a line of flavored fresh cheeses.

Laïta also produces dairy-based food ingredients, such as casein and other milk proteins, through subsidiary Laiterie Nouvelle de l'Arguenon. In 2009 Laïta processed more than 1.5 billion liters of milk produced by the members of its three cooperative shareholders, for total revenues of EUR 1.1 billion. While France remains the group's primary market, Laïta has developed a strong export operation, with sales subsidiaries in Italy, the United Kingdom, and Germany. In 2009 the company's exports accounted for 25 percent of its total sales. Jean-Bernard Solliec is Laïta's president.

ORIGINS IN COOPAGRI BRETAGNE

The creation of Laïta S.A.S. in 2009 represented a new step in the transformation of France's cooperative dairy sector, which had its roots in the 1960s. That period marked the true start toward the consolidation of France's many cooperatives in response to new pressures presented by the emergence of the supermarket sector. These pressures included the demand for new processing and packaging technologies, such as ultrahigh-temperature and corresponding long-life milk packaging, which enabled supermarkets to stock milk products for longer periods and without the need for refrigeration. At the same time, the growing negotiating power of the supermarket groups gave them the upper hand in establishing pricing. With lower margins available from traditional milk products, the dairy cooperatives sought to develop new higher-value processed dairy foods.

COMPANY PERSPECTIVES

Permanently adapting our products to market demand, our reactivity and our know-how are the keys to our success internationally.

Among the most prominent cooperatives to emerge during that time was Coopagri Bretagne, founded in 1966 upon the breakup of the Office Centrale, which had dominated the Brittany region's agricultural sector since the early part of the century. Coopagri Bretagne represented a distinct presence in the cooperative movement at the time, spanning a wide range of agricultural sectors and products.

Members of Coopagri Bretagne had begun to develop their own industrial food operations, such as the founding of a frozen vegetables plant in Landernau in 1962. The cooperative's dairy farmers joined together in 1965 to found their own production facility, Centrale Laitère de Lanrinou, also based in Landernau. This facility provided the foundation for what would become Laïta.

PAYSAN BRETON BRAND
INTRODUCED: 1969

The growth of the supermarket sector had begun to squeeze out the region's traditional small grocers by the end of the 1960s. The rising predominance of the supermarket groups also created a new demand, for the development of branded products. These were of special interest to the supermarket groups since branded products generally represented far superior profit margins in comparison to generic products or even those sold under the supermarket groups' own labels.

Coopagri Bretagne responded to this demand with the creation of its own dairy brand, Paysan Breton (literally, Brittany Farmer), in 1969. The Landernau-based dairy launched its first branded product, a molded butter, that same year. Over the next decades, the Paysan Breton brand rose to become one of France's leading butter brands. The group's marketing efforts played an important part in this success. For example, in 1972 the company introduced the famous "Vichy paper" motif on its packaging, making its butter easily identifiable on supermarket shelves. The growth of the Paysan Breton brand was also supported by a wide-ranging advertising effort, including a long line of well-received television advertisements.

The growth of Paysan Breton enabled Centrale Laitère de Lanrinou to extend its own operations, as it launched a series of mergers with dairy cooperatives throughout the Brittany region. This expansion led the company to adopt a new name, Union des Coopératives Laitière Bretonnes, or UCLAB, in 1973. At the same time, Coopagri Bretagne, like much of France's cooperative sector during this period, had begun developing a number of production partnerships with other large cooperatives in the region. An early example of this was the creation of a pork processing facility in partnership with Socopa at the end of the 1960s.

DAIRY PARTNERSHIPS

Coopagri Bretagne's dairy unit began developing its own partnerships in the second half of the 1970s. This led to another important step in the creation of Laïta, when Coopagri Bretagne teamed up with another Brittany region cooperative, Cooperative Agricole La Noëlle Ancenis (CANA), which covered a territory between the cities of Nantes and Angers. As a result, CANA opened its own butter production plant, which began producing for the Paysan Breton brand in 1977.

The following year Coopagri and CANA deepened their relationship with an agreement to construct a joint venture production unit in Irois, in the Finistere in north Brittany, for the production of cheese. This allowed the group to extend the Paysan Breton brand into the cheese category for the first time, with the launch of an Emmental cheese. The Irois cheese factory became one of the leading cheese producers in the region.

The Paysan Breton brand continued to develop strongly through the 1980s, becoming one of the country's leading national brands. Part of this success came through the extension of the brand's product family to include an extrafine butter range, starting in 1986, and a churned butter line, based on more traditional production methods, in 1989. This latter line was complemented in 1991 by the addition of a salted churned butter, incorporating salt from the Guérande region. These additions enabled the Paysan Breton brand to position itself in the high-end, higher-margin, butter category.

MILK QUOTAS IN 1984

Coopagri Bretagne developed another important partnership, and product category, during the mid-1980s. In 1986 the cooperative acquired a 50 percent stake in Regilait, the leading French producer of powdered milk. Regilait was created in 1957 by France Lait, itself formed as a union of cooperatives 10 years earlier. Regilait's production expanded into infant

KEY DATES

1969: Coopagri Bretagne launches the Paysan Breton butter brand.

1978: Coopagri Bretagne and Cooperative Agricole La Noëlle Ancenis (CANA) form a cheese production partnership.

1991: Laïta is formed as a joint marketing operation for Coopagri Bretagne and CANA dairy products.

1993: The Even cooperative joins the Laïta marketing alliance.

1995: Laïta receives its own management and headquarters.

2009: Coopagri Bretagne, Terrena (formerly CANA), and Even merge their industrial dairy operations in a new company, Laïta S.A.S.

formula in 1960. The brand gained national prominence especially after 1968, when it was featured in the first commercial ever to be broadcast on French television. Regilait expanded its product range in the 1970s, introducing a line of sweetened concentrated milk.

This product expansion formed part of Coopagri Bretagne's efforts to adapt to a major shift in the French dairy market during the 1980s. The incorporation of industrial agricultural techniques in the dairy sector starting in the 1950s had resulted in a surge of milk production in France and throughout the European Economic Community (EEC). By the early 1980s, the region was confronted with steadily growing oversupply, threatening the pricing stability of the market.

In 1983 the EEC markets were producing more than 105 million metric tons of milk, representing an oversupply of more than 20 percent compared to the actual demand. With little demand from the export market, the EEC was forced to devote considerable resources to milk storage. By the middle of the 1980s, milk storage represented nearly one-third of the EEC administration's total budget.

The EEC had made a first effort to rein in milk production in the late 1970s. These measures proved ineffective, forcing the EEC to take more draconian steps. In 1984 the EEC introduced strict quotas on dairy production, starting with a total reduction of over 4 percent in its first year. Over the next decade, France's total collection dropped by more than 10 percent. The

Brittany region was even harder hit by the quotas, seeing its total milk collection slip by 15 percent by 1995.

CREATING LAÏTA IN 1990

Despite protests from the French dairy industry, which pointed out that the massive increase in milk production had come about through the French government's own policy of encouraging intensive agriculture, the government held firm. As the then minister of agriculture suggested, the French dairy industry was expected to abide by the spirit of a free market economy, becoming as concerned with its sales volume as its production volume of milk.

Coopagri Bretagne's existing marketing efforts, spearheaded by the Paysan Breton brand, helped cushion the blow as the cooperative prepared for this new era in the dairy industry. The future of the industry lay in the development of strong branded product lines and marketing and distribution operations. This led Coopagri Bretagne and CANA, through its Val d'Ancenis dairy products unit, to deepen their already existing partnerships with the creation of a dedicated research and development facility. The following year the two cooperatives took a new step toward combining the dairy operations, founding a joint marketing company called Laïta in 1990.

Laïta took over the marketing and distribution activities for Paysan Breton, Regilait, and other brands developed by both Coopagri Bretagne and CANA. In 1991 Laïta's operation grew again when it took over the distribution for Laiterie Nouvelle de l'Arguenon (LNA), acquired by Coopagri Bretagne in October of that year. A family-owned company based in Créhen, in northern Brittany, LNA provided Laïta with an expanded range of products including soft and fresh spreadable cheeses under the King Frais brand, as well as the production of milk proteins such as casein, and other dairy-based food additives.

LNA's sales, which added approximately $80 million to Laïta's own, also allowed Coopagri Bretagne to double the amount of milk it was able to collect, to 600 million liters per year. This increase in available milk was especially important in consolidating Paysan Breton's position among France's leading butter brands. In addition, the acquisition added LNA butter production capacity of 14,000 metric tons per year.

NEW PARTNERS

Coopagri Bretagne and CANA continued to move closer to a regrouping of their dairy operations. In 1992 CANA acquired a 50 percent stake in LNA, the operation of which then came under control of Laïta. The addition of LNA helped balance Laïta's operations between the consumer and industrial markets, which each accounted for approximately half of the group's total sales of more than FRF 1.2 billion (approximately $200 million) that year.

A new opportunity for growth came in 1993 when Even, another large-scale cooperative in the region, agreed to join the Laïta partnership. Even's own operations focused heavily on dairy products, and also included a strong export business. As a result, Laïta's revenues rose to FRF 1.7 billion, including more than FRF 250 million generated from outside of France. Laïta strengthened its international sales operations through the decade, opening subsidiaries in the United Kingdom, Germany, and Italy. The company's cheeses and other dairy products soon reached more than 70 countries, and by 1995 exports represented 15 percent of the company's sales.

Laïta's own operations took on more substance in 1995. The company had initially been guided by a board of directors with representatives from its three cooperative owners. In 1995 Laïta opened its own headquarters and formed a dedicated management to oversee its future strategy and development. Laïta had 80 employees by this time.

Laïta then set out to expand its range of products. In 1997 the company launched an extension of the Paysan Breton brand, a line of spreadable flavored cheeses under the Madame Loïk name. The company thus went head-to-head with the leaders in this cheese category, St. Moret and Boursin. The company also added to its butter ranges, creating a new high-end Grande Selection line for the Paysan Breton brand. The Regilait powdered milk line also expanded with the launch of an organic brand, Regilait Bio.

INDUSTRIAL DAIRY GROUP IN 2009

Laïta's operations increasingly influenced the investment and industrial policies of its three cooperative shareholders. These included Terrena, formed through the merger of CANA with another western region cooperative, CAVAL, completed in 2003. For example, in 1999 LNA's milk production plant in Créhen was converted into a fresh cheese factory. Laïta's sales growth also led to an expansion of the Irois cheese factory.

In the new century Laïta added several new products, including its La Baguette and La Galette cheeses, launched in 2000 and 2003, respectively. Laïta also instituted a new Charte Qualité Paysan Breton, establishing a new quality standard for the milk supplied

for production of the brand's products. By 2003, nearly 75 percent of the 5,000 farmer-suppliers to the company had adopted the new quality standards.

At the middle of the decade Laïta's cooperative shareholders remained responsible for carrying out the separate industrial investments required to boost the group's production capacity. By 2006 the group had begun to take steps toward a full-scale merger of their industrial dairy operations. This included the announcement in 2006 to invest EUR 10 million to expand two of the group's factories.

In 2008 Coopagri Bretagne, Terrena, and Even announced that they had reached an agreement to merge their industrial dairy operations into a single company. This merger was completed in June 2009, forming a new company, Laïta S.A.S. In this way, the group maintained the reputation that Laïta had built up in its nearly 20 years as a major force in French dairy marketing. The new Laïta boasted a workforce of 1,850, total milk processing volumes of 1.5 billion liters, and revenues of EUR 1.1 billion.

Laïta wasted little time in expanding its product range. The company launched two new Paysan Breton cheeses at the beginning of 2010, Cream of Camembert and Cream of Brie. As the leading dairy products group in France's western region, and the third largest in France, Laïta had become a symbol of the transformation of France's dairy industry at the dawn of the 21st century.

M. L. Cohen

PRINCIPAL SUBSIDIARIES

Eurilait Ltd (UK); Fromka (Germany); Laïta Caraïbes; Laita Italia SpA; Laiterie Nouvelle de l'Arguenon.

PRINCIPAL DIVISIONS

Laïta Europe; Laïta hors Europe.

PRINCIPAL COMPETITORS

Besnier SA; Compagnie Laitiere Europeenne S.A.; Danone SA; Groupe Bel; Lactalis International S.N.C.; Senoble SA; Sodiaal SA.

FURTHER READING

Collomp, Florentin, "Le Numéro Trois du Lait Émerge en France," *Le Figaro*, June 11, 2008.

Cussonneau, Agnès, "Lait: La Qualité, Pilier de la Stratégie de Laïta," *Paysan Breton*, May 23, 2003.

Grosmolard, Anne-Laure, "Un Nouveau Grand du Lait," *LSA*, June 19, 2008.

"Laïta Engage 10 Millions d'Euros d'Investissements," *L'Usine Nouvelle*, April 4, 2006.

"Laïta Fait la Promotion de Paysan Breton," *Les Echos*, May 21, 2003, p. 16.

Leclerc, Morgan, "La Nouvelle Coopérative Laitière de l'Ouest Mettra l'Accent sur les PGC," *LSA*, January 29, 2009.

Le Gall, Frédérique, "Le Nouveau Géant du Lait S'Appelle Laïta," *Le Telegramme*, June 13, 2009.

"Les Actionnaires de Laïta Engagent 10 Millions dans Leurs Laiteries," *Les Echos*, April 10, 2006, p. 18.

Maignant, Véronique, "La Laiterie Nouvelle de l'Arguenon (LNA) Accroit sa Valeur Ajoutée," *Bretagne Economique*, February 11, 2009.

Le Creuset S.A.S.

902 rue Olivier Deguise
Fresnoy le Grand, F-02230
France
Telephone: (33 3) 23 06 22 22
Fax: (33 3) 23 09 06 62
Web site: http://www.lecreuset.fr

Private Company
Incorporated: 1925
Employees: 1,200
Sales: EUR 170 million (2008 est.)
NAICS: 332214 Kitchen Utensil, Pot, and Pan Manu-
facturing; 423440 Other Commercial Equipment
Merchant Wholesalers

■ ■ ■

Le Creuset S.A.S. produces a leading brand of high-end cookware and utensils. Its most enduring success has been the traditional cocotte (a French oven, or heat-proof dish, in which food can be cooked and served in small portions) in Volcanic Orange, which has remained a best seller for decades. The company made its name with enameled cast-iron products, which combine the heat retention properties of heavy cast iron with the advantages of a two-layer enamel coating, such as resistance to acidic foods. Available in a variety of colors, the utensils lend themselves to use as serving dishes as well as cooking vessels.

A staple of French households by the 1930s, in the mid-1990s Le Creuset abandoned mass distribution to focus on the upper end of the market. Within a few years it extended its brand into a range of culinary products including stainless steel pans, nonstick forged hard-anodized aluminum cookware, stoneware casserole dishes, silicon utensils, textiles, and enameled steel kettles. Most of these were made in Asia. Since 1991 the company has also owned the Screwpull brand of corkscrew.

Paul Van Zuydam acquired Le Creuset in 1988 and its shares were publicly traded for several years. More than 90 percent of the company's production is exported, with the largest foreign markets being the United States, the United Kingdom, Japan, and Australia. Closely identified with French cookery, Le Creuset has also introduced many vessels suited for ethnic cuisines and international markets. Outside France, Le Creuset is strongest in the United Kingdom and the United States.

ORIGINS

The 1924 meeting of Belgians Armand Desaegher and Octave Aubecq at the Brussels Fair led to the creation of one of France's most enduring export successes. Combining Desaegher's casting expertise with the enameling know-how of Aubecq, the two decided to go into business making enameled cast-iron cookware. They established a facility in the rolling farmland of Fresnoy le Grand, 120 miles northeast of Paris, at the intersection of transportation routes for critical raw materials including coal, iron, and sand.

Le Creuset produced its first cocotte, or French oven, in 1925. Between the two world wars the cocotte became a fixture in kitchens across France. In 1935 the company added other products such as cookers, hot plates, and utensils to its lineup, and intensified its marketing. World War II brought this to an abrupt halt. During wartime occupation the factory was pressed into service making grenades for the Germans.

Production resumed after World War II. The company began exporting in earnest around 1952, with half of exports slated for Europe and half for the United States. Le Creuset faced little competition until the 1970s. Le Creuset's role in French cuisine was acknowledged by celebrated food writers such as Elizabeth David. Even Marilyn Monroe owned a set of saffron cooking pots, which were auctioned by Christie's in 1999.

In 1957 Le Creuset bought its main rival, Les Hauts Fourneaux et Fonderies de Cousances aux Forges, S.A. (Cousances), which traced its origins to 1553. It was known for introducing the *doufeu,* a cocotte with a water lid used to intensify flavors in braising. After the acquisition, Cousances would provide smaller vessels at lower price points than the Le Creuset brand. However, like the Belgian-American Descoware brand Le Creuset acquired in the 1970s, this brand would ultimately disappear.

In 1970 Le Creuset bought Godin, a nearby maker of iron furnaces and foundry equipment. Based in Guise, Godin traced its origins to 1840, when it began making ovens of enameled cast iron instead of the traditional sheet metal. Godin was sold to Cheminées Philippe in 1986.

DESIGNER UPDATES

Over the years Le Creuset hired a number of eminent designers to update its iconic product, the cocotte. In 1958 Compagnie d'Esthétique Industrielle Raymond Loewy, the firm of the eminent French-American industrial designer, restyled the cocotte as the Coquelle,

which itself became an iconic product. In 1972 Italian designer Enzo Mari made a new cocotte with radically different handles, to launch the Mama series. The dishwasher-safe Futura line, designed by J. L. Barrault, made its debut in France in 1987 and appeared in the United Kingdom two years later.

At the same time, new types of vessels expanded the product lineup. Following the growing popularity of winter sports, the company brought out a fondue set in 1962. A barbeque grill followed the next year. In the early 1980s Le Creuset introduced its Jam Pot or Marmite à Confiture, as well as a cocotte adapted for steaming.

NEW OWNERSHIP IN 1988

Annual revenues were around EUR 20 million in the late 1980s. By this time, the founding families' aging heirs were reportedly squabbling and the company's profits were slipping. The company posted a loss in 1987. During the year, Prestige Group, an English manufacturer of stainless steel pressure cookers, made overtures to buy Le Creuset. The deal faced some local political opposition, inflamed by the press, from those reluctant to see one of the region's best-known enterprises slip into foreign control. There was also a one-day strike, and the government attempted to impose job security guarantees.

After Prestige's board balked, its chairman, Paul Van Zuydam, left the company and arranged his own takeover of Le Creuset in January 1988. Originally from South Africa, Van Zuydam had been with Prestige Group since 1970, when it bought his cookware company EFI Products. He had contemplated acquiring Prestige himself when it was acquired by Irish cigarette manufacturer Gallaher (then owned by American Brands) in 1984.

A U.K. subsidiary was set up shortly after the acquisition. In July 1989 Le Creuset became, as noted by Britain's *Financial Times,* only the second French company (after aerospace supplier Technofan) to be floated on London's Unlisted Securities Market. The choice of bourse made sense as it was in Van Zuydam's home base and the United Kingdom was Le Creuset's largest export market, followed by the United States. France accounted for a third of sales. The offering capitalized the company at £25 million.

Revenues were about EUR 30 million in 1990, and exports accounted for 40 percent of sales. More than half of revenues came from enameled cast-iron goods. In January Frenchman Rudy Boussemart was hired as chief executive, and within a few years the business was restructured. The cast-iron manufacturing was made

KEY DATES

1925: Le Creuset formed to make enameled cast-iron cooking vessels.
1957: Le Creuset buys its main rival, Cousances.
1974: U.S. subsidiary established near Charleston, South Carolina.
1988: U.K.-based investor Paul Van Zuydam acquires Le Creuset.
1991: Le Creuset acquires Hallen International, maker of novel Screwpull corkscrew; Japanese subsidiary is established.
1996: After seven years on the Unlisted Securities Market, Van Zuydam takes the company private again.
2005: Classic Coquelle baking dish relaunched.
2009: Traditional Volcanic Orange dish appears prominently in film *Julie and Julia.*

more efficient, and production was consolidated from several sites into two. About 10 percent of employees were laid off, and FRF 25 million was invested in new equipment. At the same time, according to *Management Today,* the company began making all of its cast-iron goods in-house, after outsourcing 60 percent of production. The company was soon posting revenues and income gains, in spite of a recession.

INTERNATIONAL DEVELOPMENT

Under new ownership, Le Creuset took more control of its distribution. It bought its U.K. distributor Kitchenware Merchants in July 1988. In the United States, the company soon replaced its agents with a sales force of its own. This resulted in increased revenues in spite of a recession early in the decade. France and the United Kingdom were the company's other largest markets.

The U.S. subsidiary, Le Creuset of America, Inc., had been established in 1974 near Charleston, South Carolina. A Japanese subsidiary was established in 1991. Le Creuset set up operations in Germany a few years later after buying Wolo, a small barbeque grill distributor. In the late 1990s it added subsidiaries in Hong Kong (1998); and Switzerland, South Africa, Brazil, and Spain (1999). Scandinavia (2003) and Italy and Canada (2004) followed within a few years. Global sales exceeded $100 million by 2000.

Le Creuset's participation in various markets and its sensitivity to cooking trends spurred the development of

new cooking vessels. The company introduced its own saffron-colored, flat-bottomed wok in 1992, a nod to the increasing popularity of Asian cuisine. In 1999 it came out with a North African tagine. Le Creuset introduced cookware for *tatin* (a French dish) in 2000; *karahi* and *balti* (Indian) and sukiyaki (Japanese) in 2002; and risotto (Italian) in 2004. The company made skillets for the American market with handles of iron instead of wood, since they were often used in the United States inside the oven as well as atop the stove.

SCREWPULL ACQUIRED IN 1991

One of Le Creuset's most important diversifications was the 1991 acquisition of Hallen International, the Houston, Texas, maker of the novel Screwpull corkscrew, for $6.75 million. Hallen's founder, Texas native Herbert Allen, had become a wine collector after a successful career inventing tools for the oil and aerospace industries. Challenged by his wife to produce a foolproof corkscrew, he introduced the Screwpull Table Model in 1979.

The Screwpull featured a Teflon-coated screw to minimize damage to the cork and a cuff to secure the device over the bottle's neck. A flood of imitators copied both of these features after the Screwpull's original patent expired in 1999. By this time, according to *Les Echos,* Le Creuset had succeeded in growing the Screwpull brand from annual sales of FRF 35 million when it was acquired to more than FRF 200 million. Le Creuset improved Screwpull's margins by bringing production of more components in-house, shifting manufacturing from the United States and the United Kingdom to its Cousances factory.

In 1995 Le Creuset's pretax profits slipped to £963,000 after a gain of £3.24 million the previous year, as revenues fell from £49.5 million to £45.1 million, noted the *Financial Times.* The company weathered labor problems in France while a strong franc hurt its export margins. At the same time, it abandoned the mass market to focus on high-end specialty retail channels.

In 1996, after seven years on London's Unlisted Securities Market, Le Creuset was taken private again when Van Zuydam's holding company, Cliden BV, acquired the 26.3 percent of shares it did not already own. Five years later, U.K. investment group Bridgepoint Capital considered a buyout but backed away. Le Creuset was reportedly valued at $200 million, or EUR 141 million. Bridgepoint had wanted to bolster its household products group, which included the Betterware brand.

BRAND EXTENSIONS AND NEW PRODUCTS

While its traditional vessels were ideally suited for braising meats and cooking rich stews, Le Creuset responded to increasing interest in health-conscious cooking by introducing ridged grill pans and stainless steel steamers. It also brought out a line of earthenware dishes to accommodate the increasingly ubiquitous microwave oven.

Le Creuset introduced a line of nonstick cast-aluminum cookware called Haute Cuisine in 1994, available in a choice of colors. The company shut this line down after four years but continued to extend the Le Creuset brand with a range of new products, most of them made in Asia. These included wood-handled silicone spatulas introduced in 1997, followed two years later with textiles and an olive oil sprayer.

By 2005, when Le Creuset relaunched its classic Coquelle baking dish, the company was making 400 different types of cast-iron items. After having some success with a heart-shaped casserole in the early 1990s, it had added a touch of whimsy with its Garden Collection of ovenproof dishes shaped like fruits and vegetables.

Meanwhile, others were encroaching on Le Creuset's turf. French rival Staub entered the U.S. consumer market in 2001 after having success with its professional cookware. Around 2006, American cast-iron heavyweight Lodge Manufacturing Company added enameled products to its lineup, having them finished in China to avoid domestic environmental laws. Soon after, Ohio-based Calphalon Corp., known for nonstick cast-aluminum cookware, introduced its own line of enameled cast-iron products.

STILL STYLISH

By then, more than 90 percent of revenues came from outside France. U.S. sales grew 25 percent in 2005. The company had added operations in India, China, Singapore, and South Korea by 2006. It also had facilities in South Africa, Brazil, Scandinavia, Germany, Spain, and Switzerland, for a total of 17 subsidiaries, all wholly owned. There were 1,200 employees around the world, 700 of them outside of France.

The company's years of diversification meant that its traditional cast-iron products accounted for only about 50 percent of total sales. The company was hiring dozens of new employees as it worked to double the main plant's capacity. It was modernizing the plant, but cast-iron production remained a labor-intensive process.

Le Creuset tweaked its marketing around 2005, seeking to court a slightly younger, more style-conscious buyer by using an updated palette with colors such as chocolate brown. Its most enduring success remained, however, the traditional cocotte in Volcanic Orange, still a best seller among its 300 different products offered in 40 colors. In 2009 a cocotte in the traditional Volcanic Orange finish appeared prominently in the American film *Julie and Julia,* an homage to Julia Child.

Revenues were reportedly up to EUR 170 million by 2008, with more than 90 percent from exports. Although the economy faltered, the company continued to invest in anticipation of a recovery in mid-2010. Le Creuset typically spent EUR 4.5 million a year in capital improvements.

Frederick C. Ingram

PRINCIPAL SUBSIDIARIES

Le Creuset Ltd. (UK); Le Creuset of America, Inc. (USA); Le Creuset France S.A.S.; Le Creuset Scandinavia (Denmark); Le Creuset GmbH (Germany); Le Creuset S.L. (Spain); Le Creuset Japon KK.

PRINCIPAL OPERATING UNITS

Europe; Americas; Asia/Pacific; Africa.

PRINCIPAL COMPETITORS

All-Clad Metalcrafters LLC; Calphalon Corp.; Godin S.A.; Groupe Staub Wilton Industries, Inc.; Lodge Manufacturing Company.

FURTHER READING

Bouillé, Julien, "La cocotte toujours en pleine forme," *L'Union* (Reims, France), August 25, 2009.

Leboucq, Valerie, "Le Creuset veut continuer à grandir en réalisant de nouvelles acquisitions," *Les Echos,* February 21, 2000.

"Le Creuset: La célèbre cocotte monte en puissance," *La Tribune,* December 6, 2006.

"Le Creuset pousse les feux à l'international," *Les Echos,* February 8, 2007, p. 18.

"Le Creuset se prépare à l'après-crise," *Les Echos,* July 6, 2009, p. 16.

Lucot, Yves-Marie, "Le Creuset veut accoître de 30% sa production en fonte," *Les Echos,* September 9, 2005, p. 16.

Porter, Thyra, and Barbara Thau, "Plenty of Plot Twists; The Tale of How the $160 Screwpull Paved the Way for a $9.99 Knockoff," *HFN—The Weekly Newspaper for the Home Furnishing Network,* May 10, 2004, p. 12.

Thau, Barbara, "Le Creuset to Take on Tabletop," *HFN—The Weekly Newspaper for the Home Furnishing Network,* August 2, 1999, p. 26.

Lekkerland AG & Company KG

———————————■———————————

Europaallee 57
Frechen, D-50226
Germany
Telephone: (49 2234) 1821-0
Fax: (49 2234) 1821-100
Web site: http://www.lekkerland.com

Private Company
Incorporated: 1960 as Lekkerland-Expres Süsswaren-
    Vertriebsorganisation GmbH
Employees: 7,361
Sales: EUR 11.6 billion ($17 billion) (2008)
NAICS: 422490 Other Grocery and Related Products
    Wholesalers; 424450 Confectionery Merchant
    Wholesalers; 422940 Tobacco and Tobacco Product
    Wholesalers; 422990 Other Miscellaneous
    Nondurable Goods Wholesalers; 422420 Packaged
    Frozen Food Wholesalers; 424430 Dairy Product
    (Except Dried or Canned) Merchant Wholesalers;
    422480 Fresh Fruit and Vegetable Wholesalers;
    422810 Beer and Ale Wholesalers; 424820 Wine
    and Distilled Alcoholic Beverage Merchant
    Wholesalers

■ ■ ■

Lekkerland AG & Company KG is one of the leading
wholesalers in the European convenience goods market.
Lekkerland delivers a broad variety of snack food and
beverages, sandwiches and baked goods, produce and
dairy products, confectionery and tobacco products, ice
cream and frozen foods, selected nonfood items, and
prepaid phone cards to approximately 134,000 gas stations, convenience stores, and other retail outlets carrying convenience and tobacco products in 11 European
countries. The goods are distributed from Lekkerland's
39 warehouses with the company's own fleet of roughly
1,000 vehicles. Tobacco products account for about
three-quarters of the company's total sales. Austria
Tabak GmbH owns 25.1 percent of Lekkerland while
the remaining 74.9 percent are owned by regional
wholesale companies.

ORIGINS

In 1955 several Dutch confectionery wholesalers merged
to form Lekkerland in the Netherlands, the word *lekker*
connoting in Dutch something delicious and enjoyable.
Five year later, 11 German confectionery wholesalers
formed a joint purchasing and marketing organization
in Cologne under the name Lekkerland-Expres
Süsswaren-Vertriebsorganisation. Lekkerland was created
to offset changes in the marketplace following the
postwar economic boom; the combined purchasing
power of its member wholesalers enabled them to
negotiate significantly lower prices with manufacturers.

Lekkerland started supplying mostly small family-
run grocery stores with a broad range of confectionery
products. In 1962 Lekkerland started adding beverages
to its line of traded goods, which was further expanded
in the following years. In the late 1960s Lekkerland
launched several promotional campaigns aimed at helping the company's customers increase their sales. Starting out with flyers advertising the latest on-sale items,
Lekkerland soon provided advertising posters, seasonal

catalogs, and promotional displays to its clients. In addition, the company helped its customers with product placement to promote impulse purchases.

Lekkerland's retail marketing strategy paid off for the company as well as for its customers who were often able to increase sales by more than 10 percent. At the same time, Lekkerland's sales increased as well. By 1969 the company was grossing DEM 365 million annually.

TARGETING GAS STATIONS BEGINS: 1974

An important step in Lekkerland's history followed in 1974 when the company recognized gas stations as a major potential growth market. Lekkerland began to work with owners or renters of gas stations who up until then had sold only spare parts and oil to motorists in their small shops, convincing a growing number of them to let the company put up extra shelves with snacks and beverages for travelers. As with its small retail store customers, Lekkerland also helped the gas stations make their shops more attractive to increase sales.

While the number of Lekkerland's gas station customers rose continuously, their in-shop sales increased as well. The gas stations in turn expanded or modernized their shops, and Lekkerland provided a rapidly growing range of convenience products. In the second half of the 1970s Lekkerland started negotiating with oil companies to supply their chains of gas stations with confectionery products. Over time, the company was able to secure long-term exclusive contracts with several oil majors.

In the mid-1980s Lekkerland started supplying kiosks and beverage stores with confectionery as well as specialty wine. The company also continued to work on optimizing the presentation of its products in the differ-

ent types of sales outlets. As the number of customers and its product line increased rapidly, Lekkerland expanded its warehouse and logistics capacity as well. As a result, Lekkerland's annual sales more than tripled during the 1970s and 1980s, reaching DEM 1.3 billion in 1989.

INTERNATIONALIZATION INTENSIFIES AFTER 1989

The opening of the Berlin Wall in 1989 set the stage for Lekkerland's expansion into Eastern Europe, where the company established subsidiaries in Hungary and the Czech Republic. Lekkerland also became active in Western European countries, including Spain and Belgium, during this time. In 1993 the company acquired several branches of Austrian wholesaler Vögro and established Austrian Lekkerland AG, which was followed by the takeover of the specialized wholesaler Janovsky, based in Ternitz near Vienna, in 1996. The following year Lekkerland, together with Zurich-based wholesaler Usego AG, founded Lekkerland (Schweiz) AG in Switzerland.

In 1997 Lekkerland entered a strategic alliance with coffee vending machine specialist Maas International Europe B.V. To optimize their business activities in the Benelux countries, the two companies established Lekkerland Benelux N.V. in the Netherlands. In the same year Lekkerland bought a 35 percent share in McLane España S.A., a joint venture with U.S.-convenience wholesaler McLane International and Spanish confectionery wholesaler Chupa Chups. By the late 1990s Lekkerland was active in more than 10 European countries where roughly half of the company's revenues were generated.

REORGANIZATION AND DIVERSIFICATION AFTER 1990

To defend its position in an increasingly competitive market, Lekkerland reorganized its domestic business, while also expanding its product range and services. In 1991 Lekkerland streamlined its organization when the existing 17 regional subsidiaries were merged under the umbrella of five new regional divisions for northern, northwestern, central, southeastern, and southern Germany. Beginning in 1994 Lekkerland added prepackaged sandwiches and salads, dairy products, and frozen foods to its product range, catering to the growing demand for these convenience snacks.

Lekkerland also added nonfood products such as cosmetics and detergents to its range and offered several hundred products under its own private labels. To stay

KEY DATES

1955: Dutch confectionery wholesalers merge under the new name Lekkerland.

1960: Lekkerland-Expres Süsswaren-Vertriebsorganisation GmbH is founded in Germany.

1974: Three tobacco product wholesalers in North Rhine Westphalia merge to form Tobaccoland GmbH & Co. KG.

1974: Lekkerland begins to supply gas stations with convenience products.

1996: Lekkerland merges with German confectionery products wholesaler Sügro.

1999: Lekkerland and Tobaccoland merge to form Lekkerland-Tobaccoland GmbH & Co. KG.

2003: Lekkerland takes over control of Spanish wholesaler McLane España.

2006: Convenience wholesalers Macromex in Romania and MILO in Poland are acquired.

ahead of the competition, Lekkerland introduced express delivery service within 24 hours and a single-item delivery option for a selected product range. The company also upgraded its fleet and storage capacity by adding refrigerated trucks and warehouses.

In the late 1990s Lekkerland was facing massive pressure in its core market, the gas stations, where the company had achieved a strong market position. On one hand, large German grocery retailers tried to get a foot in the door by offering oil companies broader product ranges at lower prices. On the other hand, the oil companies themselves tried to gain more control over the gas station business. While some oil companies were lost to competitors, Lekkerland succeeded in renegotiating long-term contracts with major customers. Although Lekkerland was not able to compete with other suppliers of freshly made foods such as sandwiches and salads, the company's highly sophisticated distribution network proved to be a major competitive advantage.

1996–99: MERGERS CREATE MARKET LEADER

In 1996 Lekkerland took a major step to strengthen itself against the growing competition when it merged with its main competitor, German confectionery products wholesaler Sügro Deutschland GmbH & Co. KG, with 18 branches in Germany. After the merger, central management functions for the whole group were carried out from Lekkerland headquarters in Frechen. To optimize cost structures, all but two of the 17 warehouses the company had taken over from Sügro were closed and several hundred Sügro products that did not fit into Lekkerland's range were delisted.

A second major move in 1996 was Lekkerland's acquisition of a majority stake in Berlin-based confectionery, beverage, and tobacco products wholesaler Kiki Petermann GmbH & Co. The company had a strong market presence in the Berlin region and generated roughly three-quarters of its revenue from servicing over 10,000 cigarette vending machines. Following through on one of Lekkerland's strategic goals to significantly increase its business with tobacco products, the company's northern German division together with Kiki and three large northern German tobacco products wholesalers founded Berlin-based CGL GmbH & Co. KG in 1996. Two years later Lekkerland's southern German division formed a similar distribution venture with tobacco products wholesaler K+S GmbH & Co. KG in Karlsruhe.

The 1999 merger of Lekkerland with tobacco product wholesaler Tobaccoland GmbH & Co. KG based in Mönchengladbach southwest of Düsseldorf, created a German market leader in convenience products with about DEM 9 billion in combined sales and roughly 4,500 employees. Founded by the merger of three tobacco product wholesalers in North Rhine Westphalia in 1974, Tobaccoland was the leading supplier of tobacco products to gas stations and other smaller retail outlets. Tobaccoland's shareholder, tobacco wholesaler Austria Tabak AG, which became the new company's sole provider of tobacco products, held 25.1 percent in the new Lekkerland-Tobaccoland GmbH & Co. KG. The remaining 74.9 percent in Lekkerland-Tobaccoland was owned by Lekkerland's shareholders.

While Lekkerland-Tobaccoland's new top management moved into brand-new headquarters in Frechen, Lekkerland's five legally independent regional companies were merged with the company's German management holding company to form a single entity. Purchasing was centralized in Frechen as well, while Lekkerland's remaining 20 regional branches and Tobaccoland's 25 branches in Germany were responsible for servicing their regional customers.

Separate companies were created for tobacco products purchasing as well as for the combined cigarette vending machine business of Lekkerland-Tobaccoland, in which Austria Tabak held a majority stake. To fulfill the requirements of the German cartel authority that approved the Lekkerland-Tobaccoland merger, the company had to give up part of its tobacco products business worth approximately DEM 450 million.

INTERNATIONAL GROWTH AND INNOVATION AFTER 2000

After the turn of the 21st century Lekkerland-Tobaccoland strengthened its presence in Western Europe and continued to expand in Eastern Europe. In 2003 the company acquired an additional 35 percent share in Spanish wholesaler McLane España from McLane International, increasing Lekkerland-Tobaccoland's stake to a 70 percent majority. One year later, the company raised its share in the Swiss Lekkerland (Schweiz) AG to 100 percent and acquired majority stakes in Lekkerland's operations in Austria and Hungary. In 2006 the company took over Polish tobacco and convenience products wholesaler MILO with 750 employees and roughly EUR 750 million in annual sales, as well as the Romanian convenience food wholesale firm Macromex. Lekkerland-Tobaccoland also formed a joint venture with convenience product wholesaler Fixmer S.à r.l. in Luxembourg.

During this time the company also began to reorganize. In 2004 Lekkerland-Tobaccoland acquired all shares in Lekkerland Europa Holding. One year later the company was renamed Lekkerland GmbH & Co. KG, omitting Tobaccoland from the company name. In 2007 Lekkerland's operative business unit in Germany was reorganized under Lekkerland Deutschland GmbH & Co. KG and separated from the renamed management holding Lekkerland AG & Co. KG.

In addition to expanding abroad and creating a streamlined organization, Lekkerland launched new ventures, innovative technologies and services to strengthen its market position and to seize additional growth opportunities. To participate in the booming mobile telecommunications market of the early 2000s, Lekkerland began to sell prepaid mobile phone cards and to provide the terminals for recharging them. Other new ventures, such as the establishment of the company's own convenience store chain, or the introduction of Lekkerland's own low-priced cigarette brand to make up for dwindling sales due to an increased tobacco tax, were put on hold.

The company also introduced new logistics optimization systems at its warehouses and started equipping its distribution centers with voice-controlled technology to enhance order fulfillment operations. When the German government imposed a deposit on beverage cans and plastic bottles in 2003, Lekkerland introduced its own recycling system.

In 2006 the company won additional gas station business in Hungary and signed a major contract with Royal Dutch Shell to provide some 2,500 gas stations in Europe with consumer goods in 2007, according to *Europe Intelligence Wire* on February 15, 2007. In 2008 Lekkerland launched its new food services division and took over complete control of the distribution of refrigerated foods to its customers in Germany and abroad, the number of which had grown to roughly 134,000 by 2010. Looking ahead, Lekkerland set its sights on expanding the company's business with fresh and preprepared microwavable frozen food under the new Food IQ label, as well as on further expanding the company's geographic reach in Eastern Europe.

Evelyn Hauser

PRINCIPAL SUBSIDIARIES

Lekkerland Deutschland GmbH & Co. KG; Lekkerland Nederland B.V. (Netherlands); Lekkerland Vending Services B.V. (Netherlands); Conway—The Convenience Company België N.V. (Belgium); Conway Vending Services N.V. (Belgium); Lekkerland Handels- und Dienstleistungs GmbH (Austria); Lekkerland (Schweiz) AG (Switzerland); Conway—The Convenience Company S.A. (Spain; 70%); Lekkerland Czeská Republika, s.r.o (Czech Republic); Lekkerland Export-Import Kereskedelmi Kft. (Hungary); Lekkerland Convenience Distributie SRL (Romania); Lekkerland Polska S.A. (Poland); Conway Fixmer S.à.r.l. (Luxembourg; 50%).

PRINCIPAL COMPETITORS

Aldi Nord GmbH & Co. oHG; Aldi Süd GmbH & Co. oHG; Edeka Group; Marketing und Convenience—Shop System GmbH; Tengelmann Warenhandelsgesellschaft KG; Metro AG.

FURTHER READING

"Convenience Is King as Consumers Eat on the Move," *Dairy Industries International,* October 1999, p. 9.

"Lekkerland Acquires Polish Wholesaler," *Europe Intelligence Wire,* February 22, 2006.

"Lekkerland entdeckt die Schweiz," *Lebensmittel Zeitung,* November 8, 1996, p. 10.

"Lekkerland Expands in Eastern Europe," *Europe Intelligence Wire,* November 17, 2005.

"Lekkerland kauft in Spanien zu," *Lebensmittel Zeitung,* December 12, 1997, p. 8.

"Lekkerland kooperiert mit BP," *Horizont,* November 27, 1997, p. 18.

"Lekkerland Signs Major Contract with Shell (Lekkerland erhält Sechs-Milliarden-Auftrag von Shell)," *Europe Intelligence*

Wire, February 15, 2007.

"Lekkerland staerkt Tabakgeschäft," *Lebensmittel Zeitung,* January 9, 1998, p. 4.

"Lekkerland-Tobaccoland Considers Own Brand Cigarette from Austria Tabak (Lekkerland denkt an eigene Billigzigarette)," *Europe Intelligence Wire,* January 16, 2004.

"Lekkerland-Tobaccoland Revises Forecast Downwards (Pflichtpfand bremst Lekkerland-Tobaccoland)," *Europe Intelligence Wire,* May 15, 2003.

"Lekkerland und Maas kooperieren," *Lebensmittel Zeitung,* March 21, 1997, p. 12.

"Lekkerland Wins New Contracts Worth an Annual HUF1 Bn," *Europe Intelligence Wire,* June 23, 2006.

"L-T Stops Construction of New Chain (Lekkerland legt Kiosk-Kette auf Eis)," *Europe Intelligence Wire,* December 9, 2004.

Rosmanith, Uwe, "Kein Weihnachtsfrieden bei Lekkerland," *Lebensmittel Zeitung,* December 8, 1995, p. 4.

"Wal-Mart wird Lekkerland-Kunde," *Lebensmittel Zeitung,* May 21, 1999, p. 10.

Solutions that Deliver

The Library Corporation

Research Park
Inwood, West Virginia 25428-9733
U.S.A.
Telephone: (304) 229-0100
Fax: (304) 229-0295
Web site: http://www.tlcdelivers.com

Private Company
Incorporated: 1974
Employees: 186
Sales: $35 million (2007 est.)
NAICS: 541512 Computer Systems Design Services;
    511210 Software Publishers

■ ■ ■

The Library Corporation (TLC) is a private company based in Inwood, West Virginia, that provides automation technology to the library market, serving about 5,000 libraries across the globe. The company's Library. Solution product is a turnkey system that provides patrons with basic circulation functions from any Internet-connected computer. A similar product is sold to the school market under the Library.Solution for Schools name, while the CARL.X system is geared toward medium to large public libraries, such as those of Los Angeles, Chicago, Denver, and Phoenix, as well as the National Library Board of Singapore.

TLC offers cataloging systems, portal and search products, an acquisitions management system, and such add-on products as EnvisionWare's print management and personal computer reservation system, the Gold Rush electronic resource management tool, the Phone-Tree messaging system, Talkingtech products that notify patrons by phone about reserved or overdue items and allow them to access their account information by phone, and the Tech Logic self-service checkout and return system.

TLC also sells patron cards and hardware, including computer servers and barcode scanning systems. In addition to its headquarters, TLC maintains offices in Denver and Singapore. The company is led by its chief executive officer, president and chair, Annette Harwood Murphy, who cofounded the company with her husband, Brower Murphy.

ORIGINS

The Library Corporation was incorporated in 1974 and moved to a research park in Inwood, West Virginia, in 1981. Two years before it was incorporated, the company had begun publishing the Library of Congress MARC (Machine Readable Cataloging) records on microfiche, MARCFICHE, and selling it to libraries, thus making it a pioneer in electronic publishing. The visionary of the founding couple was Brower Murphy. Writer Chris Andrews, who knew Murphy, described him as "an entrepreneur, gadfly, businessman, and computer nerd all in one package." Murphy also championed something called "Common Knowledge," an effort to share information for the good of humanity, a precursor to the Open Access movement to make digital content available for free on the Internet.

For his many contributions, Brower Murphy would eventually be elected to the Library Microcomputer Hall of Fame. Annette Harwood, Murphy's wife and cofounder of TLC, was accomplished in her own right. She studied systems analysis at Shepherd University, the University of Georgia, and DeKalb College, and worked as a systems analyst and consultant to develop accounting and office procedures. For TLC she played an instrumental role in administration, fiscal operations, and strategic planning.

By the early 1980s TLC was selling MARCFICHE to more than 5,000 libraries. The forward-looking Brower Murphy recognized the library market potential of personal computers (PCs) and the new CD-ROM technologies that were emerging at this time. His vision was to make catalog information available on CD-ROM. According to Andrews, "He did it with sweat, guts, and determination, after trying to get other companies to do it and being rejected. His West Virginia smarts beat Silicon Valley, Hollywood, and New York to the punch." In late 1984 Murphy became the first person to apply CD-ROM technology to data storage, and in early 1985 he sold the first system, which TLC marketed as BiblioFile Cataloging, at the American Library Association conference.

CD-ROM OPAC INTRODUCED: 1987

BiblioFile quickly became the most popular desktop cataloging tool in the history of library technical services to date, spurred in part by a subscription offer that included a PC. The product also solidified TLC's place in the library market and allowed the company to increase the number of employees 10-fold, from just 8 in 1985 to 80 in early 1990. Playing an important role in this growth was the 1987 introduction of the first multimedia CD-ROM OPAC (Online Public Access Catalog), The Intelligent Catalog, which was context-sensitive and fast searching and made use of audio help messages. The BiblioFile Circulation add-on feature was then added to complete TLC's PC-based automation system.

In the meantime, TLC was hired in 1985 by Ingram Book Company, the world's largest book wholesale distributor, to write the search software for its AnyBook CD-ROM product, which integrated book identification, electronic ordering, and acquisitions. While optical-disk databases were useful tools, they complemented rather than replaced online databases. TLC continued to help hundreds of libraries to create MARC databases, including some of the world's largest union catalogs.

Brower Murphy and TLC were also quick to see the potential of the Internet for the library market. Development began in 1990 on an indexing service that would glean information from public and private databases from around the world. In 1994 a division under the NlightN ("enlighten") name was formed and a year later the NlightN Internet-based information service was launched and offered to libraries and other institutions. This service allowed subscribers to do key word searches on a number of databases simultaneously, including 14 newswire services, the Library of Congress, the National Library of Medicine, the British Library, and U.S. patents from 1975 forward.

As an indexing service, NlightN offered a list of resources in response to a search, indicating whether the library from which the query was made had a subscription to the database holding the material or if it was in print or available on a CD in the library. The patron could then either display the full text if available or pull the desired material from the library shelves.

WINDOWS PRODUCT INTRODUCED: 1995

NlightN was not a product that proved to have staying power, but its development paved the way for other key TLC products. With the rise of PC graphical interface operating systems, in particular Microsoft's Windows, TLC revamped its BiblioFile Cataloging product. It was replaced in 1995 by ITS.For Windows, which allowed access to online MARC data from around the world using Windows and Web browser environments that many PC users had grown accustomed to.

The late 1990s brought a number of changes to TLC. Brower Murphy left the company and Annette Harwood Murphy, then using the name Annette Harwood, took over as president, chief executive officer, and chair. In February 1997 TLC built upon two decades of effort to launch Library.Solution, an integrated library management system that combined cataloging, circulation, and a Web accessible online public access catalog. It made use of the Windows NT operating system, which at the time was a bold choice because it was not until three months later that Microsoft announced a major commitment to it, earmarking about half of its sizable research and development budget to the continued development and enhancement of Windows NT.

With a head start using this platform, TLC was able to establish Library.Solution as the fastest-growing library automation system in the world. To maintain its momentum, TLC in 1999 tripled its research and development budget and hired several new senior software developers, all with more than 10 years of programming experience. Later in the year TLC looked to expand its international business, opening an office in Singapore.

CARL CORPORATION ACQUIRED: 2000

TLC continued to display an aggressive attitude as the new century dawned. At the annual conference of the American Library Association held in Chicago in July 2000, TLC caused a stir when it announced that it was acquiring a rival automation vendor, CARL Corporation. That company grew out of the integrated library automation software created for the Colorado Alliance of Research Institute (CARL) that was first marketed in 1985 under the MAGGIE III name by the Eyring Research Institute and its Eyring Library Systems subsidiary. This unit then became CARL Systems Incorporated and later took the name CARL Corporation.

In the late 1990s CARL began selling some of its products, including its UnCover document delivery service to Ingenta, and the NoveList readers' advisory tool to EBSCO, prompting speculation that the company itself was on the block. What industry observers did not know was that during this time TLC and CARL were in extended talks about a possible acquisition. Although competitors, the two companies had worked well together in the past on joint projects, TLC used CARL's card cataloging system in its own

product, and the companies even shared the new Singapore office. They also agreed on the same principles for library automation, making them a good fit. For TLC, the addition of CARL brought some of the largest public libraries in the United States as clients.

TLC made further news in the summer of 2000 by announcing a joint venture with CASPR Library Systems to distribute that company's new Web-based automation system, librarycom.com, which because it operated completely off a Web browser required no software installation at participating libraries. In 2004 TLC made another distribution deal, this one with Medialab to sell its AquaBrowser Web interface product in the United States and Canada. A year later TLC became AquaBrowser's exclusive distributor and in a matter of two years sold the product to more than 120 libraries. After R.R. Bowker LLC acquired AquaBrowser, TLC lost the product but soon introduced its own public library graphic interface, Indigo.

TLC developed other new products in the early years of the new century, including Online Selection & Acquisitions, introduced in 2003 to serve the needs of collection professionals. A year later the company unveiled CARL.X at the American Library Association conference, a next generation integrated library system offering improved search and self-service functions. An upgrade to BiblioFile was rolled out in 2006, along with Web Circ, a browser-based automation product for schools and libraries.

TECH LOGIC ACQUIRED: 2005

TLC also continued to grow by external means. In April 2005 it acquired majority control of Tech Logic Corporation. Based in White Bear Lake, Minnesota, Tech Logic manufactured book drop conveyor delivery systems, inter-library distribution systems, stand-alone and freestanding patron reserve systems, and RFID (radio-frequency identification) and bar-code check-in/checkout systems. Tech Logic was well respected in the marketplace, the first company to develop automated material handling systems exclusively for libraries.

As the economy slipped in the second half of the decade, so did library budgets, adversely impacting TLC, which saw revenues dip to about $35 million in 2007. Although CARL products experienced a difficult year, losing the Phoenix Public Library as an installation, Library.Solution, serving the largest share of the library market, held strong, adding 35 contracts to increase the number of installations to 700. It did especially well in the K-12 school market. In 2008 TLC introduced an upgraded versions of its CircIT self-checkout software, but attracted only a single major adopter, Louisiana. The Tech Logic division, on the other hand, expanded internationally, opening an office in Melbourne, Australia.

To remain competitive, TLC continued to develop new products and enhance existing ones. In 2008 the company introduced a new integrated library system platform called LS2 that would include Web, client, and mobile interfaces. The first module for the new system was LS2 PAC, a new search interface. In 2009 LS2 Kids was added, a child-friendly version of the interface. In addition, LS2 Circ was released as the successor to the company's Web Circ product. As a result of the new platform, TLC was well positioned to maintain its standing in the library automation field.

Ed Dinger

PRINCIPAL SUBSIDIARIES

TLC Carl East Pte Ltd.

PRINCIPAL COMPETITORS

Book Systems, Inc.; Polaris Library Systems; Sirsi Corporation.

FURTHER READING

Andrews, Christopher, *The Education of a CD-ROM Publisher,* Huntsville, AL: The CD-Info Company, 1993.

"Another Step toward Linked Libraries," *Washington Technology,* May 25, 1995.

Bailey, Doug, "CD-ROM Multimedia Patent Draws Fire," *Boston Globe,* November 17, 1993, p. 49.

"The Library Corporation," *Library Journal,* April 1, 2008, p. 41.

"The Library Corporation Acquires CARL Corp.," *Library Journal,* August 2000, p. 29.

Lincoln National Corporation

—■—

150 North Radnor Chester Road
Radnor, Pennsylvania 19807-5238
U.S.A.
Telephone: (484) 583-1400
Fax: (484) 583-1421
Web site: http://www.lfg.com

Public Company
Incorporated: 1905 as Lincoln National Life Insurance
    Company
Employees: 9,696
Sales: $8.5 billion (2009)
Stock Exchanges: New York
Ticker Symbol: LNC
NAICS: 524113 Direct Life Insurance Carriers; 52393
    Investment Advice

■ ■ ■

With origins in life insurance, Lincoln National Corporation has evolved into a financial services company whose principal offerings include annuities as well as life, group life, and disability insurance. Additional services include 401(k) and 403(b) plans, financial planning, and advisory services. The company, which operates under the marketing name of Lincoln Financial Group, was hit hard by the financial and economic crisis that hit the United States in 2008 and 2009. Lincoln National accepted $950 million from the U.S. government's Troubled Asset Relief Program (TARP) in 2009 while posting losses of $485 million. It sold its Delaware Investments arm in 2010 to focus on its insurance and retirement businesses.

SURVIVING A TROUBLED BEGINNING

Lincoln National Corporation traces its origins to the Lincoln Life Insurance Company, which was preceded by a troubled firm in Fort Wayne, Indiana, called the Fraternal Assurance Society of America. Its founder was Wilbur Wynant, who organized a number of supposedly nonprofit fraternal insurance companies that promised to pay benefits by leveling assessments on surviving policyholders. Wynant, who was new to Fort Wayne in 1902, persuaded a number of respected business and professional men to join him in the company, but within two years Wynant had skipped town, and his local associates were left to pick up the pieces or fold the company. The local businessmen reorganized as a legal reserve company to be capitalized at $200,000 but prepared to open for business when $100,000 in stock was sold.

Lincoln National Life Insurance Company was incorporated in Fort Wayne on May 15, 1905. A few months later the New York state investigation of the insurance industry known as the Armstrong Committee exposed widespread abuses and led to much more effective state regulation of the industry. Lincoln National was fully prepared for the more stringent regulations and used the Lincoln name and image to good effect in promoting the new company amid widespread public suspicion of all insurance companies.

Arthur Fletcher Hall, formerly an agent for Equitable Life Assurance Society of the United States, was brought in from Indianapolis to serve as secretary and manager, and for practical purposes he was the chief executive officer from the beginning, although a local businessman held the unsalaried office of president. When the company began to write policies in September 1905 it had three agents, including Hall. By 1911 the company had 106 agents and was in sound financial condition.

Arthur F. Hall was the dominant figure at Lincoln National Life Insurance for the company's first 37 years, and he did not hesitate to employ able and determined associates. In 1911 Hall hired Franklin B. Mead, the firm's first full-time actuary. Mead was much more than a numbers man. He devised careful plans for underwriting life insurance policies and for writing reinsurance policies for other companies, and he was a skilled manager. Mead provided statistical support for the company's medical director, Calvin English, and Lincoln National soon achieved a reputation for writing profitable insurance on carefully screened substandard, or undesirable, risks. While the typical insurance company rejected about 11 percent of those who applied for coverage, Lincoln National turned down only about 4 percent.

EARLY GROWTH THROUGH ACQUISITION

In 1916 the company adopted the policy of securing additional insurance in force by taking over other companies. Michigan State Life Insurance Company, acquired in 1916, was even younger than Lincoln Life, but it had grown more quickly. Michigan State Life had been a tool of Frederick L. Apps, who had involved Michigan State Life in a complex fraud. When Lincoln National purchased Michigan State Life, a web of companies set up by Apps to support the insurance company collapsed.

Michigan State Life itself was a sound purchase. The merger was so successful that Hall took over another successful midwestern firm in 1917, the Pioneer Life Insurance Company of Fargo, North Dakota. Beyond the additional insurance acquired, these mergers also greatly increased the number of experienced agents selling Lincoln National policies throughout the Midwest.

During World War I the company grew quickly. Between 1913 and 1914 Lincoln National's reinsurance more than doubled, to $2 million. By 1917 reinsurance was bringing in $9.6 million. Lincoln National did not hesitate to pick up business from large German reinsurers at this time; in 1917 the company took over Pittsburgh Life, with its $2.5 million reinsurance business.

The great influenza epidemic of 1918 and 1919 had a far greater effect on the company. Death claims almost equaled those the company had paid out over the preceding decade, and extraordinary measures were required to pay benefits. Stockholders went without dividends and the members of the executive committee personally lent $300,000 to the company, but Mead rightly predicted that deaths attributable to the war or the epidemic would increase the importance of life insurance.

CONTINUED GROWTH: 1920–29

Lincoln National was highly successful throughout the 1920s. The firm built its own offices on the southern edge of downtown Fort Wayne in 1921, part of the site it would continue to occupy until 1998, in order to accommodate the growing number of home-office employees. Hall became president in 1923, the year the headquarters building was occupied. Hall was a paternalistic chief executive and encouraged athletic and cultural activities for employees. As was typical in the 1920s, women employees were required to resign when they married, but Hall did sponsor tennis and basketball programs for single women. There was also a nine-hole putting course atop the new building, open to clerical employees as well as to management.

In 1928 Hall employed Louis A. Warren, who was establishing his reputation as a Lincoln scholar, to direct the Lincoln Historical Research Foundation. Hall had only a vague idea of doing something in line with the company's name, but Warren soon persuaded him that the company should sponsor and finance a major research library devoted entirely to the life of Abraham Lincoln. When Warren finally retired 28 years later, the company's library had grown into a national center for Lincoln scholars, called the Louis A. Warren Lincoln Library and Museum and funded entirely by the company.

Under Hall's conservative management Lincoln National avoided the extravagant financial schemes of

KEY DATES

1905: Lincoln National Life Insurance Company is incorporated in Fort Wayne, Indiana.

1916: Michigan State Life Insurance Company is purchased.

1939: Lincoln National reaches $1 billion of insurance in force.

1951: Company purchases the Reliance Life Insurance Company of Pittsburgh.

1981: First Penn-Pacific Life Insurance Company is acquired.

2006: Company acquires Jefferson Pilot Financial.

2009: Lincoln National accepts $950 million from the U.S. government's Troubled Asset Relief Program; Lincoln UK is sold.

the late 1920s. He arranged another successful merger, this time with Merchants Life Insurance Company of Des Moines, Iowa, in 1928. Hall fought off efforts to sell control of the company to interests based in New York or Chicago and announced his determination to keep Lincoln National in Fort Wayne. Its business was still entrenched in the Midwest and most of its policyholders lived on farms or in small towns.

Throughout the 1920s the company had acquired a considerable amount of farm property as a result of defaults on mortgages it held as investments. The company shifted investment emphasis from mortgages to corporate bonds before the stock market crash of 1929 and began to sell off its farm properties in 1928, sometimes at a loss rather than try to farm the land itself.

DEPRESSION AND WAR POSE SIGNIFICANT CHALLENGES

The Great Depression brought unprecedented problems for Lincoln Life and the entire insurance industry. Failed investments were more numerous than ever, and the company began to be troubled by suicides, often disguised as accidents, among policyholders. There was also an expensive problem resulting from policies written by agents desperate for business on persons who were high risks or simply unable to pay for the insurance. The company's rejection rate increased by 75 percent between 1928 and 1931. Its basic business remained sound and profitable, despite the Depression, and its reinsurance business for some 300 insurance companies was particularly successful.

Home-office employment remained stable throughout the Depression, but the proportion of men did increase significantly as the company protected the jobs of family men at the expense of unmarried women. There was not always sufficient work for all of the employees, but the company avoided layoffs and prepared for busier and more prosperous times to come.

The Depression also meant opportunities for healthy companies to acquire less successful firms, and Lincoln National took over three smaller life insurance companies between 1932 and 1933: Northern States Life Insurance Company of Hammond, Indiana; Old Line Life Insurance Company of Lincoln, Nebraska; and Royal Union Life Insurance Company of Des Moines, Iowa. The company's business was still primarily midwestern, but Lincoln National reached $1 billion of insurance in force in 1939, a goal that Hall had hoped to reach by 1930.

Franklin Mead had long been the second-ranking executive at Lincoln National and was Arthur Hall's likely successor until Mead's own death in 1933. Mead's successor as chief actuary and prospective president was Alva McAndless, known as "Mac," who had joined the company in 1919. Hall, in failing health, became chairman of the board early in 1939, and McAndless became president and chief executive officer.

His primary concern was not in writing insurance policies, which had flourished, but the low yield on the company's investments. Indiana insurance law had been changed to permit greater investment in corporate bonds, but McAndless disliked the high-yielding 30-year obligations of utilities and railroads, while few new mortgages were available on farm property and interest on government bonds slipped as low as 1.9 percent in 1940. The company turned increasingly to mortgages on urban property, particularly homes.

During World War II the company contended with higher federal taxes and a greatly altered investment climate. Labor costs were also a concern. In 1941 the company increased starting salaries for the first time since the onset of the Depression. The tight labor market also persuaded the company to relax its ban on the employment of married women. During the war there was a reduction in automobile accidents, as driving declined as a result of gasoline rationing. Life insurance companies had long escaped most federal income taxes, but wartime demand for revenue led to some changes in the laws in 1942, and the company began to pay a modest level of corporate income tax from 1943 onward.

POSTWAR EXPANSION

McAndless also planned for postwar expansion. He particularly hoped to develop Lincoln National's agency force and prod agents to sell more life insurance. By 1945 the company's profits depended more upon its extensive reinsurance business. McAndless also kept dividends moderate and built up extensive cash reserves, both to provide against emergencies, like the Depression, and to take advantage of attractive opportunities.

The company had been unable to finance an attractive acquisition during the Depression, and its leadership did not wish to be caught short again. In 1951 Lincoln National purchased the Reliance Life Insurance Company of Pittsburgh from the Mellon National Bank for $27.5 million in cash. Reliance was an exceedingly conservative firm with a strong agency force. Mellon had been forced to sell the operation in order to meet the requirements of the Bank Holding Act. It was a very large merger for the early 1950s, and Lincoln National made the most of it. It retained Reliance employees, as promised; reduced expenses; and greatly improved investment results. Reliance agents were particularly strong in the South, a region in which Lincoln National had been very weak.

McAndless was very much a detail man. He was reportedly always tight with the company's money and held a close rein on the company. Under McAndless, Lincoln National's leadership became increasingly shallow as strong managers left for positions of greater authority. McAndless died of a heart attack early in 1954 and was succeeded by another actuary, Walter O. Menge, who had worked for Lincoln National since 1937.

INTERNATIONAL EXPANSION BEGINS IN 1957

Menge was a systematic chief executive who understood how to manage a large and complex business and could delegate authority. He planned carefully and made effective use of Lincoln National's large capital base while recognizing its problems. Lincoln National faced lagging sales of ordinary life insurance and a decreasing market share in a highly competitive market. He increased efforts in group insurance and continued to seek attractive acquisitions. In 1957 Lincoln National made its first move beyond the United States, acquiring the Dominion Life Assurance Company of Waterloo, Ontario.

In 1962 Lincoln National acquired American States Insurance Company of Indianapolis, which was a property and casualty specialist, in an effort to broaden its business beyond life insurance. This was also a defensive acquisition, to help protect Lincoln National's position as the largest reinsurer of life insurance policies in the country. General Reinsurance Corporation, a large non-life reinsurance company had recently entered the life reinsurance market, and Menge believed that his firm should offer a full line of coverage in both the insurance and reinsurance markets in order to remain fully competitive.

A year later Lincoln National made its first direct move into the European reinsurance market, although it had long written reinsurance for European firms. The company established a new subsidiary in Paris, the Compagnie de Reassurance Nord-Atlantique, and soon extended its business into Asian and African markets.

REORGANIZATION: 1960–69

As Lincoln National grew larger and more complex, becoming a major competitor in the international reinsurance market, Menge and his associates began to plan a reorganization. There was no thought of leaving Fort Wayne, but there were plans for a holding company structure. Before this could be achieved Menge moved up to chairman in 1964 and was succeeded as president by actuary Henry F. Rood. Rood pushed forward with plans to form the holding company, hoping Lincoln National would become a financial department store of sorts. He established subsidiaries in the Philippines and Great Britain. The Lincoln Philippine Life Insurance Company was established for legal reasons in a nation where the company already did business, but the British market was vastly different, and Lincoln National's methods were not well received.

Rood served as president of Lincoln National for four years before becoming chairman, although he would remain chief executive officer for an additional three years. Thomas A. Watson assumed the office of president in 1968. A marketing expert in group insurance, he had joined the firm in 1945. Rood carried through the 1968 creation of the Lincoln National Corporation as the holding company for all of the firm's operating companies, but Watson had the responsibility for implementing the reorganization.

In 1969 Lincoln National Corporation was listed for trading on the New York Stock Exchange, the new name an appropriate symbol of the new holding company's wider outlook. So too was its acquisition of Chicago Title and Trust Company in 1969. However, this purchase brought unexpected problems. Title insurance was a new line of business for Lincoln National, and far more troublesome was Chicago Title's bond-brokerage subsidiary, Halsey, Stuart & Company. The bond business was completely unfamiliar to Lincoln

National, and Halsey Stuart's investment-banking salaries were far higher than those paid in the insurance industry. Thus Halsey, Stuart & Company was sold in 1973. That same year the holding company also divested its British subsidiary, which had never met expectations. Watson also withdrew from other overseas operations, for business reasons in France and to avoid local political trouble in the Philippines. At home Watson sharply increased investment in sales agencies in an effort to improve the basic life insurance business.

During this time, Watson moved to open Lincoln National's offices and agencies to female and African American employees. Commitment to community involvement was evidenced in 1973, when the company established Lincoln Life Improved Housing, to rehabilitate abandoned dwellings near its Fort Wayne headquarters.

Watson planned carefully for an early retirement and in 1977 passed the presidency to Ian M. Rolland, a Fort Wayne native who had joined Lincoln National in 1956. Like most of his predecessors, Rolland was an actuary, although he had a wide range of experience within the company.

CONTINUING TO EXPAND: 1979–89

As chief executive officer Rolland stressed systematic organization and sophisticated planning as essential for a large and complex corporation. He continued Lincoln National's policy of acquisitions, most notably Security Connecticut Life Insurance Company in 1979. Security Connecticut had no agents of its own and sold its life insurance policies entirely through independent agents and brokers. The combination of company-employed and independent agents has been successful for Lincoln National, despite the potential for conflict between agents.

In 1981 Lincoln National acquired First Penn-Pacific Life Insurance Company, an Illinois firm. First Penn-Pacific brought with it growing sales in universal life policies, which quickly became a major part of Lincoln National's life insurance business. By 1983 Lincoln National, through its various subsidiaries, had $100 billion of life insurance in force, and it continued to expand by acquiring both life and property and casualty insurance companies. The larger but less visible reinsurance business grew more by internal expansion, but the firm did acquire National Reinsurance Corporation in 1984, which brought important additions in property and casualty reinsurance. Lincoln National also cautiously reentered the British market in 1984, this time by purchasing an established British company,

Cannon Assurance Limited. The following year it sold both its Canadian life insurance subsidiary and Chicago Title and Trust, withdrawing entirely from the title insurance business.

In the mid- to late 1980s, in response to trends in the medical insurance industry, Lincoln National greatly increased its activity in group health insurance and established its own health maintenance organizations (HMOs) in Indiana and Florida. Despite early problems, the HMOs were profitable by 1990 and had grown in size and in geographical scope, expanding into Texas and California. Also during this time, the company developed a variety of investment programs, particularly individual annuities and corporate pension plans.

By the end of the 1980s Lincoln National, which then ranked as the nation's seventh-largest publicly held insurance company, organized its business along five major lines: property and casualty; group life and health; individual life; life, health, and property/casualty reinsurance; and pensions and annuities.

TRANSFORMATION: 1990–97

The 1990s brought major changes to Lincoln National's mix of businesses, as senior management determined that the company needed to pare back to those core operations in which it excelled. The company thus sold National Reinsurance in May 1990 for $316 million, in the process withdrawing by and large from the property and casualty reinsurance business. Life and health reinsurance continued as a core company offering, however. Also divested were smaller, noncore operations, including Preferred Financial Corporation, sold in 1990; Western Security Life, sold in 1991; and K & K Insurance Agency, an insurer of sports and recreational activities, sold in 1993. Next to go were the health insurance businesses, including the HMOs, as the company concluded that it could not compete with the giants of the industry, such as CIGNA and Aetna.

In 1993 Lincoln National finally began to spend some of the vast sums of money it had accumulated through these sales. That year the company's first major acquisition in six years came in the form of Citibank's life insurance operations in the United Kingdom. Citibank Life was consolidated with Cannon Assurance to form Lincoln National (UK) PLC. This subsidiary was further bolstered in 1995 through the purchase of Liberty Life Assurance Company Limited and Laurentian Financial Group PLC (renamed Lincoln Financial Group PLC), which was bought for $237 million. By this time Lincoln National (UK) had grown into the 12th-largest life insurer in the United Kingdom and also offered investment and retirement products. In other foreign activity, Lincoln National in 1997 purchased a 49 percent stake in Seguros Serfin S.A., a life insurance company based in Mexico.

FOCUSING ON FINANCIAL SERVICES

The company gradually shifted its position from traditional insurer to financial services company, a shift reflecting the impact of deregulation, which had blurred the lines between insurance companies, banks, and investment firms. As evidenced by the 1995 $510 million acquisition of Delaware Management Holdings, Inc., a specialist in mutual funds and institutional money management, Lincoln National intended to focus on asset accumulation businesses including annuities, life insurance, 401 (k) plans, mutual funds, and institutional investment management.

Subsequent acquisitions aimed to build up these areas. Meanwhile, Lincoln National exited from property and casualty insurance, which did not fit into the new strategy, when it divested American States Financial through two transactions in 1996 and 1997 that brought in nearly $3 billion. Part of the proceeds from the sale of American States went toward a late 1997 $500 million stock repurchase. Although the company had divested its property and casualty line, it retained its strong, though seemingly noncore, life and health reinsurance business.

A NEW MARKETING NAME IN 1998

Lincoln National in the late 1990s had four principal business segments: life insurance and annuities, Lincoln UK, reinsurance, and investment management. In 1998 Rolland retired after more than 20 years as CEO. His successor and the man who would lead Lincoln National into the 21st century was Jon A. Boscia, who had been president of subsidiary Lincoln National Life Insurance.

To signal the company's new focus on financial services, it adopted Lincoln Financial Group as its marketing name in 1998. It also moved company headquarters from Fort Wayne to Philadelphia, Pennsylvania. The next year, The Lincoln National Life Insurance Co. was reorganized in order to separate its life insurance and annuity businesses.

Lincoln National continued its strategy in the early years of the new millennium. In 2000, it stopped writing new business under its Lincoln UK name in order to focus on domestic operations. During 2001 it sold its

reinsurance business, Lincoln Re, to Swiss Re in a $2 billion deal. It also formed Lincoln Financial Distributors to serve as its wholesaling distribution arm for the group. In 2002 the company solidified its presence in Philadelphia by acquiring the naming rights for the National Football League's Philadelphia Eagles' new stadium.

THE JEFFERSON-PILOT DEAL: 2006

The company's next big move came in 2006 when it announced it was acquiring North Carolina-based Jefferson-Pilot Corp. Lincoln National CEO Boscia and Jefferson-Pilot CEO Dennis Glass initially began discussing merger plans in 1999 and then again in 2003 before coming to an agreement in 2005. The $7.5 billion deal was finalized in 2006 and created an integrated financial services firm with a market capitalization of $16.2 billion. Jefferson-Pilot adopted the Lincoln name, and Glass was named chief operating officer of the company. Glass assumed the CEO position when Boscia retired in 2007. Company headquarters had moved to Radnor, a suburb of Philadelphia, by early 2008.

SURVIVING AN ECONOMIC CRISIS

The economic and credit crisis that hit the United States in 2008 and 2009 left Lincoln Financial and many other life insurance companies with enormous investment losses. The International Monetary Fund estimated in 2009 that total losses to insurance industries in the United States, Europe, and Japan due to investment write-downs would exceed $300 billion. In response to the crisis, the U.S. Department of Treasury launched the Troubled Asset Relief Program (TARP) and Capital Purchase Program to aid struggling financial and insurance institutions.

Lincoln National took advantage of TARP funds, using $950 million to shore up its bottom line in 2009. It also raised funds by issuing $600 million in common shares and $500 million in senior debt. In addition, it sold its Lincoln UK subsidiary to Canada-based Sun Life Financial Inc. for $320 million. Lincoln National sold Delaware Management Holdings Inc. in early 2010 in a $451.8 million cash deal.

The company reported a net loss of $485 million for fiscal 2009 but believed it would be able to repay its TARP loan in 2010 and 2011. With a cautious outlook, Lincoln National believed it was on track for growth in the years to come by focusing on prudent investments and cost cutting, and by remaining dedicated to its core insurance and retirement businesses.

Patrick J. Furlong
Updated, David E. Salamie; Christina M. Stansell

PRINCIPAL SUBSIDIARIES

First Penn-Pacific Life Insurance Company; Lincoln Financial Advisors Corporation; Lincoln Financial Distributors, Inc.; The Lincoln National Life Insurance Company; Lincoln Life & Annuity Company of New York.

PRINCIPAL COMPETITORS

AXA; Nationwide Financial Services Inc.; Prudential Financial Inc.

FURTHER READING

Barron, Richard M., "Goodbye JP, Hello; Lincoln National," *Greensboro News & Record*, April 1, 2006.

Burton, Thomas M., "Lincoln Agrees to Buy Units from Cigna," *Wall Street Journal*, July 29, 1997, pp. A3, A8.

Connolly, Jim, "Lincoln Financial Execs Ring in the New," *National Underwriter Life & Health-Financial Services Edi-tion*, May 1, 2006.

————, "Lincoln Turns to the Task of Integrating Its Life Purchases," *National Underwriter Life & Health-Financial Services Edition*, June 8, 1998, p. 59.

David, Gregory E., "Emancipation (1994-Style)," *Financial World*, July 5, 1994, p. 24.

Fraser, Katharine, "Lincoln Plans New Push in Bank Channel after Buying Cigna Unit," *American Banker*, August 12, 1997, p. 14.

Hawfield, Michael C., *Ninety Years and Growing: The Story of Lincoln National*, Indianapolis: Guild Press of Indiana, 1995, 161 p.

"Life Insurers' Critical Condition," *Reactions*, August 3, 2009.

"Lincoln National Swings to Profit," *Best's Insurance News*, February 9, 2010.

"Lincoln Takes $950m Tarp Funds, Sells UK Arm," *Reactions*, August 3, 2009.

Lohse, Deborah, "Aetna to Sell Some Assets to Lincoln," *Wall Street Journal*, May 22, 1998, pp. A3, A6.

Neely, Mark E., Jr., *Easy to Remember: A Brief History of the Lincoln National Life Insurance Company*, Fort Wayne, IN: Lincoln National Corporation, 1980.

Panko, Ron, "A New Life Behemoth Emerges after Buying Spree," *Best's Review*, July 1, 1999.

Seism, Leslie, "Lincoln National Seeks Bigger Role in Financial Services," *Wall Street Journal*, June 10, 1997, p. B4.

LVMH Moët Hennessy Louis Vuitton S.A.

22 Avenue Montaigne
Paris, 75008
France
Telephone: (33 1) 44 13 22 22
Fax: (33 1) 44 13 21 19
Web site: http://www.lvmh.com

Public Company
Incorporated: 1987
Employees: 77,300
Sales: EUR 17.1 billion ($23.48 billion) (2009)
Stock Exchanges: New York
Ticker Symbol: MC
NAICS: 551112 Offices of Other Holding Companies;
312130 Wineries; 312140 Distilleries; 316991 Luggage Manufacturing; 316992 Women's Handbag and Purse Manufacturing; 325620 Toilet Preparation Manufacturing; 334518 Watches and Parts Manufacturing; 339911 Jewelry (Except Costume) Manufacturing; 448190 Other Clothing Stores; 448150 Clothing Accessories Stores; 446120 Cosmetics, Beauty Supplies, and Perfume Stores; 453220 Gift, Novelty, and Souvenir Stores

■ ■ ■

LVMH Moët Hennessy Louis Vuitton S.A. is the world's leading luxury goods vendor. Its fashion and leather goods division includes such prominent brands as Louis Vuitton, Kenzo, Givenchy, and Céline, while its fragrance and cosmetics group distributes brands including Parfums Christian Dior, Givenchy, and Guerlain.

LVMH's wine and spirits group includes such premium brands as Dom Pérignon, Hennessy, Krug, and Moët Chandon. Its jewelry and watch brands include TAG Heuer, Chaumet, and Hublot. The company also owns luxury retailers, including a majority stake in DFS Group Ltd., a group of duty-free stores, and Sephora, a cosmetics and perfume chain, as well as a variety of business and arts publications. Its retail network consists of more than 2,400 stores worldwide. It is a subsidiary of Christian Dior SA.

ORIGINS OF LOUIS VUITTON

Historically a supplier of luggage to the wealthy and powerful, Louis Vuitton became known for combining quality fabrication with innovative designs to reflect the needs of customers and the ever-changing modes of world travel. Louis Vuitton came to Paris in 1835 at age 15 and soon became an apprentice packer and trunk maker. During his apprenticeship, Vuitton gained experience in packing by traveling to the homes of wealthy women, where he was employed to pack their clothes before they embarked on long voyages. With his master, Monsieur Maréchal, Vuitton went regularly to the Tuileries Palace as the exclusive packers to the Empress Eugénie and her ladies-in-waiting.

In 1854 Vuitton opened his own business very close to the couture houses around Place Vendôme. His invention of flat-topped trunks, which were more easily stacked for travel than the traditional domed trunks, established his reputation as a master luggage maker. Vuitton began covering his trunks in gray Trianon canvas, which was both elegant and waterproof when varnished.

COMPANY PERSPECTIVES

The mission of the LVMH group is to represent around the world the most refined qualities of Western "Art de Vivre." LVMH must continue to be synonymous with both elegance and creativity. Our products, and the cultural values they embody, blend tradition and innovation, and kindle dream and fantasy. In view of this mission, five priorities reflect the fundamental values shared by all Group stakeholders: Be creative and innovate; Aim for product excellence; Bolster the image of our brands with passionate determination; Act as entrepreneurs; Strive to be the best in all we do.

When his original store became too small, Vuitton moved and began focusing on trunk making rather than packing. Vuitton became the supplier of luggage to many of the most famous people of the era, from King Alfonso XII of Spain to the future Czar Nicholas II of Russia. He created special trunks for Ismail Pasha, the viceroy of Egypt, for the inauguration of the Suez Canal. He also designed a trunk-bed for Pierre Savorgnan de Brazza, who discovered the source of the Congo in 1876.

The quality of the materials, the arrangement of interiors, and the finishings made Vuitton's deluxe trunks far superior to anything that had previously been produced. That success led to counterfeiting. In an attempt to discourage copying of the Trianon gray canvas, Vuitton introduced new designs in 1876 featuring red-and-beige stripes and brown-and-beige stripes to cover his trunks. By 1888 these striped canvases were being imitated, and a patented checkered material was implemented.

New modes of travel were emerging rapidly during the second half of the 19th century. A large part of the company's success was its ability to respond to the changes. Vuitton designed classic wardrobe trunks for sleeping cars and lighter versions of the suitcase traditionally used by the English aristocracy.

INTERNATIONAL EXPANSION:
1885–1918

Louis's son Georges played an important role in the managing of the business, opening the first Vuitton branch abroad in London in 1885. In 1890 Georges invented the theft-proof five-tumbler lock. This provided each customer with a personal combination to secure all of his or her luggage. Two years later, the company's first catalog presented a wide range of products, from very specialized trunks for transporting particular objects to simple bags with the typical traveler in mind.

Four years after the death of Louis Vuitton in 1892, Georges introduced a new canvas design in another attempt to thwart counterfeiters. In memory of his father, the new design featured Louis Vuitton's initials against a background of stars and flowers. It was patented and became an immediate success.

Traveling to America for the Chicago Exposition of 1893, Georges became convinced of the importance of a sales network abroad. By the end of the century, John Wanamaker began representing Louis Vuitton in New York and Philadelphia, and the London store was transferred to New Bond Street, in the heart of London's luxury commerce. The company also expanded its distribution to Boston, Chicago, San Francisco, Brussels, Buenos Aires, Nice, Bangkok, and Montreal in the early 20th century.

Anticipating the importance of the automobile as a form of transport, Georges began designing automobile trunks to protect travelers' effects from rain and dust. Contending that one should be able to take in a car what one could take on a boat or train, he created iceboxes, canteens, and light and flexible steamer bags. Other efforts to adapt to the changes in the travel industry included the manufacture of airplane and hot-air balloon trunks and cases for spare tires. In 1914 the company erected a new building on the Champs-Elysées as the center for its growing network of distribution.

During World War I production was modified as simple and solid military trunks replaced delicate and luxurious models. The company also produced folding stretchers that were loaded directly into ambulances leaving for the front. After the war, the Vuittons struggled to supply their stores from what remained of the factory. Personal orders were less common, and the factory devoted more time to producing showcases for traveling salesmen.

INNOVATIONS AND GROWTH:
1920–87

During the 1920s Louis Vuitton regained its stylish clientele and special orders increased. The workshop at Asnières produced orders for Coco Chanel, the Aga Khan, Mary Pickford, the Vanderbilts, and the president of the French Republic, among others. Charles Lindbergh ordered two suitcases from Vuitton for his return trip to America after his famous flight to France.

KEY DATES

1743: Claude Moët and his son, Claude-Louis, open Moët et Cie to sell wine.
1854: Louis Vuitton opens packing and trunk making business in Paris.
1971: Moët et Chandon merges with Jas. Hennessy & Company and is renamed Moët-Hennessy.
1984: Louis Vuitton goes public.
1987: Louis Vuitton and Moët-Hennessy merge in a $4 billion deal, creating LVMH Moët Hennessy Louis Vuitton S.A.
1990: Through Christian Dior S.A., Bernard Arnault acquires controlling interest of LVMH Moët Hennessy Louis Vuitton S.A.
1999: LVMH spends $1.5 billion to acquire 15 luxury brands.
2005: LVMH sells off several of its subsidiaries.

As economic conditions deteriorated worldwide, the Vuittons recognized the need to increase the company's profitability. Georges's son Gaston worked with his father to increase efficiency. They set up an advertising agency and created a design office to make detailed sketches of products to show customers before fabrication. By the time Georges Vuitton died in 1936, special orders had dramatically declined. The company's sales depended more than ever upon its catalog offerings, which were expanded to include trunks for typewriters, radios, books, rifles, and wine bottles.

During World War II overseas contracts were terminated and the Vuitton factory and stores closed. The postwar period involved resupplying the stores, rebuilding business to prewar levels, and restructuring operations. In 1954, the company's 100th anniversary, Louis Vuitton moved from the Champs-Elysées to Avenue Marceau.

In 1959 Gaston perfected a system of coating his motif canvases, making them more durable, waterproof, and suitable for shorter journeys. These lightweight, practical bags signified a new standard in luggage. Gaston invited well-known artists to take part in the design of accessories. From 1959 to 1965, an average of 25 new models of Vuitton luggage were created each year.

Steel magnate Henry Racamier, Gaston's son-in-law, took over management of the company in 1977. Under Racamier, the company's sales soared from $20 million in 1977 to nearly $1 billion in 1987. Racamier recognized that the major profits were in retail. He

opened Louis Vuitton stores all over the world between 1977 and 1987, and Asia became the company's principal export market. Moreover, product diversification ensued, and in 1984 the company sold stock to the public through exchanges in Paris and New York.

Under Racamier, Louis Vuitton began to acquire companies with a reputation for high quality, purchasing interests in the couturier Givenchy and the champagne house Veuve Cliquot. Louis Vuitton's takeover philosophy was personal, courteous, and discreet, rather than systematically aggressive.

ORIGINS OF MOËT-HENNESSY

Moët-Hennessy, whose product lines include Christian Dior perfume, Dom Pérignon champagne, and Hennessy X.O. cognac, is a well-established and extremely successful French enterprise. What began as the business of a talented French vintner more than 250 years ago became a world leader in the production of wines, spirits, cosmetics, and perfumes.

Claude Moët established a vineyard near Epernay in the Champagne region east of Paris, in the Marne River valley. He quickly became frustrated dealing with the *courtiers en vin,* or distributors, who took his wine to market. Instead of depending on them to sell his wine, Moët decided to buy one of the offices of *courtiers en vin* and sell the wine himself.

In 1743 Moët et Cie (Moët and Company) was formed. Joined by his son Claude-Louis, Moët quickly established customer accounts that included a number of landed gentry and nobles. In 1750 father and son established an account with Madame du Pompadour, who regularly ordered Moët champagne for the royal court at Compiègne. That same year Moët began selling champagne in Germany, Spain, Eastern Europe, and America.

Claude Moët died in 1792, leaving the company to his grandson Jean-Rémy, who laid the groundwork for the later success of Moët et Cie. Jean-Rémy expanded the base of operations at Epernay by purchasing the vineyards of the Abbey of Hautvillers, where a century earlier the Benedictine monk Dom Pérignon perfected the double fermentation of wine to create champagne.

However, it was Jean-Rémy's friendship with Napoleon that helped the company attract a loyal international following. Jean-Rémy became mayor of Epernay in 1802 and first met Napoleon two years later. Napoleon and his entourage were lavishly wined and dined by Jean-Rémy in newly built guesthouses at the firm's address, 20 Avenue de Champagne. Jean-Rémy's 10 years in the Napoleonic limelight made him the most famous winemaker in the world at that time. Moët later dedicated its Brut Imperial in Napoleon's honor.

Jean-Rémy's customer list in the early 19th century had grown to include such famous people as Czar Alexander of Russia, Emperor Francis II of Austria (Napoleon's father-in-law), the Duke of Wellington, Madame de Staël, Queen Victoria, and the Prince Royal of Russia (later to become emperor of Germany).

MOËT ET CHANDON: 1832–1970

In 1832 Jean-Rémy retired and relinquished direction of the company to his son Victor and son-in-law Pierre-Gabriel Chandon de Briailles. To reflect the new partnership, the company's name was changed to Moët et Chandon. Victor and Pierre expanded the firm's operations, and by 1879 Moët et Chandon dominated the Marne Valley with its introduction of more flavorful grapes from Cramant, Le Mesnil, Bouzy, Ay, and Verzenay.

At this time Moët et Chandon employed close to 2,000 people working as cellar men, cork cutters, clerks, vineyard farmers, tinsmiths, needlewomen, basket makers, firemen, packers, wheelwrights, and stable boys. The company had established a social security system for employees, which included free medical attention, housing assistance, pensions, maternity benefits, sick pay, and free legal aid.

Moët's average annual sales were believed to have been about 20,000 bottles during the 1820s. By 1872 that figure had risen to two million, and by 1880 it had reached 2.5 million. At the dawn of the 20th century, Moët et Chandon's clientele remained primarily within the upper echelons of society.

During World War I, bombs demolished the offices and the guesthouses where Napoleon had dined. Despite the destruction, Moët et Chandon reaffirmed its place in the market in the late 1920s by creating the Dom Pérignon brand of vintage champagne. Described by connoisseurs as the most perfect champagne available, Dom Pérignon also became the most expensive. The introduction of Dom Pérignon initiated a trend other champagne houses later followed: that of creating a premium brand, which placed other regular vintages second in status. Dom Pérignon, however, emerged as the most successful premium champagne.

Despite interruptions in its business during World War II, Moët et Chandon recovered quickly after the war, as a result of its prompt modernization of facilities. From the installation of new wine presses to a comprehensive system of work incentives, the goals of fairness and efficiency were emphasized in all aspects of production. Count Robert-Jean de Vogüé, one of France's most important wine buyers in the mid-1950s, led the company to even greater success during his tenure as president. De Vogüé transformed Moët et Chandon from a family-owned venture into a Société Anonyme, or corporation. A series of acquisitions, mergers, and diversifications expanded the company's product line.

Moët et Chandon gained control of Ruinart Père et Fils (France's oldest champagne house and Moët's chief competitor) in 1962. The company acquired Mercier, another rival champagne house, in 1970, and soon thereafter purchased an interest in Parfums Christian Dior, marking the company's first undertaking outside of the champagne business. Moët et Chandon later completed its takeover of Dior, whose perfume products include Miss Dior, Dioressence, and Eau Savage.

MOËT-HENNESSY: 1971–87

Moët et Chandon merged with Jas. Hennessy & Company, France's second-largest cognac producer, in 1971. The new company, called Moët-Hennessy, enjoyed a broader financial base and was better able to stimulate the growth of its interests abroad. The merger was brought about mainly as a result of a 1927 statute that limited the Champagne growing region to 34,000 hectares. (The statute was intended to protect the quality of French champagne by discouraging price competition.)

While fewer than 25,000 hectares were under cultivation in 1970, Robert-Jean de Vogüé believed that growing demand for champagne would exhaust the supply of land by 2000. Until other regions suitable for champagne production could be found, de Vogüé decided that diversification through a merger with Hennessy would ensure a stable future for Moët.

Moët-Hennessy established a firmer presence in the United States in 1973 when it opened the Domaine Chandon winery in Napa Valley, California, a location that proved ideal for the production of sparkling wines. Production at Domaine Chandon grew dramatically and enabled Moët-Hennessy to expand in one of its most important foreign markets. The winery also somewhat reduced demand in North America for French champagne, whose production was still restricted by law.

Alain Chevalier, a protégé of de Vogüé, was chiefly responsible for the success of Domaine Chandon. He was named chief executive officer in the mid-1970s and began transforming Moët-Hennessy into a less conservative company with more aggressive marketing strategies. After de Vogüé's death in 1976, Chevalier continued the diversification program started by his predecessor. In

1977 Moët-Hennessy purchased the Rozes companies in Portugal and France in an effort to raise demand for champagne. The following year, the company purchased Roc, a French cosmetics firm specializing in hypoallergenic makeup.

The company also acquired Delbard, a French rose company, as well as Armstrong Nurseries of Ontario, California, the largest farmer of rosebushes in America. Moët-Hennessy was trying to apply rosebush-cloning techniques to grape vines in order to produce better hybrids. As a result of these acquisitions, Moët-Hennessy became the world's leading producer of roses. Losses incurred by both Roc and Armstrong, however, depressed Moët-Hennessy's earnings. The introduction of a popular new perfume from Dior called Poison helped offset those losses.

Continuing its expansion in the United States, Moët-Hennessy acquired its American sales agent, Schieffelin & Company, one of the oldest wine and spirits distributors in North America. Moët-Hennessy was one of the first French companies to use European Currency Units (or ECUs), more stable in value against the dollar and therefore preferable for funding investments in the United States.

MERGER AND TAKEOVER: 1987–90

In June 1987 a $4 billion merger was effected between Louis Vuitton with Moët-Hennessy. The merger allowed Louis Vuitton to expand its investments in the luxury business, while saving Moët-Hennessy from the threat of takeover. Moreover, the merger respected the autonomy of each company over its own management and subsidiaries.

As Moët-Hennessy was three times the size of Louis Vuitton, its president, Alain Chevalier, was named chairperson of the new holding company, Moët-Hennessy Louis Vuitton (LVMH), and Racamier became executive vice-president. Massive disagreements and feuding followed, as management at Louis Vuitton believed that Moët-Hennessy was trying to absorb its operations. The 60 percent ownership that Racamier and the Vuitton family had held in Louis Vuitton became a mere 17 percent share of LVMH.

After several disputes and legal battles between Racamier and Chevalier over the running of the conglomerate, Racamier invited the young property developer and financial engineer Bernard Arnault to acquire stock in the company. Hoping to consolidate his position within LVMH with the help of Arnault, Racamier soon saw that Arnault had ambitions of his own. With the help of the French investment bank Lazard Frères and the British liquor giant Guinness plc, Arnault secured a 45 percent controlling interest of LVMH stock for himself.

Chevalier stepped down and an 18-month legal battle ensued between Racamier and Arnault. Despite Louis Vuitton's strong performance, accounting for 32 percent of LVMH sales, Racamier could not hold onto his stake in LVMH against Arnault, who had the support of the Moët and Hennessy families. The courts eventually favored Arnault, and Racamier stepped down to create another luxury goods conglomerate, Orcofi. Arnault weeded out Vuitton's top executives and began to bring together his fragmented luxury empire.

Structurally, LVMH became a subsidiary of Arnault's holding company, Christian Dior SA. The holding company's other major subsidiary was Christian Dior Couture. Within LVMH, other luxury brands included the fashion houses Céline, Lacroix, and Givenchy. In 1990 Arnault controlled the world's largest luxury empire, with about $5 billion in worldwide sales.

A PORTFOLIO OF LUXURY BRANDS: 1991–99

LVMH focused on growth and expansion during the decade. Purchases included cosmetics company Guerlain, Champagne brand Pommery, both the fashion and cosmetics companies of Kenzo, jeweler Fred, and leather goods specialist Loewe. In 1996 Arnault invested $2.6 billion for a 61 percent interest in DFS Group Ltd. (Duty Free Shoppers), a specialty retailer that catered to international travelers. The purchase included 180 boutiques in Asia, DFS's largest market. LVMH also invested in winery Chateau d'Yquem and purchased the fashion company Loewe.

In 1998 LVMH acquired Sephora, the French retailer of perfumes and beauty products, for $267 million, and invested in Douglas International, a German retailer of cosmetics and beauty goods. It also purchased Le Bon Marché, an exclusive specialty retailer in Paris, from the Arnault Group. LVMH also bought Marie-Jeanne Godard, a leading distributor of fragrances and cosmetics in France.

In 1999 LVMH spent $1.5 billion to acquire 15 luxury brands. It moved into watches with purchases of TAG Heuer, Chaumet, Elmo, and Zenith brands, and bought Champagne producer Krug. To expand its fragrance and cosmetics holdings, particularly in the United States, the company invested in four American beauty products companies: Hard Candy, which targeted the youth market, Bliss Spa, BeneFit Cosmetics, and Make Up for Ever.

LVMH also entered into some strategic partnerships to remain competitive in the marketplace. It partnered with Italian fashion company Prada, usually a competitor, to acquire a majority stake in fashion design house Fendi. Among LVMH's other 1999 acquisitions were a majority interest in Thomas Pink, a British shirt maker, and the purchase of Phillips Auctioneers. Each business in the company operated autonomously, with budgets set at LVMH headquarters. Arnault preferred to pay cash for the acquisitions to avoid diluting his holdings in the conglomerate.

Even as this expansion was going on, significant changes were made at Louis Vuitton to strengthen the company's star brand. The ubiquity of the brand's monogram in the mid-1980s had damaged its reputation as a status symbol, and both profits and sales had declined. Rampant counterfeiting also cut into revenues. Arnault named Yves Carcelle, a former textile executive, as president of Louis Vuitton and in 1998 brought in Marc Jacobs as creative designer.

Together they implemented the formula Arnault had used to revitalize the Christian Dior luxury brand, which first involved the pairing of creative and business talents. On the creative side, Jacobs studied the history of the brand and developed modern twists for each new collection. On the business side, Carcelle focused on improving product quality and solving distribution issues. Other components in the formula consisted of altering the product mix and targeting new customers by adding a line of ready-to-wear clothing, and public relations efforts, including endorsements by models and actresses.

GLOBAL MARKET LEADERSHIP

The early years of the new century were difficult ones for the luxury market. LVMH's sales in the United States and Europe dropped significantly in 2001 when tourism slumped following the terrorist attacks in the United States in September of that year. Profits fell 98 percent in 2001. The company responded with strong moves into China and India, and 2002 saw growth improving. That upswing ended the next year, with low tourism due to the SARS pneumonia scare and the invasion of Iraq, along with the boycott of some French products in the United States.

LVMH had sold off several of its subsidiaries by 2005, even as its flagship brands were introducing new products. It also moved to apply the Louis Vuitton/ Christian Dior formula to other of its companies. Analysts and reporters at the time questioned whether the company could make so many brands profitable while maintaining standards. Nevertheless, the very diversity of the conglomerate's offerings along with their geographical range provided a stabilizing effect.

The fashion and leather goods division was LVMH's overall leader. Year after year it generated the largest percentage of sales and of profits. Other divisions saw greater volatility, however. For example, in 2001 the wine and spirits division was the only other profitable business. In 2005 all business groups saw increased sales and increased profits. However, during the recession in 2009, profits for wines and spirits fell significantly, as they did for watches and jewelry.

SURVIVING THE GLOBAL DOWNTURN

Geographically, LVMH doubled its business in emerging markets between 2003 and 2008. By 2009 Asia (not including Japan) was generating 23 percent of sales, up from 17 percent at the beginning of the decade. This cushioned revenue declines in the United States, France, and Japan, which together accounted for 47 percent of revenue in 2009. That was down from 57 percent in 2001.

The global economy was not the only factor influencing sales. Counterfeit merchandise was a continuing threat. Low-quality merchandise undercut not only company profits but also the allure of the company's brands and the confidence of consumers in those brands. LVMH and its parent company actively pursued threats in these areas. LVMH won two lawsuits against eBay for selling counterfeit perfumes and other goods under LVMH brands.

During the decade, LVMH successfully developed and expanded its major brands. It opened new stores, hosted art exhibits, and introduced high-priced limited edition products. For example, in 2004 the Theda bag sold for $5,550. The company was also a pioneer in sustainable development. Its subsidiaries examined their carbon footprints and developed initiatives to reduce carbon emissions and save energy.

Several of the smaller subsidiaries were less successful in breaking into the upper tiers of luxury items. With the recession there was some anticipation that LVMH might sell some of its brands. However, LVMH continued to make purchases. In addition to adding new brands, including watchmaker Hublot, LVMH bought a stake in a leading Russian beauty and cosmetics retail chain, aimed at helping Sephora in that market.

LVMH's focus on quality, creativity, and innovation appeared to have helped it survive the global downturn. Its strategy of diversification among brands and regions proved successful. However, even LVMH recognized the need to cut back on extravagance. LVMH had been less dependent on the middle-class shopper than many other luxury firms. There was speculation that LVMH would take advantage of competitors' weakness and add another star brand to its portfolio. There seemed little question that LVMH was resilient. What remained to be seen in the near future was the array of its brands.

Jennifer Kerns
Updated, Mariko Fujinaka; Ellen D. Wernick

PRINCIPAL SUBSIDIARIES

Louis Vuitton Malletier; Champagne Moët & Chandon; DFS Group Ltd. (Hong Kong; 62%); Dom Pérignon; Glenmornangie Company (Scotland); Guerlain SA; Hublot S.A.; Jas Hennessy & Co.; Le Bon Marché; Parfums Christian Dior; Parfums Givenchy; Sephora Holding; TAG Heuer S.A.

PRINCIPAL COMPETITORS

Compagnie Financière Richemont SA; PPR SA; Rémy Cointreau Group.

FURTHER READING

Edmondson, Gail, Sharon Reier, and Julia Flynn, "LVMH: Life Isn't All Champagne and Caviar," *Business Week,* November 10, 1997, p. 108.

Guyon, Janet, "The Magic Touch," *CCNMoney.com,* September 6, 2004.

Heller, Richard, "Le Brand, C'est Moi," *Forbes.com,* November 27, 2000.

Monnin, Philippe, and Claude Vincent, *Guerre du luxe— l'affaire LVMH,* Paris: François Bourin, 1990.

Pasols, Paul-Gerard, *Louis Vuitton: The Birth of Modern Luxury,* New York: Abrams Books, 2005.

Sebag-Montefiore, Hugh, *Kings on the Catwalk: The Louis Vuitton and Moët-Hennessy Affair,* London: Chapmans, 1992.

Som, Ashok, "Personal Touch That Built an Empire of Style and Luxury," *European Business Forum,* Winter 2005, pp. 69–71.

"The Substance of Style," *Economist,* September 19, 2009, pp. 79–81.

Thomas, Dana, *Deluxe: How Luxury Lost Its Luster,* New York: The Penguin Press, 2007.

Vuitton, Henry L., *La malle aux souvenirs,* Paris: Editions Mengès, 1984.

Magna Steyr AG and Company KG

Magnastrasse 1
Oberwaltersdorf, A-2522
Austria
Telephone: (+43 02253) 600 0
Fax: (+43 02253) 600 1200
Web site: http://www.magnasteyr.com

Wholly Owned Subsidiary of Magna International Inc.
Incorporated: 2001
Employees: 12,000
Sales: $6.84 billion
NAICS: 336399 All Other Motor Vehicle Parts
Manufacturing

■ ■ ■

Magna Steyr AG and Company KG is Europe's largest coachbuilder, providing contract manufacturing and engineering services to the automobile industry. Austria-based Magna Steyr operates in four interconnected business areas: Complete Vehicle Production; Roof Systems; Engineering Services; and Systems & Modules. This allows the company to provide support services ranging from homologation (adapting foreign cars to the specification of different markets), to initial design phase support, to the automobile paint services, to complete vehicle manufacturing. Magna produces more than 100,000 vehicles per year and has reached peaks of more than 200,000 vehicles per year, making it the world's largest non-branded automotive manufacturer.

Magna Steyr typically handles smaller-run and niche versions, such as convertibles and specialized engine series, of common automotive models. In November 2009, for example, the company debuted the first Peugeot RCZ sports coupe. Others include the Jeep Commander, the Chrysler 300C, the BMW X3, the Saab 9-3, and the Mercedes-Benz G-Class. The company also develops and produces specialized rooftop systems, such as retractable hardtops for the Mercedes SLK and the Opel Astra, and car-top systems for the Nissan 370Z Roadster and the Infiniti G convertible.

In addition to its manufacturing services, the company provides a full range of engineering services. The company provided the engineering for the Fiat Bravo vehicle body and was also responsible for the development of the Audi TT. The company has also established a presence in China, where it provides engineering services to that country's automotive manufacturers, in part to help them raise their quality levels for a future entry into the U.S. and European markets.

Magna Steyr is a subsidiary of Canada's Magna International Inc. Magna Steyr's main manufacturing facility is in Graz, Austria. The company operates three other factories in Austria, five factories in Germany, two plants in Japan, and a manufacturing and assembly plant in Poland. The company owns engineering, product development and/or sales offices in Germany, Italy, France, Hungary, and India and operates an automotive painting facility in Ohio in the United States. Magna Steyr's revenues neared $6.85 billion in 2009. Guenther Apfalter is the company's CEO.

SMALL ARMS ORIGINS IN 1864

Magna Steyr stemmed from the former Steyr-Daimler-Puch, the Austrian industrial giant. That company's origins reach back to the mid-19th century. Its earliest component originated as a gun factory founded by Josef Werndl in Steyr, Austria, in 1864.

Steyr's tradition as an iron work and metal crafting hub reached back to the Middle Ages. By the 19th century, Steyr had gained particular prominence as the center of Austria's weapons and small arms industry. The Werndl family was already well-known as gunsmiths before Josef Wendl joined his father's business in 1855. Werndl had completed a series of apprenticeships, notably with Colt and Remington in the United States, before returning to Steyr. In 1864 Werndl founded his own company, Josef und Franz Werndl & Comp. Waffenfabriek und Sägemuhle, which launched production of its own breech loading rifle design.

By 1869 Werndl already employed 6,000 people. In that year, the company went public as the Oesterreichische Waffenfabrik Gesellschaft, Steyr (OWG). OWG went on to world-fame after Ferdinand Mannlicher joined the company and took over its small arms designs at the turn of the 20th century. By then, OWG had already begun to diversify, launching bicycle production in 1894 and then adding automobiles in 1918. The company changed its name to Steyr-werke AG in 1926, while its small arms operations became known as Steyr Mannlicher. In 1934, Steyr-werke merged with another up-and-coming automotive manufacturer, Austro-Daimler-Puchwerke.

AUTOMOTIVE PIONEERS FROM 1899

Austro-Daimler-Puchwerke itself had been founded in 1928 through the merger of two of Austria's automotive pioneers. Like many of Europe's early automakers, Puchwerke originated as a bicycle manufacturer, Erste Steiermärkische Fahrrad-Fabriks-Aktiengesellschaft (First Styrian Bicycle Factory, Inc.). Founded by Johann Puch in 1899, Puch quickly extended production beyond bicycles, however, and by 1901 had launched its first motorcycle design. This led the company into four-wheeled vehicles, with the introduction of its first automobile in 1904. By 1906, Johann Puch had already started to gain a name for himself in automotive circles, debuting the Puch Voiturette.

In 1909 one of Puch's models established a new speed record, topping 130 kilometers per hour (65 mph). This led the company to focus on developing its automobile designs, and by the outbreak of the World War I the company had already introduced 21 different models. These included a limousine model, built for the Habsburg monarchy starting in 1910. The company launched its four-cylinder Alpenwagen line in 1912. In that year, Johann Puch retired. By then, the company had already expanded to 1,100 employees, with production totals of 300 automobiles, 300 motorcycles, and 16,000 bicycles per year.

The company changed its name to Puchwerke AG in 1914. During the war, Puch's production turned to support the Austro-Hungarian war effort. With the breakup of the empire, however, Puch suddenly found its market restricted to Austria alone. As a result, the company abandoned its automobile operations in 1923. Instead, Puch's operations increasingly focused on its motorcycle production, especially its scooters and mopeds. These were based on a two-piston engine design patented by the company in 1923.

MERGER IN 1934

Five years later, Puchwerke merged with another fast-growing Austrian automotive company, Österreichische Daimler-Motoren-Gesellschaft, also known as Austro-Daimler. That company had been established in 1899 by Eduard Bierenz, who had started out as a salesman for Gottlieb Daimler's automobiles in Austria in 1890. The popularity of Daimler's designs soon outpaced the German company's production capacity. This led Bierenz to join with Eduard Fischer, who ran an engineering and manufacturing company in Wiener Neustadt to found Österreichische Daimler-Motoren-Gesellschaft Bierenz, Fischer & Co.

In 1902 Daimler acquired the Austrian company, which quickly emerged as a major part of the growing Daimler automotive empire in the new century. The company launched production of its first armored car in 1905. The following year, Ferdinand Porsche took direction of the design team for the company, which was renamed Austro-Daimler that year. Porsche introduced new aerodynamic designs and also led the company into the production of Zeppelin engines. By 1909 Austro-Daimler had begun to separate from its German parent.

KEY DATES

1864: The predecessor to Steyr-werke is founded in Wiener Neustadt, Austria.

1934: Steyr and Austro-Daimler-Puch merge to form Steyr-Daimler-Puch (SDP).

1949: SDP launches its contract manufacturing operations for the automobile sector.

1987: SDP sells off its bicycle and motorcycle production to focus on the automobile industry.

1998: Magna International acquires SDP.

2006: Magna Steyr enters the U.S. and Chinese markets.

This led to a change in name that year, to Österreichische Daimler-Motoren-AG.

Led by Porsche, Austro-Daimler enjoyed some success as an automotive manufacturer in its own right into the beginning of World War I. The company converted its production to support of the Austrian-Hungarian military effort. Like Puch, however, Austro-Daimler found it difficult to adapt to the post-empire market conditions. Another blow to the company came when Ferdinand Porsche left the company to work for Daimler in Germany in 1923. By 1928 Austro-Daimler was struggling, leading to its merger with Puchwerke.

Austro-Daimler-Puchwerke produced several more models under the Austro-Daimler name. Nevertheless, the company bore the brunt of the economic chaos of the early 1930s, leading to its merger with Steyr-werke in 1934. The company formally registered as Steyr-Daimler-Puch AG (SDP) in 1935. Following the merger, the company dropped the Austro-Daimler brand. SDP did briefly revive the Austro-Daimler name later, however, for its higher-end bicycle line in the 1970s.

POSTWAR CONTRACT MANUFACTURER

Motorcycles remained SDP's staple through the 1930s and 1940s. Into the late 1930s, the Puch brand represented some 86 percent of the total Austrian motorcycle market. SDP carried out a major expansion of its manufacturing capacity with the opening of a new plant in Graz-Thorndorf in 1941. That site ultimately became the company's primary production facility. In 1946 SDP shifted its production of roller bearings and motorcycles to the Graz plant as well.

At the end of the decade, SDP became one of the pioneers for Europe's automobile contract manufacturing sector. Unlike their U.S. counterparts, European automobile manufacturers seeking expansion were confronted with the need to develop their automobiles for a wide variety of national markets. This led to the development of a growing number of "coachbuilders," so called because many of these companies had started out building coaches for horse-drawn carriages.

Like Puch and Austro-Daimler, a good number of coachbuilders had also launched their own automotive designs in the early years of the industry. As the European automobile market narrowed, however, to a smaller number of major, largely national brands, these companies turned to providing support services to the major automobile companies. Over the next decades, these support services ranged from providing initial design and engineering services, to manufacturing systems and components, to assembly and even full vehicle manufacturing. Another important service was "homologation," that is, adapting vehicles to the specifications and regulations of a specific market.

SDP's own entry into the contract manufacturing sector came in 1949, when it began building cars for Italy's Fiat, starting with its 1100 model. Through the decade, Fiat remained a major client for the company, which launched production of the 500 in 1952, the 1400 in 1953, and the 600 in 1956. SDP also built several Fiat models under license for the Austrian market, such as the Puch 500, introduced in 1957, which it marketed under its own name through the 1970s. Also during the 1950s, SDP developed expertise in all-wheel drive vehicles, leading to the launch of the Puch Haflinger in 1958.

AUTOMOBILE FOCUS IN THE EIGHTIES

SDP continued to produce bicycles and motorcycles, particularly mopeds and scooters, until the 1980s. These included its most successful moped model of all, the Maxi, introduced in 1968. Through the 1970s, SDP's two-wheeled division remained strong, topping 270,000 mopeds and motorcycles and 350,000 bicycles. These numbers declined into the 1980s, however, and in 1987 the company sold off the Puch trademark and operations to Piaggio of Italy.

By then, SDP's automotive operations had made major gains. The company gained particular expertise in the four-wheel-drive sector, with the success of its Pinzgauer all-terrain vehicle introduced in 1970. This led to collaboration with Mercedes to design and build that company's own four-wheel-drive vehicle, the famous G series, launched in 1979. SDP continued to produce the

Mercedes G into the next century.

The Mercedes G represented another major trend in the European automotive industry, which increasingly turned to coachbuilders in order to develop and produce niche versions for their popular brands and models. SDP adapted its own operations for this market, setting up dedicated manufacturing lines for a wide range of models. These included the all-wheel-drive version of the Volkswagen T3 van, produced from 1983. The company added another Volkswagen model, the "Country" version of its highly popular Golf, in 1990.

SDP also provided non-European automakers with a lower-cost entry into the European market. The company began producing the Chrysler Voyager, as part of the Eurostar joint venture, in 1991. The company also added production of the Jeep Grand Cherokee in 1994. Other additions to SDP's line during the decade included the 4Matic version of Mercedes-Benz E class, starting in 1996.

PART OF MAGNA INTERNATIONAL IN 1996

SDP provided something of a return home for Magna International founder Frank Stronach, an Austrian native, when the Canadian automotive parts giant bought control of the company in 1998. Magna paid $312 million for nearly 67 percent of the company and then eventually increased its shareholding to 100 percent. By then, SDP had grown to include 5,200 employees, and revenues of more than EUR 1 billion. SDP changed its name to Magna Steyr in 2001.

Magna Steyr expanded rapidly as part of the Magna group, taking over Magna International's existing European businesses in Germany, Poland, Italy, and France. The company also took complete control of the Eurostar factory, located next door to its main Graz factory, in 2002. These sites were then combined, forming one of the largest automobile manufacturing centers in Europe.

The company continued to secure high-profile contracts in the new decade. In 2003, for example, Magna STEYR began producing a convertible version of the Saab 9-3. The company also received the contract to engineer and produce the new BMW X3, the first complete vehicle produced outside of that company's own factories. Then in 2005, the company also gained the contract to produce the Chrysler 300C for the European market.

ADDING JAPAN IN 2010

This flurry of activity led to a major increase in production at Magna Steyr. In 2006 the company established a new production record of 248,000 vehicles produced in a single year. In that year, the company began establishing its first non-European operations. This led to a contract with DaimlerChrysler to operate that company's paint shop as part of its Toledo, Ohio, Jeep factory. The company also added an engineering office in Shanghai, China, that year, in order to position itself as a contract services supplier to that country's fast-growing automotive sector.

Magna Steyr gained new high-profile contracts in the second half of the decade. The company began producing the new Aston Martin Rapide in 2009 and also signed a contract to produce the Porsche Boxster, slated to begin in 2012. Magna Steyr had geared up for production of the Peugeot RCZ sport coupe and a sport-utility version of the Mini, both starting in 2010.

By this time, the company was feeling the effects of the global economic crisis; its production orders plummeted through 2009, and its total production dropped to 150,000 vehicles. The company also faced the cancellation of the Boxster contract in November 2009, after Porsche, then part of Volkswagen, acquired one of Magna Steyr's rivals, Karmann.

The takeover of Karmann nonetheless provided a new growth opportunity for Magna Steyr, as that company's Japanese subsidiary was put up for sale. In February 2010, Magna Steyr announced that it had agreed to acquire Karmann Japan. The purchase came in support of a new contract, for the production of the car-top system for the new Nissan 370Z Roadster, signed in December 2009. As a key component of Magna International, Magna Steyr looked forward to new challenges along the road ahead.

M. L. Cohen

PRINCIPAL SUBSIDIARIES

Magna Car Top Systems (Bowling Green) LLC; Magna Car Top Systems GmbH (Germany); Magna Car Top Systems Poland Sp.z.o.o.; Magna International Japan Inc.; Magna Steyr Automotive Technologies (Shanghai) Ltd.; Magna Steyr Engineering Center Hungaria Ktf.; Magna Steyr France SAS; Magna Steyr Fuel Systems Ges.m.b.H.; Magna Steyr India (Pvt) Ltd.; Magna Steyr Italia (Italy); Magna Steyr Japan; Magna Uniport S.A.S.; Service Technologies GmbH & Co OHG.

PRINCIPAL DIVISIONS

Engineering Services; Complete Vehicle Production; Systems & Modules; Roof Systems.

PRINCIPAL COMPETITORS

Robert Bosch GmbH; New-Era Company Ltd.; Denso Corp.; ArvinMeritor OE L.L.C.; Aisin Seiki Company Ltd.; Adam Opel GmbH; MAN SE; ZF Friedrichshafen AG.

FURTHER READING

Auer, Georg, "Magna Gets Steyr at Last," *Automotive News*, March 30, 1998, p. 45.

——, "Magna's Growth Strategy," *Automotive News Europe*, March 11, 2002, p. 12.

Chappell, Lindsay, "Magna Steyr: Big Changes Are Needed," *Automotive News Europe*, September 4, 2006, p. 31.

Chellini, Roberto, "Magna Cum Luck," *Automotive Industries*, January 2004, p. 38.

Ciferri, Luca, "Good News That Is Bad News," *Automotive News Europe*, February 2, 2009, p. 2.

——, "How Magna Steyr Built a Coachbuilding Dynamo," *Automotive News Europe*, September 5, 2005, p. 21.

——, "Magna Steyr: A Giant with Many Talents," *Automotive News*, September 19, 2005, p. 32B.

——, "Magna Steyr Cautious about Future," *Automotive News Europe*, July 21, 2008, p. 6.

Mauerer, Gerhard, "Magna Could Lose Contract to Build the New Boxster," *Automotive News*, November 30, 2009.

Murphy, Tom, "Graz's Global Vision," *Ward's Auto*, January 1, 2006.

Turrettini, John, "Made to Order," *Forbes*, September 1, 2003, p. 78.

Webb, Alysha, "Magna Steyr Helps Chinese to Reach Europe's Markets," *Automotive News Europe*, November 26, 2007, p. 22.

Wernle, Bradford, "Magna Steyr Seeks More Work in US," *Automotive New Europe*, September 18, 2006, p. 16.

Wright, Rebecca, "Magna Makes Move into Batteries," *Automotive News Europe*, May 12, 2008, p. 18.

Magyar Villamos Muvek Zrt

Vam u 5-7
Budapest, H-1011
Hungary
Telephone: (+36 06 1) 224 6200
Fax: (+36 06 1) 202 1246
Web site: http://www.mvm.hu

State-Owned Company
Incorporated: 1992
Employees: 8,968
Sales: HUF 721.24 billion ($3.68 billion) (2008 est.)
NAICS: 221122 Electric Power Distribution

■ ■ ■

State-owned Magyar Villamos Muvek Zrt (MVM) is Hungary's national electrical power company, controlling most of the country's electricity generation, transmission, systems operation, and trading sectors. Through its Trade division, MVM serves as Hungary's central public utility wholesaler, buying electrical power for sale to the country's network of independent electric power distributors. MVM's Generation division includes its ownership of the country's only nuclear power plant, Paks, which supplies nearly 40 percent of the country's total power supply. Other generation operations include the power plants in Vertesz, Tatabánya, Miskolc, and North Buda, Budapest, as well as the Hungarowind Windpower Plant acquired in November 2009.

MVM's Transmission and Systems Operation division is centered on its ownership of Mavir, operator of the country's power grid. This network includes more than 3,500 kilometers of high-voltage power lines, as well as 25 substations. While fully owned by MVM, Mavir operates as a separate company in advance of a future spin-off in compliance with European Union (EU) regulations. Mavir is led by CEO Imre Martha. In 2008 the company reported revenues of HUF 721 billion ($3.7 billion).

EUROPEAN ELECTRICITY PIONEER

As part of the Austrian-Hungarian Empire, Hungary played an important role in the development of the electrical power industry in 19th-century Europe. In 1884 the empire became the first on the continent to install an electrical power generation plant in Temesvár (later known as Timişoara). By the end of the year, that city also became the first in Europe to install an electric streetlight grid.

Timişoara later became part of Romania, after the breakup of the Austrian-Hungarian Empire following World War I. The region of the future Hungary had developed its own electric power base by then, starting with the city of Matészalka in 1888. Budapest, the country's largest city, received electric power in 1893. This stimulated the development of a broader electrical power industry in the country's main provincial towns at the dawn of the 20th century. Among these was the Central Power Generation Plant, constructed in 1898 in Tatabanya. By 1900 Hungary boasted 40 power plants, with an average power output of 1 megawatt (MW).

The construction of the Kelenfold Thermal Power Plant in Budapest marked a new milestone in Hungary's electrical power industry. Completed in 1914, the plant provided a total power output of 30 MW, becoming the first large-scale generating facility in the country. That plant completed a number of capacity expansions over the decades, and remained in service until 2005. The construction of Hungary's power grid continued through the interwar years. By 1935 electrical power had come to nearly 1,000 cities and towns. That number had risen to 1,255 towns 10 years later.

NATIONALIZED POWER UTILITY IN 1948

Prior to World War II, Hungary's electrical power industry remained fragmented among a large number of privately held companies. These joined together to form the Hungarian Power Companies National Association, in order to promote their interests to the Hungarian government. Hungary boasted more than 300 utility operators by the beginning of World War II. However, during the war large portions of the country's power generation and transmission networks were damaged or destroyed.

The Communist takeover of Hungary following the war introduced a new era to Hungary's power industry. In 1948 the new Hungarian government nationalized the entire electricity sector, creating the National Electricity Company, predecessor to Magyar Villamos Muvek, or MVM. The following year, the government inaugurated the Industrial Center of Power Plants, which took over coordination of the country's large and medium-sized power generation facilities focused on the Budapest region. The country's provincial power distribution operations were turned over to six regional distribution companies, created in 1951.

The Hungarian government also restructured the country's electrical power infrastructure. This led to the creation of a new body, Országos Villamos Teherelosztó, or the National Power Dispatch Center, established in 1949 to govern the country's electricity transmission

operations. This company, which later became known as Mavir, then set up a grid of 60 kilovolts (kV) and 120 kV linking the country's five largest power plants. In order to build this grid, the government created a second company that year, Távvezetéképíto Nemzeti Vállalat, or the National Power Line Building Company. This company changed its name to Országos Villamostávvezeték Vállalat, or the National Power Line Company, two years later.

PART OF COMECON

Movement toward the creation of a unified electrical power body began during the 1950s. The period was marked by significant power shortages, as the government's ambitious industrialization policies strained the country's existing power capacity. The country's infrastructure was also highly vulnerable to breakdowns. For example, in 1953 the country recorded nearly 1,200 incidents in its power plants and transmission lines. As a result, Hungary faced frequent power outages. In 1954 the government set up a new Power Plant Trust. The body served to coordinate the operations of the country's power generation sector in order to ensure the power supply to Hungary's growing industrial sector.

The Hungarian government also stepped up the expansion of its network of power plants. The country launched construction of several new plants, including completion of a 130 MW plant in Matravidek, which had been started before World War II. In the middle of the 1950s the country added a 120 MW plant in Inota, and a 75 MW plant in Sztálinváros. In 1955 the country began building its largest power plant to date, a 150 MW facility to support the new industrial zone in Behence-Kazincbarcika. This was followed by a 220 MW plant in Tiszapalkonya.

As part of the Soviet Bloc, Hungary also developed a series of international cooperation agreements with the national power operators in neighboring markets, including Czechoslovakia and Yugoslavia. This led to the construction of a new network of high-voltage transmission lines, with an initial carrying capacity of 220 kV, linking Hungary to its neighbors and beyond.

Hungary had also become part of the Council for Mutual Economic Assistance, or COMECON. Although initially created by Josef Stalin in order to exploit the resources of the Soviet Union's new satellite markets, COMECON evolved into a market exchange counterpart of the early European Common Market. In the second half of the 1950s COMECON developed a body governing its members' electricity trade, called the Union of Electricity Systems of COMECON.

KEY DATES

1948: The Hungarian government nationalizes the country's electrical power industry.

1963: All electrical power operations are regrouped under Magyar Villamos Muvek Trust (MVMT).

1982: The first unit of the Paks Nuclear Power Plant comes online.

1992: MVMT is restructured as a state-owned corporation, Magyar Villamos Muvek Zrt. (MVM).

2006: MVM completes the unbundling process according to European Union regulations.

2010: MVM announces plans to upgrade the Paks nuclear power plant.

This development provided some benefits to Hungary, including the construction of a 400 kV transmission network linking Hungary to the Soviet Union in 1967. This link was expanded in 1978 with the addition of a 750 kV line. However, Hungary's position within COMECON also left it vulnerable to increasing Soviet dominance over its power generation sector. Over time, the Soviet Union gained control of the supply of as much as one-third of Hungary's electrical power needs. Nevertheless, Hungary had also begun building bridges to the West, with the construction of a 220 kV transmission link to Austria in 1968.

ELECTRICAL POWER TRUST IN 1963

Hungary's electricity network grew slowly through the postwar period. Significant parts of the country remained without any electrical power. Hungary's power grid was not completed until 1963, with arrival of electricity to the last unconnected village, Aporliget. In that year the Hungarian government adopted a new organizational structure for its electrical power sector, creating Magyar Villamos Muvek Trust (MVMT). This body then took over control of all of the country's power generation, transmission, and distribution operations.

MVMT oversaw a major expansion of Hungary's power generation capacity during the 1960s and in the 1970s. This included one of the country's largest infrastructure projects during the 1960s, the construction of a 600 MW hydroelectric plant in Gyöngyös. MVMT also constructed the Dunamenti power plant,

in Szazhalimbatta, in the 1960s. Subsequent expansion of that plant during the 1970s and 1980s raised its total capacity to nearly 1,300 MW.

In 1967 MVMT launched planning for construction of the country's first nuclear power plant. This facility, called the Paks Nuclear Power Plant, was initially slated to begin construction in 1970. However, in 1971 MVMT put the project on hold, and instead focused on building a new thermal power plant in Tisza.

Work resumed on the Paks plant in 1974, using safer and more advanced technology. The first of the plant's four units came online in 1982. The second unit, also started in 1974, launched production in 1984. By then, construction of the two remaining units, launched in 1979, had also gotten under way. When these units came online, in 1986 and 1987, the Paks nuclear power facility reached a total output of more than 1,700 MW. Further expansion of the plant raised its output to 1,900 MW by the dawn of the 21st century. The completion of the Paks facility allowed Hungary to gain almost complete independence for its electricity supply.

RESTRUCTURING THE UTILITY SECTOR

Hungary's emergence from Communist rule amid the breakup of the Soviet Union at the end of the 1980s paved the way for the restructuring of the country's energy and industrial sectors. MVMT's turn came at the beginning of 1992, when the company was reincorporated as a state-owned corporation, Magyar Villamos Muvek Zrt. (MVM). As part of this process, MVM's operations were reorganized into a network of eight power generation companies, a transmission company (Mavir), and six power distribution companies.

The next phase in MVM's restructuring came with the privatization of its six distribution companies in 1995. These were acquired primarily by foreign electricity groups, including Germany's E.ON and France's EDF. At the same time, the government sold off parts of MVM's power generation operations, starting with three plants in 1995. The government sold three more of the group's power generation facilities two years later. The restructuring left MVM in control of the Paks nuclear power plant, the country's largest, and a smaller fossil fuel-based power plant in Vertesz. Through Mavir, the company also maintained control of Hungary's transmission grid.

MVM invested heavily in expanding its transmission network during the second half of the 1990s and in the next decade, as the company began positioning itself to take part in the liberalized European electricity market at the beginning of the 21st century. By 2010 MVM had extended its high-voltage transmission network to include more than 3,500 kilometers, supported by a network of 25 substations.

POWER EXCHANGE IN 2010

While the Paks nuclear power plant remained the flagship of MVM's generation wing, the company added a number of new generation operations in the new century. These included a contract to modernize and operate several heating plants for the town of Miskolc, starting in 2001. In 2005 the group won a bid to build a gas turbine cogeneration plant in North Buda, part of Budapest. The company also gained control of the 240 MW Oroszlány Power Plant that year. By the end of the decade MVM had added renewable energy operations as well, acquiring the Hungarowind Windpower Plant in November 2009.

MVM had also been preparing for the liberalization of the Hungarian and European electrical power industry during the decade. In 2001 the company began the process of unbundling Mavir. This move was made in accordance with EU regulations, which stipulated the unbundling of the distribution, generation, and transmission operations of the EU's former electricity monopolies. By 2004 Mavir had qualified to join ETSO, the European system monitoring cross-border transmission transactions through the European power grid.

MVM completed the transfer of its transmission operations and assets to Mavir in 2006. That year also marked the creation of MVM Villamosenergia Kereskedelmi Zrt., which took over its wholesale distribution business. This meant that MVM had completed the EU unbundling requirements, even though, for the time being, the company maintained 100 percent control of both companies. The Hungarian electricity sector had been fully liberalized by that time, and opened to competition. As a result, MVM's control of the distribution market slipped back to 80 percent.

MVM began preparing for its privatization starting in 2007, announcing plans to raise quadruple its market value, to more than HUF 1 billion, before launching an initial public offering. The company hoped to achieve this before 2012. A major component of this effort involved the modernization of the Paks power plant. This upgrade was necessary in order to extend the power plant's life span. As it stood, the company's initial units were scheduled to go offline as early as 2013.

MVM also began acquiring minority positions in a number of Hungary's privatized power generation and distribution companies. For example, in 2008 the company acquired 10.54 percent of Elmu, the electricity distributor for Budapest and the surrounding region. In December 2008 the company also purchased 8.6 percent of Emasz, which operated in Hungary's industrialized northern region. At the beginning of 2010, MVM entered talks with E.ON to purchase part of the German company's generation and distribution operations in Hungary as well.

MVM announced in February 2010 that it had finalized its plans to upgrade and expand the Paks Nuclear Power Plant. This project, to be completed before 2022, was expected to extend the facility's life span by another 60 years. MVM had successfully completed its transformation from government monopoly to position itself as a power player in the liberalized European energy sector.

M. L. Cohen

PRINCIPAL SUBSIDIARIES

Hungarowind Windpower Plant Operating Ltd.; Mavir Ltd.; MIFU Miskolc Combined Heat and Power Plant Ltd.; MVM ADWEST GmbH; MVM GTER Gasturbine Power Plant Ltd.; MVM Konto Ltd.; MVM North Buda Cogeneration Power Plant Ltd.; MVM Partner Energy Trading Ltd.; MVM Trade Ltd.; National Power Line Company; Paks Nuclear Power Plant Ltd.; Vertesi Power Plant Ltd.

PRINCIPAL DIVISIONS

Generation; Transmission and Systems Operation; Trade.

PRINCIPAL OPERATING UNITS

Mavir.

PRINCIPAL COMPETITORS

Czech Power Company CEZ, a.s.; EDF Démász; E.ON Hungaria Zrt.

FURTHER READING

"EU Clamps Down on MVM," *Economist Intelligence Unit: Country ViewsWire*, June 26, 2006.

"Hungarian Power Firm MVM Plans to Multiply Market Value in Mid-Term to Get Ready for IPO," *Hungary Business News*, January 29, 2007.

"Hungary's MVM to Join RWE in USD 1.24 Billion Project," *TendersInfo*, June 27, 2008.

"Hungary's National Power Firm MVM Completes Unbundling of Electricity Wholesale Activities," *Hungary Business News*, August 3, 2006.

"Hungary's State Power Holding MVM Acquires 8.6% Stake in RWE-Controlled Utility Emasz," *Hungary Business News*, December 9, 2008.

"MVM Hungary's Biggest Energy Company in Terms of Revenue," *Hungarian News Agency*, October 16, 2006.

"A Tough Haul for Electricity Privatisation," *Economist Intelligence Unit: Country ViewsWire*, September 23, 2004.

·······T··

Makedonski Telekom AD Skopje

———•———

Orce Nikolov bb
Skopje, 1000
Macedonia
Telephone: (+389 02) 310 0200
Fax: (+389 02) 310 0300
Web site: http://www.telekom.mk

Joint Stock Company
Founded: 1997 as AD Makedonski Telekomunikacii
Employees: 1,906
Sales: MKD 18.6 billion ($433.6 million) (2008)
Stock Exchanges: Macedonia
Ticker Symbol: TEL
NAICS: 517110 Wired Telecommunications Carriers; 517212 Cellular and Other Wireless Telecommunications; 517910 Other Telecommunications; 518111 Internet Service Providers

■ ■ ■

Makedonski Telekom AD Skopje (MakTel) is the leading telecommunications services provider in the former Yugoslavian Republic of Macedonia. MakTel, the country's telecom monopoly, offers a full range of telecommunications services to the business and residential markets. These services include T-Home, providing fixed-line broadband Internet and multimedia services, such as the MaxTV Internet-based television package; T-Mobile, the leading mobile telephone provider in Macedonia; and a range of corporate products and services marketed under the T brand. MakTel also operates Macedonia's national fixed-line telephone network, providing both local and international call services.

Other MakTel operations include the IDIVIDI Web portal, providing news and interactive content. The company operates a national sales network with 29 locations, including the "T-Home and T-Mobile Shop-Café" format launched in Skopje in 2009. MakTel has also launched a series of major infrastructure investments, including the installation of a high-speed fiber-optic network as part of its "Fiber to the Home" project. MakTel is one of Macedonia's top 10 companies, generating revenues of MKD 18.6 billion ($433.6 million) in 2008. The company is controlled by Magyar Telekom, itself a subsidiary of Deutsch Telekom, while the Macedonian government retains a nearly 34 percent stake. MakTel is led by CEO Nikolai J. B. Beckers.

INDEPENDENT PTT IN 1991

The Republic of Macedonia (technically known as the former Yugoslavian Republic of Macedonia as a result of a name dispute with Greece) declared its independence in 1991. While Yugoslavia had developed a relatively modern telecommunications infrastructure, in contrast to many of the former Soviet Bloc nations, Macedonia itself had remained a largely overlooked part of the former Communist state and one of the poorest in the southern European region. As part of Yugoslavia, Macedonia's telecommunications sector was governed by the PTT, the Yugoslav post and telegraph authority.

With independence, the government of Macedonia also became responsible for reorganizing the country's telecommunications sector. This was achieved with the creation of a new body, PTT Macedonia, which operated the country's postal service, offered banking services, and also operated the country's fixed-line telephone monopoly.

The early 1990s, however, remained difficult years for Macedonia. While Macedonia successfully avoided becoming involved in the hostilities that broke out among the other former Yugoslav republics, its independence from Yugoslavia also meant the loss of its major export market. Furthermore, the naming dispute with Greece, its other major export market, led to the imposition of an embargo by Greece that lasted into the middle of the decade.

As a result, Macedonia's economy suffered a severe decline, leaving little resources available for investment in expanding and upgrading the country's telephone and telecommunications infrastructure. This situation began to change in 1994, when the Macedonian government agreed to accept financial assistance from the European Bank for Reconstruction and Development (EBRD). In exchange, the government agreed to carry out the privatization of nearly all of the many companies and industries still controlled by the state.

DEDICATED TELECOMMUNICATIONS COMPANY IN 1997

PTT Macedonia benefited directly from the EBRD aid program. In 1995 the company received a loan of nearly $42.6 million to upgrade and expand the country's fixed-line telephone network. This allowed PTT Macedonia to invest in the modernization of its network, including the installation of digital exchanges and fiber-optic cabling in the country's major cities. Modernization of the country's telecommunications sector was

seen as a crucial factor in revitalizing Macedonia's corporate and industrial sectors.

As part of its upgrade program, PTT Macedonia also set out to increase its relatively low fixed-line penetration rate. To this end, the company launched a major expansion of its network, adding nearly 80,000 new fixed-line subscribers. As part of its upgrade program, the PTT also launched Macedonia's first Internet service provider, MTNet, which began offering Internet access services in 1995.

Along with funding, EBRD had also provided the PTT with technical consulting and assistance in order to prepare the company's telecommunications division for its future privatization. The sale of the telephone monopoly formed a centerpiece of Macedonia's privatization program. This led the Macedonian government to launch its own series of investments in the PTT's telecommunications. Between 1995 and 1997, the PTT spent a reported $230 million on upgrades. These included the creation of the country's mobile telephone service, based on the GSM (Global System for Mobile Communications) standard supplied and installed by Ericsson.

In 1996 the government took a major step in its privatization effort when it passed legislation breaking up the PTT into its postal, banking, and telecommunications operations. This led to the creation of a dedicated telecommunications company, AD Makedonski Telekomunicatii (MakTel), on January 1, 1997.

PREPARING FOR PRIVATIZATION

MakTel then began preparing in earnest for its privatization, as the Macedonian government announced its plans to sell 35 percent of the company to a foreign investor before the end of 1998. A new step in this process came in March 1998, when Makedonski Telekomunicatii registered as a state-owned joint stock company. By this time, the company had launched its mobile telephone service, MobiMak. At its launch, the company's mobile service capacity was limited to just 25,000 subscribers. However, by 1999 the company had expanded the network, allowing its subscriber base to climb to 47,000.

The Macedonian government's privatization program hit a snag when its offer to sell a minority stake in MakTel failed to attract foreign investor interest. In the end, the offer received just one bid, from Greek telecom monopoly OTE. Despite a treaty signed between Macedonia and Greece in 1996 ending the Greek trade embargo, the sale of part of the country's telephone monopoly to its Greek counterpart remained a politically sensitive issue.

KEY DATES

1991: PTT Macedonia is formed to take over the telephone and postal services monopoly for the newly independent Republic of Macedonia.

1995: PTT Macedonia receives a $42.55 million European Bank for Reconstruction and Development (EBRD) loan in order to modernize its telephone network; launches Internet access service MTNet.

1997: AD Makedonski Telekomunicatii (MakTel) is split off from PTT Macedonia and becomes the country's telecommunications monopoly.

2001: Consortium led by Magyar Telecom, a subsidiary of Deutsche Telekom, acquires majority control of MakTel from the Macedonian government.

2003: MakTel launches ADSL-based Internet access.

2006: MakTel rebrands MobiMak under the T-Mobile name.

2008: MakTel rebrands its fixed-line and Internet services as T-Home; changes its name to Makedonski Telekom.

2010: MakTel launches $206 million investment to upgrade its telephone network.

Politics continued to play a role in MakTel's progress at the dawn of the new century. The war in Kosovo in 1999 forced the government to put further privatization plans on hold. On the other hand, the presence of large numbers of humanitarian aid organizations near Macedonia's region fueled demand for further expansion of its mobile telephone network. This led the EBRD to provide MakTel with a new loan of EUR 18.7 million ($15 million) to expand its capacity to handle up to 100,000 subscribers. As a result, the company's mobile telephone subscriber base rose to 86,000 by the end of 2000.

MakTel's fixed-line operations made slow progress, rising to 430,000 subscribers by 1998 and to 500,000 by 2001. Meanwhile, the company counted just 10,000 Internet customers at the time, while its mobile telephone operation represented just 4 percent of the potential mobile telephone market. MakTel itself remained tiny by European telecom standards, posting annual revenues of approximately $140 million at the beginning of the new century.

MATAV SUBSIDIARY IN 2001

The Macedonian government remained committed both to MakTel's expansion and to its privatization. In 1998 the government promised a new round of investments of more than EUR 350 million by 2002, as it continued to expand and modernize the country's telecommunications infrastructure. In 2000 the government adopted a new privatization strategy for the company, announcing its intention to sell a majority stake in MakTel by 2001.

This time, the prospect of control of Macedonia's monopoly telecommunications operator, coupled with the strong future growth potential offered by its low penetration rates, brought strong interest from the foreign investment community. In the end, the government awarded the sale to a consortium led by Hungary's Matav (Magyar Telecom Group), itself controlled by Deutsche Telekom. Through the consortium, called Stonebridge Communications, Matav offered to pay EUR 343 million for a 51 percent stake in MakTel, and also promised to spend nearly EUR 256 million in further infrastructure investments into 2003. The deal also marked the first step in Matav's own international expansion strategy.

Matav brought in a new management team to streamline and restructure MakTel. Matav's experience streamlining its own formerly bloated, commercially backward organization following its privatization gave it an edge in reorganizing MakTel, cutting staff while improving customer service. The company also rolled out a new chain of sales and service offices, opening 29 shops across the country.

In terms of infrastructure, the company began phasing out the remnants of its former party line system, as it completed the digitalization of its network. By 2002 MakTel became the first in the region to boast a fully digital telephone exchange system. The conversion to digital technology was accompanied by the rollout of its first high-speed ISDN lines to the corporate sector in 2001. (ISDN, or Integrated Services Digital Network, was a circuit-switched telephone network system allowing for the transmission of data, video, and voice.) The company had signed up nearly 42,000 ISDN subscribers by 2002.

As a result, MakTel made impressive gains in building its subscriber base. By the end of 2003, the company counted 590,000 fixed-line customers, which according to the *Financial Times* represented a 95 percent penetration rate. More impressive still was the gain in mobile telephone customers, which surged to 500,000 customers by then. The company also claimed to cover more than 95 percent of Macedonia, reaching 99 percent of the population.

INTRODUCING BROADBAND IN 2003

Despite the continued political and economic difficulties faced by Macedonia at the beginning of the 21st century, MakTel had succeeded in transforming itself into a modern telecommunications player with technology on the level of most of its European peers. The company further signaled this transition with the launch of its first ADSL-based broadband Internet services in December 2003. (ADSL, or Assymetric Digital Subscribers Line, was a type of Internet connection that split a telephone line into two channels, allowing the user to be online and on the phone at the same time.) The company followed its launch of ADSL service with the launch of a new interactive news and media portal, IDIVIDI, in 2004. The company also launched a new high-speed data service for its corporate customers, called Metro Ethernet, that year. By this time, MakTel's revenues had climbed to MKD 16.9 billion (approximately $360 million). More than 62 percent of this total came from its Internet operations.

MakTel next turned its attention toward preparing for the coming liberalization of the Macedonian telecommunications market, in keeping with the country's aspirations to join the European Union. The company launched a new streamlining and restructuring movement, called "Road To Success," which involved a further reduction of some 800 jobs. At the same time, Matav reorganized its own shareholding in MakTel, buying the share of its minority partners in Stonebridge Communications. Matav then liquidated Stonebridge, taking direct control of MakTel.

This move preceded the Macedonian government's decision, in compliance with a request from the European Union and the World Bank and International Monetary Fund, to complete MakTel's privatization. In April 2006 the government announced its intention to place a further 45.1 percent of MakTel on the Macedonian Stock Exchange. As a first step in this process, the government placed a 10 percent stake on the market, which was then acquired by MakTel itself, increasing Matav's control of the company.

REBRANDING

This led MakTel to launch a rebranding process in the second half of the decade in order to move the company closer to the Deutsche Telekom brand family. The first step in this process took place in 2006, when the company rebranded its MobiMak mobile telephone service under the T-Mobile name. In 2008 MakTel moved to bring the rest of its operations under the new brand umbrella, renaming its fixed-line and broadband services as T-Home. Similarly, its corporate services were also placed under the T brand family. Also that year, MakTel changed its own name, to Makedonski Telekom AD Skopje.

At the end of the decade, MakTel continued developing new product offerings, centered around its high-speed Internet backbone. In 2008, for example, the company began offering a new line of "Call and Surf" packages, combining fixed-line services with ADSL Internet access plans. This was followed by the launch of a new Internet-based television (or IPTV) offer, called MaxTV, in 2008. This service was also bundled into so-called "double-play" and "triple-play" packages, providing Internet and television, and Internet, telephony, and television, respectively.

In 2009 MakTel boosted its customer service offerings as well. The company's T-Mobile network began to upgrade to the new high-speed 3G standard, following the company's award of a 3G license at the end of 2008. MakTel then opened the first of a new retail chain format, combining sales both of T-Home and T-Mobile products, as well as a café offering coffee as well as Internet access, among other amenities.

At the end of 2009, MakTel announced its plan to spend nearly $206 million upgrading its telephone network in a "Fiber to the Home" program that would enable the rollout of ultra high-speed Internet access with speeds up to 100 megabits per second. In the meantime, MakTel's annual sales had risen to MKD 18.6 billion ($433 million). Makedonski Telekom had succeeded in transforming Macedonia into one of southern Europe's most modern telecom markets.

M. L. Cohen

PRINCIPAL SUBSIDIARIES

e-Makedonija; Montmak (Montenegro); T-Mobile Macedonia AD.

PRINCIPAL DIVISIONS

e-Makedonija Foundation Skopje; Makedonski Telekom AD Skopje; T-Mobile Macedonia AD Skopje; IDIVIDI.

PRINCIPAL OPERATING UNITS

Key Accounts Business Centre; Residential SoHo/SME Business Customer Centre; Sales and Provisioning Support Business Centre; Large Project Management Business Centre; Wholesale Business Centre.

PRINCIPAL COMPETITORS

Ontel AD.

FURTHER READING

"FYROM to Privatise 45.1% of MakTel for EUR 275 Mln," *Telecompaper Europe*, April 21, 2006.

"Hungary's Magyar Telekom Becomes Direct Owner of Macedonian Unit MakTel," *Hungary Business News*, November 24, 2005.

"The Internal Investigation of Magyar Telekom Revealed Thursday that Makedonski Telekom Embezzled 24 Million Euros from the Period of 2000 to 2006," *Macedonian Electronic Media Digest*, December 4, 2009.

"Macedonian Government to Sell Shares in Makedonski Telekomunikacii," *Metamorphosis*, April 19, 2006.

"Magyar Macedonian Unit Wins 3G License," *Total Telecom Online*, December 23, 2008.

"Makedonski Telecom Enhances MaxTV Product Portfolio," *DMEurope.com*, November 23, 2009.

"Makedonski Telekom Increases Internet Speeds," *Telecompaper Europe*, March 19, 2009.

"Makedonski Telekom Launches Bundled Phone, ADSL Package," *Telecompaper Europe*, September 12, 2008.

"Makedonski Telekom Opens T-Home, T-Mobile Shop-Café," *DMEurope*, January 27, 2009.

"MakTel, T-Mobile Macedonia to Merge?" *Telegeography*, September 21, 2009.

Matador Records Inc.

304 Hudson Street, 7th Floor
New York, New York 10013
U.S.A.
Telephone: (212) 995-5882
Fax: (212) 995-5883
Web site: http://www.matadorrecords.com

Private Company
Incorporated: 1989
Employees: 33
Sales: $13 million (2009 est.)
NAICS: 512220 Integrated Record Production/
  Distribution

■ ■ ■

Matador Records Inc. is one of the leading independent record companies in the United States. The firm's roster includes such alternative rock icons as Sonic Youth, Pavement, and Yo La Tengo, and its steady-selling back catalog features key releases by Interpol, Guided by Voices, Teenage Fanclub, and many more. One half of the company is owned by the U.K.-based Beggars Group, which performs worldwide marketing, and the rest is held by members of management.

BEGINNINGS

Matador Records was founded in New York in 1989 by Chris Lombardi, a young Manhattan native who had briefly worked as a sales representative for music distributor Dutch East India Trading and London-based

Fire Records. Deciding to start an imprint of his own, he secured funding from his father and brother to found Matador, which he named after a movie by the Spanish director Pedro Almodóvar. At year's end Lombardi's apartment-based label issued its first release, by Austrian rock duo H.P. Zinker.

Not long after this, Lombardi asked former Homestead Records manager Gerard Cosloy to join him as Matador's second employee. Cosloy had earned a reputation as an astute talent spotter by signing such bands as Dinosaur Jr. and Sonic Youth to Homestead, but he had quit that label in January 1990 out of frustration over internal politics. The Massachusetts native had been immersed in music since childhood, founding opinionated fan magazine *Conflict*, booking bands, working as a disc jockey, and releasing records while still in his teens. Both of Matador's principals were strongly motivated by their love of music, and, although they hoped it would turn a profit, believed that artistic integrity trumped commercial success. The bands they would sign in turn valued the artistic freedom Matador offered.

Upon joining Matador, Cosloy quickly signed a new Scottish band called Teenage Fanclub, which had been turned down by larger labels including Homestead, to a two-album contract. The small label issued the group's first record in the United States just as its popularity was beginning to skyrocket, and the band soon sought to break the contract. The ensuing yearlong dispute was resolved with Matador releasing the band to larger label Geffen in exchange for a cash settlement.

In the meantime, Matador had begun to put out records by other "indie rock" groups including Superchunk and Railroad Jerk, as well as a compilation of unknown bands called *New York Eye and Ear Control*. In one of the tightly budgeted firm's more extravagant moves, Lombardi and Cosloy flew to Europe to sign Dutch band Bettie Serveert.

PAVEMENT PROVES INDIE HIT IN 1992

In 1992 Matador released the first album by Stockton, California, rockers Pavement, *Slanted & Enchanted,* which was named album of the month in indie-rock bible *Spin* magazine before copies had even hit the streets. Although eager to capitalize on the publicity, the tiny company struggled to come up with enough cash to manufacture 15,000 copies to meet expected demand. When they finally received the first shipment of discs following a two-month funding delay, Cosloy and Lombardi found themselves locked out of their lower Broadway office for nonpayment of rent. As Lombardi raced to a bank to get a certified check, Cosloy refused police orders to leave, and the money arrived just as the locks were being changed. The Pavement album would go on to sell 80,000 copies over the next several years.

Bands were signed to a variety of deals, with some splitting the profits from a release equally with the label (as with Pavement), and others receiving an advance and then taking a royalty on sales after it was paid back. Distribution was a headache for independent labels, which tended to be paid last, if at all, by the industry's notoriously difficult middlemen. Matador tried to sell as many discs as it could directly to small mom-and-pop record stores, which gave more attention to independent labels and often served as tastemakers, and hired several employees to manage this effort. It also used distributors such as Dutch East India Trading, Caroline, Revolver, and Scat.

Although many of the firm's releases sold far fewer copies than a major label could turn a profit on, Matador was able to prosper by keeping expenses low. Recording costs were far less than for the majors (the first Pavement album was budgeted at about $600), and

the majority of releases broke even or made a profit, with only about a quarter losing money. A typical album might be produced in the low thousands at first, and eventually sell 10,000 to 15,000 copies.

DISTRIBUTION DEAL WITH ATLANTIC IN 1993

As Matador grew it began to earn the attention of larger labels that were seeking to pick up promising alternative rock acts following the success of the group Nirvana, whose first major label album, *Nevermind*, had gone multiple-platinum and beaten Michael Jackson to the top of the charts in early 1992. Such poaching of new artists by Sony, Universal, Warner-Elektra-Atlantic, Capitol, and others caused some independents to fold, while others saw the writing on the wall and sold out to the conglomerates.

After considering several suitors, Lombardi and Cosloy decided to take the offer of Atlantic Records for a nonexclusive five-year distribution deal with significant financial underwriting and no management control. About one-third of the label's 15 to 20 annual releases would be marketed and promoted by Atlantic, with the rest going through its standard channels. The first joint project was a new album by legendary British punk band The Fall.

With the label's rise in stature, talented artists began seeking it out. After Chicago-based singer/songwriter Liz Phair sent her first demo tape to Cosloy, he immediately signed her, and 1993's critically praised *Exile in Guyville* became the label's largest success to date with sales of 130,000 copies in the first year. Matador had also recently signed established Hoboken, New Jersey, indie rockers Yo La Tengo, as well as The Jon Spencer Blues Explosion.

In 1994 Matador hired a new general manager, Patrick Amory, who had a doctorate in history from Cambridge but had decided to pursue a career in the record business. Notable releases of the year included Pavement's second album and the label debut of the Pizzicato Five, a Japanese group whose first Matador release compiled material from previous albums released in their home country. In 1995 the firm began a long association with Dayton, Ohio, cult band Guided by Voices, which had chosen Matador over such high-powered suitors as Capitol and Warner Brothers.

CAPITOL BUYS STAKE IN 1996

By now the firm's deal with Atlantic had begun to sour for both parties, and in January 1996 the relationship was terminated. The move spurred a new bidding war

KEY DATES

1989: Chris Lombardi founds Matador Records in New York.

1993: Matador signs marketing/distribution deal with Atlantic Records.

1996: Capitol Records buys stake in firm; office opens in London.

1999: Matador splits with Capitol and buys back stake, giving up singer Liz Phair.

2002: Beggars Group buys 50 percent of firm, takes over marketing duties.

among the major labels, and in June it was announced that a joint venture would be formed with Capitol, which took a 49 percent ownership stake by agreeing to pay a reported $8 million to $12 million over five years to Cosloy and Lombardi. Matador's new minority shareholder would have some input into signings and distribute four or five releases a year, as per the Atlantic deal, with the first under the new arrangement being a Jon Spencer Blues Explosion disc that hit stores in October 1996.

During the year the company also opened an office in London, which Matador copresident Cosloy would head, and launched a Web site. Releases of the period included *Telephono*, the debut album by future indie stars Spoon, *A Ass Pocket of Whiskey* by bluesman R. L. Burnside, and a collaboration between rocker/visual artist Jad Fair and Yo La Tengo called *Strange but True*.

In 1998 sales hit an estimated $10 million, making it the company's best year to date. Popular acts on the label now included Cat Power, Japan's Cornelius, and Scottish group Belle & Sebastian. To spur sales, the firm dropped the price on some older "midline" titles.

SPLIT WITH CAPITOL IN 1999

As had happened with Atlantic, the firm's relationship with Capitol did not live up to expectations, and in the spring of 1999 it was announced that Matador would split from the major, with Cosloy and Lombardi buying back its stake. Liz Phair would remain with Capitol, along with her back catalog. The Jon Spencer Blues Explosion also became a free agent at this time, as its contract was up.

In May 1999 Matador signed a distribution deal with Distribution North America (DNA), although it would continue to service independent retailers

separately. During the year the label added its first hip-hop act, The Arsonists, and celebrated its 10th anniversary with a CD box set and concerts in New York and London that were streamed live on the Internet.

The company began offering music for download via EMusic.com and Napster.com in 2001. In November of that year, DNA went out of business, and the following January Matador reached an agreement with Alternative Distribution Alliance (ADA) to handle its product, although it would still sell direct to independent retailers. The firm was also seeking deals in a variety of foreign markets including Korea, where it signed Ales Music to distribute.

BEGGARS GROUP BUYS STAKE IN 2002

In August 2002 the firm sold a 50 percent ownership stake to U.K.-based Beggars Group, which was home to a number of independent labels including 4AD, XL Recordings, and Mantra. Beggars Group would handle worldwide marketing for Matador, with both firms' product distributed in the United States by ADA and Matador. Beggars Group's New York office was moved into Matador's space, and some staffers took on joint duties, although Matador would keep its own independent office in London headed by Cosloy. Co-presidents Cosloy and Lombardi, along with general manager Amory, owned the remaining 50 percent of the firm.

The music industry was now in a state of panic as sales appeared to be in free fall, having dropped by more than 25 percent from their 1999 peak of 1.16 billion units to 860 million in 2002. The decline was attributed to the rapid spread of digital file-sharing, as well as to a glut of product on the market. The major labels, which depended on blockbuster hits, were hurt the most, while independents such as Matador could still turn a profit on as few as 25,000 copies. Online file-sharing in some ways actually benefited indie labels, as it exposed people to bands that could otherwise be heard only in concert or on the relatively few radio stations that programmed alternative music.

For its part Matador continued to seek out new, cutting-edge acts and skillfully used such interactive media as its online Matablog to keep in touch with an often-passionate customer base. Although precise figures were not available, the label's attention to detail in packaging and grassroots marketing efforts appeared to make it considerably more likely that fans purchased albums rather than downloading pirated copies. The firm had long produced parallel CD and vinyl editions, and sales of the latter were increasing even as orders for

CDs dropped. Although the deluxe vinyl pressings were strictly a break-even item, even at higher retail prices than CDs, they helped build fan loyalty and make every release seem more special.

In the fall of 2003 much of Matador's music was made available through Apple's iTunes Store, and two years later the firm and Beggars Group signed an agreement with Snocap to distribute content through digital peer-to-peer services, with the latter processing royalty payments. The company also licensed tracks for use in video game Major League Baseball 2K6. Interpol, Pavement, Belle & Sebastian, and Guided by Voices were among the acts chosen.

"BUY EARLY GET NOW" LAUNCHED IN 2006

In the summer of 2006 the popular group New Pornographers' fourth album became Matador's first "buy early get now" release, in which streaming audio was made available in advance to customers who preordered a vinyl or CD copy, which they could then pick up from their local retailer about two months later. The new sales program, which would be used for many subsequent releases, offered other perks including bonus tracks and a downloadable MP3 version.

Also during the year, New York rock band Interpol signed with Capitol after its Matador contract expired. The group had sold nearly 450,000 copies of each of its first two albums for the label in 2002 and 2004, making it one of the firm's most successful ever.

The company was continuing to confront business challenges that included a steep drop in the number of independent record stores as well as the shuttering of such national music chains as Tower and Virgin. While online sales helped offset this trend somewhat, the firm had a difficult time getting its releases into the megastores such as Wal-Mart that now accounted for most music sales, many of which charged fees for stocking copies of unknown acts' albums.

In 2008 Matador began offering some recordings on AmieStreet.com, where music downloads started out free and topped out at 98 cents per track, depending on popularity. The firm also began offering some content on QTRAX.com, where free downloads were supported by ads that users had to watch first. The company's presence in the digital domain was subsequently extended via deals with imeem, which enabled users to embed streaming audio from the label's artists in social networking sites such as Facebook and MySpace, and MUZU.TV, which allowed video footage to be embedded.

SONIC YOUTH SIGNS TO MATADOR IN 2008

In September 2008 Matador scored a major coup when indie rock legends Sonic Youth signed a one-album deal with the label after nearly 20 years at Geffen. The following June *The Eternal* was released, which the band supported with a summer tour.

Matador's increasingly popular vinyl albums had been manufactured by a firm called 33 1/3 until 2006, when it went bankrupt. In the spring of 2009 it was revealed that the master tapes, sleeve art scans, and other production materials it had stored were lost, including master material from almost every vinyl pressing the firm had issued since it began. The master copies could be re-created by going back to the original artwork and session tapes, but the cost would be significant and plans to reissue several albums were delayed. While vinyl constituted only about 1 percent of U.S. music sales, it had increased by 89 percent in 2008 even as CDs were continuing to fall more than 10 percent a year.

In November Matador bought True Panther Sounds, a Brooklyn-based record label whose roster included the bands Girls, Rainbow Bridge, and Standing Nude. Notable releases of 2009 included Mission of Burma's well-received reunion disc, an effort by Belle & Sebastian offshoot God Help the Girl, and a new album by Yo La Tengo. Long-disbanded indie favorite Pavement also announced it was reuniting to record and tour in 2010. Matador had kept the group's albums in print and issued solo recordings by various members including lead singer/songwriter Stephen Malkmus.

In January 2010 the firm released *Casual Victim Pile*, a compilation of 19 local Austin, Texas, bands put together by Cosloy, who had relocated to that city from England four years earlier. Other releases of the year included a Pavement compilation and the label debut of Washington, D.C., rockers Ted Leo and the Pharmacists.

Some 20 years after Chris Lombardi started a small record company in his New York apartment, Matador Records had established itself as one of the top American independent rock music labels, with a roster of talented acts and a legacy that included many highly acclaimed releases. With backing from U.K.-based Beggars Group and guiding lights Lombardi, Cosloy, and Amory still enthusiastically involved, the company appeared well-positioned to serve music fans for some time to come.

Frank Uhle

PRINCIPAL SUBSIDIARIES

Matador Europe (UK); True Panther Sounds.

PRINCIPAL COMPETITORS

Drag City; In The Red Records; Jade Tree; Merge Records; Sub Pop Records; Touch and Go Records.

FURTHER READING

Booth, Michael, "Matador Indie Label Hits Mark," *Denver Post*, August 5, 2003, p. F1.

Cohen, Jonathan, and Chris Morris, "Beggars Purchases Half-Stake in Matador," *BPI Entertainment News Wire*, August 13, 2002.

Hirschberg, Lynn, "Gerard Cosloy Is Hipper Than You," *New York Magazine*, May 8, 1995.

"Matador Keen to Attract Local Music Lovers," *Korea Times*, January 16, 2002.

"Matador Reissues Delayed by Lost Album Masters," *Guardian*, April 23, 2009.

Morris, Chris, "Atlantic Takes Modern-Rock Bull by Horns with Matador Deal," *Billboard*, April 24, 1993, p. 1.

Morris, Chris, and Ed Christman, "Matador, Capitol Are Parting Ways," *Billboard*, April 3, 1999.

Philips, Chuck, "Capitol Wins Matador Label," *Record*, June 4, 1996, p. N12.

Powell, Austin, "Slanted & Enchanted—Matador Records' Gerard Cosloy Curates a 'Casual Victim Pile' on Red River," *Austin Chronicle*, January 22, 2010.

Mead & Hunt Inc.

———————■———————

6501 Watts Road
Madison, Wisconsin 53719-2700
U.S.A.
Telephone: (608) 273-6380
Fax: (608) 273-6391
Web site: http://www.meadhunt.com

Private Company
Incorporated: 1949
Employees: 430
Sales: $65 million (2008 est.)
NAICS: 541330 Consulting Engineer Private Practices;
541310 Consulting Architect Private Practices

■ ■ ■

Headquartered in Madison, Wisconsin, Mead & Hunt Inc. is a leading architectural and engineering firm with office locations in nine states. Privately held and employee-owned, the firm has annual billings of more than $41.7 million and is regularly ranked as a leader in its field by publications such as *Engineering News Record*. The firm has expertise in architecture and building engineering, aviation, environmental, transportation, historic preservation, municipal services, water resources, technological support, and communications.

FORMATIVE YEARS

Mead & Hunt's heritage dates back more than 100 years. The company traces its origins to 1900, when a hydroelectric engineering expert named Daniel Webster Mead established a full-time consulting practice in Chicago's First National Bank Building. A native of Rockford, Illinois, Mead began attending Cornell University in 1881, where he earned a civil engineering degree in only three years.

At the age of 23, Mead was named Rockford city engineer. In that role he was able to gain practical experience that included dealing with issues such as water supply problems. After working in that position until 1887, Mead was named chief engineer and general manager of Rockford Construction Company.

After establishing his own consulting firm, Mead specialized in water systems. He furthered his reputation by authoring expert publications and in 1904 wrote *Notes on Hydrology and the Application of Its Laws to the Problems of Hydraulic Engineering*, recognized as the first hydrology book ever published. That year, he also became a member of the engineering faculty at the University of Wisconsin-Madison, where he taught the nation's first hydrology course. At the university, Mead maintained a consulting office in the engineering building's attic.

A new office was established in downtown Madison in 1906. Charles Victor Seastone, a Purdue University sanitary engineering professor, joined the firm in 1907 as chief engineer and Madison office manager. That year, the company relocated all operations to Madison and moved to a larger space at 550 State Street. By 1908 the firm had changed its name to Mead & Seastone.

COMPANY PERSPECTIVES

Excellence. Integrity. Dedication. These are the qualities that set our firm apart.

EARLY GROWTH

During the early years of his firm, Mead worked on a number of significant projects. Among them was a two-year initiative to design a new water supply system for the Schlitz Brewing Company in Milwaukee. In addition, he designed many of Wisconsin's first hydroelectric projects and designed and built numerous dams in Michigan's Upper Peninsula.

Mead's son, Harold, joined the firm in the 1910s. In 1911 Mead established the Peninsular Power Company in partnership with other investors. The company, which also was headquartered in Madison, was formed to provide wholesale hydroelectric power to mines in Michigan and Wisconsin's Menominee range. One of its initial projects was the Twin Falls facility.

By 1913 Mead & Seastone's workforce had grown to include 23 people, and the firm's expertise had garnered worldwide recognition. The two decades that followed were marked by projects of great significance. In addition, major changes would take place at the corporate level.

IMPORTANT ENDEAVORS

Following a terrible flood in the Ohio and Miami River valleys that took the lives of approximately 500 people and caused $100 million in damage, Daniel Mead served on a commission that studied potential flood control methods for three years, ultimately resulting in construction of a $30 million system of dams and flood control that was finished in 1922. Another development around this time was the relocation of Mead & Seastone's headquarters to Madison's State Journal Building in 1919.

In 1928 President Calvin Coolidge appointed Mead to serve on a committee tasked with studying the construction of a dam that would control flooding on the Colorado River and also generate electricity. What followed was the development of Boulder Dam (renamed Hoover Dam in 1947), a national historic landmark that the American Society of Civil Engineers recognizes as one of modern civil engineering's seven wonders.

LEADERSHIP CHANGES

A major development took place in 1929 when Daniel Mead officially retired. The founder continued to provide his expertise, however, as a consultant on specific projects. Although he continued teaching courses until 1937, Mead retired from the University of Wisconsin-Madison's faculty in 1932. Following the retirement of Seastone that same year, the Mead & Seastone partnership was dissolved. However, three of its employees established a new partnership in early 1933 and the firm's legacy continued.

The partners in Mead & Seastone's successor, Mead, Ward & Hunt, were Harold Mead, Clayton Ward, and Henry Hunt. They began their tenure during the Great Depression. The firm endured a period of approximately three years during which it essentially had no work. Ultimately, programs connected with President Roosevelt's New Deal enabled the firm to survive.

In 1941, after 21 years in the same location, Mead, Ward & Hunt relocated the firm's offices. Interestingly, the firm moved back to its previous location at 550 State Street in Madison. Business began to pick up during the World War II years. One noteworthy project for the firm was the design of Camp McCoy, an Army training facility located near Sparta, Wisconsin.

CONTINUED CHANGE

Several important developments unfolded during the last half of the 1940s. In 1946 the partnership of Mead, Ward & Hunt was dissolved following the departure of Clayton Ward. A new partnership was then established between Daniel Mead and Henry Hunt. Mead was considered the leader of the firm, while Hunt served as chief engineer.

In 1948 the firm bid farewell to its founder, Daniel Mead, who died on October 13. The following year, Mead & Hunt Inc. was established when the firm formally incorporated. Following this milestone, Mead was elected president, and employees were then able to purchase stock in the organization.

In addition to providing municipalities with services related to sanitary systems, water treatment, and water supply, Mead & Hunt diversified into a variety of new areas. An architect named Harold Balch was hired in 1949, allowing the firm to expand its offerings in the architectural and building systems market. In particular, Mead & Hunt began serving dairy companies throughout Wisconsin.

Military aviation projects were another growing area for the firm following World War II. During the 1950s Mead & Hunt was involved with several noteworthy

```
┌─────────────────────────────────────────────┐
│                                               │
│              KEY DATES                        │
│          ─────────■─────────                  │
│                                               │
│  1900: Daniel Webster Mead establishes a full-time │
│        consulting practice in Chicago's First │
│        National Bank Building.                │
│  1907: Charles Victor Seastone joins the firm, lead- │
│        ing to the formation of Mead & Seastone. │
│  1932: Mead & Seastone is dissolved and the firm │
│        becomes Mead, Ward & Hunt.             │
│  1946: The partnership of Mead, Ward & Hunt dis- │
│        solves following the departure of Clayton │
│        Ward, resulting in a new partnership named │
│        Mead & Hunt.                           │
│  1949: Mead & Hunt Inc. is incorporated.      │
│  1958: Harold Mead resigns and the Mead family's │
│        connection with the firm ends.         │
│  2000: Mead & Hunt celebrates its 100th       │
│        anniversary.                           │
│                                               │
└─────────────────────────────────────────────┘
```

projects, including Madison's Truax Air Force Base. In addition, the firm's growth was prompted by work on the federal interstate system, which was considered to be crucial for the civil defense and military transportation nationwide.

PARTING WAYS

In 1955 Mead & Hunt relocated its offices to 2320 University Avenue in Madison. By this time the construction boom that followed World War II had begun to wane, impacting the firm's work load considerably. Three years later, Harold Mead resigned. For the first time in 60 years, the Mead family was no longer connected with Mead & Hunt.

Following Harold's departure, airport engineering group head Earl Kruger was named president in 1959. He took the helm at a difficult time, when the firm was forced to reduce its staff. From more than 60 employees earlier in the decade, by 1959 and Mead & Hunt employed 25 people.

During the early 1960s Mead & Hunt was involved in the development of master plans for a number of Wisconsin communities. Such plans, which addressed transportation, land use, public water and sewerage, public services, and schools, were needed following the population explosion that occurred during the 1950s. In addition, the organization also performed transportation-related planning and development work for the Wisconsin State Highway Commission.

During the mid-1960s Mead & Hunt helped to develop a master plan for the Dane County Regional Airport. The firm ended the 1960s under the leadership of five principals: Earl Kruger, Don Johnson, Leo Pratt, Ossie Knechtges, and Bob Craig.

GROWING VIA ACQUISITIONS

Mead & Hunt made its first acquisition midway through the 1970s. At that time the firm of Dane County surveyor Andrew Dahlen was acquired. From 1976 to 1979, Mead & Hunt surveyed more than 85 dams in Michigan, Illinois, and Wisconsin, under contract with the U.S. Army Corps of Engineers, as part of the national dam safety program. More growth took place in 1980, at which time the firm acquired the Appleton, Wisconsin-based engineering firm Orbison & Orbison, which had roots dating back to the early 1880s.

After serving as the firm's president for nearly 30 years, Earl Kruger retired in 1986. He was succeeded by Leo Bussan. Also serving in leadership roles were Rajan Sheth, Ashok Rajpal, Bruce Frudden, Terry Hampton, Terry Kennedy, and Al Anderson. The following year, Mead & Hunt relocated to 6501 Watts Road in Madison. The company's new facilities spanned more than 30,000 square feet and offered ample opportunity for expansion.

By the mid-1980s Mead & Hunt's workforce included more than 100 people. The company began taking advantage of advancements in computer technology, including personal computers and computer-aided drafting and design (CADD) systems. In addition, geographic information systems (GIS) also had a major impact on the firm's work, enabling engineers to analyze and manipulate a wide range of data regarding the earth's features.

By the 1990s Mead & Hunt was employing its own team of professionals devoted to environmental planning, including wetland scientists, water-quality experts, planners, and noise specialists. A significant leadership change took place in 1994 when Leo Bussan retired, ending a 39-year run with firm. He was succeeded by Rajan Sheth, a native of Amreli, India, and a University of Wisconsin-Madison graduate who had joined the organization in 1977. By this time, Mead & Hunt employed 130 people.

Another important development that took place during the mid-1990s was the acquisition of a firm in California named Larsen, Ohlinger & Holmes. The deal enabled Mead & Hunt to increase its business in the food and dairy sectors. In addition, the firm expanded its geographic footprint by establishing office locations throughout the United States. While some were full-service, others were project-based or specialized-service locations. Examples included locations in Milwaukee; Minneapolis; Washington D.C.; La Crescent, Minnesota; and Albany, New York.

EXPLOSIVE GROWTH

By the late 1990s Mead & Hunt was growing at a fervid pace. From 1995 to 1998 the company's workforce increased 20 percent and sales grew 15 percent. In 1999 the company acquired an office in Lansing, Michigan. In addition, it was recognized as Wisconsin's largest provider of historic preservation services. Mead & Hunt ended the 1990s with a workforce of 200 employees.

A major milestone was reached in 2000. In addition to celebrating the dawn of a new millennium, Mead & Hunt recognized its 100th anniversary that year. That year, the company reorganized its operations by market orientation.

Mead & Hunt continued to grow via acquisitions during the early 2000s. In 2002 it acquired Eugene, Oregon-based Boggs Aviation Associates Inc., which provided consulting services to small and medium-sized, non-hub airports. Following the deal, Mead & Hunt began conducting feasibility studies for airports that were interested in recruiting new airlines. The addition of offices in the California communities of Sacramento and Santa Rosa increased the company's workforce to 250 employees.

INDUSTRY LEADER

By 2003 Mead & Hunt employed more than 270 people. That year revenues totaled an estimated $31 million. The organization garnered recognition from a host of different engineering trade publications, which acknowledged it is one of the nation's 100 fastest-growing firms, as well as one of the 10 best to work for.

It was during the 2003 fiscal year that Ashok Rajpal stepped down from Mead & Hunt's board. The company took pride in the fact that stockholders were able to repurchase his stock quickly, without the need for a loan. One major project on the horizon in 2004 involved an initiative to route water from the Colorado River to the Baja California peninsula. That year, the number of Mead & Hunt's employee-owners increased to 68.

Midway through 2005 Mead & Hunt opened a new office in Iron Mountain, Michigan, followed by a new Milwaukee-area location in September. During the 2006 fiscal year the firm's billings reached $37.2 million, up from $12.7 million in fiscal year 1999. Mead &

Hunt's workforce increased to 300 employees, 82 of whom were stockholders. The firm's geographic footprint continued expanding in 2006, when new offices opened in the Portland, Oregon, area and in Austin, Texas.

Expansion continued at Mead & Hunt heading into the end of the first decade of the 2000s. In 2007 a new location was established in Phoenix, Arizona. From January to November, the firm saw its workforce increase by 13 percent. A variety of publications continued to recognize Mead & Hunt for its size and skill at the local, state, and national levels. Around this time the organization was involved in developing plans for a new airport terminal for the Indian Wells Valley Airport District in California. In addition, it also designed an air traffic control tower at University Park Airport for Pennsylvania State University.

By 2008 Mead & Hunt employed nearly 400 people nationwide. That year President and CEO Raj Sheth was honored by the American Society of Civil Engineers with the Edmund Friedman Professional Recognition Award. For the fiscal year ending October 31, 2008, Mead & Hunt's revenues exceeded $52 million.

Despite difficult economic conditions, the firm continued growing on a number of fronts, including employee hires, as well as mergers and acquisitions. In 2009 Mead & Hunt planned to fill more than 75 open positions. Looking to the future, Sheth indicated that, while the firm was taking a conservative financial stance, it would continue to take calculated risks that promised long-term benefits.

By 2010 Mead & Hunt's workforce had increased to 430 people. The firm had developed a global reputation for excellence in the fields of engineering and architecture. Approaching the 21st century's second decade, the firm seemed to have strong prospects for continued success.

Paul R. Greenland

PRINCIPAL COMPETITORS

HNTB Companies; CH2M HILL Companies Ltd.; URS Corporation.

FURTHER READING

Balousek, Marv, "Engineering Firm's History Spans More Than 100 Years," *Wisconsin State Journal,* January 29, 2004, p. F1.

Boorstein, Michelle, "U.S. Companies Seek Hydro Work Overseas," *Albany (NY) Times Union,* September 29, 1997, p. C7.

"City Loses Mead Suit Damages for $43,470: Famous Case Growing Out of Water Supply Decided in Engineer's Favor," *Fort Worth Luxer,* March 23, 1910.

"Final Plans for Air Traffic Control Tower Approved," *States News Service,* September 11, 2009.

Johnson, Paul, "Rajan Sheth Named to Lead Mead & Hunt; Engineering Firm Names President," *Wisconsin State Journal,* October 20, 1994, p. 1F.

Mead, Daniel W., *Report on the Dam and Water Power Development at Austin, Texas,* Madison, WI: Mead & Seastone, November 1917.

"National Firm Buys Boggs Aviation," *Eugene (OR) Register-Guard,* March 21, 2002, p. C1.

Mountaire Corp.

———————————————■———————————————

204 East 4th Street
North Little Rock, Arkansas 72114
U.S.A.
Telephone: (501) 372-6524
Fax: (501) 372-3972
Web site: http://www.mountaire.com

Private Company
Incorporated: 1914 as Hayes Grain and Commission
   Company
Employees: 6,000
Sales: $1.21 billion (2008)
NAICS: 311119 Other Animal Food Manufacturing

■ ■ ■

One of the largest private companies in the United States, Mountaire Corp., doing business as Mountaire Farms, is a diverse agricultural food processing company with a focus on poultry. With headquarters in Little Rock, Arkansas, Mountaire maintains vertically integrated poultry operations in Delaware, North Carolina, and Maryland. These include a Statesville, North Carolina, breeder operation that produces eggs for company hatcheries, which produce chicks that are raised on Mountaire-grown grains. When fully grown the chickens are processed, packaged, and shipped to retail, foodservice, and institutional customers across the United States and 40 countries.

Mountaire offers a variety of broiler chicken products, including private-label whole chickens and fresh or frozen portions; the Mountaire Black Label por-

tions for the foodservice market; BO-SAN roasters and parts for the Asian foodservice market; and the Mountaire Blue Label of whole birds and parts for the wholesale market. Mountaire also offers poultry house construction services and operates feed mills and grain elevators in Delaware, North Carolina, and Maryland for barley, corn, soybeans, and wheat. Mountaire is owned and operated by the Cameron family.

GRAIN MILL ORIGINS: 1914

Mountaire traces its lineage to 1914 and the launch of the Hayes Grain and Commission Company, a North Little Rock-based commercial feed business established by Caughey E. Hayes. It was actually several companies under one management and included the Hayes Grain Co. wholesale business in Fort Smith, Arkansas, and a buying firm operating under the same name in Oklahoma; Arkansas Grain Co. in Stuttgart, Arkansas; and locals plants Hayes-Thomas Grain Co., Argenta Grain Co., Farmer's Grain Co., Spot Cash Feed Co., and the Argenta Cash Store. In 1931 one of the minority partners, Guy Cameron, bought out Hayes and the other partners and changed the name of the business to the Cameron Feed Mill, the first step in the creation of Cameron Feeds Mills and eventually Mountaire Corporation.

Guy Cameron died in 1948 at the age of 64 and was succeeded by his son, G. Ted Cameron. It was under his leadership that the feed company branched into poultry production. In the fall of 1959 he bought into a Colorado corporation called Mountaire Farms, which he subsequently moved to Arkansas. In that same

COMPANY PERSPECTIVES

Mountaire Creed: To provide Quality and Service Consistently. To be honest and fair with everyone including customers, suppliers, community neighbors and each other. To provide an environment dedicated to personal and corporate growth. To be good stewards of all the assets God has entrusted to us.

year Mountaire Farms became one of six companies to form a joint venture under the name Mountaire Poultry Co. to breed, hatch, grow, process, and market broilers, turkeys, roasters, and other fowl.

The company also became involved in the wholesale egg business and held an interest in a hog production business. Two of the joint venture partners were Nashville Feed Mills, Inc., in Nashville, Arkansas, and Hope Feed Mills, Inc., of Hope, Arkansas, both of which were owned by Cameron. Two other partners were Cassady's Hatcher, Inc., Triangle Farms, Inc., of Nashville, Arkansas, both run by Neely Cassady. The final partner was Arkansas Poultry By-Products, Inc.

MOUNTAIRE POULTRY FORMED: 1964

With Cameron serving as president, Mountaire Poultry enjoyed strong growth, so that after five years annual revenues had reached $20 million. In December 1964 the partners decided their interests would be best served by consolidating the member corporations to create a single corporation: Mountaire Poultry, Inc. All of the businesses operated under the Mountaire name, with the exception of the Cameron Feed Mills division, which continued to produce the Prime Quality brand of livestock and poultry feeds in North Little Rock.

Ted Cameron's son, Ronald M. Cameron, joined Mountaire in 1968 as assistant area manager of Mountaire's Retail Food Division. In June 1970 he became the division's operations manager and later in the year took on an additional responsibility as the newly formed position of director of marketing. The job became necessary because in the late 1960s Mountaire had begun to diversify, leading to the introduction of new products and an increase in annual sales to $30 million. Part of the diversification effort included the 1969 acquisition of Southwestern Frozen Foods, Inc., which positioned Mountaire in the processed and cooked foods sectors.

Indicative of its diversification, Mountaire Poultry changed its name to Mountaire Corporation in 1971. In the meantime, Ronald Cameron became vice president of the Kitchens Division and then in 1973 was named executive vice president of Mountaire. Two years later he succeeded his father as chief executive officer and in 1978 became chairman as well when Ted Cameron passed away.

H&H POULTRY ACQUIRED: 1977

A major development in the history of Mountaire came in 1977 with the acquisition of Selbyville, Delaware's H&H Poultry. H&H brought with it feed mill, hatchery, and poultry processing facilities in Delaware and Maryland, supported by contract growers on the Delmarva Peninsula. H&H was renamed Mountaire Farms of Delmarva, and under Mountaire's ownership it was modernized and expanded.

The extra production capacity provided by the Delmarva operations allowed Mountaire in the early 1980s to establish a private-label chicken program with an increasing number of supermarket chains. Growth in the private-label category was initially slow, but the pace quickened in the 1990s. Sales were spurred further by the introduction of Mountaire's fresh home-style roaster line. It was followed a few years later by a private-label Seasoned Roaster product. Mountaire supplied all of the private-label poultry for the Hannaford Bros., Price Chopper, and Acme supermarket chains as well as some of the operations in the Ahold USA group. While offering consumers value, the Mountaire private-label products were high in quality, allowing it to replace many branded programs.

To keep pace with mounting demand, Mountaire doubled the production of Mountaire Farms of Delmarva in 1992. The parent company then added a North Carolina operation in 1996 by acquiring Lumber Bridge, North Carolina-based Piedmont Poultry, which became Mountaire Farms of North Carolina. Mountaire invested heavily in the operations.

A new feed mill was opened in Candor, North Carolina. The old Piedmont hatchery in Siler City, North Carolina, was updated and expanded, as was the processing plant in Lumber Bridge, North Carolina. A new processing facility was also added to produce such value-added products for supermarket retail as marinated roasters, premarinated boneless skinless chicken fillets, and the Sizzlin' Sensation Meal Kits line. When the expansion program was completed in 1999, the Lumber Bridge operation had doubled its production capacity.

Mountaire increased revenues to $320 million in fiscal 1999. To maintain its growth in the new century,

KEY DATES

1914: Hayes Grain and Commission Company is founded.
1931: Guy Cameron buys Hayes Grain.
1959: Mountaire Farms is formed.
1971: The Mountaire Corporation name is adopted.
1992: Mountaire Farms of Delmarva is established.

the company continued to upgrade its operations. In 2000 it built a new feed mill in Candor, North Carolina, and also expanded in Delaware through the purchase of Townsend Inc.'s 2,000-acre complex in Millsboro, Delaware. Acquired assets included a hatchery, poultry processing plant (also supported by Delmarva Peninsula growers), feed mill, and soybean processing operations, as well as four grain elevators in Delaware and Maryland. Rather than combine the business with Mountaire Farm of Delmarva, the new parent company elected to run it as a separate company under the name Mountaire Farms of Delaware.

TYSON ASSETS ACQUIRED: 2003

To support further sales growth and bolster its Delmarva Peninsula operations, Mountaire acquired assets from Tyson Foods Inc. in 2003. It purchased the Tyson processing plant in Berlin on the Eastern Shore of Maryland, as well as a feed mill, grain storage, and grain handling facility. Mountaire was now better able to support the contract poultry growers and grain farmers that served its Delmarva operations. Mountaire also hired a large number of the 155 growers that had been contracted by Tyson.

The expansion of the Delmarva units helped Mountaire to push sales beyond $900 million in fiscal 2004, a 35 percent increase over 2003. As a result, Mountaire became the fifth-largest private company in Arkansas, according to *Arkansas Business*. The company continued to grow as the decade unfolded. It increased the production capacity of the North Carolina operation by 50 percent in 2006. A year later Mountaire grew externally as well. It bought three grain facilities from Hostetter Grain Inc., located in Seaford, Delaware, and Trappe and Queen Anne, Maryland. In that same year Mountaire bought Greensboro Grain facilities in Greensboro, Maryland.

The year 2007 was also a time of transition for Mountaire and the Cameron family. In January the company elected to sell certain assets of its animal health business and the Mountaire Feeds, Inc., unit to Cargill Animal Nutrition, in particular the well-established Prime Quality brand of livestock and poultry feeds marketed in Arkansas, Louisiana, Mississippi, western Tennessee, eastern Oklahoma, and eastern Texas. In addition to feeds for poultry, cattle, horse, dairy, swine, and fish, Prime Quality offered rabbit and other exotic feeds as well as pet food.

What was not included in the sale was the Cameron Feed Mill in North Little Rock, which had been in operation for more than 80 years. The facility on which Mountaire was founded had been rebuilt after fires destroyed it in 1923 and again in 1957, and in the 1980s the warehouse was expanded. It was also a landmark in the community, the tallest downtown structure, known simply to locals as The Mill, but time had finally caught up to the facility. The equipment was outdated and the four-acre site on which it stood was too small to allow for expansion to keep it a viable operation.

CAMERON MILL CLOSES: 2007

The Cameron Mill was closed in 2007. A year later the structure was sold to the New Argenta Development Group, which also bought Mountaire Corporation's office building and leased it back to the firm. The mill was slowly dismantled as plans were made to redevelop the property with mixed-used facilities in what was tentatively to be called The Mill District.

While ties to its past were being severed, Mountaire continued to build for the future. Annual revenues increased to $1.15 billion in fiscal 2007, making Mountaire the sixth-largest broiler chicken company in the United States and giving it a number 3 ranking on *Arkansas Business'* list of the largest private companies in Arkansas. Ronald Cameron, who had been in charge of the company for more than 30 years, was also recognized for his achievements. In 2008 he was named an honorary life member of the National Chicken Council board of directors.

Cameron continued to build on the legacy established by his father and grandfather. The company received some unwelcome press, however, in June 2002, when an employee was killed by an ammonia leak in the processing plant at its Lumber Bridge, North Carolina, operation. Ammonia was used as a refrigerant to chill and process chicken, and if released in the air could cause both external and internal burns. A rupture developed in a high-pressure line to cause the fatal leak.

The company was cited for not having a complete risk management program in place, and in 2010 it was fined $27,410 for violating rules on sale handling and storage of hazardous materials. Nevertheless, Mountaire continued to expand, acquiring Mauney Grain in New London, North Carolina, in 2009. There was every reason to expect further growth as the new century unfolded.

Ed Dinger

PRINCIPAL SUBSIDIARIES

Mountaire Farms of Delaware Inc.; Mountaire Farms Inc.; Mountaire Feeds, Inc.

PRINCIPAL COMPETITORS

Pilgrim's Pride Corporation; Sanderson Farms, Inc.; Tyson Foods, Inc.

FURTHER READING

"Arkansas Business Rankings: Wealthiest Arkansas Families," *Arkansas Business*, July 24, 2000, p. 21.

Henderson, Bruce, "Chicken Plant Fined for Ammonia Death," *Charlotte Observer*, February 5, 2010.

Moritz, Gwen, "As Chickens Go, So Go State's Largest Firms," *Arkansas Business*, May 23, 2005, p. 1.

"Mountaire Consolidates Corporations," *Hope Star*, December 15, 1964, p. 1.

"Mountaire Poultry Company, Spawned in Colorado, Now a Big Arkansas Industry," *Hope Star*, June 13, 1963, p. 10.

Smith, D. J., "Feed Mill to Close after Eight Decades in Town," *Maumelle Monitor*, January 18, 2007.

MSE, Inc.

---

200 Technology Way
Butte, Montana 59701-9795
U.S.A.
Telephone: (406) 494-7100
Fax: (406) 494-7230
Web site: http://www.mse-ta.com

Wholly Owned Subsidiary of Montana Energy Research and Development Institute
Incorporated: 1974 as Montana Energy Research and Development Institute
Employees: 95
Sales: $69 million (2008 est.)
NAICS: 541330 Engineering Services; 541719 Research and Development in the Physical Sciences and Engineering Sciences

■ ■ ■

MSE, Inc., and its primary subsidiary, MSE Technology Applications, Inc., is a diversified research and engineering company based in Butte, Montana. MSE, in turn, is a wholly owned subsidiary of the Montana Energy Research and Development Institute (MERDI), created to spur economic development in Butte. Throughout its history, MSE has been dependent on federal budget earmarks provided by a string of U.S. senators, including Mike Mansfield, for whom MSE named its testing facility.

MSE has branched out to pursue more private-sector work. The company's engineering solutions and services personnel are involved in mine waste cleanup, site cleanup and closure, water resource and analysis, and facility modernization. MSE also employs advanced technologies to help in the aerospace industry's development of hypersonic and propulsion technologies, providing wind tunnel testing. MSE uses plasma technology to treat waste created by demilitarization, including nuclear and chemical wastes. In addition, MSE develops remote monitoring systems for dams and other industrial applications.

Customers have included the U.S. Department of Energy, the U.S. Department of Defense; the U.S. Environmental Protection Agency (EPA), all branches of U.S. military, as well as state governments, major research laboratories, and such commercial clients as Lockheed Martin Corporation and Boeing. To attract more diversified business and evolve into a more national concern, MSE in the first decade of the 21st century established branch offices in Richland, Washington; Morgantown, West Virginia; and Escondido, California.

ORIGINS: 1974

MSE grew out of the Montana Energy Research and Development Institute (MERDI), which was established in Butte, Montana, in 1974 to do work for the Department of Energy, testing and demonstrating magnetohydrodynamics (MHD), a power generation technology that allowed coal to be burned more efficiently at high temperatures. Butte at the time was very much a dying community and MERDI grew out of an existing nonprofit community development organization created to bring new types of employment to an area that had

COMPANY PERSPECTIVES

MSE Technology Applications, Inc., is a national customer-focused enterprise based on performance, quality, value, relationships, and solutions. We monitor our success through customer satisfaction, repeat business, and company growth. We strive to provide an ethical, challenging, and professional business environment, which promotes career growth for our employees.

been long dependent on copper mining. The population had been in decline since World War I and by the mid-1960s the area had suffered a collapse in real estate prices, resulting in the exodus of more people and the closure of scores of small businesses. Butte appeared to be a city caught in a spiral of decline.

Montana Senator Mike Mansfield intervened in 1968 with the Model Cities program that padded Butte's budget, and created employment by such means as repaving the streets. The relief provided by the six-year program was only temporary, however. In the early 1970s the price of copper collapsed, as did the morale of the city, which experienced a rash of arson-related fires that claimed much of the city's central district. It was against this background that MERDI was created.

The existence of MERDI was due in no small measure to the influence of its political benefactors, and the nonprofit was able to secure the MHD testing contract only because the Department of Energy (DOE) had built a testing facility (the Western Environmental Technology Office, or WETO) at an area industrial park that had been built by the federal government. In 1981 MERDI created a for-profit engineering company called Mountain States Energy, which would become MSE, Inc. The new entity hired engineers and other personnel to pursue more advanced work in MHD technology as well as new opportunities to make MERDI less dependent on its DOE contracts.

Because of its community organization roots, MSE was far from the typical for-profit company. It set up shop in the heart of the ravaged central district, neighbor to shuttered businesses and halfway houses. Rather than pay out its earnings to shareholders, it invested in scholarships and city infrastructure projects, essentially padding the city budget. Moreover, it helped to prevent the loss of talented Butte residents by providing jobs for those with technical training.

DON PEOPLES NAMED CEO: 1989

MSE branched into civil engineering to win contracts from the Department of Environmental Protection, in particular mine cleanup projects sponsored by the Superfund created by Congress in the wake of the Love Canal scandal of the 1970s that brought to light the dangers of pollution. However, the type of expertise MSE had to offer did not match the needs of Butte's Anaconda Mining Company, owned at the time by the Atlantic Richfield Company (ARCO). Instead of a high-technology approach, ARCO chose to use bulldozers to gather the toxins and bury them. Another area site, the Berkeley pit, was filled with acidic water. ARCO and the EPA agreed to simply mix in limestone to neutralize the acid and create a gelatin that could be transported to a toxic dump for monitoring.

Donald Peoples, board member of MERDI and MSE, as well as Butte's mayor, urged the company to take a different tack and make the best of the area's ecological problems by pursuing grant money to test permanent cleanup solutions at the Butte sites. The knowledge gained could then serve as a springboard for spin-off companies and create further employment for the community. Moreover, MSE could find a willing partner in Butte's Montana School of Mineral Science and Technology, a world-respected engineering school. Won over by the argument, the MSE board launched a nationwide search for a new president who could make the vision a reality. In the end, the board decided that Peoples was the man best suited for the job, and in 1989 he resigned as mayor and took charge of both MERDI and MSE.

Born and raised in Butte, Peoples was a local football star who returned in the 1960s to coach his high school team, a job he claimed he would have been happy performing for the rest of his life. Just three years later, however, he was persuaded that he could better serve the community by becoming a planner and manager in the city government.

The demonstrated competence of Peoples led in 1979 to his appointment as mayor at age 39, after his predecessor left town to take a job in Helena, Montana. His dedication to Butte and his conviction played a major role in the city's survival during an extended period of civic despair, and Peoples was repeatedly reelected to office. In 1987 he was named one of the top mayors in the United States by *U.S. News & World Report.*

Peoples brought the same energy and dedication to MSE. Under his leadership the company broadened its expertise to include the testing of a wide variety of waste treatment technologies, including biological, chemical, temperature, and physical properties. In conjunction

KEY DATES

1974: Montana Energy Research and Development Institute (MERDI) is established as a nonprofit company.

1981: MERDI creates a for-profit engineering company called Mountain States Energy (MSE).

1989: Donald Peoples is named chief executive of both MERDI and MSE.

1996: Western Environmental Technology Office testing facility is acquired.

2006: Peoples retires.

with the Montana School of Mineral Science and Technology, MSE during the first half of the 1990s studied six mineral-recovery technologies funded by DOE grants in an effort to find a profitable way to separate dissolved metals from mine water.

WETO FACILITY ACQUIRED: 1996

MSE acquired and privatized the WETO facility in 1996 and continued its research efforts. (Because of Senator Mike Mansfield's contributions to Montana and Butte in particular, WETO was renamed the Mike Mansfield Advanced Technology Center in 2001.) In the second half of the 1990s, MSE studied additional methods to "mine" water, while also using its expertise to find work in the aerospace industry. MSE also operated a profitable civil engineering business. At the dawn of the 21st century, MSE allowed the employees to buy this business, spinning it off only with a commitment that it would continue to be based in Butte.

What remained of MSE following the spin-off generated about $25 million in annual revenues, but was still highly dependent on federal earmarks. Currying favors with politicians to secure those funds caused a problem for the company in 2000 when it pleaded guilty in federal court to illegal corporate contributions to Senator Christopher Bond, a Republican from Missouri, who headed a Senate panel that oversaw some of MSE's federal contracts.

The illegal acts took place in 1998 when MSE honored 13 of its employees with checks for $750 with the understanding that they would donate the money to Bond's reelection campaign. Of the 13 employees, 12 contributed $750 to Bond, while another gave $1,000. At the time, Bond's subcommittee had approved a five-

year $7.5 million award to MSE for NASA research projects.

Some MSE employees who were not pleased with the way the money had been funneled to Bond shared their concerns with a Butte resident who filed a complaint with the Federal Election Committee. MSE cooperated with the ensuing investigation, maintaining that it had not knowingly violated campaign laws. Nevertheless, the company was fined $117,000 and its top four executives agreed to each devote 50 hours of their time over the following 22 months informing other Montana companies and groups about federal campaign finance laws.

TETRAGENICS ACQUIRED: 2002

In the new century MSE continued to secure aerospace work. In August 2000 it announced a contract to build and test a high-technology facility needed for an Air Force program. However, contract funding fell off in other areas in the amount of $4 million, prompting MSE to trim its workforce in late 2000 through early retirement incentives. To remain a viable research partner, MSE in 2002 acquired Tetragenics, an area electronic controls and monitoring company that added useful products and proprietary technology. The acquisition also preserved several jobs in Butte.

Peoples was nearing retirement age but agreed in October 2003 to remain chief executive as MSE approached a critical year during which the company would seek an extension on several contracts, most importantly for work with the DOE that had begun in 1996. Again, Montana's U.S. senators played an important role in securing the DOE extension through 2005 with annual renewals that could extend through 2009. Peoples also oversaw a shift in vision for MSE, which then sought to become a privately funded company less dependent on public money.

MSE's potential was evident in an offer made to acquire the business. Unlike other companies, MSE had a mission other than simply making money and was still very much committed to building a future for Butte. Some of its ventures were hardly typical for an engineering and research firm. For example, it spawned Center for Innovation Inc., a company that served as a small business incubator. This company was spun off in 2004 to a former MSE employee.

PEOPLES RETIRES: 2006

To drum up commercial business and take advantage of its technical expertise, MSE opened satellite offices in West Virginia, North Carolina, South Carolina,

Washington State, Alabama, and California. They were headed by MSE personnel on temporary assignment. In the end, three of the offices took root, located in Richland, Washington; Morgantown, West Virginia; and Escondido, California. Peoples retired in June 2006. Jim Kambick, who replaced Peoples as MERDI's CEO, had been with the organization since 1990. MSE's new chief executive, Jeff Ruffner, had an equally long tenure at that company.

Under new leadership, MSE embarked on a new phase in its history. The company continued to work on diversifying its customer base. In 2008 MSE posted the most profitable year in its history to date, but a year later experienced a 20 percent decrease in business due to defense cutbacks and other funding shortfalls caused by the poor economy. To keep expenses in line, the company trimmed its workforce by 20 percent to about 95. MSE viewed 2010 as a year of recovery, but its long-term prospects and ability to evolve into something more than a government contractor remained far from certain.

Ed Dinger

PRINCIPAL SUBSIDIARIES

MSE Technology Applications Inc.; MSE Infrastructure Services, Inc.

PRINCIPAL COMPETITORS

Advanced Environmental Technologies, LLC; Bechtel Group, Inc.; Parsons Corporation.

FURTHER READING

Dobb, Edwin, "Pennies from Hell," *Harper's Magazine*, October 1996, p. 39.

Langewiesche, William, "Profits of Doom," *Atlantic*, April 2001, p. 56.

Mannies, Jo, "Montana Firm Admits Illegally Funneling Cash to Bond in '98," *St. Louis Post-Dispatch*, April 26, 2001, p. A1.

McCartney, Leslie, "Butte, Mont.-Based Engineering Firm's 30th Birthday Brings Plans for Expansion," *Montana Standard*, January 17, 2005.

"MSE-MERDI Places Two at Helm," *Montana Standard*, June 7, 2006.

O'Brien, Gerard, "Don Peoples: The Man behind the Mining City," *Montana Standard*, February 3, 2008.

———, "MSE: The Quiet Company That's Making Noise," *Montana Standard*, January 13, 2008, p. D9.

Trainor, Tim, "MSE Enters Important Year," *Montana Standard*, January 24, 2001.

———, "MSE Lays Off 11," *Montana Standard*, May 1, 2009.

Mueller Water Products, Inc.

1200 Abernathy Road N.E., Suite 1200
Atlanta, Georgia 30328
U.S.A.
Telephone: (770) 206-4200
Fax: (770) 206-4235
Web site: http://www.muellerwaterproducts.com

Public Company
Incorporated: 1893 Mueller Plumbing & Heating Co.
Employees: 5,300
Sales: $1.43 billion (2009)
Stock Exchanges: New York
Ticker Symbol: MWA
NAICS: 332911 Industrial Valve Manufacturing

■ ■ ■

A New York Stock Exchange-listed company, Mueller Water Products, Inc., is a major provider of infrastructure and flow control products, serving municipal water distribution networks and treatment facilities in North America as well as the residential and commercial construction, heating and air conditioning, fire protection, and oil and gas industries. Products include valves, hydrants, pipe fittings, and ductile iron pipe.

The company is composed of three primary units, the flagship subsidiary of each dating to the 1800s. Mueller Co., based in Decatur, Illinois, is a full-line supplier of flow control products used in distribution systems for municipal potable water and natural gas. U.S. Pipe focuses on ductile iron pipe for clean water transmission and is based in Birmingham, Alabama. Anvil International, maintaining its headquarters in Portsmouth, New Hampshire, manufactures pipe fittings, hangers, and supports. The corporate headquarters for Mueller Water Products is located in Atlanta, Georgia. All told, the company operates more than 25 manufacturing facilities in the United States, Canada, and China.

ORIGINS

The man who gave Mueller Water Products its name was Hieronymus Mueller. He was born in 1832 in Baden-Wertheim, Germany, where he became a journeyman machinist. As a young man be became caught up in the Schleswig-Holstein War in which a German majority in Holstein and southern Schleswig attempted to free themselves from Danish rule. Mueller was said to have been involved in the blowing up of a bridge.

Attracted by the freedoms available in the United States, Mueller immigrated in 1850, first settling in Chicago and working as a machinist. Mueller came to Decatur, Illinois, in 1857, where he opened a gun repair shop. However, he soon left for Colorado's gold rush. Two years later he returned to Decatur with no gold in his pockets, and became a gunsmith. He also used his mechanical talents to make keys, repair sewing machines, and perform steam fitting and plumbing.

In 1871 Mueller was appointed "city tapper," charged with connecting homes to the new water mains. It was a taxing and dangerous occupation, requiring that he pound a drive stop with a sledgehammer into a pressurized main in order to insert a connector. This was far

COMPANY PERSPECTIVES

We are a "new" old company, with each of our three businesses, Mueller Co., U.S. Pipe and Anvil, manufacturing quality products for more than 100 years. We combined their strong heritage, expertise, talents and brand recognition into one company for a stronger future.

from an easy job. Water sprayed in all directions, filling the hole and threatening to drown the tapper. Mueller was determined to find an easier, safer way to complete the task, and according to company lore an idea came to him in a dream. The Mueller water tapper, which he patented in 1872, made use of a sealed chamber and thread-tapping tools to quickly and safely perform the connection.

COMPANY INCORPORATED: 1893

Mueller began manufacturing his tapping machine and set aside his gun business in 1885. He incorporated the Mueller Plumbing & Heating Co. in 1893 and opened a new plant two years later that began manufacturing other pressure devices and fluid control devices, as well as such miscellaneous items as roller skates that corporated Mueller's patented roller bearing concept. Also in 1893 H. Mueller Manufacturing Company was incorporated in Michigan to produce copper and brass plumbing products. It would eventually go its own way, becoming Mueller Industries, Inc., unrelated to Mueller Water Products.

In 1895 Mueller turned over control of the family businesses to his five sons, having become fascinated with his new automobile, a Benz made in Germany. When it arrived, the first automobile in town, it failed to run. Mueller rebuilt it, adding improvements that resulted in many patented automotive parts, including a spark plug, distributor, water-cooled radiator, and variable speed transmission. He renamed the enhanced car the Mueller Benz, and as such it won America's first car race in Chicago in 1895. Mueller worked on what he considered to be the first practical automobile gasoline engine, but in February 1900 Mueller lit a cigar while working on the engine and set his clothes aflame. His burns were severe and he died about two weeks later.

Mueller left his sons a plumbing company that generated $390,000 in annual revenues. Six years later, as the family celebrated its 50th year in business in De-

catur, that amount reached $1.5 million. As sales increased in Canada, served by a warehouse in New York, the family decided a northern plant was needed, and in 1912 a facility opened in Sarnia, Ontario. A year later Mueller landed a job that gave it international prominence: designing a valve used to protect the Panama Canal lock gates. Connected to giant chains that kept ships from straying and possibly damaging the locks, the valve provided enough play to corral the ship without snapping the chain.

REPUTATION FOR INNOVATION

Mueller's reputation for innovation continued in the 1920s. The company introduced copper plumbing and flare connections for domestic use in 1923, and a year later began using hard copper tube for indoor water supplies. The Mueller name became well established in the plumbing industry and by the end of the decade the company was manufacturing a complete line of valves and fittings. In 1930 Mueller made another significant contribution, the Streamline solder-type fittings that were stronger than the pipes they connected, leading to the development of all-copper plumbing and heating systems. In 1933 Mueller introduced gas valves that could be relubricated, followed three years later by a mechanical gas line stopper.

Hampered by the Great Depression, Mueller struggled through the early 1930s, returning to profitability by mid-decade. The company was thriving as the United States became involved in World War II in the early 1940s and military spending stimulated the economy. Mueller did its part for the war effort, manufacturing an armor-piercing shell of its own design. Following the war, William Everett Mueller retired as president in 1947, thus becoming the last Mueller to lead the company, although the family retained ownership for another 40 years.

More advances were credited to Mueller during the ensuing decades. O-ring sealed Lubroseal gas valves and O-ring sealed water/gas machines were introduced in 1949. O-ring sealed Oriseal water valves and insulated unions followed in the 1950s. The company, somewhat adrift at this stage, was reenergized when a new president, Edward Powers, former president of an IT&T subsidiary, took charge and brought in a new management team.

FAMILY OWNERSHIP ENDS: 1986

Between 1978 and 1986 Powers increased profits from $2.5 million to $21 million. In June 1986 he led a management team, with backing from a Bahrain-based

KEY DATES

1857: Hieronymus Mueller starts gun repair business in Decatur, Illinois.
1872: Mueller water tapper is patented.
1893: Mueller Plumbing & Heating Co. is incorporated.
1947: Last member of Mueller family to lead company retires.
1986: Mueller family sells company to management team.
2006: Mueller Water Products, Inc., is spun off by Walter Industries.

investment bank and other investors, and bought the company from the Mueller family for $325 million, bringing to an end six generations of Mueller family ownership. The company pursued a more aggressive growth strategy, driven by acquisitions that increased revenues 30 percent to $394 million in 1988. The new ownership group then sold Mueller to Tyco Laboratories in October 1988, tripling its investment in a mere 30 months.

Under Tyco's ownership Mueller completed a major acquisition in 1989, adding Hawes and Hersey Company, which had been established in Boston in 1859. Hawes and Hersey built that city's first steam-driven fire engine and became known for the rotary-type water meter it produced. Tyco also completed two other significant acquisitions. In 1996 Henry Pratt Company and James Jones Company became Mueller subsidiaries.

Established in 1901, Pratt had entered the valve business in 1926 when it introduced the first rubber seated butterfly valves. James Jones, established in California in the late 1800s, had started out making valves, and in 1926 began producing bronze fire hydrants. It became a major supplier of bronze valves and fittings to the western United States.

MORE CHANGES IN OWNERSHIP

While Tyco added assets to Mueller, it also cut jobs and costs while saddling the company with considerable debt. Tyco's chief executive, Dennis Kozlowski, grew Tyco at an accelerated pace in the 1990s. However, his extravagant spending eventually caught the attention of authorities, and in 2004 he was convicted of grand larceny and fraud and sent to prison.

In the meantime, debt-ridden Mueller was sold in 1999 to DLJ Merchant Banking, the private-equity arm

of Credit Suisse First Boston, for $938 million. The new management team overhauled Mueller, closing unproductive foundries while implementing leaner manufacturing methods at the remaining plants. It proved to be a fruitful approach, as revenues increased from $865 million in 2000 to $1.05 billion in 2001.

The revitalized Mueller attracted the attention of Walter Industries, a Florida-based homebuilder and water transmission products company that already owned U.S. Pipe, a Mueller competitor that generated about $500 million in annual sales. Walter was founded in Tampa, Florida, in 1936 by James W. Walter, who started out building "shell" homes, which required the buyers to finish the interior. He provided the necessary materials as part of the price and as a result acquired a number of building materials companies, including U.S. Pipe and Foundry in 1968.

Walter was acquired by New York private-equity firm Kohlberg Kravis Roberts & Co. in 1988 but asbestos liabilities soon led to bankruptcy. The company did not emerge from Chapter 11 bankruptcy until 1995, after achieving protection from the asbestos litigation. In 2003 Walter initiated a restructuring effort, selling off assets in order to focus on its home, finance, and pipe-making operations. The acquisition of Mueller fit into this strategy.

WALTER INDUSTRIES ACQUIRES MUELLER: 2005

In June 2005 Walter agreed to acquire Mueller for $860 million in cash and the assumption of $1.05 billion in debt, the largest deal in Walter's 60-year history to date. Mueller did not remain part of Walter for very long, however. By the fall of 2005 Walter was taking steps to spin off Mueller and U.S. Pipe into a separate company, some of the stock to be distributed to Walter's shareholders and the remainder to be sold in an initial public offering (IPO).

According to press accounts, the spin-off was forced by a hedge fund, Pirate Capital LLC of Norwalk, Connecticut, which owned about 8.2 percent of Walter. The hedge fund urged the breakup as a way to create value, threatening to lead a shareholder revolt and replace the board of directors if its plan was not adopted by an October 31, 2005, deadline. Walter complied and the spin-off was slated for 2006.

As Mueller Water prepared for its IPO, Walter added several assets to the company. Hunt Industries Inc., a Tennessee-based maker of water meter pits and yokes, was acquired in January 2006, followed by CCNE, LLC, a Connecticut manufacturer of check valves used in water and wastewater treatment and distribution systems. In addition, Mueller closed a valve manufacturing plant in Illinois as well as a valve and hydrant plant in Milton, Ontario, transferring the production of both to other Mueller operations. Mueller also made plans to move its corporate headquarters to Atlanta, Georgia, by year's end.

Mueller's public offering was completed in May 2006, raising $400 million and setting the stage for Walter to spin off the business. As an independent stand-alone business, Mueller soon completed an acquisition, paying $24.5 million for Fast Fabricators Inc., maker of ductile iron pipe, in a deal that closed in early 2007.

A drop in housing starts, followed by a faltering economy, hurt the company, which was forced to cut jobs in 2009. By the end of that year business began to pick up. Long-term trends favored Mueller. The water infrastructure in the United States was rapidly eroding. According to government reports, almost half of all pipes in the ground by 2020 would be in very poor condition, at the very least having exceeded their life expectancy. Hence, Mueller was positioned to enjoy robust sales for many years to come.

Ed Dinger

PRINCIPAL SUBSIDIARIES

Anvil Star, LLC; Henry Pratt Company, LLC; James Jones Company, LLC; Mueller Co. Ltd.; U.S. Pipe Valve & Hydrant, LLC.

PRINCIPAL COMPETITORS

American Cast Iron Pipe Company; McWane, Inc.; Tyco International Ltd.

FURTHER READING

Barancik, Scott, "Walter Industries to Make $1.9-Billion Buy," *St. Petersburg Times,* June 20, 2005.

Frazier, Ron, "Looking Back at Central Illinois," *Decatur (Ill.) Herald & Review*, March 27, 2000, p. B12.

Ioannou, Lori, "The LBO with the Happy Ending," *Euromoney,* February 1990, p. 78.

Reid, Tony, "A Decatur Original," *Decatur (Ill.) Herald & Review*, March 30, 2008, p. A1.

———, "Mueller CEO Predicts Rising Tide of Infrastructure Needs for Nation," *Decatur (Ill.) Herald & Review*, December 14, 2007.

———, "Mueller to Be Dynamite Company Once Again," *Decatur (Ill.) Herald & Review*, February 12, 2006, p. F1.

———, "Tapping Quality," *Decatur (Ill.) Herald & Review*, March 30, 2008, p. S1.

"What the Muellers Have Done in Decatur in Fifty Years," *Daily Review,* June 30, 2007, p. 14.

New York & Company Inc.

---

450 West 33rd Street
New York, New York 10001-2632
U.S.A.
Telephone: (212) 884-2000
Fax: (212) 884-2396
Web site: http://www.nyandcompany.com

Public Company
Incorporated: 1917 as Lorraine Stores Corporation
Employees: 8,129 (2,358 full-time)
Sales: $1.14 billion (2008)
Stock Exchanges: New York
Ticker Symbol: NWY
NAICS: 448120 Women's Clothing Stores

■ ■ ■

New York & Company Inc. (New York & Co.) is a leading specialty retailer of fashion-oriented, moderately priced women's apparel, offering an assortment of casual and work apparel and accessories, including handbags and jewelry. The target customers are fashion-conscious, value-sensitive women between the ages of 25 and 45. New York & Co. designs its own proprietary-branded merchandise and purchases it from manufacturers and buying agents, almost all of them in Asia. It is sold exclusively through its national network of retail stores and Web site. At the end of fiscal 2008 (January 31, 2009), the company operated 589 stores in 44 states.

ORIGINS

Samuel A. Lerner and his brothers Joseph J. and Michael sold blouses before founding Lorraine Stores Corporation in 1917 in New York City to sell moderately priced women's clothing. They renamed it Lerner Stores Corporation the following year. Joseph Lerner was elected president in 1929, when the company made its initial public offering (IPO) of stock, and he continued in that position until succeeding Samuel in 1952 as chairman.

The budget-conscious retail chain remained profitable during the Great Depression and had 179 stores in 40 states and the District of Columbia in 1941. A full line of children's wear first made its appearance in 1945. The Lerners were quick to exploit the population shift to the suburbs after World War II and installed outlets in many of the first suburban malls. They sold their shares around this time, and Harold M. Lane, a longtime company executive, became president in the early 1950s. Net sales rose from $50.42 million in fiscal 1941 to $204.02 million in fiscal 1961, when there were 304 stores in 39 states, the District of Columbia, and Puerto Rico.

Lane controlled about 10 percent of Lerner Stores in 1961, when these shares, plus an almost equivalent amount of other stock, were sold to the McCrory Corporation, a diversified retail chain controlled and managed by Meshulam Riklis. By the end of 1962 McCrory owned almost all the stock and had made Lerner a subsidiary. Lane continued to head Lerner's management and became a McCrory board member as well.

McCrory purchased Lerner's Lane Department Stores division in 1965.

Riklis, described in one publication as a pioneer in bootstrap finance, later explained that he had acquired Lerner Stores for very little cash by issuing debentures and warrants. Five years after the purchase, he calculated that McCrory had already tripled its $17.5 million cash investment in acquiring Lerner.

With more than 440 stores in 1974, Lerner was described as McCrory's most profitable enterprise and the nation's largest retail chain of women's and children's apparel, with an estimated market value of about $200 million. The Lerner chain continued to grow. There were 767 stores in 45 states plus the District of Columbia, Puerto Rico, and the Virgin Islands at the end of fiscal 1982, when net sales came to $717 million.

SOLD TO THE LIMITED: 1985

Lerner Stores was the nation's second-largest chain of moderate-priced women's and children's apparel stores (trailing Petrie Stores Corporation) when it was sold in 1985 to The Limited, Inc., for $297 million in cash and notes and the assumption of debt. The deal quickly went sour, however, both for its buyer and the merchants who had consigned goods to Lerner. Leslie Wexner, The Limited's founder, immediately dismissed the top Lerner managers amid reports of inventory irregularities and other indications of mismanagement. The suppliers were furious as Wexner just as quickly canceled all merchandise on order, an action that gave rise to a flurry of lawsuits.

Renamed Lerner New York in 1988, the store chain sought to foster a more fashionable image while retaining its budget-conscious core customer. The company closed or sold 140 stores, mostly in city downtown areas or aging suburban malls. The units shed also included the Puerto Rican and Virgin Islands outlets, which were sold to Petrie Stores. Fifty new stores were opened, and others were remodeled.

By 1990 Lerner's management believed it had turned the corner. Sales volume for its 814 stores had passed $900 million a year. The company opened a flagship store near Manhattan's Herald Square and an even larger one in Miami. The new look featured a peaches-and-cream decor, hand painted wallpaper, marble-floored foyers, and curvy ceilings and aisles. Smaller areas were created for both private-label and branded goods. Seeking a more prosperous customer, the chain added more-expensive, better-quality merchandise. However, its profit margin and sales per square foot remained below what Wexner considered acceptable.

Lerner's sales peaked in 1992, when its 914 stores made it the largest The Limited company in terms of number of outlets. From perhaps as high as $1.2 billion, sales volume dropped to $1.03 billion in 1994. The following year a new executive team targeted a somewhat older customer, the working woman 35 to 55 years in age. A new collection featured what was described as updated lifestyle clothing, including dresses, coats, and suits, categories that had been dropped a few years earlier. The outfits continued to retail for $100 or less. Career clothing bore the logo Metro 212. Sweatshirts and other non-work merchandise carried the logo NY & Co. A line of jewelry and accessories was named SoHo Studio.

CHANGE IN LEADERSHIP

After another year of falling operating profits and disappointing same-store sales, Lerner New York got a new chief executive: Richard P. Crystal, a longtime Macy's division chairman. The chain closed almost 100 oversized or underperforming stores during the next two years, including the Herald Square flagship, leaving its only urban downtown outlet on Chicago's State Street. Nevertheless, about half of the 100 Lerner New York stores renovated in this period featured black-and-white photos of Manhattan street scenes, while a sound system broadcast weather and traffic reports.

Lerner New York's fortunes improved in 1998, a development that was ultimately attributed largely to Charlotte Neuville, the vice-president of design brought in by Crystal. Neuville established the Manhattan-based store decor and New York & Company as the chain's brand in place of various labels previously developed by

The Limited. Sales volume was said to have passed $1 billion again in 1998.

The New York & Company (or New York & Co.) brand proved so strong that 79 Lerner New York stores in three markets, Chicago, Philadelphia, and the state of New York, reopened under that name in late 2000. For the chain as a whole, sales volume was holding steady despite downsizing in both the number of stores and the size of the stores. Between 1996 and 2004 Lerner closed 425 stores that were collectively only marginally profitable. Only 579 units remained by late 2000, and they ranged in size from 5,000 to 6,000 square feet. In contrast, the Herald Square store opened in 1990 had occupied 30,000 square feet.

UNDER BEAR STEARNS OWNERSHIP

The relative resurgence of Lerner New York did not impress its owner, however, for the chain was doing little better than breaking even. In 2002 Lerner actually lost money, and The Limited, which was then Limited Brands, Inc., sold the company to Bear Stearns Merchant Banking, the private-equity arm of the big Wall Street firm, for $153.5 million, of which no more than $78.5 million was in cash. The full amount was much lower than The Limited had paid for the chain almost 20 years earlier and less than one-fifth of its annual sales. "This was a dead business," an investment analyst told Andrew Bary of *Barron's*. "Limited wanted to get rid of it, nobody was interested, so they gave it away."

Lerner New York, which was renamed New York & Company, Inc., proved to be a bonanza for Bear Stearns. Industry observers said the chain benefited once it was freed from The Limited's bureaucracy and the perception that it was of lesser importance to its parent, whose other retail chains included Victoria's Secret, The Limited, Express, and Bath & Body Works. By late 2004 New York & Co., still under Crystal's leadership, was growing in size again. Sales for the first half of 2004 were 13 or 14 percent higher than in the same period of the previous year.

One innovation was the opening of accessory stores right next to the New York & Co. units to create a dual format. Accessories had accounted for 13 percent of company sales in 2003. The new outlets, which averaged 6,500 square feet compared to 5,500 square feet for the standard ones, numbered 58 by the end of 2005.

PUBLICLY OWNED COMPANY: 2004

In October 2004 Bear Stearns made an IPO of the common stock of New York & Company, collecting about

$105 million for about one-quarter of the shares. Other stockholders garnered about $75 million for selling their own shares at the same time. New York & Co. ended fiscal 2004 with 476 stores, net sales of $1.04 million, and net income of $17.44 million. The next year yielded even better results: 503 stores, $1.11 million in net sales, and net income of $58.49 million.

During what proved to be New York & Company's most profitable year to date, Crystal foresaw the possibility that the chain might grow to 800 stores. New York & Co. returned to Midtown Manhattan that year, planting a 14,700-square-foot outlet on the expensive Upper East Side, facing Bloomingdale's. Another addition was Boston-based Jasmine Company, Inc. This 2005 acquisition was a women's retailer of upscale and contemporary apparel, footwear, and accessories sold through its chain of 23 Jasmine Sola branded stores.

In late 2007 New York & Company opened a line of bath and body care products named City Beauty. The collection consisted of six different fragrances, all developed by International Flavors & Fragrances Inc. and bearing the names of different Manhattan neighborhoods. Each fragrance was available in five products: body mist, body lotion, body scrub, hand and body cream, and shower gel. The bottles and jars were shaped to resemble the city skyline.

Fiscal 2006 did not quite match the previous year in net income. That year New York & Company established an e-commerce store on its Web site. In fiscal 2007 the company lost $4.86 million after taking a $31.53 million charge to close the Jasmine Sola chain. The following year was marked by a worldwide financial crisis and a consequent deterioration in net sales. Comparable-store sales fell by 8.6 percent, and the company suffered a net loss of $19.81 million.

As a result of poor economic conditions, New York & Company announced in early 2009 a multiyear restructuring and cost-reduction program intended to save $175 million over the next five years. The program foresaw a permanent reduction of 12 percent of the company's field management in its existing stores and about a 10 percent reduction of corporate-office professionals. Some 40 to 50 underperforming stores would be closed.

Although women were doing less shopping and buying in 2009, New York & Company executives expressed confidence in the future. Crystal announced in January 2010 that New York & Co. planned, for the first time, to open outlet stores during the year. These 20 to 25 units would sell the same merchandise as the existing stores at first but would later include exclusive merchandise manufactured exclusively for the company.

LOOKING TO THE FUTURE

At the end of fiscal 2008 New York & Company was operating 589 stores in 44 states, with the most units in New York, California, and Texas, respectively. All of these stores, which averaged 5,594 square feet in selling space, were leased. They were typically concentrated in large population centers of the United States, in shopping malls, lifestyle centers, and off-mall locations, including urban street locations.

New York & Company's target customers were described as fashion-conscious, value-sensitive women between the ages of 25 and 45. The merchandise consisted of casual and work apparel and accessories, including pants, jackets, knit tops, blouses, sweaters, denim, T-shirts, active wear, handbags, and jewelry. The company's stores carried only New York & Co.-branded merchandise.

New York & Company was introducing new product lines for its stores six times a year: spring, summer, transition, fall, holiday, and pre-spring. These lines were being updated with selected new items every four to six weeks to keep the merchandise current. New York & Co. was purchasing apparel and accessories products from importers and manufacturers in some 20 countries, almost all in the Far East. China, Macau, and Hong Kong accounted for about 65 percent of company purchases in fiscal 2008.

All merchandise was being received, inspected, processed, warehoused, and distributed through the distribution center of Limited Brands in Columbus, Ohio. Irving Place Capital (the former Bear Stearns Merchant Banking) continued to hold 52 percent of New York & Co.'s common stock in April 2009. Corporate headquarters were in Manhattan.

Robert Halasz

PRINCIPAL COMPETITORS

Ann Taylor Stores Corporation; The Gap, Inc.; J.C. Penney Company, Inc.; Kohl's Corporation; Old Navy, Inc.; Target Corporation.

FURTHER READING

Bary, Andrew, "In Style: New York & Co. Looks Pretty for Bear Stearns," *Barron's,* October 4, 2004, p. 32.

Butler, Elisabeth, "New York & Co. Prospers after Leaving Its Parent," *Crain's New York Business,* October 25, 2004, pp. 4, 47.

Edelson, Sharon, "Bendel's Lerner: On the Mend," *WWD/ Women's Wear Daily,* May 20, 1999, p. 13.

Gault, Ylonda, "Lerner NY Looking for Un-Limited Recovery," *Crain's New York Business,* August 7, 1995, pp. 3, 37.

Struensee, Chuck, "How Lerner/NY Put the Pizzazz into the Budget," *WWD/Women's Wear Daily,* April 25, 1990, pp. 1, 6–7.

Zinn, Laura, "No Off-the-Rack Solutions Here," *Business Week,* May 25, 1992, pp. 116, 118.

Nilson Group AB

—■—

Box 508, Haerdgatan 7
Varberg, SE-432 19
Sweden
Telephone: (+46 0340) 865 00
Fax: (+46 0340) 865 51
Web site: http://www.nilsongroup.com

Private Company
Founded: 1955
Employees: 1,300
Sales: SEK 2.8 billion ($360 million) (2008 est.)
NAICS: 448210 Shoe Stores

■ ■ ■

Nilson Group AB is Sweden's leading retail shoe company. The Varberg-based company operates nearly 220 shops in Sweden across six core brands: Din Sko (literally "Your Shoe"), Skopunten, Nilson, Radical Sports, Ecco, and Jerns. With little room left to grow in Sweden, Nilson has also expanded into the broader Scandinavian market, primarily in Norway and Finland, with a small presence in Denmark. At the beginning of 2010, the company's international operations included 56 stores.

Din Sko is the company's flagship retail format. This division also operates the largest shoe chain in Sweden, with 116 stores and a 7.8 percent market share. The Din Sko chain also has 32 stores in Norway and 12 in Finland. Din Sko stores typically feature a selling space of 200 square meters and target the fashion-conscious, price-sensitive consumer market with the company's own shoe designs. Skopunkten is the company's next largest chain in terms of sales volume, generating a 7.1 percent market share from its 46 stores in Sweden. Skopunkten is also Sweden's leading discount shoe chain, generally located in out-of-town shopping centers with a sales surface of 500 square meters. The company is also expanding Skopunkten internationally, opening five stores in Norway.

The Nilson chain, named after the group's founder, Rolf Nilsson, focuses on the branded shoe segment. This division operates 47 stores in Sweden, as well as four stores in Norway, three in Finland, and one in Denmark. Many Nilson stores also include company's Radical Sports sport shoe format, which operates through 30 in-store boutiques and one self-standing store. Nilson Group also targets the high-end shoe market with the city-based Jerns chain, which operates 10 stores in Stockholm, Malmö, Göteborg and Uppsala. Lastly, Nilson Group has held the franchise license for Danish comfort brand Ecco since the 1960s. Nilson operates 42 self-standing Ecco Shops; the group's Din Sko chain plays host to 37 in-store boutiques as well.

Nilson Group does not produce its own shoes but works with manufacturers in China, Taiwan, Vietnam, and elsewhere to produce shoes according to the company's own designs. In order to maintain proximity to its suppliers, the company operates purchasing offices in Vietnam and Wenzhou, China. Nilson Group remains a privately held company controlled by the founding family. Ingemar Charleson, who joined the company at the age of 15 in 1969, is the group's chief executive officer. In 2009 Nilson Group reported total revenues of SEK 2.8 billion ($392 million).

KEY DATES

1955: Rolf Nilsson founds a wholesale footwear business in Sweden.

1961: Nilson acquires his first store and enters the retail market.

1977: Nilson regroups his retail stores under the Din Sko name.

1981: The company opens its first foreign store, in Norway.

2000: Rolf Nilsson retires, and the company restructures as Nilson Group AB.

2009: Nilson launches sourcing and product development operations in Vietnam.

FROM WHOLESALER TO RETAILER IN THE SEVENTIES

Nilson Group had its origins in the 1950s when Rolf Nilsson founded a small wholesale business supplying wooden clogs and work shoes to retailers. Nilsson established his company in Askloster, north of Varberg, near the Swedish coast. Nilsson later moved the company to Varberg itself. His success helped transform that town into the shoe capital of Sweden. By the turn of the next century, approximately 70 percent of all shoes in Sweden transited through Varberg.

Nilsson's interests soon extended beyond the work shoe segment. In 1959 he made the first of many trips to Italy, which by then had become one of the world's footwear capitals. Nilsson began importing men's and women's shoes from Italy, helping to revolutionize the Swedish footwear industry. Into the beginning of the 1960s, Nilsson was ready to move into the retail market. This was accomplished through the acquisition of a first shoe shop in 1961.

Nilsson continued to expand his retail operations through the 1960s, already building up a number of stores in Sweden. Helping to fuel the company's success was its early partnership with another fast-growing company, Denmark's Eccolet (later Ecco), which had pioneered the comfort shoe market in the 1960s. Nilsson played a major role in introducing the Ecco brand to Sweden, which grew into one of the brand's largest international markets.

These stores initially operated under various names. In 1977, however, Nilsson introduced a new brand name, Din Sko, or "Your Shoe" in Swedish. Nilsson then created a subsidiary for this operation, Din Sko

AB, and converted all of his existing stores to the new name.

INTERNATIONAL STEPS IN THE EIGHTIES

Nilsson maintained his wholesale operations alongside his fast-growing retail business through the 1980s. Nilsson's company had also become a breeding ground of sorts for Sweden's footwear industry. Over the years, a number of the company's former employees left the company to establish their own footwear and retail businesses. Many of these companies remained in Varberg, helping consolidate the town's position as Sweden's footwear capital.

While Sweden continued to offer plenty of room for building his retail chain, Nilsson also began eyeing expansion into the larger Scandinavian market in the early 1980s. The company's first move outside of Sweden came in 1981, with the launch of the Din Sko chain in Norway. That country remained Nilsson's largest international market into the next century, with nearly 50 of the company's stores, including 32 Din Sko shops.

When Ecco decided to move into the retail market in the early 1980s, Nilsson became one of its early franchise licensees. This enabled the company to build up a network of Ecco-branded shops in Sweden. Nilsson also rolled out Ecco's in-store boutique format, which became part of the Din Sko chain. Over the next two decades, Nilsson added 43 self-standing Ecco stores and 37 in-store boutiques its operations.

Nilsson also sought others areas of growth for his retail business in the 1980s. Din Sko targeted the mid-priced family footwear market and featured primarily Nilsson's own footwear designs. Nilsson, however, spotted two new market opportunities into the late 1980s. By then, the trend toward designer-label and brand-name clothing, accessories, and footwear, which had swept through much of the West from the late 1970s, had reached Sweden as well.

NEW BRANDS IN THE NINETIES

Nilsson responded by launching a second retail format, modifying his name to create the Nilson chain of stores in 1989. These shops targeted the midpriced footwear segment and offered a range of popular footwear brands. The Nilson chain grew strongly, extending its operations to 46 stores throughout Sweden.

Nilsson had also recognized the potential for developing a discount retail footwear format. This led to the launch of Skopunkten in 1989, which quickly captured a leading share of the low-priced footwear market. The Skopunkten stores differed from both the Din Sko and Nilson stores by featuring a larger selling space of up to 500 square meters, more than five times the size of the smallest Nilson shops. Skopunkten stores were typically located in out-of-town shopping areas, taking advantage of the lower rents. They also encouraged shopping by offering additional discounts for multiple purchases. The Skopunkten format became one of the company's most successful, growing into a chain of 45 shops across Sweden.

The 1990s represented a new period of strong growth for the company's retail operations. In 1991 the company decided to focus its future solely on its retail wing and sold off its wholesale business that year. This decision followed on the completion of a major acquisition, of the Oscaria BATA footwear chain, in 1991. The Oscaria brand had been founded at the dawn of the 20th century, initially as a manufacturer, and had grown into Sweden's largest footwear company before its breakup at the beginning of the 1990s. Nilsson took over 67 Oscaria stores, which it then redesigned and later incorporated into its other retail formats.

NILSON GROUP IN 2000

The Oscaria acquisition set Nilsson itself on the course to becoming Sweden's footwear leader. Into the second half of the decade, the company sought to fill a gap in its retail portfolio. This was accomplished with the takeover of high-end footwear retailer Jerns in 1997. The Jerns stores focused on Sweden's major urban markets, and under Nilsson's ownership grew to include five stores in Stockholm, as well as shops in Göteborg, Malmö, and Uppsala. The Jerns acquisition was accompanied by the acquisition of handbag and accessories retailer, Palmgrens. Nilsson later exited the accessories market, however.

Nilsson had quite completed its portfolio of retail formats, however. In 1998 the company moved to capitalize on the fast-growing sports shoe market, launching its own sporting goods brand, Radical Sport. This format existed largely as an in-store boutique within the company's Nilson chain. The company nonetheless developed a self-standing store for the Radical Sport format, opening its first shop soon after.

The end of the 1990s brought other expansion opportunities. The company strengthened its presence in Sweden in 1998, buying up the Idoff Skor chain of shoe stores. Nilsson also took its first step into Finland that year, with the opening a Din Sko there. The company added its first Nilson store in Finland the following year. Over the next decade, the company's Finnish sub-

sidiary's operations grew to 11 Din Sko stores and three Nilson shops.

The company reached another major milestone in 2000, when founder Rolf Nilsson announced his decision to retire. In his place, he named Ingemar Charleson, who had joined the company at the age of 15 in 1969. As part of the transition, the company restructured all of its operations under a new holding company, called Nilson Group AB.

SHIFTING SOURCING IN 2009

At the turn of the century, Nilson also followed another important trend in the international footwear industry, as it shifted all product sourcing to the contract manufacturing markets in China and other Asian markets. In order to gain a greater proximity to these markets, the company opened a purchasing office in Hong Kong in 1998. This was followed by a second office in Taiwan in 2000. Nilson added a sales office on the Chinese mainland as well, in Wenzhou, in 2004.

The increase in the company's purchasing scope came in support of a new push to build its international operations. In 2000 the company launched the wider rollout of its retail formats into the Scandinavian markets, with an entry into Denmark. For this, the company opened two Din Sko stores, followed by a Nilson and Radical Sports store.

Norway, however, remained the group's largest foreign market. This position was reinforced with the opening of the company's first Skopunkten shop in that country in 2005. By 2010, that brand's Norwegian network reached five stores.

Nilson maintained the pace of its expansion through much of the second half of the decade, opening 50 stores between 2006 and 2008. These included the company's new Skogalleria concept, a large-scale shoe store format featuring 40,000 pairs of shoes across 3,000 square meters over three floors. Opened in October 2007, the Skogalleria featured boutiques for all of the group's retail formats.

Nilson's operations developed strongly elsewhere as well. In 2006 the company launched its first e-commerce site, for the Skopunkten brand. The success of that venture led it to roll out a e-commerce site for Din Sko in 2008. In that year, Nilson boosted its logistics side, opening a fully automated, centralized warehouse facility in Vanberg. Nilson also continued to adapt its purchasing infrastructure to changing market conditions. This led the company to shift part of its sourcing and product development operations to Vietnam in 2009. That country was at the time in the process of becoming a challenger in the low-cost manufacturing sector.

Nilson posted strong revenue gains through the decade as well, boosting its total revenues from SEK 1.5 billion in 2003 to SEK 2.8 billion by 2009. The company had also succeeded in securing a nearly 25 percent share of the total Swedish footwear market. Nilson continued to target further expansion, despite the economic crisis of the end of the decade, while remaining committed to its status as a family-owned private company. In just over 50 years, Nilson Group had grown to become Sweden's footwear heavyweight.

M. L. Cohen

PRINCIPAL SUBSIDIARIES

Nilson Group AB, Filial I Finland; Nilson Group AS (Norway).

PRINCIPAL OPERATING UNITS

Nilson; Radical Sports; Jerns; Din Sko; Skopunkten.

PRINCIPAL COMPETITORS

Venue Retail Group AB.

FURTHER READING

"Europas Första Skogalleria Öppnar den 27 September," *Mynewsdesk*, September 20, 2007.

"Expansion Resulterade I Ras: "Vi Ska Förbättra Resultatet," *DagensPS*, April 11, 2008.

Öhman, Jan-Eric, "Skilda Världar I Skobranschen," *Veckans Affärer*, August 16, 2004.

Petersson, Jessica, "Skostaden Varberg," *Varbergsposten*, April 17, 2008.

"Swedish Businessman Dissatisfied with Proposed EU Duties on Chinese Shoes," *People's Daily*, February 25, 2006.

"Swedish Footwear Industry Lags Behind," *Cleanclothes.org*, May 2, 2009.

"Swedish Shoe Giant Builds Fully Automated Distribution Centre," *Moving.se*, January 10, 2007.

Oberthur Technologies S.A.

---

50 quai Michelet
Levallois Perret, F-92300
France
Telephone: (+33 01) 55 46 72 00
Fax: (+33 01) 55 46 72 01
Web site: http://www.oberthur.com

Private Company
Incorporated: 1985 as François-Charles Oberthur Card
   Systems
Employees: 6,000
Sales: EUR 882 million ($1.26 billion) (2008)
NAICS: 323119 Other Commercial Printing; 334419
   Other Electronic Component Manufacturing

■ ■ ■

Oberthur Technologies S.A. is one of the world's leading specialists in the development of secure technologies for smart cards, identity systems, banknote and fiduciary printing, and automated teller machine (ATM) and other cash-protection systems. Paris-based Oberthur operates through four divisions. The Card Systems division is the world second-largest developer and producer of smart cards for use in mobile telephones, banking, transportation, television set-top boxes. This division also accounted for 80 percent of Oberthur Technologies' total sales of EUR 882 million ($1.26 billion) in 2008.

The Fiduciary Printing division is the world's third-largest printer of bank notes, checks, and related financial documents, supplying governments and banks in more than 50 countries. This division generates 12 percent of the group's revenues. Oberthur also manufactures and personalizes passports, driving licenses, and other identity documents through its Identity division, adding 6 percent to sales. The group's smallest division, Cash Protection, focuses on the ATM and cash transport sector. Oberthur Technologies is a private company controlled by the founding Savare family. Thomas Savare is the group's chief executive officer, and his father, the company's founder Jean-Pierre Savare, is its chairman.

19TH-CENTURY ORIGINS

Oberthur Technologies originated as a Rennes-based printing company founded by François-Charles Oberthür in 1842. (The family later abandoned the umlaut over the letter *u*.) Born in Strasbourg in 1818, Oberthur's father, François-Jacques Oberthur, owned a printing company in partnership with Alois Senefelder, the Austrian playwright who invented the concept of lithography. In 1838 François-Charles Oberthur moved to Rennes, in France's Brittany region, where he completed his lithography training in 1842. In that year, Oberthur and a partner opened their own printing company.

That business prospered and in 1852 constructed a new and larger printing works. By 1855, Oberthur had bought out his partner, and the business became known as Imprimerie Oberthur. By then, Oberthur had already received the first of several important contracts, that of publishing the *Almanach des Postes*, the annual calendar of the French postal service. Oberthur was to retain the exclusive printing rights to the calendar for more than

100 years. Other major clients for the company included Chemins de Fer de l'Ouest, for which Oberthur became the exclusive printer. The company was also the first in France to publish a telephone directory.

Oberthur was joined by his son, Charles, and the company's name changed to Oberthur et Fils in 1865. The company later became a partnership between Oberthur's widow, Charles, and another son René, before becoming a joint stock company in 1909. Oberthur and his sons were also noted ethnologists; as a result, the company became well-known for its printing work in this area. This interest also led the company to publish the *Repetoire des Couleurs*, written by René Oberthur and Henri Dauthenay in 1904. This book became France's official color reference work, used for determining the tints required for the printing of flowers, leaves, fruits, and so on.

René Oberthur took over as head of the company after his brother's death in 1924. Through the end of the 1930s, the company's production included annual printed materials, such as the La Poste calendar and other promotional materials, and it also set up a division to produce encyclopedias, manuals, and textbooks. The German occupation of France in 1940 led Oberthur into a third area of operation, when the Banque de France contracted the company to print bank notes in order to secure its supply during the war.

This business evolved into the group's fiduciary printing division following the war, as the company became a major printer of checks, stock certificates, and other fiduciary and financial documents. Oberthur became responsible for printing a small part of the new currency for the Communaute Financiere d'Afrique (CFA), a 13-nation region formerly under French colonial control. The company also became partly responsible for printing tickets for the weekly national lottery. The fiduciary division later teamed up with Switzerland's SICPA, which acquired a 50 percent stake in the business.

REBIRTH IN 1984

Jean Oberthur and sister Marthe Cartier-Bresson took over the company's operations in the postwar period. By 1960, both had retired from the company, marking the end of the Oberthur family's involvement in the company's direction. The 1960s also marked the height of Oberthur's long history of success, as the company's payroll swelled to more than 1,400 employees.

The 1970s, however, spelled disaster for the company, which saw its fortunes decline rapidly through that decade. By 1980, the company had slipped into losses. Deeply in debt, Oberthur was forced to declare bankruptcy in 1981. After a long strike and the occupation of the company by its workers, Imprimerie Oberthur's bank creditors broke the company up into three separate companies in 1983. The former printing and publishing operations quickly found buyers. The company's small fiduciary printing unit proved more difficult to sell.

In 1984, however, François-Charles Oberthur Fiduciaire caught the eye of Jean-Pierre Savare. Son of Russian immigrants, Savare had overcome his modest origins to enter the Banque de France, where he focused on restructuring troubled companies in the shipbuilding and printing industries. Savare had also gained some experience in the printing market, having at one time operated his own company, Editions de Chiffre, which focused on printing bookkeeping supplies and check forms. In 1984, Savare was given the task of devising a rescue plan for Oberthur Fiduciaire.

Instead, Savare, then 45 years old, decided to buy the company himself, paying one symbolic franc for the purchase. Savare counted on his former printing experience, as well as his relationship with parts of the French political elite, including the conservative party and future French president Jacques Chirac. Another helpful influence was the mayor of Rennes who was then serving as a minister in the French government.

As a result, with Savare at its head, Oberthur quickly began building up a new range of printing contracts. A major break for the company came with the contract to provide all printing services for the launch of

KEY DATES

1842: François Charles Oberthur founds a printing business in Rennes, France, with a partner.

1940: Oberthur launches its first bank note printing operations for the Banque de France, forming the fiduciary division.

1981: Oberthur goes bankrupt and is broken up into three separate businesses.

1984: Jean-Pierre Savare acquires François-Charles Oberthur Fiduciaire for one symbolic franc.

1990: Oberthur acquires Banknote Corporation of America.

2008: Oberthur becomes Oberthur Technologies and goes private.

the new instant Tac-o-Tac Lottery. Soon after, Oberthur took on an even bigger job, when the Banque de France awarded the company the contract as the exclusive printer of bank notes for the entire CFA zone, supplying notes for a total population of 93 million people.

INTERNATIONAL EXPANSION IN 1990

The former Oberthur's bankruptcy status provided Oberthur Fiduciaire with significant tax advantages in its early years. Using the previous business's losses to offset its own tax requirements, Oberthur Fiduciaire posted strong profits from its fast-growing operations. Savare, however, carefully reinvested these earnings back into the company. Among Oberthur's most significant investments during the 1980s was the installation of two large-scale and state-of-the-art printing presses, giving the company the capacity to print more than two billion bank notes per year.

This printing capacity supported the international growth of Oberthur's business. The collapse of the Soviet Union brought new opportunities for the company. As the former Eastern Bloc countries claimed their independence, they also developed their own currency and other financial and fiduciary notes and documents. Oberthur gained a number of contracts during this time, printing stock certificates for Romania, bank notes for Moldova and Azerbaijan, among others.

At the same time, Oberthur had also established an international presence. This began in 1990, when the company took over Banknote Corporation of America (BCA), sold as part of the merger between American Banknote and U.S. Banknote. The addition of BCA transformed Oberthur into the largest supplier of stamps to the U.S. Postal Service. Oberthur became the world's largest stamp printer, producing more than 10 billion per year.

Savare jumped at another growth opportunity, acquiring Canada's British American Banknote as well. This acquisition provided Oberthur with a major extension of its lottery printing division, which became known as Oberthur Gaming Technologies.

PLAYING THE RIGHT CARDS IN 1999

Savare had begun extending Oberthur into other areas as well. In 1991 the company created François-Charles Oberthur Cheques et Securité, launching its first entry into the Cash Protection field. This sector had started to grow strongly in France as the country adopted ATMs into the 1990s. In 1993 Oberthur boosted this division with the purchase of Axytrans, which specialized in developing protection systems for the cash transport sector.

The Cash Protection division remained only a small part of Oberthur's overall business, which reached $100 million in sales by the early 1990s, compared to just a few hundred thousand a decade earlier. A more significant extension for the company came through Savare's recognition in the mid-1980s that the banking industry's future lay in banking cards, rather than printed checks. Savare led Oberthur into bank card production in 1985, with the creation of Oberthur Card Systems. By 1987 Oberthur had formed a joint venture with Bull, then one of France's leading electronics groups and a pioneer in developing microchips for so-called smart cards. Oberthur and Bull initially launched a temporary joint venture, in which Oberthur supplied cards embedded with Bull's microchips.

The smart card market rose dramatically during the 1990s. As Savare had predicted, banking cards had come to rival and then replace checks as payment methods. The smart card industry had also been developing a wide variety of new applications for the technology. These included SIM cards, used for mobile telephone and television set-top boxes, as both markets soared from the late 1990s. In France and elsewhere, the use of smart cards became important parts of the national health care system as well.

Oberthur established Oberthur Smart Cards as a subsidiary in 1997. In 1998 Savare's son Thomas, who had initially worked at Banknote Corporation of America before becoming the head of Oberthur's

Fiduciary division, became the new subsidiary's chief. The company next attempted to claim a larger share of the smart card market, launching a takeover offer for Germany-based rival Orga Kartensystem. The company lost this bid, however, when another Germany company, Bundesdrukeri launched a counteroffer.

Oberthur next launched a far larger, and ultimately successful, takeover attempt, for De La Rue Card Systems, the smart card operations of the United Kingdom's De La Rue Group. Oberthur paid $318 million for this acquisition, which quadrupled the company's total revenues to $490 million, making it the third-largest smart card producer in the world. Oberthur Card Systems could also boast of holding the top position in a number of categories, including Pay-TV smart cards and the production of VISA and MasterCard credit cards.

NEW MARKETS IN THE NEW CENTURY

Shrewdly, Savare spun off Oberthur Card Systems as a public company in 2000, selling only a small stake in its smart card subsidiary. Savare's timing proved fortunate, coming at the height of the technology stock cycle. As a result, the company easily recovered nearly all of the cost of the De La Rue acquisition.

Oberthur Card Systems rapidly grew to become the largest part of Oberthur's overall business, accounting for more than 60 percent of its total revenues by 2003 and up to 80 percent by the end of the decade. Part of the rise came through the company's investment drive, including the construction of new factories in the United States, and, in 2001, its entry into the fast-growing Chinese market as well. Also in 2001, Oberthur increased its European presence, buying up Spanish smart card producer Logica Impresora S.A. The following year, the group expanded its French business as well, taking over rival Rapsodia.

The expansion of Oberthur's international network continued through the decade, including the construction of a factory in Brazil in 2004, the acquisition of South Africa's Africard in 2005, and the opening of a factory in India in 2006. Next, Oberthur added operations in Asian financial capital Singapore with the purchase of I'M Technologies in 2007. For $34 million, Oberthur acquired nine factories in Asia and one of the leading smart card producers in the region. By then, Oberthur's total revenues had topped EUR 700 million.

FAMILY CONTROLLED COMPANY IN 2008

The growth of its card business prompted Oberthur to narrow its focus, and in 2007 the company sold off its

$140 million-per-year Gaming Technologies division to U.S.-based Scientific Games Corporation. Instead, Oberthur had been on the lookout for a new addition to its smart card operations. This came in February 2008, when the company reached an agreement to pay $111 million for XponCard, in Sweden. This acquisition boosted Oberthur into the global number two position, behind only Gemalto (formerly Gemplus). Oberthur's share of the market rose to 17 percent, while its revenues soared to EUR 735 million (approximately $1 billion).

Soon after the XponCard acquisition was completed, Jean-Pierre Savare announced his decision to turn over the leadership of the company to Thomas Savare. The Savare family also carried out a restructuring of their holdings in 2008, merging Oberthur Gaming Systems and François Charles Oberthur Fiduciaire into a single company called Oberthur Technologies. That company temporarily retained its listing on the Euronext Paris stock exchange, with the Savare family holding more than 71 percent of its shares. In September 2008, however, the family launched a buyout of the company's minority shareholders, then delisted the company.

Oberthur Technologies maintained its growth plans, despite the global economic downturn. The company launched a $15 million expansion of its factory in Exton, Pennsylvania, which then became its primary smart card production facility in the United States in 2009. In that year, the company launched several new technologies, particularly in the growing category of "contactless" cards. The company introduced its new Smart Lumiere card, a translucent card that signaled the completion of a transaction by lighting up, in November 2009. Oberthur also unveiled SimSense, a handset-independent SIM card with motion detection capabilities.

Oberthur international expansion continued into the start of the next decade. In January 2010, the company acquired Dyetron S.A., based in Colombia, which provided payment card personalization services for the Latin American market. This move came as part of Oberthur's effort to become a major player in the conversion of that region and others, including the United States and Eastern Europe away from the less secure magnetic-strip card technology to microchip-based smart card technology. From 19th-century printer and then bankruptcy in 1984, Oberthur Technologies had grown to become a world leader in its niche the new century.

M. L. Cohen

PRINCIPAL SUBSIDIARIES

Oberthur Technologies (USA); Oberthur Technologies AG (Switzerland); Oberthur Technologies BV (Netherlands); Oberthur Technologies de Mexico, S. de R.L. de C.V.; Oberthur Technologies Denmark AS; Oberthur Technologies Iberica; Oberthur Technologies Italia SRL (Italy); Oberthur Technologies Ltda (Argentina); Oberthur Technologies Norway A/S; Oberthur Technologies Oy (Finland); Oberthur Technologies Romania S.R.L.; Oberthur Technologies Sp. z.o.o. (Poland); Oberthur Technologies Sweden AB; Oberthur Technologies UK Ltd.

PRINCIPAL DIVISIONS

Card Systems; Identity; Fiduciary; Cash Protection.

PRINCIPAL COMPETITORS

Gemalto N.V.

FURTHER READING

Bender, Klaus W., *Moneymakers: The Secret World of Banknote Printing*, Berlin: Wiley-VCH, 2006.

Beyer, Caroline, "Thomas Savare Reprend le Flambeau," *Le Figaro*, July 7, 2008.

"Le CA Trimestriel d'Oberthur Dopé par la Téléphone et l'Asie," *Capital*, July 23, 2008.

Maury, Matthieu, "Oberthur Devient le Deuxième Fabricant Mondial de Cartes à Puce," *L'Usine Nouvelle*, April 8, 2008.

Mesitermann, Nathalie, "France's Oberthur to Buy Out Minorities," *Reuters*, September 23, 2008.

Michelson, Marcel, "Oberthur Bids for XponCard to Become Global No. 2," *Reuters*, February 19, 2008.

"Oberthur Plans to Go Private," *American Banker*, September 30, 2008, p. 12.

"Oberthur Technologies Acquires Service Center in Colombia to Expand EMV Delivery into Latin America," *Investment Weekly News*, January 30, 2010, p. 210.

"Oberthur to Become Private," *Smart Insights*, October 2, 2008.

"Oberthur Unveils EMV-in-a-Box," *American Banker*, November 5, 2009, p. 12.

Remoué, Agathe, "Jean-Pierre Savare, Père et Patron," *Le Nouvel Hebdo*, April 15, 2002.

Wolfe, Daniel, "Oberthur Launches Light-Up Card," *American Banker*, November 6, 2009, p. 6.

OGF S.A.

———— ■ ————

31 rue de Cambrai
Paris, F-75946 Cedex 19
France
Telephone: (+33 01) 55 26 54 00
Fax: (+33 01) 55 26 57 71
Web site: http://www.pfg.fr

Private Company
Incorporated: 1899 as Pompes Funèbres Générales (PFG)
Employees: 5,600
Sales: EUR 520 million ($731 million) (2008)
NAICS: 812210 Funeral Homes; 339995 Burial Casket Manufacturing

■ ■ ■

OGF S.A. is France's leading provider of funeral and burial services, a profession called *pompes funèbres* in French. The company operates nearly 400 funeral homes and 45 crematoriums, supported by a network of 1,000 sales offices throughout France. OGF provides funeral and burial services under the brand names Pompes Funèbres Générales (PFG), the oldest part of the company founded in 1844; Roblot; and Dignité Funéraire. Another subsidiary, Maison Henri de Borniol, specializes in state funerals and burials of celebrities and other notable figures.

In addition to its funeral services, OGF provides financing services through subsidiaries OGF Courtage and OGF Prévoyance. The company also operates its own casket production unit, with two factories and a subsidiary producing marble tombs and headstones.

With more than 120,000 funeral services each year, OGF claims a 25 percent share of the French market. OGF is a private company acquired in a management buyout that was financed by Astorg Partners, which remains its majority shareholder. In 2008 OGF reported total revenues of EUR 520 million ($731 million). The company is led by President Philippe Lerouge.

ORIGINS IN 1844

OGF stemmed from one of France's earliest funeral services specialists, founded by Joseph Adolphe Ferdinand Langlé and four partners in 1844. Langlé had previously gained experience in the trade as the director of Paris's Compagnie Générale des Sépultures. That company's dominance of the Parisian market led Langlé to establish his company, called Langlé et Compagnie, on the city's outskirts.

Langlé soon found himself facing competition with the appearance of a new company, Vafflard, Panis et Cie, set up by the director of the Compagnie Générale des Sépultures in 1847. The following year, however, the two companies agreed to work together, forming the Entreprise Générale des Pompes Funèbres. Langlé headed the combined operation, while Vafflard continued to lead Vafflard et Cie, as well as Compagnie Générale des Sépultures. Under terms of the partnership, Entreprise Générale des Pompes Funèbres was established for a 50-year period.

In 1852, however, Langlé and Vafflard once again found themselves going head-to-head, with Vafflard winning the bid to take over the funeral service operations for the city of Paris. Despite both companies remaining parts of Entreprise Générale des Pompes Funèbres, they now became bitter rivals. Langlé et Cie ultimately emerged triumphant. In 1899, following the end of the 50-year agreement, Entreprise Générale des Pompes Funèbres dissolved, and a new public company was created called Pompes Funèbres Générales (PFG).

MONOPOLY MARKET FROM 1904

Through the 19th century (and for most of French history before that), burials had been the exclusive province of the Catholic Church, which called upon the services of various companies and private parties in order to carry out the various stages of the burial rites and customs of the time. The name of the funeral services sector, *pompes funèbres*, underscored the somewhat theatrical nature of the French rites.

In 1904, however, as the French government prepared new legislation providing for the separation of church and state in the country, it also passed legislation removing the funeral services sector from the religious sphere. Churches controlled only the so-called interior parts of the funeral rite, that is, the religious ceremony. External services, including the operation of cemeteries, preparation and transport of the dead, and burial services, became public services under the exclusive province of the country's municipalities.

Where larger cities tended to develop their own funeral services departments, smaller towns and villages instead called upon private concessionaires, which then received the exclusive right to provide burial services in the town. PFG had placed itself in a strong position to profit from the change in legislation. In the early 20th century, the company set into place a network of more than 15 branches offices, both in the Parisian region and in the French provinces, including the city of Angers. As a result, the company quickly gained the exclusive concessions for these markets following the legislation.

In 1905 the company received a major boost when a group of 30 Parisian suburbs granted the company their funeral services concessions as well. PFG originally received a 20-year concession for these markets; the company's exclusive concession for these markets would remain in place until the early 1990s.

EXPANSION IN THE 20TH CENTURY

PFG continued adding new branches and new exclusive concessions. At the same time, the company accelerated its expansion through the acquisition of a number of existing funeral services companies. The first and most important of these came in 1906, when the company acquired Roblot. That company had built up its own network of concessions in Marseille and other communities in France's southeastern region.

PFG made a string of acquisitions following World War I, including larger groups such as Pompes Funèbres Réunies, Pompes Funèbres des Régions Libérées, Jouvin, Dumond, Lamy-Trouvain. PFG's acquisitions included many smaller locally and regionally operating companies, such as L Cornu et Cie, Pompes Funèbres Rhodaniennes, Pompes Funèbres Catalanes, and Compagnie Générale des Pompe Funèbres de Lyon. Another important acquisition made during the interwar period was that of Henri de Borniol, a company founded in 1820. De Borniol ultimately became specialized in providing services for state, celebrity, and related funerals and memorial services.

By 1930 PFG already counted more than 200 branches throughout France. This number was to rise 1,000 by the end of the century. To a large extent, PFG maintained the original names of these businesses, in part to retain a local feel to what had become a national business.

PFG also branched out into a number of related sectors. In 1919 the company founded its own industrial division, building caskets under the name Menuiserie Générale Française, which later became known as Compagnie Générale de Scierie et de Menuiserie. To this operation, the company added its own business supplying tombs and headstones, called Compagnie Générale de Marbrerie, in 1936.

FUNERAL HOMES IN THE SIXTIES

The period following World War II marked the beginning of the modernization of the French funeral services market. One of the major changes came with the replacement of the horse-drawn hearse with motorized vehicles. The first motorized hearses had already appeared in the 1930s; by the 1950s, the market had turned entirely toward motorized vehicles. Accompany-

```
┌─────────────────────────────────────────────┐
│                                               │
│               KEY DATES                       │
│                    ■                          │
│  ┌─────────────────────────────────────────┐ │
│                                               │
│  1844:  Joseph Adolphe Ferdinand Langlé and   │
│         four partners found Langlé et Cie to  │
│         provide funeral services outside of   │
│         Paris.                                │
│  1848:  Langlé joins with rival Vafflard to   │
│         form the Entreprise Générale des      │
│         Pompes Funèbres.                      │
│  1899:  The company goes public as Pompes     │
│         Funèbres Générales (PFG).             │
│  1906:  PFG acquires Roblot, based in the     │
│         southeast of France.                  │
│  1962:  Roblot becomes the first in France to │
│         introduce the funeral home concept.   │
│  1972:  OGF becomes the holding company for   │
│         PFG's operations.                     │
│  1979:  Lyonnaise des Eaux acquires OGF.      │
│  1995:  Lyonnaise des Eaux sells OGF to       │
│         United States-based Service           │
│         Corporation International (SCI).       │
│  2004:  SCI sells OGF to a management buyout  │
│         backed by Vestar Capital Partners.    │
│  2007:  Vestar sells OGF to Astorg Partners.  │
│  2010:  OGF sales network tops 1,000 sales    │
│         offices and nearly 400 funeral homes. │
│                                               │
└─────────────────────────────────────────────┘
```

ing this change was an ongoing simplification of the traditional French funeral rites.

The rising strength of the modern medical professions in the second half of the 20th century also had a profound impact on funerals in France. Until the 1960s, the vast majority of French deaths occurred at home. By the 1960s, however, an increasing number of deaths began to occur in hospitals, in large part because the vast advances made in medical treatments and technologies had made it possible to prolong people's lives in the face of disease and illness. This "medicalization" of death had a flip side, however. The custom of allowing the aged to die in their own homes became increasingly marginalized, and even something of a taboo, and the increasing number of deaths in hospitals quickly led to a shortage of morgue space in which to hold the bodies before their burial.

Hospital morgues offered little if no accommodation and comfort for grieving family members, and families were unwilling and unable to bring the dead back to their homes. At the beginning of 1960s, however, a number of PFG executives had traveled to the United States, where they were introduced to the concept of the funeral home. PFG, through its Roblot subsidiary, decided to introduce the concept to France, opening the first *athanée* in Menton, in the south of France in 1962.

By 1965 PFG itself opened the first funeral home under its own name, in Villeneuve-Saint-Georges. The company called this new structure a *funerarium*. Later, the companies adopted a French variation of the U.S. funeral home called a *maison funéraire*. These new structures operated essentially as private morgues, providing more appropriate surroundings for holding the dead and accommodating their mourners prior to the funeral.

ACQUISITION BY LYONNAISE DES EAUX IN 1979

PFG continued to open funeral homes throughout France. By the 1970s, the company's network counted nearly 400 homes. PFG also responded to the steadily growing demand for cremation services. While crematoriums were generally owned by municipalities, PFG gained the concessions to manage an increasing number of these facilities.

PFG remained a confederation of mortuary services companies until the early 1970s. In 1972 the company restructured, transferring its assets to a company called Omnium de Gestion et de Financement (OGF). As part of the transfer, PFG gained control of OGF, while OGF acquired all of PFG's property holdings as well as its industrial and other operations. These were placed under a new company, called Auxia. Other Auxia operations included a funeral financing business, a security services company, and a packaging and conditioning subsidiary.

PFG also took on a role in another important area in funeral services, that of the preservation of the body. This service had been pioneered in France by the Marette company, originally founded in 1887 as a Laundromat. By the turn of the 20th century, Marette had increasingly begun to provide after-death disinfecting services. Into the 1950s, as the need for preserving bodies before burial increased, Marette began developing its own techniques, initially based on the use of dry ice. Under the encouragement of PFG, Francis Marette, grandson of the company's family, made a tour of the European funeral sector, returning to France with a new embalming technique that the company dubbed *thanatopraxie*.

With PFG's support, Marette grew rapidly into the next decade, becoming PFG's primary subcontractor for pre-burial preservation care. Marette changed its name, becoming Hygecobel. PFG also acquired a stake in the company, becoming its largest shareholder in 1976. Hygecobel then became a subsidiary of Auxia.

PFG itself became part of a larger group in the late 1970s. With control of as much as 80 percent of France's funeral services market, PFG became an attractive acquisition target for Lyonnaise des Eaux. That company had become one of France's leading water utilities and water services operators, before launching a diversification program into other public services areas in the 1970s. The acquisition of PFG, which operated as a de facto public service, fit in with Lyonnaise des Eaux's diversification strategy. Following the acquisition, the company was restructured again, with OGF becoming the parent company of PFG as well.

LOSING THE MONOPOLY IN 1993

As part of Lyonnaise des Eaux, OGF launched an international expansion strategy during the late 1980s. The company expanded into a number of European markets, adding operations in Belgium, Switzerland, and Italy. In 1987 the company also established a small business in Singapore, as a first step toward future plans of expanding in the Southeast Asian region. In 1989 the company agreed to merge PFG with the United Kingdom's Hodgson et Kenyon, a leading player in the British funeral market. The merged businesses became known as PHK, with OGF as its major shareholder. OGF also transferred most of its international operations into the new company. Into the 1990s, PHK, which emerged as the United Kingdom's leading funeral services group, changed its name again to Plantsbrook PLC.

By then, OGF found itself under increasing pressure. On the one hand, the rising number of cremations, which tended to require fewer services and at lower costs, had begun to cut into the group's funeral services revenues. On the other hand, the group found its monopoly increasingly under pressure. Indeed, since the early 1980s and even before, efforts to break the system of monopoly concessions had long been underway.

By 1986 the French government made a first, if limited, attempt to legislate the end of the funeral monopolies. This legislation encouraged the development of a number of new competitors. The most important among these was a new funeral chain founded by a member of the Leclerc family, founders of one of France's leading supermarket and hypermarket chains. As a result, OGF's share of the market dropped back to 50 percent by 1990.

Despite the new tide in the funeral services sector, OGF's response remained largely limited to the legal front, as it contested attempts to liberalize the market. These efforts, however, proved futile. In 1993 the French government at last passed legislation completely ending the monopoly concessions altogether and liberalizing the funeral services sector.

REGROUPING IN 1998

OGF responded with a new round of acquisitions, picking up a number of smaller operations through the middle of the decade, in a belated attempt to consolidate its increasingly fragile position in France. This led the company to sell off its 46 percent stake in Plantsbrook PLC in 1994, for £81 million (approximately $130 million), enabling the company to post a net profit of £298 million for the year.

Soon after, Lyonnaise des Eaux announced that as OGF's operations no longer fit within its public services mandate, it was selling the company to United States-based Service Corporation International (SCI) in 1995 for $422 million. SCI, which had already become the leader in the U.S. market, was then in the process of a European expansion strategy. Nonetheless, the acquisitions of OGF appeared ill-timed, considering the company's era as France's dominant funeral services group already belonged to the past. Indeed, just two years after the 1993 legislation, OGF's market share had dwindled to just 30 percent.

OGF had restructured its PFG operations at the beginning of the 1990s, which were reorganized into a number of separate, regionally operating companies. In 1998 the company carried out a new reorganization, regrouping all of its operations under a new holding company, OGF S.A. Also during the decade, OGF carried out a company-wide cost-cutting effort, including the elimination of more than 1,600 jobs. At the same time, the company launched a new marketing program and developed its range of services to accommodate the increasingly diverse French society.

Despite these efforts, OGF continued to lose ground at the turn of the 21st century. By 2000 the company had replaced its top management several times. The company also suffered through a major strike by its workforce in the fall of that year. The arrival of Philippe Lerouge, who took over as CEO in 2000, appeared to put an end to this period of instability. Nonetheless, OGF continued to struggle against the decline in its market share, which slipped back to just 25 percent by the end of the decade.

NEW OWNERS IN THE NEW CENTURY

By then, SCI had already begun to revise its own expansion strategy, exiting several of its international operations. In 2003 the U.S. company announced its plan to seek a buyer for OGF as well. In 2004 SCI announced that it had agreed to sell 75 percent of OGF to a management buyout backed by Vestar Capital Partners. Under terms of the deal, Vestar agreed to pay EUR 300 million to acquire 65 percent of OGF directly, with 10 percent held by OGF's management and employees.

OGF changed ownership again in 2007, now with Astrog Partners acquiring a majority stake in the company. By then, OGF appeared to have regained some of its lost momentum, expanding its network to 1,100 sales offices, nearly 380 funeral homes, and 45 crematoriums. The company had also launched a fourth brand (alongside PFG, Roblot, and Henri de Borniol) called Dignité Funéraire. This label served as an umbrella brand for more than 250 regional and local businesses held by OGF.

OGF continued its expansion into the end of the decade. In 2006 the company launched OGF Courtage, boosting its range of funeral financing services. The company also took over rival group Parthenos in 2007, acquiring its PLM-branded operations. At the same time, the group expanded its industrial operations, including its casket-production facilities. By 2010 the group was producing more than 85,000 caskets at its Jussy, France, factory alone. OGF remained the leader of the French funeral services market, with revenues of EUR 520 million ($731 million) and a 25 percent market share. In the meantime, the aging of the French population, particularly of the baby boom generation, promised strong growth prospects for OGF in the near future.

M. L. Cohen

PRINCIPAL SUBSIDIARIES

Compagnie Générale de Marbrerie; Compagnie Générale de Scierie et de Menuiserie; OGF Prevoyance SA; OGF Courage S.A.

PRINCIPAL DIVISIONS

Funeral Services Division; Funeral Finance Division; Industrial Division.

PRINCIPAL OPERATING UNITS

Pompes Funèbres Générales (PFG); Roblot; Dignité Funéraire; Maison Henri de Borniol.

PRINCIPAL COMPETITORS

Les Pompes Funèbres de la Liberté; Roc E LeClerc S.A.

FURTHER READING

"Astorg Partners Rachète OGF," *Les Echos*, July 30, 2007.

Boissin, Olivier, and Pascale Trompette, *Les services funéraires: Du monopole public au marché concurrentiel*, DARES, Ministère des affaires sociales, du travail et de la solidarité, 2002.

Chevallard, Lucille, "Le Groupe OGF Repris par Son Management, en Partenariat avec Vestar," *Les Echos*, January 21, 2004, p. 32.

———, "Les Pompes Funèbres Générales Vont Etre Mises en Vente," *Les Echos*, June 10, 2003, p. 24.

Clemens, Monique, "L'Usine PFG de Jussey Fabrique des Cercueils Développement Durable," *Les Echos*, January 6, 2010.

Epinay, Benedicte, "La Guerre des Prix N'aura Pas Lieu," *Les Echos*, February 11, 1993, p. 16.

"Le Leader des Pompes Funèbres en France Passe Sous Pavillon Américain," *L'Expansion*, January 20, 2004.

Licata, Danièle, "La Mort au Prix Fort," *L'Expansion*, February 1, 2007.

"SCI Wins Auction for French Funerals Giant PFG," *Mergers & Acquisitions International*, July 17, 1995, p. 1.

Smith, Alex Duval, "McFunerals Storm Gallic Market," *Guardian*, July 15, 1995, p. 37.

Tillier, Alan, "US Funeral March into Europe," *European*, July 14, 1995, p. 16.

Oldcastle, Inc.

---

375 Northridge Road, Suite 350
Atlanta, Georgia 30350
U.S.A.
Telephone: (770) 804-3363
Toll Free: (800) 899-8455
Fax: (770) 804-3369
Web site: http://www.oldcastle.com

Wholly Owned Subsidiary of CRH plc
Incorporated: 1978
Employees: 39,810
Sales: $14 billion (2009 est.)
NAICS: 327331 Concrete Block and Brick Manufacturing; 327390 Other Concrete Product Manufacturing

■ ■ ■

Oldcastle, Inc., is the U.S. subsidiary of the Irish global building materials firm CRH plc. Based in Atlanta, Georgia, and serving all 50 states and four Canadian provinces, Oldcastle is made up of six units. Oldcastle Materials is a vertically integrated supplier of aggregates, asphalt, ready mix concrete, and construction and paving services. Oldcastle Architectural produces concrete masonry, paving, clay brick, and lawn and garden products, as well as packaged cement mixes, concrete roof tiles, lightweight aggregates, and bagged decorative stone and lime.

Oldcastle Precast produces such concrete structures as storm shelters, catch basins, utility vaults, drainage and septic tanks, wall panels, concrete barriers, and retaining walls. Focusing on building envelope solutions is Oldcastle Glass, which serves architects and building designers, developers and contractors, with architectural windows, skylights, entrance doors, architectural glass, and other custom-engineered products.

Also part of the Oldcastle family is Oldcastle Construction Accessories, maker of welded wire, concrete reinforcement, and anchoring systems; and Oldcastle Distribution, which distributes interior and exterior building products to both residential and commercial contractors from more than 200 locations. Because Oldcastle employs a decentralized approach to its business, most of the companies within the Oldcastle units operate under their own names, many of them run by the families that founded them.

PARENT COMPANY FORMED: 1970

Oldcastle's parent company was formed in 1970 as Cement-Roadstone Holdings (CRH) Ltd. through the merger of Ireland's two authorized cement producers: Roadstone Ltd., a family-owned company founded in the 1930s, and Irish Cement Ltd., which was controlled by Danish interests. CRH was taken public in 1973 to fund an effort to expand beyond the Irish market. A year later CRH acquired a Dutch company, marking its first international venture. Acquisitions in the United Kingdom followed in the 1970s and soon CRH began looking to the U.S. market.

The head of development for CRH, Don Godson, was dispatched to New York City in 1977 to scout for potential acquisitions and he was also responsible for setting up a U.S. subsidiary. As a name for the new company he used a village in County Meath, Ireland, called Oldcastle, where he enjoyed fishing. The business was incorporated in 1978 with Godson as its chief executive officer. In November of that year Amcor, Inc., a Utah-based company that produced concrete products from five plants in Utah, Colorado, and Idaho, was acquired. Given the western location of the operations, Godson relocated from New York City to the Los Angeles, California, suburb of Brentwood, where he established Oldcastle's first headquarters.

PRECAST UNIT FORMED: 1981

One of the Amcor plants was located in Littleton, Colorado, where Oldcastle then targeted Carder Concrete Products, producer of concrete pipe products from plants in Littleton and Casper, Wyoming. While its owner deliberated on selling the business, Oldcastle in November 1979 bought a manhole manufacturer in Colorado Springs. Carder then agreed to join up with Oldcastle, and Carder Concrete Products became part of the Oldcastle family in April 1980.

The company's next acquisition was completed in early 1981, with the purchase of Utility Vault Company (UVC), an innovative concern that produced high-quality concrete vault products that brought with it plants in Phoenix, Portland, San Francisco, and Seattle, as well as a plant under construction in Los Angeles. UVC laid the foundation for the Oldcastle Precast unit.

Although generating about $100 million in annual sales, Oldcastle was very much a regional operator. The company branched out to the eastern part of the United States in 1985. Tipped off by a Wall Street investment bank, Oldcastle acquired Albany, New York-based Callanan Industries, producer of aggregates and asphalt. Founded by an Irish American named Peter Callanan in the late 1880s, the company was among the oldest in its industry in the United States. One of Godson's protégés in the CRH development office, Liam O'Mahony, was brought in to run the business.

With a toehold in the East, Oldcastle then began to build up its assets in this portion of the country. In

1987, for example, it acquired N.C. Products, a maker of concrete products with several plants in North Carolina. Oldcastle also looked to the glass fabrication field. In 1989 the company acquired a glass fabrication company. A year later Oldcastle became the largest glass fabricator in the United States when it paid $135 million for Dallas-based HGP Industries in 1990, adding 13 plants.

REORGANIZATION IN 1990

In 1990 Oldcastle expanded its masonry business by acquiring three companies that together added more than $40.7 million in revenues. About half of that amount came from Bethesda, Maryland-based Betco Block & Products Inc., serving customers within a 200-mile radius that included Washington, D.C., and Baltimore. Betco sold directly to builders and home centers. The other acquisitions were Hatfield, Pennsylvania-based Eastern Prestressed Concrete Systems, and Greensboro, North Carolina-based Goria Enterprises Inc.

With annual sales in the $500 million range, Oldcastle reorganized its operation beginning in 1990. Instead of focusing on regions, the company was then arranged along product lines, resulting in the Materials Group, Architectural Products Group, Precast Group, and Glass Group. Due to the impact of a recession, Oldcastle did not resume its acquisition strategy until 1993, when it purchased Pennsy Supply, a Pennsylvania company.

There was a change at the helm at Oldcastle in 1994. Godson became the chief executive at CRH, and O'Mahony succeeded him as Oldcastle's head. O'Mahony continued the company's aggressive expansion, in that same year adding Lebanon Rock of Pennsylvania, Connecticut's Balf Co., Boston-area P.J. Keating and Co., as well as five asphalt plants and a pair of quarries from New York-based Sullivan Lafarge. Because so much of the company's growth since the late 1980s had been east of the Mississippi River, the company decided in 1994 to move its corporate headquarters to Atlanta, where Oldcastle was already represented.

GROWTH THROUGH
ACQUISITIONS

With the U.S. economy rapidly picking up steam, Oldcastle's expansion pace picked up in 1995 as the company reached out in a number of areas. The Materials Group, previously limited to the East, made a westward move by acquiring Utah-based Staker Paving and Construction, an asphalt, aggregates, and construction company. A year later the group paid $87 million

KEY DATES

1978: Oldcastle, Inc., founded as U.S. subsidiary of CRH plc.
1990: Company reorganized along product lines.
1994: Headquarters moved to Atlanta, Georgia.
1996: Oldcastle Distribution unit formed.
2006: Ashland Paving and Construction Inc. acquired.

for Jack P. Parson Companies, operator of quarries in Nevada, Idaho, and Utah.

The Staker-Parson combination became a platform for further roll-up acquisitions in the West, serving a similar function as Callanan on the East Coast, where several deals were completed in 1996. Oldcastle added New York-based Ritangela and Brooks Products, as well as Foster & Southeastern of Massachusetts, and the Materials Group completed Oldcastle's largest deal to date, the $254 million acquisition of Tilcon New York Inc., a roadstone company serving the northeastern United States.

In addition to growing its national footprint, Oldcastle was eager to add a fifth product group. With the help of Wall Street firm UBS, Oldcastle considered lumberyards and insulation before settling on roofing and siding. In the summer of 1996 Oldcastle paid about $121 million for a national roofing and siding distributor, New Jersey-based Allied Building Products, which formed the basis for the Oldcastle Distribution unit. As a result of the Tilcon and Allied acquisitions, Oldcastle became the largest construction materials supplier in the Northeast.

Oldcastle continued to grow both internally and externally in the latter half of the 1990s. N.C. Products, for example, opened a new pipe manufacturing plant in 1997. The Materials Group moved into the Northwest, acquiring Spokane, Washington-based CPM Development Corporation, an aggregate, concrete, and asphalt producer. In October 1997 Oldcastle added Trenwyth Industries in Pennsylvania, Akron Brick and Block in Ohio, and New York Trap Rock. In 1999 Michigan's largest asphalt and paving contractor, Thompson-McCully Cos., was brought into the fold at the cost of $422 million. Also that year, Oldcastle acquired three concrete roof tile plants located in Arizona, California, and Florida from MonierLifetile LLC.

O'Mahony left Oldcastle at the start of the new century, once again succeeding Godson, who retired as CRH's chief executive. Under O'Mahony's guidance, Oldcastle increased revenues to more than $3 billion and operating profits to $276.8 million, making it the chief contributor to CRH's balance sheet. O'Mahony was not reticent about his goals for the parent company, telling the press that he intended to double the company every five to seven years.

21ST CENTURY BRINGS RAPID EXPANSION

Oldcastle was to be the key driver behind CRH's growth, which would be achieved both organically and through acquisitions. Several new plants were under construction and came on line in 2000 and 2001, in Boston; Cleveland; Easton, Pennsylvania; Fontana, California; and Knoxville, Tennessee. Another new plant had already opened in Waco, Texas, in 1999, and was beginning to contribute to the balance sheet. On the acquisition side, Oldcastle paid $362 million in 2000 for Shelly Co., an Ohio paving contractor with integrated aggregate and asphalt operations.

A year later Oldcastle spent another $138 million on a similar company doing business in northern New Jersey and New York City, Mount Hope Rock Products. Also in 2001 Oldcastle acquired ready mix and quarry assets in the Salt Lake City market. The Oldcastle Architectural Product Group expanded in 2002 with the addition of Charlotte, North Carolina-based W.R. Bonsal Co. In that same year Monroe Inc., an aggregate business in Idaho, was acquired. In 2003 the Materials Group grew larger with the $177 million purchase of Toledo, Ohio-based SE Johnson, a major aggregate and asphalt producer in northern Ohio, southeastern Michigan, and northeastern Indiana.

Oldcastle refrained from further acquisitions until 2006, when the Materials Group completed by far the largest deal in its history to date, paying $1.3 billion for Ashland Paving and Construction Inc., the highway construction division of Ashland Inc. that included 93 aggregate production facilities, 31 ready mix concrete plants, and 226 hot mix asphalt plants. These operations combined to generate about $2.5 billion in annual revenues.

Oldcastle did not retain all of the assets, opting later in 2006 to sell six asphalt businesses for $215 million. Also in 2006 Oldcastle acquired an Oregon business, Egge Sand & Gravel, which complemented other Oregon aggregate operations the company had picked up in the early years of the decade. Foothills Concrete Pipe and Products in Platteville, Colorado, was added to complement the Littleton, Colorado, operation.

NEW GROUP FORMED: 2006

In the meantime, the parent company became involved in construction accessories and decided to pursue this field in North America as well. In April 2006 Oldcastle therefore established a base for a new Construction Accessories Group with the acquisition of MMI Products Inc., a Houston-based maker of wire-based building products serving the infrastructure, commercial, and residential construction sectors.

Oldcastle's Materials Group added Daytona Beach, Florida-based Conrad Yelvington Distributors Inc. in 2007, but business conditions were not conducive for further expansion in the short term. Contributing factors included high energy costs, a slowdown in construction due to a collapse in the housing market, and a credit crunch that had an adverse impact on the economy. Nevertheless, Oldcastle was a $14 billion business and remained well positioned for long-term growth.

Ed Dinger

PRINCIPAL DIVISIONS

Oldcastle Materials; Oldcastle Architectural; Oldcastle Precast; Oldcastle Glass; Oldcastle Construction Accessories; Oldcastle Distribution.

PRINCIPAL COMPETITORS

Compagnie de Saint-Gobain; Guardian Industries Corp.; Lafarge North America Inc.

FURTHER READING

Brooks, Tom, "Oldcastle Thrives on Demand for Landscaping PR," *Atlanta Business Chronicle,* March 13, 2000.

"CRH Boss Aims to Be the Predator Not the Prey," *Irish Times,* March 24, 2000, p. 54.

Heschmeyer, Mark, "Irish Building Materials Giant Buys Bethesda Masonry Firm," *Washington Business Journal,* February 19, 1990, p. 7.

McDonald, Sherri Buri, "Owner Sells Eugene, Ore., Sand, Gravel Business to European Conglomerate," *Eugene (Ore.) Register Guard,* November 2, 2006.

Oldenburg Group Inc.

1717 West Civic Drive
Milwaukee, Wisconsin 53209
U.S.A.
Telephone: (414) 977-1717
Fax: (414) 977-1700
Web site: http://www.oldenburggroup.com

Private Company
Incorporated: 1982
Employees: 1,200
Sales: $720 million (2008 est.)
NAICS: 333131 Mining Machinery and Equipment
Manufacturing; 335122 Commercial, Industrial,
and Institutional Electric Lighting Fixture
Manufacturing; 336612 Boat Building

■ ■ ■

Headquartered in Milwaukee, Wisconsin, Oldenburg Group Inc. is an international supplier of engineered heavy equipment and architectural lighting products. The company's services include engineering, field service, integrated logistics services, and training. During the latter years of the first decade of the 21st century, Oldenburg Group's operations included 11 ISO 9001 certified facilities, located in the United States, Canada, Mexico, and Chile.

Oldenburg Group's business is concentrated in several specific markets. Within the defense sector, the company's Oldenburg Lake Shore business supplies the U.S. Navy with a wide range of marine deck machinery, cargo weapons elevators, mooring and anchoring

systems, mobile cranes, boat davits, and refueling systems. Additionally, Oldenburg provides the U.S. Army with a mobile causeway system that is used to unload war equipment in the absence of a port facility. Within the mining sector, the company's Oldenburg Cannon business is a supplier of roof bolters, rock drills, drill jumbos, scalers, trucks, and utility vehicles. Finally, the company serves the lighting market via its Visa Lighting operation, which manufactures specification-grade, performance and decorative lighting products.

FORMATIVE YEARS

Wayne C. Oldenburg established Oldenburg Group in 1982. A mergers and acquisitions attorney whose father was a career Coast Guard officer, Oldenburg worked in the firm of Reinhart Boerner Van Deuren Norris & Rieselbach. An entrepreneur at heart, Oldenburg first acquired the Glendale, Wisconsin-based lighting fixtures manufacturer Products Engineering Co., which had 10 employees. The company marketed chandeliers, wall sconces, and other fixtures directly to engineers, architects, and interior designers.

Another acquisition followed in February 1983 when Oldenburg acquired Loehner Metal Spinning Co., which was renamed Spintech. An attempt to organize both Visa Lighting and Spintech under the Visa banner was met with resistance from VISA and MasterCard issuer Elanco Financial Services. Both of Oldenburg's companies relocated to a new facility on Bradley Road in February 1984, and were organized under a parent company named Lamanca Inc. (drawing its name from the words *labor, management,* and *capital*) three months

COMPANY PERSPECTIVES
■

From its inception in 1982, Wayne C. Oldenburg has built Oldenburg Group upon core beliefs in employee empowerment and customer satisfaction.

later. However, products continued to be marketed under the Visa Lighting brand name. The Delavan, Wisconsin-based precision component parts manufacturer Swiss Tech, which employed 125 people and served the medical technology and electronics industries, was acquired in December 1984. Unlike Spintech and Visa Lighting, Swiss Tech was not made a subsidiary of Lamanca.

INITIAL GROWTH

During the mid-1980s Lamanca developed a reputation for flexibility, innovation, and timeliness. Being operated in Milwaukee, in close proximity to a number of metalworking operations, the company did not need its own foundry. The majority of its components were purchased in the Milwaukee area, and its staff was highly skilled, allowing the company to provide architects and designers with custom fixtures if needed.

In 1986 Lamanca benefited from a $1 million industrial revenue bond, which the company devoted to a 22,000-square-foot expansion of its Bradley Road plant. By this time the company's Products Engineering subsidiary had adopted the name Visa Lighting. Based in a 15,000-square-foot facility in Milwaukee, the company's sales had increased by a factor of 10, and its workforce had expanded to include 25 staff, as well as 70 national sales representatives.

In May 1986 Oldenburg made a deal with Valley Forge, Pennsylvania-based Alco Industries Inc. for the acquisition of Milwaukee Machine Products Corp., located in Mequon, Wisconsin. However, when the business proved not to be a good fit, it was sold to the Spengler Corp. in mid-1992, which relocated operations from Mequon to Loves Park, Illinois. By this time Lamanca's name had been changed to Oldenburg Group Inc.

Another key acquisition that occurred around this time was Oldenburg's 1988 purchase of Lake Shore Mining Co. Inc., a 130-year-old shipbuilding operation. The company's focus was on the production of material-handling equipment for timber and mining operations. Like many companies, however, it had engaged in wartime production during World War II.

By late 1993 things were going very well for Visa Lighting. The company, which was growing at a compound annual rate of approximately 30 percent, relocated some of its production to the plant formerly occupied by Milwaukee Machine Products Corp. There, plans were made for new offices, as well as a research and development lab. In addition, the company announced it would build fitness centers at both Visa Lighting plants for its workers. Wayne Oldenburg indicated that use of the second facility was only temporary, until the company could find a suitable location for a new 100,000-square-foot plant.

A BROADER FOCUS

At this time Visa Lighting was preparing to generate more business from designers, engineers, and architects by stepping up its advertising efforts in trade magazines. To support this strategy, the company announced that it would triple its advertising budget in 1994. In addition, Visa Lighting prepared to publish its first catalog since 1983, the development of which had taken approximately $500,000 and two years of effort.

By 1995 Oldenburg Group had established a division devoted to the manufacture of mining equipment. The division consisted of two different companies. Millersburg, Kentucky-based Stamler Corp. concentrated on the manufacture of material fracturing and conveying equipment. Lake Shore Mining Co. Inc., which had operations in Iron River, Michigan, and Rhinelander, Wisconsin, produced equipment used to transport both people and material. Additional mining division operations were located in Australia, New Guinea, and Indonesia.

To further its international growth, Oldenburg Group began increasing efforts to conduct business with Chinese companies interested in purchasing its mining equipment. After attempting its first sales to China in 1993, Oldenburg hosted a delegation of nine officials from China in early 1995, in an effort to secure roughly $14 million in contracts. The international expansion of Oldenburg's mining business continued during the latter part of the year. In an effort to penetrate markets in Latin America, the company acquired Irapuato, Mexico-based Mecanica Industrial Tecnica S.A. (MITSA) in December.

Growth continued in early 1996, at which time Oldenburg acquired the Rapid City, South Dakota-based forest products machinery manufacturer Timberline Inc. By this time the company had grown to include 10 subsidiaries. Operations consisted of 12 distribution facilities and 9 factories. Oldenburg Group's sales totaled approximately $200 million by

KEY DATES

1982: Attorney/entrepreneur Wayne C. Oldenburg acquires lighting fixtures manufacturer Products Engineering Co.

1983: Oldenburg acquires Loehner Metal Spinning Co., which is renamed Spintech.

1984: Both companies are organized under parent company Lamanca Inc.

1995: Company acquires Irapuato, Mexico-based Mecanica Industrial Tecnica S.A.

1998: Wayne Oldenburg is named Master Entrepreneur in Ernst & Young's Wisconsin Entrepreneur of the Year awards.

2001: Oldenburg Group secures significant contracts with the U.S. Army and U.S. Navy.

2006: Oldenburg Group sells its Stamler division to Joy Global in a $118 million cash deal.

2008: The U.S. Navy awards the company contracts potentially worth more than $93 million over five years.

1998. That year, in recognition of his company's success and growth, Wayne Oldenburg was named Master Entrepreneur in Ernst & Young's Wisconsin Entrepreneur of the Year awards. In addition to successfully guiding his own enterprise, Oldenburg also promoted the hiring of minorities via the Milwaukee Employer Accords initiative, as well as the mentoring of minority entrepreneurs by leading a program called Partners for the Future.

NEW OPPORTUNITIES

Following a 20 percent sales increase in 1999, positive momentum continued at Oldenburg Group in the new millennium. At this time the company's Visa Lighting fixtures were being installed in the new Miller Park baseball stadium, which was home to Major League Baseball's Milwaukee Brewers. Due to space limitations, Visa Lighting was forced to delay the introduction of several new products.

In order to allow continued growth and expansion at Visa Lighting, operations were relocated once again. The company sold its two 45,000-square-foot plants in Mequon and Milwaukee, and relocated operations to a 154,000-square-foot plant in Glendale, Wisconsin. After purchasing the new facility from Johnson Controls Inc. in a $4.5 million deal, the company earmarked $3 mil-

lion for renovations, as well as $1.5 million for new equipment.

Building on the success of its lighting business, Oldenburg Group began pursuing further expansion of its mining equipment operations, which had grown considerably during the 1990s. In fact, the mining division represented approximately 75 percent of sales by the early years of the new century. In September 2000 the company announced that it had acquired Cannon Industries Inc. The company produced machines that sold for approximately $400,000 and were used for underground mining, construction, and tunneling. Cannon equipment enjoyed a more than 80 percent market share in certain segments of the U.S. mining industry.

A major development took place in mid-2001 when Oldenburg Group's Lake Shore business beat out nine other competitors to secure a four-year, $150 million contract to build modular causeways for the U.S. Army Tank-Automotive and Armaments Command. The causeways, which the company had been supplying since 1993, were steel pontoons that the Army could use to build floating piers, construction tugs, and work platforms.

The U.S. Army contract meant the addition of approximately 100 new jobs to the company's workforce, which at that time included about 1,500 people. In addition, it resulted in a near tripling of the company's military business, which had been growing at a healthy pace. Over the course of one year, the company had won nine military contracts.

DEFENSE FOCUS

More military business was announced in October 2001, at which time Oldenburg Group won a contract with the U.S. Navy potentially worth $156 million. The contract called for the company to supply the Navy with cargo- and weapons-handling equipment for 689-foot-long T-AKE cargo ships manufactured by San Diego, California-based National Steel and Shipbuilding Co. The new contract meant the addition of another 40 jobs at the company's facility in Rhinelander, Wisconsin.

In early 2002 Oldenburg Group secured a $100,000 training grant, along with a $500,000 loan, from the state of Wisconsin, via a Department of Commerce-administered economic development program. The funds were intended to support the company's operations in Rhinelander. Specifically, plans were made to acquire new equipment, and to make modifications to Lake Shore Inc.'s 90,000-square-foot facilities in relation to the contracts previously secured from the Army and the Navy.

By mid-2002 Oldenburg Group had won 17 multi-year defense contracts. In July the company received a

$70 million contract to supply Navy ships with 44 different types of equipment, including hose-handling devices, cable-handling devices, and winches. The contract, which was expected to be filled in approximately seven years, led to the formation of 25 new machinist and welding jobs at Lake Shore's Rhinelander plant.

Heading into 2003, Oldenburg Group was positioned to benefit from the presence of the U.S. military in Iraq. By this time the company had secured military contracts totaling more than $300 million, and its equipment was present on almost every ship in the naval fleet. Examples of the equipment manufactured for the military included mooring winches, anchor windlasses (used for lowering and raising anchors), davits (devices for lowering and raising lifeboats), and cranes for unloading and loading equipment. Wayne Oldenburg continued to oversee the company's efforts as president and CEO, and remained its sole shareholder.

In mid-2004 Joy Global Inc. signed an agreement to become Oldenburg Group's exclusive authorized mining products distributor in the emerging markets of Russia, China, India, and Poland. Joy Global officials remarked that the agreement was an initial step to a potentially larger alliance between the two companies. In November of that year, Oldenburg Group was awarded with a $5.35 million contract from the U.S. Army Tank-Automotive and Armaments Command to provide warping tugs for the modular causeway system.

In April 2006 Oldenburg Group sold its Stamler division (underground and surface coal mining equipment) to Joy Global. The $118 million cash deal included operations in Millersburg, Kentucky; Johannesburg, South Africa; and Brisbane, Australia. Following the deal, Oldenburg Group consisted of four divisions, including Lake Shore (defense equipment), Cannon (underground mining equipment), Visa Lighting (commercial lighting fixtures), and Timberline (timber harvesting equipment). In November of that year SEM-MCO Limitada was named Oldenburg Group's exclusive distributor of mining and material handling equipment in Peru and Chile.

CONTINUED SUCCESS

During the second half of the decade, Oldenburg Group benefited from continued growth within its defense business. In early 2007 the company received an additional $11 million contract from the Army in connection with its modular causeway system. In January 2008 the Navy awarded the company with contracts to produce underway replenishment systems and cargo/

weapons elevators for five supply ships. The contracts were potentially worth more than $93 million over the course of five years, and called for the addition of approximately 50 new jobs at the company's facilities in northern Michigan and Rhinelander, Wisconsin.

In October 2009 Maquinaria S.A. de C.V. (MAQSA) became the exclusive distributor of the company's Oldenburg Cannon and Oldenburg underground mining equipment in northern Mexico's Chihuahua region. MAQSA was already an authorized dealer of Caterpillar equipment. The deal allowed Oldenburg to market its United States-made products in Mexico, while ensuring that customers received quality technical support and service.

Over the course of a quarter of a century, Oldenburg Group had evolved from a lighting fixtures manufacturer with a handful of employees into a large enterprise with service and manufacturing facilities in Wisconsin, Michigan, Nevada, New Hampshire, Virginia, and Mexico. The company seemed to be positioned for continued success in the second decade of the 21st century.

Paul R. Greenland

PRINCIPAL DIVISIONS

Defense; Mining; Lighting.

PRINCIPAL SUBSIDIARIES

Oldenburg Cannon; Oldenburg Lake Shore; Visa Lighting.

PRINCIPAL COMPETITORS

Acuity Lighting Group Inc.; Metso Minerals Industries Inc.; Northrop Grumman Corp.

FURTHER READING

Balzell, Chantel, "Oldenburg Group Receives Nearly $11 Million from the U.S. Army," *Rhinelander Daily News*, January 21, 2007, p. A1.

Gallun, Alby, "Visa Lighting to Move into Glendale Plant," *Business Journal*, May 5, 2000, p. 3.

Kirchen, Rich, "Mining for Millions in China," *Business Journal-Milwaukee*, March 18, 1995, sec. 1, p. 1.

———, "Oldenburg Sells Milwaukee Machine Products," *Business Journal-Milwaukee*, June 27, 1992.

———, "Visa Lighting to Expand to Mequon," *Business Journal-Milwaukee*, September 18, 1993.

Romell, Rick, "Army Awards Oldenburg $150 Million Contract," *Milwaukee Journal Sentinel*, May 30, 2001.

Savage, Mark, "Oldenburg Buys Mexican Manufacturer. Purchase Expands Market for Mining Equipment,"

Milwaukee Journal Sentinel, December 7, 1995.

———, "Oldenburg Group Buys Machinery Maker. State, UP May Gain 100 Jobs at Existing Plants," *Milwaukee Journal Sentinel*, January 11, 1996, Business, p. 2.

Palm Breweries NV

Steenhuffedorp 3
Steenhuffel, B-1840
Belgium
Telephone: (+32 52) 31 74 11
Fax: (+32 52) 30 41 6
Web site: http://www.palmbreweries.com

Private Company
Founded: 1747 as De Hoorn Brewery
NAICS: 312120 Breweries

■ ■ ■

Palm Breweries NV is the largest independent, family-operated brewery in Belgium and the Netherlands. Palm Breweries is composed of three separate brewers, each of which produces a completely individual type of beer. The Palm Brewery of Steenhuffel, Belgium, brews seven different beers, including Palm Speciale Belge, Palm Royale, Dobbel Palm, and Palm Green, each made using the top fermentation method. The Rodenbach Brewery of Roeselare, Belgium, is the maker of the Flanders Red-Brown beers Rodenbach and Rodenbach Grand Cru, produced by mixed fermentation and aged in oak barrels for two years. The Gouden Boom Brewery in Brugge, Belgium, brews the abbey beers Steenbrugge Tripel and Steenbrugge Dubbel Bruin.

Palm Breweries also operates a joint venture with the Boon Brewery of Lembeek, Belgium. Boon makes beers using spontaneous fermentation. Products such as Boon Oude Geuze, the cherry beer Boon Oude Kriek, and the raspberry-flavored Boon Oude Framboise

exemplify some of the most unique and well-known types of Belgian beers. The Palm Brewery also brews a bock pilsner using the bottom fermentation method. Thus Palm Breweries is the only brewer in the world that produces beers using all four fermentation methods.

Outside of Belgium, Palm is popular in the Netherlands where it maintains a 2 percent market share. Since 2007 Palm has been making gradual inroads into the U.S. market as well. Beyond its role as a brewery, Palm Breweries considers itself the preserver of Belgian cultural heritage. This includes not only protecting Belgium's unusual beers from extinction, but also operating a stud farm for the endangered Belgian draft horses (pictured on the Palm Speciale logo) as well as preserving historic Diepensteyn Castle near Steenhuffel, which the brewer has completely renovated.

BREWERY ORIGINS IN STEENHUFFEL IN THE 18TH CENTURY

The breweries of Palm Breweries have a combined experience of more than 750 years of making beer in Belgium. Both sides of the family of Palm's owner, Jan Toye, have been active in beer making throughout Belgium since the middle of the 1500s. The original Palm Breweries traces its roots back to a 16th-century manor house owned by the De Hoorn family in Steenhuffel, Belgium, a town located between Belgium's two major cities, Brussels and Antwerp. Census records from 1747 mention the De Hoorn public house and brewery in the manor, and that is the date that Palm considers its founding. The brewery was established by Anne

Cornet (De Hoorn is Flemish for the French name Cornet) to brew the locally popular Brabant-style top fermented beer, a beer heavier, more flavorful, and with more alcohol than today's more popular lager beers, also known as pilsners.

Toward the end of the 19th century, the bottom fermented lagers had begun their march of conquest from the Czech-speaking areas of the Austrian Empire, through Germany, and into the rest of the world. These beers were considered so threatening by Belgian brewers that their trade group launched a competition to develop new top fermented beers. The De Hoorn brewery was one of the firms that took up the challenge. When Arthur Van Roy, himself a member of another brewing family, married into the De Hoorn family in 1908, he took over the brewery in Steenhuffel and developed a beer of his own. He called it Speciale Belge, or special Belgian, to emphasize that it was made using the traditional Belgian top fermentation methods.

DESTRUCTION AND RECONSTRUCTION IN TWO WORLD WARS

In 1914, when Germany invaded Belgium at the start of World War I, the De Hoorn brewery was completely destroyed. Belgian breweries in general suffered during the war; if they were not destroyed by bombardments, their brewing equipment was frequently seized by the German army and melted down for the war effort. The number of breweries in Belgium declined precipitously as a result of the war, dropping from more than 3,000 in 1914 to only 125 in 1920. After the war ended in 1918, Arthur Van Roy started rebuilding the De Hoorn brewery. Larger than the old one, and, despite the continuing popularity of lagers, he built it to brew top fermented beers exclusively. By the mid-1920s the brewery was back on its feet again. In 1929, Van Roy gave his Speciale Belge a new name, Palm, which, he

explained, symbolized the victory of top fermented beers over lagers.

Arnold's son, Alfred Van Roy, entered the business in 1930, working in the brewery in Steenhuffel as well as attending a technical college for brewers in Brussels. The company put its first copper brewing room into operation, a facility that was still being used in 2009. When German armies invaded France at the start of World War II they marched through Belgium again. Fortunately, the De Hoorn Brewery fared better during the second war. In 1947 it celebrated its 200th anniversary with a special Christmas beer which it called Dobbel Palm, a rich brew that was higher in alcohol content than the regular Palm. Dobbel Palm has been produced every Christmas season since then.

ESTABLISHING PALM AS THE MOST POPULAR BELGIAN BEER

Alfred continued to brew the top fermented beers that had made the brewery's name after Arthur Van Roy died in 1952. The firm's leap into the leadership of the traditional Belgian beer market got its impetus from the Brussels World's Fair of 1958. One of the areas planned by fair organizers was an "Old Belgium" market square at the heart of the fairgrounds. Sites at the square were awarded to Belgian businesses by lottery, and the De Hoorn company won the best location. Alfred Van Roy took advantage of the good fortune and built a luxurious "Palm Hof" to present his products. The Palm Court was one of the hits of the fair. It catapulted Palm to national prominence, and the beer was soon the most popular beer, except for the lagers, in Belgium.

GROWTH IN A SHRINKING MARKET

The 1960s were a crucial period for the De Hoorn brewery, which saw a wave of consolidation sweep across the Belgian brewing landscape, led primarily by Interbrew, the owner of Stella Artois, a popular Belgian lager. The first result was that numerous smaller breweries were acquired by larger breweries and then closed. The second was that regional beers with a small market simply disappeared. In the middle 1960s, Belgian young people launched a reaction against this trend, seeking out and supporting specialty beers. Consequently, despite a shrinking Belgian market for beer and declining sales for the lagers, regional brews started to bounce back strongly. Palm was one of the main beneficiaries of the trend, reporting growth rates up to 30 percent in the late 1960s and early 1970s. In 1967 the Danish brewer Carlsberg named De Hoorn its exclusive bottler in the Benelux countries.

KEY DATES

1747: First recorded mention of the De Hoorn Brewery in Steenhuffel, Belgium.
1929: Speciale Belge is renamed Palm.
1975: De Hoorn Brewery is renamed Brouwerij Palm.
1989: Brouwerij Palm B.V is founded in the Netherlands.
1990: Joint venture is established with the Boon Brewery.
2003: Palm Breweries is established.

As a response to its new popularity, De Hoorn added a second brewing room in 1972, one capable of producing 5,280 gallons of five different beers daily. Two years later, Van Roy and his wife, Aline Verleyen, brought her nephew, Jan Toye, into management to guarantee that De Hoorn remained a family-owned and operated business. By that time, the De Hoorn brewery was widely known simply as the Palm brewer. Hence, in 1975, the company officially changed its name to Brouwerij Palm. To indicate the beer's roots in the Brabant region, the image of a Brabant draft horse was added to the beer's label.

EXPANSION INTO HOLLAND AND FURTHER GROWTH IN BELGIUM

At the beginning of the 1980s, Brouwerij Palm established a significant foothold in the neighboring Netherlands. Dutch drinkers made Palm the best-selling non-lager in the country, a position the beer continued to enjoy in 2010, when Dutch beer drinkers annually consumed some 50 million bottles and cans of Palm annually. Holland became Palm's largest market outside Belgium, accounting for approximately one-third of the beer Palm brewed. With the Netherlands as Palm's most important foreign market, a Dutch subsidiary called Brouwerij Palm B.V. was established 1989. A year later Palm added another brewing room to its facilities in Steenhuffel with a modern shipping area.

The consolidation of the Belgian beer market was continuing unabated at the beginning of the 1990s, and Palm with a 5 percent share of the Belgian market was a tempting takeover target. Several times in the 1980s and early 1990s, Interbrew, the brewing conglomerate that later became part of InBev, approached Palm's owners about selling out. Van Roy and Toye refused, believing it would mean a death knell for some of their more specialized and less popular beers. To help solidify its market position in those uncertain times, Palm developed what it called a multi-niche strategy, becoming active in the brewing of other types of traditional Belgian beers. At the same time, the firm viewed this expansion as an effort to preserve old Belgian culture. It launched the first of these cultural projects in 1993 when it entered a 50-50 joint venture with the Boon Brewery of Lembeek, Belgium. Founded in 1680, Boon was the brewer of lambics. Some of the most unique and well-known types of Belgian beers, lambics were brewed by spontaneous fermentation, that is, by exposing the beer to the open air.

DIVERSE ACQUISITIONS

The strategy was further implemented in 1998 when Palm acquired the Rodenbach Brewery at Roeselare, in western Belgium. Rodenbach was an unusual beer variety, a West Flanders red-brown aged for two years or more in oak barrels, and was called by Rodenbach brewmaster Rudi Ghequire "the missing link between beer and wine." The liberal Rodenbach family played an important role in the Belgian Revolution of 1830 that established the independence of the country from France. Pedro and Regina Rodenbach founded the brewery in 1836, but it was their son Eugène who perfected the oak cask maturation process. He was also the last member of the Rodenbach family to run the brewery. In 1925 it was converted to a limited corporation and it remained so until its acquisition by Palm. Rodenbach's 294 oak barrels, many of which were more than 150 years of age, were under Flemish landmark protection. In 1998, one year after Alfred Van Roy celebrated his 70th year in brewing, Palm made an enormous leap to Eastern Europe, building the Browar Belgia, or Belgian brewery, in Kielce, Poland. It went into operation in September 1999.

A more unusual project, but one related to Belgian cultural heritage, was the acquisition of Diepensteyn Domain, a historic castle not far from Steenhuffel that dated back to the 14th century. The grounds would include another project, the Palm stud farm for Brabant draft horses, which it showed off in the Palm Cup Challenge that ran for four years at the end of the 1990s.

Brouwerij Palm took over another traditional Belgian beer maker in 2001 when it acquired the Gouden Boom Brewery. The brewer was a sometime brewery, sometime distillery in the coastal city of Brugge, Belgium, that could trace its history back to the mid-15th century. The name Gouden Boom ("golden tree" in Flemish) referred to the Brugge coat of arms. Gouden Boom specialized in the heavy abbey beers made by monks. With the acquisition, Palm established itself in another distinct sector of the Belgian beer universe. The two primary brews produced by the Gouden Boom were Brugge Blond and Brugge Tripel, the production of which was taken over later in the decade by the Palm brewery in Steenhuffel.

A NEW NAME

To reflect its international group of breweries in Belgium, the Netherlands, and Poland, Brouwerij Palm changed its name in 2003 to Palm Breweries. By then Palm was annually producing 44.9 million gallons of its various beers. Palm sold Browar Kielce, its Polish brewery, in 2007 to the Polish brewing group Kompania Piwowarska. That same year Palm, together with Latis Imports, began laying plans for the introduction of Palm Speciale Belge in the U.S. market. By 2009 the beer was available and getting rave reviews in New York City, San Diego, parts of New Jersey, Connecticut, Washington, D.C., and Boston. The success of the effort was confirmed in February 2010 when *Maxim* magazine named Palm the world's best beer. Although Palm had not yet achieved the victory of top fermented beers over lagers that Arthur Van Roy dreamed of early in the 20th century, the image of the Brabant draft horse on the Palm label represented considerable

progress and achievement in conquering the hearts and minds of beer drinkers.

Gerald E. Brennan

PRINCIPAL SUBSIDIARIES

Boon Brewery; Brouwerij Palm BV; Rodenbach Brewery.

PRINCIPAL COMPETITORS

Anheuser-Busch InBev; Brouwerijen Alken-Maes NV; Brouwerij Bosteels NV; Brouwerij De Koninck; Cantillon Brewery; Heineken NV.

FURTHER READING

Kitsock, Greg, "Another Kind of Red," *Washington Post,* July 16, 2008.

"Palm Beer Now in Bottles in the U.S.," *PR Newswire,* January 8, 2009.

"Palm Brewery Owner Tours U.S. Market," *Modern Brewery Age,* September 29, 2008.

"U.S. Reintroduction of Rodenbach Underway," *Modern Brewery Age,* March 26, 2009.

Polish & Slavic Federal Credit Union

———— ■ ————

100 McGuiness Boulevard
Brooklyn, New York 11222-3302
U.S.A.
Telephone: (718) 610-3980
Toll Free: (800) 297-2181
Fax: (718) 610-3960
Web site: http://www.psfcu.com

Private Company
Founded: 1976 as Industrial & Commercial Federal
   Credit Union
Employees: 238
Total Assets: $1.29 billion (2009)
NAICS: 522130 Credit Unions; 522210 Credit Card Is-
   suing; 522291 Consumer Lending; 522292 Real
   Estate Credit; 522310 Mortgage and Other Loan
   Brokers

■ ■ ■

The Polish & Slavic Federal Credit Union (PSFCU) is
the largest ethnic credit union in the United States.
Based in Brooklyn, it is among the top 10 credit unions
in the state of New York, as ranked by total assets. It is
the second largest in New Jersey, where it also maintains
branches. As a credit union, it is owned by its thousands
of members, all of whom have equal voting rights in
electing the board of directors that oversees its
operations. All its services are offered in Polish as well as
English.

The PSFCU performs most of the same functions
as a bank. It offers, for example, savings and checking
accounts, credit and debit cards, residential and commercial mortgages, and wire transfers. The credit union
extends business, personal, student, real estate,
automobile, and boat loans. Customers may bank by
phone or over the Internet as well as in person. There
are more than a dozen branches, almost all of them in
the New York and Chicago metropolitan areas.

ORIGINS

This financial institution was established in 1976 by the
founders of the Polish & Slavic Center, an organization
led by the Reverend Longin Tolczyk. The purpose was
to help Polish immigrants who settled in Greenpoint,
Brooklyn's northernmost neighborhood and a
stronghold of New York City's Polish American
community. Some of them wanted to buy or renovate
homes in Greenpoint but could not get loans from
banks without an established credit history. Just before
the end of 1976 the National Credit Union Administration (NCUA), a federal body, chartered the new institution as the Industrial and Commercial Federal Credit
Union. The name was changed to the Polish & Slavic
Federal Credit Union (PSFCU) in 1979.

The Polish community in Greenpoint dated from
about 1890, when immigrants began moving across the
East River from Manhattan's crowded Lower East Side.
Most of the neighborhood's housing units were built
about 1900, and very little was added thereafter. By the
1970s much of New York was in the grip of urban
decay, and in that decade the city's finances fell into
disarray. Greenpoint was a stable, if modest, working-
class neighborhood, but prospective lenders feared it
would decline.

COMPANY PERSPECTIVES

This credit union is a member-owned, democratically operated, not-for-profit organization managed by a volunteer board of directors, with the specified mission of meeting the credit and savings needs of consumers, especially persons of modest means. The purpose of this credit union is to promote thrift among its members by affording them an opportunity to accumulate their savings and to create for them a source of credit for provident or productive purposes.

A detailed study found that the seven largest savings banks in Brooklyn issued only 1,186 mortgages on owner-occupied residential properties in the borough in 1975, even though there were more than 200,000 owner-occupied housing units in Brooklyn at the time. Most of these mortgage loans were in southern Brooklyn. No more than 39, and perhaps many fewer, were issued for Greenpoint that year.

The first credit union office was at 940 Manhattan Avenue, in the heart of Greenpoint and adjacent to the canteen of the Polish & Slavic Center. In 1981 the PSFCU bought a bank building at nearby 140 Greenpoint Avenue to serve as its headquarters as well as a branch for its customers. A second branch opened in Union, New Jersey, in 1987 to serve Polish immigrants in that part of the New York metropolitan area.

By this time property values had risen markedly in much of New York. In Greenpoint, two- and three-family frame houses that could have been purchased for $50,000 a few years earlier were now commanding prices ranging from $125,000 to $300,000. Still more valuable were the brick multifamily residential buildings along Greenpoint's streets that rented ground-floor space to local businesses. These structures served as collateral for many PSFCU mortgage loans.

Perhaps 40 to 45 percent of the estimated 45,000 residents were of Polish descent at the time, but the neighborhood was being discovered by young professionals attracted by affordable rents in an area not far from Manhattan offices. Some artists also moved in, although neighboring Williamsburg proved to be a much bigger draw for them.

GROWTH AND EXPANSION

In order to join the PSFCU, applicants had to document Polish or other Slavic origin (in practice mostly Slovak, Ukrainian, or Russian) and to pay a $10 annual membership fee to one or another of the credit union's five sponsoring organizations. By 1995 there were 37,000 credit union members, up to 90 percent of whom were immigrants. The PSFCU was by now the largest Polish American financial institution in the United States. Three new branches opened during the 1990s: on Greenpoint's Kent Street in 1992 and in Borough Park, another Brooklyn neighborhood, and Clifton, New Jersey, in 1996.

PSFCU's assets, which had reached $100 million by the end of its first decade in existence, doubled again in only three years. An overwhelming proportion of its business was in the form of mortgage loans. In fact, PSFCU had in 1995 the highest concentration of mortgage loans of any credit union in the United States, with nearly 95 percent of its $136 million loan portfolio in real estate. Its return on assets was said to be consistently among the highest in its field.

Demand for other loans was low because the PSFCU's members, prone to savings rather than spending, preferred to pay up front for household purchases. "They aren't used to credit," the institution's general manager explained to James B. Arndorfer of *American Banker* in 1995, adding, "They hate credit. If they buy a refrigerator or car, they want to pay in cash." Many even avoided the institution's automated teller machines (ATMs), still unfamiliar to recent immigrants.

The PSFCU had issued its own credit card, and some one-sixth of its members had signed up. Even so, about a third of those were using a secured card because of bad credit or none at all. By contrast, the average account balance was $7,940 in 1994, much higher than that for most credit unions.

A DECADE OF FEDERAL SANCTIONS: 1991–2001

The growth of the PSFCU was marred by a series of conflicts with the NCUA. In 1991 the federal agency forced the PSFCU to sell some of its mortgages because it considered much of the credit union's real estate lending to be too commercial in nature, and hence risky, in a period of economic recession.

In 1998 the NCUA again cracked down on the PSFCU, this time more severely. The agency contended that the PSFCU was poorly managed, lacked sufficient internal controls or an appropriate investment policy, followed a risky interest-rate and liquidity position, and was violating the Bank Secrecy Act. The credit union's officers were required to take a number of corrective steps, such as hiring consultants and providing the agency with better board-meeting minutes. Because the

```
┌─────────────────────────────────────────┐
│                                         │
│             KEY DATES                   │
│                 ■                       │
│ ┌─────────────────────────────────────┐ │
│ │                                     │ │
│ │ 1976:  The Polish & Slavic Center,  │ │
│ │        which later becomes the      │ │
│ │        Polish & Slavic Federal      │ │
│ │        Credit Union (PSFCU), is     │ │
│ │        founded in Brooklyn,         │ │
│ │        New York.                    │ │
│ │ 1986:  The credit union's assets    │ │
│ │        reach $100 million.          │ │
│ │ 1999:  The PSFCU is placed under    │ │
│ │        federal conservatorship for  │ │
│ │        nearly a year.               │ │
│ │ 2006:  The assets of the PSFCU      │ │
│ │        reach $1 billion.            │ │
│ │ 2010:  The credit union expands to  │ │
│ │        the Chicago area with the    │ │
│ │        opening of two branches.     │ │
│ └─────────────────────────────────────┘ │
└─────────────────────────────────────────┘
```

agency contended that the PSFCU harbored conflicts of interest, all board members were required to disclose whether they or other family members or associates were affiliated with any contractors or vendors of the credit union.

The response to these sanctions failed to satisfy the NCUA, and consequently the federal agency placed the PSFCU under its conservatorship in the following year. It charged that the credit union's board had failed to perform its fiduciary duty and dissolved this governing body. A 17-member advisory panel was appointed to oversee the institution. The 10-month conservatorship ended in 2000, but not before the NCUA agreed to pay the U.S. Department of the Treasury a $185,000 fine to settle issues that otherwise might have cost it millions of dollars.

The PSFCU had incurred the wrath of the federal government by allowing, in violation of the Bank Secrecy Act, more than 6,000 money transfers to Poland without notification to U.S. authorities. The act required all transactions over $10,000 or those that seemed suspicious to be reported. While PSFCU's transfers were believed to consist of normal sending of funds to relatives rather than criminal activity, a Treasury enforcement group maintained that the credit union's failure to file necessary reports was intentional rather than inadvertent.

Six of the ousted nine-member PSFCU board challenged the NCUA takeover in court, but without avail. The agency proved unyielding despite political pressure from elected representatives and the picketing of its offices in Washington. The credit union's former directors took what satisfaction they could from the dismissal of the agency's lead attorney because of testimony that he had made disparaging remarks about the PSFCU staff and jokes about ethnic Poles.

CONTINUED GROWTH AND CONTINUED DISSENSION IN THE 21ST CENTURY

Elections to the board of the PSFCU resumed in 2001, when two former directors and two others were chosen by members of the credit union. Seven more directors were elected over the next two years in conformity with the NCUA order returning the credit union to its members. The PSFCU, however, was wracked by dissension over the next few years, and its governing board spent much of its time turning aside attempts to recall its members.

In 2005 a state judge ordered the credit union to restore Marcin Sar to the board. Sar had been the institution's general manager from 1987 to 1996, when he was fired. Another board member was suspended in 2006 and his seat declared vacant. Infighting reached a new level in 2007, when Alicja Malecka, the PSFCU's president and chief executive officer, was dismissed by the board. She was replaced by Bogdan Chmielewski, a former branch manager of the credit union.

In spite of these vicissitudes, the PSFCU continued to grow, reaching and passing $1 billion in assets. Moreover, there was an impressive increase in the number of branches during the first decade of the new century. Ridgewood, Queens, just east of the borough and county line, received a PSFCU branch in 2001.

Copiague, a Long Island community with a large Polish American presence, became the site of another PSFCU branch in 2004. Once heavily Italian American, this hamlet began receiving a significant number of Poles in the early 1980s and, by 2006, was home to six Polish delicatessens as well as the credit union. The local Catholic church offered two weekly Polish-language Masses, and a Saturday school was teaching 300 children Polish language and culture. In all, there were about 150,000 ethnic Poles in the two Long Island counties east of New York City.

The PSFCU opened a third Greenpoint branch on McGuiness Boulevard in 2005. Bayonne and Linden, two New Jersey cities within the New York metropolitan area, received branches in 2001 and 2003, respectively.

The PSFCU opened its 10th branch, in Maspeth, Queens, in 2007. Maspeth, like Ridgewood, was just over the Brooklyn borough and county line. This was followed by a branch in Garfield, New Jersey, in 2008, and one in Trenton, the capital of New Jersey, in 2009. The Trenton facility put the PSFCU within hailing distance of the Philadelphia metropolitan area. There was also an operations center in Fairfield, New Jersey.

The credit union entered the Chicago area, with its large Polish and Polish American population, in 2010, when branches in the northern suburbs of Mount Prospect and Norridge were opened. Interviewed by a *Credit Union Journal* reporter in 2007, Chmielewski said the institution was looking at Connecticut, Florida, Michigan, and even Arizona for possible expansion in the future.

SERVICE TO THE COMMUNITY: 2007–09

The financial crisis of 2008 led to many layoffs in the New York metropolitan area the following year, especially in the construction industry. The PSFCU established a program that allowed savers who had recently lost their jobs to withdraw long-term deposits such as CDs without penalty. Later in 2009, the credit union received a visit from Polish President Lech Kaczynski and reopened the original Greenpoint branch after a 10-month remodeling that included the installation of 1,110 safe-deposit boxes, the first ones made available to PSFCU customers.

As of January 31, 2010, the PSFCU had $1.29 billion in assets and 68,691 members. Besides its fixed branches, the institution was also fielding a mobile branch with tellers and ATMs. There were also ATMs for Polish pilgrims visiting American Czestochowa in Doylestown, Pennsylvania.

The PSFCU was also assisting about 180 Polish American organizations on the East Coast, such as schools and churches, each year. As part of a program adopted in 2001, it was contributing as much as $600,000 a year for student scholarships and donations to schools that taught Polish language and history. In 2007 the credit union gave Columbia University $100,000 to endow a chair of Polish studies. Through 2008, the PSFCU had given $1.3 million for its scholarship program. Almost $350,000 was donated in scholarships to 316 students in 2009. Also during the year the credit union donated $434,190 to 116 institutions.

Robert Halasz

PRINCIPAL COMPETITORS

Maspeth Federal Savings & Loan Association; PNA Bank; Polonia Bankcorp.

FURTHER READING

Arndorfer, James B., "Polish-Slavic Group Flourishes in Brooklyn," *American Banker,* January 30, 1995, p. 18.

Barancik, Scott, "Government Puts Pressure on N.Y. Ethnic Credit Union," *American Banker,* June 29, 1998, p. 2.

Blumenfeld, Matt, "Recession Responses," *Credit Union Journal,* February 23, 2009, p. 20.

Cerra, Francis, "A Detailed Study Charges 'Redlining' by Major Savings Banks in Brooklyn," *New York Times,* December 6, 1976, p. 37.

Muckian, Michael, "East Meets Best," *Credit Union Journal,* August 13, 2007, pp. 1, 32.

Petramala, Teresa I., "If You're Thinking of Living In: Greenpoint," *New York Times,* December 6, 1987, Sec. 8, p. 11.

"Polish & Slavic Federal Credit Union Breezes In to the Windy City," *Internet Wire,* February 12, 2010.

Roberts, Ed, "Polish & Slavic Returned; $185K Fine Is Paid," *Credit Union Journal,* February 14, 2000, p. 18.

Weiner, Caryn Eve, "Need Bread? This Credit Union's for You," *New York Newsday,* February 20, 1989, p. 23.

Praxair, Inc.

39 Old Ridgebury Road
Danbury, Connecticut 06810
U.S.A.
Telephone: (716) 879-4077
Toll Free: (800) PRAXAIR
Fax: (716) 879-2040
Web site: http://www.praxair.com

Public Company
Incorporated: 1907 as Linde Air Products Co.
Employees: 27,000
Sales: $8.96 billion (2009)
Stock Exchanges: New York
Ticker Symbol: PX
NAICS: 325120 Industrial Gas Manufacturing; 332812 Metal Coating, Engraving (Except Jewelry and Silverware), and Allied Services to Manufacturers

■ ■ ■

With operations in more than 30 countries around the world, Praxair, Inc., is one of the world's top suppliers of industrial gases. The company's Praxair Surface Technologies subsidiary applies high-performance metal coatings for a variety of industries. Formerly the Linde Division of chemical giant Union Carbide Corporation, Praxair was spun off to shareholders in 1992 as an independent company. A little less than half of the firm's sales are generated outside the United States.

The company's surface coatings business, developed in the 1950s, supplies wear-resistant and high-temperature corrosion-resistant metallic and ceramic coatings and powders to many industries. Industrial gases by far constitute the greatest portion of Praxair's operations, contributing 86 percent of 2008 sales. Industrial gas products include atmospheric gases like oxygen, nitrogen, and argon, and process gases such as helium, hydrogen, and acetylene.

Many of Praxair's largest customers, and an increasing number of smaller volume customers, use on-site distribution, wherein a dedicated plant is built on or adjacent to the customer's site to supply the product directly. On-site delivery constituted about 26 percent of Praxair's 2008 sales. Merchant liquid delivery involves transportation of medium-sized volumes of gases by tanker truck or railroad tank car to on-site storage containers owned and maintained by Praxair. This segment contributed 28 percent of the company's 2008 sales. Customers requiring small volumes of industrial gases receive them in metal cylinders or tanks. This packaged gases business constituted nearly one-third of sales in 2008.

ORIGINS

Praxair's origins can be traced back to 19th-century Germany, where a professor of mechanical engineering at the College of Technology in Munich started experiments in refrigeration. Karl von Linde's research came to fruition with the 1895 development of a cryogenic air liquefier. Von Linde built his first oxygen production plant in 1902. His continuing research led to the establishment of the first plant for the production of pure nitrogen two years later. The entrepreneur-scientist went on to build air separation plants throughout

COMPANY PERSPECTIVES

■

How does Praxair make our planet more productive? By helping our customers do more. Operate more efficiently. Save money. Grow profitably. Improve environmental performance. We do it with smarter ideas, superior technologies and highly responsive customer service. Reliability, safety and integrity are built into every customer relationship. Praxair has been advancing gas production and applications technologies for more than a century, putting our skills to work for customers as diverse as potato chip packagers and computer chip makers, oil refineries and welding shops, aircraft builders and hospitals. We're proud of our reputation as one of the most admired companies in our industry. And our financial performance is rock solid, so we are here for the long haul. What makes us different is our team's can-do spirit of creative problem solving. Praxair people take on our customers' challenges—large and small—as if they are our own. We measure our success by how well we help our customers achieve theirs.

Germany and Europe during the first decade of the 20th century.

Karl von Linde's 1907 foundation of Linde Air Products Company in Cleveland, Ohio, established the first firm in the United States to produce oxygen from air using a cryogenic process. Although oxygen distillation was relatively inexpensive, based on free raw material, the storage and transportation of gases in heavy containers was very costly. With its foundation in scientific inquiry, the Linde Air Products Company made research and development a priority. As a result, the industrial gas business evolved into a very capital-intensive enterprise. In 1992, *Chemical Week* estimated that every dollar of annual sales cost over a dollar in assets.

The Linde Company's relationship with Union Carbide started around 1911, when the two competitors undertook joint experiments regarding the production and application of acetylene. Union Carbide had been formed in 1898 to manufacture calcium carbide, a catalyst for the production of metal alloys. The partners had hoped that acetylene, a flammable, gaseous by-product of alloying calcium carbide with aluminum, could be marketed for street and household lighting.

While acetylene gas lighting was extensively used especially in rural areas and was also used for auto lights, Thomas Edison's invention and commercialization of electric incandescent lightbulbs diverted some emphasis away from acetylene gas lighting. A French researcher's discovery that acetylene could be burned in oxygen to produce a hot, metal-cutting flame launched a whole new market for the gas.

COMPANY JOINS UNION CARBIDE IN 1917

In 1917, Linde pooled its resources with National Carbon Co., Inc., Prest-O-Lite Co., Inc., Electro Metallurgical Co., and Union Carbide Co. to form Union Carbide and Carbon Corporation. The new entity was organized as a holding company, with its five members acting relatively autonomously and cooperating where their businesses converged. As a subsidiary of one of the largest chemical companies in the United States, Linde soon became one of the world's largest producers of such industrial gases as acetylene, hydrogen, and nitrogen, which formed the foundation of the petrochemical industry.

The companies' combined research efforts coincided with a national push for new technologies to help win World War I, and new applications for industrial gases came in rapid succession. Cooperative research and development among Union Carbide companies used Linde's gases to facilitate production of corrosion and heat-resistant ferroalloys used in skyscrapers, bridges, and automobiles.

Linde also earned a reputation as an innovator in the industrial gases industry by developing new applications for industrial gases, especially in conjunction with the growing chemicals operations of its parent. During the 1940s, for example, Linde participated in Union Carbide's contribution to the development of the atomic bomb. Linde scientists perfected a refining process for treating uranium concentrates through gaseous diffusion.

In the late 1940s, Union Carbide executives attempted to centralize the traditionally autonomous nature of the corporation through a reorganization. The holding company arrangement was dissolved, and subsidiaries were transformed into divisions. Each division, however, retained the word *company* in its name, suggesting that a decentralized corporate culture still endured at Union Carbide.

POSTWAR UPS AND DOWNS

The Linde division benefited from Union Carbide's mid-1950s to mid-1960s globalization and retained its

KEY DATES

1907: Linde Air Products Company is founded.
1917: Linde joins Union Carbide.
1988: Linde Division is renamed Union Carbide Industrial Gases.
1992: Praxair is spun off; company is listed on the New York Stock Exchange.
1996: CBI Industries, including subsidiary Liquid Carbonic, is acquired for $2.2 billion.
2000: William Lichtenberger, CEO since 1992, retires.
2004: Praxair buys pipeline, bulk, and packaged gas businesses in Germany from Air Liquide.
2008: Revenues reach $10.8 billion.

position as America's top producer of industrial gases through continuous innovation. The development of oxygen-fired furnaces for steel manufacture and application of nitrogen as a refrigerant increased Linde's markets during the 1960s. The industrial gas company was even able to benefit from the energy crisis of the 1970s, when the rapidly rising costs of traditional fuels made oxy-fuel an attractive alternative to air-fuel. Applications of industrial gases in the food industry during this period included the use of hydrogen in hydrogenated cooking oils and nitrogen to quick-freeze foods.

However, Linde's steady performance throughout the 1970s and 1980s was largely obscured by the succession of financial, environmental, and human disasters endured by parent company Union Carbide, including the disaster at its pesticide plant in Bhopal, India, in December 1984. Union Carbide's market value plummeted 75 percent to less than $3 billion in the aftermath, and the chemical giant was compelled to take on massive debt to repulse a takeover threat. Divestments scaled the parent company back to its three primary businesses (industrial gases, chemicals and plastics, and carbon products) in the late 1980s, but its debt load curbed research and development, diversification, and international expansion.

By the early 1980s, Linde was a $1 billion contributor to Union Carbide's $9 billion annual sales. However, over the course of the decade, Linde began to lose U.S. market share, particularly to U.S. rival Air Products and Chemicals, Inc. By the late 1980s, Linde was ranked second in nitrogen and hydrogen production and distribution.

Linde maintained its reputation for innovation, including a small, profitable business segment with the development of such coatings processes as acetylene detonation, which metallurgically bonded protective coatings to metal surfaces. High-tech acetylene detonation and diffusion processes were used in aircraft engines and rolled steel, while also having applications in the automotive industry, most notably in the production of Rolls-Royce automobiles.

In 1989, the industrial gas company introduced a technological breakthrough in its primary market, air separation. Robert Reitzes, then an analyst with New York's C.J. Lawrence, predicted that the economical, noncryogenic, vacuum pressure swing adsorption (VPSA) technology would consume 20 to 25 percent of the merchant market by 2000. In fact, by 2000 the company would estimate that more than 40 percent of the merchant liquid market was served by noncryogenic systems, of both the VPSA and membrane variety.

COMPANY SPUN OFF IN 1992

In 1988, the Linde division was renamed Union Carbide Industrial Gases, and in June 1992 its shares were distributed to Union Carbide shareholders on the basis of one share of the new Praxair, Inc., for each share of the parent. The new company maintained some ties to its former parent. Union Carbide was still one of its largest customers, and the two continued to share a common headquarters. The name Praxair was derived from the Greek *praxis*, or practical application, plus the name of the company's primary product.

Praxair emerged with over $2.5 billion in annual sales, more employees (18,600) than its former parent (16,000), and a debt-to-capital ratio of over 60 percent. Debt reduction was a high priority for CEO H. William Lichtenberger, who devised several corporate goals in the early 1990s, including reducing overhead, doubling profitability, effecting 15 percent annual net income growth, and expanding Praxair's global presence, especially in Asia and South Africa.

Expense reduction commenced immediately under a "work process improvement initiative," and the company's workforce was reduced by 10 percent in Praxair's first year of independence. The establishment of joint ventures in Indonesia and China was expected to help Praxair catch up quickly with its competitors in the region.

In 1994, Praxair earned one of the most comprehensive quality system certifications issued by the International Organization for Standardization (ISO). Covered by the ISO 9002 certificate were all 54 bulk-gas operating sites; 12 customer service centers; distribution facilities, including the company's North American

Logistics Center; plant operations centers and two pipeline control centers; and more than 250 on-site air separation plants in the United States, Canada, and Puerto Rico.

By 1995, Lichtenberger had largely delivered on the ambitious goals he set after the company was spun off in 1992. Rejecting a new share offering or a sell-off of assets, Praxair raised its margins by focusing on productivity and cost reductions, which saved an estimated $50 million to $60 million a year.

One way Praxair did this was by installing new plants more quickly at customers' sites. In the mid-1990s, the company had 100 on-site plants in the design or construction stages. It was also installing the world's largest oxygen plant for the Jindal Vijayanagar Steel Ltd.'s facility in Kamataka, India.

New or expanded uses for industrial gases contributed to Praxair's bottom line. Use of oxygen in the glass, steel, coal, and paper industries could improve quality while reducing toxic emissions. Demand for hydrogen was up from the petroleum refining industry and from NASA.

MAJOR ACQUISITION IN 1996

In early 1996, Praxair acquired CBI Industries, an Oak Brook, Illinois-based carbon dioxide provider, in a $2.2 billion hostile takeover. The purchase helped Praxair expand its Gulf Coast operations. Oil refining there was a large market for hydrogen. CBI subsidiary Liquid Carbonic was the world leader in carbon dioxide, with sales of $440 million a year and twice that figure in total gases revenues. CBI's product lines merged well with those of Praxair, formerly a stranger to the carbon dioxide business. The acquisition also expanded Praxair's presence in South America, Poland, and Thailand. In addition, Praxair was then investing in China and India.

Praxair was also making smaller acquisitions of cylinder gas operations in the United States. The company had exited the packaged gas business under Union Carbide. North American cylinder sales in 1999 were $900 million, $250 million of this due to the Liquid Carbonic acquisition. To contain costs, the packaged gas business was established as a subsidiary, Praxair Distribution.

Following an industry trend, Praxair and German chemicals giant Merck KGaA began shipping each other's products. Their geographic ranges were entirely complementary. In March 1999, Praxair and BOC Group plc of Great Britain announced plans to combine to create the world's largest industrial gas company. Praxair was outbid, however, and BOC's assets were divided between Air Liquide and Air Products in an $11 billion deal. In fact, Praxair would be one of the few industrial gases companies not involved in a merger at the dawn of the millennium.

Praxair stopped using the Linde name in 1999. In a deal brokered three years earlier, Praxair agreed to sell North American rights to the name to Linde AG of Germany for $60 million. Linde AG and its predecessors had been using the name in Europe and elsewhere in the world since its incorporation in 1895.

LICHTENBERGER RETIRES IN 2000

After the retirement of President and Chief Operating Officer (COO) Edgar Hotard in early 1999, Lichtenberger set up a temporary three-person "office of the chairman" staffed by himself, Chief Financial Officer John Clerico, and Executive Vice President Paul Bilek. Lichtenberger retired as CEO and chairman in November 2000 upon turning 65. His replacement, Dennis H. Reilley, was formerly a COO at du Pont.

Under the new leadership, a restructuring at Praxair was announced in December 2000 that would see plants closed and 750 employees laid off (3 percent of the total Praxair workforce). Hoping to exploit some specific growth markets beyond its traditional industrial gases business, including semiconductor materials, health care, metals technologies, and electronic coatings, the company nevertheless met with unfavorable economic conditions as a global recession ensued in 2001.

Another series of layoffs was announced in late 2001. Nevertheless, the company seemed to meet the challenges. Sales continued to climb as did Praxair stock prices, which outperformed the Standard & Poor's 500 Index in 2001. Early in 2002, Praxair began plans to build two new hydrogen plants to supply its Gulf Coast pipeline.

Praxair pursued a focused expansion policy, aimed chiefly at the countries it saw as having the highest growth potential. These included the United States, Canada, Mexico, Brazil, Spain, Italy, South Korea, Thailand, China, and India. The company sold off its Polish subsidiary in 2002 to BOC Group for $50 million. The next year, Praxair broke ground on a joint venture with rival Air Liquide to supply industrial gases to the chemical industry in Shanghai, China.

Praxair then added Germany/Benelux to its list of "core geographies." In 2004 the company bought certain pipeline, bulk, and packaged gas businesses in Germany from Air Liquide, which was required to divest them for antitrust reasons following its takeover of Messer

Griesheim. The price was EUR 497 million ($610 million).

The company's already sizable U.S. health care operations were boosted in 2004 with the purchase of privately held Home Care Supply Inc. for $245 million. Based in Houston, Home Care had operations in 13 states and annual revenues of $169 million.

100TH ANNIVERSARY IN 2007

In 2006, Praxair had 28,000 employees and total revenues of $8.3 billion, a record. Net income rose 24 percent in 2006 to $988 million. Top line growth continued as Praxair celebrated its 100th anniversary in 2007 as revenues climbed to $9.4 billion and income reached $1.2 billion. During the year the company bought Linde AG's Mexican industrial business and entered the Scandinavian market for the first time through a joint venture with Norway's Yara International ASA. Praxair remained the largest industrial gases supplier in North and South America and it continued its international expansion, broadening its focus somewhat.

Around this time the company also began an acquisition drive to consolidate its position in the North American packaged-gases market. In the next two years the company acquired 26 smaller distributors, 15 of them in 2008 alone. Mills Welding & Specialty Gases of Buffalo, New York, was acquired in 2007. Praxair was also investing $10 million in an upgrade of its Niagara Falls plant. In 2009 Praxair added three more distributors, in Alabama and Texas.

Company revenues continued to reach new heights in 2008, climbing 15 percent to $10.8 billion, while net income rose just 2.8 percent to $1.2 billion. A concern for some analysts was the increasing debt level, which rose $833 million to $5 billion during the year.

Praxair's overseas capital expenditures supported plans to supply electronics and LCD manufacturers in Asia as demand appeared likely to continue to grow in the emerging markets of China and India. In 2008 the company built a second on-site unit to supply Samsung's future-generation liquid-crystal display (LCD) facility in Tangjeong, South Korea. In 2009 Praxair entered a joint venture with China Petroleum & Chemical Corporation (Sinopec Corp.) to supply nitrogen and other gases from a plant in Guangzhou.

Revenues for 2009 slipped 17 percent. Part of this was due to unfavorable exchange rates. Net income was virtually flat at $1.3 billion. The company reported that its operations in Asia and South America were recovering more quickly than those in North America and

Europe. North America remained by far the largest business segment, accounting for a little more than half of revenues.

April Dougal Gasbarre
Updated, Frederick C. Ingram

PRINCIPAL SUBSIDIARIES

Liquid Carbonic Corporation; Praxair Deutschland GmbH & Co. KG; Praxair Surface Technologies, Inc.; Yara Praxair AS (Norway; 50%); Praxair (China) Investment Co., Ltd.; Praxair Distribution, Inc.; Welco-CGI Gas Technologies, LLC; Praxair Healthcare Services, Inc.; Shanghai Chemical Industry Park Industrial Gases Co., Ltd. (China; 50%); White Martins Gases Industrais Ltda. (Brazil).

PRINCIPAL DIVISIONS

North America; Europe; South America; Asia; Surface Technologies.

PRINCIPAL COMPETITORS

Airgas Inc.; Air Liquide S.A.; Air Products & Chemicals, Inc.; BOC Group plc; Linde AG.

FURTHER READING

Carter, Louis, David Ulrich, and Marshall Goldsmith, "Praxair," *Best Practices in Leadership Development and Organization Change: How the Best Companies Ensure Meaningful Change and Sustainable Leadership,* San Francisco: Pfeiffer, 2005, pp. 346–64.

Chang, Joseph, "Industrial Gas Firms to Profit from Boost in Gasoline Demand: Praxair in Running for Messer's German Gas Business," *Chemical Market Reporter,* May 31, 2004.

Chapman, Peter, "Praxair Is Entering Revived CO2 Market," *Chemical Marketing Reporter,* January 15, 1996.

Fink, James, "Praxair Expanding Operations," *Business First of Buffalo,* July 7, 2006.

Glynn, Matt, "Praxair Acquires Mills Welding; Buffalo Company Has 42 Employees," *Buffalo News,* July 3, 2007.

Moore, Samuel K., "From Cash Cow to Bull," *Chemical Week,* March 17, 1999, pp. 18–21.

———, "Praxair Hikes Prices for Bulk Products," *Chemical Week,* February 2, 2000, p. 16.

Nielsen, Karol, "Praxair Cut Jobs, Closes Plants; Takes a $150-Million Charge," *Chemical Week,* December 20, 2000, p. 12.

———, "Praxair Shuffles Management," *Chemical Week,* January 5, 2000, p. 16.

Plishner, Emily S., "Breaking Free at Carbide: Hydrogen Propels Growth of Industrial Gases Unit," *Chemical Week,* May 13, 1992.

———, "ISO 9000—Praxair: Learning from International Experience," *Chemical Week,* November 10, 1993, p. 73.

———, "Mergers and Acquisitions Become Demergers and Spinoffs," *Chemical Week*, October 7, 1992.

———, "Praxair Promises More Profits," *Chemical Week*, March 16, 1994, p. 13.

———, "Reconstructing Balance Sheets," *Chemical Week*, October 7, 1992.

———, "Unchained Melody," *Financial World*, August 29, 1995, p. 32.

"Praxair Names Reilley of DuPont to Succeed CEO Lichtenberger," *Wall Street Journal*, February 23, 2000, p. A4.

Williams, Fred O., "Praxair to Double Output of Gases at Niagara Falls Plant; Multimillion-Dollar Expansion Planned for Air Separation Facility," *Buffalo News,* April 17, 2007, p. B7.

Pulte Homes, Inc.

---

100 Bloomfield Hills Parkway, Suite 300
Bloomfield Hills, Michigan 48304
U.S.A.
Telephone: (248) 647-2750
Fax: (248) 433-4598
Web site: http://www.pulte.com

Public Company
Incorporated: 1956 as William J. Pulte, Inc.
Employees: 5,300
Sales: $4.08 billion (2009)
Stock Exchanges: New York
Ticker Symbol: PHM
NAICS: 23321 Single Family Housing Construction;
522292 Real Estate Credit

■ ■ ■

Pulte Homes, Inc., is the largest homebuilder in the United States. The company operates in 69 markets in 29 states and the District of Columbia. Its brands include Pulte Homes, Del Webb, and DiVosta Homes. Pulte secured its leading position in the homebuilding industry with the 2009 purchase of Centex Corp. The $3.1 billion deal added the Centex and Fox & Jacobs brands to its holdings. The company achieved record growth during the early years of the 21st century, but was harshly impacted by the U.S. housing crisis and economic downturn of the second half of the first decade of the 2000s. Pulte Homes posted a $1.18 billion loss in fiscal 2009. It celebrated its 60th anniversary in 2010 and planned to mark the occasion by changing its name to Pulte Group.

INCEPTION AND RAPID GROWTH: 1950–70

The company originated when William J. Pulte built his first house in Detroit, Michigan, in 1950. He incorporated his homebuilding activities in 1956 under the name William J. Pulte, Inc. In 1961 the company had one subdivision in Detroit; by 1969 it had 12 active subdivisions in six states. The company recorded $5 million in sales in 1964. That figure had nearly tripled by 1967, and sales exceeded $20 million by 1968. Pulte entered the Washington, D.C., market in 1964, the Chicago market in 1966, and the Atlanta market in 1968.

On March 4, 1969, William J. Pulte, Inc., was reincorporated through a merger with American Builders, Inc., of Colorado Springs, Colorado. The newly formed Pulte Home Corporation became a publicly owned company, and 200,000 shares of common stock were issued. The reorganization allowed Pulte entry into the low-cost Federal Home Administration (FHA) and Veterans Administration (VA) housing markets. At the same time, Pulte opened its first subdivision of medium-priced homes and began its first subdivision in the state of Virginia. The company also built high-priced conventionally mortgaged homes, student apartments, and turnkey multifamily housing. To control its construction costs, it implemented a computerized critical path program.

During 1970 Pulte evolved from primarily a supplier of high-priced single family homes to a builder of single family homes across price ranges. For the first time, the company's sales of low- and medium-priced houses exceeded those of high-priced houses in both sales dollars and units. The company completed and delivered 1,000 housing units for the first time, reaching $31.2 million in sales. The company also increased its capital base by selling preferred convertible stock for the first time.

In the early 1970s Pulte architects developed the first Quadrominium project, a single building that resembled large, custom-built, high-priced homes, but contained four separate two-bedroom units with separate entrances and garages. Pulte opened its first Quadrominiums in Chicago in 1971, providing buyers with homes for less than $20,000. To increase quality control and shorten the time between the first rough carpentry work and the closing in of the exterior against the elements, Pulte started to make extensive use of component parts. It used prebuilt trusses; prefinished cabinets, windows, and doors; and factory-built floor and wall sections.

The company expanded its presence into new housing markets and continued to grow during the 1970s and 1980s. Even as national housing starts and deliveries declined, Pulte's sales increased to nearly 5,000 units in 1980. It ranked first among all on-site builders in the United States in revenues and in homes delivered in 1985.

ADDING FINANCIAL SERVICES

One of Pulte's first financial services companies was the Intercontinental Mortgage Company, founded in 1972. Later renamed ICM Mortgage Corporation (ICM), the wholly owned subsidiary provided customers with home mortgage financing and thus made Pulte housing units more attractive to homebuyers. (Over half of all Pulte homebuyers financed through ICM in 1992.) ICM services included originating mortgage loans, placing loans with permanent investors, and servicing loans as an agent for investors. ICM posted its third consecutive year of increasing volume in 1992 as it began to focus on origination of "spot" loans for other than Pulte buy-

ers, development of core business relationships with local real estate brokerage professionals, and refinancing activities.

Other Pulte financial services companies included Pulte Financial Companies, Inc. (PFCI), which was the parent company of several bond issuing subsidiaries, and First Line Insurance Services, Inc. (First Line), which provided customers (principally Pulte homebuyers) with convenient and competitively priced insurance-related services to protect themselves and their new homes. In operation since 1981, PFCI subsidiaries engaged in the acquisition of mortgage loans and mortgage-backed securities principally through the issuance of long-term bonds. First Line was established in 1987.

On September 17, 1987, PHM Corporation was incorporated and became the publicly held parent holding company of the Pulte Home Corporation group of companies, which became the wholly owned subsidiary of Pulte Diversified Companies, Inc. In 1988 home sales were flat and one of Pulte's financing subsidiaries filed for Chapter 11 protection due to foreclosure losses. PHM saw a good opportunity to expand its financial services operations by taking advantage of the federal government's Southwest Plan to purchase five insolvent Texas savings and loan institutions.

Under the plan, the government offered excellent purchase terms, assumed the risk for any loans that went bad, and gave tax benefits for any losses generated. The acquisitions included two newly incorporated Federal Savings and Loan Insurance Corporation (FSLIC) insured institutions, First Heights and Heights of Texas. For $45 million, and with the assistance of the FSLIC, the company acquired substantially all of the five thrifts' assets of $1.3 billion and their business operations and assumed certain of their liabilities. Because Pulte was basically responsible only for loans made after the takeover, it was the Government National Mortgage Association's (Ginnie Mae) responsibility when one of the thrifts defaulted on a mortgage servicing contract only a month after the takeover. The $2.4 billion portfolio was Ginnie Mae's largest single default at that time.

Heights of Texas merged into First Heights in July 1990 and consolidated operations under the name Heights of Texas. Throughout 1991, the bank sold off home loans and securities not guaranteed against loss by the government, repaid high-priced liabilities, and made other transactions in anticipation of eventually being removed from government backing. The effect was an increase in core capital ratio. By 1992 First Heights had grown to 28 branches that offered a full range of deposit and loan services to retail and small business customers, and it had approximately $2 billion in assets.

KEY DATES

1950: William Pulte builds his first house in Detroit, Michigan.

1956: Pulte incorporates his business under the name William J. Pulte, Inc.

1969: Company is reincorporated through a merger with American Builders, Inc., and goes public as Pulte Home Corporation.

1972: Pulte forms Intercontinental Mortgage Company to provide its customers with home mortgage financing.

1993: Company is renamed Pulte Corporation; expands into Mexico.

1996: Pulte becomes nation's largest homebuilder.

2000: Pulte launches national brand development campaign and is renamed Pulte Homes, Inc.

2001: Pulte acquires Del Webb Corp., the nation's largest builder of active adult communities.

2007: Company delivers its 500,000th home; losses reach $2.3 billion.

2009: Centex Corp. is acquired.

THE "PULTE QUALITY LEADERSHIP" INITIATIVE

The homebuilding industry traditionally was one of the hardest hit by fluctuations in the economy. Factors that generally affected the housing market included national and world events that impacted consumer confidence and changes in interest rates; property taxes, energy prices, and other costs associated with home ownership; federal income tax laws; and government mortgage financing programs. PHM realized that a conservative financial philosophy, combined with delivery of good products, was not enough to ensure that the company's more than 35 years of consecutive profitability would continue. In 1989 the company launched the Pulte Quality Leadership (PQL) proactive initiative. PQL was a process to involve every employee, supplier, and subcontractor in devising ways to continuously improve all aspects of the company's operations and ensure its continued success. Since the company was already a decentralized organization, PQL further empowered divisions and subsidiaries to adapt products, services, and business strategies to meet the needs of local markets.

Under the PQL process, Pulte had more than 150 teams in the field working on improvements and innovations that would benefit the corporation's diverse

companies. Active councils represented each of Pulte's major disciplines: sales and marketing, land management, construction, and finance. Senior managers from every business unit joined to form the seven task teams of the National Quality Council (NQC) in 1990.

PQL training stressed the concept of "Seven Voices" that had to be heard and understood to become integral to decision making. They were the voices of customers, employees, suppliers, competitors, internal systems, communities, and shareholders. The NQC developed the Customer Satisfaction Measurement System, a communication link with new homebuyers that provided feedback on the expectations of customers nationwide. The system measured quality and satisfaction relative to expectations.

The Construction Council developed performance requirements for nearly 200 distinct processes involved in building a house. The council also implemented a comprehensive "building science" program that was the first in the industry. These initiatives fundamentally changed the way the company viewed the entire construction process. For example, in Charlotte, North Carolina, Pulte decided to complete garage slabs, driveways, walks, stairs, and rough grading far earlier in the construction process so realtors and brokers could show the houses to prospective customers even in bad weather. The new practice contributed to the company's local success and growth during challenging market conditions.

Additionally, the subcontractors liked the ease of entry and cleanliness of the job sites and customers were able to view their homes more conveniently. Pulte's Chesapeake operations converted to a screw system to attach gypsum and subfloors. The new system reduced drywall cracks, nail pops, and floor squeaks—three of the most frequently occurring problems in a new home. It also solved service problems that usually showed up after the customer moved in.

The Land Council changed the procedure Pulte Corporation used to acquire land. Instead of using the traditional industry "price and terms" philosophy, the corporation started to choose land based on an understanding of where targeted customers wanted to live. For instance, Pulte integrated 280 homesites with a large preserve of wetlands, streams, fields, and forests in suburban Baltimore. Boy Scouts, public school groups, and other civic organizations joined in planning and building hiking trails, bird houses, and other enhancements. The community received much praise, including designation by the Urban Wildlife Institute as an Urban Wildlife Sanctuary.

Because of the PQL initiative, ICM Mortgage Corporation switched from issuing traditional mortgage coupon books to a monthly mailing of mortgage statements. The innovation added costs up front, but reduced the number of calls to customer service, improved late charge collections, and decreased delinquencies because the system encouraged customers to communicate problems earlier.

THRIVING IN A CHANGING MARKET: 1990–95

During the economic downturn of the early 1990s, Pulte continued to enjoy record sales and profits in spite of weakened housing and troubled financial markets, enjoying the highest sales and profit per employee of any firm in the industry. While the country had the lowest number of housing starts since World War II during 1991, PHM Corporation enjoyed a 37 percent increase in earnings. The company was able to compete on the basis of reputation, price, location, design, and quality of its homes. It had more than 150 active subdivisions in 25 markets in the mid-Atlantic, central, southeast, and southwest geographic areas. Pulte Home Corporation attained its first $1 billion year in 1992, with a unit volume of more than 8,000.

Pulte was ready to respond to changing home design preferences and lifestyles. The typical home design before the 1990s was for a family of four. However, the company was discovering that a demand for a greater variety of styles existed and that, in order for it to remain competitive, it needed to not only "satisfy" but "delight" its customers, according to an article in *Crain's Detroit Business*. Consequently, the company established four different buyer profiles for which it designed homes: the traditional family; the single person; the empty nester; and the extended family. The last profile included parents with children starting college or with children in their 20s still living at home. To suit the lifestyles and wishes of its customers, Pulte engineered new home designs that decreased formal areas to provide space for larger kitchens with fireplaces, bigger family rooms, and master suites; and ranches gave way to two-story Cape Cods.

PHM Corporation was renamed Pulte Corporation on July 1, 1993, to capitalize on the public's recognition of the Pulte name. PHM Corporation was not widely known outside of financial circles, while Pulte had name recognition and identification throughout the geographic areas in which the company's subsidiaries marketed their products and services. It was thought that the change would decrease confusion, potentially increase awareness of the company and its subsidiaries' products and services, and help attract more investors.

The early 1990s also saw Pulte's expansion into the Mexican market. The company began by building small

850- and 450-square-foot units in Monterrey, which were priced between $7,000 and $13,000. Through an agreement with General Motors (GM) and Mexican builder Grupo Condak, Pulte also began building 6,000 homes for GM's Mexican employees in Juárez.

In 1994 the company reorganized into four separate operating divisions, based on geographic territory. The divisions—Pulte Home West, Pulte Home South, Pulte Home Central, and Pulte Home North—were highly autonomous, with each division in charge of making its own asset management decisions. The company also changed the way it evaluated potential land acquisitions. Whereas previously Pulte had used financial criteria to determine land purchase and use in a given market, it began to use a more consumer-driven approach.

In a January 1997 edition of *Builder*, Pulte CEO Bob Burgess explained: "Every land purchase must meet the needs of a particular TCG [targeted consumer group]. We normally begin land acquisition and house design addressing the specific needs of two to three TCGs." This approach allowed Pulte to develop standardized homes that met the needs of the consumers it was targeting, and reduced the need for customization of floor plans and features. The reorganization was part of an ambitious growth strategy, dubbed "Plan 2000." Plan 2000 called for Pulte to more than double its size by 2000. It also involved the company's focus on new segments of the market, including affordable housing and senior buyers.

LOOKING TOWARD A NEW CENTURY

Pulte's expansion efforts made it the nation's largest home-builder in 1996. The company, which was operating in 39 markets, sold 12,456 homes and had revenues of $1.93 billion in 1995 to win the number one spot. Just a few months after being named the biggest, it was also named the best. In November 1996, Pulte received the America's Best Builder award from the National Association of Homebuilders and *Builder* magazine.

In 1997 Pulte again reorganized its operations. The reorganization eliminated the geographic divisions established just three years earlier, replacing them with operating units that focused on targeting specific customer groups. One area of focus for the new operating structure was the adult/retirement segment of the market. Pulte jump-started its expansion in this high-growth segment, by partnering with an investment bank to form a new company dedicated to "acquiring and developing major active adult residential communities."

As Pulte left the 1990s behind, it remained poised at the top of its industry. Its activities as it prepared for the new century indicated that it planned to stay there. In late 2000, the company launched a new brand development program designed to make the Pulte name a byword for homebuilding throughout the nation. In a November 7, 2000, press release, Pulte's vice president of marketing, Jim Lesinski, explained the reason for the initiative: "On a national scale, there is limited brand identity associated with Pulte Homes or with any homebuilder. As companies in other industries and product categories have done, Pulte Homes can distinguish itself by establishing a solid brand identity that resonates strongly with the consumer." Tenets of the marketing plan included changing the company name to Pulte Homes, Inc., redesigning the logo, giving away a Pulte home in a national sweepstakes, and sponsoring a float in the Macy's Thanksgiving Day Parade.

An even more dramatic example of Pulte's commitment to growth, however, was its acquisition of Phoenix-based Del Webb Corp., the nation's leading builder of active adult communities. The July 2001 acquisition, which was valued at $1.8 billion, easily secured Pulte's position as the largest home-builder in the United States and gave the company a much stronger position in the fast-growing active adult market. In addition, the merger was expected to generate cost savings of up to $50 million annually by leveraging operational efficiencies and eliminating redundancies.

STELLAR PERFORMANCE, SHARP COLLAPSE: 2003–07

Richard Dugas was named president and CEO in 2003 and took over the company at a time when the housing market in the United States was experiencing rapid growth. In fact, Pulte was named one of the 100 fastest-growing companies in the United States by *Fortune* magazine in 2004. Revenues climbed to $11.5 billion that year and then grew to $14.7 billion in 2005. The company delivered a record 45,630 homes in 2005 was number 12 on *BusinessWeek* magazine's list of the Top 50 Best-Performing Companies. Its net profit for the year reached $1.5 billion.

According to the First American Loan Performance Index, the average U.S. home price almost doubled between 2000 and 2006. During what analysts called the housing bubble, mortgage requirements were less stringent and homebuyers were offered subprime mortgage loans and adjustable rate mortgages with low introductory interest rates. This practice left many homebuyers unable to pay their mortgages however, when interest rates were raised and home values began to fall. The number of foreclosures began to skyrocket and the housing market found itself in crisis.

The financial woes of U.S. banking, credit, and mortgage companies led to an economic recession that was felt across the globe. Unemployment rates rose in the United States and consumer confidence waned. The U.S. government launched the Federal Housing Tax Credit for first-time homebuyers in 2009 in an attempt to bolster home sales. Pulte's sales fell dramatically and in 2007, it reported a net loss of $2.3 billion. Despite the challenging business environment, the company delivered its 500,000th home that year.

A LOOK TO THE FUTURE

During this crisis, Pulte worked diligently to shore up its bottom line. It had sold its holdings in Mexico and Argentina in 2005, leaving it to focus on its domestic operations. While the number of foreclosures continued to rise and demand for new homes continued to fall, Pulte looked for ways to bolster its business. During 2009 the company announced its $3.1 billion acquisition of Centex Corp., a Dallas-based homebuilder with roots dating back to 1950. The union secured Pulte's position as the largest homebuilder in the United States and was expected to result in over $350 million in cost savings.

The deal also added the Centex and Fox & Jacobs brands to Pulte's holdings and gave the company a foothold in the first-time, lower-priced home market. This segment of the market was the strongest during this period due to low interest rates and tax incentives for first-time homebuyers.

While CEO Dugas expected harsh conditions to continue in the home building industry, the company remained focused on providing quality homes to its clients. In 2009 Pulte and its brands received more top rankings than any other homebuilder in the annual J.D. Power and Associates 2009 New-Home Builder Customer Satisfaction Study. Pulte Homes was also selected as the recipient of the 2009 Leadership for Energy and Environmental Design (LEED) Award for Homes and Outstanding Production Builder by the U.S. Green Building Council.

William J. Pulte announced his retirement from the board of directors in March 2010. A *Real Estate Weekly News* article from that month reported the founder's comments: "With 2010 marking six decades in business, with our merger with Centex complete and a great, proven leadership team in place, and, hopefully, with the worst of this housing cycle behind us, this feels like the right time to officially step away from the business."

While the future of the housing industry in the United States remained in question, William Pulte was optimistic. Indeed, he assured Pulte management during his retirement announcement, claiming, "I plan to remain a large shareholder of Pulte Homes and have never been more confident in the leadership and future success of the company."

Doris Morris Maxfield
Updated, Shawna Brynildssen; Christina M. Stansell

PRINCIPAL SUBSIDIARIES

Pulte Diversified Companies, Inc.; Pulte Mortgage LLC; Del Webb Corporation; Centex Corp.

PRINCIPAL COMPETITORS

D.R. Horton Inc.; KB Home; Lennar Corporation.

FURTHER READING

Donohue, Gerry, "Pulte Corp.," *Builder*, January 1, 1997, p. 302.

Hagerty, James R., and Sara Murray, "Fear of Double Dip in Housing," *Wall Street Journal*, November 19, 2009.

Halliday, Jean, "No Credit Problem Here: PHM Expected to Add Market Share," *Crain's Detroit Business*, March 16, 1992, p. 2.

Hurst, Nathan, "Pulte Grows with Centex," *Detroit News*, April 9, 2009.

King, R. J., "First House Pulte's Base for Success," *Detroit News*, June 11, 2000, p. 1.

"Pulte Homes Founder William J. Pulte Announces Plans to Retire," *Real Estate Weekly News*, March 5, 2010.

"Pulte Sells Mexico Operations to Investment Firm," *Reuters News*, December 27, 2005.

Runk, David, "Nation's Largest Homebuilder Looks for Room to Grow," *Associated Press Newswires*, June 8, 2002.

Wotapka, Dawn, "Pulte Buys Centex," *Wall Street Journal*, August 19, 2009, p. B3.

———, "Pulte Homes Inc. to Change Name to Pulte Group," *Dow Jones Business News*, February 9, 2010.

RR DONNELLEY

R.R. Donnelley & Sons Co.

111 South Wacker Drive
Chicago, Illinois 60606-4301
U.S.A.
Telephone: (312) 326-8000
Fax: (312) 326-7156
Web site: http://www.rrdonnelley.com

Public Company
Incorporated: 1890
Employees: 60,000
Sales: $11.58 billion (2008)
Stock Exchanges: NASDAQ
Ticker Symbol: RRD
NAICS: 323117 Book Printing; 323119 Other Commercial Printing; 51121 Software Publishers; 514191 Online Information Services

■ ■ ■

With sales of over $11 billion and manufacturing facilities around the globe, R.R. Donnelley & Sons Co. prints six out of the top ten consumer magazines in the United States. Donnelley began as a tiny print shop more than a century ago. In the decades since its first printing job, Donnelley has printed catalogs, magazines, books, telephone directories, and encyclopedias. In the early 21st century the company continued to diversify its printing services to capitalize on digital media and electronic business products. Donnelley's other services include document outsourcing and management, financial printing and communications, product usage documentation and in-box materials, real estate services,

retail inserts, radio-frequency identification and bar coding, and supply chain management solutions.

MODEST BEGINNINGS: 1860–97

In 1864 Richard R. Donnelley, a 26-year-old saddlemaker's apprentice from Hamilton, Ontario, moved to Chicago. There he established a print shop, called Church, Goodman, and Donnelley–Steam Printers, which became a modest success. When the shop's building and presses were destroyed in the Chicago fire of 1871, leaving Donnelley virtually penniless, he borrowed $20 for a trip to New York, where he managed to get new presses completely on credit. Nevertheless, it took Donnelley nearly two years to get the printing plant fully operational again.

Donnelley was a perfectionist who paid particular attention to both the artistic aspects of printing as well as the trade's scientific developments. His approach resulted in a high quality of printing that won the firm many customers. In a move that proved fortuitous, Donnelley began printing telephone books in 1886, a market that grew astronomically with the importance of the telephone.

The firm also pioneered the printing of mail-order catalogs, beginning with such local firms as Sears, Roebuck & Company. In 1890, under the aggressive leadership of Richard's son Thomas E. Donnelley, the firm was incorporated as R.R. Donnelley & Sons. By 1897 the company was so successful it expanded into larger quarters in another building. After the dawn of the 20th century, Donnelley began printing encyclopedias.

COMPANY PERSPECTIVES

For nearly a century and a half, RR Donnelley has been building an unequaled ability to help our customers prepare, produce, deliver, and process printed and other integrated communications. The enduring value that we bring to these relationships draws on our industry leading scale, innovation, and geographic reach. These resources are fostered by an intense focus on financial discipline in every aspect of our business—and exercised through our employees' deep commitment to operational excellence. We look forward to the challenges and opportunities that lie ahead.

PRINTING ADVANCES AND SUCCESS WITH MAGAZINES: 1900–30

Although becoming increasingly mechanized, printing was still very much a craft executed by hand before World War I. Donnelley often hired his employees right out of grade school, putting young workers through the Apprentice Training School he began in 1908, one of the first industrial training programs in the United States. Employees worked their way up through each department, learning all aspects of the printing business.

In 1921 Donnelley opened a printing plant in Crawfordsville, Indiana. The plant was built by local workers, who then helped install the equipment, and were offered jobs and training in how to use it. In 1928 Donnelley began printing one of the first of a new wave of national, mass-market magazines, titled *Time*. The following year, the onset of the Great Depression was disastrous for the printing industry, and magazine and newspaper circulations plummeted. However, with contracts such as *Time* magazine Donnelley was able to stay in business.

In 1934 magazine circulations began to increase again. Donnelley foresaw the demand for a larger format for magazines, printed on coated paper, as well as the industry's need to produce these new magazines on tight deadlines. Thus the company began developing the materials and expertise to produce such magazines at a reasonable cost. Donnelley engineers combined a rotary press with smaller printing cylinders and a high-speed folder to increase production from 6,000 to 15,000 impressions an hour.

Donnelley researchers, working with ink manufacturers, developed a heat-set process for instantly drying ink at these speeds, using a gas heater built right into the printing press. During this time, the publishers of *Time* magazine had been considering the development of a picture magazine. Shortly after they heard about Donnelley's new high-speed printing methods they awarded the firm the contract to publish the new *Life* magazine, the first issue of which came out in 1936.

WORLD WAR II AND POSTWAR BOOM: 1945–59

World War II, with its paper shortages and government-imposed restrictions on commercial printing, was a difficult time for those in the business. After the war, however, printing boomed and soon became a $3 billion-a-year industry. New technologies promised to revolutionize printing, including phototypesetting and electronic scanners for platemaking. Donnelley, already the largest commercial printer in the United States and continuing to grow, quickly invested in such technologies as they came out.

Donnelley went public in 1956 to raise capital for further expansion. By that time the company had over 160 presses, many of them huge and modern, using over 1,000 tons of paper and 20 tons of ink a day. The firm employed 7,500 people; Crawfordsville alone had 1,600 employees. Representing a rare exception in the printing industry, most Donnelley employees did not belong to a union. About 90 percent of Donnelley's executives and supervisors were graduates of the Apprentice Training School and were either college graduates who had gone through a training program or had come up through the ranks. The firm's turnover remained low.

The company's magazine printing business was its most profitable, and such nationally distributed periodicals as *Time, Life, Look, Sports Illustrated, Farm Journal, National Geographic,* and *Fortune* accounted for about half of sales. Donnelley's huge mail-order catalogs for Sears, Roebuck & Co. and Marshall Field's accounted for about 17 percent of sales. Donnelley printed over 1,000 telephone directories for subscribers throughout much of the country, accounting for about 13 percent of sales. It also printed encyclopedias, including *World Book, Encyclopedia Britannica,* and *Compton's,* as well as corporate reports, the Bible, and other religious publications. Donnelley engaged in less glamorous printing as well, such as booklets, pamphlets, menus, and the labels for packages and cans.

Donnelley mailed so many publications every day that the U.S. Post Office had employees working in the company's plants to supervise the vast mailings. Major plants, with floor space totaling nearly three million square feet, were located in Chicago; Willard, Ohio; and Crawfordsville and Warsaw, Indiana. The firm continued its role as a research and development leader in the industry, spending about $1.6 million a year. In addition to designing mechanical equipment and improving printing materials, Donnelley worked to keep up with cutting-edge electronic and photographic technology. Looking for new technologies was imperative as the costs of labor, material, and equipment were all rising, while intense competition kept prices down.

Having gone public, Donnelley grew by a total of 50 percent between 1954 and 1959, with record sales of $130.1 million in 1959. Despite a depressed economy, sales reached $149.8 million in 1961, with Time Inc. accounting for 29 percent.

CHANGING TIMES: 1960–79

During the mid-1960s, however, Donnelley's profits leveled off. The firm recovered by 1968 as magazine sales, which accounted for 41 percent of sales, broke out of a slump. By that point Donnelley's hardcover publishing had increased to represent 22 percent of sales while retail catalogs also stood at 22 percent. Printing technology changed rapidly in the late 1960s as photocomposition, computerized justification, and electronic scanning were changing the way plates were readied, and high-speed offset printing also changed the process. In 1968 Donnelley bought an RCA Videocomp, which set 4,500 characters of type per second using a cathode-ray tube. One Donnelley manager estimated that the machine could set as much type as every hot-metal typesetter in the Midwest. Simultaneously, the firm created a separate photocomposition and electronics division that employed computer programmers and electronic communications specialists instead of production staff.

As type became easier to set, however, the popular magazine market was shrinking. *Look* folded in 1971, taking $15 million of Donnelley's business with it; then *Life* cut circulation from 8.5 million to 5.5 million. As a result of these losses, Donnelley laid off 700 people, soon cutting an additional 400 people to keep its costs down. Despite its losses, however, the firm made $24 million in 1971 on sales of $340 million. With magazines suffering, most of Donnelley's growth came from catalogs and directories. To keep pace, the firm opened a plant in Lancaster, Pennsylvania, in 1972, exclusively for the printing of phone books for the mid-Atlantic states. To further offset mass market magazine losses, Donnelley worked to win jobs producing special interest periodicals, printing 24 such periodicals for Ziff-Davis Publishing alone.

In 1972 *Life* magazine stopped publishing entirely, resulting in a $3 million charge against earnings and further layoffs. Donnelley also lost its contracts with *Fortune* and *American Home.* Fortunately, the company found new customers with *Esquire* magazine, and signed 10-year contracts with *Glamour* and *Mademoiselle,* and a five-year contract with *U.S. News & World Report.* Donnelley's conservative financial practices helped it weather the storm. The firm paid low dividends on its earnings, had net working capital of $90 million, and only $3 million in long-term debt.

In 1974 the firm began shifting away from high-quality four-color extended runs, which had accounted for most of its work until then. Numerous small publishers were appearing, and others were moving toward smaller initial press runs to cut down on remainders and the costs of storage. Publishers instead wanted the ability to quickly reprint books that sold out their first edition; Donnelley was determined to change accordingly. Over the next few years the company installed a short-run plant in Crawfordsville, for producing college, professional, and trade books, and doubled capacity at its Willard, Ohio, plant. In the late 1970s the firm began building a state-of-the-art plant in Harrisonburg, Virginia, to offer overnight delivery to publisher warehouses on the East Coast.

SERVING CLIENTS BOTH LARGE AND SMALL: 1980–89

In the early 1980s, Donnelley increased its shift toward small press runs. It began an aggressive telemarketing campaign in which it contacted numerous small publishers, trying to change its image as a printing house for larger clients only. As a result, by 1983, Donnelley had between 600 and 700 book publishers as customers, and short-run books accounted for nearly 50 percent of unit sales.

Sales grew rapidly, reaching $2.2 billion in 1986. The following year Donnelley purchased Metromail Corp. for $282.6 million. Metromail provided lists to direct-mail marketers, and, as Donnelley already printed and distributed catalogs for direct-mail marketers, the acquisition was expected to complement Donnelley's existing business. It also moved into financial printing, opening a Wall Street financial printing center shortly before the stock market crash of October 1987.

In the late 1980s, Donnelley's expansion went into overdrive, culminating with the purchase of Meredith/Burda Printing for $570 million. Donnelley was also moving rapidly into such information services as computer documentation, with sales of $190 million by 1989 out of total sales for the year of $3.1 billion. The firm used electronic printing techniques and information from Metromail to help its clients gear advertising and editorial content toward different audiences. Furthermore, Donnelley was entering the markets for printing books for children, professional books, and quick-printing, with the purchase of 25 percent of AlphaGraphics, a high-end quick-printing chain.

The firm pushed expansion so hard because it believed ever-evolving technologies gave it an opportunity to capture large chunks of business from smaller companies that could not afford to keep up. Donnelley's moves into cutting-edge technology were not always successful, however; in 1984 it had made a premature, ill-fated attempt to move into electronic shopping.

HIGHS AND LOWS: 1990–96

With the U.S. economy in a recession in 1991, the firm's net income declined about 9 percent to $205 million. The following year, however, profits bounced back to $234 million and sales rose to nearly $4.2 billion. During this time, the company acquired Combined Communication Services, a trade magazine printer, and American Inline Graphics, a specialty, direct-mail printer. The firm also continued its expansion outside the United States, opening new offices and plants in the Netherlands, Scotland, Mexico, and Thailand. In addi-

tion, Donnelley increased its presence in electronic media and online services.

Such successes helped to partly offset losses in Donnelley's traditional markets. In early 1993 Sears ceased publication of its 97-year-old catalog, which Donnelley had printed since its inception. Consequently, Donnelley laid off 660 employees, took a $60 million charge against earnings, and closed its historic Lakeside Press plant. A few months later, the company announced it would begin printing the *National Enquirer* and *Star* tabloids. These publications opted to use Donnelley because its advanced printing processes allowed tighter deadlines and turnaround times of less than 40 hours.

In 1994 Donnelley scored several coups, including exclusive contracts with HarperCollins and Reader's Digest, a 51 percent stake in Editorial Lord Cochrane SA, South America's largest printing firm, as well as the development of a new state-of-the-art digital book production system first put into use in the Crawfordsville plant. Under a new program christened Donnelley Digital Architecture, the company was able to shift most printing jobs into digital form and shorten the entire publishing process, from proofing to final printing and binding. The next innovation, print-on-demand publishing, was initiated in a new 60,000-square-foot plant in Memphis, Tennessee, and accommodated print runs from mere hundreds to millions. Hoping to set a new standard for the industry, Donnelley wanted its customers to know that any print run, of any size, could be created and printed in record time.

Sales for 1994 climbed over 11 percent to just under $4.9 billion, and the following year the company acquired International Communications & Data, a direct-marketing information and list service provider; LAN Systems Inc., a systems integration company; and Corporate Software Inc., a leading reseller of business software. In the latter deal, Donnelley merged its Global Software Services division with Corporate Software, forming a new company called Stream International Inc., of which Donnelley retained an 80 percent interest.

The middle and late 1990s were also a time of concentrated international expansion, with Donnelley increasing its presence in Chile, China, India, and Poland, with operations in 21 countries. By the end of 1995 sales reached $6.5 billion, a 33 percent climb due in part to the company's global expansion. A slowdown came in the first quarter of 1996, however, when sales fell below expectations. Rather than adopt a wait-and-see posture, Donnelley announced restructuring plans that included closing its bindery in Scranton, Pennsylvania, while pouring millions into newer technologies and upgrades in other printing facilities. Despite taking some major write-downs during the year for its reorganization, Donnelley was still ranked the number one printing company in the United States by *American Printer* for 1996, and brought in sales of just over $5 billion.

ENDING ONE CENTURY, BEGINNING ANOTHER

In 1997 came a major transition with the appointment of a new chairman and CEO, William L. Davis, formerly of the St. Louis-based Emerson Electric Company. Davis replaced longtime CEO John Walter, who had left to become the new head of AT&T. The year also saw the departure of the company's legal and financial services subsidiary, Donnelley Enterprise Solutions Inc., which was spun off as a public company. Over the next few years Donnelley was intent on integrating its three print management segments into a cohesive whole while investing millions in the latest digital printing innovations and business solution products. "We recognize that our customers have a growing need to communicate effectively across a broad range of media to succeed," Chairman and CEO Davis told *Graphic Arts Monthly*'s Lisa Cross in a January 2000 article. A major step in this direction was the company's deal with Microsoft Corporation to produce and maintain an electronic bookstore, offering Internet clients hundreds of thousands of electronic book titles; while the acquisition of Omega Studios, a Texas-based desktop publishing service, was another coup for its evolving e-commerce solutions and services sector.

LOOKING TO THE FUTURE

During the early years of the new millennium, the shift from paper printing to digital media happened at breakneck speed. Donnelley and its peers in the printing industry were forced to adapt by revamping their business strategies to capitalize on emerging technologies. Donnelley opted to grow its business through acquisitions. In early 2000, the company acquired CTC Distribution Direct in a move that doubled the size of its Logistics arm. CTC was the largest mailer of business-to-home packages and print items in the United States. In 1999 the company delivered 130 million packages and 15 billion magazines, catalogs, and direct-mail items.

During 2000 the company invested in Noosh Inc., an Internet-based printing services company. It also purchased Iridio Inc., a premedia provider of digital photography and various other digital printing services. Donnelley's focus on Internet ventures and logistics

however, had not produced stellar profits and the company began to shutter underperforming businesses and implement cost-cutting initiatives including layoffs.

Meanwhile, the company continued to look for strategic acquisitions that would bolster is core printing business. During 2003 it announced plans to buy Canada's Moore Wallace Inc., a printer of business forms and labels, in a $2.8 billion deal. The two companies joined forces and created a printing powerhouse with over $8 billion in annual revenues. Moore Wallace CEO Mark Angelson took the helm of the newly merged company upon Davis's retirement. The Astron Group and OfficeTiger, both providers of business process outsourcing services, were also purchased.

OVERCOMING ECONOMIC CHALLENGES

With the U.S. economy beginning to falter, Donnelley began to feel the pinch as its clients began spending less on printing services. As such, the company tightened its focus on core operations and sold its package logistics business, including CTC Distribution that it had purchased in 2000, while keeping its print logistics business. It also moved company headquarters to a smaller location in Chicago as part of its cost-cutting efforts.

Angelson retired in 2007 and Donnelley's chief financial officer Thomas Quinlan was named his replacement. He led Donnelley through a series of acquisitions over the next two years that included Banta Corp., a Wisconsin-based provider of printing and digital imaging services. The $1.3 billion deal bolstered Donnelley's presence in U.S. markets as well as in Europe and Asia. Donnelley also purchased textbook printer Von Hoffman from Visant Corp. for $412.5 million and Perry Judd's Holdings Inc., a catalog and magazine printer. Cardinal Brands Inc., an office products manufacturer, was also purchased in 2007.

During 2008 the company bought Pro Line Printing Inc., a printer of retail inserts and circulars. It added Prospectus Central LLC, an electronic-delivery provider of financial and investment documents, to its arsenal in 2009. In early 2010 Donnelley announced the purchase of shareholder and marketing communications services firm Bowne & Co. Inc.

Tough economic conditions led to stagnant revenues in 2007 and 2008. While Donnelley worked to shore up sales and profits, it maintained a leadership position in the global printing industry thanks in part to its acquisition strategy over the past decade. While the company would no doubt face challenges in the near future, CEO Quinlan was confident Donnelley was well positioned for success in the years to come.

Scott M. Lewis
Updated, Nelson Rhodes; Christina M. Stansell

PRINCIPAL SUBSIDIARIES

Anthology, Inc.; Banta Corporation; Cardinal Brands Canada Limited; Caslon Incorporated; Check Printers, Inc.; Confort & Company, Inc.; Moore Canada Corporation; Moore Wallace North America, Inc.; OfficeTiger Holdings Inc.; R.R. Donnelley Global, Inc.

PRINCIPAL COMPETITORS

Dai Nippon Printing Co., Ltd.; Toppan Printing Co., Ltd.; World Color Press Inc.

FURTHER READING

"Acquisitions Will Benefit R.R. Donnelley, Analysts Say," *Chicago Daily Herald*, January 30, 2007.

Arndorfer, James B., "Waiting Made Deal Pricey for Donnelley," *Crain's Chicago Business*, February 23, 2004.

Corfman, Thomas A., "Printer R.R. Donnelley & Sons Leans to Move Away from Chicago River," *Chicago Tribune*, November 17, 2004.

Cross, Lisa, "Print's Hot Prospects in the Digital Economy," *Graphic Arts Monthly*, January 2000, p. 50.

"Donnelley Pushes Envelopes; Printer Putting Office Supplies in Big Boxes," *Crain's Chicago Business*, October 29, 2007.

"Donnelley to Buy Von Hoffman," *Capital Times & Wisconsin State Journal*, January 4, 2007.

Hilts, Paul, "Donnelley, Microsoft Team to Expand eBook Business," *Publishers Weekly*, November 8, 1999, p. 11.

Roth, Jill, "Top 100-Plus: The Listing," *American Printer*, July 1996, p. 29.

"R.R. Donnelley to Buy Banta in $1.3 Billion Deal," *Wall Street Journal*, November 1, 2006.

Tita, Bob, "Donnelley's Merger Momentum Gone," *Crain's Chicago Business*, October 25, 2004.

Randstad Holding nv

Diemermere 25
Diemen, 1112-TC
Netherlands
Telephone: (+31 20) 569 5911
Fax: (+31 20) 569 5520
Web site: http://www.randstad.com

Public Company
Incorporated: 1960 as Uitzendbureau Amstelveen
Employees: 34,550
Sales: $20 billion (2008)
Stock Exchanges: Euronext Amsterdam
Ticker Symbol: RAND
NAICS: 561320 Temporary Help Services; 561310 Employment Placement Agencies; 541612 Human Resources and Executive Search Consulting Services

■ ■ ■

Based in the Netherlands, Randstad Holding nv is the world's second-largest temporary staffing and employment services company in terms of revenues, trailing only Adecco S.A. Switzerland. Randstad operates in 44 countries under the Randstad and Tempo-Team brands for temporary staffing and permanent placement sector; Randstad, Randstad Care, Expectra, Sapphire, and Yacht brands for the search and placement of middle and senior management positions; Randstad and Tempo-Team for human resources services, including consulting and administration outsourcing; and Randstad and Tempo-Team for on-site in-house human resources services.

The company is one of the top three companies in its industry in nearly 29 countries, including Canada, France, Germany, India, Mexico, the Netherlands, Spain, and the United Kingdom. It also maintains a major position in Australia and the United States. Randstad is a public company with shares listed on the Euronext Amsterdam Exchange.

BEGINNINGS AND EARLY SUCCESS

In 1960 Frits J. D. Goldschmeding was working on a thesis for a master's degree at Amsterdam's Vrije Universiteit. His topic was temporary employment. He subsequently started his own temporary services agency, known as Uitzendbureau, from his dorm room. Soon he had more than three-dozen employees. Goldschmeding is said to have conceived the idea after reading a Citroën annual report.

The company was renamed Randstad Uitzendbureau in 1964. (The Randstad is a very densely populated region in the western Netherlands made up of cities, towns, and villages that encircle an area of woods and lakes.) The next year, the company's first international branch, Interlabor, opened in Belgium. In 1968 new offices in Germany followed. The 32 offices in the three countries brought in more than Nfl 47 million of revenues (in Netherlands florins) in 1970. Three years later, Randstad broached the French market.

In 1974 a contract cleaning division was established in Germany. These services were initiated in Belgium the next year, and Belglas was acquired. Contract cleaning services were expanded to the Netherlands in 1976,

---

COMPANY PERSPECTIVES

We match people with companies that will develop their potential; and we match companies with people that will take their business to the next level.

---

and Korrekt Gebäudereinigung was acquired in Germany. Randstad cleaned or serviced a variety of different types of sites, including planes, trains, and buildings. According to the company, this revenue source grew consistently because businesses believed in the motivational benefit of a clean working environment while at the same time they preferred to delegate non-core activities. Randstad supported the formation of objective quality standards in the cleaning industry and has proudly displayed its ISO certification in this area since 1992.

NAME CHANGE: 1978

In 1978 the corporate name was changed to Randstad Holding n.v. The next year, the company opened its 100th office and achieved a net income of more than Nfl 10 million. Group revenues surpassed Nfl 500 million in 1980. The decade began with the formation of Randon, the security division, which opened in the Netherlands. Besides guard and surveillance services, Randstad provided a home security alarm system through Randon Meldkamer. The company felt its insistence on professionalism made it attractive to this market.

In 1983 the company continued its expansion in the Dutch staffing market with the purchase of a mid-sized Dutch temporary services agency, Tempo-Team, which specialized in industrial and technical services, as did two other of Randstad's Dutch offices, Werknet and Otter-Westelaken. Belgium followed with training services in 1988, when automation services were added to the company's repertoire in the Netherlands. This profitable venture eventually had six offices. Software and hardware sales to financial, distribution, and transport companies added to the revenues of AICA, the computer services bureau, which also developed accounting systems.

Revenues exceeded Nfl 1 billion in time for the company's 25th anniversary in 1985. Over 1,300 staff and a daily average of 36,000 temporary employees then worked for Randstad's 257 offices in four countries. In addition, Lavold, a cleaning services company, was

bought, adding to Randstad's capacity in the Netherlands and Belgium.

Randstad began training cashiers, computer operators, telemarketers, and other personnel for its Dutch clientele in 1986. The Randstad Training Center consisted of 14 offices in 1994; Randstad also conducted these activities on-site for client companies. Offices were opened in Great Britain in 1989, when group revenues exceeded Nfl 2 billion. By 1993, the Randstad Employment there had seven offices. Randstad entered the Spanish market late in 1993, with a one-office firm Randstad Trabajo Temporal.

In the 1990s, Randstad began offering higher-trained technical staff in the Netherlands, Belgium, and Great Britain through nine specialized companies (Randstad Interim Techniek, Randstad Research & Development Services, Inter Techniek, Polydesign Nederland, Polydesign België, Interdesign, Randstad Inter Engineering, Randstad Specialist Engineering, and Technisch Bureau Visser). Randstad's technical services division was active in the machinery, transport equipment, electronics, hospitality, insurance, petroleum, and construction industries, among others.

INDUSTRY LIBERALIZATION

Beginning in the 1960s, the Netherlands provided an ideal environment for temp agencies. In the early 1990s, it was estimated that 2 percent of Dutch workers were temps, more than four times the ratio found in Germany. One-third of all Dutch workers had worked for a temporary services agency at some time in their careers. In 1994 the company had 408 offices overall in the Netherlands.

The challenge for Randstad in Europe, like that for many other companies with international aspirations, was the restrictive attitude of certain governments, particularly Germany, Spain, and Italy. In these countries, temporary employment agencies were seen as a threat to the job security of long-term employees. The "Doppeleinsatz" requirement in Germany, where Randstad Zeit-Arbeit had 31 offices, mandated temporary agencies provide two successive temporary positions for every worker.

After a group of temp agencies filed a complaint with the European Commission in 1992, Spain and Germany liberalized their markets somewhat. The Doppeleinsatz rule was waived for hard-to-place workers in Germany in 1994, and workers were allowed to work nine months as temporaries, rather than six months. A class action lawsuit was filed against Italy, that ultimately was decided by the European Court of Justice. In areas where public and private sectors controlled labor supply,

KEY DATES

1960: Frits J. D. Goldschmeding founds Uitzendbureau Amstelveen in the Netherlands.
1965: First international branch opens in Belgium.
1978: Company changes name to Randstad Holding nv.
1990: Company (the listing is the stock) is listed on the Amsterdam Stock Exchange.
2007: Randstad acquires Vedior N.V.

Randstad foresaw government agencies focusing on gathering candidates, while temporary agencies concentrated on matching the candidates to the most appropriate jobs. In 1994, legislation was passed allowing Belgians to work as long as six months as temporaries, compared to three months previously. Randstad operated under the names Interlabor Interim, Randstad Interim, and Flex Interim in Belgium.

After determining that many of its clients were seeking long-term solutions, Randstad set up several new programs. Vendor-on-Premise placed a Randstad staffing manager to support company management. Facility Staffing handled large-scale, long-term staffing needs. Outsourcing gave Randstad functional responsibility for an entire department, process, or function. Other solutions were labeled Vectoring and Temp-to-Hire.

U.S. EXPANSION: 1993

Randstad termed its processes "social technology." ISO certification gave Randstad the opportunity to highlight its systematic approach. These international quality guidelines, originally applied to manufacturing industries, were extended to service industries in 1992 in the Netherlands. Soon, Randstad had picked up a series of certifications, first as a specialist cleaning company, and later, in 1993, as the first international temporary employment agency to receive the appellation.

In 1994 Randstad operated 780 offices in seven countries, including Belgium, Germany, France, Great Britain, and Spain. Nevertheless, the Netherlands hosted the majority (495) of the company's offices, where it had a 37 percent market share. Thirty-five percent of revenues were earned outside the Netherlands. On an average day, nearly 100,000 people were employed by Randstad. This figure had tripled from 36,000 in 1985.

Most (86 percent, or Nfl 3.2 billion in 1994) of the firm's income came from temporary services.

The company's French operations, Flex and Randstad, were integrated in 1994 under the name Randstad Intérim. This move, which reduced the number of offices in France from 94 to 75, resulted in some loss of market share, but provided more efficiency and greater revenues. The acquisition of Temp Force in 1993 allowed Randstad entrée into the world's largest temporary services market: the United States. Randstad limited itself exclusively to the Southeast, a region where growth in temporary services consistently exceeded 10 percent annually and in which relatively few worked as temporaries. In spite of Randstad's tradition of hiring workers with higher than average educational backgrounds (more than 60 percent had attended postsecondary schools) they reported no problems regarding worker skills in the South, which had long had a spotty reputation for education.

Randstad acquired 12 Atlanta offices with the Temp Force purchase and instantly became the city's largest temporary employer. Nashville's Jane Jones Enterprises, Tennessee's largest independent staffing service, was bought the same year, giving Randstad a total of 25 offices in the United States. Nearly 40 new offices were opened in the next two years so that by 1995, the company had over 70 offices in the United States. Erik Vonk, a newly hired banker who specialized in mergers and acquisitions, led U.S. operations, which were named Randstad Staffing Services.

As had been its custom elsewhere, the company actively managed its acquisitions in the United States, to the chagrin of many existing managers; fewer than half stayed with the new owner more than two years. A chasm existed in most temporary agencies between recruiting temps and marketing to clients. Randstad managers, on the other hand, were responsible for both areas. The company also prided itself on its decentralized organization.

RANDSTAD SUPPLIES ATLANTA'S OLYMPIC GAMES: 1996

Randstad supported its risky U.S. start-up with an audacious marketing strategy. While bidding to supply employees for the 1996 Olympic Games, the company elected to become an official sponsor, an unprecedented position for a staffing service. The challenging contract reportedly gave the company a loss on some of its assignments but allowed it instant name recognition and a chance to display its skills. Part of the job included finding over 4,000 bus drivers for the public transportation system.

Despite the widespread problems reported in the press, some difficulties in communication between Randstad and the Atlanta Committee for the Olympic Games, and the disaster of the July 27 bombing in the Centennial Olympic Park, the company assembled the largest single peacetime flexible workforce to date and counted the experience as positive for the company. Debra Drew, Randstad's vice president and director of Olympic programs told *Workforce* magazine in 1997 that the company had expected a 30 percent staff "no-show" (employees quitting or skipping work without notice). In fact, only 4 percent of Randstad's Olympic employees did so. "The opportunity to work at the Games just changed people's lives. In the end, it wasn't just about giving people a job, it was giving them the experience of a lifetime," she said.

The exposure gained by participation in the Olympics seemed to help the company grow. In 1997 the company had reached 1,000 branches in Europe and North America. In 1998 the company expanded its North American operations by acquiring the staffing branch of its competitor AccuStaff, Inc. The $850 million cash deal boosted its U.S. presence and helped the company become one of the industry leaders in the United States. Also that year, founder Frits Goldschmeding stepped down as CEO and was succeeded by Hans Zwarts.

The turn of the century saw further growth for Randstad on both sides of the Atlantic. In 1999, the company enlarged its European operations with its acquisition of Time Power Personal-Dienstleistungen in Germany and Tempo Grup in Spain. However, 2000 saw the company with lower revenues than expected, and that year the company sold its cleaning services company Lavold. In 2001 the company once again expanded its operations in North America with its acquisition of Strategix Solutions. By acquiring Strategix, Randstad increased its locations in the United States from 89 to 478, providing the company with offices in 34 states.

Randstad also pursued e-commerce ventures that proved more of a distraction than they were worth. In May 2000 Randstad teamed up with publisher VNU nv to formed Newmonday.com, an online European recruitment portal. Revenues were so disappointing that in October 2001 Randstad withdrew. For the year, revenues decreased 11.3 percent to $5.15 billion and earnings dropped more than 70 percent to $53 million.

Not only did Randstad respond to this disappointing performance by implementing a cost-cutting program, the company installed a new chief executive and chairman, Ben Noteboom, in early 2003. A former executive with international experience at a major chemical company, Noteboom had been with Randstad since 1993, worked his way through the executive ranks, and joined the executive board in 2001. Once in charge, Noteboom returned Randstad to its core strength, providing temporary staffing to large companies. Randstad began to rebound, due in large measure to a decision to standardize its temp services, regardless of country. A concept that worked in one industry in one country was simply transferred to a new market.

VEDIOR NV ACQUIRED: 2007

By 2004 Noteboom had turned Randstad around and was looking to expand. A pair of Poland-based staffing companies, Intersource and Job Net, were acquired in 2004, as was the industrial staffing unit of Arvako Sverige AB. A year later, Randstad added another industrial staffing business, Netherlands-based Hageweld, and purchased a controlling interest in EmmayHR, an Indian recruitment firm. All of these deals, however, paled in comparison to the $5.14 billion acquisition of another Dutch company, Vedior NV, in 2007, a deal that made Randstad the world's second-largest staffing group with combined sales of more than $25 billion. As a result, Randstad held the top spot in the Netherlands, Belgium, Canada, Germany, India, Poland, and Portugal.

While smaller than Randstad, Vedior was older than its longtime rival. Founded in 1949 it was the first temporary staffing company in the Netherlands. Vedior expanded beyond the country in 1970 by opening offices in Belgium and Germany. In the mid-1990s the company began expanding through acquisitions, and in 1997 it was spun off by its corporate parent since 1980, Vendex International. In 1997 Vedior became a public company listed on the Amsterdam Stock Exchange. Access to the equity markets and the use of stock fueled further acquisitions, so that by the time Vedior joined with Randstad, it had completed 50 acquisitions in the space of seven years, while expanding from 28 to 50 countries.

The integration of Vedior and Randstad was time consuming but successfully completed in 2009 in spite of the complications presented by a global recession. Randstad was active on a number of other fronts in the meantime. In 2008 the company expanded its services in Japan by acquiring a 10 percent interest in FujiStaff Holdings, Inc., the sixth-largest staffing company in Japan, whose staffing market was the third largest in the world. Randstad also divested some operations. In 2008 Randstad Portugal was sold to Kelly Services, Inc., a move made necessary to pass regulatory muster on the Vedior acquisition. A year later Randstad sold some of its Dutch human resources services portfolio, including salary administration and payroll services, to Raet B.V. In October 2009 Randstad subsidiary CIAN, a provider of human resource and payroll outsourcing services, was sold to NorthgateArinso.

Despite difficult business conditions, Randstad performed well. Signs of economic recovery became apparent in the fourth quarter of 2009, setting the stage for the resumption of growth for the company. With the Vedior operations now fully integrated, there was every reason to expect a strong performance from Randstad as the economic climate continued to improve.

Frederick C. Ingram
Updated, Lisa Whipple; Ed Dinger

PRINCIPAL SUBSIDIARIES

Randstad Nederland bv; Randstad Belgium nv; Tempo-Team nv; Randstad Deutschland GmbH & Co KG (Germany); Yacht bv; Randstad North America LP (USA); Sesa International SA (Argentina); Randstad Pty Ltd.; Emmay HR Services Pvt. Ltd.

PRINCIPAL COMPETITORS

Adecco S.A.; Allegis Group, Inc.; Manpower, Inc.

FURTHER READING

Branningan, Martha, "Randstad Holding Agrees to Purchase Division of Accustaff for $850 Million," *Wall Street Journal*, August 28, 1998, p. B4.

Coleman, Zach, "Major Acquisition Boosts Randstad's U.S. Plans," *Atlanta Business Chronicle*, September 4, 1998, p. 16A.

DeMarco, Edward, "Randstad Will Try to Boost U.S. Temp Use," *Atlanta Business Chronicle*, May 7, 1993, p. 10A.

Dorsey, James M., "Randstad Expects to Post Surge in Profits for 1999," *Wall Street Journal Europe*, January 11, 2000, p. 6.

Dresang, Joel, "Staffing Companies' Merger Would Create New No. 2 Company," *Milwaukee Journal Sentinel*, December 3, 2007.

Flynn, Gillian, "The Summer Olympics: An HR Disaster?" *Workforce*, February 1997, pp. 25, 28.

Hiday, Jeffrey L., "Temporary Workers Reap Higher Pay, Competition, Changes in Sector Also Boost Benefits," *Wall Street Journal*, November 8, 1996, p. B14.

Laster, Kasee, "Changes in Temping Industry Varied, but Needed," *Business Ledger*, June 13, 1995, p. 14.

"Netherlands: Employment Agencies Could Merge," *New York Times*, December 4, 2007.

"Randstad Holding; CEO, Ben Noteboom," *Business Week*, June 27, 2005, p. 54.

"Randstad's Vedior Global Buys Indian HR Giant," *Financial Express*, August 10, 2008.

"Randstad to Buy Vedior for $5.1B," *UP NewsTrack*, December 3, 2007.

Rose, Robert L., and Martin du Bois, "Temporary-Help Firms Start New Game," *Wall Street Journal*, May 16, 1996, p. B4.

Salwen, Kevin G., "How a Bold Temp Agency Took Gambles—and Won," *Wall Street Journal*, July 5, 1995, p. 1S.

Van de Krol, Ronald, "The Netherlands' Invisible Army," *International Management*, March 1993, pp. 44–45.

sagt der Hausverstand.

Rewe International AG

———— ▪ ————

IZ-NOe-Sud Strasse 3, Objekt 16
Wiener Neudorf, A-2355
Austria
Telephone: (+43 02236) 600 0
Fax: (+43 02236) 600 82031
Web site: http://www.rewe-group.at

Wholly Owned Subsidiary of Rewe Zentrale AG
Incorporated: 1996 as Billa AG; 2009 as Rewe International AG
Employees: 66,000
Sales: EUR 11.55 billion ($16 billion) (2009)
NAICS: 445110 Supermarkets and Other Grocery (Except Convenience) Stores

■ ■ ■

Rewe International AG is the holding company for the international supermarket operations of German retailing giant REWE-Zentral AG, also known as REWE Group. Based in Wiener Neudorf, Austria, Rewe International was formed in 2009 as part of the restructuring of Rewe's Austrian operations and its growing businesses in Central and Eastern Europe.

Billa AG and the Billa supermarket chain remain the company's flagship, with more than 1,000 stores in Austria; the Billa chain also been the spearhead for the group's international expansion. Billa focuses primarily on the full-range supermarket sector. In 2009, however, Billa began pilot testing of a new convenience store format, Billa Box, specializing in coffee, drinks, and snacks. Rewe International's other Austrian operations

include the Merkur chain of more than 117 large-scale hypermarkets in Austria; nearly 560 BIPA perfume and cosmetics shops; and the ADEG network of more than 550 independently owned grocery stores. Altogether, Rewe International's Austrian operations generated nearly EUR 7 billion ($10 billion) in sales in 2009.

Billa has become the flagship brand for Rewe International's broader expansion into the Central and Eastern European regions. At the beginning of 2010, the company's operations in these markets included more than 500 Billa supermarkets in Bulgaria, the Czech Republic, Croatia, Romania, Russia, Slovakia, and Ukraine. Rewe International also regroups Rewe's supermarket operations in Italy, with more than 600 stores under the Billa and Unica names. Rewe International's operations outside of Austria accounted for approximately one-third of the company's total sales of EUR 11.55 billion ($16 billion). Rewe International itself represents nearly one-third of Rewe Group's total revenues. The German parent expects its foreign operations to account for as much as 60 percent of its total sales by 2015.

CHEAPER GOODS IN 1960

Billa AG, and its parent company Rewe International, stemmed from the retail empire founded by Karl Wlaschek in the early 1950s. Born in Vienna in 1917, Wlaschek had originally sought a career as a musician, performing as a jazz pianist under the stage name Charly Walker. Wlaschek became a bandleader and hoped to establish his own dance hall but lacked the funds to achieve this.

KEY DATES

1953: Karl Wlaschek founds a discount retail shop, Warenhandel Karl Wlaschek (WKW) in Vienna, Austria.
1960: WKW opens the first Billa supermarket in Vienna.
1977: The company incorporates as Billa AG, then becomes BML Gruppe.
1991: BML forms Eurobilla and begins expanding into Eastern Europe.
1996: Rewe Group acquires BML.
2009: Rewe International AG is formed in Austria as the holding company for Rewe Group's international operations.

Instead, at the age of 36, Wlaschek turned to the retail sector. Inspired by developments in the retail sector in other parts of Europe, Wlaschek opened Austria's first discount shop, called Warenhandel Karl Wlaschek, or WKW. Wlaschek initially focused on sales of cosmetics, perfumes, health and beauty products and other items, pioneering the market for low-priced goods in Austria. The discount formula proved a success in Austria, which struggled to rebuild its economy following World War II. By the end of the decade, Wlaschek had expanded WKW into a chain of 45 shops.

By then, Austria, like its European counterparts, had entered into a new period of economic prosperity. Wlaschek recognized a new opportunity to expand his growing retail empire. Through the 1960s, Austria's food retail sector remained dominated by the traditional small shops and groceries. The supermarket format, developed in the United States, had only just begun to spread through the other western European markets. Wlaschek spotted the potential for introducing the self-service supermarket format into Austria as well.

In 1961 Wlaschek unveiled Austria's first self-service supermarket. Wlaschek remained true to the discount pricing formula for the new store. This was reflected in the choice of the store's name: Billa, a contraction of *Billiger Laden*, the German for "cheaper goods."

LARGE-SCALE IN THE SEVENTIES

The Billa format became an instant success. Wlaschek not only replicated his success with WKW, but he surpassed it, and by 1963 the company had already opened 67 stores. By the end of 1965, the company's network already neared 110 stores, generating total revenues of 275 million shillings. Wlaschek also began expanding his original store format, adding departments for fresh foods and frozen foods. In 1966 the company pioneered a new larger store, featuring 1,000 square meters of selling space. The new store provided separate departments for fresh produce, as well as for fresh milk and dairy products.

Billa added meat-processing operations through the acquisition of Andert Fleischwaren AG. This allowed the company to include a butcher shop department in its stores into the 1970s. The company also opened a new headquarters, in Wiener Neudorf, a small town south of Vienna. In 1970 Billa became the first in Austria's grocery sector to launch an advertising campaign. As a result, the company's sales soared, topping one billion shillings that year. By 1975 Billa achieved a new milestone as its revenues topped the two billion shilling mark. Soon after, Wlaschek reincorporated the company as a joint-stock corporation, Billa AG, in 1977.

Wlaschek's retail interests continued to expand. A new retail format, the hypermarkets, that is, large-sized stores that combined the supermarket format with department store operations, had begun to appear in France and elsewhere in Europe in the 1960s. Wlaschek extended his own business into the area, opening the first Merkur hypermarket in 1969. Over the next decades, the company opened nearly 120 Merkur stores across Austria.

NEW SIGNS IN THE EIGHTIES

Into the 1980s, however, Billa faced new challenges as a number of other supermarket groups. Billa had established its reputation with its discount formula, which focused on a low-priced branded model. The company faced rising competition in this segment, however, with the appearance of the hard discount sector. Exemplified by such groups as Aldi, which had entered Austria through the acquisition of the Hofer supermarket chain, hard discount stores focused largely on generic and private-label brands in no-frills surroundings. Billa responded to this challenge with the creation of its own hard discount format, Mondo, launched in 1983. The company also developed its own line of private labels for its Billa supermarkets.

Billa also fought to maintain its position in the full-range supermarket sector, as other rivals, including Julius Meinl and Konsum, expanded their own retail chains into the 1980s. This led Billa to reinforce its own range of services and products, including the launch of a fine foods section, offering high-quality domestic and international products, such as cheeses and meat specialties.

During the 1980s Wlaschek extended his retail operations beyond the grocery sector. In 1981 Billa launched a specialty perfumery retail format, called BIPA. This chain became a major force in the Austrian retail perfume sector (and would grow to nearly 560 stores by 2010). Wlaschek had also been developing an interest in the retail books market, with the launch of the first Libro bookstore in 1978. During the 1980s, that chain grew into Austria's largest bookseller, with more than 250 outlets, and later extended its range to include stationery and school supplies, computer software, games, CDs, and DVDs.

ELECTRONIC OPERATIONS IN 1990

The growth of these extended operations led to the adoption of a new name for Wlaschek's retail empire: Billa-Merkur-Libro Gruppe (BML). By 1987 BML's network had topped 330 stores, employing more than 3,300 people and generating revenues of ATS 8.6 billion.

BML achieved still strong growth over the next decade. The company completed the expansion of its retail holdings throughout Austria. By the middle of the 1990s, the company counted more than 1,600 branches and sales of more than ATS 51 billion (approximately $5 billion), giving it a market share of between 26 and 28 percent of Austria's total retail market. BML had also become the country's single largest employer in the private sector, with a workforce of more than 18,000.

At the same time, BML boasted one of Austria's most modern retail operations. The company had become one of the first to introduce scanning technology and electronic point-of-sale equipment into its store networks at the beginning of the 1990s. These were backed by the implementation of a complete ERP (enterprise resource planning) system and the construction of an automated logistics and warehousing facility. On the product side, BML pioneered the organic foods sector, becoming one of the first supermarket chains in Europe to launch its own private-label organic foods line, Ja! Natuurlich (Yes! Naturally) in 1994.

JOINING REWE IN 1996

Karl Wlaschek remained in control of the retail empire he had founded 40 years earlier. Into the early 1990s, however, Wlaschek began taking steps to retire from the company. This led to the creation of a new private foundation, KW Foundation, which took over all of Wlaschek's retail holdings in 1994.

Two years later, Wlaschek reached an agreement to sell most of BML to German retail giant Rewe. With little room for growth left in Germany, Rewe had increasingly targeted international expansion to ensure its future growth. The acquisition of BML not only gave Rewe the leading retail company in Austria, it also gave it a new brand, Billa, with which to enter the greater Central and Eastern European markets.

Rewe reportedly paid Wlaschek 16 billion shillings (approximately $1.4 billion) to acquire nearly all of his retail empire. Not included in the initial sale was the Libro bookstore chain, which Wlaschek hoped to turn over to his son, Karl Jr. When the younger Wlaschek proved uninterested in that business, Wlaschek sold Libro in 1997. Despite his advanced age, Wlaschek himself had not finished his business career. Indeed, over the next decade, Wlaschek began investing his fortune in the real estate market. By 2009 Wlaschek, then 92 years old, had become one of, if not the, largest private property owners in Austria, with a personal fortune estimated at $3.2 billion.

TARGETING THE CENTRAL AND EASTERN EUROPEAN MARKETS

Under Rewe, meanwhile, the Austrian retail business was renamed Billa AG. The company continued to seek new expansion opportunities in Austria in order to consolidate its leadership position. In 1999 the company launched a takeover bid for the Julius Meinl supermarket group, then in the process of refocusing its own operations on the international markets. Billa's bid for Meinl was blocked on competition grounds. The two companies ultimately reached a modified agreement, with Billa taking over Meinl's stores in Vienna and southern Austria.

By then, Billa had already become Rewe's largest international operation, with nearly 1,600 outlets. Following the fight to take over Meinl, however, the company was forced to renounce any further ambitions for expansion in Austria. Instead, Billa became the spearhead for Rewe's expansion into the Central and Eastern European markets.

Billa had already made a start in this direction at the beginning of the 1990s, when the company created subsidiary Eurobilla AG in 1991. Through Eurobilla, Billa made its first entry into several of Austria's newly liberated neighbors, opening the first Billa stores in Poland, Hungary, the Czech Republic, and Slovakia. The company adapted its store formats for these markets, which were unfamiliar with Western-style supermarkets after decades of Communist rule. By the end of the 1990s, however, the international Billa stores had adopted the same format as their Austrian counterparts.

Billa added a number of new markets into the turn of the century. The company entered Romania in 1999 with a first store in Bucharest. Just two years later, the Billa's Romanian operations had already topped 35 stores. Billa also achieved strong growth in Bulgaria, where its first store opened in Sofia in 2000.

ACQUIRING SCALE IN 2008

Billa added Ukraine in 2000 as well, becoming the first to open a Western-style supermarket in Kiev that year. Through the next decade, the Billa brand continued its penetration of the region, adding subsidiaries and stores in Croatia, Hungary, and Russia. Billa's expansion was not entirely limited to the Eastern European markets, however, as the company began developing its supermarket network in Italy as well. In 2001 Rewe acquired the Standa supermarket group there and then launched the Billa and Bipa chains there as well.

Billa's Croatian operations received a boost in 2005, when it bought up local rival Minaco. This acquisition added 26 outlets to Billa's existing 16 stores, making it the second-largest supermarket group in Croatia. In Romania, the company continued adding new stores, reaching 42 outlets at the end of 2009. Meanwhile, the group had become one of the leading chains in Bulgaria, opening its 56th store at the end of that year.

Acquisitions remained a central part of the international expansion of the Billa store network. These included the takeover of Russia's Nyam-Nyam, which operated 12 stores in the Moscow area in 2008. Billa paid $100 million for the chain, and then launched a major rollout of the Billa brand in that country. By mid-2009, the company's Russian branch already operated 58 Billa stores. Similarly, Billa boosted its presence in Slovakia and the Czech Republic, buying up 11 stores in the former and 95 in the latter, formerly owned by Belgian supermarket group Delhaize. In Italy, meanwhile, the company bought up Unica and its 38 Uni supermarkets in the Piedmont region.

REWE INTERNATIONAL AG IN 2009

In Austria, in the meantime, Billa AG set out to maintain its dominance of the market there by launching a major upgrade of its 1,000-strong supermarket chain. As part of that effort, the company developed a new, more modern format. The company then began converting its existing stores or replacing them with new stores. Billa also responded to the increasing appeal of

the fast-food and convenience sectors to the Austrian public. In November 2009, the company launched the pilot testing of a new Billa Box concept. These small-sized shops focused primarily on offering a range of drinks, including coffee, and snacks. If the pilot shop proved successful, the company planned to extend the new format across Austria.

Billa's strong growth both at home and in its other markets led its ultimate parent company Rewe Group to restructure its international operations in 2009. As part of that process, Rewe created Rewe International AG, which replaced Eurobilla and took over as the holding company for Billa AG, the group's Central and European subsidiaries, as well as its operations in Italy. The company's Austrian operations remained the centerpiece of Rewe International, generating approximately two-thirds of its total sales of EUR 10.93 billion ($15 billion) in 2009. By then, Rewe International's Billa flagship brand had grown from being Austria's supermarket pioneer to becoming a leading ambassador for Western-style retailing in the Eastern European region.

M. L. Cohen

PRINCIPAL SUBSIDIARIES

Billa AG, Billa spol. S.R.O.; BIPA Parfumerien Gesellschaft mbH; Euro-Billa Holding AG; Merkur Warenhandels-Aktiengesellschaft.

PRINCIPAL DIVISIONS

Billa; Merkur; Bipa; Adeg.

PRINCIPAL COMPETITORS

Hofer KG; Interspar Gesellschaft mbH; Lidl Austria GmbH; Zielpunkt Warenhandel Gesellschaft mbH and Company KG; Pfeiffer HandelsgmbH; Penny GmbH; MPREIS Warenvertriebs GmbH; Wedl and Hofmann Gesellschaft mbH; Julius Meinl.

FURTHER READING

"Austrian Billa Supermarket," *Super Marketing*, February 26, 1999, p. 10.

"Austrian Supermarket Launches Airline," *Airline Industry Information*, May 5, 2004.

"Billa Set to Buy Nyam-Nyam," *Grocer*, August 30, 2008, p. 11.

Hochwarter, Thomas, "Billa Opens Three Shops in Bulgaria," *Austrian Times*, November 20, 2009.

———, "Billa Starts Small Shop Pilot Project," *Austrian Times*, November 10, 2009.

"Meinl Sheds Stores, Billa Expands," *Eurofood*, July 1, 1999.

Moreau, Sebastien, "L'Allemand Rewe Rachete la Premiere Chaine de Supermarches Autrichienne," *Les Echos*, July 19, 1996, p. 11.

Perrotta, Peter, "Welcome to the Most Modern Supermarket in the World," *Supermarket News*, July 16, 2001, p. 14.

"Rewe Group Is Trialing a New Billa Convenience Format in Vienna before Deciding Whether to Roll It Out," *Grocer*, November 14, 2009, p. 6.

"Rewe Uses Billa to Acquire Russian Njam Njam," *Austrian Times*, December 4, 2008.

Vorotnikov, Eugene, "Rewe-Owned Supermarket Chain Billa Continues Expansion in Romania," *FoodBizDaily*, November 19, 2009.

Rheem Manufacturing Company

1100 Abernathy Road, Suite 1400
Atlanta, Georgia 30328-5620
U.S.A.
Telephone: (770) 351-3000
Web site: http://www.rheem.com

Wholly Owned Subsidiary of Paloma Co., Ltd.
Incorporated: 1930
Employees: 5,000
Sales: $1 billion (2008 est.)
NAICS: 333415 Air Conditioning and Warm Air Heating Equipment and Commercial and Industrial Refrigeration Equipment Manufacturing

■ ■ ■

Atlanta, Georgia-based Rheem Manufacturing Company produces residential oil and gas furnaces, air conditioners, air handlers and cleaners, dehumidification systems, tank and tankless water heaters, solar water heaters, pool and spa heaters and pumps, and home generators. Rheem also offers commercial water heating and commercial heating and cooling systems. Products are marketed through independent contractors under a host of brands, including Raypak pool and spa, and hot water and heating products; Richmond water heaters; Prostock heating and air conditioning products; and Ruud water heaters, air conditioners, furnaces, and home generators. Rheem's domestic offices are located in Fort Smith, Arkansas; Montgomery, Alabama; and Oxnard, California. Rheem also maintains international operations in Canada, Mexico, Argentina, Brazil,

Australia, New Zealand, and Singapore. Rheem is a wholly owned subsidiary of Japan's Paloma Co., Ltd., the world's largest gas appliance company.

RHEEM'S ORIGINS

Rheem was launched by brothers Richard S. and Donald L. Rheem with financing from a third brother, William K. Rheem. In Emeryville, California, in 1925 these men formed a partnership, the Pacific Galvanizing Company, to oversee operation of a hot-dip galvanizing plant. They then formed a second partnership, Rheem Manufacturing Company, to produce sheet steel products at an adjoining plant, completed in the fall of 1926, thus creating the only company in northern California for fabricated and galvanized steel production at a single location.

Rheem mostly produced drums to serve the West Coast oil industry but in early 1930 acquired the Republic Steel Package Company, maker of underground storage tanks and other gas station equipment as well as hydro-pneumatic tanks, septic tanks, and boilers. Less than three weeks later Rheem Manufacturing Company, Ltd., was formed to acquire the two partnerships and Republic. The concern had shown remarkable growth during its first five years. With warehouses in Seattle, Portland, Los Angeles, and Phoenix, Rheem was able to distribute its products in 11 western states as well as several countries, and its steel drums were used to ship oil around the globe.

Rheem opened a new plant in Los Angeles in 1931 and in that same year became involved in the gas-fired water heater business through the acquisition of the

John Wood Manufacturing Company of Los Angeles. Rheem began to expand to the east in 1936 with the opening of a plant in Houston, Texas. A year later Rheem became a public company and established a national distribution system along with a sales office in New York City.

Over the next decade Rheem grew at an accelerated clip, both organically and through acquisitions. Two steel container companies were purchased in 1937: National Steel Barrel Co. of Cleveland, Ohio, and Meuer Steel Barrel Co. of Newark, New Jersey. A year later the Texas steel barrel business of Houston-based Wackman Welded Ware Co. was added. In the meantime, Rheem opened three plants and a research laboratory in Maryland in 1940 and expanded internationally as well. It acquired a plant in Sydney, Australia, in 1937 to produce shipping containers and household appliances, and plants in Brisbane and Melbourne soon followed.

WORLD WAR II-ERA TRANSACTIONS

By 1941 Rheem was largest manufacturer of steel shipping containers and water heaters in the United States. At the time, separate wars in Europe and the Pacific were about to be joined and sweep up the United States into the global conflict, resulting in Rheem devoting much of its capacity to defense contracting. In 1944 Rheem began preparing for the postwar era. In that year it acquired the Atlas Steel Barrel Division of Bethlehem Steel and the coal-fired stoker and furnace business of Stokermatic Co. of Salt Lake City.

After the war, Rheem in 1946 entered the water-softening equipment business by securing the water-softening process of Eugene P. Jordan. Rheem now looked to shift its focus from industrial to consumer markets and in 1946 began to advertise Rheem's

household appliances. A year later it bolstered its consumer products by acquiring the Frazer line of gas furnaces and winter air conditioners. Rheem did not neglect the industrial market, however. Strong growth in the petroleum and chemical industries created an increasing demand for Rheem's steel containers.

By the start of the 1950s Rheem was the world's largest manufacturer of steel drums and other steel containers, generating about $15 million in annual sales. A major factor in the company's success was the development of Rheemcote, a proprietary method for applying color lithography to the exterior of 55-gallon steel drums that could also be used to facilitate the lining of the inside of the drums with noncorrosive and sanitary materials to allow for the shipment of food products and corrosive fluids. At this stage Rheem's international business was served by 10 subsidiaries and associated companies in Australia, Canada, the United Kingdom, Singapore, and South America.

Rheem expanded its product lines in the 1950s. The boiler and tank business of the Wheeling Steel Corp. were acquired in 1951, as was the Wedgewood line of gas ranges from the James Graham Manufacturing Company. The Wedgewood brand was later applied to gas and electric clothes dryers. Fiber and steel-fiber drums introduced in 1953 bolstered Rheem's container business.

The company became involved in the production of springs and automobile bumpers through the 1954 acquisition of U.S. Spring and Bumper Company. In 1956 the purchase of Richmond Radiator Company brought a line of bathroom and kitchen plumbing fixtures, and the Blue Bonnet and Western-Holly line of gas ranges were added with the acquisition of the Standard Enameling Company, but they proved too regional in appeal and were divested two years later. The decade also saw the departure of the company's founders, as both Richard and Donald Rheem retired in 1958.

RUUD ACQUIRED: 1960

With 42 plants and operations in some 20 countries, Rheem improved annual sales to more than $60 million by the start of the 1960s. Rheem began the decade by completing one of the most significant acquisitions in its history, buying Ruud Manufacturing Company, a well respected brand and a pioneer in water heaters. Not only did Ruud expand Rheem's line of commercial products, it added an excellent distribution network to serve the commercial market. At the close of the 1960s Rheem acquired Minnesota-based National Heater Company to supplement its line of heating and cooling products.

In the early 1960s Rheem recorded net earnings and sold off an 80 percent stake in a semiconductor company. A year later, in 1962, Rheem sold its Electronics division and discontinued its Automotive division. After returning to profitability, Rheem began producing custom-engineered products and systems for the oil and gas industries; acquired Tipper Tire, Inc., to begin making metal closures and processing equipment for food and chemical packaging; became involved in the manufacture of plastic containers through the purchase of Aragon Products, Inc.; and in 1969 acquired New York Pressing to manufacture pressing and cleaning equipment used by dry cleaners. Also of significance, Rheem International, Inc., was formed in 1963, and in 1968 Rheem Manufacturing was purchased by City Investing Company of New York.

A major spur to growth for Rheem in the late 1960s and early 1970s was the increasing adoption of central air conditioning. In 1970 Rheem acquired Acme Industries, a Michigan manufacturer of commercial central air conditioning equipment. The water heaters business also enjoyed strong growth, due in large part to the development of a do-it-yourself market for water heaters, which now became available to consumers at the new big-box home improvement centers as well as lumber yards and hardware stores. To better serve these core operations, Rheem in 1973 established a pair of divisions, the Air Conditioning Division in Fort Smith, Arkansas, and the Water Heater Division in Chicago. In order to keep up with demand, the Air Conditioning Division added a plant in Milledgeville, Georgia, in 1978.

PALOMA INDUSTRIES ACQUIRES COMPANY: 1988

Ownership changed hands when in late 1984 Rheem was acquired by Pace Industries, Inc., a company backed by Merrill Lynch Capital and the private investment firm of Kohlberg, Kravis, Roberts and Company. Rheem next decided to exit the container business which was no longer a good fit, and in that same year, 1985, acquired Raypack, Inc., a California maker of commercial boilers and swimming pool heaters. Rheem's annual sales reached $834 million in 1986. A year later Pace Industries put the business on the block and an agreement was reached to sell Rheem to MLX Corp., the reorganized McLouth Steel Co., for $825 million in cash and stock. A stock market crash later in the year, however, prevented MLX from raising the necessary funds. A new buyer was then found, and in 1988 Rheem was sold to Paloma Industries Ltd. of Nagoya, Japan.

The water heater operation in Chicago was moved at the start of the 1990s to Montgomery, Alabama, which became the new headquarters for the Water Heater Division. A new water heater plant was also opened in Nuevo Laredo, Mexico, in 1990, supplementing production that was also conducted in Ontario, Canada. Across the board, Rheem improved its manufacturing operations, so that in 1996 all of its plants qualified for ISO 9000 certification.

Rheem also made advances on other fronts during this period. The industry's smallest gas furnace was introduced by the Air Conditioning Division in 1992. Two years later the division was the first in the industry to adapt scroll compressor technology to improve performance, and in 1998 it introduced its Modulating 90 Plus gas furnace, which was able to keep a home's temperature within one-half of a degree of the thermostat set point while eliminating cold and hot spots.

Raypak, in the meantime, transformed its industry in 1994 by introducing the RP-2100 pool and spa heater that included electronic controls, on-board diagnostics, and other advanced features that earned the product the International Forum Award for design in 1997. In that same year, Raypak introduced a new heat pump line that provided customers with a greater choice in pool heating.

The Water Heater Division enjoyed its share of achievements as well in the 1990s. In 1996 it introduced the feature-rich Rheem/Ruud Professional Series of residential gas water heaters for plumbers and contractors, and the Universal line of commercial gas water heaters. The Richmond gas and electric water heater line was completely redesigned for the retail market in 1997. A year later the division reached an important agreement to supply Home Depot stores throughout the United States and Canada with a General Electric water heater line.

NEW CENTURY REORGANIZATION

In the new century the company developed the Rheem Prostock wholesale concept and product line that replaced the Universal Parts line of heating and air conditioning products and launched a chain of dedicated parts retail stores to more effectively merchandise parts to contractors. The early 2000s also brought a reorganization of the Water Heater and Air Conditioning Division in 2007 to keep pace with changes in the plumbing and heating and air conditioning industries.

The company's chief executive officer. I. S. Farwell told the press, "My vision is to begin to build a 'New Rheem,' to take a bold step into the future and to take this great company to new heights and new levels of excellence." A year later, Farwell turned over the responsibility of completing this vision to a new chief executive officer, J. R. Jones, who succeeded him in April 2008. Jones was taking over a viable concern, one that was well positioned for ongoing success.

Ed Dinger

PRINCIPAL DIVISIONS

Heating and Cooling Products; Water Heating Products; Pool & Spa Products.

PRINCIPAL COMPETITORS

A.O. Smith Corporation; Carrier Corporation; Trane Inc.

FURTHER READING

"Another Advance in Sight for Rheem Manufacturing," *Barron's,* May 10, 1965, p. 22.

"Eastbay Firm Shows Rapid Expansion," *Oakland Tribune,* December 7, 1930, p. 50.

Gabriele, Michael C., "Paloma Plans to Purchase Rheem Mfg.," *Metalworking News,* April 4, 1988, p. 5.

Mazurkiewicz, Greg, "Rheem Embraces Retail Concept for Parts," *Air Conditioning, Heating & Refrigeration News,* April 9, 2001, p. 30.

"Rheem Co. Complete New Plant," *Oakland Tribune,* September 12, 1926, p. 46.

"Rheem Manufacturing Set to Extend Solid Rebound," *Barron's,* January 20, 1964, p. 21.

"Rheem MFG. Sales to Run Far Above Prewar," *Barron's,* January 27, 1947, p. 6.

"Rheem Reorganizes Corporate and Divisional Management," *Air Conditioning, Heating & Refrigeration News,* April 16, 2007, p. 6.

Well, Warren, "Rheem Manufacturing: Upturn in Sales and Earnings Point Toward Record Year for Company," *Barron's,* August 28, 1950, p. 16.

Royal Cup Coffee, Inc.

160 Cleage Drive
Birmingham, Alabama 35217
U.S.A.
Telephone: (205) 849-5836
Toll Free: (800) 366-5836
Fax: (205) 271-6071
Web site: http://www.royalcupcoffee.com

Private Company
Founded: 1896
Employees: 635
Sales: $198 million (2007 est.)
NAICS: 311920 Coffee and Tea Manufacturing

■ ■ ■

Royal Cup Coffee, Inc., is a privately held Birmingham, Alabama-based premium coffee and tea importer, roaster, and distributor serving the United States, Canada, Mexico, and the Caribbean. Wherever people consume coffee outside of the home the company considers its market. Royal Cup's restaurant clients include Carrabba's Italian Grill, Cracker Barrel Old Country Store, Landry's Seafood House, Outback Steakhouse, Red Lobster, Texas Roadhouse, and Waffle House.

The company also serves hospitals and such hotels and resorts as the Ritz-Carlton, Hilton Hotels, and Sea Island Resorts. Convenience stores are another major market, as are offices, which Royal Cup serves through its Café Concepts program. In addition to coffee and tea products and providing brewing systems, Café Concepts

offers other drinks and juices, water filtration products, and paper products.

Royal Cup coffee products include a variety of gourmet coffees, flavored coffees, and espresso. Tea products include green tea and decaffeinated tea, as well as iced tea bags. The company employs a team of buying agents who over the years have cultivated relationships with plantation owners and coffee brokers around the world and pay regular visits to the growing regions to personally inspect the crops for quality as well as to ensure that certain ethical and environmental standards are maintained. Royal Cup is owned and operated by the second generation of the Smith family.

19TH-CENTURY ORIGINS

Royal Cup traces its history to 1896 when a coffee company was established in Birmingham, Alabama. Ten years later it was bought out by Henry T. Batterton. Born in Kentucky in 1880, Batterton was a salesman whose line of work had brought him to Birmingham, which he recognized as a fast-growing community and a good place to own a business. Thus, he and his wife moved to Birmingham to run Batterton Coffee Company. She packaged in jars the coffee he roasted and he then sold it on the streets from a horse-drawn wagon for 10 cents a jar. According to company lore, the coffee was so flavorful that it was considered fit for royalty, leading Batterton to call the brand Royal Cup. He also sold the Garland brand of coffee.

Under Batterton's leadership the company enjoyed strong growth. An experienced salesman, Batterton was

<table>
</table>

COMPANY PERSPECTIVES

Over the past 100 years, Royal Cup has grown from its small, hometown roots to become a major importer, roaster and distributor of premium coffees and teas.

involved in the community and a member of the Rotary Club, bringing coffee to be served at meetings he attended. By 1919 he had outgrown his original Second Avenue location and moved to a new facility on First Avenue North and 24th Street. In addition to coffee, Batterton began to carry teas, as well as spices, extracts, and baking soda. By 1930 Batterton Coffee Company had grown to become the largest coffee supplier in Alabama. In 1930, however, Batterton was killed in an automobile accident in Palo Alto, California, and a local bank took charge of the business.

SMITH FAMILY BUYS COMPANY: 1950

In 1950 William E. Smith Sr. of Birmingham bought Batterton Coffee Company from the Batterton estate, and later in the decade the company name was changed to Royal Cup Coffee, Inc. Under Smith's leadership the company began to expand beyond Alabama. Another significant development during this period was the establishment in 1958 of the first routes to service restaurants and hotels. In 1968 Royal Cup launched its Office Beverage Division, a step that would transform the company and drive the company's growth across the southeastern United States in the next three decades.

Smith would not witness the rapid growth of Royal Cup, however. He died in 1968 and his 26-year-old son William E. Smith Jr. was thrust into the role as president. Although young, Smith Jr. was qualified to fill the position. Not only had he served two years as a second lieutenant in the U.S. Army Infantry, he held an MBA degree from the Harvard Business School. He was employed at General Mills in Minneapolis when he was called back to Birmingham to take charge of the family business. Another son, Hatton C. V. Smith, was 17 years old at the time and soon joined his brother at Royal Cup as well. In 1989 William Smith was named chairman of the company and Hatton Smith succeeded him as president.

SPECIALTY COFFEES GROW IN POPULARITY

With its office coffee service leading the way, Royal Cup grew at a rapid clip under the second generation of the Smith family, due in large measure to the growing popularity of specialty coffees. Royal Cup also did well in other channels, supplying coffee to such restaurant chains as McDonald's, International House of Pancakes, Waffle House, Huddle House, and Cracker Barrel; the Doubletree, Marriott, and Ritz-Carlton hotel chains; and Premiere Healthcare.

In addition, Royal Cup served convenience stores and gas stations, servicing not only coffee bars but also soft drink bars, making the company one of the largest wholesalers of Coca-Cola syrup in the United States. Although a line of Royal Cup coffee was sold on a limited basis in grocery and gourmet stores, the company was reluctant to divert its attention from its primary sales channels. By the early 1990s Royal Cup was selling about 20 million pounds of coffee a year, as well as two million pounds of tea.

A major step in the growth of the company came in 1996 when it entered the Washington, D.C., market. To serve the metropolitan area, the company opened a distribution center in Northern Virginia. Also in 1996 Royal Cup secured $7 million in revenue bonds from the city of Birmingham, and two years later completed a $10 million expansion to its main operation, adding a new 75,000-square-foot warehouse, 25,000 square feet in new office space, and a new, massive state-of-the-art roasting machine that would replace four existing roasting machines.

DINE-MOR ACQUIRED: 1998

Much of Royal Cup's success in the 1980s and into the 1990s came from working through the national licensing system of St. Louis-based Dine-Mor Foods Inc., a marketing and distribution company that worked with a group of regional coffee roasters. All told, the Dine-Mor operation included 310 distribution centers and 900 local coffee specialists. Royal Cup owned a stake in the business, and in the fall of 1998 acquired virtually all of Dine-Mor. Royal Cup at that time was primarily a Southeast brand, although earlier in the year it had expanded into the Pacific Northwest and acquired Phoenix, Arizona-based Kohl's Coffee Co., a roaster. The addition of Dine-Mor, while risky, helped to transform Royal Cup into a national concern. Dine-Mor was renamed Royal Cup Dine-Mor and its headquarters relocated to Birmingham.

The acquisition of Dine-Mor opened up new opportunities for Royal Cup. Royal Cup became the sole

```
┌─────────────────────────────────────────────────────┐
│                                                       │
│                    KEY DATES                          │
│                       ■                               │
│  ─────────────────────────────────────────────────   │
│                                                       │
│   1896:  Predecessor coffee company is founded in     │
│          Birmingham, Alabama.                         │
│   1906:  Henry T. Batterton acquires company;         │
│          renames it Batterton Coffee Company.         │
│   1930:  Local bank takes charge of the business fol- │
│          lowing Batterton's death.                    │
│   1950:  William E. Smith Sr. acquires Batterton      │
│          Coffee.                                      │
│   1968:  Royal Cup launches its Office Beverage       │
│          Division.                                   │
│   1998:  Royal Cup acquires Dine-mor Foods Inc.       │
│   2007:  Commercial sales division is established.    │
│                                                       │
└─────────────────────────────────────────────────────┘
```

coffee supplier for restaurants and room-service operations at the 15 units of Loews Hotels in the United States, Canada, and Monaco. As the new century began, Royal Cup continued to add customers, including 400 new McDonald's locations in Texas, the TGI Friday's restaurant chain, and Outback Steakhouse Inc., including its 72 Carrabba's Italian Grill Restaurants and all 574 units of the Outback Steakhouse restaurant chain. All told, Royal Cup at that time served over 25,000 customers.

ROYAL CUP SERVES RESCUE WORKERS: 2001

It was at the behest of Outback Steakhouse that Royal Cup became involved in the rescue efforts at Ground Zero in New York City following the terrorist attacks of September 11, 2001, that toppled the World Trade Center towers. Outback executives called Royal Cup asking if the company could help with the field cafeteria it had set up to feed rescue workers at the site. Some Royal Cup licensees in Pennsylvania were first dispatched but lacked the necessary supplies. A truck that normally served as a mobile showroom was loaded with 2,000 pounds of coffee and sent from Birmingham to New York City, where it was established at the city command post and began turning out 50 gallons of coffee an hour, some of which was delivered to the rescue site in five-gallon containers on all-terrain vehicles.

Despite the adverse impact on the economy created by the terrorist attacks, Royal Cup continued to grow. Sales increased from $116 million in fiscal 2000 to $125 million two years later. The trend continued as the new century unfolded. Sales improved to $136 million in 2003, $153 million in 2004, and $177 million in 2005.

To keep pace with demand, Royal Cup acquired a Rental Uniform Service building, spending about $3 million to buy and renovate the 50,000-square-foot property, as well as another $2.5 million to upgrade its existing manufacturing facility.

A pair of new roasters and a micro-roasting plant were installed that not only increased production capacity but also improved quality. In addition to high-quality specialty blends, Royal Cup could then produce sustainable, organic coffees. As a result of this expansion, in 2006 the Birmingham operation included 160,000 square feet of space on a three-building, 20-acre campus. Royal Cup expanded its operations elsewhere as well in 2006. The Charlotte, North Carolina, branch moved into a new 42,000-square-foot distribution center, more than twice the size of the previous facility.

COMMERCIAL SALES DIVISION FORMED: 2007

Royal Cup pursued new sales opportunities as the decade progressed, hoping to become the top coffee supplier in the United States. In June 2007, shortly before the close of fiscal 2007 when the company reported sales of $198 million, the company looked to take advantage of its increased capacity by establishing a commercial sales division to target such new customers as vending companies, airlines, and government agencies. Later in 2007 Royal Cup initiated a plan to invest $7 million in an effort to grow its food service and hospitality division in two of the country's largest hotel and restaurant markets by opening five facilities in Bakersfield, Los Angeles, Sacramento, San Diego, and San Francisco, California.

In addition to covering California, the new facilities would also serve the Las Vegas market. Royal Cup's new organic coffees, the company believed, were ideally suited for these new markets where a sustainable-food movement was under way. A similar expansion of the Royal Cup operations was also undertaken in the Florida and Texas markets.

Although William Smith Jr. and Hatton Smith remained very much in charge of Royal Cup, a third generation of the Smith family was being prepared to carry on the company's tradition. William Smith's sons, William E. Smith III and Jim Smith, were involved. By 2008 the former was vice president of operations while the latter served as the information technology manager. Their father was reaching retirement age and their uncle was in his late 50s. There was every reason to expect that, when the time came to turn over control of the business, the next generation would be ready to continue the growth of Royal Cup, following in the tradition established by their grandfather and Henry Batterton.

Ed Dinger

PRINCIPAL SUBSIDIARIES
Royal Cup, Inc.

PRINCIPAL COMPETITORS
Dallis Coffee, Inc.; Folger Coffee Company; Green Mountain Coffee Roasters, Inc.

FURTHER READING

Bosley, Anita S., "Royal Cup Expanding in Nevada, California," *Birmingham Business Journal,* September 14, 2007.

———, "Royal Cup Expands, Enters New Markets," *Birmingham Business Journal,* November 17, 2006.

———, "Royal Cup Launches New Division to Target Airlines, Vendors," *Birmingham Business Journal,* June 8, 2007.

———, "Royal Cup's Success Has Been Brewing for Century," *Birmingham Business Journal,* October 30, 2000.

Mahoney, Ryan, "Royal Cup Sends Coffee, Comfort to NYC," *Birmingham Business Journal,* September 20, 2001.

Pratt, Ted, "Dine-Mor Foods Buy to Boost Royal Cup Coffee," *Birmingham News,* November 1, 1998, p. 1D.

———, "Roasting Coffee Beans Going High Tech at Royal Cup," *Birmingham News,* January 10, 1999, p. 44H.

Royal Vendors, Inc.

———■———

426 Industrial Boulevard
Kearneysville, West Virginia 25430
U.S.A.
Telephone: (304) 728-7056
Toll Free: (800) 321-8637
Fax: (304) 725-4728
Web site: http://www.royalvendors.com

Wholly Owned Subsidiary of Coin Acceptors Inc.
Incorporated: 1987
Employees: 1,150
Sales: $186.5 million (2008 est.)
NAICS: 333311 Automatic Vending Machine
    Manufacturing

■ ■ ■

Royal Vendors, Inc., is a vending machine designer, manufacturer, and remanufacturer based in Kearneysville, West Virginia. A subsidiary of Coin Acceptors Inc., Royal Vendors focuses on cold-drink vending machines and is the largest supplier of vending machines for the Coca-Cola Company. To a lesser degree the company provides machines to bottlers of PepsiCo and Cadbury Schweppes Americas Beverages.

Products include the Royal Vision Vendor Next Generation, a glass-door unit with five shelves and 40 selections, featuring upright delivery of 320 12-ounce cans or 280 20-ounce bottles. The GIII Chameleon Coca-Cola beverage vendor with a vandal-resistant solid front is available in three configurations, capable of dispensing 240–360 20-ounce bottles, 250–372 half-

liter bottles, or 550–804 12-ounce cans. Royal Vendors's EZ Vender is a low-end but energy-efficient cold-drink dispenser, able to hold 348 half-liter bottles, 276 20-ounce bottles, and 480 12-ounce cans.

Royal Vendors's Merlin line of machines carry Pepsi, Dr. Pepper, Snapple, and miscellaneous cold drinks and are available in a variety of widths, capable of holding 348 20-ounce bottles and 768 12-ounce cans. In addition Royal Vendors carries the 20 Plus Triple-Depth Vendors for Coca-Cola, Pepsi, Dr. Pepper, Snapple, and generic cold beverages; and the Milk Merchandiser delivery chute line that can dispense 312 one-pint bottles of milk products. Royal Vendors machines are sold through a network of distributors across the United States and around the world.

COMPANY ORIGINS

Royal Vendors was cofounded by Roy Steeley and Coin Acceptors' chief executive office Jack E. Thomas Jr. The 68-year-old Steeley was something of a legend in the industry, known to many as "Mr. Vending Machine," and responsible for Dixie-Narco Inc. becoming one of the leading firms in the vending machine industry. The roots of Dixie-Narco dated back to a company called Victor Products, a maker of refrigerated vending equipment in Ranson, West Virginia.

In 1957 Dixie Foundry, a Tennessee maker of stoves and cooking utensils, bought Victor. In that same year, Steeley went to work for Victor. Helping to sell the machines produced by Victor was Narco Sales. Victor bought Narco in 1967 and the resulting company was renamed Dixie-Narco. In the meantime, Dixie Foundry acquired Magic Chef and both operations now conducted business under the Magic Chef name. Steeley took over as president of Dixie-Narco in 1970 and in 1979 became a Magic Chef vice president and a member of the board of directors.

Steeley was well respected in the soft-drink vending machine industry. He took over a business that generated $2 million in annual sales and oversaw its growth into a market leader that would maintain its position, primarily due to his decision to limit the product line and focus almost exclusively on Coca-Cola and Pepsi. As a result, Dixie-Narco was better able to control costs and keep track of inventory, and bottlers appreciated the approach because standardization reduced their maintenance costs.

By 1986 Dixie-Narco's annual revenues increased to $152 million, or 64 percent of a $260 million market. In 1986 Maytag Corporation acquired Magic Chef, including Dixie-Narco, and although Steeley was asked to continue running the company he quickly grew uncomfortable with the new owners. "After the merger, there were a lot of changes made, and I didn't have the same feeling for the company," Steeley told the *Washington Post*, adding, "They're more structured than I'm used to. They insisted everything be conducted through certain channels."

LEGAL CHALLENGES

Just four months after the merger, Steeley announced he planned to retire in January 1987 but also made it known that he planned to start up a vending machine company to compete against Dixie-Narco. He asked permission to recruit former employees but was denied. A week after he retired at the end of January 1987 a dinner was held in his honor. In a speech he announced his intention to start a new company and invited his former employees to join him. This offer did not sit well with Maytag, which promptly sued Steeley in federal district court in Alexandria, Virginia, alleging he had breached contractual obligations to Dixie-Narco and contending that he had been making plans for his new company while on Dixie-Narco's payroll. Maytag maintained that it had no objection to Steeley starting

his own company, as long as he had done it on his own time. Maytag asked that Steeley return about $1 million in salary, severance pay, bonuses, and stock options he received during the final six months he was employed by Dixie-Narco. Steeley's attorney, on the other hand, claimed that Maytag was simply trying to prevent a dangerous new competitor from entering the market by tying him up in litigation.

Steeley incorporated Royal Vendors, Inc., in March 1987 but was unable to attract the necessary funding to launch the business while the lawsuit was pending. Finally, in September 1987 a federal court jury ruled in his favor and also awarded him $11,000 related to a deferred compensation agreement. Although Maytag appealed the decision, Steeley was now able to proceed with his business plan. He found a financial backer in Jack Thomas, whose Coin Acceptors was looking to expand beyond the manufacturer of coinage mechanisms and bill validators used in vending machines and begin making entire units.

Thomas was a lawyer by training, a graduate of the St. Louis University School of Law. He also attended Dartmouth College, where he served as assistant dean before going to work for Coin Acceptors as general counsel after marrying the daughter of the founder, Rollyn Trieman, who started the St. Louis company in 1958. Known in the industry as Coinco, Coin Acceptors was the first company to manufacture plastic-molded coin changers and bill acceptors, instead of relying on heavy metal, as well as the first to offer an electronic coin changer and the ability to electronically record and track sales. In 1982 Trieman was killed when the Cessna jet he was piloting crashed near Mountain View, Missouri, where Coin Acceptors operated a fabricating plant. Thomas was named the new CEO and built on what his father-in-law had begun. Joining forces with Steeley to manufacture complete vending machines instead of money acceptance components was a major step in that direction.

FIRST UNITS SHIP: 1988

Royal Vendors became operational in 1988, working in an industrial park warehouse located five miles outside of Kearneysville. Thomas took care of sales, marketing, and promotions, while Steeley oversaw the manufacturing operations. The company's first vending cabinets were shipped early in 1988, and then, in a critical step for the prospects of the new company, the machines passed muster with Coca-Cola and Pepsi, leading to more orders. Vending machines were important to the beverage giants because 12 percent of soft drinks sold in the United States, amounting to some $8.3 billion, were distributed through vending machines. Moreover, the

KEY DATES

1987: Company is cofounded by Ray Steeley and Jack Thomas.
1996: Thomas buys out Steeley.
1999: New plant opens in Cleveland, Mississippi.
2001: Mississippi plant closes.
2004: Sur-Serve is acquired.

profit margin on these sales were significantly higher than those at retail outlets. With Dixie-Narco dominating the market, and its top two rivals experiencing financial difficulties, bottlers were more than willing to support Royal Vendors as a way to keep Dixie-Narco from turning into a monopoly and prevent vending machine prices, which averaged around $1,000, from skyrocketing. Roy Steeley's reputation also carried weight; Coca-Cola and Pepsi trusted him, all but ensuring that Royal Vendors would succeed.

A major spur to the growth of Royal Vendors came in 1991 with the introduction of the GII, or Generation-II, product line of "smart" vending machines. Designed by Coin Acceptors and manufactured by Royal Vendors, the GII machines were successfully tested by Coca-Cola in the Charlotte, North Carolina, market late in the year. The GII line incorporated technologies that were already in use in other vending markets but were included for the first time in soft-drink vendors, including the ability to vend products at different prices, track transactions and transfer this information to the operator through a handheld computer, and alert operators of machine malfunctions. The sales information could then be used by vendors to change product mix to optimize sales. For Royal Vendors the new machines, which sold for as much as $1,800 a piece, offered greater profits.

STEELEY SELLS STAKE: 1996

Royal Vendors's sales rose steadily in the early 1990s, resulting in a factory expansion of more than 60,000 square feet of production space in 1995. Annual sales approached $50 million, most of which came from the United States, but also from Canada, Mexico, South America, Australia, and Europe. Steeley remained the majority owner and president but in 1996 decided to retire and sell his share to Thomas, who became CEO of both Coin Acceptors and Royal Vendors. Steeley's retirement did not last long, however. A year later he designed a glass-front snack vendor and founded

Automated Merchandising Systems Inc., which would go on to produce other refrigerated food machines as well as bottle and food combination vendors.

After Steeley's departure, Royal Vendors continued to grow. To keep pace, the plant was expanded further in 1998 when 142,000 square feet of production and office space was added, including a state-of-the-art production line. The facility was now 262,000 square feet in size. Royal Vendors also looked to open a second plant. In 1998 the company settled on a site in Cleveland, Mississippi, and a year later a new 130,000-square-foot plant opened to produce non-Cola-Cola vending machines, serving the likes of Pepsi, Dr. Pepper, 7 UP, and Gatorade as well as generic vending machines. Royal Vendors's parent company in the meantime continued to look ahead. In 1998 Coin Acceptors acquired a New Zealand company that had developed "smart cards" for use in vending machines. As the decade came to a close, Coin Acceptors posted revenues of about $180 million.

In the new century, Royal Vendors remained on the cutting edge of beverage vending machine technology. The cabinets were redesigned to create greater capacity, allowing new models to hold more than 800 cans or 370 half-liter bottles. Royal Vendors also developed Econo-cool Technology, which combined energy-efficient lighting, a cooling unit, evaporator fan, and software to create a unit that saved as much as 14 percent in energy. In addition, the system used a compressor that reduced energy consumption by up to 15 percent. All new Royal Vendors units included the Econo-cool package starting in January 2002. Machines built after 1996 could also be retrofitted with the ability to include all or parts of the package. The technology received special recognition at the Environmental Protection Agency's Energy Star Awards ceremony in June 2002.

CLEVELAND PLANT CLOSES: 2001

The technical advances could not make up for the adverse impact of an economy lapsing into recession in 2001. With slowing sales, Royal Vendors found itself with far more capacity than demand for its products. The company was reluctant to close the new Mississippi plant and tried to keep it running by cutting employment and remanufacturing old vending equipment, but this was a stopgap measure. When it became apparent that sales were not likely to improve anytime soon, Royal Vendors decided in the summer of 2001 to close the plant and cease operations. All work was transferred to the company's remaining plant in West Virginia.

Royal Vendors weathered the tough times and continued to develop innovative products. The Merkin line was unveiled in late 2002, offering greater container flexibility and capacity, as well as enhanced electronics, LED display, programmable options, and electronic refrigeration. In April 2003 Royal Vendors reached an important milestone, producing its one-millionth unit, the side of which displayed the names of the company's current employees.

Royal Vendors completed an acquisition in January 2004, buying Nashville, Tennessee-based Sur-Serve, a company that refurbished vending machines. Royal Vendors did not make sales information available, but there was every indication the company was doing well as the decade proceeded, both home and abroad. According to West Virginia Department of Commerce information published in 2009, Royal Vendors entered the new markets of Portugal and United Arab Emirates during this time. In all likelihood, Royal Vendors would continue to remain in the forefront of its niche market for years to come.

Ed Dinger

PRINCIPAL SUBSIDIARIES

Royal Remanufacturing LLC.

PRINCIPAL COMPETITORS

All A Cart Manufacturing, Inc.; Crane Co.; Dixie-Narco, Inc.

FURTHER READING

Caldwell, Georgia, "Royal Vendors Manufactures Success from Obscure Locale," *State Journal,* March 1995, p. 15.

Chandler, Clay, "Battle Brews for Makers of Soda Machines," *Washington Post,* July 11, 1988, p. F1.

———, "Court Backs Ex-Official of Maytag in Rivalry Case," *Washington Post,* September 7, 1987, p. F5.

Desloge, Rick, "Coinco Makes Change, Names Condie President," *St. Louis Business Journal,* December 5, 2004.

"Jack Thomas, Royal Vendors Inc. (1996 Entrepreneur of the Year)," *St. Louis Business Journal,* June 24, 1996, p. 7B.

"Royal Vendors Builds Milestone Unit," *National Petroleum News,* June 2003, p. 39.

"Royal Vendors Hold Grand Opening Here," *Bolivar Commercial,* November 15, 1999.

"Royal Vendors to Close," *Bolivar Commercial,* June 20, 2001.

"Vending—More Than Just Small Change," *St. Louis Commerce,* December 1998, p. 18.

Rumpke Consolidated Companies Inc.

10795 Hughes Road
Cincinnati, Ohio 45251
U.S.A.
Telephone: (513) 851-0122
Toll Free: (800) 582-3107
Fax: (513) 851-2057
Web site: http://www.rumpke.com

Private Company
Founded: 1932
Employees: 2,119
Sales: $396 million (2009 est.)
NAICS: 562111 Solid Waste Collection

■ ■ ■

Rumpke Consolidate Companies Inc. is the privately owned, Cincinnati-based holding company for the waste removal and recycling businesses owned and operated by the Rumpke family. Serving portions of Ohio, Kentucky, Indiana, and West Virginia with a fleet of 1,700 trucks (including rear loaders, front loaders, roll-offs, and service trucks), the group is one of the largest independents in its field in the United States.

For residential customers, Rumpke provides curbside waste removal and recycling, as well as yard waste services. The company also caters to business and industrial customers, offering waste removal and recycling services, universal and e-waste, compost collection, portable restroom rental, and hydraulic repair services. Rumpke operates landfills at five locations in Ohio, two in Indiana, and two in Kentucky, as well as several transfer stations and recycling facilities. Rumpke is very much a family business, employing more than 50 family members through all ranks of the company.

DEPRESSION-ERA ROOTS

Rumpke's origins date to the 1930s when William F. Rumpke operated a coal delivery service and junkyard in Carthage, Ohio, on 65 acres he inherited from his grandfather. Many of his rural customers, strapped for cash because of the Great Depression, paid by barter for coal. At one point, William accepted hogs as payment. One of Rumpke's employees, Bill Brown, also raised hogs on the side, feeding them garbage he collected. In 1932 Rumpke bought Brown's hog business, creating a combination hog farm-garbage dump enterprise that marked the beginning of the Rumpke waste management companies.

A few years later Rumpke's brother, Bernard, joined him as a partner in the enterprise, although he continued to work as a fire fighter. By 1945 they owned 2,000 hogs and opened a larger operation to supply the hogs with feed on an 82-acre site they bought in Colerain Township in Hamilton County, Ohio. In 1946 a reported 200 area residents attended a hearing to discuss odors at the Rumpke site. Efforts were made over the next few years to close the dump, leading to a judge in 1954 ordering the dump to be shuttered. It remained open, however, and in November 1955 a court of appeals ruled that because there was no other place for garbage collection in the area, it was not a public nuisance but, in effect, a necessity.

The Rumpkes had other legal problems at the time. An Internal Revenue Service audit revealed the brothers had not properly reported their income for several years. They cooperated and pleaded guilty. While their attorney's argument that their lack of education and other factors entitled them to probation won the sympathy of the court, in the end the presiding judge issued a heavy fine and gave each a one-year prison sentence, insisting, "Unless the court imposes a sentence, it will be an invitation for everyone else to act dumb." During the four months the brothers were actually imprisoned, the Rumpke facility was operated by relatives.

FOCUS SHIFTS TO WASTE MANAGEMENT: 1955

It was also during this period that the Rumpkes decided to exit the hog business, following new farm legislation in 1955 that no longer allowed uncooked garbage to serve as hog slop. Instead, the Rumpke brothers began to focus on waste collection and disposal. In 1956 the son of William Rumpke (Bill) and the son of Bernard Rumpke (Thomas) became involved in the waste removal and recycling business for themselves, having collected trash and fed the hogs with their fathers since they were youngsters. Once the older of the cousins, Bill, was 16 and had a driver's license, they started up a Saturday collection route that they could run while going to high school Monday through Friday.

The Colerain Township landfill remained controversial in the 1960s. The community adopted zoning in 1962, but the Rumpke operation was able to attain a special, nonconforming use provision. The Rumpkes were convicted of stream pollution in 1968, resulting from industrial and chemical wastes leaking into state water, and a year later, after the creation of the Ohio Environmental Protection Agency, the brothers were forced to convert their operation into a sanitary landfill.

To further enhance company compliance with new and constantly changing environmental regulations, the cousins established an environmental affairs and engineering team, and enforced a mission of compliance, safety and customer service that is still an integral part of daily operations today. What started out as a massive hole gradually filled with refuse and continued to climb above ground until it exceeded 1,000 feet above mean sea level in height. Dubbed Mt. Rumpke, it became the highest point in the county. In the 1990s the company would begin to adorn it with popular lights and other decorations during the holiday season.

Like other waste facilities throughout the country, the Rumpke sanitary landfill continued to stir some controversy. In 1970 the company was sued for $3 million by 20 neighbors, and two years later a $5 million suit was filed by the state of Ohio, eventually leading to a court-mandated cleanup. A second landfill was purchased in Aurora, Indiana, in 1975, followed by another in Batesville, Indiana, in 1977. The company also expanded into some Kentucky markets during this period, officially forming Rumpke of Kentucky in 1977.

SECOND GENERATION BUYS COMPANY: 1978

Cousins Bill and Tom Rumpke formed Rumpke Container Service in 1965 and then bought Rumpke Inc. from their fathers in 1978. Of the 300 people employed by the company at this time, 80 were blood relatives, most of the subcontractors driving trucks. The second-generation owners expanded the company further, completing scores of small acquisitions in the years to come, including a fourth landfill added in Pendleton County, Kentucky, in 1980. Although complaints over the landfills decreased as the operation became more sophisticated, Colerain Township residents again went to court in an effort to close the landfill.

The Rumpke cousins also diversified the business. They founded Rumpke Hydraulics & Machining to develop their own hydraulic systems and a container shop, Rumpke Industrial Equipment Service Center. In 1984 they began working with Getty's Synthetic Fuel division, now Montauk Energy, and two years later added a gas recovery system to Colerain Township landfill to take advantage of the methane gas created by the decomposing garbage to be used as a supply of natural gas. A second gas plant would be added to the site in 1995, and a third plant was added in 2007 making the facility the largest landfill-gas-to-direct-pipeline energy system in the world.

New Ohio recycling laws in the 1980s provided another opportunity for Rumpke Inc., which acquired Pickaway County Community Action Recycling to provide curbside recycling services and in 1989 formed

KEY DATES

1932: William Rumpke starts a combination junk yard and hog farm.
1955: Legislation outlawing uncooked garbage as hog slop leads Rumpke family to exit hog business.
1978: Rumpke cousins buy out parents.
1989: Recycling division is formed.
2009: Rumpke enters northern Ohio market.

the Rumpke Recycling division. This unit subsequently opened recycling facilities in Cincinnati, Columbus, Circleville, and Dayton, Mansfield, and Hanging Rock (near Ironton) Ohio, as well as Louisville, Georgetown. and Ashland, Kentucky (Ashland is now closed). The Rumpke cousins also became involved in the portable restroom business and launched Rumpke Amusements to open a Cincinnati ballpark, Rumpke Park, where community softball and baseball teams continue to play.

In addition to the recycling division, the company's core businesses at the start of the 1990s were Rumpke Waste Inc., providing municipal and residential waste collection services to customers in Ohio, Indiana, Kentucky, and Illinois, and Rumpke Container Services, an industrial refuse collection business. Rumpke looked to expand these operations into the central Ohio market. The company also pursued a new niche, medical waste. In 1994 a medical waste division was established with the purchase of a Cincinnati incinerator. The facility required a significant investment to bring it into regulatory compliance, and although the division approached profitability after two years, Rumpke elected to sell off the business in 1996 to focus on its waste collection, disposal, and recycling operations.

LANDFILL LANDSLIDE: 1996

Rumpke had other matters that took precedent in 1996. In March of that year a landslide and fire took place at the Colerain Township landfill, resulting in fines and sanctions by the Ohio Environmental Protection Agency. A year later the company paid a $1 million fine and reorganized its management. In the meantime, Rumpke became involved in a new business that proved more suitable, yard waste services. In 1997 the company opened the NPK (Nitrogen, Phosphorous, Potassium) Compost Farm to collect leaves, grass, trees (including Christmas trees), pumpkins, and brush in the Greater Cincinnati area and process the material into compost,

mulch, and absorbent material. Not only was composting a good environmental practice, it decreased the amount of waste that went into the company's landfills and in turn reduced emissions. Landfill space was limited, and as experience proved, Mt. Rumpke could only grow so high. As the 1990s came to a close, Rumpke announced a desire to add 138 acres to the Colerain Township landfill in order to meet the company's dumping needs for an additional 30 years. The expansion area was approved by courts in 2004.

The Rumpke companies combined for more than $250 million in annual revenues as the new century dawned. Consolidation had been in effect in the waste removal industry for many years, resulting in the likes of such behemoths as Waste Management and Republic Services, yet Rumpke was able to survive and prosper, becoming one of the largest independent, family-owned companies that remained in business. A key to its success was a detailed knowledge of the needs of the communities it served. Moreover, as a private company it was free from shareholder pressure and the temptation to pursue short-term expediencies in order to meet quarterly earnings estimates.

In 2002, the company formed The William-Thomas Group to broker garbage service to chain customers throughout the United States. The division was designed to combat the loss of chain customers to third-party national brokering groups. With a network of thousands of privately owned service providers and new chains of customers including Kroger and the U.S. Postal Service this business division would continue to flourish in the years to come.

There were some challenges the Rumpke family could not overcome. In 2004, 63-year-old Thomas Rumpke succumbed to cancer, leaving his cousin Bill to carry on alone as president and chief executive, after decades of the two men serving as co-presidents and CEOs of the company. More like brothers than cousins, they had been named Entrepreneurs of the Year by Ernst & Young in 1999. There was no shortage of family members to fill the void in leadership, however. Bill Rumpke Jr. had been with the company since 1978 and was named chief operating officer in 2002, and throughout the top management ranks a Rumpke relation could be found. The company remained growth-oriented as well, as sales approached $300 million in 2005. Despite Colerain Township's denial of a zoning request to expand the Colerain Township landfill by 206 acres in November 2006, Rumpke took the matter to litigation, filing a lawsuit in Hamilton County, which remained pending several years later. In late 2008, the company was also issued a permit to expand its Brown County, Ohio Landfill by 153 acres. Later Rumpke obtained expansion approvals at its Beech Hollow Landfill in Ohio, Jackson County Indiana Landfill, Pendleton County, Kentucky Landfill and Montgomery County, Kentucky Landfill.

On other fronts, Rumpke extended its landfill gas recycling business to Kentucky, opening a facility Pendleton County in 2007. Together, Rumpke's landfill gas recovery systems possessed the capability to produce enough energy for about 30,000 homes. In late 2006 Rumpke bolstered its portable restroom business by acquiring Southern Ohio Sanitation, Inc., adding about 600 portable restroom units, four pump trucks, and more than 225 core customers. In 2007 Rumpke expanded its Central Ohio footprint by acquiring Buckeye Valley Waste, a Newark, Ohio-based private waste hauling company with more than 5,000 residential, commercial, industrial, and construction customers. Rumpke also expanded its Kentucky waste hauling business by purchasing assets from Ashland, Kentucky-based H&R Sanitation, including trucks, containers, and more than 2,000 customer accounts.

NORTHERN OHIO EXPANSION: 2009

A more significant step was taken in 2009 when Rumpke completed the largest acquisition in its history, making industry consolidation play to its benefit. In order for Republic Services Inc. to merge with Allied Waste Industries Inc. and alleviate the antitrust concerns of the U.S. Justice Department, it was ordered to divest a number of operations across the country, including some facilities in northern Ohio, a coveted new market for Rumpke. The company acquired a landfill, a pair of transfer stations, 60 vehicles and other collection assets, and 100 employees in Mansfield and Cleveland, Ohio, from Republic. Altogether, Rumpke added 39,000 residential and 3,000 commercial customers spread across 11 counties, providing the company with a significant foothold in northern Ohio. Shortly after the

deal closed in August 2009, Rumpke applied stickers to rebrand the trucks and containers it purchased, gradually repainting the equipment while continuing to serve the new markets. The company appeared to be well positioned to enjoy further growth in the years to come.

Ed Dinger

PRINCIPAL SUBSIDIARIES

Rumpke Inc.; Rumpke Waste, Inc.; Rumpke of Ohio, Inc.; Rumpke of Indiana, Inc.; Rumpke of Kentucky, Inc.; Rumpke Sanitary Landfill Inc.

PRINCIPAL COMPETITORS

Casella Waste Systems, Inc.; Republic Services, Inc.; Waste Management, Inc.

FURTHER READING

Bowen, Erin, "Mt. Rumpke: More Than Just a Dump," *Miami Student,* October 31, 2008.

"Garbage Is Family Bread and Butter," *Marysville Journal-Tribune,* April 6, 1981, p. 12.

Griggs, France, "Rags and Riches," *Cincinnati Post,* March 9, 1989, p. 1A.

Johnson, Jim, "It's in Their Blood," *Waste & Recycling News,* June 22, 2009, p. 1.

———, "Rumpke to Make Major Acquisition in NE Ohio," *Waste & Recycling News,* June 22, 2009, p. 6.

Melcer, Rachel, "Rumpke Takes Trash-Hauling Expertise Regional," *Business Courier Serving Cincinnati–Northern Kentucky,* December 8, 2000, p. 42.

Perry, Lisa, "Trash Becomes Cash," *Dayton Daily News,* January 28, 1999, p. 1.

"Prison Terms and Fines Meted to Rumpke Brothers on Tax Evasions," *Cincinnati Enquirer,* January 19, 1956, p. 1.

"Thomas Rumpke, Co-Owner of Trash Hauler," *Cincinnati Post,* January 14, 2004, p. A9.

Van Sant, Rick, "Rumpke: A Mountain of Trouble," *Cincinnati Post,* December 11, 1996, p. 1A.

Ryder System Inc.

11690 N.W. 105th Street
Miami, Florida 33178
U.S.A.
Telephone: (305) 500-3726
Fax: (305) 500-3203
Web site: http://www.ryder.com

Public Company
Incorporated: 1934 as Ryder Truck Rental System, Inc.
Employees: 23,000
Sales: $4.88 billion (2009)
Stock Exchanges: New York
Ticker Symbol: R
NAICS: 53212 Truck, Utility Trailer, and RV (Recreational Vehicle) Rental and Leasing

■ ■ ■

Ryder System Inc. provides transportation, logistics, and supply chain management services. The company's three business segments include: Fleet Management Solutions, Supply Chain Solutions, and Dedicated Contract Carriage. Through these segments, Ryder offers a variety of products and services including used vehicle sales, commercial truck rental, supply chain consulting and engineering, integrated logistics, global transportation management, warehouse facilities management, and inventory management. Ryder has operations in the United States, Canada, Mexico, the United Kingdom, Singapore, and China. Its stock is a component of the Dow Jones Transportation Average and the Standard & Poor's 500 Index.

ORIGINS OF AN INDUSTRY PIONEER

In 1932 James A. Ryder gave up his job as a straw boss in a construction firm and bought a Model A pickup truck with a down payment of $125. Ryder hauled trash from Miami beaches and delivered construction materials to Palm Beach. In 1934 he entered the truck-leasing business through a contract with a local beer distributor. At the age of 21, Ryder was the owner of the first truck-leasing firm in the United States, Ryder Truck Rental System, Inc.

In 1939 Ryder took on a partner, Roy N. Reedy, and the two men set out to build a trucking empire. Truck leasing was novel, and the company broke new ground. Highway trucking began to rival rail as a means of overland shipping, based partly on the vast network of better highways constructed during the 1930s. World War II boosted demand for trucking as the war economy stretched the existing transportation system to capacity, and Ryder's trucking and leasing operations grew.

The postwar era brought continued growth to the trucking industry as the interstate highway program further improved the efficiency of trucking. By 1952 Ryder was bringing in $3 million annually by renting 1,300 trucks. In the summer of that year news came that the Southeast's largest, most profitable trucking outfit, the Great Southern Trucking Company, was up for sale. Ryder was familiar with Great Southern; his company leased its pickup and delivery trucks. Founded in 1933 by L. A. Raulerson, it had grown into the Southeast's largest freight carrier with some routes as long as 1,100 miles. Ryder raised the $2 million asking price by December 1952. His company's revenues were then quadruple what they had been, and Ryder was a huge motor carrier, as well as a major truck-leasing concern.

RYDER SYSTEMS GOES PUBLIC IN 1955

The Great Southern acquisition put Ryder on the map. Ryder System, Inc., was created in 1955 to absorb Ryder Truck Rental and Great Southern, and the new company offered shares to the public. Shortly thereafter Ryder System bought more than 25 companies in five years. The larger companies included Baker Truck Rental, Inc., of Denver, Colorado; Barrett Truck Leasing Co., of Detroit; T.S.C. Motor Freight Lines, Inc.; the truck leasing business of Columbia Terminals Co.; Dixie Drive-It-Yourself System, of Alabama; the truck leasing business of Barrett Garages, Inc., of San Francisco; Morrison International Corporation; and International Railway Car Leasing Corporation.

This growth resulted in certain problems, however, because the company had neglected proper financial controls. By 1960 Ryder System was forced to write off $2 million in bad debt, and profits dipped from $2.7 million in 1959 to about $1 million in 1960. A central accounting system was implemented to remedy the problems, and steady growth returned in the early 1960s.

In 1965 Ryder System sold its motor carrier division to International Utilities (IU), a diversified holding company. The trucking division grew under IU's direction until its spin-off in 1982, keeping the Ryder name. Ryder System focused on the fast-growing truck-leasing business and, despite common misconceptions, had not operated as a freight carrier since 1965.

The late 1960s saw the development of new services in truck leasing and rental. In 1967 Ryder began offering one-way truck rental service. This service had been introduced and popularized by the U-Haul Company several years earlier. Ryder started with 1,000 trucks and expanded the one-way fleet to 7,630 the first year. Competition in this field grew rapidly; Hertz Corporation and E-Z Haul, a division of National Car Rental System, Inc., entered the field at the same time. As a result, the one-way market was oversupplied, and Ryder's one-way unit got off to a slow start. Ryder was intent on capturing this market, however. In 1968 the company offered to buy U-Haul International Co., a subsidiary of Americo, Inc., but no deal was ever worked out. Ryder expanded its one-way dealership network through an agreement with Budget Rent-A-Car. While many competitors dropped out in the early 1970s, Ryder did not, selling surplus vehicles when necessary, and eventually surpassed U-Haul's one-way rental in 1987.

In 1968 Ryder entered the new-automotive carriage business when it acquired M & G Convoy, Inc., and expanded it with the purchase of Complete Auto Transit, Inc., in January 1970. Ryder's automotive carriage services were used by General Motors Corporation and Chrysler Corporation for the transport of new automobiles to dealerships. Also around this time, Ryder entered the dedicated contract carriage business, in which it provided transportation and distribution services customized for its clients.

DIVERSIFICATION BREEDS PROBLEMS: 1969–75

In the late 1960s Ryder System also diversified into services unrelated to transport leasing. In late 1969 Ryder made a foray into the growing temporary help industry, initially placing office and industrial personnel, and later placing technical help. Ryder also acquired several trade schools in 1969 and 1970, offering courses in auto mechanics, truck driving, and a number of other technical fields. In 1970 Ryder purchased Mobile World Inc., a distributor of mobile homes and a mobile-home-park operator and franchiser. Also that year an insurance firm, Southern Underwriters, Inc., was acquired and a joint venture, Ryd-Air Inc., was formed to provide pickup and delivery service for 27 airlines in New York.

Although Ryder's main full-service truck leasing line remained strong in the early 1970s, the company's management was spread thin over a growing number of new service fields. The oil crisis of 1973 prompted Ryder to purchase Toro Petroleum Corporation of Louisiana to ensure a steady fuel supply for its trucks, but the acquisition proved rash. The value of Toro's oil

KEY DATES

1934: James A. Ryder establishes Ryder Truck Rental System, Inc.

1952: Ryder buys Great Southern Trucking Company.

1955: Company goes public as Ryder System, Inc.

1965: Ryder System sells its motor carrier division to International Utilities (IU).

1983: Aviation Sales Co. Inc. and its subsidiary General Hydraulics Corporation are purchased; Anthony Burns is named CEO.

1996: Company sells its consumer truck rental business.

1999: Ryder Public Transportation Services is sold.

2001: Singapore-based Ascent Logistics Pte. Ltd. is acquired.

2007: Sales and profits reach record highs.

reserves dropped as oil prices fell a few months after the purchase. Ryder had bought high and ended up with a $7 million operating loss.

Other problems—adjustments in the calculation of receivables from the education unit, tax assessments on the mobile home subsidiary, and reserve assessments on the insurance subsidiary—resulted in a 13 cents per share adjustment to Ryder stock following the company's 1973 audit. The truck leasing and rental businesses continued to borrow in order to finance an expanded fleet. Ryder's debts were more than $400 million, four times shareholders' equity. Thus, Moody's Investors Service downgraded Ryder's rating on commercial paper in late 1974. Ryder System lost $20 million, and the company's investors were deeply concerned. The board of directors began to question James Ryder's ability to guide the future of the growing concern.

The recession of 1973–74 had taken a heavy toll on Ryder's vast contract carriage and automotive carriage operations, which were heavily dependent upon the welfare of the automotive industry. Although Ryder's core business of truck leasing and rental was holding its own despite the hard times, company borrowing had gotten out of control.

Stockholders, displeased with the company's troublesome acquisitions from the early 1970s, demanded a refocusing of attention back on Ryder's basic businesses. In 1975 James Ryder, under pressure from the boardroom and his bankers, announced that

he was seeking a "more professional manager" to run the still growing company. In the summer of 1975, after disposing of such unprofitable subsidiaries as Toro Petroleum and Miller Trailers, Inc., as well as the major portion of the technical schools, James Ryder stepped down as head of the company he had founded.

A NEW CEO IN 1975

Ryder's successor was Leslie O. Barnes, former head of Allegheny Airlines. Barnes inherited a company that was tattered after weathering a great storm, and the 59-year-old CEO was intent on whipping Ryder System back into shape. The debt-to-equity ratio was quickly pared from four-to-one to three-to-one. Ryder Liftlease Inc., a small but troublesome subsidiary, was sold, as were the remainder of the technical schools.

Refocused on its primary businesses, Ryder rebounded. In 1977 the company acquired a major automobile carrier, Janesville Auto Transport Company, for $10 million in common stock. Ryder's automotive carriage operations were profitable as a result of the industry's rebound and tighter financial controls. During the 1979 downturn in the automotive markets, Ryder's automotive contract carriage unit, representing 16 percent of Ryder System's sales, made a profit.

In the late 1970s Ryder continued to grow internally and through acquisitions in the full-service truck-leasing business, in which the company continued to lead the continually expanding market. According to Barnes, only 38 percent of the U.S. private truck fleets were wholly owned by 1980, down from 60 percent in 1970. The vast majority of fleets were at least partially leased. Encouraged by the basic business's performance during the latter half of the 1970s, Ryder System once again began to seek acquisitions in new areas. Barnes, however, unlike James Ryder, was inclined to test out new ventures on a small scale before fully committing to them. In 1978 a parcel delivery service, Jack Rabbit Express, was acquired. Moreover, a small property and casualty reinsurance company, Federal Assurance Co., was added to existing insurance operations.

FIGHTING JARTRAN AND HALL: 1979–83

By the late 1970s the one-way rental market was well-established. Ryder trailed U-Haul in this field, and in 1978, a third major competitor, Jartran Inc., joined the field. "Jartran" was an acronym for James A. Ryder Transportation. Giving up a $100,000 annual stipend to get out of his noncompetition agreement with Ryder System, James Ryder founded Jartran, which made a smashing entry into the field, building a 30,000 vehicle fleet in less than 18 months. James Ryder's new company became a thorn in the side of his former company. The feisty Ryder appeared in Jartran ads as "the man who invented truck rental," and his new vehicles resembled Ryder System's enough to spark a lawsuit.

Nevertheless, Jartran had trouble making a profit. Once again, it appeared that James Ryder had grown the company too big too fast. As a downturn in the economy in 1979 killed the short-term rental market, Jartran cumulatively lost $30 million in 1979 and 1980. By July 1981 Jartran had dumped its commercial leasing division, and the company was foundering.

Ryder System, on the other hand, grew under the balanced leadership of Barnes and his new executive vice president, M. Anthony Burns. In the early 1980s, new tax laws encouraged diversification into new areas. Ryder began shopping for a financial services company in order to take full advantage of available tax credits. Insurance was the obvious choice because of Ryder's existing insurance business. In September 1981 Ryder System announced its desire to purchase the third-largest insurance broker in the United States, Frank B. Hall and Co. Hall, however, was not interested in being acquired and maneuvered to avert a takeover. In October 1981 Hall announced its intentions to purchase Jartran, Ryder System's troubled competitor, opening up potential antitrust obstacles for a takeover. Hall also filed a number of suits against Ryder.

Ryder System's pursuit of Hall continued through 1982, and by August of that year Ryder System had boosted its holdings in Hall to 9.5 percent. Jartran was on its way to bankruptcy, but Hall had bought enough time to discourage Ryder System from acquiring any more Hall stock. In 1983 Ryder sold its interest in the insurance broker for $33 million.

In 1982 a severe recession shook the North American economy. Ryder System was well-prepared, however, with a $70 million cash surplus and a very low debt-to-equity ratio. While the majority of transportation companies were devastated, Ryder System's profits increased. Burns moved up to CEO, and soon proclaimed Ryder's intention to "be more forward-thinking, more risk-taking." By slashing prices in half on one-way rentals, Ryder usurped a huge chunk of the market. By acquiring two new strategically located automobile carriage firms, Ryder improved its efficiency, reducing the number of trailers sent back empty.

ENTERING NEW MARKETS

Ryder System's long-standing desire to enter financial services was satisfied in 1983 when the company became an 80 percent partner in a pension fund specialist, Forstmann, Leff, Kimberly. The joint venture set up long-term trusts for pension fund investors. Ryder also decided to revise its in-house business information systems and offer them for sale to other transportation companies.

In its core transportation businesses, Ryder continued to make strides. Deregulation had been the industry trend since 1980. In 1983 new rules concerning single-source leasing allowed private fleet operators to secure drivers through Ryder as a part of the leasing agreement. Private shippers were also allowed to solicit outside freight business, effectively allowing direct competition with independent truckers. Ryder set up a new division to handle single-source leasing and bought three new freight packaging companies to book return loads for private shippers leasing from Ryder. In 1984, Ryder sold its Truckstops Corporation of America unit for $85 million to free managerial resources for more profitable businesses.

In the early 1980s Ryder System began to delve into another expanding transportation field—aviation leasing. In 1983 the Aviation Sales Co. Inc. and its subsidiary General Hydraulics Corporation, of Florida, an aircraft leasing firm and spare-parts firm, respectively, were acquired. In 1985 Ryder bought Aviall, Inc., a turbine engine repair and overhaul firm located in Dallas. Aviall was also a parts distributor. A number of smaller leasing and repair companies were acquired. By late 1986 aviation services made up about one-fifth of Ryder System's revenues, and in 1987 the division branched out overseas with the purchase of Caledonian Airmotive, Ltd. The Scottish subsidiary serviced the big engines on British Caledonian Airways' DC-10s and 747s, among others. Caledonian Airmotive complemented Aviall's operation both geographically and in services offered.

By 1988, just six years after entering the field, Ryder System was the world's largest jet engine overhaul and rebuilding company, the largest aviation parts distributor, and one of the largest aircraft and jet-engine leasing companies. Ryder's aviation division counted 300 commercial airlines among its clients, as well as dozens of private operators. In 1988 revenues from aviation neared $1 billion.

ACQUISITIONS LEAD TO GROWTH

Ryder's truck leasing continued to surge ahead. In 1986 a major federal tax law revision made it desirable for private fleet operators to lease their fleets rather than buy. Ryder had been determinedly expanding its truck fleet; between 1984 and 1988 it nearly doubled its fleet. More and more fleet operators turned over the hassles of fleet purchase, maintenance, and insurance to Ryder, allowing them to concentrate on manufacture and sale of their products.

In one-way rental, Ryder excelled. U-Haul, the longtime leader in the field, was distracted as family members battled among themselves for control of the business. U-Haul started renting all kinds of equipment, from rototillers to hoists, and its truck fleet quietly grew old. In 1987 the average age of a U-Haul truck was 10 years. Ryder's, on the other hand, averaged two years, and boasted all sorts of features not found at U-Haul, such as power steering, air-conditioning, AM-FM radios, fuel efficient engines, and radial tires. Ryder's market share was 45 percent, equal to U-Haul's in 1987, and surging forward.

Between 1983 and 1987 Ryder System spent $1.1 billion on 65 acquisitions. This time the company's rapid expansion was readily digested. In 1985 Ryder entered the school-bus leasing business and quickly grew to be the second-largest private student transport company in the United States. Ryder also entered into public transportation system consulting and leasing at about the same time. Dedicated contract carriage received greater attention in the late 1980s. Ryder provided trucks, drivers, and management system design to such specialty freight companies as Emery Air Freight, such retailers as Montgomery Ward, Sears, and J.C. Penney, and such newspaper publishers as Dow Jones and the Miami Herald.

In 1989 Ryder's growth flattened out, but its potential in its existing areas of operation remained strong. Late in the year the company sold its insurance operations, and, anticipating the coming recession, trimmed its fleet to better match demand. Ryder had proven its ability to manage well in tough times during the 1982 recession. As the automotive carriage and commercial truck operations were in the downside of the cycle, Ryder focused on improving market share while awaiting a general economic recovery. Its success was demonstrated in 1990 when Ryder moved 39 percent of the automobiles shipped in the United States and Canada.

A NEW PLAN: 1990–99

As Ryder System entered the 1990s, its full-service truck leasing, contract carriage, jet turbine aircraft overhaul and maintenance, and new aviation parts-distribution units were performing well; other units would eventually rebound alongside the manufacturing economy. As the 1990s, progressed, however, it became clear to company

leader Burns that fundamental changes were needed to properly position the company for long-term growth and profitability.

Burns, who had completed his ascent of the company's management ranks to preside as president, chief executive officer, and chairman, wanted to lessen the company's interests and sharpen its focus, a desire reminiscent of Ryder's mid-1970s restructuring. His intent was to adapt to changing market conditions before the trends of the future passed Ryder by. His vision was forward-looking, a perspective that he hoped would prevent Ryder from falling victim to the cyclic nature of its business.

As the "new Ryder" took shape during the mid-1990s, both recent and age-old components of the company were shed. No divestment was larger than the October 1996 sale of the company's consumer truck rental business, its famed yellow Ryder rental truck fleet. The sale of the consumer truck rental business represented a $574 million deal, stripping the company of more than $400 million in annual revenue.

Less than a year later, Burns also sold Ryder's automotive carrier business, reaching an agreement with Allied Holdings, Inc., for a $111 million sale price. With the divestiture of the consumer truck rental business and the automotive carrier business, Burns felt his company was "leaner, more focused, more disciplined, more profit-minded," and less vulnerable to the vagaries of capricious market conditions, ridding Ryder of businesses that were "seasonal, transactional, highly volatile, and in difficult markets." With these two business segments gone, along with its Ryder Public Transportation Services business sold in 1999, Burns pinned the company's hopes for the future on logistics and corporate truck leasing and rental services.

MOVING INTO THE NEW MILLENNIUM

Gregory T. Swienton joined Ryder in 1999 as president. He was tapped to continue restructuring Ryder in order to shore up profits. When Burns stepped down from the CEO post in 2000, Swienton took over and began steadily expanding the company's logistic and transportation services through strategic acquisitions both at home and abroad. In order to gain a foothold in the Asia Pacific market, the company purchased Singapore-based Ascent Logistics Pte. Ltd. in 2001.

Swienton assumed the chairmanship in 2002 and continued making strides to position Ryder favorably among its competitors. During 2003, the company added Vertex Services LLC, a fuel storage tank systems compliance firm, to its arsenal. Vertex's customer base included Costco Wholesale, U.S. Concrete, Inc., and

Waste Management, Inc. Ruan Leasing Company, a privately owned truck leasing, rental and contract maintenance company headquartered in Des Moines, Iowa, was purchased in 2004. General Car and Truck Leasing System, a commercial truck leasing, maintenance and rental company based in Davenport, Iowa, was also acquired that year.

By now, Ryder had three main business segments that included Fleet Management Solutions (FMS), Supply Chain Solutions (SCS), and Dedicated Contract Carriage. The company's largest segment, FMS, continued to offer new products and services including an on-board Global Positioning System called RydeSmart. It also launched a hybrid truck line under the name RydeGreen, which provided clients with a fuel efficient alternative.

From 2003 to 2007, Ryder's revenue had grown by nearly 37 percent while earnings from continued operations had climbed by 94 percent. With record sales and profits under its belt in 2007, Ryder's strategy during the early years of the new millennium appeared to be paying off. As the company ushered in its 75th anniversary in 2008 however, it faced significant challenges brought on by a downturn in the U.S. economy and a U.S. freight recession that had started in late 2006.

OVERCOMING CHALLENGES: 2008 AND BEYOND

In response to economic challenges, Ryder began to shutter unprofitable SCS operations in Brazil, Argentina, Chile, and portions of Europe. At the same time, it focused on growing its domestic business as well as its operations in Canada, Mexico, the United Kingdom, and Asia. SCS acquisitions in 2008 included Transpacific Container Terminal Ltd., CRSA Logistics Ltd. in Canada as well as CRSA operations in Hong Kong and Shanghai. The company bolstered its FMS business segment with four acquisitions during this period. Lily Transportation Corp., Gator Leasing Inc., and Gordon Truck Leasing were acquired in 2008 and Edart Leasing, LLC, was purchased in February 2009.

Tough operating conditions including a decrease in full-service leasing, high pension expenses, a reduction in commercial rentals, and faltering used vehicle sales forced Ryder to trim costs. Ryder cut approximately 700 jobs in the United States and issued temporary layoffs to approximately 1,300 drivers and warehouse employees.

In 2009 Ryder's net profit fell by 69 percent over the previous year while revenue from continuing operations dropped by 19 percent. As Ryder worked to remain financially stable and competitive, Swienton

believed the company was taking the necessary steps for growth in the future.

Thomas M. Tucker
Updated, Jeffrey L. Covell; Christina M. Stansell

PRINCIPAL SUBSIDIARIES

Ryder Transportation Services; Ryder Integrated Logistics, Inc.; Ryder Energy Distribution Corporation; RyderFleetProducts.com, Inc.; Ryder Fuel Services, LLC; Ryder Puerto Rico, Inc.; Ryder Truck Rental Canada, Ltd. (Canada); Ryder CRSA Logistics (Canada); Ryder Transpacific Container Terminal Logistics (Canada); Ryder Ltd. (UK); Ryder de Mexico, S.A. de R.L. de C.V. (Mexico); Ryder Europe B.V. (Netherlands); Ryder Deutschland GmbH (Germany); Ryder Polska (Poland); Ryder Argentina, S.A.; Ryder do Brasil, Ltda. (Brazil); Ryder Chile Limitada; Ryder Singapore Pte Ltd.; Ryder Capital Ireland; Ryder CRSA Logistics (HK) Ltd. (Hong Kong); Ryder Logistics Shanghai Co., Ltd. (China); Ryder System (Thailand) Co., Ltd.; Ryder System Malaysia Sdn. Bhd.

PRINCIPAL COMPETITORS

Con-way Inc.; Penske Truck Leasing Co. L.P.; Schenker Inc.

FURTHER READING

Cook, James, "Repetition Compulsion," *Forbes*, March 21, 1988.

Engardio, Pete, "Tony Burns Has Ryder's Rivals Eating Dust," *Business Week*, April 6, 1987.

"FirstGroup Shareholders Approve U.S. Buy," *National Post*, September 10, 1999.

"From Wings to Wheels," *Forbes*, September 18, 1978.

Gallagher, Thomas L., "Ryder Profit Fell 69 Percent in 2009," *Journal of Commerce Online*, February 3, 2010.

"Ryder Announces Strategic Initiatives to Increase Competitiveness and Drive Long-Term Profitable Growth," *ENP Newswire*, December 19, 2008.

"Ryder CEO to Ring NYSE Closing Bell on May 21 in Celebration of 75th Anniversary," *ENP Newswire*, May 21, 2008.

Ryder, James A., "Shooting for the Big Time—and Making It," *Nation's Business*, January 1970.

Schulz, John D., "Ryder to Close $145M Ruan Deal," *Traffic World*, March 15, 2004.

Villano, David, "A New Road for Ryder," *Florida Trend*, March 1, 2006.

Wax, Alan, "Institutions Grill Ryder over Earnings Change," *Commercial and Financial Chronicle*, April 8, 1974.

Yee, Chew Wai, "Ryder's Singapore Buy First in Asian Expansion Plans," *Lloyd's List Daily Commercial News*, January 26, 2001.

Saft Groupe S.A.

12 rue Sadi Carnot
Bagnolet, F-93170
France
Telephone: (+33 01) 49 93 19 18
Fax: (+33 01) 49 93 19 55
Web site: http://www.saftbatteries.com

Public Company
Incorporated: 1924 as Saft S.A.
Employees: 3,800
Sales: EUR 559.3 million ($839 million) (2009)
Stock Exchanges: Euronext Paris
Ticker Symbol: FR 0010208165
NAICS: 335911 Storage Battery Manufacturing; 335912
    Dry and Wet Primary Battery Manufacturing

■ ■ ■

Saft Groupe S.A. is a leading developer and producer of batteries for industrial, defense, and aerospace applications. The company claims world-leading positions in a number of categories, such as industrial Ni-Cd (nickel-cadmium) batteries for aircraft, rail travel, and emergency lighting; primary lithium batteries; and the number two position in advanced technology batteries for the defense and aerospace market. Saft has also been positioning itself as a major producer of batteries for electric vehicles. Saft, based in Bagnolet, France, operates on a global level, with 16 manufacturing facilities and subsidiaries in 18 countries.

The company's operations fall under two main divisions: Industrial Battery Group, focused on rechargeable

nickel- and lithium-based batteries for industrial use; and the Specialty Battery Group, which produces rechargeable and non-rechargeable lithium-based batteries used for such defense and aerospace applications as space satellites, missiles, torpedoes, military radios, and night vision goggles. At the beginning of 2010, the company merged a third division, Rechargeable Battery Systems, which focused on nickel-based batteries for the industrial and professional sectors, into the Industrial Battery division. Saft Groupe is listed on the Euronext Paris Stock Exchange and is led by Chairman John Searle. The company posted revenues of EUR 559 million ($839 million) in 2009.

ORIGINS: 1918

Saft Groupe traces its origins to Victor Herold, a Swiss electrochemical engineer who sought to set up a company producing Leclanché dry cell batteries, Edison-designed accumulators, and related equipment for the railway sector. In 1913 Herold decided to found a new company in Romainville, France. The outbreak of World War I put the new company on hold for the duration. By 1918, however, Herold had succeeded in founding the company, called Société des Accumulateurs Fixes et de Traction, or Saft. The company quickly scored a number of successes, including contracts to provide batteries for the railcar lighting systems for the Paris-Lyon-Marseille railroad, as well as motors, starters, and traction systems for baggage carts used in the Paris railway stations.

Saft's growth continued into the next decade. By 1924 the company had listed its shares on the Paris

COMPANY PERSPECTIVES

Our Group has a wide portfolio of technologies and a good defensive spread of products and customers, as well as a balance between replacement sales and business in emerging markets. In addition there are increasing opportunities for Saft in our Research and development-generated technologies in industrial markets of the future such as aviation, telecom networks, renewable energy systems and hybrid electric vehicles. Saft is an industry leader in traditional technologies and is also well-placed to turn today's new technologies into tomorrow's growth.

Stock Exchange, becoming Saft S.A. The company's independence proved short-lived, however. In 1928 Compagnie Générale d'Electricité (CGE), one of France's largest electric utility operations and electric product manufacturers at that time, took over Saft. The company remained part of CGE, which later became the refocused telecommunications group Alcatel, into the late 1990s.

Nationalized during World War II, CGE was privatized again in the period following the war, minus its electric utility operations, which remained under government ownership. CGE's focus then turned fully to its diversified range of products, ranging from consumer appliances to large-scale industrial and advanced technology applications. Saft itself grew to encompass CGE's fast-growing battery operations. These included a new factory in Bordeaux, opened in 1949, which became one of the first in France to develop alkaline batteries for industrial uses.

The Bordeaux site was also the home of a major Saft innovation, the Voltabloc, introduced in 1953. This product became a major success for the company, particularly after the U.S. Navy placed an order for 2,000 24-volt batteries that same year. By then, Saft had also begun to develop its international presence, having set up a sales agency in the United Kingdom in 1946.

FOCUS ON INDUSTRIAL BATTERIES

Saft remained at the cutting edge of battery technology through the next decades. The company became a major supplier of batteries to French railway operator SNCF, as well as to railway, aerospace, and defense sectors around the world. Saft's products were also in high

demand from the power generation industry, the telecommunications industry, and for a wide variety of other industrial applications. By the beginning of the 1960s, Saft had also added a consumer products division, developing batteries for a range of appliances. This led to the addition of a new subsidiary, known as Saft-Leclanché, which operated a factory in Poitiers.

In addition to batteries, Saft-Leclanché developed a wide range of battery-operated consumer products, such as flashlights and camping lamps, among others. In 1979 Saft-Leclanché began cooperating with another leading French battery and battery-operated products group, Cidel-Mazda, creating a new company, Gipelec. By 1982, Saft and Mazda merged their consumer products divisions, creating Saft Mazda. CGE had been nationalized that same year. In 1986, when the French government reprivatized CGE, Saft Mazda was sold to French business magnate Bernard Tapie, who merged the company with another major French battery brand, Wonder. As a result, Saft refocused itself as a producer of batteries for the industrial and defense sectors following its privatization.

Saft had also continued its international expansion. In 1969 the company acquired its U.K. sales agent and established a dedicated subsidiary in the United Kingdom. The company then boosted its U.K. operations in 1971 with the acquisition of Venner Accumulators. This purchase also gave Saft access to a new type of battery technology, based on a silver-zinc composition.

The company added its first operations in the United States during the 1970s. The rapid growth of the Asian market led the company to establish its first subsidiary in that region, in Singapore, during the 1980s. The company also expanded its operations into a number of European markets, including Germany and Italy, and Spain through a 50-50 joint venture with battery group Cegaso. In 1986 the company also moved into Japan, establishing a joint venture there with Japan Storage Battery, part of the Mitsubishi group, in order to produce nickel-cadmium based batteries.

A SERIES OF ACQUISITIONS

CGE became Alcatel Alsthom (and later simply Alcatel) in 1990. During this time, Saft's shares were once again listed on the Paris Stock Exchange. Alcatel nevertheless retained majority control of Saft. In the early 1990s, Alcatel changed course and repurchased 100 percent control of Saft. However, the company remained listed on the Paris Stock Exchange until 1995.

KEY DATES

1918: Victor Herold founds Société des Accumulateurs Fixes et de Traction (Saft) in Romainville, France.

1924: Saft goes public on the Paris Stock Exchange.

1928: Saft is acquired by the Compagnie Générale d'Electricité (CGE).

1946: Saft launches sales in the United Kingdom through a sales agent.

1987: Saft begins reinforcing its industrial battery operations through acquisitions, starting with Alcad.

1997: Saft enters Eastern Europe with the purchase of Ferak in the Czech Republic.

2000: Saft begins developing its specialty battery division with purchase of Tadiran in Israel.

2005: Saft goes public on the Euronext Paris Stock Exchange.

2010: Saft merges its rechargeable battery division into the industrial battery division.

By then, Saft had been growing strongly as its parent company completed a number of acquisitions in order to build its scale to compete on an international level. These included major rival Alcad, acquired in 1987, which helped boost the group's nickel-based battery capability. In 1991 the group added another competitor, Nife Power Systems, not only extending its range of battery technologies and products, but also adding a line of electronic products. That subsidiary became known as Saft Nife.

Other acquisitions during the period helped consolidate the company's international operations. At the end of 1993, the company reached an agreement to acquire the aerospace divisions of Gates Corporation and Johnson Controls in the United States, giving Saft approximately 25 percent of the market for satellite batteries. Also that year, Saft teamed up with Aerospatiale, forming a joint venture to produce thermal batteries used in tactical missiles.

The following year, Saft bought out Cegaso and took full control of the Spain joint venture. The company then expanded its Saft Nife operations in the United Kingdom with the purchase of Harmer and Simmons in 1995. After a restructuring of its operations in England, the company's U.K. subsidiary was renamed Saft Ltd. in 1998.

GROWING EMPHASIS ON SPECIALTY BATTERIES

The rising economies of the former Soviet Bloc countries provided the company with new growth opportunities in the late 1990s. Saft made its first move into Eastern Europe in 1997, when it acquired Ferak, a major industrial battery manufacturer based in the Czech Republic. Saft also reinforced its presence in the United States, opening a new factory in North Carolina in order to position itself for the surge in demand for portable rechargeable batteries. By then, the company had also added a factory in Tijuana, Mexico, and a battery assembly plant in South Korea. By the end of the 1990s, rechargeable batteries, including for portable devices, but especially for defense and industrial applications, accounted for some 70 percent of Saft's revenues.

With the arrival of devices such as personal digital assistants (PDAs) and the explosion of the mobile telephone market, the need for rechargeable batteries soared at the dawn of the new century. However, this demand brought a new range of competitors, particularly from the low-cost Asian markets, drastically reducing battery prices. These market conditions led Saft to adopt a new strategy for its rechargeable batteries division, which it then refocused around the higher-value defense and industrial sectors. As a result, Saft shut down its Tijuana plant and sold off its other portable rechargeable operations in South Korea and elsewhere.

Saft instead launched a new round of investments in order to boost its industrial battery division and to establish itself as a major player in the specialty battery sector. High-performance specialty batteries, which were largely lithium-based, were required for such demanding applications as satellites and space launching systems, military communication equipment, night vision goggles, missiles, and submarines. They were also important components in such civil applications as GPS systems, medical equipment, and utility meters.

Saft's specialty battery division expanded in 2000 with the acquisition of Israel's Tadiran from Koor Industries for $33 million. The purchase of Tadiran not only gave Saft additional manufacturing facilities in the United States, it also brought it a 50 percent stake in Sonnenschein Lithium, based in Germany. Saft quickly moved to buy out the remaining 50 percent of Sonnenschein, completing the takeover in 2001.

By the end of that year, Saft had also acquired England's Hawker Eternacell, which had been part of Invensys Power Systems. Hawker operated factories in South Shields, England, and in New Jersey in the United States, and was a major supplier to the militaries of both the United States and the United Kingdom. Saft continued to invest in expanding its specialty battery capacity. For example, in 2005 the company launched construction of a new factory in Zhuhar, China. By then, the specialty battery division had become the company's largest, generating nearly 46 percent of its total revenues of EUR 576 million.

PUBLIC AGAIN IN 2005

Saft continued to build its industrial battery division as well. In 2003 the company acquired the European non-lead battery operations from Exide Technologies. This deal gave Saft control of Germany's Friemann & Wolf Batteritechnik; the nickel-cadmium battery operations of Poland's Centra; and parts of Electro Mercantil Industrial, in Spain. After integrating these businesses, Saft turned to India, where it acquired a 51 percent stake in the industrial battery division of India's Amalgamations Pvt. Ltd. This led to the creation of a new joint venture, Amco Saft, based in Bangalore. By the end of 2005, Saft's industrial battery operations generated nearly 40 percent of the group's total revenues.

By then, Saft itself had undergone a change in ownership. In the late 1990s, Alcatel adopted its new telecommunications-based strategy. This led Alcatel to put Saft up for sale in 1999, attracting the interest of investment group Industri Kapital. The two companies failed to reach an agreement, however. With the slump in the global economy at the beginning of the next decade, Alcatel was forced to place the sale of Saft on hold.

In 2003 the group reached an agreement with another investment group, Doughty Hanson, of the United Kingdom, for EUR 410 million. The sale was completed in 2004. By the end of that year, as Saft completed its transition toward the industrial and specialty battery sectors, the company began preparing for a return to the stock exchange. This listing, completed on Euronext Paris in 2005, became a major success for Doughty Hanson, which saw Saft's value double to more than EUR 800 million. Doughty Hanson completed its exit from the company's shareholding in 2007.

TARGETING ELECTRIC AUTOMOBILES IN THE 21ST CENTURY

Growing demand for the development of viable electric and hybrid-electric automotive vehicles in the second half of the decade led Saft to step up its investments in this area. Saft had already built up its own expertise in this sector, including participating in efforts to develop batteries for electric automobiles in the United States in the early 1990s. Saft's batteries also equipped the first generation of electric cars introduced in France at the dawn of the new century.

In 2006 Saft sought to expand its presence in this market, forming a joint venture with U.S.-based Johnson Controls to form Johnson Controls-Saft Advanced Power Solutions. Saft's stake in the joint venture stood at 49 percent. That company then began developing its own lithium-ion based battery designs. This led to the construction of a dedicated factory in Nersac, France, which launched production in early 2008, supplying batteries for hybrid cars for Mercedes and BMW.

Saft's investments in the automotive sector placed it in a strong position as the United States announced a new subsidy program in order to fund the development of electric automobiles. Under that program, Saft received nearly $400 million for the construction of two factories. The company itself launched construction of a $96 million factory in Jacksonville, Florida, in 2009. At the same time, the group's Johnson Controls-Saft Advanced Power Solutions joint venture received almost $300 million to build an even larger lithium ion production unit in Holland, Michigan.

Saft nevertheless was forced to confront the global economic downturn of the end of the decade. The company's revenues began to slip, dropping back by more than 8 percent, to EUR 559.3 million in 2009. By then, the company's rechargeable battery division represented little more than 10 percent of the company's total sales. This led Saft to dissolve that division, merging its remaining business into the industrial battery division at the beginning of 2010. Saft looked forward to continued growth in the years ahead.

M. L. Cohen

PRINCIPAL SUBSIDIARIES

Advanced Thermal Batteries Inc. (USA); Aérospatiale Batteries Saft S.A. (50%); Alcad AB (Sweden); Amco-Saft India Ltd.; Eternacell Inc. (USA); Fast Jung KB (Sweden); Friwo GmbH (Germany); Johnson Controls-Saft Advanced Power Solutions LLC (USA; 49%); Saft Acquisition SAS; Saft America Inc. (USA); Saft A.S. (Norway); Saft Australia Pty Ltd.; Saft Baterias SL (Spain); Saft Batterie Italia S.r.l.; Saft Batterien GmbH (Germany); Saft Batteries Pte Ltd. (Singapore); Saft Batteries Pty Ltd. (Australia); Saft Batterijen BV (Netherlands); Saft Federal Systems Inc. (USA); Saft Ferak A.S. (Czech Republic); Saft Finance Sarl (Luxembourg); Saft Hong Kong Ltd.; Saft (Zhuhai FTZ) Batteries Co. China; Saft Ltd. (UK); Saft Nife ME Ltd. (Cyprus); Saft Sweden AB; Tadiran Batteries Ltd. (Israel).

PRINCIPAL DIVISIONS

Industrial Battery Group (IBG); Specialty Battery Group (SBG).

PRINCIPAL COMPETITORS

BYD Company Ltd.; Exide Technologies; Gillette Co.; Hyosung Corp.; Johnson Controls Inc.; Korindo Group, PT; Motorola Electronics Company Ltd.; Panasonic Electric Works Company Ltd.; Sanyo Electric Company Ltd.; Vietnam National Chemical Corp.

FURTHER READING

"Battery Powered," *Acquisitions Monthly*, November 2000, p. 35.

Betts, Paul, "Alcatel Puts Saft Back on Market," *Financial Times*, May 29, 2003, p. 28.

"French Saft Sees Business Pick-up Despite Sales Drop," *ADP News France*, January 29, 2010.

"French Saft to Get USD 400m Subsidy from US Govt.," *ADP News France*, August 7, 2009.

"JCI and Saft to Make Advanced Batteries in Michigan," *Chemical Business Newsbase*, December 23, 2009.

"Saft Batteries, Fully Charged," *Manufacturer*, February 2004.

"Saft to Float on Eurolist," *European Venture Capital Journal*, July–August 2005, p. 28.

"Saft to Supply Li-ion Batteries for Galileo Satellites," *Space Daily*, June 8, 2006.

"Saft Works on Batteries for Space Vehicles," *Professional Engineering Magazine*, June 24, 2009, p. 46.

Seppälä

Seppälä Oy

∎

Tikkurilantie 146
PO Box 234
Vantaa, FI-0153
Finland
Telephone: (+358 9) 121 7200
Fax: (+358 9) 825 1100
Web site: http://www.seppala.fi

Wholly Owned Subsidiary of Stockmann plc
Incorporated: 1988
Employees: 1,636
Sales: EUR 169 million ($248 million) (2009 est.)
NAICS: 22330 Women's, Children's, and Infants'
    Clothing and Accessories Wholesalers; 448150
    Clothing Accessories Stores

■ ■ ■

Seppälä Oy operates Finland's largest fashion clothing retail chain, with 132 stores throughout the country. Seppälä is also building an international retail network, focusing on the Baltic and Russian markets. The company operates 16 stores in Estonia, Latvia, and Lithuania; 17 stores in Russia; and 2 stores in Ukraine. Seppälä also operates a number of shop-in-shop boutiques in the department stores owned by its parent company, Stockmann plc. Altogether, Seppälä's operations included 203 stores at the beginning of 2010.

Finland remains the company's largest market, accounting for 66 percent of its revenues of EUR 169 million ($248 million) in 2009, followed by Russia and Ukraine at 18 percent, and the Baltic markets at 16

percent. Seppälä's stores sell clothing designed by its own staff of designers, as well as a number of guest designers. Ladies' clothing accounts for 64 percent of its sales, followed by children's fashions at 19 percent, and men's clothing at 13 percent. Sales of cosmetics make up the remainder.

Seppälä has been a wholly owned subsidiary of Stockmann, Finland's leading department store and retail group, since 1988. Other Stockmann operations include Hobby Hall and the Lindex retail clothing chain. Heikki Väänänen is Seppälä's managing director.

ORIGINS

Finland's textiles sector took off at the beginning of the 20th century, with the introduction of industrial production techniques. The country's independence in 1917 was another important step in the development of a truly Finnish retail clothing market, as the country slowly emerged from its long history of Swedish and Russian dominance. The country's relative isolation from other major retail markets during this period encouraged the growth of homegrown fashions and designs. By the 1930s a number of venerable names in the country's textiles and clothing sectors had appeared. These included the retail clothing business founded by Edvard Seppälä and his brothers, who opened their first shop in Kymintehdas in 1930.

The company focused from the outset on providing clothing at affordable prices. Seppälä survived World War II and Finland's slow recovery in the immediate postwar period. By the 1950s Finland's economy, like much of Western Europe, had entered a new period of booming growth. The growing consumer wealth of this period also stimulated a transition in the country's retail sector from viewing clothing as utilitarian goods to emphasizing clothing as fashion, and ultimately as a lifestyle statement.

Finland's textile sector grew strongly during the 1950s as the country became a major exporter to the Soviet Union. The existence of a large, talented, and relatively low-wage workforce enabled Seppälä to develop its own manufacturing operations, and to begin developing its own clothing fashions. Through the 1950s and 1960s, the company's clothing ranges followed the spirit of the times.

BRANDS ADDED

Seppälä also started to expand its retail operations. By 1970 the company had arrived in Kaisaniemi, Helsinki, establishing its first store in Finland's capital city. This successful opening encouraged the company to develop on a national scale, and by 1975 Seppälä had moved its headquarters to Helsinki. In order to build its retail network, Seppälä launched a franchise operation. Seppälä became one of the first companies in Finland to adopt a franchising formula, which enabled the company to open new stores quickly and at a relatively low cost. By the mid-1980s Seppälä operated 40 stores in Finland.

The 1970s brought a new trend to the retail clothing industry with the development of designer-label clothing. This trend accelerated in the 1980s, as a growing number of designers added their names to ready-to-wear and retail clothing lines. Retail groups also participated in the trend, developing their own in-house ranges. Seppälä launched several of its own branded lines in the 1970s and 1980s, including the S-Style casual wear line; Impazzivo, targeting the younger active market; and Martinelli, a line created by Italian designer Edo Martinelli, featuring classic women's and men's career clothing fashions.

The appearance of a new generation of brand-name fashion played a part in the shift in the textiles industry away from a focus on manufacturing. A major factor in the development of this trend was the rising wages in western markets. As a result, clothing companies increasingly shut down their factories and instead turned to contract manufacturers in lower-wage markets in other parts of the world. By the 1980s Seppälä had shifted its own manufacturing to the contract market, working with manufacturers in other parts of Europe and the Far East.

This internationalization of the clothing market also inspired the appearance of a new breed of internationally operating retail clothing brands, such as The Gap, Benetton, and Esprit. Seppälä also joined in this trend, opening its first international retail shop in Berlin in 1984. The company then opened two more stores in West Germany before targeting a new and even larger market: the United States. In 1987 Seppälä opened a store on the corner of New York's Third Avenue and 60th Street, featuring nearly 7,000 square feet of selling space. The company also launched a new women's clothing brand, Third Avenue, in support of the shop. Seppälä then announced plans to open a string of U.S. stores, focusing on the East Coast.

ACQUIRED BY STOCKMANN: 1988

Seppälä pulled out of the United States just one year later, however, followed soon after by an exit from Germany as well. This move was prompted in part by the Seppälä family's decision to sell the company to Finnish retail group Stockmann plc in 1988. Stockmann had been founded in Helsinki in 1862 and grew into the leading department store group in the Scandinavian region.

Stockmann's financial clout provided Seppälä with the resources it needed in order to accelerate its growth in the 1990s. Seppälä at first focused on building its presence in Finland, and by the end of the decade the company's Finnish network had expanded to 115 stores. Seppälä also shut down its franchising operations, absorbing these stores into its own network. The last of the company's franchised stores, in Seinäjoki and Kauhajoki, were taken over by Seppälä in 1998.

Stockmann had begun developing an international expansion strategy during the decade. For this the company targeted the Baltic markets, which, after emerging from decades of Soviet rule, had quickly transitioned to a free market economy. Estonia especially achieved strong growth during the 1990s, outpacing nearly all of the former Eastern Bloc markets. Estonia's proximity to Finland also made it a natural choice for

KEY DATES

1930: Edvard Seppälä and his brothers found a clothing store in Kymintehdas, Finland.
1975: Seppälä moves its headquarters to Helsinki.
1988: Stockmann plc acquires Seppälä.
1996: Seppälä opens its first store in Estonia.
2004: Seppälä enters the Russian market with a store in Moscow.
2009: Seppälä opens its second store in Ukraine.

the next international moves by Stockmann and Seppälä.

Stockmann, which had also added department stores in Russia, opened its first department store in Estonia, in Tallinn. By 1996 Stockmann had also opened a Seppälä shop in Tallinn. This store initially operated as part of Stockmann, before being transferred to Seppälä's control in 1999. Seppälä then began expanding its Estonian subsidiary as a full-fledged chain, opening three more stores in Estonia, in Parnu, Tartu, and Viljandi that year.

SWEDISH EXPERIMENT LAUNCHED: 2000

Seppälä rolled out a larger store format in 1999, opening the first of its new look shops, featuring 2,200 square meters of sales space, in Helsinki. The company had opened five large-format stores by the end of that year. The larger format helped to drive up Seppälä's revenues, especially its operating profits. While Seppälä contributed just 9 percent to Stockmann's total revenues, it was responsible for generating 25 percent of the group's profits.

In 2000 the group launched an effort to enter Sweden, opening five SPL-branded stores in the Stockholm area that year. By the end of 2001 the company had opened a total of nine stores in Sweden. This extension came as part of the company's ambitious store-opening program, which included a total of 20 new stores in 2000.

Despite this expansion, Seppälä struggled to maintain its revenue levels, in part because of the entry of a number of major international retail competitors into the Finnish market. Seppälä, meanwhile, failed to make a mark in Sweden, which was already dominated by the H&M retail chain. In 2002 Seppälä made the decision to shut down the Swedish subsidiary, a move that cost the company more than EUR 5 million.

RUSSIA ENTERED: 2004

Seppälä refocused its efforts on improving its existing operations. The company's new store opening program slowed, in favor of the launch of an effort to refurbish its existing stores. Seppälä also took steps to improve its supply chain, particularly in shortening the time it took to bring a garment from the design phase to its store shelves. The company, which focused especially on clothing sales, also began testing a shoe department that year. While Seppälä's revenues continued to slip, to EUR 132.7 million in 2002, its profits regained their momentum, climbing to EUR 10.4 million for the year.

Seppälä had established itself as the leading clothing retailer in Finland by the dawn of the 21st century. However, with nearly 130 stores across the country, the company had reached the limit on its future growth at home. Seppälä instead targeted the wider international expansion of its operations. This started in Latvia, with the opening of the company's first store in Riga in 2003. By the end of the year the company operated four stores in Latvia, including a shop in Stockmann's new 11,000-square-meter shopping mall in Riga.

Seppälä then set its sights on entering Russia, opening three stores in the Moscow area in 2004. The move into the new market, backed by the parent company's existing operations in Russia, helped the company post its first revenue gains since the end of the 1990s. Seppälä's sales climbed past EUR 143 million, while its operating profits also grew, passing EUR 16.4 million.

By the end of 2005 Seppälä operated seven stores in Russia, including its first in St. Petersburg. Seppälä also completed its expansion into the Baltic region, opening its first stores in Lithuania, in Vilnius. The company added two more Lithuanian stores through the end of 2005, and by 2007 had boosted its stores in that market to nine.

Seppälä's Russian branch had grown even more strongly in the meantime, topping 28 stores. These included a store in Novosibirsk, in the Siberia region. Seppälä's Russian strategy targeted cities with populations of at least one million. This strategy led the company to expand to such cities as Yekaterinburg, Kazan, Nizhny Novgorod, Rostov-on-Don, and Samara.

NEW COLLECTIONS LAUNCHED

If much of Seppälä's international expansion had come from following Stockmann into new markets, at the end of the decade the company also played the role of pioneer. In 2008 Seppälä opened its first store in Ukraine, in Kharkov, adding a sixth market to its own network, and the 10th for Stockmann. Stockmann by this time had completed a major restructuring of its own operations, including the acquisition of Lindex, a major Swedish retail group with operations in most of Stockmann's other markets, in 2007.

By the end of 2008 Seppälä's annual sales had soared to a new record, nearing EUR 183 million. The company expanded its Russian strategy to include cities with a population of 500,000 and more. In Finland, meanwhile, the group launched a new designer-based clothing line concept, called Seppälä By and featuring the work of noted Finnish designers. The Seppälä By collection, by Hanna Saren, was launched in September 2008, followed by Seppälä By Nykänen & Frigren, created by two of the group's in-house designers.

As the global economy slipped into deep recession, Seppälä, like most of its retail counterparts, struggled to maintain its momentum. By the end of 2009 the company's sales had dropped back by nearly 8 percent, to EUR 168 million. The group's international operations were hardest hit, posting a 14 percent loss. Nevertheless, Seppälä pursued its international expansion, opening a second Ukraine store, in Kiev in 2009. With its sales showing a small sign of recovery at the beginning of 2010, Seppälä hoped for new growth in the new decade.

M. L. Cohen

PRINCIPAL SUBSIDIARIES

AS Stockmann/Seppälä (Estonia); TOV Stockmann/Seppälä (Ukraine); ZAO Stockmann/Seppälä (Russia).

PRINCIPAL DIVISIONS

Finland; Estonia; Sweden; Russia.

PRINCIPAL COMPETITORS

Zara International Inc.; Arcadia Group plc; Baugur Group; Benetton Group S.p.A.; Debenhams plc; Diesel SpA; Esprit Holdings Limited; The Gap, Inc.; Guess?, Inc.; H&M Hennes & Mauritz AB; Otto Versand Gmbh & Co.

FURTHER READING

"Cheap Dollar Could Lower Clothing Prices at H&M Outlets," *Helsingen Sanomat*, December 1, 2004.

"Finnish Clothing Chain Expands in Sweden," *Invest in Sweden Agency*, June 11, 2001.

"Finnish Clothing Chain Seppälä Plans Major Expansion in Russia," *Helsingen Sanomat*, January 24, 2006.

Spadel S.A./NV

rue Colonel Bourg 103
Brussels, B-1030
Belgium
Telephone: (+32 02) 702 38 11
Fax: (+32 02) 702 38 12
Web site: http://www.spadel.com

Public Company
Incorporated: 1912 as S.A. Compagnie Fermière des
Eaux et des Bains de Spa
Employees: 777
Sales: EUR 207.5 million ($337 million) (2008)
Stock Exchanges: Euronext Brussels
Ticker Symbol: BE 0003798155
NAICS: 312111 Soft Drink Manufacturing

■ ■ ■

Spadel S.A./NV is Belgium's leading producer of bottled
still and sparkling minerals. The Brussels-based company
commands more than 20 percent of the Belgian still
mineral water sector, through its core Spa Reine brand.
The group also holds a 40 percent stake in the sparkling
mineral water segment through its Bru and Spa Barisart
brands. Spadel also marks an extended line of mineral
water-based soft drinks, including fruit-flavored drinks
and flavored teas. Spadel operates as the holding
company for Spa Monopole SA, which holds the
exclusive exploitation rights to the Spa springs in
Belgium's Ardennes region; and for Bru-Chevron,
which holds the rights to the Bru springs, also in the
Ardennes.

Spadel is also the leading branded mineral water
company in the Netherlands and Luxembourg, where it
markets its Spa and Bru brands. In the United
Kingdom, Spadel operates through the Brecon Beacons
Natural Waters brand, and in France the company owns
Les Grandes Sources de Wattwiller S.A.S. Listed on the
Euronext Brussels stock exchange, Spadel remains
controlled by the Du Bois family, which has operated
the Spa springs since the early 20th century and which
holds nearly 83 percent of the group's shares. Jean-
Philippe Despontin is the company's president. In 2008
Spadel posted total sales of EUR 207.5 million ($337
million).

ROMAN ERA FAVORITE

While Spadel itself was formed in the early decades of
the 20th century, the first records of the exploitation of
the Spa mineral water springs date back to the Roman
era. One of the first mentions of the Spa springs appeared in the first century of the common era, noted by
Pliny the Elder in his *Naturalis Historia*. The Romans
were also credited with providing the source with its
name, Spa, derived from the Latin for "to gush forth."

Spa remained a popular destination long after the
collapse of the Roman Empire. Over the centuries the
iron- and mineral-rich waters of the springs developed a
strong reputation for their health and curative properties, attracting visitors from across Europe. Various
legends and traditions sprang up surrounding the
springs and their waters. The Sauveniere spring, one of
the primary Spa sources, was said to have fertility
enhancing properties, for example.

In the 16th century, Spa gained even greater renown after Gilbert Lymborgh, the personal physician to the Prince-Bishop of Liège, published a thesis promoting the medicinal properties of Spa water. Lymborgh's work became translated into several languages, helping to spread Spa's fame. This in turn stimulated demand for the mineral water from France and elsewhere, leading to the first shipments of bottled Spa water in 1583.

The Spa waters soon became a major source of revenues for the Principality of Liège. This in turn led to numerous attempts at selling counterfeit bottles labeled as Spa. One method included the mixing of ordinary city water with Spa water, a practice that was outlawed in 1624. Nonetheless, the counterfeit market flourished; a major part of this trade came from the marketing of a nearby spring's water, Bru, under the Spa name.

PROTECTIVE ZONE IN 1889

Demand for Spa spread with the exploration of the world, and by 1700 Spa water had reached the New World. The need to ensure the quality and purity of the spring water over long distances and time periods encouraged the development of better bottling and corking techniques. The need to preserve the purity of the Spa source also began to become a priority during the 18th century. This led to the first laws designed to protect the Spa spring to be enacted in 1772.

The importance of the Spa springs to the local economy was underlined in the late 19th century, with the introduction of a new and more far-reaching legislation designed to protect the purity of the mineral water. Toward this end, the protective zone, of 34.6 hectares, was established around one of the principal springs, Pierre-le-Grand, in 1889.

Over the next decades, this perimeter was expanded on an ever-larger scale. By the end of the 20th century, the protective zone surrounding the Spa springs had extended to 14,000 hectares. All farming and industrial operations were banned from within the zone, while residents were prohibited from excavating deeper than

two meters. At the same time, salting the roadways, despite the area's status as one of the regions in Belgium where it snowed the most, was also prohibited, replaced by spreading sand.

MODERN PRODUCTION BEGINS IN 1912

These measures nonetheless helped preserve the purity of the Spa waters, as Spa grew into Belgium's best-selling bottled water brand. The origins of the modern Spadel company appeared soon after the turn of the 20th century, with the granting of the commercial rights to exploit the Spa springs to a company called S.A. Compagnie Fermière des Eaux et des Bains de Spa in 1912. As the company's name indicates, its operations included its function as a popular therapeutic spa resort, as well as its developing bottled water sales.

The exploitation rights passed to Chevalier de Thier in 1921, who restructured the Compagnie Fermière des Eaux et des Bains de Spa into a new company, Spa Monopole–Compagnie des Eaux de Spa. This company then launched bottling operations at what was to become the Spa spring's most iconic source, the Reine. The new Spa Reine still water brand was launched soon after, and grew to become Belgium's leading bottled water brand. This was reinforced with the introduction of the popular Pierrot character, in 1923, which became the company's most popular mascot through the century.

Soon after its founding, however, De Thier's operations ran into financial difficulties. Among De Thier's creditors was Ernst du Bois, who had made his first fortune selling carbon dioxide gas. Instead of payment, Du Bois agreed to accept shares in Spa Monopole. Before long, the Du Bois family became Spa Monopole's majority shareholders, and continued to hold more than 80 percent of the company's shares into the next century. Du Bois' other interests, grouped under his holding company Finances et Industrie, included the Frisko ice cream brand, one of the first to be produced on an industrial scale.

ADDING BRU IN 1942

Spa Monopole expanded its range of products in the 1920s, launching a line of flavored soft drinks featuring Spa water. The company also established its own research center, the Institut Henrijean, which opened in 1931. The beginning of the next decade brought new expansion opportunities, but also tribulations for the company. In the face of the German occupation of Belgium, Du Bois's family left the country for refuge in

KEY DATES

1921: Spa Monopoleis is founded to take over the bottling operations of the Spa mineral water springs; the Du Bois family become major shareholders.

1942: Spa Monopole acquires rival mineral water producer Bru-Chevron.

1956: Spa Monopole acquires the Spontin mineral water and soft-drink company.

1969: Artois (later Interbrew) acquires 36 percent of Spa Monopole.

1980: Spadel becomes the holding company for Spa, Spontin, and Bru.

1883: Spadel acquires Brecon Beacons in Wales.

2000: Interbrew sells its stake in Spadel to the Du Bois family.

2007: Spadel sells Spontin.

2009: Spa is awarded the first place prize among 2,000 European mineral water brands.

the United States for the duration of the war. Ernst du Bois stayed behind, and was later arrested by Gestapo for supporting the resistance.

In the meantime, Spa had acquired its Ardennes neighbor and longtime rival, Bru. Like Spa, Bru traced its renown to Pliny's work, and the Bru springs, in the later principality of Stavelot-Malmedy, appeared on early Roman maps of the region. Like Spa, the Bru water also featured significant iron content, and became well-known for its own therapeutic virtues. The Bru springs were exploited by a local monastery, which bottled the water in brown bottles. This was done in order to conceal the discoloration caused by the water's high iron content. (Both Spa and Bru later developed filtration methods to remove the iron from their drinking waters.)

Bru's renown grew to rival Spa's into the 17th century. Indeed, by the middle of that century, Bru sales had climbed to 150,000 liters per year, topping Spa's own output. Bru continued to sell strongly until well into the end of the 18th century, when the upheavals surrounding the French revolution put an end to its growth. Instead, property of the springs was transferred to the local community of Chevron.

The next attempt to commercialize the Bru springs came at the dawn of the 20th century, when three Antwerp-based partners were given a 30-year concession to the springs. They formed a new company, P. Lepage, and launched one of Belgium's first modern bottling

operations, marketing its mineral water under the Chevron brand. The company changed its name to Compagnie des Eaux de Chevron in 1906, then again to Compagnie Générale de Chevron in 1925. In 1942 du Bois's holding company, Finances et Industrie, took control of the Bru springs, which then became part of Spa Monopole in 1944.

BECOMING SPADEL IN 1980

Ernst du Bois died in 1947, and control of Spa Monopole was taken over by his son, Guy du Bois, who had returned from the United States in 1945. Into the 1950s, Spa sought new expansion opportunities, particularly in the fast-growing soft-drinks sector. This led the company to acquire Spontin S.A. in 1956.

Spontin, like Spa and Bru, was a village situated in the Ardennes, and had begun exploiting its own mineral water spring in 1888. This activity was formalized in 1921 with the creation of SA des Eaux Minerales de Spontin, following the spring's designation as a natural mineral water spring that year. By 1923 the company had completed construction of a spring house and bottling factory, launching the Spontin brand. Spontin's true success, however, stemmed from the late 1930s when it launched its own line of flavored soft drinks.

By the 1950s, Spontin had become the leading soft-drink brand in Belgium, a position it held until it was eclipsed by such international rivals as Coca-Cola and Pepsi into the 1970s. During this time, however, Spontin developed a strong secondary business as a bottling company, starting with Pepsi in 1966, and then for Coca-Cola in 1979. The Spontin line was extended during this time as well, particularly with the successful launch of its fruit-flavored Squash line, which grew to become a major seller in Belgium and the Netherlands.

In the meantime, the Du Bois family had opened Spa Monopole's shareholding, bringing in Belgian beer major Artois as a minority shareholder in 1969. That company, later known as Interbrew, before becoming In-Bev, held more than 36 percent of Spa until 2000. The association with Artois enabled Spa Monopole to launch an effort to expand its own sales on an international level. Over the next decades, the company launched sales of its Spa and other brands to more than 20 markets, including the United States. As part of that effort, Spa Monopole restructured in 1980, creating a new holding company, Spadel S.A.

ENTERING WALES IN 1983

Still water remained Spadel's core product category into the early 1980s, based on its flagship Spa Reine brand.

The company had sold off the Chevron brand, in part because of conflicts with the Chevron oil company over the name, in 1979. In 1981, however, Spadel regained control of the naturally carbonated Bru springs and decided to launch the new Bru brand. The company hit upon the idea of marketing Bru as a "slightly sparkling" drink, in the process creating a new mineral water category. Bru became a major hit, quickly conquering the Belgian market for sparkling water. Spadel later launched a sparkling version of Spa as well, boosting its total market share for sparkling waters to 40 percent in Belgium.

Spadel also made its first move into other markets during that decade. In 1983 the company acquired Wales-based Brecon Beacons. This small company had been started up only in 1978. As part of Spadel, Brecon Beacons grew strongly, becoming the leading bottled water brand in Wales. By the turn of the century, Brecon Beacons had also become one of the fastest-growing water brands in England.

Guy du Bois died in 1990, and Spadel's operations were taken over by his son Guy Bernard du Bois, who was joined by right-hand man Jean-Philippe Despontin. When du Bois was killed in an accident in 2000, his younger brother Marc du Bois took over as head of the family's shareholding as well as an active role in new product development, while Despontin became responsible for the group's day to day operations. In that year, Spadel bought out Interbrew's shareholding in the company, boosting the du Bois family's ownership of the company to 83 percent.

The Interbrew exit also led to a change in strategy at Spadel, as the company decided to refocus its operations around its core markets of the Benelux for the Spa and Bru brands, as well as the Brecon Beacons brand in the United Kingdom. As a result, the company abandoned its international distribution operations elsewhere.

NEW BRANDS INTO THE 21ST CENTURY

Instead, Spadel targeted a different form of international growth. Into the turn of the century, the company made plans to enter the French market, one of the largest bottled water markets in Europe. For this, the company decided to move into France directly, acquiring an established mineral water brand. In 2004 the company bought up Les Grandes Sources de Wattwiller S.A.S., which bottled still mineral water under the Wattwiller brand. That company had been founded in 1992, taking over a dormant bottling business that dated back to the early 1920s.

Spadel's new product development effort, led by Marc du Bois, had in the meantime led to the creation of new soft-drink lines under the Spa name. These included a line of fruit-flavored waters, Spa & Fruit, as well as a line of flavored teas, called Spa & Tea. With the successful expansion of the Spa brand into these new categories, Spadel decided to sell off its fading Spontin operations, completing the sale in 2007.

Spadel also extended its other brands, launching a still version of the Bru brand, and, in 2008 a sparkling version of Wattwiller. The company also experimented with packaging, introducing water in cartons instead of bottles; a 33-milliliter water bottle marketed for children; and a three-liter size "rolling" bottle in 2004.

Despite the company's expansion, Spa Reine remained the most prominent of its product stable. Into the turn of the century, Spa remained the top-selling mineral water brand in Belgium, accounting for more than 20 percent of the market. Spa's water quality also achieved international recognition, particularly in 2009 when the company was awarded the first place prize among 2,000 natural mineral water brands by the European Center for Mineral Water Research.

M. L. Cohen

PRINCIPAL SUBSIDIARIES

Brecon Beacons Natural Waters (UK); Bru-Chevron S.A.; Les Grandes Sources de Wattwiller S.A.S.; Spa Monopole S.A.; Spadel Nederland B.V.; Spadel UK.

PRINCIPAL OPERATING UNITS

Spa; Bru; Wattwiller; Brecon Carreg.

PRINCIPAL COMPETITORS

Nestlé S.A.; The Procter & Gamble Company; Unilever N.V.; PepsiCo, Inc.; Coca-Cola Company; Groupe Danone.

FURTHER READING

Bodeux, Philippe, and Alain Dewez, "Spadel N'Est Pas a Vendre!" *Le Soir*, October 19, 2001.

Dresse, Isabelle, "Bru avec ou Sans Perles," *Le Soir*, April 20, 2006.

Green, Hannah, "Taste of Success for Spadel," *FoodBev.com*, October 2, 2009.

Lambert, Eddy, "L'Eau Minérale par Excellence," *Le Soir*, January 30, 2009.

Lederer, Edouard, "Un Patron Comme un Poisson dans l'Eau," *Le Soir*, May 28, 2005.

Munster, Jean-François, "Les Perles Centenaires de l'Eau de Bru," *Le Soir*, November 29, 2003.

———, "Spadel se Mouille sur le Marché Français," *Le Soir*, January 22, 2004.

"Profile: Brecon Mineral Water," *Western Mail*, November 25, 2009, p. 4.

Renette, Eric, "Spa Monopole s'Oppose au Développement de l'Aérodrome Local," *Le Soir*, February 3, 2010.

"SPA Rolls Out a New Bottle Design," *Food Trade Review*, September 2004, p. 562.

"Still Water on a Roll," *Packaging Magazine*, September 9, 2004, p. 562.

Todd, Stuart, "Spadel Acquires Water Company Wattwiller," *just-drinks.com*, January 26, 2004.

"Toute une Vie à Se Ressourcer," *CCI Mag*, October 23, 2008.

Vandendooren, Sandrine, "Au Fil(s) de l'Eau," *La Libre Belgique*, August 6, 2005.

Williams, David, "Power Flows Back to Wales," *Western Mail*, April 5, 2006, p. 4.

StarKist Company

323 North Shore Drive, Suite 600
Pittsburgh, Pennsylvania 15212
U.S.A.
Telephone: (412) 323-7400
Toll Free: (800) 252-1587
Web site: http://www.starkist.com

Wholly Owned Subsidiary of Dongwon Industries Co., Ltd.
Incorporated: 1917 as French Sardine Co.
Employees: 5,464
Sales: $560 million (2008 est.)
NAICS: 311711 Seafood Canning

■ ■ ■

The StarKist Company is the largest producer of canned tuna in the world. The firm's products include both canned and pouch-packed tuna in regular and premium albacore varieties, as well as prepared foods like lunch kits and premixed tuna salad. Pittsburgh-based StarKist has canning operations in Ecuador and American Samoa, and its products are largely sold in the United States, where it controls nearly 40 percent of the market. For years a unit of H.J. Heinz and then Del Monte, the firm has been owned since 2008 by Korean food conglomerate Dongwon.

ORIGINS

The roots of StarKist date to 1910, when Austrian immigrant Martin Bogdanovich bought a boat and began fishing off the California coast near Los Angeles. Born in 1882 to a family that fished and operated vineyards,

Bogdanovich had served in the Austrian Imperial Navy before moving in 1908 with his wife to San Pedro, California.

In 1917 Bogdanovich partnered with five others to found the French Sardine Company. Started with an investment of $10,000, the canning venture was created to supply U.S. troops fighting in World War I. During these years Bogdanovich began to experiment with putting fish on ice while at sea to preserve the catch, and the firm eventually built up a fleet of refrigerated boats that could stay out for long periods and bring back large quantities of fish.

The use of ice helped French Sardine expand into tuna, and in the early 1940s the firm began canning it under the brand name Star-Kist. Following the U.S. entry into World War II some 60 percent of the company's output would go to military accounts, which earned it an award from the War Food Administration. The wide distribution of the Star-Kist brand during those years also helped position the company for growth after the war's end.

In 1944 company head Martin Bogdanovich died suddenly while leading a war bond rally, and control of the firm passed to his son Joseph. The younger Bogdanovich was up to the task, having received business training as well as experience serving as a production manager and boat skipper.

WORLD'S LARGEST TUNA
CANNERY OPENS: 1952

In 1951 French Sardine helped found the Canner's Cooperative Steam Company with four other Los

COMPANY PERSPECTIVES

StarKist Co. is a leading producer, distributor and marketer of shelf-stable and frozen seafood products in the United States. A category leader in innovation, StarKist was the first brand to introduce the StarKist Flavor Fresh Pouch; StarKist Tuna Creations, a line of lightly marinated tuna; and, a dolphin-safe policy. As America's favorite tuna, StarKist represents a 65-year tradition of quality, innovation and consumer trust and is well known for its charismatic brand icon, Charlie the Tuna, who swam into the hearts of tuna fans in 1961 and is still a fan favorite today.

Angeles canners to build a shared steam plant, and a year later the firm opened the largest tuna cannery in the world to date on Terminal Island in Los Angeles Harbor. Built at a cost of $1 million, it was situated on 10 acres and included specially designed machinery and docking facilities. The facility could pack more than 400 tons of tuna in a single eight-hour shift.

In 1953 French Sardine officially changed its name to Star-Kist Foods, Inc., and also began producing cat food under the name 9Lives, using tuna by-products. In 1960 the growing company opened a second cannery in Puerto Rico.

Star-Kist launched a new marketing campaign in 1961 that featured an artsy cartoon tuna named Charlie who hoped to be chosen by Star-Kist for his "good taste." The television commercials ended with a note lowered on a hook that said "Sorry, Charlie," while a voice-over explained that he had been turned down because "Star-Kist only wants tuna that tastes good." Created by ad agency Leo Burnett, Charlie helped boost sales significantly and went on to become one of the iconic advertising characters of all time.

HEINZ BUYS FIRM: 1963

In 1963 the H.J. Heinz Co. acquired a 90 percent stake in Star-Kist in a stock-swap deal, after which Joseph Bogdanovich remained in place as the firm's president. During the year Star-Kist also opened another large tuna cannery in American Samoa. Annual sales at this time were an estimated $70 million.

Charlie the Tuna was joined in 1968 by future ad icon Morris the Cat, who pitched for sister brand 9Lives. By the early 1970s 9Lives had become the cat food market leader, with nearly 20 percent of sales, and

the firm boosted production capacity to keep up with demand.

In 1973, 173,000 cans of Star-Kist tuna produced in Samoa were recalled after they were found to contain decomposed fish. Some 200 customers were sickened, and the firm and two executives were later made to pay small fines. The company subsequently tightened quality control procedures.

Star-Kist acquired tuna fleet operator Ocean Fisheries, Inc., in 1974 in a deal worth $17.5 million. The firm's sales were strong during this era, as the product's low price and ease of use proved a solid fit with the American lifestyle. During the 1970s Star-Kist also began offering tuna packed in spring water, which had a lower calorie count than the oil traditionally used.

STAR-KIST BECOMES TOP TUNA BRAND: 1983

By 1983 Star-Kist had bested rivals Chicken of the Sea and Bumble Bee to become the top-selling tuna brand in the United States. The industry at that time was facing a surge in lower-priced imports, however, which had doubled in market share to 20 percent in just five years. In the fall of 1984 the firm closed its California cannery and shifted all production to Puerto Rico and American Samoa to cut costs. Over 1,100 workers would lose their jobs, although 700 would remain on Terminal Island handling pet food production, can making, distribution, and other duties.

In 1985 Star-Kist's New Brunswick, Canada, subsidiary became the subject of controversy after reports emerged that the country's fisheries minister, under pressure from the company, had overridden inspectors who found some cans of tuna to be spoiled. The firm subsequently recalled a million cans and the minister was forced to resign. Star-Kist's Canadian market share of 39 percent quickly plummeted, and several years later the company shuttered its operation there, causing the loss of 400 jobs.

The firm bought the assets of Mississippi cat food maker Mayar in 1987, but an attempt the following year by Heinz to purchase number three tuna brand Bumble Bee for $225 million was blocked by the U.S. Justice Department over antitrust concerns. Shortly after the latter deal fell through, Heinz reorganized the firm into two units, Star-Kist Seafood Co. and Heinz Pet Products Co. The move had reportedly been made because canned pet food sales were largely limited to the United States, and Heinz wanted to boost tuna sales abroad. By this time retail sales of Star-Kist tuna were estimated at more than $500 million and the company had about 40 percent of the U.S. market.

KEY DATES

1917: Martin Bogdanovich and five partners found French Sardine Co.

1940s: Firm begins using Star-Kist brand name for canned tuna.

1952: Company opens largest tuna cannery in the world in Los Angeles Harbor.

1953: French Sardine changes name to Star-Kist Food Co., launches 9Lives cat food.

1963: Star-Kist acquired by H.J. Heinz Co.; new cannery added in American Samoa.

1990: Firm announces it will buy only tuna caught without killing dolphins.

2000: Star-Kist launches first pouch-packed tuna products.

2002: Heinz sells Star-Kist to Del Monte Foods Co.

2008: Dongwon Group buys Del Monte tuna unit, which becomes StarKist Company.

GOING DOLPHIN SAFE: 1990

For reasons unclear to even marine biologists, dolphins in the eastern Pacific Ocean from Chile to Southern California swam with tuna, and fishing boats in these waters typically used dolphins, which surfaced periodically for air, as markers for schools of tuna. Both of the commercial catching methods typically employed caused dolphin deaths. So-called drift or gill nets, which were up to 40 miles long, indiscriminately trapped and drowned anything in their path, from fish to turtles. "Purse seine" nets, which were placed around a school of fish and the bottom closed by means of a drawstring, killed fewer dolphins because fishermen could push them out, but this was not consistently done.

Although the U.S. Marine Mammal Protection Act of 1972 had established guidelines for the inadvertent killing of dolphins by American tuna fleets, the public had at this time become sensitized to the topic through high-profile news stories about dolphins, perceived to be smart and friendly, dying in conjunction with tuna fishing. With legislation in the works that would require label notification if tuna had been caught with dolphins, boycotts being threatened by environmental groups such as Greenpeace and the Earth Island Institute, and some school lunch programs considering banning tuna, the industry was rapidly being pushed into a corner.

On April 12, 1990, Star-Kist made headlines when it announced it would no longer buy tuna from suppliers whose fishing methods killed dolphins, a move that was immediately followed by Bumble Bee and Chicken of the Sea. Star-Kist deemed use of drift nets totally unacceptable, with purse seine fishing allowed in waters where dolphins did not swim with tuna. These methods were used for the more common yellowfin and skipjack types, while the premium albacore variety was generally caught with hand-baited hook-and-line methods.

Half of the 63-vessel U.S. tuna fleet worked the affected areas, and their operators bitterly protested the move, but the firm stood its ground. Soon after making the announcement, cans of StarKist tuna, as well as 9Lives Cat Food, began to carry a prominent "Dolphin Safe" label notation. Although numerous operational changes were required, the price of canned tuna was only minimally affected.

HEADQUARTERS MOVED TO KENTUCKY: 1993

In 1993 Star-Kist moved its headquarters from California to Newport, Kentucky, just outside of Cincinnati, where its operations were recombined with the Heinz pet food unit. The firm continued to hold 40 percent of the U.S. tuna market, and, with 9Lives, accounted for 10 percent of Heinz revenues. Star-Kist was the fifth-largest-selling dry grocery brand in the United States.

New products introduced during this era included a "lunch kit" that consisted of a 3.75-ounce can of tuna, crackers, mayonnaise, pickle relish, plastic dishes, and a small wooden spoon; and a line of 100 percent yellowfin "Select" tuna in regular and hickory-smoked varieties. The latter retailed for about a dollar a can, as compared with 70 cents for the regular variety and $1.40 for albacore.

The firm had dropped its standard can size from six and one-half ounces to six and one-eighth ounces, which reduced the amount of tuna in a can by about 5 percent, thus raising profitability. The brand name had also lost its hyphen to become StarKist, although the official corporate name remained Star-Kist Foods.

PUERTO RICO EXPANSION: 1995

In early 1995 Star-Kist broke ground on a new 150,000-square-foot production facility in Mayaguez, Puerto Rico, which would create 150 new jobs, and parent Heinz formed a joint venture with the government of Seychelles to operate a tuna-processing plant there for sale through the StarKist Europe unit. The company at that time had tuna-processing facilities in Puerto Rico, American Samoa, Ecuador, Portugal, France, Ghana, and Australia.

In 1996 Heinz bought several Italian tuna brands from Kraft General Foods, and a United Kingdom unit was set up. Sales of canned tuna in Europe were growing at a rate of 7 percent per year, while in the United States per-capita consumption had fallen to 11 tuna meals per year from 14 a decade earlier. During the year Star-Kist also launched a Web site and redesigned its packaging to feature a trimmer Charlie character.

Still seeking ways to cope with the shrinking canned tuna segment, in 1998 the company test marketed frozen fish fillets under the name Seaside Gourmet, which included pre-sauced salmon and cod dishes, but not tuna. A gourmet tuna line in cans was also introduced, which included garlic, smoked, and lemon and cracked pepper varieties.

In 2000 the firm's headquarters moved to Pittsburgh as Heinz restructured yet again. While about 100 employees were relocated from Kentucky, 200 more jobs were lost, in part from combining some operations with other Heinz units. Star-Kist Foods then had an estimated $1.3 billion in sales and employed 10,000 around the world.

TUNA-IN-A-POUCH DEBUTS: 2000

In June 2000 the company announced that, starting in the fall, it would offer consumers tuna in a vacuum-sealed foil pouch. Requiring little added liquid, the product was also said to taste fresher due to the reduced cooking and processing required. Three varieties were offered in seven-ounce serving sizes, which ranged in price from $1.89 to $2.79 for albacore. Star-Kist supported the introduction with a $20 million ad campaign, and later also added variations including pouch-sealed salad kits.

Shortly after unveiling the pouch, the firm sold can-making operations in Pennsylvania, California, West Virginia, Puerto Rico, and American Samoa to Impress Metal Packaging Holdings B.V. of Amsterdam. Impress signed a 10-year agreement to continue making cans for Star-Kist, which had also sold its fleet of eight tuna boats to Tri-Marine International, Inc.

With prices low due to a surplus of fish on the market, and with sales of both tuna and canned pet food falling, in March 2001 Star-Kist announced its tuna processing plant in Puerto Rico would close, eliminating 1,300 jobs. The pet food unit in California was also shuttered, with 325 jobs cut, and its operations moved to a Heinz plant in Bloomsburg, Pennsylvania.

SALE TO DEL MONTE: 2002

In June 2002 H.J. Heinz announced it would spin off Star-Kist, 9Lives, and several other lines of pet food, baby food, and soup to Del Monte Foods Co. of San Francisco. The units had combined revenue of $1.8 billion, or 20 percent of Heinz's annual sales. In the complicated deal, they were merged into a new subsidiary of Heinz that was spun off to its shareholders, after which it was immediately merged into a new Del Monte subsidiary. Heinz shareholders would subsequently hold a 75 percent ownership stake in Del Monte.

The Reverse Morris Trust structure would allow Heinz to rid itself of numerous less-profitable businesses without paying taxes on the transaction, and the acquisition would more than double Del Monte's sales to $3.1 billion, as well as helping boost that firm's presence on store shelves. About 5,000 Star-Kist workers would become Del Monte employees, with only about 100 jobs expected to be lost. Del Monte hoped to achieve nearly $40 million per year in savings by sharing some factories and distribution centers with Heinz.

In June 2004 the state of California sued Star-Kist, Bumble Bee, and Tri-Union Seafoods, maker of Chicken of the Sea, claiming that they violated a state law requiring warnings on products that exposed consumers to the toxin mercury. All seafood contained it to some degree, and concerns about mercury in tuna dated to the early 1970s. A subsequent statement from the U.S. Food and Drug Administration that pregnant women and children should limit tuna consumption brought more bad news, and during 2004 Star-Kist sales dropped more than 5 percent.

The firm responded to criticisms of tuna by noting that people would have to consume much larger than average quantities to reach a problematic mercury level, and touted tuna's high protein to fat ratio and sizable omega-3 fatty acid content, which was thought to help reduce the risk of heart disease. In May 2006 a Superior Court judge in San Francisco ruled that tuna did not have to be labeled with a warning about mercury in California.

DONGWON ACQUIRES
STAR-KIST: 2008

In June 2008 Korea-based Dongwon Group agreed to purchase the firm from Del Monte for $359 million. Founded in 1969 by a former sea captain, Dongwon's operations were largely food based but also included telecommunications and construction affiliates. The Star-Kist deal was seen as a way for its new owner to gain entry to the U.S. market for its other product lines. Dongwon controlled 75 percent of the Korean tuna market and also operated canning operations and a fleet of 36 fishing boats. Its 11 business units, including the renamed StarKist Company, had $2.3 billion in annual revenues.

After the deal was completed Dongwon would continue to run the firm's tuna processing operations in Samoa, Ecuador, and Southern California, while Del Monte would provide it with warehousing, distribution, sales, transportation, and other services for two years during the ownership transition. Del Monte would also keep the pet food lines, including 9Lives, which had long been part of Star-Kist.

Following the Dongwon purchase, company veteran Donald Binotto was named president and CEO of the firm, which would remain headquartered in Pittsburgh. StarKist's sales hit an estimated $560 million for fiscal 2008, and it claimed 37 percent of the canned tuna market in the United States.

In the summer of 2009 the firm announced it would lay off 350 workers at its American Samoa canning operation, bringing the total number of jobs lost there in the previous 18 months to 1,000. Federally mandated minimum wage increases were slated to double its payroll costs, and StarKist, the territory's largest private employer, was looking to find a way for the operation to remain economically viable even as rival Chicken of the Sea announced that a neighboring 2,172-worker facility would close in the fall. Congress began consideration of a bill that included paying subsidies to tuna processors, while Samoa extended tax incentives to the firm.

In the fall of 2009 StarKist boosted promotion of its pouch-packaged tuna products, targeting budget-conscious consumers with a $9 million marketing campaign. It also expanded the product line with new flavors and a new premixed tuna salad. The firm had approximately 85 percent of the pouch-packed tuna market.

A century after founder Martin Bogdanovich first began fishing the waters off Los Angeles, StarKist Company had grown to become the number one tuna processor in the world. The firm was struggling to remain profitable in the face of a decline in tuna sales and other challenges, but new owner Dongwon appeared committed to finding a strategy for long-term success.

Frank Uhle

PRINCIPAL SUBSIDIARIES

StarKist Samoa, Inc.

PRINCIPAL COMPETITORS

Thai Union Frozen Products Public Company Ltd.; Bumble Bee Foods, LLC; Chicken of the Sea International.

FURTHER READING

Conner, K. Patrick, "The Conversion of StarKist," *San Francisco Chronicle*, June 17, 1990.

Eig, Jonathan, and Robert Frank, "Heinz Spins Off Sluggish Units," *Wall Street Journal*, June 14, 2002, p. B4.

"$500-Million Plant Set in Puerto Rico," *Engineering News-Record*, June 17, 1991, p. 23.

"Heinz's Pet Food History," *Pittsburgh Post-Gazette*, August 25, 1996, p. C2.

Kay, Jane, "State Loses Efforts on Warnings about Tuna," *San Francisco Chronicle*, May 13, 2006, p. B1.

Lancaster, John, "3 Tuna Firms Move to Save Dolphins," *Washington Post*, April 13, 1990, p. A1.

Lindeman, Teresa F., "Former StarKist Chief Returns to Brand as Del Monte Completes Sale," *Pittsburgh Post-Gazette*, October 8, 2008.

Miller, Nick, "Not-Sorry Charlie StarKist Revives Hapless '60s Mascot," *Cincinnati Post*, June 9, 1995, p. 14C.

Sabatini, Patricia, "Heinz Bringing StarKist HQ to Pittsburgh," *Pittsburgh Post-Gazette*, October 5, 1999, p. F1.

———, "Heinz to Cut 1,900," *Pittsburgh Post-Gazette*, March 16, 2001, p. C1.

"StarKist's Uncanny New Pouch Touts Convenience," *Food & Drug Packaging*, July 1, 2000, p. 10.

Strabag SE

———————————— ■ ————————————

Triglavstrasse 9
Villach, A-9500
Austria
Telephone: (43 1) 22422-0
Fax: (43 1) 22422-2226
Web site: http://www.strabag.com

Public Company
Incorporated: 1895 as Strassenwalzenbetrieb vorm. H.
  Reifenrath GmbH
Employees: 75,548
Sales: EUR 13 billion ($18.1 billion) (2009)
Stock Exchanges: Vienna
Ticker Symbol: STR
NAICS: 234110 Highway and Street Construction;
  233310 Manufacturing and Industrial Building
  Construction; Water, Sewer, and Pipeline Construc-
  tion; 234120 Bridge and Tunnel Construction;
  234930 Industrial Nonbuilding Structure Construc-
  tion; 234990 All Other Heavy Construction;
  233320 Commercial and Institutional Building
  Construction; 233220 Multifamily Housing
  Construction

■ ■ ■

Strabag SE is one of Europe's five largest construction
companies. In addition to its core markets in Germany,
Austria, the Czech Republic, Poland, Hungary, and Slo-
vakia, Strabag SE is also active in other Eastern and
Western European countries as well as in Canada, Chile,
China, India, and in several Arab countries. Strabag

builds anything from roads and highways to airports
and railway stations, bridges and tunnels, dams and
power plants, hospitals and universities, office buildings
and hotels, shopping and convention centers, business
parks and sports stadiums, industrial and leisure-time
complexes.

The company's civil engineering division also carries out earthwork; builds wastewater systems and pipes;
and manufactures asphalt, concrete, and other construction materials. Its environmental engineering division
builds landfills, waste treatment plants, and wastewater
collection and treatment systems. Other subsidiaries
manufacture prefabricated building elements, construct
steel girders and façades, and offer construction-related
planning and engineering services as well as project
development and facility management. Strabag's primary
brands are STRABAG, Dywidag, Heilit+Woerner, and
Züblin. The Austrian Haselsteiner Group, the
Raiffeisen/UNIQUA Group, and the Russian Rasperia
Trading own roughly three-quarters of Strabag's share
capital.

1882–95: INITIAL SUCCESS WITH ROAD ROLLING

The history of Strabag dates back to the 1880s when
Heinrich Reifenrath, the owner of an iron products firm
in Germany, started focusing on road construction.
During the economic boom of the 1880s and 1890s,
which was driven by rapid industrialization, the swelling
populations of larger cities, and the rise in the number
of motorized vehicles, new roads were being built
everywhere. The technically talented entrepreneur

COMPANY PERSPECTIVES

Building Visions—Building Values—Building Europe. STRABAG is an important European construction company that developed from companies full of tradition and rooted in Europe, as well as the people thereof. With the competence, innovative power and motivation of our employees as well as a streamlined and transparent organizational structure associated therewith, we are on the way to becoming Europe's leading construction service providers. The broadness and internationality of our fields of activity in conjunction with the depth of our know-how put us on a stable economic basis, on which we continue to grow dynamically.

purchased his first 10-ton steam-engine-driven road roller in 1882 and began to rent it in nearby towns where it was mainly used for road repairs. In 1888 Reifenrath sold his firm and two years later started a new business in Niederlahnstein near Koblenz that was solely focused on road construction.

By the early 1890s Reifenrath's company had become one of Germany's leading road roller companies. He lined up additional investors to finance further expansion and established the limited liability company Strassenwalzenbetrieb vormals H. Reifenrath GmbH, Niederlahnstein, in February 1895. Five years later the founder withdrew from the business.

FAST GROWTH UNTIL WORLD WAR I

Around the turn of the 20th century Strassenwalzenbetrieb expanded its reach to other parts of western Germany. In 1903 the company carried out its first contract in Switzerland, followed by activities in Luxembourg and the Netherlands. By 1905 the company's annual sales had more than doubled to over one million reichsmark, and they almost doubled again between 1905 and 1913.

In addition to road rolling, Strassenwalzenbetrieb Niederlahnstein built a thriving road construction materials business by selling the necessary basalt, tar, and later macadam, to the company's clients. Moreover, it started selling the equipment it had built for its own needs, such as scarification equipment, sprinkler vehicles, pumps, and trailers, to outside customers as well. The company also continuously expanded its

workshop capacity and developed new road construction technologies and materials.

When World War I began in 1914, Strassenwalzenbetrieb had to turn over most of its road rollers to the military. Raw materials were also used for the war effort, and municipal road construction came to a sudden halt. The company's road rolling business dropped by one-quarter in the first year of the war but continued at a steady level during the following war years. The company's road construction equipment and repair business soared as the war progressed. Its subsidiary in Switzerland continued its business during World War I but was shut down by the Swiss after the war. Subsidiaries in France were lost as well.

With almost no demand for road construction and repair right after the war, Strassenwalzenbetrieb used some of its remaining road rollers to carry out coal transports and started repairing and building road rollers for other customers. The company also acquired a number of struggling competitors.

1923–29: SHAREHOLDER SPLIT-UP STIRS INNOVATION

On June 20, 1923, the company's owners, which, in addition to Strassenwalzenbetrieb's initial group of shareholders, included Linz-based construction material manufacturer Basalt-Actien-Gesellschaft and several road construction firms, founded Strassenbau-AG, Niederlahnstein, a stock corporation that functioned as an organizational umbrella for the company's many subsidiaries and shareholdings. Although officially still based in Niederlahnstein, the company's actual headquarters were moved to Cologne in 1924.

The introduction of a new currency in Germany in 1923 put an end to hyperinflation and initiated a revitalization of road construction. In the mid-1920s Strassenbau AG was involved in major projects that were carried out through a number of *Wegebaugesellschaften*, regional joint ventures with Basalt-Actien-Gesellschaft, its contractual supplier of raw materials. However, after a dispute between the shareholders of the two companies had caused Strassenbau AG to withdraw from the ventures, and Basalt-Actien-Gesellschaft to withdraw as a Strassenbau shareholder, the company focused on the development of innovative road construction technologies and invested considerably in its newly established research lab.

Between 1926 and 1929 Strassenbau's research and development (R&D) efforts produced new kinds of road covering mixtures of tar, bitumen, and asphalt, and the accompanying on-site mixing equipment, both of which became a huge success in Germany. Some of the

KEY DATES

1890: Entrepreneur Heinrich Reifenrath starts a road construction business.

1895: The company Strassenwalzenbetrieb vormals H. Reifenrath GmbH, Niederlahnstein is founded.

1923: Public stock corporation Strassenbau-Aktiengesellschaft, Niederlahnstein, is founded.

1931: Mixing plant subsidiary Deutag is established.

1949: Headquarters move to Cologne, company is renamed Strabag Bau-A.G., and listing is made on the Cologne Stock Exchange.

1965: The company sets up a subsidiary in Linz, Austria.

1986: Strabag's Austrian subsidiary goes public on the Vienna Stock Exchange.

1998: Austrian construction group BIBAG Bauindustrie Beteiligungs AG acquires Strabag AG.

2005: The company takes over German construction groups Walter Bau, Dywidag, and Ed. Züblin.

company's most noteworthy projects of this period included a major freeway connecting Cologne and Bonn; curved and climbing sections of the Nürburgring racetrack; and the construction of the new exhibition grounds in Cologne.

1930–33: CONSOLIDATION AND CRISIS YEARS

In the decade after its foundation, the company (adopting the shortened name Strabag) had expanded its activities into all parts of Germany as well as to other European countries. In 1930, after lengthy negotiations, Strabag took over four German *Wegebaugesellschaften* from Basalt-Actien-Gesellschaft, which had suffered major losses, in exchange for company stock. The move strengthened Strabag's market position and provided easier access to credit, since Basalt-Actien-Gesellschaft's owners, the von Oppenheims, had excellent connections in the world of finance.

However, the ripples of the Great Depression sent the German economy into another serious downturn in the early 1930s. Again, public road construction came to a sudden halt. A fierce competition broke out between construction companies for the few contracts

that were awarded, resulting in sharply dropping price levels. Strabag managed to survive this difficult period, mainly due to several large projects in Germany, Poland, Czechoslovakia, and Hungary. After suffering a major loss of 1.7 million reichsmark in 1931, Strabag remained slightly in the red until the mid-1930s.

1933: UNDER THE NAZI GOVERNMENT

After the new Nazi government had launched a major road construction program in 1933, Strabag's business began to soar again. The company was involved in many public road maintenance projects as well as in building bicycle lanes, pedestrian areas, railroad platforms, company grounds, waterways, and flood protection installations. As a result, Strabag's sales more than doubled while its workforce doubled between 1933 and 1936. However, due to the fierce competition, price levels remained fairly low, and it took until 1936 for the company to turn a considerable profit again.

The 1931 establishment of Deutsche Teer- und Asphaltschotterwerke GmbH (Deutag), a new subsidiary for the operation of mixing plants for paving materials, was a major milestone in Strabag's history. It was Deutag's new type of basalt-based concrete that came into high demand as the new government's policy of preferring domestic raw materials over mineral-oil-based products was an attempt to reduce the German economy's dependency on oil imports.

In 1936 Strabag's headquarters were moved to Berlin. After being involved in the planning stages of Adolf Hitler's *Reichsautobahn* project, a network of highways connecting major cities in all of Germany, Strabag built about 400 kilometers of highway, equaling almost 10 percent of the entire project, between 1936 and 1940. Since the new highways were mainly built with Deutag's concrete mixture, the company's sales roughly doubled within only two years and remained at a high level until the early 1940s when highway construction was discontinued due to the progressing war.

DEFENSE AND RUNWAY CONSTRUCTION DURING WORLD WAR II

Beginning in 1938 Strabag, by then Germany's largest road construction company, became increasingly involved in war-related activities. The company took part in the construction of the Siegfried Line and the Atlantic Wall, Hitler's gigantic defense installations, and built access roads and parking areas for airports, mainly in northern Germany.

Since the construction of new runways for airplanes was of critical importance during the war, Strabag engineers, using the so-called mixed-in-place technology, invented machinery that mixed the ground material with the construction material very thoroughly and evenly in a very short time. The new technology resulted in a significant increase in contracts for runways, and the company used the incoming cash flow to invest in state-of-the-art equipment but also to build massive financial reserves. All in all, the company built over 100 runways between 1936 and 1945.

After the beginning of World War II in 1939, Strabag's activities were moved into the occupied territories in Western and Eastern Europe where the company continued to build airports, roads, and bridges. As the war progressed, Strabag employed an increasing number of prisoners of war and forced laborers from many European countries, according to German economic historian Manfred Pohl in *Die Strabag*.

1945–49: RUBBLE REMOVAL AND RUNWAY RECONSTRUCTION

Thanks to Josef Oberbach, a leading Strabag engineer and a member of the executive board since 1939, the company transitioned into the postwar reconstruction period with almost no delay. Oberbach contacted the two main shareholders, Wilhelm Werhahn and Friedrich Carl Freiherr von Oppenheim, who in June 1945 authorized him to get the company up and running again. Strabag had lost 90 percent of its equipment during the war. Seven of Deutag's 13 concrete-mixing plants were expropriated by the Soviet occupation forces as were many of Strabag's subsidiaries abroad. However, due to the company's conservative financial risk management policy during the war years, Strabag was able to absorb the enormous war losses on its balance sheet.

With the remaining equipment Strabag began to build runways for airports for the Allied forces in the second half of the 1940s, after it was officially established that Werhahn and von Oppenheim had not been involved with the Nazis in any way. At the beginning of 1948 Strabag was able to sell the land and buildings of one of its remaining subsidiaries in West Berlin for a large sum, which enabled the company to invest in rebuilding the business.

In September 1949 Strabag's headquarters were moved to Cologne, and the company was formally renamed Strabag Bau-A.G. and listed on the Cologne Stock Exchange. As the company secured a number of larger contracts for removing the rubble of the war, for providing construction material, and for repairing roads, railroads, and bridges in big cities, Strabag's sales and workforce rose significantly.

Repairing and building airport runways and access roads for the Allied forces helped Strabag rebuild the business during the postwar years. Until 1953 the company worked on 28 civil and military airports in Berlin, Frankfurt, Hamburg, and Freiburg, among others. Airport construction remained a major pillar of Strabag's business in the following decades.

1950–65: POSTWAR RECONSTRUCTION BOOM

After the foundation of the Federal Republic of Germany in 1949 and the reorganization of German municipal authorities in the early 1950s, public road construction picked up speed again, and Strabag soon regained its leading position in road construction. In the following decades the company was involved in almost all major highway construction projects in West Germany and participated in the building of numerous roads and freeways. Strabag's engineers also continued to enhance road construction technologies by developing new kinds of road covering mixtures, such as the patented porous asphalt, an asphalt mixture that was particularly durable and long lasting, as well as the necessary equipment for applying it onto the road surface.

The production of construction material mixtures constituted one of Strabag's most stable and profitable activities during the 1950s and 1960s. The setting up of a tightly knit network of stationary mixing plants started in major cities of the Ruhr region in the early 1950s and was extended to all of West Germany until the mid-1970s. After the original Deutag had been liquidated in 1951, Strabag established a new mixing plant division that was merged with Basalt AG's mixing plants and spun off as Cologne-based Deutag-Mischwerke GmbH & Co. OHG in 1969.

HYDRAULIC CONSTRUCTION BEGINS IN 1950

In addition to rebuilding its core business in the 1950s, Strabag ventured into new promising markets, such as dam construction. Based on a massive R&D research program, the company developed new kinds of bituminous sealing materials for dams as well as special equipment for dam building. In 1950 Strabag acquired its first dam construction project and completed the sealant work for 15 dams and 12 reservoirs by 1967.

Beginning in 1968 Strabag expanded its dam construction activities to other countries. One of the most noteworthy projects was the bituminous insulation for one of the world's largest pumping plants and reservoirs in Ludington, Michigan, where Strabag in cooperation with the U.S.-based firm Morrison & Knudsen sealed a face area of 720,000 square meters in the early 1970s. In addition to dam construction, the company got involved in the construction of waterways, sea works, harbor installations, and water power plants.

Strabag's breakthrough occurred with an innovation in the area of open sea construction wherein the company used *Hubinseln* (elevated platforms used primarily in the open sea oil production) as equipment for setting up structures in the open sea, which greatly shortened the time needed to build such structures.

1965–75: SURFACE CONSTRUCTION AND CIVIL ENGINEERING

In the early 1960s the company was awarded a number of contracts from the federal government university construction program. In addition to universities and schools, Strabag focused on the construction of theaters and convention centers in the late 1960s and early 1970s.

Thought to be a major step into the German aboveground construction market, the mid-1960s takeover of Düsseldorf-based Allgemeine Hochbau-Gesellschaft mbH (AHI), a construction company founded in 1904, turned out to be a major setback for Strabag. Due to mismanagement, AHI produced losses in the tens of millions in the late 1960s and caused a serious financial crisis. However, after changing AHI's top management and after the company's integration into Strabag in 1972, AHI's engineers proved to be a valuable asset as Strabag evolved as a major player in civil engineering.

In addition to civil engineering, Strabag also became a major player in the area of industrial construction in the late 1960s and early 1970s. The company was involved in numerous large projects such as the construction of oil refineries, aluminum and paper manufacturing plants, chemical processing plants, nuclear power plants, large manufacturing halls, silos, and office buildings. In 1972 Strabag founded Modulent Fertighaus GmbH, a subsidiary for the manufacturing of prefabricated homes. By the mid-1970s Strabag had become Germany's third-largest construction company.

1975–89: SUCCESSES AND SETBACKS ABROAD

As early as in the 1950s Strabag had begun to acquire construction projects abroad, mainly in the Middle East and Africa. Strabag's activities abroad expanded in the 1960s when the German government funded a number of large construction projects in developing countries. During that time, Strabag, often in cooperation with other construction companies, built roads and highways in Liberia, Cameroon, Somalia, Madagascar, Gabon, Kenya, Iraq, and Thailand; bridges in Guinea; railroads and the Lomé harbor in Togo; and large dams in Syria and Morocco. While these projects helped Strabag build a reputation abroad, their financial results were mixed.

Strabag's international activities intensified in the 1970s. Among the larger projects was a highway along Oman's coast; the construction of the Tarbela Dam on the Indus River in Pakistan, the world's largest earth-filled dam; the Lagos-Ibadan highway and the runways of Lagos International Airport in Nigeria. In addition, Strabag was involved in dam building projects in Norway, Greece, and Austria, where the company set up a subsidiary in Linz in 1965.

The increasing importance of Strabag's business abroad resulted in the percentage of its performance abroad rising from barely 10 percent in 1973 to roughly 33 percent 10 years later. However, Strabag's strategic decision in 1980 to focus on large projects in politically unstable Iraq threw the company into financial turmoil for almost a decade.

EASTWARD EXPANSION AFTER 1989

The opening of the Berlin Wall in 1989 and the subsequent opening of Eastern Europe to the West also brought new geographic markets for Strabag and initiated a construction boom that lasted until 1994. The company set up a network of subsidiaries covering eastern Germany in record time and acquired several East German construction companies. As Strabag got involved in a broad variety of construction projects in eastern Germany, most importantly the renewal of the transportation and energy infrastructure, the company's business soared with total performance doubling between 1990 and 1994. Strabag built highways and railways, commercial, public, commercial and residential buildings, while the company's newly established environmental engineering division worked on building water treatment plants and sewage systems.

At the same time Strabag expanded into Eastern Europe as well. The company's Austrian arm set up a subsidiary in Hungary in 1990 that acquired highway construction, hotel and office building contracts in Budapest. In 1994 Strabag established a subsidiary in the Czech Republic. The company also acquired construction companies in Poland.

1995–99: AUSTRIAN FIRM FORMED AFTER CRISIS

In 1995 the dynamic growth of the German construction industry came to a sudden halt. As demand slowed, the existing overcapacities resulted in fierce competition and mounting price pressure. In addition, Strabag struggled with major losses from large projects where real costs were significantly higher than calculated. As a result, the company slipped into the red in 1995. To overcome the crisis, Strabag cut its eastern German workforce in half, streamlined its organization, and sold a 51 percent majority stake in Deutag to the Werhahn group. Nonetheless, the company reported a loss of over DEM 200 million in 1996.

Although Strabag was out of the red in 1997, the Wilhelm Werhahn family sold an estimated 49.9 percent share in Strabag to the Austrian company Bibag Bauindustrie Beteiligungs AG, holding company of Bau Holding AG, the predecessor of ILBAU Ges.m.b.H, a reputable, but much smaller construction company. Bau Holding's majority shareholder, Hans Peter Haselsteiner, had long been working on creating a large European construction concern. Combined with Strabag's profitable Austrian subsidiary, the new group, which was renamed Bauholding Strabag AG, became one of Europe's top 10 construction companies.

FAST GROWTH AND REORGANIZATION AFTER 2000

As the German construction market went through a severe downturn in the early 2000s, Bauholding Strabag grew rapidly by acquiring a number of large German construction firms that were struggling financially because of the crisis. In 2002 Strabag acquired Deutsche Asphalt from the insolvent construction giant Philipp Holzmann AG. In 2006 Strabag took over Preusse Bauholding, followed one year later by the acquisition of parts of the bankrupt construction group Walter Bau, including major subsidiaries of Dywidag, Heilit+Woerner Bau-AG, and Ed. Züblin AG. On the other hand, Strabag sold another 25 percent in Deutag to the Werhahn & Nauen group.

Strabag next reorganized its various business activities and subsidiaries. Strabag Societas Europaea, or Strabag SE, became the group's new holding company. Strabag's German subsidiary focused mainly on transportation infrastructure while building construction and civil engineering was outsourced to Ed. Züblin AG.

The Lenz family, which owned a 43 percent stake in Züblin, filed a lawsuit against the merger of Strabag's loss-producing high-risk construction business with Züblin. However, Germany's Federal Supreme Court ruled in favor of Strabag in 2008. The company's third division was called special divisions and concessions and included tunnel construction and global project management of mainly transportation infrastructure projects.

ACQUISITIONS AND NEW PROJECTS

In spring 2007 Strabag's shareholders sold a significant stake in the company to Russian billionaire Oleg Deripaska, a move that was intended to help Strabag generate more business in Russia. In October 2007 Strabag SE went public at the Vienna Stock Exchange. The initial public offering raised almost 900 million euros, the majority of which was earmarked for further expansion. In 2008 Strabag acquired eight companies, including the German Telekom's property and facility management subsidiary Deutsche Telekom Immobilien und Service (DeTeImmobilien), the German firms Kirchner Holding and F. Kirchhoff, and the Austrian Efkon AG, as well as smaller companies in Italy, Sweden, Switzerland and the Czech Republic, adding a total of EUR 2 billion in annual sales.

In 2010 Strabag was involved in building highways in Poland, Hungary, Denmark, Tanzania, and Kenya; the Rohtang Pass in the western Himalaya region of India; a wastewater treatment plant in Belarus; several dams in Oman; concrete foundations for an offshore wind power pilot project in the North Sea and the Leipzig city tunnel with underground railway stations in Germany; and the new Vienna Central Station in Austria, among many other construction projects worldwide. Looking ahead, the company aimed at acquiring transportation infrastructure projects on the basis of public private partnership and concession models in selected geographic markets such as Scandinavia and India.

Evelyn Hauser

PRINCIPAL SUBSIDIARIES

Strabag AG (Germany; 90%); Bau Holding Beteiligungs AG; BBS Baustoffbetriebe Sachsen GmbH (Germany); Ed. Züblin AG (Germany; 57.26%); F. Kirchhoff AG (Germany; 94.99%); Heilit+Woerner Bau GmbH (Germany); Josef Riepl Unternehmen für Hoch- und Tiefbau GmbH (Germany); STRABAG Sp. z o.o. (Poland); Polski Asfalt Spolka z Ograniczona Odopowiedzialnoscia (Poland); Strabag Epitö Zartköruen Muködo Reszvenytarsasag (Hungary); Strabag a.s. (Czech Republic); Strabag spol. s.r.o. (Slovakia); Slovasfalt spol. s.r.o. (Slovakia); Strabag AG (Switzerland); ODEN Anläggningsentreprenad AB (Sweden); Strabag za gradevinske poslove d.o.o. (Croatia); N.V. STRABAG Belgium S.A. (Belgium); Strabag Bouw en Ontwikkeling B.V. (Netherlands); Strabag EAD (Bulgaria); Strabag srl (Romania); Möbius Construction Ukraine Ltd.; Strabag z.a.o. (Russia); Shanghai Changijang-Züblin Construction & Engineering C. Ltd. (China; 75%); Strabag Inc. (Canada); Al-Hani General Construction Co. (Libya; 60%); Strabag Dubai LLC (United Arab Emirates); Strabag Oman; Dywidag Saudi Arabia Ltd.

PRINCIPAL COMPETITORS

HOCHTIEF AG; Bilfinger Berger AG; Skanska AB; Vinci S.A.

FURTHER READING

"Austria's Strabag to Invest 22.5 Bln Rubles in Building Highways in Volgograd," *Russia & CIS Business and Financial Newswire,* May 24, 2007.

"Deutsche Bank and Strabag form Russian Joint Venture (Strabag und Deutsche Bank schliessen Pakt für Russland)," *Europe Intelligence Wire,* April 5, 2007.

"German Federal Supreme Court Rules in Favor of Strabag (BGH erlaubt Umbau der Strabag-Tochter Zublin)," *Europe Intelligence Wire,* September 18, 2008.

"Lenz Family Opposes Merger Plan for Zublin (Fusionsstreit bringt Baukonzern Zublin in die Klemme)," *Europe Intelligence Wire,* June 6, 2005.

Pohl, Manfred, *Die Strabag: 1923 bis 1998,* Munich, Germany: Piper Verlag, 1998.

"Strabag Acquires Viable Activities of Walter Bau (Strabag übernimmt Teile von Walter Bau)," *Europe Intelligence Wire,* February 16, 2005.

"Strabag Gives Up Controlling Stake in Deutag (Strabag trennt sich von Asphalthersteller Deutag)," *Europe Intelligence Wire,* February 16, 2006.

"Strabag Hopes for More Deals in Russia after Deripaska's Share Purchase," *Russia & CIS Business and Financial Newswire,* May 24, 2007.

"Strabag Restructures Activities in Germany (Strabag baut Deutschlandgeschäft um)," *Europe Intelligence Wire,* January 26, 2006.

"Strabag Returns to Profit for 2002 (Strabag schreibt wieder schwarze Zahlen)," *Europe Intelligence Wire,* May 15, 2003.

"Strabag's Euros 1.35bn Flotation Plan Boosts Vienna Stock Exchange," *Financial Times,* October 9, 2007, p. 43.

"Strabag to Take Over German Holding Group (Strabag kauft Bauholding Preusse)," *Europe Intelligence Wire,* March 29, 2006.

"Strabag to Take Over Zublin (Baukonzern Strabag greift sich Zublin)," *Europe Intelligence Wire,* June 1, 2005.

StreamServe Inc.

3 Van de Graaff Drive
Burlington, Massachusetts 01803
U.S.A.
Telephone: (781) 863-1510
Toll Free: (800) 304-7312
Fax: (781) 229-6622
Web site: http://www.streamserve.com

Private Company
Incorporated: 1995
Employees: 300
Sales: $803 million (2008 est.)
NAICS: 511210 Software Publishers

∎ ∎ ∎

Headquartered in Burlington, Massachusetts, Stream-Serve Inc. is a leading enterprise document presentment solutions provider. The company, which operates from 14 locations throughout the world, offers advanced software (document composition, process automation, and enterprise output management solutions) that companies can use to produce and deliver customized documents in almost any format. The majority of StreamServe's 5,000 customers come from the manufacturing, telecommunications, distribution, utilities, and financial services industries, including companies such as BMW France and Siemens Financial.

FORMATIVE YEARS

StreamServe traces its roots to 1995, when the company was established in Stockholm, Sweden. During the

company's formative years, it enjoyed tremendous success in Europe, resulting in an annual growth rate of approximately 150 percent. Significant international expansion took place during the late 1990s. In 1998 and 1999 alone, StreamServe branched out to the United States, Germany, France, Finland, the United Kingdom, Norway, and the Netherlands.

One of StreamServe's six cofounders was Hans Otterling, who served as CEO during the company's initial years. A Fulbright scholar, Otterling earned an undergraduate degree from the Stockholm School of Economics and Business Administration, as well as an MBA from the University of Massachusetts. Prior to cofounding StreamServe he established a company named BIT-Borslistans Informationstjanst, which distributed financial information regarding Swedish companies.

In 1999 StreamServe relocated its headquarters from Sweden to Raleigh, North Carolina. European headquarters were maintained in Stockholm. At that time the company had 15 employees and was backed by $8 million in funding from the London-based venture capital firm Apax Venture & Associates, as well as a smaller group of private investors. As part of this transition, Otterling relocated to the United States, joining cofounders Per Einarsson, who then served as vice president of research and development, and Technical Director Magnus Einarsson.

Driving StreamServe's early success was its output management software, which created documents including customized invoices and shipping statements from business applications such as Baan and SAP. Distribution was possible in a variety of formats via multiple channels, including cellular phones, e-mail, fax servers, pagers, and printers. The output management software market was valued at approximately $20 billion annually at that time. StreamServe ended the 1990s with revenues of $14.7 million in 1999.

In 2000, the establishment of a midwest headquarters facility in Chicago marked StreamServe's 12th office location. By then the company served 1,500 customers worldwide in a range of industries. Among its customer base were companies such as AstraZeneca, Ingram Micro, British Steel, and Oklahoma Gas & Electric.

StreamServe introduced several new offerings for its customers in early 2000. These included a free business communications software application called StreamServe XML Enabler, which eliminated technical barriers and allowed users to connect to trading exchanges, auction sites, and portals, regardless of the enterprise software they were using. In addition, the company introduced an Arabic version of its output management software.

Midway through the year, a leading construction company named Skanska established a multinational agreement with StreamServe for the provision of customer communication and output management software. In August, StreamServe cemented a strategic alliance with Hewlett-Packard Company to cooperatively develop an advanced output management system for SAP AG, a leading enterprise resource planning software firm. The following month, the company chose Singapore-based Sun Office Management Pte Ltd. as a new distributor.

LEADERSHIP CHANGES

A major leadership change took place in mid-2001, when the company named former Hewlett-Packard executive Nick Earle as its new CEO. At this time the original founders remained with the company, which then served approximately 2,500 customers. Hans Otterling assumed the role of president. Another leadership

change followed in November when the company named Sheila Gibson as its chief marketing officer. StreamServe ended 2001 by establishing a new Singapore-based subsidiary named StreamServe Asia Pacific Pte Ltd., to support the company's growth in the region.

StreamServe's growth continued in 2002 when the company's customer base exceeded the 3,000 mark. Midway through that year the company established a strategic alliance with IBM Printing Systems focused on enterprise resource planning applications. In addition, StreamServe established a licensing agreement with the Swedish postal service, Posten Sverige AB, for the use of the company's Business Communication Platform for electronic services such as e-mail, as well as some 300 million invoices and letters annually. Another major customer addition that year occurred when StreamServe signed a three-year contract with Volvo IT. The company ended 2002 by relocating its U.S. headquarters to Burlington, Massachusetts.

In August 2003 the professional services firm Deloitte & Touche LLP added StreamServe to its Technology Fast 50 list for New England, in recognition of revenue growth in fiscal years 1998 through 2002. StreamServe's customer base continued to grow, exceeding 3,500 in 2003 and 4,000 in 2004. Several leadership changes occurred during this time. By early 2004 Otterling was again serving as CEO. In March of that year the company named former Oracle executive George Bloom to serve as president of its North American region.

In late 2004 StreamServe appointed former Hewlett-Packard executive Peter Blackmore as an adviser to its board of directors, in order to help the company execute an aggressive growth strategy. Early the following year, the company added electronics retailer Circuit City to its customer base. Circuit City chose StreamServe's Business Communication Platform to create and distribute approximately 78 million price tags throughout its chain of more than 600 stores.

Another leadership change took place in April 2005, at which time StreamServe appointed former Novell executive Chris Stone as president and CEO. Stone succeeded Otterling, who remained with the company as vice chairman. By this time StreamServe had added companies such as Bayer and KLM Royal Dutch Airlines to its customer base.

INTERNATIONAL GROWTH

Significant customer additions continued in late 2005. In September of that year StreamServe added Apoteket, the only retailer of pharmaceutical products in Sweden,

KEY DATES

1995: The company is established in Stockholm, Sweden.

1999: StreamServe relocates its headquarters from Sweden to Raleigh, North Carolina.

2000: A midwest headquarters facility is established in Chicago.

2001: Former Hewlett-Packard executive Nick Earle is named CEO; Hans Otterling assumes the role of president.

2002: StreamServe relocates its U.S. headquarters to Burlington, Massachusetts.

2003: Deloitte & Touche adds the company to its Technology Fast 50 list for New England.

2005: StreamServe appoints former Novell executive Chris Stone as president and CEO.

2006: The company begins distributing its enterprise document presentment software in the People's Republic of China through an arrangement with Carnation Software.

2009: StreamServe unveils Partner Portal, as well as its Sustainability Program.

to its customer base. As part of the arrangement StreamServe's products would be used to produce approximately 100 million documents each year. In addition to Apoteket, StreamServe also included China Light & Power, Novell, and ING among its customers by this time.

In early 2006 StreamServe began distributing its enterprise document presentment software in the People's Republic of China through an arrangement with Carnation Software. This development enabled the company to tap into a lucrative market that included 1.3 billion people, and make headway into the Chinese telecommunications, utilities, retail, manufacturing, and financial services sectors.

StreamServe's alliance with Carnation bore immediate fruit. In April 2006 the company was chosen to provide, through Carnation, its enterprise document presentment software to China Telecom subsidiary Guangzhou Telecom, which used the technology to deliver invoices to approximately 10 million subscribers in Guangdong Province. Midway through 2006 StreamServe established an international customer council. Comprising leading customers, the purpose of the council was to provide StreamServe with insight into international customer business needs, facilitate dialogue

about enterprise document presentment between customers, and receive feedback about product development.

It was around this time that StreamServe gained several high-profile customers. In June the company announced that it was working with Dutch ABP General Pension Fund, the second-largest pension fund in the world. Specifically, Dutch ABP used the company's technology to send income projections to 1.2 million people on a biannual basis. Another major customer acquisition was the Isotoner Company, the world's largest gloves, slippers, and sunglasses marketer, which joined StreamServe's client roster in August. Isotoner chose the company's technology to meet the automation requirements of a major mass-market retailer, increase productivity, and reduce printing costs. In October Scandinavia's leading construction and real estate firm, NCC, chose StreamServe's technology to automate the handling and distribution of 1.3 million invoices annually.

In early 2007 StreamServe established an agreement with Adobe Systems Inc. that focused on next-generation dynamic enterprise publishing. Specifically, the agreement involved Adobe providing support for XML Forms Architecture, which combined Extensible Markup Language (XML) technology (a flexible text format used for exchanging data) with the capabilities found in Adobe's popular PDF file format. Benefits included enhanced document security. Template designs allowed the inclusion of digital signatures, helping companies comply with government requirements pertaining to online forms.

StreamServe rolled out a private beta program in early 2008 that focused on a new Web-based document creation and administration tool named Correspondence Manager. Specifically, the new tool was aimed at companies in the communication-centered marketing, legal, and call center industries. It allowed customers to strengthen their brand identity by blending design, data, and other content. In addition to serving up transaction-based documents such as invoices, StreamServe's solutions began allowing customers to deliver marketing-based messages as well.

PARTNERSHIP FOCUS

By late 2008 StreamServe was led by President and CEO Dennis Ladd. At that time the company served more than 5,000 customers in 130 countries worldwide. Its operations were based in 14 different locations across the globe. In December StreamServe was recognized with a positive rating from Gartner in one of the research firm's MarketScope reports.

Despite difficult economic conditions, StreamServe ended 2008 on a high note. During the fourth quarter the company reported its highest quarterly license revenue to date. In order to further StreamServe's growth, new business development positions were added in several locations throughout the world, including the Asia Pacific, Benelux, and North American regions. In addition, StreamServe also added additional marketing staff in Germany and North America.

StreamServe began 2009 by intensifying its focus on new channel partnerships. The company began establishing partnerships with consulting firms and resellers that were interested in consulting about, integrating, or marketing its various solutions. New relationships were established with entities in the United Kingdom, Germany, France, Greece, Scandinavia, Switzerland, North America, Austria, South Africa, Russia, and Poland. In addition, the company expanded the scope of relationships it had with existing partners.

In support of its new partnership focus, StreamServe developed its Partner Portal. The new offering provided partners with a wide range of different tools, such as collateral templates, a demonstration platform, a program guide, partner selling kits, and more. In addition, the portal included an online forum to promote collaboration and communication between partners.

In the interest of environmental responsibility, the StreamServe Sustainability Program was introduced in mid-2009. The program offered customers best practices, tools, and research focused on eco-savings connected with StreamServe's solutions. Specifically, it focused on significantly reducing the use of electricity, paper, and ink, thereby lessening environmental impact. StreamServe initially rolled out its new program to the utilities market, with plans to expand it to other industry sectors, including manufacturing/distribution and financial services.

In August 2009 StreamServe was named a market leader in a report by the research firm IDC. The report provided a forecast and analysis for the global dynamic enterprise publishing market from 2009 to 2013. IDC projected that the dynamic enterprise publishing market would continue to achieve strong growth into the second decade of the 21st century. IDC predicted that by 2013 compound annual growth of 9.1 percent would push industry revenues to $1.4 billion.

In November 2009 StreamServe introduced a new online training environment for its partners and customers. The system provided on-demand access to training information about the company's products, as well as live expert sessions. Tools included online forums, chat rooms, video, and more.

Paul R. Greenland

PRINCIPAL COMPETITORS

Document Sciences Corporation; Elixir Technologies Corporation.

FURTHER READING

"Stone Named CEO at StreamServe," *Computerworld*, April 11, 2005.

"StreamServe Achieves Record Growth Despite Weakened Global Economy," *Business Wire*, February 25, 2009.

"StreamServe Enters into Agreement with Adobe for Next Generation Dynamic Enterprise Publishing," *Business Wire*, April 17, 2007.

"StreamServe Expands Presence in United States; Software Company Opens Midwest Headquarters Signaling Its Continued Growth as a Leading Provider of Intelligent Business Communications," *Business Wire*, May 18, 2000.

"StreamServe, Inc. to Be Named One of New England's Fastest Growing Technology Companies in Deloitte & Touche Technology Fast 50 Program," *Internet Wire*, August 18, 2003.

"StreamServe Introduces Enterprise Document Presentment to People's Republic of China with the Help of Carnation Software," *Business Wire*, April 4, 2006.

"StreamServe Launches Asia Pacific Operations to Support Global Customers," *M2 Presswire*, December 5, 2001.

"StreamServe Launches Interactive Online Training Environment," *Wireless News*, November 17, 2009.

SVP Worldwide LLC

1224 Heil Quaker Boulevard
LaVergne, Tennessee 37086
U.S.A.
Toll Free: (800) 4-SINGER
Fax: (615) 213-0994
Web site: http://www.svpworldwide.com

Wholly Owned Subsidiary of Kohlberg & Company L.L.C.
Incorporated: 2006
Employees: 4,000
NAICS: 333298 All Other Industrial Machinery
Manufacturing

■ ■ ■

SVP Worldwide LLC is the world's largest sewing machine company. SVP, an abbreviation for Singer, Viking, and Pfaff, unites three of the world's best-known sewing machine brands under one organizational roof. The company develops and produces a broad range of sewing machines, from beginner's models to sophisticated embroidery sewing machines, as well as related products in Brazil, China, and the Czech Republic. SVP sells its premium segment sewing machines in nearly every country of the world through a tightly knit network of more than 4,100 dealerships and associated distributors. The company is owned by U.S. equity-firm Kohlberg & Company L.L.C.

SINGER'S SUCCESS STORY BEGINS IN 1850

Before Isaac Merritt Singer invented the sewing machine carrying his name in 1850 that would soon take the world by storm, he had already patented a rock-drilling machine and a wood and metal-carving machine. While repairing a sewing machine at a mechanical workshop in Boston, Singer was told that if he could design a more practical and reliable machine than the ones already in the market, he could become a rich man.

The technically gifted son of German immigrants got to work immediately and built a prototype of an improved sewing machine within 11 days. Equipped with precision metal working parts, Singer's machine had a straight instead of a curved needle operating vertically from an overhanging arm, which enabled the sewing of any kind of garment. The shuttle moved in a straight instead of a circular motion, while the fabric was held in place by a presser foot with a spring. Most importantly, Singer's machine was able to perform continuous stitching.

Singer immediately applied for a patent for his invention and established his own company in Boston to manufacture it. Confronted with patent infringement charges by sewing machine inventor Elias Howe, Singer went to New York lawyer Edward S. Clark for help. In 1851 Singer received a patent for his sewing machine, and Clark became his business partner in I.M. Singer & Company.

In 1853 company headquarters of the renamed Singer Manufacturing Company were moved to New York City where a new factory started manufacturing

Singer sewing machines, which sold for $100 apiece. Since that was still a large sum for many U.S. citizens at the time, Clark came up with the idea of allowing customers to pay for their Singer machine in installments over time, then a revolutionary idea. Customers could also bring in their old sewing machines and receive a discount on a new Singer. The company also sold the marketing rights for its sewing machines to independent salesmen and businesspeople, pioneering the idea of franchising. During the 1850s and early 1860s Singer patented roughly 20 improvements to his machine, which kept the company ahead of the competition.

RAPID EXPANSION AFTER 1855

The combination of Singer's continued technical refinement with Clark's innovative marketing models resulted in Singer's rapid commercial success. By 1855, the year that a Singer machine received a first prize at the World Fair in Paris, the company had already become the world's largest sewing machine manufacturer. In 1857 company headquarters were relocated to Broadway in Manhattan while three additional plants in New York City went onstream the following year. The company's first sales office abroad was established in Glasgow, Scotland, in 1856, and was followed up by the establishment of an operation in Brazil two years later. In 1861 the company's revenues abroad exceeded sales generated in the United States for the first time.

According to the *Encyclopedia of New York State*, Isaac M. Singer retired to England in 1863 after being sued for assault by his wife and daughter, and after subsequently being pressured to step back from company management by Clark. By then, the company's factories were putting out 20,000 Turtlebacks, lightweight Grasshoppers, and other popular models of Singer's home sewing machines per year. Within the next decade the number of Singer sewing machines sold annually climbed steeply after additional production plants and sales offices had been set up in the United States, Scotland, England, and Germany. A multimillionaire, Singer died at age 63 in 1875, five

years after the red "S" trademark, one of the most recognized in the world, had been introduced.

In the late 1880s, additional production plants were built in the United States, Canada, Austria, and Scotland, some of them employing more than 10,000 workers. After the turn of the 20th century, the company also ventured into Russia where a factory was established in 1902. In 1904 the company's sales and distribution division Singer Sewing Machine Company was established. Four years later the 47-story Singer Building was completed at 149 Broadway; at 612 feet it was the world's tallest building for a short time and served as the company's headquarters for the next 54 years.

The advent of electric motors in the late 19th century resulted in Singer's first electric sewing machine in 1889. In 1892 Singer's first commercial zigzag machine was introduced. By that time the company claimed four-fifths of the world's market for sewing machines. All in all, the number of Singer sewing machines sold per year rose from 500,000 in 1880 to over 1.3 million in 1903. By 1913 the company was selling three million sewing machines per year and employed a workforce of roughly 100,000.

NEW MODELS AND SEWING INSTRUCTION BETWEEN WORLD WARS

World War I suddenly interrupted Singer's rapid growth. While the demand for household sewing machines declined, the company manufactured war goods. In the early 1920s Singer launched the first portable electric Singer and opened the first Singer Sewing Center in New York City where sewing classes were offered. In 1929 Singer took over competitor Standard Sewing Machine Company. In an attempt to generate further growth through diversification, the company introduced a Singer vacuum cleaner that did nothing to prevent declining sales during the Great Depression.

In 1933 the company launched the very successful Featherweight model that came with a suitcase-like carrying case. In the same year Singer opened new factories in Italy and France. During World War II, the company again switched production to mostly war materials. After the war Singer launched a new model capable of performing 4,000 stitches per minute in 1949, followed by the first Model 206 household zigzag machine three years later. With about 400,000 housewives attending sewing classes at the company's sewing centers per year, sales began to pick up again in the 1950s, reaching over $500 million or roughly 1.9 million sewing machines at the end of the decade.

```
┌─────────────────────────────────────────────┐
│                                               │
│              KEY DATES                        │
│                  ■                            │
│  ───────────────────────────────────────     │
│                                               │
│  1851:  I.M. Singer & Company is established  │
│         in the United States.                 │
│  1862:  Georg Michael Pfaff builds his first  │
│         sewing machine in Germany.            │
│  1872:  Rifle manufacturer Husqvarna starts   │
│         producing sewing machines in Sweden.  │
│  1930s: Pfaff's zigzag household sewing        │
│         machine becomes a worldwide best      │
│         seller.                               │
│  1975:  Singer introduces the first electronic│
│         sewing machine.                       │
│  1989:  Hong Kong businessman James H. Ting   │
│         takes over control of Singer Co.      │
│  1997:  Husqvarna is spun off from Electrolux │
│         as Viking Sewing Machines (VSM) and   │
│         is acquired by European investment    │
│         firm Industri Kapital.                │
│  2000:  VSM takes over the household sewing   │
│         machines division of Pfaff.           │
│  2004:  U.S. investment firm Kohlberg &       │
│         Company acquires Singer Sewing        │
│         Company.                              │
│  2006:  Newly established SVP Holdings takes   │
│         over VSM Group AB.                     │
│                                               │
└─────────────────────────────────────────────┘
```

DIVERSIFICATION AND INNOVATION AFTER 1960

In 1961 the company was renamed Singer Company. To offset declining sewing machine sales due to increasing competition from Japan and the fading popularity of home sewing, Singer ventured into computers with the acquisition of Packard Bell Electronics in 1966 and into defense electronics with the takeover of General Precision Equipment Corporation in 1968. Consequently, Singer's annual sales soared, passing the $1 billion mark for the first time in 1966 and reaching $2.5 billion in 1973 when the company's stock was listed on the London Stock Exchange for the first time.

Meanwhile, Singer's sewing machine division continued to develop cutting edge models which, with the advent of electronics, were more and more computerized and automated. In 1975 Singer introduced Athena 2000, the first electronic sewing machine, followed by Touchtronic 2001, the first computer-controlled home sewing machine. In 1979 company headquarters were moved to Stamford, Connecticut. Throughout the 1980s Singer continued to put out a broad variety of new and improved models with customized features and price levels for different

consumer groups. Advanced features included an unlimited number of stitch patterns, monogramming and embroidery capabilities.

REVIVAL IN ASIA AFTER 1989, BANKRUPTCY IN 1999

The acquisitions of the 1970s left Singer struggling financially. In 1988 the company was taken over by leveraged buyout specialist Paul Bilzerian. After the company's aerospace and electronics subsidiaries had been sold off, Hong Kong businessman James H. Ting, through his firm International Semi-Tech Microelectronics, acquired Singer Co. for roughly $289 million in 1989 and revived Singer's sewing machine business. Ting formed a joint venture between Singer and China's leading sewing machine company to produce domestic sewing machines at low cost for the huge Chinese market. Ting even obtained the permission of the Chinese government to offer the first installment purchase plan for Chinese consumers. In 1990 Ting's Semi-Tech also bought Singer's sewing machine business in Europe from the U.K.-based retail group European Home Products, according to the March 10, 1990, issue of *Cosmetics International.*

Singer's initial public offering (IPO) at the New York Stock Exchange in 1991 raised $1.2 billion, with which additional plants were set up in India and Brazil. The company also continued to develop more advanced models and manufactured a line of small consumer electrical appliances, such as irons and steam presses, but also blenders, coffeemakers, and rice cookers, which were sold mostly in Asia under the Singer brand.

When a severe financial crisis hit Asia in 1997, however, sales of consumer goods dropped sharply, and Ting's empire tumbled into financial turmoil. Consequently, Singer filed for bankruptcy in 1999. According to the August 5, 2002, issue of *Business Week,* the investigation that followed revealed that $1.1 billion generated by issuing Singer stocks and bonds had been transferred to Ting's Hong Kong subsidiary Akai Holdings Ltd., which led to Singer's financial failure. Another factor that contributed to Singer's bankruptcy was G.M. Pfaff, a world renowned but loss-producing German sewing machine manufacturer, which Ting had acquired in 1993 and then sold to Singer, according to *Business Week.*

PFAFF'S ORIGINS

Like Singer, Pfaff originated in the 19th century, when a sewing machine that the German brass instrument maker Georg Michael Pfaff had seen at a trade fair stirred his interest, and he began designing one himself. The skilled craftsman completed the first leather sewing machine in 1862 and kept building improved models until he sold his instrument-making business in 1866 to focus solely on making sewing machines.

Starting out with 20 workers building about 100 sewing machines per year, Pfaff's workshop in southwestern Germany quickly grew into a full-fledged steam-engine-powered factory, putting out 10 times as many machines by 1872. The repair workshop he ran enabled Pfaff to examine different sewing machine models and to make improvements to his own designs. By the early 1870s Pfaff's company, G.M. Pfaff, exported half of its output, carrying the Pfaff brand name to other European countries. The company founder's sons Georg and Jacob joined the enterprise in the 1870s and, due to Jacob Pfaff's successful marketing efforts, such as granting exclusive sales areas to selected dealers, participating in World Fairs, and setting up a sewing machine store in London, G.M. Pfaff grew by leaps and bounds.

SECOND PFAFF GENERATION
TAKES OVER IN 1893

After the premature death of his brother Jacob in 1889 and his father's death in 1893, Georg Pfaff moved the company to a much larger site nearby. The business-savvy engineer, who had spent two years in the United States studying cutting-edge production technologies firsthand, established a cast-iron foundry and an in-house machine tool construction. Around 1910 more than 1,000 workers were putting out over 25,000 Pfaff sewing machines annually which were shipped to 64 countries. Under Georg Pfaff's leadership, the company thrived until World War I put a sudden end to its dynamic growth. Instead of sewing machines, G.M. Pfaff manufactured war goods.

Georg Pfaff died in 1917, and his sister Caroline Pfaff headed the company for the next decade. The establishment of the company's own sales organization in 1924, including a network of dealerships and consumer outlets called Pfaff Houses in major German cities, and an army of door-to-door sales personnel, was a major step in regaining market share against the growing competition from Singer and other manufacturers after World War I. In 1926 the family enterprise was transformed into a privately owned stock corporation that was directed and owned by Jacob Pfaff's son Karl, an engineer, after his aunt's death in 1929.

In the late 1920s the company expanded its range of high-performance commercial sewing machines for the shoemaking and textile industries. During the Great Depression Pfaff intensified its efforts to boost sales abroad by setting up sales offices in South America and by entering the U.S. market. The company regained market share in the Middle East and India, which became Pfaff's single largest market abroad followed by Brazil. Pfaff's zigzag household sewing machine Klasse 130 launched in the 1930s became a worldwide best seller.

1929–52: THE KARL PFAFF ERA

Just before World War II, Pfaff's workforce had grown to roughly 3,500. Although the company continued to manufacture sewing machines on a small scale, Pfaff produced mainly war goods until the factory was destroyed during bombing raids in 1944. While rebuilding the factory after the war, Pfaff began producing industrial sewing machines again in 1946. Two years later the company resumed exports to the United States.

By 1950 Pfaff's factory was fully rebuilt and eventually expanded due to the postwar economic boom. With over 5,000 employees putting out more than 1,000 sewing machines per day, Pfaff's was the largest sewing machine factory on the European continent. The era of Karl Pfaff ended with his death in 1952.

POSTWAR MARKET CHANGES
AND REORGANIZATION

In 1958 Pfaff acquired a majority share in competitor Gritzner-Kayser AG in Karlsruhe-Durlach. To defend its market position, Pfaff launched its own low-priced Familia line of domestic sewing machines. In 1960 the heirs of Karl Pfaff decided to transform the company into a public stock corporation, with a listing on the Frankfurt exchange. As the German consumer market contracted in the mid-to-late 1960s, Pfaff rented larger shops in city centers and offered sewing classes, fabrics, and sewing accessories in addition to its domestic sewing machines. Nevertheless, the percentage of sales generated by the company's industrial sewing machine division continued to climb, reaching 54 percent in 1968. The result of a restructuring program that was completed in 1970 was the creation of independent companies for domestic and industrial sewing machines which, together with about 30 other subsidiaries, mostly sales organizations, were organized under the umbrella of the holding company G.M. Pfaff AG.

NEW PRODUCTS AND OWNERS
AFTER 1970

The introduction of the midpriced Pfaff 1000 line with easy-to-use one-touch program buttons and the Super-automatic 1200 line, Pfaff's first electronically controlled domestic sewing machine, as well as the launch of new types of "rapid ironers" helped the company maintain and even slightly raise sales in the stagnating domestic sewing machine market of the 1970s. In 1983 the company launched Pfaff-Creative, its first microprocessor-controlled model for home sewers.

In 1987, Pfaff's 125th anniversary year, the company's workforce of roughly 9,800 generated over DEM 1 billion in sales. One year later the Pfaff family sold a 52 percent stake in the company to German lawyer Wolfgang Schuppli, according to *Börsen-Zeitung*. In 1993 Ting's Semi-Tech acquired a majority stake in Pfaff. After Semi-Tech's bankruptcy in the late 1990s, Pfaff was separated from Singer. The research and development, sales, and spare parts divisions of Pfaff's domestic sewing machine subsidiary as well as the Pfaff brand name were consequently acquired by the European private-equity firm Industri Kapital in 2000. Industri Kapital already owned Viking Sewing Machines AB, another well-known European sewing machine manufacturer with a long tradition.

VSM ORIGINS

VSM was home to the Husqvarna and Viking sewing machine brands. Husqvarna was established as a royal arms factory in 1689. The small company manufactured guns for 80 years before its board of directors decided in 1872 to start producing sewing machines as the demand for its rifles was drying up. Husqvarna's first sewing machine was named Nordsjernan, the Northern Star. In 1883 the company launched the Freja model, which was named after the goddess of love in Norse mythology and based on its technological advancements became an instant best seller.

Husqvarna continued to introduce cutting-edge technologies in the 20th century. In 1903 the company introduced the CB model, a machine with an oscillating bobbin that ran very smoothly at 1,000 to 1,500 stitches per minute and allowed for backward sewing. While the Nordsjernan model was manufactured until 1925, the CB machines became best sellers all over the world and were produced until 1955. The 1930s brought about a change in machine design, in which machines became streamlined and functional, in sharp contrast to the lavishly embellished and artfully curved earlier models. The year 1934 saw Husqvarna's one-millionth sewing machine, as well as the company's first electrically powered model.

POSTWAR INNOVATIONS

After World War II, Husqvarna continued to improve the functionality and user-friendliness of its sewing machines, evolving as one of the world's most well-known manufacturers. The company launched the first free-arm machine with a zigzag stitch in 1947, which was successfully marketed in the United States under the Viking brand name beginning in 1949. Six years later Husqvarna introduced the Class 20 model featuring a gearshift transmission, a slow-motion gear, a jam-proof hook that did not require lubrication, and a lightweight cast-iron casing.

The Husqvarna 2000 launched in 1960 offered color-coded settings and automatic feed stitches for the then-fashionable stretch and knitwear fabrics. The 1970s saw Husqvarna introduce the Centennial model, the world's first household sewing machine with self-lubricating bearings. In 1979 the company launched its first programmable electronic sewing machine, followed by the first sewing machine that could stitch letters in 1980.

NEW OWNERS AND ACQUISITIONS AFTER 1978

The year 1979 marked a change in ownership when Husqvarna became part of the Swedish Electrolux group, an electrical appliance and sewing machine manufacturer. In 1990, however, Electrolux's sewing machine division became Husqvarna Sewing Machines AB. In 1997 that company was spun off as Viking Sewing Machines AB and acquired by European investment firm Industri Kapital. Two years later Viking Sewing Machines took over Embroidery Networks Ltd., a British developer of software that greatly enhanced the embroidery capabilities of Viking's line of computer-controlled embroidery and sewing machines.

After Industri Kapital's acquisition of Pfaff's domestic sewing machine division in 2000, the latter was integrated into Viking Sewing Machines. Moving the manufacturing of Pfaff models to the Czech Republic and Sweden and integrating the research and development, sales, and service divisions with Viking's led Pfaff back into profits. In 2002 Viking Sewing Machines was renamed VSM Group AB.

THREE WORLD BRANDS UNITE IN 21ST CENTURY

After Singer's bankruptcy in 1999 the company's sewing machine manufacturing division, which had been moved to LaVergne, Tennessee, was acquired by KSIN Holdings, an affiliate of U.S.-investment firm Kohlberg & Company in 2004. The sales price of $134 million did not include the European Singer N.V., which kept the branded consumer products retail businesses in Asia and Jamaica. Two years later Kohlberg, through the newly established SVP Holdings, took over VSM Group. At the time of the takeover, VSM Group reported annual sales of EUR 240 million and a workforce of 2,000.

Under the new structure, SVP Worldwide maintained U.S. headquarters for its Singer and Pfaff operations and Swedish headquarters for the Husqvarna Viking lines. In September 2006, Pfaff introduced Creative Vision, a cutting-edge sewing machine that sewed extremely detailed embroidery motifs with the push of a button, which could be designed via a high-resolution touch screen. The following year, SVP signed a long-term endorsement contract with Martha Stewart Living Omnimedia. With various SVP sewing machine models reaching millions of magazine readers and television viewers, and through sewing classes in 225 locations, the company was hoping to participate in a revival of home sewing in the United States. To increase profitability, SVP raised prices by 3 to 10 percent across its product lines in 2009 and announced in 2010 that in order to cut costs the manufacturing of top-of-the-line models was being moved from Sweden to China.

Evelyn Hauser

PRINCIPAL SUBSIDIARIES
Singer Sewing Co. (USA); VSM Group AB (Sweden).

PRINCIPAL COMPETITORS
Aisin Seiki Co., Ltd.; Bernina International AG; Brother Industries, Ltd.; Janome Sewing Machine Co., Ltd.; SGSB Group Co., Ltd.; Tacony Corporation.

FURTHER READING
Banks, Brian, "One Billion Buyers, Easy Credit Terms," *Canadian Business,* June 1994, p. 33.

Bissell, Don, "Singer Sewing Machine Company," *Encyclopedia of New York State,* Syracuse, NY: Syracuse University Press, 2005, p. 1414.

"EHP Sews Up Pounds 12.5 m Result at Half Time; European Home Products Pre-tax Profits," *Times* (London), September 7, 1988.

"European Home Products Sells Off Singer," *Cosmetics International,* March 10, 1990, p. 14.

"Investor nimmt Pfaff-Faden auf," *Börsen-Zeitung,* December 3, 2005, p. 9.

Miller, Matthew, Mark L. Clifford, and Susan Zegel, "Dishonored Dealmaker," *Business Week,* August 5, 2002.

125 Jahre Pfaff: 1862–1987, Kaiserslautern, Germany: G. M. Pfaff AG, 1987.

Peterson, Chris, "'Bobbin' Along: With Three Leading Sewing Machine Brands under Its Roof, SVP Worldwide Drives Its Product Lines Forward at the Request of Customers," *US Business Review,* December 2007, p. 52.

"Singer Names Thomas Noering to Head North American Operations," *PR Newswire,* October 15, 1999.

"Singer Sewing Company Sold to Affiliate of Kohlberg & Company," *PR Newswire,* October 1, 2004.

"Singer Will Obtain Small Electric Appliances Manufactured in the United States," *PR Newswire,* January 10, 1992.

"Viking Adopts New Name & Tagline," *Profitable Embroiderer,* December 1, 2002.

"VSM Deutschland GmbH/Pfaff Haushaltsnähmaschinen verkauft," *DPA–AFX,* February 14, 2006.

Wauschkuhn, Franz, "Industri Kapital ist Europa's zweitgrösste Gesellschaft für Beteiligungskapital," *Welt am Sonntag,* April 27, 2003.

"World's Largest Sewing Machine Manufacturer—SVP Worldwide—Plans to Increase Prices Globally on Its Singer, Husqvarna Viking and Pfaff Product Portfolio," *Business Wire,* September 29, 2008.

Syral S.A.S.

BP 32, Zone Industrielle et Portuaire
Marckolsheim, F-67390
France
Telephone: (+33 03) 88 58 60 60
Fax: (+33 03) 88 58 60 61
Web site: http://www.syral.com

62% Owned Subsidiary of Tereos S.A.
Incorporated: 1996
Employees: 1,400
Sales: EUR 1.36 billion ($1.9 billion) (2008 est.)
NAICS: 325188 All Other Inorganic Chemical Manufacturing

■ ■ ■

Syral S.A.S. is the third-largest producer of starch and glucose in Europe, and that market's second-largest manufacturer of starch-based sweeteners. The company operates factories in France, Belgium, Spain, and Italy, processing more than three million tons of corn and wheat to produce more than 1.8 million tons of starch-based products each year. The company also operates a distribution subsidiary in the United Kingdom and a sales office in Hong Kong.

Syral's product list includes native and modified starches; isoglucose (the European name for high-fructose corn syrup) and other glucose and dextrose syrups; maltodextrin and other dry sweeteners; polyols (artificial sweeteners), including sorbitol and malitol; and proteins derived from corn and wheat. Syral's production also generates more than 180,000 cubic

meters of food-grade alcohol, ethanol, and fuel-additive bioethanol. In addition, the company produces 200,000 tons of vegetable proteins, and 850,000 tons of products for animal feed. The processed food industry remains Syral's core market, accounting for 61 percent of the group's annual sales, which neared EUR 1.4 billion ($1.9 billion) in 2008. The "green chemistry" industry, including pharmaceutical and biofuel applications, adds 17 percent to group sales, followed by the animal feed (13 percent) and packaging (9 percent) industries.

Syral is itself a subsidiary of the Tereos S.A. cooperative group, France's number three sugar producer, which owns 61.7 percent of the company. The remaining shares are held by a group of French cereal cooperatives. This shareholding structure ensures Syral of a steady supply of raw materials.

ORIGINS

Syral started out as a subsidiary of Switzerland-based Jungbunzlauer, which built a glucose factory in Marckolsheim in France's Alsace region in 1993. Jungbunzlauer traced its own roots to a Bohemian grain distillery founded in 1867. That business later established operations in Prague under the name of Actiengesellschaft Jungbunzlauer Spiritus und Chemische Fabrik, founded in 1897. In 1901 Jungbunzlauer added an Austrian subsidiary, which became the group's headquarters after World War II.

In the postwar period, Jungbunzlauer's focus shifted from alcohol to the food additives sector, especially the production of citric acid. In the 1980s the company became a major producer of xanthan gum. In 1988

COMPANY PERSPECTIVES
■

SYRAL's winning formula is its driving principle, combined with the company's commitment to responding to your changing needs. Formulating the future means ... Flexibility.

SYRAL is renowned for developing tailor-made products and customised formulations. In extending our product range and creating new formulae for consumer taste in our Innovation Centre for Application, we demonstrate our determination to pursue innovation. Reactivity. SYRAL is young, dynamic and entrepreneurial and we are determined to respond ever faster to our customer's needs. The international and multi-cultural dimension of our company reinforces the close relationship with our clients and ensures that we offer the most suitable service. Reliability. Through its shareholdings, its industrial strength, and its professionalism, SYRAL offers its customers unrivalled guarantees in terms of: Access to cereal resources; Quality & food safety standards of its products; Innovation in product development. As a leading processor of raw agricultural materials, reliability is part of our culture, and we continue to develop this aspect on a daily basis.

Jungbunzlauer acquired the organic acids operations of Benckiser. This purchase not only boosted the company's citric acid production, but also made it one of the world's leading producers of sodium gluconate. Derived through the fermentation of glucose, sodium gluconate was an important food additive, used for the production of cheeses and other processed dairy products, herb and spice preparations, and processed meats. Sodium gluconate had a wide range of other uses, including in dental care, cosmetics, and a variety of industrial applications.

Jungbunzlauer moved its headquarters to Switzerland in 1993. In that same year, Jungbunzlauer launched construction of a new glucose fermentation factory in Marckolsheim. From the outset, the company targeted integrated operations, including production of glucose in order to ensure its supply. The Marckolsheim factory launched production of glucose by the end of 1993. By 1996, the company had completed a second production unit in Marckolsheim, where it launched production of sodium gluconate.

JOINING FORCES IN 1996

While the Marckolsheim facility ensured the supply of glucose for Jungbunzlauer's sodium gluconate production, the company soon sought a partner in order to ensure its supply of starch, derived from corn and wheat, the raw materials for its glucose production. For this, Jungbunzlauer teamed up with French farmers' cooperative Union SDA in 1996. Union SDA's own origins reached back to the 1930s and the founding of a distillery by a farmers' cooperative in Origny in 1932. That distillery was converted into a beet sugar refinery in 1951.

Over the following decades, France's sugar industry underwent a major consolidation, including the 1996 merger of two of France's largest beet growers and beet sugar cooperatives, Sucreries et Distilleries de l'Aisne and Coopérative d'Artenay. Their merger created Union SDA, which became one of France's leading sugar producers, commanding 10 percent of the domestic market. This merger also gave Union SDA the scale to launch its investment beyond its core sugar production.

Union SDA's association with Jungbunzlauer provided the company with an entry into an important and fast-growing part of the foods sector, that of the production of glucose and glucose-derived sweeteners. This category, which included such highly processed artificial sugars as high-fructose corn syrup (also called isoglucose in the European Union), manitol, and sorbitol, had been growing rapidly since the late 1980s and in the 1990s.

In order to add its own glucose production, Union SDA agreed to create a starch-production joint venture with Jungbunzlauer, called Staral, based at the Marckolsheim site. Staral's production in turn supplied the raw materials for two new factories, the first, an organic acid plant owned by Jungbunzlauer, and the second, a glucose syrup factory 100 percent owned by Union SDA. The subsidiary operating this latter facility was called Syral S.A.S.

EXPANDING THE RANGE

Syral quickly ramped up its production, topping a capacity of 100,000 metric tons of glucose by 1997. The company, which posted sales of the equivalent of EUR 40 million by 1998, also began investing in developing a wider range of glucose-derived sweeteners.

Syral launched the construction of a new wheat-starch processing plant in Marckolsheim at the dawn of the new century. The new plant, which cost the company EUR 67 million to build, was completed in 2001 and added another 150,000 metric tons of

KEY DATES

1993: Swiss company Jungbunzlauer opens a glucose factory in Marckolsheim, France.
1996: Jungbunzlauer and Union SDA form joint venture Staral for starch production; Union SDA founds subsidiary Syral to produce glucose syrup.
2003: Union SDA acquires full control of Staral, which is merged into Syral; Union SDA merges with another leading French sugar group, becoming Tereos.
2007: Syral acquires five factories from Tate & Lyle, becoming the third-largest producer of starch and glucose in Europe.
2009: Syral launches investment drive; opens new applied research center in Marckolsheim.

capacity. With these new facilities, Syral was able to market both corn-based and wheat-based starch derivatives.

By then, Union SDA had brought a new partner into the Syral operation, selling a 36 percent stake in the company to Nordzucker, one of Germany's leading sugar cooperatives. By the middle of the decade, Nordzucker had increased its share of Syral to 50 percent.

Syral continued to add to its range of products at the beginning of the new century. New products introduced at this time included maltodextrin, anhydrous dextrose, and a range of dried glucose products. Syral also expanded into the production of sugar substitutes, setting up a sorbitol production plant in Marckolsheim. This facility became operational in July 2002, with an initial capacity of 5,000 tons per year. Sorbitol represented another corn derivative. Syral also launched a new investment drive, focusing on its research and development effort in order to develop new glucose-based products.

In 2003 Jungbunzlauer decided to refocus its own operations around its core citric acid and related businesses. As a result, Union SDA acquired full control of the Staral starch production factory, which was then merged into Syral. By the end of that year, the company's total production capacity had reached 320,000 metric tons, as its revenues climbed to EUR 160 million. Union SDA itself grew that year, merging with another leading French sugar group, Eridania Beghin-Say, becoming Tereos.

By the end of 2004, the company's sales had risen to nearly EUR 177 million. The company had also completed a transformation of its product range. Where glucose syrups had formed more than 80 percent of its sales in the mid-1990s, these contributed less than one-third of the company's range by this time. Instead, Syral had successfully refocused itself as a producer of high-value-added products, such as sorbitol, high-fructose corn syrup, maltodextrin, and other sweeteners.

NEW ALLIANCE IN 2006

Syral nevertheless ran into difficulties in 2005, as the European Union instituted a new sugar regime, resulting in a drop in the price of sugar. This in turn brought down sales of sugar substitutes. By the end of the year, Syral's own revenues had fallen back to EUR 173 million, forcing the company to post a net loss of EUR 1 million for the year. Syral launched a number of cost-cutting measures at the beginning of 2006, including the elimination of 40 jobs.

The change in the sugar regime also led Nordzucker to withdraw from Syral in December 2006 in order to refocus its business on its own sugar production. Rather than take full control of Syral, Tereos sought out new partners, turning to several French cereal cooperatives, including the Theal alliance, to invest in Syral. In this way, Syral also gained a guaranteed supply of its main raw materials. Tereos itself maintained a 62 percent stake in Syral.

Syral posted new revenue gains in 2006, rebuilding its annual sales to EUR 177 million. The company also returned to profitability, posting a net income of EUR 5.3 million. In 2007 the company claimed the number four position among European glucose and starch-based sweeteners. The company nevertheless remained a small part of Tereos, which posted total revenues of more than EUR 2.3 billion.

MOVING INTO THE LEAD IN 2007

Syral's position was to change dramatically, however, in 2007. In late 2006, British sugar giant Tate & Lyle announced that it planned to sell off its own glucose and starch production units. Syral joined with U.S. rival Roquette, the world's number two glucose group, to launch a bid for the Tate & Lyle sites. Syral's part of that bid would have given it control of four of Tate & Lyle's European factories. When Roquette decided not to pursue the bid, Syral decided it to pursue it alone, this time offering EUR 310 million to take over five factories. These included production units in Nesle, France; Aalst, Belgium; Greenwich, England; Zaragoza,

Spain; and in a 50-50 joint venture with the Frandino Group, one of the largest glucose factories in Europe, in Saluzzo, Italy.

Syral completed the purchase in October 2007. Acquisition of these sites boosted the group's total payroll to more than 1,100, while multiplying its annual sales more than fivefold, to EUR 900 million. Syral then became the third-largest glucose and starch producer in Europe. The company's expansion also included a move into the production of alcohol, including ethanol, used as a fuel additive among other applications.

Syral continued to grow through the end of the decade. The company began developing a range of soluble fibers, positioning itself in the fast-growing nutraceuticals market. For example, in 2008 the company debuted its new Actilight-branded prebiotic fiber. Other company products included Meripro wheat proteins and a line of maltitol crystals and syrups.

INVESTMENT DRIVE LAUNCHED IN 2009

Syral launched a new investment drive in 2009, promising to spend EUR 160 million over the next three years. Among the group's projects was a new spray drying tower, completed in July of that year, helping to boost the group's production of dry glucose and maltodextrin in Marckolsheim. Soon after, the company opened an applied research center in Marckolsheim as well. The company also launched plans to expand its Aalst, Belgium, plant with a bioethanol production wing, as well as adding new manufacturing capacity for maltitol and proteins in its Nesle, France, factory.

This investment program also led the company to restructure part of its manufacturing base. At the end of 2009 the company shut down its U.K. manufacturing operation in Greenwich, England, maintaining that subsidiary as a distribution center. By then, the company had also made its first venture into the Asian region, setting up a sales office in Hong Kong. Syral had transformed itself into one of the world's leading producers of glucose and starch-based products, with sales of more than EUR 1.36 billion.

M. L. Cohen

PRINCIPAL SUBSIDIARIES
Syral Belgium S.A./NV; Syral SAU; Syral UK Ltd.

PRINCIPAL OPERATING UNITS
Starch Products; Native Starches; Modified Starches; Sweetening Products; Glucose Syrups; Maltodextrins and Dehydrated Glucoses; Polyols; Biofuels and Green Chemistry; Vegetable Proteins and Co-products.

PRINCIPAL COMPETITORS
Ajinomoto Co., Inc.; Archer Daniels Midland Company; Cargill Incorporated; Cerestar Companies; Corn Products International, Inc.; Gruma S.A. de C.V.; Hayashibara Co.; MGP Ingredients, Inc.; Monsanto Company; Tate & Lyle PLC; SunOpta Inc.; Penford Australia Ltd.

FURTHER READING
"A Travers Syral, Tereos Conclut Son Operations avec Tate & Lyle," *Agra Alimentation*, May 17, 2007.

Latham, Antoine, "L'Union des Sucreries et Distilleries Agricoles s'Associe au Suisse Jungbunzlauer," *Les Echos*, May 6, 1996, p. 23.

"New Centre of Excellence for Syral," *Nutraceutical Business & Technology*, March/April 2009.

"Nordzucker Cède Sa Participation au Capital de Syral," *Agra Alimentation*, December 7, 2006.

"Starch and Glucose Producer Syral Opens New Facilities at Marckolsheim," *Chemical Business Newsbase*, July 31, 2009.

"Syral Acquires Assets from Tate & Lyle," *International Food Ingredients*, June–July 2007, p. 4.

"Syral Gets the Best out of Cereals," *Nutraceutical Business & Technology*, November–December 2009, p. 17.

"Syral Investit 160 Millions sur Trois Ans," *Agra Alimentation*, June 11, 2009.

"Syral Reveals New Applied Research Centre to Customers," *Food Engineering & Ingredients*, September 2009, p. 35.

Systembolaget AB

Kungstraedgaardsgatan 14
Stockholm, S-103 84
Sweden
Telephone: (+46 08) 503 300 00
Fax: (+46 08) 503 310 00
Web site: http://www.systembolaget.se

Government-Owned Company
Incorporated: 1955
Employees: 3,232
Sales: SEK 21.30 billion ($3.03 billion) (2008)
NAICS: 445310 Beer, Wine, and Liquor Stores

■ ■ ■

Systembolaget AB operates Sweden's retail alcohol monopoly. The government-owned company serves its mandate to limit the consumption of alcoholic beverages in Sweden through the strict control of sales of all spirits, wine, and beer with alcohol levels higher than 3.5 percent. Systembolaget operates a chain of 411 stores in 322 communities across Sweden, with limited opening hours, a minimum drinking age of 20, and strict sales policies. The company refuses to sell alcohol to anyone who is already intoxicated or to people whom its sales staff believe intend to resell their products or who might be purchasing alcohol for minors. The company supports its mandate through a number of educational initiatives, largely carried out by subsidiary IQ-initiativet AB. Systembolaget's total revenues topped SEK 21.30 billion ($3.03 billion) in 2008. The company operates on a nonprofit basis, and all income

is returned to the Swedish government. Magdalena Gerger has been the company's CEO since 2009.

BANNING DISTILLERIES IN THE 16TH CENTURY

Like many of its Western counterparts, Sweden had long held a love-hate relationship with spirits before the rise of the temperance movement in the 19th century. The first efforts to control the production and consumption of alcohol appeared as early as the 15th century. Until then, beer had traditionally been the most common alcoholic beverage in Sweden, while wine remained an expensive import available only to a small number of the wealthy nobility.

The distillation process, pioneered by Genoans in Crimea, later part of Russia, reached Sweden in the early 15th century. Gunpowder, arriving from Germany and elsewhere, featured highly inflammable distilled spirits as a primary ingredient. In Russia, these spirits became known as vodka and quickly became the national drink of choice.

In Sweden, the distilled liquid's aptitude for burning led to its name, *brannvin,* which literally meant "burned wine." The distillation process itself was often referred to as burning. A number of distilleries opened in Sweden during this time. Their production at first focused especially on ensuring the supply of gunpowder. Spirits were also used as the base of medicines. The limited supply, however, left little for private consumption.

This situation changed dramatically by the 16th century as the practice of owning distilleries spread across the noble class. This practice was soon taken up by the population as a whole. During this time, a large majority of the population began what was called "subsistence" distilling, producing small quantities of spirits for personal consumption. *Brannvin* soon replaced beer as Sweden's drink of choice. The popularity of the spirits, however, drained the country's grain supply, which was particularly problematic during periods of famine.

This led King Gustavus Adolphus, who ruled from 1611 to 1632, to promulgate the first decrees ordering the suppression of the country's distilleries. Later, King Charles XII, whose reign stretched from 1697 to 1718, made a new attempt at protecting the country's grain supply by calling for the elimination of the country's distilleries. Neither was successful, however. Later attempts, including a ban on all alcohol production in 1756, proved equally unenforceable.

CROWN DISTILLERIES IN 1774

The reign of Gustavus III, who took the throne in 1771, introduced a new era in Sweden's relationship to alcohol. Gustavus's policies toward *brannvin* took their inspiration from Russia, which had long exploited the production of vodka as a significant source of state revenues. Gustavus, who had aspirations of rivaling the French Court of Versailles in splendor and influence, became determined to tap into this revenue source as well.

In 1774 Gustavus declared the production of alcohol to be a state monopoly and established a system of Crown Distilleries. Over the next decade, the crown built 60 large-scale distilleries. These attempted to take control of every aspect of the market, including wine and other imports, distillery production, and even the production and repair of distillery equipment. At the same time, the court called upon the clergy not only to help enforce the monopoly among the peasant population but also to encourage spirits consumption among the population in order to raise revenues.

The Crown Distilleries proved highly unpopular. By the early 1780s, discontent had grown widespread, lead-

ing to a series of popular uprisings. In fact, the establishment of the Crown monopoly created a new network of illicit distilleries, the creation of a black market, and a growing number of smugglers. At last, in 1787, the Crown was forced to abandon the monopoly. In an effort to appease the population, the king now drafted new legislation that established the right of every Swede to operate his own distillery for personal consumption. Tavern owners, brewers, and town freeholders were given the right to distill spirits for sale. At the beginning of the 19th century, the right to commercialize one's production was later extended to landowners, and eventually to their tenants and lodgers as well.

TEMPERANCE EFFORTS IN THE 19TH CENTURY

Consumption of *brannvin* soared in Sweden during the early decades of the 19th century. *Brannvin* consumption also spread across all classes and age groups, even children. By then, the average yearly consumption of spirits, which generally held an alcohol content of 50 percent, reached as high as 45 liters per person. This led to a growing variety of public and social problems, including public drunkenness and health problems.

The government made a number of new, if limited, attempts to rein in consumption. In 1813 the court passed a new edict forbidding drunkenness. This proved difficult to achieve in a society where distilleries were omnipresent, wages were often paid in spirits, and consumption was encouraged by the agricultural sector among others, in order to reduce the surplus of grain. In 1824 the court imposed a new system of license fees for distillery operation. These fees did little to stem the production of alcohol in the country. Indeed, by 1830 Sweden counted nearly 175,000 fee-paying distilleries. At the time, the country's total population numbered less than three million.

Sweden's rampant alcohol consumption continued to take its toll on the country's physical, social, and moral health through that decade. In 1835 the government made a new effort to control the country's alcohol problem, drafting new rules regarding distillery operations. Distilling became limited to just six months per year. At the same time, the government established a minimum value for properties on which stills were allowed to operate.

New momentum for controlling the spirits market came from members of the population itself and the creation of the Swedish Temperance Society in 1837. Members of the society pledged to abstain from the consumption of spirits (but not beer or wine). Their

KEY DATES

1850: The first local retail alcoholic beverage monopoly (*bolaget*) is created in the town of Falun, Sweden.

1955: Systembolaget is created to take over all 41 local retail alcoholic beverage monopolies in Sweden.

Mid-1970s: Sales of mid-strength beer are banned in Swedish supermarkets.

2000: Systembolaget launches a self-service format in most of its shops.

influence grew strongly over the following decade, and by 1854 their petitions to the king had resulted in the creation of a special committee to the Swedish Diet (parliament).

The committee's report resulted in the passage of the Liquor Law of 1855, which significantly restricted private distilling. Under the new laws, municipalities were granted control over issuing distillery licenses in their districts. The number of licenses issued was greatly reduced, while requirements for obtaining a license were tightened.

THE GOTHENBURG SYSTEM IN 1865

One of the provisions of the new law gave municipalities the right to award the entirety of their distillery licenses to a single company. This provision came in recognition of a growing movement in Sweden, that of the creation of local nonprofit alcoholic beverage monopolies. This movement had started in 1850, when a group of mine owners in the town of Falun established a new company, or *bolaget,* that took over all production and sales of alcohol in the town. The company was attached to the local government and operated on a nonprofit basis. All income instead was to be used for the public good.

The idea quickly caught on, and by 1852 the town of Jonkoping, in southern Sweden, had created its own alcohol monopoly. Over the next decade, the *bolaget* system slowly spread to other towns in the country. A major push in this movement came in 1860, when the Swedish government tightened its liquor regulations, finally banning private distilleries altogether. This was followed in 1863 with the imposition of the first state tax on alcohol profits, initially established at 20 percent.

The creation of an alcohol monopoly in the city of Göteborg (or Gothenburg) in 1865 marked a major milestone in the creation of the future Systembolaget. The new company especially established control over the sale of spirits in the city, with the opening of a bar staffed with employees picked by the city. The bar established new rules for purchasing and consuming *brannvin*, including establishing a minimum age requirement of 18 years. Staff was also instructed to refuse alcohol to people who already appeared under the influence or exhibited signs of unruly behavior. The company also controlled a system of liquor licenses, which it granted to the city's restaurants and taverns.

The Gothenburg System, as it became known, introduced the liquor monopoly concept to a worldwide audience. Before long, new *systembolaget* stores had opened in Sweden's other major towns, including Stockholm, Lund, and Hudiksvall. The new companies came to represent a significant source of revenues and played an important role in stimulating the country's industrial development. This was especially true after the Swedish government passed new legislation in 1871 establishing the Gothenburg System at a national level (as well as in Norway, then part of the Swedish kingdom). The new legislation also stipulated that all of the profits from the sale of alcohol be turned over to the government. Over the next decades, the system evolved into a network of 40 independently operating companies located throughout Sweden.

RATION SYSTEM IN 1914

Despite its successes, both in raising revenues and lowering alcoholic consumption, the Gothenburg System remained imperfect. Into the 20th century, the temperance movement had become more radical, with growing numbers of the population calling for total prohibition of all alcoholic beverages. Some portions of Sweden, particularly in the north, had already banned alcohol consumption. In 1909 the prohibitionist movement held a private referendum. More than 55 percent of the population voted to prohibit alcohol in the country.

While the Swedish government did not immediately act on the referendum, its results cast a pall over Sweden's distilling and brewing industries. This gave an idea to Ivan Bratt, a pediatrician who, while a member of the temperance movement, was against total prohibition. Bratt convinced several wealthy acquaintances to buy up the country's brewers, distillers, and importers, which were eager to sell amid the uncertain climate created by the referendum. By 1914, this effort had succeeded in gaining control of alcoholic beverage production and imports in Sweden. These operations were placed under a new government-owned company, called Vins och Spritcentralen (The Wine and Liquor Trust, or Vin & Sprit, or V&S).

Under Bratt's leadership, the government also set into place a new rationing system for alcoholic beverages. The system, launched in Stockholm in 1914 and then on a national level three years later, was based on a passbook system, called the *motbok*. All alcoholic beverage purchases were recorded in the booklet, with a limit of 13 gallons of spirits allowed per person each year. The system was not a fair rationing system: Women, when they were granted a *motbok* at all, were limited to just one gallon per year. The minimum drinking age was also raised to 23.

CREATING SYSTEMBOLAGET IN 1955

The rationing system, also known as the Bratt System, succeeded in cutting alcohol consumption in half over the next decade. Its success also helped thwart a new attempt at total prohibition, which was brought to a vote in 1922. The Bratt System remained in effect through World War II and into the 1950s.

The end of food rationing in Sweden in the postwar period also led to the abolition of the Bratt System. In 1955 the Swedish government decided to establish a single monopoly controlling the country's retail alcoholic beverages sector, merging the 41 local monopolies then in operation into a new company, Nya Systemaktiebolaget, later renamed Systembolaget AB. The new system abandoned the passbook system and instead developed a new retail format. Consumers were no longer required to register in order to purchase alcohol, and the age limit dropped to 21 years old.

Systembolaget was also charged with serving as a watchdog of sorts for public health. By the end of the 1950s, alcohol consumption had risen quickly, along with the number of offenses related to drunkenness, and an increase in alcohol-related health problems occurred as well. The company moved to stem these developments, adding identification requirements, establishing blacklists, and, especially, imposing successively heavy taxes on alcoholic beverages.

ADAPTING TO EUROPEAN UNION MEMBERSHIP IN 1995

Nonetheless, the company made a brief attempt at loosening its grip on the entire sector. The drinking age was lowered to 20 in 1969. The company also experimented with allowing mid-strength beer to be sold in grocery stores, starting in 1965. This was extended on a limited basis to strong beers, with higher alcohol

content, in 1967. Following a consumption increase of 1,000 percent, the trial was quickly brought to an end. By the middle of the 1970s, the government had decided to end grocery store sales of mid-strength beers as well. Only beers with alcohol content of less than 3.5 percent were then allowed to be sold outside of the Systembolaget chain.

Systembolaget's retail network continued to grow through the end of the century, reaching a peak of 575 stores by 1999. By then, however, the company's monopoly had come under fire. In order to comply for its admission into the European Union (EU) in 1995, the Swedish government had agreed to dismantle a number of its monopolies, including V&S. While the government successfully defended the continued existence of Systembolaget, it was forced to compromise in a number of areas, including allowing individuals to carry alcoholic beverages into Sweden from other European markets. Sweden initially gained an exemption allowing it to place severe limits on the country's personal import quotas.

SURVIVING SCANDALS IN 2009

By 2004, however, the country exemption had expired, and the company was forced to accept the far higher amounts allowed by the EU. In 2006 Systembolaget lost another important test to its monopoly, when the European Court ruled that it could not impose its taxes on personal imports from other countries. The following year, the European Court ruled against Systembolaget again, when the company attempted to place a ban on remote sales of alcoholic beverages, from online sites in particular, into Sweden. The company did, however, win the right to impose its own taxes on these purchases.

Systembolaget had in the meantime begun taking steps to adapt to the new market conditions. Between 1991 and 1996, it had tested a new self-service concept for its stores. In 2000 the company decided to extend the self-service throughout most of its network. The company also trimmed its number of locations back to just 411 shops in 2010. Meanwhile, Systembolaget continued to respond to shifts in alcoholic beverage consumption, adapting its catalog accordingly. As a result, Systembolaget developed one of the world's most comprehensive wine lists, as wine sales skyrocketed at the end of the century. By the end of 2009, the company had established a new record, selling more than 174 million liters of wine during that year.

Systembolaget faced other pressures in the first decade of the new century, however. In 2003 the company became mired in a major bribery scandal, in which 71 of its store managers were accused of accepting bribes from suppliers in exchange for favorable treatment. The scandal ultimate spread to the company's head office, involving three executives, including a member of its board of directors. In 2009 Systembolaget came under investigation again when it was accused of violating privacy regulations by maintain customer credit card records for as long as a decade.

Despite these setbacks, Systembolaget remained a important source of revenues for the Swedish government, posting total sales of more than SEK 21 billion ($3 billion) and net profits of SEK 774 million ($110 million) in 2008. Systembolaget prepared to watch over Sweden's health for years to come.

M. L. Cohen

PRINCIPAL SUBSIDIARIES

AB K14 Näckströmsgatan; IQ-Initiativet AB; Lagena Distribution AB.

PRINCIPAL DIVISIONS

Northern Sales Region; Southern Sales Region.

FURTHER READING

"Bribery Scandal at Sweden's Alcohol Monopoly Widens to Head Office," *AP Online*, November 19, 2003.

"End Systembolaget Control, More Drinkers Will Die," *just-drinks.com*, August 29, 2007.

Karen, Mattias, "Sweden Proposes 40 Percent Cut in Liquor Tax to Discourage Purchases Abroad," *AP Worldstream*, August 16, 2004.

Nuthall, Keith, "EU Overturns Sweden Alcohol Import Ban," *just-drinks.com*, June 5, 2007.

Sayles, Robert, "British Airways, Systembolaget and Those Supermarkets!" *Publican*, February 11, 2010.

"Sweden Bottles Up," *Economist*, February 26, 2000, p. 62.

"Sweden Heads toward New Wine Sales Record," *Local*, December 14, 2009.

"Systembolaget Hails Organic Drinks in 2007," *just-drinks.com*, March 27, 2008.

"Systembolaget Sees Sales Head South in January," *just-drinks.com*, February 11, 2008.

"V&S Admits Defeat in Systembolaget Wine Row," *just-drinks.com*, March 14, 2007.

Zanca, Salvatore, "Sweden's State-Owned Alcohol Monopoly Has Right to Ban Personal Imports," *AP Worldstream*, November 30, 2006.

Szerencsejáték Zrt.

Csalogány utca 30-32
Budapest, H-1015
Hungary
Telephone: (+36 06 1) 201 6777
Fax: (+36 06 1) 201 0219
Web site: http://www.szerencsejatek.hu

Government-Owned Company
Incorporated: 1991
Employees: 1,296
Sales: HUF 150 billion ($800 million) (2009 est.)
NAICS: 713990 All Other Amusement and Recreation
Industries

■ ■ ■

Szerencsejáték Zrt. is Hungary's largest gaming company. A state-owned company, Szerencsejáték is the monopoly operator of the country's national and instant lottery games. The company also holds the monopoly on sports betting, and operates four casinos in Hungary. Draw-based number games represent the largest part of Szerencsejáték's operations, accounting for approximately two-thirds of the group's annual revenues. Szerencsejáték's games include the 5/90 Lotto (in which players must match five numbers from a pool of 90), 6/45 Lotto, Scandinavian Lotto, Joker, Keno, the bingo-based Luxor, and Tango. Other lottery games include the Putto instant winner game, and a variety of instant scratch card-based games.

The company's sports betting games, which represent 14 percent of its annual sales, include Toto,

Goal Toto, Tippmix, and Tippmax. Szerencsejáték supports its operations through sales at its own network of nearly 300 lottery shops, as well as through online and SMS- and telephone-based sales. The company's products are also sold through more than 4,000 independent outlets throughout Hungary. Szerencsejáték's casinos include the Tropicana Budapest, and the country's only rural casinos, located in Győr, Kecskemét, and Sopron.

Altogether, Szerencsejáték's operations generated revenues of HUF 150 billion ($760 million) in 2009. Although Szerencsejáték maintains the monopoly over lottery and sports betting games, it faces competition in the Hungarian gambling market from horse betting and from a large installed base of slot machines. Nevertheless, the company controls approximately two-thirds of the Hungarian gaming market. László Varga is Szerencsejáték's chairman and the general director is Gábor Székely.

INHERITING HUNGARY'S LOTTERY IN 1991

The earliest state-operated lotteries in Hungary appeared in the late 18th century, centered around the government seat in what was then known as Buda. Lotteries and other forms of gambling remained fixtures of the region over the next two centuries. However, the modern history of Hungary's lottery and gaming market began following the end of World War II with the introduction of *totalisator*, tote-based betting pools, in 1947. This was followed by the creation of the first national lottery, a five-number draw game introduced by the government in 1957.

COMPANY PERSPECTIVES

With its fair, professional business policy, and ongoing investments for the future, Szerencsejáték Zrt endeavours to remain the largest service provider for Hungarian players. In order to achieve this objective, the company will continue to develop its games, increasingly exploit the opportunities offered by electronic commerce, and extend the services related with the games. Considered as permanent tasks, it will also continue to modernize the image of its sales network, and strengthen security. The company was prepared for the country's accession to the European Union, and is now, a recognized and reputable member of the national lottery companies of Europe and the world.

The lottery, known as the 5/90 Lotto because players picked five numbers from a pool of 90, proved hugely popular. At the end of the century, the 5/90 remained the country's single most popular form of gaming. A new type of game, the prize draw ticket, was introduced in 1967. By the end of the 1980s Hungarian gamblers were also able to purchase instant lottery tickets. Another number draw lottery game, 6/45 Lotto, was introduced in 1988.

Lottery and other gambling operations during the Communist era were governed by the Országos Takarékpénztár (OTP, the National Savings Bank). With the collapse of the Soviet Union and the introduction of democracy, the Hungarian government reorganized the gambling sector. This led in 1991 to the splitting off of the lottery and gaming operations of the National Savings Bank into a newly created independent company, called Szerencsejáték.

Szerencsejáték took over OTP's lottery and betting pools business. Szerencsejáték also inherited a network of more than 250 shops, through which much of the lottery and tote betting operations had been conducted. Szerencsejáték remained a state-owned company, placed under the supervision of the newly created Gambling Supervisory Authority. In 1991 the government also passed its first Gambling Operations Act.

COMPUTERIZED TICKETING IN 1993

As part of the transition to a free market economy, the Hungarian government had also attempted to liberalize the gambling sector. As a result, the country became

flooded with a large number of new gaming operators both from Hungary and from abroad. Szerencsejáték found itself competing against a growing amount of number draw lotteries, as well as prize draw ticket games. At the same time, changes in the previously highly restrictive casino legislation led to the appearance of a large number of new casino-type operations, far exceeding the demand for casino gaming. Slot machines, previously restricted to casinos, became a fixture in bars, restaurants, newsstands, and other outlets.

Already affected by the oversupply of lottery and related games, Szerencsejáték also suffered the consequences of the new gambling legislation, which imposed tighter tax regulations on lottery operations and winnings. This resulted in steady declines in the lottery market, in favor of other forms of gambling.

Szerencsejáték attempted to counter its slowing lottery revenues in a number of ways. In 1992 the company introduced its first instant lottery scratch cards. The company also sought to expand beyond its lottery and sports betting businesses in the early 1990s. As part of that effort, Szerencsejáték made its first investments into the casino market and also began offering horse race betting services.

The following year Szerencsejáték added several new games to its lineup, including a weekly drawing of the 6/45 Lotto game. The company also added Joker, a supplement to both the 5/90 and 6/45 games, and a new pools betting game called Goal Toto. Szerencsejáték also installed its first computerized terminals in 1993. By the following year, the company had installed computer terminals in all 260 of its lottery shops. The move into the digital era permitted the company to centralize all of its ticket processing starting in 1995.

LOTTERY MONOPOLY IN 1995

The year 1995 marked a new era for Szerencsejáték, as the government added a series of amendments to the Gambling Operations Act that introduced stricter regulations governing the gambling sector. The new legislation provided for background checks, reinforced casino licensing requirements, and legalized slot machine operations under a new tax regime. The legislation became especially important for Szerencsejáték in that it transferred monopoly control over all lottery, prize draw, and sports betting operations to the company.

The company then began developing a new daily lottery, Keno, introduced in 1996 and the first to take full advantage of the group's shift to digital technology. The company also launched a Millionaire-type instant lottery scratch card game called Telemazli that year.

Szerencsejáték also began exploring new media outlets for its lottery operations. In 1997 the company launched televised broadcasts of the 5/90 drawing, called the *Lotto Show*. Also that year, the company introduced its first telephone-based betting service, which accompanied the launch of a new sports-betting product, Tippmix. This new service offered bookmaker-style betting that provided odds-based payouts, as opposed to the company's tote-based betting products that drew the payouts from a single betting pool.

The company continued its transition to computer technology. By 1997 all of Szerencsejáték's ticket processing operations had been computerized. The company had also begun rolling out digital terminals to its wider point-of-sale network. By 2000 nearly all of the company's independent sales agents had been outfitted with computerized terminals. Szerencsejáték also launched Internet-based lottery ticket and sports betting sales, starting in 1998.

NEW PRODUCTS IN THE 21ST CENTURY

The increase in sales and processing capability permitted Szerencsejáték to continue to expand its range of gaming products. The company launched a new weekly number draw lottery, called the Scandinavian Lottery, on Wednesdays. This was followed by the introduction of Luxor, the group's first bingo-style game, introduced in 2001. Also that year, the group introduced a second Millionaire-type lottery game, called Golyoderbi.

Szerencsejáték's casino investments also expanded at the beginning of the new century. In May 2000 the company opened its first casino, the Tropicana Buda-

pest. This was followed by its first rural casino, which opened for business in January 2001 in Sopron. By the middle of the decade, Szerencsejáték had opened two more rural casinos, in Győr and Kecskemét. This positioned Szerencsejáték as the sole operator of casinos outside of Budapest. The company also claimed a 50 percent share of the total Hungarian casino market.

Lottery operations nevertheless remained Szerencsejáték's core business, accounting for the majority of its revenues. The company especially benefited from the popularity of its 5/90 Lotto, which established new prize records. For example, in 1999 the company awarded its first HUF 1 billion jackpot. The company then established a new jackpot record, of nearly HUF 3 billion, in 2002. This record was soon surpassed, with a drawing for nearly HUF 5 billion in 2003.

The rapid growth of the mobile telephone market in Hungary led Szerencsejáték to introduce an SMS-based sports betting service in 2003. The company hoped this would attract a growing number of young gamblers. The company also extended its Joker game to the Scandinavian Lottery that year. The following year, the company began taking bets by telephone. Also in 2004, Szerencsejáték extended its online sales platform to include the sale of sporting and other events tickets. The group began offering online scratch-type lotteries at the same time. The company then added a new member to its lottery family, Putto, an instant winner game featuring drawings every five minutes.

REAFFIRMING STATE-OWNED STATUS IN 2004

Szerencsejáték faced a number of new threats as Hungary prepared for its entry into the European Union. In 2003 the liberal government at the time announced a plan to sell a minority stake in Szerencsejáték, ahead of its eventual privatization. However, that plan was quickly put on hold.

In the meantime, Szerencsejáték found its monopoly under attack as a number of foreign gambling groups, including U.K.-based Sportingbet and Active Lotto 24 of Germany, began promoting their online services to Hungarians, despite the country's ban on cross-border lotteries. Part of the company's difficulties stemmed from the lack of a coherent European Union policy governing the gambling industry. The number of online operators continued to proliferate through the end of the decade. As a result, Szerencsejáték saw a significant drop-off in its sports betting business.

Despite the uncertainty surrounding its future as a state-owned company, and the potential loss of revenues to cross-border online gambling sites, Szerencsejáték continued to make strong gains. The passage of new legislation in 2005 played a part in the company's growth, boosting the percentage of winning scratch-type lottery cards to 60 percent. As a result, the company posted strong revenue gains through the middle of the decade, nearing HUF 132 billion in 2005. By the end of 2008, the company's total sales had risen past HUF 159 million.

By that time, the Hungarian parliament, dominated by the socialist MSZP party, had confirmed Szerencsejáték's status as a state-owned monopoly when it voted against a proposal to privatize the company in 2007. At the same time, the government introduced new changes in its tax laws, including eliminating income tax payments on winnings from bookmaker-type gambling. Szerencsejáték, which had been responsible for making the tax payments, promised to put these savings into higher payouts. This move was expected to help revive the company's flagging sports betting business.

By 2010 the global economic crisis had caught up both to the Hungarian economy, which had grown strongly during the previous decade, and to Szerencsejáték. As a result, the company posted a dip in revenues, which barely topped HUF 150 billion for the year. As a state-owned company and the holder of Hungary's lottery monopoly, Szerencsejáték looked forward to new gains in the future.

M. L. Cohen

PRINCIPAL SUBSIDIARIES

Casino Gyor Kft.; Casino Kecskemét Kft.; Casino Sopron Kft.

PRINCIPAL DIVISIONS

Lottery Games; Sports Betting Games; Instant Games; Casinos.

PRINCIPAL COMPETITORS

Belvárosi Kaszinó Kft.; Hrvatska Lutrija; Las Vegas Casino Kft.; Polski Monopol Loteryiny; Sazka AS.; Sportna Loterija; Tipos AS.; Totalisator Sportowy; Totolotek SA; Várkert Kaszinó Kft.

FURTHER READING

"Changes to Gambling Law Boost Revenue of State Lottery Company," *Hungarian News Agency*, October 17, 2005.

"Hungarian Lottery Operator Szerencsejáték Expects Increased '08 Revenues on Positive Tax Changes," *Hungary Business News*, December 28, 2007.

"Hungary's Lottery Firm to Boost Revenues by HUF 1 Bln annually Following Internet Launch," *Hungary Business News*, June 26, 2006.

Olah, Peter, "Gaming Firms Expect Boost from Nationwide Arcade Hookup," *Budapest Business Journal*, September 8, 2003.

———, "SMS Betting Service Targets Youth," *Budapest Business Journal*, September 8, 2003.

"State Seeks to Sell Minority Stake in Lottery Operator Szerencsejáték RT," *Hungary Business News*, October 3, 2003.

"State-Owned Gambling Company Revenues to Fall from HUF 159bn to HUF 150bn in 2009," *Hungarian News Agency*, December 23, 2009.

"Szerencsejáték Sees Revenue of More than HUF 150bn in 2009," *Hungarian News Agency*, December 14, 2009.

☰ techno trans

Technotrans AG

———— ■ ————

Robert-Linnemann-Strasse 17
Sassenberg, D-48336
Germany
Telephone: (+49 02583) 3 01 0
Fax: (+49 02583) 3 01 1030
Web site: http://www.technotrans.de

Public Company
Incorporated: 1985 as Technotrans Böhnensieker GmbH
Employees: 823
Sales: EUR 141.67 million ($208 million) (2008)
Stock Exchanges: Frankfurt
Ticker Symbol: TTR
NAICS: 333298 All Other Industrial Machinery
Manufacturing

■ ■ ■

Technotrans AG is the worldwide leader in the manufacture of industrial printing peripherals, commanding as much as 50 percent of the global market. Based in Sassenberg, Germany, Technotrans operates through a network of subsidiaries spanning 18 countries, including the United Kingdom, the United States, Japan, China, Brazil, Singapore, France, Italy, and Russia. In addition to its main production facility in Sassenberg, Technotrans operates manufacturing facilities in the United States, Brazil, and China. Germany remains the company's single largest market, with 47.5 percent of sales of EUR 142 million ($208 million) in 2008. The rest of Europe adds 25.7 percent

to sales, followed by the Americas at 16.2 percent, and Asia at 10 percent.

Technotrans operates through two primary divisions: Technology and Service. The Technology division is the company's largest, generating 73 percent of its revenues. This division develops and manufactures the company's production line, which focuses on the following areas: dampening solution circulation and ink roller temperature control; ink supply; cleaning systems/blanket cleaners; spray dampening systems; cleaning and filtration; central cooling systems; and varnish preparation. The company's peripherals are typically installed by printing press manufacturers prior to delivery to the end customer. The Service division then provides maintenance and support to this customer base. Technotrans is listed on the Frankfurt Stock Exchange.

COMPANY FOUNDED: 1970

Technotrans AG was founded in Sassenberg, Germany, by Franz Böhnensieker in 1970 as an equipment manufacturer called FB-Apparatebau Böhnensieker. The company started out with just two employees, and by the end of its first year in business had recorded DEM 200,000 in sales.

By 1973 Böhnensieker's annual sales had topped DEM 1 million. That year also marked the launch of production of the company's first equipment for the printing and audio industries. The company's initial ventures into these markets included the components for the production of vinyl LPs. The company also launched the production of ultraviolet (UV) sterilization machinery in 1973.

Böhnensieker entered the industrial printing peripherals market in 1977 with the introduction of its first dampening solution preparation assembly. The success of this launch helped establish Böhnensieker as an up-and-coming force in fluids handling and control technology, an important component in the printing process. Böhnensieker began focusing more of its printing peripherals research and development effort on developing automated controls and other preparation assemblies for the handling of dampening solution. This led the company to form a separate division dedicated to this product line in 1981. The company's focus helped it to gain a growing share of this niche market in Germany, and then in the rest of the world.

By 1985 Böhnensieker's revenues had grown to DEM 7 million. The company had also developed a new business area, the production of CD (and later DVD) manufacturing and processing equipment. In this way, the company maintained its position in the audio media industry despite the phasing out of vinyl records.

MANAGEMENT BUYOUT IN 1990

By this time, Franz Böhnensieker had begun to withdraw from the company's day-to-day operations. These were increasingly turned over to a new management team, including Heinz Harling, who joined the company in 1980. Underscoring this transition was a change in the company's name, to Technotrans Böhnensieker GmbH, in 1985.

Technotrans moved to streamline its business focus in the second half of that decade. The company decided to focus its operations around two areas, printing peripherals and audio media processing. As a result, the company sold off its UV sterilizing equipment manufacturing operations in 1987. A major factor behind this decision was the successful launch of the company's first temperature control system for ink rollers. This launch enabled Technotrans to position itself as a leading controls manufacturer for both of the primary fluids used by the printing industry.

Harling became managing director of Technotrans in 1988. Over the next two years, Harling successfully expanded the business. By the end of the decade the company's revenues had risen above DEM 18 million and the company's workforce had grown to 70 people. In 1990 Franz Böhnensieker made the decision to retire from the company altogether, and agreed to sell the company to a management buyout led by Harling and four other company managers. Hannover Financial and West LB provided financial backing for the buyout.

INTERNATIONAL EXPANSION

With the buyout completed, Technotrans began seeking new expansion opportunities. This led the company to make its first move into the international market, founding subsidiary Technotrans Graphics Ltd. in Colchester, England. This not only provided the company with new sales and marketing strength in the United Kingdom, but also gave Technotrans its first foreign manufacturing facility.

The move into England was soon followed by the addition of subsidiaries in a number of other international markets. The company entered France in 1993, establishing a sales and service subsidiary there. Two years later, Technotrans moved into the United States, founding Technotrans Inc. based in Atlanta, Georgia. The company boosted its manufacturing operations again in 1997 with the creation of its first Chinese subsidiary, in Beijing. At the end of the decade the company added sales and service operations in Italy as well, founding Technotrans Italia in 1999. The company entered the Southeast Asia market that year as well, establishing a subsidiary in Singapore. This addition also backed the company's entry into the Australian market.

The international expansion of Technotrans came in support of its rapidly building market share. By the beginning of the 1990s, Technotrans had become one of the top three producers of dampening solution preparation equipment. In 1990, the company developed a new component-based peripherals concept, enabling it to present coordinated ink roller temperature control and dampening fluid preparation equipment.

The new concept quickly impressed two of the world's leading offset printing press manufacturers, Heidelberg and MAN-Roland, both based in Germany. In 1992 both companies signed on Technotrans as the original equipment supplier for their respective Speedmaster and 700 presses. Before the end of the decade, the company had signed up the third of the big three offset printing press manufacturers, KP, also a German company. As a result, Technotrans grew into the dominant supplier of fluids handling technology to the printing industry, claiming a 43 percent market share by 1998. The company's market share ultimately rose to nearly 50 percent in the next century.

KEY DATES

1970: Franz Böhnensieker founds FB-Apparatebau Böhnensieker in Sassenberg, Germany.

1977: The company launches its first dampening solution preparation assembly for the printing industry.

1985: The company changes its name to Technotrans Böhnensieker GmbH.

1990: Heinz Harling leads a management buyout of Technotrans.

1998: Technotrans goes public on the Frankfurt Stock Exchange's Neuer Markt.

2000: Technotrans completes its first U.S. acquisition, of Ryco Graphic Manufacturing.

2007: Technotrans acquires Rotoclean GmbH in Germany.

2010: Technotrans receives orders to supply components for two printing presses in China.

ACQUISITION DRIVE

The company's revenues rose strongly through the 1990s, topping DEM 71 million in 1996 and then DEM 88 million the following year. The company and its investors began preparing a public offering that year, reincorporating the company as a joint stock company (*aktiengesellschaft* or AG). The company then went public in 1998, becoming one of the first companies to list its shares on the Frankfurt Stock Exchange's Neuer Markt index. The company had listed over half of its shares by 2000.

The proceeds from the public offering fueled the next growth phase for Technotrans. The company began targeting a series of acquisitions at the end of the 1990s and into the next decade. These acquisitions became a major component in the group's efforts to gain market share in its core fluid handling category as well as to expand its range of printing press peripherals technologies.

Technotrans completed its first acquisition in 1998, buying up BVS Grafische Technik GmbH, based in Augsburg, Germany. BVS brought the company its world-leading production of offset roller ink delivery systems. The addition of BVS helped boost the company's total sales above DEM 123 million (approximately $60 million). Following its acquisition, BVS was renamed Technotrans Systems. In 1999 Technotrans Systems was merged into Technotrans itself.

The company next attempted a move into the Internet, acquiring Globalprint, based in the United Kingdom, which operated one of the first Web sites with content developed specifically for the global printing industry. Technotrans acquired Globalprint in 1999, hoping to generate as much as EUR 5 million in yearly revenues from the site. However, the company's Internet experiment failed to make an impression. By the end of 2003, the company decided to shut down the site.

EXPANSION INTO THE UNITED STATES: 2000

Despite the difficulties at Globalprint, that operation remained only a minor part of the company's operations. By 2000, the group's sales had grown again, approaching the DEM 150 million mark. By then, more than 79 percent of the group's sales came through its printing peripherals technologies, and were complemented by the strong growth of the company's services division, which added another 14.4 percent to its revenues. The company's CD and DVD equipment, which shared similar technologies with its printing components, added the remaining 6 percent to its revenues. However, the company began phasing out this division in the new decade in order to focus its operations fully on its print technologies.

Technotrans launched a drive to expand its operations in the North American market in the new century. In 2000 the company completed its first acquisition in the United States, of Ryco Graphic Manufacturing Inc., based in Illinois. The purchase provided Technotrans with Ryco's expertise in spray dampening systems and silicon applicators, used especially in the production of self-adhesive printing products. The Ryco addition added another $15 million in sales, as well as a second U.S. manufacturing facility, while also expanding the scope of the company's printing peripherals technology.

Technotrans continued to build its technology portfolio, announcing the acquisition of California-based The Steve Barberi Company and its subsidiary Farwest Graphic Technology LLC in October 2000. Farwest expanded the U.S.-based manufacturing capacity of Technotrans with its own production of water cooling and ink tempering systems. At the same time, The Steve Barberi Company added new coatings technologies to the company's lineup, and particularly its industry-leading expertise in UV-based coatings applications. The new acquisition also complemented a partnership agreement formed between Technotrans and Germany's IST that year to develop UV and other cooling technologies for coatings applications.

STRUGGLING IN THE 21ST CENTURY

Technotrans maintained its momentum in the new decade. In 2001 the company acquired Toolex International B.V.'s Sweden-based Electroforming Division, which formed the base for the company's new subsidiary, Technotrans Scandinavia. Also that year, Technotrans added sales and service subsidiaries in Kobe, Japan, and in Hong Kong.

By the end of the year, however, the company found itself struggling amid a sharp downturn in the global printing industry, brought on in part by the terrorist attacks against the United States of September 11, 2001. As a result, the company saw its revenues fall sharply, dropping back to EUR 131 million ($120 million), and then again to EUR 117 million by the end of 2002. In response, the company launched a restructuring, including shutting down the manufacturing arm of its U.K. subsidiary. By the end of 2003, the company's sales had slipped again, to EUR 106 million. The company also posted a net loss that year, of EUR 11 million.

The difficult market nevertheless offered potential for new expansion. In 2003 the company reached an agreement to acquire one of its main U.S. rivals, Baldwin Technology Company, for $37.5 million. However, the resurgence of the printing sector at the beginning of 2004, along with Baldwin's share price, put an end to the agreement. Complicating matters for the two companies was a dispute centering around Baldwin's claim that Technotrans had infringed on certain of its patents. Nevertheless, thanks to the return to growth of the printing sector, by the end of 2004 the company's revenues had recovered from their slide, climbing back up to EUR 117 million, for a net profit of nearly EUR 7 million.

STREAMLINING IN 2005

Technotrans reorganized in 2005, streamlining its structure into two main divisions, Technology, which absorbed the company's remaining microtechnology operations, and Service. The latter division became an increasingly important part of the company's overall business, and by the end of the decade had become responsible for nearly 25 percent of its total revenues.

During this period, Technotrans continued making progress toward becoming a full-range printing peripherals producer. In 2005 the company entered a new product category, cleaning systems, with the launch of its Contex.c blanket cleaner system. By 2007 the company had successfully completed the installation of its first Contex.c unit. Also in that year, the company further expanded its cleaning technology offering, acquiring fellow German company Rotoclean GmbH.

Technotrans expanded its German production capacity in 2005, adding a new factory in Gersthofen, near its Augsburg operations. This was followed by a move to streamline its U.S. production in 2006, which was combined into a single location at its Illinois factory that year.

The company also raised its international profile during the second half of the decade. In 2006 the company established a dedicated sales and service subsidiary for the Latin American market, in São Paulo, Brazil. This was followed by the opening of a sales office in Madrid, Spain, that same year. In 2007, the company added subsidiaries in Dubai and in Moscow, and sales and service offices in Melbourne, Australia, and in Shanghai, China.

SURVIVING THE GLOBAL DOWNTURN

Technotrans made steady revenue gains as well, reaching a new peak of EUR 153 million in 2007. However, the company was hit by a new sales slump the following year as the world entered a severe economic downturn. As a result, the company's revenues slipped back again to just EUR 141 million at the end of 2008. After several years of profits, the group also reported a new loss, of EUR 2.8 million. By then, Heinz Harling had announced his decision to retire as the company's chairman, effective in May 2008.

The company remained vulnerable to the difficulties confronting the global printing industry through 2009. By the end of the year, the company's revenues had dropped by more than 40 percent, as the company revised its sales forecast for the year to just EUR 85 million. In order to reduce its exposure, the company took steps to streamline its manufacturing base, moving most of its production to its main Sassenberg facility in June 2009. In a further effort to reduce its costs, Technotrans also established new headquarters for the Asian region, combining the administrative and support operations for all of its operations in the region at a single Hong Kong location.

Moving into 2010, Technotrans appeared buoyed by signs of the gradual recovery of the global economy. In January 2010, for example, the company received two major orders to install several key components, including the dampening solution preparation and ink supply units, as well its Contex.c blanket cleaning system in two presses to be delivered to the *Beijing Daily* and *Tianjin Daily* newspapers. As the dominant producer of printing press peripherals, Technotrans looked forward to new growth in the years ahead.

M. L. Cohen

PRINCIPAL SUBSIDIARIES

Globalprint AG; Technotrans América Latina Ltda. (Brazil); Technotrans America, Inc.; Technotrans China Limited; Technotrans France s.a.r.l; Technotrans Graphics Limited (UK); Technotrans Italia S.r.l.; Technotrans Japan K.K.; Technotrans Middle East FZ-LLC (Dubai); Technotrans Printing Equipment (Beijing) Co. Ltd.; Technotrans Rus 000; Technotrans Scandinavia AB (Sweden); Technotrans Technologies Pte Ltd. (Singapore); Technotrans Trading (Shanghai) Co. Ltd.

PRINCIPAL DIVISIONS

Technology; Service.

PRINCIPAL COMPETITORS

Delphax Technologies Inc.; Gunther International Ltd.; Koenig & Bauer AG; Komori Corp.; Presstek Inc.

FURTHER READING

"Baldwin and Technotrans End Patent Dispute," *Biotech Week*, October 14, 2009.

"Growth Continues at Technotrans," *Europe Intelligence Wire*, August 9, 2006.

Marsh, Peter, "Keeping Fluidity in the Industry," *Financial Times*, May 18, 2000, p. 6.

"Technotrans AG: Board of Management Completes Generation Shift," *DGAP Regulatory Newsfeed*, December 17, 2009.

"Technotrans Confirms Targets," *Europe Intelligence Wire*, November 5, 2008.

"Technotrans to Increase Production Capacity," *Europe Intelligence Wire*, October 9, 2004.

"Technotrans to Step up Cost-Saving," *Europe Intelligence Wire*, October 17, 2008.

Tenneco Inc.

500 North Field Drive
Lake Forest, Illinois 60045-2595
U.S.A.
Telephone: (847) 482-5000
Fax: (847) 482-5940
Web site: http://www.tenneco.com

Public Company
Founded: 1940 as Tennessee Gas and Transmission
   Company
Employees: 21,000
Sales: $4.65 billion (2009)
Stock Exchanges: New York
Ticker Symbol: TEN
NAICS: 336399 All Other Motor Vehicle Parts
   Manufacturing

■ ■ ■

Tenneco Inc. makes emissions control and ride control components for the automotive industry. Sales to original equipment manufacturers account for most of its revenues, but the company is increasing its share of the aftermarket business. Tenneco is one of the 40 largest global automotive suppliers. At one time Tenneco was one of the largest diversified companies in the world, ranking among the 30 largest industrial companies in the United States and among the top 100 worldwide. By the end of the 1990s Tenneco had divested many of its holdings.

The company remained a giant even after selling off its non-core operations, with the Tenneco name carried on by the automotive operations. By 2008 revenues approached $6 billion, two-thirds of which came from outside North America. Although sales slipped by one-fifth in 2009 as U.S. passenger vehicle production plummeted, Tenneco was supplying a number of programs in China and other growing economies. The company had more than 80 manufacturing facilities, most of them located outside the United States.

ORIGINS

Much of the company's early success was attributed to its first director, Henry Gardiner Symonds. Acquiring a degree in geology from Stanford University in 1924 and an MBA from Harvard three years later, Symonds began his career in Chicago as a banker with what eventually became the Continental Illinois Bank and Trust Company. In 1930, Symonds began work with a small investment firm and bank subsidiary called the Chicago Corporation, and his success there led to his appointment as vice president of the division in 1932.

In 1938, oil was discovered on land near Corpus Christi, Texas, that the Chicago Corporation had purchased for natural gas deposits, and Symonds was dispatched to Texas to manage the property. Later that year, he became a board member of the firm. The Chicago Corporation was unable to fully exploit the large reserves of natural gas it had developed in Texas, due to national shortages of pipeline materials essential for gas transmission.

When a shortage of fuel for defense plants in West Virginia developed in 1943, the Chicago Corporation

COMPANY PERSPECTIVES

Tenneco has emerged as strong standalone company and has positioned itself as a sound global automotive supplier. From Day One, Tenneco has had a disciplined focus, an employee culture of teamwork and execution, and a commitment to customer service—all characteristics of a great company. Given this, Tenneco faces the future with confidence in its financial success, growth opportunities and market leadership.

was able to obtain a Federal Power Commission (FPC) license to operate a pipeline, in addition to a priority order for pipeline materials. Symonds was placed in charge of the construction of a 1,265-mile pipeline, which linked the gas fields of the Gulf Coast states with factories in the eastern United States.

A company called the Tennessee Gas and Transmission Company, founded in 1940 and acquired by the Chicago Corporation in 1943, was placed in charge of the pipeline. The project was completed in October 1944. However, the day after the pipeline went into operation, the FPC moved to regulate the pipeline and ordered the company to reduce its transmission rates. Symonds protested, contending that the FPC had led him to believe that the Chicago Corporation would be allowed to operate without such regulations.

Regarding the FPC's actions as unfair, Symonds declared that he would never again become involved in projects subject to government regulation. Nevertheless, when the Chicago Corporation promptly divested itself of Tennessee Gas after World War II, Symonds remained with the company and was subsequently named its president. Tennessee Gas continued to add pipelines to its network, planning 3,840 additional miles in 1946.

OIL AND CHEMICAL ACQUISITIONS: 1950–66

Symonds used profits from the pipeline operations to establish a separate but complementary subsidiary business in oil and gas exploration. He advocated the acquisition of existing oil companies during the 1950s, including Sterling Oil, Del-Rey Petroleum, and Bay Petroleum, and oversaw acquisitions of several petrochemical companies, diversifying the product base and involving Tennessee Gas in industrial plastics.

Fifteen Oil, acquired in 1960, was one of several subsidiaries engaged in oil and gas exploration and production in places as diverse as Alaska, Canada, Latin America, and Africa. A subsidiary called the Tenneco Corporation was formed that year to coordinate the management of several company subsidiaries.

In February 1961, a corporate restructuring occurred that placed the company's non-utility subsidiaries, principally Tennessee Gas and Bay Petroleum, under the managerial authority of Tenneco. Acquisitions in the chemical industries continued through the 1960s and included the Heyden Newport Chemical Corporation, which formed the core of what later became Tenneco Chemicals, Inc., in March 1965. Moreover, the Tenneco division added a new line of business in June 1965 when it purchased the Packaging Corporation of America, a manufacturer of paperboard and packaging materials, with over 400,000 acres of timberland resources. Between September 1950 and March 1966, Tennessee Gas had acquired 22 companies.

A second corporate restructuring took place in April 1966, in which Tenneco assumed control over all the assets of Tennessee Gas, which then became a Tenneco subsidiary. Symonds was promoted from president and board chairman positions in which he had served since 1958, to chief executive officer and chief policy officer, in addition to being named the company's chairperson "for life."

Tenneco's most significant acquisition under Symonds came in August 1967, when it purchased the Kern County Land Company for approximately $430 million. Kern was established in California around 1850 by two lawyers from Kentucky, Lloyd Tevis and James Ben Ali Haggin, who intended to purchase land for resale to prospectors drawn to California in search of gold. Although the scheme failed, the subsequent development of irrigation systems transformed the 2.5 million acres of arid wasteland into arable cropland. Moreover, some of the land was later found to contain oil deposits.

While the Kern Company lacked the expertise to develop these oil deposits, Tenneco was perfectly suited to develop the sites. At the same time, Tenneco had no immediate interest in Kern's agricultural businesses. However, as those businesses were profitable, they could easily be assimilated into Tenneco's existing land management group. The acquisition also included Kern's 53 percent interest in J.I. Case, a manufacturer of farm and construction machinery located in Wisconsin, and Walker Manufacturing, which produced automotive exhaust systems.

KEY DATES

1944: Tennessee Gas Transmission Company, precursor of Tenneco Corp., completes natural gas pipeline linking gas fields of Gulf Coast states with factories in the eastern United States.

1967: Kern County Land Company, owner of farm equipment manufacturer J.I. Case, is acquired for $430 million.

1968: Newport News Shipbuilding & Drydock Company is acquired for $140 million.

1986: Five insurance companies are sold to I.C.H. Corporation for $1.5 billion.

1990: Total revenues reach $13 billion.

1995: Tenneco adds Mobil Corporation's plastics division to packaging unit for $1.27 billion.

1996: Newport News Shipbuilding is spun off.

1997: After 33 years in Houston, Tenneco relocates headquarters to Connecticut.

1999: Tenneco Packaging is spun off as Pactiv Corp., leaving Tenneco Automotive as stand-alone company.

2005: Tenneco Automotive is renamed Tenneco Inc.

2008: Tenneco acquires Italy's Gruppo Marzocchi, supplier of suspension components for two-wheeled vehicles.

NEWPORT NEWS SHIPBUILDING ACQUIRED: 1968

After the acquisition, Tenneco divided its subsidiaries along geographical lines, resulting in Tenneco West (formerly Kern) and Tenneco Virginia, which had grown out of the company's gas transmission business. In September 1968, Tenneco Virginia purchased Newport News Shipbuilding & Drydock Company for about $140 million. Newport News was engaged in the construction of nuclear-powered submarines and aircraft carriers, as well as merchant and commercial ships. The company also repaired and reconditioned ships, and refueled nuclear vessels. The nation's largest privately owned shipyard, Newport News was also in serious financial trouble.

Symonds died of a heart ailment on June 2, 1971. His method of expansion through diversification had been based on three rules: seeing that the company he wished to acquire would benefit from Tenneco management; choosing companies whose operations would complement those of Tenneco; and enforcing standards which kept each division autonomous. Under Symonds's successor, James Lee Ketelsen, Tenneco continued to operate on these precepts, but the number and size of subsequent acquisitions were noticeably reduced.

The application of Tenneco management methods to Newport News had transformed the shipbuilding division into a successful venture by 1971. Over a period of several years, Tenneco invested nearly $100 million in the company, and by 1973 the division had accumulated an order backlog of $1 billion. As a result of increased demand for imported petroleum products, Newport News engaged in the construction of large ships capable of carrying crude oil and liquefied natural gas.

In the course of restructuring Newport News Shipbuilding, Tenneco encountered strong opposition from organized labor and the Occupational Safety and Health Administration (OSHA). Eventually, after a three-month strike, all 16,500 employees of Newport News gained representation by the United Steelworkers. OSHA levied a fine of $786,190 on Newport News, citing 617 cases of deficient medical care, unsafe working conditions, and excessive noise. It was the largest fine OSHA had ever imposed on any company.

Wall Street analysts had consistently advised Tenneco to sell Newport News, warning that the division would require costly modernization and reorganization. Despite such problems, however, Tenneco officials recognized the subsidiary's potential, particularly after Navy Secretary John Lehman declared his intention to establish a 600-ship navy in 1981. Thereafter, Newport News abandoned commercial shipbuilding in favor of government defense contracts.

A GROWING CONGLOMERATE: 1968–90

Between 1968 and 1976, Tenneco made an additional 13 acquisitions, including an initial stake in the British chemical company Albright & Wilson Ltd., and consolidated its ownership of J.I. Case. The automotive parts division of Tenneco experienced strong growth during the 1970s through the acquisition of AB Starlawerken of Sweden in 1974, Monroe Auto Equipment (best known for their line of shock absorbers) in 1977, and Lydex, a Danish company, in 1978. Tenneco started to purchase insurance companies in 1978, including Philadelphia Life and Southwestern Life Insurance.

During the early 1980s, Tenneco sold its petrochemical and polyvinyl chloride production facilities to Occidental Petroleum. In 1984, to combat low gas prices and the adverse trends in the gas industry, Tenneco formed a new subsidiary called Tenngasco, which was responsible for sales of spot market gas in unregulated intrastate markets. Also that year, the Tenneco Packaging Corporation of America acquired Ecko Housewares and Ecko Products from the American Home Products Corporation.

In 1985, Tenneco purchased the farm machinery division of International Harvester, which had been forced to restructure as a result of a severe crisis in the American farming industry. Paying $430 million for the division, Tenneco then combined these operations with its Case subsidiary, which was also losing money. Tenneco officials believed that Case could benefit from Harvester's broader product line and stronger dealer network. The new combined group commanded a 35 percent market share for large tractors, a figure second only to Deere & Company's 42 percent. As a result of restructuring efforts and the temporary closure of several tractor plants, the new Case division registered a modest profit by the end of the year.

Having survived a 1982 attempt by stockholders to separate and sell the company's various divisions, the company was again considered a prime takeover target in 1987, given its high debt, rich assets, and record of underperformance. The company had previously insisted on paying stock dividends rather than reducing its debt or, in some other way, reducing its exposure to corporate raiders. In the late 1980s, Tenneco began boosting its stock through massive repurchasing programs and debt retirement. From 1988 to 1990, the company bought back 26.3 million shares and paid off $5 billion in long-term and short-term debt.

OUT OF INSURANCE: 1986

In 1986, Tenneco divested its five insurance companies to I.C.H. Corporation for about $1.5 billion. The company's late 1980s efforts to refocus its business interests included the sale of all its precious metals operations, the agricultural operations of Tenneco West, Tenneco Oil Company, and the retail muffler shops of Tenneco Automotive. At the same time, a new holding company, Tenneco Inc., was organized to serve as the corporation's principal financing vehicle. Revenues reached $13.3 billion in 1990.

Fine-tuning continued through the early 1990s under new leadership. In August 1991, Tenneco replaced James L. Ketelsen, who had led the company for 13 years, with Michael H. Walsh. The new president, who soon became CEO as well, found a company in far worse shape than he had been led to believe. Earnings and cash flow were falling short of targets in nearly every division, and debt stood at 70 percent of capital, "unacceptable" results, as Walsh's 1991 letter to shareholders observed.

By the end of the year, Walsh had instituted a $2 billion action plan that incorporated several retrenchment initiatives in the face of a lingering global recession. Walsh, dubbed a "tough boss for tough times" by *Business Week*, cut Tenneco's dividend in half, eliminated 8,000 jobs, divested three short-line railroads and other non-core assets, issued $512 million in new equity, and reduced capital spending for the two-year period by $300 million.

Walsh instituted additional reorganization measures in 1992, focusing on divestments and consolidation. Tenneco Minerals Company was sold for $500 million, and Albright & Wilson's pulp chemicals business was spun off to Sterling Chemicals. Although the latter sale brought $202 million to the corporation, it also eliminated 54 percent of Albright & Wilson's annual profit. Tenneco's plans for the ensuing three years included consolidation and "resizing" of production capacity, divestment of unprofitable product lines, and privatization of company-owned retail outlets. After just 18 months at Tenneco's helm, Walsh had reversed potentially dangerous trends and instilled a "no excuses" policy in its corporate culture.

In January 1993, Walsh announced that he had been diagnosed with inoperable brain cancer. Walsh elected to stay on at Tenneco and see the conglomerate through the reorganization he had begun. He designated a new recruit, Dana G. Mead, head of the Case Corporation subsidiary, as his successor and began delegating more authority to Mead and the rest of Tenneco's senior management. In February 1994, Walsh yielded Tenneco's presidency and chief executive officership to Mead and accepted the post of chairman. By that time, Tenneco was a $13 billion business, having gone from two successive years of losses totaling over $2 billion to a 1993 net income of $426 million and having reduced its debt from 70 percent of capitalization to 49.3 percent. Mike Walsh died in May 1994.

DIVESTMENTS AND ACQUISITIONS: 1994–99

Major divestments and a few acquisitions reshaped Tenneco in the second half of the decade. The company reduced its holdings in the capital-intensive J.I. Case unit through an initial public offering in June 1994 and subsequent secondary stock offerings. The Albright & Wilson chemicals business was divested in 1995. Newport News Shipbuilding was spun off the next year.

In 1995 Tenneco bolstered its packaging unit with the $1.27 billion acquisition of Mobil Corporation's plastics division. This included well-known plastic bag brand names Hefty and Baggies and made Tenneco Packaging the fourth largest in the industry. Tenneco sold its energy division to El Paso Energy Corporation for $4 billion in 1997. After 33 years in Houston, company headquarters moved to Connecticut. CEO Dana Mead explained that there was better access to capital on the East Coast.

Tenneco had been building its automotive business as the sprawling conglomerate was dismantled, adding Clevite Elastomers in 1996. Tenneco opened a vehicle exhaust factory in Shanghai in 1998, taking a 55 percent interest in a joint venture with Shanghai Tractor & Engine Co. It opened a new elastomers plant in Shanghai in 2005 and had an existing facility in Reynosa, Mexico.

Following an industry trend, Tenneco had formed a joint venture with ITT Automotive in 1996 to produce complete corner modules, combining chassis parts, suspension, and brakes. Several years later, however, it lost out on a bid to acquire ITT Automotive. According to *Crain's Chicago Business,* analysts believed that the newly slimmed Tenneco was vulnerable to takeover in a rapidly consolidating industry. Indeed, Tower Automotive Inc., a Grand Rapids, Michigan, auto parts supplier, nearly acquired Tenneco in early 1999, reported *Automotive News.* Southfield, Michigan's Federal-Mogul Corp. was also said to be a likely suitor. However, Tenneco opted to proceed independently.

In April 1999 Chicago venture capital firm Madison Dearborn Partners Inc. acquired a 55 percent interest in Tenneco's containerboard subsidiary, Packaging Corp. of America. The rest went with Tenneco Packaging when it was spun off as Pactiv Corp. in November 1999.

FOCUS ON AUTOMOTIVE IN THE 21ST CENTURY

After the packaging spin-off, the auto parts unit was left as a stand-alone company, Tenneco Automotive. Based in the Chicago suburb of Lake Forest, the company had revenues of $3.5 billion in 2000 and about 24,000 employees. The name was shortened to Tenneco Inc. in 2005. Revenues were $4.4 billion for the year; original equipment manufacturer (OEM) parts made up all but $1 billion of this. *Automotive News* ranked the company the 40th-largest global supplier. By this time, the number of employees had fallen to 19,000.

Mark Frissora, who had headed the company since its spin-off, left in July 2006 to lead Hertz Corp. His replacement was Gregg Sherrill, formerly head of Johnson Controls Inc.'s extensive automotive battery business. Increasing environmental regulation around

the world promised to fuel the emissions-control side of the business for some time to come. Tenneco perceived room to grow in Asia, where it had little market penetration. The company also wanted to increase aftermarket sales, which then accounted for a little more than one-fifth of revenues.

Tenneco was attempting to claim its share of the emerging market for emissions controls for diesel agricultural and construction equipment. It became a designated aftermarket supplier to Caterpillar Inc. in 2008. Also during that year Tenneco acquired Italy's Gruppo Marzocchi, a supplier of suspension components for two-wheeled vehicles.

In 2008 two-thirds of revenues of nearly $6 billion came from outside North America. The global credit crisis that began in the fall of 2008 furthered the auto industry's decline. Tenneco responded by restructuring in a bid to be more efficient. It shifted more of its engineering work from its Edenkoben, Germany, research center to its own facilities in lower cost countries such as Poland and India. However, the extent of the slowdown prompted the company to defer some of its plans for two years.

Revenues slipped 21 percent in 2009 to $4.65 billion. The net loss was narrowed to $73 million from $415 million the previous year. Car and truck sales production was down in North America and Europe, but still growing in China. In the midst of a challenging economic environment, Tenneco's CEO Sherrill remained optimistic, stating in the company's 2008 annual report that management would focus on reducing costs and generating cash, and expressing confidence that Tenneco would emerge stronger, more profitable, and in a leadership position in its industry.

Updated, April Dougal Gasbarre; Frederick C. Ingram

PRINCIPAL SUBSIDIARIES

Clevite Industries Inc.; Fric-Rot S.A.I.C. (Argentina; 99%); Heinrich Gillet GmbH (Germany); Monroe Australia Pty. Limited; Shanghai Tenneco Exhaust System Co., Ltd. (China; 55%); Tenneco (Beijing) Ride Control System Co., Ltd. (China; 65%); Tenneco Marzocchi S.r.l. (Italy); Tenneco RC India Private Limited; Walker Australia Pty. Limited; Walker Manufacturing Company.

PRINCIPAL OPERATING UNITS

Europe OE EC; Europe OE RC; North America OE EC; North America OE RC and Aftermarket; South America; Tenneco Asia; India; Australia; Japan.

PRINCIPAL COMPETITORS

Tower Automotive Inc.; Bridgestone APM Company; Federal-Mogul Corporation.

FURTHER READING

Bremner, Brian, "Tough Times, Tough Bosses," *Business Week,* November 25, 1991.

Daniels, Steve, "Northern Suburb Inherits Tenneco Leftovers: Auto Parts Next Acquisition Target?" *Crain's Chicago Business,* May 3, 1999, p. 4.

Donlon, J. P., "A Work in Progress," *Chief Executive* (U.S.), January 1996.

Huey, John, "Mike Walsh Takes on Brain Cancer," *Fortune,* February 22, 1993, pp. 76–77.

Jewett, Dale, "Tenneco Expects Stability at Top Despite Losing CEO," *Automotive News,* July 17, 2006, p. 29.

Meyer, Bruce, "A Full Agenda; Tenneco Deals with China, Transplants, Big Three," *Rubber & Plastics News,* June 25, 2007, p. 10.

Palmeri, Christopher, "Back on Course," *Forbes,* August 28, 1995.

Plishner, Emily, "Tenneco's New Business," *Journal of Business Strategy,* November/December 1996.

Richards, Don, "Tenneco, a Houston Force, Out of Chemicals, and Town," *Chemical Market Reporter,* January 13, 1997.

Sherefkin, Robert, "Tenneco's Auto Balancing Act: Spinoff Plans Acquisitions and Internal Growth," *Automotive News,* May 3, 1999.

Sobel, Robert, *The Age of Giant Corporations,* Westport, CT: Greenwood, 1972.

"Supplier Profile: Tenneco," *Supplier Business,* September 1, 2009.

Tenneco's First 35 Years, Houston: Tenneco Inc., 1978.

Treece, James B., "Tenneco Takes on Tokyo; As Big Three Struggle, Parts Maker Looks to Asia," *Crain's Chicago Business,* March 5, 2007.

Thermotech

1302 South Fifth Street
Hopkins, Minnesota 55343-7877
U.S.A.
Telephone: (952) 933-9400
Toll Free: (800) 735-1888
Fax: (952) 933-9412
Web site: http://www.thermotech.com

Wholly Owned Subsidiary of Pioneer Plastics, Inc.
Incorporated: 1949 as Thermotech Industries, Inc.
Employees: 650
Sales: $65 million (2009 est.)
NAICS: 326199 All Other Plastics Product Manufacturing

■ ■ ■

A subsidiary of Pioneer Plastics, Inc., Hopkins, Minnesota-based Thermotech is a contract manufacturer of custom injection-molded products, specializing in parts and components that have mission critical applications and therefore require engineering-grade thermoplastic and thermoset materials. The company serves three major markets: automotive, medical, and electronics. Automotive applications include electronics, such as sensors, connectors, brush holders, and motor gearboxes; fuel systems, including pump and vapor management components, injector bobbins, and canisters; and braking components, including antilock brake modules, speed sensors, and pistons.

Thermotech's medical applications include diagnostic devices, such as glucose meter components, cell scrapers, cuvette trays, and site probe kits; surgical supplies, including surgical staplers, heart valve packaging, and heart valve sizing devices; and the filters, heat exchangers, pump components, and other parts required in infusion systems. Electrical and electronic applications include bezels, bobbins and coil forms, solenoid and sensor components, molded interconnect devices, switch components, and transformer components.

Aside from manufacturing parts and components, Thermotech assists customers through all the steps of product development, production, and final assembly. In addition to its main 120,000-square-foot plant in Hopkins, the company maintains two plants in Mexico: a 60,500-square-foot facility in Juarez and a 54,000-square-foot facility in Queretaro. All three plants are ISO 9001-2000 Certified and ISO/TS 16949 Certified.

ORIGINS

Bob Booker and Victor Wallestad founded Thermotech in Minnesota in 1949 as Thermotech Industries, Inc., a plastic injection molding company. Two years earlier, Booker had established the Booker Co. to produce plastic fish baits. He was then joined by Wallestad, a North Dakota farmer who had become involved in the tool and die industry. In 1949 they formed Juno Tool Co. in addition to Thermotech, but sold off this business in 1951.

The following year Thermotech formed the Booker & Wallestad division to manufacture custom molded parts to serve the needs of semiconductor manufacturers, this new business the result of a referral from du Pont. The Delco Radio subsidiary of General Motors had made some rough semiconductor wafer carriers out of Teflon blocks to produce solid-state radio circuits and asked du Pont if it knew of a molding company that could do a better job. Thermotech was then recommended by du Pont.

Thermotech enjoyed success with semiconductor wafer carriers, leading to the 1957 creation of the Thermoset Molding division of Booker & Wallestad, which also used its expertise in molding Teflon to produce lab ware, such as tanks and beakers. As sales of these Teflon products increased in the early 1960s it became apparent that the operation, involved in a kind of molding different from the thermoplastics produced by the rest of Thermotech, needed to be independent. In 1966 the unit was spun off as Fluoroware, with Wallestad serving as the sole owner. It became a very successful business in its own right, spinning off operations, and eventually taking the name of Entegris, Inc.

Thermotech opened a plant in the St. Petersburg, Florida, area in 1961, which in addition to thermoplastics processed thermosets. The process produced stable products with a strong chemical resistance, but proved more abrasive on tooling, and most of the resulting products were not recyclable. Nevertheless, it was a viable niche and the Florida plant enjoyed steady growth.

COMPANY SOLD TO ITT: 1970

Thermotech moved its headquarters and main plant to a new facility in Hopkins, Minnesota, in 1969. A year later the company was acquired by International Telephone & Telegraph (ITT), along with two subsidiaries located in Golden Valley, Minnesota: Rainbow Plastic Products, Inc., maker of miscellaneous plastic products; and Cosum Corporation, which produced Frisbee knockoffs known as Flying Saucers. The operations then formed ITT's Thermotech Division.

ITT had been established in 1920 as a holding company for telephone companies in Cuba and Puerto Rico, and it soon developed a major business in Europe. In the 1960s the company turned its attention to the

United States, launching an acquisition spree that transformed it into a conglomerate. Notable purchases included the Avis car rental company, Sheraton Hotels, and Continental Baking Co., maker of Wonder Bread, Morton potpies, and Hostess snack cakes.

As part of ITT, Thermotech closed the Rainbow and Cosum plant in November 1973 and consolidated all operations in a new facility at Lakeview, Minnesota. In 1976 a new president and general manager took over, Robert Radunz, who had been with Thermotech for 18 years. He reaped the benefits of an owner with deep pockets in 1978 when ITT acquired a plant in Monson, Massachusetts, for Thermotech. ITT then acquired Anglo American Mold and Engineering Co. of Tustin, California, in 1983 and folded the operation into the Thermotech division.

By this time, however, a new chairman of the board at ITT had begun to sell off assets to pay down debt. Continental Baking was divested in 1984, and a year later ITT sold a dozen industrial equipment manufacturers, including Thermotech, for $408 million to Forstmann Little & Company, an investment banking firm that specialized in leveraged buyouts. Forstmann Little had been in business for only a short period, but had already made a splash by acquiring Dr. Pepper Co. and Topps Co. in 1984. Thermotech and the other former ITT units were placed under a holding company called FL Industries Inc.

ANOTHER CHANGE IN OWNERSHIP

Thermotech's tenure with Forstmann Little was short-lived, however, as was that of the other former ITT companies. Thermotech was sold to Wisconsin-based Menasha Corporation in 1988, and the others were divested four years later as Forstmann Little cashed out with hefty profits. Thermotech's new owner was one of the oldest privately held manufacturing companies in the United States, its origins dating to 1849 when a pail factory, aptly called the Pail Factory, was started in Menasha, Wisconsin. It later became the Menasha Wooden Ware Company and at the dawn of the 20th century began to acquire timberlands and became involved in the production of wood fiber products.

In the 1920s Menasha began producing corrugated containers, an industry that turned to the new plastic materials in the 1950s. Menasha, as a result, became involved in all manner of plastic manufacturing, acquiring a variety of companies in the field over the ensuing decades. Hence, Thermotech found a ready home in Menasha's Plastics Group, one of six primary business groups that made up Menasha at the time, along with Forest Products, Packaging, Promotional Graphics,

```
┌─────────────────────────────────────────┐
│  ┌───────────────────────────────────┐  │
│  │                                   │  │
│  │           KEY DATES               │  │
│  │                 ■                 │  │
│  ├───────────────────────────────────┤  │
│  │  1949:  Thermotech Industries, Inc., is formed.  │
│  │  1970:  ITT acquires company.              │
│  │  1985:  Investment firm buys Thermotech.   │
│  │  2001:  Plant opens in Mexico.             │
│  │  2007:  Pioneer Plastics acquires Thermotech. │
│  └───────────────────────────────────┘  │
└─────────────────────────────────────────┘
```

Information Graphics, and Material Handling. Within the Plastics Group, Thermotech's sister companies included Appleton Manufacturing, Molded Products, Traex, and Poly Hi. They formed working groups within their ranks to provide support and diversity to the whole, while at the same time each retained its autonomy.

EL PASO PLANT OPENS: 1995

Despite two changes in ownership, Radunz continued to head Thermotech. Under Menasha's ownership, the company expanded its connection to the automotive industry, following vehicle manufacturers to the Southwest by opening a new plant in El Paso, Texas, in 1995, to serve the maquiladora area near the Mexican border. Like the Florida plant, it processed thermosets as well as thermoplastics, and included 14 thermoplastic presses and six thermoset presses. The 50,000-square-foot facility produced precision bobbins, connectors, and under-the-hood parts for Tier One automotive suppliers and other customers, as well as molding small engine and aircraft components.

Radunz turned 60 in 1996, and after four decades at Thermotech, 22 of them in charge, he decided in early 1997 to retire, turning over the reins to John Bonham, a 15-year Menasha veteran who had previously served as general manager of the molded products division in Watertown, Wisconsin. Bonham inherited a company that generated sales of $68.2 million in 1996, an amount that placed it 71st among North America's largest injection molders according to trade publication *Plastics News*. All three plants were ISO 9002/QS 9000 certified, and the company had well-established relationships with a multitude of customers, as demonstrated by the quality awards it had received over the years from such companies as Eaton, Baxter, Hitachi, Honeywell, Phillips Technologies, United Technologies, and Recovery Engineering.

MEXICO PLANT OPENS: 2001

Revenues held steady into the new century, but like the plastics industry as a whole, Thermotech felt the impact of a downturn in the economy in 2001. In April of that year Thermotech opened a new 54,000-square-foot plant in Queretaro, Mexico. Not only would it be better located to serve customers with operations in Central Mexico, it could offer low-cost manual assembly. The Florida plant, in the meantime, ceased to be economically viable. The smallest of the Thermotech plants, it was no longer ideally located to serve its customers, who had moved their operations elsewhere. As a result, sales that peaked at $12.5 million in 1998 dwindled to less than $7 million in 2000. Management made the decision to shut down the operation at the end of 2001.

In addition to the Florida closing, Thermotech invested in new technologies to maintain a competitive edge, including precision gearing, micromolding, and MuCell microstructural foam technologies. Because of these capabilities and the new plant in Mexico, Thermotech was able to increase sales to $73 million in 2002 and $74 million in 2003. Management was eager to expand further, especially overseas, but found that the company was no longer a good fit for Menasha, which over the past few years had been undergoing a multiyear restructuring program.

The forest products business was spun off in 2001, and other assets were soon to follow as Menasha elected to devote its limited financial resources to its core packaging operation, which accounted for three-quarters of its revenues. In late 2002 Menasha sold the Thermotech division to a management group and Audax Management Co. LLC, a Boston-based private-equity group formed in 1999 with more than $1 billion of capital under management. The CEO of Nash Elmo Industries, one of Audax's portfolio companies, was a member of Thermotech's board of directors and had suggested the deal.

A few weeks after Audax acquired Thermotech, the company announced that it would close the El Paso plant and in the spring of 2004 moved the operation to a facility in nearby Ciudad Juarez. The same customers would be served in the maquiladora region, but the cost of labor would be greatly reduced, providing Thermotech with more of a competitive edge.

ANOTHER NEW OWNER: 2007

Ownership of Thermotech again changed hands in late 2007 when another Minnesota-based company, Pioneer Plastics, Inc., acquired the business. Pioneer was younger than Thermotech, established in a Minneapolis suburb in 1985. It remained very much a small start-up operation until the mid-1990s when it began to win contracts from area *Fortune* 500 companies, allowing it to add employees and equipment. In 2001 Pioneer moved to a new headquarters and plant in Eagan, Minnesota, and a year later initiated an acquisition program to generate further growth.

The addition of Thermotech was part of this strategy, and the company became a key Pioneer asset, along with the Eagan facility, Group Tool Inc. and its two Illinois operations, a manufacturing plant in China, and distribution centers in Ireland, Hungary, and Singapore. In 2009 Thermotech celebrated its 60th anniversary and as a part of Pioneer Plastics appeared to have finally found a home where it could flourish in the years to come.

Ed Dinger

PRINCIPAL COMPETITORS

Blow Molded Products; Don Evans, Inc.; Lomont Molding, Inc.

FURTHER READING

MacFadyen, Kenneth, "Audax Acquires Thermotech," *Buyouts,* January 19, 2004.

Pryweller, Joseph, "Menasha Sells Thermotech to Private Equity Firm Audax," *Plastics News,* January 26, 2004, p. 3.

Renstrom, Roger, "Thermotech's Radunz Ending 40-Year Career," *Plastics News,* January 5, 1997, p. 31.

"Thermotech Celebrates Its 60th Anniversary," *Pioneer Xpress,* Summer 2009, p. 1.

"Thermotech Closing Texas Site," *Plastics News,* February 16, 2004, p. 7.

Wilson, Jon, "Tyrone Plastics Company to Close," *St. Petersburg Times,* October 17, 2001, p. 1.

Thousand Trails Inc.

3801 Parkwood Boulevard, Suite 100
Frisco, Texas 75034-8648
U.S.A.
Telephone: (214) 618-7200
Toll Free: (800) 205-0606
Fax: (214) 618-7324
Web site: http://www.1000trails.com

Wholly Owned Subsidiary of Equity LifeStyle Properties, Inc.
Incorporated: 1991 as USTrails, Inc.
Employees: 2,400
Sales: $89 million (2005 est.)
NAICS: 721211 Recreational Vehicle (RV) Parks and Campgrounds; 721214 Recreational and Vacation Camps

■ ■ ■

Thousand Trails Inc. operates more than 80 membership-based campgrounds under the Thousand Trails, NACO, and Leisure Time banners. The company's camping facilities are located in 22 states and in British Columbia, serving more than 130,000 member customers. These include about 18,000 campsites on 10,000 acres, and feature amenities such as pools and lodges.

ORIGINS

The precursor of Thousand Trails was incorporated in 1969. Milton Kuolt II created the first Thousand Trails campground in Chehalis, Washington, a 90-minute drive from Seattle. Kuolt, in his mid-40s at the time and a 20-year Boeing Company veteran, believed he could make his fortune selling campground memberships, a concept grounded on the premise that Americans would flock to secure, affordable, and well-maintained campground sites for their vacations. For the price of a single extended vacation to Hawaii, for instance, Thousand Trails customers could make a down payment on a lifetime membership, entitling them to visit a variety of locations whenever they chose.

Kuolt's immediate need after establishing the first campground was to develop more sites. At each Thousand Trails campground he wanted to establish a suitable mixture of the pristine outdoors and the security and amenities of a private resort. Typically, two-thirds of the acreage included within a campground was left untouched. The remaining third was developed for the member campers. Recreational vehicle (RV) sites were created, some with electrical and sewer hookups, sheltered from each other by curtains of trees. Clubhouses were built, serving as activity centers for the member campers, many of whom were retirees, and security measures were implemented. The camping complexes were gated, patrolled 24 hours a day by guards.

Providing a controlled environment in a natural setting required considerable development money. Kuolt quickly found himself strapped for cash. In 1976, when Kuolt was attempting to build his portfolio of camping properties, an opportunity arose that revealed the company's dire need for money. Kuolt was presented with the chance to buy 199 acres of defaulted property,

COMPANY PERSPECTIVES

Some campers come just for a fun weekend with their families, while others may camp for weeks, touring the country and enjoying our hospitality from coast to coast. Our members have full access to all of the premium amenities each time they stay with us. Dedicated staff and a loyal membership are two of the reasons for our success. While we are a members-only network, we always welcome new visitors. We invite you to visit soon—it is the only way to appreciate the truly peaceful and beautiful experience at a Thousand Trails preserve.

its mortgage held by a banker who offered to sell it to Kuolt for $1 million. Kuolt believed the acreage was worth half the amount, but the banker stipulated that if Thousand Trails acquired the property for $1 million, the bank would extend the company a $2.5 million credit line.

In an April 11, 1983, interview with *Forbes* magazine, Kuolt explained that the asking price was unacceptable, but he was forced to agree to the terms because of the precarious financial state of his company: "My closest advisers pulled me right out of this room and said, 'Kuolt, we don't give a damn if you push the whole goddamn piece of land into Puget Sound. You sign that ... deal with this banker. You need the cash.'"

FINANCIAL WOES PERSIST

Kuolt was forced to capitulate to the banker's offer, but the $2.5 million credit line did not resolve his company's financial problems. As the expansion of Thousand Trails continued, Kuolt again found himself in need of capital. In 1979, he took Thousand Trails public, turning to an initial public offering (IPO) for a fresh supply of cash. At the time of the company's IPO, liabilities exceeded assets by more than $2 million.

In his 1983 *Forbes* interview, Kuolt conceded, "We were technically bankrupt," but the $5.7 million raised from the IPO relieved the pressure only temporarily. Within a year, Thousand Trails again stood on the brink of financial failure. Marketing expenses had stripped the company of its IPO proceeds. To stay the company's collapse, Kuolt searched for an institution willing to extend Thousand Trails more credit. In 1980, First National Bank of Boston emerged as the company's savior, granting it $10 million of credit, an offer that

Kuolt was forced to accept at 2 percent over the prime rate.

As the 1980s began, Thousand Trails was heavily in debt and suffering from a recurring problem. Escalating operating costs had hamstrung the company, forcing Kuolt to take a new approach to the problem. Instead of treatment, the company needed a cure, which led Kuolt to look at the company's operation from a more detached, objective view. As befitted his candid, no-holds-barred demeanor, Kuolt cast the finger of blame directly on himself.

"You've got to pull yourself away and say, 'Now what's wrong with the company?'" he explained in his 1983 *Forbes* interview, adding that the chairman was "fouling it up." Kuolt stepped down from the chairman's office in 1981, sacrificing himself as a last resort to save Thousand Trails. Later in the year, Kuolt started a new airline company named Horizon Air, while the person he selected to head Thousand Trails grappled with the profound problems hobbling the company's progress.

NEW LEADERSHIP IN 1981

Jim Jensen, a self-described "new age" manager, moved into Kuolt's office in 1981. During the previous two years, Jensen had taken a hiatus from corporate life to pursue readings in metaphysics and psychology and to take a trip to Brazil, where he met with a Brazilian psychic who performed psychokinesis, mental telepathy, and telekinesis. Jensen's avid interest in seeking alternative methods of self-improvement dovetailed with his method of management.

Before his two-year self-exploratory sojourn, Jensen had cemented his reputation as an effective leader at Grantree Furniture Rental, the principal subsidiary of Oregon-based Grantree Corp. Instilling what he called "whole brain" communications in his employees, Jensen spearheaded prolific growth. During his six-year term as president and chief operating officer of Grantree Furniture Rental, Jensen transformed the subsidiary from a 183-employee, $6 million-in-sales operation to a $72 million-in-sales enterprise that employed 1,400 workers.

Jensen's achievements at Grantree Furniture Rental had impressed Kuolt, convincing Kuolt that he had found the person capable of resolving the fundamental problem facing Thousand Trails. The company was suffering because it consistently spent more money than it collected. Lifetime memberships were priced at an average of $6,000, but the middle-income campers who purchased the memberships usually made a down payment equal to only 40 percent of the full price. The

```
┌─────────────────────────────────────────────────────┐
│                                                       │
│                   KEY DATES                           │
│                       ■                               │
│  ─────────────────────────────────────────────────   │
│                                                       │
│  1969:  Thousand Trails, Inc., is formed by Boeing    │
│         veteran Milton Kuolt.                         │
│  1979:  Thousand Trails completes initial public      │
│         offering.                                     │
│  1981:  Kuolt steps down as chairman of the           │
│         company.                                      │
│  1991:  Thousand Trails and NACO are acquired by      │
│         USTrails, Inc.                                │
│  1996:  USTrails changes its name to Thousand Trails, │
│         Inc.                                          │
│  1999:  Thousand Trails acquires Leisure Time         │
│         Resorts of America, Inc.                      │
│  2002:  Headquarters are moved from Dallas to         │
│         Frisco, Texas.                                │
│  2003:  Thousand Trails is acquired by private-equity │
│         firm Kohlberg & Co.                           │
│  2004:  Equity LifeStyle Properties Inc. buys real    │
│         estate holdings of Thousand Trails.           │
│  2006:  Privileged Access buys membership business    │
│         of Thousand Trails.                           │
│  2008:  Equity LifeStyle Properties Inc. buys         │
│         Thousand Trails from Privileged Access.       │
│                                                       │
└─────────────────────────────────────────────────────┘
```

company, which recorded partial payments at the full membership price as revenue on its balance sheet, was spending 45 percent of sales on marketing, rendering it incapable of meeting its cash flow needs. The only way to overcome this obstacle was to borrow money or to sell portions of the company to equity investors, a tactic that could not be used in the long term.

Despite the financial crisis, Jensen pressed ahead with expansion. He inherited 14 campgrounds when he took control in 1981 and over the next two years increased the number of properties to 21. To tide the company over financially, he continued to seek outside sources for infusions of cash, doing what Kuolt had done since the company's birth. When sales reached $56 million in 1982, Jensen brokered a $25 million credit line from a Phoenix-based, state-regulated savings and loan association named Western Savings. In return, Western Savings gained a 24 percent ownership stake in the company. The credit line from Western Savings was dedicated to property acquisition and development, while commercial credit lines, which amounted to another $25 million in 1983, were used to supply working capital.

STRUGGLING WITH DEBT

Thousand Trails was falling deeper and deeper in debt, but as Jensen looked ahead from his vantage point in 1983, his forecast was optimistic. He believed that within two years, the company's ever-growing receivables would collect enough in repayments to finally pay down the company's debt. In the interim, the company was forced to finance its aggressive expansion by continuing to borrow against receivables, further deteriorating its financial health. In 1984, when the company announced a record $19.1 million in earnings, it used $52 million more cash than it produced.

The following year earnings plunged 90 percent to $1.8 million after a considerable number of members dropped out of the company's system before paying for their full memberships, stripping Thousand Trails of revenues it had prematurely recorded. Marketing expenses at this point were two times greater than down payments, saddling the company with a cash shortage of $55 million. When the first-quarter results of 1986 revealed a nearly $2 million loss, expansion came to a stop. Again, company officials endeavored to reduce marketing costs. Debt by the beginning of 1986 represented 244 percent of shareholders' equity.

In 1986 and 1987, Thousand Trails lost a total of $67 million, still unable to generate positive cash flow without the help of financing. The company's financial performance moderately improved in the late 1980s, but by the beginning of the 1990s Thousand Trails stood on the verge of bankruptcy. The company at that time operated one of the largest of membership campground resort systems in the nation, comprising 39 campgrounds situated in 15 states and in British Columbia, but its financial problems were grave.

In 1990 the company obtained financing from only one source, NACO Finance Corp. (NFC), which itself was mired in financial problems. NFC had been created by Southmark Corp. in 1987 to finance some of its subsidiaries, which included Thousand Trails. By 1990, a Southmark subsidiary that owned 68.8 percent of Thousand Trails was in Chapter 11 bankruptcy reorganization, making the position of Thousand Trails that much more untenable. The company managed a $1 million profit on revenues of $100 million in the 1990 fiscal year.

FRESH START IN 1991

For a brief period, a familiar figure emerged as a possible savior for Thousand Trails. Milt Kuolt, who had sold Horizon Air to Alaska Airlines in 1986, had moved on to become chairman of Delta Campground Management Corp., which in November 1990 announced its intention to buy a controlling interest in Thousand

Trails from Southmark's ailing subsidiary, San Jacinto Savings Association of Houston. Kuolt and his company later backed away from the deal, but another deal soon took its place.

In 1991, as part of its own Chapter 11 reorganization efforts, NFC acquired National American Corporation (NACO), a manager of timeshare facilities and full service resorts, and 69 percent of Thousand Trails. The new company was named USTrails, Inc., which operated as the parent company of Thousand Trails. USTrails acquired the remaining interest in Thousand Trails in 1994. Two years later, the entire organization was renamed Thousand Trails, Inc.

Against the backdrop of these significant corporate maneuvers, important changes were made in the way Thousand Trails operated. In April 1992, after years of suffering losses from rising marketing costs, the company suspended its sales program. No new campground memberships were sold, and, in fact, by the fall of 1992, the company began helping its members to sell their memberships in the secondary market. By May 1994, the company was ready to renew its marketing efforts and implemented a sales program to build up its membership base.

Initially, with USTrails governing the operations of Thousand Trails, memberships were sold on a limited basis, but in May 1995 the company introduced a range of new membership options. Before halting its sales program in 1992, the company sold campground memberships for prices up to $8,000, but in 1995 marketing efforts began focusing on a greater number of membership options, available for a wide range of prices. Membership packages were offered that gave customers the option of using one system, either Thousand Trails or NACO, or both, for prices ranging between $495 and $2,495. By 1996, when all of the entities operated under one corporate banner, the average price paid by members for a membership package was $779.

FITFUL PROGRESS

By 1996, after the final merger that created a multifaceted Thousand Trails, the scope of the company's operations comprised several networks of properties. Under the Thousand Trails logo, there were 35 campgrounds, complementing the 23 campgrounds operating under the NACO banner. The 58 campgrounds controlled by the company comprised 19,300 campsites, which were used by 81,000 Thousand Trails members and 47,000 NACO members. In addition, a subsidiary named UST Wilderness Management managed 35 public campgrounds for the U.S. Forest Service,

a service it began providing in 1994.

By the late 1990s, after years of fitful progress, the company continued to be beleaguered by the realities of its business. By the end of the decade, the number of campgrounds controlled by Thousand Trails had been reduced to 53, scattered among 17 states and British Columbia. Sales were on the wane, as was net income, although the company had recorded 10 consecutive quarters of profit by the first quarter of 2000. As Thousand Trails prepared for the future, the emphasis was on increasing its membership base.

Toward this end, the company entered into a joint marketing agreement in 1997 with Fleetwood Industries, Inc., the largest U.S. manufacturer of RVs. Under the terms of the arrangement, purchasers of new Fleetwood RVs received temporary Thousand Trails memberships. In another bid to increase sales, Thousand Trails acquired Leisure Time Resorts of America, Inc., in December 1999, paying $7.7 million in cash and assuming debt of $2.3 million. Leisure Time had been incorporated in 1984 and owned and operated 10 membership campground resorts in Oregon and Washington.

Total revenues were $79.4 million in fiscal 2000–01. In fiscal 2001–02, the last year for Thousand Trails as a public company, revenues reached $89.2 million as net income doubled to $13.2 million. The company had 59 campgrounds with 18,000 campsites on 10,000 acres in 17 states and British Columbia, used by 112,000 members. There were about 70,000 members in the Thousand Trails program, plus 29,000 in NACO, and 13,000 in Leisure Time. New memberships sold for an average of about $3,300, plus annual dues of $400. In addition, the subsidiary Thousand Trails Management Services, Inc., ran 240 public campgrounds on behalf of the U.S. Forest Service and others. Another subsidiary called Resorts Parks International, Inc., operated a reciprocal program involving 64,000 members and 280 facilities.

TAKEN PRIVATE IN 2003

In 2002, lured by local tax incentives, the company relocated its headquarters from Dallas, its home since 1994, to nearby Frisco, Texas. The move affected about 100 employees. Private-equity firm Kohlberg & Co. LLC soon acquired the company for $113 million in 2003. John Malone, formerly a restaurant-industry executive, succeeded Bill Shaw as president and CEO of Thousand Trails in March 2004.

Manufactured Home Communities Inc. (MHC) acquired the real estate holdings of Thousand Trails in November 2004, paying $160 million. MHC aimed to develop 3,000 acres of vacant land included in the purchase. MHC was a real estate investment trust (REIT) based in Chicago that was a spin-off of Sam Zell's real estate empire, publicly traded since 1993. It was renamed Equity LifeStyle Properties, Inc., soon after the acquisition.

At the time, there was a boom in RV use due in part to affluent Americans preferring to vacation closer to home to avoid the hassles and security threats of international airline travel. Thousand Trails invested in upgrading its facilities to suit those who chose to use the parks as destinations in their own right. For those without RVs, in September 2004 the company introduced its Getaway Club, with access to dozens of rental facilities near tourist destinations such as Disney World. The company averaged about $2 million per year in capital improvements, but doubled this in 2005.

CHANGES IN OWNERSHIP

In 2006, Privileged Access, a company founded by former Thousand Trails Chairman Joe McAdams, bought the membership business of Thousand Trails. McAdams had formed Privileged Access in October 2005 after leaving the board of Equity LifeStyle Properties. He had previously been CEO of Affinity Group Inc. of Ventura California. According to *RV Business*, his aim was to expand the number of parks in the Thousand Trails system to more than 100 and to provide more-flexible membership options.

Nearly half of the members of Thousand Trails were senior citizens. The company continued to introduce novel marketing initiatives in order to expand its appeal. In 2007 it announced a plan to team with the Official NASCAR Members Club (ONMC) to provide 15 properties for use as ONMC sites during NASCAR auto-racing events, which were known for attracting large numbers of RVs. In the same year, its Club Blazer program sought to lure children away from sedentary indoor activities and into the outdoors.

In 2008 Equity LifeStyle Properties bought Thousand Trails from Privileged Access. McAdams also became head of Equity LifeStyle Properties during the year. Thousand Trails laid off about 240 employees, most of them administrative, after it was acquired. Acquisitions of new properties were a priority, particularly in Pennsylvania, Michigan, and Florida.

While the economic downturn of 2008 slowed RV sales by a third, the company continued to invest in the upkeep of its properties. In the winter of 2009–10

alone, Thousand Trails spent $2 million to improve roads and upgrade hundreds of campsites.

Jeffrey L. Covell
Updated, Frederick C. Ingram

PRINCIPAL SUBSIDIARIES

MHC TT Memberships Limited Partnership; MHC LTR Memberships Limited Partnership; MHC MAR Memberships Limited Partnership; MHC NAC Memberships Limited Partnership; MHC ODW Memberships Limited Partnership; MHC TT (Canada) Holdings, Inc.; MHC Resort Parks Limited Partnership; Thousand Trails Management Services, Inc.

PRINCIPAL OPERATING UNITS

Thousand Trails; NACO; Leisure Time.

PRINCIPAL COMPETITORS

Kampgrounds of America, Inc.; International Leisure Hosts, Ltd.; Outdoor Resorts of America, Inc.; Affinity Group Holding, Inc.

FURTHER READING

Crider, Jeff, "Joe McAdams' New Privileged Access Buys Thousand Trails Business," *RV Business*, June 2006, pp. 7, 62.

———, "Manufactured Home Communities Inc. Acquires Thousand Trails Properties," *RV Business*, October 2004, pp. 7, 58.

———, "Thousand Trails' Rebound: Membership Firm Is Seeing Profits with a New, No-Nonsense Business Strategy," *RV Business*, October 1998, p. 20.

———, "Thousand Trails Remains in Strong Expansion Mode," *RV Business*, December 2005, p. 105.

Holman, Kelly, "Thousand Trails to Go Private," *Daily Deal*, May 1, 2003.

Kuolt, Lois Petit, *We Called It Thousand Trails: The True Story of a Family's Dream Come True*, Wilsonville, OR: BookPartners, 2000.

McGough, Robert, "Flying High on Debt," *Forbes*, April 11, 1983, p. 93.

"Minding His Business," *Inc.*, November 1983, p. 120.

Neurath, Peter, "Thousand Trails Not Resorting to Real Estate Sales," *Puget Sound Business Journal*, June 11, 1993, p. 13.

———, "Thousand Trails Strives to Fend Off Bankruptcy," *Puget Sound Business Journal*, November 12, 1990, p. 12.

"Not-So-Happy Trails," *Forbes*, July 14, 1986, p. 13.

Perez, Christine, "Cash Lures Thousand Trails to Frisco," *Dallas Business Journal*, May 27, 2002.

Pratte, Bob, "Thousand Trails: No Specific Site, but Members Are Guaranteed of a Place for Camping," *Bend (Ore.) Bulletin*, October 21, 1978, p. 8.

The Timken Company

————■————

1835 Dueber Avenue S.W.
Canton, Ohio 44706
U.S.A.
Telephone: (330) 438-3000
Fax: (330) 458-6006
Web site: http://www.timken.com

Public Company
Incorporated: 1899 as Timken Roller Bearing Axle
  Company
Employees: 16,667
Sales: $3.14 billion (2009)
Stock Exchanges: New York
Ticker Symbol: TKR
NAICS: 332991 Ball and Roller Bearing Manufacturing

■ ■ ■

The Timken Company is a leading manufacturer of friction management and power transmission products, and alloy steels and steel components for such major markets as aerospace, automotive, construction, defense, energy, industrial equipment, heavy industry, machine tool, power generation, and rail. The company's flagship product is the tapered rolling bear, for which the company's founder received a pair of patents in the late 1880s.

Timken also offers other types of bearings, power transmission components and systems, alloy steel and steel components, engineered surfaces and coatings, motion control systems, seals, and bearing lubricants. Maintaining its headquarters in Canton, Ohio, Timken operates 61 plants, nearly half of which are ISO certified, 15 distribution centers, and a dozen technology centers spread across the world. Timken is a *Fortune* 500 company listed on the New York Stock Exchange, controlled by the fifth generation of the Timken family.

ORIGINS

Henry Timken founded the earliest form of The Timken Company in St. Louis in 1899. Timken had entered the carriage business as an apprentice 40 years earlier at the age of 16. By the time he was 24, Timken had opened his own carriage shop. In 1877 Timken received the patent for the Timken Buggy Spring, the first of his 13 patents. His spring design became widely used throughout the country, and was produced on a royalty basis by a number of companies. As a result of the spring's success, Timken became well known across the United States, and his carriage business flourished. Around 1895 Timken took an interest in the problems created by friction in wagon design. In 1898 the patent was issued for the Timken tapered roller bearing. The new bearing was a dramatic improvement over the ball bearings and straight roller bearings that had previously been used. The following year, the founder and his two sons, William and Henry (H. H.) Timken, organized the Timken Roller Bearing Axle Company. It produced axles that used the new bearing in their design.

Within the next couple of years, the axle business began to outgrow its allotted space in the St. Louis carriage plant, and in 1902 the company relocated to Canton, Ohio. Canton was seen as an ideal midpoint between Detroit, home of the automotive industry, and

Pittsburgh, a major steel-producing city. By that time, the Timkens had recognized the future importance of the automobile, and worked to develop bearings tailored to the needs of that young industry. When Henry Ford introduced the automobile assembly line and the Model T that it produced in 1908, the demand for Timken bearings and axles grew exponentially.

HENRY TIMKEN DIES: 1909

In 1909 the Timken brothers moved the axle division to Detroit, launching the new Timken-Detroit Axle Company with William Timken as its president. The Canton operation continued to manufacture bearings, and its name was changed to The Timken Roller Bearing Company. By 1909, the year Henry Timken died, the company was turning out over 850,000 bearings a year, and it employed about 1,200 people.

Timken began to produce its own steel in 1915 as a way to ensure an adequate supply for its manufacturing in the face of shortages created by World War I. That year, the company added a steel tube mill to its Canton facilities. A year later a melt shop was added. With the inclusion of these steel works, Timken became the first bearing manufacturer to act as its own supplier of steel for its products. The company was soon producing steel in quantities far greater than its own manufacturing needs. It therefore began marketing its alloy steel to outside buyers, with such companies as Mack Truck among its early regular customers. In 1919 the Industrial Division was organized, taking the place of the company's Farm Implement and Tractor Division. The mission of the Industrial Division was to develop bearings for a wide variety of industrial uses, including electric motors, elevators, and printing presses.

The market for Timken bearings and steel continued to expand quickly throughout the 1920s. In 1920 the company opened the Columbus Bearing Plant,

its first facility outside of Canton. The same year, a waste treatment plant was built at the Canton facility. Timken stock went on sale to the public for the first time in 1922, and the company opened an assembly plant in Canada that year.

Timken bearings found their way into the railroad industry in 1923, when bearings specially designed by Timken were tested first on an intercity streetcar running between Canton and Cleveland, and later that year in a boxcar on the Wheeling and Lake Erie Railroad. By 1926, other railroads recognized that the tapered bearings would allow the speed of their trains to increase. A large order was placed by the Chicago, Milwaukee, St. Paul & Pacific railroad for use in its high-speed trains, such as the Burlington Zephyr and the Santa Fe Super Chief.

EXPANSION: 1925–29

Timken began acquiring smaller companies in the mid-1920s. In 1925 the company purchased the assets of Gilliam Manufacturing Co., a Canton-based roller bearing producer. The Bock Bearing Co. of Toledo, Ohio, was acquired the following year. In 1927 Timken purchased a large interest in British Timken Ltd. from Vickers Ltd., which had been manufacturing Timken bearings and axles under license since 1909. Timken went on to acquire the remainder of the British operation in 1959. The Weldless Steel Company's Wooster, Ohio, piercing mill was purchased in 1928. That year also brought the creation of Société Anonyme Française Timken (SAFT), a French subsidiary of British Timken. In 1929 Timken purchased a 177-acre block of land adjacent to the company's existing facilities in Canton and opened two new plants, the Gambrinus Steel Plant and the Gambrinus Bearing Plant.

In spite of the Great Depression, Timken continued to grow steadily through the 1930s. During the early 1930s the company developed bearings for propeller driveshafts, thereby expanding its customer base to include shipbuilders and the U.S. Navy. In 1932 Timken began manufacturing removable rock bits for construction and mining equipment. The production of the rock bits provided a much needed outlet for the company's steel in the face of a badly depressed steel market. By that year, British Timken had stretched to another continent, opening a manufacturing subsidiary in South Africa in 1932. In 1934 William Umstattd became president of Timken, succeeding H. H. Timken, who stayed on as chairman of the board. The company's Mt. Vernon Rock Bit Plant opened the following year. When H. H. Timken died in 1940, his son, H. H. Timken Jr. became the chairman of Timken's board of directors.

KEY DATES

1899: Timken Roller Bearing Axle Company is founded.
1954: The patented AP bearing is introduced.
1970: The Timken Company name is adopted.
1975: Latrobe Steel Company is acquired.
1989: Plant modernization effort begins.
2000: Restructuring program is launched.
2003: Torrington Company is acquired.
2007: Automotive Group is eliminated.

The onset of World War II provided the momentum for Timken's continued growth in the 1940s. To meet increasing wartime demand for its products, Timken opened several new facilities in Ohio during this period. In 1941, for example, the Timken Ordnance Company was built in Canton, where about 80,000 gun tubes were manufactured over the next couple of years. The Zanesville Bearing Plant was opened in 1943. Other new locations included Columbus and Newton Falls. During the war, the company's output more than doubled its previous peak. In 1948 Timken began experimenting with automation, beginning a pilot project at a plant in Bucyrus, Ohio. The project was an instant success, and a brand-new plant was built in 1950.

Meanwhile, Timken was the subject of an antitrust suit brought by the Justice Department around the same time. After several levels of appeals, the Supreme Court ruled in 1951 that Timken had conspired with its foreign affiliates (British and French Timken) in restraint of trade. The case, initiated in 1947, came about as a result of agreements between the companies regarding sales territories, price coordination, exchange of exclusive information, and other practices. The Court's ruling indicated that a company must compete with other companies in which it holds a substantial interest if that company is not a legal subsidiary.

POSTWAR EXPANSION

In 1954 Timken introduced the "AP" bearing, an innovation that would have a great impact on the railroad industry. The AP was a preassembled, prelubricated, self-contained bearing that was inexpensive and easily integrated into nearly any type of railroad car. The new bearing was credited with dramatically reducing the number of freight car set-outs. The AP bearing was initially produced at Timken's Columbus plant. So quickly did demand for it grow, however, that by 1958, the new Columbus Railroad Bearing Plant was opened. In 1956 the Bucyrus Distribution Center was opened. The Distribution Center was a huge warehouse, from which bearings were shipped to customers throughout the United States, as well as to the company's foreign plants. In 1958 Australia became the fourth continent on which Timken operations took place, with the opening of a bearing plant at Ballarat, Victoria. That year, SAFT was officially merged into Timken, and its name was changed to Timken France. Timken purchased the remaining shares of British Timken the following year.

Around this time, Timken began its expansion into South America. A sales subsidiary was established in Argentina in 1959. The next year saw the opening of the São Paulo Bearing Plant in Brazil. Also in 1960, W. Robert Timken (another son of H. H. Timken) replaced Umstattd as company president. Timken's sales continued to grow steadily through the first half of the 1960s, climbing from $240 million in 1961 to $393 million in 1966.

In 1963 production began at the company's new Colmar Plant in France. Timken Research, a sprawling research and development center located near the Akron-Canton Airport, was completed in 1966. Railroad companies continued to grow in importance as customers during this period. By 1968, more than 90 percent of the new freight cars being built used tapered roller bearings, and more than 60 percent of those bearings were made by Timken.

FOREIGN SALES TRIPLE

During the second half of the 1960s, Timken's sales leveled off, and net income actually shrank, from $49 million in 1966 to $29 million in 1970. The portion of this income that came from foreign sales tripled between 1967 and 1970. In 1968 a continuous casting plant was added to the company's steelmaking facilities. By 1969 the plant had a capacity of 850,000 tons. The company's Ashland Plant was opened in 1969 as well. Timken had a total of 16 plants in operation by 1971, seven of which were in Ohio. Tapered roller bearings and rock bits accounted for about 80 percent of Timken's revenue that year, with specialty steels generating the rest of the company's sales. At that time, about 35 different types of roller bearings were being produced in over 11,000 sizes at its facilities.

H. H. Timken Jr. died in 1968, and was succeeded as chairman by his brother W. Robert Timken. The company presidency was assumed by Herbert Markley, who had joined the company as an accountant nearly 30 years earlier. In 1970 the corporation's name was officially shortened to The Timken Company. The following year, the Gaffney Bearing Plant, a highly automated facility in South Carolina, was opened. Timken was hurt in 1970 by strikes at General Motors and in the trucking industry. By 1972, however, sales were once again strong in the automotive industry, which, as a whole, was the purchaser of nearly half of the bearings sold by Timken. As a result, Timken's sales began to grow once again, reaching a company record of $470 million in 1972. In 1974 a wholly owned sales subsidiary, Nihon Timken K.K., was formed in Japan.

W. R. TIMKEN TAKES CHARGE: 1975

W. Robert Timken stepped down in 1975, and was replaced as chairman of the board by his son, W. R. Timken Jr. That year Timken acquired Latrobe Steel Company, a Pennsylvania-based producer of specialty steel and alloys. For 1975 Timken was able to post record sales of $804 million, in spite of a terrible year in the automobile industry. In 1978 construction was completed on the company's Canton Water Purification Plant.

Timken introduced the UNIPAC bearing in 1979. These prelubricated and preadjusted bearings made assembly operations much easier for vehicle, industrial machinery, and construction equipment manufacturers. Timken also opened the Lincolnton Bearing Plant that year. The Lincolnton plant, located 50 miles north of Gaffney in North Carolina, featured such advanced automation as driverless trains that transported parts between departments. Markley faced mandatory retirement as company president in 1979. He was succeeded by Joseph F. Toot Jr., a Timken employee since 1962.

As the 1980s began, Timken was still the dominant force in the American bearing industry, controlling about 25 percent of the U.S. bearings market, and 75 percent of the market for tapered roller bearings. In 1981 the company earned $101 million on sales of $1.4 billion. The 1980s proved to be a difficult decade for Timken, however. The company reported a loss of $3 million in 1982, its first unprofitable year since the Depression.

Part of the problem was the flood of low-cost bearings entering the United States from Europe and Japan. Nevertheless, Timken did not stop investing in its facilities during this time. In 1983 an expansion project that doubled the size of Timken Research was completed. The company's $450 million Faircrest Steel Plant went into production in 1985. Upon the opening of the plant, which was situated not far from Canton, Timken's steelmaking capacity increased by 50 percent to 1.5 million tons.

In 1986 Timken reorganized its corporate structure, cutting costs by consolidating departments and eliminating personnel. The Rock Bit Division was sold off entirely. A new division, the Original Equipment–Bearings group, was formed by combining the Industrial Division with the Automotive and Railroad Divisions. In addition, all Research and Development functions and computer operations were organized into a newly created Technology Center.

After six years of showing little or no profit, Timken rebounded in 1988, earning $65.9 million on net sales of $1.55 billion. During that year offices were opened in Italy, Korea, Singapore, and Venezuela. The following year, a 37-day strike by steelworkers prevented a significant continuation of the rally. Nevertheless, a $1 billion multiyear investment program was launched in 1989 to modernize and expand the company's plants. In 1990 Timken paid $185 million for MPB Corporation, a manufacturer of superprecision bearings (used in sensitive machinery such as aircraft, computer disk drives, and medical equipment) based in Keene, New Hampshire, with annual sales of $120 million.

LATE-CENTURY RETOOLING

Timken's sales declined slightly in both 1991 and 1992, largely due to reduced demand caused by the global recession. For 1991, the company recorded a net loss of $36 million. Through an active streamlining program, Timken was able to turn a modest profit of $4.45 million in 1992 without making any gains in sales. In April 1993 the company announced the formation of a steel sales unit in Europe, its first such steel operation outside of the United States. Efforts to improve manufacturing efficiency and to reduce costs throughout the corporation continued. In 1993 the company began operations at a steel parts plant in Eaton, Ohio. Latrobe Steel planned to open a new facility in Franklin, Pennsylvania, in 1994.

That same year, Timken's most advanced plant to date opened in Asheboro, North Carolina, at a cost of $120 million. Its automated features allowed the company to produce small batches of custom bearings in a matter of days, rather than weeks, reported *Forbes*. Another new factory was opened in Singapore to produce the minuscule bearings used in computer disk drives. Even as these facilities were being constructed, the company's annual earnings were reaching their highest levels since 1988, although the company had lost money in 1991 and 1993. By 1996 earnings had risen to $138.9 million. Analysts attributed the performance to reducing production costs and finding niches outside the company's traditional, cyclical lines of business.

In late 1997 Toot retired as president and CEO. Chairman William R. Timken Jr., great-grandson of the company founder, took over Toot's duties. After an all-time record first quarter, the Asian financial crisis resulted in reduced orders for farm equipment and less business for Timken in the second half of 1998. For the year, income fell from $171 million to $114 million, on sales of $2.7 billion. Timken's share price also fell during the year, from $41 to $13.

NEW CENTURY TRANSFORMATION

In the face of excess industry capacity, Timken trimmed 1,700 jobs as the 1990s came to a close. At the dawn of the millennium the company launched a restructuring effort to better position Timken for the next century by focusing on value-added products and services for its global customers. It was so radical a departure that it was dubbed internally as "the transformation." As part of a plan to cut annual costs by $120 million and embrace a trend towards smaller, more specialized factories, a bearing plant in England was closed, as was a railroad bearing plant in Columbus, Ohio, and a tooling plant in Ashland, Ohio, was put on the block. Although sales of excess steel made up one-third of Timken's revenues, the company relied more heavily on outside sources as it expanded production into such countries as China and India. The company also adopted more efficient processes, opting for hot-forging over metal-cutting in some instances.

Changes in the top management ranks were in the offing as well. With William Timken approaching the mandatory retirement age of 65, the board of directors elected James W. Griffith to succeed him as chief executive officer in the summer of 2002. The 48-year-old Griffith had been with the company since 1984 and held a number of positions throughout the company before being named president, chief operating officer, and director in 1999. William Timken remained chairman of the board until 2003 when he reached age 65 and became nonexecutive chairman. In 2005 Ward J. Timken succeeded him as chairman and William Timken, a major donor to President George W. Bush, was named U.S. ambassador to Germany.

TORRINGTON COMPANY ACQUIRED: 2003

Soon after Griffith took over as CEO, Timken engineered the largest acquisition in its history, reaching an agreement to buy Torrington Company from Ingersoll-Rand Co. for $700 million in cash and $140 million in stock. The deal, which closed in February 2003, made Timken the third-largest company among global bearings makers and bolstered its position in Asia, Europe, India, and Latin America. The Torrington operation included 27 manufacturing plants in 24 countries.

While the automotive markets struggled, Timken experienced strong sales with industrial customers, leading to the company reaching the $5 billion mark in revenues in 2005. The transform of the company was far from complete, however. In 2007 a major reorganization was instituted. The Auto Group was eliminated, leaving the Bearings and Power Transmission Group and the Steel Group. The operations of the Auto Group were now folded into the Mobile Industries division of the new Power Transmission group, part of an effort to reduce the company's exposure to the problems of the automotive industry. The changes were made to streamline decision making to improve financial performance as well as trim expenses by another $10 million to $20 million.

Timken's industrial business, especially in Asia, was becoming the key driver of growth. In 2008 new plants opened in Chennai, India, and Chengdu, China, to support the company's expansion in the global industrial markets. Timken also looked for new opportunities, such as the growing wind market which used massive turbines that relied on the kinds of bearings and components that were Timken's strong suit. In 2008 a South Carolina plant was expanded to serve this market, and in 2009 a new plant in China to produce large bore bearing for the Chinese wind energy market was opened in conjunction with Xiangtan Electric Manufacturing Co., Ltd. At the time, the sale of windmill components generated less than $50 million a year, but it was expected to soon emerge as Timken's fastest-growing sector.

Wind energy component sales were especially welcome because of a global recession that reduced earnings in 2009 and led to cuts in the workforce. Timken also continued to reduce its exposure to the auto industry. In 2009 the company sold its needle roller bearing division in Canton for $330 million. Because of its long-term reorganization, Timken was not only well positioned to weather rough conditions, it was poised to take advantage of lean times to acquire assets at reasonable prices that could bring new competencies to drive future growth.

Robert R. Jacobson
Updated, Frederick C. Ingram; Ed Dinger

PRINCIPAL DIVISIONS

Bearings and Power Transmission Group; Steel Group.

PRINCIPAL COMPETITORS

NSK Ltd.; Aktiebolaget SFK; United States Steel Corporation.

FURTHER READING

Byrne, Harlan S., "Timken Co.: It Spends Big to Compete in Global Bearings Market," *Barron's*, August 6, 1990, pp. 31–32.

Dix, R. Victor, "Steel Industry Still Competitive, Timken Boasts," *Wooster (Ohio) Daily Record*, May 6, 1997, p. B1.

From Missouri to Mars—A Century of Leadership in Manufacturing, Canton: The Timken Company, 1998.

Gerdel, Thomas W., "Timken Abandons Tradition," *Cleveland Plain Dealer*, May 3, 2001, p. 1C.

———, "Timken Marks First Century," *Cleveland Plain Dealer*, April 24, 1999, p. 1C.

Hardy, Eric S., "The Soul of an Old Company," *Forbes*, March 13, 1995, p. 70.

History of the Timken Company, Canton: Timken Company, 1990.

Irwin, Gloria, "CEO Upbeat as Bearing Manufacturer Timken Increases Hiring," *Akron Beacon*, September 25, 2004.

Mackinnon, Jim, "Timken Adopts New Strategies," *Akron Beacon*, February 21, 2008.

———, "Timken Plans Major Reorganization," *Akron Beacon*, August 14, 2007.

Marsh, Peter, "Making Bearings a Family Affair," *Financial Times*, June 30, 1999, p. 7.

Rozic, Jeff, "W. R. 'Tim' Timken," *Inside Business*, October 2001, p. B54.

Sacco, John, "Timken Hands the Wheel to James Griffith," *American Metal Market*, August 1, 2002, p. 4.

———, "Timken Reducing Work Force in Refocus," *American Metal Market*, April 18, 2001, p. 12.

Shingler, Dan, "Japanese Firm Buys Timken Arm, Bets on Autos," *Crain's Cleveland Business*, January 18, 2010, p. 6.

Siuru, Bill, "Timken's 100 Years: From Buggies to Boxsters," *Ward's Auto World*, August 1999, pp. 65–66.

Thomas, Dana L., "Rough to Smooth," *Barron's*, March 6, 1972, p. 3.

Weiss, Gary, "Timken's Folly?" *Barron's*, November 25, 1985, p. 13.

Wilder, Clinton, "Timken: A Big Step for an Old-Line Industry," *Informationweek*, September 13, 1999, p. 50.

Tipiak S.A.

——————●——————

CP 1011
Saint-Herblain, F-44806 Cedex
France
Telephone: (+33 02) 23 03 09 30
Fax: (+33 02) 28 03 99 60
Web site: http://www.tipiak.fr

Public Company
Incorporated: 1967
Employees: 1,190
Sales: EUR 154.68 million ($220 million) (2009)
Stock Exchanges: Euronext Paris
Ticker Symbol: 066482 (TIPI)
NAICS: 311412 Frozen Specialty Food Manufacturing;
    311812 Commercial Bakeries; 311813 Frozen
    Bakery Product Manufacturing

■ ■ ■

Tipiak S.A. is a leading French specialty foods producer operating in both the dry grocery and frozen foods sectors. Historically known as a tapioca importer, Tipiak has evolved into diversified food groups producing a range of products from food starch, thickeners, and other additives, to high-end frozen ready meals. The company operates through two main divisions, Dry Foods and Cold Foods. The Cold Foods division is its largest, generating two-thirds of the group's annual sales of EUR 155 million ($220 million) in 2009. This division include the frozen ready meals business unit, known especially for its scallops and other seafood-based meals; and cocktail products, featuring a range of sweet and savory snacks.

The Dry Foods division includes the group's historic dry grocery unit, which includes the production of tapioca, breadcrumbs, semolina for couscous, quinoa, and other pulse and grain preparations. This unit also produces additives for the food industry, including starches and texturizers. Bread products, the smallest business unit, includes the group's line of croutons as well as ready-made bread-based products such as crepes and piecrusts.

Tipiak is present across a broad spectrum of sales channels. The major supermarket chains account for 31 percent of sales. Most of the group's sales are made under the Tipiak brand name. The company also generates 12 percent of sales through the production of private and discount label foods. The retail frozen foods distribution sector, made up of supermarket chains and delivery services that specialize in frozen food products, accounts for 36 percent of the group's revenues. The company also supplies the restaurant and industrial foods sectors.

Tipiak is also present on the international market and includes a U.S.-based sales and marketing subsidiary. Tipiak operates eight factories, primarily located in France's west coastal region. The company's headquarters are located in Saint-Herblain, near Nantes. Tipiak is listed on the Euronext Paris Stock Exchange. The company is led by CEO Hubert Groues. The founding Groult and Billard families each maintain a 37 percent share of Tipiak.

TAPIOCA IMPORTERS IN THE 19TH CENTURY

For many French people, tapioca represented the start of their day and remained a fixture on the French breakfast table throughout most of the 20th century. Tapioca, derived from the manioc root, had been a staple part of the diet of many of the indigenous peoples in the Caribbean and in Central and South America, as well as other parts of the world. French colonial expansion during the early part of the 19th century brought France into contact with tapioca and other new pulses, such as arrowroot. The import of these and other products from the French colonies, including cacao, coffee, sugar, and spices, developed into a major industry during the 18th and 19th centuries. This period also saw the growth of most of the country's great family-owned trading houses.

The Groult family's involvement in the colonial food trade began in 1830 when Thomas Groult founded a business in Paris. In 1831 Groult acquired a retail shop called the Bazar des Comestibles in the French capital that featured, among other products, a range of flours, grains, and other starches. Groult began building a network of suppliers and agents in a number of countries, including the French colonies, as well as in other regions. By 1836 Groult had also established contacts with Brazil. That country became one of Groult's most important trade markets.

Another prominent trading family appeared on the scene in the second half of the 19th century. By then, Nantes, near France's west coast, had emerged as a major center of the country's foreign trade. In 1879 Georges Billard founded a new company, Etablissements Billard, which began importing a range of products from France's colonial empire, including sugar, cocoa, spices, and tapioca. The country's colonial phase reached its peak toward the end of the century, epitomized by its famous clipper ships, including the *Belem*, launched in 1896.

The launch of that vessel inspired Billard to create its own brand, called Petit Navire, or Little Ship,

introduced that same year. The brand name evolved into Veritable Petit Navire, and the triple-mast clipper ship was to remain a company symbol into the 21st century. Billard's business continued to expand in the 20th century, with the company adding its first industrial operations, including a sugar refinery.

MERGING FAMILIES IN 1967

By the 1930s both Billard and Groult focused more and more on the tapioca market. By then, tapioca had become an important ingredient for a large number of food preparations. At the same time, tapioca had become a staple of the French breakfast, touted not only for its health benefits but also as an inexpensive way to fill the stomach. This became especially important amid the food shortages during and following World War II. As a result, the tapioca market expanded steadily into the 1950s. By 1955 Billard alone claimed to sell as many as 70,000 boxes of tapioca per day.

Demand for tapioca began to taper off in the 1960s, however. This was in large part because the rising affluence of French society had made a variety of new breakfast foods more affordable. At the same time, the food industry had begun to develop a variety of new food additives capable of replacing tapioca in a growing number of recipes. By the middle of the 1960s, tapioca had begun losing ground, bought by just 50 percent of French consumers. By the 1970s, that figure had dropped to one-third.

The tapering off of the tapioca market led its two leaders, Billard and Groult, to merge in 1967. The new company, which set up headquarters in Nantes, took the name of Tipiak, based on the Amazon Indian name for tapioca. The company maintained its Veritable Petit Navire brand for its tapioca, rice, and other products. Tapioca remained the company's major product, at 50 percent of its annual sales.

DIVERSIFICATION STRATEGY

Tipiak set into motion a new strategy of diversification as the tapioca market continued to shrink in the 1970s. The company sought out new product categories, leading to the launch of production of semolina for couscous, a popular dish in France introduced as a result of its former colonial presence in Algeria and Morocco. Tipiak's entry into semolina sales enabled the company to build and hold a leadership position in this niche market in France.

The success of its semolina operation led Tipiak to invest further in developing a new dry grocery products division. Rather than create its new division entirely

KEY DATES

1830: Thomas Groult founds a trading business in Paris.

1879: Georges Billard launches a trading business in Nantes.

1967: Billard and Groult merge to form Tipiak, based in Nantes.

1984: Tipiak launches a U.S. sales subsidiary.

1988: Tipiak goes public on the Paris Stock Exchange.

1996: Tipiak adds sweet and savory cocktail snacks through the addition of Duteil.

2000: Tipiak launches its fourth business unit, bread products, through the acquisition of Gesnoin.

2008: Tipiak moves its headquarters to Saint-Herblain.

from scratch, however, Tipiak moved to take over an existing producer, Naux-Hardiau, also based in Nantes. That company had been founded in 1884 and had long specialized in the production of dried legumes, as well as spices, coffee, and manioc. By the end of the century, Tipiak's market share in certain of its dry grocery categories in the supermarket sector reached near-monopoly status.

Tipiak also moved to take control of its tapioca production. In 1978 the company built its own factory, in Saint-Aignan de Grand-Lieu, near Nantes. There the company introduced industrial manufacturing methods which helped drive down the costs of tapioca production. At the same time, the group developed a wider range of tapioca-based products, from larger grains to finer powders. In this way, the company reduced the effects of the declining consumer market by boosting its range of tapioca-based ingredients and additives for the food industry.

Tipiak's success in France led the company to develop its sales in the international market as well. Toward this end the company created a sales team covering Germany, the United Kingdom, and beyond. The company also created a new subsidiary, Tipiak Inc., in Connecticut in the United States, in 1984. In the next century, the company extended its sales reach to some 40 countries. However, Tipiak's International division accounted for less than 10 percent of the group's total sales.

PUBLIC OFFERING IN 1988

France remained Tipiak's core market. However, the company faced new pressures in the 1980s as the rise of the large-scale distribution groups, such as Auchan, LeClerc, Carrefour, and Casino, created a major shift in French shopping habits and in consumption trends as well. The rise of the two-job family became another important factor in the changing French kitchen, as more and more people sought alternatives to home cooking. This trend was encouraged by the major distribution groups, which eagerly promoted higher-margin prepared foods to their customers.

As a result, French consumers increasingly abandoned home cooking, leading to new declines in the dry grocery segment. Tipiak responded in a number of ways, including developing new formulations and packaging for its semolina and other products in order to make them easier to prepare. At the same time, Tipiak recognized the opportunities offered by the large-scale supermarket groups and particularly their ever-expanding frozen foods aisles. A move into frozen foods also offered a second growing distribution channel, that of frozen foods home delivery by such groups as Agrigel and Picard, which had appeared with the arrival of the first home freezers in the 1950s.

Tipiak began developing its own range of frozen foods starting in 1984. This effort hit its stride at the end of the decade as the company completed two major acquisitions: Charrongel, based in Marans, and Celva, based in Quimper. These purchases also helped guide the direction of the group's frozen food operations, which turned toward the production of high-end seafood ready meals such as scallops.

In order to provide fuel for this expansion, the company went public in 1988, listing its shares on the Paris Stock Exchange's Secondary Market. As a result, the founding Groult and Billard families reduced their own shareholdings to 37 percent each. Neither family remained active in the company's direction, however. Instead, CEO Alain Bouleau led the group's growth during the 1980s. Under his leadership, Tipiak launched a major investment drive through the end of the decade.

By 1990 the company had spent more than FRF 150 million, including the construction a new frozen foods factory in Marans. This effort allowed the company quickly to claim a 13 percent share of the total market. By the end of that year, the company's sales neared FRF 450 million (approximately $60 million).

TIPIAK BRAND ESTABLISHED

Tipiak's investments had given the group's new frozen foods division a running start, but had also saddled the company with a debt burden of more than FRF 260 million. Despite the group's rising revenues, its profits plummeted, and at the end of 1990 Tipiak posted a net loss of more than FRF 21 million. The company's financial difficulties soon led to rumors that it might be sold.

That fate was avoided, however, through financial restructuring. Tipiak also brought in a new general manager, Herbert Groues, to lead a restructuring of the group's operations. Groues had gained experience with another major Nantes-region food company, Biscuiteries Nantaises. Under Groues, the company reorganized, eliminating a number of jobs, and focused its growth efforts more solidly on expanding its frozen foods operations. At that time, the company created a new two-division structure based around its dry grocery and frozen foods operations.

Groues, who became the company's CEO in 1992, also led a revamping of the company's product lines, and particularly its frozen foods specialties. By 1994 the company had revised or replaced all of its frozen foods products, targeting the higher end and seeking a higher-quality image. Concurrent with this effort, the company, which had retained its Veritable Petit Navire brand for its dry grocery business, set out to establish Tipiak as a new national, and even international, brand name for the first time. Toward this end, the company rolled out a massive advertising campaign, including print, radio, and television spots, starting in 1992. The effort was singularly successful, and by the dawn of the new century the company claimed recognition rates of more than 90 percent across France.

NEW BUSINESSES IN THE 21ST CENTURY

By the middle of the 1990s Tipiak had succeeded in reducing its debt load to FRF 88 million, while rebuilding its annual sales past FRF 450 million. The company had also returned to profits, making a net gain of 14 million in 1994. By then, tapioca sales represented just 7 percent of the group's total.

Through the first half of the 1990s, Tipiak had concentrated on its restructuring effort and on expanding distribution of its existing food lines. With its return to growth, the company began seeking new expansion opportunities. This led the company to make a new acquisition in 1996, of Société Nouvelle Duteil, based in Malville, not far from Nantes. The addition of Duteil gave the company a new line of sweet and savory cocktail snacks, including both fresh and frozen specialties. This new operation then provided the basis

for a third company business unit, cocktail products. Duteil also added nearly FRF 30 million to Tipiak's revenue base.

Under Tipiak, the cocktail products business grew rapidly, more than doubling in scale by 1999. The particularly strong growth of its fresh food products encouraged the company to expand its capacity in this segment. For this, Tipiak acquired a factory in Saint-Herblain formerly owned by Unilever. This factory was converted to the production of so-called "surprise" breads and other savory cocktail foods. In 2002 the group began construction of a second factory, dedicated to the production of sweet pastries, in Pont Château.

By then, with the purchase in 2000 of Gesnoin, based in Normandy, Tipiak had added its fourth business unit, bread products. Gesnoin not only added nearly EUR 15 million to the group's total sales, but also its line of crusty bread products, including croutons and ready-made pie shells. Tipiak's rebranded crouton operations quickly gained a near monopoly in France's large-scale distribution sector. Tipiak's frozen foods business unit also grew during this time, with the purchase of the Gourmandise de Fanny brand in 2001.

NEW HEADQUARTERS IN 2008

Tipiak had achieved a good balance among its various operations by the end of the decade. The group's frozen prepared foods, cocktail products, and dry grocery business units each represented approximately one-third of the group's total revenues, complemented by the smaller bread products division. The company's annual sales remained relatively stable during the decade, topping EUR 135 million in 2001 and reaching a high of EUR 162.8 million ($223 million) in 2008.

Tipiak continued to invest in expanding its manufacturing capacity through the decade. In 2004 the group decided to concentrate part of its frozen food production into a single, larger factory in Fouesnant. This was followed by factory expansions in Saint-Herblain in 200 and in Pont-Château in 2007. In 2008 Tipiak moved to new headquarters in Saint-Herblain.

Also in 2008, Tipiak announced its intention to seek new acquisitions in order to expand its bread products sales to meet the level of its three larger foods operations. Through 2009, however, as the global economic crisis of the period intensified, Tipiak was forced to put this expansion effort on hold. Indeed, by the end of the year, the downturn had caught up to the company, forcing its own revenues down to less than EUR 155 million for the year. Tipiak, which continued to feature the clipper ship as part of its logo, hoped for smoother sailing in the years to come.

M. L. Cohen

PRINCIPAL SUBSIDIARIES

Gesnoin Espana; Tipiak Epicerie; Tipiak Inc. (USA); Tipiak Panification; Tipiak Plats Cuisinés Surgelés; Tipiak Traiteur Pâtissier.

PRINCIPAL DIVISIONS

Dry Foods; Cold Foods.

PRINCIPAL OPERATING UNITS

Tipiak Cocktail Products; Tipiak Crusty Bread Products; Tipiak Dry Grocery; Tipiak Frozen Ready Meals; Tipiak International.

PRINCIPAL COMPETITORS

Associated British Foods PLC; Danisco A/S; Danish Crown AmbA; Dr. August Oetker KG; McCain GmbH; Nestlé S.A.; Orkla ASA; Unilever N.V.

FURTHER READING

Guimard, Emmanuel, "Tipiak Investit 30 Millions pour Renforcer Ses Moyens Industriels," *Les Echos*, May 2, 2006, p. 24.

"L'Appetit de Tipiak Ne Tarit Pas," *Journal du Net*, February 27, 2007.

LeGoff, Y., "Tipiak en Recul de 5%," *LSA*, February 5, 2010.

Lewis, Robyn, and Rachel Potter, "Selling France to the British," *Grocer*, March 29, 2008, p. 37.

"A New Plant for Tipiak," *Les Echos*, July 3, 2002.

"Tipiak Prêt à des Acquisitions pour Equlibrer Ses Activités," *LSA*, April 10, 2008.

"Tipiak's Q3 Helped by Recovery in September," *Flexnews*, October 21, 2009.

"Tipiak, une Entreprise Ouverte sur l'Atlantique," *LSA*, April 20, 2000.

Todd, Stuart, "Tipiak Embarks on Investment Programme," *just-food.com*, March 26, 2007.

Town Pump Inc.

600 South Main Street
Butte, Montana 59702
U.S.A.
Telephone: (406) 497-6700
Fax: (406) 497-6704
Web site: http://www.townpump.com

Private Company
Incorporated: 1959
Employees: 1,800
Sales: $1.48 billion (2008 est.)
NAICS: 424720 Petroleum and Petroleum Products
    Merchant; 713210 Casinos (Except Casino Hotels)

■ ■ ■

Town Pump Inc. is a Butte, Montana-based company that houses the business interests of the Kenneally family. At the core of the company are about 80 independently owned and operated Town Pump convenience stores spread across Montana, many of them in small and midsize towns. About 20 are larger units located on major highways and serve as truck stops and travel plazas, offering such driver amenities as television lounges and showers. Town Pump has also built upon its convenience store chain to take advantage of Montana's gambling laws that permit bars and taverns to operate as many as 20 video poker and keno gaming devices.

Town Pump has courted controversy by opening Montana-style "casinos" as adjuncts to their convenience stores. They are operated under a variety of banners, including Lucky Lil's, Montana Lil's, Magic Diamond Casino, Lady Lil's, and Lucky Logger, as well as the Suds 'n Fun Casino Laundromat. Additionally, Town Pump operates about 10 hotels, including franchises from such chains as Super 8, Comfort Inn, and Town-house Inn; a chain of about 20 independently owned and operated car washes; and a propane delivery service. Subsidiary Northwest Petroleum Co. supplies Town Pump convenience stores and other fuel retailers in the greater Rocky Mountain and northwestern United States with branded and unbranded gasoline, diesel, and propane.

COMPANY FOUNDED: 1953

Town Pump grew from a single gas station opened by Thomas F. Kenneally Sr. and his wife Mary Ann. A native of Butte born in 1924, Kenneally earned an engineering degree from Montana State University and worked as an industrial engineer for Texaco, but he harbored a desire to go into business for himself. The Kenneallys saved $5,000 over the course of five years and in 1953 constructed a spare A-frame gas station next to the Butte Civic Center, which they opened under the Town Pump name.

The name held special significance for Kenneally. As a child he spent some of his summers in Helmville, Montana, a ranching community that shared a single source of water: a hand-operated pump in the center of town that also offered a trough for horses, a pair of buckets, and a drinking cup. Radiating from the pump were a general store and post office, the local school, and a church. The importance and the spirit behind the town pump impressed the youngster, and as an adult he appropriated it as an apt symbol for his business, albeit the pump dispensed gasoline instead of water.

Kenneally never lacked for energy or ambition. Many years before the advent of quick lubrication services, Kenneally made his mark by offering customers a three-minute oil change. As part of the full service that all gas stations offered, Kenneally checked a customer's oil, and should the oil be low or dirty and the customer was in a hurry, he made his pitch for an oil change: no labor charge and if it took him longer than three minutes the oil was free. He even removed his wristwatch and handed it to the customer to time him. Kenneally never failed the challenge, having mastered a choreographed routine that allowed him to drain the old oil and pour in the new in the allotted time. Although he charged no labor, Kenneally reaped the benefits of increased oil sales through volume purchasing.

COMPANY INCORPORATED: 1959

In 1959 Kenneally incorporated Town Pump Inc. in Montana. He opened a second Butte service station the following year called Up-town Pump, operated by George Shea at the corner of Montana and Gold Streets. A third station on East Mercury Street followed in the fall of 1962. By this stage, Kenneally was selling propane gas in a number of Montana communities. Also during the 1960s Kenneally found a way to save money, reduce prices, and increase sales when he became the first to bring self-service gas pumps to Montana, many of them operating under the Gas For Less name.

At the time, allowing customers to pump their own gas was considered dangerous. Moreover, Butte ordinances required attendants to pump gas and those attendants were unionized and fought against self-service. Kenneally eventually won out and began to build a chain of self-service gas stations, which included pumps that included bill acceptors. Some of the units also began to carry groceries, a precursor to the switch to a convenience store format.

By the end of the 1960s, Kenneally was operating nine Town Pump stations in Butte and 35 overall in the state. Just two years later that number increased to 53 independently owned and operated service stations spread across Montana. However, the company faced a challenge that threatened to put it out of business: finding someone to sell it gasoline. Kenneally complained to Montana's U.S. senators and the press, stating in September 1972 that at least some of his stations had been out of gasoline more than 100 times in the previous three months. He also claimed that 49 companies had refused to sell him fuel.

Town Pump's annual consumption was 20 million gallons. What especially upset Kenneally was that while Montana's gasoline consumption was 275 million gallons a year, the state's refineries produced 941 million gallons of gasoline a year. He maintained that none of Montana's refineries would sell to him because his stations undercut the prices of the service station chains operated by the major oil companies, which pressured the refineries to shut him out.

The major oil companies soon found themselves in a similar situation when in the fall of 1973 the Organization of Petroleum Exporting Countries (OPEC) instituted an oil embargo on the United States and other countries for their military support of Israel. Even before this action, Montana had been forced to adopt rationing measures in response to a petroleum shortage. Matters grew so bad that in 1974 Town Pump and the 48 stations that remained in operation were fortunate to stay in business. Kenneally helped his case by making a trip to Washington, D.C., to lobby the Department of Energy for the right to import gasoline from Canada whenever product was not available in the United States.

GROWTH RESUMES

Eschewing any attempts at growth, Town Pump hung on through the rest of the 1970s. A sudden surplus of petroleum changed the company's fortunes in the 1980s, however. Confident that it possessed a reliable supply of gasoline, Town Pump began embracing the convenience store format. Service stations were upgraded and converted, and liquor licenses were obtained in order to sell beer, a critical component in the convenience store business.

After nearly four decades of effort, Kenneally, aided greatly by his wife and six children, took Town Pump in a number of directions in the 1990s. In answer to customer demand, in 1990 the company began opening car washes, which like the convenience stores were independently owned and operated. Town Pump also

```
┌─────────────────────────────────────────────┐
│                                               │
│              KEY DATES                         │
│                    ◼                           │
│  ─────────────────────────────────────────    │
│  1953:  First Town Pump gas station opens in Butte, │
│         Montana.                               │
│  1960:  Second gas station opens.              │
│  1973:  Gas shortages pose challenge.          │
│  1990:  Town Pump begins opening car washes.   │
│  1991:  First casino opens.                    │
│  1997:  Casino opening is thwarted in Big Timber, │
│         Montana.                               │
│  2007:  4B's restaurant chain is acquired.     │
│                                               │
└─────────────────────────────────────────────┘
```

became involved in the hospitality industry, opening several motels through franchise agreements with Super 8, Comfort Inn, and Townhouse Inn, some at the request of small communities that lacked needed lodging. Further ventures included Laundromats, delis, and quick-serve restaurants, but the most lucrative and controversial were the new gaming establishments Town Pump began to open in 1991.

Montana had allowed some form of legalized gambling since 1937 when the state legislature passed the Hickey Act, permitting certain table games at specified locations at the discretion of each county. Although slot machines and punchboards were eventually deemed illegal, the legislature passed a law in 1973 that allowed card games, bingo, raffles, and sports pools. Three years later the Montana Supreme Court legalized video keno, maintaining that it was a form of bingo. (In keno, a player selects 10 numbers and the machine selects 20 from a pool of 80 numbers, and winnings are based on the number of matches.) In 1985 the legislature addressed video poker, passing a law that allowed the operation of five poker machines per liquor license and an unlimited number of keno machines. In 1991 the Montana legislature limited the number of gambling machines allotted to each liquor license, in any combination of keno or poker, to 20.

TOWN PUMP ADDS CASINOS: 1991

Montana lawmakers anticipated that taverns and restaurants might house a few video poker and video keno machines, and several Town Pump stores used their liquor licenses to add one or two gaming machines. In 1991 the Kenneally family decided to take full advantage of Montana law to open adjuncts to their stores, essentially casinos, which operated the full complement of 20 gambling machines. The first of these

establishments, taking the name Lucky Lil's, opened in Butte in 1991.

Tom Kenneally maintained that Town Pump was simply "responding to what people want." In lieu of an interview, Kenneally had made written responses to questions posed by the *Great Falls Tribune* in 1999. Regarding the origin of the new casinos, he wrote, "We thought we would take the risk and make an investment in a new kind of business, because we perceived a demand by the public for a product offering that was better than what was being offered by most of our competitors."

FACING CONTROVERSY

Video gaming became even more attractive to Montanans in 1993 when the maximum payout in video poker was increased from $100 to $800. Lucky Lil's and the other Town Pump casinos that followed enticed gamblers by increased paybacks. Instead of the state-mandated 80 percent payback, Town Pump casinos offered paybacks of at least 90 percent and as high as 94 percent. Moreover, players were given free drinks while they played.

Town Pump steadily opened more casinos, mostly under the Lucky Lil's and Magic Diamond labels. The company's embrace of gaming earned it a host of critics, including antigambling and community activists, but also competitors, many of whom simply imitated Town Pump's successful formula. "I kind of think of it as a giant vacuum cleaner," State Senator Lorents Grosfield of Big Timber, Montana, told the *Great Falls Tribune* regarding Town Pump and the other large casino operators. "You have this huge vacuum cleaner going to all of the towns in Montana, sucking cash out of these towns, and sucking it to the ownership of the casino, which is generally not in the same town."

It was the residents of Big Timber who in 1997 were able to block the opening of a Lucky Lil's casino by protesting the transfer of the required liquor license. The antigaming forces in the community presented an indictment of gambling in rural Montana to the state's Department of Revenue, but in the end their moral argument carried no weight, given that Town Pump operated within the state's gambling laws. The casino opening was thwarted because of a technicality, an improper liquor license transfer.

The residents of Wolf Point, Montana, also protested a liquor license in the fight against a proposed Town Pump casino. After a nearly decade-long fight, the company prevailed and opened a Lucky Lil's in that community in 1998. Town Pump maintained, conversely, that it dropped a number of casino projects in view of local opposition, and in many cases Town

Pump worked well with communities in opening much-needed motels and other businesses.

21ST-CENTURY GROWTH

In the new century, Town Pump continued to grow and diversify. In 2003 the company purchased a 67-acre property in Belgrade, Montana, the site of a former Louisiana Pacific lumber mill. After an effort to restrict the opening of new casinos in Belgrade failed, Town Pump received permission to use three of those acres to open a convenience store, gas station, and casino, and another 12 acres for mall retail development. The company also looked to make use of the site for a light-manufacturing business.

In 2007 Town Pump added to its holdings by acquiring six 4B's restaurants founded and owned by the Hainline family. More casinos were also to follow. In 2009, for example, a former Krispy Kreme donut store in Billings was acquired and renovated to house a new Montana Lil's Casino. Known to be hardworking and far from ostentatious, the Kenneally family showed no signs that their drive to continue to build Town Pump would slow any time soon.

Ed Dinger

PRINCIPAL SUBSIDIARIES

Propane Services Inc.; Northwest Petroleum Co.

PRINCIPAL COMPETITORS

The Best Bet; ConocoPhilips; Wyndham Worldwide Corporation.

FURTHER READING

Dennison, Mike, "Butte Family Runs Montana Empire," *Great Falls Tribune,* August 8, 1999, p. 1B.

———, "Gas, Groceries, Gambling, Lodging—and Controversy," *Great Falls Tribune,* August 8, 1999, p. 1A.

———, "The Kenneally Empire," *Great Falls Tribune,* August 8, 1999, p. 7A.

———, "Tom Kenneally Sr.," *Great Falls Tribune,* December 19, 1999, p. 34MC.

Falstad, Jan, "4B's Eatery in Prime Location to Close," *Billings Gazette,* April 6, 2007.

Nicholes, Erin, "Town Pump Gets Zone Change," *Bozeman Daily Chronicle,* July 9, 2004.

"Town Pump Adds to Its Portfolio," *Convenience Store News,* April 26, 2007.

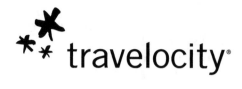

Travelocity.com LP

3150 Sabre Drive
Southlake, Texas 76092
U.S.A.
Telephone: (210) 521-5871
Toll Free: (888) 872-8356
Web site: http://www.travelocity.com

Wholly Owned Subsidiary of Sabre Holdings
Founded: 1996 as Travelocity
Employees: 2,000
Sales: $10 billion (2006 est.)
NAICS: 454110 Electronic Shopping and Mail-Order
    Houses; 514191 On-Line Information Services

■ ■ ■

Travelocity.com LP operates a leading online travel Web site where travelers can take control of their bookings and reservations and research information about potential destinations. The site provides reservation information for hundreds of airlines, more than 17,000 hotels, and dozens of car rental companies. It also offers vacation packages as well as tour and cruise departures. Internationally, Travelocity.com operates Web sites for customers in Canada in both French and English, as well as in the United Kingdom and Germany. In 2001, it launched Travelocity Europe in partnership with Otto, a German direct-marketing firm. In that year the company logged more than $3.1 billion in gross travel bookings and posted revenue of $301.8 million.

The industry-wide slowdown after the September 11, 2001, terrorist attacks on the United States forced the company to innovate. The company shifted more of its business to a merchant model and in 2004 launched a marketing campaign based around a traveling garden gnome mascot. In 2002, Sabre Holdings Corp., the computer reservation service, bought out the remaining shares in Travelocity it did not already own. Sabre became a private company in 2007. By that time, Travelocity had total bookings in excess of $10 billion and annual revenues of $1 billion.

LAUNCH FOLLOWED BY STEADY GROWTH: 1996–98

Travelocity.com was launched in March 1996 as a joint venture of two travel companies, Sabre Interactive and Worldview Systems Corp. Sabre Interactive was a unit of AMR Corp., the parent company of American Airlines, while Worldview was a partnership formed by publisher Random House and Ameritech, a regional Bell operating company. Sabre was the leading travel reservation system used by travel agents. Its principal business was to develop and install travel agents' computer reservation systems. Sabre booked Travelocity.com's airline reservations, while Worldview provided travel-related content for the site.

At first Travelocity's strategy was to offer compelling content and sell airline tickets. Destination information provided at the site included hotel recommendations, restaurant reviews, entertainment listings, weather reports, video clips, photos, maps, news, chat forums, and other information about specific destinations. Travelocity provided this information on its Web site directly from Worldview's databases. After Sabre Interactive

COMPANY PERSPECTIVES

We here at Travelocity believe that you deserve great travel experiences. That's why we created our own Travelocity Customer Bill of Rights and realigned our entire organization so that our products, policies and employees protect them. It's on the foundation of this work, strengthened by our commitment to continually get better at what we do, that we offer the Travelocity Guarantee. The Travelocity Guarantee is our seal on your traveler rights, a promise to our customers that we'll do our utmost to take care of you—that when you book with Travelocity, "you'll never roam alone." This promise extends to your entire trip experience; it even includes a low price guarantee to assure that you're getting a great deal for the travel you want.

bought out Worldview's interest in Travelocity in February 1997, Worldview remained the featured content provider for the Travelocity Web site.

In its first three months of operation, Travelocity reported 1.2 million visits and had 144,000 people register at the site. Registration was required to make a purchase through Travelocity. The site soon added more features, including hotel reservations, car rentals, and vacation packages. It was able to provide street maps for specific U.S. attractions through an agreement with Vicinity Corp. The Travelocity site was refined to make it easier to use, and by the end of 1996 it offered travel information for more than 200 destinations internationally and had more than 400,000 registered members. During 1996, Travelocity was selected to be the travel content provider for Time Warner's experimental online service, Road Runner.

Travelocity grew steadily during its first two years in business. Together with Expedia, an online travel site launched by Microsoft Corp. in October 1996, it was one of the leading travel sites on the Internet. While purchases were made online, tickets were delivered either to a local travel agency or through Travelocity's own travel agency, the Travelocity Service Center. Sabre and Travelocity built 12,000 customized Web sites for travel agents to help them handle online bookings. This helped position Travelocity as an ally, rather than a competitor, to travel agents. Travelocity was a key component in Sabre's strategy to capture the biggest possible share of overall travel bookings, both on and off the Web. For 1997, Travelocity handled more than $100 million in gross travel bookings, a significant percentage

of the estimated $900 million booked in online travel reservations that year.

MERGER AND DRAMATIC GROWTH: 1999–2000

In October 1999, Travelocity announced it would merge with Preview Travel, another leading online travel service. The new combined company was called Travelocity.com, Inc., and was headquartered in Fort Worth, Texas. The merger made Travelocity.com a category leader in online travel services. It also had the effect of making Travelocity.com a public company, with access to public-equity markets, because Preview Travel was already a public company.

Following the merger, which was completed in March 2000, Travelocity was separated from its parent company, Sabre. Sabre retained a 70 percent ownership interest in Travelocity, while Preview shareholders owned the remaining 30 percent. Sabre also continued to be Travelocity's principal technology partner, handling its online transactions. In the future Sabre would also provide technology for other online travel services, including Priceline.com and Hotwire.

As a result of the merger Travelocity was the third-most-visited electronic commerce site in the world following Amazon.com and eBay. The new Travelocity had about 17 million registered members and eight million monthly visitors. It was the preferred travel provider for all of the major Internet portals, including America Online, Excite, Go Network, Lycos, Netscape, USA Today, and Yahoo!

Prior to their merger, both Travelocity and Preview Travel were pursuing a strategy of building market share. As a result, both companies sustained losses in 1998 and 1999, with Travelocity reporting a loss of $21 million in 1998 and Preview a loss of $27 million. For 1999, Travelocity and Preview Travel reported combined revenues of $90.9 million and a combined loss of $49.8 million. Competing travel site Expedia went public in November 1999 and, according to Media Metrix, had slightly more traffic than Travelocity during the 1999 holiday season.

Around this time, Travelocity and Preview Travel entered into an agreement with Priceline.com, the name-your-own-fare online service. Together, the three companies agreed to refer customers to each other's sites and collect referral fees when purchases were made. The arrangement enabled Travelocity and Preview Travel to expand its audience and serve customers who were looking for the cheapest fares. Expedia countered by announcing it would develop its own name-your-own-price plan for airline tickets.

KEY DATES

1996: Travelocity.com is launched as a joint venture of Sabre Interactive and Worldview Systems Corp.

1999: Travelocity.com announces merger with on-line travel provider Preview Travel; launches first international sites in United Kingdom and Canada.

2000: Travelocity.com becomes a public company when its merger with Preview Travel closes.

2002: Sabre Holdings buys out remaining shares in Travelocity; Travelocity acquires last-minute travel site Site59.com.

2005: Sabre Holdings acquires European travel site Lastminute.com for $1 billion.

2006: Total bookings exceed $10 billion and revenues reach $1 billion.

2007: Sabre Holdings Corp. is taken private through $5 billion acquisition by Texas Pacific Group and Silver Lake Partners.

INTERNATIONAL EXPANSION

Once the merger between Travelocity and Preview Travel closed in March 2000, the new Travelocity launched a $50 million print and television advertising campaign to gain new customers. The ad campaign positioned Travelocity as the place where people could take control of their travel arrangements. The radio spots noted that Travelocity's online site listed 45,000 hotels, 700 airlines, and 50 car rental companies. Meanwhile, Travelocity had combined online traffic of more than eight million visitors in February 2000, according to Media Metrix, making it the top online travel site in terms of traffic. Expedia had 5.3 million visitors, while Travelocity by itself had 5.1 million.

By mid-2000, Travelocity completed its integration with Preview Travel and introduced a redesigned Web site. New features included a group shopping tool that made travel planning for groups easier. Also added to the site were customer reviews and a message board. The home page was redesigned, and wireless travel services were offered. At the end of June 2000, Travelocity had 21.6 million registered members, up from 19.2 million at the end of March.

In the second half of 2000, Travelocity and American Airlines Publishing launched *Travelocity Magazine*, a bimonthly periodical with a controlled circulation of 250,000. The new magazine was part of Travelocity's strategy to extend its brand, and it enhanced the company's position as a provider of tools for travelers who wanted to take control of their travel planning. The company sold its 10 millionth airline ticket in October 2000.

To serve customers outside of the United States, Travelocity supported Web sites in Canada, the United Kingdom, and Germany by the end of 2000. The company first began serving international customers in September 1997, when it gained the infrastructure to support global pricing and taxation. At first international customers were served by Travelocity's main online site in the United States, with tickets delivered through Sabre's international network of more than 10,000 travel agents.

The company ventured into the U.K. market in mid-1998 and established a customer service center in Cardiff, Wales. The following year it partnered with a U.K. travel agency to develop a Web site specifically for British customers. Travelocity Canada was established in April 1999, followed by a bilingual customer service center in Ottawa and then English and French Web sites for Canadian customers. Travelocity then launched Travelocity Germany, and in 2000 the company entered into an agreement with Japan Airlines, All Nippon Airways, and 11 other international carriers to launch Travelocity Japan in 2001.

SEEKING PROFITABILITY

Travelocity's gross travel bookings reached $2.5 billion in 2000, more than double that of 1999 and more than 22 percent of the estimated $11 billion spent in online travel during 2000. At the beginning of 2001, Travelocity was the top-ranked online travel provider with 8.72 million visitors in January, equal to an 18 percent market share, according to Nielsen/NetRatings and Harris Interactive. The other top-four online travel providers in terms of visitors were Southwest Airlines with 5.1 million visitors; Expedia, with 4.8 million visitors; Priceline.com, with 3.4 million visitors; and Delta Airlines, with 3 million visitors.

Travelocity began 2001 by predicting it would achieve profitability by the end of the year. During 2001, the company faced new competition from the airlines, which launched two new online ticketing services, http://www.Hotwire.com and http://www.Orbitz.com. The airlines also capped commissions at $10 per ticket for all airline tickets sold online or of-fline, and some airlines, notably Northwest and KLM, eliminated commissions for airline tickets sold online. In March 2001, Travelocity stopped booking flights on Southwest Airlines after the two companies experienced customer service problems. Travelocity also began charging customers $10 commissions on Northwest and KLM tickets.

Part of Travelocity's strategy to achieve profitability was to introduce new services during the year. For its fifth anniversary in March 2001, it launched several new services, including the Travelocity Preferred Traveler travel club, and Goodbuy, a negotiated fare service for 20 airlines and rooms at 2,500 hotels. Option Finder was a new feature that searched for alternate airports and departure dates.

For the first quarter ending March 31, 2001, Travelocity reported a pro forma profit of $618,000 before special items and a positive cash flow. However, special items totaling $26.4 million resulted in a quarterly net loss of $22.1 million, compared to a net loss of $9 million for the same quarter in 2000. Nevertheless, Travelocity's stock rallied on the news and increased more than 134 percent from January through the end of April 2001. Travelocity's second quarter of 2001 was also profitable on a pro forma basis, excluding the write-off of goodwill.

TERRORIST ATTACKS TAKE A TOLL

During the rest of the year, Travelocity added more new products and services. Through an investment in Viator, Travelocity added a database of sightseeing tours, attractions, and other destination activities in 33 countries. A partnership with American Classic Voyages Co. enabled Travelocity to offer Hawaiian cruises. In July, Travelocity introduced its Bon Voyage e-mail service, which recommended activities, events, and personalized special offers to its members. A new specialty content area for golf travel was added, and later in the year a new content area for ski and snowboarding vacations was introduced. The company also increased its offline support, opening a third customer service center in Virginia and improving the technology in all of its customer service centers.

Internationally, Travelocity entered into agreements with Lufthansa and British Airways, and it began offering the entire range of 73 European rail passes. The company announced it would acquire Air Tickets Direct, a U.K.-based online travel agency that also had a dedicated call center for offline customer support. Before the end of the year it finalized arrangements with Otto, a German direct-marketing firm, to launch Travelocity Europe.

For the third quarter ending September 30, Travelocity reported a pro forma profit of $4.9 million before special items. Membership increased to 30.4 million. While the online travel industry was the best performing sector of the Internet economy for the first eight months of 2001, the terrorist attacks of September 11, 2001, against the United States had a devastating effect on online travel providers. Online bookings dropped to only 30 to 40 percent of their previous levels. At the beginning of October Travelocity announced it would close its call center in Sacramento, California, and reduce its workforce by 19 percent, or 320 jobs. The company had about 1,700 employees before the cutbacks and planned to institute a hiring freeze.

The economic slowdown of 2001 and the lingering effects of the September 11 terrorist attacks made the fourth quarter of 2001 a difficult one. Travelocity's gross travel bookings for the quarter were $630.2 million, down 9.5 percent for the same quarter of 2000. For 2001, Travelocity reported gross travel bookings of $3.1 billion, an increase of 27 percent over 2000. While the company was able to report a pro forma quarterly profit of $4.9 million, it recorded a net loss of $24.4 million for the fourth quarter, more than double the loss of the same quarter in 2000. For all of 2001, Travelocity had a net loss of $85 million. While Travelocity did not achieve profitability in 2001, it was able to report pro forma net income of $15.6 million for the year, and membership at the end of the year rose to 32 million.

SHIFT TO RETAIL IN 2002

In April 2002, Sabre Holdings Corp. bought out the remaining shares in Travelocity it did not already own. The next month Travelocity founder Terrell Jones was replaced as CEO by Sam Gilliand, a longtime Sabre executive and then its chief marketing officer. Gilliand became president and CEO of Sabre in December 2003.

The lingering industry-wide slowdown forced the company to innovate. There was also opportunity, as thousands of traditional travel agencies folded. Travelocity began selling travel insurance and developed several features to improve the functionality of its Web sites by offering more information.

Travelocity generally lagged behind rivals in offering vacation packages, but it developed an interest in spur-of-the-moment travel plans, which offered higher margins. In April 2002 it acquired Site59.com, a site for last-minute travel packages, for $43 million. The company later tapped its head, Michelle Peluso, as its own CEO.

Around September 2002 the company shifted to the merchant model of buying at wholesale and selling at retail for hotel rooms as well as airline seats and travel packages. In 2004 Travelocity bought Allstate Ticketing, which sold tickets for shows and bus tours out of 20 kiosks in the Las Vegas area.

Revenues inched up 2.2 percent in 2002 to $308 million as parent company Sabre's slipped 3.5 percent to $2 billion. Revenues were $395 million in 2003. The company posted a $55 million loss for the year and was leapfrogged as the leading online travel agency by Expedia Inc. Travelocity then had about 2,000 employees. In early 2004 Travelocity outsourced some of its call-center functions to India, closing a call center in Virginia and laying off a total of 300 U.S. workers.

ROAMING WITH THE GNOME IN 2004

To encourage brand loyalty among comparison-shopping–driven customers, the company launched a series of whimsical ads to create an emotional connection to a service that was utilitarian in nature. In 2004 it kicked off the $80 million campaign, its largest to date and the first to feature its garden gnome mascot (an allusion to the French film *Amélie*). The tagline was, "You'll never roam alone."

Travelocity hired Alan Whicker, host of 1970s travelogues, to represent the brand in the United Kingdom in a series of "Hello World" ads in 2004. However, Travelocity remained a niche player in Europe, noted *Marketing Week,* and parent company Sabre Holdings opted to build market share in 2005 via the $1 billion acquisition of London-based Lastminute.com, which continued to operate under its own brand.

TAKEN PRIVATE IN 2007

Travelocity's total bookings exceeded $10 billion in 2006 as revenues rose 31 percent to $1.1 billion. Private-equity firms Texas Pacific Group and Silver Lake Partners acquired Sabre Holdings for $5 billion in March 2007, making it a private company. Michelle Peluso stepped down as CEO in February 2009. Former AMR Corp. and Sabre executive Hugh Jones succeeded her.

Customers became especially frugal following the worldwide economic slump that followed the mortgage crisis of 2008. Like other online agencies, Travelocity rolled back flight-booking fees. In October 2009 it began guaranteeing its hotel reservations as the lowest available, offering to credit travelers the difference if they found lower rates.

An enduring and potentially very expensive issue remained to be resolved. A wave of lawsuits had been gathering for years among municipal governments eager for a slice of the differential between what Travelocity and other firms had been collecting in room tax, based on retail rates, and what they had been paying local authorities, the latter based on wholesale prices. The agencies claimed that since they did not own or operate the rooms, the responsibility for the difference fell to the hotels themselves.

David P. Bianco
Updated, Frederick C. Ingram

PRINCIPAL OPERATING UNITS

Travelocity.com; Travelocity.co.uk; Travelocity.ca.

PRINCIPAL COMPETITORS

Expedia, Inc.; Orbitz Worldwide, Inc.; Priceline.com, Inc.

FURTHER READING

Bittle, Scott, "Travelocity Site Gets Lots of Bites," *Travel Weekly*, July 11, 1996, p. 15.

Blakey, Elizabeth, "Travelocity Cuts Jobs, Closes Call Centers," *E-Commerce Times*, October 5, 2001.

Butterman, Eric, "Profits for Travelocity and Expedia Put More Pressure on Orbitz Debut," *Travel Agent*, April 30, 2001, p. 4.

Fredericks, Alan, "Old-Fashioned Service," *Travel Weekly*, September 13, 2001, p. 82.

Goodridge, Elisabeth, "Travelocity Overcomes Barriers in Its Global Expansion," *Information Week*, December 11, 2000, p. 76.

Harwood, Jonathan, "Travelocity: The Road Less Travelled," *Marketing Week* (UK), February 9, 2006, p. 31.

Hibbard, Justin, "Airlines, Online Agencies Battle for Customers," *Information Week*, November 9, 1998, p. 30.

"Japanese Airlines Join with Travelocity.com on New Web Venture," *Airline Industry Information*, August 16, 2000.

Kornik, Joseph, "Sabre Interactive Buys Travelocity," *Travel Weekly*, February 6, 1997, p. 1.

McGee, William J., "Travelocity-Preview Merger Creates On-line Powerhouse," *Travel Agent*, October 11, 1999, p. 8.

Tedeschi, Bob, "As Domestic Sales Slow, Travel Sites Go Global," *New York Times,* July 9, 2007, p. C6.

———, "In the Pursuit of Face-to-Face Sales and Web Site Traffic, Expedia and Travelocity.com Open Shops in Tourist Areas," *New York Times,* January 17, 2005, p. C4.

"Travelocity Buys Stake in Viator," *Travel Weekly*, May 21, 2001, p. 8.

"Where the Net Delivers: Travel," *Business Week*, June 11, 2001, p. 142.

Wilson, David, "Internet Travel Sites Take Flight amid Internet Chaos," *Los Angeles Business Journal*, May 7, 2001, p. 40.

vandemoortele

Vandemoortele S.A./NV

■

Ottergemsesteenweg zuid 806
Ghent, B-9000
Belgium
Telephone: (+32 09) 240 18 00
Fax: (+32 09) 240 18 30
Web site: http://www.vandemoortele.com

Private Company
Incorporated: 1914 as Société en nom collectif Adhémar
    en Edgard Vandemoortele
Employees: 5,600
Sales: EUR 1.23 billion ($1.72 billion) (2008 est.)
NAICS: 311225 Fats and Oils Refining and Blending;
    311813 Frozen Bakery Product Manufacturing

■ ■ ■

Vandemoortele S.A./NV is Belgium's largest food
processing company and one of Europe's leading
producers of edible lipids and frozen baked goods. Vandemoortele's Lipids Division produces vegetable oils,
margarine, frying fats, and other products for the food
industry and for private labels for the European retail
market. The company also maintains a small consumer
goods operation in Belgium, producing mayonnaise and
other products under the Vandemoortele and Vitelma
brand names, among others. The Lipids Division generated 39 percent of the group's sales of EUR 1.23 billion
($1.7 billion) in 2008.

The Bakery Division oversees the company's
production of frozen breads, pastries, and dessert
products. These are semifinished products sold to bak-

ers, supermarkets, and other foodservice outlets. The
Bakery Division generated 38 percent of the group's
sales in 2008. In 2009 Vandemoortele sold off a third
division, Alpro, a producer of soy-based food products,
to Dean Foods Group.

In addition to production facilities in Belgium,
Vandemoortele operates in France, Germany, Poland,
Italy, the Netherlands, the United Kingdom, and Spain.
Vandemoortele remains under the control of the founding family, led by CEO Jean Vandemoortele. In 2009
the company brought in the Gimv investment fund as a
minority shareholder.

ORIGINS IN ANIMAL FEEDS: 1899

Vandemoortele started out as a small company producing animal feeds based on rapeseed and linseed. The
company was founded by Constant Vandemoortele and
his son Adhémar in 1899, who opened a factory in Izegem, in the northern Flemish region of Belgium. The
company grew strongly at the beginning, and the factory was expanded in 1901 and again in 1909. In 1914
the company incorporated as Société en nom collectif
Adhémar en Edgard Vandemoortele.

However, World War I put an end to the
company's growth. By the end of the war, parts of the
factory had been confiscated, and the equipment that
remained was outdated. Vandemoortele soon regained
its footing, building a new oil press in 1919. This extension enabled the company to establish a dedicated oil
production subsidiary, NV Oliefabrieken Vandemoortele, in 1921. The company then added a new

oil factory in 1922, and expanded that facility again in 1928.

Vandemoortele's oil production initially focused on the industrial sector. However, in 1934 the company began importing peanuts and soybeans from China, from which it initially produced animal feeds. The introduction of peanuts also provided the company with an opportunity to convert its operations to the production of edible oils. This was accomplished with the construction of an oil refinery in 1936. Vandemoortele then launched its own brand of table oils.

MARGARINE PRODUCTION ADDED

The company continued to extend its production capacity through the 1940s. The group opened an extraction and hydrogenation facility in 1942, followed by soy oil extraction capacity in 1944. Vandemoortele boosted its table oil business, launching a line of bottled oils in 1947. In 1950 the company added glycerin production as well. By then, Vandemoortele had expanded beyond its home region, with sales throughout Belgium.

The 1950s were also marked by a number of acquisitions. Among these was the takeover of a neighboring factory in Kahn-Dreyfus, which allowed the company to extend its original linseed factory. Another acquisition, of Lier-based Firma Albers in 1951, provided Vandemoortele with the extension into a new food area, margarine. In 1955 Vandemoortele boosted its logistics operations with the creation of a dedicated transport subsidiary, Metro N.V.

The extension into margarine provided a platform for Vandemoortele's move into a wider variety of consumer oils and fats in the 1960s. The company added deep fryer fats in 1962, followed by disposable oil packages, and the production of mayonnaise, sauces, and dressings by 1967. In 1969 the company bought Germany's Meyer Lippinghausen, expanding its margarine operations while also adding a new international element.

INTERNATIONAL EXPANSION

The diversification of Vandemoortele's business led to a restructuring of the group's operations. As part of this, the company created a new subsidiary, Vamo Mills, which took over its oilseed extraction operations in 1974. Vandemoortele also launched another extension of its business during the decade, when it began manufacturing products specifically for the professional bakery sector. This led to the formation of a dedicated subsidiary, Vamix, in 1978. Vamix soon began to focus especially on the frozen baked goods market. This involved producing semifinished breads, pastries, and desserts, which the company supplied to bakers, restaurants, and others for cooking and final preparation.

Vandemoortele added another pillar to its operations in 1980, forming Alpro. This subsidiary took over Vandemoortele's production of soy drinks and other soy products, a category just beginning to build scale in Europe. Alpro remained an important part of Vandemoortele's operations into the 21st century.

Through the 1980s Vandemoortele focused on expanding its operations into the broader European market. Acquisitions formed a major part of this strategy, leading the company to build up a range of businesses in France, Germany, Italy, Spain, and the Netherlands. In France these included a pastry producer in Reims in 1986, and a bread production unit in Somain in 1989. The company added rival Belgian mayonnaise producer Vleminckx, based in Herent, in 1989.

Vandemoortele's international expansion continued in the 1990s, starting with the launch of a subsidiary and the construction of a factory in England in 1991. The company raised its Netherlands presence in 1992, buying Comexol from that country's Bunge group. The company added operations in the former Soviet Bloc the following year, buying up Maro Rostock, including three mayonnaise factories in Dresden, Riesa, and Dommitzsch, in the former East Germany. Vandemoortele added other operations in the East European region, moving into the Czech Republic and Slovakia.

OIL MILLING SOLD OFF: 1997

By 1997 Vandemoortele's revenues had grown to the equivalent of $2 billion per year. The company had

KEY DATES

1899: Constant Vandemoortele and his son Adhémar launch an animal feed company in Izegem, Belgium.

1951: The company acquires Lier-based Firma Albers and begins producing margarine.

1978: The company launches a bakery products subsidiary, Vamix.

1998: Vandemoortele refocuses its operations on lipids, frozen bakery, and soy products.

2009: Vandemoortele sells its Alpro soy operations; Gimv becomes a minority shareholder.

grown into one of Europe's top oilseed crushing and refining businesses, with a diversified line of finished products ranging from margarine and mayonnaise, to frozen breads, to soy drinks. However, in the late 1990s the company launched a strategic review of its operations. This resulted in the group's decision to refocus its operations on categories in which it could claim a position among the European top two.

Amid pressures surrounding the European oilseed market, Vandemoortele had begun to restructure its oil milling interests earlier in the decade. The company brought in a new financial partner, France's Soprol SA, which acquired a 15 percent stake in the company's Vamo Mills subsidiary. Soprol's subsidiary Saipol operated four oil mills in France, located in Bordeaux, Chalon-sur-Saone, Dieppe, and Rouen. In 1995 Vandemoortele and Soprol reached a deal to merge Saipol into Vamo Mills. The company then became the third-largest European edible oil refiner in Europe, trailing Archer Daniels Midland and Cargill, with 10 mills in Belgium, France, and Germany, and a total refining capacity of 350,000 tons. Under terms of the deal, Soprol gained a 49 percent stake in Vamo Mills.

In the second half of the decade oil milling had become even more competitive, and more difficult to achieve profitability. A major factor behind this change came from the globalization of the industry and the rise of lower-cost manufacturers in South America, China, and elsewhere in the Asian region. In order to compete on a global level, Vandemoortele, which remained a family-owned company, would have been required to invest heavily in expansion beyond the European region.

Despite its strong presence in Europe, Vandemoortele recognized that it would have been hard-pressed to compete against the heavyweights in the global industry. Instead, Vandemoortele reached an agreement to sell all of its upstream oil crushing and milling operations to Cargill in 1997. This move effectively slashed the company's total revenues by more than half, with its sales dropping to just above $800 million.

STREAMLINING IN THE 21ST CENTURY

Vandemoortele's streamlining continued into the next decade. In 2000 the company refocused its bakery division entirely around frozen dough products. This led to the sale of Vamix's bakery ingredients operations, based in Ghent, Belgium, to DSM in February of that year. Vandemoortele next targeted an exit from the bottled oils sector. The group decided to abandon its mayonnaise and dressings business at the same time, keeping only the Belgian operations of this division. The international operations were sold to Germany's Heinrich Hamker Lebensmittlewerke at the end of 2003.

As a result of its restructuring, Vandemoortele's revenues, which had risen to EUR 900 million in 2002, dropped again to EUR 800 million. Nevertheless, the company had refocused itself around three core products areas, frozen bread dough, margarines and fats, and soy products. In the five-year period since the beginning of Vandemoortele's restructuring, these divisions had posted growth of nearly 45 percent.

ACQUIRING SCALE

The sale of its noncore operations provided Vandemoortele with a treasury with which to launch a new acquisition campaign in order to solidify the European leadership positions of its three remaining divisions. For example, in December 2004 the company acquired France's Cottes SA, based in Le Foussat, in the country's Ariège region. Cottes had originated as a small bakery before launching industrial-scale production of breads and pastries in 1978.

In the 1990s Cottes adapted to new demands of the supermarket industry by converting its production to frozen bread dough, and then opened a second factory serving the Spanish market. With competition rising in the frozen bread dough market, Cottes decided to specialize in the leavened bread category in 1997, gaining an 80 percent share of that market niche with its Pérènes brand. As part of Vandemoortele, Cottes soon launched an expansion of its operations, investing EUR 18 million to expand its two factories. Vandemoortele followed the Cottes purchase with that of Belgian doughnut manufacturer Colombus Food, helping the company position itself as a leading producer of "American" frozen bread dough specialties.

In 2006 Vandemoortele raised its profile in the Netherlands, acquiring pastry products group Erkens Bakkerijen and tofu and meat replacer SoFine Foods. Vandemoortele also added operations in Spain, through a 25 percent stake in edible oils and fats producer Lipidos Santiga.

Vandemoortele then moved into Poland, buying up the frozen bread and pastries business of Gourmand Poland, part of Dossche Group. A small company with annual sales of just $4 million, Gourmand nevertheless provided the company with a distribution network reaching into the Czech Republic, Hungary, and other Central and Eastern European markets.

Vandemoortele remained on the lookout for opportunities to build its frozen breads division. This led the company to its next major acquisition, of Panavi, the leading frozen breads producer in France. Panavi added more than EUR 300 million ($480 million) to Vandemoortele, as well as a national network of 22 factories, thus raising Vandemoortele to the top of the European bread sector.

SOY OPERATIONS SOLD: 2009

By 2008 the company's Bakery and Lipids divisions each contributed nearly 40 percent to the company's total sales, which topped EUR 1.23 billion for the year. With both divisions ranked at the top of their industries, Vandemoortele announced its intention to sell off its Alpro soy operations that year. This led the company to reach an agreement with U.S.-based Dean Foods Company, which paid EUR 325 million to take over Alpro in June 2009.

Vandemoortele celebrated 110 years as a family-owned company that year. The company remained under family leadership, in the form of Jean Vandemoortele, grandson of the founder. Vandemoortele nevertheless did not rule out the possibility of a public offering in the future, should it require additional capital to expand its operations. In the meantime, the group opened its shareholding for the first time in 2009, selling a minority stake to investment fund Gimv, in exchange for EUR 75 million. Vandemoortele had suc-

cessfully negotiated its change of strategy as it targeted new growth in the 21st century.

M. L. Cohen

PRINCIPAL SUBSIDIARIES

Cottes SA (France); Croustifrance Benelux NV; Erkens Bakkerijen BV; Hobum Öle und Fette GmbH (Germany); JB Schmidt Söhne GmbH & Co. KG (Germany); Lipidos Santiga SA; Metro N.V.; Paindor SAS (France); Panavi SAS (France); Safinco Nederland BV; SoFine Foods BV (Netherlands); Vamix NV; Vamix Slovenska Republika s.r.o.; Vamo Mills NV; Vandemoortele Deutschland GmbH; Vandemoortele France SA; Vandemoortele GmbH (Austria); Vandemoortele Hungary Ltd.; Vandemoortele Iberica SA (Spain); Vandemoortele Italia S.p.A.; Vandemoortele NV (Netherlands); Vandemoortele Polska Sp.z o.o.; Vandemoortele Rückversicherung AG (Switzerland); Vandemoortele UK Ltd.

PRINCIPAL DIVISIONS

Bakery; Lipids.

PRINCIPAL COMPETITORS

Arla Foods amba; Lantmänne Unibake A/S; Unilever N.V.

FURTHER READING

"Belgium's Vandemoortele Buys Local Bakery Firm," *just-food. com*, August 22, 2007.

Crosskey, Peter, "Vandemoortele to Invest EUR 25m in Bread Plant," *just-food.com*, November 28, 2007.

Smedts, Sjoukje, "Vandemoortele Heeft Europese Ambities," *Trends/Cash*, November 27, 2008.

"Topman Groep Vandemoortele Wordt Baron," *Het Nieuwsblad*, July 19, 2006.

"Vandemoortele Bevestigt Zoektocht naar 100 Miljoen," *De Tijd*, September 14, 2008.

"Vandemoortele Buys Baker Panavi," *just-food.com*, June 6, 2008.

"Vandemoortele: Geven en Nemen," *Trends/Cash*, February 27, 1995.

"Vandemoortele Wordt Europese Gigant in Diepvriesbakkerij," *Trends/Cash*, June 12, 2008.

Van Ypersele, Nathalie, "Vandemoortele Van Haver Tot Gort," *Trends/Cash*, June 15, 2000.

"Wie Is Jean Vandemoortele?" *Trends/Cash*, May 13, 2004.

VDL Groep B.V.

Hoevenweg 1
Eindhoven, 5652 AW
Netherlands
Telephone: (+31 40) 292 50 00
Fax: (+31 40) 292 50 50
Web site: http://www.vdlgroep.com

Private Company
Incorporated: 1957 as Metaalindustrie P. v.d. Leegte NV
Employees: 6,100
Sales: EUR 1.7 billion ($2.3 billion) (2008)
NAICS: 336370 Motor Vehicle Metal Stamping; 336211 Motor Vehicle Body Manufacturing; 421740 Refrigeration Equipment; 421730 Warm Air Heating and Air Conditioning Equipment; 326199 All Other Plastics Product Manufacturing; 333513 Machine Tool (Metal Forming Types); 336999 All Other Transportation Equipment Manufacturing

■ ■ ■

The VDL Groep B.V. is a Netherlands-based international conglomerate. With roots in metalworking, the VDL Groep produces a broad of finished and semifinished products, each of which are manufactured by one or more of the group's 78 subsidiaries in 14 different countries. VDL's philosophy is to allow each subsidiary to operate autonomously with a minimum of interference from the group's headquarters. The group's activities are concentrated in the Netherlands and Belgium, where in 2008 about 90 percent of its workforce was employed. The company has customers in 115 countries throughout the world.

VDL maintains three divisions: Subcontracting, Buses & Coaches, and Finished Products. The Subcontracting division provides semifinished metal goods to other manufacturers, about 50 of which are in the automotive, construction, semiconductor, medical systems, alternative energy, and mechanical engineering industries. The other activities of the division include surface treatment services, the production of mechatronic systems for solar cell makers, and the production of plastic items.

VDL's Buses & Coach division manufactures buses, coaches, and their parts for public and commercial transportation purposes. The Finished Products division produces a wide variety of products that include production automation equipment, agricultural systems, container handling equipment, sunbeds and auto roof carriers, and machines for the production of cigars. However, heat exchangers and suspension systems for automobiles constitute about 60 percent of the division's production. In 2008 Buses & Coaches accounted to 39 percent of the VDL Groep's revenues, Subcontracting for 34 percent, and Finished Products for 27 percent.

SMALL BEGINNINGS 1953-63

VDL was founded in December 1953 by Pieter van der Leegte, whose name would eventually provide the initials for the company's name. Born in the Netherlands in 1919, van der Leegte completed an apprenticeship at Philips Machinefabrieken in Eindhoven, where he was later employed. While still at Philips, van der Leegte, his brother Steef, and a friend started doing their own metal-working jobs on the side, at first producing metal fasteners for folding beds, and later offering galvanization services. Pieter soon grew frustrated working for others, and left to launch his own company, Metaalindustrie en Constructiewerkplaats P. v.d. Leegte, in Eindhoven just before Christmas 1953.

The start-up was financed with money borrowed from van der Leegte's in-laws, as well as with support from his former employer Philips, which generously provided both financing and advice. Van der Leegte was also fortunate in securing as his first customers two major firms, Philips and DAF Trucks, both of Eindhoven. The company's five employees performed turning, milling, and drilling jobs as well as punching, welding, and soldering.

After five years, just before New Year's 1958, the company was incorporated and given a new name Metaalindustrie P. v.d. Leegte NV. By then van der Leegte had started developing his own products. One was a simple but efficient electric washing machine. He called it De Vlinder, or the Butterfly, and it was popular right from the start. Unfortunately, larger companies that could manufacture more inexpensively and in greater quantities reacted by bringing out similar products and drove De Vlinder from the market. More successful for the firm was a metal oven that burned oil rather than coal to heat a room. That proved to be a long-term best seller for the company.

GROWTH, REORGANIZATION, AND CHALLENGES

In 1962, following a sizable order from Honda, the company moved its production to larger facilities in the Dutch city of Hapert, near Eindhoven. In the end, however, the Honda order was much smaller than originally anticipated, and the company had to shift gears in the mid-1960s and start producing a line of stainless steel kitchen and household utensils, such as pots, pans, bed warmers, butter dishes, and egg cups. In 1964 van der Leegte founded a subsidiary, VEM, the Vereinigte Eindhovense Metaalindustrie or the United Metal-Working Industries of Eindhoven. The new company united six different operations under a single administrative roof to organize sales more efficiently.

One year after the consolidation, however, the firm found itself in a financial crisis with losses totaling NLG 110,000 in 1965; the subsequent year the losses were even higher, reaching NLG 150,000. VEM required an influx of cash, and Pieter van der Leegte responded by investing NLG 100,000. Needing new business, van der Leegte negotiated a deal with the company Artola, another Dutch manufacturer. By then van der Leegte was some NLG 250,000 in debt. As part of their contract, Artola agreed to cover those losses. The deal, however, turned over 50 percent of the shares in van der Leegte's firm to Artola and tied up the remaining 50 percent as collateral on the NLG 250,000 loan. The deal rescued the company, but in doing so put its independence at risk.

NEW LEADERSHIP IN TROUBLED TIMES

The pressure was mounting on Pieter van der Leegte. Since founding the company, he had had the ultimate responsibility for nearly every phase of its operations, including general management, accounting, sales, and purchasing. The workload proved to be too much for a single person. Given too his company's recent financial worries and a personal loss of NLG 70,000, his breakdown in 1966 was regarded as almost inevitable. Van der Leegte's 19-year-old son Wim was called into the breech. One month he was training as an intern at the company; three months later he was running the entire firm. One year later, Pieter van der Leegte withdrew from the day-to-day management of the company.

The company's problems continued at first. Some of the worst involved key products. A particularly unfortunate example was a metal hot water bottle that had been a perennially popular item. Quality control difficulties arose when the adhesive that held the bottle's two main components together was unable to withstand the changes between heat and cold and eventually the parts separated. Thousands of the bottles were returned to stores, and the firm was forced to take a loss. Moreover, new products were being developed (electric heating pads and hot water bottles made of rubber) that, together with the growing prevalence of central heating in Dutch homes, made the company's bottles

KEY DATES

1953: Metaalindustrie en Constructiewerkplaats P. v.d. Leegte is founded.
1967: Wim van der Leegte takes over company.
1977: Open management organizational plan is implemented.
1979: VDL makes its first acquisition, TIM.
1993: DAF Bus International is acquired.

obsolete almost overnight. By 1968 the market for the metal hot water bottles had evaporated completely, and the firm had to junk its remaining stocks.

In 1971 Artola made its move, attempting to parlay its holdings in Metaalindustrie P. v.d. Leegte into a takeover of the troubled firm. Only with the efforts of Wim van der Leegte was the company able to reach an agreement with Artola and maintain its independence. Following van der Leegte's successful avoidance of the crisis, he was given all company stock that had been held by his father in order to concentrate ownership in the hands of the company head.

The elder van der Leegte remained with the firm, but in the capacity of a technical consultant. He was thus also able to dedicate himself to his first loves: solving technical problems and inventing. He enjoyed great success, developing products that the firm produced for the Dutch army, such as a new gas mask design and a cup that the military purchased for nearly 20 years. Suffering a heart attack at the end of the 1970s, Pieter van der Leegte eventually retired, although he remained a director of the company until his death in 1991.

NEW COMPANIES AND A NEW ORGANIZATIONAL STRUCTURE

If his father was technically adept, Wim van der Leegte proved a good businessman. By the mid-1970s as the manufacture of metal household goods was becoming increasingly unprofitable, Wim steered the company away from the production of finished, consumer products and toward parts for the production processes of other firms. The first subsidiaries were founded around this time. Lerosta, for example, was established as a marketing and sales organization, headed by Wim van der Leegte, who called on potential customers personally.

A far-reaching reorganization of the firm went into effect in 1977. Three basic principles were introduced.

The first was a simplification of the decision-making and execution process. From then on there were to be no more than three organizational levels in total between upper management and the factory floor. Second, all positions in the company received clear job descriptions to provide a transparent division of responsibilities. Third, the workforce itself was to maintain a certain balance between production and service areas, with five workers in the former for everyone in the latter.

In addition, to improve communication and create a greater sense of employee identification with the company, biweekly meetings were introduced that were attended by sales people, production and other department heads, quality-control people, and the foremen from the company's various production areas. The reorganization was extremely successful, so much so (in particular for organizations with no more than 150 workers) that it was adopted by the group's subsidiaries as well. The name of the parent company was changed at the same time to VD Leegte Metaal. In 1979 revenues topped NLG 4 million for the first time and one year later grew to NLG 5 million.

CONSTANT GROWTH THROUGH NEW ACQUISITIONS

With the start of the 1980s, the VDL Groep, as it would soon be known, entered a period of steady growth that would last for the next 30 years. One new strategy Wim van der Leegte had established for the firm was to take over underperforming companies. VDL's first acquisition was made in 1979 when it acquired a 50 percent share in TIM (Technische Industrie Metaalwerken, or Technical Metal Works for Industry), a company established by Pieter van der Leegte in 1971 for his youngest son Piet.

In 1981 VDL purchased the Dutch company VDS, a competitor that produced fully automatic metal-working equipment, a new element for VDL's product palette. A second major addition to the group was concluded two years later with the acquisition of Hoeks, a paint, injection molding, and enamel specialist.

By 1984 there were five companies in the VDL Groep, as it was by then known. Other would soon follow. VDL next looked to purchase finished-goods companies that could also use the parts VDL was supplying to other firms. In that way the company could hedge its bets and protect itself from order cancellations and other unpleasant surprises from companies with which it did business. VDL was also limiting its interest to companies with a workforce of 150 or less, as van der Leegte believed that larger companies did not function as well. If a larger company did join the group, it was immediately broken up into smaller units.

A family tragedy led to further organizational changes at the VDL Groep. Until 1984 van der Leegte had been VDL's sole director. The sudden death of Piet van der Leegte, the head of TIM, emphasized the serious impact such a loss could have on a company. As a result, the board of the VDL Groep was expanded to four members with Wim van der Leegte its chairman. An advisory board was established at the same time, chaired by Pieter van der Leegte Sr.

In 1984 VDL International was founded for the sale of finished products including a successful line that consisted of products for industrial livestock breeding. The acquisition of the Belgian company DENIES in 1986 led to VDL's first work for the automaker Volvo. DENIES was later reorganized into VDL Belgium, the company's first foreign subsidiary.

BUS MANUFACTURING BEGINS

In 1990 a financial crisis hit many Dutch firms, including VDL customers Philips and DAF. VDL's revamped organization had made it stronger and more flexible; in fact, its financial health was so good that was in a position to help the stricken firms get back on their feet again. VDL also acquired some of the troubled companies and added them the VDL Groep. Among the most important additions at that time were NSA Apparatenbouw and NSA Metaalindustrie, both of which were manufacturers of high-quality technical equipment. Their addition in 1991 led to a sharp increase in the size of the VDL Groep workforce. In 1993 it acquired DAF Bus International, later reorganized into VDL Bus & Coach. This division would eventually become one of the group's largest and most profitable subsidiaries.

By 1996 the group had grown to include 20 companies, a total workforce of more than 2,000, and annual revenues surpassing EUR 200 million. BOVA, a manufacturer of luxury buses based in Eindhoven, was acquired in 2003. Three years later the group made the largest acquisition in its history when it purchased the Philips Enabling Technologies Group, formerly known as Philips Machinefabrieken, the company where Pieter van der Leegte had started his career in the 1930s.

Through the first decade of the 2000s the VDL Groep set new annual sales records regularly. Between 2006 and 2007, for example, sales increased by more than 30 percent. Despite worldwide economic downturn in 2008, VDL turned a profit of about $140 million for the year. These results were achieved despite the fact that VDL continued to buck a growing trend in manufacturing; Wim van der Leegte refused to transfer his production capacity from the Netherlands and Belgium to low-wage countries in the Far East and Eastern Europe to save money, convinced that it would lead to unacceptable drops in product quality and efficient delivery.

Gerald E. Brennan

PRINCIPAL SUBSIDIARIES

VDL Nederland BV; VDL Holding Belgium NV; VDL International BV; VD Leegte Beheer BV; VDL Bus & Coach BV; VD Leegte Metaal BV; VDL Gereedschapmakerij BV; VDL TIM Hapert BV; VDL Belgium NV; VDL Kunststoffen BV.

PRINCIPAL DIVISIONS

Subcontracting; Buses & Coaches; Finished Products.

PRINCIPAL COMPETITORS

AB Volvo; Airwell-Fedders North America, Inc.; Alfa Laval AB; Comau S.p.A.; Daimler AG; Delta PLC; Denso Corporation; Fu Yu Corporation Limited; Robert Bosch GmbH.

FURTHER READING

Adong, Ton, *Kracht Door Samenwerking, Deel 1: Ontstann en groei de VDL Groep, 1953–1997*, VDL Groep, 1997.

Bueters, Philip, "Wim van der Leegte: 'Ik wil mijn mensen hier houden,'" *FEM Business and Finance*, December 20, 2008.

"VDL boekt recordwinst, maar verwacht een moeilijker jaar," *NRC Handelsblad*, January 18, 2008.

Vecellio Group, Inc.

———— ■ ————

101 Sansbury's Way
West Palm Beach, Florida 33411
U.S.A.
Telephone: (561) 793-2102
Fax: (561) 798-3778
Web site: http://www.vecelliogroup.com

Private Company
Incorporated: 1948 as Vecellio & Grogan, Inc.
Employees: 1,200
Sales: $422 million (2008 est.)
NAICS: 237310 Highway, Street, and Bridge Construction

■ ■ ■

Vecellio Group, Inc., is a West Palm Beach, Florida-based set of heavy/highway contracting, mining, and energy services firms. In addition to road and bridge construction, the group is involved in such areas as asphalt contracting and paving, limestone aggregate production, underground utilities, site development, golf course construction, environmental reclamation, and biodiesel production.

The flagship subsidiary is Vecellio & Grogan, Inc., a West Virginia contractor doing business throughout the Mid-Atlantic and southeastern United States. It also includes White Rock Quarries, a Florida producer of limestone aggregates; and Sharpe Brothers, a North Carolina provider of grading, paving, and utilities services. Another subsidiary, Ranger Construction, offers many of the same services as Vecellio & Grogan, focus-

ing on the Florida market, and includes Ranger Golf, which builds and renovates golf courses in Florida and throughout the country.

Vecellio Group's energy services are tucked into the Vecenergy subsidiary, which includes Vecenergy BIDA, a joint venture with Biodiesel de Andalucia that constructs biodiesel production facilities; Vecenergy Resources, a provider of fuel additives to major oil companies; and Vecenergy Logistics, which constructs port terminals for petroleum and fuel products. Other Vecellio Group units include South Florida Petroleum Services, a Port Everglades, Florida, provider of offloading services for petroleum products, and South Florida Materials, operator of a liquid asphalt and diesel terminal at the Port of Palm Beach and a large terminal in Port Everglades near Fort Lauderdale, both in southeast Florida.

Vecellio Group consistently ranks among the Top 400 Contractors compiled by *Engineering News-Record,* listed among the Top 25 in Transportation, Top 25 in Highways, and Top 20 in Airports. Vecellio Group is owned and operated by the Vecellio family, including members of the fourth generation.

ORIGINS

The origins of Vecellio Group can be traced to a native of northern Italy named Enrico Vecellio who immigrated to the United States. A stonemason by trade, he was in his mid-20s when he found his way to Northfork in West Virginia's McDowell County in 1900, although he did not stay there for long. He did stone and masonry work as a contractor for coal mines and moved his family from place to place to find work. He also moved from partnership to partnership and drifted into road building along the way.

It was during the 1920s that Vecellio and his partners at Gilbert Construction, organized in 1923, became the top highway construction firm in the state. After taking his family to virtually every part of the state, Vecellio finally settled in Beckley, West Virginia, in 1930, after he came to the community to build the Raleigh-Shady Spring road. According to a 1999 profile of Vecellio & Grogan that appeared in the *State Journal* of Charleston, West Virginia, "After moving 29 times in 29 years, Enrico's wife put her foot down and refused to move again."

Another employee of Gilbert Construction was a young man named Eugene G. Grogan, who hailed from Martinsville, Virginia, and came to Beckley in 1930. In 1934 he married Vecellio's daughter, Erma, a graduate of the West Virginia Business College at Fairmont who at the age of 20 began keeping the books at Gilbert Construction. Vecellio's son, Leo, completed his public schooling in Beckley and attended Greenbrier Military School before enrolling at Virginia Polytechnic Institute and State University (Virginia Tech), where he was a star football player and graduated with honors from the engineering department. He also received a commission as a second lieutenant in the Army reserves.

Upon graduation in 1938, Leo Vecellio, his father, and Grogan formed a partnership called Vecellio & Grogan Construction Co. to take on paving projects. Erma Grogan provided office support. The new venture soon landed its first contract, a street-paving job valued at $6,942, and quickly found a steady stream of road paving contracts.

VECELLIO & GROGAN INCORPORATED: 1948

Leo Vecellio remained a lieutenant in the Army Reserve, and after the United States entered World War II, he was called to active duty in May 1942. He was assigned to an airfield construction division in Virginia before being transferred to the Pacific theater, where he built highways and airfields in Burma, China, and India. His father, sister, and Grogan managed to keep the business running until his discharge. Following the war, Vecellio & Grogan was incorporated in 1948, and a year later Vecellio Corporation was chartered.

Grogan was forced into partial retirement due to a rheumatic arthritis condition, which also cost the company the services of his wife, who took a leave of absence to care for him. His health continued to deteriorate, and Grogan passed away at the age of 50 in a Rochester, Minnesota, hospital in December 1949, due to a second attack of jaundice. Five years later, Enrico Vecellio passed away as well. While vacationing in Florida with his family in February 1954, he became ill and lingered in a Miami hospital for a month before succumbing.

During the post-World War II era, the Cold War between the United States and the Soviet Union led to the 1956 passage of the National Interstate and Defense Highways Act, which resulted in the creation of the expansive U.S. interstate highway system, developed not only to help the country move troops and materials in time of war, but also to speed the delivery of goods and services to support the economy on an everyday basis. Vecellio & Grogan received its share of highway projects, winning its first interstate highway contract in 1959.

Also during this period, the company became involved in coal mining, operating through Ranger Fuel Corporation and Sterling Smokeless Coal Company, pursuing both underground mining and surface mining, commonly known as strip mining. The latter form of mining came under fire for the ravaged landscape it left behind. Leo Vecellio was a pioneer in reclaiming surfaces after the removal of coal. He used a ready-mix concrete truck to blend seed and fertilizer and then spread the mixture from a helicopter. In all, he seeded 6,000 acres for ground cover, the largest such reclamation project ever completed in the United States.

Vecellio & Grogan elected to exit the coal business in 1970. After selling a 30 percent stake in Ranger Fuel to Eastern Associated Coal Corp. in January 1970, the company sold the remainder of the business to Pittston Company at the end of the year. Sterling Smokeless was also sold to Eastern Associated. Vecellio & Grogan would reenter the coal business in the mid-1970s but a decade later exited the field for good.

EXPANSION BEYOND WEST VIRGINIA

By necessity, Vecellio & Grogan expanded beyond West Virginia in order to invest in new equipment and keep its people employed. In addition to highway construc-

KEY DATES

1938: Vecellio & Grogan Construction Co. is founded in Beckley, West Virginia.
1954: Founder Enrico Vecellio dies.
1959: Vecellio & Grogan wins its first interstate highway contract.
1979: Vecellio Contracting Corporation, a holding company, is formed to do business in Florida.
1996: Leo Vecellio Jr. becomes third-generation CEO.
2004: Vecenergy energy division is formed.

tion, Vecellio & Grogan became involved in railroad projects in the early 1960s, taking on three major contracts in Kentucky at the same time. It was a watershed moment for the company, which met the challenge and emerged a stronger company, gaining a reputation in the marketplace that would serve it well in the years to come. In the 1970s Vecellio & Grogan was able to use its good name to expand beyond Appalachia.

The 1970s also brought the third generation of the family into the business in the form of Leo Vecellio Jr., who had graduated with a civil engineering degree from Virginia Tech in 1968. He earned a master's degree from Georgia Tech University and served in the military, working on construction projects for the U.S. Air Force. After a four-year stint, in 1973 he joined his father and aunt at Vecellio & Grogan. Erma Vecellio Grogan retired in 1977.

Already familiar with the business, having accompanied his father to job sites all of his life and working for him during summers, the younger Vecellio soon made his mark. At his behest, the company in 1979 formed a holding company, Vecellio Contracting Corporation, to do business in Florida, acquiring West Palm Beach-based heavy/highway contractor Rubin Construction, a company founded in the 1940s and subsequently renamed Ranger Construction Industries.

In that same year, Ranger Golf was launched and constructed most of the courses at PGA National in Palm Beach Gardens. Over the next 20 years the subsidiary would build about 40 courses, mostly in the Mid-Atlantic and southeastern United States. Famed golfer Arnold Palmer, as well as Jack Nicklaus Design, Tom Fazio, Ed Seay, Pete Dye, Gene Bates, and others, designed many of the courses. Ranger Construction, in the meantime, expanded beyond Palm Beach County,

adding operations that spread from Central Florida to the Florida Keys.

WHITE ROCK QUARRIES ADDED: 1986

Vecellio & Grogan added to its Florida holdings in 1986 by starting White Rock Quarries in Miami to provide its area businesses with aggregate. The materials were much in demand. During the 1980s Vecellio & Grogan completed a $20 million contract to build 13 bridges for the I-95 interchange at Jupiter, Florida. Later Ranger Construction received a resurfacing contract for that portion of the interstate highway and interchange. Vecellio & Grogan also expanded its operations in the Mid-Atlantic region during this period. In 1985 the company began building highways in North Carolina, and continued the work into the 1990s. In addition, it landed a contract in 1995 to expand the Greenville-Spartanburg International Airport in South Carolina.

In April 1996 Leo Vecellio Sr. died at the age of 80, leaving his son as the chairman and chief executive of the Vecellio Group of companies. Under his leadership the company continued to grow in the late 1990s, despite a shortage of skilled workers. A notable project during this time was a "smart road" contract from the Virginia Department of Transportation, a 1.7-mile stretch of two-lane road where new transportation technology could be tested.

21ST CENTURY BRINGS FOURTH GENERATION

In the new century the fourth generation of the Vecellio family became involved in the business when the sons of Leo Vecellio Jr., Christopher and Michael, joined their father. It was also during the early years of the 21st century that the Vecellio Group was formed to house the family businesses, which continued to secure major highway and construction projects. In 2003, for example the company won a $67 million contract for work on I-540 in North Carolina. Also in that area, Vecellio & Grogan was awarded three contracts at the Piedmont Triad International Airport worth $73.5 million to provide better service for Federal Express at the airport. In 2009 Ranger completed the largest contract in its history to date, $108 million for an elevated highway section project north of Orlando.

Vecellio Group also upgraded operations and diversified into new areas. An expansion at White Rock in 2004 doubled the facility's production capacity. In that same year, a new energy division was formed under the Vecenergy name. It began with an asphalt terminal at the Port of Palm Beach and expanded to Port Everglades in Fort Lauderdale and included fuel offloading services, petroleum storage and distribution, and fuel additization services. Later in the decade, Vecenergy joined forces with Biodiesel de Andalucia (BIDA), a European company that worked with the University of Cordoba, to form Vecenergy BIDA to build and operate biodiesel production facilities in Europe and potentially in the United States. Vecellio Group also grew through acquisition, purchasing North Carolina-based Sharpe Brothers in 2006.

As the decade progressed, the number of available transportation contracts began to dwindle, due to government cutbacks brought on by a sputtering economy that was hard hit by a slowing residential real estate market. A credit crunch in 2009 made matters worse, but with the election of a new administration in Washington, funds were appropriated to stimulate the economy, a significant portion of which were earmarked for road projects, helping to improve the fortunes of the Vecellio Group. The company appeared well positioned to continue a record of success, and with a fourth generation of the Vecellio family in place, there was every reason to believe it would remain an independent, family owned and operated business for many years to come.

Ed Dinger

PRINCIPAL SUBSIDIARIES

Vecellio & Grogan, Inc.; Sharpe Bros.; Ranger Construction; Vecenergy.

PRINCIPAL COMPETITORS

Colas Inc.; CW Matthews Contracting Co. Inc.; Skanska USA Civil Inc.

FURTHER READING

Arrington, Scott, "Vecellio & Grogan Expanding Beckley Roots Nationwide," *Charleston (W.Va.) State Journal*, February 22, 1999, p. 15.

"Firm Founder Dies at 80," *Charleston Daily Mail*, April 20, 1996, p. 3C.

Maurice, Johanna, "Vecellio ... People Made the Difference in Beckley," *Beckley Post-Herald*, November 4, 1977, p. 17.

"Surface Mine Operators Presented Awards," *Beckley Post-Herald Raleigh Reporter*, December 22, 1968, p. 4.

"Vecellio Rites Set Tentatively, Body to Arrive Today," *Beckley Post-Herald*, March 27, 1954, p. 9.

Vinci S.A.

---

1 cours Ferdinand-de-Lesseps
Rueil-Malmaison, 92851 Cedex
France
Telephone: (+33 1) 47 16 35 00
Fax: (+33 1) 47 51 91 02
Web site: http://www.vinci.com

Public Company
Incorporated: 1899 as Giros et Loucheur
Employees: 163,494
Sales: $48.13 million (2008)
Stock Exchanges: Euronext Paris
Ticker Symbol: DG
NAICS: 237990 Other Heavy and Civil Engineering
Construction; 237310 Highway, Street, and Bridge
Construction; 812930 Parking Lots and Garages

■■■

Vinci S.A. is a French construction and engineering conglomerate that divides its operations among four sectors: construction, roads, concessions, and energies. Vinci Construction is comprises three main subsidiaries in France, Germany, and the United Kingdom, involved in the construction of commercial and industrial buildings, schools, bridges, tunnels, and highways.

Vinci's road sector is conducted through the Eurovia subsidiary, which operates primarily in Europe and to a lesser extent in the United States, and is involved in transport infrastructure projects such as road, airport,

and light rail; industrial production, including about quarries, binder plants, coating plants, recycling facilities, and road equipment manufacturing plants; and maintenance and services of road, rail networks, and urban transport infrastructure.

Vinci Concession operates a variety of transport infrastructure concessions, including toll roads, tunnels, bridges, and parking facilities. Vinci Energies offers energy and information technology services to power generation and distribution companies, manufacturers, transport and telecommunications operators, and local authorities. Vinci, the largest company of its kind in the world, is a public company listed on the Euronext Paris stock exchange.

LATE 19TH-CENTURY ORIGINS

Vinci traces its origins to the beginning of the 20th century. In 1899 Alexandre Giros and Louis Loucheur formed Giros et Loucheur, a small construction company dedicated to public works projects. The company quickly became known as Girolou, which served as the company's telephone number. Giros and Loucheur eyed greater growth in the early 1900s, as France prepared to enter a period of modernization. The restructuring of the country's infrastructure, spurred on the growing use of electricity, automobiles, and other new inventions of the late 19th and early 20th century created new demands for large-scale public works projects and for the companies that could build them. In 1908 Giros and Loucheur changed the name of their company to the more imposing Société Générale des

---

COMPANY PERSPECTIVES

Created in 1899 by French engineers Alexandre Giros and Louis Loucheur, Vinci has become the largest company in construction and related services worldwide.

Entreprises (SGE) and set out to become one of France's largest construction companies.

SGE participated in a number of France's most important public works projects, ranging from the construction of factories, such as the building of the Comines factory in 1922, to the works for the hydroelectric industry, such as the construction of the Chastang dam on the river Dordogne, completed in 1955. SGE also branched out into other areas related to the construction industry, such as electrical installations and power generation. These diversified activities brought the company under the sway of Compagnie Générale d'Electricité, one of France's largest companies and eagerly seeking to expand its own construction and public works operations since the French government had nationalized the electrical power industry in the late 1940s.

Compagnie Générale d'Electricité began the process of transforming SGE into a holding company for its varied construction, public works, and related projects. In 1970 SGE received control of the engineering, construction, and public works activities of its parent company, while Compagnie Générale d'Electricité took over SGE's electrical business and added it to its CGEE-Alsthom subsidiary. Ten years later, Compagnie Générale d'Electricité once again expanded SGE on a grand scale, merging it with another of its subsidiaries, Sainrapt et Brice. The new company, which took the form of a holding company overseeing the extensive operations of both companies, became known as SGESB.

By then, SGE had already added an important new component, that of highway construction and toll road concessions, as France began construction of its Autoroute network. SGE took part in the formation of Cofiroute, later building a majority share, and took over the operations and concessions of the A10 Paris-Poitiers highway and the A11 Paris-Le Mans highway. Cofiroute was to extend its highway operations through the 1970s and 1980s, becoming one of France's top toll road operators.

SAINT GOBAIN ASSUMES CONTROL: 1984

While many of France's industries were undergoing an ambitious nationalization program under the government led by François Mitterrand, the country's major companies were playing a particularly French form of musical chairs, as the companies transferred their shareholding positions among a number of entities, including SGESB. As such, by 1984 SGESB had come under the majority control of a new owner, diversified conglomerate Saint Gobain, which had achieved its majority position through the transfer of the main pieces of its "Enterprise" division. By the mid-1990s, SGE had res-implified its name and added a number of new company names to its list of holdings, including Saunier Duval, Tunzini, Wanner Isofi, and Sobea.

This last company, a construction and public works specialist, had originally been founded as Etablissements Girault in 1878. In 1918, after coming under control of the Pont-a-Mousson group (itself later merged into Saint Gobain), the company took on the name Eau et Assainissement. The company went on to develop expertise in hydraulics and civil engineering projects as well as major construction projects. After its merger with another water services company, Socoman in 1961, it took on the new name of Socea, before becoming the lead company of the newly merged Saint Gobain-Pont-a-Mousson group's Entreprises et Services in 1970. The addition of rival Balency-Briard, in 1979, gave the company a new name, Sobea.

In 1985 the newly enlarged SGE merged its existing construction and public works subsidiary, SGE-BTP, with its new Sobea assets, creating the new company Sogea, one of the world's top 10 construction companies. Three years later, SGE was to find itself under new management and expanded to a new scale. The acquisition of majority control of SGE by the French industrial and water services group Générale des Eaux (later Vivendi) was accompanied by two immediate steps. The first was the purchase, by Générale des Eaux, of Saint Gobain's insulation and heating and air conditioning subsidiary, G+H Montage, which not only added its expertise, but gave SGE a strong entry into its new subsidiaries German domestic market. The second move by Générale des Eaux was to transfer its own construction and public works subsidiaries, including Viafrance, Campenon Bernard, and Freyssinet, to SGE.

Freyssinet had taken its name from civil engineering genius Eugène Freyssinet. One of 20th-century France's leading bridge and industrial building designers, Freyssinet had also developed a new form of prestressed concrete that made possible new types of large scale construction techniques. The Freyssinet company,

KEY DATES

1899: The Giros et Loucheur construction company is established.
1908: Company changes name to Société Générale des Entreprises (SGE).
1966: SGE is acquired by Compagnie Générale d'Electricité (CGE).
1970: SGE acquires parent CGE's engineering, construction, and public works operations.
1988: Générale des Eaux (later Vivendi) gains control.
2000: Vivendi sells most of stake; SGE is renamed Vinci.
2007: Vinci Park enters U.S. market.

bridges, the company also became a prominent builder of nuclear power facilities, as well as developing expertise in constructing tunnels and viaducts.

INTERNATIONAL EXPANSION

Campenon Bernard became a spearhead for SGE's expanded construction and public works holdings. In 1992 SGE transferred its Sogea subsidiary's operations to Campenon Bernard, which then became known as Campenon Bernard SGE. By then, SGE had been undergoing its own international expansion drive in the run-up to the unification of the European Union's economic interests. In 1989 SGE acquired 55 percent of the United Kingdom's Norwest Holst, a position the company was to increase to 100 percent control in 1991, after expanding Norwest Holst in 1990 with the addition of fellow U.K. company Rosser & Russell.

SGE also looked across the French border to Germany, where it acquired OBG and VU, the first a construction company, the latter a roadworks company, both based in the former East Germany. SGE continued to acquire companies in that part of Germany, taking over MLTU and OBAG in 1992. SGE's German acquisitions were to continue into the mid-1990s, with the takeovers of Controlmatic and Klee.

Back home in France, SGE was also expanding its holdings, notably with the purchase of highway group Moter, based in the south of France. Through its Campenon Bernard SGE subsidiary, SGE was meanwhile posting a number of construction triumphs, such as the 17-kilometer-long Vasco de Gama bridge in Lisbon, the first nuclear power plant built in China's Daya Bay, and the completion of the Normandy bridge in 1995. That year also marked the award of the contract to conceive and build the Stade de France in Paris, which was completed for the Soccer World Cup in 1998. In 1997 Campenon Bernard SGE took control of the French and European operations of the construction business of CBC, another Générale des Eaux subsidiary, giving SGE a greater balance between its construction and civil engineering operations, while also strengthening its international presence. Nonetheless, nearly 95 percent of SGE's business came from Europe, and some 75 percent of its business was generated among France, Germany, and the United Kingdom.

originally known as the Société Technique pour l'Utilisation de la Précontrainte (Stup), was formed in 1943 in order to exploit an exclusive right to use the prestressed concrete.

Stup quickly expanded onto the international scene, and became known worldwide for such construction projects as the Caracas Viaducts in Venezuela, the bridge over Lake Pontchartrain in the United States, and a series of bridges over the Marne River. The loss of the company's prestressed concrete monopoly encouraged Stup (renamed Freyssinet) to diversify its activities in the 1960s and 1970s, in particular into the construction subcontracting category. The company's diversification continued into the 1980s, leading to the construction of nuclear power facilities, the Gladesville bridge in Australia, the Montreal Olympics complex, and more.

When Freyssinet came under control of Générale des Eaux, it found itself in the company of another Générale des Eaux subsidiary, Campenon Bernard (which had joined in the founding of Stup). Campenon had been founded in the 1920s by Edmé Campenon and André Bernard. The company presented diversified interests from its start, with construction projects ranging from railroad and highway construction to industrial facilities. Campenon Bernard was also largely responsible for the building of structures for the famed Maginot Line defense system. The company's diversified interests enabled it to become one of pre-World War II France's largest public works companies. In the postwar period, Campenon Bernard was highly active in helping to reconstruct the damage to France's infrastructure, before turning its attention to international expansion. Apart from construction of many of the world's largest

The transition from SGE to Vinci began in earnest in the late 1990s. In 1997 Générale des Eaux began a reorganization process that was to transform it into Vivendi. As part of this process, SGE was refocused on its core construction, public works, conjcessions, and related services operations, and a number of its assets, including its waste management subsidiaries, water distribution operations, real estate—were transferred to Générale des Eaux. At the same time, Générale des Eaux shifted a number of its holdings under SGE, including its GTIE and Santerne electric works subsidiaries. The transfer increased Générale des Eaux's holding in SGE to more than 85 percent, which Générale des Eaux then reduced to just over 50 percent by the end of that year.

LATE CENTURY REORGANIZATION

As Générale des Eaux became Vivendi, SGE itself was preparing to be launched as an independent company for the first time since the mid-1960s. In 1998 and 1999, SGE began its own restructuring of its holdings, grouping its subsidiaries under four divisions: Concessions, Equipment (which then became Energy and Information), Road Works, and Construction. SGE accompanied its reorganization with a new commitment to external growth. Beginning in 1998, the company's subsidiaries began to make a series of important acquisitions, including Freyssinet's purchase of Terre Armée Internationale in 1998; three fire protection companies, Calanbau, Mecatiss, and Vraco in 1999; and then Ménard Soltraitement, Teerbau, the German roadworks leader, and lastly, the French parking garage and parking lot leader Sogeparc.

In February 2000, Vivendi (which, after its merger with Universal and acquisition of Seagrams, was in the process of redefining itself as a world-leading communications and entertainment company) substantially reduced its remaining holding in SGE, selling another 32 percent of its shares, reducing its holding to just 17 percent. By the end of that year, Vivendi had all but exited from SGE's capital. The company's newly acquired independent status, as well as its increasing interest in global development, led it to change its name to Vinci in May 2000.

With the change in name also came a change in strategy. Vinci sought to become less dependent on the cyclical construction industry and more involved in the concession sector with its recurring business and more predictable revenue streams. The company pursued France's toll motorway business, the car park business in both Europe and the United States, and the global airport services market. At the same time, Vinci remained committed to the construction sector. Vinci was able to meet its dual needs by acquiring the French construction and concession company GTM Group in a $1.7 billion stock deal completed in late 2000 that created the world's largest construction company, generating annual sales of EUR 17 billion.

Vinci beefed up its non-construction assets through other deals in 2000. It acquired Baker Support Services, Inc., an American company that provided facility management, maintenance, and support services. Vinci also acquired a car park company in Spain, Aparcamientos Vallerhermoso, operator of seven public and five residential car parks, and won the contract to operate three car parks in Prague, Czech Republic. In Slovakia, in the meantime, Vinci's roadworks subsidiary acquired a roadworks contractor.

VINCI PARK: 2002

Expansion into businesses with recurring income continued in the early 2000s. In 2001 Vinci acquired Energilec, a manager of residential buildings and office towers. World Flight Services, an airport services group, was also acquired that year. A year later Vinci added to its facilities management business with the acquisition of Crispin & Borst, a U.K. company serving both public and private sector clients in the London market. Additionally, Vinci reorganized its car park business, forming the Vinci Park umbrella brand for its operations in 12 countries that included 900 car parks. In 2003 Vinci Park expanded at an accelerated pace, completing further acquisitions and winning new contracts that added 70,000 parking spaces to its inventory.

On other fronts, Vinci Energies acquired the Dutch company Netlink in 2004 to expand its European footprint in energy and information technology. The business network was bolstered further with the acquisition of a German company, NK Networks & Services, a network infrastructure integration, Internet telephony, and network security company. It brought with it operations in nine German cities.

While Vinci was enjoying strong growth it also had to contend with internal strife. In June 2005 chairman and chief executive officer Antoine Zacharias agreed to turn over the latter position to Xavier Hulliard, a senior vice president, who took over in January 2006. Although Zacharias had recruited Hulliard in 1996, the two men soon fell out. Following a successful acquisition, Zacharias attempted to award himself a $10.3 million bonus, according to French press reports, only to have Hulliard object and accuse Zacharias of "enriching himself beyond all reason."

In a letter written to Vinci's board of directors, Hulliard claimed that between 2000 and the start of 2006, Zacharias had awarded himself stock options worth $320 million. Moreover, Hulliard stated, "I realize now that I have been the honest façade for a man who has progressively set about enriching himself beyond all reason on the back of Vinci." Zacharias tried to have Hulliard removed but failed to win the necessary support from the board of directors. He subsequently tendered his resignation, and this time the board complied and replaced him with Yves-Thibault de Silguy, a former Suez senior executive and member of the European Commission for economic affairs.

MOVE INTO U.S. MARKET: 2007

French water utility Veolia Environnement SA made a friendly takeover bid for Vinci in June 2006, but the offer was quickly rejected. Vinci remained independent and continued to expand under Hulliard's direction. Vinci Energies completed a dozen acquisitions in 2006 to widen in footprint in Europe. A year later Vinci Park entered the United States by acquiring a half-interest in LAZ Parking, a Connecticut-based firm that managed more than 225,000 parking spaces in 77 U.S. cities, including Atlanta, Boston, Chicago, Dallas, Miami, New York City, and Washington, D.C. Also in 2007 Vinci Park acquired a German company, NETPARK GmbH, adding 25 car parks in that country. Vinci Park's presence in the United States grew further in 2009 when LAZ Parking acquired Ultimate Parking in Boston, a major valet parking operator.

Vinci's strategy of bolstering the concession sector with its recurring business paid dividends in 2009 when a global recession adversely impacted most of the company's activities. The concession division's revenues increased 2.4 percent in a year in which overall revenues fell 4.6 percent. Construction revenues fell 7.5 percent, but it remained Vinci's primary business, contributing about half of all revenues. While there was little doubt it would remain the core operation, the contributions from Vinci's other operations would be counted on to smooth out the rough patches in the years to come.

M. L. Cohen
Updated, Ed Dinger

PRINCIPAL DIVISIONS

Vinci Concessions; Vinci Roads; Vinci Energy; Vinci Construction.

PRINCIPAL COMPETITORS

Bouygues S.A.; Eiffage S.A.; Skanska AB.

FURTHER READING

"French Builders to Merge," *New York Times,* July 14, 2000, p. C4.

Le Goff, Delphine, "La Renaissance de la SGE," *Strategies,* June 16, 2000.

"Le nouveau groupe Vinci-GTM va jouer la carte des concessions à l'international," *La Tribune,* July 18, 2000.

Niyoyita, Aloys, "Veolia Environment Drops Plan for Vinci Tie-Up," *America's Intelligence Wire,* June 17, 2006.

"Record Sales for Vinci," *Construction Europe,* March 2004, p. 9.

"Vinci Chairman Resigns in Board Showdown over Fat-Cat Accusations," *America's Intelligence Wire,* June 1, 2006.

"Vinci nouveau numéro un mondial de la construction," *Le Figaro Economie,* July 13, 2000.

"Vinci to Launch Bid for GTM in Euro 1.83 Billion, All-Share Deal," *Wall Street Journal,* July 14, 2000.

"Vinci Woos Nervous Investors with Stable Credit Ahead of Debut Euro-Sterling Issue," *Euroweek,* July 5, 2002, p. 4.

Warsteiner Group

——————————●——————————

Domring 4-10
Warstein, D-59581
Germany
Telephone: (49 2902) 88-0
Fax: (49 2902) 88-1219
Web site: http://www.warsteiner.com

Wholly Owned Subsidiary of Haus Cramer Holding KG
Incorporated: 1898 as Warsteiner Bierbrauerei Casp.
   Cramer, Warstein
Employees: 2,200
Sales: EUR 560 million ($778 million) (2009 est.)
NAICS: 312120 Breweries

■ ■ ■

The Warsteiner Group, under the corporate umbrella of Haus Cramer Holding KG, is one of the largest privately owned brewery groups in Germany. The company's main product, the Pilsner Warsteiner Premium Verum, is one of Germany's most popular beer brands and is also being produced abroad under license by a number of partner breweries. In addition, Warsteiner puts out a nonalcoholic version of its flagship brand and produces a variety of mixed beer-and-soda-pop beverages under the Warsteiner label.

The Warsteiner group holds major stakes in six other German breweries that put out a range of wheat beers, dark ales, and Pilsner beers, and distributes the Guinness and Kilkenny brands of the British Diageo group in Germany. The company owns the Casa Isenbeck brewery in Argentina and operates joint ventures with the French Castel Group in Cameroon, Nigeria, and Gambia. Based in Warstein in the Sauerland region, the group, which consists of over 120 different companies, exports more than one-quarter of its total output to about 60 countries around the globe. Warsteiner is owned and managed by the eight and ninth generations of the Cramer family.

HOME BREWERY GROWS IN 18TH CENTURY

The first record of the Cramer family's brewing tradition goes back to the farmer Antonius Cramer who was required to pay taxes for the first time in 1753 for his home-brewed beer. In the following years Cramer continued to grow his side business, serving beer to guests in his home in Warstein in the western German Sauerland region. After his son, Johannes Vitus Cramer, married the daughter of a local brewer, Antonius Cramer handed down the business to him.

Johannes Vitus continued to develop the home-based brewing business in the second half of the 18th century. Centrally located right across the street from the Old Church in Warstein's uptown, his home soon became a popular meeting place for churchgoers who quenched their thirst before or after mass with Cramer's home brew. Cramer's beer also became a staple at local events such as dances, weddings, baby showers, and funerals. However, some of his fellow citizens begrudged the well-connected, business-savvy farmer and brewer his success. As the story goes, malicious neighbors set a fire to Cramer's barn in 1792, wiping out a whole year's grain harvest.

COMPANY PERSPECTIVES

We work together. The Warsteiner Group is a company that has values and tradition. Our Group has a high standard: to develop quality, produce quality and guarantee quality. A very important source of this quality is the dedication of our employees—that's why teamwork, continuing education, training and career advancement have always been part and parcel of the corporate philosophy. *Philosophy.* This might be the place to mention the extraordinary taste of WARSTEINER beers, but ultimately you can only experience this for yourself—with every sip. Thanks to the latest brewing technology, the Warsteiner Group guarantees top quality in all categories and varieties. The reasons for this include the original, particularly soft brewing water, resource-conserving use of other valuable ingredients such as hops and malt, and above all the extreme dedication of our employees from all parts of the company—production, distribution, marketing and administration—to the art of brewing.

After another fire on New Year's Eve destroyed the whole city in 1802, Johannes Vitus together with his son Caspar Cramer built a larger house for his family and business in Warstein's city center. As home of the Domschänke Inn, it featured a tavern on the main floor and several guest rooms along with the family's private rooms on the upper floors, and included a brewery in the basement. Centrally located in downtown, the Cramers' inn quickly regained its popularity and survived the next 200 years in its original structure and style.

FROM TRADITIONAL BREWING TO INDUSTRIAL PRODUCTION

After taking over the family business, Caspar Cramer, together with his son Johann Matthias, continued his father's work into the 19th century. With further growth in mind, he acquired several pieces of land bordering the Domschänke Inn as well as additional farming land in Warstein. Johann Matthias Cramer inherited the family business in 1835 and married the widowed and wealthy daughter of Petronella Cramer, one of the company founder's granddaughters. One of their sons, Caspar Josef Cramer, who married the daughter of an innkeeper in 1868, continued to run the family brewery in the second half of the 19th century.

After the newly built St. Pancratius Church opened its doors to worshippers right next-door to the Domschänke Inn in 1853, the Cramers' brewery flourished again. Until that time, the process of brewing beer had not changed much. Filling large amounts of boiling water into big vats while constantly stirring the hops-and-malt mixture for over an hour with wooden sticks, emptying and refilling the vats with buckets, mixing in the yeast, and finally filling the beer from the vats into barrels with large pitchers, was all done by hand.

However, a number of groundbreaking inventions revolutionized the brewing trade in the second half of the 19th century. Refrigeration technology allowed for longer storage and long-distance transportation, and the breeding of specialized yeast cultures made the fermentation process controllable and enabled brewers to produce many batches of beer with the same characteristics and taste. Industrialization attracted a growing number of people to Warstein who worked in stone quarries, iron ore mines, and iron and steel works, and also populated the city's taprooms.

With these fundamental changes under way, Caspar Josef Cramer's sons Albert and August took the plunge and transformed the traditional home brewery into an industrial enterprise. After he learned the maltster craft and graduated from brewing school in Worms in 1896, the 22-year-old Albert Cramer persuaded his brother August and his father to invest in state-of-the-art brewing equipment. Stretching the family's financial resources to the limits, the Cramers invested in a brand-new mechanized brew house with steam-engine driven water and beer pumps and replaced the wooden fermentation barrels with metal kegs. In 1898 the brewery was incorporated as Warsteiner Bierbrauerei Casp. Cramer, Warstein.

SUITABLE SPRINGWATER DISCOVERED BETWEEN WORLD WARS

It took 10 years for the company to pay back the debt incurred for the investment in an industrial enterprise. At the beginning of World War I the company was transformed from a general partnership into a limited liability company. On September 25, 1915, August Cramer died on the battlefield. Albert Cramer continued to manage the business, which by then employed ten workers, a master brewer, and three clerks. Despite the brewery's high technical standard, the company had to work hard to defend its customer base against the competition of large breweries from the nearby Ruhr region. Warsteiner's annual output increased from 3,000 hectoliters in 1897 to more than double that in 1924.

KEY DATES

■

1753: Farmer Antonius Cramer starts paying taxes for his home-brewed beer.

1803: Caspar Cramer builds a brewery in Warstein's city center.

1928: The company starts specializing in brewing Pilsner beer using selected local springwater.

1978: Production is moved to a newly built brewery in Warstein.

1983: The company starts exporting Warsteiner Pilsner to the United States.

1984: Warsteiner is Germany's largest private brewery by output.

1991: The company takes over the Paderborner Brewery.

2001: Warsteiner acquires a stake in the Bavarian König Ludwig brewery.

A major problem Warsteiner brewery was struggling with was the hard water used for brewing, which resulted in a beer of less satisfactory quality. The calciferous water also clogged pipelines and machinery, resulting in higher maintenance costs. Realizing that the future of the business depended heavily on a high-quality product, Albert Cramer started searching for new water supplies and finally found what he was looking for.

In 1928 a spring was discovered in a nearby forest that yielded particularly soft water which was highly suitable for brewing beer. Soon after, Warsteiner started brewing Pilsner beer, a top-fermented beer of light-yellow color that was becoming increasingly popular. Named after the so-called Kaiserquelle or Emperor's Spring, the new beer was named Warsteiner Kaiserbräu, Warsteiner Emperor's Brew.

Although Warsteiner Kaiserbräu was bottled in the 1920s and 1930s, the majority of the brewery's output was still sold in barrels and transported to its customers by horse carriage and later by truck. While beer consumption dropped in the early 1930s due to the Great Depression, Warsteiner brewery managed to defend its core market against a rising number of competitors. In 1937 the company modernized and expanded production facilities and started producing nonalcoholic beverages such as soda pop.

During World War II Warsteiner's production was put under state control. The brewery put out a beer-like beverage during that time, using whey instead of malt,

which was not available as raw material, and started supplying customers of Dortmunder Brauerei, one of the company's main competitors which had been heavily damaged by bombings, in the Sauerland region. Three sons, Albert Cramer Jr., Willi Cramer, and August Cramer Jr., and seven brewery employees were killed during the war.

MASSIVE GROWTH AFTER WORLD WAR II

It took much effort by the Cramer family and the remaining employees to prevent the Allied forces' military administration from confiscating the company's brewhouse, to repair the war damage, and to get the company up and running again after World War II. However, Warsteiner started producing beer and nonalcoholic beverages again as early as in 1945. The brewery became a supplier to the British, Canadian, and U.S. troops to whom Warsteiner was delivered in custom-designed aluminum cans. In 1952 the company also started manufacturing apple juice.

Albert Cramer oversaw the family business until his sudden death in 1953 and was succeeded by his sons Paul and Josef Cramer. With the postwar economic boom in Germany in full swing, Warsteiner grew by leaps and bounds during the 1950s. Under Paul Cramer as technical director, the brewery as well as its fleet of delivery vehicles was constantly modernized and expanded. A new building in Warstein's city center housed the company's filling plant and shipping division.

As the competition from large breweries in the Ruhr grew stronger again in the 1950s, Warsteiner intensified its marketing efforts. Under Josef Cramer's direction, the company established a new sales division, launched promotional campaigns, and supported its customers from the hospitality trade in setting up and growing their businesses. Within one decade Warsteiner's output grew fivefold, from roughly 18,000 hectoliters in 1950 to 94,000 hectoliters in 1959. Finally, the company passed the 100,000 hectoliter mark in 1960, joining the ranks of Germany's largest breweries.

SUCCESS WITH BRAND STRATEGY AFTER 1960

After Josef Cramer's early death in 1962, his brother Paul was responsible for steering the company through another period of rapid growth. In 1968 he was joined by his son Albert, who had studied business administration and who took care of the brewery's marketing activities, and later by Josef Cramer's son Claus, who assumed responsibility for administration and finances. After Claus Cramer died in an accident in 1985, Albert Cramer became the company's sole owner.

As early as the 1930s Warsteiner had advertised its Pilsner in movie theaters. As the postwar boom in Germany faded in the 1960s, the company intensified its marketing efforts. Warsteiner Pilsner was advertised in newspapers and popular magazines and on television. To emphasize the brand's upscale appeal, the company introduced the slogan "a queen among beers" in the early 1960s. In the 1970s the brewery introduced a gift delivery service that shipped decorative gift cartons with a dozen or so bottles of Warsteiner Pilsner and coasters or small party-sized kegs anywhere in Germany.

Although the country's beer market started shrinking in the 1970s, Warsteiner's sales continued to soar, pushing the company to the limits of the existing production and distribution capacity. In the middle of the decade Warsteiner began to move operations to new company grounds near the Kaiserquelle spring. By 1978 the move was completed, and Warsteiner was one of Europe's most technically sophisticated breweries.

In the 1970s the company also streamlined its product portfolio. The brewery discontinued the production of stout and bock beer, Kaiser-Bräu Export, and malt beer as well as the filling of soda pop and table water, until by 1977 Warsteiner Pilsner remained the company's sole product. Supported by massive advertising and promotion campaigns, the one-brand strategy became a success. Having already tripled between 1970 and 1979, the company's output more than doubled again until 1989. By 1984 Warsteiner had become Germany's largest private brewery.

ACQUISITIONS AND VENTURES ABROAD AFTER 1990

As the German beer market went into decline in the 1990s, competition among breweries became increasingly intense. To defend its market position in Germany and to generate further growth, Warsteiner acquired a number of regional specialty breweries and intensified efforts to expand abroad. The year 1991 saw the acquisition of Paderborner Brewery in Paderborn, about 25 miles northeast of Warstein, where the company started producing the nonalcoholic Warsteiner Premium Fresh and the low-calorie Premium Light varieties along with other local brands.

After entering the U.S. market in 1983, sales of Warsteiner Premium grew rapidly during the 1990s. According to the *Beer Handbook*'s 2000 edition, Warsteiner importers' shipments in the United States more than doubled between 1994 and 1999. In 1994 Warsteiner

established the Casa Isenbeck brewery in Argentina and started business ventures in Cameroon, Nigeria, and Gambia in the 1990s that were continued as joint ventures with the French Castel group in 2008. In 2002 the company entered a partnership with Turkish beverage group Efes, which started producing Warsteiner premium Pilsner in its brewery in Moscow for the Russian market. In 2005 the brewery started distributing the Guinness and Kilkenny brands of the British Diageo group in Germany.

Warsteiner also continuously expanded its foreign sales organizations and partnerships with local importers and distributors. Italy and the Netherlands became major export markets in Western Europe. Warsteiner added Chile and Uruguay to its growing list of export countries in the early 2000s. All in all, the company's exports grew roughly fivefold between 1990 and 2009. After the turn of the 21st century Warsteiner acquired major stakes in three regional German breweries, including the Bavarian König Ludwig Schlossbrauerei Kaltenberg in 2001, Düsseldorf-based dark ale brewery Frankenheim in 2005, and the Westphalian premium Pilsner brewery Herforder Brauerei that was taken over in 2007.

REORGANIZATION, NEW PRODUCTS AFTER 2000

While these activities added to Warsteiner's revenues and boosted exports, the company's flagship brand witnessed a significant downturn in its core market in Germany. With the output of Premium Verum roughly cut in half from an all-time high of almost six million hectoliters in 1995 to about 3.5 million hectoliters a decade later, the company lost its market leadership in the premium Pilsner segment. In an attempt to reverse the trend, Warsteiner took a variety of measures.

The company launched promotional and advertising campaigns, reorganized and strengthened its sales organization, and intensified contacts with retail accounts. As the trend of decreasing sales and shrinking market share in Germany persisted, Warsteiner affirmed the commitment to its premium segment strategy, stopped supplying discount stores and even raised prices for its flagship brand, which resulted in diminished sales but increased profitability. The company streamlined its product portfolio and production capacities, reduced its workforce, brought in new management, and introduced a new corporate structure by establishing four operational holding companies under the umbrella of Haus Cramer Holding KG.

On the other hand, Warsteiner modernized its brand and product design and, according to the new umbrella brand concept. The company successfully introduced several varieties of beer mixed with soda pop as well as the Warsteiner Premium Alkoholfrei with no alcohol. In the United States the company launched the calorie-reduced HiLight, the dark beer Premium Dunkel, and the seasonal Oktoberfest varieties under the Warsteiner label. To strengthen the brewery's market position in Germany, the company intensified efforts to establish the low-priced Pilsner Paderborner as a major brand at the lower end of the market.

In 2006 Albert Cramer's youngest daughter Eva-Catharina joined her father as managing partner of the Warsteiner group of companies, the number of which had grown to over 120 by 2010. Confirming to the press repeatedly that the company was not for sale, the Cramer family continued to work on realizing the vision of building up Warsteiner Premium as a European brand, as well as on establishing their enterprise as a diverse international beverage concern.

Evelyn Hauser

PRINCIPAL SUBSIDIARIES

Warsteiner Brauerei Haus Cramer KG; Warsteiner International KG; Warsteiner Distribution KG; Haus Cramer Assets KG; König Ludwig GmbH & Co. KG Schlossbrauerei Kaltenberg; Herforder Brauerei GmbH & Co. KG; Paderborner Brauerei GmbH & Co. KG; Frankenheim GmbH & Co. KG; C.A.S.A. Isenbeck (Argentina).

PRINCIPAL COMPETITORS

Anheuser-Busch InBev; Bitburger Braugruppe GmbH; Brau Holding International GmbH & Co. KGaA; Carlsberg A/S; Karlsberg Brauerei KG Weber; Krombacher Brauerei Bernhard Schadeberg GmbH & Co. KG; Radeberger Gruppe KG.

FURTHER READING

"Frischer Wind im Hause Warsteiner," *Welt am Sonntag,* October 21, 2007.

"Germany: Warsteiner Lines Up Brewer Purchase," just-drinks. com, 2007.

"Ich verkaufe nicht!" *Focus,* March 1, 2003, p. 172.

"Image Means Everything," *Modern Brewery Age,* July 13, 1992, p. 46.

Scheffran-Pieper, Barbara, *Das einzig wahre Warsteiner. Tradition und Innovation 1753–2003,* Warstein, Germany: Warsteiner Brauerei, 2003.

Vossen, Manfred, "Warsteiner leidet noch," *Lebensmittel Zeitung,* January 20, 2006, p. 22.

"Warsteiner Adds Another Brewery," *Modern Brewery Age,* March 4, 1991, p. 1.

"Warsteiner Announces Brand Expansion, 1st Quarter Sales Increase," *Modern Brewery Age,* May 10, 1993, p. 3.

"Warsteiner bündelt mit Castel," *Lebensmittel Zeitung,* August 15, 2008, p. 15.

"Warsteiner Gives Priority to Profitability," *Europe Intelligence Wire,* July 28, 2003.

"Warsteiner Importers Shipments, 1994–1999," *Beer Handbook,* Bev-AL Communications, Inc., 2000, p. 132.

"Warsteiner Reinforces Brand Strategy with New Product Design," *Business Wire,* July 29, 2009.

"Warsteiner to Boost Sales with Cheap Brand," *Europe Intelligence Wire,* March 21, 2005.

"Warsteiner to Increase Prices to Meet Business Costs," *Europe Intelligence Wire,* November 11, 2002.

Winn-Dixie Stores, Inc.

5050 Edgewood Court
Jacksonville, Florida 32254-3699
U.S.A.
Telephone: (904) 783-5000
Fax: (904) 370-7224
Web site: http://www.winn-dixie.com

Public Company
Incorporated: 1928 as Winn & Lovett Grocery Company
Employees: 50,000
Sales: $7.37 billion (2009)
Stock Exchanges: NASDAQ
Ticker Symbol: WINN
NAICS: 445110 Supermarkets and Other Grocery (Except Convenience) Stores

■ ■ ■

Based in Jacksonville, Florida, Winn-Dixie Stores, Inc., is one of the nation's largest food retailers, with 515 stores in the southeastern states of Florida, Alabama, Louisiana, Georgia, and Mississippi. The *Fortune* 500 company tracks consumer trends via a Customer Reward Card program. In addition to its stores, Winn-Dixie has distribution centers in Jacksonville, Miami, and Orlando, Florida; Hammond, Louisiana; and Montgomery, Alabama, as well as several food and beverage plants.

EARLY HISTORY

Winn-Dixie's founder, William M. Davis, was the owner of an old-fashioned charge-and-deliver general store in Idaho before World War I. The advent of self-service, cash-and-carry chain stores after the war drove many old-fashioned independent grocers out of business. Davis, however, saw the potential of this new kind of grocery store. He moved his family to Miami, Florida, borrowed $10,000, and entered the self-service grocery business. He bought his first store, the Rockmoor Grocery, in the Miami suburb of Lemon City in 1925. Davis, his wife, and their four sons ran the store. The Davis family went on to lead the company for many decades.

In the early years Davis found it difficult to expand. Three times he attempted to open a second store and three times the store failed. Chain stores had demonstrated their ability to deliver a wider variety of high-quality goods at lower prices than had ever before been possible, but many consumers still preferred the old way of doing business. After consumers' initial resistance was overcome, however, it became evident that supermarkets were the wave of the future. By 1927 the Rockmoor Grocery had expanded to five stores, which were renamed Table Supply Stores that year. Having expanded to Tampa in 1931 with the $10,000 purchase of Lively Stores, the company operated 34 stores in south Florida by 1934, the year W. M. Davis died.

Davis's four sons took control of the company at their father's death and set out on a course of further expansion. In 1939 they acquired control of the 78 stores of the Winn & Lovett Grocery Company of Florida and Georgia. In 1944 the company established its headquarters in Jacksonville, Florida, and officially adopted the Winn & Lovett name.

The war years brought a lull in the supermarket industry. Food rationing, labor shortages, and price increases forced supermarkets to tighten their belts with the rest of the nation. Winn & Lovett, along with most of the supermarket industry, cooperated with the government by maintaining a lid on prices during and immediately following the war. During this time nonfood products filled what would otherwise have been empty shelves, and began to assume a more prominent place in supermarkets. The higher profit margins on nonfood products allowed supermarkets to maintain food prices at relatively low levels without jeopardizing overall profitability.

MERGER WITH DIXIE HOME STORES CREATES WINN-DIXIE: 1955

Once the economy had returned to normal, Winn & Lovett picked up where it had left off before the war. In 1945 the company expanded into Kentucky with the purchase of 31 Steiden Store units. An additional 46 Florida stores were gained in 1949 through the acquisition of Margaret Ann Stores. Winn & Lovett became the first Florida industrial corporation to gain a listing on the New York Stock Exchange in 1952. Three years later the company added several more grocery chains to its company rolls, including Penney Stores in Mississippi and two South Carolina chains, Ballentine Stores and Eden Stores.

Later in 1955, Winn & Lovett merged with Dixie Home Stores of Greenville, South Carolina, which operated 117 stores, and changed its name to Winn-Dixie Stores, Inc. With this merger, Winn-Dixie broke into the top 10 supermarket chains and from the mid-1950s to the mid-1960s was the most profitable company in the industry. Profits in the supermarket industry are more dependent on high volume than high-profit margins, but Winn-Dixie's profit margins in this period were exceptionally high. This was due to both an increase in sales (fourfold between 1954 and 1964) and lower labor costs in the nonunion South. Winn-Dixie continued to expand and prosper in the late 1950s and early 1960s.

In 1956 alone, Winn-Dixie acquired 24 North Carolina stores from Ketner-Milner Stores, Inc.; 42 Hill Store units in the New Orleans area; and 9 Kings outlets in Georgia. In 1962 the company acquired Hill Grocery Co., Inc., and its 35 stores in the Birmingham, Alabama, area. In addition to acquiring more retail outlets, Winn-Dixie also branched out into processing, manufacturing, and distribution, producing a wide variety of store brand products from these support facilities. With profits increasing each year and with 23 consecutive years of cash dividend increases, Chairman J. E. Davis (one of W. M. Davis's sons) could confidently predict in the *Wall Street Journal* in 1966 that Winn-Dixie would shatter all previous sales and profit records in fiscal 1967.

TROUBLES WITH THE FTC: 1966

The year 1966 also brought some bad news, however. The Federal Trade Commission (FTC) had been investigating the increasing concentration in the supermarket industry and had concluded that mergers and acquisitions in the industry had unfairly limited competition, in violation of the Clayton Anti-Trust Act. Winn-Dixie, as the most profitable and one of the fastest-growing chains, was an obvious target. The investigation showed that, in fact, a third of Winn-Dixie's increase in sales over the previous 10 years had been generated by stores acquired during that period. As a result, the FTC ruled that for 10 years Winn-Dixie was forbidden to acquire any retail grocery stores in the United States without FTC approval.

The ruling was not as much a punishment of Winn-Dixie as it was a settlement between the firm and the FTC, and the company hoped it would serve to alleviate challenges to all previous acquisitions and mergers. All that was required of Winn-Dixie was obedience to the ruling. Winn-Dixie used the 10-year period for "internal" expansion, adding stores by leasing new stores and improving existing retail and support facilities. Winn-Dixie did acquire 11 City Market stores in the Bahamas that were not covered by the FTC order.

When the ban was lifted in 1976, Winn-Dixie acquired the 135 stores and the support facilities of Kimbell, Inc., in Texas, Oklahoma, and New Mexico. The stores in New Mexico, which were unionized, posed a problem for the traditionally nonunion Winn-Dixie. After the company refused to negotiate with the union and a pro-union boycott began, Winn-Dixie sold its New Mexico stores in 1979.

INCREASED COMPETITION

In 1983 J. E. Davis stepped down as chairman of Winn-Dixie, and a member of the third generation of

KEY DATES

■

1925: William M. Davis enters the self-service grocery business through the purchase of Rockmoor Grocery in a suburb of Miami, Florida.

1939: The company gains control of the Winn & Lovett Grocery Company, which operates 78 stores in Florida and Georgia.

1944: The company adopts the Winn & Lovett name and moves its headquarters to Jacksonville, Florida.

1952: The company lists its stock on the New York Stock Exchange.

1955: Dixie Home Stores of Greenville, South Carolina, is acquired; the company changes its name to Winn-Dixie Stores, Inc.

1966: The Federal Trade Commission forbids Winn-Dixie from acquiring any retail grocery stores in the United States for 10 years.

1976: Kimbell, Inc., and its 135 stores in Texas, Oklahoma, and New Mexico are acquired.

1984: The first Winn-Dixie Marketplace store opens.

1995: Winn-Dixie acquires the Thriftway Food Drug chain, operator of 25 outlets in the greater Cincinnati area.

2000: The company launches a major restructuring involving the closure of more than 110 stores and the elimination of 11,000 workers from the payroll.

2004: Winn-Dixie's stores are impacted when four hurricanes hit Florida in less than six weeks; the company's stock reaches a 10-year low of $3.95 and Winn-Dixie is removed from the S&P 500 stock index.

2005: Winn-Dixie files for Chapter 11 bankruptcy protection in February; proceeds to close 245 underperforming stores and sell 81 others.

2006: Winn-Dixie emerges from bankruptcy with $725 million in financing from Wachovia Corp., as well as a new board of directors.

the Davis family, Robert D. Davis, assumed control. Robert's five years at the helm were marked by a virtually flat rate of growth in gross profits, although net earnings did not suffer because of lower tax rates. Winn-Dixie faced increasing competition in the 1980s, not

only from its traditional competitors, the other large chains, but also from convenience stores, which made a large dent in the market. In 1988 Robert stepped down as chairman (but remained vice chairman) and his cousin, A. Dano Davis, was elected to succeed him.

Dano Davis's new management team implemented measures to cut operating costs and raise gross profit margins. Management costs were also pared, and 60 management positions were eliminated. Winn-Dixie began selling off its smaller, less efficient stores and also unloaded some of its less productive baking facilities. The prevailing trend was toward larger, more modern stores offering more merchandise.

Despite these very positive moves, Winn-Dixie faced some problems in the late 1980s. It was notified by the Environmental Protection Agency that it was a PRP (potentially responsible party) for the cleanup of two dumping grounds designated as "Superfund sites" in Florida. The company estimated cleanup costs at about $200,000. Winn-Dixie also spearheaded a battle between grocery retailers and large producers of packaged goods over who would determine the shape of the market for retail food. Winn-Dixie announced in 1988 that it would no longer accept promotion allowances for products on a market-by-market basis, but only chain wide.

Winn-Dixie demanded a consistent national pricing policy from major suppliers such as Campbell Soup, General Mills, Quaker, and Procter & Gamble. The companies initially refused to meet Winn-Dixie's demands and Winn-Dixie retaliated by dropping certain of their products from its inventory. According to *Fortune*, Winn-Dixie's crusade was a response to the declining profitability of the preceding five years. Winn-Dixie negotiated with each of the producers separately, hoping to solve the impasse and preserve its market position.

EMPHASIS ON LOW PRICES AND LARGER STORES

In January 1990 Winn-Dixie abandoned the acquisition of 24 B&B Cash Grocery Stores in the Tampa, Florida, area that had been announced the previous October. The FTC was concerned about the antitrust implications of the deal, which could have provided Winn-Dixie a virtual monopoly in several southern Florida counties, and launched an investigation. The deal was called off when both parties became concerned about the cost of complying with the FTC's inquiry.

By the early 1990s, Winn-Dixie had essentially won the producers over to its position, a victory that was crucial to the company's emphasis on chain wide low prices that began in 1991. The chain quickly became the "low price leader" within the markets it served. Keeping prices low helped Winn-Dixie compete in the increasingly crowded markets it served.

That accomplished, Winn-Dixie next aimed to attain a further leg up on the competition by increasing the size of its stores. During the previous decade, the company had increased average store size from 22,000 square feet in 1982 to 30,000 square feet in 1989. It had also introduced larger, 44,000-square-foot Marketplace stores, which were grocery stores with the addition of such services as pharmacies and photofinishing. After the first had been opened in Valdosta, Georgia, in 1984, about 55 Marketplace stores had been built by the end of the 1980s. Starting in 1991, Winn-Dixie increased its store sizes even further, renovated or closed hundreds of its older and smaller stores, and altered the layout and conception of the Marketplace stores, some of which were as large as 55,000 square feet.

By 1996 average store size was up to 38,800 square feet. Although Winn-Dixie did open a number of new stores during this period and also early in 1995 acquired the Thriftway Food Drug chain, which had 25 units in the greater Cincinnati area, overall Winn-Dixie had fewer stores in its chain in 1996 (1,178) than in 1991 (1,207), because of the large number of older stores it closed. The company spent large sums of money on renovations and new store openings—$650 million in fiscal 1994 alone—and converted more and more of its stores to the new Marketplace design.

SALES DECLINE

By 1996 there were 504 Marketplace stores in the chain (compared to 634 Winn-Dixie stores), and many of these larger format stores included a "Food Pavilion," which was a large single aisle featuring a bakery, produce, deli, a combination meat-seafood service area, and a sit-down eating area. The Food Pavilion aimed to offer customers a convenient layout and more convenience food, especially targeted for the more time-stressed customer. Also in 1996, Winn-Dixie began experimenting with self-checkout lanes.

After net income hit a peak of $255.6 million in the fiscal year ending in June 1996, Winn-Dixie saw its earnings steadily erode in the face of heightening competition. In addition to its traditional rival Publix Super Markets, Inc., which was aggressively targeting many of Winn-Dixie's main markets, Winn-Dixie saw two new competitors enter its territory in the late 1980s. These were Food Lion, Inc., which expanded into Florida, and Wal-Mart Stores, Inc., which began a

massive move into the grocery trade through its combination discount and grocery outlets that were eventually dubbed Supercenters. Given that the Arkansas-based Wal-Mart's main territory was in the South, Winn-Dixie was hit particularly hard by the discount giant's food foray.

Despite Winn-Dixie's shift to the Marketplace format, same-store sales were constantly on the decline in the late 1990s. During fiscal 1999, the company's 52-year streak of increasing its dividends came to an end, and the following year the company's overall revenues fell for the first time in more than 60 years. Further bad news came in mid-1999 when the company reached an agreement to spend $33 million to settle a class-action discrimination lawsuit. The suit was similar to suits filed against other large grocery chains, charging the companies with systematically discriminating against female and African American workers in hiring and promotion.

RESTRUCTURING IN THE 21ST CENTURY

Late in 1999 Dano Davis relinquished his position as chief executive to Allen Rowland, who was named president and CEO, with Davis remaining chairman. The first Winn-Dixie leader ever to be hired from outside the company, Rowland had been president and COO of Smith's Food & Drug Centers, Inc. Just a few months later, in April 2000, Winn-Dixie announced a major restructuring involving the shuttering of more than 110 underperforming stores, the slashing of the workforce by 8 percent (or 11,000 employees), the closure of paper bag and detergent manufacturing plants, and the consolidation of some division offices and warehouse facilities.

The company also centralized its procurement, marketing, and merchandising, and it began a $144 million remodeling program to overhaul about 650 of the remaining 1,000-plus stores. Winn-Dixie also wanted to exit from the Texas and Oklahoma markets, where operations were only marginally profitable and market share was falling, but a deal to sell the 74 stores in those states to the Kroger Co. was nixed by the FTC, which was concerned about the potential erosion in competition in the Fort Worth, Texas, market. In connection with the restructuring, Winn-Dixie recorded charges of $396 million. As a result, Winn-Dixie suffered a net loss of $228.9 million for fiscal 2000.

At the same time that this strategic downsizing was being implemented, Winn-Dixie took the unusual step of expanding through two acquisitions. In October 2000 nine supermarkets in the Orlando, Florida, area were acquired from Gooding's Supermarkets, Inc., and in January 2001 Winn-Dixie spent $85 million to acquire 68 grocery stores from the bankrupt Jitney Jungle Stores of America, Inc. The latter outlets were located in Mississippi, Alabama, and Louisiana, and that deal also included gas stations that operated in conjunction with 32 of the stores.

Later in 2001 Winn-Dixie announced that it was slashing its dividend from $1.02 per share to 20 cents in order to improve earnings and free up cash for debt reduction and reinvesting in the business. In October 2001 the company launched a new advertising campaign called "The Real Deal" that touted "real good food, from real good people, at a real good price." The next year Winn-Dixie followed an industry trend by launching a customer loyalty card.

CHANGES IN LEADERSHIP

During the early years of the decade Winn-Dixie converted more than 50 of its stores to the Save Rite Grocery Warehouse format. Typically located in lower-income neighborhoods, Save Rite stores sold a limited selection of low-priced groceries in sparsely furnished stores. The biggest shift to this format was in Atlanta, where 38 locations began sporting the Save Rite banner in 2002. Also in 2002 the manufacturing operations were reduced still further with the sale of Deep South Products, Inc., operator of a cheese plant in Gainesville, Georgia, to Schreiber Foods, Inc. Winn-Dixie also divested its troubled operations in Texas and Oklahoma, which included 76 stores, a dairy plant, and a distribution center. This cut the workforce by another 5,300 jobs and also resulted in a $172.8 million net loss from discontinued operations, which cut net earnings for fiscal 2002 to $86.9 million.

At this time, Winn-Dixie aimed to increasingly tailor its stores to the particular neighborhoods in which they were located. This was a growing trend among food retailers attempting to differentiate themselves from the likes of Wal-Mart. The Save Rite chain was a step in this direction, as were newer more upscale Winn-Dixie outlets serving more affluent communities that included special features such as sushi bars, full-time wine stewards, and organic food sections. Early in 2003 the company said that it would accelerate its development of new stores, with this neighborhood-focused strategy in mind. In June of that year Rowland retired from the company. Rowland had succeeded in stabilizing the company's financial position, but observers were not entirely convinced that Winn-Dixie had been turned around fully.

Winn-Dixie's new president and CEO was Frank Lazaran, whom Rowland had brought onboard as COO

a little more than a year earlier. Lazaran had previously been president of Randalls Food Markets, Inc., a division of Safeway Inc. Net earnings of $239.2 million for fiscal 2003 represented the company's best showing since 1996. In June 2003 Winn-Dixie also announced that it would consolidate its private-label product lines from the more than 60 brands that had been in use to just three: the premium-quality Prestige line; the new Winn-Dixie brand, which would be used for moderately priced items; and the value-priced Thrifty Maid brand.

DIFFICULT TIMES

Conditions worsened at Winn-Dixie during the second half of calendar 2003. Competition from the likes of Wal-Mart and Publix intensified, and the company continued to lose market share. In October Winn-Dixie's shares fell to $8 apiece, the lowest since 1985. Under Lazaran, a restructuring initiative was announced that involved doing away with non-core assets, ceasing operations at some 156 locations, and eliminating 10,000 jobs. In addition, the company began stepping up advertising efforts and revamping many locations. Winn-Dixie ended its 2004 fiscal year (June 2004) with a loss of $100.4 million.

Natural disasters exacerbated already difficult conditions in 2004, when four hurricanes hit Florida in less than six weeks. Following Hurricane Charley in August, damage resulted from Hurricanes Frances, Ivan, and Jeanne in September. Winn-Dixie's stock continued to plummet, reaching a 10-year low of $3.95. Two months later the company shuttered its distribution facilities in Raleigh, North Carolina, and Sarasota, Florida, as part of a cost-cutting move. Insurance deductibles alone cost Winn-Dixie $10.3 million. In December 2004, Winn-Dixie was removed from the S&P 500 stock index. Unsatisfied with the company's performance, the board replaced President and CEO Lazaran with former Albertson's president and chief operating officer, Peter L. Lynch.

Winn-Dixie filed for Chapter 11 bankruptcy protection in February 2005 and proceeded to close 245 underperforming stores and sell 81 others. Winn-Dixie also revealed plans to close or sell eight manufacturing facilities and three distribution centers, and trim about 500 jobs from its workforce. Around this time the company established agreements to sell 102 of its stores to 30 different buyers. In addition, Winn-Dixie arranged to sell pharmacy records at 62 of its closed stores to 10 different buyers, including Walgreens, CVS, and Target, for approximately $16.5 million. Winn-Dixie's

1.1 million-square-foot, $26.6 million warehouse in Charlotte, North Carolina, was put up for sale, and the company auctioned off its Chek Beverage and Astor Products private-label products and manufacturing operations.

A NEW BEGINNING

In early 2006 Winn-Dixie revealed it would close an additional 35 stores, as well as its supermarkets in the Bahamas. After filing a restructuring plan midway through the year, the company emerged from bankruptcy on November 21 with $725 million in financing from Wachovia Corp., as well as a new board of directors. On December 21, Winn-Dixie's new common stock began trading under the symbol WINN on the NASDAQ. Post-bankruptcy, Winn-Dixie was a leaner organization. Compared to 920 stores in eight states and the Bahamas, the new organization consisted of 522 stores in five states. One other development that took place in late 2006 was the addition of freestanding walk-in medical clinics in some Winn-Dixie stores, which the company arranged through an alliance with Wellspot Medical Clinics Inc.

On the leadership front, Winn-Dixie named Dan Portnoy as its senior vice president and chief merchandising and marketing officer in mid-2007. In September of that year, the company reopened Store #1439 in the Industrial Canal section of New Orleans, which had been closed since Hurricane Katrina in 2005. On September 27, CEO Peter Lynch rang the NASDAQ opening bell remotely from the New Orleans store. Two months later, the company held its first post-bankruptcy annual shareholders' meeting. Other noteworthy developments in 2007 included New York investor Richard Perry acquiring a 5.02 percent stake in Winn-Dixie, as well as an initiative to remodel 75 stores.

Winn-Dixie began introducing a variety of new offerings for its customers during the later years of the decade. In 2008 the company teamed with Mayo Clinic to offer customers healthful recipes, as well as health and wellness information via the Winn-Dixie Web site. The following year, plans were made to expand an existing Visa-branded prepaid debit card program to all 520 of the company's stores. Also in 2009, Winn-Dixie partnered with Blue Cross and Blue Shield of Florida to offer health insurance at 353 Winn-Dixie and Save-Rite stores in Florida. In 2010, Winn-Dixie remained one of the nation's largest food retailers. Despite difficult economic conditions and some challenging years, the company seemed to have good prospects for success in the second decade of the 21st century.

Robin Carre
Updated, David E. Salamie; Paul R. Greenland

PRINCIPAL SUBSIDIARIES

Deep South Products, Inc.; Winn-Dixie Logistics, Inc.; Winn-Dixie Montgomery, LLC; Winn-Dixie Procurement, Inc.; Winn-Dixie Raleigh, Inc.; Winn-Dixie Supermarkets, Inc.; Winn-Dixie Stores Leasing, LLC; Winn-Dixie Properties, LLC; WIN General Insurance, Inc.

PRINCIPAL COMPETITORS

Publix Super Markets, Inc.; Sweetbay Supermarket; Wal-Mart Stores, Inc.

FURTHER READING

Albright, Mark, "FTC Rejects Winn-Dixie Store Sale," *St. Petersburg (Fla.) Times*, June 3, 2000, p. 1E.

———, "Is Winn-Dixie Next on Shopping List?" *St. Petersburg (Fla.) Times*, August 22, 1999, p. 1H.

Basch, Mark, "New York Investor Buys into Winn-Dixie," *Florida Times-Union* (Jacksonville), February 14, 2007.

Daniels, Earl, "Winn-Dixie to Exit Two States," *Florida Times-Union* (Jacksonville), May 7, 2002, p. F1.

Dowdell, Stephen, "Winn-Dixie's New Blueprint," *Supermarket News*, March 1, 1993.

Finotti, John, "What's Eating Winn-Dixie?" *Florida Trend*, March 1999.

Giovis, Jaclyn, "Winn-Dixie Files Restructuring Plan," *South Florida Sun-Sentinel*, June 30, 2006.

Hamstra, Mark, "Winn-Dixie Shares Hit New Low," *Supermarket News*, September 6, 2004, p.6.

Johnsen, Michael, "Winn-Dixie, Mayo Clinic Partner on Web Initiative," *Drug Store News*, November 17, 2008, p. 12.

Merrefield, David, "Winn-Dixie's Next Battle," *Supermarket News*, December 7, 1992.

Richards, Gregory, "Is Winn-Dixie Turned Around?" *Florida Times-Union* (Jacksonville), May 5, 2003.

———, "Winn-Dixie's New CEO Plans to Build on Store's Progress," *Florida Times-Union* (Jacksonville), May 8, 2003, p. D1.

———, "Winn-Dixie Stores Consolidate, Revamp Private Label Products," *Florida Times-Union* ++(Jacksonville), June 28, 2003, p. D1.

Springer, Jon, "Winn-Dixie Goes on the 'Offensive,'" *Supermarket News*, October 15, 2007.

———, "Winn-Dixie Loses $100M, Upgrades Remodel Effort," *Supermarket News*, August 23, 2004, p. 1.

Spurgeon, Devon, "Winn-Dixie to Close Stores, Cut 11,000 Jobs," *Wall Street Journal*, April 21, 2000, p. A3.

"Winn-Dixie Bids Adieu to Chap. 11," *MMR*, December 11, 2006, p. 3.

"Winn-Dixie Broadens Prepaid Card Plan," *American Banker*, February 23, 2009, p. 9.

"Winn-Dixie Partners with Blue Cross and Blue Shield to Offer Health Insurance," *Food & Beverage Close-Up*, November 5, 2009.

"Winn-Dixie Stores Inc.," *Notable Corporate Chronologies*, Farmington Hills, MI: Gale Group, 2010.

"Winn-Dixie, Two Others Add Clinics," *MMR*, November 13, 2006, p.1.

Zimmerman, M., *The Supermarket: A Revolution in Distribution*, New York: McGraw-Hill, 1955.

Zwiebach, Elliot, "Winn-Dixie Completes Thriftway Buy," *Supermarket News*, April 3, 1995.

———, "Winn-Dixie to Close 114 Stores, Cut 11,000 Jobs," *Supermarket News*, May 1, 2000.

Zep Inc.

1310 Seaboard Industrial Boulevard
Atlanta, Georgia 30318
U.S.A.
Telephone: (404) 352-1680
Fax: (404) 603-7958
Web site: http://www.zepinc.com

Public Company
Incorporated: 1937 as Zep Manufacturing Company
Employees: 2,200
Sales: $501 million (2009)
Stock Exchanges: New York
Ticker Symbol: ZEP
NAICS: 325612 Polish and Other Sanitation Goods Manufacturing

■ ■ ■

Zep Inc. is an Atlanta, Georgia-based provider of specialty chemicals, serving the cleaning and maintenance needs of institutional, industrial, and retail customers. Product categories include cleaners and degreasers, bathroom care, vehicle care, food sanitation, odor control, laundry, pest control, floor and carpet care, and hand care. All told, Zep manufactures more than 3,500 products to meet the needs of about 300,000 customers. In addition to the Zep brand, products are sold under the Zep Commercial, Zep Professional, Enforcer Products, Armor All Professional, and National Chemical labels. Spun off by Acuity Brands, Inc., in 2007, Zep is a public company listed on the New York Stock Exchange.

DEPRESSION-ERA ORIGINS

Zep Inc. was founded as Zep Manufacturing Co. in Atlanta in 1937 by Mandle Zaban, along with his brother Sam, William Eplan, and Sam Powell. The initial letters of their last names were used to coin the Zep name. Mandle Zaban financed the janitorial supply company by taking out a $6,000 loan on his life insurance policy. It proved to be a wise investment as Zep survived the Great Depression and then prospered, developing a complete line of cleaning and sanitation products.

Also helping to launch the business was Mandle Zaban's 15-year-old son, Erwin, who dropped out of high school to go to work for his father. In 1942 he became an officer of the company, and four years later succeeded his father as president at the age of 24. In 1962 he sold Zep to Atlanta's National Linen Service, headed by a neighbor, Milton N. Weinstein. Erwin Zaban continued to run Zep for what was then known as National Service Industries Inc. (NSI) and four years later he became NSI's president.

NSI was founded in Atlanta in 1919 by Weinstein's father, Isadore M. Weinstein. As an employee of a towel supply company, he had been sent to open a branch in Atlanta, but decided instead to start his own towel business. His plans were delayed by military service in World War I, during which he was wounded. He drew inspiration from the French hospital where he recuperated, impressed by the stacks of fresh sheets and uniforms in addition to towels. Hence, he decided to expand the purview of the company he subsequently launched, calling it Atlanta Linen Supply Company.

COMPANY PERSPECTIVES

Our mission is to deliver superior solutions to our customers. Guided always by the needs and preferences of our customers, Zep Inc. will strive to deliver long-term financial performance as measured by consistent, profitable growth and an industry leading return on invested capital.

With the opening of a branch in Birmingham, Alabama, three years later, the firm was renamed Southern Linen Service Corporation, and more branches throughout the south were to follow. In 1928 the company was taken public as National Linen Service Corporation and in 1944 secured a listing on the New York Stock Exchange. During the post-World War II era, under the leadership of Milton Weinstein, National Linen became such a dominant force in its highly fragmented field that the U.S. Department of Justice filed an antitrust suit against the company, a matter settled in 1956.

It was against this backdrop that National Linen looked to diversify into businesses unrelated to linens and uniforms. Zep became National Linen's first acquisition outside of its industry. As would be the case with subsequent acquisitions, NSI relied almost entirely on shares of stock to finance the transactions.

SELIG CO. ACQUIRED: 1968

NSI became involved in envelopes and insulation services through acquisitions in the 1960s, and also built up Zep and its specialty chemicals division. In 1968 another Atlanta company was added, Selig Co., founded in 1896 by 16-year-old Simon S. Selig, who used a bicycle to sell disinfectants and cleaning supplies to industrial customers door to door. In 1919 he hired a New York chemist in order to manufacture his own soap, and later added disinfectants.

In 1923 Selig opened the first branch office, in Dallas, Texas, followed by others strategically located across the United States and Puerto Rico. After Selig's death in 1943, his brother Albert took charge, serving as president until 1955 when Simon Selig Jr. took charge. He ran the business until NSI acquired it and changed the name to Selig Chemical Industries. As part of NSI's Chemical Division, Selig would offer 300 industrial soaps, disinfectants, degreasers, lubricants, and deodorants.

In 1972 Erwin Zaban became NSI's chief executive officer. A few months earlier a new president had taken charge of Zep, Harry Maziar, who began his career at Zep in 1960 as a sales representative. A prolific salesman who had peddled goods since childhood, he became Zep's first director of sales before assuming the presidency. Maziar then inspired the ranks of Zep's sales representatives to perform at ever-higher levels. An important factor in his success was his requirement that every branch across the country conduct weekly meetings. Furthermore, twice a year everyone came together for sales meetings where the sales representatives could directly address management.

When Maziar took charge, Zep was generating $30 million in annual sales. Fifteen years later, that amount had increased to over $150 million. More than just salesmanship, the key to Zep's growth was its responsiveness to the needs of its customers. It developed experimental products, the "X" line, based on specific features not offered by existing Zep products, often resulting in new revenue streams. For example, Zep created the Pre-Soak solution to solve the problem of mechanical car wash brushes scratching car exteriors. By the time it celebrated its 50th anniversary, Zep had more than 1,000 products to offer.

While Maziar was growing Zep, Zaban was expanding the parent company. Like his predecessor, he bought companies run by friends, avoiding companies in need of a turnaround in favor of those with solid management teams that were devoted and eager to remain after the acquisition. Not every deal worked out, however, and Zaban was quick to divest unprofitable lines, such as furniture, packaging, and a recreation division that came and went. Core product lines, on the other hand, were supported with increasing investments. NSI's lighting equipment division was the prime example of this approach, and by the early 1990s it contributed nearly 40 percent of NSI's revenues and about 30 percent of operating income. Zep and the other members of the chemical division, in the meantime, provided less than 18 percent of sales but 25.4 percent of operating income.

ENFORCER PRODUCTS
ACQUIRED: 1997

Zaban retired as NSI's CEO in 1987 and as chairman in 1992 (although he briefly served as interim chairman before completely retiring in 1994). Also in 1992, to further grow the chemical division, NSI completed a pair of acquisitions, adding Graham Group, Europe's second-largest specialty chemicals company, and Canadian specialty chemical manufacturer Kleen Canada, Inc. In 1997 the Enforcer line of products was brought into the fold with the $20 million acquisition of Emerson, Georgia-based Enforcer Products, Inc., maker of home pesticide and cleaning products as well as pet care products. Moreover, the deal provided entry into the chemical retail channel. Another specialty chemical company, Pure Corporation, was also acquired, followed a year later by another overseas business, Calman Australia Pty Ltd.

NSI made acquisitions in other sectors as well, but in doing so accumulated considerable debt. As a result, investors bid down the price of the company's stock as the 1990s came to a close. A worsening economy led NSI to make an attempt in 2001 to sell off two units, National Linen Service and Atlantic Envelope. Receiving no acceptable offers, NSI elected instead to spin off its two largest divisions, Lithonia Lighting Group and NSI Chemicals Group, into a new public company under the name of Acuity Brands. Zep became part of Acuity Specialty Products, Inc., when the spin-off was completed in November 2001.

Acuity Brands, which also included Acuity Brands Lighting, Inc., struggled to gain traction during the difficult economic conditions of the early years of the 21st century. Restructuring efforts eventually paid off, and in 2006 Acuity Brands earned $107 million on $2.4 billion in sales. Management then decided in 2007 to split the business into two separate companies as a way to unlock the value of the underlying assets. Thus, Acuity Specialty Products was spun off in the fall of 2007 as Zep Inc., leaving Acuity Brands as the holding company for Acuity Brands Lighting.

ZEP INDEPENDENT AGAIN: 2007

Zep Inc. began trading on the New York Stock Exchange as an independent company on November 1, 2007. It was a development embraced by its employees. Chief Financial Officer Mark Bachmann told the *Atlanta Journal-Constitution,* "Now every dollar of profit

in the chemical business, we will decide how to invest that in the chemical business." Led by Chairman and CEO John K. Morgan, Zep planned to grow sales to big-box retailers such as Home Depot and Wal-Mart, as well as to industrial distributors such as HD Supply and W.W. Grainger, Inc. The industrial segment was especially attractive, because it represented 45 percent of the $16 billion U.S. cleaning chemicals maintenance market. When fiscal 2007 came to a close, Zep reported $565.9 million in sales and more than $14 million in net income.

In an effort to increase sales through industrial distributors, Zep introduced the Zep Professional line of professional-strength general purpose cleaners, degreasers, disinfectants, floor care, bathroom care, hand care, odor control, and others products catering to a wide range of markets, including manufacturing, health care, food service, hospitality, schools, and government. In 2008 Zep unveiled a new line of Zep Commercial products targeting small auto repair shops and independent mechanics as well as do-it-yourself consumers. The line included a concentrated hand cleaner, lubricating spray, and degreasers.

Zep recorded $574.7 million in sales for the fiscal year ending August 31, 2008, and net income improved to $16.3 million, but ominous signs were developing. The cost of raw materials soared as the economy began to soften. To offset a sudden drop in orders, Zep implemented some cost-cutting measures in December 2008, including a reduction in its non-sales headcount. It also revamped its sales program to include a more robust employee review process to help spur improved performance. Zep fared better than most companies, due in large part to the continued need for cleaning products despite the poor economy.

In the spring of 2009 Zep introduced a new line of biodegradable detergents and cleansers designed to serve the requirements of food service customers whose need for cleaning products was undiminished, including supermarkets, restaurants, and institutional kitchens. Although revenues fell to $501 million in fiscal 2009, Zep turned a net profit of $9.26 million, a good performance given the conditions. A month after the fiscal year closed, Zep struck an important deal with Advance Auto Parts, Inc., which agreed to carry a line of Zep Commercial Auto Aftermarket products at its 3,400 stores and through its Web site. The initial products included hand cleaners and an instant hand sanitizer.

Ever since it was spun off, Zep had planned to grow through acquisitions, especially targeting expansion into Eastern Europe. Difficult business conditions forced the postponement of that pursuit, but in early 2010 Zep made its first foray into external growth by paying $64.4

million for Amrep Inc., a leading maker of maintenance chemicals for the automotive aftermarket. Other acquisitions were likely to follow as Zep continued to forge an independent path.

Ed Dinger

PRINCIPAL SUBSIDIARIES

Acuity Specialty Products, Inc.

PRINCIPAL COMPETITORS

Ecolab Inc.; JohnsonDiversey, Inc.; NCH Corporation.

FURTHER READING

Elie, L. Eric, "Zep Zips Out New Product Every 5 Years," *Atlanta Journal-Constitution,* February 16, 1987, p. C11.

Paul, Péralte C., "Zep Cleans Up, Cuts Costs amid Downturn," *Atlanta Journal-Constitution,* January 7, 2010, p. A8.

———, "'Zep Reps' Safe, but Cutbacks Will Flow," *Atlanta Journal-Constitution,* December 11, 2008, p. B1.

———, "Zep to Go Shopping for Future Growth," *Atlanta Journal-Constitution,* October 30, 2009, p. A19.

Saporta, Maria, "Acuity Brands Spinoff Makes NYSE Debut Today," *Atlanta Journal-Constitution,* November 1, 2007, p. C2.

Walker, Tom, "Almost a Century Later, Selig Co., Products Still Help Industry Clean Up," *Atlanta Journal-Constitution,* December 21, 1986, p. M5.

Cumulative Index to Companies

African Rainbow Minerals Ltd., 97 17–20

Africare, 59 7–10

After Hours Formalwear Inc., 60 3–5

Aftermarket Technology Corp., 83 16–19

AG Barr plc, 64 9–12

Ag-Chem Equipment Company, Inc., 17 9–11 *see also* AGCO Corp.

Ag Services of America, Inc., 59 11–13

Aga Foodservice Group PLC, 73 18–20

AGCO Corp., 13 16–18; 67 6–10 (upd.)

Agence France-Presse, 34 11–14

Agere Systems Inc., 61 17–19

Agfa Gevaert Group N.V., 59 14–16

Aggregate Industries plc, 36 20–22

Aggreko Plc, 45 10–13

Agilent Technologies Inc., 38 20–23; 93 28–32 (upd.)

Agilysys Inc., 76 7–11 (upd.)

Agland, Inc., 110 6–9

Agnico-Eagle Mines Limited, 71 11–14

Agora S.A. Group, 77 5–8

AGRANA *see* Südzucker AG.

Agri Beef Company, 81 5–9

Agria Corporation, 101 9–13

Agrigenetics, Inc. *see* Mycogen Corp.

Agrium Inc., 73 21–23

AgustaWestland N.V., 75 18–20

Agway, Inc., 7 17–18; 21 17–19 (upd.) *see also* Cargill Inc.

AHL Services, Inc., 27 20–23

Ahlstrom Corporation, 53 22–25

Ahmanson *see* H.F. Ahmanson & Co.

AHMSA *see* Altos Hornos de México, S.A. de C.V.

Ahold *see* Koninklijke Ahold NV.

AHP *see* American Home Products Corp.

AICPA *see* The American Institute of Certified Public Accountants.

AIG *see* American International Group, Inc.

AIMCO *see* Apartment Investment and Management Co.

Ainsworth Lumber Co. Ltd., 99 18–22

Air & Water Technologies Corporation, 6 441–42 *see also* Aqua Alliance Inc.

Air Berlin GmbH & Co. Luftverkehrs KG, 71 15–17

Air Canada, 6 60–62; 23 9–12 (upd.); 59 17–22 (upd.)

Air China Limited, 46 9–11; 108 15–19 (upd.)

Air Express International Corporation, 13 19–20

Air France–KLM, 108 20–29 (upd.)

Air-India Limited, 6 63–64; 27 24–26 (upd.)

Air Jamaica Limited, 54 3–6

Air Liquide *see* L'Air Liquide SA.

Air Mauritius Ltd., 63 17–19

Air Methods Corporation, 53 26–29

Air Midwest, Inc. *see* Mesa Air Group, Inc.

Air New Zealand Limited, 14 10–12; 38 24–27 (upd.)

Air Pacific Ltd., 70 7–9

Air Partner PLC, 93 33–36

Air Products and Chemicals, Inc., I 297–99; 10 31–33 (upd.); 74 6–9 (upd.)

Air Sahara Limited, 65 14–16

Air T, Inc., 86 6–9

Air Wisconsin Airlines Corporation, 55 10–12

Air Zimbabwe (Private) Limited, 91 5–8

AirAsia Berhad, 93 37–40

Airborne Freight Corporation, 6 345–47; 34 15–18 (upd.) *see also* DHL Worldwide Network S.A./N.V.

Airborne Systems Group, 89 39–42

AirBoss of America Corporation, 108 30–34

Airbus Industrie *see* G.I.E. Airbus Industrie.

Airgas, Inc., 54 7–10

Airguard Industries, Inc. *see* CLARCOR Inc.

Airlink Pty Ltd *see* Qantas Airways Ltd.

Airstream *see* Thor Industries, Inc.

AirTouch Communications, 11 10–12 *see also* Vodafone Group PLC.

Airtours Plc, 27 27–29, 90, 92

AirTran Holdings, Inc., 22 21–23

Aisin Seiki Co., Ltd., III 415–16; 48 3–5 (upd.)

Aitchison & Colegrave *see* Bradford & Bingley PLC.

Aiwa Co., Ltd., 30 18–20

Ajegroup S.A, 92 1–4

Ajinomoto Co., Inc., II 463–64; 28 9–11 (upd.); 108 35–39 (upd.)

AK Steel Holding Corporation, 19 8–9; 41 3–6 (upd.)

Akamai Technologies, Inc., 71 18–21

Akbank TAS, 79 18–21

Akeena Solar, Inc., 103 6–10

Akerys S.A., 90 17–20

AKG Acoustics GmbH, 62 3–6

Akin, Gump, Strauss, Hauer & Feld, L.L.P., 33 23–25

Akorn, Inc., 32 22–24

Akro-Mills Inc. *see* Myers Industries, Inc.

Aktiebolaget SKF, III 622–25; 38 28–33 (upd.); 89 401–09 (upd.)

Akzo Nobel N.V., 13 21–23; 41 7–10 (upd.); 112 1–6 (upd.)

Al Habtoor Group L.L.C., 87 9–12

Al-Tawfeek Co. For Investment Funds Ltd. *see* Dallah Albaraka Group.

Alabama Farmers Cooperative, Inc., 63 20–22

Alabama National BanCorporation, 75 21–23

Aladdin Knowledge Systems Ltd., 101 14–17

Alain Afflelou SA, 53 30–32

Alain Manoukian *see* Groupe Alain Manoukian.

Alamo Group Inc., 32 25–28

Alamo Rent A Car, 6 348–50; 24 9–12 (upd.); 84 5–11 (upd.)

ALARIS Medical Systems, Inc., 65 17–20

Alascom, Inc. *see* AT&T Corp.

Alaska Air Group, Inc., 6 65–67; 29 11–14 (upd.)

Alaska Communications Systems Group, Inc., 89 43–46

Alaska Railroad Corporation, 60 6–9

Alba-Waldensian, Inc., 30 21–23 *see also* E.I. du Pont de Nemours and Co.

Albany International Corporation, 8 12–14; 51 11–14 (upd.)

Albany Molecular Research, Inc., 77 9–12

Albaugh, Inc., 105 9–12

Albemarle Corporation, 59 23–25

Alberici Corporation, 76 12–14

The Albert Fisher Group plc, 41 11–13

Albert Heijn NV *see* Koninklijke Ahold N.V. (Royal Ahold).

Albert Trostel and Sons Company, 113 5–9

Albert's Organics, Inc., 110 10–13

Alberta Energy Company Ltd., 16 10–12; 43 3–6 (upd.)

Alberto-Culver Company, 8 15–17; 36 23–27 (upd.); 91 9–15 (upd.)

Albertson's, Inc., II 601–03; 7 19–22 (upd.); 30 24–28 (upd.); 65 21–26 (upd.)

Albtelecom Sh. a, 111 1–5

Alcan Aluminium Limited, IV 9–13; 31 7–12 (upd.)

Alcatel-Lucent, 9 9–11; 36 28–31 (upd.); 109 12–17 (upd.)

Alco Health Services Corporation, III 9–10 *see also* AmeriSource Health Corp.

Alco Standard Corporation, I 412–13

Alcoa Inc., 56 7–11 (upd.)

Alderwoods Group, Inc., 68 11–15 (upd.)

Aldi Einkauf GmbH & Co. OHG, 13 24–26; 86 10–14 (upd.)

Aldila Inc., 46 12–14

Aldus Corporation, 10 34–36 *see also* Adobe Systems Inc.

Aleris International, Inc., 110 14–17

Alès Groupe, 81 10–13

Alex Lee Inc., 18 6–9; 44 10–14 (upd.)

Alexander & Alexander Services Inc., 10 37–39 *see also* Aon Corp.

Alexander & Baldwin, Inc., 10 40–42; 40 14–19 (upd.)

Alexander's, Inc., 45 14–16

Alexandra plc, 88 5–8

Alexandria Real Estate Equities, Inc., 101 18–22

Alexon Group PLC, 107 6–10

Alfa Corporation, 60 10–12

Alfa Group, 99 23–26

Alfa-Laval AB, III 417–21; 64 13–18 (upd.)

Alfa Romeo, 13 27–29; 36 32–35 (upd.)

Alfa, S.A. de C.V., 19 10–12

Alfesca hf, 82 1–4

Alfred A. Knopf, Inc. *see* Random House, Inc.

Alfred Dunhill Limited *see* Vendôme Luxury Group plc.

Faber-Castell *see* A.W. Faber-Castell Unternehmensverwaltung GmbH & Co.

Fabri-Centers of America Inc., 16 197–99 *see also* Jo-Ann Stores, Inc.

Facebook, Inc., 90 184–87

Facom S.A., 32 183–85

FactSet Research Systems Inc., 73 148–50

Faegre & Benson LLP, 97 164–67

FAG—Kugelfischer Georg Schäfer AG, 62 129–32

Fair Grounds Corporation, 44 177–80

Fair, Isaac and Company, 18 168–71

Fairchild Dornier GmbH, 9 205–08; 48 167–71 (upd.)

Fairclough Construction Group plc, I 567–68

Fairfax Financial Holdings Limited, 57 135–37

Fairfax Media Ltd., 94 202–08 (upd.)

Fairfield Communities, Inc., 36 192–95

Fairmont Hotels & Resorts Inc., 69 161–63

Faiveley S.A., 39 152–54

Falcon Products, Inc., 33 149–51

Falconbridge Limited, 49 136–39

Falke Group, 113 141–45

Fallon Worldwide, 22 199–201; 71 157–61 (upd.)

Family Christian Stores, Inc., 51 131–34

Family Dollar Stores, Inc., 13 215–17; 62 133–36 (upd.)

Family Golf Centers, Inc., 29 183–85

Family Sports Concepts, Inc., 100 160–63

Famous Brands Ltd., 86 144–47

Famous Dave's of America, Inc., 40 182–84

Fannie Mae, 45 156–59 (upd.); 109 225–31 (upd.)

Fannie May Confections Brands, Inc., 80 114–18

Fansteel Inc., 19 150–52

Fanuc Ltd., III 482–83; 17 172–74 (upd.); 75 137–40 (upd.)

FAO Schwarz, 46 187–90

Farah Incorporated, 24 156–58

Faribault Foods, Inc., 89 212–15

Farley Northwest Industries Inc., I 440–41

Farley's & Sathers Candy Company, Inc., 62 137–39

Farm Family Holdings, Inc., 39 155–58

Farm Journal Corporation, 42 131–34

Farmacias Ahumada S.A., 72 126–28

Farmer Bros. Co., 52 117–19

Farmer Jack Supermarkets, 78 109–13

Farmer Mac *see* Federal Agricultural Mortgage Corp.

Farmers Insurance Group of Companies, 25 154–56

Farmland Foods, Inc., 7 174–75

Farmland Industries, Inc., 48 172–75

Farnam Companies, Inc., 107 112–15

FARO Technologies, Inc., 87 164–167

Farouk Systems, Inc., 78 114–17

Farrar, Straus and Giroux Inc., 15 158–60

Fastenal Company, 14 185–87; 42 135–38 (upd.); 99 158–163 (upd.)

FASTWEB S.p.A., 83 147–150

Fat Face Ltd., 68 147–49

Fatburger Corporation, 64 122–24

FATS, Inc. *see* Firearms Training Systems, Inc.

Faultless Starch/Bon Ami Company, 55 142–45

Faurecia S.A., 70 91–93

FAvS *see* First Aviation Services Inc.

FAW Group *see* China FAW Group Corporation.

Faygo Beverages Inc., 55 146–48

Fazoli's Management, Inc., 27 145–47; 76 144–47 (upd.)

FC Bayern München AG, 111 128–31

Featherlite Inc., 28 127–29

Fechheimer Brothers Company, Inc., 110 147–50

Fedders Corporation, 18 172–75; 43 162–67 (upd.)

Federal Agricultural Mortgage Corporation, 75 141–43

Federal Deposit Insurance Corporation, 93 208–12

Federal Express Corporation, V 451–53 *see also* FedEx Corp.

Federal Home Loan Mortgage Corp. *see* Freddie Mac.

Federal-Mogul Corporation, I 158–60; 10 292–94 (upd.); 26 139–43 (upd.)

Federal National Mortgage Association, II 410–11 *see also* Fannie Mae.

Federal Paper Board Company, Inc., 8 173–75

Federal Prison Industries, Inc., 34 157–60

Federal Signal Corp., 10 295–97

Federated Department Stores Inc., 9 209–12; 31 190–94 (upd.) *see also* Macy's, Inc.

Fédération Internationale de Football Association, 27 148–51

Federation Nationale d'Achats des Cadres *see* FNAC.

Federico Paternina S.A., 69 164–66

FedEx Corporation, 18 176–79 (upd.); 42 139–44 (upd.); 109 232–41 (upd.)

FedEx Office and Print Services, Inc., 109 242–49 (upd.)

Feed The Children, Inc., 68 150–52

FEI Company, 79 168–71

Feld Entertainment, Inc., 32 186–89 (upd.)

Feldmühle Nobel AG, III 692–95 *see also* Metallgesellschaft.

Fellowes Inc., 28 130–32; 107 116–20 (upd.)

Fenaco, 86 148–51

Fender Musical Instruments Company, 16 200–02; 43 168–72 (upd.)

Fenwick & West LLP, 34 161–63

Ferolito, Vultaggio & Sons, 27 152–55; 100 164–69 (upd.)

Ferrara Fire Apparatus, Inc., 84 115–118

Ferrara Pan Candy Company, 90 188–91

Ferrari S.p.A., 13 218–20; 36 196–200 (upd.)

Ferrellgas Partners, L.P., 35 173–75; 107 121–25 (upd.)

Ferrero SpA, 54 103–05

Ferretti Group SpA, 90 192–96

Ferro Corporation, 8 176–79; 56 123–28 (upd.)

Ferrovial *see* Grupo Ferrovial

Ferrovie Dello Stato Societa Di Trasporti e Servizi S.p.A., 105 163–67

FHP International Corporation, 6 184–86

Fiat SpA, I 161–63; 11 102–04 (upd.); 50 194–98 (upd.)

FiberMark, Inc., 37 139–42; 53 24

Fibreboard Corporation, 16 203–05 *see also* Owens Corning Corp.

Ficosa *see* Grupo Ficosa International.

Fidelity Investments Inc., II 412–13; 14 188–90 (upd.) *see also* FMR Corp.

Fidelity National Financial Inc., 54 106–08

Fidelity Southern Corporation, 85 124–27

Fieldale Farms Corporation, 23 191–93; 107 126–30 (upd.)

Fieldcrest Cannon, Inc., 9 213–17; 31 195–200 (upd.)

Fielmann AG, 31 201–03

Fiesta Mart, Inc., 101 183–87

FIFA *see* Fédération Internationale de Football Association.

Fifth Third Bancorp, 13 221–23; 31 204–08 (upd.); 103 163–70 (upd.)

Le Figaro *see* Société du Figaro S.A.

Figgie International Inc., 7 176–78

Fiji Water LLC, 74 111–13

Fila Holding S.p.A., 20 216–18; 52 120–24 (upd.)

FileNet Corporation, 62 140–43

Fili Enterprises, Inc., 70 94–96

Filipacchi Medias S.A. *see* Hachette Filipacchi Medias S.A.

Film Roman, Inc., 58 122–24

Filtrona plc, 88 87–91

Fimalac S.A., 37 143–45

FINA, Inc., 7 179–81 *see also* Total Fina Elf S.A.

Finarte Casa d'Aste S.p.A., 93 213–16

Findel plc, 60 122–24

Findorff *see* J.H. Findorff and Son, Inc.

Fingerhut Companies, Inc., 9 218–20; 36 201–05 (upd.)

Finisar Corporation, 92 115–18

The Finish Line, Inc., 29 186–88; 68 153–56 (upd.)

FinishMaster, Inc., 24 159–61

Finlay Enterprises, Inc., 16 206–08; 76 148–51 (upd.)

Finmeccanica S.p.A., 84 119–123

Finnair Oy, 6 87–89; 25 157–60 (upd.); 61 91–95 (upd.)

Manufactured Home Communities, Inc., 22 339–41

Manufacturers Hanover Corporation, II 312–14 *see also* Chemical Bank.

Manulife Financial Corporation, 85 235–38

Manutan International S.A., 72 219–21

Manville Corporation, III 706–09; 7 291–95 (upd.) *see also* Johns Manville Corp.

MAPCO Inc., IV 458–59

Mapfre S.A., 109 394–98

MAPICS, Inc., 55 256–58

Maple Grove Farms of Vermont, 88 249–52

Maple Leaf Foods Inc., 41 249–53; 108 327–33 (upd.)

Maple Leaf Sports & Entertainment Ltd., 61 188–90

Maples Industries, Inc., 83 260–263

Marathon Oil Corporation, 109 399–403

Marble Slab Creamery, Inc., 87 304–307

Marc Ecko Enterprises, Inc., 105 288–91

March of Dimes, 31 322–25

Marchesi Antinori SRL, 42 245–48

Marchex, Inc., 72 222–24

marchFIRST, Inc., 34 261–64

Marco Business Products, Inc., 75 244–46

Marcolin S.p.A., 61 191–94

Marconi plc, 33 286–90 (upd.)

Marcopolo S.A., 79 247–50

Marco's Franchising LLC, 86 264–67

The Marcus Corporation, 21 359–63

Marelli *see* Magneti Marelli Holding SpA.

Marfin Popular Bank plc, 92 222–26

Margarete Steiff GmbH, 23 334–37

Marie Brizard et Roger International S.A.S., 22 342–44; 97 276–80 (upd.)

Marie Callender's Restaurant & Bakery, Inc., 28 257–59 *see also* Perkins & Marie Callender's Inc.

Mariella Burani Fashion Group, 92 227–30

Marine Products Corporation, 75 247–49

MarineMax, Inc., 30 303–05

Mariner Energy, Inc., 101 326–29

Marion Laboratories Inc., I 648–49

Marion Merrell Dow, Inc., 9 328–29 (upd.)

Marionnaud Parfumeries SA, 51 233–35

Marisa Christina, Inc., 15 290–92

Marisol S.A., 107 260–64

Maritz Holdings Inc., 38 302–05; 110 305–09 (upd.)

Mark IV Industries, Inc., 7 296–98; 28 260–64 (upd.)

Mark T. Wendell Tea Company, 94 299–302

The Mark Travel Corporation, 80 232–35

Märklin Holding GmbH, 70 163–66

Marks and Spencer p.l.c., V 124–26; 24 313–17 (upd.); 85 239–47 (upd.)

Marks Brothers Jewelers, Inc., 24 318–20 *see also* Whitehall Jewellers, Inc.

Marlin Business Services Corp., 89 317–19

The Marmon Group, Inc., IV 135–38; 16 354–57 (upd.); 70 167–72 (upd.)

Marquette Electronics, Inc., 13 326–28

Marriott International, Inc., III 102–03; 21 364–67 (upd.); 83 264–270 (upd.)

Mars, Incorporated, 7 299–301; 40 302–05 (upd.)

Mars Petcare US Inc., 96 269–72

Marsh & McLennan Companies, Inc., III 282–84; 45 263–67 (upd.)

Marsh Supermarkets, Inc., 17 300–02; 76 255–58 (upd.)

Marshall & Ilsley Corporation, 56 217–20

Marshall Amplification plc, 62 239–42

Marshall Field's, 63 254–63 *see also* Target Corp.

Marshalls Incorporated, 13 329–31

Martek Biosciences Corporation, 65 218–20

Martell and Company S.A., 82 213–16

Marten Transport, Ltd., 84 243–246

Martha Stewart Living Omnimedia, Inc., 24 321–23; 73 219–22 (upd.)

Martha White Foods Inc., 104 284–87

Martignetti Companies, 84 247–250

Martin-Baker Aircraft Company Limited, 61 195–97

Martin Franchises, Inc., 80 236–39

Martin Guitar Company *see* C.F. Martin & Co., Inc.

Martin Industries, Inc., 44 274–77

Martin Marietta Corporation, I 67–69 *see also* Lockheed Martin Corp.

Martini & Rossi SpA, 63 264–66

MartinLogan, Ltd., 85 248–51

Martins *see* Grupo Martins.

Martin's Super Markets, Inc., 101 330–33

Martz Group, 56 221–23

Marubeni Corporation, I 492–95; 24 324–27 (upd.); 104 288–93 (upd.)

Maruha Group Inc., 75 250–53 (upd.)

Marui Company Ltd., V 127; 62 243–45 (upd.)

Maruzen Company Ltd., 18 322–24; 104 294–97 (upd.)

Marvel Entertainment, Inc., 10 400–02; 78 212–19 (upd.)

Marvell Technology Group Ltd., 112 268–71

Marvelous Market Inc., 104 298–301

Marvin Lumber & Cedar Company, 22 345–47

Mary Kay Inc., 9 330–32; 30 306–09 (upd.); 84 251–256 (upd.)

Maryland & Virginia Milk Producers Cooperative Association, Inc., 80 240–43

Maryville Data Systems Inc., 96 273–76

Marzotto S.p.A., 20 356–58; 67 246–49 (upd.)

The Maschhoffs, Inc., 82 217–20

Masco Corporation, III 568–71; 20 359–63 (upd.); 39 263–68 (upd.); 111 295–303 (upd.)

Maserati *see* Officine Alfieri Maserati S.p.A.

Mashantucket Pequot Gaming Enterprise Inc., 35 282–85

Masland Corporation, 17 303–05 *see also* Lear Corp.

Mason & Hanger Group Inc., 110 310–14

Masonite International Corporation, 63 267–69

Massachusetts Mutual Life Insurance Company, III 285–87; 53 210–13 (upd.)

Massey Energy Company, 57 236–38

MasTec, Inc., 55 259–63 (upd.)

Mastellone Hermanos S.A., 101 334–37

Master Lock Company, 45 268–71

Master Spas Inc., 105 292–95

MasterBrand Cabinets, Inc., 71 216–18

MasterCard Worldwide, 9 333–35; 96 277–81 (upd.)

MasterCraft Boat Company, Inc., 90 290–93

Matador Records Inc., 113 247–51

Matalan PLC, 49 258–60

Match.com, LP, 87 308–311

Material Sciences Corporation, 63 270–73

The MathWorks, Inc., 80 244–47

Matra-Hachette S.A., 15 293–97 (upd.) *see also* European Aeronautic Defence and Space Company EADS N.V.

Matria Healthcare, Inc., 17 306–09

Matrix Essentials Inc., 90 294–97

Matrix Service Company, 65 221–23

Matrixx Initiatives, Inc., 74 177–79

Matsushita Electric Industrial Co., Ltd., II 55–56; 64 255–58 (upd.)

Matsushita Electric Works, Ltd., III 710–11; 7 302–03 (upd.)

Matsuzakaya Company Ltd., V 129–31; 64 259–62 (upd.)

Matt Prentice Restaurant Group, 70 173–76

Mattel, Inc., 7 304–07; 25 311–15 (upd.); 61 198–203 (upd.)

Matth. Hohner AG, 53 214–17

Matthews International Corporation, 29 304–06; 77 248–52 (upd.)

Mattress Giant Corporation, 103 254–57

Matussière et Forest SA, 58 220–22

Maui Land & Pineapple Company, Inc., 29 307–09; 100 273–77 (upd.)

Maui Wowi, Inc., 85 252–55

Mauna Loa Macadamia Nut Corporation, 64 263–65

Maurices Inc., 95 255–58

Maus Frères SA, 48 277–79

Maverick Ranch Association, Inc., 88 253–56

Maverick Tube Corporation, 59 280–83

Maverik, Inc., 103 258–61

Max & Erma's Restaurants Inc., 19 258–60; 100 278–82 (upd.)

Norinchukin Bank, II 340–41

Norm Thompson Outfitters, Inc., 47 275–77

Norrell Corporation, 25 356–59

Norsk Hydro ASA, 10 437–40; 35 315–19 (upd.); 109 421–27 (upd.)

Norske Skogindustrier ASA, 63 314–16

Norstan, Inc., 16 392–94

Nortek, Inc., 34 308–12 *see also* NTK Holdings Inc.

Nortel Networks Corporation, 36 349–54 (upd.)

North American Galvanizing & Coatings, Inc., 99 303–306

North Atlantic Trading Company Inc., 65 266–68

North Carolina National Bank Corporation *see* NCNB Corp.

The North Face, Inc., 18 375–77; 78 258–61 (upd.)

North Fork Bancorporation, Inc., 46 314–17

North Pacific Group, Inc., 61 254–57

North Star Steel Company, 18 378–81

The North West Company, Inc., 12 361–63

North West Water Group plc, 11 359–62 *see also* United Utilities PLC.

Northeast Utilities, V 668–69; 48 303–06 (upd.)

Northern and Shell Network plc, 87 341–344

Northern Foods plc, 10 441–43; 61 258–62 (upd.)

Northern Rock plc, 33 318–21

Northern States Power Company, V 670–72; 20 391–95 (upd.) *see also* Xcel Energy Inc.

Northern Telecom Limited, V 308–10 *see also* Nortel Networks Corp.

Northern Trust Corporation, 9 387–89; 101 366–72 (upd.)

Northland Cranberries, Inc., 38 332–34

Northrop Grumman Corporation, I 76–77; 11 363–65 (upd.); 45 304–12 (upd.); 111 343–53 (upd.)

Northwest Airlines Corporation, I 112–14; 6 103–05 (upd.); 26 337–40 (upd.); 74 204–08 (upd.)

Northwest Natural Gas Company, 45 313–15

NorthWestern Corporation, 37 280–83

Northwestern Mutual Life Insurance Company, III 321–24; 45 316–21 (upd.)

Norton Company, 8 395–97

Norton McNaughton, Inc., 27 346–49 *see also* Jones Apparel Group, Inc.

Norwegian Cruise Lines *see* NCL Corporation

Norwich & Peterborough Building Society, 55 280–82

Norwood Promotional Products, Inc., 26 341–43

Notations, Inc., 110 342–45

Nova Corporation of Alberta, V 673–75

NovaCare, Inc., 11 366–68

Novacor Chemicals Ltd., 12 364–66

Novar plc, 49 292–96 (upd.)

Novartis AG, 39 304–10 (upd.); 105 323–35 (upd.)

NovaStar Financial, Inc., 91 354–58

Novell, Inc., 6 269–71; 23 359–62 (upd.)

Novellus Systems, Inc., 18 382–85

Noven Pharmaceuticals, Inc., 55 283–85

Novo Nordisk A/S, I 658–60; 61 263–66 (upd.)

NOW *see* National Organization for Women, Inc.

NPC International, Inc., 40 340–42

The NPD Group, Inc., 68 275–77

NPM (Nationale Portefeuille Maatschappij) *see* Compagnie Nationale à Portefeuille.

NPR *see* National Public Radio, Inc.

NRG Energy, Inc., 79 290–93

NRJ Group S.A., 107 300–04

NRT Incorporated, 61 267–69

NS *see* Norfolk Southern Corp.

NSF International, 72 252–55

NSK *see* Nippon Seiko K.K.

NSP *see* Northern States Power Co.

NSS Enterprises, Inc., 78 262–65

NSTAR, 106 324–31 (upd.)

NTCL *see* Northern Telecom Ltd.

NTD Architecture, 101 373–76

NTK Holdings Inc., 107 305–11 (upd.)

NTL Inc., 65 269–72

NTN Buzztime, Inc., 86 308–11

NTN Corporation, III 595–96; 47 278–81 (upd.)

NTTPC *see* Nippon Telegraph and Telephone Public Corp.

NU *see* Northeast Utilities.

Nu-kote Holding, Inc., 18 386–89

Nu Skin Enterprises, Inc., 27 350–53; 31 386–89; 76 286–90 (upd.)

Nucor Corporation, 7 400–02; 21 392–95 (upd.); 79 294–300 (upd.)

Nufarm Ltd., 87 345–348

Nuplex Industries Ltd., 92 280–83

Nuqul Group of Companies, 102 311–14

NuStar Energy L.P., 111 354–57

Nutraceutical International Corporation, 37 284–86

The NutraSweet Company, 8 398–400; 107 312–16 (upd.)

Nutreco Holding N.V., 56 256–59

Nutrexpa S.A., 92 284–87

NutriSystem, Inc., 71 250–53

Nutrition 21 Inc., 97 307–11

Nutrition for Life International Inc., 22 385–88

Nuveen *see* John Nuveen Co.

NV Umicore SA, 47 411–13

NVIDIA Corporation, 54 269–73

NVR Inc., 8 401–03; 70 206–09 (upd.)

NWA, Inc. *see* Northwest Airlines Corp.

NYK *see* Nippon Yusen Kabushiki Kaisha (NYK).

NYMAGIC, Inc., 41 284–86

NYNEX Corporation, V 311–13 *see also* Verizon Communications.

Nypro, Inc., 101 377–82

NYRG *see* New York Restaurant Group, Inc.

NYSE *see* New York Stock Exchange.

NYSEG *see* New York State Electric and Gas Corp.

O

O&Y *see* Olympia & York Developments Ltd.

O.C. Tanner Co., 69 279–81

Oak Harbor Freight Lines, Inc., 53 248–51

Oak Industries Inc., 21 396–98 *see also* Corning Inc.

Oak Technology, Inc., 22 389–93 *see also* Zoran Corp.

Oakhurst Dairy, 60 225–28

Oakleaf Waste Management, LLC, 97 312–15

Oakley, Inc., 18 390–93; 49 297–302 (upd.); 111 358–65 (upd.)

Oaktree Capital Management, LLC, 71 254–56

Oakwood Homes Corporation, 13 155; 15 326–28

OAO AVTOVAZ *see* AVTOVAZ Joint Stock Co.

OAO Gazprom, 42 261–65; 107 317–23 (upd.)

OAO LUKOIL, 40 343–46; 109 428–36 (upd.)

OAO NK YUKOS, 47 282–85

OAO Severstal *see* Severstal Joint Stock Co.

OAO Siberian Oil Company (Sibneft), 49 303–06

OAO Surgutneftegaz, 48 375–78

OAO Tatneft, 45 322–26

Obagi Medical Products, Inc., 95 310–13

Obayashi Corporation, 78 266–69 (upd.)

Oberoi Group *see* EIH Ltd.

Oberthur Technologies S.A., 113 277–81

Oberto Sausage Company, Inc., 92 288–91

Obie Media Corporation, 56 260–62

Obrascon Huarte Lain S.A., 76 291–94

Observer AB, 55 286–89

Occidental Petroleum Corporation, IV 480–82; 25 360–63 (upd.); 71 257–61 (upd.)

Océ N.V., 24 360–63; 91 359–65 (upd.)

Ocean Beauty Seafoods, Inc., 74 209–11

Ocean Bio-Chem, Inc., 103 308–11

Ocean Group plc, 6 415–17 *see also* Exel plc.

Ocean Spray Cranberries, Inc., 7 403–05; 25 364–67 (upd.); 83 284–290

Oceaneering International, Inc., 63 317–19

Ocesa *see* Corporación Interamericana de Entretenimiento, S.A. de C.V.

O'Charley's Inc., 19 286–88; 60 229–32 (upd.)

Piaggio & C. S.p.A., 20 426–29; 100 348–52 (upd.)

PianoDisc *see* Burgett, Inc.

PIC International Group PLC, 24 386–88 (upd.)

Picanol N.V., 96 335–38

Picard Surgeles, 76 305–07

Piccadilly Cafeterias, Inc., 19 299–302

Pick 'n Pay Stores Ltd., 82 280–83

PictureTel Corp., 10 455–57; 27 363–66 (upd.)

Piedmont Investment Advisors, LLC, 106 369–72

Piedmont Natural Gas Company, Inc., 27 367–69

Pier 1 Imports, Inc., 12 393–95; 34 337–41 (upd.); 95 336–43 (upd.)

Pierce Leahy Corporation, 24 389–92 *see also* Iron Mountain Inc.

Piercing Pagoda, Inc., 29 382–84

Pierre & Vacances SA, 48 314–16

Pierre Fabre *see* Laboratoires Pierre Fabre S.A.

Piggly Wiggly Southern, Inc., 13 404–06

Pilgrim's Pride Corporation, 7 432–33; 23 383–85 (upd.); 90 334–38 (upd.)

Pilkington Group Limited, II 724–27; 34 342–47 (upd.); 87 375–383 (upd.)

Pillowtex Corporation, 19 303–05; 41 299–302 (upd.)

Pillsbury Company, II 555–57; 13 407–09 (upd.); 62 269–73 (upd.)

Pillsbury Madison & Sutro LLP, 29 385–88

Pilot Air Freight Corp., 67 301–03

Pilot Corporation, 49 328–30

Pilot Pen Corporation of America, 82 284–87

Pinault-Printemps-Redoute S.A., 19 306–09 (upd.) *see also* PPR S.A.

Pindar *see* G A Pindar & Son Ltd.

Pinguely-Haulotte SA, 51 293–95

Pinkerton's Inc., 9 406–09 *see also* Securitas AB.

Pinnacle Airlines Corp., 73 261–63

Pinnacle West Capital Corporation, 6 545–47; 54 290–94 (upd.)

Pinskdrev Industrial Woodworking Company, 110 367–71

Pioneer Electronic Corporation, III 604–06; 28 358–61 (upd.) *see also* Agilysys Inc.

Pioneer Hi-Bred International, Inc., 9 410–12; 41 303–06 (upd.)

Pioneer International Limited, III 728–30

Pioneer Natural Resources Company, 59 335–39

Pioneer-Standard Electronics Inc., 19 310–14 *see also* Agilysys Inc.

Piper Jaffray Companies, , 22 426–30 ; 107 357–63 (upd.)

Pirelli & C. S.p.A., V 249–51; 15 353–56 (upd.); 75 326–31 (upd.)

Piscines Desjoyaux S.A., 84 310–313

Pitman Company, 58 273–75

Pitney Bowes Inc., III 156–58, 159; 19 315–18 (upd.); 47 295–99 (upd.); 111 389–96 (upd.)

Pittsburgh Brewing Company, 76 308–11

Pittsburgh Plate Glass Co. *see* PPG Industries, Inc.

Pittsburgh Steelers Sports, Inc., 66 255–57

The Pittston Company, IV 180–82; 19 319–22 (upd.) *see also* The Brink's Co.

Pittway Corporation, 9 413–15; 33 334–37 (upd.)

Pixar Animation Studios, 34 348–51

Pixelworks, Inc., 69 298–300

Pizza Hut Inc., 7 434–35; 21 405–07 (upd.)

Pizza Inn, Inc., 46 346–49

PKF International, 78 315–18

PKZ Burger-Kehl and Company AG, 107 364–67

Placer Dome Inc., 20 430–33; 61 289–93 (upd.)

Plain Dealer Publishing Company, 92 311–14

Plains All American Pipeline, L.P., 108 385–88

Plains Cotton Cooperative Association, 57 283–86

Planar Systems, Inc., 61 294–97

Planet Hollywood International, Inc., 18 424–26; 41 307–10 (upd.); 108 389–95 (upd.)

Planeta *see* Grupo Planeta.

Plantation Pipe Line Company, 68 290–92

Plante & Moran, LLP, 71 280–83

Plantronics, Inc., 106 373–77

Platinum Entertainment, Inc., 35 341–44

PLATINUM Technology, Inc., 14 390–92 *see also* Computer Associates International, Inc.

Plato Learning, Inc., 44 344–47

Play by Play Toys & Novelties, Inc., 26 374–76

Playboy Enterprises, Inc., 18 427–30

PlayCore, Inc., 27 370–72

Players International, Inc., 22 431–33

Playmates Toys, 23 386–88

Playskool, Inc., 25 379–81 *see also* Hasbro, Inc.

Playtex Products, Inc., 15 357–60

Pleasant Company, 27 373–75 *see also* American Girl, Inc.

Pleasant Holidays LLC, 62 274–76

Plessey Company, PLC, II 81–82 *see also* Marconi plc.

Plexus Corporation, 35 345–47; 80 287–91 (upd.)

Pliant Corporation, 98 315–18

PLIVA d.d., 70 223–25

Plow & Hearth, Inc., 104 379–82

Plum Creek Timber Company, Inc., 43 304–06; 106 378–82 (upd.)

Pluma, Inc., 27 376–78

Ply Gem Industries Inc., 12 396–98

PMC Global, Inc., 110 372–75

The PMI Group, Inc., 49 331–33

PMP Ltd., 72 282–84

PMT Services, Inc., 24 393–95

The PNC Financial Services Group Inc., II 342–43; 13 410–12 (upd.); 46 350–53 (upd.)

PNM Resources Inc., 51 296–300 (upd.)

Pochet SA, 55 307–09

PODS Enterprises Inc., 103 327–29

Pogo Producing Company, 39 330–32

Pohang Iron and Steel Company Ltd., IV 183–85 *see also* POSCO.

Polar Air Cargo Inc., 60 237–39

Polaris Industries Inc., 12 399–402; 35 348–53 (upd.); 77 330–37 (upd.)

Polaroid Corporation, III 607–09; 7 436–39 (upd.); 28 362–66 (upd.); 93 345–53 (upd.)

Polartec LLC, 98 319–23 (upd.)

Policy Management Systems Corporation, 11 394–95

Policy Studies, Inc., 62 277–80

Poliet S.A., 33 338–40

Polish & Slavic Federal Credit Union, 113 300–03

Polk Audio, Inc., 34 352–54

Polo/Ralph Lauren Corporation, 12 403–05; 62 281–85 (upd.)

Polski Koncern Naftowy ORLEN S.A., 77 338–41

PolyGram N.V., 23 389–92

PolyMedica Corporation, 77 342–45

PolyOne Corporation, 87 384–395 (upd.)

Pomare Ltd., 88 304–07

Pomeroy Computer Resources, Inc., 33 341–44

Ponderosa Steakhouse, 15 361–64

Poof-Slinky, Inc., 61 298–300

Poore Brothers, Inc., 44 348–50 *see also* The Inventure Group, Inc.

Pop Warner Little Scholars, Inc., 86 335–38

Pope & Talbot, Inc., 12 406–08; 61 301–05 (upd.)

Pope Cable and Wire B.V. *see* Belden CDT Inc.

Pope Resources LP, 74 240–43

Popular, Inc., 41 311–13; 108 396–401 (upd.)

The Porcelain and Fine China Companies Ltd., 69 301–03

Porsche AG, 13 413–15; 31 363–66 (upd.)

The Port Authority of New York and New Jersey, 48 317–20

Port Imperial Ferry Corporation, 70 226–29

Portal Software, Inc., 47 300–03

Portillo's Restaurant Group, Inc., 71 284–86

Portland General Corporation, 6 548–51

Portland Trail Blazers, 50 356–60

Portmeirion Group plc, 88 308–11

Portucel *see* Grupo Portucel Soporcel.

Portugal Telecom SGPS S.A., 69 304–07

Sun Pharmaceutical Industries Ltd., 57 345–47

Sun-Rype Products Ltd., 76 336–38

Sun Sportswear, Inc., 17 460–63

Sun Television & Appliances Inc., 10 502–03

Sun World International, LLC, 93 426–29

SunAmerica Inc., 11 481–83 *see also* American International Group, Inc.

Sunbeam-Oster Co., Inc., 9 484–86

Sunburst Hospitality Corporation, 26 458–61

Sunburst Shutters Corporation, 78 370–72

Suncor Energy Inc., 54 352–54

Suncorp-Metway Ltd., 91 463–66

Sundstrand Corporation, 7 502–04; 21 478–81 (upd.)

Sundt Corp., 24 466–69

SunGard Data Systems Inc., 11 484–85

Sunglass Hut International, Inc., 21 482–84; 74 323–26 (upd.)

Sunkist Growers, Inc., 26 466–69; 102 399–404 (upd.)

Sunoco, Inc., 28 438–42 (upd.); 83 373–380 (upd.)

SunOpta Inc., 79 406–10

SunPower Corporation, 91 467–70

The Sunrider Corporation, 26 470–74

Sunrise Greetings, 88 385–88

Sunrise Medical Inc., 11 486–88

Sunrise Senior Living, Inc., 81 380–83

Sunshine Village Corporation, 103 415–18

Sunsweet Growers *see* Diamond of California.

Suntech Power Holdings Company Ltd., 89 432–35

Sunterra Corporation, 75 354–56

Suntory Ltd., 65 328–31

Suntron Corporation, 107 421–24

SunTrust Banks Inc., 23 455–58; 101 458–64 (upd.)

Super 8 Motels, Inc., 83 381–385

Super Food Services, Inc., 15 479–81

Supercuts Inc., 26 475–78

Superdrug Stores PLC, 95 390–93

Superior Energy Services, Inc., 65 332–34

Superior Essex Inc., 80 364–68

Superior Industries International, Inc., 8 505–07

Superior Uniform Group, Inc., 30 455–57

Supermarkets General Holdings Corporation, II 672–74 *see also* Pathmark Stores, Inc.

SUPERVALU INC., II 668–71; 18 503–08 (upd.); 50 453–59 (upd.)

Suprema Specialties, Inc., 27 440–42

Supreme International Corporation, 27 443–46 *see also* Perry Ellis International Inc.

Suramericana de Inversiones S.A., 88 389–92

Surrey Satellite Technology Limited, 83 386–390

The Susan G. Komen Breast CancerFoundation, 78 373–76

Susquehanna Pfaltzgraff Company, 8 508–10

Sutherland Lumber Company, L.P., 99 431–434

Sutter Home Winery Inc., 16 476–78 *see also* Trinchero Family Estates.

Suzano *see* Companhia Suzano de Papel e Celulose S.A.

Suzuki Motor Corporation, 9 487–89; 23 459–62 (upd.); 59 393–98 (upd.)

SVB Financial Group, 109 521–25

Sveaskog AB, 93 430–33

Svenska Cellulosa Aktiebolaget SCA, IV 338–40; 28 443–46 (upd.); 85 413–20 (upd.)

Svenska Handelsbanken AB, II 365–67; 50 460–63 (upd.)

Svenska Spel AB, 107 425–28

Sverdrup Corporation, 14 475–78 *see also* Jacobs Engineering Group Inc.

Sveriges Riksbank, 96 418–22

SVP Worldwide LLC, 113 384–89

SWA *see* Southwest Airlines.

SWALEC *see* Scottish and Southern Energy plc.

Swales & Associates, Inc., 69 336–38

Swank, Inc., 17 464–66; 84 380–384 (upd.)

Swarovski International Holding AG, 40 422–25 *see also* D. Swarovski & Co.

The Swatch Group Ltd., 26 479–81; 107 429–33 (upd.)

Swedish Match AB, 12 462–64; 39 387–90 (upd.); 92 349–55 (upd.)

Swedish Telecom, V 331–33

SwedishAmerican Health System, 51 363–66

Sweet Candy Company, 60 295–97

Sweetbay Supermarket, 103 419–24 (upd.)

Sweetheart Cup Company, Inc., 36 460–64

The Swett & Crawford Group Inc., 84 385–389

SWH Corporation, 70 307–09

Swift & Company, 55 364–67

Swift Energy Company, 63 364–66

Swift Transportation Co., Inc., 42 363–66

Swinerton Inc., 43 397–400

Swire Pacific Ltd., I 521–22; 16 479–81 (upd.); 57 348–53 (upd.)

Swisher International Group Inc., 23 463–65

Swiss Air Transport Company Ltd., I 121–22

Swiss Army Brands, Inc. *see* Victorinox AG.

Swiss Bank Corporation, II 368–70 *see also* UBS AG.

The Swiss Colony, Inc., 97 395–98

Swiss Federal Railways (Schweizerische Bundesbahnen), V 519–22

Swiss International Air Lines Ltd., 48 379–81

Swiss Reinsurance Company (Schweizerische Rückversicherungs-Gesellschaft), III 375–78; 46 380–84 (upd.)

Swiss Valley Farms Company, 90 400–03

Swisscom AG, 58 336–39

Swissport International Ltd., 70 310–12

Sybase, Inc., 10 504–06; 27 447–50 (upd.)

Sybron International Corp., 14 479–81

Sycamore Networks, Inc., 45 388–91

Sykes Enterprises, Inc., 45 392–95

Sylvan, Inc., 22 496–99

Sylvan Learning Systems, Inc., 35 408–11 *see also* Educate Inc.

Symantec Corporation, 10 507–09; 82 372–77 (upd.)

Symbol Technologies, Inc., 15 482–84 *see also* Motorola, Inc.

Symrise GmbH and Company KG, 89 436–40

Syms Corporation, 29 456–58; 74 327–30 (upd.)

Symyx Technologies, Inc., 77 420–23

Synaptics Incorporated, 95 394–98

Synchronoss Technologies, Inc., 95 399–402

Syneron Medical Ltd., 91 471–74

Syngenta International AG, 83 391–394

Syniverse Holdings Inc., 97 399–402

SYNNEX Corporation, 73 328–30

Synopsys, Inc., 11 489–92; 69 339–43 (upd.)

SynOptics Communications, Inc., 10 510–12

Synovus Financial Corp., 12 465–67; 52 336–40 (upd.)

Syntax-Brillian Corporation, 102 405–09

Syntel, Inc., 92 356–60

Syntex Corporation, I 701–03

Synthes, Inc., 93 434–37

Sypris Solutions, Inc., 85 421–25

SyQuest Technology, Inc., 18 509–12

Syral S.A.S., 113 390–93

Syratech Corp., 14 482–84

SYSCO Corporation, II 675–76; 24 470–72 (upd.); 75 357–60 (upd.)

System Software Associates, Inc., 10 513–14

Systemax, Inc., 52 341–44

Systembolaget AB, 113 394–98

Systems & Computer Technology Corp., 19 437–39

Sytner Group plc, 45 396–98

Szerencsejáték Zrt., 113 399–402

T

T-Netix, Inc., 46 385–88

T-Online International AG, 61 349–51

T.J. Maxx *see* The TJX Companies, Inc.

T. Marzetti Company, 57 354–56

T. Rowe Price Associates, Inc., 11 493–96; 34 423–27 (upd.)

TA Triumph-Adler AG, 48 382–85

TAB Products Co., 17 467–69

Telephone and Data Systems, Inc., 9 494–96

TelePizza S.A., 33 387–89

Television de Mexico, S.A. *see* Grupo Televisa, S.A.

Television Española, S.A., 7 511–12

Télévision Française 1, 23 475–77

TeliaSonera AB, 57 361–65 (upd.)

Telkom S.A. Ltd., 106 460–64

Tellabs, Inc., 11 500–01; 40 426–29 (upd.)

Telsmith Inc., 96 429–33

Telstra Corporation Limited, 50 469–72

Telxon Corporation, 10 523–25

Tembec Inc., 66 322–24

Temple-Inland Inc., IV 341–43; 31 438–42 (upd.); 102 410–16 (upd.)

Tempur-Pedic Inc., 54 359–61

Ten Cate *see* Royal Ten Cate N.V.

Ten Thousand Villages U.S., 108 483–86

Tenaris SA, 63 385–88

Tenedora Nemak, S.A. de C.V., 102 417–20

Tenet Healthcare Corporation, 55 368–71 (upd.); 112 407–13 (upd.)

TenFold Corporation, 35 421–23

Tengasco, Inc., 99 444–447

Tengelmann Group, 27 459–62

Tennant Company, 13 499–501; 33 390–93 (upd.); 95 415–20 (upd.)

Tenneco Inc., I 526–28; 10 526–28 (upd.); 113 408–13 (upd.)

Tennessee Valley Authority, 50 473–77

TenneT B.V., 78 392–95

TEP *see* Tucson Electric Power Co.

TEPPCO Partners, L.P., 73 335–37

Tequila Herradura *see* Grupo Industrial Herradura, S.A. de C.V.

Ter Beke NV, 103 442–45

Teradyne, Inc., 11 502–04; 98 398–403 (upd.)

Terex Corporation, 7 513–15; 40 430–34 (upd.); 91 475–82 (upd.)

Tergal Industries S.A.S., 102 421–25

The Terlato Wine Group, 48 390–92

Terra Industries, Inc., 13 502–04; 94 420–24 (upd.)

Terra Lycos, Inc., 43 420–25

Terremark Worldwide, Inc., 99 448–452

Terrena L'Union CANA CAVAL, 70 320–22

Terumo Corporation, 48 393–95

Tesco plc, II 677–78; 24 473–76 (upd.); 68 366–70 (upd.)

Tesoro Corporation, 7 516–19; 45 408–13 (upd.); 97 411–19 (upd.)

Tessenderlo Group, 76 345–48

The Testor Corporation, 51 367–70

Tetley USA Inc., 88 399–402

Teton Energy Corporation, 97 420–23

Tetra Pak International SA, 53 327–29

Tetra Tech, Inc., 29 463–65

Teva Pharmaceutical Industries Ltd., 22 500–03; 54 362–65 (upd.); 112 414–19 (upd.)

Texaco Inc., IV 551–53; 14 491–94 (upd.); 41 391–96 (upd.) *see also* Chevron Corp.

Texas Air Corporation, I 123–24

Texas Industries, Inc., 8 522–24

Texas Instruments Incorporated, II 112–15; 11 505–08 (upd.); 46 418–23 (upd.)

Texas Pacific Group Inc., 36 472–74

Texas Rangers Baseball, 51 371–74

Texas Roadhouse, Inc., 69 347–49

Texas Utilities Company, V 724–25; 25 472–74 (upd.)

Textron Inc., I 529–30; 34 431–34 (upd.); 88 403–07 (upd.)

Textron Lycoming Turbine Engine, 9 497–99

TF1 *see* Télévision Française 1

TFM *see* Grupo Transportación Ferroviaria Mexicana, S.A. de C.V.

Tha Row Records, 69 350–52 (upd.)

Thai Airways International Public Company Limited, 6 122–24; 27 463–66 (upd.)

Thai Union Frozen Products PCL, 75 370–72

Thales S.A., 42 373–76

Thames Water plc, 11 509–11; 90 404–08 (upd.)

Thane International, Inc., 84 394–397

Thanulux Public Company Limited, 86 393–96

Theatre Development Fund, Inc., 109 539–42

Thermadyne Holding Corporation, 19 440–43

Thermo BioAnalysis Corp., 25 475–78

Thermo Electron Corporation, 7 520–22

Thermo Fibertek, Inc., 24 477–79 *see also* Kadant Inc.

Thermo Fisher Scientific Inc., 105 443–54 (upd.)

Thermo Instrument Systems Inc., 11 512–14

Thermo King Corporation, 13 505–07 *see also* Ingersoll-Rand Company Ltd.

Thermos Company, 16 486–88

Thermotech, 113 414–17

Things Remembered, Inc., 84 398–401

Thiokol Corporation, 9 500–02 (upd.); 22 504–07 (upd.)

Thistle Hotels PLC, 54 366–69

Thomas & Betts Corporation, 11 515–17; 54 370–74 (upd.)

Thomas & Howard Company, Inc., 90 409–12

Thomas Cook Travel Inc., 9 503–05; 33 394–96 (upd.)

Thomas Crosbie Holdings Limited, 81 384–87

Thomas H. Lee Co., 24 480–83

Thomas Industries Inc., 29 466–69

Thomas J. Lipton Company, 14 495–97

Thomas Nelson Inc., 14 498–99; 38 454–57 (upd.)

Thomas Publishing Company, 26 482–85

Thomaston Mills, Inc., 27 467–70

Thomasville Furniture Industries, Inc., 12 474–76; 74 339–42 (upd.)

Thomsen Greenhouses and Garden Center, Incorporated, 65 338–40

The Thomson Corporation, 8 525–28; 34 435–40 (upd.); 77 433–39 (upd.)

THOMSON multimedia S.A., II 116–17; 42 377–80 (upd.)

Thor Equities, LLC, 108 487–90

Thor Industries Inc., 39 391–94; 92 365–370 (upd.)

Thorn Apple Valley, Inc., 7 523–25; 22 508–11 (upd.)

Thorn EMI plc, I 531–32 *see also* EMI plc; Thorn plc.

Thorn plc, 24 484–87

Thorntons plc, 46 424–26

ThoughtWorks, 90 413–16

Thousand Trails Inc., 33 397–99; 113 418–22 (upd.)

THQ, Inc., 39 395–97; 92 371–375 (upd.)

Threadless.com *see* skinnyCorp, LLC.

365 Media Group plc, 89 441–44

3Com Corporation, 11 518–21; 34 441–45 (upd.); 106 465–72 (upd.)

The 3DO Company, 43 426–30

3i Group PLC, 73 338–40

3M Company, 61 365–70 (upd.)

Thrifty PayLess, Inc., 12 477–79 *see also* Rite Aid Corp.

Thrivent Financial for Lutherans, 111 452–59 (upd.)

Thumann Inc., 104 442–45

ThyssenKrupp AG, IV 221–23; 28 452–60 (upd.); 87 425–438 (upd.)

TI Group plc, 17 480–83

TIAA-CREF *see* Teachers Insurance and Annuity Association-College Retirement Equities Fund.

Tianjin Flying Pigeon Bicycle Co., Ltd., 95 421–24

Tibbett & Britten Group plc, 32 449–52

TIBCO Software Inc., 79 411–14

TIC Holdings Inc., 92 376–379

Ticketmaster, 13 508–10; 37 381–84 (upd.); 76 349–53 (upd.)

Tidewater Inc., 11 522–24; 37 385–88 (upd.)

Tiffany & Co., 14 500–03; 78 396–401 (upd.)

TIG Holdings, Inc., 26 486–88

Tiger Aspect Productions Ltd., 72 348–50

Tiger Brands Limited, 112 420–24

Tigre S.A. Tubos e Conexões, 104 446–49

Tilcon-Connecticut Inc., 80 373–76

Tilia Inc., 62 363–65

Tillamook County Creamery Association, 111 460–63

Tilley Endurables, Inc., 67 364–66

Tillotson Corp., 15 488–90

TIM *see* Telecom Italia Mobile S.p.A.

Tim-Bar Corporation, 110 459–62

Tim Hortons Inc., 109 543–47 (upd.)

Viewpoint International, Inc., 66 354–56

ViewSonic Corporation, 72 365–67

Viking Office Products, Inc., 10 544–46 *see also* Office Depot, Inc.

Viking Range Corporation, 66 357–59

Viking Yacht Company, 96 446–49

Village Roadshow Ltd., 58 356–59

Village Super Market, Inc., 7 563–64

Village Voice Media, Inc., 38 476–79

Villeroy & Boch AG, 37 415–18

Vilmorin Clause et Cie, 70 344–46

Vilter Manufacturing, LLC, 105 475–79

Vin & Spirit AB, 31 458–61 *see also* V&S Vin & Sprit AB.

Viña Concha y Toro S.A., 45 432–34

Vinci S.A., 27 54; 43 450–52; 113 455–59 (upd.)

Vincor International Inc., 50 518–21

Vinmonopolet A/S, 100 434–37

Vinson & Elkins L.L.P., 30 481–83

Vintage Petroleum, Inc., 42 421–23

Vinton Studios, 63 420–22

Vion Food Group NV, 85 438–41

Virbac Corporation, 74 379–81

Virco Manufacturing Corporation, 17 515–17

Virgin Group Ltd., 12 513–15; 32 491–96 (upd.); 89 479–86 (upd.)

Virginia Dare Extract Company, Inc., 94 447–50

Viridian Group plc, 64 402–04

Visa Inc., 9 536–38; 26 514–17 (upd.); 104 464–69 (upd.)

Viscofan S.A., 70 347–49

Vishay Intertechnology, Inc., 21 518–21; 80 401–06 (upd.)

Vision Service Plan Inc., 77 473–76

Viskase Companies, Inc., 55 379–81

Vista Bakery, Inc., 56 365–68

Vista Chemical Company, I 402–03

Vistana, Inc., 22 537–39

VistaPrint Limited, 87 451–454

Visteon Corporation, 109 572–76

VISX, Incorporated, 30 484–86

Vita Food Products Inc., 99 478–481

Vita Plus Corporation, 60 315–17

Vital Images, Inc., 85 442–45

Vitalink Pharmacy Services, Inc., 15 522–24

Vitamin Shoppe Industries, Inc., 60 318–20

Vitasoy International Holdings Ltd., 94 451–54

Viterra Inc., 105 480–83

Vitesse Semiconductor Corporation, 32 497–500

Vitro Corp., 10 547–48

Vitro Corporativo S.A. de C.V., 34 490–92

Vivarte SA, 54 409–12 (upd.)

Vivartia S.A., 82 407–10

Vivendi, 46 438–41 (upd.); 112 462–68 (upd.)

Vivra, Inc., 18 545–47 *see also* Gambro AB.

Vizio, Inc., 100 438–41

Vlasic Foods International Inc., 25 516–19

VLSI Technology, Inc., 16 518–20

VMware, Inc., 90 428–31

VNU N.V., 27 498–501

VNUS Medical Technologies, Inc., 103 485–88

Vocento, 94 455–58

Vodacom Group Pty. Ltd., 106 481–85

Vodafone Group Plc, 11 547–48; 36 503–06 (upd.); 75 395–99 (upd.)

voestalpine AG, IV 233–35; 57 399–403 (upd.)

Voith Sulzer Papiermaschinen GmbH *see* J.M. Voith AG.

Volcan Compañia Minera S.A.A., 92 403–06

Volcom, Inc., 77 477–80

Volga-Dnepr Group, 82 411–14

Volkert and Associates, Inc., 98 452–55

Volkswagen Aktiengesellschaft, I 206–08; 11 549–51; 32 501–05 (upd.); 111 519–25 (upd.)

Volt Information Sciences Inc., 26 518–21

Volunteers of America, Inc., 66 360–62

Von Maur Inc., 64 405–08

Vonage Holdings Corp., 81 415–18

The Vons Companies, Inc., 7 569–71; 28 510–13 (upd.); 103 489–95 (upd.)

Vontobel Holding AG, 96 450–53

Voortman Cookies Limited, 103 496–99

Vornado Realty Trust, 20 508–10; 112 469–74 (upd.)

Vorwerk & Co. KG, 27 502–04; 112 475–79 (upd.)

Vosper Thornycroft Holding plc, 41 410–12

Vossloh AG, 53 348–52

Votorantim Participaçoes S.A., 76 375–78

Vought Aircraft Industries, Inc., 49 442–45

VSE Corporation, 108 533–36

VSM *see* Village Super Market, Inc.

VTech Holdings Ltd., 77 481–84

Vueling Airlines S.A., 97 445–48

Vulcabras S.A., 103 500–04

Vulcan Materials Company, 7 572–75; 52 392–96 (upd.)

W

W + K *see* Wieden + Kennedy.

W.A. Whitney Company, 53 353–56

W. Atlee Burpee & Co., 27 505–08

W.B Doner & Co., 56 369–72

W.B. Mason Company, 98 456–59

W.C. Bradley Co., 69 363–65

W.H. Brady Co., 16 518–21 *see also* Brady Corp.

W. H. Braum, Inc., 80 407–10

W H Smith Group PLC, V 211–13

W Jordan (Cereals) Ltd., 74 382–84

W.L. Gore & Associates, Inc., 14 538–41; 60 321–24 (upd.)

W.P. Carey & Co. LLC, 49 446–48

W.R. Berkley Corporation, 15 525–27; 74 385–88 (upd.)

W.R. Grace & Company, I 547–50; 50 522–29 (upd.)

W.S. Badcock Corporation, 107 461–64

W.W. Grainger, Inc., V 214–15; 26 537–39 (upd.); 68 392–95 (upd.)

W.W. Norton & Company, Inc., 28 518–20

Waban Inc., 13 547–49 *see also* HomeBase, Inc.

Wabash National Corp., 13 550–52

Wabtec Corporation, 40 451–54

Wachovia Bank of Georgia, N.A., 16 521–23

Wachovia Bank of South Carolina, N.A., 16 524–26

Wachovia Corporation, 12 516–20; 46 442–49 (upd.)

Wachtell, Lipton, Rosen & Katz, 47 435–38

The Wackenhut Corporation, 14 541–43; 63 423–26 (upd.)

Wacker-Chemie AG, 35 454–58; 112 480–85 (upd.)

Wacker Construction Equipment AG, 95 438–41

Wacoal Corp., 25 520–24

Waddell & Reed, Inc., 22 540–43

Waffle House Inc., 14 544–45; 60 325–27 (upd.)

Wagers Inc. (Idaho Candy Company), 86 416–19

Waggener Edstrom, 42 424–26

Wagon plc, 92 407–10

Wah Chang, 82 415–18

Wahl Clipper Corporation, 86 420–23

Wahoo's Fish Taco, 96 454–57

Wakefern Food Corporation, 33 434–37; 107 465–69 (upd.)

Wal-Mart de Mexico, S.A. de C.V., 35 459–61 (upd.)

Wal-Mart Stores, Inc., V 216–17; 8 555–57 (upd.); 26 522–26 (upd.); 63 427–32 (upd.)

Walbridge Aldinger Co., 38 480–82

Walbro Corporation, 13 553–55

Waldbaum, Inc., 19 479–81

Waldenbooks, 17 522–24; 86 424–28 (upd.)

Walgreen Co., V 218–20; 20 511–13 (upd.); 65 352–56 (upd.)

Walker Manufacturing Company, 19 482–84

Walkers Shortbread Ltd., 79 464–67

Walkers Snack Foods Ltd., 70 350–52

Wall Drug Store, Inc., 40 455–57

Wall Street Deli, Inc., 33 438–41

Wallace Computer Services, Inc., 36 507–10

Walsworth Publishing Company, Inc., 78 445–48

The Walt Disney Company, II 172–74; 6 174–77 (upd.); 30 487–91 (upd.); 63 433–38 (upd.)

Walter E. Smithe Furniture, Inc., 105 484–87

Walter Industries, Inc., III 765–67; 22 544–47 (upd.); 72 368–73 (upd.)

Western Union Company, 54 413–16; 112 492–96 (upd.)

Western Wireless Corporation, 36 514–16

Westfield Group, 69 366–69

Westin Hotels and Resorts Worldwide, 9 547–49; 29 505–08 (upd.)

Westinghouse Electric Corporation, II 120–22; 12 544–47 (upd.) *see also* CBS Radio Group.

WestJet Airlines Ltd., 38 493–95

Westmoreland Coal Company, 7 582–85

Weston Foods Inc. *see* George Weston Ltd.

Westpac Banking Corporation, II 388–90; 48 424–27 (upd.)

WestPoint Stevens Inc., 16 533–36 *see also* JPS Textile Group, Inc.

Westport Resources Corporation, 63 439–41

Westvaco Corporation, IV 351–54; 19 495–99 (upd.) *see also* MeadWestvaco Corp.

Westwood One Inc., 23 508–11; 106 490–96 (upd.)

The Wet Seal, Inc., 18 562–64; 70 353–57 (upd.)

Wetterau Incorporated, II 681–82 *see also* Supervalu Inc.

Weyco Group, Incorporated, 32 510–13

Weyerhaeuser Company, IV 355–56; 9 550–52 (upd.); 28 514–17 (upd.); 83 454–461 (upd.)

WFS Financial Inc., 70 358–60

WFSC *see* World Fuel Services Corp.

WGBH Educational Foundation, 66 366–68

WH Smith PLC, 42 442–47 (upd.)

Wham-O, Inc., 61 390–93

Whataburger Restaurants LP, 105 493–97

Whatman plc, 46 462–65

Wheaton Industries, 8 570–73

Wheaton Science Products, 60 338–42 (upd.)

Wheelabrator Technologies, Inc., 6 599–600; 60 343–45 (upd.)

Wheeling-Pittsburgh Corporation, 7 586–88; 58 360–64 (upd.)

Wheels Inc., 96 458–61

Wherehouse Entertainment Incorporated, 11 556–58

Whirlpool Corporation, III 653–55; 12 548–50 (upd.); 59 414–19 (upd.)

Whitbread PLC, I 293–94; 20 519–22 (upd.); 52 412–17 (upd.); 97 468–76 (upd.)

White & Case LLP, 35 466–69

White Castle Management Company, 12 551–53; 36 517–20 (upd.); 85 458–64 (upd.)

White Consolidated Industries Inc., 13 562–64 *see also* Electrolux.

The White House, Inc., 60 346–48

White Lily Foods Company, 88 435–38

White Martins Gases Industriais Ltda., 111 526–29

White Mountains Insurance Group, Ltd., 48 428–31

White Rose, Inc., 24 527–29

White Wave, 43 462–64

Whitehall Jewellers, Inc., 82 429–34 (upd.)

Whiting Petroleum Corporation, 81 424–27

Whiting-Turner Contracting Company, 95 446–49

Whitman Corporation, 10 553–55 (upd.) *see also* PepsiAmericas, Inc.

Whitman Education Group, Inc., 41 419–21

Whitney Holding Corporation, 21 522–24

Whittaker Corporation, I 544–46; 48 432–35 (upd.)

Whittard of Chelsea Plc, 61 394–97

Whole Foods Market, Inc., 20 523–27; 50 530–34 (upd.); 110 479–86 (upd.)

WHX Corporation, 98 464–67

Wickes Inc., V 221–23; 25 533–36 (upd.)

Widmer Brothers Brewing Company, 76 379–82

Wieden + Kennedy, 75 403–05

Wienerberger AG, 70 361–63

Wikimedia Foundation, Inc., 91 523–26

Wilbert, Inc., 56 377–80

Wilbur Chocolate Company, 66 369–71

Wilco Farm Stores, 93 490–93

Wild Oats Markets, Inc., 19 500–02; 41 422–25 (upd.)

Wildlife Conservation Society, 31 462–64

Wilh. Werhahn KG, 101 491–94

Wilh. Wilhelmsen ASA, 94 459–62

Wilhelm Karmann GmbH, 94 463–68

Wilkinson Hardware Stores Ltd., 80 416–18

Wilkinson Sword Ltd., 60 349–52

Willamette Industries, Inc., IV 357–59; 31 465–68 (upd.) *see also* Weyerhaeuser Co.

Willamette Valley Vineyards, Inc., 85 465–69

Willbros Group, Inc., 56 381–83

William Grant & Sons Ltd., 60 353–55

William Hill Organization Limited, 49 449–52

William Jackson & Son Ltd., 101 495–99

William L. Bonnell Company, Inc., 66 372–74

William Lyon Homes, 59 420–22

William Morris Agency, Inc., 23 512–14; 102 448–52 (upd.)

William Reed Publishing Ltd., 78 467–70

William Zinsser & Company, Inc., 58 365–67

Williams & Connolly LLP, 47 445–48

Williams Communications Group, Inc., 34 507–10

The Williams Companies, Inc., IV 575–76; 31 469–72 (upd.)

Williams Scotsman, Inc., 65 361–64

Williams-Sonoma, Inc., 17 548–50; 44 447–50 (upd.); 103 515–20 (upd.)

Williamson-Dickie Manufacturing Company, 14 549–50; 45 438–41 (upd.)

Willis Group Holdings Ltd., 25 537–39; 100 456–60 (upd.)

Willkie Farr & Gallagher LLPLP, 95 450–53

Willow Run Foods, Inc., 100 461–64

Wilmar International Ltd., 108 537–41

Wilmer Cutler Pickering Hale and Dorr L.L.P., 109 600–04

Wilmington Trust Corporation, 25 540–43

Wilson Bowden Plc, 45 442–44

Wilson Sonsini Goodrich & Rosati, 34 511–13

Wilson Sporting Goods Company, 24 530–32; 84 431–436 (upd.)

Wilsons The Leather Experts Inc., 21 525–27; 58 368–71 (upd.)

Wilton Products, Inc., 97 477–80

Winbond Electronics Corporation, 74 389–91

Wincanton plc, 52 418–20

Winchell's Donut Houses Operating Company, L.P., 60 356–59

WinCo Foods Inc., 60 360–63

Wincor Nixdorf Holding GmbH, 69 370–73 (upd.)

Wind River Systems, Inc., 37 419–22

Windmere Corporation, 16 537–39 *see also* Applica Inc.

Windstream Corporation, 83 462–465

Windswept Environmental Group, Inc., 62 389–92

The Wine Group, Inc., 39 419–21

Winegard Company, 56 384–87

Winmark Corporation, 74 392–95

Winn-Dixie Stores, Inc., II 683–84; 21 528–30 (upd.); 59 423–27 (upd.); 113 465–71

Winnebago Industries, Inc., 7 589–91; 27 509–12 (upd.); 96 462–67 (upd.)

WinsLoew Furniture, Inc., 21 531–33 *see also* Brown Jordan International Inc.

Winston & Strawn, 35 470–73

Winterthur Group, III 402–04; 68 402–05 (upd.)

Wintrust Financial Corporation, 106 497–501

Wipro Limited, 43 465–68; 106 502–07 (upd.)

The Wiremold Company, 81 428–34

Wirtz Corporation, 72 374–76

Wisconsin Alumni Research Foundation, 65 365–68

Wisconsin Bell, Inc., 14 551–53 *see also* AT&T Corp.

Wisconsin Central Transportation Corporation, 24 533–36

Wisconsin Dairies, 7 592–93

Wisconsin Energy Corporation, 6 601–03; 54 417–21 (upd.)

Wisconsin Public Service Corporation, 9 553–54 *see also* WPS Resources Corp.

Index to Industries

Accounting

American Institute of Certified Public
   Accountants (AICPA), 44
Andersen, 29 (upd.); 68 (upd.)
Automatic Data Processing, Inc., III; 9
   (upd.); 47 (upd.)
BDO Seidman LLP, 96
BKD LLP, 96
CPP International, LLC, 103
CROSSMARK, 79
Deloitte Touche Tohmatsu International,
   9; 29 (upd.)
Ernst & Young Global Limited, 9; 29
   (upd.); 108 (upd.)
FTI Consulting, Inc., 77
Grant Thornton International, 57
Huron Consulting Group Inc., 87
JKH Holding Co. LLC, 105
KPMG International, 33 (upd.); 108
   (upd.)
L.S. Starrett Co., 13
McLane Company, Inc., 13
NCO Group, Inc., 42
Paychex, Inc., 15; 46 (upd.)
PKF International 78
Plante & Moran, LLP, 71
PRG-Schultz International, Inc., 73
PricewaterhouseCoopers International
   Limited, 9; 29 (upd.); 111 (upd.)
Resources Connection, Inc., 81
Robert Wood Johnson Foundation, 35
RSM McGladrey Business Services Inc.,
   98
Saffery Champness, 80
Sanders\Wingo, 99
Schenck Business Solutions, 88
StarTek, Inc., 79
Travelzoo Inc., 79

Univision Communications Inc., 24; 83
   (upd.)

Advertising & Business Services

ABM Industries Incorporated, 25 (upd.)
Abt Associates Inc., 95
Accenture Ltd., 108 (upd.)
AchieveGlobal Inc., 90
Ackerley Communications, Inc., 9
ACNielsen Corporation, 13; 38 (upd.)
Acosta Sales and Marketing Company,
   Inc., 77
Acsys, Inc., 44
Adecco S.A., 36 (upd.)
Adelman Travel Group, 105
Adia S.A., 6
Administaff, Inc., 52
Advertising Council, Inc., The, 76
Advisory Board Company, The, 80
Advo, Inc., 6; 53 (upd.)
Aegis Group plc, 6
Affiliated Computer Services, Inc., 61
AHL Services, Inc., 27
Allegis Group, Inc., 95
Alloy, Inc., 55
Amdocs Ltd., 47
American Building Maintenance
   Industries, Inc., 6
Amey Plc, 47
Analysts International Corporation, 36
aQuantive, Inc., 81
Arbitron Company, The, 38
Ariba, Inc., 57
Armor Holdings, Inc., 27
Asatsu-DK Inc., 82
Ashtead Group plc, 34
Associated Press, The, 13

Avalon Correctional Services, Inc., 75
Bain & Company, 55
Barrett Business Services, Inc., 16
Barton Protective Services Inc., 53
Bates Worldwide, Inc., 14; 33 (upd.)
Bearings, Inc., 13
Berlitz International, Inc., 13; 39 (upd.)
Bernard Hodes Group Inc., 86
Bernstein-Rein, 92
Big Flower Press Holdings, Inc., 21
Billing Concepts, Inc., 26; 72 (upd.)
Billing Services Group Ltd., 102
BISYS Group, Inc., The, 73
Booz Allen Hamilton Inc., 10; 101 (upd.)
Boron, LePore & Associates, Inc., 45
Boston Consulting Group, The, 58
Bozell Worldwide Inc., 25
BrandPartners Group, Inc., 58
Bright Horizons Family Solutions, Inc., 31
Brink's Company, The, 58 (upd.)
Broadcast Music Inc., 23; 90 (upd.)
Bronner Display & Sign Advertising, Inc.,
   82
Buck Consultants, Inc., 55
Bureau Veritas SA, 55
Burke, Inc., 88
Burns International Services Corporation,
   13; 41 (upd.)
Cambridge Technology Partners, Inc., 36
Campbell-Ewald Advertising, 86
Campbell-Mithun-Esty, Inc., 16
Cannon Design, 63
Capario, 104
Capita Group PLC, 69
Cardtronics, Inc., 93
Carmichael Lynch Inc., 28
Cash Systems, Inc., 93
Cazenove Group plc, 72
CCC Information Services Group Inc., 74

National Equipment Services, Inc., 57
National Media Corporation, 27
Navigant Consulting, Inc., 93
NAVTEQ Corporation, 69
Neopost S.A., 53
New England Business Services Inc., 18; 78 (upd.)
New Valley Corporation, 17
NFO Worldwide, Inc., 24
Norrell Corporation, 25
Norwood Promotional Products, Inc., 26
NPD Group, Inc., The, 68
O.C. Tanner Co., 69
Oakleaf Waste Management, LLC, 97
Obie Media Corporation, 56
Observer AB, 55
OfficeTiger, LLC, 75
Ogilvy Group, Inc., The, I
Olsten Corporation, 6; 29 (upd.)
Omnicom Group, I; 22 (upd.); 77 (upd.)
On Assignment, Inc., 20
1-800-FLOWERS.COM, Inc., 26; 102 (upd.)
Opinion Research Corporation, 46
Oracle Corporation, 67 (upd.)
Orbitz, Inc., 61
Orchard Enterprises, Inc., The, 103
Outdoor Systems, Inc., 25
Paris Corporation, 22
Paychex, Inc., 15; 46 (upd.)
PDI, Inc., 52
Pegasus Solutions, Inc., 75
Pei Cobb Freed & Partners Architects LLP, 57
Penauille Polyservices SA, 49
PFSweb, Inc., 73
Philip Services Corp., 73
Phillips, de Pury & Luxembourg, 49
Pierce Leahy Corporation, 24
Pinkerton's Inc., 9
Plante & Moran, LLP, 71
PMT Services, Inc., 24
Posterscope Worldwide, 70
Priceline.com Incorporated, 57
Publicis Groupe, 19; 77 (upd.)
Publishers Clearing House, 23; 64 (upd.)
Quintiles Transnational Corporation, 68 (upd.)
Quovadx Inc., 70
R&R Partners Inc., 108
@radical.media, 103
Randstad Holding n.v., 16; 43 (upd.)
RedPeg Marketing, 73
RedPrairie Corporation, 74
RemedyTemp, Inc., 20
Rental Service Corporation, 28
Rentokil Initial Plc, 47
Research Triangle Institute, 83
Resources Connection, Inc., 81
Rewards Network Inc., 70 (upd.)
Richards Group, Inc., The, 58
Right Management Consultants, Inc., 42
Ritchie Bros. Auctioneers Inc., 41
Robert Half International Inc., 18; 70 (upd.)
Roland Berger & Partner GmbH, 37
Ronco Corporation, 15; 80 (upd.)
Russell Reynolds Associates Inc., 38

Saatchi & Saatchi, I; 42 (upd.)
Sanders\Wingo, 99
Schenck Business Solutions, 88
Securitas AB, 42; 112 (upd.)
ServiceMaster Company, The, 6; 23 (upd.); 68 (upd.)
Servpro Industries, Inc., 85
Shared Medical Systems Corporation, 14
Sir Speedy, Inc., 16
Skidmore, Owings & Merrill LLP, 13; 69 (upd.)
SmartForce PLC, 43
SOS Staffing Services, 25
Sotheby's Holdings, Inc., 11; 29 (upd.); 84 (upd.)
Source Interlink Companies, Inc., 75
Spencer Stuart and Associates, Inc., 14
Spherion Corporation, 52
SR Teleperformance S.A., 86
SSI (U.S.) Inc., 103 (upd.)
Steiner Corporation (Alsco), 53
Superior Uniform Group, Inc., 30
Sykes Enterprises, Inc., 45
Synchronoss Technologies, Inc., 95
TA Triumph-Adler AG, 48
Taylor Nelson Sofres plc, 34
TBA Global, LLC, 99
TBWA/Chiat/Day, 6; 43 (upd.)
Thomas Cook Travel Inc., 33 (upd.)
Ticketmaster, 13; 37 (upd.); 76 (upd.)
TMP Worldwide Inc., 30
TNT Post Group N.V., 30
Towers Perrin, 32
Trader Classified Media N.V., 57
Traffix, Inc., 61
Transmedia Network Inc., 20
Treasure Chest Advertising Company, Inc., 32
TRM Copy Centers Corporation, 18
True North Communications Inc., 23
24/7 Real Media, Inc., 49
Tyler Corporation, 23
U.S. Office Products Company, 25
Unica Corporation, 77
UniFirst Corporation, 21
United Business Media plc, 52 (upd.)
United News & Media plc, 28 (upd.)
Unitog Co., 19
Valassis Communications, Inc., 37 (upd.); 76 (upd.)
ValleyCrest Companies, 81 (upd.)
ValueClick, Inc., 49
Vebego International BV, 49
Vedior NV, 35
Vertis Communications, 84
Vertrue Inc., 77
Viad Corp., 73
W.B Doner & Co., 56
Wackenhut Corporation, The, 14; 63 (upd.)
Waggener Edstrom, 42
Warrantech Corporation, 53
WebEx Communications, Inc., 81
Welcome Wagon International Inc., 82
Wells Rich Greene BDDP, 6
Westaff Inc., 33
Wieden + Kennedy, 75

William Morris Agency, Inc., 23; 102 (upd.)
Williams Scotsman, Inc., 65
Workflow Management, Inc., 65
WPP Group plc, 6; 48 (upd.); 112 (upd.)
Wunderman, 86
Xerox Corporation, III; 6 (upd.); 26 (upd.); 69 (upd.)
Young & Rubicam, Inc., I; 22 (upd.); 66 (upd.)
Ziment Group Inc., 102
Zogby International, Inc., 99

Aerospace

A.S. Yakovlev Design Bureau, 15
Aerojet-General Corp., 63
Aeronca Inc., 46
Aerosonic Corporation, 69
Aerospatiale Group, The, 7; 21 (upd.)
AeroVironment, Inc., 97
AgustaWestland N.V., 75
Airborne Systems Group, 89
Alliant Techsystems Inc., 30 (upd.)
Allison Gas Turbine Division, 9
Antonov Design Bureau, 53
Arianespace S.A., 89
Aviacionny Nauchno-Tehnicheskii Komplek im. A.N. Tupoleva, 24
Aviall, Inc., 73
Avions Marcel Dassault-Breguet Aviation, I
B/E Aerospace, Inc., 30
BAE Systems plc, 108 (upd.)
Ballistic Recovery Systems, Inc., 87
Banner Aerospace, Inc., 14
BBA Aviation plc, 90
Beech Aircraft Corporation, 8
Bell Helicopter Textron Inc., 46
Boeing Company, The, I; 10 (upd.); 32 (upd.); 111 (upd.)
Bombardier Inc., 42 (upd.); 87 (upd.)
British Aerospace plc, I; 24 (upd.)
CAE USA Inc., 48
Canadair, Inc., 16
Cessna Aircraft Company, 8; 27 (upd.)
Cirrus Design Corporation, 44
Cobham plc, 30
CPI Aerostructures, Inc., 75
Daimler-Benz Aerospace AG, 16
DeCrane Aircraft Holdings Inc., 36
Derco Holding Ltd., 98
Diehl Stiftung & Co. KG, 79
Ducommun Incorporated, 30
Duncan Aviation, Inc., 94
EADS SOCATA, 54
Eclipse Aviation Corporation, 87
EGL, Inc., 59
Elano Corporation, 14
Empresa Brasileira de Aeronáutica S.A. (Embraer), 36
European Aeronautic Defence and Space Company EADS N.V., 52 (upd.); 109 (upd.)
Fairchild Aircraft, Inc., 9
Fairchild Dornier GmbH, 48 (upd.)
Finmeccanica S.p.A., 84
First Aviation Services Inc., 49
G.I.E. Airbus Industrie, I; 12 (upd.)

Agribusiness & Farming

Airlines

Automotive

Volkswagen Aktiengesellschaft, I; 11 (upd.); 32 (upd.); 111 (upd.)

Wagon plc, 92

Walker Manufacturing Company, 19

Webasto Roof Systems Inc., 97

Wilhelm Karmann GmbH, 94

Winnebago Industries, Inc., 7; 27 (upd.); 96 (upd.)

Woodward Governor Company, 13; 49 (upd.); 105 (upd.)

Yokohama Rubber Company, Limited, The, V; 19 (upd.); 91 (upd.)

ZF Friedrichshafen AG, 48

Ziebart International Corporation, 30; 66 (upd.)

Beverages

A & W Brands, Inc., 25

A. Smith Bowman Distillery, Inc., 104

Adolph Coors Company, I; 13 (upd.); 36 (upd.)

AG Barr plc, 64

Ajegroup S.A., 92

Allied Domecq PLC, 29

Allied-Lyons PLC, I

Anadolu Efes Biracilik ve Malt Sanayii A.S., 95

Anchor Brewing Company, 47

Andrew Peller Ltd., 101

Anheuser-Busch InBev, I; 10 (upd.); 34 (upd.); 100 (upd.)

Apple & Eve L.L.C., 92

Asahi Breweries, Ltd., I; 20 (upd.); 52 (upd.); 108 (upd.)

Asia Pacific Breweries Limited, 59

August Schell Brewing Company Inc., 59

Bacardi & Company Ltd., 18; 82 (upd.)

Baltika Brewery Joint Stock Company, 65

Banfi Products Corp., 36

Baron de Ley S.A., 74

Baron Philippe de Rothschild S.A., 39

Bass PLC, I; 15 (upd.); 38 (upd.)

Bavaria S.A., 90

BBAG Osterreichische Brau-Beteiligungs-AG, 38

Belvedere S.A., 93

Ben Hill Griffin, Inc., 110

Berentzen-Gruppe AG, 113

Beringer Blass Wine Estates Ltd., 22; 66 (upd.)

Bernick Companies, The, 75

Bitburger Braugruppe GmbH, 110

Blue Ridge Beverage Company Inc., 82

Boizel Chanoine Champagne S.A., 94

Bols Distilleries NV, 74

Boston Beer Company, Inc., The, 18; 50 (upd.); 108 (upd.)

Brauerei Beck & Co., 9; 33 (upd.)

Britannia Soft Drinks Ltd. (Britvic), 71

Bronco Wine Company, 101

Brooklyn Brewery, The, 109

Brown-Forman Corporation, I; 10 (upd.); 38 (upd.)

Brouwerijen Alken-Maes N.V., 86

Budweiser Budvar, National Corporation, 59

Cadbury Schweppes PLC, 49 (upd.)

Cains Beer Company PLC, 99

California Dairies Inc., 111

Cameron Hughes Wine, 103

Canandaigua Brands, Inc., 13; 34 (upd.)

Cantine Giorgio Lungarotti S.R.L., 67

Caribou Coffee Company, Inc., 28; 97 (upd.)

Carlsberg A/S, 9; 29 (upd.); 98 (upd.)

Carlton and United Breweries Ltd., I

Casa Cuervo, S.A. de C.V., 31

Central European Distribution Corporation, 75

Cerveceria Polar, I

Chalone Wine Group, Ltd., The, 36

Charmer Sunbelt Group, The, 95

City Brewing Company LLC, 73

Clearly Canadian Beverage Corporation, 48

Clement Pappas & Company, Inc., 92

Click Wine Group, 68

Coca Cola Bottling Co. Consolidated, 10

Coca-Cola Company, The, I; 10 (upd.); 32 (upd.); 67 (upd.)

Coffee Holding Co., Inc., 95

Companhia de Bebidas das Américas, 57

Compania Cervecerias Unidas S.A., 70

Constellation Brands, Inc., 68 (upd.)

Corby Distilleries Limited, 14

Cott Corporation, 52

D.G. Yuengling & Son, Inc., 38

Dairylea Cooperative Inc., 111

Dallis Coffee, Inc., 86

Daniel Thwaites Plc, 95

Davide Campari-Milano S.p.A., 57

Dean Foods Company, 21 (upd.)

Delicato Vineyards, Inc., 50

Deschutes Brewery, Inc., 57

Desnoes and Geddes Limited, 79

Diageo plc, 79 (upd.)

Direct Wines Ltd., 84

Distillers Company PLC, I

Double-Cola Co.-USA, 70

Dr Pepper/Seven Up, Inc., 9; 32 (upd.)

Drie Mollen Holding B.V., 99

Drinks Americas Holdings, LTD., 105

E. & J. Gallo Winery, I; 7 (upd.); 28 (upd.); 104 (upd.)

Eckes AG, 56

Edrington Group Ltd., The, 88

Embotelladora Andina S.A., 71

Empresas Polar SA, 55 (upd.)

Energy Brands Inc., 88

F. Korbel & Bros. Inc., 68

Faygo Beverages Inc., 55

Federico Paternina S.A., 69

Ferolito, Vultaggio & Sons, 27; 100 (upd.)

Fiji Water LLC, 74

Florida's Natural Growers, 45

Foster's Group Limited, 7; 21 (upd.); 50 (upd.); 111 (upd.)

Freixenet S.A., 71

Frucor Beverages Group Ltd., 96

Fuller Smith & Turner P.L.C., 38

G. Heileman Brewing Company Inc., I

Gambrinus Company, The, 40

Gano Excel Enterprise Sdn. Bhd., 89

Gatorade Company, The, 82

Geerlings & Wade, Inc., 45

General Cinema Corporation, I

Glazer's Wholesale Drug Company, Inc., 82

Gluek Brewing Company, 75

Golden State Vintners, Inc., 33

Gosling Brothers Ltd., 82

Grand Metropolitan PLC, I

Green Mountain Coffee Roasters, Inc., 31; 107 (upd.)

Greenalls Group PLC, The, 21

Greene King plc, 31

Grands Vins Jean-Claude Boisset S.A., 98

Groupe Danone, 32 (upd.); 93 (upd.)

Grupo Industrial Herradura, S.A. de C.V., 83

Grupo Modelo, S.A. de C.V., 29

Gruppo Italiano Vini, 111

Guinness/UDV, I; 43 (upd.)

Hain Celestial Group, Inc., The, 43 (upd.)

Hansen Natural Corporation, 31; 76 (upd.)

Heineken N.V., I; 13 (upd.); 34 (upd.); 90 (upd.)

Heublein, Inc., I

High Falls Brewing Company LLC, 74

Hindustan Lever Limited, 79

Hiram Walker Resources, Ltd., I

Hite Brewery Company Ltd., 97

illycaffè S.p.A., 50; 110 (upd.)

Imagine Foods, Inc., 50

Interbrew S.A., 17; 50 (upd.)

Irish Distillers Group, 96

Ito En Ltd., 101

J.J. Darboven GmbH & Co. KG, 96

J. Lohr Winery Corporation, 99

Jacob Leinenkugel Brewing Company, 28

JD Wetherspoon plc, 30

Jim Beam Brands Worldwide, Inc., 58 (upd.)

John Dewar & Sons, Ltd., 82

Jones Soda Co., 69

Jugos del Valle, S.A. de C.V., 85

Karlsberg Brauerei GmbH & Co KG, 41

Kemps LLC, 103

Kendall-Jackson Winery, Ltd., 28

Kikkoman Corporation, 14

Kirin Brewery Company, Limited, I; 21 (upd.); 63 (upd.)

Kobrand Corporation, 82

König Brauerei GmbH & Co. KG, 35 (upd.)

Krombacher Brauerei Bernhard Schadeberg GmbH & Co. KG, 104

L. Foppiano Wine Co., 101

Labatt Brewing Company Limited, I; 25 (upd.)

Lancer Corporation, 21

Langer Juice Company, Inc., 107

Latrobe Brewing Company, 54

Laurent-Perrier SA, 42

Lion Brewery, Inc., The, 86

Lion Nathan Limited, 54

Löwenbräu AG, 80

Macallan Distillers Ltd., The, 63

Madeira Wine Company, S.A., 49

Maison Louis Jadot, 24

Marchesi Antinori SRL, 42

Bio-Technology

Chemicals

Construction

Containers

Drugs & Pharmaceuticals

Education & Training

Electrical & Electronics

Ramtron International Corporation, 89
Raychem Corporation, 8
Raymarine plc, 104
Rayovac Corporation, 13; 39 (upd.)
Raytheon Company, II; 11 (upd.); 38 (upd.); 105 (upd.)
RCA Corporation, II
Read-Rite Corp., 10
Redback Networks, Inc., 92
Reliance Electric Company, 9
Research in Motion Ltd., 54
Rexel, Inc., 15
Richardson Electronics, Ltd., 17
Ricoh Company, Ltd., III; 36 (upd.); 108 (upd.)
Rimage Corp., 89
Rival Company, The, 19
Rockford Corporation, 43
Rogers Corporation, 61; 80 (upd.)
S&C Electric Company, 15
SAGEM S.A., 37
St. Louis Music, Inc., 48
Sam Ash Music Corporation, 30
Samsung Electronics Co., Ltd., 14; 41 (upd.); 108 (upd.)
Sanmina-SCI Corporation, 109 (upd.)
SANYO Electric Co., Ltd., II; 36 (upd.); 95 (upd.)
Sarnoff Corporation, 57
ScanSource, Inc., 29; 74 (upd.)
Schneider Electric SA, II; 18 (upd.); 108 (upd.)
SCI Systems, Inc., 9
Scientific-Atlanta, Inc., 45 (upd.)
Scitex Corporation Ltd., 24
Seagate Technology, 8; 34 (upd.); 105 (upd.)
SEGA Corporation, 73
Semitool, Inc., 79 (upd.)
Semtech Corporation, 32
Sennheiser Electronic GmbH & Co. KG, 66
Sensormatic Electronics Corp., 11
Sensory Science Corporation, 37
SGI, 29 (upd.)
Sharp Corporation, II; 12 (upd.); 40 (upd.)
Sheldahl Inc., 23
Shure Inc., 60
Siemens AG, II; 14 (upd.); 57 (upd.)
Sierra Nevada Corporation, 108
Silicon Graphics Incorporated, 9
Siltronic AG, 90
SL Industries, Inc., 77
Sling Media, Inc., 112
SMART Modular Technologies, Inc., 86
Smiths Industries PLC, 25
Solectron Corporation, 12; 48 (upd.)
Sony Corporation, II; 12 (upd.); 40 (upd.); 108 (upd.)
Spansion Inc., 80
Spectrum Control, Inc., 67
SPX Corporation, 10; 47 (upd.); 103 (upd.)
Square D, 90
Sterling Electronics Corp., 18
STMicroelectronics NV, 52
Strix Ltd., 51

Stuart C. Irby Company, 58
Sumitomo Electric Industries, Ltd., II
Sun Microsystems, Inc., 7; 30 (upd.); 91 (upd.)
Sunbeam-Oster Co., Inc., 9
SunPower Corporation, 91
Suntech Power Holdings Company Ltd., 89
Suntron Corporation, 107
Synaptics Incorporated, 95
Syneron Medical Ltd., 91
SYNNEX Corporation, 73
Synopsys, Inc., 11; 69 (upd.)
Syntax-Brillian Corporation, 102
Sypris Solutions, Inc., 85
SyQuest Technology, Inc., 18
Taiwan Semiconductor Manufacturing Company Ltd., 47
Tandy Corporation, II; 12 (upd.)
Tatung Co., 23
TDK Corporation, II; 17 (upd.); 49 (upd.)
TEAC Corporation 78
Tech-Sym Corporation, 18
Technitrol, Inc., 29
Tektronix, Inc., 8
Teledyne Technologies Inc., 62 (upd.)
Telxon Corporation, 10
Teradyne, Inc., 11; 98 (upd.)
Texas Instruments Inc., II; 11 (upd.); 46 (upd.)
Thales S.A., 42
Thomas & Betts Corporation, 11; 54 (upd.)
THOMSON multimedia S.A., II; 42 (upd.)
THQ, Inc., 92 (upd.)
Titan Corporation, The, 36
TiVo Inc., 75
TomTom N.V., 81
Tops Appliance City, Inc., 17
Toromont Industries, Ltd., 21
Trans-Lux Corporation, 51
Trimble Navigation Limited, 40
TriQuint Semiconductor, Inc., 63
TT electronics plc, 111
Tweeter Home Entertainment Group, Inc., 30
Ultimate Electronics, Inc., 69 (upd.)
Ultrak Inc., 24
Uniden Corporation, 98
Unisys Corporation, 112 (upd.)
United Microelectronics Corporation, 98
Universal Electronics Inc., 39
Universal Security Instruments, Inc., 96
Varian, Inc., 12; 48 (upd.)
Veeco Instruments Inc., 32
VIASYS Healthcare, Inc., 52
Viasystems Group, Inc., 67
Vicon Industries, Inc., 44
Victor Company of Japan, Limited, II; 26 (upd.); 83 (upd.)
Vishay Intertechnology, Inc., 21; 80 (upd.)
Vitesse Semiconductor Corporation, 32
Vitro Corp., 10
Vizio, Inc., 100
VLSI Technology, Inc., 16

Vorwerk & Co. KG, 112 (upd.)
VTech Holdings Ltd., 77
Wells-Gardner Electronics Corporation, 43
Westinghouse Electric Corporation, II; 12 (upd.)
Winbond Electronics Corporation, 74
Wincor Nixdorf Holding GmbH, 69 (upd.)
WuXi AppTec Company Ltd., 103
Wyle Electronics, 14
Xantrex Technology Inc., 97
Xerox Corporation, III; 6 (upd.); 26 (upd.); 69 (upd.)
Yageo Corporation, 16; 98 (upd.)
York Research Corporation, 35
Zenith Data Systems, Inc., 10
Zenith Electronics Corporation, II; 13 (upd.); 34 (upd.); 89 (upd.)
Zoom Telephonics, Inc., 18
Zoran Corporation, 77
Zumtobel AG, 50
Zytec Corporation, 19

Engineering & Management Services

AAON, Inc., 22
Aavid Thermal Technologies, Inc., 29
Acergy SA, 97
AECOM Technology Corporation, 79
Alliant Techsystems Inc., 30 (upd.)
Altran Technologies, 51
AMEC plc, 112
Amey Plc, 47
American Science & Engineering, Inc., 81
Analytic Sciences Corporation, 10
Arcadis NV, 26
Arthur D. Little, Inc., 35
Austin Company, The, 8; 72 (upd.)
Autostrada Torino-Milano S.p.A., 101
Babcock International Group PLC, 69
Balfour Beatty plc, 36 (upd.)
BE&K, Inc., 73
Bechtel Corporation, I; 24 (upd.); 99 (upd.)
Birse Group PLC, 77
Bowen Engineering Corporation, 105
Brown & Root, Inc., 13
Bufete Industrial, S.A. de C.V., 34
C.H. Heist Corporation, 24
Camp Dresser & McKee Inc., 104
CDI Corporation, 6; 54 (upd.)
CH2M HILL Companies Ltd., 22; 96 (upd.)
Charles Stark Draper Laboratory, Inc., The, 35
Coflexip S.A., 25
CompuDyne Corporation, 51
Cornell Companies, Inc., 112
Corrections Corporation of America, 23
CRSS Inc., 6
Dames & Moore, Inc., 25
DAW Technologies, Inc., 25
Day & Zimmermann Inc., 9; 31 (upd.)
Donaldson Company, Inc., 16; 49 (upd.); 108 (upd.)
Doosan Heavy Industries and Construction Company Ltd., 108

Entertainment & Leisure

Financial Services: Banks

Financial Services: Excluding Banks

Food Services, Retailers, & Restaurants

Health, Personal & Medical Care Products

Health Care Services

Information Technology

Insurance

Legal Services

Chadbourne & Parke, 36
Cleary, Gottlieb, Steen & Hamilton, 35
Clifford Chance LLP, 38
Coudert Brothers, 30
Covington & Burling, 40
CRA International, Inc., 93
Cravath, Swaine & Moore, 43
Davis Polk & Wardwell, 36
Debevoise & Plimpton, 39
Dechert, 43
Dewey Ballantine LLP, 48
DLA Piper, 106
Dorsey & Whitney LLP, 47
Drinker, Biddle and Reath L.L.P., 92
Faegre & Benson LLP, 97
Fenwick & West LLP, 34
Fish & Neave, 54
Foley & Lardner, 28
Fried, Frank, Harris, Shriver & Jacobson, 35
Fulbright & Jaworski L.L.P., 47
Gibson, Dunn & Crutcher LLP, 36
Greenberg Traurig, LLP, 65
Heller, Ehrman, White & McAuliffe, 41
Hildebrandt International, 29
Hogan & Hartson L.L.P., 44
Holland & Knight LLP, 60
Holme Roberts & Owen LLP, 28
Hughes Hubbard & Reed LLP, 44
Hunton & Williams, 35
Jenkens & Gilchrist, P.C., 65
Jones, Day, Reavis & Pogue, 33
Kelley Drye & Warren LLP, 40
King & Spalding, 23
Kirkland & Ellis LLP, 65
Lambda Legal Defense and Education Fund, Inc., 106
Latham & Watkins, 33
LeBoeuf, Lamb, Greene & MacRae, L.L.P., 29
LECG Corporation, 93
Legal Aid Society, The, 48
Mayer, Brown, Rowe & Maw, 47
Milbank, Tweed, Hadley & McCloy, 27
Morgan, Lewis & Bockius LLP, 29
Morrison & Foerster LLP 78
O'Melveny & Myers, 37
Oppenheimer Wolff & Donnelly LLP, 71
Orrick, Herrington and Sutcliffe LLP, 76
Patton Boggs LLP, 71
Paul, Hastings, Janofsky & Walker LLP, 27
Paul, Weiss, Rifkind, Wharton & Garrison, 47
Pepper Hamilton LLP, 43
Perkins Coie LLP, 56
Phillips Lytle LLP, 102
Pillsbury Madison & Sutro LLP, 29
Pre-Paid Legal Services, Inc., 20
Proskauer Rose LLP, 47
Quinn Emanuel Urquhart Oliver & Hedges, LLP, 99
Robins, Kaplan, Miller & Ciresi L.L.P., 89
Ropes & Gray, 40
Saul Ewing LLP, 74
Seyfarth Shaw LLP, 93
Shearman & Sterling, 32
Sidley Austin Brown & Wood, 40

Simpson Thacher & Bartlett, 39
Skadden, Arps, Slate, Meagher & Flom, 18
Slaughter and May, 112
Snell & Wilmer L.L.P., 28
Sonnenschein Nath and Rosenthal LLP, 102
Southern Poverty Law Center, Inc., 74
Strook & Strook & Lavan LLP, 40
Sullivan & Cromwell, 26
Troutman Sanders L.L.P., 79
Vinson & Elkins L.L.P., 30
Wachtell, Lipton, Rosen & Katz, 47
Weil, Gotshal & Manges LLP, 55
White & Case LLP, 35
Williams & Connolly LLP, 47
Willkie Farr & Gallagher LLP, 95
Wilmer Cutler Pickering Hale and Dorr L.L.P., 109
Wilson Sonsini Goodrich & Rosati, 34
Winston & Strawn, 35
Womble Carlyle Sandridge & Rice, PLLC, 52

Manufacturing

A.O. Smith Corporation, 11; 40 (upd.); 93 (upd.)
A.T. Cross Company, 17; 49 (upd.)
A.W. Faber-Castell Unternehmensverwaltung GmbH & Co., 51
AAF-McQuay Incorporated, 26
Aalborg Industries A/S, 90
ACCO World Corporation, 7; 51 (upd.)
Acme United Corporation, 70
Acme-Cleveland Corp., 13
Acuity Brands, Inc., 90
Adolf Würth GmbH & Co. KG, 49
AEP Industries, Inc., 36
Aga Foodservice Group PLC, 73
Agfa Gevaert Group N.V., 59
Ahlstrom Corporation, 53
Aktiebolaget Electrolux, 22 (upd.)
Albert Trostel and Sons Company, 113
Alfa Laval AB, III; 64 (upd.)
Alliance Laundry Holdings LLC, 102
Allied Defense Group, Inc., The, 65
Allied Products Corporation, 21
Alltrista Corporation, 30
ALSTOM, 108
Alvis Plc, 47
American Cast Iron Pipe Company, 50
American Equipment Company, Inc., 104
American Homestar Corporation, 18; 41 (upd.)
American Locker Group Incorporated, 34
American Seating Company 78
American Tourister, Inc., 16
American Woodmark Corporation, 31
Amerock Corporation, 53
Ameron International Corporation, 67
AMETEK, Inc., 9
Ampacet Corporation, 67
Anchor Hocking Glassware, 13
Andreas Stihl AG & Co. KG, 16; 59 (upd.)
Andritz AG, 51
Applica Incorporated, 43 (upd.)

Applied Films Corporation, 48
Applied Materials, Inc., 10; 46 (upd.)
AptarGroup, Inc., 69
Arc International, 76
Arçelik A.S., 100
Arctic Cat Inc., 16; 40 (upd.); 96 (upd.)
AREVA NP, 90 (upd.)
Ariens Company, 48
Aristotle Corporation, The, 62
Armor All Products Corp., 16
Armstrong Holdings, Inc., III; 22 (upd.); 81 (upd.)
Art's Way Manufacturing Co., Inc., 101
Ashley Furniture Industries, Inc., 35
Assa Abloy AB, 112
Atlantis Plastics, Inc., 85
Atlas Copco AB, III; 28 (upd.); 85 (upd.)
Atwood Mobil Products, 53
Austin Powder Company, 76
AZZ Incorporated, 93
B.J. Alan Co., Inc., 67
Babcock & Wilcox Company, The, 82
Badger Meter, Inc., 22
Baldor Electric Company, 21; 97 (upd.)
Baldwin Technology Company, Inc., 25; 107 (upd.)
Ballantyne of Omaha, Inc., 27
Bally Manufacturing Corporation, III
Baltimore Aircoil Company, Inc., 66
Bandai Co., Ltd., 55
Barmag AG, 39
Barnes Group Inc., 13; 69 (upd.)
Barry-Wehmiller Companies, Inc., 90
Bassett Furniture Industries, Inc., 18; 95 (upd.)
Bath Iron Works, 12; 36 (upd.)
Baxi Group Ltd., 96
Beckman Coulter, Inc., 22
Beckman Instruments, Inc., 14
BEI Technologies, Inc., 65
Bekaert S.A./N.V., 90
Belleek Pottery Ltd., 71
Benjamin Moore & Co., 13; 38 (upd.)
Benninger AG, 107
Berger Bros Company, 62
Bernina Holding AG, 47
Berwick Offray, LLC, 70
Bianchi International (d/b/a Gregory Mountain Products), 76
BIC Corporation, 8; 23 (upd.)
Bing Group, The, 60
Binks Sames Corporation, 21
Binney & Smith Inc., 25
BISSELL Inc., 9; 30 (upd.)
Black & Decker Corporation, The, III; 20 (upd.); 67 (upd.)
Blodgett Holdings, Inc., 61 (upd.)
Blount International, Inc., 12; 48 (upd.)
Blyth, Inc., 18; 74 (upd.)
Bodum Design Group AG, 47
Bombril S.A., 111
Borrego Solar Systems, Inc., 111
Borroughs Corporation, 110
Boston Scientific Corporation, 37; 77 (upd.)
Boyds Collection, Ltd., The, 29
BPB plc, 83
Brady Corporation 78 (upd.)

Furukawa Electric Co., Ltd., The, III
G.S. Blodgett Corporation, 15
Gaming Partners International
 Corporation, 93
Ganz, 98
Gardner Denver, Inc., 49
Gates Corporation, The, 9
Gaylord Bros., Inc., 100
GEA AG, 27
Geberit AG, 49
Gehl Company, 19
Gelita AG, 74
Gemplus International S.A., 64
General Bearing Corporation, 45
General Cable Corporation, 40; 111
 (upd.)
General Housewares Corporation, 16
geobra Brandstätter GmbH & Co. KG,
 48
George F. Cram Company, Inc., The, 55
Gerber Scientific, Inc., 12; 84 (upd.)
Getrag Corporate Group, 92
Gévelot S.A., 96
Giant Manufacturing Company, Ltd., 85
Giddings & Lewis, Inc., 10
Gildemeister AG, 79
Gleason Corporation, 24
Glen Dimplex 78
Glidden Company, The, 8
Global Power Equipment Group Inc., 52
Glock Ges.m.b.H., 42
Goodman Holding Company, 42
Gorman-Rupp Company, The, 18; 57
 (upd.)
Goulds Pumps Inc., 24
Graco Inc., 19; 67 (upd.)
Gradall Industries, Inc., 96
Graham Corporation, 62
Great Dane L.P., 107
Greatbatch Inc., 72
Greene, Tweed & Company, 55
Griffon Corporation, 34
Grinnell Corp., 13
Groupe Genoyer, 96
Groupe Guillin SA, 40
Groupe Herstal S.A., 58
Groupe Legis Industries, 23
Groupe SEB, 35
Grow Group Inc., 12
Groz-Beckert Group, 68
Grunau Company Inc., 90
Grundfos Group, 83
Grupo Cydsa, S.A. de C.V., 39
Grupo IMSA, S.A. de C.V., 44
Grupo Lladró S.A., 52
GT Solar International, Inc., 101
Gund, Inc., 96
Gunite Corporation, 51
Gunlocke Company, The, 23
Guy Degrenne SA, 44
H.O. Penn Machinery Company, Inc., 96
Hach Co., 18
Hackman Oyj Adp, 44
Haeger Industries Inc., 88
Haier Group Corporation, 65
Hammond Manufacturing Company
 Limited, 83
Hamon & Cie (International) S.A., 97

Hansgrohe AG, 56
Hardinge Inc., 25
Harnischfeger Industries, Inc., 8; 38
 (upd.)
Hartmann Inc., 96
Hasbro, Inc., III; 16 (upd.); 43 (upd.)
Haskel International, Inc., 59
Haworth Inc., 8; 39 (upd.)
Headwaters Incorporated, 56
Hearth & Home Technologies, 107
Henkel Manco Inc., 22
Henley Group, Inc., The, III
Herman Goldner Company, Inc., 100
Herman Miller, Inc., 8; 77 (upd.)
Hexagon AB 78
Hilding Anders AB, 102
Hillenbrand Industries, Inc., 10; 75 (upd.)
Hills Industries Ltd., 104
Hitchiner Manufacturing Co., Inc., 23
HMI Industries, Inc., 17
HNI Corporation, 74 (upd.)
Holland Group, Inc., The, 82
Hollander Home Fashions Corp., 67
Holson Burnes Group, Inc., 14
Home Products International, Inc., 55
HON INDUSTRIES Inc., 13
Hooker Furniture Corporation, 80
Hoover Company, The, 12; 40 (upd.)
Howden Group Limited, 111
Huhtamäki Oyj, 64
Hunt Manufacturing Company, 12
Hunter Fan Company, 13; 98 (upd.)
Hydril Company, 46
Hyster Company, 17
IDEX Corp., 103
IdraPrince, Inc., 76
Igloo Products Corp., 21; 105 (upd.)
Illinois Tool Works Inc., III; 22 (upd.); 81
 (upd.)
IMI plc, 9
Imo Industries Inc., 7; 27 (upd.)
In-Sink-Erator, 66
Industrie Natuzzi S.p.A., 18
Ingersoll-Rand Company Ltd., III; 15
 (upd.); 55 (upd.)
Insilco Corporation, 16
Insituform Technologies, Inc., 83
Interco Incorporated, III
Interlake Corporation, The, 8
Internacional de Ceramica, S.A. de C.V.,
 53
Interstate Batteries, 110
Intevac, Inc., 92
Ipsen International Inc., 72
iRobot Corporation, 83
Irwin Toy Limited, 14
Itron, Inc., 64
J.I. Case Company, 10
J.M. Voith AG, 33
Jacuzzi Brands Inc., 23; 76 (upd.)
JAKKS Pacific, Inc., 52
James Avery Craftsman, Inc., 76
James Hardie Industries N.V., 56
James Purdey & Sons Limited, 87
Jarden Corporation, 93 (upd.)
Jayco Inc., 13
JD Group Ltd., 110
Jeld-Wen, Inc., 45

Jenoptik AG, 33
Jervis B. Webb Company, 24
Johns Manville Corporation, 64 (upd.)
Johnson Outdoors Inc., 28; 84 (upd.)
Johnstown America Industries, Inc., 23
Jotun A/S, 80
JSP Corporation, 74
Jungheinrich AG, 96
Kaman Corporation, 12; 42 (upd.)
Kansai Paint Company Ltd., 80
Karsten Manufacturing Corporation, 51
Kaydon Corporation, 18
KB Toys, Inc., 35 (upd.); 86 (upd.)
Kelly-Moore Paint Company, Inc., 56;
 112 (upd.)
Kennametal Inc., 68 (upd.)
Keramik Holding AG Laufen, 51
Kewaunee Scientific Corporation, 25
Key Technology Inc., 106
Key Tronic Corporation, 14
Keystone International, Inc., 11
KHD Konzern, III
KI, 57
Kit Manufacturing Co., 18
Klein Tools, Inc., 95
Knape & Vogt Manufacturing Company,
 17
Koala Corporation, 44
Koch Enterprises, Inc., 29
Kohler Company, 7; 32 (upd.); 108
 (upd.)
Komatsu Ltd., 113 (upd.)
KONE Corporation, 27; 76 (upd.)
Korg, Inc., 111
KraftMaid Cabinetry, Inc., 72
Kreisler Manufacturing Corporation, 97
KSB AG, 62
Kwang Yang Motor Company Ltd., 80
L-3 Communications Holdings, Inc., 48
L.A. Darling Company, 92
L.B. Foster Company, 33
L.S. Starrett Company, 64 (upd.)
La-Z-Boy Incorporated, 14; 50 (upd.)
Lacks Enterprises Inc., 61
LADD Furniture, Inc., 12
Ladish Company Inc., 30; 107 (upd.)
Lakeland Industries, Inc., 45
Lane Co., Inc., The, 12
Le Creuset S.A.S., 113
Leatherman Tool Group, Inc., 51
Leggett & Platt, Inc., 11; 48 (upd.); 111
 (upd.)
Leica Camera AG, 35
Leica Microsystems Holdings GmbH, 35
Lennox International Inc., 8; 28 (upd.)
Lenox, Inc., 12
Liebherr-International AG, 64
Linamar Corporation, 18
Lincoln Electric Co., 13
Lindsay Manufacturing Co., 20
Lionel L.L.C., 16; 99 (upd.)
Lipman Electronic Engineering Ltd., 81
Little Tikes Company, 13; 62 (upd.)
Loctite Corporation, 8
Lodge Manufacturing Company, 103
Longaberger Company, The, 12; 44 (upd.)
LSB Industries, Inc., 77
Lucas Industries PLC, III

Materials

North Pacific Group, Inc., 61
Nuplex Industries Ltd., 92
OmniSource Corporation, 14
Onoda Cement Co., Ltd., III
Otor S.A., 77
Owens-Corning Fiberglass Corporation, III
Pacific Clay Products Inc., 88
Pilkington Group Limited, III; 34 (upd.); 87 (upd.)
Pioneer International Limited, III
PMC Global, Inc., 110
PolyOne Corporation, 87 (upd.)
PPG Industries, Inc., III; 22 (upd.); 81 (upd.)
PT Semen Gresik Tbk, 103
Redland plc, III
Rinker Group Ltd., 65
RMC Group p.l.c., III; 34 (upd.)
Rock of Ages Corporation, 37
Rogers Corporation, 80 (upd.)
Royal Group Technologies Limited, 73
Rugby Group plc, The, 31
Scholle Corporation, 96
Schuff Steel Company, 26
Sekisui Chemical Co., Ltd., III; 72 (upd.)
Severstal Joint Stock Company, 65
Shaw Industries, 9
Sherwin-Williams Company, The, III; 13 (upd.); 89 (upd.)
Siam Cement Public Company Limited, The, 56
SIG plc, 71
Simplex Technologies Inc., 21
Siskin Steel & Supply Company, 70
Smith-Midland Corporation, 56
Solutia Inc., 52
Sommer-Allibert S.A., 19
Southdown, Inc., 14
Spartech Corporation, 19; 76 (upd.)
Ssangyong Cement Industrial Co., Ltd., III; 61 (upd.)
Steel Technologies Inc., 63
Strongwell Corporation, 110
Sun Distributors L.P., 12
Symyx Technologies, Inc., 77
Taiheiyo Cement Corporation, 60 (upd.)
Tarmac Limited, III, 28 (upd.); 95 (upd.)
Tergal Industries S.A.S., 102
Thermotech, 113
Tilcon-Connecticut Inc., 80
Titan Cement Company S.A., 64
Tong Yang Cement Corporation, 62
TOTO LTD., III; 28 (upd.)
Toyo Sash Co., Ltd., III
Tuscarora Inc., 29
U.S. Aggregates, Inc., 42
Ube Industries, Ltd., III; 38 (upd.); 111 (upd.)
United States Steel Corporation, 50 (upd.)
USG Corporation, III; 26 (upd.); 81 (upd.)
Usinas Siderúrgicas de Minas Gerais S.A., 77
Vicat S.A., 70
voestalpine AG, 57 (upd.)
Vulcan Materials Company, 7; 52 (upd.)
Wacker-Chemie AG, 35; 112 (upd.)

Walter Industries, Inc., III; 22 (upd.); 72 (upd.)
Waxman Industries, Inc., 9
Weber et Broutin France, 66
White Martins Gases Industriais Ltda., 111
Wienerberger AG, 70
Wolseley plc, 64
ZERO Corporation, 17; 88 (upd.)
Zoltek Companies, Inc., 37

Mining & Metals

A.M. Castle & Co., 25
Acindar Industria Argentina de Aceros S.A., 87
African Rainbow Minerals Ltd., 97
Aggregate Industries plc, 36
Agnico-Eagle Mines Limited, 71
Aktiebolaget SKF, III; 38 (upd.); 89 (upd.)
Alcan Aluminium Limited, IV; 31 (upd.)
Alcoa Inc., 56 (upd.)
Aleris International, Inc., 110
Alleghany Corporation, 10
Allegheny Ludlum Corporation, 8
Allegheny Technologies Incorporated, 112 (upd.)
Alliance Resource Partners, L.P., 81
Alrosa Company Ltd., 62
Altos Hornos de México, S.A. de C.V., 42
Aluar Aluminio Argentino S.A.I.C., 74
Aluminum Company of America, IV; 20 (upd.)
AMAX Inc., IV
AMCOL International Corporation, 59 (upd.)
Ampco-Pittsburgh Corporation, 79
Amsted Industries Incorporated, 7
Anglo American Corporation of South Africa Limited, IV; 16 (upd.)
Anglo American PLC, 50 (upd.)
Aquarius Platinum Ltd., 63
ARBED S.A., IV, 22 (upd.)
Arcelor Gent, 80
ArcelorMittal, 108
Arch Coal Inc., 98
Arch Mineral Corporation, 7
Armco Inc., IV
ASARCO Incorporated, IV
Ashanti Goldfields Company Limited, 43
Atchison Casting Corporation, 39
Aubert & Duval S.A.S., 107
Barrick Gold Corporation, 34; 112 (upd.)
Battle Mountain Gold Company, 23
Benguet Corporation, 58
Bethlehem Steel Corporation, IV; 7 (upd.); 27 (upd.)
BHP Billiton, 67 (upd.)
Birmingham Steel Corporation, 13; 40 (upd.)
Boart Longyear Company, 26
Bodycote International PLC, 63
BÖHLER-UDDEHOLM AG, 73
Boliden AB, 80
Boral Limited, III; 43 (upd.); 103 (upd.)
British Coal Corporation, IV
British Steel plc, IV; 19 (upd.)

Broken Hill Proprietary Company Ltd., IV, 22 (upd.)
Brush Engineered Materials Inc., 67
Brush Wellman Inc., 14
Bucyrus International, Inc., 17; 103 (upd.)
Buderus AG, 37
California Steel Industries, Inc., 67
Cameco Corporation, 77
Caparo Group Ltd., 90
Carpenter Technology Corporation, 13; 95 (upd.)
Chaparral Steel Co., 13
Charter Manufacturing Company, Inc., 103
China Shenhua Energy Company Limited, 83
Christensen Boyles Corporation, 26
Cleveland-Cliffs Inc., 13; 62 (upd.)
Coal India Ltd., IV; 44 (upd.)
Cockerill Sambre Group, IV; 26 (upd.)
Coeur d'Alene Mines Corporation, 20
Cold Spring Granite Company Inc., 16; 67 (upd.)
Cominco Ltd., 37
Commercial Metals Company, 15; 42 (upd.)
Companhia Siderúrgica Nacional, 76
Companhia Vale do Rio Doce, IV; 43 (upd.)
Compañia de Minas Buenaventura S.A.A., 93
CONSOL Energy Inc., 59
Corporacion Nacional del Cobre de Chile, 40
Corus Group plc, 49 (upd.)
CRA Limited, IV
Cyprus Amax Minerals Company, 21
Cyprus Minerals Company, 7
Daido Steel Co., Ltd., IV
De Beers Consolidated Mines Limited/De Beers Centenary AG, IV; 7 (upd.); 28 (upd.)
Degussa Group, IV
Diavik Diamond Mines Inc., 85
Dofasco Inc., IV; 24 (upd.)
Dynatec Corporation, 87
Earle M. Jorgensen Company, 82
Echo Bay Mines Ltd., IV; 38 (upd.)
Engelhard Corporation, IV
Eramet, 73
Evergreen Energy, Inc., 97
Evraz Group S.A., 97
Falconbridge Limited, 49
Fansteel Inc., 19
Fluor Corporation, 34 (upd.)
Freeport-McMoRan Copper & Gold, Inc., IV; 7 (upd.); 57 (upd.)
Fried. Krupp GmbH, IV
Gencor Ltd., IV, 22 (upd.)
Geneva Steel, 7
Georg Jensen A/S, 110
Gerdau S.A., 59
Glamis Gold, Ltd., 54
Gold Fields Ltd., IV; 62 (upd.)
Goldcorp Inc., 87
Grupo Mexico, S.A. de C.V., 40
Gruppo Riva Fire SpA, 88

Personal Services

Petroleum

Publishing & Printing

Real Estate

Retail & Wholesale

Ulta Salon, Cosmetics & Fragrance, Inc., 93
Ultimate Electronics, Inc., 18; 69 (upd.)
Ultramar Diamond Shamrock Corporation, 31 (upd.)
Uni-Marts, Inc., 17
United Rentals, Inc., 34
United States Shoe Corporation, The, V
United Stationers Inc., 14
Universal International, Inc., 25
Uny Co., Ltd., V; 49 (upd.)
Upper Deck Company, LLC, The, 105
Urban Outfitters, Inc., 14; 74 (upd.)
Uwajimaya, Inc., 60
Vallen Corporation, 45
Valley Media Inc., 35
Value City Department Stores, Inc., 38
Value Merchants Inc., 13
ValueVision International, Inc., 22
Vann's Inc., 105
Vans, Inc., 47 (upd.)
Variety Wholesalers, Inc., 73
VBA - Bloemenveiling Aalsmeer, 88
Venator Group Inc., 35 (upd.)
Vendex International N.V., 13
Venture Stores Inc., 12
Vermont Country Store, The, 93
Vermont Teddy Bear Co., Inc., The, 36
Viewpoint International, Inc., 66
Viking Office Products, Inc., 10
Viterra Inc., 105
Vivarte SA, 54 (upd.)
Volcom, Inc., 77
Von Maur Inc., 64
Vorwerk & Co. KG, 27; 112 (upd.)
W.B. Mason Company, 98
W.S. Badcock Corporation, 107
W.W. Grainger, Inc., V; 26 (upd.); 68 (upd.)
Waban Inc., 13
Wacoal Corp., 25
Wal-Mart de Mexico, S.A. de C.V., 35 (upd.)
Wal-Mart Stores, Inc., V; 8 (upd.); 26 (upd.); 63 (upd.)
Waldenbooks, 17; 86 (upd.)
Walgreen Co., V; 20 (upd.); 65 (upd.)
Wall Drug Store, Inc., 40
Walter E. Smithe Furniture, Inc., 105
Warners' Stellian Inc., 67
WAXIE Sanitary Supply, 100
Weiner's Stores, Inc., 33
West Marine, Inc., 17; 90 (upd.)
Wet Seal, Inc., The, 18; 70 (upd.)
Weyco Group, Incorporated, 32
WH Smith PLC, V; 42 (upd.)
White House, Inc., The, 60
Whitehall Jewellers, Inc., 82 (upd.)
Wickes Inc., V; 25 (upd.)
Wilco Farm Stores, 93
Wilkinson Hardware Stores Ltd., 80
Williams Scotsman, Inc., 65
Williams-Sonoma, Inc., 17; 44 (upd.); 103 (upd.)
Wilsons The Leather Experts Inc., 21; 58 (upd.)
Wilton Products, Inc., 97
Windstream Corporation, 83

Winmark Corporation, 74
Wolohan Lumber Co., 19
Wolverine World Wide, Inc., 59 (upd.)
Woolworth Corporation, V; 20 (upd.)
Woolworths Group plc, 83
World Duty Free Americas, Inc., 29 (upd.)
Yamada Denki Co., Ltd., 85
Yankee Candle Company, Inc., The, 37
Yingli Green Energy Holding Company Limited, 103
Young's Market Company, LLC, 32
Younkers, 76 (upd.)
Younkers, Inc., 19
Zale Corporation, 16; 40 (upd.); 91 (upd.)
Zany Brainy, Inc., 31
Zappos.com, Inc., 73
Zara International, Inc., 83
Ziebart International Corporation, 30
Zion's Cooperative Mercantile Institution, 33
Zipcar, Inc., 92
Zones, Inc., 67
Zumiez, Inc., 77

Rubber & Tires

AirBoss of America Corporation, 108
Aeroquip Corporation, 16
Avon Rubber p.l.c., 108
Bandag, Inc., 19
BFGoodrich Company, The, V
Bridgestone Corporation, V; 21 (upd.); 59 (upd.)
Canadian Tire Corporation, Limited, 71 (upd.)
Carlisle Companies Incorporated, 8
Compagnie Générale des Établissements Michelin, V; 42 (upd.)
Continental AG, V; 56 (upd.)
Continental General Tire Corp., 23
Cooper Tire & Rubber Company, 8; 23 (upd.)
Day International, Inc., 84
Elementis plc, 40 (upd.)
General Tire, Inc., 8
Goodyear Tire & Rubber Company, The, V; 20 (upd.); 75 (upd.)
Hankook Tire Company Ltd., 105
Kelly-Springfield Tire Company, The, 8
Kumho Tire Company Ltd., 105
Les Schwab Tire Centers, 50
Myers Industries, Inc., 19; 96 (upd.)
Pirelli S.p.A., V; 15 (upd.)
Safeskin Corporation, 18
Sumitomo Rubber Industries, Ltd., V; 107 (upd.)
Trelleborg AB, 93
Tillotson Corp., 15
Treadco, Inc., 19
Ube Industries, Ltd., III; 38 (upd.)
Yokohama Rubber Company, Limited, The, V; 19 (upd.); 91 (upd.)

Telecommunications

A.H. Belo Corporation, 30 (upd.)
Abertis Infraestructuras, S.A., 65
Abril S.A., 95

Acme-Cleveland Corp., 13
ADC Telecommunications, Inc., 10; 89 (upd.)
Adelphia Communications Corporation, 17; 52 (upd.)
Adtran Inc., 22
Advanced Fibre Communications, Inc., 63
AEI Music Network Inc., 35
AirTouch Communications, 11
Alaska Communications Systems Group, Inc., 89
Albtelecom Sh. a, 111
Alcatel S.A., 36 (upd.)
Alcatel-Lucent, 109 (upd.)
Allbritton Communications Company, 105
Alliance Atlantis Communications Inc., 39
ALLTEL Corporation, 6; 46 (upd.)
América Móvil, S.A. de C.V., 80
American Tower Corporation, 33
Ameritech Corporation, V; 18 (upd.)
Amstrad plc, 48 (upd.)
AO VimpelCom, 48
AOL Time Warner Inc., 57 (upd.)
Arch Wireless, Inc., 39
ARD, 41
ARINC Inc., 98
ARRIS Group, Inc., 89
Ascent Media Corporation, 107
Ascom AG, 9
Aspect Telecommunications Corporation, 22
Asurion Corporation, 83
AT&T Bell Laboratories, Inc., 13
AT&T Corporation, V; 29 (upd.); 68 (upd.)
AT&T Wireless Services, Inc., 54 (upd.)
Avaya Inc., 104
Basin Electric Power Cooperative, 103
BCE Inc., V; 44 (upd.)
Beasley Broadcast Group, Inc., 51
Belgacom, 6
Bell Atlantic Corporation, V; 25 (upd.)
Bell Canada, 6
BellSouth Corporation, V; 29 (upd.)
Belo Corporation, 98 (upd.)
Bertelsmann A.G., IV; 15 (upd.); 43 (upd.); 91 (upd.)
BET Holdings, Inc., 18
Bharti Tele-Ventures Limited, 75
BHC Communications, Inc., 26
Blackfoot Telecommunications Group, 60
Bonneville International Corporation, 29
Bouygues S.A., I; 24 (upd.); 97 (upd.)
Brasil Telecom Participaçoes S.A., 57
Brightpoint Inc., 18; 106 (upd.)
Brite Voice Systems, Inc., 20
British Broadcasting Corporation Ltd., 7; 21 (upd.); 89 (upd.)
British Columbia Telephone Company, 6
British Telecommunications plc, V; 15 (upd.)
Broadwing Corporation, 70
BT Group plc, 49 (upd.)
C-COR.net Corp., 38
Cable & Wireless HKT, 30 (upd.)
Cable and Wireless plc, V; 25 (upd.)

Textiles & Apparel

Transport Services

Utilities

Waste Services

Geographic Index

Albania

Albtelecom Sh. a, 111

Algeria

Sonatrach, IV; 65 (upd.)

Argentina

Acindar Industria Argentina de Aceros
  S.A., 87
Adecoagro LLC, 101
Aerolíneas Argentinas S.A., 33; 69 (upd.)
Alpargatas S.A.I.C., 87
Aluar Aluminio Argentino S.A.I.C., 74
Arcor S.A.I.C., 66
Atanor S.A., 62
Coto Centro Integral de Comercializacion
  S.A., 66
Cresud S.A.C.I.F. y A., 63
Grupo Clarín S.A., 67
Grupo Financiero Galicia S.A., 63
IRSA Inversiones y Representaciones S.A.,
  63
Ledesma Sociedad Anónima Agrícola
  Industrial, 62
Loma Negra C.I.A.S.A., 95
Mastellone Hermanos S.A., 101
Molinos Río de la Plata S.A., 61
Nobleza Piccardo SAICF, 64
Penaflor S.A., 66
Petrobras Energia Participaciones S.A., 72
Quilmes Industrial (QUINSA) S.A., 67
Renault Argentina S.A., 67
SanCor Cooperativas Unidas Ltda., 101
Sideco Americana S.A., 67
Siderar S.A.I.C., 66
Telecom Argentina S.A., 63
Telefónica de Argentina S.A., 61
YPF Sociedad Anonima, IV

Australia

ABC Learning Centres Ltd., 93
Amcor Limited, IV; 19 (upd.), 78 (upd.)
Ansell Ltd., 60 (upd.)
Aquarius Platinum Ltd., 63
Aristocrat Leisure Limited, 54
Arnott's Ltd., 66
Austal Limited, 75
Australia and New Zealand Banking
  Group Limited, II; 52 (upd.)
AWB Ltd., 56
BHP Billiton, 67 (upd.)
Billabong International Limited, 44; 112
  (upd.)
Blundstone Pty Ltd., 76
Bond Corporation Holdings Limited, 10
Boral Limited, III; 43 (upd.); 103 (upd.)
Brambles Industries Limited, 42
Broken Hill Proprietary Company Ltd.,
  IV; 22 (upd.)
Burns, Philp & Company Ltd., 63
Carlton and United Breweries Ltd., I
Cochlear Ltd., 77
Coles Group Limited, V; 20 (upd.); 85
  (upd.)
Colorado Group Ltd., 107
Commonwealth Bank of Australia Ltd.,
  109
CRA Limited, IV; 85 (upd.)
CSL Limited, 112
CSR Limited, III; 28 (upd.)
David Jones Ltd., 60
Elders IXL Ltd., I
Fairfax Media Ltd., 94 (upd.)
Foster's Group Limited, 7; 21 (upd.); 50
  (upd.); 111 (upd.)
Goodman Fielder Ltd., 52
Harvey Norman Holdings Ltd., 56

Hills Industries Ltd., 104
Holden Ltd., 62
James Hardie Industries N.V., 56
John Fairfax Holdings Limited, 7
Lend Lease Corporation Limited, IV; 17
  (upd.); 52 (upd.)
Lion Nathan Limited, 54
Lonely Planet Publications Pty Ltd., 55
Macquarie Bank Ltd., 69
McPherson's Ltd., 66
Metcash Trading Ltd., 58
MYOB Ltd., 86
National Australia Bank Ltd., 111
News Corporation Limited, IV; 7 (upd.);
  46 (upd.)
Nufarm Ltd., 87
Orica Ltd., 112
Pacific Dunlop Limited, 10
Pioneer International Limited, III
PMP Ltd., 72
Publishing and Broadcasting Limited, 54
Qantas Airways Ltd., 6; 24 (upd.); 68
  (upd.)
Repco Corporation Ltd., 74
Ridley Corporation Ltd., 62
Rinker Group Ltd., 65
Rural Press Ltd., 74
Santos Ltd., 81
Sims Metal Management, Ltd., 109
Smorgon Steel Group Ltd., 62
Southcorp Limited, 54
Suncorp-Metway Ltd., 91
TABCORP Holdings Limited, 44
Telecom Australia, 6
Telstra Corporation Limited, 50
Village Roadshow Ltd., 58
Washington H. Soul Pattinson and
  Company Limited, 112
Wesfarmers Limited, 109

Germany

United States

National TechTeam, Inc., 41
National Thoroughbred Racing
    Association, 58
National Weather Service, 91
National Wildlife Federation, 103
National Wine & Spirits, Inc., 49
NationsBank Corporation, 10
Nationwide Mutual Insurance Company,
    108
Native New Yorker Inc., 110
Natori Company, Inc., 108
Natrol, Inc., 49
Natural Alternatives International, Inc., 49
Natural Grocers by Vitamin Cottage, Inc.,
    111
Natural Ovens Bakery, Inc., 72
Natural Selection Foods, 54
Natural Wonders Inc., 14
Naturally Fresh, Inc., 88
Nature Conservancy, The, 28
Nature's Sunshine Products, Inc., 15; 102
    (upd.)
Naumes, Inc., 81
Nautica Enterprises, Inc., 18; 44 (upd.)
Navarre Corporation, 24
Navigant Consulting, Inc., 93
Navigant International, Inc., 47
Navigators Group, Inc., The, 92
Navistar International Corporation, I; 10
    (upd.)
NAVTEQ Corporation, 69
Navy Exchange Service Command, 31
Navy Federal Credit Union, 33
NBBJ, 111
NBD Bancorp, Inc., 11
NBGS International, Inc., 73
NBTY, Inc., 31
NCH Corporation, 8
NCI Building Systems, Inc., 88
NCL Corporation 79
NCNB Corporation, II
NCO Group, Inc., 42
NCR Corporation, III; 6 (upd.); 30
    (upd.); 90 (upd.)
Nebraska Book Company, Inc., 65
Nebraska Furniture Mart, Inc., 94
Nebraska Public Power District, 29
Nederlander Producing Company of
    America, Inc., 108
Neenah Foundry Company, 68
Neff Corp., 32
NeighborCare, Inc., 67 (upd.)
Neiman Marcus Group, Inc., The, 12; 49
    (upd.); 105 (upd.)
Nektar Therapeutics, 91
Neogen Corporation, 94
NERCO, Inc., 7
NetCracker Technology Corporation, 98
Netezza Corporation, 69
Netflix, Inc., 58
NETGEAR, Inc., 81
NetIQ Corporation 79
NetJets Inc., 96 (upd.)
Netscape Communications Corporation,
    15; 35 (upd.)
Network Appliance, Inc., 58
Network Associates, Inc., 25
Network Equipment Technologies Inc., 92

Newark Group, Inc., The, 102
Neuberger Berman Inc., 57
NeuStar, Inc., 81
Neutrogena Corporation, 17
Nevada Bell Telephone Company, 14
Nevada Power Company, 11
Nevamar Company, 82
New Balance Athletic Shoe, Inc., 25; 68
    (upd.)
New Belgium Brewing Company, Inc., 68
New Brunswick Scientific Co., Inc., 45
New Chapter Inc., 96
New Dana Perfumes Company, 37
New England Business Service Inc., 18;
    78 (upd.)
New England Confectionery Co., 15
New England Electric System, V
New England Mutual Life Insurance
    Company, III
New Jersey Devils, 84
New Jersey Manufacturers Insurance
    Company, 96
New Jersey Resources Corporation, 54
New Line Cinema, Inc., 47
New Orleans Saints LP, 58
New Piper Aircraft, Inc., The, 44
New Plan Realty Trust, 11
New School, The, 103
New Seasons Market, 75
New Street Capital Inc., 8
New Times, Inc., 45
New Valley Corporation, 17
New World Pasta Company, 53
New World Restaurant Group, Inc., 44
New York & Company Inc., 113
New York City Health and Hospitals
    Corporation, 60
New York City Off-Track Betting
    Corporation, 51
New York Community Bancorp Inc., 78
New York Daily News, 32
New York Health Care, Inc., 72
New York Life Insurance Company, III;
    45 (upd.)
New York Restaurant Group, Inc., 32
New York Shakespeare Festival
    Management, 93
New York State Electric and Gas, 6
New York Stock Exchange, Inc., 9; 39
    (upd.)
New York Times Company, The, IV; 19
    (upd.); 61 (upd.)
New York Yacht Club, Inc., 103
Neways Inc., 78
Newcor, Inc., 40
Newegg Inc., 107
Newell Rubbermaid Inc., 9; 52 (upd.)
Newfield Exploration Company, 65
Newhall Land and Farming Company, 14
Newly Weds Foods, Inc., 74
Newman's Own, Inc., 37
Newmont Mining Corporation, 7; 94
    (upd.)
Newpark Resources, Inc., 63
Newport Corporation, 71
Newport News Shipbuilding Inc., 13; 38
    (upd.)
News America Publishing Inc., 12

News Communications, Inc., 103
News Corporation, 109 (upd.)
Newsday Media Group, 103
NewYork-Presbyterian Hospital, 59
Nexstar Broadcasting Group, Inc., 73
Nextel Communications, Inc., 10; 27
    (upd.)
NextWave Wireless Inc., 112
NFL Films, 75
NFO Worldwide, Inc., 24
NGC Corporation, 18
Niagara Corporation, 28
Niagara Mohawk Holdings Inc., V; 45
    (upd.)
Nichols Research Corporation, 18
Nicklaus Companies, 45
Nicole Miller, 98
Nicor Inc., 6; 86 (upd.)
Nielsen Business Media, Inc., 98
NIKE, Inc., V; 8 (upd.); 36 (upd.); 75
    (upd.)
Nikken Global Inc., 32
Niman Ranch, Inc., 67
Nimbus CD International, Inc., 20
Nine West Group, Inc., 11; 39 (upd.)
99¢ Only Stores, 25; 100 (upd.)
NIPSCO Industries, Inc., 6
NiSource Inc., 109 (upd.)
Nitches, Inc., 53
NL Industries, Inc., 10
Nobel Learning Communities, Inc., 37;
    76 (upd.)
Noble Affiliates, Inc., 11
Noble Roman's Inc., 14; 99 (upd.)
Noland Company, 35; 107 (upd.)
Nolo.com, Inc., 49
Noodle Kidoodle, 16
Noodles & Company, Inc., 55
Nooter Corporation, 61
Norcal Waste Systems, Inc., 60
NordicTrack, 22
Nordson Corporation, 11; 48 (upd.)
Nordstrom, Inc., V; 18 (upd.); 67 (upd.)
Norelco Consumer Products Co., 26
Norfolk Southern Corporation, V; 29
    (upd.); 75 (upd.)
Norm Thompson Outfitters, Inc., 47
Norrell Corporation, 25
Norstan, Inc., 16
Nortek, Inc., 34
North American Galvanizing & Coatings,
    Inc., 99
North Atlantic Trading Company Inc., 65
North Face, Inc., The, 18; 78 (upd.)
North Fork Bancorporation, Inc., 46
North Pacific Group, Inc., 61
North Star Steel Company, 18
Northeast Utilities, V; 48 (upd.)
Northern States Power Company, V; 20
    (upd.)
Northern Trust Corporation, 9; 101
    (upd.)
Northland Cranberries, Inc., 38
Northrop Grumman Corporation, I; 11
    (upd.); 45 (upd.); 111 (upd.)
Northwest Airlines Corporation, I; 6
    (upd.); 26 (upd.); 74 (upd.)
Northwest Natural Gas Company, 45

Owens & Minor, Inc., 16; 68 (upd.)
Owens Corning, III; 20 (upd.); 98 (upd.)
Owens-Illinois, Inc., I; 26 (upd.); 85 (upd.)
Owosso Corporation, 29
Oxford Health Plans, Inc., 16
Oxford Industries, Inc., 8; 84 (upd.)
P&C Foods Inc., 8
P & F Industries, Inc., 45
P.C. Richard & Son Corp., 23
P.F. Chang's China Bistro, Inc., 37; 86 (upd.)
P.H. Glatfelter Company, 8; 30 (upd.); 83 (upd.)
P.W. Minor and Son, Inc., 100
Paccar Inc., I; 26 (upd.); 111 (upd.)
Pacer International, Inc., 54
Pacer Technology, 40
Pacific Clay Products Inc., 88
Pacific Coast Building Products, Inc., 94
Pacific Coast Feather Company, 67
Pacific Coast Restaurants, Inc., 90
Pacific Ethanol, Inc., 81
Pacific Enterprises, V
Pacific Gas and Electric Company, V
Pacific Mutual Holding Company, 98
Pacific Sunwear of California, Inc., 28; 104 (upd.)
Pacific Telecom, Inc., 6
Pacific Telesis Group, V
PacifiCare Health Systems, Inc., 11
PacifiCorp, V; 26 (upd.)
Packaging Corporation of America, 12; 51 (upd.)
Packard Bell Electronics, Inc., 13
Packeteer, Inc., 81
PacketVideo Corporation, 112
Paddock Publications, Inc., 53
Paging Network Inc., 11
PaineWebber Group Inc., II; 22 (upd.)
Palace Sports & Entertainment, Inc., 97
Pall Corporation, 9; 72 (upd.)
Palm Harbor Homes, Inc., 39
Palm Management Corporation, 71
Palm, Inc., 36; 75 (upd.)
Palmer & Cay, Inc., 69
Palmer Candy Company, 80
Palomar Medical Technologies, Inc., 22
Pamida Holdings Corporation, 15
Pampered Chef, Ltd., The, 18; 78 (upd.)
Pan American World Airways, Inc., I; 12 (upd.)
Pan-American Life Insurance Company, 48
Panamerican Beverages, Inc., 47
PanAmSat Corporation, 46
Panattoni Development Company, Inc., 99
Panavision Inc., 24; 107 (upd.)
Pancho's Mexican Buffet, Inc., 46
Panda Restaurant Group, Inc., 35; 97 (upd.)
Panera Bread Company, 44
Panhandle Eastern Corporation, V
Pantone Inc., 53
Pantry, Inc., The, 36
Papa Gino's Holdings Corporation, Inc., 86

Papa John's International, Inc., 15; 71 (upd.)
Papa Murphy's International, Inc., 54
Papetti's Hygrade Egg Products, Inc., 39
Pappas Restaurants, Inc., 76
Par Pharmaceutical Companies, Inc., 65
Paradies Shops, Inc., The, 88
Paradise Music & Entertainment, Inc., 42
Parallel Petroleum Corporation, 101
Parametric Technology Corp., 16
Paramount Pictures Corporation, II; 94 (upd.)
PAREXEL International Corporation, 84
Paris Corporation, 22
Parisian, Inc., 14
Park Corp., 22
Park-Ohio Industries Inc., 17; 85 (upd.)
Parker Drilling Company, 28
Parker-Hannifin Corporation, III; 24 (upd.); 99 (upd.)
Parlex Corporation, 61
Parsons Brinckerhoff, Inc., 34; 104 (upd.)
Parsons Corporation, The, 8; 56 (upd.)
Party City Corporation, 54
Patch Products Inc., 105
Pathmark Stores, Inc., 23; 101 (upd.)
Patina Oil & Gas Corporation, 24
Patrick Cudahy Inc., 102
Patrick Industries, Inc., 30
Patriot Transportation Holding, Inc., 91
Patterson Dental Co., 19
Patterson-UTI Energy, Inc., 55
Patton Boggs LLP, 71
Paul Harris Stores, Inc., 18
Paul, Hastings, Janofsky & Walker LLP, 27
Paul Mueller Company, 65
Paul Reed Smith Guitar Company, 89
Paul Revere Corporation, The, 12
Paul Stuart Inc., 109
Paul, Weiss, Rifkind, Wharton & Garrison, 47
Paul-Son Gaming Corporation, 66
Paxson Communications Corporation, 33
Pay 'N Pak Stores, Inc., 9
Paychex, Inc., 15; 46 (upd.)
Payless Cashways, Inc., 11; 44 (upd.)
Payless ShoeSource, Inc., 18; 69 (upd.)
PayPal Inc., 58
PBSJ Corporation, The, 82
PC Connection, Inc., 37
PCA International, Inc., 62
PCC Natural Markets, 94
PDI, Inc., 52
PDL BioPharma, Inc., 90
PDQ Food Stores, Inc. 79
PDS Gaming Corporation, 44
Peabody Coal Company, 10
Peabody Energy Corporation, 45 (upd.)
Peabody Holding Company, Inc., IV
Peak Technologies Group, Inc., The, 14
Peapod, Inc., 30
Pearle Vision, Inc., 13
Peavey Electronics Corporation, 16; 94 (upd.)
PECO Energy Company, 11
Pediatric Services of America, Inc., 31
Pediatrix Medical Group, Inc., 61

Peebles Inc., 16; 43 (upd.)
Peet's Coffee & Tea, Inc., 38; 100 (upd.)
Pegasus Solutions, Inc., 75
Pei Cobb Freed & Partners Architects LLP, 57
Pelican Products, Inc., 86
Pella Corporation, 12; 39 (upd.); 89 (upd.)
Pemco Aviation Group Inc., 54
Pendleton Grain Growers Inc., 64
Pendleton Woolen Mills, Inc., 42
Penford Corporation, 55
Penn Engineering & Manufacturing Corp., 28
Penn National Gaming, Inc., 33; 109 (upd.)
Penn Traffic Company, 13
Penn Virginia Corporation, 85
Pennington Seed Inc., 98
Pennsylvania Blue Shield, III
Pennsylvania Power & Light Company, V
Pennwalt Corporation, I
PennWell Corporation, 55
Pennzoil-Quaker State Company, IV; 20 (upd.); 50 (upd.)
Penske Corporation, V; 19 (upd.); 84 (upd.)
Pentair, Inc., 7; 26 (upd.); 81 (upd.)
Pentech International, Inc., 29
Penton Media, Inc., 27
Penzeys Spices, Inc. 79
People Express Airlines, Inc., I
People's United Financial Inc., 106
Peoples Energy Corporation, 6
PeopleSoft Inc., 14; 33 (upd.)
Pep Boys—Manny, Moe & Jack, The, 11; 36 (upd.); 81 (upd.)
Pepper Construction Group, LLC, The, 111
Pepper Hamilton LLP, 43
Pepperidge Farm, Incorporated, 81
Pepsi Bottling Group, Inc., The, 40
PepsiAmericas, Inc., 67 (upd.)
PepsiCo, Inc., I; 10 (upd.); 38 (upd.); 93 (upd.)
Perma-Fix Environmental Services, Inc., 99
Perdue Farms Inc., 7; 23 (upd.)
Performance Food Group, 31; 96 (upd.)
Perini Corporation, 8; 82 (upd.)
PerkinElmer Inc. 7; 78 (upd.)
Perkins & Marie Callender's Inc., 22; 107 (upd.)
Perkins Coie LLP, 56
Perot Systems Corporation, 29
Perrigo Company, 12; 59 (upd.)
Perry Ellis International, Inc., 41; 106 (upd.)
Perry's Ice Cream Company Inc., 90
Perseus Books Group, The, 91
Pet Incorporated, 7
Petco Animal Supplies, Inc., 29; 74 (upd.)
Pete's Brewing Company, 22
Peter Kiewit Sons' Inc., 8
Peter Pan Bus Lines Inc., 106
Peter Piper, Inc., 70
Peterbilt Motors Company, 89
Petersen Publishing Company, 21